BUSINESS MATH
Brings You

- **Real-world business applications to apply math concepts**
- **Contemporary topics such as consumer loans, inventory and investing**
- **Correlation to NBEA Standards for Business Education**
- **Correlation to Jump$tart National Standards in Personal Finance**
- **Basic Math Skills**
- **Algebra Connection**
- **A wealth of activities**
- **Ongoing review and assessment**
- **Integrated technology**
- **Comprehensive coverage of personal and business math topics**

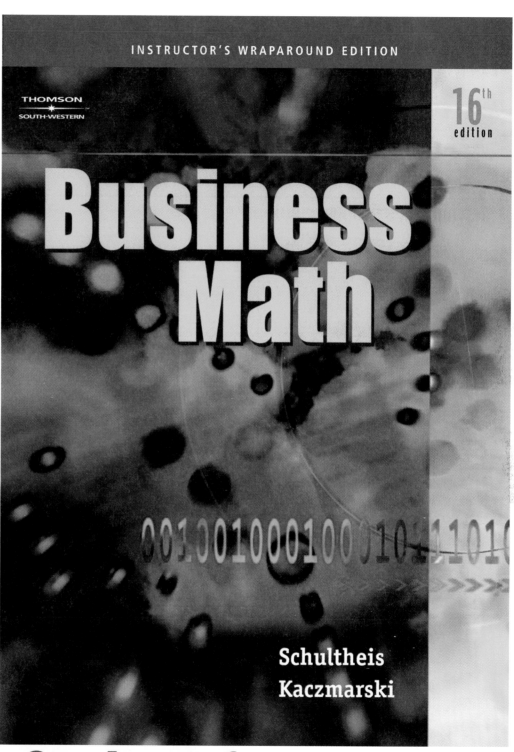

INSTRUCTOR'S WRAPAROUND EDITION

THOMSON
SOUTH-WESTERN

16th edition

Business Math

0010010001000100101011010

Schultheis
Kaczmarski

Prepare Your Students for Tomorrow's World.

CREATE A LEARNING ENVIRONMENT WITH INSTRUCTOR RESOURCES

INSTRUCTOR'S WRAPAROUND EDITION

THOMSON SOUTH-WESTERN

16th edition

Business Math

001001000100.10:11010

Schultheis
Kaczmarski

INSTRUCTOR'S RESOURCE BOX

ADOBE EBOOK

EXAMVIEW CD

DATA CD

INSTRUCTOR'S RESOURCE CD

LESSON PLANS

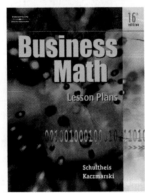

CHAPTER TEST MASTERS AND ANSWERS

WORKBOOK INSTRUCTOR'S EDITION

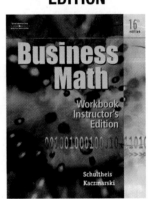

EXPLORE ALGEBRA AND GEOMETRY ACTIVITIES

TECHNOLOGY ACTIVITIES

COMPETITIVE EVENTS GUIDE

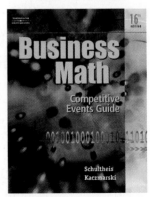

ALL THE SUPPORT YOU'LL EVER NEED

Teaching Tools provide support for the challenges you face with different learning styles, infusing technology, using media and the Internet, assessment, study skills, block scheduling, and encouraging parent involvement.

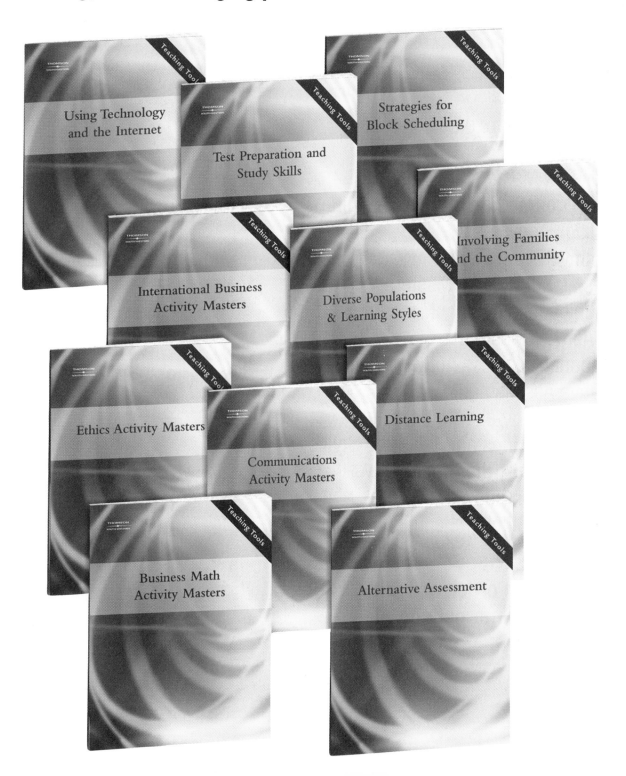

Business Math

Student Edition	0-538-44052-X
Instructor's Wraparound Edition	0-538-44053-8
Workbook	0-538-44054-6
ExamView CD	0-538-44055-4
Data CD	0-538-44056-2
Instructor's Resource CD	0-538-44431-2
Instructor's Resource Box	0-538-44231-X

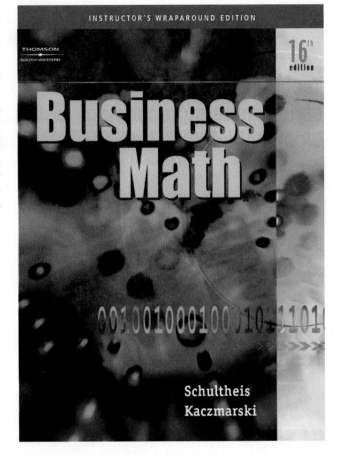

Includes

Workbook Instructor's Edition
Lesson Plans
Chapter Test Masters and Answers
Explore Algebra and Geometry Activities
Technology Activities
Competitive Events Guide
Business Math Activity Masters
Communications Activity Masters
Ethics Activity Masters
International Business Activity Masters
Alternative Assessment
Using Technology and the Internet
Diverse Populations and Learning Styles
Involving Families the Community
Test Preparation and Study Skills
Strategies for Block Scheduling
Distance Learning

**For information or to order, call 800-354-9706.
Or you can visit our Internet site at
www.swlearning.com.**

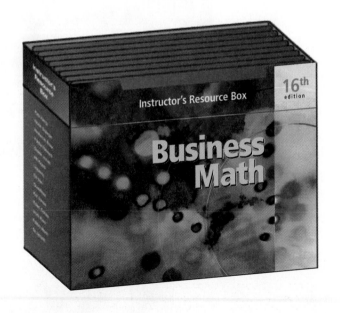

National Business Education Association Standards
The Role of Computation in Business Education

A hallmark of the business education curriculum is its relevance to everyday applications. As such, the curriculum, as a whole and the development of computation skills, in particular, are essential in helping students fulfill their future roles as citizens, consumers, employees, employers, investors, inventors, and entrepreneurs.

Computation skills, as defined in these standards, are more than just the skills needed to make quantitative and precise calculations. Rather, these skills encompass the ability to solve mathematical problems, analyze and interpret data, and apply sound decision-making skills.

The business education curriculum offers multiple opportunities to develop, use, and integrate computations skills into consumer education, economics, personal finance, marketing, management, information technology, accounting, career development, basic business, and entrepreneurship. In addition, specific courses in business and consumer mathematics help students develop the computation skills needed to solve business- and consumer-related problems.

The standards in this section demonstrate a developmental approach to the acquisition of computation skills. The first five standards address the development of general mathematical skills. In the sixth standard, these skills are utilized in problem solving applications.

I. MATHEMATICAL FOUNDATIONS
Achievement Standard: Apply basic mathematical operations to solve problems.

Level 1 Performance Expectations	
Determine mathematical processes to use for various problem situations. Use formulas when appropriate.	Chapters 1–14
Select and use appropriate tools when solving problems.	Chapters 1–14
Define and use appropriate mathematical symbols for given problems.	Chapters 1–14
Round numbers for estimation and other purposes.	Chapters 1–14
Estimate and then calculate answers to problems using addition, subtraction, multiplication, and division.	Chapters 1–14
Compare computed result with the result to determine the reasonableness of the solution.	Chapters 1–14
Explain relationship between mathematical processes.	Chapters 1–14
Communicate understanding through oral and written means.	Chapters 1–14

II. NUMBER RELATIONSHIPS AND OPERATIONS
Achievement Standard: Solve problems involving whole number, decimals, fractions, percents, ratios, averages, and proportions.

Level 1 Performance Expectations	
Solve problems that involve whole numbers, decimals, and fractions and use appropriate conversions.	Chapters 1–14

Level 2 Performance Expectations	
Solve problems that involve percents, ratios, averages, and proportions and use appropriate conversions.	Chapters 1–14

III. PATTERNS, FUNCTIONS, AND ALGEBRA
Achievement Standard: Use algebraic operations to solve problems.

Level 1 Performance Expectations	
Recognize, describe and predict patterns of data.	pp. 2, 38, 82, 130, 188, 220, 280, 344, 384, 422, 464, 500, 554, 590, Lessons 6.8, 12.3, 12.4, 13.2, 13.5
Construct and solve an algebraic equation for a given problem.	pp. 29, 115, 159, 163, 367, 534, 573, 600, 612
Solve for an unknown variable in an equation.	pp. 29, 115, 159, 163, 367, 534, 573, 600, 612
Apply the order of operations when using mathematical processes.	Chapters 1–14

Level 2 Performance Expectations	
Identify multiple applications for using algebraic equations to solve problems.	Chapters 10–12

IV. MEASUREMENTS
Achievement Standard: Use common international standards of measurement when solving problems.

Level 1 Performance Expectations	
Identify standard U.S. units of measurement and show relationships.	Lessons 14.3, 14.4–14.5
Identify standard metric units of measurement and show relationships.	Lessons 14.3, 14.4–14.5
Determine units of time and show relationships.	Lesson 14.2

Level 2 Performance Expectations	
Identify currency measurements for countries other than the United States.	Lesson 14.1
Solve problems using various types of measurements.	Chapter 14
Solve problems using conversion calculators on the Internet.	Chapter 14

Level 3 Performance Expectations	
Estimate and convert U.S. units of measurements to metric measurements and vice versa.	Lessons 14.3, 14.4
Estimate and convert the U.S. dollar to currency of other countries and vice versa.	p. 591, Lesson 14.1

Reprinted with permission from the National Standards for Business Education copyright 2001 by National Business Education Association, 1914 Association Drive, Reston, Virginia 20191-1596.

V. STATISTICS AND PROBABILITY
Achievement Standard: Analyze and interpret data using common statistical procedures.

Level 2 Performance Expectations	
Construct, read, and interpret tables, charts, and graphs.	pp. 2, 38, 82, 130, 188, 220, 280, 344, 384, 422, 464, 500, 554, 590, Chapter 8
Make inferences about data from tables, charts, and graphs.	Chapter 8
Estimate and calculate measures of central tendency.	Lesson 8.1
Level 3 Performance Expectations	
Construct frequency distributions.	Lesson 8.1
Use probability concepts to solve problems involving uncertainty.	Lesson 8.2
Level 4 Performance Expectations	
Calculate measure of dispersion.	Lesson 8.1
Calculate probability using the appropriate probability distribution.	Lesson 8.2
Calculate point and interval estimates of population parameters based on sample statistics.	Lessons 8.5, 12.5
Conduct one-and two-sample hypothesis tests to make objective decisions about population parameters.	Lesson 12.5

VI. PROBLEM-SOLVING APPLICATIONS
Achievement Standard: Use mathematical procedures to analyze and solve business problems.

A. TAXATION

Level 3 Performance Expectations	
Compute individual income taxes.	Lesson 2.3–2.4
Calculate property tax, assessed value, or the tax rate when one of the three variables is unknown.	Lesson 6.3
Level 4 Performance Expectations	
Calculate corporate income taxes.	Chapter 13
Calculate estate and other taxes.	Lessons 5.1, 6.5, 13.3

B. SAVINGS AND INVESTMENTS

Level 1 Performance Expectations	
Calculate the purchase price of a stock transaction.	Lesson 7.1
Level 2 Performance Expectations	
Compute compound interest and the resulting compound amount at the maturity date for savings and investments.	Lessons 3.6–3.7
Use compound interest calculators on the Internet to computer compound interest and compound amounts.	Chapters 3, 4, 7
Calculate the price of a bond, stock or mutual fund given a recent quotation.	Lessons 7.4–7.7
Level 3 Performance Expectations	
Compute and compare the rates of return for various instruments to make decisions.	Lesson 7.8, 13.5
Calculate the amount, compound interest, and present value for a simple annuity.	Lessons 3.6, 3.7
Determine and verify the periodic payment required to finance a sinking fund and prepare a sinking fund schedule.	Chapter 7
Determine total amount deposited and interest earned on a sinking fund.	Chapter 7
Calculate earnings per share.	Lesson 7.6
Determine current yield on a bond.	Lesson 7.4–7.5
Calculate pension income from social security, company or union plans, or retirement accounts.	Lesson 7.9
Calculate penalties for early withdrawal and minimum withdrawals from an IRA.	Lesson 7.9
Calculate penalties for early withdrawal from a certificate of deposit.	Lesson 3.7
Calculate the net income from real estate investment.	Lesson 7.8
Calculate the rent needed to earn a desired net income from real estate investments.	Lesson 7.8
Use calculators on the Internet to solve problems pertaining to annuities, bonds, stocks, IRAs, and real estate investments.	Chapters 3, 7
Level 4 Performance Expectations	
Calculate present value of an investment with compound interest.	Lesson 7.9
Use calculators on the Internet to solve problems pertaining to present value.	Chapter 7

C. PAYROLL AND HUMAN RESOURCE MANAGEMENT

Level 1 Performance Expectations	
Calculate gross earnings.	Chapter 1
Level 2 Performance Expectations	
Calculate payroll withholdings, social security, and Medicare deductions, other deductions, and net earnings.	Chapter 2

Level 3 Performance Expectations	
Maintain payroll register and individual earnings record.	Chapter 2, Lessons 10.2–10.3
Complete the employers' quarterly federal tax return, which includes the calculations for employee and employer taxes.	Lessons 2.3, 10.2–10.3
Calculate fringe benefits.	Lessons 2.2, 10.2
Calculate wage and salary increase plans.	Chapter 1, Lesson 10.2
Calculate the costs of recruiting, placing, and training employees.	Lessons 10.1, 10.3

D. CASH MANAGEMENT

Level 1 Performance Expectations	
Maintain check records.	Chapter 5
Calculate income and expense for a given time period.	Lesson 2.2

Level 2 Performance Expectations	
Calculate fixed and variable costs, analyze data, and estimate the projected total income and total expenses for a given time period.	Lessons, 2.2, 2.5–2.6
Prepare a budget.	Lesson 2.6

Level 3 Performance Expectations	
Reconcile the bank statement with the check register.	Lessons 3.4, 3.5
Reconcile and replenish petty cash fund and cash drawer.	Lesson 2.6
Maintain a columnar cash record.	Lesson 2.5

E. FINANCIAL MANAGEMENT

Level 3 Performance Expectations	
Calculate net sales, costs of goods sold, gross profit, operating expenses, and net profit for the income statement.	Chapter 13
Calculate total assets, liabilities, and owner's equity for the balance sheet.	Chapter 13
Calculate the distribution of profit/loss to the proprietor, partners, or stockholders.	Lesson 13.3
Calculate bankruptcy distribution rate and amounts.	Lesson 13.6

Level 4 Performance Expectations	
Apply generally accepted business ratios such as current ratio, debt ratio, and equity ratio to accounting data in order to make decisions.	Lesson 13.5
Calculate the cash flow and determine cash sufficiency for a given time period.	Lesson 13.2, 13.5
Calculate the change in equity for the statement of change of owner's equity or retained earnings statement.	Lesson 13.5

F. CREDIT MANAGEMENT

Level 2 Performance Expectations	
Using the simple interest equation, $I = PRT$, solve for one of the variable and find maturity value, maturity date, and days between dates.	Chapter 4
Calculate bank discount and proceeds on a discounted note.	Lesson 4.2

Level 3 Performance Expectations	
Determine the outstanding amount for installment purchases.	Lesson 4.4
Determine finance/additional charges, periodic payment, total costs, and APR on an installment contract.	Chapter 4
Compare cash price to installment price in order to make a purchasing decision.	Lesson 4.7
Calculate the effects of early payoff of an installment plan.	Lesson 4.5
Determine periodic payment, interest, and total amount required to pay to amortize a loan.	Lessons 4.3, 4.4
Prepare a simplified amortization schedule.	Lesson 6.1–6.4
Calculate finance charges on credit card balances and cash advances.	Lesson 4.7–4.8
Calculate a down payment, closing costs, and mortgage loan amount.	Lesson 6.1
Calculate the interest saved by early mortgage repayment or shorter mortgage terms.	Lesson 6.1
Calculate the savings from refinancing a mortgage.	Lesson 6.1
Use calculators on the Internet to solve problems pertaining to installment loans, mortgages, mortgage refinancing and loan prepayment.	Chapters 4, 6

Level 4 Performance Expectations	
Calculate present value of a simple interest loan.	Lessons 4.1–4.3
Use spreadsheets and calculators on the Internet to solve problems pertaining to present value.	Chapters 4, 6

G. PURCHASES

Level 1 Performance Expectations	
Calculate the total purchase price given the number of units and unit price.	Lesson 5.3

Level 2 Performance Expectations	
Calculate net business purchases with discounts and purchase returns and allowances.	Lessons 10.4–10.6, 12.1–12.4

Level 3 Performance Expectations	
Compare the cost of renting, leasing, and buying equipment.	Lessons 9.1, 11.5
Use calculators on the Internet to compare the cost of renting, leasing, and buying equipment.	Lessons 9.1, 11.5
Calculate the cost of buying and maintaining a new and used car.	Lesson 6.5–6.7

H. SALES

Level 1 Performance Expectations	
Determine the dollar amount of cost, markup, or selling price when one of the three variables is unknown.	Lessons 5.4, 12.4
Determine the dollar amount of markdown, regular selling price, or reduced price when one of the three variables is unknown.	Lessons 5.4, 12.4

Level 2 Performance Expectations	
Calculate the total sales and the sales tax for a sales transaction.	Lesson 6.1–6.2

Level 3 Performance Expectations	
Compute net sales with sales/returns allowances and sales discount.	Lessons 12.1–12.4
Compute the percent of markup when based on the cost of when based on the selling price.	Lessons 12.1–12.4
Compute the percent of markdown given the regular selling price and the reduced price.	Lessons 12.1–12.4
Calculate sales projections and market share.	Lessons 12.6–12.7
Calculate advertising costs.	Lessons 12.8

Level 4 Performance Expectations	
Calculate the operating profit or loss, absolute loss, and breakeven point.	Chapters 11–12

I. INVENTORY RECORDS

Level 3 Performance Expectations	
Determine inventory valuation according to different plans including LIFO, FIFO, specific identification, and weighted average.	Lessons 10.4–10.6
Determine costs of goods sold for a given period using different inventory valuation methods.	Lessons 10.4–10.6
Determine gross profit for a given period using different inventory valuation methods.	Lessons 10.4–10.6
Calculate economic order quantity and reorder points.	Lessons 10.4–10.6
Calculate shipping costs.	Lesson 10.4

Level 4 Performance Expectations	
Calculate inventory turnover at cost and at retail for a given period.	Lesson 10.5

J. DEPRECIATION, COST RECOVERY, AND DEPLETION

Level 3 Performance Expectations	
Calculate the depletion of natural resources.	Lesson 11.1
Calculate book value.	Lesson 11.3
Calculate average annual depreciation.	Lesson 11.4
Calculate the rate of depreciation.	Lesson 11.4

Level 4 Performance Expectations	
Calculate the annual accumulated depreciation or cost recovery of plant assets.	Chapter 11
Prepare depreciation and cost recovery schedules.	Chapter 11
Calculate the amortization of intangible assets.	Chapters 11, 13

K. COMPUTERS, INFORMATION TECHNOLOGY, AND THE INTERNET

Level 2 Performance Expectations	
Calculate and compare the cost of connecting to the Internet.	Lesson 5.5
Calculate and compare the cost of online connections.	Lessons 5.5, 9.4
Calculate and compare speeds of file transfers.	Lesson 5.5

Level 3 Performance Expectations	
Calculate and compare the costs of cell phone ownership.	Lesson 9.5
Compare the costs of renting, leasing, and buying computer equipment.	Lesson 9.1
Compare the costs of various options for acquiring software.	Lesson 9.2

L. MANUFACTURING AND OFFICE COSTS

Level 3 Performance Expectations	
Calculate total factory and office costs.	Chapter 11
Allocate factory expenses.	Chapter 11
Calculate total, average, and unit costs of factory and office equipment, supplies, space, and labor.	Chapter 11

M. INSURANCE

Level 3 Performance Expectations	
Calculate benefits, claims, and premiums on real estate, health, disability, life, and auto insurance.	Lesson 6.4, 6.7, 7.1–7.3, 7.8
Compare costs of insurance coverage with different options.	Lesson 6.4, 6.7, 7.1–7.3, 7.8

16th edition

Business Math

Robert A. Schultheis

•

Raymond M. Kaczmarski

THOMSON

SOUTH-WESTERN

Australia · Brazil · Canada · Mexico · Singapore · Spain · United Kingdom · United States

THOMSON

SOUTH-WESTERN

Instructor's Wraparound Edition

Business Math 16th Edition

by Robert A. Schultheis and Raymond M. Kaczmarski

VP/Editorial Director:
Jack W. Calhoun

VP/Editor-in-Chief:
Karen Schmohe

VP/Educational Marketing:
Carol Volz

Executive Editor:
Eve Lewis

Project Manager:
Enid Nagel

Production Project Manager:
Diane Bowdler

Marketing Manager:
Nancy Long

Editorial Assistant:
Linda Keith

Manufacturing Coordinator:
Kevin Kluck

Production House:
Better Graphics

Art Director:
Stacy Jenkins Shirley

Internal Designer:
Joseph R. Pagliaro

Cover Designer:
Beckmeyer Design, Inc.

Cover Image:
(c) Getty Images

Printer:
Courier
Kendallville, IN

For more information about our
products, contact us at:

Thomson Higher Education
5191 Natorp Boulevard
Mason, OH 45040
USA

Don't Settle for the Status Quo

ENGAGE STUDENTS IN THE REAL WORLD

CHAPTER 5

Spend Wisely

5.1 Sales Tax
5.2 Sales Receipts
5.3 Unit Prices
5.4 Comparative Shopping
5.5 Personal Internet Access

Statistical Insights

State Sales Tax Rates
January 1, 2004

State	Sales/Use Tax, %	State	Sales/Use Tax, %	State	Sales/Use Tax, %
Alabama	4	Louisiana	4	Ohio	6
Arizona	5.6	Maine	5	Oklahoma	4.5
Arkansas	6	Maryland	5	Pennsylvania	6
California	6	Massachusetts	5	Rhode Island	7
Colorado	2.9	Michigan	6	South Carolina	5
Connecticut	6	Minnesota	6.5	South Dakota	4
Florida	6	Mississippi	7	Tennessee	7
Georgia	4	Missouri	4.225	Texas	6.25
Hawaii	4	Nebraska	5.5	Utah	4.75
Idaho	6	Nevada	6.5	Vermont	6
Illinois	6.25	New Jersey	6	Virginia	3.5
Indiana	6	New Mexico	5	Washington	6.5
Iowa	5	New York	4.25	West Virginia	6
Kansas	5.3	North Carolina	4.5	Wisconsin	5
Kentucky	6	North Dakota	5	Wyoming	4

Note: Alaska, Delaware, Montana, New Hampshire and Oregon have no statewide sales taxes.

Use the data shown above to answer each question.
1. How many states listed have a statewide tax that is greater than 6.5%? Name each state.
2. What is the average statewide tax percent for the states listed?

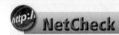 NetCheck

Shopping Online Smartly

Online purchases require the use of a credit card and access to the Internet. Care must be taken when using a credit card online. You should only purchase from Internet web sites that offer a secure checkout system or will allow you to establish an account or will ship goods C.O.D. Many web sites use special encryption software to safeguard your credit card number.

The Internet is also an excellent source for getting information about a product, checking its availability in your area, and locating a retailer with the best price. Consider the total cost of the purchase, including shipping costs, before making a decision to buy online.

Taxing Online Purchases

Many online sellers have a billing system that allows sales tax to be collected from customers if required by the state where the online customers live. The sellers collect the correct amount of tax and forward it to the state tax office.

If the seller does not collect state sales taxes, customers still have a responsibility to pay the sales taxes due their state. This may be done by reporting the amount due on a state income tax return or by using some other required process.

How Times Have Changed

Forty years ago the Internet did not exist. Today, well over 100 million Internet hosts are sending information over the major backbones of the network at speeds greater than 2 billion bits per second.

Research to discover a significant event in 1957 that relates to the history of the Internet.

Internet traffic moves at 1.544 mbps. **1988**

Internet traffic moves at 44.736 mbps. **1991**

Internet traffic moves at 2.488 gbps. **1999**

1950 1960 1970 1980 1990 2000

1969
The Internet is born when four universities are connected via the ARPANET, a computer network commissioned by the U.S. Department of Defense.

1986
The NSFNET replaces ARPANET as the backbone of the Internet. Internet traffic moves over the backbone at a speed of 56 kbps.

1995
America Online and other companies begin to provide dial-up Internet access.

189

STATISTICAL INSIGHTS
Data Analysis

Presents real-world data that is relevant to the business and math topics of the chapter.

NETCHECK
Internet Feature

Suggests ways to get information and assistance for business topics relevant to the chapter.

HOW TIMES HAVE CHANGED
Timeline Feature

Provides interesting historical details relevant to the business topic of the chapter. Taking a look at events, inventions, and technology from the past gives you a clearer understanding and appreciation for the way business is done today.

FEATURES ENHANCE LEARNING

TEAM MEETING

You and your team members are to conduct a survey of 200 people to determine what they think about a movie. First, select a relatively new movie that would appeal to a wide audience. Then construct a simple questionnaire to determine whether the respondents like or do not like the movie, or have not seen the movie. Demographic data should be the age of the respondent in five-year segments, such as 13–17, 18–22, and so on. Also ask for the number of movies seen in a year within these categories: once a week, once a month, less than once a month.

Tabulate the data from the survey of your 200-person population. Then randomly select 20 surveys and tabulate their results. Compare the results of the population and sample surveys. Discuss the reasons for any differences you find in the results.

TEAM MEETING
Cooperative Learning Activities

Provides group activities where you can put into practice the business topics you are learning.

COMMUNICATION
Written and Spoken Language Activities

Communication, both written and spoken, is vital to being successful in business. These features provide you opportunities to use various methods of communication.

COMMUNICATION

Write a brief paragraph you might include in an e-mail to a friend who works explaining why it is important for the friend to file a tax return.

There are three important guidelines that should be followed when sending e-mail.

1. Your e-mail should cover only one topic.
2. Your message should be brief.
3. Be courteous and professional in your message.

Remember, once the e-mail is sent, you cannot get it back.

WORKPLACE WINDOW

FINANCIAL ADVISOR Investigate the job of financial advisor in your state. Described the typical duties of the job. Identify the typical education requirements, if any. Check to see if your state requires any licensing, testing, or certification of people with that job title. Use the resources of the Web. Some tips: go to the Web sites for the Dictionary of Occupational Titles, the Certified Financial Planner Board of Standards, and the National Association of Securities Dealers Regulation. Prepare a report of your findings and list your sources of information.

WORKPLACE WINDOW
Career Awareness Activities

Each skill taught is applied within the business world. Some careers use a skill more extensively than others. These features bring to your attention some career options that you may want to consider as you look to the future.

ALGEBRA CONNECTION
Basic Algebra Activities

When the skill you are studying can be related to algebra, an algebra connection will provide you with an alternative way to look at a problem.

Algebra Connection

An *approximate* annual percentage rate can be calculated for monthly level-payment loans without the use of tables using this formula:

$$\text{APR} = \frac{24F}{P(N + 1)}$$

F = Finance charge amount

P = Original principal

N = Number of payments per year

Revisit this Algebra Connection after completing the exercises. Enter the information from Exercise 19, find the APR to the nearest tenth percent, and compare your results to the answer to Exercise 19 you got using the table. Which gave a higher percent, the table or the formula? What was the amount of the difference? Would you rely on the formula to find the APR?

UNDERSTANDING CHECKPOINTS

GOALS
Student goals

Clear and concise description of what you will learn in the lesson.

START UP
Engages Students

Provides a real-world situation that motivates learning in the chapter.

MATH SKILL BUILDER
Integrated Basic Math Review

Provide review of basic math skills needed in the lesson.

1.4 Commission

Goals

- Calculate straight commission earnings
- Calculate commission earnings based on quota
- Calculate graduated commission earnings
- Find the rate of commission

Start Up

Two sales jobs are advertised in the newspaper. The first job pays a commission of 3.5% on all sales, and sales usually average $52,000 a month. The second job pays a commission of 4% on sales up to $5,000 and 12% on sales over $5,000, and sales usually average $25,000 a month. Based on the usual monthly sales average, which job pays more?

Math Skill Builder

Review these math skills and solve the exercises that follow

1 **Rewrite** a percent as a decimal.
Rewrite this percent. 50% = 0.5

1a. 12%

1b. 18.6%

1c. 2.5%

2 Find a **percent of a number**.
Find the percent. 1% of $1,956 = 0.01 × $1,956 = $19.56

2a. 14% of $500   2b. 3.5% of $1,200

3 **Rewrite** a decimal as a percent.
Rewrite this decimal. 0.25 = 25%

3a. 0.08   3b. 0.75

3c. 0.01   3d. 0.1825

4 Find **what percent** one number is of another number.
Find the percent. $10 ÷ $80 = 0.125 or 12.5%

4a. $15 ÷ $75   4b. $4,800 ÷ $32,000

20 ■ Chapter 1 Gross Pay

THROUGHOUT EACH LESSON

■ Sales Slip Totals

Sales slip totals are found by adding the extensions to get the subtotal. If there is a sales tax and it is applied to all items sold, the tax rate is multiplied by the subtotal to find the tax amount. Then the subtotal and tax amount are added to find the total amount of the sales slip.

Subtotal = Sum of Extensions

Sales Tax Amount = Subtotal × Sales Tax Rate

Total of Sales Slip = Subtotal + Sales Tax Amount

To simplify matters, all items sold in this lesson will be subject to sales taxes.

EXAMPLE 2

A shopper bought 3 pairs of gloves @ $15.89 and 2 pair of shoes @ $78.98. There was a state sales tax of 4.75%. What was the total of the cash register receipt?

SOLUTION

Multiply the quantities by the prices to find the extensions.

$3 \times \$15.89 = \$47.67$ $2 \times \$78.98 = \$157.96$

Add the extensions to find the subtotal for the sale.

$\$47.67 + \$157.96 = \$205.63$ subtotal

Find the sales tax.

$\$205.63 \times 0.0475 = \$9.77$ sales tax

Add the subtotal and sales tax.

$\$205.63 + \$9.77 = \$215.40$ receipt total

■ CHECK YOUR UNDERSTANDING

C. Alexis Bakov bought 3 boxes of recycled kraft envelopes @ $3.89 and 5 boxes of recycled kraft clasp envelopes @ $5.79. The sales tax rate was 3.85%. What was the sales slip total?

D. Sonia Alvarez bought 2 doz. team T-shirts @ $139.89 and 2 boxes of baseball caps @ $89.99 for the Little League team she manages. There was a state sales tax of 5% and a city sales tax of 2.5%. What was the cash register receipt total?

Wrap Up

People often fail to safeguard sales slip. They are commonly left at the gasoline pump and dropped on store floors. This carelessness allowed thieves to steal the slips and use the credit card numbers. In the case of online ordering systems, displaying x's for all but the last four numbers prevents passersby from obtaining the number.

BUSINESS TIP

Items bought in large quantities may be priced by the *gross (12 dozen)*, *hundred (C)*, *thousand (M)*, *hundred pounds* or *hundredweight (cwt)*, and *ton (T)*.

CALCULATOR TIP

To find the subtotal: press the M+ key after finding each extension. To display the subtotal press the MR/C key. Multiply the subtotal in the display by the sales tax rate and press M+. Pressing MR/C now displays the total of the sales slip. Clear the memory by pressing the MR/C again before starting the next problem.

EXAMPLES
Show work step-by-step

Each lesson has worked out examples. The example explains step-by-step how to solve the problem. The text in blue helps you identify what you calculated.

CHECK YOUR UNDERSTANDING
Practice for example

Allows you to practice before continuing. The questions are like the example and will help you know if you understand the skills being taught.

WRAP UP
Concludes Start Up

You will already have formed an opinion and answer about the Start Up question. This paragraph gives you an opportunity to check your answer and your reasoning.

ABUNDANT EXERCISES

EXERCISES
Practice for basic and business math

Exercises start with basic math skills followed by the business math taught in the examples.

Integrating Your Knowledge

You will use skills that were taught in more than one lesson.

Decision Making

You will analyze a process or computation and then make a recommendation.

Critical Thinking

Asks you to apply critical thinking to the basic math concepts.

Best Buy

You will need to perform calculations for two different situations and then determine the better choice.

Stretching Your Skills

The numbers may be larger or your answer may not be as easy to arrive at, but the skills you use are the same.

MIXED REVIEW
Reviews basic and business math

You will work exercises from previous lessons that provide ongoing review and assessment.

EXERCISES

Find the result.
1. $98.62 + $978.22 − $34.15 − $98.18
2. $789.23 + $98.21 − $44.63 − $641.09

Find the product.
3. $879.43 × 0.00526
4. $2,097.46 × 0.0002978

5. The October credit card statement for Genaro Rios had a previous balance of $175.30, new purchases and fees of $108.85, and payments and credits of $125. The card's annual percentage rate is 21% and the previous balance method is used to figure the finance charge. What is Genaro's finance charge for October and new balance?

10. **INTEGRATING YOUR KNOWLEDGE** You have two credit cards. The Banker's Card has a previous balance of $301.55, carries an APR of 18%, and uses the previous balance method of figuring finance charges. The MallCard lists a previous balance of $260.61 and payments and credits of $175. It uses the adjusted balance method to find finance charges and carries an APR of 21%. Find the finance charge on both cards.

11. **DECISION MAKING** Your credit card statement shows a previous balance of $231.86, payments and credits of $125, and purchases and fees of $175.66. Your current card company uses an APR of 15% and the adjusted balance method. Another credit card company that sent you an application in the mail also uses an APR of 15% but uses the previous balance method. Should you switch companies? Why or why not?

12. When Gorica Batic received her May credit card statement she found these two wholesale firms. The Trill Company offers a cabinet for $800, less 40%. Pender Products offers the same cabinet for $650, less 30%. From which firm should Pearl buy the cabinet in order to get the lowest price? How much less will the lower price be?

29. **CRITICAL THINKING** Name three things that you consider when you buy a product and rank them in order of importance. Next list three things that you think a business considers when it buys a product and rank them in order of importance. What are the similarities and differences between the lists and the rankings?

STRETCHING YOUR SKILLS On November 6, Owen Tormo bought $28,000 worth of goods with terms of 3/10, n/30. To pay the invoice on November 16 and get the 3% discount, Owen borrowed the cash price of the invoice at his bank for 20 days at 12%, ordinary interest.

30. What was the cash price of the invoice?

31. What was the cost of interest on the loan?

32. What cash discount did Owen receive?

MIXED REVIEW

34. Write 1.93 as a percent.

35. Find $\frac{2}{5}$ of 550.

36. Estimate: $3,016 \div 18$

37. $\frac{2}{3} \div 48$

38. Find the quotient of $9.5 \div 2.4$ to the nearest hundredth.

39. The Bremmers want to buy a home. They estimate these home operating expenses: property tax, $3,400; insurance, $485; utilities, $1,480; maintenance, $1,200; mortgage interest, $6,400; lost interest on down payment, $420. Their estimated income tax savings are $1,800. What will be the net cost of owning the home in the first year?

INTEGRATED TECHNOLOGY

TECHNOLOGY WORKSHOP
Spreadsheet Activities

A template task is provided for you to enter information and learn how spreadsheets work. You answer questions about the results and the template. Then you design your own spreadsheet to fit a situation or data given.

Notice how the social security tax, total deductions, an
These changes show what would happen if the social s
from 6.2% to the higher 6.5%.

Answer these questions about your updated payroll s
6. What is the formula used in cell F16? What arithme
7. What is the formula used in cell G6? What arithme
8. What is the formula used in cell H6? What arithme
9. What is the formula used in cell J13? What arithme
10. Why did changing cell E18 change the amounts thr
spreadsheet?

Task 3: Design a Job Benefits Sprea

Design a spreadsheet that will allow you to compare
The spreadsheet for Task 1 includes formulas that use s
the SUM function. Create a spreadsheet that will use the
the situation below. The spreadsheet should allow you
net benefits. Assume that each job is for a 40-hour wee
spreadsheet should contain a row for each of the items
should enter row or column labels and formulas to calc
pension benefits, total job benefits, total job expenses, a

DATA: You receive two job offers. The expenses and benefits for each job are shown at the right.

Task 4: Analyze the Spreadsheet Output

Answer these questions about your completed spreadsheet.
11. How did you calculate annual pension benefits?
12. What were the total job benefits of Offer 1? Offer 2?
13. Which job offered the highest net benefits? How much higher?
14. Which job benefits package do you think is better?
15. If you were to (a) change the pension percentage rate for Job 1 to 7%, (b) change the hourly rate to $12.50 for Job 1, and (c) eliminate life insurance as a benefit from both jobs, what is the difference in net benefits between the two offers?

	Offer 1	Offer 2
Salary Information		
Hourly Rate	$11.25	$12.05
Annual Benefits		
Health Insurance	$2,500	
Life Insurance	$250	$325
Health Club		
Membership	——	$550
Pension*	8%	6%
Free Parking	$650	——
Expense Information		
Commuting Costs	$777	$955
Dues	$98	$150
Tools	——	$380
Uniforms	——	$425
*Stated as a percent of annual salary.		

Technology Workshop

Task 1: Enter Data In A Payroll Sheet Template

Complete a template that calculates the social security tax, Medicare tax, and net pay for each employee of the Bainbridge Company.
Open the spreadsheet for Chapter 2 (tech2-1) and enter the data shown in blue (cells D6-E15). Social security taxes, Medicare taxes, and net pay are calculated for each employee. Your finished spreadsheet should look like the one shown.

	A	B	C	D	E	F	G	H	I	J	K
1					Bainbridge Company						
2					Payroll Sheet for January 15, 20—						
3							Deductions				
4	Employee No.	Name	Allow-ances	Mar-ried	Gross Wages	Income Tax	Social Security	Medicare	Other	Total Deductions	Net Pay
6	1	Ajanaku	1	N	421.02	40.00	26.10	6.10	35.45	107.65	313.37
7	2	Bell	1	N	435.89	42.00	27.03	6.32	37.84	113.19	322.70
8	3	Cole	0	Y	502.54	39.00	31.16	7.29	49.75	127.20	375.34
9	4	Dern	1	N	399.50	36.00	24.77	5.79	31.54	98.10	301.40
10	5	Evers	2	Y	575.64	32.00	35.69	8.35	58.97	135.01	440.63
11	6	Ford	5	Y	449.54	0.00	27.87	6.52	50.02	84.41	365.13
12	7	Gomez	0	Y	557.76	46.00	34.58	8.09	57.64	146.31	411.45
13	8	Huang	2	Y	450.89	18.00	27.96	6.54	38.19	90.69	360.20
14	9	Isom	0	N	438.27	51.00	27.17	6.35	37.17	121.69	316.58
15	10	Jackson	3	Y	580.24	25.00	35.97	8.41	61.55	130.93	449.31
16		Totals			4,811.29	329.00	298.30	69.76	458.12	1,155.18	3,656.11
18		Social Security Rate		0.062							
19		Medicare Rate		0.0145							

Task 2: Analyze the Spreadsheet Output

Answer these questions about your completed payroll sheet.
1. Which employee had the largest net pay for the period?
2. Which employee had the largest amount of deductions?
3. Which employee had the greatest number of allowances?
4. Which employees paid more in combined social security taxes and Medicare taxes than they paid in income taxes?
5. What was the total amount of income taxes withheld from wages for the week?

Now move the cursor to cell E18, labeled Social Security. Enter the rate 0.065.

76 ■ Chapter 2 Net Pay

Chapter 2 Technology Workshop ■ 77

How To Use This Book ■ ix

ASSESSMENT AND REVIEW

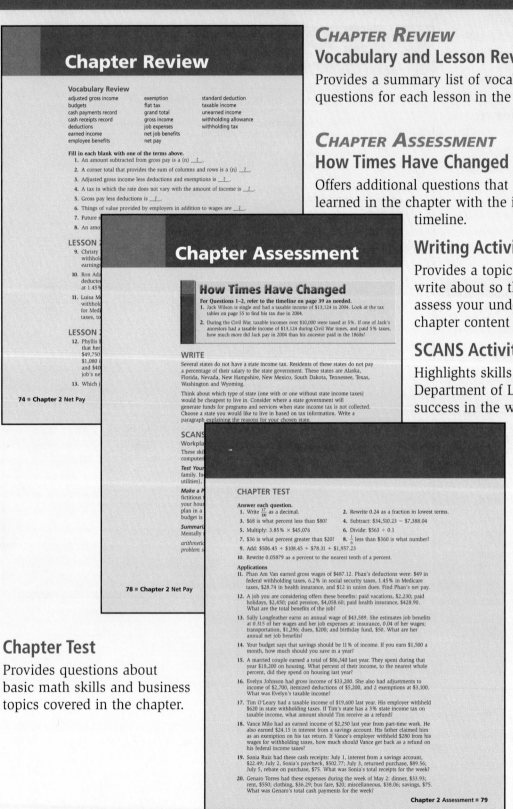

CHAPTER REVIEW
Vocabulary and Lesson Review
Provides a summary list of vocabulary terms and review questions for each lesson in the chapter.

CHAPTER ASSESSMENT
How Times Have Changed
Offers additional questions that integrate what you have learned in the chapter with the information in the timeline.

Writing Activity
Provides a topic or task that you can write about so that your teacher can assess your understanding of the chapter content through your writing.

SCANS Activity and Assessment
Highlights skills identified by the U.S. Department of Labor as critical for success in the workplace. Each chapter focuses on one of SCANS competencies.

Chapter Test
Provides questions about basic math skills and business topics covered in the chapter.

Chapters 1-2 Cumulative Review

MULTIPLE CHOICE

Select the best choice for each question.

1. Last week Sarah Carver worked 4 overtime hours at time-and-a-half pay. Her regular pay rate is $8.70 per hour. What was her overtime pay for the week?
   A. $13.05   B. $52.20   C. $52.50
   D. $69.60   E. $400.20

2. Last year Jose Inez's tax gross income was $24,685. She had adjustments to income of $3,640. What was Jose's adjusted gross income last year?
   A. $21,045   B. $22,185   C. $25,825
   D. $28,325   E. $30,825

3. Carmen Rielly is paid piece-rate for each of the 268 items she produces in a week and she receives gross wages of $469. What is Carmen's per piece rate?
   A. $1.50
   D. $1.75

4. Gary Kersting has tax
   1.5% on taxable inco
   A. $346.72
   D. $5,200.80

5. Maureen Ritter is pai
   sales last week were
   A. $273.28
   D. $2,732.80

6. Jan Morrison's annua
   A. $1,897.51
   D. $18,975.10

7. Jontay Mays works 8
   for one week if he ea
   A. $78.72
   D. $383.60

8. Morgan Born is paid
   are 33% of her wage
   A. $165.76
   D. $7,687.68

9. Dean Stroble is marri
   wage is $448. His wi
   A. $396.73
   D. $499.27

10. Kim Lui is paid an a
    What is her gross pay
    A. $551.54
    D. $1,434

OPEN ENDED

11. Last week Jason Fields worked: Monday, 7.2 hours; Tuesday, 8.3 hours; Wednesday, 8 hours; Thursday, 8 hours; Friday, 7.4 hours. He is paid $8.90 per hour. What was Jason's gross pay last week?

12. LaDonna Ekwilugo has sales last month of $86,400. Her total earnings for the month were $5,156, which included $1,700 for her monthly salary. What rate of commission was LaDonna paid?

13. A shipping department has five workers: a supervisor who is paid $484 a week, and four other workers who are paid $390, $410, $425, and $430 a week. What is the average weekly pay for shipping department workers?

14. Janice Barton is an assembler in a factory and is paid $1.25 for each hand-held radio she assembles. During one week, Janice assembled these radios: 65 on Monday, 72 on Tuesday, 70 on Wednesday and 68 on Thursday. How many radios must Janice assemble on Friday to earn $425 for the week?

QUANTITATIVE COMPARISON

Compare the quantity in Column A with the quantity in Column B. Select the letter of the correct answer from these choices:
A if the quantity in Column A is greater;
B if the quantity in Column B is greater;
C if the two quantities are equal;
D if the relationship between the two quantities cannot be determined from the given information.

Column A	Column B

15. Chris Beltsos is paid a salary of $280 a week and a commission of 5.5% on all sales. His sales last week were $5,025.

Chris' weekly salary	Chris' commission last week

16. Alvin Barr's taxable income last year was $25,800. Jamaal White's taxable income last year was $29,600. Their state income tax rates were 5% for Alvin and 4% for Jamal.

Alvin's state income tax	Jamaal's state income tax

17. Krista Egan worked 4 overtime hours at time-and-a-half pay. Her regular hourly rate is $9.85. Haley Kale worked 2.5 overtime hours at double-time pay. Her regular hourly rate is $11.82 per hour.

Krista's overtime pay	Haley's overtime pay

CONSTRUCTED RESPONSE

18. A friend has just graduated from high school and is looking at two job offers. One pays $12.50 an hour for a 40-hour week. The other pays $14 an hour for a 40-hour week. The friend thinks the choice is a no-brainer. The $14 an hour job pays more and so he should take that job. Write a letter to your friend to explain what other job factors should be examined before making the decision.

CUMULATIVE REVIEW

Multiple-choice

Presents questions in the five-choice format found on most standardized tests.

Open-ended

Presents questions where you provide the answer.

Quantitative Comparison

Presents questions in a testing format where you must calculate two different problems and then compare those answers.

Constructed Response

Presents a question where your response will include both a calculation and an explanation.

CONTENTS

Skills Workshops

Skills Workshop 1

PLACE VALUE AND ORDER

EXAMPLE 1 Write 2,345,678.9123 in words.

millions	hundred thousands	ten thousands	thousands	hundreds	tens	ones	.	tenths	hundredths	thousandths	ten thousandths
2	3	4	5	6	7	8	.	9	1	2	3

The place-value chart shows the value of each digit. The value of each place is ten times the place to the right.

SOLUTION The number shown is *two million, three hundred forty-five thousand, six hundred seventy-eight and nine thousand one hundred twenty-three ten-thousandths.*

EXAMPLE 2 Use < or > to make this sentence true. 6 ■ 2

SOLUTION Numbers can be graphed on a number line. The number farther to the right is the larger number. Remember, < means "less than" and > means "greater than".

Six is greater than two. 6 > 2

Write each number in words.

1. 3,647

2. 6,004,300.002

3. 0.9001

4. 17.049

5. 40,372

6. 6,071.435

1. three thousand, six hundred forty-seven
2. six million, four thousand, three hundred and two thousandths
3. nine thousand one ten-thousandths
4. seventeen and forty-nine thousandths
5. forty thousand, three hundred seventy-two
6. six thousand, seventy-one and four hundred thirty-five thousandths

Write each of the following as a number.

7. two million, one hundred fifty thousand, four hundred seventeen
   2,150,417
8. five thousand, one hundred twenty and five hundred two thousandths
   5,120.502
9. nine million, ninety thousand, nine hundred and ninety-nine ten-thousandths
   9,090,900.0099
10. four hundred sixty-eight thousand, forty-six and fourteen thousandths
    468,046.014

Use < or > to make each sentence true.

11. 9 ■ 8   >

12. 164 ■ 246   <

13. 63,475 ■ 6,435   >

14. 52 ■ 50   >

15. 5.39 ■ 9.02   <

16. 43.94 ■ 53.69   <

17. 1.75 ■ 1.25   >

18. 1,476 ■ 1,467   >

19. 847.05 ■ 846.75   >

Skills Workshop 2

ROUNDING WHOLE NUMBERS AND DECIMALS

When rounding whole numbers, first locate the digit in the place value to which you are rounding. If the digit to the right of it is 5 or greater, increase the digit in the specified place by 1. If the digit to the right of it is less than 5, the digit in the specified place remains the same. All digits to the right of the place value to which you are rounding become zero.

EXAMPLE 1 Round 4,782 to the nearest hundred.

SOLUTION Find the hundreds place. 4,792   7 is in the hundreds place.

The digit to the right of 7 is 9.

Since 9 is greater than 5, round 7 up to 8.

So, 4,792 rounds to 4,800.   All digits to the right of the hundreds place become zero.

When rounding decimals, follow the same procedure for rounding whole numbers except no zeros are needed if they are to the right of the place to which you are rounding and to the right of the decimal point. This is because they are not significant digits.

EXAMPLE 2 Round 8.243 to the nearest tenth.

SOLUTION Find the tenths place. 8.243   2 is in the tenths place.

The digit to the right of 2 is 4.

Since 4 is less than 5, 2 remains the same.

So, 8.243 rounds to 8.200.   All digits to the right of the tenths place are dropped.

8.200 can be written as 8.2

Round each number to the indicated place value.

1. 429 to the nearest ten 430

2. 9,058 to the nearest thousand 9,000

3. 36,815 to the nearest hundred 36,800

4. 85,726 to the nearest thousand 86,000

5. 48,280 to the nearest ten thousand 50,000

6. 392,682 to the nearest ten thousand 390,000

7. 6,329,451 to the nearest hundred thousand 6,300,000

8. 9,583,507 to the nearest thousand 9,584,000

9. 93,487,991 to the nearest hundred thousand 93,500,000

10. 4,540,597 to the nearest million 5,000,000

11. 0.38 to the nearest tenth 0.4

12. 6.849 to the nearest hundredth 6.85

13. 62.9042 to the nearest hundredth 62.90

14. 601.584 to the nearest tenth 601.6

15. 3.9015 to the nearest thousandth 3.902

16. 42.3952 to the nearest thousandth 42.395

17. 9.00391 to the nearest ten-thousandth 9.0039

18. 0.92403 to the nearest ten-thousandth 0.9240

19. 18.670308 to the nearest hundred-thousandth 18.67031

20. 3.0040916 to the nearest hundred-thousandth 3.00409

Skills Workshop 3

ADD AND SUBTRACT WHOLE NUMBERS AND DECIMALS

To add or subtract whole numbers and decimals, write the digits so the place values line up. Add from right to left, renaming when necessary. When adding or subtracting decimals, be sure to place the decimal point directly below the aligned decimals in the problem.

EXAMPLE 1

Find the sum of 0.058, 25.39, 6,346, and 1.57.

The answer is called the **total** or **sum**.

SOLUTION

```
      1  2
     0.058    The red zero is used to
    25.39     show there are no ones.
 6,346.       The decimal point is at
 +   1.57     the end of whole numbers.
 6,373.018    Add from right to left.
```

EXAMPLE 2

Find the difference between 10,049 and 5,364.

The answer is called the **difference**.

SOLUTION

```
    9 10 14
  10,049      Rename as needed to
 -  5,364     subtract.
   4,685
```

EXAMPLE 3

Subtract 6.37 from 27.

The smaller number is subtracted from the larger.

SOLUTION

```
   6 10 10
  27.00       Add a decimal point and
 - 6.37       zeros if that helps you
  20.63       complete the subtraction.
```

Add or subtract.

1. 23.146 + 17.215   40.361

2. 46.48 − 6.57   39.91

3. 52 − 1.95   50.05

4. 0.86 + 0.75   1.61

5. 83 − 82.743   0.257

6. 9.45 + 13.2   22.65

7. 14.5 − 9.684   4.816

8. 6.4 + 54.2 + 938.05 + 3.7 + 47.3   1,049.65

9. 913.03 − 79   834.03

10. 1,765.36 + 1,587.50 + 1,400   4,752.86

11. 0.8523 − 0.794   0.0583

12. 51,876.36 + 48,156.95 + 1,417.86   101,451.17

13. 17,347.85 − 12,516.90   4,830.95

14. 76.2 + 80 + 56 + 9.321   221.521

15. 107,285 − 61,500.25   45,784.75

16. 567.1 + 6 + 13.452 + 100   686.552

17. 6.013 + 39 + 14.09   59.103

18. 4.621 + 372.14   376.761

19. 1,468,329 − 370,418.5   1,097,910.5

20. 472.13 + 1,695.006 + 27.127   2,194.263

Skills Workshop 4

MULTIPLY WHOLE NUMBERS AND DECIMALS

To multiply whole numbers, find each partial product and then add.

The red zeros are added to help align the answers.

Add. Then rewrite the answer with commas.

EXAMPLE 1 Multiply 5,754 by 236.

SOLUTION	5,754	factor
	× 236	factor
	34524	5,754 × 6
	172620	5,754 × 30
	1150800	5,754 × 200
	1357944	Add.
	1,357,944	product

When multiplying decimals, locate the decimal point in the product so that there are as many decimal places in the product as the total number of decimal places in the factors.

EXAMPLE 2 Multiply 2.6394 by 3,000.

SOLUTION	2.6394	4 decimal places
	× 3,000	0 decimal places
	7,918.2000	4 decimal places
	or 7,918.2	

Zeros at the end (far right) *after* the decimal point can be dropped because they are not *significant digits*.

EXAMPLE 3 Multiply 3.92 by 0.023.

SOLUTION	3.92	2 decimal places
	× 0.023	+3 decimal places
	1176	
	7840	
	0.09016	5 decimal places

The red zero is added *before* the nine, so the product will have five decimal places.

Multiply.

1. 36 × 45
   1,620
2. 500 × 30
   15,000
3. 17,000 × 230
   3,910,000
4. 6.2 × 8
   49.6
5. 950 × 1.6
   1,520
6. 3.652 × 20
   73.04
7. 179 × 83
   14,857
8. 257 × 320
   82,240
9. 8,560 × 275
   2,354,000
10. 467 × 0.3
    140.1
11. 2.63 × 183
    481.29
12. 0.758 × 321.8
    243.9244
13. 49.3 × 1.6
    78.88
14. 6.859 × 7.9
    54.1861
15. 794.4 × 321.8
    255,637.92
16. 0.08 × 4
    0.32
17. 0.062 × 0.5
    0.031
18. 0.0135 × 0.003
    0.0000405
19. 21.6 × 3.1
    66.96
20. 8.76 × 0.005
    0.0438

Skills Workshop 5

DIVIDE WHOLE NUMBERS AND DECIMALS

Dividing whole numbers and decimals involves a repetitive process of estimating a quotient, multiplying, and subtracting.

EXAMPLE 1 Find 239 ÷ 7.

SOLUTION

$$
\begin{array}{r}
34 \\
7\overline{)239} \\
-21\downarrow \\
\hline
29 \\
-28 \\
\hline
1
\end{array}
$$

3 × 7
Subtract. Bring down the 9.
4 × 7

> **MATH TIP**
>
> In Example 1, 239 is the dividend, 7 is the divisor, 34 is the quotient, and 1 is the remainder.

EXAMPLE 2 Find 283.86 ÷ 5.7.

SOLUTION When dividing decimals, move the decimal point in the divisor to the right until it is a whole number. Move the decimal point in the dividend the same number of places that you moved the decimal point in the divisor. Then place the decimal point in the answer directly above the new location of the decimal point in the dividend.

$$
5.7.\overline{)283.8.6} \rightarrow
\begin{array}{r}
49.8 \\
57\overline{)2838.6} \\
-228 \\
\hline
558 \\
-513 \\
\hline
45\ 6 \\
-45\ 6 \\
\hline
0
\end{array}
$$

If answers do not have a remainder of 0, you can add 0's after the last digit and continue dividing.

Divide.

1. 72 ÷ 6   12
2. 6,000 ÷ 2   3,000
3. 26,568 ÷ 8   3,321
4. 5.6 ÷ 7   0.8
5. 120 ÷ 0.4   300
6. 936 ÷ 12   78
7. 3.28 ÷ 4   0.82
8. 0.1960 ÷ 5   0.0392
9. 1968 ÷ 0.08   24,600
10. 16 ÷ 0.04   400
11. 1525 ÷ 0.05   30,500
12. 109.94 ÷ 0.23   478
13. 0.6 ÷ 24   0.025
14. 7.924 ÷ 0.28   28.3
15. 32.6417 ÷ 9.1   3.587
16. 24 ÷ 0.6   40
17. 1,784.75 ÷ 29.5   60.5
18. 0.01998 ÷ 0.37   0.054
19. 7.8 ÷ 0.3   26
20. 12,000 ÷ 0.04   300,000
21. 820.94 ÷ 0.02   41,047
22. 121.55 ÷ 18.7   6.5
23. 29,000 ÷ 1,450   20
24. 5929.52 ÷ 9.4   630.8
25. 618.03 ÷ 12.6   49.05
26. 22.1616 ÷ 34.2   0.648
27. 235,083.36 ÷ 67.09   3,504

Skills Workshop 6

AVERAGE OF A GROUP OF NUMBERS

An **average**, or **mean**, is a measure of central tendency. To find the average of a group of numbers, find the sum of the numbers, and then divide the sum by the number of items in the group.

EXAMPLE 1 Find the average of $36, $49, $22, $48, $39, $40, and $18.

SOLUTION Find the sum of the numbers.
$36 + $49 + $22 + $48 + $39 + $40 + $18 = $252
Count how many items are in the group.
Divide the sum by 7 since there are 7 items.
$\frac{\$252}{7} = \$36$
The average of the set of numbers is $36.

EXAMPLE 2 Find the average of the following set of numbers.
3.2, 4.2, 6.05, 9.25, 5, 7.1, 9.8, 12.4, 3.3

SOLUTION Find the sum of the numbers.
3.2 + 4.2 + 6.05 + 9.25 + 5 + 7.1 + 9.8 + 12.4 + 3.3 = 60.3
Count how many items are in the group.
Divide the sum by 9 since there are 9 items.
$\frac{60.3}{9} = 6.7$
The average of the set of numbers is 6.7.

Find the average of each set of numbers.

1. 85, 60, 72, 68, 95, 83, 97, 84 80.5

2. $125, $149, $135, $146 $138.75

3. 260, 362, 302, 381, 295, 332, 280 316

4. 37, 28, 33, 30, 25, 15 28

5. 32,052, 33,559, 30,129, 34,058 32,449.5

6. 1.1, 1.5, 1.8, 2.7, 1.6 1.74

7. 6, 8, 9, 6, 3, 4, 6, 8, 7, 8, 6, 5, 9, 9, 8 6.8

8. $17, $24, $28, $16, $28, $17, $18, $24, $22, $25, $29, $25 $22.75

9. $625, $501, $399, $572, $459, $680, $377, $540 $519.13

10. 2.5, 3.5, 2.6, 2.8, 2.4, 3.2, 2.3, 3.1 2.8

11. 24.5, 20.5, 22.4, 28.2, 25, 23.7 24.05

12. $10.25, $12.32, $11.24, $13.08, $14.48, $10.76, $15.30 $12.49

13. 135.05, 241.62, 452.13, 105.95, 261.48 239.246

14. 9.1, 9.4, 9.9, 8.9, 9.3, 9.1, 9.1, 9.4, 8.8, 9.4 9.24

15. $545, $425, $600, $562, $399, $457 $498

16. $135.06, $132.29, $145.92, $162.37, $127.55, $144.26, $150.05, $138.42 $141.99

Skills Workshop 7

MULTIPLY AND DIVIDE FRACTIONS

To multiply fractions, multiply the numerators and then multiply the denominators. Write the answer in simplest form.

EXAMPLE 1 Multiply $\frac{2}{5}$ and $\frac{7}{8}$.

SOLUTION $\frac{2}{5} \times \frac{7}{8} = \frac{2 \times 7}{5 \times 8}$

$$= \frac{14}{40}$$

$$= \frac{7}{20}$$

To divide by a fraction, multiply by the reciprocal of that fraction. To find the reciprocal of a fraction, invert (turn upside down) the fraction. The product of a fraction and its reciprocal is 1. Since $\frac{2}{3} \times \frac{3}{2} = \frac{6}{6}$ or 1, $\frac{2}{3}$ and $\frac{3}{2}$ are reciprocals of each other.

EXAMPLE 2 Divide $1\frac{1}{5}$ by $\frac{2}{3}$.

SOLUTION $1\frac{1}{5} \div \frac{2}{3} = \frac{6}{5} \div \frac{2}{3}$ Write the mixed number as a fraction.

$$= \frac{6}{5} \times \frac{3}{2}$$ Rewrite division as multiplication by the inverse of the divisor.

$$= \frac{6 \times 3}{5 \times 2}$$ Multiply and simplify.

$$= \frac{18}{10}$$

$$= 1\frac{4}{5}$$

Multiply or divide. Write each answer in simplest form.

1. $\frac{2}{3} \div \frac{5}{6}$ $\frac{4}{5}$

2. $\frac{3}{5} \times \frac{10}{12}$ $\frac{1}{2}$

3. $\frac{5}{8} \div \frac{1}{4}$ $2\frac{1}{2}$

4. $\frac{1}{2} \times \frac{2}{3}$ $\frac{1}{3}$

5. $\frac{2}{3} \times \frac{1}{2}$ $\frac{1}{3}$

6. $\frac{3}{4} \times \frac{5}{8}$ $\frac{15}{32}$

7. $\frac{1}{2} \div \frac{2}{3}$ $\frac{3}{4}$

8. $\frac{2}{3} \div \frac{1}{2}$ $1\frac{1}{3}$

9. $\frac{3}{4} \div \frac{5}{8}$ $1\frac{1}{5}$

10. $2\frac{2}{3} \div 1\frac{3}{5}$ $1\frac{2}{3}$

11. $1\frac{1}{5} \times 2\frac{1}{4}$ $2\frac{7}{10}$

12. $3\frac{1}{3} \times 1\frac{1}{10}$ $3\frac{2}{3}$

13. $5\frac{2}{5} \div 2\frac{4}{7}$ $2\frac{1}{10}$

14. $2\frac{4}{7} \div 5\frac{2}{5}$ $\frac{10}{21}$

15. $2\frac{4}{7} \times 5\frac{2}{5}$ $13\frac{31}{35}$

16. $1\frac{7}{8} \div 1\frac{7}{8}$ 1

17. $\frac{3}{4} \times \frac{2}{3} \times 1\frac{5}{8} \times 2\frac{2}{3}$ $2\frac{1}{6}$

18. $\frac{1}{8} \times \frac{3}{4} \times 1\frac{2}{3} \times \frac{7}{10}$ $\frac{7}{64}$

19. $5\frac{1}{8} \times 3\frac{4}{5}$ $19\frac{19}{40}$

20. $1\frac{4}{7} \div 7\frac{5}{6}$ $\frac{66}{329}$

21. $6\frac{3}{4} \times 9\frac{7}{8}$ $66\frac{21}{32}$

Skills Workshop 8

ADD FRACTIONS

To add fractions with a common denominator, add the numerators and write the sum over the denominator they have in common. Then write the answer in simplest form.

EXAMPLE 1 Add $\frac{7}{8}$ and $\frac{3}{8}$.

SOLUTION

$$\begin{array}{r} \frac{7}{8} \\ +\frac{3}{8} \\ \hline \frac{10}{8} \end{array}$$

Add the numerators.
Use the common denominator.

$$\frac{10}{8} = 1\frac{2}{8} = 1\frac{1}{4}$$

To add fractions without a common denominator, first find a common denominator by finding the least common multiple of the denominators. Next, rename each fraction with an equivalent fraction using the common denominator. Then add the numerators and write the sum over their common denominator. Write the answer in simplest form.

EXAMPLE 2 Add $\frac{3}{4}$ and $\frac{5}{6}$.

SOLUTION

$$\begin{array}{rcl} \frac{3}{4} = \frac{3}{4} \times \frac{3}{3} = & \frac{9}{12} \\ +\frac{5}{6} = \frac{5}{6} \times \frac{2}{2} = & +\frac{10}{12} \\ \hline & \frac{19}{12} \end{array}$$

Add the numerators.
Use the common denominator.

Then simplify. $\quad \frac{19}{12} = 1\frac{7}{12}$

Add. Write each answer in simplest form.

1. $\frac{1}{5} + \frac{2}{5}$ $\frac{3}{5}$ ✓

2. $\frac{2}{3} + \frac{1}{3}$ 1

3. $\frac{8}{9} + \frac{4}{9}$ $1\frac{1}{3}$

4. $\frac{11}{15} + \frac{4}{15}$ 1

5. $\frac{1}{5} + \frac{1}{10}$ $\frac{3}{10}$

6. $\frac{5}{8} + \frac{3}{4}$ $1\frac{3}{8}$

7. $\frac{16}{21} + \frac{2}{21}$ $\frac{6}{7}$

8. $\frac{6}{7} + \frac{1}{3}$ $1\frac{4}{21}$

9. $\frac{11}{14} + \frac{3}{4}$ $1\frac{15}{28}$

10. $2\frac{1}{2} + 3\frac{1}{2}$ 6

11. $6\frac{5}{8} + 3\frac{7}{8}$ $10\frac{1}{2}$

12. $3\frac{2}{3} + 4\frac{1}{2}$ $8\frac{1}{6}$

13. $6\frac{1}{2} + 5\frac{7}{9}$ $12\frac{5}{8}$ $12\frac{5}{18}$

14. $7\frac{2}{3} + 6\frac{1}{5}$ $13\frac{13}{15}$

15. $11\frac{4}{5} + 9\frac{1}{4}$ $21\frac{1}{20}$

16. $4\frac{3}{8} + 2\frac{1}{6}$ $6\frac{13}{24}$

17. $11\frac{2}{5} + 9\frac{4}{9}$ $20\frac{38}{45}$

18. $5\frac{3}{10} + 13\frac{7}{8}$ $19\frac{7}{40}$

19. $3\frac{1}{2} + 9\frac{4}{5} + 2\frac{2}{5}$ $15\frac{7}{10}$

20. $1\frac{1}{5} + 2\frac{1}{3} + 5\frac{1}{4}$ $8\frac{47}{60}$

21. $10\frac{7}{8} + 3\frac{3}{4} + 6\frac{1}{2} + 2\frac{5}{8}$ $23\frac{3}{4}$

Skills Workshop 9

SUBTRACT FRACTIONS

To subtract fractions with a common denominator, subtract the numerators and write the difference over the common denominator. Then write the answer in simplest form.

EXAMPLE 1 Find the difference of $\frac{7}{8} - \frac{3}{8}$.

SOLUTION
$$\begin{array}{r} \frac{7}{8} \\ -\frac{3}{8} \\ \hline \frac{4}{8} \end{array}$$

To subtract fractions without a common denominator, first find a common denominator by finding the least common multiple of the denominators. Next, rename each fraction with an equivalent fraction using the common denominator. Then subtract the numerators and write the difference over the common denominator. Write the answer in simplest form.

EXAMPLE 2 Subtract $1\frac{3}{5}$ from $5\frac{1}{2}$.

SOLUTION
$$\begin{array}{r} 5\frac{1}{2} = \quad 5\frac{5}{10} = \quad 4\frac{15}{10} \\ -1\frac{3}{5} = -1\frac{6}{10} = -1\frac{6}{10} \\ \hline 3\frac{9}{10} \end{array}$$

You can not subtract $\frac{6}{10}$ from $\frac{5}{10}$, so rename again.

Subtract. Write each answer in simplest form.

1. $\frac{6}{7} - \frac{2}{7}$ $\frac{4}{7}$

2. $\frac{4}{9} - \frac{2}{9}$ $\frac{2}{9}$

3. $\frac{7}{16} - \frac{3}{16}$ $\frac{1}{4}$

4. $\frac{9}{11} - \frac{6}{11}$ $\frac{3}{11}$

5. $\frac{3}{4} - \frac{1}{3}$ $\frac{5}{12}$

6. $\frac{5}{8} - \frac{1}{4}$ $\frac{3}{8}$

7. $\frac{7}{12} - \frac{1}{6}$ $\frac{5}{12}$

8. $\frac{9}{10} - \frac{3}{4}$ $\frac{3}{20}$

9. $\frac{15}{16} - \frac{5}{8}$ $\frac{5}{16}$

10. $\frac{7}{8} - \frac{1}{5}$ $\frac{27}{40}$

11. $\frac{5}{8} - \frac{1}{12}$ $\frac{13}{24}$

12. $\frac{3}{5} - \frac{7}{12}$ $\frac{1}{60}$

13. $2\frac{3}{4} - 1\frac{1}{4}$ $1\frac{1}{2}$

14. $5\frac{1}{8} - 3\frac{7}{8}$ $1\frac{1}{4}$

15. $1\frac{1}{3} - \frac{2}{3}$ $\frac{2}{3}$

16. $8\frac{1}{10} - 5\frac{2}{3}$ $2\frac{13}{30}$

17. $6\frac{1}{2} - 5\frac{3}{5}$ $\frac{9}{10}$

18. $10\frac{5}{8} - 9\frac{3}{4}$ $\frac{7}{8}$

19. $10\frac{1}{4} - 9\frac{5}{7}$ $\frac{15}{28}$

20. $15\frac{5}{6} - 13\frac{2}{3}$ $2\frac{1}{6}$

21. $5\frac{1}{2} - 3\frac{4}{11}$ $2\frac{3}{22}$

22. $24\frac{4}{7} - 8\frac{5}{12}$ $16\frac{13}{84}$

23. $8\frac{4}{9} - 8\frac{3}{10}$ $\frac{13}{90}$

24. $37\frac{7}{8} - 33\frac{8}{9}$ $3\frac{71}{72}$

Skills Workshop 10

FRACTIONS, DECIMALS, AND PERCENTS

Percent means *per hundred*. Thus, 35% means 35 out of 100. Percents can be written as equivalent decimals and fractions.

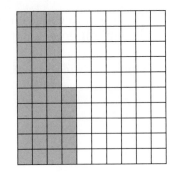

$$35\% = 0.35 \quad \text{Move the decimal point two places to the left.}$$

$$35\% = \frac{35}{100} \quad \text{Write the fraction with a denominator of 100.}$$

$$= \frac{7}{20} \quad \text{Then simplify.}$$

EXAMPLE Write $\frac{3}{8}$ as a decimal and as a percent.

SOLUTION $\frac{3}{8} = 0.375$ To change a fraction to a percent, first divide and write the answer as a decimal. Then change the decimal to a percent

$0.375 = 37.5\%$ by moving the decimal point two places to the right and adding a percent symbol.

Percents greater than 100% represent whole numbers or mixed numbers.

$$200\% = 2 \text{ or } 2.00 \qquad 350\% = 3.5 \text{ or } 3\frac{1}{2}$$

Complete each table. Write all fractions in simplest form.

	Fraction	Decimal	Percent		Fraction	Decimal	Percent
1.	$\frac{1}{2}$	0.5	50%	**8.**	$\frac{3}{4}$	0.75	75%
2.	$\frac{63}{100}$	0.63	63%	**9.**	$\frac{2}{5}$	0.4	40%
3.	$\frac{1}{10}$	0.10	10%	**10.**	$1\frac{1}{2}$	1.5	150%
4.	$\frac{1}{4}$	0.25	25%	**11.**	$2\frac{7}{20}$	2.35	235%
5.	$\frac{3}{20}$	0.15	15%	**12.**	$3\frac{7}{8}$	3.875	387.5%
6.	$\frac{3}{25}$	0.12	12%	**13.**	$1\frac{3}{5}$	1.6	160%
7.	1	1	100%	**14.**	$10\frac{1}{8}$	10.125	1012.5%

Skills Workshop 11

PERCENT

To find a percent of a number, first write the percent as a decimal by moving the decimal point two places to the left. Then multiply the given number by this decimal.

EXAMPLE 1 Find 20% of 275.

SOLUTION Write 20% as a decimal.

20% = 0.2

Multiply.

$$\begin{array}{r} 275 \\ \times\ 0.2 \\ \hline 55.0 \end{array}$$

So 20% of 275 is 55.

To find what percent a number is of another number, write a fraction where the numerator is the part and the denominator is the whole. Reduce the fraction if possible. Then divide to change the fraction to a decimal. Finally change the decimal to a percent.

> **MATH TIP**
>
> The *whole* is the number that comes after the word *"of."*

EXAMPLE 2 What percent of 50 is 16?

SOLUTION Write a fraction and reduce. $\frac{16}{50} = \frac{8}{25}$

Divide.

$$\begin{array}{r} 0.32 \\ 25\overline{)8.00} \\ \underline{75} \\ 50 \\ \underline{50} \\ 0 \end{array}$$

0.32 = 32%

So, 16 is 32% of 50.

Find each percent.

1. 2% of 18 0.36
2. 21% of 54 11.34
3. 85% of 400 340
4. 25% of 384 96
5. 27% of 12.2 3.294
6. 82% of 55 45.1
7. 34% of 2,200 748
8. 72.5% of 340 246.5
9. 6% of 12,500 750

Find the following.

10. What percent of 60 is 42? 70%
11. What percent of 5 is 2? 40%
12. 9 is what percent of 36? 25%
13. What percent of 45 is 36? 80%
14. What percent of 125 is 32? 25.6%
15. 81 is what percent of 3,600? 2.25%
16. 28 is what percent of 32? 87.5%
17. What percent of 63 is 63? 100%
18. What percent of 112 is 21? 18.75%
19. 114 is what percent of 475? 24%

Skills Workshop 12

ESTIMATION SKILLS

You can round numbers to find the estimated sum, difference, product, or quotient. Round the numbers to the highest place value they have in common and then perform the operation.

EXAMPLE 1 Find the estimated difference of $6,452 - 2,806$.

SOLUTION Round each number to the nearest thousandth.

$$6,000 - 3,000 = 3,000 \quad \text{The difference is about 3,000.}$$

You can use **front-end estimation** to find an estimated sum, difference, product, or quotient. Use only the front digit of each number and the rest of the digits become zero.

EXAMPLE 2 Find the estimated product of 842×67 using front-end estimation.

SOLUTION
$$
\begin{array}{r} 842 \\ \times\ 67 \end{array} \longrightarrow
\begin{array}{r} 800 \\ \times\ 60 \\ \hline 48,000 \end{array} \quad \text{The product is about 48,000.}
$$

You can use **adjusted front-end estimation** by looking at more than the front digits to get an answer that is more accurate.

EXAMPLE 3 Find the estimated sum of $4,367 + 5,735$ using adjusted front-end estimation.

SOLUTION
$$
\begin{array}{r} 4,\boxed{367} \\ +\ 5,\boxed{735} \\ \hline 9,000 \end{array} \longrightarrow \text{about } 1,000
$$

$9,000 \quad + \quad 1,000 = 10,000 \quad$ The sum is about 10,000.

Estimate by rounding the numbers.

1. $395 + 842$ 1,200
2. $9,940 - 2,504$ 7,000
3. 459×34 13,800
4. $837 \div 38$ 21
5. $34,651 + 84,648$ 110,000
6. $668,345 - 229,048$ 500,000
7. $\$338 \times 22$ $6,800
8. $\$39,648 \div 196$ $198
9. $\$75,045 - \$8,654$ $66,000

Use front-end estimation to perform each operation.

10. 248×49 8,000
11. $6,482 + 8,248$ 14,000
12. $946 \div 305$ 3
13. $8,459 - 6,218$ 2,000
14. $84,516 + 3,811$ 83,000
15. $\$735 \times 63$ $42,000
16. $\$245,364 - \$19,563$ $190,000
17. $946 + 358 + 205$ 1,400
18. $\$6480 \div 231$ $30

Use adjusted front-end estimation to perform each operation.

19. $5,638 + 3,281$ 9,000
20. $867 - 311$ 550
21. 326×284 90,000
22. $2,942 + 9,133$ 12,000
23. 649×48 32,500
24. $81,506 - 9,408$ 71,000
25. $\$3,945 - \$3,108$ $800
26. $\$1,235 \times 72$ $84,000
27. $948 + 629 + 755 + 371$ 2,700

ELAPSED TIME

The amount of time that passes between two given times is called elapsed time. You can find elapsed time by finding the difference in the earlier time and the later time.

EXAMPLE 1 Find the elapsed time from 9:15 A.M. to 10:55 A.M.

SOLUTION Subtract the earlier time from the later time.

$$
\begin{array}{r}
10:55 \\
-\ 9:15 \\
\hline
1:40
\end{array}
$$

The elapsed time is 1 hour and 40 minutes.

Sometimes you are not able to subtract the number of minutes in the earlier time from the number of minutes in the later time. When this happens, rewrite the later time with 1 less hour and 60 more minutes.

If one of the times is A.M. and the other is P.M., add 12 hours to the later time before finding the difference.

EXAMPLE 2 Find the elapsed time from 11:40 A.M. to 3:30 P.M.

SOLUTION Subtract the earlier time from the later time. / Rewrite 3:30 as 2:90 / Add 12 hours to 2:90 since one time is A.M. and the other is P.M.

$$
\begin{array}{r}
3:30 \\
-11:40 \\
\hline
\end{array}
\qquad
\begin{array}{r}
2:90 \\
-11:40 \\
\hline
\end{array}
\qquad
\begin{array}{r}
2:90 + 12:00 \\
-\ 11:40 \\
\hline
\end{array}
\qquad
\begin{array}{r}
14:90 \\
-11:40 \\
\hline
3:50
\end{array}
$$

The elapsed time is 3 hours and 50 minutes.

Find the elapsed time.

1. from 5:00 P.M. to 11:00 P.M.
   6 hours
2. from 6:15 A.M. to 9:15 A.M.
   3 hours
3. from 2:10 P.M. to 7:33 P.M.
   5 hours 23 minutes
4. from 12:30 P.M. to 8:45 P.M.
   8 hours 15 minutes
5. from 8:00 A.M. to 5:00 P.M.
   9 hours
6. from 1:42 P.M. to 3:17 P.M.
   1 hour 35 minutes
7. from 2:55 A.M. to 9:45 A.M.
   6 hours 50 minutes
8. from 8:15 P.M. to 2:30 A.M.
   6 hours 15 minutes
9. from 11:00 A.M. to 9:00 P.M.
   10 hours
10. from 11:47 A.M. to 12:45 P.M.
    58 minutes
11. from 4:12 P.M. to 1:33 A.M.
    9 hours 21 minutes
12. from 7:10 A.M. to 9: 30 P.M.
    14 hours 20 minutes
13. from 3:30 P.M. to 3:50 A.M.
    12 hours 20 minutes
14. from 9:33 P.M. to 4:08 A.M.
    6 hours 35 minutes
15. from 7:34 A.M. to 4:18 P.M.
    8 hours 44 minutes
16. from 1:42 P.M. to 3:37 A.M.
    13 hours 55 minutes
17. from 4:18 P.M. to 2:03 A.M.
    9 hours 45 minutes
18. from 7:56 A.M. to 5:12 P.M.
    9 hours 16 minutes

PROBLEM SOLVING: 4-STEP PLAN

When solving word problems it is helpful to follow a 4-step plan.

1. **Understand** Read the problem and determine what information is given and what it is you are to find.

2. **Plan** Determine the method or strategy you will use to solve the problem.

3. **Solve** Carry out your plan to find an answer to the problem.

4. **Look Back** Go back over the problem and your answer to determine if your answer makes sense and make sure your computations are correct.

EXAMPLE 1 Jessica is buying two sheets of $0.34 stamps from a vending machine. There are 20 stamps on each sheet. If she needs to put the exact amount of money in the vending machine, how much money does she need?

SOLUTION **Understand** It is given that Jessica is buying 2 sheets of 20 stamps. Each stamp costs $0.34. You are to find the total cost.

Plan First find the cost of one sheet. Then double this amount to find the cost of both sheets.

Solve $0.34 × 20 = $6.80   The cost of one sheet of stamps is $6.80
$6.80 × 2 = $13.60

The exact amount of money Jessica needs for the stamps is $13.60.

Look Back You can use estimation to determine if your answer makes sense. Round the amount of one stamp to $0.30.

$0.30 × 20 = $6.00
$6.00 × 2 = $12.00

Since the stamps are slightly more than $0.30, the answer $13.60 makes sense.

Use the 4-step plan to solve each problem.

1. Latoya earns $1.75 an hour for each child she baby-sits. How much does she earn if she baby-sits 3 children for 4 hours? $21

2. James works at a department store and receives a 25% discount on his purchases. He purchases some new clothes at the store and his total before the discount is $145.20. What is James's total after the discount? $108.90

3. Kegan borrows $78 from his sister. He will pay her back over a 4-week period. If he pays the same amount each week, how much will he have paid back after the third week? $58.50

4. Ashley stops by the grocery to pick up a few items. She buys a loaf of bread for $1.09, a pound of turkey for $4.59, 2 cans of soup for $0.79 each, and 4 oranges for $0.27 each. How much money does Ashley spend at the grocery? $8.34

5. Jackie buys a one-way ticket to Nevada and a one-way ticket back home. Each way costs $118. Joe buys a round-trip ticket to Nevada for $227. Whose ticket is less? By how much? Joe's ticket; $9

Skills Workshop 15

METRIC MEASURES

The basic metric units are meter (length), liter (capacity), and gram (mass or weight). All measurements can be expressed in terms of these three basic units. However, prefixes are used with the basic units to avoid dealing with very large and very small numbers.

The same prefixes are used for length, capacity, and mass.

1,000 m	100 m	10 m	1 m	0.1 m	0.01 m	0.001 m
kilo-meter	hecto-meter	deca-meter	meter	deci-meter	centi-meter	milli-meter
km	hm	dam	m	dm	cm	mm

1,000 L	100 L	10 L	1 L	0.1 L	0.01 L	0.001 L
kilo-liter	hecto-liter	deca-liter	liter	deci-liter	centi-liter	milli-liter
kL	hL	daL	L	dL	cL	mL

1,000 g	100 g	10 g	1 g	0.1 g	0.01 g	0.001 g
kilo-gram	hecto-gram	deca-gram	gram	deci-gram	centi-gram	milli-gram
kg	hg	dag	g	dg	cg	mg

EXAMPLE 1 Change 0.68 meters to centimeters

SOLUTION Think: 1 meter = 100 centimeters
So 0.68 meters = 68 centimeters   Move the decimal point to the right 2 spaces.

EXAMPLE 2 Change 8000 grams to kilograms

SOLUTION Think: 1000 grams = 1 kilogram
So 8000 grams = 8 kilometers   Move the decimal point to the left 3 spaces.

EXAMPLE 3 Change 5.2 liters to milliliters

SOLUTION Think: 1 liter = 1000 milliliters
So 5.2 liters = 5200 milliliters   Move the decimal point to the right 3 spaces.

Change each measurement to the named unit.

1. 76 grams to centigrams 7,600
2. 88 milliliters to liters 0.088
3. 200 meters to millimeters 200,000
4. 34 kiloliters to centiliters 3,400,000
5. 123 milligrams to grams 0.123
6. 7,065 liters to kiloliters 7.065
7. 4.35 grams to hectograms 0.0435
8. 0.98 meters to centimeters 98
9. 12.5 kilograms to grams 12,500
10. 44 decimeters to millimeters 4,400
11. 600 kilograms to centigrams 60,000,000
12. 0.025 liters to kiloliters 0.000025

Gross Pay

Chapter Overview

Chapter 1 reviews the math skills of addition, subtraction, multiplication, division, rounding, fractions, and percents. These skills are used to calculate gross pay for hourly, salary, commission, piece-rate, per diem, or tip employees.

Lesson 1.1 Hourly Pay and Salary
Students learn to find the gross pay for hourly-rate and salaried employees.

Lesson 1.2 Average Pay
Students use gross pay amounts to calculate simple and grouped-data averages and find the unknown item in a set of data.

Lesson 1.3 Regular and Overtime Pay
Students calculate the number of overtime hours, overtime pay rates, and regular and overtime pay.

Lesson 1.4 Commission
Students learn to find straight, quota-based, and graduated commissions and the rate of commission.

Lesson 1.5 Other Wage Plans
Students calculate the gross wages of employees paid on a piece-rate, per diem, and tip basis.

Statistical Insights

Category	Examples	Range of Hourly Compensation
White Collar	engineers, nurses, accountants, insurance agents, cashiers, hotel clerks, computer operators	$14.34–$33.12
Blue Collar	carpenters, electricians, truck drivers, material handlers, stockers, production inspectors	$12.07–$22.12
Service	security guards, nursing aides, janitors, barbers, food service	$5.65–$10.61

Use the data shown above to answer each question.
1. Is the data presented in a way that an average overall income can be figured? Explain. No. The wages are given as a range. Also, the number of workers is not given.
2. Explain one reason why white collar compensations differ by $18.78 and service compensations differ by only $4.96. Answers will vary. Possible answer: the education and experience levels of white collar workers vary greatly resulting in a broader range of wages.

Statistical Insights

Workers are often referred to as blue collar or white collar. Have students look at the examples of job titles of both types of workers and draw a general conclusion about the difference in their work. Also ask students if, given the range of hourly compensation, it is possible for a blue-collar worker to earn more than a white-collar worker and a service worker to earn more than a blue-collar worker.

NetCheck

Online Career Search

Today, in addition to looking for a job in the want ads or having an agency provide assistance, help is available on the Internet. Career search web sites help to locate job openings. Someone looking for a job can post a resume, and a summary of job qualifications, on the site. Potential employers can then view the resumes. When employers find a person whose qualifications match those required by their company, they can contact the person.

Is the Income Fair?

If someone finds a job in another part of the country, the pay being offered needs to be in line with the cost of living in that region. Many Internet web sites allow you to select a city and state and then compare the cost of living between two cities. Average income information is also available at these web sites.

Teaching Resources

Lesson Plans, Ch. 1
Chapter 1 Test Forms A and B
Workbook, Ch. 1
Explore Algebra and Geometry
   Activities
Technology Activities
Competitive Events Prep
Data Activities CD, Ch. 1
ExamView® Pro CD, Ch. 1

NetCheck

Online Career Search Work with students on searches for Internet job posting web sites. Suggest keywords such as jobs, find a job, job postings, careers, and help wanted to get them started. Have them review any requirements the web site has regarding the format of data to be posted, length of posting, security, and any costs connected with the posting.

Have students make notes of their findings and share them with others in class discussion.

Is the Income Fair? Help students find and use web sites that contain comparative wage data. Also have students select a city and see if it has a web site that provides information about employment potential and wages. Some keywords are comparative wages and municipal web sites.

How Times Have Changed

The minimum wage does not automatically rise with inflation. It is up to Congress to determine when and how much to raise the minimum wage. The 25-cent minimum wage set by Congress in 1938 seems extraordinarily low by today's standards. However, when taking inflation into account, 25 cents in 1938 had the buying power of $3.35 in 2004.

Massachusetts enacts the earliest minimum wage law in the U.S. **1912**

Minimum wage: $0.40/hour (effective Oct. 24) **1945**

Minimum wage: $2.65/hour **1978**

Research to find the minimum wage introduced in 1991.

1900　1920　1940　1960　1980　2000

1938 The federal government sets the minimum wage at $0.25/hour.

1968 Minimum wage: $1.60/hour

1981 Minimum wage: $3.35/hour

1997 Minimum wage: $5.15/hour

Answer to research item:

The minimum wage was raised to $4.25 an hour on April 1, 1991.

The U.S. Department of Labor provides a CPI inflation calculator at its web site:
http://www.bls.gov/bls/inflation.htm

3

HOW TIMES HAVE CHANGED

Possible questions to ask:
What is the current minimum wage? ($5.15 in 2004) When was the last minimum wage increase? (1997) When do you think the next minimum increase will be? Do you think the minimum wage will go up or down in the future? Why do you think

minimum wages are necessary?
Turn the students' attention to the timeline. Have them do their own research to find the minimum wage introduced in April 1991. See page 36 for assessment questions related to the timeline.

Hourly Pay and Salary

GOALS

- Calculate gross pay for hourly-rate employees
- Calculate gross pay for salaried employees

Start Up

Sarah has a new job as an assistant manager in a shoe department. She will work 54 hours each week and earn $15 an hour. For this work schedule and rate of pay, is it possible for Sarah's gross pay for one month to be at least $3,750?

Math Skill Builder

Review these math skills and solve the exercises that follow.

1 **Add** money amounts.
Find the sum. $430 + $95 = $525

  1a. $450 + $76 $526   **1b.** $1,600 + $14,750 $16,350

2 **Multiply** money amounts by whole numbers.
Find the product. 24 × $9 = $216

  2a. 35 × $8 $280   **2b.** 52 × $355 $18,460

3 **Multiply** numbers with end zeros.
Find the product. 20 × $310 = $6,200

  3a. 40 × $12 $480   **3b.** 50 × $460 $23,000

4 **Multiply** numbers with decimals.
Find the product. 8 × $9.42 = $75.36

  4a. 7 × $8.15 $57.05   **4b.** 6.5 × $11.46 $74.49

> **MATH TIP**
>
> Write whole dollar amounts in your answers as whole numbers without decimals. For example, write $525, not $525.00.

■ Gross Pay for Hourly-Rate Employees

Most people earn money by working for others. Those who work for others are called **employees**. The person or company an employee works for is called an **employer**.

An employee who is paid by the hour works for an **hourly rate**, which is a certain amount for each hour worked. The total amount of money that an employee is paid is called **gross pay** or *gross wages*. Gross pay may also be called total earnings or total pay.

The gross pay earned by employees who are paid by the hour is found by multiplying the pay per hour by the hours worked.

Hourly Rate × Number of Hours Worked = Gross Pay

EXAMPLE 1

Mark Willow works as a customer service representative and is paid $9.10 per hour. He worked 38 hours last week. Find his gross pay.

SOLUTION
Multiply the hours worked by the hourly rate.

$38 \times \$9.10 = \$345.80$

Mark's gross pay for last week was $345.80.

■ CHECK YOUR UNDERSTANDING

A. Kenny Walker works as a shopping mall security guard and is paid $7.50 an hour. Find his gross pay when he works 46 hours a week. $345

B. Cassie Boland earns $16.25 an hour. What gross wages did she earn last week by working 25 hours? $406.25

CALCULATOR TIP

When you use a calculator, the decimal point will be placed correctly automatically. This feature is called *floating decimal point.* Your calculator will show 345.8. To write the answer, add the 0 and a dollar sign.

EXAMPLE 2

Sharon Medal is paid $7 an hour. Last week Sharon worked 8 hours a day for 5 days. Find her gross pay for last week.

SOLUTION
$5 \times 8 = 40$ hours worked in last week

$40 \times \$7 = \$280$ gross pay for last week

■ CHECK YOUR UNDERSTANDING

C. Rosa Mendez works 8 hours Monday through Friday as a legal assistant. Her hourly wage is $18.75. Find how many hours she worked in one week and her gross pay for that week. 40, $750

D. Vincent O'Malley worked the following schedule one week: Monday, 8 hours; Tuesday, 6 hours; Wednesday, 7 hours; Thursday, 6 hours; Friday, 5 hours. He was paid $9 an hour. How many hours did Vincent work that week and what was his gross pay? 32, $288

■ Gross Pay for Salaried Employees

Some employees are paid a **salary**, which is a fixed amount of money for each time period worked, such as a day, week, month, or year. They are referred to as *salaried employees.* To find their gross pay, multiply their pay for a time period by the number of time periods worked.

Pay per Time Period × Number of Time Periods Worked = Gross Pay

Lesson 1.1 Hourly Pay and Salary ■ 5

■ **ONGOING ASSESSMENT**
Ask students to read the examples. They are to identify what is to be solved and then select the facts that are needed to solve the problem.

■ **Teach Goal 2**

Explain that salaried employees get paid the same amount regardless of how many hours they work. Salaried employees often work more than 40 hours a week.

Caution students to read salary problems carefully so they are clear as to the time periods for which pay is given and to be calculated.

■ **Apply Goal 2**

Work through Example 3 at the board with students completing the math at their desks. Write the numbers on the board and ask students to tell you which labels you should write next to the numbers.

Assign Check Your Understanding problems E and F for class work. Circulate through the classroom and examine student work for any difficulties they may be having and whether they are labeling their problems.

Note: The feature *Check Your Understanding Solutions* show the work need to solve the Check Your Understanding questions. Often space only allows for one of each pair to be shown.

■ *CHECK YOUR UNDERSTANDING SOLUTIONS*

A. $46 \times \$7.50 = \$345$

B. $25 \times \$16.25 = \$390$

C. $8 \times 5 = 40 \times \$18.75 = \$750$

D. $(8 + 6 + 7 + 6 + 5) = 32; 32 \times \$9 = \$288$

E. $2 \times \$680 = \$1,360$

F. $52 \times \$540 = \$28,080$

Wrap Up

Review the Start Up. Have students verify the gross pay calculations. Explain that math calculations are often used to answer questions or make decisions.

WORKPLACE WINDOW

Help students draft the questions they should ask, including follow-up questions. Students may pair off and interview each other to get practice at interviewing. Advise students not to ask people how much they earn.

Assign

Assignment: Exercise 1–24, 26–30. Start with the basic arithmetic problems at the beginning to insure that students understand the underlying arithmetic in the exercises.

EXAMPLE 3

Albert Meyer is paid a salary of $465 a week. How much gross pay does Albert receive for 4 weeks of work?

SOLUTION

$465	pay for 1 week
$\times\ 4$	weeks worked
$1,860	gross pay for 4 weeks

MATH TIP

1 year = 12 months

1 year = 52 weeks

1 year = 365 days

■ CHECK YOUR UNDERSTANDING

E. Tek Research pays its office manager a weekly salary of $680. What gross pay will the office manager receive every 2 weeks? $1,360

F. Tom works as a dispatcher and is paid a weekly salary of $540. What gross pay will Tom earn for one year of work? $28,080

Wrap Up

Look back at the Start Up question. Sarah's weekly gross pay is $810. A month has anywhere from 4 weeks to about $4\frac{1}{2}$ weeks. So, Sarah's monthly pay will be between $3,240 and $3,645. It is not possible for her to earn $3,750 a month working 54 hours a week.

WORKPLACE WINDOW

Interview two people you know who work full time. Choose one person who is paid a salary, and another who is paid by the hour. Find out each person's job title and list his or her job responsibilities.

Ask each person if they like the method by which they are paid. For example, ask the salaried employee whether he or she would rather be paid hourly. Ask the hourly employee whether he or she would prefer to be paid a salary. Be sure to ask them for their reasons.

As a class, make a complete list of all job titles, job responsibilities, and methods of payment. Discuss reasons why salaried and hourly paid employees liked and disliked their methods of payment. Look for general trends among the types of jobs that are salaried and the types that are paid hourly.

EXERCISES

Find each sum.

1. $8 + 7 + 6.5 + 7 + 8$ 36.5
2. $7 + 6.5 + 7.5 + 8 + 6$ 35
3. $1,500 + $723 $2,223
4. $680 + $72 $752

Find each product.

5. $38 \times $12 $456
6. $40 \times $9.80 $392
7. $25 \times $412 $10,300
8. $7.5 \times $8.10 $60.75
9. $7.75 \times $418 $3,239.50
10. $10 \times $1,200 $12,000

DIFFERENT LEARNING STYLES Kinesthetic Learners

Have students copy the gross pay formula at the top of page 5 and enter beneath the formula the data and arithmetic operators for Example 1 and Check Your Understanding Problems A and B.

11. Francesco Jardin earns $7 an hour at his part-time job. Last week he worked 16 hours. What was his gross pay for the week? $112

12. Shannon Burke is a substitute teacher. On the days she works she is paid $85 a day. What is Shannon's pay for 3 days of work? $255

13. Caroline Gracely works 8 hours a day Monday through Friday as an engineer. Find her gross pay for one week. She is paid $20.15 an hour. $806

14. Tom Page earns $368 a week. Tom is paid every two weeks. What gross pay does he receive each payday? $736

15. Jacob Tenoever works 10 hours a day Monday through Thursday as a factory worker. Find his gross pay for one week. He is paid $11.40 an hour. $456

16. An employee earns $2,300 each pay period. He is paid on the first and fifteenth of each month. How much does he earn in one year? $55,200

17. Eldon Cavanaugh is paid a weekly salary of $562. How much would Eldon earn in 4 weeks of work? $2,248

18. Use Eldon's information from Exercise 17 to find how much would he earn in one year, assuming that he works 50 weeks and is paid for 2 weeks of vacation? $29,224

19. Edmund Jasik earned $274.50 last week at his regular job. Last week he also worked 11 hours at his part-time job that pays him $8.25 an hour. What total pay did he earn from both jobs last week? $365.25

The chart below shows the hourly pay and hours worked for Trilton Company's four employees. Copy and complete the chart.

	Employee	Hourly Pay	Hours Worked	Gross Pay
20.	Rick Wilson	$9.25	40	$370
21.	Art Dillart	$9.45	32	$302.40
22.	Letitia Reed	$9.75	42	$409.50
23.	Alice Boehm	$9.50	36	$342
24.	Total			$1,423.90

25. **CRITICAL THINKING** Look at the Start Up problem for this lesson. Assume that Sarah feels that she must have a monthly gross pay of at least $3,750 to meet her expenses. What advice would you give to Sarah about the choices she might need to make? Answers will vary. Possible answer: ask for a raise.

MIXED REVIEW

26. $680 + $302
$982

27. 52 × $826
$42,952

28. 40 × $7.80
$312

29. 7.5 × $9.42
$70.65

30. Marion Polk worked 9 days in two weeks. He worked 8 hours each day and was paid $7.10 an hour. What gross pay did he earn for the two weeks? $511.20

Lesson 1.1 Hourly Pay and Salary ■ 7

SELECTED SOLUTIONS
13. (5 × 8) × $20.15 = $806
18. (50 + 2) × $562 = $29,224
19. $274.50 + (11 × $8.25) = $365.25
23. 36 × $9.50 = $342
30. 9 × 8 = 72 × $7.10 = $511.20

Assess

Ask students to give the formula for finding gross pay. **Gross pay = number of hours × hourly rate.**

Check student answers to the exercises by calling on them in class, collecting and grading selected exercises, or by observing student work at their desks.

Reteach

STUDENT WORKBOOK If students need help with finding gross pay for hourly employees, work through Exercise 2, weeks 1 and 2, in the workbook with them. Then have them find the gross pay in Exercise 2, weeks 3 and 4.

If students need help with finding gross pay for salaried employees, complete Exercise 4 in the workbook with them. Then have them solve Exercise 5.

Enrich

Discuss Exercise 25, Critical Thinking. If students think only of income-related options such as asking for a raise or getting another job, remind them to look at the expense side of the problem for possible solutions.

Close

Ask students to identify the arithmetic processes used to find gross pay for hourly and salaried workers. Read the bolded terms to the class and ask students to give definitions in their own words.

NOTE: The feature *Selected Solutions* shows work for a few select exercises.

1.2 Average Pay

GOALS

- Calculate simple averages
- Calculate averages from grouped data
- Find the unknown item in a set of data

Start Up

A six-figure income is a total yearly earnings amount that most people will never receive. A part-time grocery clerk once joked that her annual pay of $8,000 showed she had a six-figure income of $8,000—if you count the cents. In reality, a six-figure income means that a person has annual earnings from $100,000 to $999,999. If one person earning $100,000 and another earning $999,999 annually were paid each week, what would be their gross pay each week, rounded to the nearest dollar?

Math Skill Builder

Review these math skills and solve the exercises that follow.

1 **Divide** money amounts.
Find the quotient. $95 \div 5 = \$19$

   1a. $450 \div 5$ $90   **1b.** $18,000 \div 12$ $1,500

2 **Round** to the nearest cent.
Round this amount to the nearest cent. $9.287 = \$9.29$

   2a. $8.765 $8.77

   2b. $9.996 $10

   2c. $7.097 $7.10

3 **Multiply** money amounts by whole numbers.
Find the product. 8 @ $8.25 = \$66

   3a. 7 @ $7.25 $50.75   **3b.** 4 × $178 $712   **3c.** 4 @ $76 $304

> **MATH TIP**
>
> The symbol @ means at. It means the same as multiply.

■ Simple Averages

An **average** is a single number used to represent a group of numbers. The most commonly used average is the simple average.

A *simple average* is found by adding several numbers and dividing the sum by the number of items added. Another name for a simple average is the *mean*.

CONNECTION TO ECONOMICS

Tell students that statistical data published by many sources often refers to averages. Reports often describe such data as average family size, average household income, average selling prices of homes, average number of years completed in school, and average number of cars per household.

EXAMPLE 1

Tricia Willard earned these amounts for the 5 days she worked last week: Monday, $82; Tuesday, $91; Wednesday, $96; Thursday, $80; Friday, $86. What was her average pay for the 5 days?

SOLUTION

Add daily amounts to find total pay.

$82 + $91 + $96 + $80 + $86 = $435   total pay

Divide the sum by the number of days to find the average pay per day.

$435 ÷ 5 = $87   average pay per day

■ **CHECK YOUR UNDERSTANDING**

A. Monica Wilkes earned these amounts last week at her part-time job: Friday, $18; Saturday, $58; Sunday, $32. What was her average daily pay for the 3 days she worked? $36

B. A clothing designer earned these amounts in four consecutive months: $2,400, $3,200, $1,500, $1,700. What average monthly earnings did the designer have for these 4 months? $2,200

EXAMPLE 2

Valeria Mishkov earns $18,000 per year as assistant manager at a local store. Find her average pay per hour (to the nearest cent) if she works 37.5 hours for 50 weeks per year and gets 2 weeks paid vacation.

SOLUTION

Find total weeks for which pay is received.

50 + 2 = 52 weeks

Find total hours for which she is paid in 1 year.

37.5 × 52 = 1,950   total hours

Divide the total earnings by the number of hours. Round the final answer to the nearest cent.

$18,000 ÷ 1,950 = $9.2308, or $9.23   average pay per hour

MATH TIP

In solving problems in this book, round to the nearest cent all answers involving money amounts unless you are directed otherwise.

■ **CHECK YOUR UNDERSTANDING**

C. Last month Antoine Beal earned $264 by working 38 hours at his part-time job. What average hourly pay did he earn last month, to the nearest cent? $6.95

D. LaKeisha Jones earned $35,800 in the first year of her new job. After receiving a promotion she earned $47,000 in the second year. What were her average earnings for the two years? $41,400

Lesson 1.2 Average Pay ■ **9**

■ **Apply Goal 1**

Work through Examples 1 and 2 on the board with students completing the math at their desks. Be sure to point out the Math Tip while working Example 2.

Assign Check Your Understanding problems A through D for completion in class. Circulate in the classroom and check student work at their desks.

■ **ONGOING ASSESSMENT**

Write on the board the number of points the school's basketball team scored in its first game of either this season or last season. Ask whether the number is an average. Now write the points scored in the second game and add the two sets of points and divide by two. Ask students if the result is an average. Have students explain why both numbers are averages.

■ *CHECK YOUR UNDERSTANDING SOLUTIONS*

A. $18 + $58 + $32 = $108; $108 ÷ 3 = $36

B. $2,400 + $3,200 + $1,500 + $1,700 = $8,800 ÷ 4 = $2,200

C. $264 ÷ 38 = $6.95

D. $35,800 + $47,000 = 40,500 ÷ 2 = $20,250

■ **Teach Goal 2**

Demonstrate the Calculator Tip to find an average from grouped data for Example 3.

Also show how the same result would occur if the amounts earned for each of the five months were listed individually and a simple average was taken of their total.

■ **Apply Goal 2**

Work through Example 3 on the board with students completing the math at their desks.

Assign Check Your Understanding problems E and F for completion in class. Check student work at their desks for any difficulties they may have in solving the assigned problems.

■ **Teach Goal 3**

Explain to students how the value of items and the number of items are related to an average, and how any missing element may be calculated.

You may also set the facts in Example 4 into an equation where x represents the unknown. Thus, $400 + $410 + $460 + x = 4 \times$ $433.

■ **Apply Goal 3**

Work through Example 4 on the board with students completing the math at their desks.

■ Averages in Grouped Data

A number or rate can occur more than once in a set of data. When that happens, you can find the sum quickly by grouping the common numbers.

EXAMPLE 3

Brandon Chin sell t-shirts at the beach. During the first month of the season, he earned $600. In each of the next three months he earned $1,050 per month. In the last month of the season, Brandon earned $180. What were his average earnings per month for those five months?

SOLUTION
Find his total earnings for months worked.

1 month @ $600 = $600

3 months @ $1,050 = $3,150

1 month @ $180 = $180

5 total months = $3,930   total earnings

Divide the total earnings by the months worked.

$3,930 ÷ 5 = $786   average monthly earnings

> **CALCULATOR TIP**
>
> To use grouped data with a calculator, press the M+ key (instead of the Equal or Enter key) to complete the multiplication for each line and store the product. Press MR/C to recall the total. Then divide by the number of items.

■ **CHECK YOUR UNDERSTANDING**

E. The Runwell Company has 8 employees. Five of the employees earn $12 an hour, two earn $9 an hour, and 1 earns $11 an hour. What is the average amount per hour that the employees are paid? $11.13

F. Rosalind Jeszko repairs vending machines. She earned these amounts in the first 4 weeks of the year: Week 1, $280; Week 2, $315; Week 3, $424; Week 4, $265. What were her average earnings for the 4 weeks, rounded to the nearest dollar? $321

■ Unknown Items in a Set of Data

If one item in a group or set of data is unknown, you may have to find it. Averages are used often in finding the value of the unknown item.

EXAMPLE 4

The weekly pay of four picture frame assemblers in a company averages $433 per employee. The weekly pay amounts of three of the four employees are $400, $410, and $460. What is the weekly pay of the fourth employee?

SOLUTION
Multiply the average employee pay to find the total pay of 4 employees.

4 × $433 = $1,732   total pay

Add to find the total pay of the known employees.

$400 + $410 + $460 = $1,270   total pay of 3 employees

COMMON ERRORS

When working with problems that involve grouped data, students may not divide by the correct number. For instance in Example 3 on this page, students might divide by 3 rather than 5. Remind students that there are 3 months at $1,050 each plus 2 other months, so the divisor must be 5.

Subtract the totals to find the missing weekly pay item.

$1,732 − $1,270 = $462   weekly pay of fourth employee

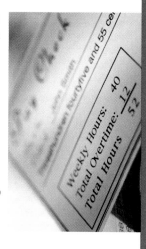

G. Your daily pay for the first 4 days of the week was $68, $80, $75, and $79. How much do you have to earn on the fifth day to average $77 a day in earnings for the 5-day week? $83

H. Hank Borden was paid $420 for 5 days work. For 4 of those days, his average pay was $86. Find his pay for the fifth day. $76

Wrap Up

The two ends of the six-figure income range must be divided by 52 weeks to calculate the average weekly pay. A person earning $100,000 a year would have weekly earnings of $1,923. The person earning $999,999 would earn $19,231 weekly. Because the weekly pay figures are rounded, the answers are approximate.

TEAM MEETING

A company can have as few as one employee to as many as tens of thousands of employees. This class activity will simulate a company's weekly payroll for hourly-rate employees. You need two boxes. Mark one Dollars and the other Cents. Place in the Dollar box slips of paper marked from $5 to $11. In the Cents box place slips marked from $0.55 to $0.95 in multiples of 0.05. Each student randomly chooses an hourly pay rate by drawing one slip from each box. Then, complete these steps.

1. List all hourly rates. Record the number of students at each rate.
2. Find the average hourly pay rate for all class members.
3. Calculate the total weekly gross pay for all students for a 40-hour week using the hourly rate drawn.
4. Find the average weekly gross pay of the class.

EXERCISES

Find the quotient or product.

1. $4,500 ÷ 12 $375

2. $620 ÷ 40 $15.50

3. 12 × $1,578 $18,936

4. 4 @ $12.75 $51

Round to the nearest cent.

5. $406.439 $406.44

6. $10.407 $10.41

7. Ben's earnings for work he did from Monday through Saturday were: $78, $94, $115, $108, $67, $78. What was his average daily pay for the days he worked? $90

Lesson 1.2 Average Pay ■ **11**

■ ***CHECK YOUR UNDERSTANDING SOLUTIONS***

E. (5 × $12) + (2 × $9) + (1 × $11) = $89; $89 ÷ 8 = $11.13

G. $77 × 5 = $385; $68 + $80 + $75 + $79 = $302; $385 − $302 = $83

Check student answers to the exercises by calling on them in class, collecting and grading selected problems, or by observing student work at their desks.

Ask students to define the bolded and italicized terms in the lesson and use them in sentences.

STUDENT WORKBOOK If students need help with simple averages, work Exercise 1 in the workbook with them individually or as a group. Then have them complete Exercise 2 independently during class time so you may help them individually, as necessary.

If students need help with averages from grouped data, work Exercise 6 in the workbook with them. Then assign Exercise 7 to be completed independently.

Complete Exercise 10 in the workbook with students who need help in finding the unknown item in a set of data. Follow up by having them complete Exercise 11 independently.

Two years ago Randi earned $18,400. Last year she earned $19,700. Suppose she earns $21,600 this year.

8. What total amount will Randi have earned for the three years? $59,700

9. What will be her average earnings per year? $19,900

10. Four employees are paid a monthly salary as follows: Wilma, $1,820; Mavis, $1,615; Martha, $1,977; Tom, $1,560. What average salary per month are these employees paid? $1,743

11. Emma has been offered a job that pays $38,950 for working a 52-week year training software users. What average amount does the job pay per month? per week? $3,245.83 $749.04

Rashad earned $662 by working five days a week at his full-time job. He earned $118 for 12 hours of work at his part-time job.

12. What average pay per day did he earn from full-time work? $132.40

13. What average amount per hour did he earn from part-time work? $9.83

Three weeks ago James worked 46 hours and earned $414. Two weeks ago he earned $333 by working 37 hours. Last week he worked 42 hours for $378.

14. For the three weeks how many hours did James work? 125 hours

15. What were his total earnings? $1,125

16. What were his average hourly earnings? $9/hour

17. What were his average weekly earnings? $375

18. At her job of grooming horses, Polly Yaskovich worked 8 hours a day on Monday and Tuesday and earned $69 each day. On Wednesday, she earned $82. On Thursday and Friday, she earned $78 a day. What was Polly's average daily pay for the 5 days she worked? $75.20

19. The Willis Avenue Door Company gave its employees bonuses. Six employees received a bonus of $940 each; 4 employees received a bonus of $820 each; 5 employees were paid a bonus of $1,150 each. What was the average bonus paid to these employees? $978

20. The owner of Mid-Town Rapid Delivery plans to spend no more than $980 a day for employees' wages. The owner now has 8 employees who earn an average of $108 a day. Another employee must be hired. What is the most the new employee can be paid without spending more money than planned? $116

12 ■ **Chapter 1** Gross Pay

SELECTED SOLUTIONS

8. $18,400 + $19,700 + $21,600 = $59,700

9. $59,700 ÷ 3 = $19,900

19. (6 × $940) + (4 × $820) + (5 × $1,150) = $14,670; $14,670 ÷ 15 = $978

20. $980 − (8 × $108) = $116

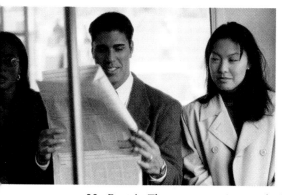

Yi Chin was offered a new job. For the first 3 months she works, she will be paid a monthly salary of $1,600. Her monthly pay for the next 3 months will be $1,760. For the next 6 months after that, Yi's monthly salary will be $1,936.

21. How much will Yi earn during a full year? $21,696

22. What average pay per month will she receive if she works a full year? $1,808

23. Beatrix Thompson owns a craft shop and plans to sell 260 ceramic vases this year. She earns $25 for every vase sold. For the first 8 months of this year, she sold an average of 16 vases a month and had total earnings of $3,200. How many vases must she sell, on average, in each of the remaining 4 months to reach her goal? 33

24. STRETCHING YOUR SKILLS Marsha's scores on seven tests were: 82, 78, 77, 93, 85, 91, and 86. What was her average score on the tests, rounded to the nearest whole number? 85

25. STRETCHING YOUR SKILLS The owner of a small business bought 5 cases of copier paper for $14 each, 8 cases for $13.50, and 11 cases for $12.75. What average price did the owner pay for each case, to the nearest cent? $13.26

26. CRITICAL THINKING The owner of a business has two skilled employees who each earn $160 a day and 12 unskilled employees who each earn $56 a day. Find the average daily pay for the 14 employees. Does the average show what the "average" worker is paid? $70.86, no

27. DECISION MAKING The daily cost of public transportation to get you to and from your current job is $5. You regularly work 8 hours a day Monday through Friday and 4 hours on Saturday. You have been offered a new job close to home where you could walk to and from work each day. The new job pays $0.75 less an hour than your current job. You will work an average of 44 hours a week. Will you make or lose money by taking the new job? You will lose $3.

MIXED REVIEW

28. Find the quotient: $31,920 ÷ 12 $2,660

29. Find the product: $235 × 4 $940

30. What is $12.655 rounded to the nearest cent? $12.66

31. Carmella Petrocelli earns a weekly salary $1,352 as a web site designer. If she works at this pay rate for a year, what will be her total annual earnings? $70,304, Lesson 1.1

32. Sol Levin sold 22 pairs of shoes each day, Monday through Wednesday, 28 pairs on Thursday, and 31 on Friday. How many shoes must he sell on Saturday to average 29 pairs sold for the 6 days he worked during the week? 49, Lesson 1.2

Lesson 1.2 Average Pay ■ 13

DIFFERENT LEARNING STYLES Print Learners

Before doing the Mixed Review, write the bolded terms from Lessons 1.1 and 1.2 on the board under the heading "important terms:" employees, employer, hourly rate, salary, and average. Ask students to copy the list and review the definitions of the terms.

Start Up

Have students read the Start Up. Ask them to identify the different scenarios under which the gross pay of Victor and George would be the same while they work a different number of hours.

Point out to students that companies often have different pay plans among different categories of workers.

Math Skill Builder

The skills of addition and multiplication of decimals are used in this lesson, as are the rewriting of fractions as decimals and the rounding of money amounts.

Complete all exercises in Math Skill Builder 1–4.

1.3 Regular and Overtime Pay

GOALS

- Compute overtime pay rates
- Calculate regular and overtime pay

Start Up

Victor and George are employed by the same company. Victor worked 40 regular hours last week and earned $480. In the same week George worked 38 total hours, including 4 overtime hours. He also earned $480. How is this possible?

Math Skill Builder

Review these math skills and solve the exercises that follow.

1 **Rewrite** fractions and mixed numbers as their decimal equivalents.
Rewrite as a decimal. $1\frac{1}{2} = 1.5$

1a. $\frac{3}{4}$ 0.75   **1b.** $\frac{1}{2}$ 0.5   **1c.** $6\frac{3}{4}$ 6.75   **1d.** $48\frac{3}{4}$ 48.75

2 **Add** decimals.
Add. $6.25 + 4.75 + 7.5 = 18.5$

2a. $5.5 + 7.25 + 8 + 7 + 6.75$ 34.5   **2b.** $8.4 + 9.1 + 7.7$ 25.2

3 **Multiply** decimals. Remember to round to the nearest cent.
Multiply. $\$18.30 \times 6.5 = \$118.95$

3a. $\$12.80 \times 1.5$ $19.20   **3b.** $\$11.63 \times 40.5$ $471.02   **3c.** $\$9.87 \times 45.7$ $451.06

4 **Round** to the nearest cent.
Round. $\$1,874.898 = \$1,874.90$

4a. $24.373 $24.37   **4b.** $99.995 $100   **4c.** $537.307 $537.31

■ Recording Hours Worked

Many companies keep an exact record of the number of hours their employees work. They record the times people arrive at work, take breaks, and leave for the day.

Most larger companies electronically record time worked. As employees arrive at work or leave, they pass a *magnetic stripe card* through a reader. Time is recorded in a computer connected to the reader.

TEACHING STRATEGIES Cooperative Learning

Have two students work together to complete the exercises in this lesson. One student should tell the other how to solve the problem. The second student records the exercises solution and does the calculations. Students reverse roles after each exercise is solved.

Other companies use a *time card* to record the work time of employees. As they arrive or leave, employees manually insert the time card into a slot on a time clock where the current time is printed. Smaller companies simply write the times employees work on a payroll form called a *time sheet*.

Computers are almost always used to figure the total time worked for a pay period regardless of the method used to record time worked. Computers also apply any penalties for employees who are late to work or leave early.

TIME BY QUARTER HOURS   Some companies record time worked in 15-minute segments so that any part of an hour would show as $\frac{1}{4}$, $\frac{1}{2}$, or $\frac{3}{4}$ hours. In decimal form the part of an hour would be shown as 0.25, 0.5, or 0.75 hours. An employee that worked seven and one-half hours in a day would have their work time recorded as $7\frac{1}{2}$, or 7.5, hours.

The time worked for a day or week would also include any penalties for being late. For example, a company that records time in quarter hours may penalize a worker 15 minutes for arriving more than 3 minutes late to work or leaving more than 3 minutes before the end of scheduled work time. Similar penalties also apply to scheduled breaks or lunch.

TIME BY TENTHS OF HOURS   Most companies record work time in tenths of an hour. Since an hour has 60 minutes, one tenth of an hour is 6 minutes. Parts of an hour would be shown as: 6 minutes = 0.1 hour; 12 minutes = 0.2 hour; 18 minutes = 0.3 hour; and so on. Penalties in 6-minute segments are deducted from time worked for employees who arrive late or leave early throughout the day.

■ Overtime and Overtime Pay Rates

Companies record regular hours of work and overtime, which is time worked beyond the regular working day or week. Daily overtime is based on a regular working day, such as an 8-hour day. So, an employee who works 10 hours in one day will be paid for 8 hours regular time and 2 hours overtime.

If the regular working week is 40 hours, then an employee who works 45 hours in a week is paid for 40 regular hours and 5 overtime hours.

OVERTIME RATES   Overtime pay is often figured at one and a half times ($\times$ 1.5) the regular-time rate and is called time-and-a-half pay. Sometimes double-time pay is given for work over a certain number of hours, or for work on weekends and holidays. Double-time pay is twice ($\times$ 2) the regular-time pay rate.

To find a time-and-a-half pay rate, multiply the regular pay rate by 1.5.

1.5 × Regular Pay Rate = Time-and-a-Half Rate (Do NOT round.)

To find the double-time pay rate, multiply the regular rate by 2.

2 × Regular Pay Rate = Double-Time Rate

Lesson 1.3 Regular and Overtime Pay ■ 15

■ Teach Goal 1

When discussing with students how companies record time worked, relate the magnetic stripe card used for payroll purposes to a credit card. Also point out that employees that are paid a salary usually do not have to record the time they arrive for work or when they leave.

Review the decimal equivalents for quarter-hour fractions that may be used to report time worked.

Remind students that the overtime rate is not rounded. It is one of the exceptions to the practice in the textbook of rounding money amounts to the nearest cent. Only the final calculations of overtime pay and regular-time pay are rounded to the nearest cent.

CONNECTION TO ECONOMICS

Students may wonder why a company requires employees to work overtime instead of hiring more employees. One reason is the cost of employee benefits, which is a hidden expense of hiring employees. Students should understand that it is often difficult to find qualified employees, and that training new employees takes time and money. Also, overtime is usually worked only during peak periods.

Work through Example 1 at the board with students completing the math at their desks.

Assign Check Your Understanding problems A and B for class work. Inform students that the five-steps referred to in the directions refer to the steps listed on page 16 and used in the example. Circulate in the classroom and examine student work for any difficulties.

Write on the board abbreviations for Monday through Friday and these hours beneath the days: 8, 11, 8, 6, and 10. Show the differences in calculating regular-time hours and overtime hours for the 8-hour day and 40-hour week pay plans.

Demonstrate the use of the Calculator Tip in changing fractions to decimals.

EXAMPLE 1

Paul Mears' regular pay is $10.73 an hour. His employer pays overtime at 1.5 of the regular rate and double time at twice the regular rate of pay. What are Paul's time-and-a-half and double-time pay rates?

SOLUTION

$1.5 \times \$10.73 = \$16.095$ time-and-a-half rate

$2 \times \$10.73 = \$21.46$ double-time rate

■ **CHECK YOUR UNDERSTANDING**

A. Find time-and-a half and double-time rates for these regular-time pay rates.

1) $7.51 $11.265; $15.02   **2)** $8.76 $13.14; $17.52   **3)** $13.67 $20.505; $27.34

B. Emilio's regular-time pay rate is $11.25 per hour. What time-and-a-half and double-time rates would he earn for overtime work? $16.875; $22.50

■ Regular and Overtime Wages

To find gross wages for an employee who has worked both regular time and overtime, use these five steps.

Step 1: Find the number of regular-time and overtime hours worked.

Step 2: Find the overtime pay rate or rates.

Step 3: Find the regular-time pay by multiplying the regular-time hourly rate by the number of regular-time hours worked.

Step 4: Find the overtime pay by multiplying the overtime hourly rate by the number of overtime hours worked. Match time-and-a-half overtime hours and rate; match double-time overtime hours and rate.

Step 5: Add the regular-time pay and the overtime pay.

EXAMPLE 2

Stanley Bartlett's time is recorded in quarter hours. He worked these hours last week: Monday, $7\frac{1}{4}$; Tuesday, 10; Wednesday, $9\frac{1}{2}$; Thursday, 8; Friday, 9. Stanley is paid based on an 8-hour day with time-and-a-half for daily overtime. If Stanley's regular-time pay rate is $9.50 per hour, what gross wages did he earn last week?

SOLUTION

Step 1: $7.25 + 8 + 8 + 8 + 8 = 39.25$ regular-time hours
        $2 + 1.5 + 1 = 4.5$ time-and-a-half overtime hours

Step 2: $1.5 \times \$9.50 = \$14.25$ time-and-half rate

Step 3: $39.25 \times \$9.50 = \$372.88$ regular-time pay

Step 4: $4.5 \times \$14.25 = \$64.125 \approx \$64.13$ time-and-a-half pay

Step 5: $\$372.88 + \$64.13 = \$437.01$ gross wages

> **CALCULATOR TIP**
>
> It is often easier to work with decimals than fractions. To change a fraction such as $\frac{3}{4}$ to a decimal, use $3 \div 4 = 0.75$

16 ■ **Chapter 1** Gross Pay

DIFFERENT LEARNING ABILITIES At-Risk Learners

Students may have difficulty following a generic list of instructions such as the five-step process for calculating gross pay. Relate Step 1 of the Example 2 solution to the Step 1 written instruction. Repeat for each step in the instructions.

EXAMPLE 3

Olivia Ricardo works on a 40-hour week basis, and her work time is recorded in tenths of hours. She is paid time-and-a-half for all hours worked over 40 hours in a week. Olivia's regular-time pay is $12.87 an hour. She worked these hours in a week: Monday, 8.4, Tuesday, 7.8, Wednesday, 8.0, Thursday, 9.2; Friday, 8.5. What gross wages did Olivia earn last week?

SOLUTION

Step 1: $8.4 + 7.8 + 8.0 + 9.2 + 8.5 = 41.9$ total hours worked

$41.9 - 40.0 = 1.9$ overtime hours is hours over 40

Step 2: $1.5 \times \$12.87 = \$19.305$ time-and-a-half rate

Step 3: $40 \times \$12.87 = \$514.80$ regular-time pay

Step 4: $1.9 \times \$19.305 = \$36.679$, or $\$36.68$ overtime pay

Step 5: $\$514.80 + \$36.68 = \$551.48$ gross wages

■ CHECK YOUR UNDERSTANDING

C. Xavier Centor works on an 8-hour day. He is paid $13.69 an hour for regular-time work and time-and-a-half for any hours over 8 hours a day. Xavier worked these hours last week: Monday, $9\frac{3}{4}$; Tuesday, 8; Wednesday, 6; Thursday, $8\frac{1}{2}$; Friday, 8. Complete all five steps to find Xavier's gross wages for last week.   38, 2.25, $520.22, $46.20, $566.42

D. Diedra McKenney works on a 40-hour week basis with time-and-a-half paid for overtime work. Her regular-time hourly rate is $17.50. Last week she worked 45.3 hours from Monday through Thursday and 8.1 hours on Friday. Complete all five steps to find Diedra's gross wages for last week.   40, 13.4, $700, $351.75, $1,051.75

Wrap Up

Companies pay more for overtime work than for regular-time work. Victor earned his pay of $480 by working 40 hours at $12 an hour. George earned only $408 ($34 \times \$12$) from regular-time work but made up the difference by working 4 hours overtime at an overtime pay rate of $18 an hour.

TEAM MEETING

Imagine you are responsible for supervising a small group of workers and have been assigned to write guidelines for them. The company you work for expects employees to be on time for work and not leave early. The penalty for employees who break this work rule is a loss of pay.

What rules would you have about paying employees who are ill or need time off from work to take care of personal business? Will the rules be different for new employees or the same as those rules for people who have been with the company longer? Be fair to your employees, to yourself, and to the company when writing the guidelines. As a class discuss everyone's guidelines. Make a list of the rules the class generally agrees on.

■ *CHECK YOUR UNDERSTANDING SOLUTIONS*

C. Step 1: $8 + 8 + 6 + 8 + 8 = 38$ regular-time hours; $1.75 + 0.5 = 2.25$ overtime hours

Step 2: $1.5 \times \$13.69 = \$20.535$ time-and-a-half rate

Step 3: $38 \times \$13.69 = \$520.22$ regular-time pay

Step 4: $2.25 \times \$20.535 = \$46.20$ overtime pay

Step 5: $\$520.22 + \$46.20 = \$566.42$ gross wages

EXERCISES

Add decimals.

1. $8.5 + 9.75$ 18.25

2. $6.75 + 6.75 + 8$ 21.5

Rewrite as decimals.

3. $\frac{1}{2}$ 0.5

4. $\frac{3}{4}$ 0.75

5. $43\frac{1}{2}$ 43.5

6. $40\frac{1}{4}$ 40.25

Multiply decimals.

7. 1.5×11.63 17.445

8. 1.5×9.87 14.805

Round to nearest cent.

9. $78.438 $78.44

10. $298.987 $298.99

11. $419.097 $419.10

Jaci Welk is paid $11.95 an hour with time-and-a-half pay for all hours she works over 40 hours a week. Last week she worked $45\frac{1}{2}$ hours.

12. How many overtime hours did Jaci work?   5.5

13. What was her overtime rate? $17.925

14. What was her overtime pay? $98.59

Steve Gaimes is paid overtime for all time worked past 40 hours in a week. His regular-time pay rate is $12 an hour, and his overtime pay rate is $18 an hour. Last week Steve worked 47.3 hours.

15. How many regular-time hours did Steve work last week?   40

16. How many overtime hours did he work last week?   7.3

17. What was Steve's regular-time pay last week? $480

18. What was his overtime pay last week? $131.40

19. What was Steve's gross or total pay last week? $611.40

20. Alberta Doan worked 6 hours at time-and-a-half pay and $3\frac{1}{4}$ hours at double-time pay. Her regular pay rate was $9.72 an hour. What was Alberta's total overtime pay for the week? $150.66

Ike Phillips worked 6.7 hours at time-and-a-half pay and 3.4 hours at double-time pay last week. His regular earnings for the week were $454.80 figured on a regular pay rate of $11.37 an hour.

21. What were Ike's time-and-a-half and double-time pay rates? $17.055; $22.74

22. What amounts did he earn for time-and-a-half and double-time work? $114.27; $77.32

23. What was Ike's total gross pay for the week? $646.39

18 ■ Chapter 1 Gross Pay

SELECTED SOLUTIONS

13. $1.5 \times \$11.95 = \$17.925$

16. $47.3 - 40 = 7.3$

20. $(1.5 \times \$9.72) \times 6 = \$87.48$; $(2 \times \$9.72) \times 3.25 = \$63.18$; $\$87.48 + \$63.18 = \$150.66$

24. **CRITICAL THINKING**   At the end of an interview you are offered a job. You would start at $7.50 an hour and work an average of 45 hours a week. At the end of six months with a positive evaluation, your hourly pay would increase to $8. The job pays overtime at a time-and-a-half rate, based on a $37\frac{1}{2}$ hour regular work week. What total earnings could you expect to make by working a full year? $19,646.25

25. **CRITICAL THINKING**   Why do jobs, or even the same type of job at different companies, have different rates of pay?   experience, background, education, and years of experience

26. **DECISION MAKING**   You are offered a job by two companies. Both companies pay overtime based on a 40-hour week. The Aztec Company's regular hourly rate is $8.60 and workers are penalized 15 minutes if they arrive at work more than 3 minutes late or leave more than 3 minutes early. The Wolfson Company pays a regular hourly rate of $8.35 and the 15-minute pay deduction is based on employees arriving no more than 6 minutes late or leaving no more than 6 minutes early. Use only the information provided to decide which company's offer will you accept and why?   Answers will vary, but if on time Aztec at $8.60 is the best offer.

MIXED REVIEW

27. $24 \times \frac{3}{4}$ $18

28. $\frac{2}{5} + \frac{2}{3}$ $1\frac{1}{15}$

29. 115% × $30 $34.50

30. $34,000 ÷ $10,000   3.4

31. What is 20% more than 50?   60

32. What is 1% of $2,593? $25.93

Solve each proportion.

33. $\frac{1}{2} = \frac{?}{30}$ 15

34. $\frac{2}{?} = \frac{14}{49}$ 7

35. $\frac{3}{5} = \frac{45}{?}$ 75

Tina Colbert's annual pay is $34,320. What is her average gross pay?   Lesson 1.2

36. per month? $2,860

37. per week? $660

38. per day $94.03

Last week, Greg Derkaz worked 4 hours a day Monday through Friday at his after-school job. He is paid $8.20 an hour.

39. How may hours did Greg work last week?   20

40. What was his gross pay for the week? $164, Lesson 1.1

41. Sallie Woo worked these hours last week: Monday, 10; Tuesday, $8\frac{1}{4}$; Wednesday, $9\frac{1}{2}$; Thursday, 6; Friday, 8; Saturday, 5. Sallie is paid $11.40 per hour for regular hours, time and a half for overtime during the week, and double time for weekend hours. If Sallie works on an 8-hour day basis, what was her pay for the week? $616.33, Lesson 1.3 $611.33

42. The Caloto.com Company has 5 employees whose average weekly pay is $890. The weekly pay amounts of 4 of the employees are: $760, $910, $825, and $1,200. What is the weekly pay of the fifth employee? $755, Lesson 1.2

43. Mary Lynn Bower worked 8 hours a day, Monday through Wednesday, 8.8 hours on Thursday, and 8.7 hours on Friday. She works an 8-hour day at a regular-time rate of $16.48 and overtime at time-and-a-half. What was her gross pay for the week? $696.28, Lessons 1.2, 1.3

44. Ida Taylor is paid a monthly salary of $2,800. What will be her earnings for 1 year at this pay rate? $33,600, Lesson 1.1

Lesson 1.3 Regular and Overtime Pay ■ 19

ENRICHING SELECTED SOLUTIONS

After students solve Exercise 26, Decision Making, you might ask them if they would take the Aztec offer considering the emphasis that Aztec places on its employees arriving on time.

19

Start Up

Have students read the Start Up. Ask students for suggestions on how the Start Up problem could be solved. Have students test their approaches by calculating a solution that they believe will yield the correct answer. Have students who had the correct answer share their solution with the class.

Math Skill Builder

The skills of rewriting percents as decimals and vice versa are used in this lesson. Also used are the skills of finding a percent of a number and the percent that a number is of another number.

Complete all exercises in Math Skill Builder 1–4.

1.4 Commission

Goals

- Calculate straight commission earnings
- Calculate commission earnings based on quota
- Calculate graduated commission earnings
- Find the rate of commission

Start Up

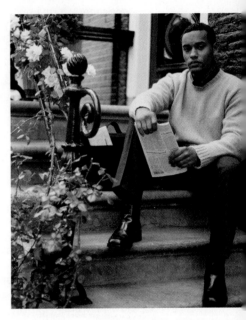

Two sales jobs are advertised in the newspaper. The first job pays a commission of 3.5% on all sales, and sales usually average $52,000 a month. The second job pays a commission of 4% on sales up to $5,000 and 12% on sales over $5,000, and sales usually average $25,000 a month. Based on the usual monthly sales average, which job pays more?

Math Skill Builder

Review these math skills and solve the exercises that follow

1. **Rewrite** a percent as a decimal.
   Rewrite this percent. 50% = 0.5

   1a. 12% 0.12

   1b. 18.6% 0.186

   1c. 2.5% 0.025

2. Find a **percent of a number**.
   Find the percent. 1% of $1,956 = 0.01 × $1,956 = $19.56

   2a. 14% of $500 $70   **2b.** 3.5% of $1,200 $42

3. **Rewrite** a decimal as a percent.
   Rewrite this decimal. 0.25 = 25%

   3a. 0.08 8%   **3b.** 0.75 75%

   3c. 0.01 1%   **3d.** 0.1825 18.25%

4. Find **what percent** one number is of another number.
   Find the percent. $10 ÷ $80 = 0.125 or 12.5%

   4a. $15 ÷ $75 20%   **4b.** $4,800 ÷ $32,000 15%

20 ■ Chapter 1 Gross Pay

CONNECTION TO MANAGEMENT

Those who work as auto salespersons, real estate agents, and sports agents are often paid a straight commission. The idea behind straight commission is an employer's desire to pay salespeople only when they are productive and make sales that generate income for their employer. Paying commissions based on sales rewards individual effort and keeps employees highly motivated to be on task.

■ Straight Commission

■ Teach Goal 1

Some salespeople earn a commission instead of a fixed salary or hourly pay. A commission may be an amount for each item sold, or it may be a percent of the dollar value of sales. A higher commission may be earned for goods that are harder to sell than for goods that are easy to sell. Both a salary and a commission may be earned.

Salespeople whose earnings come only from commission work on a straight commission basis. When the rate of commission is an amount for each item sold, multiply the number of items by the rate to find the commission.

Quantity Sold × Rate of Commission = Commission

EXAMPLE 1

Maxwell Lytle sells decorative notepads and is paid a straight commission of $0.80 on each notepad he sells. During December, he sold 750 notepads. Find his commission.

SOLUTION
750 × $0.80 = $600   commission

■ CHECK YOUR UNDERSTANDING

A. Lorraine Wilk is paid a commission of $1.30 for each hand-painted tile she sells. What commission did she earn by selling 74 tiles last week? $96.20

B. Leo Margolis receives a $0.075 commission for each newspaper he sells at his newsstand. What commission would he earn by selling 1,200 newspapers? $90

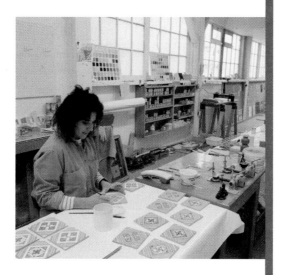

When the rate of commission is a percent, multiply the amount of the sales by the rate to find the commission.

Sales × Rate of Commission = Commission

EXAMPLE 2

Huey Gaines is paid a straight commission of 6% on his sales. During February, his sales were $38,000. What was his commission?

SOLUTION
$38,000 × 0.06 = $2,280   commission

■ CHECK YOUR UNDERSTANDING

C. Melvin's sales last month of a new tile cleaner were $9,500. If he receives a commission rate of 15% of all sales, what commission did he earn? $1,425

D. Jacqueline earns 15% commission on sales. Her sales for three months were: $2,870, $3,150, and $3,940. What was her total commission for the three months? $1,494

Lesson 1.4 Commission ■ 21

■ Teach Goal 1

Ask students if they know of any instance where they or someone they know was paid on a straight commission basis. You may find someone in class who delivers newspapers and is paid a certain amount for each paper delivered. Students may also have sold items for a fund-raiser where a certain amount per unit or a percent of the total order is kept by the organization. That amount is commonly called a share of the profits, but is really a commission on sales.

■ Apply Goal 1

Work through Examples 1 and 2 at the board with students completing the math at their desks.

Assign Check Your Understanding problems A through D for class work. Move about the classroom and examine student work for any difficulties.

After students complete Problem D, point out that for this problem they could get the same answer by adding the monthly sales figures and taking a percent of the total or by finding the commission for each month and then take their total.

Explain that it is possible for two answers to differ slightly when solving problems because of the rounding of intermediate answers.

■ ONGOING ASSESSMENT
Ask students to state how percents are changed to decimals, using 2.4% as an example. Also ask them to explain how many places the decimal point is moved in the product in paper-and-pencil calculations when sales are multiplied by the decimal 0.024.

■ *CHECK YOUR UNDERSTANDING SOLUTIONS*

A. 74 × $1.30 = $96.20

C. 0.15 × $9,500 = $1,425

E. $2,890 − $2,000 × 0.03 = $26.70; $26.70 + $125 = $151.70

Emphasize that no commission is earned until sales exceed the quota amount. So, in solving problems, the quota has to be subtracted from total sales before commission is calculated.

A salary is often combined with this type of commission to provide a salesperson with some income until the quota is reached.

Work through Example 4 at the board with students completing the math at their desks.

Assign Check Your Understanding problems G and H for class work. Circulate in the classroom and examine student work for any difficulties.

Tell students that a graduated commission pay system is used to motivate salespersons to achieve higher sales. In this way, the employee gains more income and the employer has greater total sales and profits.

Alternatively, you may ask students why such a plan is used instead of giving them the information.

Work through Example 4 at the board with students completing the math at their desks.

Assign Check Your Understanding problems G and H for class work. Circulate in the classroom and examine student work for any difficulties.

■ Commission Based on Quota

Some salespersons may be paid a commission that is a percent of their sales above a certain amount. This fixed amount is called a **quota**. Salespersons may also be paid a salary in addition to commission.

EXAMPLE 3

Leona Bahr is paid a commission of 12% on all sales above $7,000 for the week. She is also paid a weekly salary of $380. What are her total earnings for a week in which her sales were $9,800?

SOLUTION

Sales	$9,800	Salary	$380
Quota	−7,000	Commission	+336
Sales over Quota	$2,800	Total Earnings	$716

Commission: 12% of $2,800 = $336
Leona's total earnings were $716

■ CHECK YOUR UNDERSTANDING

E. Colby Richards is paid a salary of $125 a week and a 3% commission on all sales he makes above $2,000 for the week. What total earnings did he have for a week in which his sales were $2,890? $151.70

F. Lula Krobo is paid a 7% commission on all sales over $15,000 in a month and a monthly salary of $2,300. Her last month's sales were $29,700. What were Lula's total earnings for the month? $3,329

■ Graduated Commission

Some salespersons are paid a **graduated commission**. This means their rate of commission increases as their sales increase. For example, the rate may be 3% on the first $12,000 of sales; 4% on the next $6,000; and 5% on sales over $18,000. Graduated commissions may also be based on the number of units sold.

EXAMPLE 4

Lamont Cotton is paid 4% commission on the first $10,000 of monthly sales and 10% on all sales over $10,000. Last month his sales were $38,000. What was his commission?

SOLUTION

Commission on first $10,000: $10,000 × 0.04 = $400

Sales over $10,000: $38,000 − $10,000 = $28,000

Commission on sales over $10,000: $28,000 × 0.10 = $2,800

Total commission: $400 + $2,800 = $3,200

COMMON ERRORS

Students may calculate graduated commission incorrectly by applying either the first or last rate given to all sales. Caution students to read the problems carefully and account for all numbers in the solutions except those that are not needed and which occur in "too much information" problems.

G. Morgan Lee is paid a commission of 3% on the first $100,000 of monthly sales and 5% on any sales above that amount. What commission did he earn if his sales for a month were $120,000? $4,000

H. Janice Corrudo is paid a commission of 15% of her yearly sales up to $85,000 and 18% of any sales above $85,000. Her total sales for last year were $112,000. What total commission did she earn last year? $17,610

■ Rate of Commission on Sales

To find the rate of commission, divide the amount of commission paid on total sales by the total sales amount.

Rate of Commission = Amount of Commission ÷ Sales

> **CALCULATOR TIP**
>
> If your calculator has a % key, you can find the percent directly by following these steps: key 120, press ÷, key 3000, press %. Be sure to add the percent symbol to your answer.

EXAMPLE 5

A salesperson sold a laptop computer and software for $3,000 and received a $120 commission. What percent commission did the salesperson receive?

SOLUTION

$120 ÷ $3,000 = 0.04 = 4%

■ CHECK YOUR UNDERSTANDING

I. Marc received a commission of $448 for selling $6,400 in goods in the past two weeks. What rate of commission did he earn? 7%

J. Nedra's sales last month were $54,000 for which she received a commission of $3,240. What rate of commission was Nedra paid? 6%

Wrap Up

The first sales job would pay monthly commission of $1,820. The second job would pay commission of $200 on the first $5,000 of sales and $2,400 on the $20,000 of sales over $5,000 in a month. Total monthly commission for the second job would be $2,600. The second sales job pays more.

COMMUNICATION

A company is considering changing the way in which it pays its sales staff. The company now pays a straight commission of 15% of all monthly sales. Sales now average $24,000 a month per salesperson.

The company wants to switch to a plan that pays a monthly salary of $1,500 and a 22% commission on all sales over $15,000 a month. Team up with another student to figure what would be the increase or decrease in the annual wages of salespeople by using the new plan compared to the old plan. Write your answer in sentence form.

Lesson 1.4 Commission ■ 23

■ **Teach Goal 4**

Point out to students that they may have already studied problems similar to finding the rate of commission. As an example, ask students how they would calculate the percent of the days in a month with rain. So, if in a month of 30 days there were 3 rainy days, it would have rained on 10% (3 ÷ 30) of the days.

Also demonstrate to students how to use the Calculator Tip to find percents directly.

■ **Apply Goal 4**

Work through Example 5 at the board with students completing the math at their desks.

Assign Check Your Understanding problems I and J for class work. Circulate in the classroom and examine student work for any difficulties.

Wrap Up

Review the Start Up. Through the Start Up activity students already know that the second sales job pays more. Ask students what else they would want to know about the commission plan before they took the higher-paying job. Students ought to consider whether the commission rate will change and whether sales are likely to stay the same or increase, but not decrease.

COMMUNICATION

Remind students that they are to write about their results and not just do the calculations. Sentences must be written with proper grammar, spelling, and punctuation.

■ *CHECK YOUR UNDERSTANDING SOLUTIONS*

G. $100,000 × 0.03 = $3,000;
($120,000 − $100,000) × 0.05 = $1,000;
$3,000 + $1,000 = $4,000

I. $448 ÷ $6,400 = 7%

Assign

Assignment: Exercises 1–24, 27–34. Start with the basic arithmetic problems to insure that students understand the underlying arithmetic in the problems.

Assess

Check student answers to the exercises by calling on them in class, collecting and grading selected problems, or by observing student work at their desks.

Reteach

STUDENT WORKBOOK If students need help with solving problems in this lesson, work through with students the workbook exercises indicated below followed by independent work on assigned workbook exercises.

For straight commission, work Exercise 1 with students. Then have them work Exercise 2. Check their work after they find the commission for each fountain.

For commission earnings based on quota, work Exercise 5a with students. Then have them calculate only the commission earnings in 5b and 5c.

For graduated commissions, work Exercise 6 with students. Assign Exercise 7 for independent work.

For the rate of commission, work Exercise 10a with students. Give them the amount of commission for 10b and have them calculate the rate of commission. If they calculate the rate correctly, have them verify the commission amount you provided.

EXERCISES

Rewrite as a decimal.

1. 9.25%   0.0925

2. 16.2%   0.162

3. 0.5%   0.005

Find the amount.

4. 12% of $800 $96

5. 7.5% of $13,000 $975

6. 4.2 % of $569 $23.90

Find the percent.

7. $1.26 ÷ $7   18%

8. $1.20 ÷ $8   15%

9. $90 ÷ $2,000   4.5%

Rewrite as a percent.

10. 0.08   8%

11. 0.11625   11.625%

12. 0.0025   0.25%

13. Dan Pawlik is paid a straight commission of $5.75 for each item he sells. Last month he sold 103 items. Find his estimated and exact commissions. $600; $592.25

14. A student who sells subscriptions for a magazine that costs $35 a year makes a commission of $5.25 on each subscription. What percent commission does the student make?   15%

15. Paul Batik earns a commission of 9% on sales. Last week he had sales of $646.70, $237.58, $1,984.89, $658.66, and $953.73. Find his total commission to the nearest cent. $403.34

16. Jo Ann White is paid a salary of $410 a week and a commission of 5.6% on all sales. Her sales last week were $6,700. Find her total earnings for the week. $785.20

17. Sheldon Cole earns a salary of $150 a week and a commission of 7% on all sales. If Cole's sales for one week were $6,890, what were his total weekly earnings? $632.30

18. Roosevelt Quinn receives a weekly salary of $600 plus $\frac{1}{2}$% commission on all sales in excess of $12,500 a week. Last week his sales were $48,370. What were his total earnings for the week? $779.35

19. Alice Miller works for a paint manufacturer. She is paid 3% commission on her first $20,000 of monthly sales and 8% commission on all sales over $20,000. In March her sales were $54,500; in April, her sales totaled $47,300. What were the total commissions she earned for the 2 months? $6,144

20. Olivia Thoms sells surplus books to bookstores. She is paid a weekly commission of $1.50 each on the first 50 books she sells, $1.75 each on the next 100 books, and $2 on any books she sells over 150. Last week she sold 225 books. What was her commission for the week? $400

21. Ludmilla Pavel is paid a commission on all sales over $3,000 a week. Last week she earned a commission of $420 on sales of $16,000. What rate of commission was she paid to the nearest tenth percent?   3.2%

24 ■ Chapter 1 Gross Pay

DIFFERENT LEARNING STYLES Visual Learners

Display a transparency of the solutions to Exercises 16, 18, and 19. These exercises represent one problem for each lesson goal.

Martin Ellis sells a line of cooking pots. He is paid a salary of $1,150 a month plus a commission on all sales. Each month his employer pays $120 of the cost of a health insurance plan. Last month his sales were $35,000, and he earned a total salary and commission of $3,250.

22. How much commission was Martin paid? $2,100

23. What rate of commission was he paid? 6%

24. CRITICAL THINKING When a new inkjet printer model is introduced salespeople may be paid a larger commission by their store for each old printer model they sell. Why would the store's manager offer such an incentive to salespeople? Answers will vary. Possible answer: to get rid of old model

25. CRITICAL THINKING Write two paragraphs that explain the advantages and disadvantages of working on commission. The first paragraph should be from an employee's viewpoint, the second from the viewpoint of an employer.
Check students' work.

26. DECISION MAKING You see ads on an Internet job listing service from two companies looking for salespeople. Both companies market a weight-loss system. The Slo-Loss Company pays a weekly salary of $100 and a commission of 14.5% on sales. The Slim-Now Company pays a straight commission of 30% of sales. Both companies expect you to be able to have sales of $1,000 in the first month and reach sales of $5,000 at the end of six months. List the reasons in outline form why you want to get one job over the other. Answers will vary.

MIXED REVIEW

27. Find $\frac{1}{4}$% of $28,000 $70

28. $97,398 × 1% $973.98

29. 60 is 15% of what number? 400

30. 20% more than $18 is what amount? $21.60

31. $250 decreased by what percent of itself is $235? 6%

32. Marc Bullard has two part-time jobs. At one job he worked 12 hours last week and was paid $8.15 an hour. Marc worked 6.25 hours last week at his second job that pays $7 an hour. What was his gross pay last week from both jobs? $141.55, Lesson 1.1

33. Nola Potter earns a salary of $1,200 a month and a commission of 7.5% on all sales over $4,000. This month her sales were $21,400. Find her total earnings for the month. $2,505, Lesson 1.4

34. Carolyn Mills does maintenance work at a golf course. She earned these amounts last season: April, $1,505; in each of the next four months, $1,806; September, $901. What were her average earnings per month for these 6 months? $1,605, Lesson 1.2

Lesson 1.4 Commission ■ 25

Enrich

Have 3 to 4 students read the paragraphs they wrote for Exercise 25, Critical Thinking. List on the board the advantages and disadvantages they mention. Ask other students to provide additional items not listed. Check to see if any advantage cited has an opposite viewpoint in the disadvantage listing. If so, remind students that employers and employees look at issues from different perspectives.

For Exercise 26, Decision Making, have students calculate what commission earnings might be given some assumed level of sales. Discuss the results. Then discuss reasons, other than income, why students would prefer one job to the other.

You may also show students how to find an unknown sales amount when the amount and rate of commission are known.

Close

Ask students to identify the arithmetic processes used to find commission earnings for straight, quota, and graduated commission pay plans. Read the bolded terms to the class and ask students to define the terms.

1.5 Other Wage Plans

GOALS

- Calculate gross pay for piece-rate employees
- Calculate gross pay for per diem employees
- Calculate gross pay for tip employees

Start Up

Employees, such as food service staff, whose pay varies widely, may need to estimate or project annual gross income based on current earnings. Assume that a waiter's monthly earnings from hourly wages and tips for the first quarter of the year are as follows: January, $1,367; February, $1,845; March, $2,398. What is the projected annual gross income for the waiter based on the first quarter's earnings?

Math Skill Builder

Review these math skills and solve the exercises that follow.

1. **Add** whole numbers and money amounts.
   Find the sum. 34 + 25 + 31 + 37 + 28 = 155

   1a. 78 + 92 + 101 + 86 357   **1b.** $135 + $176 + $157 $468

2. **Multiply** money amounts by whole numbers.
   Find the product. 347 × $0.81 = $281.07

   2a. 181 × $1.24 $224.44   **2b.** 5 × $98 $490

3. **Multiply** money amounts by percents.
   Find the product. 15% × $54 = 0.15 × $54 = $8.10

   3a. 20% × $26 $5.20   **3b.** 5% of $20.45 $1.02   **3c.** 10% of $60 $6

■ Piece-Rate Employees

Employers use a variety of ways to pay their employees. Some employees are paid for each item or *piece* they produce. Their wages are paid on a **piece-rate** basis. To figure their gross pay, you must multiply their pay per piece by the number of pieces produced. If employees are paid only for usable pieces produced, they get no pay for the pieces that are rejected.

Number of Pieces Produced × Piece Rate = Gross Pay

26 ■ Chapter 1 Gross Pay

CONNECTION TO ECONOMICS

Even though piece-rate employees are paid only for production that meets standards, both the employees and the employer lose when defective items are made. A defective product still requires materials, tools, and machines to be produced. The materials may have to be discarded, the tools wear out, and valuable machine time is lost.

EXAMPLE 1

Helen Burchett is paid $1.30 for each usable picture frame she produces. What was Helen's gross pay for last week if she produced the following quantities of usable frames:

Monday	52
Tuesday	47
Wednesday	54
Thursday	50
Friday	45

SOLUTION

$52 + 47 + 54 + 50 + 45 = 248$ usable frames produced

$248 \times \$1.30 = \$322.40$ gross pay

■ CHECK YOUR UNDERSTANDING

A. Louise Schubert is paid $18 for each computer she installs at customer offices. She installed these numbers of computers in 5 days last week: 7, 6, 9, 8, 5. What gross pay did Louise earn for the week? $630

B. Trevor Sherr is paid $1.20 for each hand-painted dish he produces. He is not paid for dishes that are not acceptable. On Monday, he painted 56 dishes; on Tuesday, he painted 44 dishes. For the two days 6 dishes contained slight errors and were unacceptable. What gross pay did Trevor earn for the two days? $112.80

■ Per Diem Employees

Some people are paid on a per diem basis. **Per diem** means "by the day." Per diem employees are paid a fixed daily amount by their employer. Many per diem employees are temporary employees provided to a company by temporary help agencies.

Self-employed persons may charge a per diem rate for their services. These people may provide a specialized service to their clients. Self-employed persons work for themselves instead of for employers.

The gross pay of someone paid by the day is found by multiplying the per diem rate by the number of days worked.

Per Diem Rate × Number Of Days = Gross Pay

EXAMPLE 2

Shawn Traylor worked 5 days last week as a temporary computer operator. His per diem pay rate was $120. What gross pay was Shawn paid for the week?

SOLUTION

$5 \times \$120 = \$600$ gross pay for the week

Lesson 1.5 Other Wage Plans ■ **27**

■ Apply Goal 1

Work through Example 1 at the board with students completing the math at their desks.

Assign Check Your Understanding problems A and B for class work. Circulate in the classroom and examine student work for any difficulties.

■ Teach Goal 2

Point out that many per diem employees are usually placed in jobs by a temporary help agency. They get paid only for the days they work even if they are willing and available to work each day.

Some per diem employees are independent contractors who make their own arrangements for employment.

Explain to students that employers often like the flexibility with which per diem workers may be hired or let go.

■ Apply Goal 2

Work through Example 2 at the board with students completing the math at their desks.

Assign Check Your Understanding problems C and D for class work. Walk around the classroom to examine student work and provide assistance as needed.

■ ONGOING ASSESSMENT

Ask students to explain the difference between salary and per diem. Have them calculate the daily pay of a salaried worker who earns $525 a week **[$105]** and the weekly pay of a per diem worker who gets $76.15 a day **[$380.75]**

■ *CHECK YOUR UNDERSTANDING SOLUTIONS*

B. $56 + 44 = 100$; $100 - 6 = 94$;
$94 \times \$1.20 = \$112.80$

C. $180 \times \$425 = \$76,500$

E. 1) $0.15 \times \$10.20 = \$1.53$;
2) $\$10.20 + \$1.53 = \$11.73$

Make sure that students understand that there are traditional units on which tip income is calculated. For example, a bellman receives a tip for each bag carried to a hotel room and not a percentage of the cost of renting the room. Give other examples, as well.

Tell students that tips based on a percent of a bill are usually rounded up to some greater amount. Also tell them that the suggested tips described in the chart may not be given by customers if the employee provides poor service.

Also point out that wait staff may agree to pool their tips and divide them equally or share part of their tips with others who bus tables or provide other direct help to them.

■ Apply Goal 3

Work through Example 3 at the board with students completing the math at their desks.

Assign Check Your Understanding problems E and F for class work. Circulate through the classroom and examine student work for any difficulties.

■ CHECK YOUR UNDERSTANDING

C. Sherry McCoy is a tax consultant. She charges $425 per diem for her services. If she worked 180 days last year, what was her gross income for the year? $76,500

D. Charlie's neighbors are often out of town and they hire him to house-sit. They pay Charlie $20 for each day they are gone. If they were out of town 57 days last year, what was Charlie's income from house sitting? $1,140

■ Tip Employees

Many workers receive income in the form of tips. A **tip** is an amount of money given to someone for services they provide. The person receiving the service pays tips voluntarily.

A tip, also called a *gratuity*, is often calculated as a percentage when there is a dollar value attached to the service. A waiter, for example, may receive a tip of 15% of the total restaurant bill.

Tip Percent × Total Bill = Tip Amount

An airport skycap on the other hand, may receive a specific amount for each piece of luggage handled.

Tip Per Unit × Number of Units = Tip Amount

Tipping practices vary considerably. The table below suggests guidelines for tipping certain types of workers. Most people round tips to the nearest quarter, or even dollar amount.

	Suggested Tipping Amounts
Airport skycap	$1 per bag
Hair stylist	15% of cost, minimum $1
Hotel chambermaid	$5 to $9 a night
Pizza delivery person	$1 to $5 depending on distance
Waiter/waitress	15-20% of total bill
Buffet waitstaff	5-10% of total bill
Taxi driver	15% of fare

EXAMPLE 3

After the Sutton family finished their meal at a local restaurant, the waiter brought them a check for $46.86. If Mrs. Sutton leaves a 20% tip, what amount of tip wages will the waiter receive for serving dinner to the Suttons? What will be the total meal cost to the Sutton's?

TEACHING STRATEGIES Cooperative Learning

Have a group of students form a team to list other workers who may earn tip income. These may include newspaper carriers, valet parking attendants, golf caddies, and street entertainers.

SOLUTION

The check amount is multiplied by the tip percentage to find the amount of the tip. The tip is added to the check amount to find the meal's total cost.

$20\% \times \$46.86 = 0.2 \times \$46.86 = \$9.372$ round tip to $9.50

$\$9.50 + \$46.86 = \$56.36$ total meal cost

■ **CHECK FOR UNDERSTANDING**

E. Jack orders the lunch special and a beverage. His check comes to $10.20.

   1) How much will the waitress receive if a 15% tip is left? $1.53, about $1.50

   2) What is the total cost of the meal to Jack? $11.73, about $11.75

F. Lydia and Sarah share a cab ride to work. Their fare is $7.60.

   1) At 15%, how much should they tip the driver? $1.14, about $1.25

   2) What is their total cost to ride the cab? $8.74, about $8.85

Wrap Up

A waiter's total earnings for the first 3 months, or one quarter year, are $5,610. Since there are 4 quarters in a year, multiply the total earnings for three months by 4 to find the total gross income for the year. So, $5,610 × 4 = $22,440 total annual gross income.

Algebra Connection

Write the formula an employer uses to calculate a piece-rate gross pay where *n* represents the number of completed units, *r* represents the pay rate per unit, and *G* represents gross pay. Use the formula to find gross pay for 415 envelopes stuffed at a rate of $0.20 each. $G = rn$, $83

The formula may also be used to find the gross pay for per diem employees. Test the formula by finding gross pay for a food demonstrator who works 4 days a month at a rate of $65 a day. $260

EXERCISES

Find the sum.

1. $40 + 38 + 39 + 45 + 41$ 203

2. $\$135 + \$18.60$ $153.60

Find the product.

3. $87 \times \$1.12$ $97.44   4. $3 \times \$97$ $291   5. $15 \times \$3 \times 5$ $225

Find the product.

6. $5\% \times \$38$ $1.90   7. $20\% \times \$187$ $37.40   8. $\$425 \times 22$ $9,350

Assess

Check student answers to the exercises by calling on them in class, collecting and grading selected problems, or by observing student work at their desks. If you notice that students are not labeling results, remind them to do so.

Reteach

STUDENT WORKBOOK If students need help with piece-rate problems, work through Exercise 1 in the workbook with them. Then have them recalculate gross pay using 27 unacceptable pieces and a piece rate of $1.17. The gross pay is $533.52.

If students need help with calculating per diem problems, work with them to find the gross pay of the first employee in Exercise 3. Then have them work independently to find gross pay of the second per diem employee.

Work with students to solve the tip portion of Exercise 4 in the workbook if they have difficulty with tip problems. Have student rework the problem using 17 homes and an average tip of $2.35 per stop. The gross pay for Saturday would be $71.95.

9. An airport skycap handled 520 bags in a weekend. His average tip per bag was $1.25. What total earnings did he have from tips for the weekend? $650

10. A waitress in an exclusive restaurant presented a food and beverage check in the amount of $340 to customers at a table. The customers decided to leave a 20% tip. What tip amount did the waitress receive? $68

11. Sandra Mitchell worked 22 days last month as a temporary employee in the Purchasing department. Her per diem pay was $95. What were Sandra's total earnings for the month? $2,090

12. To meet a shortage of medical staff, a doctor agreed to work 6, 24-hour shifts in the emergency room of a hospital during the next year. She is paid $950 for each shift worked. What total pay will the doctor receive for the 6 days of emergency room work? $5,700

13. Lu Ying works at the Wilkins Bike Shop and is paid $3.25 for every bike he assembles. The shop owner charges customers $20 for this service. During the five working days of one week, Lu assembled these numbers of bikes: 27, 33, 29, 27, 31. What was Lu's gross pay for that week? $477.75

For each of these piece-rate employees at Dover Industries, find the total pieces produced and the gross pay for the week. Copy and complete the chart.

	Name	M	T	W	T	F	Total pieces	Rate per piece	Gross Pay
14.	Zinke, T	54	55	59	62	60	290	$1.60	$464.00
15.	Bello, V.	24	28	30	31	27	140	$2.80	$392.00
16.	Dixon, S.	63	69	59	62	50	303	$1.55	$469.65
17.	Maier, B.	68	65	72	74	75	354	$1.18	$417.72

18. **DECISION MAKING** You and your partners are just starting a business. Since you are the manager, the partners are letting you decide whether to hire only regular, full-time employees or per diem employees who will work full time. Your other business partners told you that it may be less expensive for the first year of operation to hire per diem employees. You have to explain your decision to your partners. What will you tell them about your decision? Check students' work.

30 ■ Chapter 1 Gross Pay

ENRICHING SELECTED SOLUTIONS

In Exercise 11, Sandra Mitchell worked 22 days as a temporary employee. Ask students whether it is true that Sandra worked about the same number of days as a full-time employee would have worked. Prove that this is true by multiplying the usual days worked per week, 5, by the number of weeks in a year, 52, and dividing by the number of months, 12. The answer rounded to the nearest day is 22 days.

19. CRITICAL THINKING Steve took a taxi from the airport to his hotel across town. The fare came to $19.30. Steve handed the driver a $20 bill and told him to keep the change. Do you think Steve gave the driver a generous tip, an adequate tip, or not enough tip to express his appreciation for good service? No, only 4%.

INTEGRATING YOUR KNOWLEDGE Fred must make a decision about keeping his current job, which he dislikes, or accepting an offer for a new job, which he thinks he would enjoy. His current job pays an hourly rate of $12. Fred works 40 hours a week.

At the new job, Fred would earn $0.80 for each item he produces up to 125 pieces per day. For each piece over 125 produced in a day, Fred would receive $0.85. The average production rate is 15 pieces an hour. Because of his experience and skill, Fred believes that he can produce 18 an hour. At the new job, Fred would work 8 hours a day, 5 days a week.

20. What is the average weekly pay received by employees at the new job? $480

21. How much does Fred expect to make each week at the new job? $580.75

22. What is Fred's weekly pay at his current job? $480

23. Create a chart, like the one shown, that will allow you to compare both jobs by estimated daily, weekly, and annual earnings based on Fred's predictions that he will produce 18 pieces an hour.

	Current Job	New Job
Daily Earnings	$96	$116.15
Weekly Earnings	$480	$580.75
Annual Earnings	$24,960	$30,199

MIXED REVIEW

24. $1\frac{5}{8} + 2\frac{3}{4}$ $4\frac{3}{8}$ **25.** $15 \div \frac{5}{8}$ 24

26. What number increased by 8% of itself equals 1,944? 1,800

27. Bob Turnquist works 42 hours a week at a pay rate of $12.50 an hour. What amount will Bob earn in 4 weeks? $2,100, Lesson 1.1

Brenda Peoples earned $43,680 last year. Her usual work schedule is 50 hours a week. What were her average earnings Lesson 1.2
28. per month? $3,640   **29.** per week? $840   **30.** per hour? $16.80

31. Danny Mills receives a salary of $660 a month and a 7.5% commission on all sales above his monthly sales quota of $15,000. His sales for February totaled $32,000. What was Danny's total income for February? $1,935, Lesson 1.4

32. A waitress at a Sunday brunch served 50 customers in a 4-hour period. The total of all the food and beverage checks she wrote for customers was $1,500. Her customers left an average tip of 8%. What is her tip income for Sunday? $120, Lesson 1.5

Lesson 1.5 Other Wage Plans ■ **31**

SELECTED SOLUTIONS
9. 520 × $1.25 = $650
12. 6 × $950 = $5,700

14. 54 + 55 + 59 + 62 + 60 = 290;
290 × $1.60 = $464

Chapter Summary

Lesson 1.1 Hourly Pay and Salary

- Multiply hours worked by the hourly pay rate to find gross pay.

- Multiply salary by periods worked to find gross pay.

Lesson 1.2 Average Pay

- Add numbers and divide their total by the number of items to find an average.

- Add individual numbers and the product of grouped data and divide their total by the number of items to find an average.

- Multiply the average by the number of items and subtract known amounts from that total to find an unknown amount.

Lesson 1.3 Regular and Overtime Pay

- Multiply the hourly rate by 1.5 to find the time-and-a-half rate.

- Multiply the hourly rate by 2 to find the double-time rate.

- Based on the usual work schedule, count hours worked over 8 hours in a day or 40 hours in a week to find overtime hours.

- Multiply regular hours by the regular rate to find regular-time gross pay.

- Multiply overtime hours by the overtime rate to find overtime pay.

- Add regular-time pay and overtime pay to find total gross pay.

Chapter Review

Vocabulary Review

average	hourly rate	salary
commission	overtime	straight commission
double-time pay	piece rate	time-and-a-half pay
graduated commission	per diem	tip
gross pay	quota	

Fill in each blank with one of the terms above. Use each term only once.

1. The total amount of an employee's earnings is called __?__. gross pay

2. Pay that is 1.5 times the regular hourly pay rate of an employee is called __?__. time-and-a-half pay

3. An amount of money, often calculated as a percent, given to someone for service they provide is called (a, an) __?__. tip

4. A fixed amount of pay for a week or a month is called __?__. salary

5. Salespeople who receive a specific percent of the sales they make are paid on (a, an) __?__ basis. straight commission

6. One number that represents a group of numbers is called (a, an) __?__. average

7. Time worked beyond the end of a usual working day is called __?__. overtime

8. A wage rate based on the amounts produced by an employee is called __?__. piece-rate

9. Employees that are paid a fixed amount daily are called __?__ employees. per diem

LESSON 1.1

10. Raphael Winston is paid $15.60 for each hour he works. What is his gross pay for a week in which he works 43 hours? $670.80

11. Karolyn Yoder is paid a salary of $4,600 a month. What are her total annual earnings? $55,200

LESSON 1.2

12. The gross earnings of 6 employees in a picture framing shop for a week were: $620, $524, $715, $670, $588, and $675. What was the average amount earned for the week by these employees? $632

13. For the 9 warmest months of the year Kendrick Beachom installed chain link fences and earned $3,500 a month. For the remaining 3 months of the year he earned these monthly amounts by working several part-time jobs: $2,450, $1,785. $3,025. What were his average monthly earnings for the year? $3,230

14. The average annual pay of 4 construction workers is $46,800. Three of the workers earned these annual amounts of pay: $44,200, $47,450, and $45,900. What was the annual pay of the fourth worker? $49,650

DIFFERENT LEARNING ABILITIES Limited English Learners

Students whose dominant language is other than English may use a translating dictionary to provide the meanings of the key words in the Vocabulary Review. Enlist the aid of the ESL teacher in providing appropriate translations for these key terms if they do not appear in the student's dictionary.

LESSON 1.3

15. Monique Valla is paid an hourly rate of $17.63 for regular-time work. What will be her time-and-a-half and double-time hourly pay rates for overtime work? $26.445, $35.26

16. Raul Pina worked these hours in five days: $8\frac{1}{4}$, $7\frac{1}{2}$, 10, $8\frac{3}{4}$ and 8 hours. Overtime is based on an 8-hour workday. How many regular hours and overtime hours did he work in the five days? $39\frac{1}{2}$ regular hours, 3 overtime hours

17. Penelope Schoenberg's overtime is figured on a 40-hour week. Last week she worked 45.6 hours. This week she worked 9.7 hours on Monday, 8.3 hours on Tuesday, 8 hours on Wednesday, 9.1 hours on Thursday, and 8.6 hours on Friday. How many overtime hours did she work in the two weeks? 9.3

18. Eddie Fantin is paid every two weeks. For the first week of his pay period he worked 42 hours, 4 of which were overtime hours. In the second week he worked 40 regular hours and 7 overtime hours. His regular pay rate is $14.40 an hour with time-and-a-half for overtime. What are his regular, overtime, and total wages for the two weeks? $1,123.20, $237.60, $1,360.80

19. Marcel Ouimet is paid $9.80 an hour for regular time work and $14.70 overtime pay for all hours worked beyond 40 hours in a week. He is paid every two weeks. During Week 1 he worked 46 hours; in Week 2 he worked $42\frac{1}{4}$ hours. What was his total gross pay for the two weeks? $905.28

LESSON 1.4

20. Gaston Kohl is paid a straight commission of 6.5% on all sales. In March his sales were $105,000. What were his commission earnings in March? $6,825

21. A company pays sales staff a monthly commission of 4% on the first $15,000 of sales, 6% on the next $20,000 of sales, and 7.5% on all sales above $35,000. What amount would Tony Renshaw earn if his sales for a month were $41,000? $2,250

22. Irene Ogan earned a commission of $5,130 on sales of $90,000. What rate of commission was she paid? 5.7%

23. Doris Bommarito is paid a commission of 1.4% on all monthly sales above $80,000. Her sales for November were $382,000. What commission amount did she earn for the month? $4,228

LESSON 1.5

24. Steven Kahn is paid $4.25 for each wooden duck he paints that passes inspection. What is his pay on a day when he paints 38 ducks, 2 of which were rejected? $153

25. Tammy Scott-Hogan charges $350 a day to develop a personal training program for her clients. What amount did she earn last month if she worked 17 days? $5,950

26. What tip will Brady get if a customer adds a 15% tip to his $18.52 meal cost? $2.78

27. Amanda delivers newspapers to subscription customers. She receives an average annual tip of $12 from her 156 customers. What is her tip income for the year? $1,872

Chapter 1 Review ■ 33

Lesson 1.4 Commission
- Multiply sales by the rate of commission to find commission pay.
- Multiply sales over quota by the rate of commission to find commission pay.
- Multiply sales amounts by the appropriate commission rates and add their products to find total graduated commission pay.
- Divide the commission by sales to find the rate of commission.

Lesson 1.5 Other Wage Plans
- Multiply the piece-rate by the number of acceptable pieces to find gross pay.
- Multiply the daily pay rate by days worked to find the gross pay of per diem workers.
- Multiply the total bill by a tip percentage to find tip earnings.
- Multiply the tip per unit by the number of units to find tip earnings.

TEACHING STRATEGIES Cooperative Learning

Without referring to the body of the text, have students scan the exercises for Lesson 1.1 and identify the purpose of each problem. The purpose of Exercise 10 is to find the gross pay for an employee paid hourly. Repeat for all exercises in the Chapter Review.

The Tasks

Students need spreadsheet file tech1-1.xls for Tasks 1 and 2.

Task 1 Students enter data into a payroll detail spreadsheet.

Task 2 Students answer questions about the results of Task 1. They also change data and answer questions about the results.

Task 3 Students design and create a spreadsheet that calculates monthly earnings of salespersons paid on a graduated commission basis.

Task 4 Students answer questions about how the spreadsheet was designed and tested and how it could be changed to calculate average commissions. They also change data and answer a question about the calculation.

Teach and Apply Task 1

Show students how to open the spreadsheet. Inform students that all but the blue spreadsheet cells are protected from changes.

Have students enter the hours worked for Friday, Saturday, and Sunday for the first employee. Explain that if zero hours are worked on a day and the cell's contents are set to 0.00, no data has to be entered for that day. Have students enter hours worked for all employees.

When students complete data entry, ask them to check the total of all gross wages with the textbook solution. If the grand totals do not agree, the data entered should be verified.

Technology Workshop

Task 1: Enter Data Into A Payroll Detail Template

You are to complete a template that calculates the weekly gross wages for each employee of the Bainbridge Company. All employees receive regular hourly pay for time worked and overtime pay for hours worked beyond 40 hours in a week.

Open the spreadsheet for Chapter 1 (tech1-1.xls). Next, enter into the spreadsheet the hours worked by each employee for the three days shown in blue cells (cells G5-I14). The spreadsheet will calculate regular, overtime, and total gross wages for each employee. When finished, your spreadsheet should look like the one shown below.

	A	B	C	D	E	F	G	H	I	J	K	M	N	O	P
1							**Bainbridge Company**								
2							**Payroll Detail Sheet for January 8, 20—**								
3	Employee			Daily Hours Worked						Total Hours		Hourly	Gross Wages		
4	No.	Name	M	T	W	T	F	S	S	Reg	O.T.	Rate	Reg	O.T.	Total
5	1	Ajanaku	8.00	8.00	7.80	8.00	8.00	0.00	0.00	39.80	0.00	10.46	416.31	0.00	416.31
6	2	Bell	8.00	8.00	4.50	8.00	8.00	0.00	0.00	36.50	0.00	11.15	406.98	0.00	406.98
7	3	Cole	8.00	10.00	10.00	10.00	8.10	0.00	0.00	40.00	6.10	12.23	489.20	111.90	601.10
8	4	Dern	7.70	8.00	8.00	8.00	8.00	4.10	2.00	40.00	5.80	10.15	406.00	88.31	494.31
9	5	Evers	8.00	9.80	8.10	8.00	8.00	0.00	0.00	40.00	1.90	12.85	514.00	36.62	550.62
10	6	Ford	7.10	8.00	8.00	8.00	8.00	4.10	0.00	40.00	3.20	10.46	418.40	50.21	468.61
11	7	Gomez	8.00	8.00	8.00	8.00	8.00	3.90	2.00	40.00	5.90	12.35	494.00	109.30	603.30
12	8	Huang	8.00	9.30	8.00	8.00	8.00	0.00	0.00	40.00	1.30	11.70	468.00	22.81	490.82
13	9	Isom	8.00	8.00	5.40	8.00	8.00	0.00	0.00	37.40	0.00	11.32	423.37	0.00	423.37
14	10	Jackson	8.00	8.00	10.00	8.10	8.40	0.00	0.00	40.00	2.50	13.20	528.00	49.50	577.50
15		Totals											4,564.25	468.65	5,032.90
16															
17										Pay Raise Factor		1.000			

Task 2: Analyze the Spreadsheet Output

Answer these questions about your completed payroll sheet.
1. What hourly pay rate did Dern have? $10.15
2. Which employee had the largest gross pay for the week? Gomez, $603.30
3. Which employee worked the least regular-time hours? Bell, 36.5
4. Which employee worked the most overtime hours? Cole, 6.1
5. What was the total amount paid to all employees for overtime work? $468.65
6. What total gross pay was paid to employees for the one-week pay period? $5,032.90

Now move the cursor to cell M17, labeled Pay Raise Factor. The current entry in the cell should be 1.000. Now enter the 1.021. This change shows what would happen if the Bainbridge Company gives its employees a 2.1% pay increase. The increase would raise wages to 102.1%, or 1.021, of their current level. Notice how the hourly rate and the regular, overtime, and total gross wages figures changed for all workers.

34 ■ Chapter 1 Gross Pay

DIFFERENT LEARNING ABILITIES Hearing Impaired Learners

When presenting Task 1, turn your book to face a hearing impaired student and point to the line or cells you are talking about. You may also point to the line on a transparency, to a cell on a projection of your computer screen, or to the cell on the student's screen.

Answer these questions about your updated payroll sheet.

7. What is the formula used in Cell N5? What does the formula calculate? J5*M5, regular wages

8. What is the formula used in Cell O7? What arithmetic is done in the cell? K7*(M7*1.5), multiplication

9. What is the formula used in Cell P12? What does it do? N12+O12, adds regular and overtime wages for employee in Row 12

10. What hourly rate does Dern now earn? How much more per hour is Dern paid after the raise was calculated? $10.36, $0.21

11. Find the difference between the original and the new total gross wages, then calculate the percent increase to the nearest tenth percent. What does your answer show? Percent increase of 2.1% was constant throughout the spreadsheet.

Task 3: Design a Sales Commission Spreadsheet

You are to design a spreadsheet that will compute the monthly earnings of salespersons that are paid monthly on a graduated commission basis.

The spreadsheet for Task 1 includes formulas that use subtraction, multiplication, the IF function, and the SUM function. Create a spreadsheet that will use similar math operators and functions. The spreadsheet should allow you to calculate the gross pay for a month for all employees listed. Your spreadsheet should contain a row for each employee. The column formulas should calculate the amount of commission earned by each employee for each commission level and the total gross wages for all employees.

> *SITUATION:* You are the payroll clerk in the office of the Betadyne Company. The company pays its salespeople a commission on their sales. It does not pay them any salary. The employee names and their April sales are shown below on the left. Shown below on the right are the sales levels and rates by which your company figures commission payments.

Salesperson	April Sales	Betadyne Company Commission Structure
Boyce, Thad	$53,000	1.5% on all sales
Elkins, James	$48,000	3.4% of the first $50,000 of sales
Kubik, Lucy	$92,000	4.6% of all sales above $50,000
Mays, Nora	$64,000	

Task 4: Analyze the Spreadsheet Output

Answer these questions about your completed spreadsheet.

12. How did you figure the commission on all sales? commission rate × sales

13. How did you test the spreadsheet to make sure the calculations were correct? Used a calculator to compute the answers first.

14. How would you change the spreadsheet to calculate the average gross commissions earned by employees? Add formula: total gross wages ÷ number of employees

Chapter 1 Technology Workshop ■ 35

Teach and Apply Task 2

Assign Questions 1–6. Make sure students answer Questions 1–6 before they enter new data for Questions 7–11.

Teach and Apply Task 3

Assign Task 3. Students may work in teams of 2–3 if desired.

Students may find it helpful to plan the design of the spreadsheet on paper, including formulas, before using a computer.

Suggest to students that they calculate and display amounts for each commission structure in separate columns before calculating the total monthly earnings.

Teach and Apply Task 4

Assign Questions 12–15. Advise students to write concise, yet complete answers to Questions 12–14. If they need help with question 15, remind them that the phrase "how much more" implies a comparison, so they will have to calculate total earnings using 1.5% and 2% commissions on all sales.

Students might submit disks with their completed spreadsheets, printouts of the results of the data for Question 15, and written answers to Questions 11–14.

TEACHING STRATEGY Task 3

After students complete the design of their spreadsheet to calculate sales commissions, have them calculate the answers to use as a guide for writing formulas and to check the accuracy of the output of their spreadsheet after it is entered.

1. $40 \times \$0.40 + 4 \times \$0.60 =$ $\$18.40$
If the year is 1945, his gross wages are $18.40.
$40 \times \$4.25 + 4 \times \$6.375 =$ $\$195.50$
If the year is 1991, his gross wages are $195.50.

2. $\$5.15 \times 40 \times 52 = \$10,712$
A full-time minimum wage employee in 2004 makes $10,712.

3. $\$0.38 > \$0.25$
The 2004 minimum wage has $0.13 more buying power.

■ **WRITE**
Students need additional information about both jobs to compare the total earnings of both jobs if their decision is to be based on earnings alone. The value of benefits for the caregiver job must be determined. For the medical assistant job, the information needed includes the number of hours worked per week, the overtime pay rate, and the value of potential benefits.

Students may calculate comparative earnings for both jobs and their work may be checked for accuracy and the reasonableness of their assumptions.

■ **SCANS**
The students' work should be evaluated on its organization and the extent to which all directions were followed. The work should be supported by evidence that research sources and techniques were used.

■ **ONGOING ASSESSMENT**
STUDENT WORKBOOK The Integrated Project found in the workbook provides a comprehensive assessment activity for the goals of this chapter.

Chapter Assessment

How Times Have Changed

For Questions 1–2, refer to the timeline on page 3 as needed.

1. Cedric Jacobie works on a 40-hour week basis with time-and-a-half paid for overtime work. He is new at his job and is paid the minimum wage. One week in December he works 44 hours. If the year is 1945, what are his gross wages for the week? If the year is 1991, what are his gross wages for the week?

2. How much does a full-time (40 hr/wk, 52 wk/yr) minimum-wage employee make per year in 2004?

WRITE

Suppose that you live in Chicago, Illinois and interview for both of the jobs described in the classified advertisements shown below. Both companies are strong financially with equal growth potential and each offers you the job. Explain and show the computations that you need to make in order to decide which company is the best choice for you.

> CAREGIVERS—$100 signing bonus! Full-time work with individuals that have special medical needs. Travel to patients' homes. Annual salary range: $32–$38K depending on experience. Excellent benefits. For more information, please call 555-700-8000.

> MEDICAL ASSISTANT needed for busy doctor's office. Seeking high-energy person to work full-time to assist with patients. Must have previous experience. Hourly-rate is $16.85 with the possibility of overtime. Please fax resume to 555-700-1111, attn: Kim.

SCANS

Workplace Skills—*Acquiring and Evaluating Information*

These skills include the ability to see when information is needed, to gather information from a variety of sources, and to evaluate the usefulness of the information.

Test Your Skills Identify three jobs or industries that interest you. Look at a variety of resources such as job ads, the Internet, professional journals, library materials or direct contact with companies. Determine job titles. Name potential employers. List the skills each job requires. Mark each skill with either 1 (have the skill) or 2 (need to develop the skill).

Make a Plan From your three jobs or industries, choose the one that interests you the most. Create a plan that includes short-term goals and long-term goals to prepare you for a career in your chosen field.

Summarize Prepare in writing a speech that you could give that would influence an employer to hire you. Include references to your abilities in any of the following mathematical skills and how they apply to your ability to do this job.

multiplication   *division*   *estimation*   *rounding*
grouping data   *calculating pay*   *using spreadsheets*   *writing formulas*

PORTFOLIO ASSESSMENT

You may wish to have students find the cost per mile of operating a car since the caregiver job requires the employee to travel to patient's homes. Student may use the Internet to research the topic at the IRS web site, www.IRS.gov. They may also search key words such as car costs, car operating costs, or mileage reimbursement. Have students summarize their research and prepare a simple map of their Internet research for their portfolio.

Chapter-Test Correlation

Question	Lesson
12	1.1
13	1.1
14	1.2
15	1.2
16	1.3
17	1.3
18	1.3
19	1.4
20	1.5

CHAPTER TEST

Answer each question.

1. Add: $8\frac{1}{4} + 9 + 7\frac{1}{2} + 8 + 10\frac{1}{4}$ 43

2. Subtract: $47.3 - 37.5$ 9.8

3. Multiply: $38\frac{3}{4} \times \$13.35.$ $517.31

4. Divide: $\$85,956 \div 52$ $1,653

5. Rewrite 1.0567 as a percent. 105.67%

6. $30 \div \frac{5}{8} = ?$ 48

7. What is 1.25% of $34,500? $431.25

8. 120 is $\frac{1}{4}$ greater than what number? 96

9. Write 5.68% as a decimal rounded to the nearest hundredth. 0.06

10. Round $0.8794 to the nearest cent. $0.88

11. What number increased by 20% of itself equals $103.20? $86

Applications

12. Fiona Wolfe was paid $9 an hour for 46 hours of work last week at her full-time job. She also worked 7 hours last week at a part-time job that pays $11 an hour. What total gross pay did she earn last week from both jobs? $491

13. Zygmund Oleksik is paid a salary of $800 a week to manage a party store. What amount will he make in one year working at this job? $41,600

14. Rosie Belin worked these total weekly hours in four weeks of work: 45, 38, 42, 43. Her job pays $14 for each hour she works. What average gross pay did she earn per week for these four weeks of work? $588

15. The six employees in the security department of a company average $120 gross pay a day. Three of the employees earn $125 per day. Two others earn $116.50 a day. How much does the sixth employee earn per day? $112

16. Frank Camp's regular hourly pay rate is $11.87 an hour. His overtime pay rate is time-and-a-half. How much is Frank paid per hour for overtime work? $17.805

17. Justine Gilbert worked these hours last week: Monday, 8; Tuesday, $10\frac{1}{4}$; Wednesday, $8\frac{1}{2}$; Thursday, 9; Friday, $7\frac{3}{4}$. She works on an 8-hour day with time-and-a-half being paid for overtime work. Her regular gross pay rate is $17.10 an hour. What was Justine's overtime pay amount for last week? $96.19

18. Barney Mullins' regular pay rate is $14.85 an hour. He is paid time-and-a-half for hours worked over 40 hours in a week, including weekend work. He worked these hours from Monday through Saturday last week: 8.2, 8.9, 10.1, 9.6, 8.8, 6.7. What was his gross pay for the week? $867.98

19. Tiffany Penfield is paid a salary of $750 a month at her sales job. She also earns a commission on her sales in this way: 2% on all sales up to $34,000 in a month and 8% on all higher sales. What were Tiffany's total earnings for a month where her total sales were $80,000? $5,110

20. All employees of the Crafton Company are paid $0.375 for each wrench set they pack. How much would Kenny Pace earn if he packed 1,740 wrench sets in one week of work? $652.50

Chapter 1 Assessment ■ **37**

TEACHING STRATEGIES Chapter Test

Since this is the first chapter test, it is important to emphasize that solutions must be presented in an organized manner with parts clearly labeled. When the problems are checked, examine whether numbers are written dis-tinctly and whether labels are legible, concise, and spelled correctly. Deductions may be taken from students' final scores if they had been told that such factors would be considered for scoring purposes.

Chapter 2 reviews the math skills of horizontal addition, subtraction, multiplication, percents, rounding, and division. These skills are used to solve business and consumer problems of payroll deductions, net pay, job benefits and expenses, cash receipts, cash payments, and budgets.

Lesson 2.1 Deductions from Gross Pay
Students learn to find federal withholding taxes, calculate social security and Medicare taxes, and find net pay.

Lesson 2.2 Benefits and Job Expenses
Students calculate fringe benefits, total job benefits, job expenses, and net job benefits.

Lesson 2.3 Federal Income Taxes
Students calculate adjusted gross and taxable income, tax due, and refunds for single dependents.

Lesson 2.4 State and City Income Taxes
Students calculate state and city income taxes using flat and graduated tax rates.

Lesson 2.5 Cash Receipts and Payments Records
Students learn to find total receipts and keep a columnar cash payments record with grand totals.

Lesson 2.6 Budgets
Students prepare budgets and calculate the percent of income spent on expenses.

CHAPTER 2

Net Pay

2.1 Deductions from Gross Pay
2.2 Benefits and Job Expenses
2.3 Federal Income Taxes
2.4 State and City Income Taxes
2.5 Cash Receipts and Payments Records
2.6 Budgets

Statistical Insights

	Average Monthly Social Security Benefits for Retired Workers 1940–2002		
Year	Average for All Recipients	Average for Men Only	Average for Women Only
1940	$22.71	$23.26	$18.38
1945	25.11	25.71	19.99
1950	29.03	30.16	22.98
1955	69.74	75.86	56.05
1960	81.73	92.03	63.26
1965	82.69	90.89	68.78
1970	123.82	136.80	103.67
1975	196.42	220.35	160.50
1980	321.10	374.00	244.90
1985	432.00	509.60	322.20
1990	550.50	654.60	403.30
1995	671.70	794.30	505.80
2000	844.00	951.00	730.00

Use the data shown above to answer each question.
1. Social Security Benefits are paid to retired individuals once they reach 62 years of age and have paid social security taxes while they were employed. How can you use the data to estimate annual benefits? Multiply number from chart by 12.
2. Between what two rows did the benefits more than double for men, women, and all recipients? 1950 and 1955

Statistical Insights

Ask students how long it takes for the average social security recipient to recover all the money contributed while working. You might also ask what percent, on average, social security income is of total retirement income for recipients. Web search keywords might be: recover social security contributions, social security income.

NetCheck

Personal Finance Software

Many people keep financial information on their home computer. Several companies market such programs. Although each may look different and offer unique features, they all basically perform the same tasks. Keeping financial records on a computer makes it easy to keep information up-to-date and prevents calculation errors. Often software companies will allow you to try their software before you purchase it. Downloadable versions of these software programs may be available on the Internet.

Do State Tax Rates Differ?

State income tax rates differ among the states. Some states do not require their residents to pay state income taxes. States need money to operate and provide services. If a state has a higher income tax rate, other state taxes may be less. Or, if a state has a lower income tax rate, they may charge a higher sales tax rate. Information is available on the Internet that will allow you to compare state tax rates and other costs of living.

How Times Have Changed

The federal income tax has an enormous impact on the economy, both on the society at large and the individual workers. Although taxes tend to increase over time, the last couple of decades have seen income taxes decrease.

The high costs of the Civil War lead to the first federal income tax. **1861**

The 1894 tax law is ruled unconstitutional. **1895**

The 16th Amendment to the Constitution gives Congress the right to tax personal income. **1913**

Research to discover a significant event that happened in 1981 that relates to income taxes in the United States.

1894 Congress imposes a flat federal income tax.

1943 The withholding tax is introduced.

1850 — 1880 — 1910 — 1940 — 1970 — 2000

39

2.1 Deductions from Gross Pay

GOALS

- Find federal withholding tax deductions
- Calculate social security and Medicare tax deductions
- Calculate total deductions and net pay

Start Up

Janice is single and has just graduated from community college. She needs at least $480 each week to pay for her rent and other living expenses to afford to live alone. If she earns $13 an hour and works 40 hours each week, will she earn enough to pay her expenses?

Math Skill Builder

Review these math skills and solve the exercises that follow.

1 Add money amounts.
Find the sum.
$35.62 + $12.65 + $87.61 + $27.59 = $163.47

1a. $77.12 + $18.92 + $40.56 + $9.21 $145.81

1b. $53.07 + $3.76 + $21.98 + $82.16 $160.97

2 Subtract money amounts from money amounts.
Find the difference. $540.09 − $62.72 = $477.37

2a. $3,145.00 − $809.12 $2,335.88

2b. $723.82 − $129.04 $594.78

2c. $235.88 − $13.48 $222.40

3 Rewrite percents as decimals.
Rewrite 7.52% as a decimal. 7.52% = 0.0752

3a. 4% 0.04   **3b.** 5.2% 0.052   **3c.** 10.5% 0.105   **3d.** 4.34% 0.0434

4 Multiply money amounts by percents and round the product to the nearest whole cent.
Find the product. $387.25 × 7% = $387.25 × 0.07 = $27.1075, or $27.11

4a. $1,249.00 × 4% $49.96

4b. $478.53 × 7.2% $34.45

4c. $809.42 × 1.45% $11.74

> **MATH TIP**
>
> To rewrite a percent as a decimal, move the decimal point two places to the left and drop the percent sign.

40 ■ Chapter 2 Net Pay

■ Federal Withholding Tax Deduction

Deductions are subtractions from gross pay. The federal government, as well as many states and cities, require employers to deduct money from employee wages for income taxes, or **withholding taxes**, plus social security and Medicare taxes.

The amount of withholding tax depends on a worker's wages, marital status, and number of withholding allowances claimed. A **withholding allowance** is used to reduce the amount of tax withheld. Workers may claim one withholding allowance for themselves, one for a spouse, and one for each child or dependent.

To find the amount withheld from a worker's wages, you can use an income tax withholding table prepared by the government. Use the tables shown to find federal withholding taxes on weekly wages. First determine whether the person is single or married. Then using the table for the employee's marital status, read down the *if the wages are*—column at the left until you reach the correct wage line. Next, read across to the column headed by the number of withholding allowances claimed by the employee.

BUSINESS TIP

Congress changes the federal income tax rates from time to time. You can find the latest federal withholding tax rates at www.irs.gov.

Single Persons—Weekly Payroll Period

(For Wages Paid Through December 2004)

If the wages are—		And the number of withholding allowances claimed is—										
At least	But less than	0	1	2	3	4	5	6	7	8	9	10
		The amount of income tax to be withheld is—										
350	360	39	30	21	13	7	1	0	0	0	0	0
360	370	40	31	22	14	8	2	0	0	0	0	0
370	380	42	33	24	15	9	3	0	0	0	0	0
380	390	43	34	25	17	10	4	0	0	0	0	0
390	400	45	36	27	18	11	5	0	0	0	0	0
400	410	46	37	28	20	12	6	0	0	0	0	0
410	420	48	39	30	21	13	7	1	0	0	0	0
420	430	49	40	31	23	14	8	2	0	0	0	0
430	440	51	42	33	24	15	9	3	0	0	0	0
440	450	52	43	34	25	17	10	4	0	0	0	0
450	460	54	45	36	27	18	11	5	0	0	0	0
460	470	55	46	37	29	20	12	6	0	0	0	0
470	480	57	48	39	30	21	13	7	1	0	0	0
480	490	58	49	40	32	23	14	8	2	0	0	0
490	500	60	51	42	33	24	15	9	3	0	0	0
500	510	61	52	43	35	26	17	10	4	0	0	0
510	520	63	54	45	36	27	18	11	5	0	0	0
520	530	64	55	46	38	29	20	12	6	0	0	0
530	540	66	57	48	39	30	21	13	7	1	0	0
540	550	67	58	49	41	32	23	14	8	2	0	0

Married Persons—Weekly Payroll Period

(For Wages Paid Through December 2004)

If the wages are—		And the number of withholding allowances claimed is—										
At least	But less than	0	1	2	3	4	5	6	7	8	9	10
		The amount of income tax to be withheld is—										
440	450	30	23	17	11	5	0	0	0	0	0	0
450	460	31	24	18	12	6	0	0	0	0	0	0
460	470	33	25	19	13	7	1	0	0	0	0	0
470	480	34	26	20	14	8	2	0	0	0	0	0
480	490	35	27	21	15	9	3	0	0	0	0	0
490	500	37	28	22	16	10	4	0	0	0	0	0
500	510	39	30	23	17	11	5	0	0	0	0	0
510	520	40	31	24	18	12	6	0	0	0	0	0
520	530	42	33	25	19	13	7	1	0	0	0	0
530	540	43	34	26	20	14	8	2	0	0	0	0
540	550	45	36	27	21	15	9	3	0	0	0	0
550	560	46	37	29	22	16	10	4	0	0	0	0
560	570	48	38	30	23	17	11	5	0	0	0	0
570	580	49	40	32	24	18	12	6	0	0	0	0
580	590	51	42	33	25	19	13	7	1	0	0	0
590	600	52	43	35	26	20	14	8	2	0	0	0
600	610	54	45	36	27	21	15	9	3	0	0	0
610	620	55	46	38	29	22	16	10	4	0	0	0
620	630	57	48	39	30	23	17	11	5	0	0	0
630	640	58	49	41	32	24	18	12	6	0	0	0

Lesson 2.1 Deductions from Gross Pay ■ **41**

■ **Teach Goal 1**

Explain how to use the withholding tables to find the withholding tax.

Point out that withholding tables will change often in the next few years because of recent changes Congress has made in the tax law. Help students find the latest tables using the IRS web site: www.irs.gov.

■ **Apply Goal 1**

Work through Example 1 at the board with students completing the math at their desks.

Assign Check Your Understanding problems A and B for class work. Circulate through your classroom and examine student work to identify student problems.

■ **ONGOING ASSESSMENT**

Name a series of weekly incomes and number of dependents for single and married people that fit the tables in the lesson. As you do so, call on students to use the tables to find the withholding tax that applies.

DIFFERENT LEARNING ABILITIES At-Risk Learners

Students may have difficulty finding the withholding tax for a gross income such as $440 because it is listed twice in withholding tables. Make sure they can differentiate between "At least" and "Less than."

EXAMPLE 1

A single receptionist's weekly wages are $380 with 1 withholding allowance. What federal income tax is withheld?

SOLUTION

Use the table for single persons. The wages, $380, are on the fourth line of this part of the table. Read across to find the column under 1 withholding allowance. The amount of tax is $34.

■ **CHECK YOUR UNDERSTANDING**

A. Jared Brown is a single hospital technician with weekly wages of $458. He claims 1 withholding allowance. What amount should be deducted from his wages for federal withholding taxes? $45

B. Imy Berstein is a married worker earning $514 each week. She claims 2 withholding allowances. What amount should be deducted from her weekly earnings for federal withholding taxes? $24

On many calculators, you can multiply by a percent directly without rewriting it. Enter the number to be multiplied ($562), press the multiplication symbol (×), enter the percent (6.2) and press the percent sign (%). The answer, 34.844 will appear in the calculator display.

■ Social Security and Medicare Tax Deductions

The tax for social security is part of the Federal Insurance Contributions Act and is also called the FICA tax. The FICA benefits include:

■ *disability benefits* for workers who are disabled and unable to work

■ *Medicare*, which provides hospital insurance for some disabled people and for people over 65

■ *retirement benefits* for people who are at least 62

■ *survivors' benefits*, which are paid to spouses and dependent children when a social security recipient dies

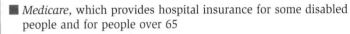

FICA tax rates and the maximum wages on which the taxes are charged are set by Congress and may change from time to time.

The overall tax rate of 7.65% is used in this text. This rate is made up of the social security tax rate of 6.2% applied to a maximum wage of $87,900 and the Medicare tax rate of 1.45%, applied to all wages.

If one earns more than $87,900 a year from one job, the employer does not deduct social security tax after the wages exceed $87,900. If one earns more than $87,900 a year from several jobs, each employer withholds 6.2% social security tax to the maximum $87,900 earning limit. The taxpayer must apply for a return of the overpayments when a federal income tax return is filed.

BUSINESS TIP

People who work for themselves must also pay FICA taxes on yearly net earnings. The tax rates for the self-employed are twice the rates paid by employees because the self-employed person must pay the employee and employer shares.

42 ■ Chapter 2 Net Pay

■ *CHECK YOUR UNDERSTANDING SOLUTIONS*

A. The weekly wage, $458, is found on the 11th line of the Single Persons table. Read across to the 1 withholding allowance column. The amount of tax is $45.

C. $24,000 × 0.062 = $1,488 $24,000 × 0.0145 = $348; $1,488 + $348 = $1,836

E. $460 × 0.0765 = $35.19

■ **Teach Goal 2**

Make sure students know how to rewrite the social security and Medicare percent rates as decimals.

Point out that the retirement benefits provided through FICA provide supplementary income and are not meant to be one's total retirement income.

Stress that Congress changes FICA rates and taxable income limits often.

Point out that the US population is living longer and the demands on the social security system will increase.

Explain that there are two parts to the FICA tax rate: (1) the Old Age, Survivors, and Disability Insurance rate (social security rate) and (2) the Hospital Insurance Plan rate (Medicare rate). Each rate is applied to different annual income maximums.

■ **Apply Goal 2**

Work through Example 2 and Example 3 at the board with students completing the math at their desks.

Assign Check Your Understanding problems C through H for completion in class. Move about the classroom and examine student work to identify student errors or difficulties.

EXAMPLE 2

Find the total FICA tax on incomes of $35,000, $80,000, and $92,000.

SOLUTION

Income	Social Security	Medicare	Total FICA
$35,000	$35,000 × 6.2% = $2,170	$35,000 × 1.45% = $507.50	$2,677.50
$80,000	$80,000 × 6.2% = $4,960	$80,000 × 1.45% = $1,160	$6,120.00
$92,000	$87,900 × 6.2% = $5,449.80	$92,000 × 1.45% = $1,334	$6,783.80

■ CHECK YOUR UNDERSTANDING

Find the FICA tax on each income. **C.** $24,000 $1,836   **D.** $89,000 $6,740.30

FICA taxes owed by workers are collected by their employers. Employers deduct the tax from each employee's earnings. Employers must also pay a FICA tax equal to the FICA taxes they deduct from their employees' earnings.

EXAMPLE 3

Sarah Fellows earned $562 during the last week of January. Find the total FICA taxes her company deducted from her wages.

SOLUTION

Since Sarah's wages are paid in January, you are sure that her wages have not exceeded the social security earning limit. She is taxed on both social security and Medicare. Use 7.65% as the tax rate.

7.65% = 0.0765   Rewrite as a decimal.

562 × 0.0765 = $42.993   Multiply the weekly wages by the decimal rate.

The total FICA tax amount deducted from Sarah's wages was $42.99.

■ CHECK YOUR UNDERSTANDING

Find the total FICA tax amount on each weekly wage.

E. $460 $35.19   **F.** $712.44 $54.50   **G.** $1,087.30 $83.18   **H.** $375.88 $28.75

■ Total Deductions and Net Pay

In addition to withholding, social security, and Medicare taxes, other deductions may also be subtracted from gross pay, such as union dues, health and life insurance, and government bonds. After all deductions are subtracted from total wages, or gross pay, an amount remains that is called **net pay**, or *take-home pay*.

Gross Pay − Deductions = Net Pay

Statement of Employee Earnings and Payroll Deductions											

	EARNINGS			DEDUCTIONS							
WEEK ENDED	REGULAR	OVER-TIME	TOTAL	FED. WITH.	SOC SEC.	MEDI CARE.	LIFE INS.	HEALTH INS.	OTHER	TOTAL	NET PAY
2/4	375.00		375.00	33.00	23.25	5.44	12.50	56.45	13.75	144.39	230.61

NO. 4798

Lesson 2.1 Deductions from Gross Pay ■ 43

COMMON ERRORS

When using a calculator to find FICA taxes, students may enter 7.65% as 0.765 instead of 0.0765. Review the use of a calculator with students before assigning exercises for independent practice.

Wrap Up

Review the Start Up. Work through the arithmetic of Janice's problem with the class. Have students complete work at the board and discuss each step. Since Janice cannot live alone on her salary, discuss what changes she might make to achieve her goal.

TEAM MEETING

Help teams draft questions for their interviews. Use the board to combine the lists that students prepare. Discuss the types of deductions they found and the range of percents each deduction type represented.

EXAMPLE 4

Mary Mendosa earned gross pay of $426 last week. Federal withholding taxes of $40, social security taxes of 6.2%, Medicare taxes of 1.45%, health insurance premiums of $45.80, and union dues of $12.56 were deducted from her gross pay. Find Mary's net pay.

SOLUTION

Multiply the gross pay by each tax rate.

$426 \times 0.062 = \$26.41$ $426 \times 0.0145 = \$6.18$

$\$40 + \$26.41 + \$6.18 + \$45.80 + \$12.56 = \$130.95$ Add to get the total deductions.

$\$426.00 - \$130.95 = \$295.05$ Subtract the total deductions from gross pay.

Mary Mendosa's net pay for the week was $295.05.

■ CHECK YOUR UNDERSTANDING

I. Jay Panetta earned gross pay of $410 last week. From his gross pay the following were subtracted: federal withholding tax, $39; social security tax, 6.2%; Medicare tax, 1.45%, health insurance, $34.88, and $40 for his savings plan. Find Jay's net pay. $264.75

J. Last week, Rose Petropolis earned gross pay of $820. Her employer deducted $118 in federal withholding taxes, 6.2% in social security taxes, 1.45% in Medicare taxes, $74 in health insurance, and $45 in union dues. What was Rose's net pay? $520.27

Wrap Up

Look back at the Startup Question. Janice earns $520 a week ($13/hr × 40 hr). Using the federal withholding tax table for single persons with 1 withholding allowance, her tax on $520 is $55. In addition, social security taxes are $38.44 and Medicare taxes, $7.54. Even if she had no other deductions from her gross pay, her net pay is only $419.02. This amount is not enough to cover the $480 she needs to live alone.

TEAM MEETING

Form a team with two other students. Each team member should interview one person who receives a paycheck. Each team member should prepare a three-column report of the interview. Make the first column show required deductions; the second, personal or optional deductions; the third, percent of paycheck. Compare lists. Then combine the lists into one, three-column report. When deductions from two or more lists match, show the percents of paycheck as a range of percents using the lowest and highest percents found for that deduction.

■ *CHECK YOUR UNDERSTANDING SOLUTIONS*

I. $410 × 0.062 = $25.42 $410 × 0.0145 = $5.95
$39 + $25.42 + $5.95 + $34.88 + $40 = $145.25
$410 − $145.25 = $264.75

J. $820 × 0.062 = $50.84
$820 × 0.0145 = $11.89
$118 + $50.84 + $11.89 + $74 + $45 = $299.73
$820 − $299.73 = $520.27

Find the sum.

1. $34 + $15.23 + $65.01 + $23.85 $138.09   **2.** $87 + $32.71 + $48.14 + $12.09 $179.94

Find the difference.

3. $523.19 − $106.42 $416.77   **4.** $4,456.12 − $98.76 $4,357.36

5. $389.28 − $79.52 $309.76   **6.** $2,107.88 − $278.43 $1,829.45

Rewrite percents as decimals.

7. 8% 0.08   **8.** 2.4% 0.024   **9.** 12.06% 0.1206

10. 3.67% 0.0367   **11.** 89.145% 0.89145   **12.** 145% 1.45

Find the product.

13. $498 × 5.6% $27.89   **14.** $826 × 3.456% $28.55

Find the withholding tax in each exercise using tables given.

	Total Wages	Marital Status	Withholding Allowances			Total Wages	Marital Status	Withholding Allowances
15.	$390.00	Single	1 $36		**16.**	$487.00	Married	2 $21
17.	$411.00	Single	0 $48		**18.**	$444.00	Single	4 $17
19.	$528.97	Married	5 $7		**20.**	$612.81	Married	3 $29
21.	$457.07	Single	1 $45		**22.**	$438.88	Single	9 $0

Find the social security tax and Medicare tax on each weekly wage. Use a 6.2% social security tax rate on a maximum of $87,900 gross wages and a 1.45% Medicare tax rate on all wages.

23. $475.00 $29.45, $6.89   **24.** $556.34 $34.49, $8.07

25. $249.40 $15.46, $3.62   **26.** $497.45 $30.84, $7.21

27. $749.23 $46.45, $10.86   **28.** $180.04 $11.16, $2.61

29. $289.48 $17.95, $4.20   **30.** $863.78 $53.55, $12.52

Copy and complete the table below. Use a 6.2% social security tax rate on a maximum of $87,900 gross wages and a 1.45% Medicare tax rate on all wages.

	Name	Allow-ances	Marital Status	Gross Wages	Income Tax	Social Secur.	Medi-care	Other	Total Deduc.	Net Wages
31.	Ahern	1	Single	467.29	46.00	28.97	6.78	82.12	163.87	303.42
32.	Brown	0	Single	399.62	45.00	24.78	5.79	56.45	132.02	267.60
33.	Cali	3	Married	578.21	24.00	35.85	8.38	31.51	99.74	478.47
34.	Devon	6	Married	459.65	0.00	28.50	6.66	75.21	110.37	349.28
35.	Ezeka	2	Married	538.76	26.00	33.40	7.81	48.22	115.43	423.33

Lesson 2.1 Deductions from Gross Pay ■ **45**

Ali Zaheer is married with 3 withholding allowances. Each week his employer deducts federal withholding taxes, social security taxes, Medicare taxes, and $38.12 for health insurance from his gross pay. His gross weekly wage is $578.

36. Find the total deductions $106.34

37. Find his net pay. $471.66

Josh Logan is paid a monthly salary of $7,500.

38. Estimate his social security taxes for May. $480

39. Find the exact social security taxes he paid for the month of March. $465

40. Find the social security taxes he paid in December. $334.80

41. What Medicare taxes did he pay for the year? $1,305

Rachel Radcliff earns an annual salary of $126,000.

42. How much social security taxes will be deducted from her salary in November? $0.00

43. How much social security taxes will be deducted from her salary in May? $651

44. How much Medicare taxes will be deducted from her salary for the year? $1,827

45. **CRITICAL THINKING** What is the relationship between income, tax, and the number of withholding allowances? Why would less money be taken out when more allowances are claimed? Taxes go up with income, go down with allowances; exemptions are greater.

46. **DECISION MAKING** Your employer allows you to deduct money each week from your gross wages to be placed in a savings plan of your choice. Should you have this deduction taken from your wages each week? By deducting savings before you receive it, you are not tempted to spend the money.

MIXED REVIEW

47. $25.60 × $1\frac{1}{4}$ $32

48. $\frac{1}{4} + 6\frac{3}{4} + 8\frac{1}{2}$ $15\frac{1}{2}$

49. $5\frac{1}{4} - 3\frac{1}{2}$ $1\frac{3}{4}$

50. $8 × 0.1 $0.80

51. $\frac{1}{4}$ more than 40 50

52. $25,600 × 12.5% $3,200

Cory Mathis is married with 4 withholding allowances. Each week his employer deducts $21 in federal withholding taxes, 6.2% in social security taxes, 1.45% in Medicare taxes, and $58.77 for health insurance from his gross pay. His gross weekly wage is $609.

53. Find the total deductions. $126.36, Lesson 2.1

54. Find his net pay. $482.64, Lesson 2.1

55. Faye Rivera worked these hours last week: Monday, 8 hours; Tuesday, 6 hours; Wednesday, 7 hours; Thursday, 8 hours; Friday, 7 hours. If she is paid $12 an hour, what was Faye's gross pay for the week? $432, Lesson 1.1

56. Tyrone Wilson's yearly pay for the last three years was: $24,800, $25,900, and $29,760. What was Tyrone's average yearly pay? $26,820, Lesson 1.2

SELECTED SOLUTIONS

38. $8,000 × 0.06 = $480

39. $7,500 × 0.062 = $465

44. $126,000 × 0.0145 = $1,827

49. $5\frac{1}{4} - 3\frac{1}{2} = \frac{21}{4} - \frac{7}{2} = \frac{21}{4} - \frac{14}{4} = \frac{7}{4} = 1\frac{3}{4}$

56. $24,800 + $25,900 + $29,760 = $80,460
$80,460 ÷ 3 = $26,820

2.2 Benefits and Job Expenses

GOALS

- Find total job benefits
- Find net job benefits
- Compare the net job benefits of jobs

Start Up

Sally's uncle asked her to help with a remodeling job that will take 10 days to complete. He said he would pay Sally $60 a day or start with $1 for the first day and double her pay each day. Which wage do you think will earn Sally the most money?

Math Skill Builder

Review these math skills and solve the exercises that follow.

1 **Add** money amounts.
Find the sum. $43,112 + $3,078 + $1,087 + $466 = $47,743

1a. $19,208 + $189 + $2,417 + $25 $21,839

1b. $78,297 + $35 + $108 + $3,108 $81,548

2 **Subtract** money amounts.
Find the difference. $39,087 − $8,648 = $30,439

2a. $98,085 − $13,498 $84,587   **2b.** $29,337 − $2,073 $27,264

2c. $101,882 − $24,938 $76,944   **2d.** $289,108 − $57,650 $231,458

3 **Multiply** money amounts.
Find the product. $8.75 × 40 = $350

3a. $12.88 × 36 $463.68   **3b.** $15.39 × 38 $584.82

3c. $10.82 × 40 $432.80   **3d.** $10.10 × 32 $323.20

> **BUSINESS TIP**
>
> Health insurance is often too costly for many workers. Some companies provide health insurance at a lower cost as a benefit to their workers.

■ Total Job Benefits

In addition to wages, many employers provide other things of value called **employee benefits** or *fringe benefits*. For example, employers may provide low-cost health and accident insurance, life insurance, and pensions. They may also provide paid holidays, sick leave, and vacation time, the use of a car, a credit union, uniforms, parking, discounts for purchases of merchandise, recreational facilities, child care, and education or training.

Lesson 2.2 Benefits and Job Expenses ■ 47

Start Up

Have students read Sally's offers in the Start Up and choose one pay plan. Then have students calculate the options and save them to discuss in the lesson Wrap Up.

Math Skill Builder

The skills of adding, subtracting, and multiplying money amounts are used in this lesson.

Complete all exercises in Math Skill Builder 1–3.

■ Teach Goal 1

Have students make a list of job benefits they would like to receive or use the one developed in the Start Up. Next to each item, have them estimate the cost of each benefit and give a reason why an employer might want to offer such a benefit to their employees.

Point out that rising health care costs have driven up costs of providing health care to employees and that some employers are asking employees to pay a greater share of health insurance costs.

COMMON ERRORS

Students may confuse fringe benefits, total job benefits, and net job benefits. Total job benefits include both base salary and fringe benefits. Net job benefits are found by subtracting job expenses from total job benefits.

■ **Apply Goal 1**

Work through Example 1 at the board while students complete the math at their desks.

Assign Check Your Understanding problems A and B for completion in class. Circulate through your classroom and examine student work to identify errors and problems.

■ **Teach Goal 2**

Make sure students realize that all jobs have expenses and that finding net job benefits is a way to compare jobs economically in a fairer manner. An often-overlooked job expense is childcare.

■ **ONGOING ASSESSMENT**
Name some job benefits and expenses and ask students to classify them as one or the other.

Employee benefits are an important part of a job's total value. Benefits can be worth from 15% to 40% of the amount paid in wages. Benefits may be stated in money amounts or as a percent of gross pay.

Benefit 1 + Benefit 2 = Total Employee Benefits

Benefit Rate × Gross Pay = Total Employee Benefits

When you are considering a job offer, the value of employee benefits should be added to the amount of wages to find the *total job benefits*.

Gross Pay + Employee Benefits = Total Job Benefits

EXAMPLE 1

Kirby Rosen is a manager with Durable Products, Inc. Last year Kirby earned gross pay of $34,800 and these benefits: paid pension, $2,784; health insurance, $1,892; paid vacation, $1,338; paid holidays, $2,007; and free parking, $425. What total job benefits did Kirby receive last year?

> **CALCULATOR TIP**
>
> Add the benefits first to find the total benefits package. Then add the gross pay to the benefits package to get total job benefits.

SOLUTION
Gross pay: $34,800

Benefits:	Paid pension	$2,784	Health insurance	$1,892
	Paid vacation	1,338	Paid holidays	2,007
	Free parking	425		

Total employee benefits: $8,446

Total job benefits: $34,800 + $8,446 = $43,246

■ **CHECK YOUR UNDERSTANDING**

A. Vi Schashack estimated her yearly fringe benefits last year to be: health insurance, $2,580; paid vacations and holidays, $3,133; paid pension, $2,545. Vi's gross pay was $31,807 last year. (1) What were Vi's total benefits for last year? (2) What were Vi's total job benefits for last year? $8,258; $40,065

B. Lin Ping earned gross pay of $28,089 last year. Her yearly benefits are 33% of her gross pay. (1) What were Lin's total benefits for last year? (2) What were her total job benefits for last year? $9,269.37; $37,358.37

■ Net Job Benefits

Almost every job has expenses. Some examples of **job expenses** are union or professional dues, commuting expenses, uniforms, licenses, and tools. To find **net job benefits**, subtract total job expenses from total job benefits.

Total Job Benefits − Job Expenses = Net Job Benefits

EXAMPLE 2

Rita Espinosa had total job benefits of $32,620. Her job expenses were $1,624 for commuting, $135 for a required license, $275 for professional dues, and $75 for the company birthday fund. Find her net job benefits.

■ *CHECK YOUR UNDERSTANDING SOLUTIONS*

A. (1) $2,580 + $3,133 + $ 2,545 = $8,258
(2) $8,258 + $31,807 = $40,065

B. $28,089 × 0.33 = $9,269.37
$28,089 + $9,269.37 = $37,358.37

SOLUTION

Total job benefits: $32,620

Job expenses: Travel + License + Professional Dues + Birthday Fund
$1,624 + $135 + $275 + $75 = $2,109

Total expenses: $2,109

Net job benefits: $32,620 − $2,109 = $30,511

■ **CHECK YOUR UNDERSTANDING**

C. Ben Asimov found that his job expenses for last year were: Uniforms, $329; licenses, $278; professional dues, $475; commuting costs, $1,077. His total job benefits for the same period were $56,102. Find his net job benefits. $53,943

D. Nicki's total job benefits for the previous year were estimated to be $78,299. However, her job expenses for the same job were: licenses, $580; commuting costs, $1,793; technical books, $2,057. What were her net job benefits for the year? $73,869

■ Comparing Net Job Benefits

When you compare jobs you should consider many features about each job, not just the net job benefits offered by each job. For example, you should consider how much you like the job, the chances for raises and promotions, the chances of layoffs, and job security.

EXAMPLE 3

Iko Moro's job pays $33,750 in yearly wages and 26% of her wages in yearly benefits. She estimates that yearly job expenses are $2,354. Another job that she is looking at pays $32,590 in yearly wages and has estimated yearly benefits of 29%, with job expenses of $2,080. Which job offers the greater net job benefits, and how much greater?

SOLUTION

Rewrite Iko's estimated benefit percent as a decimal and then multiply her yearly wages by the decimal rate to get the benefits of the job.

Then add the benefits and yearly wage amounts and subtract the job expenses to find the net job benefit of the job.

Iko's current job   *The other job she is considering*

$33,750 × 0.26 = $8,775 $32,590 × 0.29 = $9,451.10

$33,750 + $8,775 − $2,354 = $40,171 $32,590.00 + $9,451.10 − $2,080.00 = $39,961.10

Subtract the net job benefits of the other job from the net job benefits of the Iko's current job.

$40,171.00 − $39,961.10 = $209.90

Iko's current job offers her the greatest net job benefits, by $209.90.

■ **Apply Goal 2**

Work through Example 2 at the board while students complete the math at their desks.

Assign Check Your Understanding problems C and D for completion in class. Circulate through the room and examine student work for difficulties.

■ **Teach Goal 3**

Stress that comparing jobs on only gross pay is inaccurate because of the value of fringe benefits and job expenses.

Re-emphasize that job choice should include factors other than economic ones, such as liking your work, liking your fellow workers, and job security.

■ **Apply Goal 3**

Work through Example 3 at the board while students complete the math at their desks.

Assign Check Your Understanding problems E and F for completion in class. Circulate through your classroom and examine student work for difficulties.

■ CHECK YOUR UNDERSTANDING SOLUTIONS

C. $329 + $278 + $475 + $1,077 = $2,159
$56,102 − $2,159 = $53,943

D. $580 + $1,793 + $2,057 = $4,430
$78,299 − $4,430 = $73,869

■ **CHECK YOUR UNDERSTANDING**

E. Ted Roberts earned a salary of $41,700 last year. His benefits were 32.5% of his salary. His job expenses totaled $3,180. Ted is looking at another job that offers $45,260 in wages and 24% in benefits. His job expenses for the other job total $3,740. Which job offers the greatest net job benefits, and how much greater? 2nd; $309.90

F. Amy Weir had these job expenses last year: union dues, $650; tools, $1,890; uniforms, $375; licenses, $480. She earned $49,500 in wages and received benefits worth 29% of her wages. She has been offered another job at another company that will pay $45,200 in wages and 34% in benefits. Amy's job expenses for the other job are: commuting, $2,560; licenses, $480; tools, $590; parking, $380. Which job offers the greatest net job benefits, and how much greater? 1st; $3,902

Wrap Up

Look back at the Start Up problem posed at the beginning of this lesson. Sally would receive $600 ($60 per day × 10 days) in the first offer. The second offer would pay her $512. Isn't it amazing how quickly doubling your daily pay starting with only $1 can add up?

WORKPLACE WINDOW

BENEFITS CLERK   Benefits clerks are part of a larger group of workers called human resource specialists. Benefits clerks work in the human resource departments of organizations. Their job is to keep records about the benefits that organizations can provide to employees, the benefits organizations make available to employees, and the benefits actually selected by employees. Benefits clerks also answer employee questions about the benefits a firm provides, fill out benefits application forms, and handle employee claim forms. They may also contact physicians, hospitals, and employees about claims.

Usually benefits clerks maintain benefit records in a computer system that uses human resource information system software. Because their job is so specialized, benefits clerks are usually found only in large organizations or in firms that manage employee benefits for other organizations.

1. What education and experience are usually required of beginning benefits clerks?

2. What is the job outlook for benefits clerks?

3. What types of organizations are most likely to hire benefits clerks?

50 ■ Chapter 2 Net Pay

■ *CHECK YOUR UNDERSTANDING SOLUTIONS*

E. 2nd job

$41,700 × 0.325 = $13,552.50

$41,700 + $13,552.50 = $55,252.50;

$55,252.50 − $3,180 = $52,072.50

$45,260 × 0.24 = $10,862.40

$45,260 + $10,862.40 = $56,122.40;

$56,122.40 − $3,740 = $52,382.40

Find the sum.

1. $1,034 + $215 + $65,901 + $819 $67,969

2. $82,298 + $3,725 + $406 + $616 $87,045

Find the difference.

3. $45,823 − $41,637 $4,186

4. $35,789 − $30,479 $5,310

5. $52,907 − $48,278 $4,629

6. $156,980 − $75,345 $81,635

Rewrite percents as decimals.

7. 56.4%   0.564

8. 3.8%   0.038

9. 23.6%   0.236

10. 13.723%   0.13723

Find the product.

11. $44,098 × 25.7% $11,333.19

12. $52,491 × 31.8% $16,692.14

13. $29,926 × 23.245% $6,956.30

14. $31,044 × 15.5% $4,811.82

John Bellows earned gross pay of $26,888 last year. He estimates his yearly benefits to be: paid pension, $1,828; health and life insurance, $1,654; paid vacations and holidays, $2,582; free parking, $237.

15. What were John's total estimated benefits for last year? $6,301

16. What were his total job benefits for last year? $33,189

17. Thomasina Serling had the following job expenses for last year: union dues, $529; licenses, $178; commuting costs, $2,709. Her total job benefits for the same period were $46,192. Find her net job benefits. $42,776

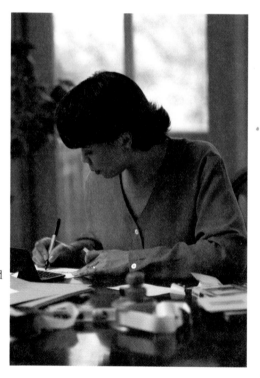

BEST BUY   Jorge Conseco can work for ABM, Inc. for $437 per week or Zeda, Inc. for $1,408 per month. Benefits average 19% of yearly wages at ABM and 25% at Zeda. Job expenses are estimated to be $1,096 per year at ABM and $636 per year at Zeda.

18. Which job would give Jorge more net job benefits for a year?   1st

19. How much more? $5,461.56

20. **CRITICAL THINKING**   The value of some benefits, such as paid holidays, can be figured very accurately. However, the value of other benefits, such as free recreation facilities, can only be estimated. If you were offered a benefit package that included use of a free gymnasium, how would you estimate its dollar value?   Answers will vary but should include membership price in fitness club.

Lesson 2.2 Benefits and Job Expenses ■ **51**

Assign

Assignment: Exercises 1–19, 21–40. Start with the basic arithmetic problems at the beginning to insure that students understand the underlying arithmetic in the Exercises.

Assess

Check student answers to the exercises by calling on them in class, collecting and grading selected problems, or by observing student at work.

Ask students to define the bolded and italicized terms in the lesson and use them in sentences.

Reteach

STUDENT WORKBOOK If students need help with job benefits, complete Exercise 1 in the workbook with them. Then have them complete Exercise 2.

If students need help with job expenses and net job benefits, complete Exercise 3 in the workbook with them. Then have them complete Exercise 4.

If students need help comparing net job benefits, complete Exercise 5 in the workbook with them. Then have them finish Exercise 6.

SELECTED SOLUTIONS

15. $1,828 + $1,654 + $2,582 + $237 = $6,301;
$26,888 + $6,301 = $33,189

18. 1st job

19. $437 × 52 = $22,724;
$22,724 × 0.19 = $4,317.56;
$22,724 + $4,317.56 = $27,041.56

$27,041.56 − $1,096 = $25,945.56
$1,408 × 12 = $16,896;
$16,896 × 0.25 = $4,224;
$16,896 + $4,224 = $21,120
$21,120 − $636 = $20,484;
$25,945.56 − $20,484 = $5,461.56

Assign and discuss with students Exercise 20, Critical Thinking. One way to estimate the value of the gym is to find the cost of membership in a health club with similar facilities.

After students solve Exercises 18–19, Best Buy, have them discuss whether they have enough information to decide which job Jorge should take.

Have students invent their ideal job. Caution students to develop a realistic salary and benefits package, based on current practices. Have students identify non-monetary factors in their ideal job.

Bring in job ads. Have students compare their lists of job benefits in their ideal job with actual job benefits advertised in ads.

INTEGRATING YOUR KNOWLEDGE   Nora Bertram works at Radnor Products, Inc. and is paid a salary of $25,000 plus 5% commission on all her sales. Last year her sales were $200,000. Nora's benefits were: paid pension, $3,150; health insurance, $2,400; paid vacations and holidays, $3,365. Her job expenses are $3,007. She is considering a job offer from B-Tree, Inc. that pays a salary of $30,000 plus 6% commission on all sales over $100,000. She estimates her benefits at B-Tree to be $8,489 and her job expenses to be $2,050.

21. If Nora's sales at B-Tree were $200,000, which job would give her more net job benefits?   B-Tree

22. Use your answer from Exercise 22 to determine how much more the net job benefits would be? $1,531

MIXED REVIEW

Change to percents.

23. 1   100%   24. 2.85   285%   25. 0.39   39%   26. $\frac{4}{5}$ 80%

Change to decimals.

27. $\frac{3}{8}$ 0.375   28. 87.6%   0.876

29. 0.5%   0.005   30. $\frac{1}{4}$%   0.0025

Change to fractions or mixed numbers and simplify.

31. 25% $\frac{1}{4}$ 32. 250% $2\frac{1}{2}$ 33. 10% $\frac{1}{10}$

34. Ursala Thomas had the following job expenses for last year: union dues, $388; licenses, $109; commuting costs, $1,478. Her total job benefits for the same period were $39,256. Find her net job benefits. $37,281, Lesson 2.2

David Allen is paid $11.80 an hour for an 8-hour day, time and a half for time past 8 hours per day, and double time on weekends. Last week he worked these hours: Mon., 9; Tues., 8; Wed., 6; Thurs., 11; Fri., 8; Sat., 5. Deductions were: $48 in withholding, 6.2% in social security, 1.45% in Medicare, and $46 in union dues.

35. What is David's regular pay? $448.40, Lesson 1.3

36. What is his overtime pay? $188.80, Lesson 1.3

37. What amount is withheld from David's pay for FICA taxes? $48.75, Lesson 2.1

38. What is his net pay? $494.45, Lesson 2.1

39. Natasha Dubcek works on a piece-rate basis. She produced these numbers of items last week: Monday, 65; Tuesday, 48; Wednesday, 69; Thursday, 68. How many items must Natasha produce Friday to average 63 items per day?   65, Lesson 1.2

40. Cromwell, Inc. employs 5 people at a branch office. Their weekly wages are: Fred, $423.34; Erin, $479.14; Bob, $378.98; Susan, $528.20; and James, $462.93. What is the average weekly wage at the branch office? $454.52, Lesson 1.2

CONNECTION TO ECONOMICS

Students should understand the economic consequences of fringe benefits. They are a cost to employers and reduce profits unless they are recovered by raising prices or reducing profits. A result of higher prices can be falling sales and employee layoffs. Another is that not enough is invested in the business to keep it competitive, and it fails.

2.3 Federal Income Taxes

GOALS

- Calculate adjusted gross income and taxable income
- Calculate the income tax due
- Calculate the income tax refund for single dependents

Start Up

Sven Tole is a high school student who worked during summer vacation. He noticed that federal income taxes were withheld from his paychecks. He didn't think it was fair for him to pay taxes when he made so little during the year. Is he right?

Math Skill Builder

Review these math skills and solve the exercises that follow.

1 **Add** money amounts.
Find the sum. $2,509 + $1,090 + $56 + $398 = $4,053

  1a. $1,907 + $3,763 + $78 + $189
  $5,937
  1b. $5,007 + $208 + $976 + $92
  $6,283

2 **Subtract** money amounts.
Find the difference. $32,459 − $4,108 = $28,351

  2a. $3,766 − $791
  $2,975
  2b. $28,067 − $1,448
  $26,619
  2c. $107,390 − $65,288
  $42,102

3 **Multiply** money amounts.
Find the product. $2,600 × 2 = $5,200

  3a. $2,789 × 4 $11,156   **3b.** $3,188 × 6 $19,128   **3c.** $1,572 × 10 $15,720

■ Adjusted Gross Income and Taxable Income

Employers deduct money for federal income tax from worker's pay. This is called *a withholding tax*. The amounts withheld are estimates of the tax owed at year's end.

The tax year for individuals ends on December 31. You must calculate and pay any federal income tax due by April 15 of the next calendar year. Income earned and taxes due are reported on *a federal income tax return*.

A completed return shows how much you owe in federal income taxes. If the amount withheld from wages was larger than what was owed, you should claim a refund. If the withholding taxes paid were less than what you owed, you pay the difference.

BUSINESS TIP

Self-employed people must estimate their income taxes for the year. They then pay part of that estimated tax each quarter.

Lesson 2.3 Federal Income Taxes ■ 53

Start Up

Have students read the Start Up. Then discuss with them the probability of Sven paying taxes. Students who work are usually listed as dependents on their parents' tax returns. However, their total yearly incomes are usually so low that they owe little or no actual federal income tax. Since their employers withhold federal income taxes from their wages, they should file a tax return to get a refund on those taxes.

Math Skill Builder

The skills of adding, subtracting, and multiplying money amounts are used in this lesson.

Complete all exercises in Math Skill Builder 1–3 to have students review these skills.

■ Teach Goal 1

Point out that there are legal definitions of acceptable tax deductions and that these may change. Also emphasize the importance of keeping good records of income and deductions.

This text uses simplified amounts for exemptions and the standard deduction. The actual amounts allowed change periodically. However, the arithmetic processes associated with these amounts do not. You may wish to have students substitute current amounts for those used in the text problems.

CONNECTION TO ECONOMICS

Students should understand some of the impacts of a graduated income tax on the economy. One such impact is that wealthier taxpayers pay more tax. Since wealthier people have more discretionary income to invest, there will be less money for investment. On the other hand, tax-payers with less money will pay less tax. A greater percentage of their income is spent on necessities adding to consumer spending. Consumer spending constitutes about two-thirds of our economy.

■ Apply Goal 1

Work through Example 1 with students completing the math at their desks.

Assign Check Your Understanding problems A and B for completion in class. Walk about your classroom and examine student work for errors and problems.

Gross income is the total income in a year and includes income from wages, salaries, commissions, bonuses, tips, interest, dividends, prizes, pensions, the sale of stock, and profit from a business.

From gross income, you may be eligible to subtract *adjustments to income*. These include business losses, payments to approved retirement plans, alimony, and certain penalties. The amount left is called **adjusted gross income**.

Adjusted Gross Income = Gross Income − Adjustments to Income

From adjusted gross income you subtract the deductions and exemptions for which you qualify. The result is your taxable income. **Taxable income** is the income on which you actually pay tax.

Taxable Income = Adjusted Gross Income − Deductions and Exemptions

Deductions are expenses that reduce the amount of your taxable income. You may deduct interest paid on a home mortgage, property taxes, state and local income taxes, medical and dental expenses, casualty and theft losses, and contributions to charities. You may claim a fixed amount called a **standard deduction**. Or, if your actual deductions are more than the standard deduction, you list all your deductions on your tax return under *itemized deductions*.

An **exemption** is an amount of income per person that is free from tax. You may claim one exemption for yourself unless you are claimed as a dependent on another person's tax return. You can also claim one exemption for a spouse and one exemption for each dependent. For example, a couple with two dependent children can claim four exemptions. A single person with a dependent parent can claim two exemptions.

The amounts allowed for the standard deduction and exemptions change often. In this text, the standard deduction is $4,850 for a person filing an income tax return as an individual and $9,700 for married people filing a return together, or *jointly*. The amount used for each exemption is $3,100.

EXAMPLE 1

a. Clara Shane is single and has a gross income of $32,600. She pays $2,600 into an approved retirement plan. Clara has deductions of $6,900. She has one exemption for herself. What is her taxable income?

b. Andy Cross and his spouse have a gross income of $33,000. They file jointly. They make payments into an approved retirement plan of $3,000. Their itemized deductions were only $4,300. So, they will take the standard deduction of $7,800. They claim two exemptions. What is their taxable income?

SOLUTION

	a. Clara Shane	b. The Crosses
Gross Income	$32,600	$33,000
Adjustments to Income	− 2,600	− 3,000
Adjusted Gross Income	$30,000	$30,000
Deductions	− 6,900	− 9,700
	$23,100	$20,300
Exemptions	− 3,100	− 6,200
Taxable Income	$20,000	$14,100

COMMON ERRORS

Students may misread information given in tables. Suggest that students place a blank piece of paper below the row with the amount they need to find and then carefully select the correct column to find the required data.

A. Tyronne Gilkey is single and has an adjusted gross income of $65,000. Tyronne has deductions of only $2,900 and so decides to take the standard deduction. He claims one exemption for himself. What is his taxable income? $57,050

B. Alice Greer and her spouse have an adjusted gross income of $50,000. file jointly. Their itemized deductions are $10,500 and they claim three exemptions. What is their taxable income? $30,200

■ Income Tax Due

Employers withhold money for income taxes from employee paychecks during the year. The amount of tax paid in withholding is an estimate and is probably more or less than the tax the employee actually owes.

To find the tax due, you must complete a tax return. If too much withholding or self-employment tax has been paid, the government will pay back, or *refund* the difference. If too little tax has been paid, you must pay the difference to the government. If taxable income is less than $100,000, a tax table must be used to find the tax. Parts of a recent tax table are shown below.

If your taxable income is—		And your filing status is—			
At least	But less than	Single	Married filing jointly	Married filing separately	Head of a household
				Your Tax is—	
13,000					
13,000	13,050	1,596	1,303	1,596	1,444
13,050	13,100	1,604	1,308	1,604	1,451
13,100	13,150	1,611	1,313	1,611	1,459
13,150	13,200	1,619	1,318	1,619	1,466
13,200	13,250	1,626	1,323	1,626	1,474
13,250	13,300	1,634	1,328	1,634	1,481
13,300	13,350	1,641	1,333	1,641	1,489
13,350	13,400	1,649	1,338	1,649	1,496
13,400	13,450	1,656	1,343	1,656	1,504
13,450	13,500	1,664	1,348	1,664	1,511
13,500	13,550	1,671	1,353	1,671	1,519
13,550	13,600	1,679	1,358	1,679	1,526
13,600	13,650	1,686	1,363	1,686	1,534
13,650	13,700	1,694	1,368	1,694	1,541
13,700	13,750	1,701	1,373	1,701	1,549
13,750	13,800	1,709	1,378	1,709	1,556
13,800	13,850	1,716	1,383	1,716	1,564
13,850	13,900	1,724	1,388	1,724	1,571
13,900	13,950	1,731	1,393	1,731	1,579
13,950	14,000	1,739	1,398	1,739	1,586

If your taxable income is—		And your filing status is—			
At least	But less than	Single	Married filing jointly	Married filing separately	Head of a household
				Your Tax is—	
23,000					
23,000	23,050	3,096	2,739	3,096	2,944
23,050	23,100	3,104	2,746	3,104	2,951
23,100	23,150	3,111	2,754	3,111	2,959
23,150	23,200	3,119	2,761	3,119	2,966
23,200	23,250	3,126	2,769	3,126	2,974
23,250	23,300	3,134	2,776	3,134	2,981
23,300	23,350	3,141	2,784	3,141	2,989
23,350	23,400	3,149	2,791	3,149	2,966
23,400	23,450	3,156	2,799	3,156	3,004
23,450	23,500	3,164	2,806	3,164	3,011
23,500	23,550	3,171	2,814	3,171	3,019
23,550	23,600	3,179	2,821	3,179	3,026
23,600	23,650	3,186	2,829	3,186	3,034
23,650	23,700	3,194	2,836	3,194	3,041
23,700	23,750	3,201	2,844	3,201	3,049
23,750	23,800	3,209	2,851	3,209	3,056
23,800	23,850	3,216	2,859	3,216	3,064
23,850	23,900	3,224	2,866	3,224	3,071
23,900	23,950	3,231	2,874	3,231	3,079
23,950	24,000	3,239	2,881	3,239	3,086

If your taxable income is—		And your filing status is—			
At least	But less than	Single	Married filing jointly	Married filing separately	Head of a household
				Your Tax is—	
0	5	0	0	0	0
5	15	1	1	1	2
15	25	2	2	2	2
25	50	4	4	4	4
50	75	6	6	6	6
75	100	9	9	9	9
100	125	11	11	11	11
125	150	14	14	14	14
150	175	16	16	16	16
175	200	19	19	19	19
200	225	21	21	21	21
225	250	24	24	24	24
250	275	26	26	26	26
275	300	29	29	29	29
300	325	31	31	31	31
325	350	34	34	34	34
350	375	36	36	36	36
375	400	39	39	39	39
400	425	41	41	41	41
425	450	44	44	44	44
450	475	46	46	46	46
475	500	49	49	49	49
500	525	51	51	51	51
525	550	54	54	54	54
550	575	56	56	56	56
575	600	59	59	59	59
600	625	61	61	61	61
625	650	64	64	64	64
650	675	66	66	66	66
675	700	69	69	69	69

To use a tax table, find your taxable income in the "At least . . . but less than" columns. Then read across that line to the column that shows the filing status: single, married filing jointly, etc. The amount where that line and column meet is your tax.

■ **Teach Goal 2**

Students should understand that the amount withheld for taxes seldom corresponds exactly with the amount of taxes owed. Taxpayers must file an income tax return at the end of the year so that their actual tax liability and the underpayment or overpayment may be reported.

You may wish to use current tax tables for exercises in this lesson.

Many people have their tax returns professionally prepared. Caution students that the liability for the correctness of the return is still the taxpayer's, not the preparer's.

■ **ONGOING ASSESSMENT**

Call out taxable income amounts and number of dependents for single and married people that fit the table in the lesson. As you do so, ask students to name the amount of income tax that fits each case.

■ *CHECK YOUR UNDERSTANDING SOLUTIONS*

A. $65,000 − ($4,850 + $3,100) = $57,050

B. $50,000 − ($10,500 + $9,300) = $30,200

Apply Goal 2

Work through Example 2 with students completing the math at their desks.

Assign Check Your Understanding problems C and D for completion in class. Circulate through the room and examine student work for errors or problems.

Teach Goal 3

Make sure students understand why they cannot claim themselves as an exemption if their parents claim them as an exemption. This would allow them to be counted as an exemption twice.

Federal tax laws, rates, and tax tables change frequently, but the basic procedures presented in this lesson remain unchanged. Explaining the basic procedures should help students understand how to compute their federal tax liability regardless of constant amendments to federal tax law.

EXAMPLE 2

a. Bea O'Shea is single, has taxable income of $13,200, and her employer deducted $2,340 in withholding taxes for the year. Find Bea's tax due and any refund or amount owed. Use the tax tables shown on the previous page.

b. Vince Tagliani is married and files a joint return. He and his wife had a taxable income of $23,425 last year. The amount withheld from their wages was $2,669 during the year. Find the tax due and refund or amount owed for the Taglianis. Use the tax tables.

BUSINESS TIP

A head of household is an unmarried or legally separated person who pays more than half the cost of keeping a home for a dependent father, mother, or child.

SOLUTION

	a. O'Shea	b. Taglianis
Income tax due from table	$1,626	$2,799
Amounts withheld during year	$2,340	$2,669
Tax owed	—	$130
Refund due	$714	—

■ CHECK YOUR UNDERSTANDING

C. Bill Reston is single and has taxable income of $13,576. His employer deducted $1,827 in withholding taxes for the year. Find Bill's tax due and any refund or amount owed. $1,679; $148 refund

D. Vera Yates is married and files a joint return. Vera and her spouse had a taxable income of $23,901 last year. The amount withheld from their wages was $2,509 during the year. Find their tax due and refund or amount owed. $2,874; $365 due

■ Income Tax Refunds for Single Dependents

Many young, single people, such as students, are listed as dependents on someone else's income tax even though they are employed. They are required to pay income taxes on their earnings, even though the tax they actually owe is usually very low. That means that usually the federal income taxes withheld from their paychecks are greater than the federal income taxes they owe.

To claim a refund on taxes paid, you must file an income tax return. The rules for dependents filing returns are different than for people who are not dependents.

A dependent's income is grouped into two categories: earned income and unearned income. **Earned income** is from the dependent's own labor, such as wages, salaries, and tips. Everything else is **unearned income**, including interest and dividends.

A single dependent who is not blind and under 65 can claim as a standard deduction the higher of these two amounts:

a. $800

b. The amount of earned income, plus $250, up to $4,850 (This is the standard deduction used in this text.)

■ *CHECK YOUR UNDERSTANDING SOLUTIONS*

C. From table, tax is $1,679; $1,827 − $1,679 = $148 refund

D. From table, tax is $2,874; $2,874 − $2,509 = $365 tax due

EXAMPLE 3

Jack Valente is a senior at Bayview High School and his parents claimed him as a dependent on their tax return. Jack worked last summer and earned $2,385. His employer deducted $320 in withholding taxes from his pay. Jack also earned $302 in interest on his savings account and had no adjustments to income. Jack claimed the standard deduction. What was the amount of Jack's refund?

SOLUTION

Find the amount of allowable deduction: $2,385 + $250 = $2,635.

Since $2,635 > $800 and $2,635 < $4,850, Jack's allowable deduction is $2,635

Find the amount of adjusted gross income: $2,385 + $302 = $2,687

Find the amount of taxable income: $2,687 − $2,635 = $52

Find the tax due or refund amount.   *from chart on pg. 57*

$320 − $9 = $311   Jack's refund

6 ← $314

> **MATH TIP**
>
> The symbol > means greater than. The < means less than.

■ CHECK YOUR UNDERSTANDING

E. Tina Moore is a junior who earned $3,510 working at a card shop. Her employer deducted $468 in withholding taxes. She has no adjustments to her income or additional income. Her mother claims her as a dependent. How much will Tina receive as a refund? $468

F. Kim Chung worked for his uncle during the summer. He was paid $2,897 but no withholding tax was deducted. He earned $57 in interest on his savings account. He has no adjustments to his income and his parents claim him on their tax return. How much does he owe in federal income taxes? $0

Wrap Up

Young, single, dependent people, such as students, often have federal income taxes withheld from their paychecks, even though they make very little money during a year. Most will pay only a small amount in income taxes and receive a refund when they file their tax return.

COMMUNICATION

Write a brief paragraph you might include in an e-mail to a friend who works explaining why it is important for the friend to file a tax return.

There are three important guidelines that should be followed when sending e-mail.

1. Your e-mail should cover only one topic.
2. Your message should be brief.
3. Be courteous and professional in your message.

Remember, once the e-mail is sent, you cannot get it back.

■ *CHECK YOUR UNDERSTANDING SOLUTIONS*

E. $3,510 < $4,700; allowable deduction is $3,510; $468 − $0 = $468 refund

F. $57 < $250; ($2,897 + $57) < $4,700; allowable deduction is $2,954; $0 tax due

Work through Example 3 with students completing the math at their desks. Point out the meaning of the < and > signs. Also point out that the symbol always opens to the larger number.

Assign Check Your Understanding problems E and F for completion in class. Circulate through your classroom and examine student work for difficulties.

Wrap Up

Review the Start Up. Use the Wrap Up problem to help students realize that they are likely to get all of the withholding taxes they pay back IF they file a return. Some students never file returns because they believe that filing a return means paying more taxes or because they do not understand the process.

COMMUNICATION

Discuss with the class the points that should be included in the e-mail before assigning the problem. Have some students read their e-mails and have the class evaluate the e-mails using the three criteria listed in the problem.

Assign

Assignment: Exercises 1–35, 37–44. Start with the basic arithmetic problems at the beginning of the exercises to insure that students understand the underlying arithmetic in the exercises.

Assess

Check student answers to the exercises by calling on them in class, collecting and grading selected problems, or by observing student work as you circulate.

Ask students to define the bolded and italicized terms in the lesson and use them in sentences.

Reteach

STUDENT WORKBOOK If students need help with adjusted gross or taxable income, complete Exercises 1 and 2 in the workbook with them. Then have them complete Exercises 3–5.

If students need help finding the tax due, complete Exercises 6a–6c in the workbook with them. Then have them complete Exercises 6d, 6e, and 7–10.

If students need help finding the tax refund for dependents, complete Exercise 11 in the workbook with them. Then have them finish Exercises 12–13.

EXERCISES

Find the sum.

1. $2,683 + $5,094 + $94 + $625 $8,496
2. $8,262 + $853 + $493 + $77 $9,685

Find the difference.

3. $4,228 − $735 $3,493
4. $63,163 − $15,926 $47,237
5. $73,997 − $16,398 $57,599
6. $125,370 − $73,920 $51,450

Find the product.

7. $3,034 × 7 $21,238
8. $6,517 × 23 $149,891
9. $2,183 × 7 $15,281
10. $7,525 × 18 $135,450

11. Bo and Dan Brady's income last year was: net income from business, $35,838.67; dividends, $2,312.98; interest, $3,517.45; rental income, $2,672. Adjustments to income totaled $4,628.83. Find their adjusted gross income. $39,712.27

12. In one year, Nestor Ortiz's wages totaled $29,450. His wife, Maria Gomez had a salary of $31,572 and a bonus of $500. The Gomezes also received $2,519 in interest, and $953.37 in dividends. They paid $4,850 into a retirement fund and were penalized $52 for removing money from a savings plan early. What was their adjusted gross income that year? $60,092.37

Dee Goer is single and had an adjusted gross income last year of $16,457. Dee's itemized deductions were $5,452 She claimed one exemption of $3,100.

13. What was Dee's estimated taxable income? $8,000

14. What was Dee's actual taxable income? $7,905

In preparing their tax return, the Rossinis, a married couple, claimed 5 exemptions at $3,100 each, and the standard deduction. Their adjusted gross income was $45,208.

15. Estimate the Rossini's taxable income. $20,000

16. What was the Rossini's exact taxable income? $20,008

Use the tax tables in this lesson to find the tax.

17. Beth and Ira Stein are married and file a joint tax return. Their taxable income is $23,378. What is their tax? $2,791

18. Nicki O'Shea is 25 years old and is single. Her gross income last year was $21,455 and her taxable income was $13,926. Find her tax. $1,731

19. How much tax does a head of household with taxable income of $23,798 owe? $3,056

20. Jim Bouche is married but is filing a separate tax return. His taxable income is $23,624. Find the amount of his tax. $3,186

21. Tien Chou's tax return for last year shows a total tax of $8,278. Tien's employer withheld $8,450 from her wages during the year. What refund should Tien receive? $172

22. Kumar Panday paid $16,118 in federal withholding. Kumar's total tax shown on his tax return was $17,448. What amount of tax did he owe? $1,330

58 ■ Chapter 2 Net Pay

SELECTED SOLUTIONS

13. $16,000 − ($5,000 + $3,000) = $8,000
23. $26,820 + $5,495 + $1,466 = $33,781
24. $2,000 + $19 = $2,019
25. $33,781 − $2,019 = $31,762
26. $31,762 − ($4,850 + $3,100) = $23,812

27. Tax from table, $3,216
28. $3,985 − $3,216 = $769 refund
29. $100 < $250; $250 + $100 < $4,850; $250 + $100 = $350

On his federal income tax return, Benito Silva, a single taxpayer, reported income from wages, $26,820; tips, $5,495; and interest earned, $1,466. Benito had these adjustments to income: payments to a retirement plan, $2,000; penalty for early with-drawal of savings, $19. His employer withheld $3,985 from his pay for federal income tax. Benito claims the standard deduction of $4,850 and an exemption of $3,100.

23. What was Benito's gross income? $33,781

24. Find the total of his adjustments to income. $2,019

25. Find Benito's adjusted gross income. $31,762

26. What was his taxable income? $23,812

27. What is his amount of tax due? $3,216

28. Does he owe or get a refund? How much? $769 refund

For Exercises 29–35, assume that each person claims the standard deduction, is under age 65, not blind, had no adjustments to income, and is listed on the parents' return as a dependent. Use the tax tables found in this lesson when needed.

Find each dependent's standard deduction.

Earned Income	Unearned Income	Standard Deduction		Earned Income	Unearned Income	Standard Deduction
29. $250	$100	$800	**30.**	$1,950	$600	$2,200
31. $4,875	$300	$4,850	**32.**	$5,175	$0	$4,850

33. Last summer, Troy Yaeger earned $2,855. His employer withheld $240 of his wages for income taxes. What is the amount of Troy's tax refund? $240

34. Carmen Reyes worked part time last year while attending college and earned $4,288. The total withholding taxes she paid were $450. Carmen also earned $78 in interest and $16 in dividends. How much tax refund should she receive? $450

35. Jon Kent's parents subtracted $3,100 from their adjusted gross income when they listed him as an exemption on their tax return. Jon's taxable income was $148. He paid $277 in withholding taxes. What amount should he expect as a tax refund? $263

36. DECISION MAKING Molly and Dan Shashack claim one less withholding allowance than they are legally entitled to. They do this so that they always get a large refund when they file their federal income tax return. Is this a good idea? Why or why not? Answers will vary. Students need to defend their answer, however a good point to include is that the Shashacks are allowing the government to hold their extra money during the year. They could be making interest from this "extra" money.

MIXED REVIEW

37. Find 11% of $250. $27.50

38. Find $\frac{1}{2}$% of $4,800. $24

39. 180 is what percent less than 240? 25%

40. What percent of $90 is $270? 300%

41. 432 × 0.001 0.432

42. 9.053 ÷ 0.001 9,053

43. Bea Rosenthal is single with a taxable income of $23,616. Her employer withheld $3,796 from her wages for income tax during the year. Using tax tables in this lesson, find how much her refund should be. $610, Lesson 2.3

44. Jerry Blanchard sells computers. The average price of the computers is $1,248. His rate of commission is $12\frac{1}{2}$%. How many computers would he have to sell to make $624 a week? 4, Lesson 1.4

Lesson 2.3 Federal Income Taxes ■ 59

Start Up

Have students read the Start Up. Have them name services that cities, counties, and states typically provide to their citizens.

Math Skill Builder

The addition and multiplication of money amounts are skills that are used in the lesson. So is the ability to rewrite percents as decimals.

Have students complete all exercises in Math Skill Builder 1–3.

■ **Teach Goal 1**

State and city income taxes may be based on the same taxable income used in the federal tax, or adjustments in taxable income may have to be made.

Remind students of the need for 100% accuracy, especially when dealing with tax issues in either personal or business life.

GOALS

- Calculate state and city income taxes using a flat tax rate
- Calculate state and city income taxes using a graduated tax rate table

Start Up

What are the major uses of city, village, or town taxes in your area? If you live outside a city, village or town, what are the major uses of your county taxes? Make a list of services that your city, village, town, or county provides using tax money.

Math Skill Builder

Review these math skills. Solve the exercises that follow.

❶ **Add** money amounts.
Find the sum. $150 + $280 + $450 + $580 = $1,460

   1a. $45 + $108 + $289 + $310 $752   **1b.** $308 + $467 + $589 + $612 $1,976

❷ **Rewrite** percentages as decimals.
Rewrite 5.6% as a decimal. 5.6% = 0.056

   2a. 4.7% 0.047   **2b.** 7.14% 0.0714   **2c.** 0.8% 0.008   **2d.** 14.9% 0.149

❸ **Multiply** money amounts by decimals and **round** products to the nearest cent.
Find the product. $54,109 × 0.035 = $1,893.815, or $1,893.82

   3a. $24,780 × 0.07 $1,734.60   **3b.** $47,090 × 0.048 $2,260.32

   3c. $35,100 × 0.127 $4,457.70   **3d.** $249,410 × 0.0345 $8,604.65

■ State and City Flat Income Taxes

Some states and cities tax personal income as a percent of federal taxable income. Some tax personal income as a percent of gross income. Some use a fixed, or flat tax rate no matter how much taxable income a person has. That is, the tax rate is the same for every person, regardless of the amount of income they earn in a year.

EXAMPLE 1

Allyson Greve has calculated her federal taxable income to be $45,300. She pays a state income tax rate of 3% on her federal taxable income. Find her state income tax.

TEACHING STRATEGIES Cooperative Learning

Have small student teams research the various types of county and local taxes that are used to support the services that students identified in the Start Up problem. Have teams prepare visual or verbal reports on their findings. Those reports should include lists of taxes and matching services.

SOLUTION

Rewrite the tax rate as a decimal rate: $3\% = 0.03$

Multiply the federal taxable income by the decimal tax rate: $\$45,300 \times 0.03 = \$1,359$

Allyson's state income tax is $1,359.

■ **CHECK YOUR UNDERSTANDING**

A. LaDonna Traube has to pay a city income tax of 1.5% of her federal taxable income. Last year her federal taxable income was $34,100. What amount of city income tax did she pay? $511.50

B. The state in which Angel Soto lives charges a 2.8% income tax based on a person's federal taxable income. If Angel's federal taxable income last year was $29,900, how much state income tax did he pay? $837.20

■ State and City Graduated Income Taxes

Some states and cities use a *graduated* income tax rate like the federal government. In a graduated tax system, the tax rate gets higher as taxable income gets larger. A portion of a graduated tax rate schedule that might be used by a state is shown below.

For taxable income		
Over —	**But not over —**	**The tax is —**
$ -0-	$8,000	2% of taxable income
8,000	16,000	$160 plus 3% of taxable income over $8,000
16,000	24,000	$400 plus 4% of taxable income over $16,000
24,000	32,000	$720 plus 5% of taxable income over $24,000
32,000	40,000	$1,120 plus 6% of taxable income over $32,000
40,000	48,000	$1,600 plus 7% of taxable income over $40,000
48,000	56,000	$2,160 plus 8% of taxable income over $48,000
56,000	64,000	$2,800 plus 9% of taxable income over $56,000
64,000	72,000	$3,520 plus 10% of taxable income over $64,000

COMMUNICATION

Which do you favor: A flat tax or a graduated tax? Your local government is considering charging an income tax on the taxable incomes of its citizens. Write a letter to your mayor in which you recommend either a flat income tax or a graduated income tax. Your letter should defend your choice of income tax.

Lesson 2.4 State and City Income Taxes ■ 61

■ **Apply Goal 1**

Work through Example 1 with students completing the math at their desks.

Assign Check Your Understanding problems A and B for completion in class. Examine student work at their desks for errors or problems.

■ **Teach Goal 2**

If your city or state has applicable income taxes, you may wish to have students solve some problems using those rates.

Make sure that students don't forget to add the tax on the base amount in the graduated income tax table after finding the tax on income over the base amount.

■ **Apply Goal 2**

Work through Example 2 with students completing the math at their desks.

Assign Check Your Understanding problems C and D for completion in class. Circulate through your classroom and examine student work for difficulties.

■ **ONGOING ASSESSMENT**

Have students reread Check Your Understanding problem C. Then call on students to describe the steps they must take to solve the problem. Ask each student called upon to describe one step.

COMMUNICATION

Discuss the reasons for and against both flat income taxes and graduated income taxes. List the reasons on the board as students name them.

Wrap Up

Review the Start Up. Call on students to provide their ratings of each service. Have students with different ratings justify their ratings.

Assign

Assignment: Exercises 1–28.
Start with the basic math exercises at the beginning to make certain that students can handle the arithmetic used in the exercises.

Assess

Check student answers to the exercises by calling on them in class, collecting and grading selected problems, or by observing student work as you circulate.

Ask students to define the bolded and italicized terms in the lesson and use them in sentences.

Reteach

STUDENT WORKBOOK If students need help with flat tax problems, complete Exercise 1 in the workbook with them. Then have them complete Exercise 2.

If students need help with graduated tax problems, complete Exercises 3a–3b in the workbook with them. Then have them complete Exercises 3c, 3d, and 4.

EXAMPLE 2

Your taxable income last year was $25,800. What was your state income tax?

SOLUTION

Find the income ($25,800) in the table shown on the previous page. It is in the column for over $24,000 but under $32,000.

Find the tax on taxable income up to $24,000: $720

Find the taxable income over $24,000: $25,800 − $24,000 = $1,800

Find the tax on $1,800 at a tax rate of 5%: $1,800 × 0.05 = $90

Find the total state income tax on $25,800: $720 + $90 = $810

■ **CHECK YOUR UNDERSTANDING**

C. Jennifer Robler's taxable income last year was $43,600. Use the table given on the previous page to find her state income tax. $1,852

D. San-li Pyeon had a taxable income last year of $38,200. Using the table given on the previous page, what is his state income tax? $1,492

Wrap Up

Look back at your list of the uses of local taxes from the beginning of the lesson. Rate the importance of each of the services to you. Place a "1" next to the tax use that is most important to you, a "2" next to the next more important use, and so on.

EXERCISES

Find the sum.
1. $120 + $270 + $375 + $489 $1,254
2. $240 + $597 + $812 + $956 $2,605

Rewrite as decimals.
3. 7.2% 0.072
4. 14.7% 0.147
5. 24.98% 0.2498
6. 0.5% 0.005

7. Renatta Versan pays a city income tax of 3.7% on her taxable income. Her taxable income last year was $58,390. What city income tax amount did she pay? $2,160.43

8. Jason Wiley lives in a state that charges an income tax of 4.52% on all taxable income. Last year Jason's taxable income was $42,189. What state income tax did he pay that year? $1,906.94

9. In addition to federal and state income taxes, Rue Lange also has to pay a city income tax. The city income tax rate is $2\frac{1}{2}$% of his taxable income. If his taxable income is $2,345, what is his city income tax? $58.63

10. The City of Beacon charges its residents an income tax of $\frac{1}{2}$% of their taxable income. Dora Feldman lives in Beacon and has taxable income of $34,676. What is her city income tax? $173.38

■ **CHECK YOUR UNDERSTANDING SOLUTIONS**

C. From the $40,000–$48,000 line of table, $1,600
$43,600 − $40,000 = $3,600;
$3,600 × 0.07 = $252
$1,600 + $252 = $1,852

D. From the $32,000–$40,000 line of table, $1,120
$38,200 − $32,000 = $6,200
$6,200 × 0.06 = $372
$1,120 + $372 = $1,492

For Exercises 11–18 use the graduated tax tables given.

11. Oren Bradley's taxable income last year was $25,890. What was his state income tax? $814.50

12. Lea Kristen's state income tax return shows taxable income of $39,350. What is the state income tax on that amount? $1,561

13. Wayne Delvica's income subject to state income tax is $22,690. What is his state income tax? $667.60

Bill Stark has taxable income of $26,600. He pays a city income tax of 2% on taxable income in addition to state and federal taxes.

14. What is Bill's city tax? $532   15. What is his state tax? $850

16. What is Bill's total city and state tax? $1,382

17. Ellen Donald pays city tax of 2.5% on taxable income, in addition to state income tax. Her taxable income last year was $42,870. What was her total state and city income tax? $2,872.65

18. Helmut Schmidt pays a city income tax of $2\frac{1}{4}$% on his taxable income of $28,834. In addition, he pays both state and federal income taxes on the same taxable income. If his federal tax last year was $4,538, what was the total of his federal, state, and city income taxes last year? $6,148.47

INTEGRATING YOUR KNOWLEDGE Alma Ruforio is a medical technician. Last year, her employer withheld $520 from her wages for state income tax. When she prepared her tax return, Alma showed gross income of $32,400 less $4,850 as a standard deduction and one exemption for herself.

19. What was Alma's taxable income? $24,450

20. What was her correct state tax for the year? $742.50

21. How much is her refund or tax due? Tax due: $222.50

MIXED REVIEW

22. $4\frac{2}{5} + 6\frac{1}{2}$ $10\frac{9}{10}$ 23. $17\frac{1}{4} - 6\frac{1}{3}$ $10\frac{11}{12}$ 24. $8\frac{1}{2} \times 5\frac{1}{3}$ $45\frac{1}{3}$

25. The Carter's taxable income last year was $43,780. They paid a state tax of 3.6% and a city tax of 1.35% on that income. What was the total of the state and city taxes they paid? $2,167.11, Lesson 2.4

26. Terry Jansen works on a piece-rate basis. He completed 70 pieces on Monday, 68 on Tuesday, 74 on Wednesday, and 72 on Thursday. He is paid $1.20 for each piece. How many pieces must he complete on Friday so that his earnings for the 5 days will average $84 a day? 66, Lesson 1.5

27. Valerie Bassett is paid 5% commission on all sales up to and including $25,000, and 7% on all sales over $25,000 in any month. Last month Valerie's sales were $45,250. What was the amount of her total commission? 2,667.50, Lesson 1.4

28. Last year the Pavlos earned $72,800 from salaries. They also earned $1,280 in interest and $2,789 in dividends. The Pavlos paid $6,240 into a retirement fund. What was their adjusted gross income for the year? $70,629, Lesson 2.3

Lesson 2.4 State and City Income Taxes ■ **63**

SELECTED SOLUTIONS

8. $42,189 × 0.0452 = $1,906.94

14. $26,600 × 0.02 = $532

15. $26,600 − $24,000 = $2,600;

$2,600 × 0.04 = $104;
$720 + $104 = $824

16. $532 + $824 = $1,356

GOALS

- Keep a cash receipts record
- Keep a columnar cash payments record

Start Up

What do you spend your weekly allowance and other income for? List the amounts you spend on each type of payment during a typical week.

Math Skill Builder

Review these math skills and solve the exercises that follow.

1 Add each column.

	1a.	**1b.**	**1c.**
4	53	17.48	$533.71
6	72	48.46	393.67
3	28	91.10	416.83
+9	+17	+32.74	+862.42
22	170	189.78	$2,206.63

MATH TIP

You can add faster by mentally combining two or three numbers that total 10, then adding that 10 to the other numbers. When you add from the top down, think "10, 20, 30, 40, 48." When you check your work by adding from the bottom up, think "8, 18, 28, 38, 48."

$$5 \atop 5 {\Big]}10$$
$$2 \atop 3 {\Big]}10 \atop 5$$
$$10{\Big[} {9 \atop 4} \atop {1 \atop 6}{\Big]}10$$
$$8 \over 48$$

2 Add each row and each column. The sum of the row totals and the sum of the column totals should be equal.

6 + 4 + 5 = 15	**2a.** 34 + 56 = 90	**2b.** 24 + 33 + 53 = 110
3 + 6 + 7 = 16	21 + 39 = 60	51 + 27 + 22 = 100
+ 8 + 5 + 2 = 15	16 + 85 = 101	33 + 96 + 56 = 185
17 15 14 46	71 180 251	108 156 131 395

■ Cash Receipts Record

Cash receipts records are written records of money received. Cash receipts records can be of great help to persons, families, organizations, and businesses when planning how to use money and when filling out income tax forms. Cash receipts records may be kept manually or with a computer, using accounting, spreadsheet, or database software.

EXAMPLE 1

Amy and Forrest Tracer receive weekly pay from their full-time jobs. Amy also receives pay from a part-time job. They keep track of all their cash receipts manually using a cash receipts record shown below. Copy and complete the form for the Tracers.

The Tracer Family • Cash Receipts Record				
Date		Explanation	Amount	
20—, July	5	Amy's part-time pay for week	200	00
	6	Refund for state income tax	235	45
	6	Insurance dividend	23	87
	8	Forrest's full-time pay for week	520	75
	9	Amy's full-time pay for week	600	00
		Total		

SOLUTION

Copy the cash receipts record on your paper. Be sure to include the heading and column headings before you enter the cash receipts.

Total the cash receipts by adding the amount column. The Tracers cash receipts totaled $1,580.07 for the week of July 5, 20--.

■ CHECK YOUR UNDERSTANDING

A. Louisa and Jose Medina had these cash receipts for the week: May 1, interest from a savings account, $27.89; May 2, Louisa's birthday gifts, $75; May 3, Jose's paycheck, $745.98; May 3, Louisa's paycheck, $635.78; May 5, rebate on printer purchase, $50. Create a cash receipts record. Find the total receipts for the week. $1,534.65

B. Jill West is the treasurer of the senior class of Eastbrook High School. She received the following cash during the week: April 4, senior class car wash, $154.50; May 4, senior class bake sale, $83.75; May 5, food sales at baseball game, $190.45; May 8, sales of class caps, $275.90; May 8, food sales at baseball game, $150.80. Create a cash receipts record. Find the total receipts for the week. $855.40

> **MATH and CALCULATOR TIP**
>
> Check addition by *reverse addition*. Either manually or with a calculator, add a column in the opposite direction from the way you added it the first time. This will give you new combinations of numbers.

■ Columnar Cash Payments Record

Cash payments records are written records of money paid out. Together with cash receipt records, cash payments records can help you plan how to use money and complete income tax forms.

Like cash receipts records, cash payments records can be kept manually or electronically with computer systems. A *columnar cash payments record* uses special money columns to place every payment into categories, such as housing, food, and auto.

■ *CHECK YOUR UNDERSTANDING SOLUTIONS*

A. $27.89 + $75 + $745.98 + $635.78 + $50 = $1,534.65

B. $154.50 + $83.75 + $190.45 + $275.90 + $150.80 = $855.40

Work through Example 2 with students completing the math at their desks.

Use the rows in the Illustration on p. 66 to show students how to implement the Calculator Tip on this page. If students have calculators in class, demonstrate the tip to students while they perform the operations at their desks.

Assign Check Your Understanding problems C and D for completion in class. Move about your classroom and check student work for difficulties.

■ **ONGOING ASSESSMENT**
Ask students to look at the columnar cash journal on p. 66. Then ask them how they might check the arithmetic that was done in the journal. The answers might include adding each column up, adding each row to from right to left, adding each column and row twice using a calculator, and asking another student to check the arithmetic. One answer that must not be overlooked in the student responses is to ensure that the grand total is correct at both the row and column levels.

EXAMPLE 2

The Tracers also keep a record of the cash they spend using a columnar cash payments record. The cash payments record for the Tracer family for the week of July 5 is shown below. Find the totals for each column.

The Tracer Family
Cash Payments Record for the Month of July

Date		Explanation	Housing	Food	Clothing	Entertainment	Transportation	Miscellaneous	Savings	Total Payments
20–July	5	Power bill for June	125.68							125.68
	6	Gift for friend						50.00		50.00
	7	Home mortgage payment	831.55							831.55
	7	Auto loan payment					247.59			247.59
	8	Groceries		184.58						184.58
	9	Auto repair					95.00			95.00
	9	Savings							100.00	100.00
		Totals								$1,634.40

SOLUTION

Copy the cash payment record on your paper.

The Tracers entered a date, explanation, and amount each time they paid out cash. They placed the payment amount in the column that matched the payment. For example, the power bill and home mortgage payments were entered in the "Housing" column. The payment for a gift was placed in the "Miscellaneous" column. Each payment was entered twice: Once in a "Type of Payment" money column and again in the "Total Payment" column.

Add the money columns to find out how much they spent on each payment category and how much they spent totally.

Check the accuracy of the record. The sum of the "Type of Payment" columns totals should equal the sum of the "Total Payments" column. When you add the row totals in the "Total Payments" column, you should get $1,634.40. When you add the totals of each "Type of Payment" column, you should also get $1,634.40. Because the two totals matched, the arithmetic in the cash payments record is correct.

The total, $1,634.40 is called a corner total or **grand total** and is used in business often to check the accuracy of work.

CALCULATOR TIP

Find the grand total using the memory keys. Find the sum of the first column or row. Then press the memory plus M+ key. Next, clear the screen, find the sum of the next row or column, and press the memory plus key again. Repeat for each row or column. When all rows or columns have been summed, press the memory recall MR key. The display should show the grand total.

■ CHECK YOUR UNDERSTANDING

C. The cash payments for Consuelo Valdez for the week of May 14 are: May 14, dinner out $27.88; May 15, groceries $95.85; May 15, movie rental $4.50; May 17, telephone bill $54.91; May 18, clothing purchase $135.67; May 19, lawn mowing service $25; May 20, gift $47.89. Complete a columnar cash payments record and find the total payments for the week. $391.70

CONNECTION TO ACCOUNTING

Have a team of students interview an accounting teacher to learn other ways that businesses record cash payments. Other teams might interview the marketing educa-tion teacher on the same topic. Each team should prepare a short written report.

D. Vince Bartolemo uses a spreadsheet program to keep his cash payments records. His spreadsheet shows these expenses: March 1, rent, $700; March 2, groceries, $123.83; March 3, clothing, $62.28; March 4, car license, $70; miscellaneous, $52.76; savings, $100. Complete a columnar cash payments record for the Week of March 1 and find the total payments for the week. $1,108.87

Wrap Up

Look back at the list of expenses you made at the beginning of the lesson. Find the total amount of your typical weekly payments. Then find the percent each type of payment is of that total. On what payments do you feel you spend too much money each week? Does your list of payments include savings?

TEAM MEETING

As a class have a brief discussion about why people, organizations, and business firms find records with multiple columns helpful.

While classmates speak, be sure to listen actively. Listening is more important to a person at work than any other communication skill. The average employee spends 45% of all communication time listening to others. Here are some tips to improve your active listening skills.

- Adopt a positive attitude toward the speaker.
- Be responsive to the speaker.
- Shut out distractions that may come between you and the speaker.
- Listen for the speaker's purpose.

Often, even if you do not agree with the speaker, you can still pick up on facts and opinions that are useful. Listen to all speakers during the class discussion.

EXERCISES

Add each column.

1. 3	**2.** 13	**3.** 67.23	**4.** $357.31
8	75	28.58	923.17
7	50	32.10	515.53
2	47	41.32	682.62
4	25	72.17	108.97
+ 7	+ 68	+ 53.79	+ 397.64
31	278	295.19	$2,985.24

Add each column and row. Check your work by finding the grand total.

5. 7 + 9 + 3 + 1 = 20
5 + 5 + 6 + 8 = 24
3 + 8 + 2 + 5 = 18
4 + 4 + 2 + 7 = 17
19   26   13   21   79

6. 93 + 122 = 215
237 + 154 = 391
593 + 47 = 640
134 + 89 = 223
1,057   412   1,469

7. 123 + 39 + 221 = 383
140 + 66 + 84 = 290
155 + 31 + 219 = 405
79 + 51 + 106 = 236
497   187   630   1,314

Wrap Up

Review the *Start Up.* Then assign the Wrap Up problem. Write student expense types on the board and compare the percentages given for each type of payment. Discuss with students why they felt that they spent too much money on some types of payments.

TEAM MEETING

You might have one or more students read aloud to the class newspaper items from the local paper that you have selected because they relate to the chapter topics. After each student has read an item, have students identify the facts from the opinions in the item.

Assign

Assignment: Exercises 1–11 and 13–24. Start with the basic arithmetic problems at the beginning of the exercises to insure that students understand the underlying arithmetic in the exercises.

Assess

Check student answers to the exercises by calling on them in class, collecting and grading selected problems, or by viewing their work as you move about the room.

Ask students to define the bolded and italicized terms in the lesson and use them in sentences.

■ *CHECK YOUR UNDERSTANDING SOLUTIONS*

C. $27.88 + $95.85 + $4.50 + $54.91 + $135.67 + $25 + $47.89 = $391.70

D. $700 + $123.83 + $62.28 + $70 + $52.76 + $100 = $1,108.87

For Exercises 8 and 9, create a cash receipts record.

8. Roberta Arthur had the following receipts for the week of April 12: April 12, $50 gift; April 12, $25 rebate; April 13, $2.45 refund of deposit on aluminum cans returned; April 14, $299.89 weekly pay from her regular job; April 16, $75 pay from her part-time job. Find Roberta's total receipts for the week. $452.34

9. For the week of August 7 Rick Sutton received: August 7, $274.89 weekly pay; August 8, $32.34 interest on savings; August 9, $498.23 reimbursement check for travel expenses; August 10, $50 loan repayment from a friend; August 11, $45.29 refund purchase. Find Rick's total receipts for the week. $900.75

For Exercises 10 and 11, create a columnar cash payments record.

10. The cash payments for Carla Stern for the week of October 4 are: October 4, lunch out $14.88; October 5, groceries $125.75; October 6, movie $7.50; October 7, cell phone bill $43.91; October 8, savings $125; October 9, power bill $215; October 20, mortgage payment $878.99. Find Carla's total cash payments for the week. $1,411.03

11. Alan McCully uses a spreadsheet program to keep his cash payments records. During the week his spreadsheet shows these expenses: January 20, groceries, $219.54; January 21, clothing, $201.95; January 23, rent, $650; January 24, transportation, $71.36; January 25, computer printer to use to work at home, $238.96; savings, $100. Find Alan's total cash payments for the week. $1,481.81

12. **CRITICAL THINKING** Why must the grand total obtained from the horizontal addition be the same as the grand total obtained from the vertical addition? You are adding the same numbers, but in a different order.

13. **STRETCHING YOUR SKILLS** An auto service station had these cash receipts for a week: auto parts, $527.98; repairs, $2,079.65; fuel, $25,108.23; car wash, $419.53; car detailing, $598.12; other cash receipts, $244.98. What were the total receipts for the week? $28,978.49

14. **STRETCHING YOUR SKILLS** Movie Palace, a video store, had these cash receipts for a week: Monday, $208.55; Tuesday, $419.39; Wednesday, $527.19; Thursday, $388.58; Friday, $839.94; Saturday, $942.53; Sunday, $617.11. What were the total receipts for the week? $3,943.29

MIXED REVIEW

15. 7.7% of $23,560   16. $35,290 − $1,549   17. $3\frac{1}{8} + 14\frac{2}{5}$
$1,814.12 $33,741 $17\frac{21}{40}$

In the number 7,385, what digit is in each of these places?

18. tens place 8   19. ones place 5

20. thousands place 7   21. hundreds place 3

Calli Burns was paid $14.56 an hour for 37.5 hours last week.

22. What was Calli's gross pay for the week? $546, Lesson 1.1

23. How much was deducted for social security taxes at 6.2% $33.85, Lesson 2.1

24. Olaf Svenson worked 8 hours on Monday and Tuesday, 9 hours on Wednesday, and 10 hours on Thursday and Friday. Olaf is paid $12 an hour and time-and-a-half for time past 40 hours in a week. What was Olaf's gross pay for the week? $570, Lesson 1.3

SELECTED SOLUTIONS

8. $50 + $25 + $2.45 + $299.89 + $75 = $452.34

10. $14.88 + $125.75 + $7.50 + $43.91 + $125 + $215 + $878.99 = $1,411.03

13. $527.98 + $2,079.65 + $25,108.23 + $419.53 + $598.12 + $244.98 = $28,978.49

2.6 Budgets

GOALS

- Calculate the percent of income spent on expenses
- Prepare a budget

Start Up

Choose a club or organization in which you participate. What types of income and expenses are typical of that club? What are the actual or estimated annual amounts for each income and payment type? Make a list of the types and amounts of the income and expenses.

Math Skill Builder

Review these math skills and solve the exercises that follow.

1 **Divide** to the nearest hundredth.
Find the quotient. $12,600 ÷ $56,230 = 0.22407, or 0.22

1a. $10,500 ÷ $35,400   **1b.** $5,200 ÷ $24,700   **1c.** $3,740 ÷ $67,390
0.30   0.21   0.06

2 **Rewrite** decimals as percents.
Rewrite as a percent. 0.5234 = 52.34%

2a. 0.67 67%   **2b.** 0.245 24.5%   **2c.** 0.5698 56.98%   **2d.** 0.2791 27.91%

3 **Change** to a fraction in its simplest form.
Find the fraction in its simplest form. $\frac{\$5,000}{\$10,000} = \frac{1}{2}$

3a. $\frac{\$3,500}{\$7,000}$ $\frac{1}{2}$ **3b.** $\frac{\$3,000}{\$15,000}$ $\frac{1}{5}$ **3c.** $\frac{\$8,000}{\$32,000}$ $\frac{1}{4}$

4 **Multiply** and **round** to the nearest dollar.
4a. $56,000 × 14%   **4b.** $73,400 × 25%   **4c.** $29,700 × 12.5%
$7,840 $18,350 $3,713

■ Expense Percentages

It is very helpful to summarize and analyze your income and expenses for the previous year. That way, you can determine how much you spent on each type of expense. You can also compare your past spending to other peoples' spending and you can use the percents to plan your future spending.

Cash receipts and payments records can be used to identify your past income and expenses. The Tracer family developed a cash record summary. After writing in the December amounts, they totaled and ruled the summary.

Lesson 2.6 Budgets ■ 69

Start Up

Have students answer the Start Up problem at the desks. Have them work in teams if there are students who have never been part of a club. Call on students to give the types of income and expenses they listed. Make a frequency tabulation (卌) to identify those types that are the most common to all clubs.

Math Skill Builder

Assign all exercises in the Math Skill Builder 1–4 to prepare students for the division, multiplication, rounding, rewriting and fraction simplification used in the lesson. You may also use it to get the class started while attendance is taken or while materials are handed out.

COMMON ERRORS

Students make errors by writing figures poorly or arranging them carelessly. Give students practice in careful writing and arrangement by dictating exercises to them and inspecting their work. Using graph paper is often helpful for students who have problems being neat. Place one number or character in each square.

Emphasize that careful records of receipts and payments are not only helpful to complete tax forms, they are also helpful in developing a budget.

Ask students to examine the Tracer Family Cash Record on this page and suggest additional categories of payments that the family might consider.

Ask students why the Tracer family uses separate columns for the various payments they make. How do these columns make it easier for the family to examine their spending?

■ Apply Goal 1

Work through Example 1 with students completing the math at their desks.

Assign Check Your Understanding problems A and B for completion in class. Roam the classroom and check student work for errors and problems.

The Tracer Family Cash Record Summary									
						Types of Payments			
20– Month	Receipts	Payments	Housing	Food	Clothing	Entertain- ment	Transpor- tation	Miscel- laneous	Savings
Jan.	6,324.58	5,108.48	1,578.21	738.21	168.78	102.52	684.12	1,056.64	780.00
Feb.	6,210.90	5,617.38	1,645.29	794.12	315.78	301.24	845.28	845.67	870.00
Nov.	6,523.78	5,310.87	1,668.59	812.02	498.20	288.43	711.97	481.66	850.00
Dec.	6,428.84	5,672.68	1,790.86	824.54	218.23	201.87	698.54	1,169.64	850.00
Total	75,888.10	63,930.69	19,801.95	9,521.85	3,001.95	2,161.42	8,939.91	10,753.61	9,750.00

Some people keep track of their expenses using very specific categories, such as house insurance, home maintenance, housing expenses, and taxes. Others use broader categories. The Tracers use broad categories. Their housing expense category include mortgage payments, property taxes, home insurance, and home maintenance expenses.

To analyze their previous expenses, the Tracer family calculated what percent of income each type of expense represented.

EXAMPLE 1

Find the percent of income that the Tracers spent for food.

SOLUTION
Divide food expense for the year by total receipts, or income. Round the result to the nearest tenth percent.

$9,521.85 \div $75,888.10 = 0.12547$, or 12.5%

The Tracers can use these percents to compare how they spend their money with other people and to identify expenses that are higher or lower than they would like them to be.

■ **CHECK YOUR UNDERSTANDING**

A. The Ping family expects to save $6,400 of their annual income in an account for their son's college fees. Their annual income is $128,000. What percent of their income is being saved in the son's college fund? 5%

B. Last year Allon Company's expenses totaled $475,000. If $338,200 was spent for salaries, what percent of the total expenses was salary expense to the nearest whole percent? 71%

■ *CHECK YOUR UNDERSTANDING SOLUTIONS*

A. $6,400 ÷ $128,000 = 0.05; or 5%   **B.** $338,200 ÷ $475,000 = 0.711, or 71%

Budgeting

Budgets are your future spending plans. They help you allocate your future income to meet your future needs and save for the things you want.

One way to begin a budget is to project next year's expenses based on the percent of income spent in the previous year. To do this, you multiply the expected income by the percent spent for each type of expense last year.

EXAMPLE 2

Last year the Tracers spent 12.5% on food. If they estimate that they will spend the same percent of their income for food next year, how much should they budget for food if their income is expected to be $78,500?

SOLUTION
Rewrite the expense percent as a decimal: 12.5% = 0.125

Multiply by the estimated income: $0.125 \times \$78,500 = \$9,812.50$

The Tracers should budget $9,812.50 for food next year.

■ CHECK YOUR UNDERSTANDING

C. Tri-county Supply budgets 5% of the previous year's total revenue for utilities. The receipts from last year showed revenue of $4,500,000. How much will be budgeted for utilities? $225,000

D. The news reports that next year, gasoline prices will increase. Mr. Jones knows that he needs to increase the auto budget to 2.5% of his monthly income to cover the increase. Mr. Jones' gross pay each month is $5,489. What will his monthly auto budget be to the nearest dollar? $137

To develop a budget you must identify not only your past income and expenses but estimate your expected future income and expenses. You should include income and expenses that will occur on a regular basis, such as weekly paychecks and monthly rent, and those that may happen periodically, such as gifts or semiannual insurance payments.

You should also try to plan for income and expenses that cannot be scheduled or accurately predicted, such as income tax refunds and car repairs.

Budgets include *fixed income* and *expenses* and *variable income* and *expenses*. With fixed income and expenses, a set amount of money is allocated each month for that income or expense.

Fixed income may include weekly wages or monthly salary. Fixed expenses may include money set aside to pay the insurance, mortgage, rent, car payment, or a savings plan.

Other expenses, such as telephone bills, transportation expenses, and personal expenses, while they occur regularly, vary in amount. Those expenses are called variable, or *flexible*, expenses.

> **CALCULATOR TIP**
>
> On many calculators, you can multiply by a percent directly without rewriting it. Enter the number to be multiplied ($78,500), press the multiplication sign (×), enter the percent (12.5) and press the percent sign (%). The answer, $9,812.50 will appear in the calculator display.

■ Teach Goal 2

Point out that a budget is designed to shift you from a day-to-day spending perspective to planning and managing your cash flow over longer periods. By setting aside money on a regular basis to cover periodic payments and unexpected expenses, such as major auto repairs, people should have an easier time handling unexpected expenses.

Emphasize that most financial advisors recommend that we "pay ourselves first" by budgeting for savings. Budgeted savings allow people to save for things they want and to handle unexpected expenses.

■ Apply Goal 2

Work through Example 2 with students completing the math at their desks.

Assign Check Your Understanding problems C and D for completion in class. Check student work at their desks for errors or problems.

■ ONGOING ASSESSMENT
With the textbook closed, call on students to name possible income and expense headings for a budget a family.

■ *CHECK YOUR UNDERSTANDING SOLUTIONS*

C. $4,500,000 × 0.05 = $225,000   **D.** $5,489 × 0.025 = $137

Wrap Up

Review the Start Up. Prepare the answer for the Wrap Up as a completed budget form and make a transparency of it. When students have completed their work, display the transparency so students can check their work. Discuss any problems they encountered in creating their budgets.

COMMUNICATION

After students complete the paragraph, call on them and make a list of factors they have identified on the board. Discuss the factors and how they might impact a budget forecast. You might also collect the paragraphs and grade them for completeness, grammar, and clarity.

Assign

Assignment: Exercises 1–24
Start with the basic arithmetic problems at the beginning of the exercises to insure that students understand the underlying arithmetic in the exercises.

Assess

Check student answers to the exercises by calling on them in class, collecting and grading selected problems, or by observing student work at their desks.

Ask students to define the bolded and italicized terms in the lesson and use them in sentences.

Wrap Up

Look at the list you prepared for the school club or organization at the start of this lesson. Assume that the club will have a 5% growth in total income. Prepare a budget for the next school year for the club. Allocate amounts to each budget item as you wish but make sure that the budgeted total does not exceed 105% of last year's total.

COMMUNICATION

Write a brief paragraph explaining why using last year's income and expenses is usually not adequate for preparing a budget for next year. In your paragraph, identify other factors, besides last year's expense percents, that should be considered.

EXERCISES

Divide to the nearest hundredth.

1. $6,750 ÷ $36,250 0.19

2. $15,730 ÷ $44,900 0.35

Rewrite decimals as percents.

3. 0.39 39%

4. 0.641 64.1%

5. 0.705 70.5%

6. 1.089 108.9%

Change to a fraction in its simplest form.

7. $\dfrac{\$48,000}{\$64,000}$ $\dfrac{3}{4}$

8. $\dfrac{\$10,756}{\$26,890}$ $\dfrac{2}{5}$

9. $\dfrac{\$27,400}{\$82,200}$ $\dfrac{1}{3}$

10. $\dfrac{\$9,850}{\$59,100}$ $\dfrac{1}{6}$

Multiply and round to the nearest dollar.

11. $36,500 × 12% $4,380

12. $27,300 × 45% $12,285

13. $87,400 × 14.7% $12,848

14. $205,645 × 21.6% $44,419

Use the data from the Tracer family's cash record summary to answer Exercises 15–18.

15. What fractional part of their annual savings were the Tracers' January payments for savings? $\dfrac{2}{25}$

16. To the nearest whole percent, what percent of the Tracer's annual receipts were their payments for housing? 26%

17. To the nearest whole percent, what percent of the Tracer's annual receipts were their payments for transportation? 12%

18. To the nearest whole percent, what percent of the Tracer's annual receipts were their payments for savings? 13%

72 ■ Chapter 2 Net Pay

DIFFERENT LEARNING ABILITIES Gifted Learners

Have a team(s) of students use a spreadsheet program to develop a spreadsheet template for the illustration on p. 70. To test the accuracy of their formulas, have them enter $100 in each row in the Receipts column and $10 in each row of the Types of Payments columns. The total for the Receipts column then should be $1,200. The total of the Payments column should be $840. The total of each row of the Payments column should be $70.

19. **STRETCHING YOUR SKILLS** Last year Tylon Company's expenses totaled $951,600. If $677,446 was spent for salaries, what percent of the total expenses was salary expense, to the nearest whole percent? 71%

20. **STRETCHING YOUR SKILLS** Relco Internet Services, Inc., had total sales for one year of $1,891,720. Their advertising expenses were $114,740. Find the percent of total sales, that advertising expenses were to the nearest tenth of a percent. 6.1%

Use the data from the Tracer family's cash record summary to answer Exercises 21–24.

The Tracer family expects their income next year to be $81,500. Assume that they budget the same percents for each expense category as they did last year. Show the percent, rounded to the nearest half percent, and the amount of money they will spend during the year for each of the following.

21. Food 12.5%, $10,187.50

22. Clothing 4%, $3,260

23. Entertainment 3%, $2,445

24. Miscellaneous 14%, $11,410

25. **DECISION MAKING** Suppose the Tracers decide they want to adjust their budget so they can save for a special summer vacation that will cost $5,000. How would you suggest they go about revising their budget to meet their goal? Answers will vary.

26. **CRITICAL THINKING** Why should items not usually paid monthly, such as insurance and taxes, be included in a monthly budget? They need to be included so the money is not spent and will be in the account when payments are due.

27. **CRITICAL THINKING** Tyrone's net annual income is $28,000 a year. On his 25th birthday, he spent $1,500 to celebrate with friends and family. Rosita makes $200,000 a year. When she celebrated her 50th birthday, she spent $5,000 for her party. Which one of them do you think overspent for the party? Explain your answer. Answers will vary. Tyrone spent 5.4% of his salary. Rosita spent 2.5% of her salary.

Mixed Review

28. Multiply $3\frac{1}{3}$ by $2\frac{1}{6}$. $7\frac{2}{9}$ 29. Subtract $3\frac{1}{2}$ from $7\frac{1}{8}$. $3\frac{5}{8}$

30. $2\frac{3}{4} + 6\frac{1}{2} + 3\frac{2}{3}$ $12\frac{11}{12}$ 31. $3\frac{3}{5} \div \frac{2}{3}$ $5\frac{2}{5}$

32. 344 increased by 20% of itself is what number? 412.8

33. $324 increased by $\frac{1}{2}$ of itself equals what amount? $486

34. $350 is what percent of $500? 70%

35. Regis Computer Supply, Inc., had total sales of $2,975,000 last year and spent $1,950,000 on salaries and wages. What percent, to the nearest percent, of total sales was the amount they spent on salaries and wages? 66%, Lesson 2.6

36. Regina Wilson goes to college and works a part-time job. February 1 is on a Monday. In February, she earned $225 each week from her job and was paid each Friday. She earned $20 baby-sitting on February 13 and $25 on February 26. She received $100 from her parents on February 15. A scholarship check of $250 came in the mail on the February 10. Prepare a cash receipts record for the month of February for Regina. $1,295, Lesson 2.5

Lesson 2.6 Budgets ■ 73

Reteach

STUDENT WORKBOOK If students need help with percent of income spent on expenses problems, add the Receipts and Food columns in Exercise 1 in the workbook with them and calculate the percent food expenses were of total receipts. Then have them complete the rest of Exercises 1 and 2 independently during class time so you can be available for help.

If students need help with fractional expense parts of cash receipts problems, complete Exercise 3a in the workbook with them. Then have them complete Exercises 3b–3e during class.

If students need help in budgeting, complete Exercise 4a with them and then have them complete Exercise 4 during class.

Enrich

Assign Exercises 25–27 and discuss the student responses.

Make a transparency of the school district budget for the year and display it. Discuss the format of the budget (percentages, pie chart, etc.). If percentages are not presented, have students calculate the percent each budgeted expense is of the total revenue for the school district.

Close

Select one or more problems from the textbook or workbook from the lesson and call on students to describe how they would solve each part of the problems.

If you haven't already done so, call on students to define and use in a sentence each of the bolded and italicized terms in the lesson.

SELECTED SOLUTIONS

16. $19,801.95 ÷ $75,888.10 = 0.260, or 26%

19. $677,446 ÷ $951,600 = 0.711, or 71%

21. $9,521.85 ÷ $75,888.10 = 0.1254, or 12.5%; $81,500 × 0.125 = $10,187.50

Chapter Review

- Locate withholding taxes in a federal withholding tax table.

- Multiply gross pay by the social security tax rate to find social security taxes.

- Multiply gross pay by the Medicare tax rate to find Medicare taxes.

- Add deductions to find total deductions.

- Subtract total deductions from gross pay to find net pay.

Lesson 2.2 Benefits and Job Expenses

- Add fringe benefits to find total fringe benefits.

- Multiply gross pay by fringe benefit rate to find total fringe benefits.

- Add total fringe benefits to gross pay to find total job benefits.

- Subtract job expenses from total job benefits to find net job benefits.

- Compare net job benefits of jobs.

Lesson 2.3 Federal Income Taxes

- Calculate adjusted gross income by subtracting adjustments to income from gross income

- Calculate taxable income by subtracting deductions and exemptions from adjusted gross income.

- Calculate the income tax due using a tax table.

Vocabulary Review

adjusted gross income	exemption	standard deduction
budgets	flat tax	taxable income
cash payments record	grand total	unearned income
cash receipts record	gross income	withholding allowance
deductions	job expenses	withholding tax
earned income	net job benefits	
employee benefits	net pay	

Fill in each blank with one of the terms above.

1. An amount subtracted from gross pay is a (n) __?__. deduction

2. A corner total that provides the sum of columns and rows is a (n) __?__. grand total

3. Adjusted gross income less deductions and exemptions is __?__. taxable income

4. A tax in which the rate does not vary with the amount of income is __?__. flat tax

5. Gross pay less deductions is __?__. net pay

6. Things of value provided by employers in addition to wages are __?__. employee benefits

7. Future spending plans are called __?__. budgets

8. An amount of income per person that is free from tax is called a (n) __?__. exemption

LESSON 2.1

9. Christy Bellows is a married worker earning $612.83 each week. She claims 3 withholding allowances. What amount should be deducted from her weekly earnings for federal withholding taxes? $29

10. Ron Adams earns $450 in gross wages on January 10. How much is deducted from Ron's gross wages for social security at 6.2% and Medicare at 1.45%? $27.90; $6.53

11. Luisa Medina is paid $556 a week. Her employer deducts $56 for federal withholding tax, $54.78 for insurance, 6.2% for social security taxes, and 1.45% for Medicare taxes. For the week, what are her social security and Medicare taxes, total deductions, and net pay? $34.47; $8.06; $153.31, $402.69

LESSON 2.2

12. Phyllis Regan's job pays $46,350 plus 24% of wages in benefits. She estimates that her yearly job expenses are $2,256. A job she has been offered pays $49,750 with these estimated benefits: $3,980 in pensions, $450 in free parking, $1,080 in paid vacation, $1,560 in paid holidays, $2,100 in health insurance, and $400 in tools. The job has job expenses of $2,624. What are her current job's net job benefits? What are the other job's net job benefits? $55,218; $56,696

13. Which job offers the greater net job benefits? How much greater? 2nd; $1,478

DIFFERENT LEARNING STYLES Kinesthetic Learners

Have students write the words that complete each vocabulary question 3 times on their answer sheet to help them remember the word and how it is spelled.

LESSON 2.3

14. Freida Werner earned gross income of $45,600 last year. She made payments into an approved retirement plan of $3,600. What was her adjusted gross income last year? $42,000

15. Jorge Viscano had $38,000 in adjusted gross income last year. He took the standard deduction of $4,850 and one exemption for himself for $3,100. What was his taxable income for the year? $30,050

16. Ben Uris is single, has taxable income of $23,500, and his employer deducted $3,640 in withholding taxes. Find Ben's tax due and any refund or amount owed. $3,171; $469 refund

17. Elena Alvarez is a high school student and her parents claim her as a dependent on their tax return. Elena works part time and earned $2,490 last year. Her employer deducted $320 in withholding taxes. Elena also earned $270 in interest on a savings account and had no adjustments to income. Elena wants to file for a refund and claim the standard deduction instead of itemizing deductions. What is the amount of Elena's refund? $318

LESSON 2.4

18. Alan Grey has federal taxable income of $31,500. He pays a state income tax rate of 2.5% on his federal taxable income. Find his state income tax. $787.50

19. Haru Umeki's taxable income is $44,200. Find her state income tax. $1,894

LESSON 2.5

20. Joe Palucci had these cash receipts for the week: April 1, interest from a savings account, $17.89; April 2, birthday gift, $65; April 3, paycheck, $445.88; April 5, rebate, $50. Complete a cash receipts record. Find Joe's total receipts for the week. $578.77

21. Maggie Ryan had these expenses during the week of June 2: dinner out, $43.93; clothing, $72.95; rent, $875; toll coupons, $70; miscellaneous, $18.96; savings, $150. Complete a columnar cash payments record and find the total payments for the week. $1,230.84

LESSON 2.6

22. Jon Marlow's total income last year was $31,300. Of that amount, he spent $7,900 for food. What percent of Jon's total income did he spend for food? 25%

23. Cesar Guerra's total income last year was $35,000. He expects to earn 10% more this year and wants to budget 24% of that income for food. What yearly amount should Cesar budget for food? $9,240

24. What yearly amount is Cesar's transportation budget if it is 17% of his income? $6,545

25. What yearly amount does Cesar put into savings if it is 13% of his income? $5,005

(Lesson 2.3 cont'd)
- Calculate the tax refund or tax due by subtracting the income tax withheld from the tax due.

- Calculate the adjusted gross income for dependents by adding all income amounts.

- Calculate the standard deduction for dependents by adding earned income and $250.

- Calculate the taxable income for dependents by subtracting the standard deduction from adjust gross income.

- Calculate the income tax refund for dependents by subtracting the income tax withheld from the tax due.

Lesson 2.4 State and City Income Taxes
- Calculate state and city income taxes using a flat tax rate.

- Calculate state and city income taxes using a graduated tax rate table.

Lesson 2.5 Cash Receipts and Payments Records
- Keep a cash receipts record

- Keep a columnar cash payments record

Lesson 2.6 Budgets
- Find the percent spent on a budget category by dividing the amount spent by the total income.

- Find the total amount to be budgeted for a category by multiplying the total income by the percent allotted.

TEACHING STRATEGY Cooperative Learning

Have students work in teams of two to complete the Chapter Review exercises. When both team members have completed the exercises for one lesson, have them check each other's work. The checker should make sure that the answer is correct, the solution is correct, and that the solution items are properly labeled.

Task 1 Students enter data into a payroll spreadsheet template.

Task 2 Students answer questions about the results of Task 1. They also change data and answer questions about the results.

Task 3 Students design and create a spreadsheet that calculates net job benefits.

Task 4 Students answer questions about the data entered and about how the sheet was designed. They also change data and answer questions about the new results.

Teach and Apply Task 1

Remind students that all but the blue spreadsheet cells are protected from changes.

Point out that placing social security and Medicare rates in separate cells, rather than including them in each row's formulas, lets you change rates quickly and see the impact on employee net pay.

Show how to open the spreadsheet and how only blue cells allow entry. Enter gross wage and income tax data for employee 1 while students do so at their stations. When students complete data entry, ask them to check their grand total with the textbook.

Technology Workshop

Task 1: Enter Data In A Payroll Sheet Template

Complete a template that calculates the social security tax, Medicare tax, and net pay for each employee of the Bainbridge Company.

Open the spreadsheet for Chapter 2 (tech2-1) and enter the data shown in blue (cells D6-E15). Social security taxes, Medicare taxes, and net pay are calculated for each employee. Your finished spreadsheet should look like the one shown.

	A	B	C	D	E	F	G	H	I	J	K
1					Bainbridge Company						
2					Payroll Sheet for January 15, 20—						
3	Employee No.	Name	Allow-ances	Mar-ried	Gross Wages	Deductions					
4						Income Tax	Social Security	Medicare	Other	Total Deductions	Net Pay
5											
6	1	Ajanaku	1	N	421.02	40.00	26.10	6.10	35.45	107.65	313.37
7	2	Bell	1	N	435.89	42.00	27.03	6.32	37.84	113.19	322.70
8	3	Cole	0	Y	502.54	39.00	31.16	7.29	49.75	127.20	375.34
9	4	Dern	1	N	399.50	36.00	24.77	5.79	31.54	98.10	301.40
10	5	Evers	2	Y	575.64	32.00	35.69	8.35	58.97	135.01	440.63
11	6	Ford	5	Y	449.54	0.00	27.87	6.52	50.02	84.41	365.13
12	7	Gomez	0	Y	557.76	46.00	34.58	8.09	57.64	146.31	411.45
13	8	Huang	2	Y	450.89	18.00	27.96	6.54	38.19	90.69	360.20
14	9	Isom	0	N	438.27	51.00	27.17	6.35	37.17	121.69	316.58
15	10	Jackson	3	Y	580.24	25.00	35.97	8.41	61.55	130.93	449.31
16		Totals			4,811.29	329.00	298.30	69.76	458.12	1,155.18	3,656.11
17											
18		Social Security Rate		0.062							
19		Medicare Rate		0.0145							

Task 2: Analyze the Spreadsheet Output

Answer these questions about your completed payroll sheet.
1. Which employee had the largest net pay for the period? 10
2. Which employee had the largest amount of deductions? 7
3. Which employee had the greatest number of allowances? 6
4. Which employees paid more in combined social security taxes and Medicare taxes than they paid in income taxes? 5, 6, 8, 10
5. What was the total amount of income taxes withheld from wages for the week? $329

Now move the cursor to cell E18, labeled Social Security. Enter the rate 0.065.

DIFFERENT LEARNING ABILITIES Visually Impaired Learners

Show students how the spreadsheets in Excel can be enlarged on the screen. Make sure that the Standard toolbar is visible (click on View, Toolbars, Standard). Then move to the Zoom box.

100% ▼

Either type in a larger percent into the box or click the down arrow and select a preset size. You can also click Select from the down arrow list and it will resize just the cells you have selected.

Notice how the social security tax, total deductions, and net pay amounts all change. These changes show what would happen if the social security tax rate was updated from 6.2% to the higher 6.5%.

Answer these questions about your updated payroll sheet.

6. What is the formula used in cell F16? What arithmetic is done in the cell?
   SUM(F6:F15); withholding taxes are totaled
7. What is the formula used in cell G6? What arithmetic is done in the cell?
   ROUND(E6*E18,2); gross wages multiplied by soc. sec. tax rate and rounded to nearest cent
8. What is the formula used in cell H6? What arithmetic is done in the cell?
   ROUND(E6*E19,2); gross wages multiplied by Med. tax rate and rounded to nearest cent
9. What is the formula used in cell J13? What arithmetic is done in the cell?
   SUM(F13:I13); deductions from income tax to other are totaled
10. Why did changing cell E18 change the amounts throughout the rest of the spreadsheet? soc. tax rate in E18 used in formulas in column G, that affected total deductions and net pay for each employee

Task 3: Design a Job Benefits Spreadsheet

Design a spreadsheet that will allow you to compare net job benefits.
The spreadsheet for Task 1 includes formulas that use subtraction, multiplication, and the SUM function. Create a spreadsheet that will use these same types of formulas for the situation below. The spreadsheet should allow you to compare the jobs based on net benefits. Assume that each job is for a 40-hour week and 52-week year. Your spreadsheet should contain a row for each of the items shown. In addition, you should enter row or column labels and formulas to calculate annual gross pay, pension benefits, total job benefits, total job expenses, and net benefits.

DATA: You receive two job offers. The expenses and benefits for each job are shown at the right.

	Offer 1	Offer 2
Salary Information		
Hourly Rate	$11.25	$12.05
Annual Benefits		
Health Insurance	$2,500	
Life Insurance	$250	$325
Health Club		
Membership	——	$550
Pension*	8%	6%
Free Parking	$650	——
Expense Information		
Commuting Costs	$777	$955
Dues	$98	$150
Tools	——	$380
Uniforms	——	$425
*Stated as a percent of annual salary.		

Task 4: Analyze the Spreadsheet Output

Answer these questions about your completed spreadsheet.

11. How did you calculate annual pension benefits? pension percentage × annual salary

12. What were the total job benefits of Offer 1? Offer 2? $27,797, $25,532.84

13. Which job offered the highest net benefits? How much higher? 1st, $2,264.16

14. Which job benefits package do you think is better? Answers will vary.

15. If you were to (a) change the pension percentage rate for Job 1 to 7%, (b) change the hourly rate to $12.50 for Job 1, and (c) eliminate life insurance as a benefit from both jobs, what is the difference in net benefits between the two offers? Job 1's net benefits of $30,095 are $4,887.16 greater than Job 2's net benefit of $25,207.84.

TEACHING STRATEGIES Task 3

An example solution to Task 3 is provided in the file tech2-3.xls. You may wish to display the design used in tech2-3.xls and have students make suggestions for improving the readability, ease of data entry, and organization of the spreadsheet rather than having the class review another student's work. Examine with students the formulas in the cells critically and ask for suggestions for improvement. For example, students may suggest that E5 containing the pension rate be expanded to 3 decimal points to allow for pension rates like 7.5%.

Assess

■ HOW TIMES HAVE CHANGED

1. $1,611

2. $13,124 × 0.05 = $656.20
$1,611 − $656.20 = $954.80

■ WRITE

Student work should recognize that states must pay for services some way, if not through income taxes, then through other taxes, such as sales taxes. The question is really what type of taxes would you like to pay and that usually depends on how much you earn and what you own. High-income taxpayers like low income taxes and high sales taxes; low-income taxpayers like the reverse. Those who own homes usually prefer taxes other than property taxes.

■ SCANS

Students' work should demonstrate that they have tested the accuracy of their spreadsheets. The spreadsheets should be easy to read and cells not requiring data entry should be protected.

■ ONGOING ASSESSMENT

STUDENT WORKBOOK The Integrated Project found in the workbook provides a broad, ongoing assessment activity for the goals of this chapter.

How Times Have Changed

For Questions 1–2, refer to the timeline on page 39 as needed.

1. Jack Wilson is single and had a taxable income of $13,124 in 2004. Look at the tax tables on page 55 to find his tax due in 2004.

2. During the Civil War, taxable incomes over $10,000 were taxed at 5%. If one of Jack's ancestors had a taxable income of $13,124 during Civil War times, and paid 5% taxes, how much more did Jack pay in 2004 than his ancestor paid in the 1860s?

WRITE

Several states do not have a state income tax. Residents of these states do not pay a percentage of their salary to the state government. These states are Alaska, Florida, Nevada, New Hampshire, New Mexico, South Dakota, Tennessee, Texas, Washington and Wyoming.

Think about which type of state (one with or one without state income taxes) would be cheapest to live in. Consider where a state government will generate funds for programs and services when state income tax is not collected. Choose a state you would like to live in based on tax information. Write a paragraph explaining the reasons for your chosen state.

SCANS

Workplace Skills—*Organizing and Maintaining Information*

These skills include the ability to organize, process, and maintain written or computerized data in an understandable and systematic form.

Test Your Skills Prepare a spreadsheet that includes a budget for a fictitious family. Include gross income, taxes paid, and expenses of housing (including utilities), food, transportation, savings, and other expenses.

Make a Plan Using your budget, create a plan that you would share with your fictitious family on how the family will stay on budget. Check with the head of your household to determine if your budget is practical. Prepare your budget and plan in a format that will be easy to understand. Include reasons why staying on budget is important. Set a family goal.

Summarize Reflect on the process and time you spent on this assignment. Mentally note which of the following skills you used.

arithmetic	*speaking*	*listening*	*decision making*
problem solving	*responsibility*	*selects technology*	*uses technology*

TEACHING STRATEGIES Write

You may wish to allow students to explore the income tax versus sales and property taxes in depth. Using the tax terms just named, students might browse the Internet to find documents that present arguments for or against each of those taxes. Students might then be asked to select a single tax type and write a summary of the arguments for and against it.

CHAPTER TEST

Answer each question.

1. Write $\frac{17}{100}$ as a decimal. 0.17

2. Rewrite 0.24 as a fraction in lowest terms. $\frac{6}{25}$

3. $68 is what percent less than $80? 15%

4. Subtract: $34,510.23 − $7,388.04 $27,122.19

5. Multiply: 3.85% × $45,076 $1,735.43

6. Divide: $563 ÷ 0.1 $5,630

7. $36 is what percent greater than $20? 80%

8. $\frac{1}{6}$ less than $360 is what number? $300

9. Add: $506.45 + $108.45 + $78.31 + $1,957.23 $2,650.44

10. Rewrite 0.05879 as a percent to the nearest tenth of a percent. 5.9%

Applications

11. Phan Am Van earned gross wages of $487.12. Phan's deductions were: $49 in federal withholding taxes, 6.2% in social security taxes, 1.45% in Medicare taxes, $28.74 in health insurance, and $12 in union dues. Find Phan's net pay. $360.12

12. A job you are considering offers these benefits: paid vacations, $2,230; paid holidays, $2,450; paid pension, $4,058.60; paid health insurance, $428.90. What are the total benefits of the job? $9,167.50

13. Sally Longfeather earns an annual wage of $43,589. She estimates job benefits at 0.315 of her wages and her job expenses at: insurance, 0.04 of her wages; transportation, $1,296; dues, $200; and birthday fund, $50. What are her annual net job benefits? $54,029.98

14. Your budget says that savings should be 11% of income. If you earn $1,500 a month, how much should you save in a year? $1,980

15. A married couple earned a total of $86,340 last year. They spent during that year $18,200 on housing. What percent of their income, to the nearest whole percent, did they spend on housing last year? 21%

16. Evelyn Johnson had gross income of $33,200. She also had adjustments to income of $2,700, itemized deductions of $5,200, and 2 exemptions at $3,100. What was Evelyn's taxable income? $19,100

17. Tim O'Leary had a taxable income of $19,600 last year. His employer withheld $620 in state withholding taxes. If Tim's state has a 3% state income tax on taxable income, what amount should Tim receive as a refund? $32

18. Vance Milo had an earned income of $2,250 last year from part-time work. He also earned $24.15 in interest from a savings account. His father claimed him as an exemption on his tax return. If Vance's employer withheld $280 from his wages for withholding taxes, how much should Vance get back as a refund on his federal income taxes? $280

19. Sonia Ruiz had these cash receipts: July 1, interest from a savings account, $22.49; July 2, Sonia's paycheck, $502.77; July 3, returned purchase, $89.56; July 5, rebate on purchase, $75. What was Sonia's total receipts for the week? $689.82

20. Genaro Torres had these expenses during the week of May 2: dinner, $33.93; rent, $550; clothing, $36.29; bus fare, $20; miscellaneous, $38.06; savings, $75. What was Genaro's total cash payments for the week? $753.28

Chapter 2 Assessment ■ 79

Chapter-Test Correlation

Question	Lesson
11	2.1
12	2.2
13	2.2
14	2.6
15	2.6
16	2.3
17	2.4
18	2.3
19	2.5
20	2.5

PORTFOLIO ASSESSMENT

The spreadsheet, plan, and summary from the SCANS activities need to be prepared for students to include in their portfolios. Also, have students review the materials they have created in this chapter and select those they wish to place in their portfolios.

Cumulative Review–Lesson Correlation

Question	Lesson
1	1.3
2	2.3
3	1.5
4	2.4
5	1.4
6	2.1
7	1.1
8	2.2
9	2.1
10	1.1
11	1.1
12	1.4
13	1.2
14	1.5
15	1.4
16	2.4
17	1.3
18	2.2

Chapters 1-2 Cumulative Review

MULTIPLE CHOICE

Select the best choice for each question.

1. Last week Sarah Carver worked 4 overtime hours at time-and-a-half pay. Her regular pay rate is $8.70 per hour. What was her overtime pay for the week? B
   - **A.** $13.05
   - **B.** $52.20
   - **C.** $52.50
   - **D.** $69.60
   - **E.** $400.20

2. Last year Jose Inez's tax gross income was $24,685. She had adjustments to income of $3,640. What was Jose's adjusted gross income last year? A
   - **A.** $21,045
   - **B.** $22,185
   - **C.** $25,825
   - **D.** $28,325
   - **E.** $30,825

3. Carmen Rielly is paid piece-rate for each of the 268 items she produces in a week and she receives gross wages of $469. What is Carmen's per piece rate? D
   - **A.** $1.50
   - **B.** $1.70
   - **C.** $1.74
   - **D.** $1.75
   - **E.** $2.75

4. Gary Kersting has taxable income of $34,672. He pays a city income tax of 1.5% on taxable income. What is Gary's city tax? C
   - **A.** $346.72
   - **B.** $490.83
   - **C.** $520.08
   - **D.** $5,200.80
   - **E.** $34,151.92

5. Maureen Ritter is paid $275 a week and a commission of 7% on all sales. Her sales last week were $3,904. What were her total earnings for the week? B
   - **A.** $273.28
   - **B.** $548.28
   - **C.** $558.28
   - **D.** $2,732.80
   - **E.** $3,007.80

6. Jan Morrison's annual salary is $30,605. What is Jan's social security tax? A
   - **A.** $1,897.51
   - **B.** $1,989.32
   - **C.** $4,340
   - **D.** $18,975.10
   - **E.** $28,707.49

7. Jontay Mays works 8 hours a day Monday through Friday. What is his gross pay for one week if he earns $9.84 per hour? E
   - **A.** $78.72
   - **B.** $314.88
   - **C.** $344.40
   - **D.** $383.60
   - **E.** $393.60

8. Morgan Born is paid $11.20 an hour for a 40-hour week. Her estimated benefits are 33% of her wages. What is the value of her total yearly job benefits? D
   - **A.** $165.76
   - **B.** $595.84
   - **C.** $1,989.12
   - **D.** $7,687.68
   - **E.** $7,956.48

9. Dean Stroble is married and claims 2 withholding allowances. His gross weekly wage is $448. His withholding is $17 and FICA is $34.27. What is his net pay? A
   - **A.** $396.73
   - **B.** $431
   - **C.** $389.22
   - **D.** $499.27
   - **E.** $465

10. Kim Lui is paid an annual salary of $28,680. She is paid every other week. What is her gross pay for each pay period? B
    - **A.** $551.54
    - **B.** $1,103.08
    - **C.** $1,195
    - **D.** $1,434
    - **E.** $2,390

TEACHING STRATEGIES Cumulative Review

Assigning the Cumulative Review exercises allows students to refresh their knowledge and skills acquired in this and the previous chapter. Keeping student knowledge and skills current improves student retention of those capabilities and should improve their performance on periodic tests, such as quarter and semester tests.

OPEN ENDED

11. Last week Jason Fields worked: Monday, 7.2 hours; Tuesday, 8.3 hours; Wednesday, 8 hours; Thursday, 8 hours; Friday, 7.4 hours. He is paid $8.90 per hour. What was Jason's gross pay last week? $346.21

12. LaDonna Ekwilugo has sales last month of $86,400. Her total earnings for the month were $5,156, which included $1,700 for her monthly salary. What rate of commission was LaDonna paid? 4%

13. A shipping department has five workers: a supervisor who is paid $484 a week, and four other workers who are paid $390, $410, $425, and $430 a week. What is the average weekly pay for shipping department workers? $427.80

14. Janice Barton is an assembler in a factory and is paid $1.25 for each hand-held radio she assembles. During one week, Janice assembled these radios: 65 on Monday, 72 on Tuesday, 70 on Wednesday and 68 on Thursday. How many radios must Janice assemble on Friday to earn $425 for the week? 65

QUANTITATIVE COMPARISON

Compare the quantity in Column A with the quantity in Column B. Select the letter of the correct answer from these choices:
A if the quantity in Column A is greater;
B if the quantity in Column B is greater;
C if the two quantities are equal;
D if the relationship between the two quantities cannot be determined from the given information.

Column A	Column B
Chris' weekly salary	Chris' commission last week
Alvin's state income tax	Jamaal's state income tax
Krista's overtime pay	Haley's overtime pay

15. Chris Beltsos is paid a salary of $280 a week and a commission of 5.5% on all sales. His sales last week were $5,025. A

16. Alvin Barr's taxable income last year was $25,800. Jamaal White's taxable income last year was $29,600. Their state income tax rates were 5% for Alvin and 4% for Jamal. A

17. Krista Egan worked 4 overtime hours at time-and-a-half pay. Her regular hourly rate is $9.85. Haley Kale worked 2.5 overtime hours at double-time pay. Her regular hourly rate is $11.82 per hour. C

CONSTRUCTED RESPONSE

18. A friend has just graduated from high school and is looking at two job offers. One pays $12.50 an hour for a 40-hour week. The other pays $14 an hour for a 40-hour week. The friend thinks the choice is a no-brainer. The $14 an hour job pays more and so he should take that job. Write a letter to your friend to explain what other job factors should be examined before making the decision. Check students' work.

Chapter 2 Cumulative Review ■ 81

TEACHING STRATEGIES Cumulative Review

The Cumulative Review exercises provide students with opportunities to apply the knowledge and skills acquired in this and the previous chapter in a setting similar to standards tests used in many school districts and states. Such opportunities help students face standard tests with more experience and confidence.

Chapter 3 reviews the math skills of addition, subtraction, percents, multiplication, fractions, and rounding to solve check register and interest problems.

Lesson 3.1 Checking Accounts
Students prepare deposit slips and find account balances.

Lesson 3.2 Electronic Banking
Students record electronic bank transactions and find account balances.

Lesson 3.3 Online Banking
Students calculate the account balance needed to make electronic payments.

Lesson 3.4 Check Register Reconciliation
Students reconcile check registers and bank statements.

Lesson 3.5 Other Reconciliation Problems
Students complete a more complex reconciliation of check registers and bank statements.

Lesson 3.6 Savings Accounts
Students calculate simple and compound interest.

Lesson 3.7 Money Market and CD Accounts
Students calculate the interest earned on money market and CD accounts, early withdrawal penalties, and the effective rate of interest.

CHAPTER 3

Banking Services

3.1 Checking Accounts
3.2 Electronic Banking
3.3 Online Banking
3.4 Check Register Reconciliation
3.5 Other Reconciliation Problems
3.6 Savings Accounts
3.7 Money Market and CD Accounts

Statistical Insights

Leading U.S. Commercial Banks as of March 31, 2004		
Bank	**Headquarters**	**Consolidated Assets (Millions of Dollars)**
Bank of America	Charlotte, NC	690,573
J.P. Morgan Chase Bank	New York, NY	648,692
Citibank	New York, NY	606,191
Wachovia Bank	Charlotte, NC	364,474
Wells Fargo Bank	Sioux Falls, SD	347,560
Bank One	Chicago, IL	256,701
Fleet National Bank	Providence, RI	195, 323

Use the data shown above to answer each question.

1. Write the assets of Bank of America in standard form. $690,573

2. What is the difference between the banks with the highest and lowest assets? $495,250

3. Which banks have less than $20,000,000,000 difference in their revenues? Wachovia and Wells Fargo

Statistical Insights

Show students how to write out in full the data in the millions of dollars in revenue column. Ask how they would write out revenue figures of 10, 8.5, and 0.7 if they represent millions of dollars. Show how multiplying the revenue figures by $1,000,000 yields the correct result. Thus, $10 \times \$1,000,000 = \$10,000,000$ and $0.7 \times \$1,000,000 = \$700,000$.

NetCheck

Online Banking Services Search

Most major banks offer online account access to their customers. The level of service available online differs with the bank and the type of accounts established. In many cases you are simply able to get account balances and loan payoff information, while other banks allow you to conduct all of your banking business online. It is no longer necessary to do business with your nearby bank. Research the web sites of several banks, and determine the level of service offered. Consider how much banking you would want to do online: all, a little, or none.

Current Interest Rates

When choosing to deposit money into savings, you should look for the best interest rates and the most flexibility to access your money. The Internet makes shopping for current rates easy and up-to-date. Locate a web site that provides general economic indicators so that you can compare the interest of your selected bank with national averages.

Just as interest rates paid to customers change frequently, so do interest rates charged to customers who borrow money. Make sure the web site you located above also provides current rates for borrowing money.

How Times Have Changed

When ATMs were first introduced, each machine was installed at a single bank location, and customers could only access their accounts from that location. Today customers can use ATMs all around the world.

The Bankograph, which allows customers to pay utilities without a teller, is installed in New York's First National City Bank.
1960

The first magnetically encoded plastic cards are used at an ATM.
1969

Research to discover a significant event in 1974 that led to the worldwide use of ATMs.

1960   1965   1970   1975   1980   1985

1967
The first cash dispenser is installed in a Barclay's Bank outside London.

1971
The Docutel Corporation introduces the Total Teller, the first bank ATM.

1980s
Banks begin charging ATM fees to customers who use another owner's ATM.

83

GOALS

- Prepare a deposit slip
- Record entries in a check register

Start Up

A 23-year-old college student who lives at home buys two money orders a month to pay her bills. A 42-year old, single mother gets six bills each month. She also pays by money order. If neither of them have a checking account, should they open one to save the cost of buying money orders?

Math Skill Builder

Review these math skills and solve the exercises that follow.

❶ Add money amounts.
Find the sum. $17 + $5.25 + $632.19 = $654.44

  1a. $5.60 + $67.49 $73.09   **1b.** $294.43 + $123 $417.43

❷ Subtract money amounts.
Find the difference. $832.02 − $76.98 = $755.04

  2a. $900.35 − $298.37 $601.98   **2b.** $1,264.43 − $634.06 $630.37

❸ Multiply a money amount.
Find the product. 5 × $20 = $100

  3a. 15 × $10 $150   **3b.** 13 × $0.50 $6.50

■ Deposit Slip

Many people deposit their cash receipts in a checking account at a bank and make their payments by check. A checking account is safe and easy to use. The canceled checks returned to you by the bank provide you with a record of your payments. A **deposit slip** has been filled in for Sherry and Jamal Taylor to deposit their paychecks and other monies.

Cash deposits of *bills* and *coins* are listed on the line labeled CASH. Each check is listed on a separate line in the space for checks.

If there are more checks than lines available on the front of the deposit slip, list the additional checks separately on the back of the deposit slip.

84 ■ Chapter 3 Banking Services

COMMON ERRORS

Remind students that unlike addition, subtraction is neither commutative nor associative. So, 5 − 3 is not equal to 3 − 5. Addition and subtraction should be done from left to right, in order. Thus, 33 − 18 − 5 = 15 − 5 = 10. Watch for students who think that 33 − 18 − 5 = 33 − 13 = 20. The latter is the solution of 33 − (18 − 5).

The total of those checks is entered on the *Total from Other Side* line on the front of the deposit slip. Then, all the amounts are added to find the sum, which is written on the *Subtotal* line.

To receive *cash back* from the bank, write the amount wanted on the *Less Cash Received* line below the subtotal. Cash back is the amount that you want returned to you in cash.

MATH TIP

Check all subtraction. The best way to check subtraction is to add the amount subtracted and the difference. The answer should equal the top number.

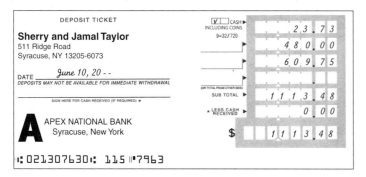

Find the *Total Deposit* by subtracting the cash received from the subtotal. The total deposit is sometimes called the *net deposit*. You only sign the deposit slip if you receive cash back and the bank requires a signature.

EXAMPLE 1

Alisha Reed made a deposit to her checking account: (bills) 6 twenties, (coins) 40 quarters, (checks) $457 and $18.10. She received 10 one-dollar bills in cash back. Complete a deposit slip.

SOLUTION
Fill in each line with the appropriate amount.

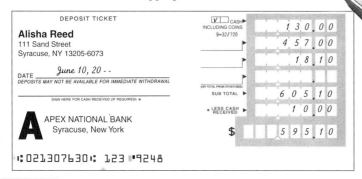

■ CHECK YOUR UNDERSTANDING

A. Shirley Poe deposited these items into her account at a bank: (bills) 14 twenties; (coins) 21 quarters, 6 dimes; (checks) $322.94, $1.45. She received 100 one-dollar bills in cash back. What was the amount of Shirley's deposit?
$510.24

B. Charles Gray made a deposit for the booster club at his school. He deposited: (bills) 17 twenties, 18 tens, 9 fives, 37 ones; (coins) 49 quarters, 12 dimes; (checks) $39.86, $3.83. Charles received no cash back. Find the total deposit.
$659.14

Lesson 3.1 Checking Accounts ■ **85**

■ Apply Goal 1

Work through the math of Example 1 at the board or use a transparency to explain why items are entered in certain places on the deposit slip. Have students complete the math at their desks. Point out that deposit slips they may use in the future may look different, but will contain the same basic elements.

Assign Check Your Understanding problems A and B for class work. Observe student work at their desks to identify any student errors or difficulties they have in solving the problems.

■ *CHECK YOUR UNDERSTANDING SOLUTIONS*

A. $(14 \times \$20) + (21 \times \$0.25) + (6 \times \$0.10) +$
$\$322.94 + \$1.45 - \$100 = \$510.24$

B. $(17 \times \$20) + (18 \times \$10) + (9 \times \$5) + (37 \times \$1) +$
$(49 \times \$0.25) + (12 \times \$0.10) + \$39.86 + \$3.83 =$
$\$659.14$

You may wish to discuss the various parts of the check and review how to fill out a check correctly including how to write the amount in words and numerals in a way that prevents the check from being altered.

Remind students of the need for 100% accuracy in completing the check register.

Work through Example 2 at the board or on a transparency with students completing the math at their desks.

Remind students that addition and subtraction are inverse operations. Show how the deposit amount may be subtracted from the running balance to arrive at the previous balance.

Assign Check Your Understanding problems C and D for class work. Remind students to write numbers and transaction descriptions legibly. Circulate in the classroom and examine student work for any difficulty they may be having with the problems.

■ Check Register

When you write a check you direct the bank to make a payment from your checking account. Checks are numbered to make it easy to keep track of checks.

The Taylors record each deposit made and check written in their **check register**, shown below. The check register is part of the checkbook in which deposits and checks are recorded. A new balance, called a *running balance*, is calculated after each entry. Each deposit is added to the previous balance. Each check is subtracted from the previous balance. The **balance** is the amount of money in the account.

		CHECK REGISTER						
NUMBER	DATE	DESCRIPTION OF TRANSACTION	PAYMENT/DEBIT (-)	√ T	FEE (IF ANY) (-)	DEPOSIT/CREDIT (+)	BALANCE $	1500 00
1341	7/6	Omnisat	$ 25 75		$	$		1474 25
	7/6	Sherry's Paycheck				480 00		1954 25
1342	7/7	Syracuse Electric	98 32					1855 93
1343	7/7	APEX Mortgage	772 33					1083 60
1344	7/8	Mid-town Appliance	165 98					917 62
	7/10	Jamal's Pay Check				609 75		1527 37

EXAMPLE 2

On October 18, Rico Ortez made a deposit of $250 to his checking account that had a previous balance of $1,288.43. He also wrote Check 67 to Mick's Catering for $78.50 and Check 68 to Bev's Tires for $143.78. Record each transaction and a running balance. What was the final balance in his check register?

		CHECK REGISTER			
CHECK NO.	DATE	TRANSACTION	PAYMENT/DEBIT	DEPOSIT/CREDIT	BALANCE
	10/17	Previous Balance			1288 43
	10/18	Deposit		250 00	1538 43
67	10/18	Mick's Catering	78 50		1459 93
68	10/18	Bev's Tires	143 78		1316 15

SOLUTION
The final balance is $1,316.15.

DIFFERENT LEARNING ABILITIES Visually Impaired Learners

Some students with visual problems may have difficulty in completing check registers. Some check registers have gray shading on every other row. This allows for a larger section for writing words and numbers by using a combined white and gray row as a single row.

C. Edwina Moss' check register showed a previous balance of $2,583.45 at the beginning of the week. During the week she made a deposit of $1,220 to her account and wrote checks for $825, $96.40, and $12.78. What final balance did her check register show? $2,869.27

D. Alex Devine made deposits of $500 and $1,236 to his account. He wrote checks for $196, $950, and $87.83. His previous balance before these transactions was $129.74. What was the new balance of his account? $631.91

GROSS AND NET Gross and net are common business terms. For example, the subtotal you find on a deposit slip may be thought of as the *gross* deposit. The deposit amount you get after subtracting cash received may also be called the *net* deposit.

A *gross* amount is the larger amount—the amount before anything is deducted. A *net* amount is the smaller amount that you get when you deduct or subtract something from a larger, gross amount.

Wrap Up

Every financial service is provided at a cost. Money orders are available for a fee and may be bought at a variety of places. Banks offer a variety of checking accounts that have some sort of cost or requirement attached to them, so they also are not free. Both women need to compare the monthly cost of buying money orders and using checking accounts. If the decision is made considering only cost, the student and the single mother should choose the plan that is least expensive for them individually.

TEAM MEETING

Join a team of four to six students. Each student in the group must contact a different bank, including credit unions and savings and loans institutions. Many institutions offer several types of checking account. Find the features and costs of checking accounts available at the bank you contact. Choose two accounts that you prefer and prepare a short summary or chart to share with your team members.

A good summary has the following content.

- ■ It covers the highlights or main points that are important for decision-making.

- ■ It summarizes and is not filled with detail.

- ■ It is no longer than one page.

The team needs to review all the information provided by each team member. Make comparisons and as a group decide which checking accounts they would want to use.

Lesson 3.1 Checking Accounts ■ 87

■ ONGOING ASSESSMENT
Have students use the inverse relationship of addition and subtraction to check their work by subtracting the amounts added and adding the amounts subtracted.

Wrap Up

Review the Start Up. Have students who volunteered to find money order costs report their findings.

TEAM MEETING

Have team members share their reports with the class and decide on the least expensive checking account available. Compare the costs of checking accounts with the costs of money orders reported in the Wrap Up.

■ *CHECK YOUR UNDERSTANDING SOLUTIONS*

C. $2,583.45 + $1,220 − $825 − $96.40 − $12.78 = $2,869.27

D. $129.74 + $500 + $1,236 − $196 − $950 − $87.83 = $631.91

EXERCISES

Do the indicated operation.

1. $458.59 + $312.03 $770.62

2. $1,098.45 + $17.31 $1,115.76

3. $1,492.49 − $231.56 $1,260.93

4. $248.72 − $9.87 $238.85

5. 14 × $10 $140

6. 12 × $20 $240

7. Eva Lanier deposited these checks into her account: $384.39, $12.44, $284.12. She received no cash back. What was her deposit total? $680.95

8. June Wilson's account had a beginning balance of $288.43. She made a deposit of $627 and wrote two checks for $35.87 and $263.56. What was the final balance in her check register? $616

9. The Singer family had a moving sale. The next day they made this deposit with no cash back: 25 twenties, 19 tens, 28 fives, 18 ones; 15 quarters; and checks for $25, $20, $85. What was the amount of their deposit? $981.75

10. On May 1 Rufus Knight's check register showed a balance of $505.23. Rufus had these transactions: May 4, check written for $34.66; May 7, check written for $98.62; May 9, deposit of $259.34; May 10, check written for $112.97. What was his check register's balance on May 10? $518.32

11. Yolanda Downey's checking account balance was $182.63. She made a deposit of $218.55 and wrote checks for $25, $30.17, and $46.07. What was the new balance in Yolanda's check register? $299.94

12. Donela Boyd's checking account balance was $3,060.65. A deposit of $1,603.48 was made and checks for $1,780.44, $22.74, $9.10, and $125 were written. What was the new balance of her account? $2,726.85

13. **STRETCHING YOUR SKILLS**   All-Sports Trophies made this deposit: 6 hundreds, 14 fifties; and checks for $85, $23.50, $32, $45, $17.50, $147, $17.27, $32.25, $65. They got cash back of 50 one-dollar bills, 20 five-dollar bills, 10 ten-dollar bills and 8 twenty-dollar bills. Find the total deposit. $1,354.52

14. **CRITICAL THINKING**   Assume you have a checking account that returns your canceled checks to you with a monthly statement. If the bank offers you a discount on your checking account charges if you agree not to have the checks returned, would you take advantage of such an offer to save money? Explain your response. Answers will vary. Be sure explanations defend the decision.

15. **CRITICAL THINKING**   Your bank gives you a choice of ordering either 200 or 400 checks at a time. The cost of 400 checks is double the cost of 200 checks, so there is no cost saving. You write about 14 checks a month. How many checks would you order at one time? Why? Answers will vary. Sample answer: 400, save on shipping costs

SELECTED SOLUTIONS

13. (6 × $100) + (14 × $50) + $85 + $23.50 + $32 + $45 + $17.50 + $147 + $17.27 + $32.25 + $65 = $1,764.52 gross deposit;

(50 × $1) + (20 × $5) + (10 × $10) + (8 × $20) = $410 cash back;
$1,764.52 − $410 = $1,354.52 net deposit

16. **STRETCHING YOUR SKILLS** The Floral Place made this deposit: 72 twenties, 126 tens, 57 fives, 235 ones; 287 quarters, 312 dimes, 48 nickels, 347 pennies; and checks for $124.68, $132.08, $1.29, $5.79. They received no cash back. Find the total of the deposit. $3,592.66

INTEGRATING YOUR KNOWLEDGE Stuart Rosenblatt earned a gross salary of $800 in one week. He received a paycheck that showed that taxes and other deductions of $206.75 were subtracted from his gross salary. Stuart also received an $82 purchase refund check and a $200 check from the sale of an old washer and dryer. His previous checking account balance was $502.87.

17. What was the net amount of Stuart's paycheck? $593.25

18. Stuart deposited all the checks and got $35 cash back. What was his net deposit? $840.25

19. What was Stuart's checking account balance after making the deposit and then writing a check to City Garage for $143.65? $1,199.47

MIXED REVIEW

Do the indicated operation.

20. $24,900.53 + $3,102.87 $28,003.40

21. $\frac{1}{3} + \frac{1}{2} + \frac{1}{8}$ 23/24

22. $2,348.81 − $5.99 $2,342.82

23. $8\frac{1}{4} − 3\frac{1}{6}$ 5 $\frac{1}{12}$

24. 249.88 ÷ 1,000 0.24988

25. 0.14859 × 100 = 14.859

26. Find the value of N, to the nearest cent: $N = $352.98 ÷ 100$ $3.53

27. A subway station's four cashiers collected these amounts in one work shift: $4,384.56, $6,398.20, $5,261.38, $4,900.15. What was the total amount of the cash collected? $20,944.29, Lesson 2.5

28. Regina Charren's job pays $45,300 in annual wages and 31% of annual wages in benefits. Her job expenses are estimated to be $3,300 a year. Regina interviewed for another job that pays $47,000 in yearly wages, average benefits of 29.5%, and estimated yearly job expenses of $3,750. Which job offers Regina the greater job benefits, and how much greater? second job, $1,072, Lesson 2.2

29. Elmer Hartley is paid a salary of $710 a week. What total salary does Elmer earn in one year? $36,920, Lesson 1.1

30. At the end of a craft show, Luma Villa deposited her receipts in a checking account: (bills) 19 twenties, 53 tens, 14 fives, 83 ones; (coins), 17 quarters, 1 nickel; (checks) $64.50 and $49.25. She got back in cash 3 fifties and $5 in dimes. What was her total deposit? $1,026.05, Lesson 3.1

31. Elrod York is paid a 5% commission on all monthly sales. His monthly sales average $82,000. What total commission is he likely to earn for the year? $49,200, Lesson 1.4

32. The city in which Leah Zang-Clouse works has a 1.25% tax on all income. What total city income taxes must she pay if her income for a year is $38,200? $477.50, Lesson 2.4

Lesson 3.1 Checking Accounts ▪ 89

Reteach

STUDENT WORKBOOK If students need help completing deposit slips, work Exercise 1 in the workbook with them. Then have them do Exercises 2 and 3.

Some students may need help in recording entries in check registers. Work Exercise 4 with them and assign Exercises 5 and 6 for independent work.

Enrich

Ask students to find out what "FDIC insured" means. (The Federal Deposit Insurance Corporation was created in 1933. If a bank is a member of FDIC, depositors are protected in case the bank fails or goes bankrupt. Usually, depositors are insured for up to $100,000 per account.)

Close

Have students share their understanding of how a checking account works and what the columns in a check register are used for.

Ask students to name advantages of paying by check instead of cash. The answers may include: safer than carrying large amounts of cash; creates a written record of payment.

Emphasize that checks must be used when making payments by mail and that cash should never be sent through the mail.

TEACHING STRATEGIES Cooperative Learning

Ask students how safe they or adults they know feel about withdrawing cash through ATMs. Have small groups of students prepare lists of precautions to take when withdrawing cash from ATMs.

Start Up

Have students read the Start Up. Ask questions to determine if students already know the difference between charge and debit transactions. Emphasize that Marc and Lenore may have legitimate reasons for the way they pay for purchases, and that there is usually no one, correct approach to handling personal finances.

Math Skill Builder

The addition and subtraction of money amounts are skills used in this lesson.

Complete all exercises in Math Skill Builder 1–2.

3.2 Electronic Banking

GOALS

- Record electronic banking transactions
- Find account balance when banking electronically

Start Up

Marc uses his charge card to pay for almost everything he buys. Lenore pays for most of her purchases with a debit card. Which approach is best?

Math Skill Builder

Review these math skills and solve the exercises that follow.

1 **Add** money amounts.
Find the sum. $15.98 + $3.42 + $70 = $89.40

  1a. $32,982.78 + $3,481.65 $36,464.43   **1b.** $3.50 + $12.75 + $2.75 $19

2 **Subtract** money amounts.
Find the difference. $54,857 − $34,298 = $20,559

  2a. $2,384.73 − $1,395.45 $989.28   **2b.** $30 − $28.96 $1.04

■ Electronic Banking

All banks use computers to process transactions electronically. Electronic banking allows bank customers to use telephones, computers, and other technologies in place of paper transactions such as writing checks and making loan payments.

ELECTRONIC FUNDS TRANSFER Banks use computers to transfer deposits and checks, or "funds," from person to person and bank to bank. This process is called **Electronic Funds Transfer**, or *EFT*.

Banks print the account numbers of customers and the bank identification number in *Magnetic Ink Character Recognition*, or *MICR*, form at the bottom of deposit slips and checks. This lets special computer equipment read the MICR data and update bank accounts and transfer funds from account to account electronically.

Each bank has its own, unique identification, or *routing number*.

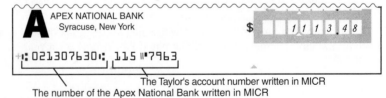

APEX NATIONAL BANK
Syracuse, New York

$ | | | 1 1 3 . 4 8

⑆021307630⑆ 115 ⑈7963

The Taylor's account number written in MICR
The number of the Apex National Bank written in MICR

DIFFERENT LEARNING ABILITIES Limited English Learners

Electronic terms are not likely to appear in a translation dictionary. To assist the LEP learner, obtain definitions beforehand from teachers who work with LEP students.

When using a technical term for the first time, print the term and its abbreviation on the board and repeat its pronunciation several times.

Individuals can also transfer funds electronically when they use an **Automatic Teller Machine**, or **ATM**. By using an ATM card issued by your bank, you can withdraw or deposit money, see account balances, or make transfers between your accounts. These transactions can be made at ATMs at any time of the day. ATMs are found at shopping malls, grocery stores, airports, and other convenient places.

Your bank's ATM card also allows you to withdraw money at another bank's ATM if it displays the same network logo shown on your card. The network logo is a brand name symbol that identifies an ATM network. You will have to pay an ATM-use fee when you use another bank's ATM. The fee and the withdrawal will be electronically deducted from your account and appear on your bank statement.

A *Personal Identification Number*, or *PIN*, that is known only to you is entered into the ATM before your transaction is processed. The PIN provides protection against unauthorized use of your ATM card.

EFTs may also be used to pay your monthly bills, such as utility bills. You can instruct your bank to transfer funds automatically each month from your bank account to the account of your utility provider. No checks are written or mailed.

Some companies use EFT to pay their employees by transferring funds directly into their employees' bank accounts without writing any checks to the employees. This is called **direct deposit**.

DEBIT CARD   Many people use a special form of EFT called a **debit card**. Debit cards allow you to pay for your purchases without using cash. You insert your debit card into a special computer terminal at stores that offer this type of service. The computer system subtracts the amount of each purchase automatically from your checking account and adds the same amount to the store's bank account. You may also use your debit card to withdraw cash from your account. Debit cards are sometimes called check cards.

At many banks, the ATM card is also the debit card. The ATM card is used for bank transactions. The debit card is used to pay for purchases. Fees may be charged for using this card.

■ Recording Electronic Transactions

When you use a debit card you get a receipt of the transaction. Save the receipt and immediately record the payment or cash withdrawal in your check register.
You may record the payment by writing the word "Debit" and adding a short description as well.

You also get a receipt when you use an ATM terminal. To record the transaction in your check register, you may write ATM-WD to describe a withdrawal or write ATM-DEP to describe a deposit.

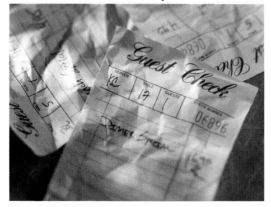

Lesson 3.2 Electronic Banking ■ 91

CONNECTION TO PERSONAL FINANCE

Inform students that some banks charge fees for teller-assisted transactions, checks written, and even for electronic transactions such as use of the bank's ATM and debit cards. Some of these charges are revealed to customers when accounts are opened. Bank customers are notified of other fees added over time through notices sent with bank statements. Consumers need to analyze continually what banking costs they pay and shop for better terms.

EXAMPLE 1

Wan-ying Kuo's checking account had a balance of $512.45 on April 4. Over the next three days she had these electronic transactions: a direct deposit of her weekly pay of $782.50 on 4/5, ATM cash withdrawal of $100 on 4/6, and a debit card clothing purchase of $90.27 on 4/7. What was her final check register balance?

SOLUTION

		CHECK REGISTER			
CHECK NO.	DATE	DESCRIPTION	PAYMENT/DEBIT	DEPOSIT/CREDIT	BALANCE
	4/4	Previous Balance			512.45
	4/5	Direct Deposit		782.50	1294.95
	4/6	ATM-WD	100.00		1194.95
	4/7	Debit (Clothes)	90.27		1104.68

■ **CHECK YOUR UNDERSTANDING**

A. Fred Wilhelm began the day with a $782.88 balance in his checking account. During the day he used his debit card to pay $85 for car repairs and $86.54 for a clothing purchase. Fred also withdrew $50 from his account at an ATM machine. What was the balance of Fred's checking account at the end of the day? $561.34

B. In one day Katrina Woll deposited her $890.50 paycheck at an ATM and withdrew $200 in cash. She also made two debit card purchases for $12.87 and $118.94. If she started the day with a bank balance of $1,248.40, what was her balance at the end of the day? $1,807.09

Wrap Up

Either way of payment is acceptable to the bank. Marc is spending money now that he doesn't have, but hopes to have when his charge bill is due. If he doesn't pay his charge bill on time, he will be charged interest. Lenore, on the other hand, in using the debit card is spending only the money she already has on deposit in her checking account. By only spending money that she has, Lenore is using good personal financial skills.

COMMUNICATION

Banks ask you to select your PIN when they issue an ATM or debit card. Often you don't have much time to think of something that is easily remembered. Assume that your bank asks you to choose a PIN that is six characters long and is alphanumeric, a combination of letters and numbers.

Write guidelines that offer advice to customers that banks should hand out when someone needs to create a personal PIN that cannot easily be guessed by someone who has stolen your card. Be sure to include do and don'ts in your guidelines. Share your guidelines with the rest of the class in an open discussion.

92 ■ **Chapter 3 Banking Services**

■ *CHECK YOUR UNDERSTANDING SOLUTIONS*

A. $782.88 − $85 − $86.54 − $50 = $561.34   B. $1,248.40 + $890.50 − $200 − $12.87 − $118.94 = $1,807.09

Find the sum or difference.

1. $54.38 + $0.86 + $120.37 $175.61

2. $10,076.01 + $67.43 $10,143.44

3. $12,938.38 − $5,987.29 $6,951.09

4. $700 − $579.86 $120.14

5. On Tuesday Henry St. John used a debit card to pay for: garden tools, $83.12; work clothing, $46.75; groceries, $54.79. If Henry's bank balance was $437.01 at the start of the day, what is his new balance at the end of the day? $252.35

6. After work Gladys Schroeder used the ATM to deposit her paycheck for $638.77 and to withdraw $200 cash. If her starting bank balance was $418.03, what is her new balance? $856.80

7. Adlise Leiber started the day with a bank balance of $343.64. She used another bank's ATM to withdraw $100 cash. The charge for using the ATM was $2.50. Adlise then used her card to make purchases of $85.10, $23.95, and $8.47. Find the balance in her account after the bank processed these transactions. $123.62

8. Gilbert Conroy withdrew $200 from his bank's ATM. On a shopping trip he bought an office chair for $120.87 in cash and paid $75.11 cash for groceries. He then used his ATM card to pay for $136.50 in painting supplies and $66.52 for lawn mower repair. What amount was left in Gilbert's account if it had a balance of $740.12 at the start of the day? $337.10

9. **CRITICAL THINKING** Molly Abrams will begin receiving social security monthly benefits that the law requires be paid by direct deposit. Molly is used to getting a paper paycheck and going to a bank to cash her check. Molly would prefer to receive her benefits in a paper check. What advantages of direct deposit could you tell Molly about that might convince her that direct deposit is better? Answers will vary, but may include that it is easy, the deposit is made on time, and eliminates the theft of a check.

MIXED REVIEW

10. Write 6.25% as a decimal. 0.0625

11. Rewrite $\frac{3}{5}$ as a decimal 0.6

12. Of a total budget of $48,000 for a year, the Ford family budgets $3,500 for medical costs. What percent of their total budget did the Fords budget for medical costs, to the nearest percent? 7%, Lesson 2.7

13. Vito Carletti paid a social security tax rate of 6.2% and a Medicare tax rate of 1.45% on his gross pay of $1,280. What total FICA tax did he pay? $97.92, Lesson 2.1

14. The Sunflower Nursery paid these amounts for its electric bills in the first half of the year: $258.38, $290.26, $358.24, $346.87, $310.43, $400.34. What was the average electric bill per month? $327.42, Lesson 1.2

15. Nina Talbot is paid a regular hourly rate of $14.67 and time-and-a-half for overtime. What is her overtime pay rate? $22.005, Lesson 1.3

Lesson 3.2 Electronic Banking ■ 93

SELECTED SOLUTIONS

6. $418.03 + $638.77 − $200 = $856.80

7. $343.64 − $100 − $2.50 − $85.10 − $23.95 − $8.47 = $123.62

12. 3,500 ÷ 48,000 = 0.072; 7%

14. $258.38 + $290.26 + $358.24 + $346.87 + $310.43 + $400.34 = $1,964.52; $1,964.52 ÷ 6 = $327.42

Start Up

Have students read the Start Up. Lead the students to discuss how consumers often buy a product, such as a new food item, to try it out. For software-based products, it is possible to use a trial version for a limited time without buying it or to try a simulated version, which is one alternative Ronald may use to make a decision.

Math Skill Builder

The addition and subtraction of money amounts are skills used in this lesson.

Complete all exercises in Math Skill Builder 1–2.

3.3 Online Banking

GOAL

- Calculate account balance needed to make online payments

Start Up

Your friend, Ronald Billings, received a letter from his bank inviting him to enroll in the bank's online banking program. Ronald thinks he would like to use this service. He also wonders whether the monthly charge of $5.95 for online banking is worth the cost. What would you say to Ronald that might help him decide what to do?

Math Skill Builder

Review these math skills and solve the exercises that follow.

1 **Add** money amounts.
Find the sum. $873.12 + $12 = $885.12

$ 2,903.69

1a. $18 + $357.38 $375.38   **1b.** $2,874 + $29.69 $2,904.69

2 **Subtract** money amounts.
Find the difference. $1,738 − $622.98 = $1,115.02

2a. $734 − $719.87 $14.13   **2b.** $287 − $165.45 $121.55

■ Online-Account Access

Many people regularly use electronic banking services such as ATM, debit cards, automatic bill payment, and direct deposit. They like the convenience of having 24-hour, everyday access to their bank accounts.

The use of another type of electronic banking service, called online banking, is rapidly growing. **Online banking** allows you to do your banking by using your personal computer and the Internet.

Each bank designs its own Internet website. What you see on your screen and how you use an online banking system differs among banks. Yet, the online banking services at most banks allow you to:

1. have access to your account 24 hours day, 7 days a week.
2. transfer money between your accounts.
3. have bills sent to you electronically instead of through the mail.
4. make payments to companies you select.
5. reorder checks and send messages to bank staff.
6. look at the history of your accounts.

94 ■ Chapter 3 Banking Services

DIFFERENT LEARNING ABILITIES At-Risk Learners

Some learners may not have access to a home computer. To assist such learners, make arrangements to use a computer lab for some lessons or activities that require use of computers. You may also encourage the at-risk learner to ask friends or relatives who have computers to provide assistance, or schedule time before or after school when a school computer might be available.

APEX National Bank *online banking*

Checking Account: 115 7953

YOUR ACCOUNTS		
View Accounts		
Download Your Recent Activity		
Transfer Money		
Payees		
Payment		
Electronic Payments		
CUSTOMER SERVICE		
Read message		
Send message		
Update personal information		
Reorder Check		

Last Statement Date	11/20/2001	Balance Last Statement $55.71
Current Balance	$216.95	Interest YTD $2.54
Available Balance	$216.95	Interest Rate 1.24%

Activity sorted by Date

Date	Description	Amount	Type
11/30/2001	CHECK #1017	-$100.00	CHK
11/29/2001	ONLINE TRANSFER FROM SAVINGS	$800.00	DEP
11/29/2001	ATM WITHDRAWAL	-$20.00	W/D
11/22/2001	TORINO MARKETS	-$16.57	DEB
11/22/2001	ATM DEPOSIT	$20.00	DEP
11/18/2001	METROPAGE, INC	-$22.19	EBL

■ **Teach Goal 1**

Have students examine the list of online banking services that appear on page 94 and identify those that do not require use of a computer. For example, an ATM or telephone provides access to bank accounts and allows the account owner to transfer money between accounts. Also, arrangements can be made with a bank to provide automatic bill payment.

Next, have students identify those services that allow customers the convenience of making transactions while at home.

Many banks offer "free online banking" to their customers. This free service allows customers to look at their account balances and make transfers between accounts. The online bill payment option is available for a monthly fee. A sample online banking screen is shown above.

The sample screen shows the *available balance* of the checking account. This is the amount that is available to spend. Knowing the balance helps you plan future online and check payments. Checks may have to be written if the person or company to whom the check is written does not have EFT capabilities.

The *account activity* section of the online screen shows the items that have been processed since the last statement date. It includes EFT transactions, as well as regular checks.

MAKING DECISIONS ABOUT ONLINE ACCOUNTS When selecting a bank at which to do online banking, the most convenient choice is the bank you now use. You should also evaluate the systems at other banks. Select the system that best meets your needs, is easiest to use, and does so at the least cost.

After selecting an online bank, some planning is needed to use the online accounts. You must identify sources of deposits to the account and decide who will be paid online. You will also have to determine the dates on which bills are due and the usual amount of the bill if it changes from month to month.

Online banking simplifies the banking process, yet is very similar to using a regular checking account. Both require making decisions to manage the account. To help her to plan and make decisions, Annie Clark made a worksheet that shows the transactions she expects will take place in March. The worksheet is shown on the next page.

Lesson 3.3 Online Banking ■ 95

CONNECTION TO ECONOMICS

Students should be made aware that online banking systems provide banks with an opportunity to reduce costs and increase profits. The more online customers a bank has, the less need the bank has to buy or build branches and hire teller and management staff. The reductions would offset the costs of developing online software and setting up and maintaining the online network. Emphasize that such a business strategy is considered to be long term.

Work through Example 1 with students at the board or on a transparency. Point out that several items in the worksheet are likely to be the same from month-to-month, except for their amounts.

Point out that the reason Annie may want to keep a minimum balance of $100 in the checking account is to cover checks to payees who do not accept online payments and provide a cushion for a week when debit purchases exceed $280. Account holders may also maintain a minimum balance to avoid paying a service charge that some banks levy on accounts with less than certain balance amounts.

Remind students that an insufficient funds charge will be made if the account does not contain enough money to cover checks that are written.

Assign Check Your Understanding problems A and B for class work and help students who have difficulty solving the problems.

■ ONGOING ASSESSMENT

Have students study the sample online banking screen and identify the items and terms that are similar to those they encountered while recording checking account transactions.

DIRECT DEPOSIT: $690 each Fri on dates: 03/01, 03/08, 03/15, 03/22, 03/29	ATM Cash withdrawal of $150 each Saturday	DEBIT CARD Purchases each Fri average $280 weekly	OTHER CHARGES None
EXPECTED PAYMENTS			
Electric bill	$ 53.00	due 03/06	
Natural gas bill	115.00	due 03/22	
Local phone bill	35.00	due 03/13	
Long distance phone bill	17.00	due 03/19	
Medical Insurance	108.00	due 03/24	
Internet service	18.95	due 03/05	
Car payment	312.40	due 03/13	
Home improvement loan	367.00	due 03/06	
House payment	842.00	due 03/20	

EXAMPLE 1

On Tuesday, March 5 Annie Clark decides to pay all bills listed in the "expected payments" section that are due by March 11. Before she makes any payments on March 5, Annie reviews her account balances: checking, $423.90; savings, $1,513. Her last deposit was the March 1 direct deposit.

Will Annie have enough money in her checking account to make the online payments on March 5 and have a balance of at least $100 in the account? If not, how much money will she have to transfer to checking from savings?

SOLUTION

	PAYMENT PLAN WORKSHEET, MARCH 5		
1	Checking Account Balance, March 5		423.90
2	Deposits made after March 1		+ 0.00
3	Subtotal (Line 1 + Line 2)		423.90
4	Online payments, debits, paper checks, ATM withdrawals		
5	Electric bill	53.00	
6	Internet service	18.95	
7	Home improvement loan	367.00	
8	Subtotal of all payments	− 438.95	
9	Difference (Line 3 − Line 8)		(15.05)

Line 1   Enter last available checking account balance.
Line 2   Enter 0.00 to show that no deposits were made after March 1.
Line 3   Add lines 1 and 2.
Line 4   An instruction line that directs you to list any online payments you wish to make, any checks you will write, and any expected ATM withdrawals.

TEACHING STRATEGIES Cooperative Learning

Have students work in teams to develop a list of payments that families are likely to make each month, quarter, or year. They may wish to use some of the data from their study of budgeting in Lesson 2.6. Have them identify which payments could be made online and calculate what percent of total transactions the probable online payments represent.

Lines 5–7   Enter bills due from March 5–11. These include the electric bill, Internet service bill, and home improvement loan. (Add more lines as needed.)

Line 8   Take a subtotal of all payments.

Line 9   When Line 8, $438.95, is subtracted from Line 3, $423.90, the result is a negative number, shown in parentheses as (15.05). There is not enough money to make the payments listed and maintain a minimum balance of $100 in the account. A total of $115.05 ($15.05 + $100) will have to be transferred to checking from savings.

■ CHECK YOUR UNDERSTANDING

A. The balance of Annie Clark's checking account on March 7 was $100 and her savings account balance was $1,413. Use Annie's worksheet to determine if on March 12 she can make online payments for all bills due from March 12 through March 18 and still leave a minimum balance of $100 in the account? If not, how much must she transfer to checking from savings? (Hint: Be sure to include in your calculations any deposits, ATM withdrawals, and debit purchases since the last online payment.)   No, $87.40

B. After making his online payments a week ago, Brian Hurley's checking account balance was $67. In the past seven days, he had these transactions in his checking account: deposit, $728; debit card purchases of $36.90 and $112.85; two checks written for $270 and $15. Today Brian is making online payments for boat insurance, $128; charge card, $89.23; medical bill, $45.50. What will be the balance of his checking account after all the transactions and online payments are entered? $97.52

Wrap Up

Ronald's bank may have a demonstration program of its online service for him to try. He may also talk with users of online banking to find out what their experience has been. Since he wants to try online banking, he ought to, even for a short time. If it doesn't work out, he can always switch back to the bill payment method he now uses.

TEAM MEETING

As a class, make a list of area banks, credit unions, and savings and loans that offer online banking services. Class members with Internet access should each choose an institution.

Research the web sites of these banks, credit unions, and savings and loans. Print screen captures that show how the sites function and also list the services provided online.

The entire class should then review the printouts and list the features common to all institutions, and then identify those features that are unique to specific banks, credit unions, or savings and loans.

Wrap Up

Review the Start Up. Have students compose a list of questions that Ronald may wish to ask online banking users to get information that would help him make a decision.

TEAM MEETING

As students review online banking screen captures and other data about online services, point out that different institutions may use different terms to describe the same feature or service.

Assign

Assignment: Exercises 1–13. Have students begin with the basic arithmetic problems at the beginning of the exercises since they review the underlying arithmetic in the exercises.

Assess

Ask students to name services that many banks offer online. **Access to account 24/7, transfer money between accounts, bills sent electronically, make payments, reorder checks, send messages to staff, see history of account.**

■ *CHECK YOUR UNDERSTANDING SOLUTIONS*

A. $100 + $690 − $150 − $280 − $35 − $312.40 = $12.60 balance;
$100 − $12.60 = $87.40 transfer from savings

B. $67 + $728 − $36.90 − $112.85 − $270 − $15 − $128 − $89.23 − $45.50 = $97.52

Reteach

STUDENT WORKBOOK Some students may need more practice to learn how to find the account balance needed to make online payments. If so, work Exercise 1 with them. Assign Exercises 2–4 for independent solution. Provide individual help as needed.

Enrich

Have students calculate how online checking costs may be partially offset by keeping a greater average balance in savings than in checking and earning more interest as a result. For example, a customer has an average monthly balance in a savings account of $2,000. The savings account earns 2% interest annually. How much of a monthly online banking cost of $5 would be offset by the interest earned from the savings account?

average monthly interest rate:

$2\% \div 12 \text{ months} = 0.1\overline{6}\%$

average monthly interest:

$\$2,000 \times 0.1\overline{6} \approx \$3.33$

The monthly online banking cost would be offset by the $3.33 interest earned in the savings account.

Close

Ask students how online and regular checking accounts differ and how they would organize a payments worksheet.

■ **STUDENT PORTFOLIO**
Have students consider including in their portfolio some of the problems they solved in this lesson or their research for the Team Meeting.

Check Your Understanding Problem A provides evidence of skill in planning and managing online payments.

EXERCISES

Find the sum or difference.

1. $12,873.29 + $2,498.32 $15,371.61

2. $387 + $28.07 $415.07

3. $1,483.87 − $842.38 $641.49

4. $248.09 − $74.83 $173.26

5. **DECISION MAKING** Your bank's online banking web site takes 15 seconds longer to load than that of a competing bank, yet costs $1 less per month than a competitor's system. Will you switch banks and gladly pay $1 more a month to get faster service? no

6. Toni Nicolet's checking account balance on Monday, April 13, is $540; her savings balance is $980. On Tuesday, April 14 she made an ATM withdrawal of $86. On April 15, Toni plans to make these online payments: income tax bill, $823, utility bill, $98, charge account bill, $127. How much money, if any, will Toni have to transfer into her checking account from savings to cover the online payments and leave a balance of $50 in the checking account? $644

7. Kwei-tseng Kuo plans to make these online payments: store charge account, $160; charitable donation, $40; rent, $550; cable bill, $42.01. She began the day with a checking account balance of $16.83. Later that same day she estimated her online payments and transferred $800 into checking from savings to cover the expected payments. What will be the balance of her checking account after the online payments are made? $24.82

8. Andrew Galen had a checking balance of $1.39 Monday morning. His net wages of $512.89 were transferred by direct deposit at 11:00 a.m. to his checking account. Later that evening, Andrew made online payments of $3.24, $18.30, $38.96, $100.34, and $314.78. His goal is to keep only a $10 balance in his checking account and have most of his money in savings. How much money was available in Andrew's checking account to be transferred to savings after all the transactions were completed? $28.66

MIXED REVIEW

9. Divide: $8,008 \div 13$ 616

10. Multiply: $2\frac{2}{9} \times 8\frac{3}{5}$ $19\frac{1}{9}$

11. Jeanne Williams sells welding equipment and is paid a commission of 9.5% on the first $25,000 of sales in a month and 12.4% of sales from $25,001 to $70,000 in a month. A commission of 15.1% is paid on all sales over $70,000 in a month. Her sales last month were $43,000 and $54,000 this month. What total commission earnings did Jeanne have for the two months? $10,578, Lesson 1.4

12. Justin Niklas made this deposit to the Breakfast Book Club's checking account: (bills) 43 ones, 13 fives; (coins) 9 quarters, 3 half-dollars, 5 dimes, 4 nickels, 12 pennies; (checks) $397.42, $192.81. Find the amount of the deposit. $702.80, Lesson 3.1

13. The city of Dubline has this income tax schedule for earnings of $46,000 to $58,000: $460 plus 1.25% of earnings over $46,000. What income tax will Jules Rubin have to pay on earnings of $53,400? $552.50, Lesson 2.4

98 ■ Chapter 3 Banking Services

SELECTED SOLUTIONS

6. $86 + $823 + $98 + $127 = $1,134 payments;
$1,134 − $540 = $594 cash short; $594 + $50 = $644 transfer from savings

12. Bills = $43 + 13($5) = $108
Coins = 9($0.25) + 3($0.50) + 5($0.10) + 4($0.05) + 12($0.01) = $4.57
Checks = $297.42 + $192.81 = $590.23
Deposit = $108 + $4.57 + $590.23 = $702.80

3.4 Check Register Reconciliation

GOALS

- Reconcile a bank statement
- Reconcile and correct a check register

Start Up

Two people are discussing a historical event. The more they talk, the more they disagree about when the event took place, the parties involved, and the outcome. You are asked to settle, or reconcile, the dispute. How would you do this?

Math Skill Builder

Review these math skills and solve the exercises that follow.

1 **Add** money amounts.
Find the sum. $23,487 + $15.34 $23,502.34

1a. $20.08 + $832.58 $852.66 **1b.** $85.82 + $70.18 $156

2 **Subtract** money amounts.
Find the difference. $76.28 − $5.39 $70.89

2a. $900 − $2.08 $897.92   **2b.** $175.29 − $38.43 $136.86

■ Reconcile the Bank Statement

Banks keep track of checking account transactions and send a monthly report, called a bank statement, to depositors. A sample bank statement for Gerald Booth is shown on the next page.

BANK STATEMENT   The bank statement shown lists (1) nine *checks* paid by the bank; (2) four *deposits*, including interest earned, (3) and two *other charges*, an ATM withdrawal and a service charge.

Interest earned is money paid to customers for the use of their money. A service charge is a deduction made by the bank for handling the checking account.

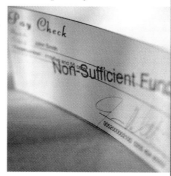

TRANSACTIONS OUTSTANDING   With his September bank statement Gerald Booth received several canceled checks. A *canceled check* is a check that the bank has paid and then marked so it can't be used again.

Lesson 3.4 Check Register Reconciliation ■ 99

Start Up

Have students read the Start Up. To dramatize the Start Up, you might show an item such as a travel poster to the class for ten seconds. Put the poster away and have students write a description of the poster's message, colors, size, scene depicted, etc. Then select two students to read their descriptions and have the class identify and resolve the differences between the two observations that are in dispute.

Math Skill Builder

Students use the skills of addition and subtraction of money amounts in this lesson.

Complete all exercises in Math Skill Builder 1–2.

Gerald Booth compared the bank statement and the canceled checks with his check register. On the bank statement he placed a check mark next to the number of the check when both records agreed.

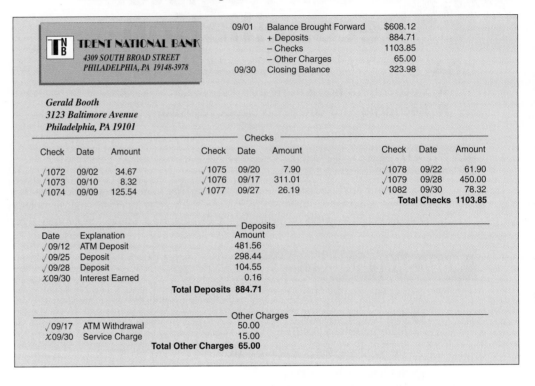

Gerald found two checks (numbers 1080 and 1081) that were not returned by the bank. These checks are called **outstanding checks**. This means that the checks have not yet been received or paid by the bank.

Gerald also placed a check mark next to each deposit shown on the statement that appeared in his check register. Since all deposits were accounted for, there were no *outstanding deposits*. An outstanding deposit occurs when a deposit is made after the closing date of the bank statement and the deposit is recorded in the check register.

Gerald also placed a check mark next to the ATM withdrawal because it was recorded in his check register. The letter "X" was placed next to the interest earned and the service charge, items that were not recorded in the check register. Gerald's statement shown above is already marked.

RECONCILIATION FORM   When Gerald Booth looked in his check register, he found his last recorded balance for September to be $196.89. The final balance on his bank statement was $323.98. The difference in the balances was the result of the outstanding checks, interest earned, and the service charge.

To bring both balances into agreement and to make sure the bank's records were correct, Gerald Booth has to *reconcile* both records. This is a two-step process. The first step is to reconcile the bank statement. To help him, Gerald has to complete the reconciliation form printed on the back of the bank statement.

COMMON ERRORS

Students may not understand that different terms often represent the same idea. For example, they may not know that a direction to reconcile the account means the same as reconcile the checking account and bank statement.

EXAMPLE 1

Prepare a reconciliation form for Gerald Booth to reconcile the bank statement.

SOLUTION
Complete the reconciliation form.

Reconciliation Form				
Follow these steps:			Outstanding Checks	
1 Enter Closing Balance from Statement	$ 323.98		1080	$48.65
2 Add any deposits outstanding	+ 0.00		1081	$93.28
3 Add lines 1 and 2	= 323.98			
4 Enter total of Checks Outstanding	− 141.93			
5 Subtract line 4 from line 3. This amount should equal your check register balance.	$ 182.05		Total	$141.93

Follow these steps to complete the form:

1. List separately the outstanding checks in the "Outstanding Checks" column. Find their total, $141.93, and write it in Line 4.

2. Write the closing bank statement balance of $323.98 on Line 1.

3. Write 0.00 on Line 2 to show no "Deposits Outstanding."

4. Do the addition shown on Line 3.

5. Do the subtraction shown on Line 5. The result, $182.05, is the "reconciled" bank balance. Since $182.05 does not agree with Gerald Booth's check register balance of $196.89, he will have to also reconcile the check register.

■ CHECK YOUR UNDERSTANDING

A. Maria Greeley's bank statement showed a closing balance of $1,383.53, no outstanding deposits, and two outstanding checks for $129.45 and $87.39. Reconcile her bank statement. $1,166.69

B. Xavier Allasandro had a closing balance of $793.57 in his bank statement. The outstanding items were: a deposit of $312.09, Check 278 for $174.85, and Check 280 for $32.78. Reconcile his bank statement. $898.03

■ Reconcile the Check Register

After reconciling his bank statement balance, Gerald Booth found that it still did not agree with the check register balance. The next step is to reconcile his check register.

■ Apply Goal 1

Work through Example 1 using a transparency of the bank statement and the reconciliation form to demonstrate how the two forms are interrelated.

Show students how the known items (closing balance and out-standing checks and deposits) may be entered first into the reconciliation form followed by calculations.

Assign Check Your Understanding problems A and B for class work. Circulate through the classroom and examine student work for any difficulties they may be having.

Provide students with copies of the reconciliation form. If they draw their own form, check that their work reflects a format similar to that of the reconciliation form in the textbook.

■ ONGOING ASSESSMENT
Use the reconciliation form in Example 1. Point to Lines 2 and 4 and ask why outstanding deposits must be added and outstanding checks subtracted from the closing balance. Ask if they would get the same answer if the checks were subtracted first and then the deposits were added.

BUSINESS TIP

Outstanding items (checks and deposits) are items that you have recorded in your check register but the bank has not yet received. That means they have not subtracted outstanding checks from the bank balance nor added outstanding deposits to the bank balance. These are two reasons why your balance doesn't match the bank's balance.

■ *CHECK YOUR UNDERSTANDING SOLUTIONS*

A. $1,383.53 − $129.45 − $87.39 = $1,166.69   B. $793.57 + $312.09 − $174.85 − $32.78 = $898.03

■ **Teach Goal 2**

Remind students that the second step of reconciliation is to correct the check register by entering any transactions that appeared on the bank statement but did not appear in the check register.

■ **Apply Goal 2**

Work through Example 2 at the board with students. Write the check register entries on the board and have students calculate the running balance. Have them compare the check register final balance with the final total of the reconciliation form in Example 1 to verify that the two records agree.

Assign Check Your Understanding problems C and D for class work. Remind students to write the check descriptions and amounts clearly. Check student work at their desks.

Wrap Up

Review the Start Up and the Wrap Up solution. Have students relate the reconciliation process to the resolution of a dispute. This approach may be used: identify the facts in dispute (bank statement and check register do not agree); do research (find the items unaccounted for in each record); resolve the dispute (do the reconciliation).

EXAMPLE 2

Record transactions from the bank statement in Gerald Booth's check register to reconcile the register.

SOLUTION

CHECK REGISTER							
CHECK NO.	DATE	DESCRIPTION	PAYMENT/DEBIT		DEPOSIT/CREDIT	BALANCE	
	9/30	Previous Balance				196	89
	9/30	Interest Earned			0 16	197	05
	9/30	Service Charge	15	00		182	05

The $0.16 interest earned was added to the account by the bank so it also must be added to the balance in the check register. The $15 service charge was deducted from the account by the bank. The service charge must also be deducted from the check register.

The final balance of $182.05 shown in the check register agrees with the final balance of $182.05 shown on the bank's Reconciliation Form. The account is reconciled.

■ **CHECK YOUR UNDERSTANDING**

C. Mildred Galin's previous check register balance was $727.92. Her bank statement showed a service charge of $18.90 and interest earned of $1.60. Reconcile her check register. $710.62

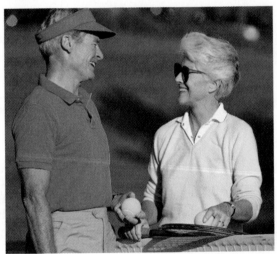

D. Ludwik Sirros had a balance of $457.38 in his check register. His checking account does not pay interest. His bank statement showed a $7.68 service charge. Reconcile his check register. $449.70

Wrap Up

One way to settle disagreements is to collect and present the facts. Historical records contain information about the event. Presenting the facts to the people who do not agree is a way to begin reconciling the disagreement.

■ *CHECK YOUR UNDERSTANDING SOLUTIONS*

C. $727.92 − $18.90 + $1.60 = $710.62   D. $457.38 − $7.68 = $449.70

WORKPLACE WINDOW

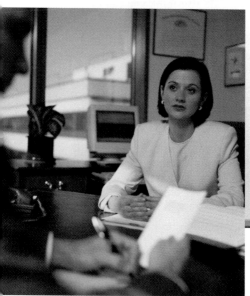

BANK MANAGERS oversee the operation of bank branches. They coordinate the work of bank tellers, loan officers, and other personnel. They are also responsible for the accuracy of financial reports and the cash flow of the branch.

Managers must use their organizational skills and banking knowledge to implement strategies that will achieve the bank's long-term goals and to make sure that the policies of the bank are followed. A college degree in finance and accounting is often required.

Managers must have good communication skills to interact effectively with customers, employees, and personnel from other banks. Strong computer, analytical, and problem-solving skills are also required of bank managers.

The employment outlook for bank managers is generally good, but the responsibilities of managers may change as the banking industry continues to encourage customers to make greater use of electronic banking.

WORKPLACE WINDOW

Ask students to describe what the long-term goals of a bank might be and give examples of policies that a bank may have in place. Ask whether they agree that an increase in electronic banking is likely to decrease the need for personnel in branch offices.

Assign

Assignment: Exercises 1–8, 10, and 12–24. Remind students to begin with the basic arithmetic problems.

EXERCISES

Find the sum or difference.

1. $874.20 + $392.29 $1,266.49

2. $125.62 + $1.23 + $72.76 $199.61

3. $17,800.23 − $2,893.98 $14,906.25

4. $274.65 − $110.38 $164.27

5. The bank statement of Dottie Weigand showed a closing balance of $3,150.18. The transactions outstanding included three checks for $12.87, $39.47, and $840. Reconcile Dottie's bank statement. $2,257.84

6. Roger Korsak's check register balance was $745.84. His bank statement showed an ATM deposit of $82.67 that was not recorded in his check register, interest earned of $0.87, and a $18 charge for printing new checks. Reconcile Roger's check register. $811.38

7. Phoebe Duncan's check register balance on November 30 was $984.09. Her November 30 bank statement showed a balance of $1,462.25. Checks outstanding were 207 for $298.12, 209 for $86.73, and 210 for $105.03. The bank service charge for November was $12.80 and the interest earned was $1.08. Reconcile Phoebe's check register. $972.37

Lesson 3.4 Check Register Reconciliation ■ **103**

SELECTED SOLUTIONS

6. $745.84 + $82.67 + $0.87 − $18 = $811.38

8. $906.57 − $170.13 − $103.89 − $13.16 − $4.68
= $614.71 bank statement balance
$612.91 − $8.20 + $10 = $614.71 check register balance

12. $\overset{1}{\cancel{3}}_{1} \times \frac{\cancel{8}\,2}{\cancel{15}\,5} = \frac{2}{5}$

13. $12\frac{3}{4} - 3\frac{1}{8} = 12\frac{6}{8} - 3\frac{1}{8} = 9\frac{5}{8}$

STUDENT WORKBOOK If students need help reconciling check registers, work the check register portion of Exercise 1 with them. Then have them complete Exercise 2.

Other students may need help in completing a reconciliation form. Work through the Exercise 1 reconciliation form with them and assign the Exercise 3 reconciliation form to be done as individual work.

Assign Exercise 9, Critical Thinking. Have students discuss the difference between writing a check when you know there is not enough money in the account and making an honest error.

Assign Exercise 11, Decision Making. Point out how an income deduction may be taken for the contribution in the year the check was written even though the check may be cashed in the following year.

8. When Yoko Doi got her bank statement on April 30 it showed a balance of $906.57, a service charge of $8.20, and a $10 credit in her favor for an error the bank had made. Outstanding checks were: 267, $170.13; 268, $103.89; 269, $13.16; 271, $4.68. Her checkbook showed a balance of $612.91 on April 30. Reconcile Yoko's bank statement and check register. $614.71

9. **CRITICAL THINKING** Do you know what it means to "bounce" a check? Write your understanding of the term. How do you think you can avoid "bounced" checks? keep track of account balance

10. Hajit Khanna opened a checking account on July 1 with a deposit of $500. On October 31 his bank statement balance was $1,061.74 and his check register balance was $628.59. Hajit's statement showed six checks, two ATM deposits, a service charge of $6.20, an ATM withdrawal, and interest earned of $2.78. A comparison of the register and statement showed these outstanding checks: 5114 for $96.72, 5115 for $301.56, and 5117 for $38.29. Reconcile Hajit's checking account. $625.17

11. **DECISION MAKING** Suppose you made a contribution to a charity by check in December. You just received your March bank statement and found the check to be outstanding. If the check is outstanding for several months, can it still be cashed by the charity? Do you need to take any action? Possibly not since many banks honor checks up to 6 months after they are written.

MIXED REVIEW

12. $\frac{3}{4} \times \frac{8}{15} =$ $\frac{2}{5}$

13. $12\frac{3}{4} - 3\frac{1}{8} =$ $9\frac{5}{8}$

14. Rewrite 0.8 as a fraction $\frac{4}{5}$

15. Find 75% of 140 $105

16. Estimate the quotient: 6,132 ÷ 42 150

17. Divide to the nearest hundredth: 995 ÷ 7.4 134.46

18. Round 5,437 to the nearest 10, and then to the nearest 100. 5,440, 5,400

19. Kristin Thomas' job expenses last year were: tools, $1,250; work supplies, $180; work clothes, $360; union dues, $480; truck expenses, $3,800. Her total job benefits for the year were $48,000. Find Kristin's net job benefits. $41,930, Lesson 2.2

20. The owner of a hospital supply company bought four new trucks of different sizes. Their purchase prices were $28,430, $21,692, $22,572, and $25,870. What average price per truck did the owner pay? $24,641, Lesson 1.2

21. McCarther Williams, a waiter, wrote $430 in breakfast checks one morning. His tips average 11% of the total checks. What was his tip income for the morning? $47.30, Lesson 1.5

22. Elva Rainey is single and has taxable income of $23,810. Her employer deducted $3,718 in withholding taxes for the year. Find Elva's tax due and any refund or amount owed. Use the tax tables in Chapter 2. $3,216; $502 refund, Lesson 2.3

23. The Garth family's income is $45,200. They estimate they will spend $1,800 on vacations and $500 on other entertainment this year. What percent of their income will be spent on vacations, to the nearest percent? 4%, Lesson 2.6

24. Walker Levin is paid a 2.75% commission on all sales over $5,500 each week. Last week his sales were $12,650. On how much of his sales did he earn commission and what was the amount paid to him in commission? $7,150, $196.63; Lesson 1.4

CONNECTION TO PERSONAL FINANCE

Inform students that reconciling checking accounts is a way to update and correct the check register, but it is a process that takes place after the fact. Remind students that it is important to keep the check register accurate throughout the month to avoid NSF (not sufficient funds) charges. The charges are the same regardless of whether the account owner overdraws the account intentionally or accidentally.

Other Reconciliation Problems

GOAL

- Reconcile a checking account with outstanding transactions and other errors

Start Up

Vernon thinks it is too much work to reconcile a checking account. Instead, he just assumes the bank statement is correct because he says the computers used by banks do not make errors. Vernon's most recent statement showed that his balance was $591.42. Vernon's check register showed his balance as $519.42. Is it a good idea for Vernon to simply add the $72.00 difference into his account so that he can spend it?

Math Skill Builder

Review these math skills and solve the exercises that follow.

1 **Multiply** to find money amounts.
Find 5% of $1,837. $0.05 \times \$1,837 = \$91.85$

  1a. 8% of $953 $76.42   **1b.** 24% of $150.09 $36.02

2 **Subtract** money amounts.
Find the difference. $\$2,832.45 - \$929.78 = \$1,902.67$

  2a. $789.39 − $719.87 $69.52   **2b.** $80.01 − $9.98 $70.03

■ Reconcile the Checking Account

Sometimes you must reconcile a bank statement and check register balances when deposits, checks, and EFT transactions are not recorded and when other errors are made.

To understand this process, use Rena Jackson's July bank statement dated August 6. The bank statement is shown on the next page. When Rena compared her check register balance of $1,181.39 with the bank statement's closing balance of $632.31, the two amounts did not agree. She had to reconcile the account.

To begin, Rena compared each item in the check register with each item on the bank statement. On the bank statement she placed a check mark next to the items when the two records agreed.

An "X" was placed next to those items that needed to be investigated. Rena's bank statement is already marked.

Lesson 3.5 Other Reconciliation Problems ■ 105

Start Up

Have students read the Start Up. Have students relate Vernon's thoughts to what they already know about how errors may occur in check records. Ask if there might be a situation where it would be possible for Vernon to simply add the $72 and be correct. One possibility would be that Vernon did not record a deposit of exactly $72 in his check register and had no other adjustments.

Math Skill Builder

In this lesson, students use the skills of subtracting money amounts and finding a percent of money amounts.

Complete Exercises 1–2 in the Math Skill Builder.

■ Teach Goal 1

Point out that there are many more items that have to be checked and reconciled before bank statements and check registers totals agree.

Review the use of the √ to identify items that appear on both documents and the X to label items that require attention or correction.

TEACHING STRATEGIES Cooperative Learning

The problems in this lesson include additional and more complex variables for students to consider in reconciling checking accounts. You may wish to have students work in pairs to solve the problems in this lesson. Where possible, pair a student who may benefit from one-on-one dialog with a student you feel might provide good explanations.

Work through Example 1 with students using a transparency to correlate the bank statement to Rena's notes that appear in the solution to Example 1.

Provide an overview for students by showing how items 9 and 10 on Rena's list on page 106 are accounted for in the reconciliation form.

Have students participate in the explanation of how the check register entries relate to the explanations by line number that follow.

Assign Check Your Understanding problems A and B for class work. Examine student work by circulating about the classroom.

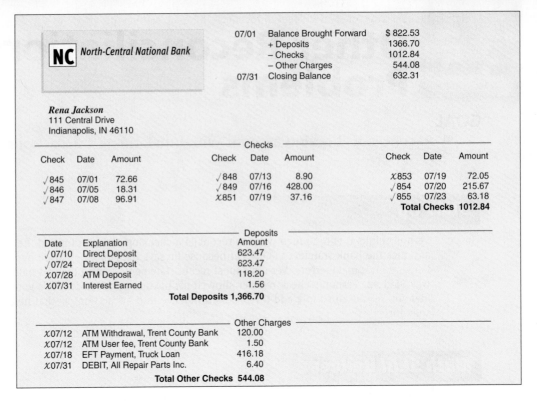

	07/01	Balance Brought Forward	$ 822.53
		+ Deposits	1366.70
		– Checks	1012.84
		– Other Charges	544.08
	07/31	Closing Balance	632.31

NC North-Central National Bank

Rena Jackson
111 Central Drive
Indianapolis, IN 46110

————— Checks —————

Check	Date	Amount	Check	Date	Amount	Check	Date	Amount
√845	07/01	72.66	√848	07/13	8.90	✗853	07/19	72.05
√846	07/05	18.31	√849	07/16	428.00	√854	07/20	215.67
√847	07/08	96.91	✗851	07/19	37.16	√855	07/23	63.18
							Total Checks	**1012.84**

————— Deposits —————

Date	Explanation	Amount
√07/10	Direct Deposit	623.47
√07/24	Direct Deposit	623.47
✗07/28	ATM Deposit	118.20
✗07/31	Interest Earned	1.56
	Total Deposits	**1,366.70**

————— Other Charges —————

Date	Explanation	Amount
✗07/12	ATM Withdrawal, Trent County Bank	120.00
✗07/12	ATM User fee, Trent County Bank	1.50
✗07/18	EFT Payment, Truck Loan	416.18
✗07/31	DEBIT, All Repair Parts Inc.	6.40
	Total Other Checks	**544.08**

EXAMPLE 1

Reconcile Rena Jackson's bank statement and check register.

SOLUTION

Step 1: Compare the bank statement to the check register and note any differences between them.

Rena's notes about the items where she found a problem are listed.

1. Check 851 for $37.16 was cashed on 7/19, but not recorded and subtracted in the register.

2. Check 853 for $72.05 was recorded as $27.05 in the register.

3. An ATM deposit of $118.20 made 7/28 was not recorded in the register.

4. Interest of $1.56 was earned on the account but not recorded in the register.

5. An ATM withdrawal of $120 on 7/12 from the Trent County Bank's ATM was not recorded in the register.

6. A fee of $1.50 charged by the Trent County Bank for the use of its ATM on 7/12 was not recorded in the register.

7. An EFT loan payment of $416.18 was not recorded in the register.

8. A debit charge of $6.40 was subtracted from the bank balance but not from the check register balance.

9. Checks 850 for $8.12 and 852 for $34.28 were outstanding.

10. A deposit of $85 made on 8/1 was recorded in the register but deposited after 7/31, the closing date for July's bank statement.

DIFFERENT LEARNING ABILITIES Visually Impaired Learners

If students have difficulty reading Rena Jackson's bank statement, provide them with a photocopy of the statement that greatly increases the size of the print.

Step 2: Prepare a reconciliation form to reconcile the bank statement.

Reconciliation Form				
Follow these steps:		Outstanding Checks		
1 Enter Closing Balance from Statement	$ 632.31	850	$ 8.12	
2 Add any deposits outstanding	+ 85.00	852	$34.28	
3 Add lines 1 and 2	= 717.31			
4 Enter total of Checks Outstanding	− 42.40			
5 Subtract line 4 from line 3. This amount should equal your check register balance.	$ 674.91	Total	$42.40	

The August 1 deposit of $85 not on the July 31 bank statement was added and the two outstanding checks subtracted from the closing balance to reconcile the bank statement.

Step 3: Reconcile the check register.

	CHECK NO.	DATE	DESCRIPTION OF TRANSACTION	PAYMENT/DEBIT (-)	√ T	FEE (IF ANY) (-)	DEPOSIT/CREDIT (+)	BALANCE
			Check Register					
LINE 1			Previous Balance	$		$	$	1181 39
LINE 2			Ck 851, July 19	37 16				1144 23
LINE 3			Ck 853 (wrong amount)				27 05	1171 28
LINE 4			Ck 853 (correct amount)	72 05				1099 23
LINE 5			ATM-DEP				118 20	1217 43
LINE 6			Interest earned				1 56	1218 99
LINE 7			ATM-WD	120 00				1098 99
LINE 8			ATM user fee	1 50				1097 49
LINE 9			EFT payment, truck loan	416 18				681 31
LINE 10			Debit	6 40				674 91

Line 1   The previous balance of $1,181.39 is the last balance in the check register before the reconciliation begins.

Line 2   Record unrecorded Check 851 for $37.16.

Line 3   Check 853 was recorded incorrectly as $27.05. The $27.05 had to be added back into the check register to cancel the error.

Line 4   The correct amount for Check 853 was recorded as $72.05.

Line 5   Record the unrecorded ATM deposit of $118.20.

Line 6   Add interest earned of $1.56 to the register.

Line 7   Record the unrecorded ATM withdrawal of $120 in the register as a payment.

Line 8   Record the unrecorded ATM user fee of $1.50 in the register as a payment.

Line 9   Record the unrecorded EFT payment of $416.18 in the check register.

Line 10   Record the debit charge of $6.40 in the register as a payment.

The final balance of $674.91 shown in the Reconciliation Form agrees with the final balance of $674.91 shown in the check register. The checking account is reconciled.

■ ONGOING ASSESSMENT
Obtain samples of reconciliation forms from several banks. Have students examine the differences between the forms and use one of the forms in the solution of the exercises.

■ STUDENT PORTFOLIO
Students should consider including in their portfolio the bank reconciliation problems they solved in this lesson.

COMMON ERRORS

Students may add outstanding checks to the bank statement balance rather than subtract them. It may help if you explain that the bank records and customer records are parallel. Deposits are added to the bank's record of your account just as they are added to the check register.

Similarly, checks are subtracted in both records. Thus, checks already subtracted in the check register must be subtracted from the bank statement balance if they are outstanding.

Wrap Up

Review the Start Up. Since students know why bank and check register balances disagree, ask them for their opinion about the practice of writing checks ahead of an expected deposit while knowing that there is not enough money in the account when the check is written and mailed.

Point out that such checks are probably written and mailed often. There is likely to be a 1 or 2 day period between the mailing of a check and its charge against the checking account. This practice could backfire if the unexpected happens.

■ CHECK YOUR UNDERSTANDING

A. On January 30, your check register balance is $107.87 and your bank statement balance is $161.96. Interest earned of $0.43 and an ATM deposit of $56 also appeared on the statement but had not been recorded in the register. You also find that check 307 for $35.29 had been entered in the register as $32.95. Reconcile the checking account. $161.96

B. At the end of October, Allen Springer's check register balance was $812.45. His bank statement balance was $624.77. An examination of his statement and check register showed that an ATM withdrawal of $200 had not been entered in the register, check 201 for $92.49 was outstanding, and check 202 for $80.17 was cashed but not recorded in the register. Reconcile the checking account. $532.28

Wrap Up

Vernon needs to reconcile his account. If the mistake is on the part of the bank, once it is discovered, the money will be deducted from Vernon's account. It is good practice to reconcile a checking account when the statement arrives. Not doing so means the balance of the account is not really known. This makes it more likely for checks to be written against money that is not available in the account.

COMMUNICATION

Many employers rely on a Standard Operating Procedure (SOP), which is a guide for all employees to follow in making decisions and completing tasks. The SOP is generally used so that the everyday activities of a company are done consistently even when personnel changes.

The Standard Operating Procedures must be clearly and precisely written. Procedures that are unclear can lead to misunderstandings between the expectations of employers and the performance of employees. The procedures may also define how employees are to interact with customers. Misunderstandings with customers can lead to a damaged business relationship and a loss of sales.

Prepare a Standard Operating Procedure on how to reconcile a checking account. Assume that you manage a team of bookkeepers and all accounts must be reconciled in the same manner. Your Standard Operating Procedure will serve as guidelines for all who work for you.

108 ■ Chapter 3 Banking Services

■ CHECK YOUR UNDERSTANDING SOLUTIONS

A. $107.87 + $0.43 + $56 + $32.95 − $35.29 = $161.96

B. $812.45 − $200 − $80.17 = $532.28 check register balance; $624.77 − $92.49 = $532.28 bank statement balance

Find the sum or difference.

1. $12.45 + $8.30 + $127.87 $148.62

2. $15.34 + $99.18 + $2.08 $116.60

3. $10,471.48 − $6,284.92 $4,186.56

4. $874.19 − $249.87 $624.32

For Exercises 5–10 reconcile both the check register and bank statement unless you are directed otherwise.

5. Theresa Penfield's December 31 bank statement balance was $381.36. Her outstanding checks were for these amounts: $45.71, $9.45, $24.90. A January 1 ATM withdrawal of $100 and a January 5 ATM deposit of $85 were recorded in her check register but did not appear on the bank statement. Reconcile the bank statement. $286.30

6. Walter Singletree's check register balance was $829.76 on June 30. When comparing his check register and the June bank statement, he found these items were not recorded in the register: service charge of $5.67, ATM deposit of $135, and a debit for $55.78. He also found that Check 203 for $28.98 was recorded as $28.89. Reconcile Walter's check register. $903.22

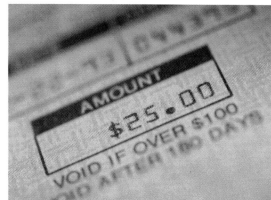

7. On May 31, Sue Ware's check register balance was $289.30 and her bank statement balance was $375.37. Checks outstanding were: 543, $86.24; 543, $12.82; 547, $57.67. A late deposit on June 1 for $68.50 was not on the statement. The statement showed an ATM-use service fee of $2.50 and interest earned of $0.34. $287.14

8. On March 31, Goro Hayashi's check register balance was $277.37 and his bank statement balance was $289.23. The statement showed an ATM-use service charge of $1.25. Checks 85 for $5.37 and 90 for $73.09 were outstanding. Goro also found that he had recorded Check 87 for $20.75 twice in the check register and did not record Check 93 for $86.10. $210.77

9. On May 30, Amy Millard's check register showed a balance of $700.61. Her bank statement balance on that date was $1,143.90. The "other charges" part of the statement showed that an EFT car loan payment of $250 was not recorded in the register. Checks outstanding were: 834 for $48.33, 837 for $21.19, 838 for $161.77. A direct deposit of $480 was not recorded in the check register. Check 836 for $86.40 was recorded as $68.40. $912.61

10. Brad Meyer's check register balance on June 30 was $503.45. His June bank statement showed a balance of $458.16 on the same date. When Brad examined the statement he found an ATM-use service charge of $2.75 and interest earned of $0.78. He also found that check 467 for $12.98 had been recorded in the check register as $12.89. An ATM withdrawal of $60 and a debit card purchase of $105.11 had not been recorded in the check register. Checks outstanding were: 477 for $64 and 478 for $57.88. $336.28

Lesson 3.5 Other Reconciliation Problems ■ **109**

Assign

Assignment: Exercises 1–26. Have students solve the basic arithmetic problems before completing the rest of the exercises. Provide students with duplicated copies of reconciliation forms and check registers to be used to complete the exercises.

Assess

Collect student solutions and examine their errors. Prepare a list of the transactions that appear to be the most difficult for students to complete accurately.

SELECTED SOLUTIONS

7. $289.30 − $2.50 + $0.34 = $287.14 check register balance; $375.37 − $86.24 − $12.82 − $57.67 + $68.50 = $287.14 bank statement balance

9. $700.61 − $250 + $480 + $68.40 − $86.40 = $912.61 check register balance; $1,143.90 − $48.33 − $21.19 − $161.77 = $912.61 bank statement balance

11. **CRITICAL THINKING** When an amount is incorrectly recorded in the check register, you may correct the error by finding and recording the difference between the amounts. If a check for $34 had been recorded in the register as $43, would you add or subtract the difference from the last balance? Why? add. Because too much was taken out

12. **CRITICAL THINKING** Your bank issued you an ATM card that may be used at all the bank's ATM locations. You may use the ATM card at the automated teller machines of other banks that display the same network symbol as shown on your card. The charge for this service may range from $1.50 to $7. Why is such a charge made? Is it a fair charge? Answers will vary.

MIXED REVIEW

Find the product or quotient.

13. $156 \times \$0.10$ $15.60

14. $1,874 \times 1¢$ $18.74

15. $\frac{2}{5} \times \$815$ $326

16. $\$241.78 \div 100$ $2.4178

17. $\$85 \div 1.00$ $85

18. $\$630 \div \frac{1}{3}$ $1,890

19. What is $580 increased by $\frac{1}{5}$ of itself? $696

20. $\frac{3}{4} \div \frac{2}{3}$ $1\frac{1}{8}$

21. Of her annual income of $26,000 last year, Margot spent $800 on car repairs. What percent of her annual income was spent on car repairs, to the nearest tenth percent? 3.1%, Lesson 2.6

22. Arrange 21¢, $0.35, $0.15, 11¢ from lowest to highest order, writing all numbers in dollar form. $0.11, $0.15, $0.21, $0.35

23. In addition to salary of $3,570, Mary Holt is paid a commission of 4.5% of all sales over $18,000 in a month. In February her sales were $21,500. What commission did she earn for the month? $157.50, Lesson 1.4

24. An assistant chef is paid $120 for every day she works. What is her gross pay for a month in which she works 25 days? $3,000, Lesson 1.5

25. Ricky DeWitt is a high school student. His parents claim him as a dependent on their income tax return. Ricky earned $2,780 at his part-time job. His employer deducted $336 in withholding taxes from his wages. Ricky earned $53 interest on his savings account and had no adjustments to income. He wants to claim the standard deduction on his tax return when he files for a tax refund. What refund will Ricky get? $336, Lesson 2.3

26. The average number of newspapers delivered by four carriers is 135. Three of the carriers delivered 118, 140, and 129 newspapers. How many papers did the fourth carrier deliver? 153, Lesson 1.2

CONNECTION TO PERSONAL FINANCE

Present a situation to students of a person who works in an office complex and uses an ATM that does not belong to his/her bank four times a week. The ATM-use charge is $1.50 per transaction. The person enjoys the convenience of getting cash-in-a-minute. Have students calculate the annual cost of ATM withdrawals and suggest alternatives the person might consider to save money.

3.6 Savings Accounts

Goals

- Calculate simple interest on savings deposits
- Calculate compound interest on savings deposits
- Calculate interest using a compound interest table

Start Up

Have students read the Start Up. In addition to answering the question raised, ask students to describe the kind of protection banks offer.

Math Skill Builder

Students use the skills of multiplying money amounts by decimals and factions, as well as multiplying percents by fractions.

Complete Exercises 1–3 in the Math Skill Builder.

■ Teach Goal 1

Tell students that interest rates are annual rates, or rates for one year. Simple interest is figured by the formula $I = PRT$.

Review with students that time may be expressed as a fraction. For example, interest paid quarterly is paid 4 times a year or every 3 months. Time for one quarter is $\frac{3}{12}$ or $\frac{1}{4}$ of a year. The time for semiannual interest for one half year is $\frac{6}{12}$, or $\frac{1}{2}$.

Start Up

Banks provide protection for your money when you open a saving account. They also pay you interest. Why do they pay you interest?

Math Skill Builder

Review these math skills and solve the exercises.

1 **Multiply** money amounts by decimals and round.
Find the product. $1,200.56 \times 0.065 = 78.036, or $78.04

1a. 965×0.043 $41.50   **1b.** 870×0.0125 $10.88

2 **Multiply** money amounts by fractions.
Find the product. $23.876 \times \frac{1}{2} = 11.938, or $11.94

2a. $12.836 \times \frac{1}{4}$ $3.21   **2b.** $8.3598 \times \frac{1}{2}$ $4.18

3 **Multiply** percents by fractions.
Find the product. $6\% \times \frac{1}{4} = 1.5\%$

3a. $5\% \times \frac{1}{4}$ 1.25%   **3b.** $8\% \times \frac{1}{2}$ 4%

■ Simple Interest

One reason people open savings accounts is to keep their money safe. Another reason is that they earn interest on their money. Interest is money paid to an individual or institution for the privilege of using their money.

As with a checking account, you may deposit money into or withdraw money from your savings account. The bank teller may give you a receipt, which is an official record of the transaction. A transaction is something that happens that has to be recorded, such as a deposit or withdrawal.

INTEREST ON SAVINGS ACCOUNTS There are several types of savings accounts. In a passbook account, simple interest is often figured *quarterly*, or four times a year, on the balance of the account at the end of each quarter. The interest is paid on the first day of the next quarter, or on January 1, April 1, July 1, and October 1. Sometimes interest is paid twice a year, or in *semiannual* periods (six months, or one-half year).

Lesson 3.6 Savings Accounts ■ **111**

CONNECTION TO PERSONAL FINANCE

Point out to students that passbook savings accounts are also referred to as regular savings accounts or statement accounts. The owner of the account is provided with a printed record of account transactions since the last statement. Previously, passbook account owners were given a small book in which tellers recorded deposits, withdrawals, interest, and the running balance. The advent of computers made the need for passbooks virtually obsolete.

Work through Example 1 on the board with students completing the math at their desks. Emphasize that the intermediate calculation of interest for one year is not rounded because the result must be multiplied by time to complete the calculation in the formula $I = PRT$.

Assign Check Your Understanding problems A and B for completion in class. Check student work at their desks to identify difficulties they may have with solving the problems.

■ ONGOING ASSESSMENT
Have students write the letters P, R, or T above the numbers in the solutions to Example 1 and Check Your Understanding problems A and B to identify the factors of the interest formula.

■ Teach Goal 2

Explain that interest on savings is usually compounded, which means that interest is calculated on the principal and any interest that has been earned previously.

■ Apply Goal 2

Work through Example 2 at the board with students completing the math at their desks. Clearly label all parts of the solution including individual factors of the interest formula.

Assign Check Your Understanding problems C and D for completion in class. Circulate about the classroom to observe student work and whether they are solving the problems correctly.

Since interest rates change over time, some of the interest rates used in this book may be different than current interest rates. Some computations involving lower interest rates often will not reveal any difference between compound interest and simple interest, thereby lacking significant instructional value.

To find the simple interest for any period, first find the interest on the deposit for a full year. Then multiply that amount by the fraction of a year, such as $\frac{1}{4}$ or $\frac{1}{2}$ for which you want to find interest.

EXAMPLE 1

Find the interest for six months on $400.60 at $1\frac{1}{2}\%$ annual interest paid semiannually.

SOLUTION

$0.015 \times \$400.60 = \$6.009$ interest for one year (do not round)

$\frac{1}{2} \times \$6.009 = \$3.0045$, or $\$3.00$ interest for six months

You may find simple interest by using a formula.

Interest = Principal × Rate × Time ($I = PRT$)

In the formula $I = PRT$, I is the amount of interest, P is the principal amount, R is the annual percentage rate, and T is time in years.

Interest = Principal × Rate × Time

$I = \$400.60 \times 0.015 \times \frac{1}{2} = \$3.0045$, or $\$3.00$ interest for six months

■ **CHECK YOUR UNDERSTANDING**

A. What interest is paid for three months on $860 at $2\frac{1}{4}\%$ annual interest paid quarterly? $4.84

B. Find the interest for six months on $350 at 3.1% annual interest paid semiannually. $5.43

■ Compound Interest

At the end of each interest period, the interest due is calculated and added to the previous balance in the savings account. The new balance then becomes the principal on which interest is calculated for the next period, if no deposits or withdrawals are made. When you calculate interest and add it to the old principal to make a new principal on which you calculate interest for the next period, you are *compounding interest*. Most banks pay interest compounded either daily or quarterly.

Regardless of how interest is earned, the total money in the savings account at the end of the last interest period is called the **compound amount**, assuming that no deposits or withdrawals have been made. The total interest earned, called **compound interest**, is the difference between the original principal and the compound amount.

EXAMPLE 2

On January 1, Peter Monroe made an ATM deposit of $800 in a savings account that pays 2% interest, compounded quarterly. He made no other deposits or withdrawals. If interest is calculated and paid on April 1 and July 1, find the account balance (compound amount) and the compound interest on July 1.

■ *CHECK YOUR UNDERSTANDING SOLUTIONS*

A. $\$860 \times 0.0225 \times \frac{1}{4} = \$4.837$, or $4.84

C. $\$700 + (\$700 \times 0.03 \times \frac{1}{4}) = \$700 + \$5.25 =$ $705.25; \$705.25 + (\$705.25 \times 0.03 \times \frac{1}{4}) =$ $705.25 + \$5.29 = \$710.54

D. $\$400 + (\$400 \times 0.025 \times \frac{1}{2}) = \$400 + \$5 = \$405;$ $405 + (\$405 \times 0.025 \times \frac{1}{2}) = \$405 + \$5.06 =$ $410.06; \$410.06 - \$400 = \$10.06

SOLUTION

$800 \times 0.02 \times \frac{1}{4} = \$4$ interest for first quarter

Find the new account balance.

$800 + \$4 = \$804$ new balance, or new principal, on April 1

$804 \times 0.02 \times \frac{1}{4} = \$4.02$ interest for second quarter

Find the new account balance.

$804 + \$4.02 = \$808.02$ new balance on July 1

Find the difference between the July 1 balance and the original principal.

$808.02 - \$800 = \$8.02$ compound interest for two interest periods

The account balance (compound amount) on July 1 was $808.02. The compound interest for the two quarters is $8.02.

■ **CHECK YOUR UNDERSTANDING**

C. Your bank pays 3% interest compounded quarterly on October 1 and January 1. You had $700 on deposit on July 1 and made no additional deposits or withdrawals. Find the account balance on January 1. $710.54

D. You deposited $400 on July 1 and kept your money on deposit for one year. You made no deposits or withdrawals. If your bank pays 2.5% interest compounded semiannually, what compound interest will you earn in one year? $10.06

■ Compound Interest Tables

When you calculate compound interest for several interest periods, you can use a compound interest table such as one shown below. The table shows the value of one dollar ($1) after it is compounded for various interest rates and periods.

Interest Periods		1%	$1\frac{1}{4}$%	$1\frac{1}{2}$%	2%	$2\frac{1}{2}$%	4%	5%
Annual	1	1.010000	1.012500	1.015000	1.020000	1.025000	1.040000	1.050000
	2	1.020100	1.025156	1.030225	1.040400	1.050625	1.081600	1.102500
	3	1.030301	1.037971	1.045678	1.061208	1.076891	1.124864	1.157625
	4	1.040604	1.050945	1.061364	1.082432	1.103813	1.169859	1.215506
	5	1.051010	1.064082	1.077284	1.104081	1.131408	1.216653	1.276282
	6	1.061520	1.077383	1.093443	1.126162	1.159693	1.265319	1.340096
	7	1.072135	1.090850	1.109845	1.148686	1.188686	1.315932	1.407100
	8	1.082857	1.104486	1.126493	1.171659	1.218403	1.368569	1.477455
	9	1.093685	1.118292	1.143390	1.195093	1.248863	1.423312	1.551328
	10	1.104622	1.132270	1.160541	1.218994	1.280084	1.480244	1.628895
	11	1.115668	1.146424	1.177949	1.243374	1.312086	1.539453	1.710339
	12	1.126825	1.160754	1.195618	1.268242	1.344888	1.601032	1.795856
Daily	30	—	—	—	1.001668	1.002085	1.003339	1.004175
	90	—	—	—	1.005012	1.006269	1.010050	1.012578
	180	—	—	—	1.010050	1.012578	1.020200	1.025313
	365	—	—	—	1.020484	1.025670	1.041387	1.051998

The table has two parts. The top part is used to calculate annual interest. It may also be used to calculate quarterly and semiannual interest. The bottom part is used to calculate daily interest.

■ **Teach Goal 3**

Point out that tables are often used in business since it is easier to look up a multiplier in a table than to calculate the interest for several consecutive periods.

Show students how to use the table by giving them various rates and interest periods and having them find the multiplier.

Repeat the process for rates and time periods not in the table and explain that an inverse operation is required. If the rate is divided, the number of periods must be multiplied.

COMMON ERRORS

When compounding interest, students may forget to add the interest to create a new principal for the next interest period. To help such students, remind them to add the interest calculated for the period to the old principal and label the result (the compound amount) as "new balance, or new principal" as is shown in the example.

Work through Examples 3 and 4 on the board. Have students complete the math at their desks.

Assign Check Your Understanding problems E through H for completion in class. Observe student work at their desks making suggestions as needed.

To calculate annual interest, locate the column and row where the interest rate and the number of interest periods meet. The number you find is called the *multiplier*. For example, the multiplier for daily interest at 2% for 90 days is 1.005012. You multiply the deposit amount by the multiplier to find the compound amount. Subtract the original principal from the compound amount to find compound interest. Follow this procedure to find both annual and daily compound interest.

EXAMPLE 3

Find the compound interest paid on a $400 deposit that earns interest at an annual rate of $2\frac{1}{2}$% for 12 years.

SOLUTION
Find the multiplier in the compound interest table: 1.344888

$400 × 1.344888 = $537.9552, or $537.96   compound amount

Find the difference between the compound amount and the original deposit.

$537.96 − $400 = $137.96   compound interest

■ **CHECK YOUR UNDERSTANDING**

E. What compound interest is paid on a $1,100 deposit earning 1.25% annual interest for 3 years? $41.77

F. A deposit of $720 earns 1% annual interest for 7 years. What compound interest will the deposit earn? $51.94

When interest is compounded quarterly, you use the multiplier in the table for *four times* the number of annual periods and *one fourth* the rate. When interest is compounded semiannually, you use the multiplier for *twice* the number of annual periods and *one half* the rate.

EXAMPLE 4

A $1,200 deposit earns annual interest of 4% compounded quarterly. Find the compound interest the deposit will earn in 3 years.

SOLUTION
Since 4% is an annual rate, take one-fourth of that rate to find the equivalent quarterly rate. Then multiply the deposit term by 4 to find the number of quarterly periods.

$\frac{1}{4} × 4\% = 1\%$ quarterly rate $4 × 3 = 12$ interest periods

Find the multiplier in the compound interest table: 1.126825

$1,200 × 1.126825 = $1,352.19   compound amount

Find the difference between the compound amount and the original deposit.

$1,352.19 − $1,200 = $152.19   compound interest for 3 years

■ *CHECK YOUR UNDERSTANDING SOLUTIONS*

E. 1.037971 × $1,100 = $1,141.77;
$1,141.77 − $1,100 = $41.77

F. 1.072135 × $720 = $771.94;
$771.94 − $720 = $51.94

G. 1.104486 × $850 = $938.81;
$938.81 − $850 = $88.81

H. 1.050945 × $1,600 = $1,681.51;
$1,681.51 − $1,600 = $81.51

G. An $850 savings deposit is on deposit for 2 years and earns 5% annual interest compounded quarterly. What will be the compound amount in the account in two years? What interest will have been earned? $938.81, $88.81

H. An account in which interest is compounded semiannually pays 2.5% annual interest. What interest will be earned in this account if $1,600 is left on deposit for 2 years? $81.51

Wrap Up

Banks pay interest to you as an incentive to deposit your money. In turn, the banks lend your money to someone else at a higher interest rate than you are paid. The difference between the amount paid to you and collected from the borrower is profit that the bank keeps.

Algebra Connection

The dictionary has many definitions for formula. One definition is a general fact, rule, or principle. Formulas are commonly used in algebra courses because they state a mathematical or geometrical rule using variables. For each specific situation, the variables are replaced in the formula with given values so that a value can be assigned to the rule.

The formula $I = prt$ is used to calculate simple interest. Now find the formula to calculate compound interest either at the library or through an Internet search. Test the formula by reworking the compound interest problems you've already solved. Explain any differences you may find between the formula's answers and your hand-calculated answers.

EXERCISES

Find the sum.

1. $842 + $32.89 $874.89

2. $430 + $16.13 $446.13

Find the product and round.

3. $1,286 × 0.0125 $16.08

4. $984 × 0.026 $25.58

5. $67.20 × $\frac{1}{12}$ $5.60

6. $189.78 × $\frac{1}{4}$ $47.25 4 47.45

Lesson 3.6 Savings Accounts ■ 115

Wrap Up

Review the Start Up and the answer provided in the Wrap Up. Discuss with students that not all the money on deposit is lent or invested by banks. Banks are required to keep a percentage of their savings on hand to take care of withdrawals.

Ask students whether banks would make risky loans or investments with their depositor's funds. You may wish to mention the bailout of Savings and Loan banks that resulted partly from making bad loans.

Algebra Connection

Point out that there are many ways in which savings institutions calculate compound interest. The most common way uses the formula $B = p(1 + \frac{r}{n})^n$ where B is the balance in the account after interest is added, p is the principal (or amount in the account before interest is added), r is the annual rate, and n is the number of times a year that interest is compounded.

Assign

Assignment: Exercises 1–40. Exercises may be completed after all goals are taught or they may be assigned for additional practice after each example and the related Check Your Understanding problems are completed. Exercises 7–10 relate to Example 1, Exercises 17–20 to Example 2, Exercises 11–14 to Example 3, and Exercises 15–16 to Example 4.

TEACHING STRATEGIES Cooperative Learning

Students may not know how to use their calculator to apply the compound interest formula they located through their Algebra Connection search. Have students form teams to arrive at the most efficient calculator procedures for the compound interest calculation.

Check student answers to the exercises. Exercises 21–23, Stretching Your Skills, require students to compute interest on minimum balances on deposit in a period. Write and work through the solution for the problem on the board. You may wish to change the facts and present a similar problem for additional practice.

Reteach

STUDENT WORKBOOK If students encounter difficulty with simple interest calculations, work Exercise 1a and 1b with them. Then assign Exercises 1c–1j for independent work.

Work Exercises 2 and 6 with students who are not successful in calculating compound interest. Assign Exercises 3 and 7–9 for class work to be completed independently.

If students need work on figuring compound interest using tables, complete Exercises 10 and 14 with them. Then assign class work of Exercises 11–13 and 15–18.

Find the simple interest for one quarter.

7. $300 at 5% a year $3.75

8. $750 at 3% a year $5.63

9. $217.66 at 1.5% a year $0.82

10. $1,400 at 0.9% a year $3.15

Use the compound interest table to solve Exercises 11–16.

	Principal	Rate	Time	Compounded	Compound Amount	Compound Interest
11.	$1,000	1.25%	4 years	Annually	$1,050.95	$50.95
12.	700	1.0%	11 years	Annually	$780.97	$80.97
13.	900	2.5%	90 days	Daily	$905.64	$5.64
14.	1,000	2%	180 days	Daily	$1,010.05	$10.05
15.	600	5%	3 years	Quarterly	$696.45	$96.45
16.	800	3%	5 years	Semiannually	$928.43	$128.43

Your bank pays 4% annual interest compounded quarterly on January 1, April 1, July 1, and October 1. You deposited $840 on April 1 and made no other deposits or withdrawals.

17. Find your savings account balance on January 1 of the next year. $865.45

18. How much interest did you earn for these nine months? $25.45

19. Flora Kenyon made a deposit of $1,600 to her savings account on July 1. For the next year she made no other deposits or withdrawals. Her bank pays annual interest of 3.1% compounded quarterly. Find the estimated and actual interest earned by Flora by July 1 of the next year. $1,600 × 3% = $48 estimated; $50.18 actual.

20. Seamus Keane made a $600 deposit on April 1 in the Mac-Oak Bank. The bank pays an annual rate of 2.6% compounded quarterly on the first day of January, April, July, and October. On July 1, Seamus deposited $200 more to his account. He made no other deposits or withdrawals. Find his balance on October 1. $809.13

STRETCHING YOUR SKILLS Some banks pay interest only on the minimum or smallest balance on deposit during an interest period. Helen Lamb had a balance of $783 in such an account on July 1. Annual interest is 2.7% compounded quarterly. She withdrew $170 on August 17 and deposited $200 on September 12.

21. What was Helen's minimum balance during the quarter? $613

22. How much interest was she paid on October 1? $4.14

23. How much did Helen have on deposit on October 1? $817.14

24. CRITICAL THINKING Some people explain compound interest as a way to earn interest on interest. Others say that interest earned is simply added to the previous balance to make a new balance on which interest is computed. Is either view more accurate that the other? Check students' work.

25. CRITICAL THINKING Look at the compound interest table. Why are the amounts in the table not rounded to the nearest cent since all money amount answers are rounded to the nearest cent? Answers will vary. Rounding to the nearest cent can increase amounts significantly over the life of loan. This method is more fair to the consumer.

116 ■ Chapter 3 Banking Services

SELECTED SOLUTIONS

9. $217.66 × 0.015 × $\frac{1}{4}$ = $0.816, or $0.82

13. 1.006269 × $900 = $905.64;
$905.64 − $900 = $5.64

15. 1.160754 × $600 = $696.45;
$696.45 − $600 = $96.45

20. $600 × 0.026 × $\frac{1}{4}$ = $3.90;

$600 + $3.90 + $200 = $803.90;

$803.90 × 0.026 × $\frac{1}{4}$ = $5.23;

$803.90 + $5.23 = $809.13

26. $\frac{4}{5} + \frac{1}{4} + \frac{1}{2}$ $1\frac{11}{20}$ 27. $\frac{2}{5} \times 20$ 8

28. $\frac{8}{9} - \frac{2}{3}$ $\frac{2}{9}$ 29. $\frac{4}{7} \div 16$ $\frac{1}{28}$

30. $100 \times \$26.50$ $2,650   31. $100,000 \times \$32.18$ $3,218,000

32. 15 is what percent of 200? 7.5%

33. 18 is what percent of 240? 7.5%

34. Find the average of $9.14, $3.83, $1.94, and $4.13. $4.76

35. Find the average of $0.90, $0.42, $0.78, $0.13, and $1.25 to the nearest cent.
$0.70; Lesson 1.2

36. Eva and Trent Blum, a married couple, file a joint tax return for their gross income of $53,000 and claim two exemptions. Their itemized deductions are $3,680. The standard deduction they may use is $9,700. What is their taxable income? $37,100, Lesson 2.3

37. Lynn is paid $2.08 for every usable machine part she makes. During one week, she made 220 parts, 14 of which were unusable. What was Lynn's gross pay for the week? $428.48, Lesson 1.5

38. Della Lynch is married and earns $470 a week. She claims three withholding allowances. What amount should be deducted from her weekly earnings for federal withholding taxes? $14, Lesson 2.1

39. Eduardo Rivas works in sales for straight commission. His gross pay of $680 last week was based on his sales of $13,600. What rate of commission was Eduardo paid? 5%, Lesson 1.4

40. Emma's bank statement's closing balance on March 31 is $683. There were three checks outstanding for: $12.33, $8.32; $19, and $274.90. Reconcile Emma's bank statement.
$368.45, Lesson 3.4

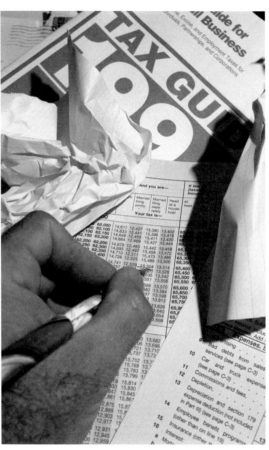

Lesson 3.6 Savings Accounts ■ 117

CONNECTION TO PERSONAL FINANCE

Ask students for their reaction to a savings plan where a savings account owner withdraws and spends the interest earned on savings. The account owner always deposits money to earn the highest interest rate possible and never withdraws the principal. The owner is proud of his/her money management skills of making sure that the money is always in a safe place.

Money Market and CD Accounts

GOALS

- ■ Calculate interest earned on special savings accounts
- ■ Calculate the penalty for early withdrawals from CD accounts
- ■ Compare the interest earned on savings accounts
- ■ Calculate the effective rate of interest

Start Up

Banks often pay a higher interest rate on savings accounts to customers who keep their money on deposit for a fixed period of time, such as a year, and not make any withdrawals. Name reasons why banks encourage people to use such savings accounts.

Math Skill Builder

Review these math skills and solve the exercises that follow.

1 **Subtract** money amounts.
Find the difference. $705.46 − $700 = $5.46

   1a. $870 − $8.78 $861.22   **1b.** $265.38 − $187.46 $77.92

2 **Multiply** money amounts by a percent and round.
Find the product. 2.13% × $673 = 0.0213 × $673 = $14.334, or $14.33

   2a. 4.7% × $547 $25.71   **2b.** 2.9% × $992 $28.77

3 **Multiply** money amounts by a fraction and round.
Find the product. $\frac{1}{4}$ × $27.34 = $6.835, or $6.84

   3a. $\frac{1}{2}$ × $68.46 $34.23   **3b.** $\frac{1}{12}$ × $56.89 $4.74

■ Special Savings Accounts

In addition to regular passbook savings accounts, many banks also offer special savings accounts for long-term savers. The interest rates paid on these special savings accounts are higher than the rates paid on regular savings accounts.

CERTIFICATE OF DEPOSIT The **certificate of deposit** is widely referred to as a CD. The CD is also known as a *time deposit* or a *savings certificate*. Some government rules apply to certificate of deposit accounts.

CONNECTION TO ECONOMICS

Emphasize to students that many federal and state laws apply to banks to ensure the safety of the funds customers have on deposit. Federal rules place special restrictions on time-deposit accounts such as CDs, especially in regard to the penalty imposed on early withdrawal of deposits. Explain that the penalty was imposed to encourage consumers not only to save money but to also keep their funds on deposit for a specific time. This action lends stability to the banking system by minimizing the daily outflows of money from banks.

In addition, most banks require depositors to meet certain requirements.

- Deposit a minimum amount. This may be $500, $1,000, $5,000, or $10,000.

- Leave the money on deposit for a minimum time. The time may be specified in number of days, months, or years. The minimum time is called the **term**. The date that marks the end of the term is the **maturity date**.

- Pay a penalty if money is withdrawn before the end of the term.

MONEY MARKET ACCOUNTS   Like certificates of deposit, money market accounts offer higher interest rates than regular accounts. Special rules apply:

- A minimum balance must be kept in the account for the term specified. More money may be added to the account at any time.

- The interest rate paid is fixed for short periods of time.

- A small number of checks may be written against the account.

Banks usually pay a higher interest rate for larger minimum balances. Money may be withdrawn as long as the minimum balance is maintained. If the minimum balance is not kept, a lower interest rate will be paid.

In both certificates of deposit and money market accounts, interest does not have to be compounded. Some banks pay simple interest at the end of the term, other banks compound interest daily, monthly, or quarterly. The interest rate paid usually changes at the end of the term.

EXAMPLE 1

Nick Bolger kept $1,200 on deposit for six months in a three-month money market account that pays simple interest. For the first 3 months, the account paid 2.5% annual interest. For the next 3 months, an annual interest rate of 2.15% was paid. What total interest did Nick earn for the six months?

SOLUTION
Multiply the principal by the interest rate and by the time to find interest for the first 3-month term.

$1,200 \times 0.025 \times \frac{3}{12} = \$7.50$ interest for first 3-month period

Multiply the principal by the interest rate and by the time to find interest for the second 3-month term.

$1,200 \times 0.0215 \times \frac{3}{12} = \$6.45$ interest for second 3-month period

Add the interest earned for each 3-month term.

$7.50 + \$6.45 = \$13.95$ total interest earned for six months

■ CHECK YOUR UNDERSTANDING

A. Rose Bannon deposited $10,000 in a three-year certificate of deposit that pays simple interest at a fixed annual rate of 5.4%. What total interest will Rose have earned at the end of three years? $1,620

B. Alex Nugent had $2,000 on deposit for March and April in a one-month money market account. Interest in the account is not compounded. In March, the account paid 1.4% annual interest. In April, an annual interest rate of 1.32% was paid. What total interest did Alex earn for the two months? $4.53

Lesson 3.7 Money Market and CD Accounts ■ 119

■ *CHECK YOUR UNDERSTANDING SOLUTIONS*

A. $10,000 \times 0.054 \times 3 = \$1,620$

$2,000 \times 0.0132 \times \frac{1}{12} = \$2.20$ April interest;

B. $2,000 \times 0.014 \times \frac{1}{12} = \$2.333$, or $2.33 March interest;

$2.33 + \$2.20 = \$4.53$ total interest

■ **Apply Goal 1**

Work through Example 1 on the board pointing out that the simple interest formula is used in the solution. Students should complete the math at their desks.

Tell students that the same procedure would have been used even if the money on deposit had been in a CD account instead of a money market account.

Assign Check Your Understanding problems A and B for completion in class. Check student work at their desks.

■ Teach Goal 2

Emphasize that the penalty for early withdrawal of funds applies only to CDs and is required by law. Stress that the penalty is figured only on the amount withdrawn.

■ Apply Goal 2

Work through Example 2 on the board with students completing the math at their desks.

Assign Check Your Understanding problems C and D for completion in class. Check student work to be sure the penalty is based on the correct amount and time period.

■ Teach Goal 3

Emphasize that comparisons are valid only when the same time periods are compared. Interest may not be figured for a quarter, for example, and compared to interest figured for a year.

Point out to students that they may not assume that the higher rate will always yield the greatest interest. A lower compound rate may earn more interest than a higher simple interest rate, especially over long periods of time.

■ Penalties on Certificates of Deposit

By law, banks must charge depositors a penalty for withdrawing money early from a certificate of deposit. Each bank sets its own penalty for early withdrawals. The penalty usually varies with the term of the certificate. For example, a 1-year CD may carry a penalty of 3 months' interest; a 5-year CD may have a 12 months' interest penalty.

The penalty is calculated on the money withdrawn from the certificate of deposit account before the end of its term. The penalty amount is usually deducted from the money withdrawn. It is possible for the penalty to be greater than the interest earned. When that happens, the difference is usually deducted from the money on deposit.

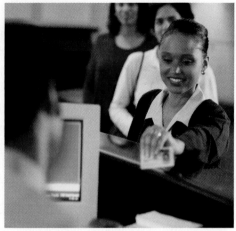

EXAMPLE 2

Ella Trane invested $5,000 in a 4-year CD that paid 5.2% annual interest. When she withdrew $800 at the end of 3 years, her early withdrawal penalty was 6 months' interest. What was the amount of the penalty and what was Ella's net withdrawal?

SOLUTION

Multiply the amount withdrawn by the interest rate and by the penalty time period of the early withdrawal.

$$\$800 \times 0.052 \times \frac{6}{12} = \$20.80 \qquad \text{six months' interest penalty for early withdrawal}$$

Find the difference between the withdrawal amount and the interest penalty.

$$\$800 - \$20.80 = \$779.20 \qquad \text{net withdrawal amount}$$

■ CHECK YOUR UNDERSTANDING

C. Neil Richards has $2,000 in a one-year time-deposit account that pays an annual interest rate of 2%. He withdrew $500 before the end of the term. The bank charged Neil 3 months' interest for the early withdrawal. What penalty will Neil pay? $2.50

D. Noelle Hastings' 5-year savings certificate pays an annual interest rate of 4.7%. At the end of the first year she withdrew $1,000 of the $12,000 she had on deposit and paid a penalty of 12 months' interest. What net amount did she withdraw? $953

■ Compare Savings Accounts

Savings accounts are often compared by the interest earned in each account. To compare, calculate the interest that would be earned by each type of account for the same time period.

COMMON ERRORS

Students may not understand that the early withdrawal penalty applies only to the amount withdrawn and calculate the penalty on the total deposit. Encourage them to think of the CD deposit and withdrawal as separate amounts. Have them write two $I = prt$ formulas, each with a different principal and possibly a different time, and label them "calculate interest" and "calculate penalty."

EXAMPLE 3

In one year, you could earn $18.44 interest on a $900 deposit in a passbook account paying 2% daily interest. The $900 could also be deposited in a one-year CD paying simple interest at an annual rate of 2.7%. How much more interest could you earn in 1 year by placing your money in a CD instead of a passbook account?

SOLUTION

Passbook account: $18.44   one-year's interest

CD: $900 × 0.027 × 1 = $24.30   one year's interest

Find the difference between the interest earned on each account.

$24.30 − $18.44 = $5.86   more interest earned by CD

■ CHECK YOUR UNDERSTANDING

E. A six-month time deposit account pays 2.35% simple interest. Dora has already calculated that she could earn $15.13 in six months on a $1,400 deposit in a passbook savings account earning 2.15% daily interest. How much more interest could Dora earn if she deposited the $1,400 in the time deposit account instead of a savings account for 6 months? $1.32

F. Jim Russell's $1,500 deposit could earn $31.37 in 9 months in a passbook account paying 2.76% daily interest. How much more interest could Jim earn in a 3-month CD that pays 3.26% simple interest every 3 months during the 9-month period? $5.31

■ Effective Rate of Interest

The effective rate of interest is the rate you actually earn by keeping your money on deposit for one year. The annual rate and the effective rate you earn can be different. The effective rate is sometimes referred to as the *annual percentage yield*.

$$\frac{\text{Amount of Interest Earned for One Year}}{\text{Amount of Money on Deposit}} = \text{Effective Rate of Interest}$$

EXAMPLE 4

Find the effective rate of interest to the nearest hundredth percent on $1,000 deposited in an account that pays 5% annual interest, compounded quarterly. Use the compound interest table given in Lesson 3.6.

SOLUTION

Find the multiplier in the compound interest table: 1.050945

Multiply the deposit amount by the multiplier.

$1,000 × 1.050945 = $1,050.945, or $1,050.95   compound amount

Find the difference between the deposit and the compound amount.

$1,050.95 − $1,000 = $50.95   interest earned in one year

Divide the interest earned for one year by the principal. Round as directed.

$50.95 ÷ $1,000 = 0.05095, or 5.10%   effective rate of interest

Lesson 3.7 Money Market and CD Accounts ■ **121**

■ **Apply Goal 3**

Work through Example 3 at the board with students completing the math at their desks.

Assign Check Your Understanding problems E and F for completion in class. Check student work at their desks.

■ **Teach Goal 4**

Point out that the annual interest rate paid is a simple interest rate. The effective rate of interest reflects compounded interest, and will always be greater than the simple interest rate.

■ **Apply Goal 4**

Work through Example 4 at the board with students completing the math at their desks.

Assign Check Your Understanding problems G and H for completion in class. Check student work at their desks followed by an explanation of the solutions at the board.

■ *CHECK YOUR UNDERSTANDING SOLUTIONS*

C. $500 × 0.02 × $\frac{1}{4}$ = $2.50

D. $1,000 × 0.047 × 1 = $47; $1,000 − $47 = $953

E. $1,400 × 0.0235 × $\frac{1}{2}$ = $16.45;
   $16.45 − $15.13 = $1.32

F. $1,500 × 0.0326 × $\frac{1}{4}$ = $12.23;
   3 × $12.23 = $36.68; $36.68 − $31.37 = $5.31

Wrap Up

Review the Start Up. Reemphasize that banks are in business to earn profits for their owners. If banks were not able to lend the money on deposit, they would not be able to pay interest to depositors.

G. A deposit of $2,000 is kept in an account that pays 4% annual interest, compounded quarterly. Find the effective rate of interest to the nearest hundredth percent if the money is on deposit for 1 year. Use the compound interest table. 4.06%

H. A CD pays 5% yearly interest and compounds interest semiannually. Find the effective rate of interest to the nearest tenth percent if $6,000 was on deposit for 1 year. Use the compound interest table. 5.1%

Wrap Up

When an account has a fixed term, such as a year, banks spend less money on personnel and other costs of processing withdrawals or deposits. In turn, the bank can lend the money to a borrower for a longer period of time since they know the money on deposit is not likely to be withdrawn during the term of the deposit.

COMMUNICATION

Remind students that certificates of deposit are also called time deposits, and perhaps by other names as well. The results of their research should show that CDs with longer terms offer higher interest rates. If you wish, have the students determine if a relationship exists between the size of the minimum deposit amount and interest rates paid.

COMMUNICATION

Visit a local bank or the Internet site of a bank not in your area to find the types of certificates of deposit offered. Create an overhead transparency that shows the bank name, term of deposit, interest rate, and minimum deposit amount. Write a sentence about the relationship of the length of the term and the interest rate.

When preparing visual presentations, keep in mind the following hints:

- Keep your design simple.
- Include only one bank per visual.
- To maximize effectiveness, be selective in how much information you include on the page.
- Proofread visuals carefully.
- Make sure visuals are large enough to be seen by the entire audience.
- Avoid distorting facts on visuals; be clear and concise.
- When presenting at the overhead, position yourself so the audience may clearly view the visual.
- Make an effort to talk about the data rather than read your visual line by line.

Assign

Assignment: Exercises 1–20
Begin with the basic arithmetic problems to insure that students understand the underlying arithmetic in the exercises.

Assess

Call on students to state the formula of the Effective Rate of Interest in their own words. **Amount of interest earned in one year divided by the amount on deposit.**

EXERCISES

Find the sum or difference.

1. $7.58 + $8.34 = $15.92

2. $1,430.67 + $78.34 $1,509.01

3. $7,757.82 − $257.82 $7,500

4. $45.63 − $28.08 $17.55

Find the product and round to the nearest cent.

5. 4.26% × $720 $30.67

6. 2.78% × $1,570 $43.65

7. $\frac{1}{2}$ × $27.83 $13.92

8. $\frac{1}{12}$ × $87.65 $7.30

122 ■ Chapter 3 Banking Services

■ CHECK YOUR UNDERSTANDING SOLUTIONS

G. 1.040604 × $2,000 = $2,081.21;

$2,081.21 − $2,000 = $81.21;

$81.21 ÷ $2,000 = 0.040604, or 4.06%

H. $6,000 × 0.05 × $\frac{1}{2}$ = $150;

$6,000 + $150 = $6,150;

$6,150 × 0.05 × $\frac{1}{2}$ = $153.75;

$6,150 + $153.75 = $6,303.75;

$6,303.75 − $6,000 = $303.75;

$303.75 ÷ $6,000 = 0.0506, or 5.1%

9. A money market account paid annual interest of 4.8% in June and 4.91% in July. A two-month, time-deposit account pays 4.87% annual interest. Neither account compounds interest. Which account would have earned more interest if $15,000 were left on deposit in each account for 2 months? How much more? time deposit, $0.37 more

10. Magda Saleto had a three-month savings certificate that paid simple interest at 2.67% on her $12,000 deposit. At the end of three months she invests the original $12,000 in another certificate with a one-month term that pays 2.83%. What total interest will she have earned from both certificates at the end of four months? $108.40

see below

11. A $500 investment in a 12-month CD with an interest rate of 4.89% compounded monthly, earns $25 interest in one year. What effective rate of interest does this investment earn? 5%

$\frac{25}{500} = 0.05 = 5\%$

12. **CRITICAL THINKING** A money market account may pay interest of 3.25% provided that a minimum balance of $2,500 is kept on deposit. A deposit that falls below the minimum, to $2,498 perhaps, earns 1% interest. Why is there such a large difference in the rates? Answers will vary. The bank uses higher rates to get customers to deposit more money.

13. **DECISION MAKING** You sold your house with net cash received of $40,000. You did not need the money for at least two months. You could deposit the $40,000 in a 12-month CD that pays 4.2% simple interest and has an early withdrawal penalty of two-months' interest. You could also deposit the money in a money market account that pays 2.1% interest, compounded monthly. In which account would you deposit your money to earn the most interest if you plan to withdraw the money at the end of the second month? money market earns $140.12; CD earns $0 after penalty

MIXED REVIEW

14. 907 + 48 + 412 + 62 1,429

15. $867.38 − $20.09 $847.29

16. Write 0.0345 as a percent. 3.45%

17. $4\frac{2}{3} \div 1\frac{1}{9}$ $4\frac{1}{5}$

18. A corner food vendor had these cash receipts in five days: $328.50, $410.40, $379, $326.25, $387.75. What were the vendor's total cash receipts for the five days? $1,831.90, Lesson 2.5

19. A truck farmer brought 200 pints of berries to sell in a market during each week of the growing season. She sold 80% of the berries the first week and 90% the second week. She sold all the berries in each of the next three weeks. What average number of pints of berries did the farmer sell per week during the five-week period? 188, Lesson 1.2

20. Jack Nesbitt worked 52.5 hours last week. He is paid $11.29 per hour for regular-time work and time-and-a-half overtime for hours worked past 40 hours in a week. What gross pay did he earn last week? $663.29, Lesson 1.3

Lesson 3.7 Money Market and CD Accounts ■ 123

123

Lesson 3.1 Checking Accounts
- Add cash and check deposits and subtract cash received to find the net deposit.

- Add deposits and subtract checks and other payments from a previous balance to find a new balance.

Lesson 3.2 Electronic Banking
- Add and subtract electronic transactions to find account balances.

Lesson 3.3 Online Banking
- Add and subtract manual, EFT, and online transactions to calculate account balances and make online banking decisions.

CHAPTER REVIEW

VOCABULARY REVIEW

Automated Teller Machine, ATM	deposit slip	online banking
balance	direct deposit	outstanding checks
bank statement	debit card	reconciliation form
certificate of deposit	Electronic Funds Transfer, EFT	service charge
check register	interest	term
compound amount	maturity date	transaction
compound interest		

Fill in the blanks with one of the terms above. Terms are used only once.

1. An electronic method allowing you to pay bills using your home computer is ___?___. online banking

2. The amount of money in a checking account is called (a, an) ___?___. balance

3. The total in a savings account at the end of a period after interest is added is called the ___?___. compound amount

4. A printed report of bank transactions given to a depositor is called (a, an) ___?___. bank statement

5. A savings plan also known as a time deposit or savings certificate is called (a, an) ___?___. certificate of deposit

6. A record you keep of deposits made and checks written is called (a, an) ___?___. check register

7. When employers send the pay of employees to their bank account instead of issuing a paper check, they are making (a, an) ___?___. direct deposit

8. The movement of money from one bank's computer to another computer is called ___?___. Electronic Funds Transfer

9. The fixed period of time money is on deposit in a savings account is called the ___?___. term

LESSON 3.1

10. Justin Nucci listed these items on his deposit slip: (bills) 8 one-hundreds, 27 fifties, 83 fives, 141 ones; (coins) 13 quarters, 117 nickels; (checks) $317.94, $57.89, $527.24, $77.49. He received cash back of 30 twenties and 11 tens. What total deposit did he make? $2,985.66

11. Zora Omar had a balance of $1,189.17 in her checking account. She wrote checks for $62.41, $224.14, $12.92, and $357.16. Her deposits were $197.34 and $879.13. What was Zora's new bank balance? $1,609.01

LESSON 3.2

12. At the start of the day, Grace Williams' checking account had a $201.87 balance. She used her debit card to pay $56.12 for groceries and $28.45 for cleaning. Grace then transferred $150 to her checking account from savings using her bank's ATM. She also directed her bank to transfer funds electronically from her checking account to pay a charge account bill of $187.12. What was the balance of Grace's checking account at the end of the day? $80.18

124 ■ **Chapter 3 Banking Services**

TEACHING STRATEGIES Chapter Review

Have students close their textbook and give an impromptu, ungraded spelling test. Have students check their own spelling against the list in the Vocabulary Review. Remind students that it is important to know what business terms mean and how they are spelled. Ask students to complete the Vocabulary Review. When they finish, call on various students for their answers.

LESSON 3.3

13. Basil Tomlin's online checking account had a balance of $371.07. The balance did not include a direct deposit of $672.80 that will be transferred to the checking account by Basil's employer at 11:00 a.m. Basil's bank will automatically deduct a house payment of $720 at the end of the business day. Basil plans to make online payments for $34.85, $90.29, and $368.20. How much money does Basil need to transfer to complete these transactions and still have a balance of $100? $269.47

LESSON 3.4

14. Giselle Mulroon's bank statement shows a balance of $539.22. Checks outstanding were #841 for $29.67, #843 for $89.02, and #844 for $9.76. A $130 deposit was outstanding. Reconcile Giselle's bank statement. $540.77

15. Elva Mayberry's check register balance was $641.18. Her bank statement listed several items that did not appear in Elva's check register. These include interest earned of $0.48, a service charge of $2.80, and two ATM withdrawals of $300 each. Reconcile Elva's check register. $38.86

LESSON 3.5

16. Henry Sokol's bank statement balance on June 30 was $845.43. His check register balance was $247.62. His comparison of the two records showed a check for $85 was recorded twice in the register, a check for $138.11 was recorded as $183.11, and an ATM deposit of $368 and a debit card purchase for $81.10 were not recorded in the register. Also, an ATM withdrawal of $50 and interest earned of $0.82 were not recorded. Three checks were outstanding: $191.22; $23.87; $15. Reconcile Henry's bank statement and check register. $615.34

LESSON 3.6

17. Bob Rowinski made a $4,000 deposit to a savings account paying 1.6% annual interest compounded semiannually. If he kept the money on deposit for 6 months, what would his account balance be after the interest payment is made? $4,032

$$I = prt$$
$$I = 4000 \cdot 0.016 \cdot \frac{6}{12}$$
$$I = \$32$$
$$4000 + 32 =$$

18. On April 1, Preston McCord deposited $1,400 in a passbook savings account that pays annual interest of 3.2% compounded quarterly. If he made no deposits or withdrawals in the account, what interest could he earn by keeping his money on deposit until October 1? $22.49 22.40

$$Apl - Oct 1 = \frac{3}{4}$$
$$I = prt$$
$$I = 1,400 \cdot 0.032 \cdot \frac{1}{2}$$
$$I = \$22.40$$

LESSON 3.7

19. Sonya Lister's 6-month CD pays 5.3% simple interest. Her deposit to the CD was $4,500. At the end of each 6-month period, Sonya withdraws the interest earned and renews the CD on its original terms. What total interest will Sonya have earned at the end of one year? $238.50

$$I = prt$$
$$I = 4,500 \cdot 0.053 \cdot \frac{1}{2}$$
$$I = \$119.25 = 1st 6 mo.$$
$$1 y = 119.2$$

20. Dale Lawrence had $80,000 on deposit in a six-month CD paying 2.72% simple interest. At the end of three months, Dale withdrew $4,000. The penalty for early withdrawal of money from this CD is one-month's interest. What was the amount of the penalty Dale had to pay? $9.07

$$4,000 \cdot 0.0272 \cdot \frac{1}{12}$$
$$9.06 \approx \$9.07$$

$$I = prt$$
$$I = 4,500 \cdot 0.053 \cdot \frac{1}{2}$$
$$I = 119.25 = 2nd 6 mo$$
$$+ 119.25 = \$238.50$$

TEACHING STRATEGIES Chapter Review

Have students complete each problem in the Chapter Review. After students complete the problems for each lesson, check the results. Have students who got the correct answers place their work on the board. If some students did not remember the process for solving a problem, refer them to the example in the lesson where the process was explained.

Students need spreadsheet file tech3-1.xls for Tasks 1 and 2.

Task 1 Students enter data into a spreadsheet template that compares interest on savings accounts. The spreadsheet can calculate interest for daily through annual interest periods.

Task 2 Students answer questions about Task 1 results. They change data and answer questions about the results.

Task 3 Students design and create a spreadsheet to reconcile a checking account.

Task 4 Students answer questions about the results of calculations and the process used in the spreadsheet.

Teach and Apply Task 1

Task 1 Remind students they may enter data only in blue cells.

Point out that the number of interest periods is derived from the compounding period. If interest is compounded monthly, then there are 12 interest periods in a year. There would be 365 interest periods in a year when interest is compounded daily.

Teach and Apply Task 2

Assign questions 1–5 and have students write their answers.

Discuss the answers. Point out that a wrong answer might result from incorrect data entry or a spreadsheet design error.

Remind students to change the data in Cell C4 before answering questions 6–8. They may use the spreadsheet to recalculate answers to the exercises.

Technology Workshop

Task 1: Comparing the Interest Earned on Savings Accounts

Enter data into a template that calculates the compound interest earned by two savings deposits. Use the results to compare the interest earned by different savings plans.

Open the spreadsheet for Chapter 3 (tech3-1.xls) and enter the data shown in blue (cells B4-7 and C4-7) into the spreadsheet. The compound amount and compound interest of two savings deposits will be calculated and also the difference in the amount of interest earned by the deposits. Your computer screen should look like the one shown below when you are done.

	A	B	C	D
1	COMPARING INTEREST EARNED IN SAVINGS ACCOUNTS			
2				
3	ACCOUNT INFORMATION:	ACCOUNT A	ACCOUNT B	DIFFERENCE
4	Interest Rate (%)	4.00	4.00	
5	Interest Periods in a Year	12	4	
6	No. of Periods on Deposit	12	4	
7	Amount of Deposit	$1,500.00	$1,500.00	
8	INTEREST INFORMATION:			
9	Compound Amount	$1, 561.11	$1,560.91	
10	Less Original Deposit	$1,500.00	$1,500.00	
11	Interest Earned	$61.11	$60.91	
12	DIFFERENCE: (ACCOUNT A − ACCOUNT B)			$0.20

Task 2: Analyze the Spreadsheet Output

Answer these questions about the interest calculations.
1. What number of years was the money on deposit in both accounts? 1 year

2. How much money was on deposit in both accounts? $1,500

3. What compounding period was used to compute interest in Account A? a month

4. What was the total interest earned by the deposit in Account B? $60.91

5. Which account earned the most interest, and how much more did it earn? Account A, $0.20

Now move the cursor to cell C4, which holds the Account B interest rate. Enter a new interest rate of 4.1% without the percent symbol.

6. What is the new difference between Account A and Account B? ($1.34)

7. What does it mean when a number is enclosed in parentheses? the result of subtraction is a negative number

8. If the result in Cell D12 shows a negative number, is there something wrong with the result? No, it simply means that the interest earned in Account B is greater than the interest earned in Account A.

Now use the spreadsheet to calculate the answers to interest problems you have already solved or to compare the terms of savings plans.

126 ■ Chapter 3 Banking Services

TEACHING STRATEGIES Task 1

Display the file tech3-1.xls. Have students identify the cells that contain the factors found in the $I = prt$ formula. Display the cells that contain a formula and have students review them. Allow students to make suggestions as to how the spreadsheet could have been designed differently.

Task 3: Design a Bank Reconciliation Spreadsheet

You are to design a spreadsheet that will reconcile the bank statement balance and the check register balance.

The spreadsheet for Task 3 may be solved by using addition and subtraction. The spreadsheet should have two sections, placed side-by-side, one for the bank statement and the other for the check register. Place all the items to be added or subtracted in one column with the balance labeled at the bottom. You may want to indicate that a number is to be subtracted by placing a minus sign before the number when it is entered, but do so sparingly.

The information shown below lists the usual adjustments necessary to complete the reconciliation of the bank statement and check register. Add any other adjustment items you think are necessary. Be sure to allow enough lines so that all data may be entered.

SITUATION: Your bank statement and check register balances do not agree. The following shows what was found when the bank statement and check register were compared. Prepare a spreadsheet that will result in both the bank statement and check register balances being in agreement.

Bank Statement		Check Register	
Closing Balance	$498.36	Last Balance	$483.41
Late Deposit	$0.00	Deposit Outstanding	$0.00
Outstanding Checks	$75.30	Other Credit	$20.00
Outstanding Checks	$32.57	Interest Earned	$0.56
		Check, Debit, or ATM withdrawal	$91.28
		Check, Debit, or ATM withdrawal	$15.00
		Check Error	*
		Service Charge	$4.50
		Other Charge	$2.25

*Check #764 for $17.50 was recorded incorrectly in the check register as $17.05.

Task 4: Analyze the Spreadsheet Output

Answer these questions about your completed spreadsheet:

9. What was the reconciled balance? $390.49
   The checks were deducted from the check register and must also be deducted on the statement.
10. Why are outstanding checks deducted from the bank statement balance?
    The incorrect amount was added back into the register balance; the correct amount was then deducted.
11. How was the error made in Check #764 corrected?
    Find the difference, $0.49, and deduct it from the check register.
12. In what other way could you have corrected the Check #764 error?

Continue testing the spreadsheet by entering the data from reconciliation problems you have already solved.

Teach and Apply Task 3

Assign Task 3. Suggest to students that the completed spreadsheet should resemble the layout of the table in the textbook. Separate columns are to be provided for the amounts. Formulas are to be used to do calculations whenever possible.

Teach and Apply Task 4

Assign Task 4. Have students make sure the bank statement and check register balances have the same amount. Remind them to answer questions 10–12 using complete sentences.

TEACHING STRATEGIES Task 3

An example solution is provided in the file tech 3-3.xls. Display the solution and have students compare the example solution to theirs. Have them identify similarities between the spreadsheets and any features they found especially worthwhile.

$3.50 \times 52 = $182

She will pay $182 in ATM fees for the year.

$983.20 - $240.00 = $743.20

■ **WRITE**
Students should form teams to design the flyer. The flyer content should include the items listed in the directions and the results of interest calculations that show the financial benefits of compound interest or higher interest rates.

■ **SCANS**
Each student should reflect on the contributions made by members of the team in regard to how each of their strengths and abilities were used to create the flyer. Each student is to compose a narrative assessing their contributions to the team and write a brief report on how team members shared work.

■ **ONGOING ASSESSMENT**
STUDENT WORKBOOK The Integrated Project found in the workbook provides a broad, ongoing assessment activity for the goals of this chapter.

Chapter Assessment

How Times Have Changed

For Questions 1–2, refer to the timeline on page 83 as needed.

1. Kami Jones uses an ATM that is not owned by her bank. Her bank charges a fee of $1.50 for each transaction, and the ATM owners charge her $2.00 for each transaction. If she uses this ATM to withdraw $100 every week for one year, how much will she pay in ATM fees for the year?

2. Morgan Tinsley deposited a check for $983.20 in an ATM at his bank. He also withdrew $240 from the same account. What is the net increase of his account?

WRITE

Create a promotional flyer that a bank would use to persuade customers to open a special savings account such as a CD or money market account. Include information about the benefits of saving money in these types of accounts. To ensure an effective promotional campaign, keep in mind these helpful hints:

- keep your design simple
- avoid distorting facts
- be concise and accurate
- provide information about how to get questions answered
- be sure to include the who, where, and how information
- color can make a visual more appealing, but use color selectively

SCANS

Workplace Skills—*Allocate Human Resources*

These skills assess the knowledge and skills of yourself and others and then distribute work accordingly to the strengths of the workers. Evaluating performances and providing feedback is also included in human resources. The ability to assess your own skills can be a powerful tool in building your career. You can match your skills to those needed by potential employers. Many businesses include self-appraisals as part of the system they use to evaluate employees, establish performance goals, and determine raises and promotions.

Test Your Skills Identify two skills that you learned in this chapter. Make a checklist of the knowledge and work processes involved in performing each skill. On a scale of 1–5 (5 being the highest) rate your understanding and ability to perform the work for each element on your checklist.

Make a Plan Review your self-assessment. For the knowledge and work processes on which you scored below 3, determine what is needed for at least a ranking of 4.

Summarize Write a paragraph explaining why you gave yourself each rating and your plans for improvement. You may want to include references to the following skills in your summary.

arithmetic	decision making	problem solving	responsibility
reasoning	self-management	integrity/honesty	speaking

TEACHING STRATEGIES Write

Select a few reports that best illustrate how the flyer design was solved by teamwork. Have the students who wrote the reports present them to the class.

Chapter Test

Answer each question.

1. $237.10 + $76 + $0.56 + $2.48 $316.14

2. $745.28 − $237.30 $507.98

3. $850 × 0.00368 $3.13

4. 6.7% × $\frac{1}{4}$ 1.675% *or 0.01675*

5. $268.44 × $\frac{1}{12}$ $22.37

6. 2.37% × $1,200 $28.44

7. $2\frac{3}{8} - 1\frac{1}{2}$ $\frac{7}{8}$

8. 54 is what percent of 360? 15%

9. 350 increased by $\frac{1}{5}$ of itself is? 420

10. $288 is $\frac{6}{5}$ of what number $240

Applications

11. Stuart Terril listed these items on his checking account deposit slip: (bills) 47 ones, 3 fives; (coins) 129 quarters, 74 dimes; one check for $8. His cash received consisted of 2 twenties and 1 ten. What total deposit did Stuart make? $59.65.

12. The Yearbook Club's checking account balance was $8,411.13 on Monday. Three checks from the sale of ads for $200, $110, and $65 were deposited. A check was written on Thursday for $650 for graphics design. What is the new balance of the checking account? $8,136.13

13. On Friday, Carlotta Rowe's checking account balance was $173.56. During the day Carlotta's employer deposited her $516.45 pay directly to her checking account. At lunchtime, she wrote checks for $172, $86.43, and $9.05, and made an ATM withdrawal from checking of $150. What is the balance of Carlotta's checking account at the end of the day? $272.53

14. The bank statement sent to Abigail Ochs did not show checks for $158.23, $12.89, and $71.27, and an outstanding deposit of $75 that were listed in the check register. The balance printed on the statement was $289.07. What is the reconciled bank statement balance? $121.68

15. The bank statement of Jake Hansen showed a balance of $356.93. His check register showed a balance of $308.34. When Jake compared the two records he found several differences. The bank statement listed these items not recorded in the register: ATM withdrawal, $50; ATM user fee, $2.25; direct deposit of paycheck, $624.70; checks for $287.23, $180.11, and $72.89. A check for $85.89 was recorded in the register as $58.89. The items not listed on the bank statement included checks for $72.44, $9.76, and $113.57; and a $50 deposit made after the statement closing date. Debit card purchases of $85.67 and $16.73 appeared on the statement but not in the register. Reconcile Jake's bank statement and check register. $211.16

16. Find the interest that a $510 deposit will earn in 3 months at 4.25% simple interest. $5.42

    I = prt
    I = 510 · 0.0425 · $\frac{3}{12}$
    I = 5.41875 ≈ 5.42

17. The daily interest multiplier for a savings account paying 2% annual interest for 180 days is 1.010050. What compound amount will be in a savings account if $5,000 is on deposit in the savings account for 180 days? $5,050.25

    Amt · multiplier
    5000 · 1.010050 = 5,050.25

18. A 2-month CD pays 2.1% simple interest for the term of the deposit. A passbook account pays 1.65% annual interest compounded monthly. In which account will a $3,600 investment earn the most interest for two months, and how much more? CD pays $2.69 *2.70*
    more interest

    CD I = prt
    I = 3,600 · 0.021 · $\frac{2}{12}$
    I = $12.60

    passbk I = prt
    I = 3600 · 0.0165 · $\frac{2}{12}$
    I = $9.90

    12.60
    − 9.90
    $2.70

Chapter 6 Assessement ■ 129

Chapter-Test Correlation

Question	Lesson
11	3.1
12	3.1
13	3.2
14	3.4
15	3.5
16	3.6
17	3.6
18	3.7

Test Taking Strategies

Exercise 17 Estimation may be used to determine if the answer is reasonable. The multiplier is 1.010050. If you multiply $5,000 by a rounded multiplier of 1, you get a compound amount of $5,000. Since the actual multiplier is greater than 1, the actual compound amount must be greater than $5,000.

PORTFOLIO ASSESSMENT

Students should include in their portfolios the promotional flyer that they created. In their evaluation of their work, have them include comments on how and why they incor- porated the six helpful hints. Also, have them explain why they did not include or address any of the helpful hints.

Chapter Overview

Chapter 4 reviews addition, subtraction, multiplication, percents, fractions, rounding, and division. These math skills are used to solve business and consumer problems related to loans and credit card transactions.

Lesson 4.1 Promissory Notes
Students find interest on notes using exact and ordinary interest methods. They also learn to calculate the rate of interest.

Lesson 4.2 Discounted Promissory Notes
Students calculate interest and the proceeds for discounted notes, and find the true rate of interest on discounted notes.

Lesson 4.3 Interest Tables
Students use simple interest tables to calculate interest. They also find the due date of a note and the days between dates.

Lesson 4.4 Installment Loans
Students calculate the installment price and finance charges on installment purchases. They also find the number and amount of monthly payments, the payments for interest and principal, and the new balance on installment loans.

Lesson 4.5 Early Loan Repayments
Students find how much interest must be refunded to borrowers and the amount borrowers must pay when Rule of 78 installment loans are paid off early.

CHAPTER 4

Loans and Credit Cards

4.1 Promissory Notes
4.2 Discounted Promissory Notes
4.3 Interest Tables
4.4 Installment Loans
4.5 Early Loan Repayments
4.6 Annual Percentage Rates
4.7 Credit Card Costs
4.8 Credit Card Finance Charges

Statistical Insights

Percent of Families Holding Specific Debt		
By Age of Head of Family		
Age of Head of Family	**Installment Loans**	**Credit Card Balance**
Under 35 years old	60.0%	50.7%
35–44 years old	53.3%	51.3%
45–54 years old	51.2%	52.5%
55–64 years old	37.9%	45.7%
65–74 years old	20.2%	29.2%
75 years old and older	4.2%	11.2%
By Family Income		
Family Income	**Installment Loans**	**Credit Card Balance**
Less than $10,000	25.7%	20.6%
$10,000–$24,999	34.4%	37.9%
$25,000–$49,999	50.0%	49.9%
$50,000–$99,999	55.0%	56.7%
$100,000 or more	43.2%	40.4%

Use the data shown above to answer each question.

1. Using the *By Family Income* data, rank the income levels in order from the group with the greatest to the least credit card debt. $50,000-$99,999, $25,000-$49,999, $100,000 or more, $10,000-$24,999, less than $10,000.
2. Why does it seem reasonable that in the *By Age of Family Head* data, the installment loan debt is decreasing as age increases? Answers will vary but may include that as people get older they make fewer long-term purchases.

Statistical Insights

There are non-profit agencies that help consumers confront high indebtedness. These agencies may help a person budget their income and expenses to meet their debt. They also may help people find lenders who will lend them money to pay off their credit card debts at rates lower than credit card companies typically charge. Students could be assigned to find several of these companies on the Web, and list the typical services that they provide.

NetCheck

Borrowing Money

Borrowing money will cost you money. Before you make a purchase with borrowed money you should investigate exactly how much you will pay to borrow the money. Locate an Internet web site that offers a loan calculator. Imagine that you are planning to make a purchase of a big screen television that costs approximately $2,500. Enter the amount into the calculator and assume a 2-year loan at 14%. Some web sites will provide a total cost for the loan, while others only return a monthly payment amount. When looking at the total cost of borrowing money, be sure to add any processing fees and note the cost of making late payments.

Shopping for the Best Rate?

Borrowing money is just like making other purchases. Comparison shopping is a good idea. Use a web search engine to develop a list of 10 national banks and their web addresses. Visit each web site and look for current rate information and criteria to get approved to borrow money. See if you can find a place that offers the best service at the lowest rate. Remember that borrowing money is a serious financial decision, and costs should always be investigated prior to making a commitment to get the cash.

How Times Have Changed

Credit was used in ancient civilizations more than 3,000 years ago, and ever since then merchants have been introducing new ways for customers to pay with credit. Some have used informal tally systems; others have issued specific objects like metal or wooden cards that customers carry with them; and others have used the honor system.

Research to find a significant event in 1950 that relates to the history of credit cards in the United States.

The Interbank Card Association (ICA) issues the MasterCharge card, known today as MasterCard.
1966

Supermarkets begin accepting credit cards.
1990s

1950　1960　1970　1980　1990　2000

1958
The Bank of America issues BankAmericard, known today as Visa.

1974
Magnetic strips are first used on credit cards.

131

Start Up

Have students read the Start Up. Discuss that if someone defaults on a car loan, the bank can take back the car and resell it. They have no security on the vacation loan. So, the bank has less risk of total loss with the car loan.

Math Skill Builder

The skills of multiplying by percents, whole numbers, and fractions are used in this lesson. Also used are writing percents as decimals and simplifying fractions.

Complete all exercises in Math Skill Builder 1–5.

4.1 Promissory Notes

GOALS

- Calculate interest on interest-bearing promissory notes
- Calculate interest using the exact interest method
- Calculate interest using the ordinary interest method
- Calculate the rate of interest

Start Up

Jamal wants to borrow money for a vacation and also to buy a new car. He thinks that since the vacation loan is for less money than the car loan, he will get a better interest rate on that loan. Do you think he is correct?

Math Skill Builder

Review these math skills and solve the exercises that follow.

1 **Write** percents as decimals.
Write 67% as a **decimal**. 67% = 0.67

   1a. 45% 0.45   **1b.** 150% 1.5   **1c.** 0.5% 0.005   **1d.** 1.89% 0.0189

2 **Multiply** money amount by percents.
Find 4% of $3,500. 4% = 0.04; 0.04 × $3,500 = $140

   2a. 3% of $2,580 $77.40   **2b.** 6.5% of $6,340 $412.10   **2c.** 5.07% of $855 $43.35

3 **Multiply** money amounts by whole numbers and fractions.
Find the product: $3,000 × 2% × $\frac{1}{2}$; 0.02 × $3,000 = $60; $60 × $\frac{1}{2}$ = $30

   3a. $5,000 × 4% × $\frac{1}{4}$ $50   **3b.** $7,520 × 6.2% × $1\frac{1}{2}$ $699.36

   3c. $8,356 × 4.25% × 3 $1,065.39   **3d.** $2,698 × 1.42% × $3\frac{1}{3}$ $127.71

4 **Calculate** a percent.
What percent of $350 is $14? $14 ÷ $350 = 0.04, or 4%

   4a. $15 is what percent of $750? 2%

   4b. $25 is what percent of $860? 2.9%

   4c. $1,170 is what percent of $4,500? 26%

5 **Simplify** fractions.
Simplify $\frac{24}{48}$. $\frac{24 \div 24}{48 \div 24} = \frac{1}{2}$

   5a. $\frac{180}{360}$ $\frac{1}{2}$ **5b.** $\frac{260}{360}$ $\frac{13}{18}$ **5c.** $\frac{126}{360}$ $\frac{7}{20}$

   5d. $\frac{240}{365}$ $\frac{48}{73}$ **5e.** $\frac{165}{365}$ $\frac{33}{73}$ **5f.** $\frac{170}{365}$ $\frac{34}{73}$

132 ■ **Chapter 4** Loans and Credit Cards

DIFFERENT LEARNING STYLES Visual Learners

Get blank promissory notes from local banks or office supply stores and make transparencies of them. Display the transparencies and have students compare the notes you display to the note illustrated on p. 133 for items that are the same or similar, missing, or different.

■ Interest-Bearing Promissory Notes

When you borrow money, you usually sign a promissory note. A **promissory note** is your written promise, or IOU, that you will repay the money to the lender on a certain date. Usually you also have to pay for using the lender's money. That cost is called **interest**. A note that requires you to pay interest is called an *interest-bearing note*.

Lenders may require a borrower to deposit or pledge property as security for a loan. This property is called *collateral*. Types of collateral that are often used to secure loans are cars, stocks, bonds, and life insurance.

Many lenders offer *home equity loans* to home owners. *Home equity* is the difference between what the home could be sold for and what is owed on it. To get a home equity loan, the borrower pledges the equity in the home as collateral for the loan.

If the loan is not repaid, the lender can seize the collateral and sell it to recover the borrowed money.

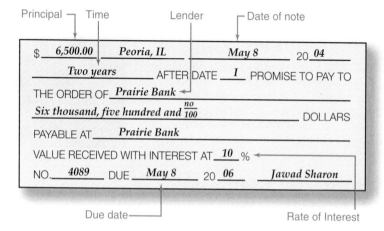

The amount borrowed on a promissory note is the *face*, or **principal**. The date the note was signed is called the *date of the note*. The time for which the money is borrowed is called the **time**. The date on which the money must be repaid is the *due date*, or *maturity date*. The rate of interest to be paid is the **rate of interest**. The money that must be paid on the due date is the *maturity value* or the amount due.

To calculate interest on a note, you use the same formula as you used to calculate simple interest paid on savings.

Interest rates are stated as rates *per year*. The interest you pay on a loan is proportional to the time for which you borrow the money. For a loan of three months, or $\frac{1}{4}$ of a year, the interest is one year's interest multiplied by $\frac{1}{4}$. For a loan of 2 years, the interest is one year's interest multiplied by 2.

To find the amount due on the due date, you add the interest to the principal.

Lesson 4.1 Promissory Notes ■ 133

EXAMPLE 1

On May 8, 2004, Jawad Sharon borrowed $6,500 from his bank to buy a boat, which he used as collateral for the loan. Jawad signed a 2-year promissory note at a 10% interest rate. Find the amount of interest Jawad must pay. Then find the total amount he must repay when the note is due.

SOLUTION

Rewrite the interest rate as a decimal: $10\% = 0.10$

Substitute known values in the formula.

$\$6,500 \times 0.10 \times 2 = \$1,300$ Use $PRT = I$.

Add to find the amount due at end of 2 years.

$\$6,500 + \$1,300 = \$7,800$

■ **CHECK YOUR UNDERSTANDING**

A. On May 8, 2004, Leslie Regis borrowed $2,500 from her bank to pay for a cruise. Leslie signed a 6-month promissory note at 11% interest. Find the amount of interest Leslie must pay. Then find the total amount she must repay to her bank when the note is due. $137.50; $2,637.50

B. Raanan Beilin borrowed $3,500 for 18 months from his bank to have his house repainted. Raanan signed a promissory note that carried 12% interest. Find the amount of interest Raanan must pay. Then find the total amount he must repay to his bank on the due date. $630; $4,130

■ Exact Interest Method

When the time of a note is shown in days, interest may be calculated by the **exact interest method**. Exact interest uses a 365-day year. The exact interest method is used by the United States government and by many banks and other businesses.

To find exact interest, you show the time as a fraction with 365 as the denominator. For example, you would show 83 days as $\frac{83}{365}$.

EXAMPLE 2

Rosa Chavez borrows $1,000 at 6% exact interest for 85 days.

SOLUTION

Rewrite the interest rate as a decimal: $6\% = 0.06$

Write and simplify the time fraction: $\frac{85}{365} = \frac{17}{73}$

$\$1,000 \times 0.06 \times \frac{17}{73} = I$ Use $PRT = I$.

$\$1,\!\overset{10}{\cancel{000}} \times \frac{6}{\underset{1}{\cancel{100}}} \times \frac{17}{73} = \frac{1020}{73} = \$13.97$

CALCULATOR TIP

To use a calculator:
Enter	1000
Press	$\times$
Enter	.06
Press	$=$
Press	$\times$
Enter	85
Press	$=$
Press	$\div$
Enter	365
Press	$=$

134 ■ **Chapter 4** Loans and Credit Cards

■ ***CHECK YOUR UNDERSTANDING SOLUTIONS***

A. $\frac{6}{12} = \frac{1}{2}$; $\$2,500 \times \frac{1}{2} \times 0.11 = \$137.50$;
$\$2,500 + \$137.50 = \$2,637.50$

B. $\frac{18}{12} = 1.5$; $\$3,500 \times 1.5 \times 0.12 = \$630$;
$\$3,500 + \$630 = \$4,130$

C. Ana Lopez borrows $5,000 for 75 days at 8% exact interest. Find how much interest she must pay on the loan and how much will be due at maturity. $82.19; $5,082.19

D. Albert O'Malley signs a promissory note for $3,500 for 150 days at 9% exact interest. Find the interest he must pay and the total amount due on the due date. $129.45; $3,629.45

■ Ordinary Interest Method

The **ordinary interest method**, or *banker's interest method* is used in place of the exact interest method by some businesses. With this method of finding interest, a year has only 360 days. The 360-day year has 12 months of 30 days each and is known as the *banker's year*. Of course, there really is no such year. It is used because it is easier to calculate with than a 365-day year.

EXAMPLE 3

Rosa Chavez borrows $1,000 at 6% ordinary interest for 85 days.

SOLUTION

$$\$1,000 \times 0.06 \times \frac{85}{360} = I \quad \text{Use } PRT = I.$$

$$\$\cancel{1,000} \times \frac{\cancel{6}}{\cancel{100}} \times \frac{85}{\cancel{360}} = \frac{85}{6} = \$14.17$$

■ CHECK YOUR UNDERSTANDING

E. Ikuko Kimura signed a promissory note for $5,900 at 12% ordinary interest for 180 days. Find the interest and amount due she will pay when the note is due. $354; $6,254

F. On May 6, Solomon Kaufman borrowed $4,000 signing a promissory note at his bank. The note carries 9% ordinary interest and is due in 4 months. Find the interest and amount due that Solomon must pay at maturity. $120; $4,120

■ Rate of Interest

If you know the principal and the amount of interest for one year, you can find the rate of interest by dividing the interest by the principal.

Rate of Interest ÷ Interest for One Year ÷ Principal

If the interest given in the problem is not for a year, you must first find how much the interest would be for one year.

EXAMPLE 4

Ella Stein paid $30 interest on a loan of $1,000 for 3 months. Find the rate of interest she paid.

Lesson 4.1 Promissory Notes ■ **135**

■ Teach Goal 3

Point out to students that the only difference between exact interest and ordinary interest is the number of days in a year.

Note to students that by using a 360-day year, banks earn more interest. Ask students to compute interest on $100 borrowed for 60 days at 10% using both exact and ordinary interest and compare the results. Exact interest generates $1.64 in interest but ordinary interest earns $1.67.

Stress that when time is given in months, the formula $I = PRT$ is still used and T is written as a fraction.

■ Apply Goal 3

Work through Example 3 at the board with students doing the math at their desks.

Assign Check Your Understanding problems E and F for in-class work. Walk about the room and examine student work to identify student errors or difficulties.

■ Teach Goal 4

Stress that interest rates, unless otherwise specified, are always stated as a yearly rate.

■ *CHECK YOUR UNDERSTANDING SOLUTIONS*

C. $5,000 × $\frac{75}{365}$ × 0.08 = $82.19;
$5,000 + $82.19 = $5,082.19

E. $\frac{180}{360} = \frac{1}{2}$; $5,900 × $\frac{1}{2}$ × 0.12 = $354;
$5,900 + $354 = $6,254

G. 12 ÷ 4 = 3; $320 × 3 = $960;
$960 ÷ $8,000 = 0.12, or 12%

Work through Example 4 at the board with students doing the math at their desks.

Assign Check Your Understanding problems G and H for in-class work. Walk about the room and examine student work to identify student errors or difficulties.

Wrap **Up**

Review the Start Up. Using collateral to secure loans reduces risk to banks and lowers interest rates to borrowers. But point out to students that using home equity to pay for a vacation loan raises risk to the borrower. If you lose your job and can't make the loan payments, you will lose your home.

TEAM MEETING

You might ask a banker to visit the class after the teams have listed and collated their reasons. Have teams ask the banker how effective their reasons might be.

SOLUTION

Find the amount of interest for one year by finding the number of 3-month periods in one year.

12 months ÷ 3 months = 4   number of 3-month periods in one year

$30 × 4 = $120   interest for one year

$120 ÷ $1,000 = 0.12, or 12%   rate of interest

■ **CHECK YOUR UNDERSTANDING**

G. Trish Newcomb must pay $320 in interest on a promissory note for $8,000 due 4 months from the date of the note. Find the rate of interest she will pay. 12%

H. Susilo Wahyudi paid $450 in interest on a 3-month note for $12,000. Find the rate of interest he paid. 15%

Wrap **Up**

To answer the questions posed in the Start Up, you needed to know about collateral and different types of loans. If Jamal gets a car loan and a personal loan, the car loan will have the lower interest rate because collateral is used for that loan. If Jamal uses a home equity loan to get money for his vacation, the interest may be as good or better than the car loan. In the case of the home equity loan, his home becomes the collateral for the vacation loan.

TEAM MEETING

Lenders usually charge higher interest rates on loans that have no collateral than on loans that are secured with collateral. The interest rate on an auto loan or a home equity loan is usually less than a personal loan for a vacation. Organize a team of 2-3 members and identify reasons that could be used to convince a bank to lower the rate of interest on a personal loan. To gather ideas for reasons, call or visit one or more neighborhood banks. You might also search the Web for reasons. These keywords might help get you started: credit risk, cosigning notes, credit rating.

Prepare a list of the reasons you found to convince a bank to lower the interest rate on a personal loan. As a follow up, someone from your team may want to question bank personnel to determine if your list is accurate and complete.

EXERCISES

Find the product.

1. 2% of $4,689 $93.78   **2.** 150% of $84 $126   **3.** $2,200 × 6% × 5 $660

Find the percent.

4. 75 as a percent of 3,000 2.5%   **5.** $150 as a percent of $1,200 12.5%

6. Write these as a decimal: 2.3%, 230%, 23% 0.023, 2.3, 0.23

TEACHING STRATEGIES Cooperative Learning

In lieu of the Team Meeting project, have students work in teams to identify banks in the area and determine (a) the home equity interest rates and (b) the car loan interest rates they charge. Have the teams report orally in class and list the rates found in two columns on the board. Discuss the possible reasons for the differences in rates they found.

Find the interest to be paid for each promissory note.

	Principal	Rate	Time in Years	
7.	$2,500	0.15	2	$750
8.	$12,500	0.12	$3\frac{1}{2}$	$5,250
9.	$500	0.08	$\frac{1}{2}$	$20

Find the interest and the amount due at maturity for each note.

	Face of Note	Time	Rate	Interest	Amount Due at Maturity
10.	$500	3 yr	12%	$180	$680
11.	$150	3 mo	18%	$6.75	$156.75
12.	$920	$2\frac{1}{4}$ yr	$5\frac{1}{2}$%	$113.85	$1,033.85

13. To finance the remodeling of her kitchen, Rosa borrowed $26,400 on an 18-month home equity loan. She signed a promissory note bearing interest at $7\frac{1}{2}$%. What total amount did Rosa pay on the due date? $29,370

14. Rondel Wilson borrowed $2,000 for a vacation trip to Mexico. The promissory note he signed was for 3 months at $15\frac{1}{4}$% interest. How much did Rondel have to pay when the note came due? $2,076.25

Find the exact interest to the nearest cent. Then find the ordinary interest to the nearest cent.

15. $360 @ 14% for 210 days $29.00, $29.40

16. $1,500 @ 15% for 36 days $22.19, $22.50

17. $1,200 @ 6% for 240 days $47.34, $48

18. $2,400 @ 9% for 60 days $35.51, $36

19. $450 @ 12% for 146 days $21.60, $21.90

20. $1,450 @ 7% for 100 days $27.81, $28.19

Tara Long borrowed $10,000 for 180 days. She paid exact interest at an annual rate of 12%.

21. Estimate the interest Tara owed. Estimates will vary; $600

22. What is the exact amount of interest she had to pay? $591.78

23. What total amount did she have to repay? $10,591.78

Bill Rich signed a 180-day note for $1,250. He repaid the loan when due with interest at an annual rate of 12% using a banker's year.

24. How much interest did Bill pay? $75

25. What total amount did he pay? $1,325

26. Kelly Bullock borrowed $4,800 for 6 months and paid $264 interest. What rate of interest did she pay? 11%

27. Tony Colito paid $19.50 in interest on a loan of $2,600 for 1 month. What rate of interest did he pay? 9%

Lesson 4.1 Promissory Notes ■ **137**

SELECTED SOLUTIONS

13. 18 mos. = 1.5 yrs.;
$26,400 × 1.5 × 0.075 = $2,970;
$26,400 + $2,970 = $29,370

21. $\frac{180}{360} = \frac{1}{2}$; $10,000 × $\frac{1}{2}$ × 0.12 = $600

24. $1,250 × $\frac{180}{360}$ × 0.12 = $75

33. $9,000 + $1,875 = $10,875;
$150,000 − $10,875 = $139,125;
$139,125 ÷ $150,000 = 0.927, or 93%

28. Khalil Hamid Ali borrowed $12,000 and paid $1,890 in exact interest when the loan came due $1\frac{1}{2}$ years later. What rate of interest did Khalil pay? 10.5%

29. Lynn Wessel borrowed $2,500 for 18 months. The total interest she paid was $315. What rate of interest did Lynn pay? 8.4%

30. **CRITICAL THINKING** Look at your answers to Check Your Understanding problems B, E, and Exercises 11, 21, and 24. What relationship do you see between the amount of interest and time? Short times usually mean higher interest rates.

DECISION MAKING You can borrow $5,600 at 12% interest for 90 days from a lender that uses the exact interest method. You can borrow $5,600 at 12% for 90 days from a lender that uses the ordinary interest method.

31. Which lender offers the loan with the lowest interest? exact interest lender

32. How much less interest will you pay? $2.30

33. **STRETCHING YOUR SKILLS** A family sells their home for $150,000 through a real estate agent who deducts $9,000 commission. Other costs they were charged to complete the sale totaled $1,875. What percent of the sale price did the family receive, to the nearest whole percent? 93%

MIXED REVIEW

34. 632.7 + 25.23 + 0.17 658.1

35. 4.15 × 0.822 3.4113

36. Write $5\frac{7}{8}$% as a decimal. 0.05875

37. $80 is $6\frac{1}{2}$% of what amount? $1,230.77

38. $5.32 is 5% less than what amount? $5.60

39. Julio Navarro began the day with $65. During the day he received $25 for mowing a lawn and spent $19.75 for gas, $6 for a movie, $25 for some CDs, and $6.75 for lunch. How much money did Julio have at the end of the day? $32.50, Lesson 3.2

40. Ellen Carson's sales for 5 months were $26,908, $28,386, $28,730, $27,290, and $29,009. What must be her sales next month if she wants her monthly sales average to be $28,000 for the 6 months? $27,677, Lesson 1.2

41. Klaus Reinhardt, a secretary, is paid a yearly salary of $24,960. This is equal to how much a week? $480, Lesson 1.1

42. On April 31, Steve Daley's balances were checkbook, $339.11, and bank statement, $394.62. A service charge of $1.74 had not been deducted in the checkbook. Checks outstanding were 134, $41.32; 135, $3.18; 137, $12.75. Prepare a reconciliation statement for Steve. $337.37, Lesson 3.4

138 ■ **Chapter 4 Loans and Credit Cards**

CONNECTION TO ECONOMICS

Have students investigate (a) what the Federal Reserve System is and (b) what impact the Federal Reserve has on interest rates. Students may use the Internet, the school's economics texts, or other sources to prepare a brief report of their findings.

4.2 Discounted Promissory Notes

GOALS

- Calculate the interest and proceeds for discounted promissory notes
- Calculate the true rate of interest on a discounted promissory note

Start Up

Have students read the Start Up. Have students find the interest to be paid. Then ask them the Start Up question—will the note provide Fernando enough money for his European vacation? This should lead directly into the lesson topic, discounted promissory notes.

Start Up

Fernando Morrero is planning a vacation to Europe next year. He estimates that the vacation will cost him about $3,000. His bank offers to lend him the money if he signs a 6-month, $3,000, discounted promissory note with a rate of 15%. Will this note provide him with enough money for his trip?

Math Skill Builder

The skills of multiplying money amounts and percents are used in this lesson as are rewriting and calculating percents and simplifying fractions.

Complete all exercises in Math Skill Builder 1–5.

Math Skill Builder

Review these math skills and solve the exercises that follow.

1. **Write** percents as decimals.
   Write 39% as a **decimal**. 39% = 0.39

   1a. 45% 0.45   **1b.** 150% 1.5

   1c. 0.5% 0.005   **1d.** 1.89% 0.0189

2. **Multiply** money amount by percents.
   Find the product. 15% of $8,500. 0.15 × $8,500 = $1,275

   2a. 13% of $4,800 $624   **2b.** 18.07% of $950 $171.67

3. **Multiply** money amounts by whole numbers and fractions.
   $8,500 × 5% × $\frac{1}{2}$. 0.05 × $8,500 = $425; $425 × $\frac{1}{2}$ = $212.50

   3a. $15,000 × 14% × 4 $8,400

   3b. $1,720 × 9.2% × $1\frac{1}{2}$ $237.36

   3c. $9,686 × 13.25% × $\frac{1}{4}$ $320.85

4. **Calculate** a percent.
   What percent of $800 is $56? $56 ÷ $800 = 0.07, or 7%

   4a. $35 is what percent of $1,250? 2.8%

   4b. $627 is what percent of $1,650? 38%

   4c. $29,700 is what percent of $44,000? 67.5%

5. **Simplify** fractions.
   Simplify $\frac{124}{648}$. $\frac{124 \div 4}{648 \div 4} = \frac{31}{162}$
   5a. $\frac{120}{560}$ $\frac{3}{14}$ **5b.** $\frac{380}{1,260}$ $\frac{19}{63}$ **5c.** $\frac{56}{860}$ $\frac{14}{215}$

> **SPREADSHEET TIP**
>
> To enter and display fractions and mixed numbers in an Excel cell, enter the whole number first, then a space, then the fraction.
>
> To enter $14\frac{1}{4}$, enter 14, space, 1, slash, 4.
>
> To enter $\frac{1}{4}$ only, enter 0 (as the whole number), space, 1, slash 4.
>
> If you simply enter 1/4 your entry will be read as a date: January 4.

Lesson 4.2 Discounted Promissory Notes ■ 139

COMMON ERRORS

When dealing with discounted notes, students may become confused and add bank discount to the face of the note to find the proceeds. Remind students that the bank discount is subtracted, not added.

■ Discounted Promissory Notes

Banks and other lenders may lend money to businesses and people for short periods of time, such as 30, 60, or 90 days. These loans are called short-term loans.

When a bank makes a short-term loan, it may require the borrower to sign a note and pay the interest when the loan is made. When interest is collected in advance this way, it is known as a **bank discount**. Because the interest is paid in advance, the note itself does not show any interest rate, and it is called a *noninterest-bearing note*.

The bank collects the bank discount by deducting it from the principal, or face of note. The amount the borrower gets is the principal of the note less the discount. When the loan is due, only the principal of the note is paid. Obtaining a loan in this way is known as *discounting a note*.

The percent of discount charged by the bank is the *rate of discount*. The amount of money that the borrower gets is the *proceeds*.

Principal × Rate of Discount = Bank Discount

Principal − Bank Discount = Proceeds

EXAMPLE 1

A lender discounted a $3,500 note for Risa DeWitt at 15% interest for 3 months. Find the proceeds of the note that Risa receives.

SOLUTION

Rewrite the rate of bank discount as a decimal: 15% = 0.15

3 months ÷ 12 months = $\frac{1}{4}$ time of note as fraction of a year

Multiply the principal by the rate of bank discount and time of note.

$3,500 × 0.15 × $\frac{1}{4}$ = $131.25 bank discount (interest)

Subtract the bank discount from the principal.

$3,500 − $131.25 = $3,368.75   Risa received as proceeds

Note that three months later, Risa would repay the lender $3,500.

■ CHECK YOUR UNDERSTANDING

A. A bank discounted a $9,600 noninterest-bearing note for Jason Williams at 10% interest for 9 months. Find the proceeds of the note that Jason receives. $8,880

B. Yang Sun discounted her $12,800, 3-month, noninterest-bearing note at 13% at her bank. Find the proceeds of the note. $12,384

■ True Rate of Interest

When you discount your own noninterest-bearing note, you pay a rate of interest based on the principal. However, you do not get the full principal because interest is deducted in advance. To find the true rate of interest you paid, you must divide the interest paid (bank discount) by the amount you actually received (proceeds).

■ *CHECK YOUR UNDERSTANDING SOLUTIONS*

A. $9,600 × $\frac{9}{12}$ × 0.10 = $720;

$9,600 − $720 = $8,880

C. 12 ÷ 6 = 2; $25,000 − $23,250 = $1,750; $1,750 × 2 = $3,500; $3,500 ÷ $23,250 = 0.1505, or 15.1%

True Rate of Interest = Interest $\left(\begin{smallmatrix}\text{Bank}\\\text{Discount}\end{smallmatrix}\right)$ ÷ Actual Amount Borrowed (Proceeds)

If the interest paid is for less than one year, you must first find the interest for one year. For example, if the interest paid is for 6 months, multiply that interest by 2 to find the interest for one year ($12 \div 6 = 2$).

EXAMPLE 2

Find the true rate of interest, rounded the nearest tenth of a percent, on Risa DeWitt's note in Example 1.

SOLUTION

12 months ÷ 3 months = 4   periods of 3-months in the year

Multiply the interest for 3 months by 4 to find the interest for one year.

$131.25 × 4 = $525   interest (bank discount) for 1 year

Subtract the interest (bank discount) from the principal of the note.

$3,500 − $131.25 = $3,368.75   amount actually borrowed (proceeds of note)

$\frac{\$525}{\$3,368.75}$ = 0.1558, or 15.6%   true interest rate Risa paid

■ CHECK YOUR UNDERSTANDING

C. Julius Amani signed a $25,000 noninterest-bearing note on March 22. He discounted the note at 14% and paid the principal back 6 months later. He received $23,250 as proceeds. What true rate of interest, to the nearest tenth percent, did Julius pay on the note? 15.1%

D. Your bank discounted your 4-month, $2,600, noninterest-bearing note. The discount rate was 12%. You received $2,496 as proceeds. What true rate of interest, to the nearest tenth percent, did you pay on the note? 12.5%

Wrap Up

Look back at the Start Up question at the beginning of this lesson. If Fernando took the bank's offer, he would only receive $2,775 in proceeds. The bank would deduct the interest in advance. This would leave him $225 short for his vacation.

COMMUNICATION

Call or visit at least 3 banks in your area. Gather from them the interest rates they charge for unsecured promissory notes, unsecured noninterest-bearing notes that are discounted, car loans, and home equity loans. Prepare a chart containing the names of the banks, the types of loans, and the interest rates for each type of loan.

Prepare a short presentation for your chart. Explain to the class what information you gathered from banks and how you displayed that information on your chart.

Lesson 4.2 Discounted Promissory Notes ■ 141

■ Apply Goal 2

Work through Example 2 at the board while students complete their computations at their desks.

Assign Check Your Understanding problems C and D for completion in class. Check student work for difficulties by walking around the room.

Wrap Up

Review the Start Up. Ask students to find what amount Fernando should borrow to receive $3,000 in proceeds

(15% ÷ 2 = 7.5%;

100% − 7.5% = 92.5%;

$3,000 ÷ 0.925 = $3,243.24)

COMMUNICATION

Assign the Communication problem. Have some students give brief reports of their findings. Or, prepare a master chart of student findings at the board while students provide data from their assignments at their desks.

COMMON ERRORS

When computing the true rate of interest, students may forget to convert the bank discount into an annual amount first. Another error commonly made is that students divide by the principal instead of dividing by the proceeds.

Assign

Assignment: Exercises 1–38.
Start with the basic arithmetic problems at the beginning to insure that students understand the underlying arithmetic in the Exercises.

Assess

Check student answers to the exercises by calling on them in class, collecting and grading selected problems, or by observing student at work.

Ask students to distinguish between simple interest and bank discount. Then ask them to explain the term true rate of interest for a discounted promissory note.

Reteach

STUDENT WORKBOOK If students need help with finding bank discount and proceeds, complete Exercise 2 in the workbook with them. Then have them complete Exercise 4.

If students need help finding the true rate of interest, complete Exercise 3 in the workbook with them. Then have them complete Exercise 5.

EXERCISES

Write as a decimal.

1. 2.3% 0.023
2. 250% 2.5
3. 0.75% 0.0075

Find the product.

4. 4.2% of $4,689 $196.94
5. 150% of $84 $126
6. $2,200 × 6% × 5 $660
7. $3,800 × 8.5% × $1\frac{1}{2}$ $484.50

Find the percent.

8. 75 as a percent of 3,000? 2.5%
9. $150 as a percent of $1,200 12.5%

Find the proceeds of each noninterest-bearing note. Each note was discounted on the same day as the date of the note.

	Date of Note	Face	Time	Discount Rate	Proceeds
10.	Mar. 1	$3,000	3 months	9%	$2,932.50
11.	Oct. 5	$8,400	2 months	15%	$8,190
12.	Jan.12	$5,700	4 months	17%	$5,377
13.	May 15	$15,000	6 months	12%	$14,100
14.	Nov. 25	$900	1 month	10%	$892.50

MATH TIP

Don't forget to subtract the amount of discount from the principal or face of the note.

On June 12, the bank discounted Ehud Ben-Ami's 12%, 3-month noninterest-bearing $995 note.

15. Estimate the bank discount. Estimates may vary. $30

16. What was the actual bank discount? $29.85

17. What were the actual proceeds of the note? $965.15

18. Julie Frey signed a $5,400 noninterest-bearing note. She discounted the note at 12% and paid the principal back 3 months later. She received $5,238 as proceeds. What true rate of interest, to the nearest tenth percent, did Julie pay on the note? 12.4%

19. Farouk Alwash received $8,410.50 in proceeds from an $8,900 noninterest-bearing note that he discounted at his bank. The bank discount rate was 11%. He repaid the principal 6 months later. Find his true rate of interest, to the nearest tenth percent. 11.6%

INTEGRATING YOUR KNOWLEDGE On February 24, Lake County Bank discounted Elmore Corporation's note for $20,000. The note was dated October 21, due in 3 months, and it carried no interest. The rate of discount was 15%.

20. What was the amount of the bank discount? $750

21. What proceeds did Elmore receive? $19,250

22. What true rate of interest, to the nearest tenth of a percent, did Elmore pay? 15.6%

SELECTED SOLUTIONS

15. $1,000 × 0.12 ÷ 4 = $30 or
$1,000 × 0.10 ÷ 4 = $25
18. 12 ÷ 3 = 4; $5,400 − $5,238 = $162;
$162 × 4 = $648; $648 ÷ $5,238 = 0.1237, or 12.4%

20. $\frac{3}{12} = \frac{1}{4}$; $20,000 × 0.15 × $\frac{1}{4}$ = $750
21. $20,000 − $750 = $19,250
22. $750 × 4 = $3,000; $3,000 ÷ $19,250 = 0.1558, or 15.6%

INTEGRATING YOUR KNOWLEDGE   The bank discounted Fusako Komuro's 6-month noninterest-bearing note for $8,400. The rate of discount was 14%.

23. What was the amount of the bank discount? $588

24. What proceeds did Fusako receive? $7,812

25. How much did Fusako pay her bank on the maturity date? $8,400

26. What true rate of interest, to the nearest tenth of a percent, did Fusako pay? 15.1%

DECISION MAKING   You need to borrow $2,000 for a vacation trip. You can borrow the money from one lender who will ask you to sign a 6-month promissory note for $2,000 at 18% interest. A second lender asks you to sign a noninterest-bearing, 6-month note for $2,000. The second lender will discount the note at 17%.

27. Which bank offers the lowest true interest rate? 1st lender

28. Which bank's offer will you take and why? 1st, 2nd doesn't provide enough money for trip

MIXED REVIEW

29. $25,498.12 − $19,008.08 $6,490.04

30. What is 139 divided by 27, rounded to the nearest hundredth? 5.15

31. $\frac{3}{4} \div \frac{7}{8}$ $\frac{6}{7}$

32. $1\frac{1}{2} + 3\frac{1}{4} + 5\frac{5}{6}$ $10\frac{7}{12}$

33. Write 0.005 as a fraction in simplest form. $\frac{1}{200}$

34. Jaron received $11,371.50 in proceeds from a $12,600 noninterest-bearing note that he discounted at his bank. The bank discount rate was 13%. He repaid the principal 9 months later. Find his true rate of interest, to the nearest tenth percent. 14.4%, Lesson 4.2

35. Amelia signed a promissory note for $15,800 at 12% interest for 3 months. Find the interest and amount she will pay when the note falls due.
$474, $16,274, Lesson 4.1

36. Doug Palen started the day with a bank balance of $389.34. He used an ATM to deposit a check for $150 and his debit card to make these purchases: $45.09, $12.88, $81.06, and $23.91. What is his bank balance after these transactions are processed by the bank?
$376.40, Lesson 3.2

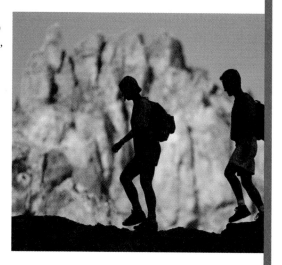

The Belino family had a total income last year of $89,500. They spent $1,790 on entertainment and $18,795 on housing. Lesson 2.6

37. What percent of their total income was spent on entertainment? 2%

38. What percent of their total income was spent on housing? 21%

Lesson 4.2 Discounted Promissory Notes ■ 143

TEACHING STRATEGIES Multicultural Connections

Consider having students use the Web to find the current exchange rates for the Mexican peso and French franc. Then with your students, convert the Integrating Your Knowledge Exercise at the top of p. 143 into first pesos, and then francs, and find the answers to Exercises 23 and 24 in both currencies.

GOALS

- Calculate interest using simple interest tables
- Find the due date of a note
- Find the number of days between dates

Start Up

You started a marathon race at 9:15 a.m. and finished at 3:08 p.m. What was your elapsed time for running the race?

Math Skill Builder

Review these math skills and solve the exercises.

1 **Divide** by 100.
Find the quotient. $7,200 ÷ $100 = 72

1a. $890 ÷ $100
8.9

1b. $12,089 ÷ $100
120.89

1c. $103,278 ÷ $100
1,032.78

2 **Multiply** money amounts by decimals and round to nearest cent.
Find the product. $475 × 0.6283 = $298.442, or $298.44

2a. $1,800 × 0.4186
$753.48

2b. $943 × 0.5289
$498.75

2c. $11,093 × 0.3752
$4,162.09

3 **Add** and **Subtract** whole numbers.
Find the sum. 16 + 31 = 47
Find the difference. 31 − 9 = 22

3a. 30 − 12
18

3b. 31 − 16
15

3c. 5 + 31 + 28
64

3d. 15 + 30 + 31 + 8
84

■ Simple Interest Tables

Most banks use computers or specially programmed calculators to find interest and calculate payment amounts on loans. However, some lenders use interest tables (like the one shown on the next page) as a quick reference chart.

The table shows the interest on $100 for a 365-day year. To find the interest on any amount of money using the table, follow these steps:

1. To find the number of hundreds of dollars in the principal, divide the principal by $100. Simply move the decimal in the principal two places to the left.

2. Use the number from the chart that matches your interest rate and time and multiply it by the number of hundreds in the principal.

SIMPLE INTEREST TABLE

Interest on $100 for a 365-Day Year

Time (Days)	8%	8½%	9%	9½%	10%	10½%	11%	11½%	12%	12½%
1	0.0219	0.0233	0.0247	0.0260	0.0274	0.0288	0.0301	0.0315	0.0329	0.0342
2	0.0438	0.0466	0.0493	0.0521	0.0548	0.0575	0.0603	0.0630	0.0658	0.0685
3	0.0658	0.0699	0.0740	0.0781	0.0822	0.0863	0.0904	0.0945	0.0986	0.1027
4	0.0877	0.0932	0.0986	0.1041	0.1096	0.1151	0.1205	0.1260	0.1315	0.1370
5	0.1096	0.1164	0.1233	0.1301	0.1370	0.1438	0.1507	0.1575	0.1644	0.1712
6	0.1315	0.1397	0.1479	0.1562	0.1644	0.1726	0.1808	0.1890	0.1973	0.2055
7	0.1534	0.1630	0.1726	0.1822	0.1918	0.2014	0.2110	0.2205	0.2301	0.2397
8	0.1753	0.1863	0.1973	0.2082	0.2192	0.2301	0.2411	0.2521	0.2630	0.2740
9	0.1973	0.2096	0.2219	0.2342	0.2466	0.2589	0.2712	0.2836	0.2959	0.3082
10	0.2192	0.2329	0.2466	0.2603	0.2740	0.2877	0.3014	0.3151	0.3288	0.3425
11	0.2411	0.2562	0.2712	0.2863	0.3014	0.3164	0.3315	0.3466	0.3616	0.3767
12	0.2630	0.2795	0.2959	0.3123	0.3288	0.3452	0.3616	0.3781	0.3945	0.4110
13	0.2849	0.3027	0.3205	0.3384	0.3562	0.3740	0.3918	0.4096	0.4274	0.4452
14	0.3068	0.3260	0.3452	0.3644	0.3836	0.4027	0.4219	0.4411	0.4603	0.4795
15	0.3288	0.3493	0.3699	0.3904	0.4110	0.4315	0.4521	0.4726	0.4932	0.5137
16	0.3507	0.3726	0.3945	0.4164	0.4384	0.4603	0.4822	0.5041	0.5260	0.5479
17	0.3726	0.3959	0.4192	0.4425	0.4658	0.4890	0.5123	0.5356	0.5589	0.5822
18	0.3945	0.4192	0.4438	0.4685	0.4932	0.5178	0.5425	0.5671	0.5918	0.6164
19	0.4164	0.4425	0.4685	0.4945	0.5205	0.5466	0.5726	0.5986	0.6247	0.6507
20	0.4384	0.4658	0.4932	0.5205	0.5479	0.5753	0.6027	0.6301	0.6575	0.6849
21	0.4603	0.4890	0.5178	0.5466	0.5753	0.6041	0.6329	0.6616	0.6904	0.7192
22	0.4822	0.5123	0.5425	0.5726	0.6027	0.6329	0.6630	0.6932	0.7233	0.7534
23	0.5041	0.5356	0.5671	0.5986	0.6301	0.6616	0.6932	0.7247	0.7562	0.7877
24	0.5260	0.5589	0.5918	0.6247	0.6575	0.6904	0.7233	0.7562	0.7890	0.8219
25	0.5479	0.5822	0.6164	0.6507	0.6849	0.7192	0.7534	0.7877	0.8219	0.8562
26	0.5699	0.6055	0.6411	0.6767	0.7123	0.7479	0.7836	0.8192	0.8548	0.8904
27	0.5918	0.6288	0.6658	0.7027	0.7397	0.7767	0.8137	0.8507	0.8877	0.9247
28	0.6137	0.6521	0.6904	0.7288	0.7671	0.8055	0.8438	0.8822	0.9206	0.9589
29	0.6356	0.6753	0.7151	0.7548	0.7945	0.8342	0.8740	0.9137	0.9534	0.9932
30	0.6575	0.6986	0.7397	0.7808	0.8219	0.8630	0.9041	0.9452	0.9863	1.0274
31	0.6795	0.7219	0.7644	0.8068	0.8493	0.8918	0.9342	0.9767	1.0192	1.0616

EXAMPLE 1

Find the interest on $850 for 20 days at 12%.

SOLUTION

Find the interest on $100 for 20 days at 12%

$0.6575   interest from the table

$850 ÷ $100 = 8.5   the number of $100s in the principal

Multiply the interest by the number of 100s.

$0.6575 × 8.5 = $5.588, or $5.59

■ CHECK YOUR UNDERSTANDING

A. Find the interest on $620 for 12 days at 10%. $2.04

B. Find the interest on $550 for 28 days at $9\frac{1}{2}$% $4.01

Lesson 4.3 Interest Tables ■ 145

CONNECTION TO SPREADSHEETS

Have students work in teams to create a simple interest table like the one on p. 145 using a spreadsheet. You may have them create a table that provides interest on $100 for more than 31 days.

145

Point out to students that finding the due date of a note in days or months is basically the same as finding the date on which a two-week assignment must be completed.

Be sure students understand that if the term of a note is stated in months and occurs on the 31st of a month, the due date of the note is then the last day of the month in which it matures even if that month has less than 31 days.

When the number of days you want is not shown in the table, you must combine multipliers to get the number.

EXAMPLE 2

Find the interest on $450 for 35 days at 8%.

SOLUTION

$0.6575   interest on $100 for 30 days at 8%

$0.1096   interest on $100 for 5 days at 8%

Add the interest for 30 days and 5 days

$0.6575 + $0.1096 = $0.7671   interest on $100 for 35 days

$450 ÷ $100 = 4.5   the number of $100s in the principal

Multiply the interest for 35 days by the number of 100s in the principal.

$0.7671 × 4.5 = $3.452, or $3.45

Interest for a rate not shown on the table can be found in much the same way. For example, the interest on $100 @ $18\frac{1}{2}$% for 20 days is the sum of the amount for 9% ($0.4932) and the amount for $9\frac{1}{2}$% ($0.5205).

■ **CHECK YOUR UNDERSTANDING**

C. Find the interest on $1,320 for 40 days at 10%. $14.46

D. Find the interest on $740 for 62 days at 12%. $15.08

E. Find the interest on $350 for 30 days at 16%. $4.60

■ Due Dates

When the time of a note is shown in months, you find the due date by counting that number of months forward from the date of the note. The due date is the same day in the month you stop with as the date of the note. If the date is the last day of the month, the note is due on the last date of the month in which the note is due. For instance, a 1-month note issued on January 31 would be due February 28 (or February 29 in a leap year).

The time of a note may be shown in days. In this case, you can find the due date by counting forward, from the date of the note, the number of days shown on the note.

■ *CHECK YOUR UNDERSTANDING SOLUTIONS*

C. $1,320 ÷ $100 = 13.2;
$0.5479 × 2 × 13.2 = $14.464, or $14.46

D. $740 ÷ $100 = 7.4;
$1.0192 × 2 × 7.4 = $15.084, or $15.08

E. $350 ÷ $100 = 3.5; $0.6575 × 2 × 3.5 = $4.602, or $4.60

EXAMPLE 3

Find the maturity date of a 90-day note dated June 28.

SOLUTION

	90 days	length of note
June	−2 days	days left in June
	88 days	
July	−31 days	days in July
	57 days	
Aug.	−31 days	days in August
	26 days	Sept. 26 Maturity date

■ **CHECK YOUR UNDERSTANDING**

F. Find the due date of a 3-month note dated March 6. 6/6

G. Find the due date of a 2-month note dated March 31. 5/31

H. Find the due date of a 60-day note dated January 15. 3/16

■ Days Between Dates

Sometimes you may need to find the number of days between two dates.

EXAMPLE 4

Find the number of days from June 14 to August 23.

SOLUTION

June 14 to June 30 =	16 days
July 1 to July 31 =	31 days
August 1 to 23 =	+ 23 days
Total	70 days

■ **CHECK YOUR UNDERSTANDING**

I. Find the number of days from January 28 to March 29. 60 days

J. Find the number of days from July 3 to September 1. 60 days

Wrap Up

Look back at the Start Up questions in this lesson. The elapsed time you found should have been 5 hours and 53 minutes. What does "elapsed time" mean? Explain the steps you took to determine elapsed time. Why do you need to find the elapsed time? Work with a partner. Have one person name a starting time or date and an ending time or date and the other find the elapsed time. Exchange roles and repeat.

SPREADSHEET TIP

Spreadsheets can display dates in many different formats, such as 12/25/04 and December 25, 2004. You can choose an alternate format if you do not like the default format used by your software.

SPREADSHEET TIP

Spreadsheets can be used to find the days between dates. Enter the first date in B1 and the other date in B2. Then in B3 enter: =B2 − B1. Next format B3 to display a *number* with *no decimal places.*

■ **Apply Goal 2**

Work through Example 3 with students completing the math at their desks.

Assign Check Your Understanding problems F, G, and H for completion during class. Move through the aisles to help students with problems.

■ **Teach Goal 3**

Ask students to think of situations in their own lives when finding the days between dates is useful (e.g., number of days until a holiday, until an assignment is due).

■ **Apply Goal 3**

Work through Example 4 with students completing the math at their desks.

Assign Check Your Understanding problems I and J for completion in class. Circulate through your classroom and examine student work for difficulties.

Wrap Up

Review the Start Up. Ask students to describe the steps to find elapsed time in hours and minutes. Then ask them to describe the steps to find the elapsed time in days and months.

■ *CHECK YOUR UNDERSTANDING SOLUTIONS*

F. 1st mo. = April 6, 2nd mo. = May 6, 3rd mo. = June 6.

H. 60 days − 16 days in Jan. = 44; 44 − 28 days in Feb. = 16 left; due date = March 16.

I. 1/28 − 1/31 = 3 days; 2/1 − 2/28 = 28 days; 3/1 − 3/29 = 29 days; 3 + 28 + 29 = 60 days

COMMUNICATION

Search the Web to find at least 4 calculators that you can use online. Include simple interest and compound interest calculators, Then, test each calculator by solving these two problems with them:

1. Find the simple interest on $1,200 for $\frac{1}{2}$ year at 12%. $72
2. Find the compound interest on $1,200 for 1 year at 5% compounded monthly. $61.39

Prepare a report containing the name of each calculator, the major types of calculations it can handle, its Web address, the ease with which you can understand how to use it, and whether it answered the problems above correctly.

EXERCISES

Find the product or quotient.

1. $418 ÷ 100
   $4.18
2. $297 × 0.2851
   $84.67
3. $310,790 ÷ $100
   3,107.90
4. $5,300 × 0.9184
   $4,867.52
5. $51,280 ÷ $100
   512.80
6. $31,627 × 0.5028
   $15,902.06

Find the sum or difference.

7. 735 − 382 353
8. 49 − 26 23
9. 9 + 31 + 30 70
10. 12 + 28 + 31 + 23 94

Use the Simple Interest Table to find the interest to the nearest cent.

11. $500 @ 8% for 20 days $2.19
12. $380 @ 12% for 12 days $1.50
13. $6,150 @ 9% for 25 days $37.91
14. $275 @ $12\frac{1}{2}$% for 20 days $1.88
15. $400 @ $9\frac{1}{2}$% for 45 days $4.68
16. $725 @ 11% for 60 days $13.11
17. $270 @ 18% for 120 days $15.98
18. $540 @ 21% for 20 days $6.21
19. $2,500 @ 20% for 30 days $41.10
20. $900 @ 17% for 16 days $6.71

Lucia Flores borrowed $1,700 on a note for 60 days with interest at 12%.

21. Using the Simple Interest Table, what interest did she pay? $33.53

22. What total amount did she owe when the note was due? $1,733.53

Find the number of days between the given dates.

23. January 5 to March 12 66 days

24. May 6 to August 22 108 days

25. February 23 to May 5 71 days

26. November 12 to January 29 78 days

27. September 6 to January 4 120 days

28. July 29 to August 8 10 days

148 ■ Chapter 4 Loans and Credit Cards

SELECTED SOLUTIONS

17. $270 ÷ $100 = 2.7;
    $0.7397 × 2.7 × 2 × 4 = $15.977, or $15.98

21. $1,700 ÷ $100 = 17;
    $0.9863 × 17 × 2 = $33.534, or $33.53

23. 1/5 − 1/31 = 26 days; 2/1 − 2/28 = 28 days;
    3/1 − 3/12 = 12 days; 26 + 28 + 12 = 66 days

31. 1 mo. = 4/30; 2 mo. = 5/31; 3 mo. = 6/30;
    4 mo. = 7/31

Find the due date for each note. Assume February has 28 days.

	Date Issued	Time		Date Issued	Time
29.	February 12	1 month 3/12	**30.**	November 14	2 months 1/14
31.	March 31	4 months 7/31	**32.**	March 31	3 months 6/30
33.	March 5	30 days 4/4	**34.**	January 29	60 days 3/30
35.	January 30	45 days 3/16	**36.**	April 14	75 days 6/28
37.	December 28	80 days 3/18	**38.**	June 9	120 days 10/7

INTEGRATING YOUR KNOWLEDGE On March 5, Jake Lowry signed a note for $15,000 at 15% exact interest. He paid the note on June 3.

39. For how many days was interest due? 90 days

40. What amount of interest did Jake owe? $554.79

41. What was the total amount due on June 3? $15,554.79

42. On July 13, Rosa D'Lario borrowed $9,000 to buy a new car for $14,500. She signed a note with exact interest at 8%. If she paid 100% of the note off on September 24, what total amount did she owe? $9,144

43. DECISION MAKING You can borrow $2,500 at 15% exact interest for 6 months from one lender. Another lender offers you a loan of $2,500 at 14% exact interest for 8 months. Which loan is the better deal? Justify your decision. Answers will vary; 1st = $2,687.50; 2nd = $2,733.33; difference of $45.83 buys you two more months

MIXED REVIEW

44. $\frac{1}{8} + \frac{1}{6}$ $\frac{7}{24}$ **45.** $2,078.01 - 43.098$ 2,034.912 **46.** $12\frac{1}{4} - 3\frac{1}{2}$ $8\frac{3}{4}$

47. What amount is $2\frac{1}{4}$% of $900? $20.25

48. What amount is $5\frac{3}{5}$% of $1,200? $67.20

49. Find the due date of a 75-day note dated May 25. August 8; Lesson 4.3

50. Find the due date of a 3-month note dated July 31. 10/31

51. Sandra Rollins discounted her $2,890, 3-months, noninterest-bearing note at 14% at her bank on January 10. Find the proceeds of the note. $2,788.85, Lesson 4.2

52. The interest on a loan of $8,600 for 3 months is $258. What is the rate of interest? 12%, Lesson 4.1

53. Jeanne Dixon is paid $2.25 for each fan she assembles. During the five days of last week, she assembled these fans: 27, 28, 33, 30, 31. What was Jeanne's gross pay for the week? $335.25, Lesson 1.4

54. Find the interest on $745 for 25 days at 8% using the Simple Interest Table. $4.08, Lesson 4.3

55. Residents that live in Devon have an average annual taxable income of $38,445. The city's income tax rate is $\frac{7}{8}$%. How much does the average resident pay in city tax each year? $336.39; Lesson 2.4

Lesson 4.3 Interest Tables ■ **149**

If students need help finding the due date of a note, complete Exercises 14a and 15a in the workbook with them. Then have them complete Exercises 14 and 15 and 16–22.

If students need help finding the days between dates, complete Exercise 23a in the workbook with them. Then have them do Exercises 23 and 24–35.

Enrich

Ask area banks to supply copies of interest tables to your class.

Have students play a calendar game. Separate the pages of a yearly calendar, and place any six consecutive months on the floor to form a 3 by 2 rectangle. Students toss two markers onto the rectangle and find the number of days between the two dates on which the markers land.

There are many calculators that find the days between two dates. Ask students to find one of the calculators and redo some of the problems using the calculator to check their work.

Assign Exercise 43, Decision Making. Have students debate and identify reasons why a longer-term loan with more interest might be (a) helpful (easier on monthly budget) and (b) less helpful (more expensive).

Close

Review steps for finding the due date and days between dates.

■ **STUDENT PORTFOLIO**
If students solve exercises using actual interest tables from area banks, these tables may be placed in the students' portfolios.

CONNECTION TO BUSINESS

Students may not use the correct row or column. They may not copy the numbers correctly or input them correctly when using a calculator. They may not round answers correctly. Remind students of the necessity of 100% accuracy for people in business, and encourage students to check that their answers are reasonable.

GOALS

- Calculate the installment price and finance charge on an installment plan purchase
- Calculate the number and amount of monthly payments
- Calculate the interest, principal payment, and new balance on an installment loan

Start Up

Darrel just graduated from high school. He needs a car to get a job but he also needs a job to get a car. What choices does Darrel have to solve his problem?

Math Skill Builder

Review these math skills and solve the exercises that follow.

1 **Add** and **subtract** dollar amounts.
Find the sum. $109.45 + $29.01 = $138.46
Find the difference. $244.21 - $62.09 = $182.12

1a. $1,905.34 + $804.23 $2,709.57   **1b.** $15,378.82 + $598.38 $15,977.20

1c. $5,074 - $2,985 $2,089   **1d.** $56.89 - $12.98 $43.91

2 **Multiply** dollar amounts by whole numbers and decimals.
Find the products. $34.19 × 6 = $205.14 and $106.80 × 0.015 = $1.602, or $1.60

2a. $537 × 8 $4,296   **2b.** $1,790 × 0.2 $358   **2c.** $450 × 0.045 $20.25

3 **Divide** dollar amounts by whole numbers and dollar amounts.
Find the quotients. $340 ÷ 8 = $42.50 and $56.30 ÷ $500 = 0.1126

3a. $1,080 ÷ 12 $90   **3b.** $36 ÷ $1,200 0.03   **3c.** $171 ÷ $3,800 0.045

■ Installment Price and Finance Charge

Sound systems, boats, cars, furniture, and many other items are often bought on an installment plan, also called a time payment plan. When you buy on an *installment plan*, you are borrowing money and paying it back in part payments.

You may have to make a **down payment**, or part of the purchase price. You may also have to sign an *installment contract* in which you agree to pay the unpaid balance.

COMMON ERRORS

When figuring the total installment price of a purchase, students often forget to add the down payment with the total amount of the monthly installment payments.

Emphasize to students that the down payment must be included with the total monthly payments to arrive at a correct installment price.

The installment price is higher than the cash price because the seller adds a **finance charge** to the cash price. This charge pays the seller interest on the money and covers the extra cost of doing business on the installment plan. The finance charge is the difference between the installment price and the cash price.

EXAMPLE 1

A desktop computer system has a cash price of $1,200. To buy it on an installment plan, you pay $100 down and $38 a month for 36 months. Find the finance charge. By what percent is the installment price greater than the cash price?

SOLUTION

Add the total of the monthly payments and the down payment to find the installment price.

$38 × 36 = $1,368   total monthly payment

$1,368 + $100 = $1,468   installment price

Subtract the cash price from the installment price to find the finance charge.

$1,468 − $1,200 = $268   finance charge

Divide the finance charge by the cash price to find the percent that the installment price is greater than the cash price.

$268 ÷ $1,200 = 0.22\overline{3}$, or $22\frac{1}{3}$% percent greater

■ CHECK YOUR UNDERSTANDING

A. You can buy a watch for $125 cash or pay $25 down and the balance in 12 monthly payments of $9. What is the installment price? By what percent would your installment price be greater than the cash price? $133, 6.4%

B. A digital audio player that sells for $169.95 can be bought for $20 down and $26.17 a month for 6 months. What is the installment price? By what percent, to the nearest tenth, does the installment price exceed the cash price? $177.02, 4.2%

■ Monthly Installment Payments

Sometimes you may know the installment price and down payment and need to find the amount of the monthly payment or the number of months to pay.

EXAMPLE 2

The installment price of a set of water skis is $190. You must pay $50 down and make payments for 16 months. What will be your monthly payments?

SOLUTION

Subtract the down payment from the installment price to find the remaining amount to pay.

$190 − $50 = $140   remainder to pay

Divide the remaining amount to pay by the number of months to pay to find the monthly payment.

$140 ÷ 16 = $8.75   monthly payment

■ *CHECK YOUR UNDERSTANDING SOLUTIONS*

A. $9 × 12 = $108; $108 + $25 = $133;
$133 − $125 = $8; $8 ÷ $125 = 0.064, or 6.4%

B. $26.17 × 6 = $157.02; $157.02 + $20 = $177.02;
$177.02 − $169.95 = $7.07;
$7.07 ÷ $169.95 = 0.0416, or 4.2%

C. $175 − $25 = $150; $150 ÷ 15 = $10

D. $1,044 − $100 = $944; $944 ÷ $59 = 16

Point out to students that they can find the annual interest rate by multiplying the monthly rate by 12. For instance, a monthly rate of 1.5% is the same as an annual rate of 1.5% × 12, or 18%.

Encourage students to talk about items that they or adults in their homes have bought on time. For those who are willing to disclose the information, use real-life data to have students find the finance charges paid.

■ CHECK YOUR UNDERSTANDING

C. A scuba diver's wetsuit costs $175 on the installment plan. You must make a down payment of $25 and make payments for 15 months. What will be your monthly payments? $10

D. A refrigerator sells for $1,044 on the installment plan. After making a down payment of $100, you pay $59 a month. How many months will it take to pay for the refrigerator? 16

■ Installment Loans

Rather than pay a retail store a down payment and monthly payments, you can obtain an *installment loan* from a bank or credit union. When you borrow on an installment loan, you receive the full amount of the principal. You repay the principal in installments, usually monthly.

Many lenders calculate payments so that each payment is the same amount. This payment method is called the *level payment plan*. From each payment, the interest due for that month is deducted. The payment amount remaining after deducting the interest is applied to the principal.

If the interest rate on the loan is 1.5% a month, this rate is equal to 18% a year (1.5 × 12 = 18). Sometimes a service charge is added to the cost of the loan.

Below is a schedule of payments on a one-year, $500 loan at 18%. The loan was repaid in 12 equal monthly payments of $45.84.

BUSINESS TIP

There are many loan calculators on the Web. You enter the principal, annual interest rate, and time of the loan. What is returned to you is the amount of the level monthly payment. Search for "loan calculator."

Loan Repayment Schedule				
Month	Monthly Payment	Interest Payment	Applied to Principal	Balance
1	45.84	7.50	38.34	461.66
2	45.84	6.92	38.92	422.74
3	45.84	6.34	39.50	383.25
4	45.84	5.75	40.09	343.15
5	45.84	5.15	40.69	302.46
6	45.84	4.54	41.30	261.16
7	45.84	3.92	41.92	219.24
8	45.84	3.29	42.55	176.68
9	45.84	2.65	43.19	133.50
10	45.84	2.00	43.84	89.66
11	45.84	1.34	44.50	45.16
12	45.84	0.68	45.16	0.00
Totals	550.08	50.08	500.00	

SPREADSHEET TIP

The spreadsheet function *PMT* lets you compute the monthly payment needed in a level payment loan. In Excel, the function for a $500 loan for 1 year at 18% is
=PMT (0.18/12,12,500,0)
0.18/12 is the monthly interest rate. The number of months is 12. The principal is 500 and 0 means the monthly payment is made at the end of the month. A 1 would mean the monthly payment is made at the beginning of the month.

TEACHING STRATEGIES Cooperative Learning

Have teams of two students each develop a spreadsheet that will produce the loan repayment schedule found on p. 152. Then have each team swap their spreadsheet with another team to have their spreadsheet audited. Auditing should include making sure that the most efficient formu- las or functions are used, that the data in the loan repayment schedule when entered produces the results found on p. 152, that the non-variable cells are protected, and that the format of the spreadsheet is clear and easy to understand.

Notice that the interest paid in any month is the amount you get by multiplying the unpaid balance by the monthly interest rate. A loan that uses this method of allocating interest is called a *simple interest installment loan*.

EXAMPLE 3

The Winstons borrowed $500 on a one-year simple interest installment loan at 18% interest. The monthly payments were $45.84. Find the amount of interest, amount applied to the principal, and the new balance for the first monthly payment.

SOLUTION

Calculate the monthly interest rate: $18\% \div 12 = 1.5\%$

Multiply the principal by the monthly interest rate: $\$500 \times 0.015 = \$7.50$

Subtract the interest from the monthly payment: $\$45.84 - \$7.50 = \$38.34$

Subtract the amount applied to principal from the previous balance.

$\$500.00 - \$38.34 = \$461.66$ new balance

■ CHECK YOUR UNDERSTANDING

E. Benito Diaz borrowed $1,000 on a one-year simple interest installment loan at 15% interest. The monthly payments were $90.26. Find the amount of interest, amount applied to the principal, and the new balance for the first monthly payment. $12.50, $77.76, $922.24

F. Lillian Dish signed a $2,500, 6-month simple interest installment loan at 18% interest. The monthly payments were $438.81. Find the amount of interest, amount applied to the principal, and the new balance for the first two monthly payments. 1st mo.: $37.50, $401.31, $2,098.69; 2nd mo.: $31.48, $407.33, $1,691.36

Wrap Up

Look back at the problem described at the start of this lesson. Darrel is going to have to borrow money to purchase a car. He can borrow the money from the auto dealer, buying the car on the installment plan. Or, he can borrow the money through an installment loan from another lender, such as a bank, credit union, or finance company. Since Darrel probably doesn't have other collateral for the loan, he will have to use the car he is buying as collateral. That means that if Darrel fails to make his loan payments, the lender can take back, or *repossess* the car.

TEAM MEETING

With two other students, investigate the borrowing terms of lenders for car loans. Check out the interest rates and monthly payments they would charge for a four-year, $15,000 auto loan. The lenders should include (a) an auto dealer, (b) a bank, (c) a credit union, and (d) a finance company.

Prepare a comparison chart that includes the following for each lender.

- interest rate
- total payments
- monthly payments
- finance charge

■ **Apply Goal 3**

Work through Example 3 with students completing the math at their desks.

Stress that interest rates are always stated as annual rates, unless otherwise specified. Emphasize that annual rates must be divided by 12 to find the monthly rates applied to the balance.

Assign Check Your Understanding problems E and F for class work. Examine student work at their desks for problems.

■ **ONGOING ASSESSMENT**

Ask students to find the monthly interest rates for the following annual rates: 6%, 12%, 15%, 18%, 24% (0.5%, 1%, 1.25%, 1.5%, 2%).

Wrap Up

Review the Start Up and the list developed. Discuss with students the pros and cons of each lender and the type of loan Darrel should get.

TEAM MEETING

Suggest that some students check out auto loan terms from online lenders in addition to area lenders.

■ CHECK YOUR UNDERSTANDING SOLUTIONS

E. $0.15 \div 12 = 0.0125$; $\$1,000 \times 0.0125 = \$12.50$;
$\$90.26 - \$12.50 = \$77.76$;
$\$1,000 - \$77.76 = \$922.24$

F. $0.18 \div 12 = 0.015$; $\$2,500 \times 0.015 = \$37.50$;
$\$438.81 - \$37.50 = \$401.31$;

$\$2,500 - \$401.31 = \$2,098.69$;
$\$2,098.69 \times 0.015 = \$31.48$;
$\$438.81 - \$31.48 = \$407.33$;
$\$2,098.69 - \$407.33 = \$1,691.36$

Assign

Assignment: Exercises 1–19, 21–38. Start with the basic math exercises at the beginning to make certain that students can handle the arithmetic used in the exercises.

Assess

Check student answers to the exercises by calling on them in class, collecting and grading selected problems, or by observing student work as you circulate.

Reteach

STUDENT WORKBOOK If students need help with installment price and finance charge problems, complete Exercise 1 in the workbook with them. Then have them complete Exercise 2.

If students need help with finding the number and amount of monthly payments, complete Exercises 3 and 8 in the workbook with them. Then have them complete Exercises 4–7 and 9–12.

If students need help with finding the interest, principal payments, and new balances, complete Exercise 13 in the workbook with them. Then have them complete Exercise 14.

EXERCISES

Find the sum or difference.

1. $2,500 + $89.15 $2,589.15

2. $159.95 + $12.28 $172.23

3. $650 − $75 $575

4. $1,079.34 − $418.73 $660.61

Find the product or quotient.

5. $2,450 × 0.18 $441

6. $389.67 × 2.5 $974.18

7. $157 × 9 $1,413

8. $4,584 ÷ 6 $764

9. $81.60 ÷ $4,800   0.017

10. $1,000 ÷ 10 $100

Find the installment price and finance charge for each item.

Item	Cash Price	Installment Terms
11. Digital Camera $1,793.68; $293.68	$1,500	$100 down; $70.57 a mo. for 24 mos.
12. Sleeper Sofa $1,089.80; $139.80	$950	$50 down; $51.99 a mo. for 20 mos.
13. Computer System $2,280.60; $130.60	$2,150	$225 down; $228.40 a mo. for 9 mos.

14. You buy an MP3 changer for a car's audio system for $25 down and a total installment price of $297.34. You pay $30.26 per month. For how many months will you have to make payments?
9 months

15. A novelty watch that sells for $60 cash may be bought for $6 down and $5.76 a month for 10 months. By what percent is the installment price greater than the cash price?   6%

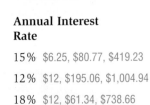

16. You can buy aluminum louvers for the rear window of your car for $180 cash or pay $45 down and the balance in 12 monthly payments of $13.50. By what percent would your installment price be greater than the cash price?   15%

Find the monthly interest payment, amount applied to principal, and new balance for the first month for each simple interest installment loan.

	Amount Financed	Number of Payments	Monthly Payment	Annual Interest Rate	
17.	$500	6	$87.02	15%	$6.25, $80.77, $419.23
18.	$1,200	6	$207.06	12%	$12, $195.06, $1,004.94
19.	$800	12	$ 73.34	18%	$12, $61.34, $738.66

20. **CRITICAL THINKING**   Look at the Loan Repayment Schedule chart. If the interest rate is 18% per year, why is the total of the interest payments less than $90, or $500 × 0.18?   The full $500 principal was not borrowed for a year; the amount borrowed was reduced each month.

SELECTED SOLUTIONS

11. $70.57 × 24 = $1,693.68 + $100 = $1,793.68;
$1,793.68 − $1,500 = $293.68

14. $297.34 − $25 = $272.34; $272.34 ÷ $30.26 = 9

15. $5.76 × 10 = $57.60; $57.60 + $6 = $63.60;
$63.60 − $60 = $3.60; $3.60 ÷ $60 = 0.06, or 6%

17. 0.15 ÷ 12 = 0.0125; $500 × 0.0125 = $6.25;
$87.02 − $6.25 = $80.77;
$500 − $80.77 = $419.23

A member of a credit union borrows $920 on a simple interest installment loan at 12% agreeing to repay it in 12 equal monthly payments of $81.74.

21. What was the total finance charge on the loan? $60.88

22. What was the interest paid for the first month? $9.20

23. What was the amount applied to principal at the end of the first month? $72.54

24. What was the new balance at the end of the first month? $847.46

Kay borrowed $400 from a finance company on a simple interest installment loan and repaid it in 6 monthly payments of $70.81. The finance charge rate was 21%.

25. What was the total finance charge on the loan? $24.86

26. What was the interest paid for the first month? $7

27. What was the amount applied to principal at the end of the first month? $63.81

28. What was the new balance at the end of the first month? $336.19

29. **DECISION MAKING** You can buy a flat panel computer screen for $720 in cash or $50 down and 12 monthly payments of $60.47 on the installment plan from the dealer. You can also obtain a simple interest installment loan from another lender by signing a promissory note and using your car as collateral. The face of the note would be for $720 and would be payable, along with interest at 12%, one year later. If you do not have the cash but want the screen now, which loan would be the best for you? Why? Installment plan; interest is $55.64; interest on note is $86.40

MIXED REVIEW

30. $43,109 \times 150$ 6,466,350

31. $7,082 \div 1,000$ 7.082

32. $2\frac{2}{5} \times 5\frac{1}{8}$ $\frac{123}{10}$, $12\frac{3}{10}$, 12.3

33. What is $36\frac{1}{2}\%$ as a decimal? 0.365

34. Find the simple interest on $2,812 for 1 month at 9% annually. $21.09

35. The town of Glen Gary charges its residents an income tax of $\frac{1}{2}\%$ of their taxable income. Julio Gonzalez lives in Glen Gary and has a taxable income of $120,560. What is his income tax? $602.80, Lesson 2.4

36. Tom Ridley invested $10,000 in a certificate of deposit. He withdrew $1,000 before the end of the certificate's term. The penalty for early withdrawal was 1 month's interest at 6% annual percentage rate. What was the amount of the penalty? $5, Lesson 3.7

37. You have $500 on deposit in a one-year certificate of deposit that pays 6% annual interest compounded quarterly. What is the effective annual interest rate, to the nearest tenth percent? 6.1%, Lesson 3.6

38. Ann Quinland bought a set of golf clubs on the installment plan for $395. She paid $45 down and the balance in equal monthly installments of $25 each. How many months did it take Ann to pay for the set? 14 months, Lesson 4.4

Lesson 4.4 Installment Loans ■ **155**

GOALS

- Calculate finance charges on Rule of 78 loans
- Calculate early loan repayment amounts on Rule of 78 loans

Start Up

Eva Lewis borrowed $500 on a 6-month installment loan at 18% interest. At the end of the first month, she decided to repay the loan. Her bank told her that the amount needed to repay the loan was $512.86. Eva thought it should be $507.50. Who is right, Eva or the bank?

Math Skill Builder

Review these math skills and solve the exercises that follow.

1 **Rewrite** percentages as decimals.
Rewrite 84% as a decimal. 84% = 0.84

   1a. 52.9% 0.529   **1b.** 253% 2.53

   1c. 0.6% 0.006   **1d.** 7.76% 0.0776

2 **Subtract** dollar amounts.
Find the difference. $42,648.29 − $35,763.11 = $6,885.18

   2a. $25,754 − $22,904   **2b.** $169.29 − $75.98
       $2,850 $93.31

3 **Multiply** dollar amounts by whole numbers and decimals.
Find the product. $390.30 × 0.027 = $10.538, or $10.54

   3a. $6,572 × 3 $19,716   **3b.** $31,290 × 0.3 $9,387   **3c.** $145 × 0.074 $10.73

BUSINESS TIP

The rule of 78 method is considered unfair by some and is illegal to use in 17 states. In others, it can be used only for short-term loans, such as loans for less than 5 years. The rule of 78 is widely used in many states for personal and auto loans.

■ Earned and Unearned Finance Charges

DIFFERENCE IN REPAYMENT AMOUNTS In a simple interest installment loan, the monthly interest rate is applied to the unpaid balance of the loan. If you pay the loan off early, you simply pay the unpaid balance plus the interest on the unpaid balance up to the payoff date.

Many lenders calculate finance charges using the *Rule of 78*. The Rule of 78 gets its name from the fact that the sum of the numbers 1–12, the number of months in a one-year loan, is 78. For a loan of 12 months, Rule of 78 loans allocate 12/78 of the total finance charge to the first month, 11/78 to the second, and so on.

156 ■ Chapter 4 Loans and Credit Cards

DIFFERENT LEARNING STYLES At-Risk Learners

The instructions for calculating early loan repayments has been broken down into (1) finding earned and unearned finance charges and (2) finding the amount that will pay off a Rule of 78 loan early. This was done to make the topic easier for students. Students are first taught to find what part of the total finance charge has not been earned by the lender. Then students are taught how to use that information to find amount needed to repay the loan.

If you do not pay off the loan before it is due, the total finance charge will not change. But, if you repay the loan early, you will be charged more in finance charges in the early months than in a simple interest installment loan.

Suppose you have a $500, one-year, 18% loan with a total finance charge of $90. If you repay it at the end of one month, you will pay $13.85 in finance charges if the lender uses the Rule of 78. If the loan is a simple interest installment loan, you will pay only $7.50 in finance charges for that one month.

$$\$500 \times 0.18 \times \frac{12}{78} = \$13.85 \quad \text{one-month Rule of 78 finance charge}$$

$$\$500 \times 0.18 \times \frac{1}{12} = \$7.50 \quad \text{one-month simple interest charge}$$

To repay the Rule of 78 loan, you need $513.85. To repay the simple interest installment loan, you need $507.50.

EARNED AND UNEARNED FINANCE CHARGES The total finance charge for the Rule of 78 loan is $500 × 0.18, or $90. Of that amount, the first month's finance charge, $13.85, was *earned* by the lender because you borrowed the money for one month. The rest, or $76.15, of the finance charge is *unearned* because you paid back the loan early.

The unearned finance charge is called the *finance charge refund* by lenders. When lenders lend you money, they expect that the loan will last its full term. So, they expect to receive the full amount of the finance charge. If you repay the loan early, they consider that the unearned interest has been lost to them, and treat it as a refund.

To calculate the earned and unearned finance charges when a Rule of 78 loan is repaid early, use the finance charge refund schedule shown. This schedule shows the percent of the total finance charge that is *unearned* by the lender.

BUSINESS TIP

The finance charge refund schedule does not show how much the borrower will get back if a loan is paid early. It shows the amount of the total finance charge that has been lost to the lender because the loan was repaid early.

■ **Teach Goal 1 (cont.)**

Point out to students that if the Rule of 78 loan is for more or less than 12 months, the sum of the years used as the denominator must change. For a 3-month loan, the denominator is 6. For an 18-month loan, the denominator is 171.

	Finance Charge Refund Schedule for Early Repayment of Installment Loan							
	Percent of Finance Charges Refunded							
Elapsed Time of Loan in Months	**Original Term of Loan in Months**							
	3	**6**	**9**	**12**	**15**	**18**	**21**	**24**
1	50.00%	71.43%	80.00%	84.62%	87.50%	89.47%	90.91%	92.00%
2	16.67%	47.62%	62.22%	70.51%	75.83%	79.53%	82.25%	84.33%
3	0.00%	28.57%	46.67%	57.69%	65.00%	70.18%	74.03%	77.00%
4		14.29%	33.33%	46.15%	55.00%	61.40%	66.23%	70.00%
5		4.76%	22.22%	35.90%	45.83%	53.22%	58.87%	63.33%
6		0.00%	13.33%	26.92%	37.50%	45.61%	51.95%	57.00%
7			6.67%	19.23%	30.00%	38.60%	45.45%	51.00%
8			2.22%	12.82%	23.33%	32.16%	39.39%	45.33%
9			0.00%	7.69%	17.50%	26.32%	33.77%	40.00%
10				3.85%	12.50%	21.05%	28.57%	35.00%
11				1.28%	8.33%	16.37%	23.81%	30.33%
12				0.00%	5.00%	12.28%	19.48%	26.00%
15					0.00%	3.51%	9.09%	15.00%
18						0.00%	2.60%	7.00%
21							0.00%	2.00%

Lesson 4.5 Early Loan Repayments ■ **157**

COMMON ERRORS

Students are likely to forget to include current payment as part of the total remaining payments. If a 9 month loan is to be repaid early on the date that the 5th payment is due, the borrower must repay the total of 5th, 6th, 7th, 8th, and 9th payments less the unearned finance charge. Many students will multiply the payments by 4 (9 − 5 = 4) to find the amount remaining to be paid instead of 5 (9 − 4 = 5).

■ Apply Goal 1

Work through Example 1 at the board while students work it at their desks.

Assign Check Your Understanding problems A and B for completion in class. Roam about your classroom and check student work for errors and problems.

■ Teach Goal 2

The second part of the lesson shows students how to find the amount that must be paid when a Rule of 78 loan is repaid early.

Stress to students that when you repay a 12-month loan on the due date of the 6th payment, the remaining number of payments is 7 because only 5 payments have been made to date.

Have student teams search the web or other resources to determine if the state in which they live allows Rule of 78 loans or places restrictions on them. Have teams report their results to the class orally. They should identify the sources of the information they included in their report.

■ Apply Goal 2

Work through Example 2 at the board while students complete the example at their desks.

Assign Check Your Understanding problems C and D for class work. Check student work for difficulties by observing them at work.

EXAMPLE 1

Vera Goode had a $500, 12-month Rule of 78 loan. The total finance charge was $80. Vera repaid the loan on the day the third monthly payment was due. Find the amount of finance charge the lender earned and the amount that was unearned.

SOLUTION

Find the unearned finance charge refund percentage in the finance charge refund schedule and change it to a decimal.

$57.69\% = 0.5769$ finance charge refund decimal rate
(3 months of loan have elapsed)

Multiply the loan's total finance charge by the refund decimal rate.

$\$80 \times 0.5769 = \$46.152$, or $\$46.15$ unearned finance charge

Subtract the unearned finance charge from the total finance charge.

$\$80 - \$46.15 = \$33.85$ earned finance charge

■ CHECK YOUR UNDERSTANDING

A. Mario Mineto bought a large TV and paid for it with a 6-month Rule of 78 installment loan. The total finance charge for the loan was $130. He decided to repay the loan at the end of the third month. What was the amount of his earned and unearned finance charges? $37.14, $92.86

B. Emily Polinski repaid a 9-month, $2,000 Rule of 78 installment loan at the end of 6 months. The total finance charge for the loan was $225. How much were the lender's earned and unearned finance charges? $29.99, $195.01

■ Early Loan Repayments

To find the amount to repay a Rule of 78 loan early, find the total of the remaining payments. Subtract from that amount the unearned finance charge on the loan.

EXAMPLE 2

Sy Bauer has a 12-month, $3,600 Rule of 78 installment loan. The total finance charge for the loan is $420. The monthly installment payments are $335. Sy has made 5 monthly installment payments and wants to repay the balance when the sixth payment is due. How much will Sy owe?

SOLUTION

Multiply the monthly payment amount by the number of monthly payments yet to be made to find the total of the remaining payments.

$\$335 \times 7 = \$2,345$ total amount of remaining payments

Find the finance charge refund percentage and change it to a decimal.

$26.92\% = 0.2692$

Multiply to find the unearned finance charge.

$\$420 \times 0.2692 = \$113.06$ unearned finance charge

Subtract to find the amount needed to repay the loan.

$\$2,345 - \$113.06 = \$2,231.94$ amount needed to repay loan

158 ■ Chapter 4 Loans and Credit Cards

■ *CHECK YOUR UNDERSTANDING SOLUTIONS*

A. $130 \times 0.2857 = \$37.14$; $130 - \$37.14 = \$92.86$ **B.** $225 \times 0.1333 = \$29.99$; $225 - \$29.99 = \$195.01$

Notice that 7 payments were remaining. Sy had only made 5 payments so far. Instead of making the sixth payment, he paid off the loan. However, the bank had lent him the money for a full 6 months. So, he owed finance charges on all 6 months.

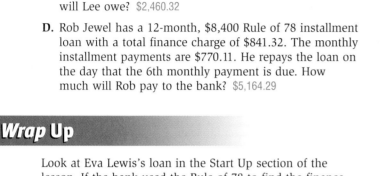

■ **CHECK YOUR UNDERSTANDING**

C. Lee Ivor repays a 9-month, $5,300 Rule of 78 installment loan on the day that the 6th monthly payment is due. The total finance charge for the loan is $336.70. The monthly installment payments are $626.30. How much will Lee owe? $2,460.32

D. Rob Jewel has a 12-month, $8,400 Rule of 78 installment loan with a total finance charge of $841.32. The monthly installment payments are $770.11. He repays the loan on the day that the 6th monthly payment is due. How much will Rob pay to the bank? $5,164.29

Wrap Up

Look at Eva Lewis's loan in the Start Up section of the lesson. If the bank used the Rule of 78 to find the finance charge on the loan, she would need $512.86 to repay it. The principal plus finance charges at 18% for the full term of the loan are $545. The finance charge refund rate is 0.7143, and the unearned finance charge is $32.14. The finance charge for the first month is $45 − $32.14 = $12.86. A simple interest installment loan would have charged $7.50 interest for one month.

Algebra Connection

Suppose you had a 12-month Rule of 78 installment loan with a finance charge of $300. You want to pay off the loan at the end of 3 months. Instead of the Refund Schedule, you can use the following formula to find the refund decimal.

$$\frac{U(U + 1)}{T(T + 1)} = \text{Rule of 78 refund decimal}$$

U = The unelapsed term of the loan. In a 12-month loan paid off in 3 months, it is 9 months.

T = The term of the loan. In the example loan, it is 12 months.

F = The finance charge. In the example loan, it is $300.

Substitute the values from the example loan into the formula.

$$\frac{9(9+1)}{12(12+1)} = 0.576923, \text{ or } 0.5769 \quad \text{Round to the nearest ten thousandth.}$$

Compare the decimal found by the formula to the one in the Refund Schedule.

Lesson 4.5 Early Loan Repayments ■ **159**

■ **CHECK YOUR UNDERSTANDING SOLUTIONS**

C. $626.30 × 4 = $2,505.20;
$336.70 × 0.1333 = $44.88;
$2,505.20 − $44.88 = $2,460.32

D. $770.11 × 7 = $5,390.77;
$841.32 × 0.2692 = $226.48;
$5,390.77 − $226.48 = $5,164.29

Assign

Assignment: Exercises 1–19.
Start with the basic arithmetic problems at the beginning of the exercises to insure that students understand the underlying arithmetic in the exercises.

Assess

Ask students to explain the Rule of 78 and why it was named that. **The Rule of 78 gets its name from the fact that the sum of the numbers 1–12 is 78. It is a method of calculating finance charges where 12/78 of the finance charge is allocated to the first month, 11/78 to the second month, and so on.**

Reteach

STUDENT WORKBOOK If students need help with finding unearned interest for Rule of 78 loans, complete Exercise 1 in the workbook with them. Then have them complete Exercise 2–7.

To help students with finding the payoff amount for a Rule of 78 loan paid off early, do Exercise 8 in the workbook with them. Then have them do Exercise 9.

Enrich

Assign Exercise 19 for in-class discussion. Students should recognize that lenders get greater amounts of interest using Rule of 78 loans when they are repaid early than when they use simple interest installment loans.

Close

Call on students to describe the steps to find (a) unearned interest and (b) the payoff amount for a Rule of 78 loan repaid early. Each student called upon should provide one step only.

Rewrite as a decimal.

1. 245.6%.   2.456

2. 0.35%.   0.0035

Perform the indicated operation.

3. $4,208 − $3,489 $719

4. $63,418.36 − 48,897.57 $14,520.79

5. $189.87 × 12 $2,278.44

6. $45.63 × 3.148 $143.64

7. Rachel Carr has a 9-month, Rule of 78 installment loan. The total finance charge for the loan is $450. She decides to repay the loan on the day that the third monthly payment is due. What is the unearned finance charge? $210.02

8. Levi Stein's 24-month, Rule of 78 installment loan has a total finance charge of $675. He decides to repay the loan on the day that the twelth payment is due. How much is the unearned finance charge? $175.50

Terry O'Doole has an 18-month installment loan for $1,700 at 12% annual interest. Interest is computed using the Rule of 78. Terry decides to pay back the loan at the end of one month.

9. What is the total finance charge on the loan? $306

10. What is the unearned finance charge? $273.78

11. What is needed to repay the loan? $1,732.22

BEST BUY Lucy Smola can borrow $2,500 at 18% for 12 months from lender A who uses the Rule of 78. She can also borrow $2,500 at 18% from a lender B, who uses the simple interest method.

12. Which loan has the largest finance charge?   both have $450

13. Which loan has the highest finance charge for the first month and by how much?   A, $31.73

14. How much would it cost Lucy to pay back the loan from lender B at the end of the first month? $2,537.50

15. **CRITICAL THINKING**   Why do you think Rule of 78 loans are so widely used for short-term loans? Why are Rule of 78 loans illegal in some states? Is the refund shown in the Refund Schedule really a refund?   See Enrich section for answer.

MIXED REVIEW

16. Round 29,458 to the nearest hundred.   29,500

17. Estimate the product of $34.56 × 24.8. $750

18. What is the average of $35.12, $36.20, $32.98, and $33.56? $34.47

19. The cash price of a large color TV was $2,400. Dee Hart bought it for $240 down and 12 monthly payments of $196. By what percent did the installment price exceed the cash price?   8%, Lesson 1.2

SELECTED SOLUTIONS

7. $450 × 0.4667 = $210.02
9. 18 ÷ 12 = 1.5; $1,700 × 0.12 × 1.5 = $306
10. $306 × 0.8947 = $273.78

11. $1,700 + $306 = $2,006;
$2,006 − $273.78 = $1,732.22

4.6 Annual Percentage Rates

GOAL

- Calculate the APR on a loan

Start Up

Have students read the Start Up. Call on students to answer the Start Up problem and discuss their answers. The problem refers to lenders quoting the annual interest rate on original principal of installment loans. Since the full principal is borrowed for only one month, the simple interest rate is not an accurate measure of the rate of interest paid.

Start Up

An auto dealer gives you a verbal quote for an interest rate on an installment loan for a car that you think is just terrific. Your friend thinks you are probably paying a higher interest rate. Who is probably right, you or your friend?

Math Skill Builder

Review these math skills and solve the exercises that follow.

1. **Round** dollar amounts to the nearest cent.
   Round $0.2978 to the nearest cent. $0.2978 = $0.30

   1a. $3.985 $3.99   **1b.** $2.0793 $2.08   **1c.** $8.0049 $8   **1d.** $0.455 $0.46

2. **Multiply** dollar amounts by 10, 100, and 1,000.
   Find the product. $489.43 × 100 = $48,943

   2a. $189 × 100 $18,900   **2b.** $208.97 × 1,000 $208,970   **2c.** $790.72 × 10 $7,907.20

3. **Divide** dollar amounts by dollar amounts to the nearest thousandth.
   Find the quotient to the nearest thousandth. $500 ÷ $3,000 = 0.1666, or 0.167

   3a. $420 ÷ $1,600 0.263   **3b.** $1,241 ÷ $8,560 0.145   **3c.** $2,445 ÷ $16,308 0.15

Math Skill Builder

Assign all exercises in the Math Skill Builder 1–3 to prepare students for the math used in the lesson.

Teach Goal 1

Stress that since the principal is not being borrowed for the full term of the loan, an annual interest rate applied to the original principal will not generate the true interest paid. The true interest rate (APR) is usually higher.

More than likely a computer program used by a lender will calculate the APR on an installment loan. However, students can also find the APR using the table in the lesson.

You might ask an area lender to provide your class with copies of an APR table that includes more time periods and APR rates than those shown in the table in the lesson.

Note that there is another APR table in Lesson 4-6 of the workbook.

Annual Percentage Rate (APR)

To find the rate of interest on a single-payment loan for one year, you divide the interest paid in a year by the principal. Finding the rate of finance charges on an installment loan is not as easy. The cost of borrowing money may include more than interest. It may also include service charges. Also, since you make payments on the loan each month, you are not borrowing the whole principal for the full time of the loan.

So the *Truth in Lending Act* makes the lender tell the borrower what annual rate is charged on the loan. The rate is called the annual percentage rate (APR). It is usually higher than the interest rate of your loan. The amount you are actually borrowing is called the *amount financed*. This might be the sale price of a car less the down payment.

The easiest way to find the annual percentage rate is to use tables like the ones shown on the next page. To use the tables, you need to know the number of monthly payments for the loan and the finance charge per $100 of the amount financed.

Lesson 4.6 Annual Percentage Rates ■ 161

DIFFERENT LEARNING STYLES Gifted Learners

Have student teams investigate the Truth in Lending Act and identify its major features. Then have them examine an installment loan contract obtained from an area lender to find the parts of the contract that reflect the features of the Act.

■ **Apply Goal 1**

Work through Example 1 with students completing the math at their desks.

Assign Check Your Understanding problems A and B to do in class. Roam the classroom and check student work for errors and problems.

■ **ONGOING ASSESSMENT**
With the textbook closed, call on students to spell out the steps for finding the APR on an installment loan. Ask each student called to name only one step.

To find the *finance charge per $100* of the amount financed, divide the finance charge by the amount financed. Then multiply the quotient by 100.

$$\text{Finance Charge per \$100 of Amount Financed} = \frac{\text{Finance Charge}}{\text{Amount Financed}} \times \$100$$

After you have found the finance charge per $100, you can use the tables to find the annual percentage rate

Number of Payments	Annual Percentage Rate										
	$12\frac{3}{4}$%	13%	$13\frac{1}{4}$%	$13\frac{1}{2}$%	$13\frac{3}{4}$%	14%	$14\frac{1}{4}$%	$14\frac{1}{2}$%	$14\frac{3}{4}$%	15%	$15\frac{1}{4}$%
	Finanace Charge per $100 of Amount Financed										
3	2.13	2.17	2.22	2.26	2.30	2.34	2.38	2.43	2.47	2.51	2.55
6	3.75	3.83	3.90	3.97	4.05	4.12	4.20	4.27	4.35	4.42	4.49
9	5.39	5.49	5.60	5.71	5.82	5.92	6.03	6.14	6.25	6.35	6.46
12	7.04	7.18	7.32	7.46	7.60	7.74	7.89	8.03	8.17	8.31	8.45
15	8.71	8.88	9.06	9.23	9.41	9.59	9.76	9.94	10.11	10.29	10.47

Number of Payments	Annual Percentage Rate										
	$15\frac{1}{2}$%	$15\frac{3}{4}$%	16%	$16\frac{1}{4}$%	$16\frac{1}{2}$%	$16\frac{3}{4}$%	17%	$17\frac{1}{4}$%	$17\frac{1}{2}$%	$17\frac{3}{4}$%	18%
	Finanace Charge per $100 of Amount Financed										
6	4.57	4.64	4.72	4.79	4.87	4.94	5.02	5.09	5.17	5.24	5.32
12	8.59	8.74	8.88	9.02	9.16	9.30	9.45	9.59	9.73	9.87	10.02

Number of Payments	Annual Percentage Rate										
	$18\frac{1}{4}$%	$18\frac{1}{2}$%	$18\frac{3}{4}$%	19%	$19\frac{1}{4}$%	$19\frac{1}{2}$%	$19\frac{3}{4}$%	20%	$20\frac{1}{4}$%	$20\frac{1}{2}$%	$20\frac{3}{4}$%
	Finanace Charge per $100 of Amount Financed										
6	5.39	5.46	5.54	5.61	5.69	5.76	5.84	5.91	5.99	6.06	6.14
12	10.16	10.30	10.44	10.59	10.73	10.87	11.02	11.16	11.31	11.45	11.59

EXAMPLE 1

The finance charge for a 6-month, $1,200 installment loan is $72. Find the annual percentage rate on the loan.

SOLUTION
Divide the finance charge by the amount financed.

$72 ÷ $1,200 = 0.06

0.06 × $100 = $6   Multiply the result by $100.

The finance charge per $100 of amount financed is $6.

Use the Annual Percentage Rate Tables. Read across the rows for 6 payments until you come to the amount closest to $6. Since $5.99 is the closest amount, use the rate, $20\frac{1}{4}$%.

The annual percentage rate is $20\frac{1}{4}$%.

> **MATH TIP**
> When necessary, round the finance charge to the nearest cent.

■ **CHECK YOUR UNDERSTANDING**

A. Melina Cavaletti borrowed $800 on a loan with a finance charge of $78. Find the finance charge per $100 of the amount financed. $9.75

B. Chris Mathers borrowed $250 on a 12-month loan that had a finance charge of $20. Find the finance charge per $100 of the amount financed and the annual percentage rate. $8, $14\frac{1}{2}$%

■ *CHECK YOUR UNDERSTANDING SOLUTIONS*

A. $78 ÷ $800 = 0.0975; 0.0975 × $100 = $9.75

B. $20 ÷ $250 = $0.08; $0.08 × $100 = $8; $8 is closest to $8.03 on 12 payment line of table; $14\frac{1}{2}$%

The auto dealer is probably quoting you an annual interest rate based on the original amount you financed. Since you are paying back part of the amount financed each month, your interest rate is higher. You need to find the annual percentage rate on the car loan and compare that with the quote from the auto dealer.

Algebra Connection

An *approximate* annual percentage rate can be calculated for monthly level-payment loans without the use of tables using this formula:

$$APR = \frac{24F}{P(N + 1)}$$

F = Finance charge amount

P = Original principal

N = Number of payments per year

Revisit this Algebra Connection after completing the exercises. Enter the information from Exercise 19, find the APR to the nearest tenth percent, and compare your results to the answer to Exercise 19 you got using the table. Which gave a higher percent, the table or the formula? What was the amount of the difference? Would you rely on the formula to find the APR? Table = 13.25%; Formula = 16.8%, Formula was higher by 3.55%, No; Formula result is too different

EXERCISES

Round to the nearest cent.
1. $4.5627 $4.56
2. $105.3978 $105.40

Find the product.
3. $98,208 × 100 $9,820,800
4. $389.74 × 1,000 $389,740
5. $1,078.43 × 10 $10,784.30
6. $38.95 × 100 $3,895

Find the quotient to the nearest thousandth.
7. $186 ÷ $828 0.225
8. $482 ÷ $4,298.18 0.112

9. Find the finance charge per $100 on a loan of $3,200 with a finance charge of $480. $15

10. Find the finance charge per $100 on a loan of $12,600 with a finance charge of $1,638. $13

Find the annual percentage rate for the following loans.
11. Finance charge of $5.75 per $100 for 9 payments. $13\frac{1}{2}$%

12. Finance charge of $2.50 per $100 for 3 payments. 15%

13. Finance charge of $8.85 per $100 for 15 payments. 13%

14. **CRITICAL THINKING** What specific pieces of information should you look for in any loan contract? Why is this information important? See Enrich section on the next page of Teacher's Edition for a detailed answer.

Lesson 4.6 Annual Percentage Rates ■ **163**

Wrap Up

Review the Start Up. Have students discuss why an annual interest rate applied to the original interest on an installment loan is not an accurate measure of the true rate of interest on the loan.

Algebra Connection

Stress that the formula given for finding the APR is approximate, as the results of the example illustrate. Use of the table provides an accurate APR.

Assign

Assignment: Exercises 1–13, 15–36. Start with the basic arithmetic exercises to insure that students understand the underlying arithmetic in the exercises. Exercises 9–13 and 15–21 develop student skill with finance charges per $100 of the amount financed and finding the APR.

Assess

Check student answers to the exercises by calling on them in class, collecting and grading selected problems, or by observing student work at their desks.

Ask students to define the bolded and italicized terms in the lesson and use them in sentences.

SELECTED SOLUTIONS

9. $480 ÷ $3,200 = 0.15; 0.15 × $100 = $15
11. $5.75 is closest to $5.71 on 9 payment line of table; $13\frac{1}{2}$%
15. $232 × 12 = $2,784; $2,784 − $2,600 = $184;

16. $184 ÷ $2,600 = 0.07076; 0.07076 × $100 = $7.076, or $7.08
17. $7.08 is closest to $7.04 on 12 payment line of table; $12\frac{3}{4}$%

Reteach

STUDENT WORKBOOK Use Exercise 1 in the workbook to redemonstrate how to find the finance charge per $100 of the amount financed. Then assign Exercise 2a–2c for in class work.

Use Exercises 2d to redemonstrate how to use the APR table to find the APR. Then assign Exercises 3–5 for in class work.

Enrich

Assign Exercise 14 and discuss the student responses. These should include the amount of the loan, the total of the finance charges, a breakdown of the finance charges to disclose fees other than interest, the APR, the monthly payment, the term of the loan, the total of the payments, the amount of any down payment, when payments start, any grace period for late payments, any special fees, such as late payment fees, collection fees, application fees, etc.; the collateral, if any, used to secure the loan.

Close

Review Exercises 22–26 and discuss the answers and steps to their solution with students.

You borrow $2,600 and repay the loan in 12 monthly installments of $232.

15. What was the finance charge on your loan? $184

16. What was the finance charge per $100 of the amount financed? $7.08

17. What was the annual percentage rate? $12\frac{3}{4}\%$

Olga Pozinski borrowed $1,300 and repaid it in 12 monthly payments of $116.

18. What was the finance charge on the loan? $92

19. What was the finance charge per $100 of amount financed? $7.08

20. What was the annual percentage rate? $12\frac{3}{4}\%$

21. Charles repaid a loan of $1,600 in 15 monthly installments of $116.40 each. Find the APR on his loan. $13\frac{1}{4}\%$

INTEGRATING YOUR KNOWLEDGE Violeta Ramos borrowed $4,000 and agreed to repay the loan in 12 equal monthly payments. To find the total finance charge, the lender calculated simple interest of 8% on the $4,000.

22. What is the simple interest on $4,000 for 1 year at 8%? $320

23. Find the total amount Violeta will pay over the life of the loan. $4,320

24. How much will Violeta's monthly payments be? $360

25. What is the finance charge per $100 of amount financed? $9

26. What is the annual percentage rate? $16\frac{1}{4}\%$

MIXED REVIEW

27. $788 × 100 = $78,800

28. $9.75 × 1,000 = $9,750

29. $10.78 × 10 = $107.80

30. $3.97 × 100 = $397

31. Write $\frac{1}{4}$ as a ratio. 1:4

32. Rewrite $12\frac{5}{8}$ as a percent. 1,262.5%

33. On January 31, Edith Nagel's bank statement balance was $516.24. Her check register showed that a deposit for $382.10 was outstanding. The following checks were also outstanding: #108, $45.93; #109, $108.12; #111, $6.87. What was the corrected bank statement balance? $737.42, Lesson 3.5

34. Rhonda Peterson pays a city tax of 1.5% on her taxable income. She also pays a state tax of 3.25% on her taxable income. What total city and state income taxes does she pay if her taxable income is $38,109? $1,810.18, Lesson 2.4

35. Hector Vadillo is a waiter and had these total food and beverage checks for the week: Tues., $245.19; Wed., $299.74; Thurs., $349.73; Fri., $612.50; Sat., $575.33. If Hector received an average of 15% for tips during the week, how much money did he receive in tips? $312.37, Lesson 1.5

36. Find the exact interest on $1,050 at 14% for 126 days. $50.75, Lesson 4.1

CONNECTION TO ECONOMICS

Invite a consumer economics teacher, a bank loan officer, or a credit union loan officer to address the class on the impact of the Truth in Lending Act and the percentage rate (APR) on businesses and consumers.

4.7 Credit Card Costs

GOALS

- Identify important information found on credit card statements
- Verify transactions on credit card statements
- Calculate the cost of using a credit card

Start Up

When Robert receives his credit card statement each month, he simply mails a check for his payment. He decided the time it takes to verify the charges was not worth it. His feeling is that a computer prints out the statement so there will be no errors. What are the dangers in using a credit card as Robert does?

Math Skill Builder

Review these math skills and solve the exercises that follow.

1 **Divide** money amounts and decimals by whole numbers.
Find the quotients. $366 \div 30 = \$12.20$ $18.25 \div 365 = 0.05$

1a. $480 \div 31$ 15.48 **1b.** $24 \div 12$ 2 **1c.** $745 \div 30$ 24.83

2 **Multiply** money amounts by whole numbers and decimals.
Find the product. $500 \times 25 \times 0.00056 = \$7$

2a. $150 \times 20 \times 0.000872$ 2.62 **2b.** $868 \times 30 \times 0.00096$ 25

3 **Add** and **subtract** money amounts.
Find the sum or difference. $\$3.45 + \$25 = \$28.45$; $\$3,298 - \$725 = \$2,573$

3a. $\$52.19 + \$78.42 + \$1.89$ 132.50 **3b.** $\$189 + \$92.09 + \$3.87$ 284.96

3c. $\$4,098.34 - \$871.36$ $3,226.98$ **3d.** $\$1,830.43 - \$792.19$ $1,038.24$

4 **Rewrite** percents as decimals.
Rewrite 45.6% as a decimal. 0.456

4a. 89.08% 0.8908 **4b.** 0.0736% 0.000736 **4c.** 0.0287% 0.000287

■ Information on a Credit Card Statement

Midori Masami's credit card company sent her the statement shown on the next page. Find each italicized word below on the statement:

Transactions are events that need to be recorded on the statement. These events include *purchases*, *payments* made, and any *fees* Midori has been charged or *credits* made to her account.

Lesson 4.7 Credit Cards Costs ■ 165

Start Up

Have students read the Start Up. Encourage students to provide incidents related to the Start Up question from family and friends.

Math Skill Builder

Assign all exercises in the Math Skill Builder 1–4 to prepare students for the basic math processes used in the lesson.

■ Teach Goal 1

Point out that credit cards are convenient to use and accepted in a wide variety of locations. They may be more easily accepted than personal checks. There are also advantages of being able to pay a bill without cash in an emergency, being able to take advantage of sales, not having to carry large amounts of cash, and having written records of transactions for tax purposes.

However, stress that there is also the danger of overspending your budget by using your card irresponsibly.

Explain that there are many types of credit cards, including bank cards, such as MasterCard and Visa; travel and entertainment cards, such as American Express and Diners Club; oil company cards to pay for fuel and automobile repairs; and department and chain store cards.

DIFFERENT LEARNING STYLES Kinesthetic Learners

Call on students to define or explain the italicized and bolded words in the lesson. As students listen to the definition or explanation, have them write the words 3 times on a sheet of paper to help them remember the word and how it is spelled.

Emphasize to students that they will be likely to receive many offers from credit card companies in the mail. While it is tempting to accept these offers, studies show that the more cards a person has the more consumer debt he or she has on the cards.

Caution students that credit card offers received in the mail and not accepted should be torn up or shredded to avoid someone using the offer materials to start a card in your name.

Notice that Midori purchased some clothes on 2/1 from Gale's Fashions. While the sale was made on 2/1, the card company did not record, or *post* the sale to the statement until 2/3.

The statement shows that the *previous balance* from Midori's last statement was $316.15. On 2/28, the card company received Midori's check for the previous balance. Although she paid it in full, her check was received after the due date, February 22, and she was charged a $25 *late fee*. Many card companies allow a cushion of 3-5 days before charging a late fee.

The card company allows Midori to carry a maximum balance of $5,000. If she spends more than that *credit limit*, the company will charge her an *over-the-limit fee*.

OneBank Card

Acct. No. 1200 1200 0000 1200
Statement Closing Date: 02/28/--
Credit Limit: $5,000.00

For customer service call: 1-800-555-5600
Cash Advance Limit: $1,500.00
Payment Must Be Received By: 03/25/--

Trans-action Date	Post Date	Reference	Transaction Description		Payments & Credits	Loans, Fees, & Purchases
2/1	2/3	T970R194	Gale's Fashions	Peoria, IL		139.89
2/5	2/7	297B9875	Superfast Gas	Peoria, IL		15.68
2/10	2/12	N978T125	Pasta Garden Restaurant	Peoria, IL		18.25
2/15	2/16	M5980922	Gale's Fashions-Return	Peoria, IL	15.99	
2/17	2/18	9780H142	Boulevard Music Store	Springfield, IL		11.31
2/20	2/20	91089478	Annual membership fee			25.00
2/28	2/28	41978573	Payment Thank You		316.15	
2/28	2/28	41827753	Late fee			25.00

Previous Balance	Purchases & Fees	Payments & Credits	Finance Charge	New Balance	Minimum Payment Due On Due Date	APR 18.9% Monthly Periodic Rate 1.575%
316.15	235.13	332.14	0.00	219.14	6.57	

On 2/15, a *credit* occurred when Midori *returned* part of the clothes she had bought from Gale's Fashions. Credits, like payments, are amounts that are subtracted from Midori's card balance.

The statement shows that Midori can borrow up to $1,500 from the company on a *cash advance*. Midori did not take any cash advances during February.

TEACHING STRATEGIES Cooperative Learning

Midori paid no *finance charges* on the previous month's balance. That's because she paid her balance in full. You are usually given a *grace period* of 25 days from the *statement closing date* to pay your credit card balance in full.

The statement closing date is the last date on which transactions are posted to the statement. That date is 2/28 for Midori.

OneBank's finance charge rate is shown in the bottom right corner of the statement. The *annual percentage rate* is 18.9%. The *monthly periodic rate* is the annual percentage rate divided by 12, or 1.575%.

Midori's *new balance* is $219.14. If she had had an unpaid balance from the previous month, it would have been added to the new balance. The *minimum payment due* that Midori must make to the card company is $6.57. Since she doesn't want to pay a finance charge, she plans to pay the new balance in full by the due date, 3/25.

EXAMPLE 1

Midori Masami received the statement shown on the previous page. What is her new balance? How much of the new balance must she repay by the due date? What is the highest balance Midori is permitted to have?

SOLUTION

Midori's new balance is $219.14. She must make a minimum payment of $6.57. The highest balance Midori may have is $5,000.

■ **CHECK YOUR UNDERSTANDING**

A. Look at Midori's statement. What is the due date for paying the balance? What was the amount of her last payment? 3/25, $316.15

B. Look at Midori's statement. What is the periodic interest rate she will pay on any unpaid balance? What is the total amount of her new purchases and fees for the month? 1.575%, $235.13

■ Verify Transactions

Each month Midori saves her credit card sales slips, like the one shown at the right. When she receives her credit card statement, she compares the sales slips with the statement transactions. She looks for purchases that are listed but were not made by her. These are called *unauthorized* purchases. She also checks to see if the sales slip amounts agree with the amounts listed on the statement.

Unauthorized purchases may occur when the credit card company mistakenly posts someone else's sales slips to her statement. Unauthorized purchases may also happen if someone has used her credit card illegally.

Midori also checks that her payments and any purchase returns are listed. Finally, she checks to make sure that there are no unauthorized fees listed.

If Midori finds errors in amounts or unauthorized purchases or fees, she will contact her credit card company immediately, before she sends any payment.

> **BUSINESS TIP**
>
> If your credit card is used by someone else illegally, you can be held responsible for up to $50 per card. If your card is lost or stolen and you notify the card company before any purchases are made, you are not liable for any unauthorized purchases.

> Sales Receipt
>
> Gale's Fashions, Inc.
> 2678 Furth St., Peoria, IL 61612
> (309) 555-2525
> THANK YOU
>
> MERCHANT ID: 346184688345854
> One Bank Card Sale/Swiped
> Acct: ***********1200 Exp: 10/12
> **Midori Masami**
>
> **Amount $ 139.89**
>
> X *Midori Masami*
> _____
>   Midori Masami
>
> Date: 02/01/-- Day: WED Time: 14:36
> Authorized ticket: 564638
>
> TOP COPY-MERCHANT
> BOTTOM COPY-CUSTOMER

Lesson 4.7 Credit Card Costs ■ **167**

■ **Apply Goal 1**

Work through Example 1 with students completing the math at their desks.

Have students complete Check Your Understanding problems A and B in class. Roam the classroom and check student work for errors and problems.

■ **ONGOING ASSESSMENT**
Make a transparency of a recent credit card statement, blocking out the account number and other identifying information about the cardholder. Then, with the textbook closed, have students find the items identified in the lesson on the statement.

■ **Teach Goal 2**

Stress to students that errors can often occur on credit card statements. Common errors are that the amount posted differs from the sales slip and that posted transactions were not authorized transactions.

Show students how to correct errors in posted amounts on statements: subtract the wrong amount and add the correct amount. This procedure avoids errors that occur when students try to find the difference and whether they should subtract or add the difference to the balance.

■ **Apply Goal 2**

Work through Example 2 with students completing the math at their desks.

Have students do Check Your Understanding problems C and D in class. Check student work at their desks for errors or problems.

■ **Teach Goal 3**

Point out to students that card companies, in an effort to get more cardholders, often waive certain fees for an initial period. To encourage you to switch from another card to theirs, card companies often waive the balance transfer fee when you start the card.

Finance charges are provided in this lesson. In the next lesson, students will learn to calculate the finance charges.

■ **Apply Goal 3**

Work through Example 3 with students completing the math at their desks.

Have students do Check Your Understanding problems E and F in class. Check student work at their desks for errors or problems.

EXAMPLE 2

Midori compared her sales slips with the statement transactions. She found sales slips for 2/1, 2/5, 2/10, and 2/15 and noted that the amounts were correct. She didn't find a sales slip for the 2/17 transaction and knew she did not buy anything in Springfield during February. The 2/28 payment listed agreed with her checkbook register and she knew that her check was sent late. She also verified that her membership fee was due. What is Midori's correct new balance?

SOLUTION

Subtract the unauthorized purchase from the new balance on the statement.

$219.14 − $11.31 = $207.83   corrected new balance

■ **CHECK YOUR UNDERSTANDING**

C. When Vondel Bradshaw checked his credit card statement, he found that a sales slip dated 3/2 for $12.49 was posted as $12.99. He also found that a purchase for $56.29 dated 3/19 was unauthorized. If the new balance on the statement was $491.23, what is the correct new balance? $434.44

D. Sonja Erickson checked her credit card statement and found a sales slip for $48.99 that was unauthorized. She also found that a sales slip for $17.89 had been listed as $18.79. If the new balance shown on her statement was $208.66, what is her correct new balance? $158.77

■ Cost of Credit Card Use

The finance charges and fees you pay on your credit card can add up. You should calculate the total cost of your credit card to see if using one is of value to you and to compare the cost of your current card to other cards.

EXAMPLE 3

Danny O'Hare switched from the Clarion credit card to the First Bank credit card in April. When he did, he paid an annual membership fee of $50. He also paid a balance transfer fee of 2% of his old card's $420 balance. During the next 12 months, he paid an average monthly finance charge of $33.80 on his unpaid balance. What was Danny's total cost for using his credit card for the year?

SOLUTION

Multiply the monthly finance charge by 12 months.

$12 \times \$33.80 = \$405.60$ total finance charge for year

Multiply the Clarion card balance by the balance transfer fee rate.

$\$420 \times 0.02 = \$8.40$ balance transfer fee

Add the total finance charge, balance transfer fee, and membership fee.

$\$405.60 + \$8.40 + \$50 = \$464$ total cost of credit card for year

> **BUSINESS TIP**
>
> Stores are charged a fee by the credit card company for accepting credit card purchases. The fee may range between 1.5%–6% of the sale. The store may also be charged a fee for every credit card transaction.

168 ■ **Chapter 4** Loans and Credit Cards

■ **CHECK YOUR UNDERSTANDING SOLUTIONS**

C. $491.23 − $12.99 + $12.49 − $56.29 = $434.44   **D.** $208.66 − $48.99 + $17.89 − $18.79 = $158.77

E. Lili Favre opened a SkyMail credit card in January. She paid a membership fee of $45 and a balance transfer fee of $29 when she moved the balance of her old card to her SkyMail card. During the year, she paid these finance charges: Jan., $2.68; Feb., $7.28; June, $9.22; Oct., $3.98. What was the total annual cost of the card to Lili? $97.16

F. Derwood Kant's credit card statement for May showed a membership fee of $25, a late fee of $29, a finance charge of $3.15, and an over-the-limit fee of $16. What was the total cost of the card to Derwood in May? $73.15

Wrap Up

Look at the Start Up question at the beginning of this lesson. As you have seen by following Midori's verification process, Robert may be paying for charges he did not make or fees he should not have to pay. Even though a computer does print the statements, unauthorized use of a credit card does occur. Robert should always check his statements.

WORKPLACE WINDOW

CREDIT CARD AUTHORIZERS review digital transactions from retailers and return an approval code that allows a retail store to allow you to purchase an item using a credit card. You have probably noticed how a cashier will swipe a credit card, then wait for a receipt to print that has an authorization code printed on it.

1. What other job titles may a credit card authorizer have?

2. What skills are necessary for a credit card authorizer?

3. What is the job outlook for credit card authorizers?

EXERCISES

Perform the indicated operation.

1. $660 ÷ 26
$25.38

2. $38.41 + $93.26 + $9.52
$141.19

3. $252 + $63.14 + $6.62
$321.76

4. 48 ÷ 8
6

5. $478 × 30 × 0.000628
$9.01

6. $350 × 15 × 0.000491
$2.58

7. $1,060 ÷ 20
$53

8. $2,617.84 − $491.53
$2,126.31

9. $3,205.33 − $1,493.59
$1,711.74

Rewrite as a decimal.

10. 9.17% 0.0917

11. 0.0316% 0.000316

12. Lannie Ickerson checked her credit card statement and found a sales slip for $27.79 that was unauthorized. She also found that a sales slip for $11.29 had been listed as $12.19. If the new balance shown on her statement was $107.09, what is her correct new balance? $78.40

Lesson 4.7 Credit Card Costs ■ **169**

Wrap Up

Review the Start Up. Discuss the measures that credit card companies take to protect card users against errors and unauthorized use such as a $50 liability limit, 800 number to report errors or unauthorized use, and fraud detection programs that review your transactions for anomalies.

WORKPLACE WINDOW

Warn students that they should not let credit cards out of their sight. Thieves at restaurants and other stores can use small, hand held card readers to get their credit card data. They then use that data to charge purchases against your card.

Assign

Assignment: Exercises 1–22, 24–32. Don't overlook the basic math problems at the beginning of the exercises. These serve as an informal test to see if students are ready for the rest of the exercises.

■ *CHECK YOUR UNDERSTANDING SOLUTIONS*

E. $45 + $29 + $2.68 + $7.28 + $9.22 + $3.98 = $97.16

F. $25 + $29 + $3.15 + $16 = $73.15

Assess

Check student answers to the
exercises by calling on them in
class, collecting and grading
selected problems, or by observing
student work at their desks.

Reteach

STUDENT WORKBOOK Use
Exercise 3 in the workbook to
demonstrate to students how to
verify a credit card statement and
find the correct balance. Then have
them complete Exercises 4–6 during class so you can be available
for help.

Use Exercise 7 in the workbook to
demonstrate how to find the cost
of using a credit card. Then have
them complete Exercises 8–10
during class.

13. John Rawlings credit card statement for June 30 showed a previous balance of $248.67 and new purchases of $59.89 on 6/10, $15 on 6/15, $28.97 on 6/17, and a new balance of $352.53 for the month. John found that the slip dated 6/10 was for $58.99 and that there was no slip dated 6/17. He was certain this purchase was unauthorized by him. What is John's correct new balance? $322.66

Use the credit card statement for Ana Guzman to answer Exercises 14–16.

UniBank Card

Acct. No. 0200 0200 0000 0200
Statement Closing Date: 11/30/--
Credit Limit: $3,500

Ana Guzman
123 Presidents Place
El Paso, Tx 79915

Trans-action Date	Post Date	Reference	Transaction Description		Payments & Credits	Loans, Fees, & Purchases
11/3	11/4	592k9781	Crestwood Gym	El Paso, TX		49.99
11/7	11/9	297B9875	Broadway Videos	El Paso, TX		12.79
11/10	11/12	N978T125	The Corner Gas Station	El Paso, TX		24.59
11/17	11/18	M5980922	Regal Department Store-Return	El Paso, TX	38.29	
11/21	11/23	91089478	Annual membership fee			45.00
11/24	11/24	41978573	Payment Thank You		100.00	
11/30	11/30	41827753	Balance from Transcredit Card			267.88
11/30	11/30	41827756	Balance transfer fee			29.00

For customer service call: 1-800-555-7800
Cash Advance Limit: $1,000.00
Payment Must Be Received By: 12/25/--

Previous Balance	Purchases & Fees	Payments & Credits	Finance Charge	New Balance	Minimum Payment Due On Due Date	APR 18.0% Monthly Periodic Rate 1.5%
249.25	429.25	138.29	3.74	543.95	10.88	

14. By what date must she make the minimum payment? What was the date and amount of her last payment? What is her credit limit? 12/25, 11/24, $100, $3,500

15. How much finance charge does she owe? How much money did she transfer from the Transcredit card to her UniBank card? What fee did she pay for the balance transfer? $3.74, $267.88, $29

16. When Ana Guzman checked her credit card statement, she found that a sales slip dated 11/7 for $11.79 was posted as $12.79. She also found that a purchase for $24.59 dated 11/10 was unauthorized. The new balance on the statement was $543.95. What is her correct new balance? $518.36

17. Sandra Beal opened a new credit card in January. She paid a membership fee of $15 and a balance transfer fee of $20 when she moved the balance of her old card to her new card. During the year, she paid these finance charges: Feb., $3.56; May, $5.82; July, $4.92; Sept., $2.18. What was the total annual cost of the card to Sandra. $51.48

170 ■ Chapter 4 Loans and Credit Cards

SELECTED SOLUTIONS

13. $352.53 − $59.89 + $58.99 − $28.97 = $322.66

16. $543.95 − $12.79 + $11.79 − $24.59 = $518.36

17. $15 + $20 + $3.56 + $5.82 + $4.92 + $2.18 = $51.48

18. Rick Chandler's credit card statements for the year showed a membership fee of $75, two late fees of $25, and an average finance charge of $23.75 a month. What was the total annual cost of the card to Rick? $410

19. Heng-che Pai's credit card statement for May showed a previous balance of $289.16, new purchases of $107.99, a membership fee of $35, a finance charge of $5.96, and a payment of $100. What is her new balance? $338.11

20. The credit card of Salizar Mendoza for April listed a previous balance of $419.65, new purchases of $283.15, a payment of $300, a finance charge of $7.23, and a late fee of $20. What is his new balance? $430.03

21. **STRETCHING YOUR SKILLS** BankNote Credit Card Company must pay a store $409,800 this month for sales the store's customers made using the BankNote credit card. Before paying, BankNote will deduct from the store's check a 3.5% merchant discount fee from the totals sales. BankNote will also deduct a $0.20 transaction processing fee for each of the 21,283 BankNote credit card transactions made at the store during the month. What net amount will the store receive from BankNote? $391,200.40

22. **STRETCHING YOUR SKILLS** Roslynn Rheinhart bought a wood chipper priced at $575 and received a 4% discount for paying cash instead of using a credit card. What did Roslynn pay for the chipper? $552

23. **CRITICAL THINKING** Think about what you have learned about interest in this chapter. What common elements are there between interest paid on savings accounts and interest owed on loans? *I = PRT*, compounding

MIXED REVIEW

24. 5 + 894 + 1.9 + 34.6 935.5

25. Write $302\frac{1}{4}\%$ as a decimal. 3.0225

26. $4.90 is what percent greater than $4.20? $16\frac{2}{3}\%$

27. What amount is $62\frac{1}{2}\%$ smaller than $88? $33

28. Gary Feliciano borrowed $720 from a finance company and repaid the loan in 18 monthly payments of $50.80 each. What was the finance charge? $194.40, Lesson 4.4

29. Carmen Dize used an ATM to deposit a check for $361.90 and to withdraw $250 in cash. If her starting bank balance was $739.18, what is her new balance? $851.08, Lesson 3.2

30. On June 30, Tina Nader's check register balance was $452.88 and her bank statement balance was $697.55. Checks outstanding were 561, $39.28; 562, $121.31; 564, $83.19. The statement showed earned interest of $0.89. Reconcile the check register and bank statement. $453.77, Lesson 3.5

31. Ira Morganstein's tax return last year showed gross income of $56,312 and adjustments to income of $2,184. What was Ira's adjusted gross income last year? $54,128, Lesson 2.3

32. **DECISION MAKING** Assume you have $15,000 earning interest in a 3-year time-deposit savings account compounded yearly at the rate of 6%. You want to buy a car for $15,000. A car manufacturer's special offer is a 3-year car loan with no money down at a 4% APR. Should you borrow the money or pay cash using your savings account? Why? Borrow; Loan costs $1,800 interest; savings will earn $2,865.24 in interest, Lesson 4.6

Lesson 4.7 Credit Card Costs ■ 171

Enrich

Assign Exercises 23 and discuss the student responses.

Have students write a report on the safe use of credit cards. Included should be topics such as when not to give out your credit card number, where to keep the physical card, what to do if your home is robbed or your purse or wallet is stolen, and what to do if you find unauthorized purchases on a statement.

Close

Have students review Check Your Understanding problems C and E. Then call on students to describe how they would solve each problem.

If you haven't already done so, call on students to define and use in a sentence each of the bolded and italicized terms in the lesson.

SELECTED SOLUTIONS

18. $23.75 × 12 = $285;
$285 + $75 + $25 + $25 = $410

21. $409,800 × 0.035 = $14,343;
21,283 × $0.20 = $4,256.60;
$409,800 − ($14,343 + $4,256.60) = $391,200.40

22. $575 × 0.04 = $23; $575 − $23 = $552

31. $56,312 − $2,184 = $54,128

GOALS

- Calculate finance charges using previous balance method
- Calculate finance charges using adjusted balance method
- Calculate finance charges using average daily balance method
- Calculate the finance charge on cash advances

Start Up

Holly Winter's credit card balance for April is $250. The minimum amount that she is required to repay of that balance is $3.75. The monthly finance charge on the same balance is 2%. If she continues to pay the minimum amount on her monthly balance, how many months will it take her to pay off the balance?

Math Skill Builder

Review these math skills and solve the exercises that follow.

1. **Add** and **subtract** money amounts.
   Find the sum. $209.34 + $345.12 + $16.54 − $516.89 − $28.76 = $25.35

   1a. $507.22 + $397.28 − $44.20 − $579.93 $280.37

   1b. $183.02 + $97.38 − $88.73 − $38.99 $152.68

2. **Multiply** money amounts by decimals.
   Muliply: $62.58 × 0.0021 = $0.13

   2a. $398.77 × 0.000673 $0.27   **2b.** $220.81 × 0.01975 $4.36

   2c. $710.29 × 0.2978 $211.52   **2d.** $1,297.55 × 0.008271 $10.73

■ Previous Balance Method

If you don't pay your card balance in full by the due date, you will be assessed a finance charge. You also will lose the *grace period* for new purchases. Finance charges will be charged on new purchases from the day they are made.

A credit card finance charge is found by multiplying the card balance by the finance charge rate, or **periodic rate**. The finance charge rate is typically a daily or monthly rate found by dividing the annual percentage rate (APR) by either 365 or 12. Thus, an APR of 24% is a daily periodic rate of 0.0658% (rounded to the nearest ten thousandth) or a monthly periodic rate of 2%.

> **BUSINESS TIP**
>
> The monthly finance charge rate on a credit card balance is often called the *periodic rate*. The month for which you are billed is often called the *billing period*.

The amount of the finance charge depends on how the card company figures the balance in your account. This balance can be found by several methods.

Laura Solon's credit card statement is shown below. The finance charge, new balance, and minimum payment due boxes in the statement are gray because these amounts will vary with the method used to find the balance on which the finance charge will be applied.

Trans-action Date	Post Date	Reference	Transaction Description		Payments & Credits	Loans, Fees, & Purchases
10/3	10/4	3165813T	Cardinal Shoe Stores, Inc.	Detroit, MI		128.99
10/7	10/9	4381R211	Vorax Gas Stations, Inc.	Detroit, MI		21.89
10/10	10/12	4Y659762	The Pasta Barn, Inc.	Detroit, MI		27.79
10/17	10/18	4897W544	Cardinal Shoe Stores-Return	Detroit, MI	35.99	
10/18	10/19	81976534	Annual membership fee			35.00
10/24	10/24	94681322	Payment Thank You		75.00	

Previous Balance	Purchases & Fees	Payments & Credits	Finance Charge	New Balance	Minimum Payment Due On Due Date	APR 18.000% Monthly Periodic Rate 1.5%
225.60	213.67	110.99				

The **previous balance method** charges interest on the balance in the account on the last billing date of the previous month. Any payments, credits, or new purchases in the current month are not included in the previous balance. Use the formula below to find the new balance.

Finance Charge = Previous Balance × Periodic Rate

New Balance =
  Previous Balance + (Finance Charge + New Purchases + Fees) − (Payments + Credits)

EXAMPLE 1

Laura Solon's card company uses the previous balance method to find the balance and to figure the finance charge. Find the finance charge for the month and the new balance.

SOLUTION
Rewrite the monthly periodic rate as a decimal and multiply by the previous balance to find the finance charge.

$0.015 \times \$225.60 = \$3.384$, or $\$3.38$ finance charge for month

Add to find the new balance.

$\$225.60 + \$3.38 + \$213.67 - \$110.99 = \$331.66$

Lesson 4.8 Credit Card Finance Charges ■ **173**

■ **Teach Goal 1**

Emphasize that card companies differ in finance charges largely for two reasons: (1) the finance charge rates they levy, and (2) how they figure the balance against which the finance charge rate is applied.

Make sure that students understand that the previous balance method simply applies the periodic rate to the final balance on the last statement. Any purchases, fees, payments, or credits in the current month are not used to find the balance on which the finance charge is calculated.

Point out that the APR is converted to a monthly or daily periodic rate by dividing the APR by 12 or 365.

■ **Apply Goal 1**

Use Example 1 to demonstrate to students how to find the finance charge on a previous balance. Have students complete the math with you at their desks.

Assign Check Your Understanding problems A and B for completion in class. Roam the classroom and check student work for errors and problems.

CONNECTION TO CONSUMER ECONOMICS

Students should understand that if they pay their card balances in full each month by the due date, they will not be charged any interest or fees. That means they were able to borrow money for purchases from the card company without paying interest. However, if they don't pay the full balance, not only will they pay interest on the unpaid balance, but the card company will charge interest from the day every new charge is posted. That means they will pay interest on all their purchases from the day they make them. That increases the true price of all their purchases.

173

Teach Goal 2

Point out that the adjusted balance method usually results in the lowest finance charges for cardholders. The card company subtracts payments and credits received in the current billing period from the previous balance, but does not add purchases and fees.

Stress that the features of any card are advantageous only when they fit a cardholder's use of the card. For example, if the cardholder always pays off the balance in full, a low APR is relatively unimportant and the size of the annual fee becomes more important.

Apply Goal 2

Demonstrate the solution of Example 2. Have students follow you by completing the math at their desks.

Assign Check Your Understanding problems C and D for completion in class. Check student work at their desks for errors or problems.

■ CHECK YOUR UNDERSTANDING

A. John Olden's credit card statement for April showed a previous balance of $309.20, new purchases and fees of $128.45, and payments and credits of $75. The card's annual percentage rate is 24%. What is John's finance charge for April and new balance using the previous balance method? $6.18, $368.83

B. Sandra Minoro's credit card company uses the previous balance method to calculate finance charges. Its APR is 21%. Sandra's credit card statement for June showed a previous balance of $488.32, new purchases and fees of $264.89, and payments and credits of $300. What is Sandra's finance charge for June and her new balance? $8.55, $461.76

■ Adjusted Balance Method

The **adjusted balance method** subtracts payments and credits during this month from the balance at the end of the previous month. Purchases and fees made during the current month are not included in the adjusted balance.

Adjusted Balance = Previous Balance − (Payments + Credits)

Finance Charge = Adjusted Balance × Periodic Rate

New Balance = Adjusted Balance + Finance Charge + New Purchases + Fees

EXAMPLE 2

Suppose that Laura's card company uses the adjusted balance method to find the balance and figure the finance charge. Find the finance charge for the month and the new balance.

SOLUTION

Subtract the payments and credits from the previous balance to find the adjusted balance.

$225.60 − $110.99 = $114.61   adjusted balance

Write the monthly APR as a decimal and multiply by the adjusted balance to find the finance charge.

0.015 × $114.61 = $1.719, or $1.72   finance charge

Add the adjusted balance, finance charge, and new purchases and fees to find the new balance.

$114.61 + $1.72 + $213.67 = $330   new balance

■ CHECK YOUR UNDERSTANDING

C. Yossi Hussein uses a credit card that carries an 18% APR and uses the adjusted balance method for calculating finance charges. Yossi's statement listed these facts: previous balance, $310.33; purchases, $219.67; fees, $75; payments, $150; credits, $62.69. What is Yossi's finance charge and new balance? $1.46, $393.77

D. Ricky Luciano's credit card statement showed a previous balance of $166.98, purchases and fees of $201.88, and payments and credits of $75. If his card carried an APR of 21% and used the adjusted balance method to calculate finance charges, what is Ricky's finance charge and new balance? $1.61, $295.47

174 ■ Chapter 4 Loans and Credit Cards

■ *CHECK YOUR UNDERSTANDING SOLUTIONS*

A. 24% ÷ 12 = 2%; $309.20 × 0.02 = $6.18
$309.20 + $6.18 + $128.45 − $75 = $368.83

C. $310.33 − ($150 + $62.69) = $97.64;
18% ÷ 12 = 1.5%; $97.64 × 0.015 = $1.46;
$97.64 + $1.46 + $219.67 + $75 = $393.77

Average Daily Balance Method

The **average daily balance method** is the most commonly used method for calculating the finance charge. When this method is used, the periodic rate is applied to the average daily balance in the account during the billing period. The dates used are the *post* dates. The card company starts with the beginning balance for each day.

The company subtracts any payments or credits posted during that day from the beginning balance. New purchases and fees posted for that day are added to the balance. The ending balances for every day are then totaled and divided by the number of days in the billing period to get the *average daily balance*.

Daily Balance = Beginning Balance − (Payments + Credits) + (Purchases + Fees)

$$\text{Average Daily Balance} = \frac{\text{Sum of Daily Balances}}{}$$

Finance Charge = Average Daily Balance × Monthly Periodic Rate

New Balance = Beginning Balance − (Payments + Credits) + (Finance Charges + New Purchases + Fees)

EXAMPLE 3

Suppose that Laura's card company uses the average daily balance method to figure the finance charge. Find the finance charge for the month and the new balance.

SOLUTION

Create a chart like the one below. A transaction is either a payment or a credit and subtracted from the balance, or purchase or fee and added to the balance. The balance at end of a day is the previous balance plus or minus any additions or deductions. The Number of Days is the number of days that the balance is in effect. The Sum of Daily Balances is the balance multiplied by the number of days.

Post Date	Transactions	Balance at End of Day	Number of Days	Sum of Daily Balances
10/1 (Bal.)	0.00	225.60	1	225.60
10/2–10/3	225.60	225.60	2	451.20
10/4	+128.99	354.59	1	354.59
10/5–10/8	0.00	354.59	4	1,418.36
10/9	+21.89	376.48	1	376.48
10/10–10/11	0.00	376.48	2	752.96
10/12	+27.79	404.27	1	404.27
10/13–10/17	0.00	404.27	5	2,021.35
10/18	−35.99	368.28	1	368.28
10/19	+35.00	403.28	1	403.28
10/20–10/23	0.00	403.28	4	1,613.12
10/24	−75.00	328.28	1	328.28
10/25–10/31	0.00	328.28	7	2,297.96

CONNECTION TO SPREADSHEETS

Calculating the average daily balance becomes drudgery if there are many transactions or if students are asked to do many problems. A way to lighten the task is for students to use the spreadsheet available in the Technology Workshop. However, this solves the complete problem. Instead, ask student teams to create a spreadsheet like the chart in Example 3 on p. 175. This spreadsheet wouldn't generate the finance charge and new balance, but would calculate the average daily balance so that students could do the rest of the problem more quickly.

Emphasize that cash advances on your credit card are really short-term loans. Interest will be charged from the day of the loan until the day it is paid off. A one-time cash advance fee is also commonly charged.

Point out to students that some merchants may ask customers to provide personal information, such as address, phone number, etc. Some states prohibit recording of personal information on a sales slip and American Express, Visa, and Master Charge prohibit it as a condition of a sale.

Visa and Master Charge also prohibit a merchant from requiring a minimum purchase, such as $25, to use their cards.

Add the column, "Sum of Daily Balances," and divide by 31, the number of days the statement covers.

$225.60 + $451.20 + $354.59 + $1,418.36 + $376.48 + $752.96 + $404.27 + $2,021.35 + $368.28 + $403.28 + $1,613.12 + $328.28 + $2,297.96 = $11,015.73

$11,015.73 ÷ 31 = $355.346, or $355.35   average daily balance

Write the monthly periodic rate as a decimal and multiply by the average daily balance: 0.015 × $355.35 = $5.33   finance charge

Subtract the payments and credits, and add the finance charges, purchases, and fees to previous balance.

$225.60 − ($35.99 + $75) + ($5.33 + $213.67) = $333.61   new balance

■ **CHECK YOUR UNDERSTANDING**

E. Jade Hameed's credit card statement for August showed these items: 8/1, previous balance, $108.15; 8/5, purchase, $56.89; 8/10, purchase, $61.88; 8/14, purchase, $190.23; 8/25, payment, $150. Jade's card company uses a 1.6% monthly periodic rate and the average daily balance method. What is Jade's finance charge for August and the new balance? $4.45, $271.60

F. The credit card statement of Gloria Herrera for January listed these items: 1/1, previous balance, $89.27; 1/5, purchase, $159.34; 1/9, purchase, $108.45; 1/24, payment, $150; 1/28, fee, $25. The card company uses the average daily balance method and a daily periodic rate of 0.000575. What is Gloria's finance charge for January and what is her new balance? $4.87, $236.93

> **PROBLEM SOLVING TIP**
>
> If your card company charges a daily periodic rate, the formula for figuring the finance charge is: Finance Charge = Average Daily Balance × Number of Days in Billing Period × Daily Periodic Rate.

■ Cash Advances

You can get cash from an ATM using your credit card. However, you are borrowing money from the credit card company. Transactions of this type are called **cash advances**. Your credit card company will charge you a finance charge on the cash advance starting from the day you withdraw the money. There is no grace period for cash advances.

> **PROBLEM SOLVING TIP**
>
> Remember that finance charges include interest plus fees.

Card companies often charge you a one-time fee for the cash advance in addition to the finance charge. They often charge a higher periodic rate for cash advances than for regular balances.

To find the interest, multiply the amount of the advance (principal) by the daily periodic interest rate (rate) and number of days of the loan (time). To find the finance charge, add the interest to any fees paid. The cash advance and finance charge are added to find the amount needed to pay off the cash advance.

Interest = Cash Advance × Daily Periodic Rate × Term of Advance in Days

Finance Charge = Interest + Fees

Payoff Amount = Cash Advance + Finance Charge

■ *CHECK YOUR UNDERSTANDING SOLUTIONS*

E. Average daily balance = $278.20;
$278.20 × 0.016 = $4.45;
$108.15 + $56.89 + $61.88 + $190.23 − $150 + $4.45 = $271.60

F. Average daily balance = $273.03;
$273.03 × 0.000575 × 31 = $4.866, or $4.87
$89.27 + $159.34 + $108.45 − $150 + $25 + $4.87 = $236.93

G. $200 × 0.000487 × 25 = $2.435, or $2.44;
$2.44 + $5 = $7.44

EXAMPLE 4

Benito Moya borrowed $500 for 20 days on his credit card using a cash advance. His card company charged a cash advance fee of $29 and a daily periodic interest rate of 0.0573%. What was the total finance charge on the cash advance?

SOLUTION

Multiply the amount borrowed by the number of days for the advance and daily periodic rate to find the interest on the loan.

$500 × 20 × 0.000573 = $5.73   interest on cash advance

Add to find the total finance charge.
$5.73 + $29 = $34.73

■ **CHECK YOUR UNDERSTANDING**

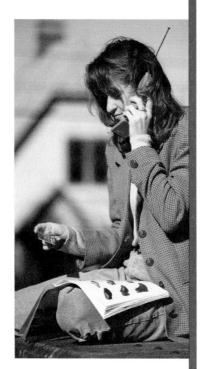

G. Vera Millay used her credit card in an ATM to borrow $200 on a cash advance. Her card company charged a cash advance fee of $5 and a daily periodic interest rate of 0.0487%. If Vera paid the loan back at the end of 25 days, what was the total finance charge on the cash advance? $7.44

H. Akbar Assam borrowed $150 on a cash advance from his credit card company. The card company charged a cash advance fee of $20 and a daily periodic interest rate of 0.058% for the 35 days the loan ran. What total amount did Akbar need to pay off the loan? $173.05

■ **Apply Goal 4**

Demonstrate the solution of Example 4. Have students follow you by completing the math at their desks.

Assign Check Your Understanding problems G and H for class work. Check student work at their desks for errors or problems.

Wrap Up

Look at the Start Up problem at the beginning of the lesson. The monthly finance charge on Holly's balance is $5 (2% × $250). Her minimum required payment is only $3.75. Her minimum payment does not even fully cover the finance charge. At that rate, Holly's balance will grow each month and she will never pay it off.

Wrap Up

Review the Start Up. Discuss why credit card companies permit such low minimum payments. Students should understand that interest on card balances is a major source of income for the card companies. Some companies even notify you that you can "skip" this month's payment or reduce the minimum payment. All the while, the companies are charging interest on the unpaid balance.

TEAM MEETING

In most bank lobbies, there is a place where brochures about bank services are available free to the public. Among these brochures is usually a stack of brochures explaining how to apply for a credit card, including the credit card features and terms. With two other students,

■ Obtain copies of these brochures from several banks or visit bank websites for information.

■ After reading the brochures, make a chart listing the features common to all credit cards offered by these banks, such as balance transfer fees, late charges, and the method of calculating the bank balance and finance charge.

■ Create columns to let you enter data for each credit card's features.

■ Prepare a brief explanation of the chart that includes a discussion of the differences among the cards.

TEAM MEETING

Select the charts from one or more student teams and make transparencies of the charts. Then have the teams use the transparencies to report their findings to the class.

COMMON ERRORS

When finding finance charges on cash advances, students may change the daily rate to a decimal incorrectly, especially dropping or adding a zero in the rate. They may also forget to multiply by the number of days. Remind students to check the reasonableness of their work. An annual rate of 21% will generate a monthly rate of less than 2%; a daily periodic rate of 1.8% is less than 2%.

Assignment: Exercises 1–9, 11–29. Start with the basic arithmetic problems at the beginning of the exercises to insure that students understand the underlying arithmetic in the exercises.

Assign half the class to find the finance charge using the first card company's terms. Assign the other half the second company's terms. Call on students for the answers and discuss them.

Check student answers to the exercises by calling on them in class, collecting and grading selected problems, or by observing student work at their desks.

Ask students to define the bolded and italicized terms in the lesson and use them in sentences.

Reteach

STUDENT WORKBOOK Use Exercise 1 to reteach finding finance charges and new balances based on the previous balance. Assign students Exercise 2 for practice.

Use Exercise 3 to reteach finding finance charges and new balances using on the adjusted balance method. Assign students Exercise 4 for practice.

Use Exercise 5 to reteach finding finance charges and new balances using the average daily balance method. Assign Exercise 6 for practice.

Use Exercise 7 to reteach finding the finance charge on cash advances. Assign Exercises 8 and 9 for practice.

EXERCISES

Find the result.

1. $98.62 + $978.22 − $34.15 − $98.18 $944.51

2. $789.23 + $98.21 − $44.63 − $641.09 $201.72

Find the product.

3. $879.43 × 0.00526 $4.63

4. $2,097.46 × 0.0002978 $0.62

5. The October credit card statement for Genaro Rios had a previous balance of $175.30, new purchases and fees of $108.85, and payments and credits of $125. The card's annual percentage rate is 21% and the previous balance method is used to figure the finance charge. What is Genaro's finance charge for October and new balance? $3.07, $162.22

6. Toni Bando's credit card has an APR of 18% figured on the previous balance. The previous balance on Toni's credit card statement for July was $308.88. During July she had new purchases and fees of $276.49, and payments and credits of $400. What is her finance charge for July and her new balance? $4.63, $190

7. Otto Schein's credit card company charges an APR of 21% and applies it to the previous balance. Otto's December statement showed: previous balance, $397.90; new purchases, $341.89; fees, $55; payments, $500; purchase return, $56.99. What is his finance charge for December and new balance? $6.96, $244.76

8. A credit card company uses an APR of 15% and the adjusted balance method of computing finance charges. A credit card statement from the company lists the following: previous balance, $601.87; purchases, $209.88; fees, $75; payments, $400; credits, $25. What was the finance charge for the month and new balance? $2.21, $463.96

9. June Christo has a credit card statement that shows a previous balance of $598.61, new purchases and fees of $127.88, and payments and credits of $250. Her card company charges an APR of 12% on the adjusted balance. What is June's finance charge and new balance? $3.49, $479.98

10. **INTEGRATING YOUR KNOWLEDGE**   You have two credit cards. The Banker's Card has a previous balance of $301.55, carries an APR of 18%, and uses the previous balance method of figuring finance charges. The MallCard lists a previous balance of $260.61 and payments and credits of $175. It uses the adjusted balance method to find finance charges and carries an APR of 21%. Find the finance charge on both cards. $4.52, $1.50

11. **DECISION MAKING**   Your credit card statement shows a previous balance of $231.86, payments and credits of $125, and purchases and fees of $175.66. Your current card company uses an APR of 15% and the adjusted balance method. Another credit card company that sent you an application in the mail also uses an APR of 15% but uses the previous balance method. Should you switch companies? Why or why not? No, finance charge is less ($1.34) in first; second is $2.90

12. When Gorica Batic received her May credit card statement she found these items listed: 5/1, previous balance, $281.59; 5/7, purchase, $168.99; 5/10, purchase, $57.98; 5/25, payment, $200. Gorica's card company uses a 1.8% monthly periodic rate and the average daily balance method. What is Gorica's finance charge for May and her new balance? $7.45, $316.01

SELECTED SOLUTIONS

5. 21% ÷ 12 = 0.0175; $175.30 × 0.0175 = $3.067, or $3.07; $175.30 + $108.85 − $125 + $3.07 = $162.22

8. $601.87 − ($400 + $25) = $176.87; 15% ÷ 12 = 0.0125; $176.87 × 0.0125 = $2.21; $176.87 + $209.88 + $75 + $2.21 = $463.96

12. Average daily balance = $413.86; $413.86 × 0.018 = $7.449, or $7.45; $281.59 + $168.99 + $57.98 − $200 + $7.45 = $316.01

13. The credit card statement of Luiz Lopea for June listed these items: 6/1, previous balance, $193.29; 6/11, purchase, $175.39; 6/15, purchase, $71.84; 6/24, payment, $75. The card company uses the average daily balance method and a daily periodic rate of 0.056%. What is Luiz's finance charge for June and what is his new balance? $5.56, $371.08

14. Jareen Knabe borrowed $800 for 30 days from her credit card company using a cash advance. The daily finance charge was 0.0543%. What was the finance charge on her loan? $13.03

Yvonne Clark used her credit card in an ATM for a $325 cash advance. Her card company charges a daily periodic interest rate of 0.06% and charged a cash advance fee of $19. Yvonne repaid the loan in 15 days.

15. What total finance charge did Yvonne pay for the cash advance? $21.93

16. How much did she pay to the card company to end the loan? $346.93

Isabel Aponte borrowed $150 on a cash advance from her credit card company. The company charges a cash advance fee of $20 and a daily periodic interest rate of 0.045%. If Isabel borrowed the money for 26 days

17. What was the total finance charge on the cash advance? $21.76

18. What total amount did Isabel pay to end the loan? $171.76

MIXED REVIEW

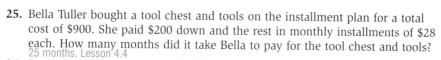

19. Divide 21.5% by 365, to the nearest hundredth. 0.06%

20. $4,298 × 50 × 0.00042 $90.26

21. Find the average of these numbers: 8, 9, 11, 7, 8. 8.6

22. Write the ratio of 16 to 236 as a fraction. $\frac{4}{59}$

23. Write $\frac{8}{24}$ as a percent. $33\frac{1}{3}$%

24. Write 175% as a decimal. 1.75

25. Bella Tuller bought a tool chest and tools on the installment plan for a total cost of $900. She paid $200 down and the rest in monthly installments of $28 each. How many months did it take Bella to pay for the tool chest and tools? 25 months, Lesson 4.4

26. Rosa Rinaldi's total job benefits for the previous year were estimated to be $62,976. However, her job expenses for the same job were: licenses, $475; commuting costs, $2,108; tools, $197. What were her net job benefits for the year? $60,196, Lesson 2.2

27. Maria Hernandez deposited these items on January 11: (bills) 15 twenties, 11 tens, 20 fives, 89 ones, (coins) 35 quarters, 65 dimes, 135 pennies, (checks) $53.69, $138.98. She received one $100 bill back. What was her net deposit? $708.27, Lesson 3.1

28. Sheila Wiggins' regular-time pay rate is $12.60 an hour, time-and-a-half for overtime, and double time for work on Saturdays or Sundays. What is her overtime rate? What is her double-time rate? $18.90, $25.20, Lesson 1.3

29. Lung Shen used his credit card in an ATM to borrow $300 on a cash advance. His card company charged a cash advance fee of $15 and a daily periodic interest rate of 0.049%. Lung paid the loan back at the end of 15 days. What was the total finance charge on the cash advance? $17.21, Lesson 4-8

Lesson 4.8 Credit Card Finance Charges ■ 179

SELECTED SOLUTIONS

14. 0.0543% = 0.000543;
$800 × 30 × 0.000543 = $13.032, or $13.03

17. 0.045% = 0.00045;
$150 × 26 × 0.00045 = $1.755, or $1.76;
$20 + $1.76 = $21.76

18. $150 + $21.76 = $171.76

28. Overtime rate: $12.60 × 1.5 = $18.90
Double time rate: $12.60 × 2 = $25.20

- Multiply principal by interest rate by time to find interest on promissory note.

- Add interest to principal to find amount due on due date.

- Divide one-year interest by principal to find interest rate.

Lesson 4.2 Discounted Promissory Notes
- Multiply principal by bank discount rate and time of note to find amount of discount.

- Subtract amount of bank discount from principal to find net proceeds.

- Divide bank discount by net proceeds to find true rate of interest.

Lesson 4.3 Interest Tables
- Divide loan amount by 100 to find number of $100s in loan principal.

- Multiply table interest by number of $100s in principal to find interest.

- Combine table multipliers when interest rate or time of loan isn't in table.

- Find note due date by counting forward number of days or months from date of note.

- Find days between two dates by adding number of days remaining in current month to days in each of succeeding months, up to due date.

Chapter Review

Vocabulary Review

adjusted balance method	exact interest method	principal
annual percentage rate	finance charge	promissory note
average daily balance method	interest	rate of interest
bank discount	ordinary interest method	time
cash advance	periodic rate	
down payment	previous balance method	

Fill in each blank with one of the terms above.

1. A way to find interest that uses a 365 day year is ___?___. exact interest method

2. Interest on a promissory note collected in advance is ___?___. bank discount

3. Interest, fees, and other charges paid on an installment loan or purchase is the ___?___. finance charge

4. The true rate of interest on an installment loan is called ___?___. annual percentage rate

5. The rate of interest on a credit card balance is called ___?___. periodic rate

6. When you apply the periodic rate to the balance from the last statement and ignore purchases, fees, and payments from the current period, you are using the ___?___. previous balance method

7. The amount charged for the use of money is called ___?___. interest

8. The amount that is borrowed is called the ___?___. principal

LESSON 4.1

9. Phyllis Snow borrowed $3,200 to pay for a cruise. She signed a 6-month promissory note at 12% interest. Find the amount of interest Phyllis must pay. Then find the amount she must repay to her bank when the note comes due. $192; $3,392

10. Oki Saga signed a promissory note for $1,500 at 8% interest for 90 days. Find the interest and amount due she will pay when the note is due using a) ordinary interest and b) exact interest. a) $30, $1,530, b) $29.59, $1,529.59

11. Mohamed Jatmiko paid $420 in interest on a 6-month note for $5,600. Find the rate of interest he paid. 15%

LESSON 4.2

12. A bank discounted a $2,600 noninterest-bearing note for Reba Deconcini at 12% interest for 6 months. Find the proceeds of the note. $2,444

13. Your bank discounted your 3-month, $1,800, noninterest-bearing note. The discount rate was 15%. You received $1,732.50 as proceeds. What true rate of interest, to the nearest tenth percent, did you pay on the note? 15.6%

LESSON 4.3

14. Find the interest on: a) $470 for 10 days at 9%; b) $470 for 40 days at 10%. a) $1.16, b) $5.15

15. Find the due date of: a) a 3-month note dated May 31; b) a 20-day note dated Oct. 21. a) Aug. 31, b) Nov. 10

DIFFERENT LEARNING STYLES Auditory Learners

Have students spell the words out loud as they write the words that complete each vocabulary question to help them remember the word and how it is spelled.

16. Find the number of days from January 13 to March 15. 61 days

LESSON 4.4

17. You can buy a DVD player for $250 cash or pay $50 down and the balance in 12 monthly payments of $18. What is the installment price? By what percent would your installment price be greater than the cash price? $266; 6.4%

18. A stove costs $525 on the installment plan. You must make a down payment of $75 and make payments for 15 months. What will be your monthly payments? $30

19. Hector Morales borrowed $2,400 on a one-year simple interest installment loan at 12% interest. The monthly payments were $220. Find the amount of interest, amount applied to the principal, and the new balance for the first monthly payment. $24; $196; $2,204

LESSON 4.5

20. Lisa Valente bought a TV and paid for it with a 6-month Rule of 78 installment loan. The total finance charge for the loan was $120. She repaid the loan at the end of the third month. Find the amount of Lisa's earned and unearned finance charges. $85.72; $34.28

21. Rawal Jarish has a 12-month, $6,300 Rule of 78 installment loan with a total finance charge of $945. The monthly installment payments were $603.75. He repays the loan at the end of 6 months. How much will Rawal pay to the bank? $3,971.86

LESSON 4.6

22. Maria Medina borrowed $400 on a 12-month loan with a finance charge of $39. Find the finance charge per $100 of the amount financed and the annual percentage rate. 9.75, $17\frac{1}{2}$%

LESSON 4.7

23. Derek Wilson checked his credit card statement and found a sales slip for $26.99 that was unauthorized. He also found that a sales slip for $35.89 had been listed as $38.59. If the new balance on his statement was $140.68, what is his correct new balance? $110.99

24. Loni Dramin's credit card statement for April showed a membership fee of $55, a late fee of $25, a finance charge of $6.45, and an over-the-limit fee of $12. What was the total cost of the card to Loni in April? $98.45

LESSON 4.8

25. Juan Mendoza's credit card statement for October showed a previous balance of $239.80, new purchases and fees of $174.50, and payments and credits of $95. The card's annual percentage rate is 24% and daily periodic rate is 0.06575%. What is Juan's finance charge and new balance for October using these methods: a) previous balance, b) adjusted balance? c) average daily balance? a) $4.80; $324.10 b) $2.90; $322.20 c) $7.01; $326.31

26. Ula Johan borrowed $250 on a cash advance from her credit card company. She was charged a cash advance fee of $14 and a daily periodic interest rate of 0.053% for the 25 days the loan ran. What was the total amount Ula had to pay to end the loan? $267.31

Chapter 4 Review ■ 181

Lesson 4.4 Installment Loans
• Add down payment and monthly payments to find installment price.

• Subtract cash price from installment price to find finance charge.

• Divide finance charge by cash price to find percent installment price is greater than cash price.

• Subtract down payment from installment price to find remaining amount to pay.

• Divide remaining amount to pay by number of months to pay to find monthly payment.

• Subtract interest from monthly payment to find amount applied to principal.

• Subtract amount applied to principal from previous balance to find new balance.

Lesson 4.5 Early Loan Repayments
• Multiply total finance charge by refund decimal rate to find unearned finance charge.

• Subtract unearned finance charge from total finance charge to find earned finance charge.

• Find total of remaining payments on a Rule of 78 loan.

• Find finance charge refund percentage in loan refund table. Multiply total finance charge by that percent to find unearned finance charge.

• Subtract unearned finance charge from total remaining payments to find amount needed to repay loan.

(cont. on p. 186)

TEACHING STRATEGIES Chapter Review

If the Chapter Review is assigned as class work, have selected students work at the board so that seated students can compare the steps they used to solve the problem with others. As students finish at the board, discuss each board solution in terms of the answer and the steps used to solve it. Try to select students for board work that you are reasonably sure will do the problem correctly.

Students need spreadsheet file tech4-1.xls for Tasks 1 and 2.

Task 1 Students enter data into an average daily balance spreadsheet template. The table can be used for either monthly or daily periodic rates by selecting either D19 or E19 to enter the decimal rate.

Task 2 Students answer questions about the results of Task 1. They also change data and answer questions about the results.

Task 3 Students design and create a spreadsheet that calculates cash advance finance charges.

Task 4 Students answer questions about the data entered and about how the sheet was designed. They also change data and answer questions about the new results.

Remind students to enter data only in the blue spreadsheet cells.

Stress that the first day of the next month must be the last entry in the date column so that the spreadsheet can find the total number of days in the month.

Ask students to suggest another way to calculate the days in a month. (D20 and E20 might look at the data in cell A5 and then use a nested set of if statements for months 30 or 28 days long with the "else" being 31.)

Technology Workshop

Task 1: Enter Data Into An Average Daily Balance Finance Charge Template

Complete a template that calculates the average daily balance, the finance charge, and the new balance for a credit card statement.

Open the spreadsheet for Chapter 4 (tech4-1.xls) and enter the data shown in blue (cells A5-B12 and D19) into the spreadsheet. The values you enter are from Example 3 in Lesson 4-8. Your computer screen should look like the one shown when you are done.

The spreadsheet will calculate the:

1. Balance at the end of each day

2. Number of days in which balance is in effect

3. Sum of the daily balances

4. Total of the sum of the daily balances

5. Number of days in the month

6. Average daily balance

7. Finance charge

8. New balance

	A	B	C	D	E
1			**Average Daily Balance**		
2			**Finance Charge Calculator**		
3	Date	Transaction	**Balance at**	**Number**	**Sum of Daily**
4			**End of Day**	**of Days**	**Balances**
5	10/1	225.60	225.60	3	676.80
6	10/4	128.99	354.59	5	1,772.95
7	10/9	21.89	376.48	3	1,129.44
8	10/12	27.79	404.27	6	2,425.62
9	10/18	-35.99	368.28	1	368.28
10	10/19	35.00	403.28	5	2,016.40
11	10/24	-75.00	328.28	8	2,626.24
12	11/1	0.00	403.28	0	0.00
13			Sums	31	11,015.73
14					
15	*When the last transaction is entered, enter the first day of the*				
16	*next month in the Date .*				
17					
18				**Monthly**	**Daily**
19		**Periodic Rate**		0.015	0.00000000
20		**Number of Days in Month**		31	31
21		**Average Daily Balance**		355.35	355.35
22		**Finance Charge**		5.33	0.00
23		**New Balance**		408.61	403.28

The template can be used for either a monthly periodic rate or a daily periodic rate. To calculate values for a daily periodic rate, enter the daily periodic rate in cell E19.

After you enter the last transaction for the month, enter the first day of the next month in the next blank Date cell. In Task 1, this required you to enter the first day of the next month, in cell A12.

182 ■ Chapter 4 Loans and Credit Cards

TEACHING STRATEGIES Task 1

Before students enter data into the average daily balance finance charge spreadsheet, display the contents of those cells that contain formulas (C5, C6, D5, E5, D13, E13,

D20-23, and E20-23). Discuss with students the formulas in these cells in terms of the math processes that are occurring.

Task 2: Analyze The Spreadsheet Output

Move the cursor to row 19 and column D, the cell for Monthly Periodic Rate. Enter the rate 0.02. Notice how the finance charge changed. This change shows what would happen if the monthly periodic rate were raised from 1.5% to 2%. Move to cell A11 and change the date to 10/25. Notice how the sums of the daily balances, total sums of daily balances, the finance charge, and the new balance have changed.

Answer these questions about your updated spreadsheet.
1. What function is used in cell E13? sum function

2. What arithmetic is done in cell E13? values in cells E5 through E12 are added

3. What is the formula used in D21? E13 ÷ D20

4. What arithmetic is done in cell D21? sum of daily balances is divided by no. of days

5. What formula is used in cell D22? D21 × D19

6. What arithmetic is done in cell D22? ave. daily balance is multiplied by monthly periodic rate.

7. What arithmetic is done in cell D23? finance charge is added to end of month balance

Task 3: Design a Cash Advance Finance Charge Spreadsheet

You are to design a spreadsheet that will calculate the interest, total finance charge, and total amount needed to payoff a cash advance.

SITUATION: You want to borrow $500 on a cash advance for 20 days using your credit card. Your card company charges a cash advance fee of $15 and a daily periodic interest rate of 0.045%. You want to know how much interest and finance charges you must pay and what amount will be needed to pay off the loan.

Task 4: Analyze the Spreadsheet Output

Answer these questions about your completed spreadsheet:
8. How did you calculate the interest on the cash advance?
   Amount of cash advance × interest rate × time in days
9. What would the interest be on the loan? $4.50

10. What would the finance charge be on the loan? $19.50

11. What amount is needed to payoff the loan in 20 days? $519.50

12. If you were to (a) change the interest rate to 0.07%, (b) change the cash advance fee to $20, and (c) extend the loan to 30 days, what would be the interest, finance charge, and payoff amount? $10.50, $30.50, $530.50

Chapter 4 Technology Workshop ■ 183

Teach and Apply Task 2

Assign Questions 1–7 and discuss the results.

Point out to students that all questions refer to the spreadsheet after the changed data were entered.

Discuss the logic of the formulas used to find the number of days. (cells D5-D12)

Teach and Apply Task 3

Assign Task 3. You may wish to have students work in groups.

Students may wish to plan the format of the spreadsheet on paper first.

Suggest to students that they consider organizing their spreadsheet roughly into two areas: input cells and output or results cells.

Remind students that if a cell is formatted to display only so many decimal places, it still contains the unformatted amount. To round the cell contents, they must use the ROUND function.

Teach and Apply Task 4

Assign Questions 8–12. Make sure students answer Questions 8–11 before they enter new data for Question 12.

TEACHING STRATEGIES Task 3

An example solution to Task 3 is provided in the file tech4-3.xls. You may wish to display the design used in tech4-3.xls and have students make suggestions for improving the readability, ease of data entry, and organization of the spreadsheet rather than having the class review another student's work. Examine with students the formulas in the cells critically and ask for suggestions for improvement. For example, students might suggest that the spreadsheet be reorganized so that part payments can be treated.

■ **HOW TIMES HAVE CHANGED**
$1,000,000,000,000 \div$
$84,000,000 \approx \$11,904.76$

The average credit card spending
is about $11,904 per household.

■ **WRITE**
Students should include reasons
for the purchase that are not trivial
or that emphasize satisfying a want
rather than a need. Students may
want to include more than one way
to raise the funds to repay the
loan. A cosigner is likely to ask
what will happen if the first money
source doesn't work out.

■ **SCANS**
Students' letters should include a
solid explanation of the need for
the purchase, should demonstrate
that they know the costs of the
loan, and should include a list of
reasonable methods of raising the
money. The letters should also be
clear, neat, grammatically correct,
and in an acceptable format.

■ **ONGOING ASSESSMENT**
STUDENT WORKBOOK The
Integrated Project found in the
workbook provides a broad, ongoing assessment activity for the
goals of this chapter.

Chapter Assessment

How Times Have Changed

For the following question, refer to the timeline on page 131 as needed.

If 84 million American households have at least one credit card, and they spend a total of 1 trillion dollars annually using credit cards, what is the average annual credit card spending for each of the 84 million households?

WRITE

Consider a purchase that you would like to make but do not have the money for. List reasons why you want to make this purchase and why it is important to buy it now. Also list reasons why you do not want to wait until you have saved the money to make the purchase. Describe how you will raise the money to repay the loan.

Now compose a letter to an adult that you would ask to co-sign a loan for you. Explain the purchase, your need for this item and why it is important enough that you want to borrow money. Be sure that you back up your request with reasons from your lists above. Also be sure to include information that makes it clear that you are aware of the costs of borrowing money and that you have accounted for those costs in your plan to earn the money.

SCANS

Workplace Skills—*Allocating and Managing Time*

Time management skills include the ability to select relevant activities, set priorities, and create a plan and schedule for achieving goals. This chapter is about the relationship between time and money.

Test Your Skills Think about your life's financial goals. Identify those that are realistic. Select one that you hope to reach by the age of thirty.

Make a Plan Write down steps you can take to achieve this goal. Include in your plan information that shows you understand the basic principals of saving and borrowing money over time.

Summarize Based on your steps, how long do you think it will take to achieve your goal? Reflect on the goal and your plan to reach it. Can your plan be modified to help you reach your goal more quickly? Mentally note which of the following skills you will use to follow through with your plan.

arithmetic	*speaking*	*understanding systems*	*decision making*
self-management	*responsibility*	*selecting technology*	*monitoring performance*

PORTFOLIO ASSESSMENT

Students should prepare their spreadsheet and plan for their portfolios. After they have completed a self-evalua-tion on their work, have them review it with an adult member of their family. The adult should make comments on the feasibility of the plan and what aspect would most likely be successful if the plan was implemented.

Chapter Test

Answer each question.

1. Rewrite 0.06% as a decimal. 0.0006

2. Simplify: $\frac{36}{64} \cdot \frac{9}{16}$

3. Multiply: $\$540 \times 3.5\% \times \frac{1}{4}$. $4.73

4. Multiply: $\$398.77 \times 0.000673$. $0.27

5. Multiply: $\$426 \times 0.057\% \times 30$. $7.28

6. Find what percent $35 is of $140. 25%

7. Divide: $720.15 \div 100$. 7.2015

8. Divide: $\$2,400 \div \$48$. 50

9. Add and subtract: $209.34 + $345.12 + $16.54 − $516.89 − $28.76. $25.35

10. Divide and round to the nearest tenth of a percent: $25.6\% \div 12$. 2.1%

Applications

11. Cora Fear borrowed $1,500 for 18 months from her bank. Cora signed a promissory note that carried 15% interest. Find the amount of interest Cora must pay. Then find the amount she must repay to her bank on the due date. $337.50; $1,837.50

12. Ted Nash must pay $1,600 in interest on a promissory note for $40,000 due 4 months from the date of the note. Find the rate of interest he will pay. 12%

13. Chao-cheng Su discounted her $2,900, 3-month, noninterest-bearing note at 12% at her bank. Find the proceeds of the note. $2,813

14. Find the due date of a 4-month note dated February 6. June 6

15. You can buy a product for $750 cash or pay $150 down and the balance in 12 monthly payments of $61.25. What is the installment price? By what percent would your installment price be greater than the cash price? $885; 18%

16. Rita Mercado has a 12-month, $1,800 Rule of 78 installment loan with a total finance charge of $378. The monthly installment payments were $181.50 She repays the loan at the end of 3 months. The Finance Charge Refund Schedule shows that 57.69% of the finance charge should be refunded. How much will Rita pay to the bank? $1,596.93

17. Don Crawitz borrowed $780 on a loan with a finance charge of $68. Find the finance charge per $100 of the amount financed. $8.72

18. Dee Mallory's credit card statement for August showed a membership fee of $75, a late fee of $20, a finance charge of $6.85, and an over-the-limit fee of $21. What was the total cost of the card to Dee in August? $122.85

19. Levy Bell's credit card has an APR of 21% figured on the previous balance. The previous balance on Levy's credit card statement for February was $268.18. During February, he had new purchases and fees of $147.29, and payments and credits of $100. What is his finance charge for February and his new balance? $4.69; $320.16

20. Mary Kelly borrowed $380 for 20 days from her credit card company using a cash advance. The card company charged her a cash advance fee of $20 and daily periodic rate of 0.044%. What was the finance charge on her loan? $23.34

Chapter 4 Assessment ■ 185

Handwritten notes in margin:

$61.25 × 12 = 735, +150 = $885
885 − 750 = $135 = finance chg
135 ÷ 750 = 0.18 ≈ 18%

Chapter-Test Correlation

Question	Lesson
11	4.1
12	4.1
13	4.2
14	4.3
15	4.4
16	4.5
17	4.6
18	4.7
19	4.8
20	4.8

TEACHING STRATEGIES Chapter Test

Make sure that students understand that they are to show all their work. Assign points to the test for neatness and completeness of labeling of solutions. Make these points in addition to the points earned for correct answers.

(cont. from p. 181)

Lesson 4.6 Annual Percentage
Rates
- Multiply finance charge by $100
  and divide by amount financed
  to find finance charge per $100.

- Find amount closest to finance
  charge per $100 of amount
  financed in tables to find annual
  percentage rate.

Lesson 4.7 Credit Card Costs
- Subtract unauthorized sales
  slips from card balance.

- Add or subtract amounts from
  card balance to correct errors in
  sales slips.

- Add finance charges and fees to
  find total cost of credit card for
  month or year.

MULTIPLE CHOICE

Select the best choice for each question.

1. Lu Yang expects to earn $64,700 next year. Last year he saved 12% of his income. If he saves the same percent this year, how much will Lu save? B

   A. $6,470   **B.** $7,764   **C.** $7,864
   D. $7,876   **E.** $7,964

2. Olga Kirosky deposited these items in a bank: (bills) 12 twenties, (coins) 11 quarters, 16 dimes; (checks) $125.99, $41.65. She received 100 one-dollar bills in cash back. What was the net amount of her deposit? A

   A. $311.99   **B.** $319.99   **C.** $399.99
   D. $411.99   **E.** $419.99

3. You discount a 6-month, noninterest-bearing note for $3,000 at a bank at 14%. What true rate of interest, to the nearest tenth percent do you pay? C

   A. 3%   **B.** 7%   **C.** 7.5%
   D. 14%   **E.** 24.5%

4. The bank statement sent to Abigail Ochs did not show checks for $158.23, $12.89, and $71.27, and an outstanding deposit of $75 that were listed in the check register. The balance printed on the statement was $289.07. What is the reconciled bank statement balance? A

   A. $121.68   **B.** $167.39   **C.** $28.32
   D. $456.46   **E.** $606.46

OPEN ENDED

5. A note, dated July 15, has a term of 3 months, what is the due date of the note? Oct. 15

6. The bank statement of Jake Hansen showed a balance of $356.93. His check register showed a balance of $308.34. When Jake compared the two records he found several differences. The bank statement listed these items not recorded in the register: ATM withdrawal, $50; ATM user fee, $2.25; direct deposit of paycheck, $624.70; checks for $287.23, $180.11, and $72.89. A check for $85.89 was recorded in the register as $58.89. The items not listed on the bank statement included checks for $72.44, $9.76, and $113.57; and a deposit made after the statement closing date. Debit card purchases of $85.67 and $16.73 appeared on the statement but not in the register. Reconcile Jake's bank statement and check register. $211.16

7. Justin Niklas made this deposit to the Breakfast Book Club's checking account: (bills) 43 ones, 13 fives; (coins) 9 quarters, 3 half-dollars, 5 dimes, 4 nickels, 12 pennies; (checks) $397.42, $192.81. Find the amount of the deposit. $702.80

8. After work Gerry Mathews used the ATM to deposit her paycheck for $868.39 and to withdraw $400 in cash. If her starting bank balance was $1,528.93, what is her new balance? $1,997.32

TEST TAKING STRATEGIES Cumulative Review

Multiple-choice questions often provide clues to their answers. Students should look for agreement between the words in the questions and those in the answers. For example, a question might state, "the answer is an _____." If only one of the choices begins with a vowel, the answer has been flagged for the student.

9. Drew Moro's check register balance was $349.64. His bank statement showed an ATM deposit of $59.39 that was not recorded in his check register, interest earned of $1.27, and an $15 charge for printing new checks. Reconcile Drew's check register. $395.30

10. Etta Warnicke deposited $20,000 in a three-year certificate of deposit that pays simple interest at a fixed annual rate of 4.9%. What total interest will Etta have earned at the end of three years? $2,940

11. A bank discounted a $3,200 noninterest-bearing note for Larry Pons at 12% interest for 9 months. Find the proceeds that Larry receives from the note. $2,912

12. Yoko Soga borrowed $450 on a loan with a finance charge of $94.50. Find the finance charge per $100 of the amount financed. $21

QUANTITATIVE COMPARISON

Compare the quantity in Column A with the quantity in Column B. Select the letter of the correct answer from these choices:

A if the quantity in Column A is greater;
B if the quantity in Column B is greater;
C if the two quantities are equal;
D if the relationship between the two quantities cannot be determined from the given information.

Column A	Column B
13. New balance on an account that had a beginning Balance of $43.65 with checks written for $2.98, $78.23 and deposits of $211.86, $12.45	New balance on an account that had a beginning balance of $215.44 with checks written for $56.89, $112.90 and a deposit of $85 A
14. 1 twenty dollar bill, 6 fives, 12 dimes, and 25 pennies	4 ten dollar bill, 8 ones, 12 quarters and 9 nickels C
15. simple interest on a $1,250 loan for 2 years at 12.5% interest rate	simple interest on a $3,200 loan for 2.5 years at 4.5% interest rate B

CONSTRUCTED RESPONSE

16. A friend can borrow $1,000 at 18% for 6 months from a bank that uses simple interest. He can also borrow the same amount at the same terms from a bank that uses the Rule of 78 to allocate interest. Write a memo to your friend explaining why, if he paid off the loan in the first month, he would pay more in interest on the Rule of 78 loan than at the simple interest loan. $\frac{6}{21} \times \$90$ is more than $1.5\% \times \$90$

Chapter 4 Cumulative Review ■ 187

Lesson 4.8 Credit Card Finance Charges
- Multiply previous balance by periodic rate to find finance charge.

- Add finance charge, new purchases, fees; subtract payments and credits from previous balance to find new balance.

- Subtract payments and credits from previous balance to find adjusted balance.

- Multiply adjusted balance by periodic rate to find finance charge.

- Add new purchases, fees, finance charge to adjusted balance to find new balance.

- Add daily purchases and fees to and subtract daily payments and credits from daily beginning balances to find new daily balances.

- Divide sum of daily balances by number of days in billing period to find average daily balance.

- Multiply average daily balance by daily periodic rate and number of days in billing period to find finance charge.

- Multiply average daily balance by monthly periodic rate to find finance charge.

- Add purchases, fees, finance charge to and subtract payments, credits from beginning balance to find new balance.

- Multiply cash advance principal by daily periodic rate and number of days of loan to find interest on cash advance.

- Add interest and fees to find finance charge on cash advance.

- Add finance charge and cash advance principal to find payoff amount.

TEST TAKING STRATEGIES Cumulative Review

Outlining a memo or letter makes it easier to arrange ideas logically. It also makes it easier to spot missing topics or unnecessary topics in the document.

Chapter 5 includes the math skills of addition, subtraction, multiplication, percents, fractions, rounding, and division. These skills are applied to problems involving consumer purchases of goods and services and Internet access.

Lesson 5.1 Sales Tax
Students calculate sales tax on purchases. They also calculate sales tax on purchases where some items are not taxed.

Lesson 5.2 Sales Receipts
Students calculate extensions, sales taxes, and total sales.

Lesson 5.3 Unit Prices
Students calculate and compare unit prices. They also find unit prices from group prices.

Lesson 5.4 Comparative Shopping
Students learn to compare prices at sales, from different vendors, and in different product quantities. They also compare costs of rental options as well as the costs of renting vs. buying.

Lesson 5.5 Personal Internet Access
Students compare Internet access costs and speeds.

CHAPTER 5
Spend Wisely

5.1 Sales Tax
5.2 Sales Receipts
5.3 Unit Prices
5.4 Comparative Shopping
5.5 Personal Internet Access

Statistical Insights

State Sales Tax Rates
January 1, 2004

State	Sales/Use Tax, %	State	Sales/Use Tax, %	State	Sales/Use Tax, %
Alabama	4	Louisiana	4	Ohio	6
Arizona	5.6	Maine	5	Oklahoma	4.5
Arkansas	6	Maryland	5	Pennsylvania	6
California	6	Massachusetts	5	Rhode Island	7
Colorado	2.9	Michigan	6	South Carolina	5
Connecticut	6	Minnesota	6.5	South Dakota	4
Florida	6	Mississippi	7	Tennessee	7
Georgia	4	Missouri	4.225	Texas	6.25
Hawaii	4	Nebraska	5.5	Utah	4.75
Idaho	6	Nevada	6.5	Vermont	6
Illinois	6.25	New Jersey	6	Virginia	3.5
Indiana	6	New Mexico	5	Washington	6.5
Iowa	5	New York	4.25	West Virginia	6
Kansas	5.3	North Carolina	4.5	Wisconsin	5
Kentucky	6	North Dakota	5	Wyoming	4

Note: Alaska, Delaware, Montana, New Hampshire and Oregon have no statewide sales taxes.

Use the data shown above to answer each question.
1. How many states listed have a statewide tax that is greater than 6.5%? Name each state. 3; Mississippi, Rhode Island, Tennessee
2. What is the average statewide tax percent for the states listed? 5.32%

Statistical Insights

Ask students to compare the sales tax rate of their state with the rate of the nearest city in a neighboring state. Discuss the impact of the difference, if any, on the businesses in both states. Economic impacts might include product pricing, the types of items carried or not carried, source of customer service clerks, and advertising area covered by businesses.

Teaching Resources

Lesson Plans, Ch. 5
Chapter 5 Test Forms A and B
Workbook, Ch. 5
Explore Algebra and Geometry
    Activities
Technology Activities
Competitive Events Prep
Data Activities CD, Ch. 5
ExamView® Pro CD, Ch. 5

Shopping Online Smartly

Online purchases require the use of a credit card and access to the Internet. Care must be taken when using a credit card online. You should only purchase from Internet web sites that offer a secure checkout system or will allow you to establish an account or will ship goods C.O.D. Many web sites use special encryption software to safeguard your credit card number.

The Internet is also an excellent source for getting information about a product, checking its availability in your area, and locating a retailer with the best price. Consider the total cost of the purchase, including shipping costs, before making a decision to buy online.

Taxing Online Purchases

Many online sellers have a billing system that allows sales tax to be collected from customers if required by the state where the online customers live. The sellers collect the correct amount of tax and forward it to the state tax office.

If the seller does not collect state sales taxes, customers still have a responsibility to pay the sales taxes due their state. This may be done by reporting the amount due on a state income tax return or by using some other required process.

NetCheck

Shopping Online Smartly Point out to students that when a secure checkout system is available, the safest method of purchasing on the net may be with a credit card. This is because some card companies will cover the full cost of any fraud arising from use of the card over the Internet. Some cards also provide warranty features beyond those of the vendor.

Point out to students that purchasing online often requires paying shipping costs and that these costs may offset the savings obtained through online purchasing.

Taxing Online Purchases Inform the students that Congress has not renewed the ban on state sales taxes for Internet purchases, so state sales taxes may be levied on Internet purchases.

How Times Have Changed

Forty years ago the Internet did not exist. Today, well over 100 million Internet hosts are sending information over the major backbones of the network at speeds greater than 2 billion bits per second.

Answer to research item:

The speeds given in the timeline refer to how fast data can be transmitted through the major arteries of the Internet superhighway system. These backbone speeds are generally faster than connection speeds. Refer students to pages 209–210 for more about connection speeds.

TE Note: Originally, the NSFNET was restricted to research and education. This ban was lifted in 1991, paving the way for commercial uses like ordering pizzas and Internet banking.

189

HOW TIMES HAVE CHANGED

Lead the class into a discussion about the history of the Internet. Possible questions to ask:

How old is the Internet? (began in 1969)

For how long have people been using e-mail? (since early 1970)

Turn the students' attention to the timeline. Have them do their own research to discover a significant event that happened in 1957 that relates to the history of the Internet.

See page 218 for assessment questions related to the timeline.

Start Up

Have students read the Start Up problem. Then, ask students to use the web to find out if and how their state and local governments tax retail sales. Also have students find out if their state and local governments tax Internet purchases. Students should identify the tax rates and items taxed by each governmental level.

Math Skill Builder

The skills of adding money, multiplying money amounts by percents, rewriting percents as decimals, and rounding money amounts to the nearest cent are used in this lesson.

Complete all exercises in Math Skill Builder 1–2.

■ Teach Goal 1

Instead of sales taxes, some states have excise taxes on certain items. If your state has excise taxes instead of sales taxes, have the opening discussion concern excise taxes. Then, discuss the impact of sales or excise taxes on the cost of goods, the places people shop, and the types and quantities of items people buy.

■ Apply Goal 1

Demonstrate the solution to Example 1 at the board with students completing it at their desks.

Assign Check Your Understanding problems A and B for class work. Check student work to identify student problems.

5.1 Sales Tax

GOALS

- Calculate sales tax on purchases
- Calculate sales taxes when some items are not taxed

Start Up

Are some items excluded from sales taxes in your city or state? Why might some items be taxed and others not? How do sales taxes affect what and where people buy items?

Math Skill Builder

Review these math skills and solve the exercises.

1 **Add** money amounts.
Find the sum. $1.09 + $98.81 + $431.99 = $531.89

1a. $45.98 + $12.87 + $319.08 $377.93

1b. $512.44 + $5.89 + $29.98 $548.31

2 **Multiply** money amounts by percents.
Rewrite the percent and find the product. 4% × $24 = 0.04 × $24 = $0.96
2a. 8% × $56 $4.48   **2b.** 4.3% × $84.89 $3.65   **2c.** 8.25% × $15.99 $1.32

■ Sales Taxes on Purchases

Many states, cities, and counties charge a sales tax on certain items you buy. **Sales tax** is a percentage of the price of an item or a percentage of the total of all taxable items. Sellers collect the sales tax from consumers for the government. Sales tax rates differ from community to community and state to state.

Sales Tax Rate × Price of Item = Sales Tax

Sales tax is rounded to the nearest cent. If more than one tax is charged, the tax rates are often combined into one rate. For example, if there is a state tax of 5% and a city tax of 3%, the tax collected is 8%. The buyer pays the price of the item plus the sales tax.

Price of Item + Sales Tax = Total Cost of Item

EXAMPLE 1

Ellie Kramer purchased a chain saw priced at $285.99. The state in which she lived charges a 6.5% sales tax on purchases. What sales tax is paid and what is the total cost of the chain saw to Ellie?

190 ■ Chapter 5 Spend Wisely

TEACHING STRATEGIES Cooperative Learning

Have teams of two students outline what they consider to be the problems to online businesses of levying sales taxes on Internet purchases. Then the team members should propose possible solutions to these problems.

Encourage students to use web search engines to identify problems and solutions for businesses taxing Internet sales. Search terms might include sales tax, Internet sales tax, and Internet tax issues.

SOLUTION

Multiply price by rate as a decimal.

6.5% = 0.065; 0.065 × \$285.99 = \$18.58935, or \$18.59

\$285.99 + \$18.59 = \$304.58   price + sales tax

■ CHECK YOUR UNDERSTANDING

A. Software that turns your computer into a phone system sells for \$89.99. You buy it in a state that charges a 4.5% sales tax. What is the sales tax paid? What is the total cost of the software? \$4.05; \$94.04

B. Jane Ellis buys an exercise bike for \$369.89 in a state with a 3.5% sales tax and in a city with a 1.8% sales tax. How much sales tax did she pay on the bike? What total amount did she pay? \$19.60; \$389.49

■ Nontaxable Items

Some cities and states do not tax certain items, such as food, prescription drugs, and charges for labor, or services. To find the sales tax when some items are not taxable, first find the subtotal of all taxable items. Then calculate the sales tax on that portion of the bill only. To find the total bill, find the subtotal of all nontaxable items and add the subtotals of nontaxable and taxable items, and the sales tax.

> **MATH TIP**
> A **subtotal** is a partial total.

Sales Tax = Sales Tax Rate × Subtotal of Taxable Items

Total = Subtotal of Taxable Items + Subtotal of Nontaxable Items + Sales Tax

EXAMPLE 2

A service station mechanic took 3 hours to repair a car. The service charge was \$65 an hour. Two parts were replaced at a cost of \$117.98 and \$49.39. The state has a sales tax of 4% charged on goods, but not on labor. Find the total bill.

SOLUTION

\$65 × 3 = \$195   cost of nontaxable labor

Add the cost of the taxable parts: \$117.98 + \$49.39 = \$167.37

Multiply the sales tax rate by the subtotal of taxable items.

\$167.37 × 0.04 = \$6.694, or \$6.69   sales tax

Add to find the total bill.

\$195 + \$167.37 + \$6.69 = \$369.06   nontaxable labor + taxable items + sales tax

■ CHECK YOUR UNDERSTANDING

C. A neighbor replaced her hot water heater with an energy-efficient one. She paid \$309.59 for the heater and \$56 more to have it installed. A sales tax of 5.25% was added to the cost of the heater but not the installation. What was the sales tax and what was the total cost of the heater to the neighbor? \$16.25; \$381.84

D. A handyman installed 8 sections of cedar fencing in Jose Velez's back yard. Jose was charged \$462.53 for the sections and \$225 for the installation. A sales tax rate of 6.75% was charged on goods but not labor. What sales tax did Jose pay? How much was his total bill for the fence? \$31.22; \$718.75

■ **ONGOING ASSESSMENT**

Read, one at a time, these percentages: 2%, 2.5%, 2.08%; 0.8% and have students rewrite them as decimals. Then have students multiply \$400 by each decimal. Check their answers by calling on students.

■ **Teach Goal 2**

Ask students to use the web or contact city and state taxing bodies to find items that are not subject to sales taxes in their city and state.

Have students discuss why some purchases are taxed while others are not taxed.

Emphasize that sales tax be calculated only on the total of taxable items. So the total bill is the sum of total taxable items, total nontaxable items, and the appropriate sales tax.

■ **Apply Goal 2**

Work through Example 2 at the board with students completing the math at their desks.

Assign Check Your Understanding problems C and D to be completed in class. Move about the classroom and examine student work to identify student errors or difficulties.

■ *CHECK YOUR UNDERSTANDING SOLUTIONS*

A. 4.5% = 0.045; \$89.99 × 0.045 = \$4.049, or \$4.05; \$89.99 + \$4.05 = \$94.04

B. 3.5% + 1.8% = 5.3%; 5.3% = 0.053; \$369.89 × 0.053 = \$19.604, or \$19.60; \$369.89 + \$19.60 = \$389.49

C. \$309.59 × 0.0525 = \$16.253, or \$16.25; \$309.59 + \$56 + \$16.25 = \$381.84

E. \$462.53 × 0.0675 = \$31.220, or \$31.22; \$462.53 + \$225 + \$31.22 = \$718.75

Wrap Up

Review the Start Up. Ask students to report on their web search findings about sales tax rates, items taxed, and Internet purchases. Place answers on the board as students answer your queries.

WORKPLACE WINDOW

Have students report on their findings. List the education and experience requirements on the board as they respond.

Assign

Assignment: Exercises 1–16, 18–30. Start with the basic arithmetic problems to be sure that students understand the underlying arithmetic in the exercises.

Assess

Ask students these questions:

1. How do you rewrite a percent as a decimal? **Drop the % sign and move the decimal point two places to the left.**

2. What steps do you follow to calculate sales tax? **Convert percents to decimals and then multiply the decimal by the price of the taxable items.**

3. What steps do you take to find the sales tax on an item when more than one governmental unit taxes it? **Add the tax rates for the governmental units. Then multiply the total tax rate by the item price.**

Look back at the Start Up questions in this lesson. Many cities and states do not apply a sales tax to prescription drugs and food. Prescription drugs and food are often not taxed to reduce the cost of these items to people with limited incomes. If people live near city or state borders, they may cross these borders to avoid paying sales taxes. They may also try to avoid sales taxes by buying goods over the Internet.

WORKPLACE WINDOW

TELEMARKETERS work for an industry that can reach almost every household with a telephone. Telemarketers make phone calls to individuals or businesses to sell a product or service. Like other salespeople, telemarketers must know a lot about the product or service they sell. Some telemarketers, such as those who sell extended warranties on an appliance the customer owns, take orders directly from customers. Other telemarketers only determine the potential customer's interest in a product and arrange a time for a salesperson to call. This may be done for a product such as replacement windows that requires measurements and a personal inspection by a trained salesperson.

1. What education and experience are required to be a successful telemarketer?
2. What are the job prospects for interested individuals?
3. What types of products or services are often sold using telemarketers?

EXERCISES

Find the sum.
1. $34.89 + $1.97 + $211.03 $247.89
2. $108.67 + $0.98 + $19.98 $129.63

Find the product.
3. $45.39 × 4.9% $2.22
4. $1,509.38 × $4\frac{1}{4}$% $64.15

5. Rachel Seyval wants to buy a computer printer priced at $275.89. If the state sales tax is 5%, what sales tax will she pay? $13.79

6. Where Tony Berio lives, the state sales tax is 5.5% and the city sales tax is 2%. What amount of sales tax must he pay on a $167 purchase? $12.53

Find the sales taxes on each of the items below.

	Item	Price	Sale Tax Rate	Sales Tax
7.	Computer scanner	$99.99	5.8%	$5.80
8.	Garden tractor	$1,568.89	3.5%	$54.91
9.	Golf club set	$635.18	2.9%	$18.42
10.	Antique dresser	$498.89	4.6%	$22.95

192 ■ **Chapter 5 Spend Wisely**

COMMON ERRORS

Students may automatically apply a sales tax to the total purchase, even when the problem states that certain items are not taxed. Remind students to read each problem carefully before starting any computations.

11. **BEST BUY** Mona Allen wants to buy a bed that costs $695. The city sales tax rate is 7%. In a nearby city the sales tax rate is 4%. How much less would the bed cost if Mona bought it in the nearby city? $20.85

12. Rollie Gusewelle has his auto dealer install auto seat covers on his used car. The seat covers costs $189.99 and installation another $45.89. The sales tax rate is 4.7% but is not applied to labor. What is the total cost of the seat covers to Rollie? $244.81

LaVernn Johnson had a new 36 square yard wall-to-wall rug installed in her home. The rug cost $15.99 a square yard, the padding cost $3 a square yard, and the rug was installed for $4 a square yard. The sales tax rate is 4.9%, and it is not applied to labor.

13. What was the cost of the carpeting and padding? $683.64

14. What was the cost of the installation? $144

15. What was the sales tax? $33.50

16. What was the total cost of the purchase? $861.14

17. **CRITICAL THINKING** Some people oppose sales taxes because they believe they are unfair to those with limited incomes. Can you think of a reason why they think that sales taxes are unfair to the "poor" and fair to the "rich"? Others think they are fair. Can you think of an argument that would support sales taxes as fair to all? Answers will vary.

MIXED REVIEW

18. $5,297.12 ÷ 100 $52.97

19. $91.78 ÷ 1,000 $0.09

20. $\frac{3}{4} \times \frac{1}{8}$ $\frac{3}{32}$

21. $\frac{2}{3} \times \frac{5}{6}$ $\frac{5}{9}$

22. Rewrite $\frac{3}{8}$ as a decimal. 0.375

23. Rewrite $1\frac{3}{4}$ as a decimal. 1.75

24. Rewrite 4.978% as a decimal. 0.04978

25. Rewrite 0.0589% as a decimal. 0.000589

26. Divide 4,688 by 59 to the nearest hundredth. 79.46

27. Tyrone Bingham signed a 9-month, noninterest-bearing promissory note for $4,300 that he discounted at his bank at 12%. What were the net proceeds that Tyrone received? $3,913, Lesson 4.2

28. Zena Cranshaw's previous credit card balance was $289.14. Her credit card statement for May also showed a payment of $150 and a purchase of $98.99. The card company's APR is 18% and it uses the adjusted balance method to find the finance charge. What was Zena's finance charge for the month? $2.09, Lesson 4.8

Yancy Guzmone saves money for his son's college fund. The account has a balance of $400 on June 1. His bank pays 4% compound interest monthly on the account. He makes no deposits or withdrawals. Lesson 3.6

29. What interest will he earn at the end of the first month? $1.33

30. What interest will he earn at the end of the second month? $1.34

Lesson 5.1 Sales Tax ■ **193**

SELECTED SOLUTIONS

11. $695 × 0.07 = $48.65; $695 × 0.04 = $27.80; $48.65 − $27.80 = $20.85

13. $15.99 + $3 = $18.99; $18.99 × 36 = $683.64

14. $4 × 36 = $144

15. $683.64 × 0.049 = $33.498, or $33.50

16. $683.64 + $144 + $33.50 = $861.14

Start Up

Have students read the Start Up question. Then ask them to list possible answers on a sheet of paper. Collect the papers for discussion at the end of the lesson.

Math Skill Builder

Have students do all exercises in Math Skill Builder 1–3 to review the skills of adding and multiplying decimals, rewriting percents as decimals, and rounding. These skills will be used in this lesson.

■ Teach Goal 1

Many students have had or know of someone who has had the experience of being overcharged at a checkout counter. Have them relate these experiences as a means of emphasizing the importance of checking sales receipts.

Ask students if they think computer generated sales slips are more reliable than other sales slips. Point out that data entry errors are easy to make and that formula errors can be made in computer programs.

GOALS

■ Calculate extensions
■ Calculate sales slip totals

Start Up

Many sales slips that were paid by credit card no longer display the whole credit card number. Online ordering computer screens also frequently do not display the whole credit card number you punch in. Only the last four digits of the card number are shown. Why have companies chosen not to display the whole number?

Math Skill Builder

Review these math skills and solve the exercises that follow.

1 **Rewrite** percentages as decimals.
Rewrite as a decimal. $5.7\% = 0.057$

   1a. 3.9% 0.039   **1b.** 4.7% 0.047   **1c.** 6.25% 0.0625   **1d.** 7.75% 0.0775

2 **Add** money amounts.
Find the sum. $\$12.89 + \$35.99 + \$19.98 = \$68.86$

   2a. $\$87.79 + \$2.19 + \$35.71$ $125.69   **2b.** $\$7.08 + \$1.89 + \$3.99$ $12.96

3 **Multiply** money amounts by decimals. Round to the nearest cent.
Find the product. $\$129.89 \times 0.056 = \$7.273$, or $\$7.27$

   3a. $\$452.98 \times 0.065$ $29.44   **3b.** $\$299.18 \times 0.046$ $13.76

■ Sales Slip Extensions

Most store employees give customers a *cash register receipt*, or *sales slip*, after a transaction is completed. Customers may use these slips to check that all the items bought were received and that the prices and calculations were correct. Sales slips can also be used as expense records for business travelers or serve as proofs of purchase if items are returned.

Like the sales slip shown on the next page, most sales slips show the

■ number of units, or quantity, and a description of each item.

■ *unit price*, or the price of one item or group of items treated as one. For example, a box of paper is treated as one unit even though each box contains 10 reams of paper and each ream contains 500 sheets of paper.

CONNECTION TO LANGUAGE ARTS

Have students write a short paper explaining the possible consequences facing the store and the store clerk when errors are made on sales slips. Students should outline their paper before they begin to write. Student responses may include loss of customers, cuts in pay, and loss of jobs. Have students submit both their outlines and their papers.

- **extension**, or the unit price multiplied by the quantity of each item. For example, the amount, $95.97 on the sales slip, is the extension of 3 boxes of printer paper at $31.99 for each box.
- *subtotal*, or the sum of the extensions.
- sales tax.
- total sale, or the sum of the subtotal and the sales tax.

The total price of each quantity on a sales slip is the extension. To find the extension of an item, multiply the quantity by the unit price.

Extension = Quantity × Unit Price

"At" or "@" means the price of a single unit. For example, 1 dozen pens @ $4.99 means 12 pens are priced at $4.99 in a group of one dozen. But a price of "3 dozen pens, $14.97" means that the price is $14.97 for all 3 dozen pens.

EXAMPLE 1

Find the product of the quantities and unit prices below.

a. 12 batteries @ $0.75

b. 3 dozen batteries @ $3

c. 2 M (thousand) light bulbs @ $450

d. 2 C (hundred) ergonomic mouse pads @ $358

SOLUTION

a. 12 × $0.75 = $9   cost of batteries

b. 3 × $3 = $9   cost of batteries in groups of a dozen

c. 2 × $450 = $900   cost of light bulbs in groups of 1,000

d. 2 × $358 = $716   cost of mouse pads in groups of 100

■ **CHECK YOUR UNDERSTANDING**

A. You can buy file folders in boxes of 100 for $8.99. If you bought 600 file folders, what is the price? $53.94

B. Julie Firsch buys 300 fancy desk calendars to give to her clients as gifts. The calendars are priced at $85.99 per C. What was the total price of the calendars? $257.97

Sales Receipt

COMPUTER VILLAGE
2401 Barksdale Road, San Diego, CA 92119-2401
619-555-3900

SOLD TO: *Calvin Thomas*
STREET: *398 Grimbel Avenue*
DATE: *May 15* 20---   CITY, STATE, ZIP: *San Diego, CA 92104*

| SOLD BY *TJ* | CASH | CHARGE √ | C.O.D. | DELIVERY BY *Taken* |

QUANTITY	DESCRIPTION	UNIT PRICE	AMOUNT
3 boxes	Printer paper	31 99	95 97
1	Speaker set	28 98	28 98
1 box	Zip diskettes	98 57	98 57

Everything You Ever Wanted in Electronics!

SUBTOTAL	——|——	223 52
SALES TAX	7.5%	16 76
TOTAL	——|——	240 28

PROBLEM SOLVING TIP

Estimate your extensions before finding the exact amounts. Compare the exact amounts to the estimates to see if the exact amounts are reasonable.

■ **Apply Goal 1**

Work through Example 1 at the board while students complete the math at their desks.

Assign Check Your Understanding problems A and B for completion in class. Circulate through the classroom and examine student work to identify errors and problems.

■ ***CHECK YOUR UNDERSTANDING SOLUTIONS***

A. 600 ÷ 100 = 6; 6 × $8.99 = $53.94

B. 300 ÷ 100 = 3; 3 × $85.99 = $257.97

■ **Teach Goal 2**

Point out to students that the process used in this lesson to find sales taxes is the same as the process they used in the previous lesson.

If students have calculators, work through the Calculator Tip on page 196 with them.

■ **ONGOING ASSESSMENT**
Write gross, C, M, cwt, and T on the board and ask students to identify the full name of each measure and its value (144, 100, 1,000, 100, 2,000)

■ **Apply Goal 2**

Work through Example 2 at the board while students complete the math at their desks.

Have students estimate the extensions in Example 2 before you calculate them at the board.
$3 \times \$16 = \$48$;
$2 \times \$80 = \$160$.

Assign Check Your Understanding problems C and D for completion in class. Circulate through the room and examine student work for difficulties.

Wrap **Up**

Review the Start Up. Ask students to read items from their lists completed in the Start Up problem. Discuss the results with them.

The main reason is security. People leave, lose, or drop receipts at gas station pumps and stores where others can pick them up. Passersby may look over people's shoulders and view the numbers on the computer screen.

Sales slip totals are found by adding the extensions to get the subtotal. If there is a sales tax and it is applied to all items sold, the tax rate is multiplied by the subtotal to find the tax amount. Then the subtotal and tax amount are added to find the total amount of the sales slip.

Subtotal = Sum of Extensions

Sales Tax Amount = Subtotal × Sales Tax Rate

Total of Sales Slip = Subtotal + Sales Tax Amount

To simplify matters, all items sold in this lesson will be subject to sales taxes.

BUSINESS TIP

Items bought in large quantities may be priced by the *gross* (12 dozen), *hundred (C)*, *thousand (M)*, *hundred pounds* or *hundredweight (cwt)*, and *ton (T)*.

EXAMPLE 2

A shopper bought 3 pairs of gloves @ $15.89 and 2 pair of shoes @ $78.98. There was a state sales tax of 4.75%. What was the total of the cash register receipt?

SOLUTION
Multiply the quantities by the prices to find the extensions.

$3 \times \$15.89 = \$47.67$ $2 \times \$78.98 = \$157.96$

Add the extensions to find the subtotal for the sale.

$\$47.67 + \$157.96 = \$205.63$ subtotal

Find the sales tax.

$\$205.63 \times 0.0475 = \$9.77$ sales tax

Add the subtotal and sales tax.

$\$205.63 + \$9.77 = \$215.40$ receipt total

CALCULATOR TIP

To find the subtotal: press the M+ key after finding each extension.
To display the subtotal press the MR/C key. Multiply the subtotal in the display by the sales tax rate and press M+. Pressing MR/C now displays the total of the sales slip. Clear the memory by pressing the MR/C again before starting the next problem.

■ **CHECK YOUR UNDERSTANDING**

C. Alexis Bakov bought 3 boxes of recycled kraft envelopes @ $3.89 and 5 boxes of recycled kraft clasp envelopes @ $5.79. The sales tax rate was 3.85%. What was the sales slip total? $42.18

D. Sonia Alvarez bought 2 doz. team T-shirts @ $139.89 and 2 boxes of baseball caps @ $89.99 for the Little League team she manages. There was a state sales tax of 5% and a city sales tax of 2.5%. What was the cash register receipt total? $494.24

Wrap **Up**

People often fail to safeguard sales slip. They are commonly left at the gasoline pump and dropped on store floors. This carelessness allowed thieves to steal the slips and use the credit card numbers. In the case of online ordering systems, displaying x's for all but the last four numbers prevents passersby from obtaining the number.

CONNECTION TO MARKETING

Invite students who are in or have completed their co-op assignments to share their experiences making change, writing sales slips, and making errors. Also have them discuss store policies about sales slip errors.

Use the Web to find the city sales tax rates in your area and bordering areas. Make a chart displaying the state sales tax rates, the city sales tax rates, and the combined sales tax rates. Compare the state and city with the highest sales tax rate to the state and city with the lowest. Prepare a report that includes your charts. The report should describe possible reasons why the states and cities differ so much in their sales tax rates.

EXERCISES

Rewrite as a decimal.

1. 4.85% 0.0485   **2.** 6.25% 0.0625   **3.** 2.9% 0.029   **4.** 7.5% 0.075

Find the sum.

5. $35.29 + $191.56 + $3.12 $229.97

6. $29.58 + $4.56 + $514.16 $548.30

Find the product.

7. $458.29 × 6.3% $28.87

8. $280.12 × 7.75% $21.71

Find the extension for each purchase.

9. 5 M @ $118.98 $594.90

10. 3 doz. @ $76.12 $228.36

11. 6 reams @ $42.89 $257.34

12. 12 C @ $12.99 $155.88

13. 8 tons @ $65.21 $521.68

14. 25 sets, $213.78 $213.78

15. Chad Lauer bought 3 doz. golf tees @ $2.19 and 4 doz. golf balls @ $19.99. The city sales tax was 6%. What was the sales slip total? $91.72

16. Frieda Hausen purchased 6 tons of sand @ $42.88 and 5 cubic yards of mulch @ $28.58. The state sales tax was 4.5%. What was the cash register receipt total? $418.19

Bob Jeffries bought these items at an office supply store: 2 doz. pencils @ $1.99, 8 boxes of cellophane tape @ $5.99, 3 cartons of envelopes @ $9.83. The store applied a 7.2% sales tax to the subtotal.

17. What was the subtotal? $81.39

18. What was the state sales tax amount? $5.86

19. What was the total of the sales slip? $87.25

20. **BEST BUY** At a discount store in state A, you can buy 3 doz. antivirus programs @ $191.89, and pay a sales tax rate of 6.3%. At a department store in the adjoining state B, you can buy 3 doz. of the same programs @ $180.19, and pay a sales tax rate of 7.75%. In which state will the sales slip total be lower? State B

Lesson 5.2 Sales Receipts ■ 197

SELECTED SOLUTIONS

17. 2 × $1.99 = $3.98; 8 × $5.99 = $47.92;
3 × $9.83 = $29.49;
$3.98 + $47.92 + $29.49 = $81.39
18. $81.39 × 0.072 = $5.860, or $5.86
19. $81.39 + $5.86 = $87.25

20. (A) 3 × $191.89 = $575.67;
$575.67 × 0.063 = $36.267, or $36.27;
$575.67 + $36.27 = $611.94
(B) 3 × $180.19 = $540.57;
$540.57 × 0.0775 = $41.894, or $41.89;
$540.57 + $41.89 = $582.46; State B.

■ COMMUNICATION

Assign the Workplace Window problem. Have the authors of one or more of the best reports present their findings to the class.

■ STUDENT PORTFOLIO

Students should consider placing their reports and charts from the Communication assignment in their portfolios.

Assign

Assignment: Exercises 1–35. Start with the basic arithmetic problems at the beginning.

Assess

Check student answers to the exercises by calling on them in class, collecting and grading selected problems, or by observing students at work.

Ask students to define the bolded and italicized terms in the lesson and to use them in sentences.

Reteach

STUDENT WORKBOOK
Redemonstrate how to find extensions by doing line 1 of the sales slip in Exercise 1 with them. Have them finish the rest of the extensions in the sales slip.

Reteach how to find subtotals, taxes, and totals of sales slips by completing the sales slip in Exercise 1 with them. Then have them verify the extensions, sales taxes, subtotals, and totals in Exercises 2–4.

■ STUDENT PORTFOLIO

Students should consider placing the completed sales slips from Workbook Exercises 1–4 in their portfolios.

21. Divide 54.972 by 3.4 to the nearest thousandth. 16.168

22. Estimate the product of 32 × 109. 3,000

23. $\frac{5}{8} \div \frac{1}{2} = 1\frac{1}{4}$

24. 18. Rewrite 0.05 as a fraction. $\frac{1}{20}$

25. 22 is 25% of what amount? 88

26. Maude Regan began the day with $23.98 in cash. During the day she received $20 from a friend to repay a loan. Maude spent these amounts during the same day: $3.78, $2.19, $0.88, and $15.45. How much cash did she have at the end of the day? $21.68, Lesson 2.6

27. On July 31, LaVonn Dugan's check register balance was $742.16. When she balanced her account, she had not recorded a service charge of $4.50, a deposit of $37.50, and a check for $9.15. Find her correct check register balance. $766.01, Lesson 3.5

28. Ta-pei Han's taxable income last year was $73,840. His state's income tax rate is 4.7% of taxable income. The city in which he works also applies an income tax of 2% on taxable income earned in the city. What total state and city income taxes did Ta-pei pay last year? $4,947.28, Lesson 2.4

29. Carlita Renoso's average daily credit card balance for July was $208.37. Her credit card company charged her interest at an annual percentage rate of 18% on the balance. How much interest did Carlita pay on her credit card balance? $3.13, Lesson 4.8

30. Esmat Hussein wants to buy a set of videos on the Civil War priced at $75.89. If the state sales tax is 4%, what total amount will he pay for the videos? $78.93, Lesson 5.1

31. A washing machine sells for $562 in a state that charges a 5.3% sales tax and in a city that charges a 2% sales tax. What is the total cost of the washing machine? $603.03, Lesson 5.1

32. Ed Smoller is paid $0.95 for every framed picture he assembles. He assembles 50 on Monday, 54 on Tuesday, 53 on Wednesday, and 49 on Thursday. How many pictures must he assemble on Friday to average 55 pictures a day? 69, Lesson 1.5

33. The senior class of Ekersville High School ran a dart game at the town's 3-day homecoming event. The class collected $250.50 on Friday, $242.75 on Saturday, and $224.25 on Sunday. What was the average amount collected by the class each day? $239.17, Lesson 1.3

34. A salesperson is paid 3% commisson on all sales and 5% commission on sales over $10,000 in a week. Last week the salesperson had sales of $13,568. What was the salesperson's total commission for the week? $478.40, Lesson 1.4

35. Yoko Mari's tax return last year showed gross income of $23,412 and adjustments to income of $1,690. What was Yoko's adjusted gross income last year? $21,722, Lesson 2.3

COMMON ERRORS

Some students may not understand the concept of units. Stress that a unit price is the price for whatever "unit" you are buying the product in. For example, you don't buy individual eggs; you buy a dozen. So, eggs are priced by the unit, which is by the dozen.

5.3 Unit Prices

Goals

- Calculate and compare unit prices
- Calculate unit prices from group prices

Start Up

You can buy Product A in a 12-oz. package that sells for $2.99 and competing brand, Product B, in a $1\frac{1}{2}$-lb. package that sells for $4.59. Describe two ways that you can compare the prices of these products.

Math Skill Builder

Review these math skills and solve the exercises that follow.

1 **Subtract** money amounts, and round to the nearest cent.
Find the difference. $0.587 − $0.438 = $0.149, or $0.15

    1a. $2.56 − $2.39 $0.17   **1b.** $0.946 − $0.813 $0.13   **1c.** $4.12 − $3.78 $0.34

2 **Divide** money amounts by whole numbers and decimals.
Find the quotient. $2.99 ÷ 4.6 = $0.65

    2a. $4.99 ÷ 6.3 $0.79   **2b.** $1.39 ÷ 6.2 $0.22   **2c.** $21.87 ÷ 10.5 $2.08

■ Unit Price Comparisons

Many items are packaged in ways that make it difficult to compare them easily with competing brands. For example, one product may be packaged in an 8-oz jar while another brand uses a 12-oz jar.

To help shoppers compare the costs of products, many stores post unit prices on their shelves. The unit price is the price of one item or one measure of the item. It may be an ounce, a pound, a quart, a dozen, a hundred feet, or some other measure. If unit prices are not posted, you have to calculate them to compare the costs.

MATH TIP

1 lb = 16 oz
1 T = 2,000 lb
1 ft = 12 in.
1 yd = 3 ft
1 qt = 2 pt
1 gal = 4 qt

EXAMPLE 1

Gelo toothpaste costs $1.28 for a 6-oz tube. GloWite toothpaste costs $1.99 for a 4.6-oz tube. Which brand costs more per ounce? How much more?

SOLUTION
Divide Gelo price by 6 to find price per ounce: $1.28 ÷ 6 = $0.213

Divide GloWite price by 4.6 to find price per ounce: $1.99 ÷ 4.6 = $0.433

TEACHING STRATEGIES Metric Measures

Some items purchased may be packaged in metric quantities; e.g., liter bottles of soda. If different sizes and different brands are all in the same measure (e.g., liters), the process of finding per unit costs is the same as that used when the products are packaged in customary quantities: divide the price by the unit of measure. Make sure that students understand this concept. The metric system is treated in Chapter 14.

Subtract the per-ounce cost of Gelo from the per-ounce cost of GloWite.

$0.433 − $0.213 = $0.22   difference in cost per ounce

Dividing prices ($1.99) by units (4.6) may not result in an even number of cents. To compare the unit price of products, it is usually sufficient to round off the unit price to the nearest tenth of a cent ($0.433).

■ CHECK YOUR UNDERSTANDING

A. A store sells an 18-oz. box of National Mills corn flakes for $3.29 and a 24-oz. box of Keller's corn flakes for $3.99. Which box sells for less per ounce? How much less per ounce? Kellers; $0.02

B. You can buy a package of four D batteries for $5.99 or a package of two D batteries for $3.49. Which package costs less per battery? How much less per battery? 1st package; $0.25

■ Group Pricing

Stores may have one price for a single unit and another price for a group of two or more units. For example, soup may be sold for 89¢ a can or 3 cans for $2.60. If you buy 3 cans, you pay less than 87¢ a can ($2.60 ÷ 3 = $0.86 $\frac{2}{3}$). In this way, vendors encourage consumers to buy more of their products.

To compare prices of items priced by the group, find their unit price by dividing the group price by the number of units in the group. If there is a fraction of a cent left over, *round up*, or count it as a whole cent.

EXAMPLE 2

Corn is selling at 3 cans for $1. What is the unit price of a can of corn?

SOLUTION

Divide the group price by the number of units to find the price for one unit.

$1 ÷ 3 = $0.333, or $0.34   price of one can of corn

■ CHECK YOUR UNDERSTANDING

C. A store is selling 3 oranges for $0.97. What is the price of one orange? $0.33

D. At a sale, shirts are being sold at 5 for $53. What is the sale price per shirt? $10.60

Wrap Up

Look again at the Start Up question at the beginning of this lesson. You could compare the products by stating the price of Product A in terms of pounds or by stating the price of Product B in terms of ounces.

■ Teach Goal 2

Make sure students round up when finding a unit price from a group price.

■ ONGOING ASSESSMENT
Call out these group prices and have students find the unit prices and round them up, to the nearest tenth of a cent: 3 for $8.26 **($2.753)**, 12 for $5.69 **($0.474)**.

■ Apply Goal 2

Work through Example 2 with students completing the math at their desks.

Have students do Check Your Understanding problems C and D in class. Walk around the room and examine student work for errors or problems.

Wrap Up

Review the Start Up. Have students read their answers to the Start Up problem they completed earlier. The two ways are to convert Product A to pounds or convert Product B to ounces. The answer is basically the old saying: "You can't compare apples to oranges."

COMMUNICATION

Discuss with the class the unit types and examples on their lists. Write the types of units on the board when students respond.

■ *CHECK YOUR UNDERSTANDING SOLUTIONS*

A. $3.29 ÷ 18 = $0.1827, or $0.183;
$3.99 ÷ 24 = $0.1662, or $0.166;
larger box sells for less; $0.183 − $0.166 = $0.017, or $0.02

B. $5.99 ÷ 4 = $1.497, or $1.50; $3.49 ÷ 2 = $1.745, or $1.75; package of 4 costs less; $1.75 − $1.50 = $0.25

C. $0.97 ÷ 3 = $0.323, or $0.33

D. $53 ÷ 5 = $10.60

COMMUNICATION

Prepare a list of types of units in which items are sold, such as dozen, ream, and gross. Consider the following types of retail stores: lumber yard, hardware store, grocery store, drugstore, garden or landscaping firm, and office products store. For each type of unit you find, provide one example and the type of store where used. Organize your list to make finding a type of unit easier.

EXERCISES

Find the difference or quotient.

1. $29.16 − $24.09 $5.07   2. $1.45 − $1.34 $0.11   3. $0.68 − $0.49 $0.19

4. $3.98 ÷ 7.3 $0.55   5. $12.99 ÷ 18.5 $0.70   6. $0.98 ÷ 3.5 $0.28

Find the unit price. Round up to the next higher cent.

7. 4 batteries for $5.99 $1.50   8. 3 rolls of film for $12.99 $4.33

9. 3 large cans of dog food for $2.00 $0.67   10. 5 cans of tuna for $2.19 $0.44

11. 16-oz box of dog treats for $1.79 $0.12   12. 5 suit hangers for $2.29 $0.46

13. 5 tons of sand for $104.99 $21   14. 46-oz. can of apple juice for $1.99 $0.05

15. 50-oz. bottle of liquid detergent for $3.49 $0.07

16. 10 cubic yards of garden mulch for $64.99 $6.50

17. 5 M copies of 1-page reprint for $25.80 $5.16

18. **BEST BUY** A 13-oz. dispenser of Coral moisturizing lotion sells for $7.29. A 12-oz. dispenser of Dino moisturizing lotion sells for $6.99. Which is less expensive? How much less expensive per ounce? Coral, $0.02

19. **BEST BUY** You can buy a bottle of 250 Vitamin C pills for $11.99 or a bottle of 100 Vitamin C pills of a competing brand for $5.99. Which cost less, the larger or the smaller bottle? How much less per pill? larger; $0.01

MIXED REVIEW

20. Divide $35,109 by 1,000. $35.11   21. Divide 4.109 by 100. 0.04109

22. Todd Lyle worked Mon. through Fri. from 8:30 A.M. to 5:00 P.M. with an hour off for lunch. He is paid $11.34 an hour. Find his earnings for the week. $425.25, Lesson 1.1

23. Adele Mirsham earns a salary plus commission. Her total earnings last year were $47,600, of which $16,800 was salary. Her total sales last year were $616,000. What was her rate of commission? 5%, Lesson 1.4

24. Andy Vane's check register balance on June 1 was $811.16. He found a check for $17 was recorded in the register as $11.60 and he had not recorded a service charge of $6.50 or a deposit of $32.74. Find Andy's correct check register balance. $832, Lesson 3.5

Lesson 5.3 Unit Prices ■ **201**

Assign

Assignment: Exercises 1–24. Make sure that students solve correctly the basic arithmetic problems at the beginning of the exercises before assigning the word problems.

Assess

Check student answers to the exercises by calling on them in class, collecting and grading selected problems, or by observing student work as you circulate.

Reteach

STUDENT WORKBOOK To redemonstrate finding and comparing unit prices, use Exercise 1. Then have students complete Exercises 2–3.

Use Exercise 4a to redemonstrate finding unit prices from group prices. Then have students complete Exercises 4b–4g.

Enrich

Have students go to a grocery store and write down the size and price of three brands of the same product, such as canned corn. Ask students to find the unit prices to the nearest tenth of a cent and the price differences among the three brands (or sizes). Call on students to hear and discuss their findings.

Close

Call on students to describe the steps used to solve the problems in Examples 1 and 2.

SELECTED SOLUTIONS

15. $3.49 ÷ 50 = $0.0698, or $0.07
18. $7.29 ÷ 13 = $0.5607, or $0.561;
$6.99 ÷ 12 = $0.5825, or $0.583; Coral sells for less per ounce; $0.583 − $0.561 = $0.022, or $0.02

19. $11.99 ÷ 250 = $0.0479, or $0.048;
$5.99 ÷ 100 = $0.060; Larger bottle sells for less per ounce; $0.060 − $0.048 = $0.012, or $0.01

GOALS

- Compare prices at sales, at different stores, and in different amounts
- Compare the cost of rental options
- Compare the cost of renting vs. buying

Start Up

You can buy a set of floor mats for a car for $89.99 at a discount store in a nearby city or for $98.88 at a local auto supply store. Why might you choose to buy the floor mats locally, even at a higher cost?

Math Skill Builder

Review these math skills and solve the exercises that follow.

1 **Multiply** dollar amounts by whole numbers and decimals.
Find the product. $12 \times \$0.95 = \$11.40$

  1a. $\$1.23 \times 144$ 177.12 **1b.** $\$45.99 \times 3$ $\$137.97$ **1c.** $\$1.89 \times 5.2$ $\$9.83$

2 **Subtract** dollar amounts.
Find the difference. $\$45.99 - \$39.89 = \$6.10$

  2a. $\$1.49 - \$1.28$ $\$0.21$ **2b.** $\$25.89 - \$19.88$ $\$6.01$

3 **Divide** dollar amounts by whole numbers and decimals and round the quotients to the nearest cent.
Find the quotient. $\$2.98 \div 5.2 = \$0.573$, or $\$0.57$

  3a. $\$3.89 \div 5$ $\$0.78$ **3b.** $\$12.79 \div 6.2$ $\$2.06$

4 **Find** what percent one number is of another.
Find what percent $\$2.40$ is of $\$12.80$. $\$2.40 \div \$12.80 = 18.75\%$

  4a. $\$15.80 \div \$63.20$ 25% **4b.** $\$3.90 \div \$9.75$ 40%

■ Prices at Sales, Different Stores, and in Different Amounts

To save money, you should know how to calculate the amount you can save by buying in large amounts or at discount stores. Many of the items you buy come in different sizes and at different prices. Unit prices allow you to compare prices and identify the lowest-priced item.

DIFFERENT LEARNING ABILITIES Attention Deficit Disorder

When you are working through an example with students, ask quick, simple questions of randomly chosen students to keep their attention. For example, you can have students help you with what you are writing on the board by asking them what is the next step in the solution, what the label should be for an amount, what amount should be written on the board for a given step, or what arithmetic process sign should be written. In other words, don't write anything on the board without asking students what to write first.

EXAMPLE 1

How much will you save by buying a case of motor oil at All-Mart's Discount Store for $19.99 rather than buying it at Power Auto Supply for $27.98?

SOLUTION

$27.98 − $19.99 = $7.99   Subtract the lower price from the higher price.

■ **CHECK YOUR UNDERSTANDING**

A. How much is saved by buying a case of brownie mixes for $15.67 rather than a case for $16.29? 62¢

B. How much is saved by buying a pack of 10 T-shirts for $33.49 rather by buying two packs of 5 T-shirts for $18.25 each? $3.01

EXAMPLE 2

How much will you save by buying 12 rolls of film now at $3.98 rather than buying 1 roll at $4.39 at a time?

SOLUTION

Multiply the quantity by the unit price to find the total price of buying the specified number of products.

12 × $3.98 = $47.76   cost at $3.98 each

12 × $4.39 = $52.68   cost at $4.39 each

Subtract the lower total price from the higher total price.

$52.68 − $47.76 = $4.92

Amount saved by buying the larger quantity is $4.92.

■ **CHECK YOUR UNDERSTANDING**

C. A 53.7 square foot roll of Country paper towels costs $1.49. An 80.6 square foot roll of the same paper towels costs $1.89 on sale. Which is less expensive per square foot, the small or large roll? Large

D. After the holidays you can buy boxes of greeting cards @ 2 for $32. The same boxes sold during the season for $23.99 each. If you bought 6 boxes after the holidays, how much would you save? $47.94

■ Rental Options

You can rent items you do not use often or only need for a short amount of time. For example, since a homeowner is not likely to refinish the floors in a home very often, renting a floor sander instead of buying it makes sense.

Rental companies offer different rental rates for different time periods, such as hourly, daily, weekly, and monthly. To determine the best rental option, you should know how long you will need the item and then find the most economical rate.

Lesson 5.4 Comparative Shopping ■ 203

■ Apply Goal 1

Work through Examples 1 and 2 while students do the math at their desks.

Ask students why they might still buy one roll at a time in Example 2 (spoilage of film if kept too long) even though the larger quantity is cheaper per roll.

Assign Check Your Understanding problems A–D to do in class. Check student work at their desks for errors or problems.

■ Teach Goal 2

Ask students to describe items their families or friends have rented and what problems or benefits they had with the rental experience. For example, it may have been inconvenient to rent equipment for a half day since it meant returning it quickly, driving it a long distance, or loading it into a small car.

Note to students that half-day rentals are usually for 4 hours. However, students should know that rental firms might let you return a half-day rental the next day if you rent it for the afternoon. Likewise they might let you return a rental on Monday if you rent it for Saturday because they are not open on Sunday.

203

■ Apply Goal 2

Do Example 3 at the board with students doing the math at their desks.

Assign Check Your Understanding problems E and F to do in class. Check student work at their desks for difficulties.

■ ONGOING ASSESSMENT
Have students reread Check Your Understanding problem E or F. Then ask students to describe the steps necessary to solve the problem. Ask each student called upon to describe one step.

■ Teach Goal 3

Point out that some costs apply to both renting and buying, such as the cost of fuel for a mower.

Use the web to locate online ads for renting and buying a product, such as a long ladder or chipper. Have student use these data to identify the break-even points for the products.

■ Apply Goal 3

Do Example 4 with students while they do the math at their desks.

Assign Check Your Understanding problems G and H to do in class. Circulate in your room to see if students need help with their work.

■ ONGOING ASSESSMENT
Have students explain how they would find the number of months or years it would take for a rental fee to equal or exceed the purchase price of a product.

EXAMPLE 3

A floor sander can be rented for $7 an hour or $40 a full day. If you estimate that it will take you 6 hours to sand the floors in two rooms, which rate would be the least expensive?

SOLUTION
Calculate the cost of renting the item by the hourly rate.

6 hours × $7 = $42   hourly rate total

Find the amount saved by renting at the least expensive rate.

$42 − $40 = $2   amount saved by renting at the full-day rate

In this case, it is more economical to choose the day rate.

■ CHECK YOUR UNDERSTANDING

E. Cary wants to rent a large screen video projection system to see games 3, 4, and 5 of the World Series. The projection system rental price by the day is $130 and by the week, it is $600. If the three games are played over 4 days, which rental rate will be the least expensive for him? Daily rental rate

F. Jill Sun plans to paint her garage and estimates that it will take about 5 hours to do it with a paint sprayer. She can rent a sprayer at an hourly rate of $18, at a half-day rate of $56, or a full-day rate of $80. Which is the least expensive rental rate for the task? Day rate

■ Rent or Buy

If you need something on a regular basis, it may be less expensive to buy than rent. To make this decision, you need to:

- ■ Calculate the annual cost of renting the equipment.
- ■ Calculate how many years it would take for the rental price to equal or exceed the purchase price.

EXAMPLE 4

You rent a rug-cleaning machine four days a year at a cost of $25 a day. You see a rug cleaner on sale for $225. Do you think you should buy the rug cleaner or continue to rent?

SOLUTION
4 × $25 = $100   cost of renting the cleaner each year

Divide the cleaner's purchase price by the annual rental cost to find the number of years it would take for the cost of the rental to equal or exceed the cost of the purchase.

$225 ÷ $100 = 2.25   years to cover purchase price

BUSINESS TIP

There are other factors to consider in any decision to rent or buy. In this case, you may want to consider purchasing the rug cleaner because in about two years you would "break even" on the purchase. But, if you don't have room to store the cleaner or if the machine is likely to break down after 1 or 2 years, you may decide to continue renting.

■ *CHECK YOUR UNDERSTANDING SOLUTIONS*

E. $130 × 4 = $520; daily rental rate is cheaper than weekly rate of $600

F. $18 × 5 = $90; day rate of $80 is least expensive

G. $169.99 ÷ $25 = 6.79, or 6.8 days

H. $23.99 × 4 = $95.96; $349.99 ÷ $95.96 = 3.64, or 3.6 years

G. A backpack leaf blower rents for $25 a day. The same leaf blower sells new for $169.99. Meka Jackson thinks she will use the leaf blower for 5 days a year to clean her garage of dust and dirt and her yard of leaves. How many days of renting, to the nearest tenth of a day, will it take for the rental cost to equal or exceed the purchase price? 6.8 days

H. Joe Fiorelli rents a 40-foot extension ladder for a total of 4 days each year to clean the windows in his home in the spring and fall. The daily rental for the ladder is $23.99. The same ladder costs $349.99 new. How many years, to the nearest tenth of a year, would it take for the rental charges to equal or exceed the cost of buying the ladder? 3.6 years

Wrap Up

Look back at the Start Up question at the beginning of this lesson. You might buy the floor mats locally because it is convenient to do so and it will save you time. The quality of the floor mats in the local store might be better than in the discount store. You may also need advice about the product and you think that you will get better service locally than at a discount store. You may also want to support local businesses.

TEAM MEETING

With a team of one or two other students, develop a comparison of rental prices in your area for a home or garden product. For example, you might compare rental prices on floor waxers or garden tillers. Your comparison should describe the stores visited, the differing features of the product found at each store, the different rental terms offered, and the prices charged. Terms might include time of day, length of rental, and whether supplies are included in the rental price. Prepare a presentation for the class.

EXERCISES

Find the product.
1. $4.69 × 8 $37.52
2. $5.39 × 5.5 $29.65
3. $12.77 × 12 $153.24

Find the difference.
4. $45.29 − $38.39 $6.90
5. $139.26 − $108.66 $30.60

Find the quotient, rounded to the nearest cent.
6. $2.59 ÷ 3.8 $0.68
7. $83.66 ÷ 8 $10.46

Find the percent, rounded to the nearest percent.
8. $8.38 ÷ $98.84 8%
9. $14 ÷ $79.99 18%

Lesson 5.4 Comparative Shopping ■ 205

Wrap Up

Review the Start Up. Ask students to read the Wrap Up and then call on them to provide factors on their lists that are different from those listed in the Wrap Up.

TEAM MEETING

Help student teams pick a product and develop a checklist for comparing rental offers. Select one or more teams to make a presentation to the class.

Assign

Assignment: Exercises 1–27, 29–34. Start with the basic math exercises at the beginning to make certain that students can handle the arithmetic used in the exercises.

COMMON ERRORS

Students may forget or overlook multiplying $23.99, the daily rental rate in Check Your Understanding problem H, by 4 to find the yearly rental. So they may accidentally divide $349.99 by $23.99 instead of the actual yearly rental rate of $95.96.

Reteach

STUDENT WORKBOOK To show students how to solve comparative shopping problems again, complete Exercise 1a with them. Then have them complete Exercises 1b–1e.

To show students how to solve rental option problems again, do Exercise 2a with them. Then have them do Exercise 2b.

To show students how to solve rent vs. buy problems again, do Exercise 3a with them. Then have them do Exercises 3b–3c.

10. One radial tire sells for $89.99. A set of 4 is priced at $305.96. How much would you save if you bought a set of 4 now instead of one tire at a time over the next few months? $54

11. A digital camera is priced at $369.89 at a department store. The same camera can be bought for $310.88 plus $12.50 shipping and handling over the Internet. How much would you save by buying the camera over the Internet? $46.51

A queen-size mattress and box springs set that regularly sells for $1,499 is on sale for $1,349.10.

12. How much would you save by buying the set on sale? $149.90

13. What percent of the original price would you save? 10%

14. Tricia Lanley can buy DVD movies at the regular price of $14.95 each, or at a sale price of 5 for $66.95. How much would she save by buying five movies now instead of one at a time? $7.80

15. Carl Mueller found an automatic washer priced at $549 and a dryer for $399. They are on sale for only $849 for the set. How much can Carl save if he buys the items as a set? $99

16. At an end of season sale, Vicky Charles bought a room air conditioner that was reduced from $398.99 to $349.99 and a fan that was reduced from $39.95 to $32.99. What total amount did she save? $55.96

An airline offers senior citizens a courtesy discount of 10% on all flights. Rudy Brown, a senior citizen, buys a ticket regularly priced at $295.99.

17. What is the estimated amount of Rudy's discount? $30

18. What exact amount does Rudy pay for the ticket? $266.39

Sandra Wilson tills her garden once each year. She rents a garden tiller for one day at $57 per day to do the job. She pays 5% tax on the rental price and uses 4 gallons of gas at $1.65 per gallon.

19. What is her total cost for using the tiller? $66.45

20. If a similar tiller costs $346.99 including tax, for how many days, to the nearest whole day, could Sandra rent it before renting would cost more than buying? 6 days

---

SELECTED SOLUTIONS

13. $149.90 ÷ $1,499 = 0.1, or 10%

15. $549 + $399 = $948; $948 − $849 = $99

17. $300 × 0.10 = $30

21. $1\frac{1}{4}$ = 1.25; $4.39 ÷ 1.25 = $3.512, or $3.51;

$1\frac{1}{2}$ = 1.5; $4.69 ÷ 1.5 = $3.127, or $3.13;

$3.51 − $3.13 = $0.38

A $1\frac{1}{4}$-lb box of Brand A cereal sells for $4.39. A $1\frac{1}{2}$-lb box of Brand B cereal sells for $4.69.

21. What is the difference in the price per pound? $0.38

22. Which brand costs less per pound? Brand B

23. Yang Su needs a trailer to move her furniture and other things from her old apartment to a new one in another city. She estimates that loading and unloading the trailer will take about three days, including travel time. Yang can rent a trailer for $49 a day or $250 a week. Which rental rate will be the least expensive for Yang? daily rental rate

24. LaVonda Jones can rent a 20 horsepower wood chipper from a rental agency at $136 a day. The same chipper can be bought new for $1,789. For how many days, to the nearest tenth day, could LaVonda rent the chipper before renting would cost more than buying? 13.2 days

BEST BUY   A notebook computer can be rented for $105.95 a week or $29.89 a day. You need the computer for 4 days.

25. At which rate, daily or weekly, would it be cheaper to rent? weekly rate

26. How much would you save by renting it at that rate? $13.61

27. If a similar computer costs $1,997 to buy, for how many full weeks could you rent the computer at the weekly rate before renting would cost more than buying? 19 weeks

28. **STRETCHING YOUR SKILLS**   A friend sees an ad that would allow him to rent a large screen TV for $20 a week, for 152 weeks. At the end of the rental period, he would own the TV. He could buy the same TV at the store for $2,000. He thinks the rent-to-own price is a good buy. You don't. What are two comparisons between renting and buying the TV that you can make to support your position? cost, percentage increase in cost, how much could be saved by saving and then buying

MIXED REVIEW

29. Find the average of 13, 15, 14, 19, and 20. 16.2

30. Subtract $\frac{1}{4}$ from $\frac{5}{8}$. $\frac{3}{8}$

31. How many days are there between July 12 and September 23? 73

32. Billy Pinkus worked a total of 50 hours in one week. Of that time, 40 hours was at the regular rate of $11.25 an hour and 10 hours was at time-and-a-half for overtime. What was Billy's gross pay for the week? $618.75, Lesson 1.3

33. Josie Lamas earns an annual wage of $63,470. Josie estimates her benefits at 32% of her wages. She also estimates that her job expenses are insurance, 6% of wages; commuting, $438; dues, $175; other, $225. Find her annual net job benefits. $15,664.20, Lesson 2.2

34. On October 1, Maria Moya's bank statement balance was $372.57, and her check register balance was $307.65. While comparing the statement and her check register, she found a service charge of $4.23; earned interest of $0.25; and outstanding checks for $17.87, $2.97, $45.33, and $1.19. Prepare a reconciliation statement for Maria. $303.67, Lesson 3.4

Lesson 5.4 Comparative Shopping ■ **207**

Enrich

Assign Exercise 28 and have students find and compare the price for renting and buying the TV. Then have students identify the reasons why buying the TV outright is better than renting to own.

Have students contact area rental stores and gain information needed to make up their own problems related to renting vs. buying furniture or equipment.

Close

Using the board or a blank transparency, ask students questions that lead them through the solution to selected problems that they prepared in the above Enrich activity. If you did not assign them that task, obtain a rental ad and a purchase ad from the Internet for an item, such as a rug cleaner, paint sprayer, or garden tiller, etc. Make transparencies of the ads and have students compare purchasing vs. renting the item.

DIFFERENT LEARNING ABILITIES Limited English Learners

Help a student whose primary language is not English rewrite Exercises 25–27 in his or her primary language, or have a language arts teacher help the student. Then have the student display the rewritten exercises on a transparency to the class and solve them in the primary language at the board. Be sure the student labels each step in the solution.

GOALS

- Calculate and compare the costs of connecting to the Internet
- Calculate and compare speeds of online connections

Start Up

Etta Williams wants to connect to the Internet. She sees ads for different types of connections at prices ranging from $10 to $80 in her newspaper. She wonders, "How can I tell which type of connection I should get?" What factors might she consider in making her decision?

Math Skill Builder

Review these math skills and solve the exercises that follow.

1 **Add** dollar amounts.
Find the sum. $79.89 + $529.89 + $49.99 = $659.77

  1a. $29.99 + $280 + $16 $325.99   **1b.** $358 + $125 + $15.98 $498.98

2 **Multiply** dollar amounts and decimals by whole numbers.
Find the product. $24.99 × 12 = $299.88 and 46.5 × 8 = 372

  2a. $19.99 × 12 $239.88   **2b.** 84.2 × 8 673.6

  2c. $49.89 × 12 $598.68   **2d.** 1,340,000 × 8 10,720,000

3 **Divide** whole numbers by whole numbers. Round quotients to the nearest tenth.
Find the quotient. 544,000 ÷ 128,000 = 4.25, or 4.3

  3a. 139,200 ÷ 42,000 3.3   **3b.** 58,900,000 ÷ 256,000 230.1

■ Internet Connection Costs

To connect your home computer system to the Internet, you must open an account with an **Internet service provider**, or ISP. This is an organization that provides access to the Internet in your area.

ISPs charge a variety of fees, including installation or set-up fees, fees for special equipment, and monthly **access fees** to connect you to the Internet. Access fees vary depending on which Internet service plan you choose.

ISPs may offer several ways to connect to the Internet. The most common way is using a modem to connect through your telephone system. This type of connection is called a *dial-up connection*. Faster speeds can be obtained by other ways, such as a *cable connection*, a *digital subscriber line connection*, or a *satellite connection*.

There may be other connection costs. You may install a second telephone line so that you can make and receive voice calls while you are online. ISPs may charge you extra for more than one e-mail account or for having your own web page.

You should protect your computer from viruses and from *hackers*. To do so, many people use antivirus programs and *firewall* hardware and/or software. Firewalls protect your system from unauthorized access by others who are online. Access to your computer may let others steal your files or data, such as credit card numbers and passwords. The cost of the antivirus and firewall software usually includes free updates for a limited time, such as a year. You need to update the software regularly because new viruses are created every day.

EXAMPLE 1

TeleMet is an ISP that offers Clara Figueroa a dial-up connection to the Internet. TeleMet charges a set-up fee of $15 and an access rate of $12 a month. Clara also pays $29.95 a year to another firm for antivirus software. What will be Clara's total cost of connecting for one year?

SOLUTION

$12 \times \$12 = \$144$ Multiply the monthly fee by 12 to find yearly access fees.

Add the yearly access fees to the set-up charge and other costs to find the total annual cost of the connection.

$\$144 + \$15 + \$29.95 = \$188.95$ total annual cost of the connection

■ CHECK YOUR UNDERSTANDING

A. Sal Bonacci paid for a cable connection to AreaNET, an ISP. The ISP charged a $25 installation fee, $75 for a network connection card for his computer, a monthly rental fee of $5 for a modem, and a monthly online access fee of $39.95 for an unlimited connection. Sal also bought antivirus software for $36.99. What will be Sal's total cost to connect to the Internet for the first year? $676.39

B. Townetwork, an ISP, offers you free installation of a digital subscriber line and unlimited connection to the Internet. Access fees are $40 per month, $450 for a whole year, or $875 for 2 years. How much will you save by paying a 2-year access fee instead of the monthly access fee? $85

■ Internet Speeds

The cost of your Internet connection usually depends on the speed of the connection. The faster the connection, the higher the price will be. For people who connect to web sites that contain lots of images or who transfer large documents over the Internet, speed can be very important. For those whose primary use of the Internet is sending and receiving short e-mail messages, speed is not as important.

■ Apply Goal 1

Use the board or a transparency to do Example 1 with students while they complete the math at their desks.

Assign Check Your Understanding problems A and B for completion in class. Roam about your classroom and check student work for errors and problems.

■ Teach Goal 2

Review bits and bytes at this point, and the various prefixes to bytes, such as kilo, mega, and giga.

Point out to students that a kilobyte really represents 1,024 bytes. Thus, a file of 12 KB is really 12,288 bytes ($12 \times 1,024$). However, 1,000 is commonly used ($12 \times 1,000 = 12,000$ bytes) to make calculations easier and still give an adequate estimate of upload and download speeds.

Lesson 5.5 Personal Internet Access ■ 209

■ *CHECK YOUR UNDERSTANDING SOLUTIONS*

A. $\$5 \times 12 = \$60$; $\$39.95 \times 12 = \$479.40$;
$\$25 + \$75 + \$60 + \$479.40 + \$36.99 = \$676.39$

B. $\$40 \times 24 = \$960$; $\$960 - \$875 = \$85$

Work through Example 2 while students complete the math at their desks.

Point out that you must write out in bytes file sizes stated in KB or MB before multiplying by 8 to find the total number of bits; e.g., write 45.3 KB as 45,300 bytes and then multiply by 8.

Assign Check Your Understanding problems C and D for completion in class. Move about your classroom and check student work for difficulties.

■ **ONGOING ASSESSMENT**

After students complete Check Your Understanding problems C and D, ask them to tell you how many:

a. bits are in a byte **(8)**

b. bytes are in a kilobyte **(1,000)**

c. bits are in a kilobyte **(8,000)**

d. KB are in a MB **(1,000)**

e. bits are in a MB **(8,000,000)**

The speed of your connection is usually stated in *thousands* or *millions* of bits per second, or **kbps** and **mbps**. That is because computers reduce all the letters, numbers, spaces, commas, and other information you enter into a document into *bits*. When you send a document over the Internet, you are really sending a bunch of bits.

The speed of your connection may be faster when you **download**, or receive files over the Internet than when you **upload**, or send a file to another person. For example, a digital subscriber line's upload speed may be 128 kbps, but its download speed may be six times faster at 768 kbps.

Two download speeds commonly available for each type of home Internet connection include:

Dial-up	33 kbps, 56 kbps
Cable	128 kbps, 256 kbps
DSL	144 kbps, 768 kbps
Satellite	150 kbps, 500 kbps

You rarely get the full speed shown in the rate. For example, you may only get a true speed of 40-45 kbps on a 56 kbps dial-up line. A number of factors reduce line speed. Speed also may vary during a day because more people may use the lines at certain times.

While speeds on the Internet are measured in bits, most computer systems use 8 bits, or a *byte* to represent a single letter, number, or other item of data, such as a space, comma, or plus sign. The size of a downloaded document, image, or sound is usually shown in bytes. For example, the size of a letter to a friend may be 12,000 bytes, or 12 KB.

To find how much time it will take to download or upload a file on the Internet you convert the file's size from bytes into bits.

EXAMPLE 2

You want to download a document that is 45.3 KB in size from the Internet. If you have a true Internet connection speed of 42 kbps, how long will it take to download the file?

SOLUTION

Multiply the size of the document by 8 to find the number of bits it contains.

45,300 bytes $\times$ 8 = 362,400 bits

Write out the speed of the connection:
42 kbps = 42,000 bits per second

Divide the size of the file in bits by the connection speed in bits to find the number of seconds needed to transfer the file. Round off to the nearest tenth of a second.

362,400 $\div$ 42,000 = 8.62, or 8.6   seconds needed to transfer file

COMMON ERRORS

Students may forget to convert bytes into bits. They may also have difficulty converting KB and MB into kb and mb.

Review how to convert bytes into bits before students start Exercises 14–17.

C. Tony's cable Internet connection gives a true speed of 350 kbps. A software program that he wishes to buy and download from the Internet is 1.65 MB in size. How many seconds, rounded to the nearest tenth of a second, will it take to download the file? 37.7 seconds

D. Jamie Kirk changes from a dial-up Internet connection rated at 56 kbps to a cable connection rated at 256 kbps. How many times faster, to the nearest whole number, is the new connection than the old? 5

Wrap Up

What speed Etta needs depends on how she intends to use the Internet. If she only sends and receives short e-mail messages to and from friends, a dial-up connection is adequate. If she wants to view web pages with lots of images, she will probably want a faster connection than dial-up offers. If she downloads large files or attaches them to e-mail messages, she probably also will want a faster connection. She should look at the size of the files she is likely to upload and download and then calculate how fast those files transfer at different connection speeds to make her decision.

COMMUNICATION

Use the Web to find two national and two local Internet service providers. Make a chart with rows listing the features provided by the ISPs and the columns showing which of the features each ISP offers. Features might include the number of free e-mail accounts, the free space provided for your own web pages, and speed ranges.

Make another chart showing the one-time fees and the monthly fees charged by each ISP. Then answer these questions:

1. What types of workers would most benefit from a national ISP account? mobile workers, such as sales representatives
2. Why might you want a local ISP account instead of a national one? It is usually less expensive

EXERCISES

Perform the indicated operation.

1. $34.98 + $16 + $288 $338.98   **2.** 38,285 × 8 306,280

3. 1,890,200 ÷ 128,000 14.77   **4.** 452,880 ÷ 45 10,064

Vincent Trucano can get an ISP account with WorldVu. The standard plan costs $9.99 a month and the premiere plan costs $14.99 a month.

5. What is the annual cost of the standard plan for the first year? $119.88

6. What is the annual cost of the premiere plan for the first year? $179.88

Lesson 5.5 Personal Internet Access ■ **211**

An ISP sells Sara Janes an unlimited, 256 kbps connection to the Internet for a $39.99 monthly access fee, rental of a cable modem for $3.50 a month, and an installation fee of $125. Sara also spends $19.95 for antivirus software and $29.99 for firewall software.

7. What are the monthly costs of the connection? $43.49

8. What is the total of the other connection costs? $174.94

Arif Filani paid $600 for a satellite dish antenna and modem and $199 for their installation to StarNet, a satellite ISP. The company offers access fees of $69.99 a month or $469.95 a year for unlimited access

9. If Arif chooses a monthly access fee, what will be his total cost for Internet access for the first year? $1,638.88

10. How much could Arif save by paying the access fee annually? $369.93

11. Julio Rivera buys Internet access from his telephone company. He pays $85 in installation fees, $199 for a modem kit, and a monthly fee of $49.95 for 768 kbps, unlimited access to the Internet. The access fee also includes one voice telephone line. So, he cancels one of his existing telephone lines costing $18.95 a month. What is the net cost for Internet access for the first year? $656

BEST BUY Ben Morganstein could pay an ISP $27 for a set-up fee for a dial-up Internet connection. He also would need to pay his telephone company a $29 activation fee for a second phone line for the dial-up connection. His monthly fees would include $15.89 for the phone line and $19.95 for a 56 kbps unlimited use Internet connection. His cable company offers him free installation, and a $45 monthly access fee for a 256 kbps connection that includes rental of the cable modem.

12. Which plan would provide the least total costs? dial-up

13. How many times faster is the cable connection than the dial-up connection? Round your answer to the nearest whole number. 5

14. Ursala Christo has a cable connection that offers true upload speeds of 100 kbps and true download speeds of 490 kbps. If she sends a 1.5 MB file to a friend, how many seconds will it take? 120 sec or 2 min

Barry Convers has a dial-up connection with a true download speed of 40 kbps. How long will it take him to download the following files?

15. a scanned image file of 624 KB 124.8 sec

16. a sound file of 36 KB 7.2 sec

17. a program file of 1.2 MB 240 sec

18. **DECISION MAKING** June Wolack has a cable Internet connection at 256 kbps that costs $23.95 a month. What other purchases might June consider making? antivirus and firewall software

SELECTED SOLUTIONS

11. $49.95 × 12 = $599.40; $18.95 × 12 = $227.40; $85 + $199 + $599.40 − $227.40 = $656

12. $15.89 × 12 = $190.68; $19.95 × 12 = $239.40; $27 + $29 + $190.68 + $239.40 = $486.08 $45 × 12 = $540; dial up costs less

13. 256 ÷ 56 = 4.57, or 5 times faster

16. 36 KB = 36,000 bytes; 36,000 × 8 = 288,000 bits; 288,000 ÷ 40,000 = 7.2 seconds

17. 1.2 MB = 1,200,000 bytes; 1,200,000 × 8 = 9,600,000 bits; 9,600,000 ÷ 40,000 = 240 seconds

19. Round $0.9607 to the nearest cent. $0.96

20. Round $10.3049 to the nearest cent. $10.30

21. Estimate the quotient: $1,200,000 \div 128,000$. 10

22. Find the product: $\frac{5}{8} \times \frac{2}{3}$. $\frac{5}{12}$

23. What percent is 56 of 256, to the nearest tenth? 21.9%

24. What is the average of these numbers: 42, 45, 46, 39, and 44? 43.2

25. Van Drueke is an accountant who works for a temporary help agency. He is paid $196 per diem. Last month he worked 18 days as an account temp. What was his gross pay for the month? $3,528, Lesson 1.5

Molly O'hara's gross pay in the second week of January was $1,120. Lesson 2.1

26. What was her social security deduction at 6.2%? $69.44

27. What was her Medicare deduction at 1.45% $16.24

28. Suroyo Wahyudi deposited $3,500 in a money market account that pays interest compounded quarterly. For the first 3 months, the account paid 4.3% annual interest. For the next 3 months, an annual interest rate of 4% was paid. What total interest did Suroyo earn for the six months? $73.01, Lesson 3.7

29. A 90-day promissory note is dated March 15. What is the due date of the note? June 13, Lesson 4.3

30. Micaela Rodrigo bought a router table priced at $69.99 in a state with a sales tax of 6.25% and a city with a sales tax of 1.5%. What is the total amount Micaela paid for the router table? $75.41, Lesson 5.1

Find the extension for each item. Lesson 5.2

31. 8 gross @ $34.89. $279.12

32. 12 pair @ $19.99 $239.88

33. 50 reams @ $29.89 $1,494.50

34. Cans of Tasty Vittles cat food sell at 6 for $3.99. Cans of Cat's Delight sell at 5 for $3.39. Which cat food sells at a lower price per can? How much lower per can? Tasty Vittles; 1¢, Lesson 5.3

35. Luis Franco is a collector for a candy machine operator. He makes collections for the week: M, $598.29; T, $388.78; W, $612.89; Th $508.19; F, $659.22. What are his total collections for the week? $2,767.37, Lesson 2.5

36. Jessica Watson's check register balance was $1,093.25. Her bank statement showed an ATM deposit of $136.00 that was not recorded in her check register, $1.83 of interest earned, and a $9 monthly service charge. Reconcile Jessica's check register. What is Jessica's current balance? $1,222.08; Lesson 3.4

Ask students to identify the typical costs associated with an Internet connection. Discuss the answers.

Ask students to identify popular Internet access methods and common speeds associated with those methods.

■ **STUDENT PORTFOLIO**

Consider having students place the chart produced for the Communications assignment or the brief report produced in the Cooperative Learning assignment in their portfolios to demonstrate their knowledge of Internet topics.

Lesson 5.5 Personal Internet Access ■ **213**

TEACHING STRATEGIES Communication

Have each student write a memo to another student describing the steps needed to calculate how much time in seconds a 2.6 MB file would take to download using a 56 kbps dial-up connection. Each step should be numbered. Students should have another student read and test the steps in the memo to make sure the steps are clear and accurate.

Lesson 5.1 Sales Tax
- Multiply the purchase price of an item by the sales tax rate to find the sales tax amount.

- Add the sales tax to the purchase price to find the total cost of the item.

- Multiply the subtotal of taxable items by the sales tax rate to find the sales tax amount.

- Add the sales tax, the subtotal of the taxable items, and the subtotal of the nontaxable items to find the total of the sales receipt.

Lesson 5.2 Sales Receipts
- Multiply the quantity by the unit price to find the extension.

- Add the extensions to find the subtotal.

- Multiply the subtotal of taxable items by the sales tax rate to find the sales tax.

- Add the subtotal and sales tax amount to find the total amount of the sales receipt.

Lesson 5.3 Unit Prices
- Divide the price for an item by the number of units it contains to find the unit price.

- Subtract one unit price from another to find how much more or less one product costs per unit than another.

- Divide the group price of a product by the number of units to find the price for one unit. If there is a remainder, round up to the next whole cent.

Chapter Review

Vocabulary Review

access fees	kbps	subtotal
download	mbps	unit price
extension	online	upload
internet service provider	sales tax	

Fill in the blanks with the word or words that best completes the statement.

1. A partial total, or total of extensions is called (a, an) __?__. subtotal

2. The quantity of product times unit price is called (a, an) __?__. extension

3. An item charged by states and cities on consumer purchases is (a, an) __?__. sales tax

4. An organization that provides access to the Internet is called (a, an) __?__. Internet service provider

5. Amounts charged to connect to the Internet are called (a, an) __?__. access fees

6. The Internet allows you to send, or __?__ files to others on the Internet. upload

7. The price of a single item is called the __?__. unit price

8. When __?__, people should take care to protect their computers from unauthorized access. online

9. A 56 thousand bits per second Internet connection speed may be stated as 56 __?__. kbps

10. The Internet allows you to copy, or __?__ files to your computer from the Internet. download

LESSON 5.1

11. A piano is priced at $2,589 in a state with a 4.5% sales tax. What is the sales tax amount? What is the total cost of the piano? $116.51, $2,705.51

12. A piano tuner replaced two strings and four felts in a piano and then tuned it. He charged $10.35 each for the strings and $3.45 each for the felts. He also charged $75 to tune the piano. A state tax rate of 5.5% was applied to everything but the tuning. What was the sales tax? What was the total bill? $1.90; $111.40

13. Henry Schultz wants to buy a car that costs $18,980 in a state with a 6.25% sales tax. How much sales tax will he pay? $1,186.25

LESSON 5.2

14. What is the extension of 5 boxes of paper @ $32.99? $164.95

15. What is the extension of 34 sets of dishes @ $129.85? $4,414.90

16. You bought 3 T-shirts @ $14.95 and 4 sweatshirts @ $39.99 in a state with a sales tax rate of 2.7%. What was the total amount of the sales receipt? $210.34

DIFFERENT LEARNING STYLES Auditory Learner

If you go over the Chapter Review materials in class after students have completed them, call on students for the answers to the Vocabulary Review questions. When you do, have each student say the answers. Then have the student cover the page and spell the answer.

LESSON 5.3

17. A 12-oz bottle of cleaning fluid costs $3.89. What is the unit price, to the nearest tenth of a cent? $0.324

18. One box of 15 holiday cards costs $15.99. Another box of 20 cards costs $18.99. Which box costs less per card? How much less per card? 20 cards; $0.12

19. A store sells 3 cans of tomato sauce for $0.44. What is the price of one can? $0.15

20. What is the price per foot of cloth that sells for $3.59 a yard? $1.20

21. A 19-oz bottle of a dishwashing liquid sells for $1.49. A 25-oz bottle of the same liquid sells for $2.99. Which size sells at a lower per ounce price? the 19-oz size

LESSON 5.4

22. You can buy 2, 16-oz. jars of pasta sauce on sale for $1.99. Each 16-oz. jar regularly sells for $1.29. How much will you save if you buy 6 jars on sale? $1.77

23. 1-qt. cans of paint are on sale for 2 @ $11.98. A gallon can of the same paint costs $19.89. What is the unit cost of the 1 qt. cans? What is the price per quart for the gallon cans? How much will you save if you buy 2-gallon cans of the paint instead of 8 1-qt. cans? $5.99; $4.97; $8.14

24. A trencher can be rented for $27 an hour or $145 a day. If you need the trencher for 6 hours, how much will you save by renting it for the day instead of for 6 hours? $17

25. Leslie Wickam can rent an air compressor for $240 a week or buy it for $1,499.99. How many weeks of renting, to the nearest tenth of a week, will it take for the rental cost to equal or exceed the purchase price? 6.2 weeks

26. Tommy Voran needs a loudspeaker system for a town homecoming event that will last $3\frac{1}{2}$ days. He can rent the system for a daily rate of $75 daily or a weekly rate of $275. Which rental rate will be the least expensive for him? weekly

LESSON 5.5

27. Val Myer's ISP charged a $20 installation fee, $95 for a network connection card, a monthly rental fee of $3 for a modem, and a monthly access fee of $49.95 for an unlimited connection. In addition, Val bought antivirus and firewall software for $39.98 total. What will be Val's total cost to connect to the Internet for the first year? $790.38

28. A dial-up Internet connection gives a true speed of 35 kbps. A file you wish to download from the Internet is 650 KB in size. How many seconds, rounded to the nearest tenth of a second, will it take to download the file? 148.6 seconds

Chapter 5 Review ■ 215

Lesson 5.4 Comparative Shopping
- Compare prices of similar items sold in different quantities and prices by finding the unit prices of each item.

- Subtract the lower total price from the higher total price to find the amount saved.

- Compare the cost of renting items by different time periods by multiplying the different rates by the different time periods.

- Subtract the smaller rental cost from the larger rental cost to find the amount saved.

- Compare buying vs. renting an item by finding how many days, weeks, months, or years it will take for the rental costs to equal or exceed the purchase price.

Lesson 5.5 Personal Internet Access
- Multiply the monthly access fee by 12 to find the yearly access fee.

- Add the access fee to the installation and other fees and charges to find the total annual cost of an Internet connection.

- Multiply the size of a file by 8 to find the number of bits it contains.

- Divide the file size in bits by the connection speed in bits to find the number of seconds needed to transfer the file. Round to the nearest tenth of a second.

DIFFERENT LEARNING ABILITIES At Risk Learners

Make transparencies of the math steps found in the Chapter Summary side column of the Teacher's Edition, and use them to solve the problems in each lesson. When students have completed the Chapter Review problems, reteach the solutions to those problems they had difficulty with by displaying these steps and working through the solutions with them.

The Tasks

Students need spreadsheet file tech5-1.xls for Tasks 1 and 2.

Task 1 Students enter data into a rent or buy spreadsheet template.

Task 2 Students answer questions about the results of Task 1. They also change data and answer questions about the results.

Task 3 Students design and create a spreadsheet that calculates the extensions for each line item on a sales slip, and then finds the subtotal, sales taxes, and total of the sales slip.

Task 4 Students answer questions about the data entered and about how the spreadsheet was designed. They also change data and answer questions about the new results.

Teach and Apply Task 1

Show how to open the spreadsheet and how only blue cells allow entry. Enter the rental rates for the year, week, day, and hour and the item cost while students do the same at their stations. When students complete data entry, ask them to check the result displayed in cells B12, B13, and B14 with the textbook.

Teach and Apply Task 2

Assign Questions 1–4.

Ask students to save the spreadsheet as tech5-1A.xls. Then show them how to unprotect the spreadsheet (Tools, Protection, Unprotect Sheet). Have them add a line after row 6 for half-day rental rates and to create a row after row 13 for calculating the half-day rent.

Task 1: Enter Data Into A Rent or Buy Template

Complete a template that calculates when the total rental payments made for an item equals the item's purchase price.

	A	B	C
1	**Rent or Buy Template**		
2			
3	**Description**	**Amount**	
4			
5	Rent per year	0.00	
6	Rent per week	75.00	
7	Rent per day	25.00	
8	Rent per hour	6.00	
9	Cost of item	349.99	
10			
11	Rent per year equals or exceeds cost in:	0.00	Years
12	Rent per week equals or exceeds cost in:	4.67	Weeks
13	Rent per day equals or exceeds cost in:	14.00	Days
14	Rent per hour equals or exceeds cost in:	58.33	Hours

Open the spreadsheet for Chapter 5 (tech5-1.xls) and enter the data shown in the blue cells (cells B5 through B9). Your computer screen should look like the one shown above when you are done.

The spreadsheet will calculate when the rental payments made per day, week, month, or year exceeds the purchase price of the item.

For example, suppose that the rental price for a 40-foot extension ladder is $6 an hour, $25 a day, and $75 a week. The spreadsheet calculations show that it will take 58.33 hours, 14 days, or 4.67 weeks for the rental payments to equal the purchase price of the ladder, $349.99.

Task 2: Analyze The Spreadsheet Output

Move the cursor to row 9 and column B, the cell for Cost of item. Enter a new price for the extension ladder, $279.89. Notice how the number of hours, days, and weeks needed to equal the purchase price changed. This change shows what would happen if the price of the ladder were reduced from $349.99 to $279.89. Move to cell B7 and change the daily rental rate to $29. Notice how the number of days needed to equal the purchase price changes.

TEACHING STRATEGIES Task 1

Have students insure that cell B5 contains a zero. Then show students the purpose of the formula phrase **"=IF(B5>0"** by having them delete the phrase from cell B11 and view the result: **#DIV/0!**. The result tells students that the spreadsheet cannot divide cell B9, the *Cost of item*, by the zero in cell B5. To avoid these results, the original formula in cell B11 divided only if cell B5 was greater than zero. Students must unprotect the spreadsheet to make the changes. To avoid damaging the original spreadsheet, have them save the spreadsheet to a copy named tech5-1demo.xls.

Answer these questions about your updated spreadsheet.

1. If you rented the ladder for 3 days in the spring and 4 days in the fall of a year, how many years it would take for the total rental payments to equal the purchase price? 2

2. What arithmetic is done in cell B12? Value in cell B9 is divided by value in cell B6

3. What does "= IF(B6 > 0" mean in the formula found in cell B12? IF clause is used to determine when the weekly rental rate cell contains a value

4. What does "B9/B6" found in cell B12 calculate? Divides the purchase price by weekly rental

Task 3: Design a Sales Receipt and Sales Tax Calculator

Design a spreadsheet that will calculate the extensions, subtotal, sales tax, and total amount for a sale receipt.

> *SITUATION:* Simon Brava has his lawn treated by a local lawn service company. They apply 6 bags of fertilizer @ $9.99, 6 bags of lime @ $15.89, and 6 bags of weed killer @ $10.95. They also charge $79.88 for labor. There is state sales tax of 5.8% on the chemicals but not the labor. Find the total amount that is spent on each chemical, all the chemicals together, on the sales tax, and the total lawn treatment.

Task 4: Analyze the Spreadsheet Output

Answer these questions about your completed spreadsheet:

5. How did you calculate the extension for each chemical? Quantity × unit price

6. What is the subtotal of the cost of the chemicals? $220.98

7. What is the sales tax on the subtotal? $12.82

8. What amount is needed to pay for the entire treatment? $313.68

9. If you were to: a) change the price of the lime to $13.99 a bag and; b) change the sales tax rate to 6.5%. What would be the total cost for the entire treatment? $303.08

Teach and Apply Task 3

Assign Task 3. You may wish to have students work in groups and plan the spreadsheet format on paper first.

Suggest to students that they consider organizing their spreadsheets to look like the sales slip illustrated in the textbook, excluding the top part and starting with the quantity, description, unit price, and amount line.

Remind students how to display and print spreadsheet formulas Ctrl + `.

Teach and Apply Task 4

Assign Questions 5–9. Make sure students complete Questions 5–8 before they enter new data for Question 9.

Students can submit disks with their spreadsheets, printouts of the results of the data for Questions 5–8 and 9, and a printout of the spreadsheet formulas.

TEACHING STRATEGIES Task 3

Some students may wish to use their spreadsheet skills to duplicate the entire sales slip in the textbook, including the top part of the sales slip. You might use this as an extra-credit project for those who finish Tasks 1–4 more quickly than the rest of the class.

■ HOW TIMES HAVE CHANGED

1. 56 kbps = 56,000 bps
1.544 mbps = 1,544,000 bps
1,544,000 ÷ 56,000 ≈ 27.57
Internet traffic moved about 28 times faster in 1988 than in 1986.

44.736 mbps = 44,736,000 bps
44,736,000 ÷ 56,000 ≈ 798.86
Internet traffic moved about 800 times faster in 1991 than in 1986.

2.488 gbps = 2,488,000,000 bps
2,488,000,000 ÷ 56,000 ≈ 44,428.57
Internet traffic moved about 45,000 times faster in 1999 than in 1986.

2. 56,000 × 178,571 = 9,999,976,000 bps
9,999,999,976 bps = 9.999999976 gpbs
Internet traffic moved at about 10 gbps over the Abilene Network in 2003.

■ WRITE

Encourage students to relate their experiences described in the Write section. A typical experience might be purchasing a faddish item of clothing and having the fad fade quickly. Discuss with students how wise buying practices described in Ch. 5 and also budgeting described in Ch. 2 might have helped.

■ SCANS

Help students locate online sources of job descriptions.

Suggest to students that the scene they are to develop might involve an external customer who is receiving rude service or is returning a product that proved unsatisfactory or didn't work.

Have the class evaluate each team's presentation using as criteria the skills listed in the Summarize paragraph.

■ ONGOING ASSESSMENT

STUDENT WORKBOOK The Integrated Project found in the workbook provides a broad, ongoing assessment activity for the goals of this chapter.

How Times Have Changed

For Questions 1–2, refer to the timeline on page 189 as needed.

1. How much faster did Internet traffic move in 1988 than it did in 1986? How much faster did Internet traffic move in 1991 than it did in 1986? How much faster did Internet traffic move in 1999 than it did in 1986?

2. In 2003, the Abilene Network transmitted data at a backbone speed that was 178,571 times faster than the speed in 1986. At how many gigabits per second did the Abilene Network transfer data?

WRITE

Describe a time in your life when you look back and now know that you made a purchase that was not thought through carefully and resulted in your spending more money than you should have. What knowledge did you learn in this chapter that would have been helpful to you at that time. If you do not have such an experience, describe a time when you have witnessed a similar situation.

SCANS

Workplace Skills – *Serving Customers*

A customer is someone who must be satisfied with the product or service provided. Some businesses refer to external customers and internal customers. External customers are the people who buy a product or service. In many companies the job of a group of people within an organization is to provide a service to other groups within the same organization. For example an advertising department creates advertising campaigns under the direction of the marketing department. The marketing people are the internal customers of the advertising department.

Satisfying customers requires the ability to listen, ask meaningful questions that help you understand what someone needs, communicate in a clear and positive manner, handle complaints, obtain information and solve problems.

Test Your Skills Since this chapter covers information about shopping and receiving services, now is also a good time to consider the needs of customers. Work in groups. List at least five jobs where people deal with customers on a daily basis. Answer these questions for each job: 1) Who are the internal and external customers of an employee? 2) What do the customers need? 3) What kinds of customer service issues does an employee face?

Make a Plan Select one job profile and one customer service issue. Prepare a scene where one person plays a customer and another person plays the person profiled. Be prepared to present your scene to the class.

Summarize After several groups have acted out their scenes, have a class discussion about what you have learned about customer service. Explain which of the following skills will be useful to those who work with customers daily and why.

listening	*speaking*	*creative thinking*	*decision making*
reasoning	*responsibility*	*monitoring performance*	*integrity/honesty*

218 ■ **Chapter 5** Spend Wisely

PORTFOLIO ASSESSMENT

Ask students to review the materials they have created in this chapter and select those they wish to place in their portfolios. If you assign the spreadsheet design Task 3 in the Technology Workshop or the Write task in the Chapter Assessment sections of the chapter, suggest that they consider the products of these activities for their portfolios as well as the other work completed in the chapter.

Chapter Test

Find the cost of each purchase.

1. 6 cans of olives @ 2 for $1.19 $3.57

2. 32 yards of fabric @ $0.587 per yd $18.78

3. 44,200 lb. of gravel at $42.98 per ton $949.86

4. 25 ft. of cable @ $1.98 per yard $16.50

5. 6,500 corner braces at $12 per M $78

Find the unit price of each purchase.

6. 3 frozen meals for $14.98 $5.00 each

7. 6-oz can of tuna, $0.89 $0.15 per oz

8. 8-oz package of seasoned salt, $2.29 $0.29 per oz

9. 6 cubic yards of mulch for $49.89 $8.32 per cu yd.

10. Box of 10 pencils for $2.69 $0.27 per pencil

11. High-density computer diskettes, regularly priced at $3.99 a box, are on sale, 3 boxes for $1.99. How much would you save by buying 12 boxes at the sale price? $39.92

12. Find the total cost of a $148.99 chain saw purchased in a state with 4.25% sales tax and in a city with 1.5% sales tax. $157.56

Rachel Moreno had her lawn mower repaired by Rivlin Equipment Co. Rivlin charged her $5.96 for an air filter, $16.65 for a fuel bowl filter, and $1.99 for a spark plug. They also charged $42 in labor. There is a 3.5% state sales tax on products only.

13. What is the sales receipt subtotal for parts? $24.60

14. What is the sales tax amount? $0.86

15. What is the total amount of the sales receipt? $25.46

A camcorder can be rented for $35 a day, or $125 a week. You need it for 6 days.

16. How much cheaper is it to rent it for a week instead of by the day? $85

17. If you could buy the camcorder for $1,089, how long would it take, to the nearest tenth of a week, for the weekly rental charges to equal or exceed the purchase price? 8.7

18. An ISP's access fees are $14.99 a month or $159.99 a year. How much would you save over three years by buying the 1-year deal than a monthly deal? $59.67

19. Will Brandt purchases an Internet connection from an ISP that charges $16.99 a month for unlimited dial-up access. He also pays $21 for a start-up fee, $19.89 for antivirus software, and $79.99 for a modem to connect his computer to his phone line. What is the total cost of the Internet connection for the first year? $324.76

20. June Rizel sends a 525 KB file over her Internet connection, which has a true upload speed of 30 kbps. How many seconds will it take her to transfer the file? 140

Chapter 5 Assessment ■ 219

Chapter-Test Correlation

Question	Lesson
1	5.2
2	5.2
3	5.2
4	5.2
5	5.2
6	5.3
7	5.3
8	5.3
9	5.3
10	5.3
11	5.4
12	5.1
13	5.1
14	5.1
15	5.1
16	5.4
17	5.4
18	5.5
19	5.5
20	5.5

Test Taking Strategies

Have students estimate parts of the answers for problems 1–10 to make sure that the answers they worked out are fairly close. For example, in the first problem, students should divide 6 by 2 to get 3, then multiply 3 × $1 to get $3 as an estimated answer.

TEACHING STRATEGIES Chapter Test

If you are concerned that the students in your class may not be able to finish the Chapter Test in one period, have them omit completing one or more of problems 4, 6, 8, and 10. Alternatively, you might break up the test into two parts: problems 1–10 and problems 11–20 and give each part in a separate class period.

Chapter 6 reviews the math skills of addition, subtraction, division, multiplication, percents, and rounding to solve home and car ownership problems.

Lesson 6.1 Borrowing to Buy a Home
Students calculate home purchase costs and total interest paid on a mortgage loan.

Lesson 6.2 Renting or Owning a Home
Students compare the costs of owning and renting a home.

Lesson 6.3 Property Taxes
Students calculate decimal tax rates and property taxes.

Lesson 6.4 Property Insurance
Students calculate premiums for homeowners and renters and the amount collected on claims.

Lesson 6.5 Buying a Car
Students find the MSRP of new cars and the delivered price and balance due for car purchases.

Lesson 6.6 Depreciating a Car
Students calculate the amount and rate of car depreciation.

Lesson 6.7 Car Insurance
Students calculate car insurance premiums.

Lesson 6.8 Car Purchases and Leases
Students calculate total payments and finance charges for car loans, compare costs of leasing and buying cars, and consider the costs of operating a car.

CHAPTER 6

Own a Home or Car

6.1 Borrowing to Buy a Home
6.2 Renting or Owning a Home
6.3 Property Taxes
6.4 Property Insurance
6.5 Buying a Car
6.6 Depreciating a Car
6.7 Car Insurance
6.8 Car Purchases and Leases

Statistical Insights

Most Popular Colors of Vehicles

Type of Car	Color Preference, Percent									
Luxury cars	Silver, 14.8	Lt. Brown, 12.9	White, 10.3	Black, 9.4	Med./ dk gray, 8.3	Gold, 7.0	Med./dk green, 6.1	Med. red, 6.0	White metallic, 5.8	Med./ dk blue, 4.9	Other, 14.5
Full size/ intermediate cars	White, 15.4	Silver, 14.1	Lt. Brown, 14.0	Med./ dk green, 13.9	Black, 11.7	Med./dk blue, 6.4	Med. Red, 5.7	Bright red, 4.9	Med./ dk gray, 4.3	Gold, 1.8	Other, 7.8
Compact/ sports car	Silver, 16.2	Black, 14.7	White, 14.0	Med./dk green, 12.4	Lt. Brown, 8.5	Med./dk blue, 8.5	Bright red, 7.5	Med. Red, 7.0	Dk red, 4.5	Lt. Green, 1.7	Other, 5.0
Light trucks and vans	White, 26.2	Black, 11.2	Med./dk green, 11.0	Med./ dk blue, 8.4	Silver, 7.7	Med. Red, 7.4	Lt. Brown, 6.2	Bright red, 6.1	Med, dk gray, 3.2	Dk red, 3.1	Other, 9.5

Use the data shown above to answer each question.

1. What color is favored among light truck and van owners? white

2. If you were the person responsible for placing the order for the compact and sports cars that are to be sold from a dealer's lot, what three car colors would you order most? silver, black, white

3. What color is among the top three favored colors for all vehicles? white

4. Fifteen black vehicles in each category are ordered and arrive at a dealer's lot on the same day. Assuming each type of vehicle sells at about the same rate, which type of black vehicle would sell out first? Which type of black vehicle would sell out last? compact/sports, luxury

Statistical Insights

About 26% of the buyers of vans and light trucks choose the color white. Ask students to give a reason for this color preference. One reason might be that many trucks are purchased by businesses, and white provides a good background on which to paint the company name, phone number, and an advertising message.

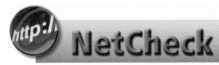

NetCheck

Shopping for a Car Online

All carmakers have web sites. You can visit these web sites to get information about the vehicles they sell and features such as:

- Engine and transmission options
- Gas mileage
- Safety and security systems
- Interior and exterior trim packages
- Exterior colors
- Sound systems
- Warranties
- Financing

Shop among the carmakers to find comparable models. Compare the models' features, warranties, and performances.

Get the Best Deal Possible

Web sites geared to assist the consumer in negotiating with car dealers are available. You should locate as much information as possible about the dealer's cost, destination charges, option packages, and special financing available before deciding where and when to negotiate a new car deal. Use keywords such as the make and model of your desired car, best deal, list price, sticker price, and markup to search for consumer information sites about cars. Do not rely on the first site you find or only one site. Plan to have several browsing sessions before you make a decision.

How Times Have Changed

The percentage of American households that own homes is the homeownership rate. At the beginning of the 20th century, this rate was below 50%. By the end of the century, the homeownership rate was above 67%.

The homeownership rate is 45.9%.
1910

The Great Depression begins. The housing finance system eventually collapses with $10 billion of mortgage debt in default.
1929

World War II ends. Low-interest 30-year mortgages ignite a homeownership boom.
1945

1900   1920   1940   1960   1980   2000

Research to find the homeownership rate in 1940.

1950
The homeownership rate is 55.0%.

1980
The homeownership rate is 64.4%.

2003
The homeownership rate is 68.3%.

221

Start Up

Have students read the Start Up. Ask students what they might find undesirable about living near a school bus parking lot. Ask if they made any assumptions about the home located several blocks away regarding its location and the surrounding area.

Math Skill Builder

Students use the skills of adding, subtracting, and multiplying money amounts in this lesson.

Complete all exercises in Math Skill Builder 1–4.

■ Teach Goal 1

Point out to students that the down payment and closing costs represent money needed prior to signing a mortgage loan. Inform them that the lender specifies the minimum down payment required for a certain type of loan, and that a greater down payment may be made, if desired.

Explain that mortgage loans are usually obtained from banks, savings and loan associations, and mortgage companies.

Inform students that mortgage loans are not automatically approved just because the buyer has money for the down payment. Lenders are interested in the finances of the borrower including having a steady income sufficient to repay the loan and a good credit history.

6.1 Borrowing to Buy a Home

GOALS

- Calculate the down payment, closing costs, and mortgage loan amount
- Calculate the total interest cost of a mortgage loan
- Calculate the savings from refinancing mortgages

Start Up

A home located near a school bus parking lot may cost less to buy than a similar home located several blocks away. Why might this be true?

Math Skill Builder

Review these math skills. Solve the exercises.

1. **Add** money amounts.
   Find the sum. $127 + $258 + $98 = $483
   1a. $956 + $32 + $128 $1,116
   1b. $125 + $85 + $275 $485

2. **Multiply** whole numbers.
   Find the product. 20 × 12 = 240
   2a. 30 × 12 360
   2b. 25 × 12 300

3. **Multiply** money amounts by whole numbers and percents.
   Find the product. 240 × $416.70 = $100,008
   3a. 300 × $316.98 $95,094
   3b. 360 × $501.05 $180,378
   Find the product. 15% × $49,000 = 0.15 × $49,000 = $7,350
   3c. 20% × $115,800 $23,160
   3d. 25% × $78,200 $19,550

4. **Subtract** money amounts.
   Find the difference. $95,600 − $42,000 = $53,600
   4a. $106,892 − $41,985 $64,907
   4b. $3,582 − $1,284.34 $2,297.66

■ Down Payments and Closing Costs

The total cost of buying a home includes the purchase price, the cost of borrowing money for the purchase, and closing costs.

Most people make a cash **down payment**, or a percentage of the total cost of the house paid at the time of purchase, to their lender. Some lenders require no down payment; others ask for as much as 30%. The more money you can put as a down payment, the less you need to borrow.

CONNECTION TO ECONOMICS

Have students investigate census or other data that shows the number of people residing in various types of dwellings. Students may be especially interested in finding the percentage of people who live in homes they own or are buying compared to those who rent.

The balance of the purchase price (after the down payment) is usually borrowed through a **mortgage loan** taken with a bank or other lender. The money borrowed is called the **principal**. Interest must be paid on the mortgage loan. A mortgage gives the lender the right to take the property if the loan is not repaid as agreed. The length and terms of mortgages vary; 15-, 20-, and 30-year mortgages are common.

Closing costs are fees and expenses paid to complete the transfer of ownership of a home. Closing costs may range from 3% to 6% of the purchase price of the home. Typical closing costs include legal fees, recording fees, title insurance, loan application fees, appraisal and inspection fees, land surveys, prepaid taxes, and prepaid interest charges known as *points*. Interest rates and closing costs vary among lenders, so it pays to compare when you are looking for a lender.

To calculate the amount of the loan you need, subtract the down payment from the purchase price.

Mortgage Loan = Purchase Price − Down Payment

To calculate the amount of money you need to buy a home, add the down payment and the closing costs.

Cash Needed to Buy a Home = Down Payment + Closing Costs

BUSINESS TIP

At the time you pay the down payment and closing costs, you must also provide proof that you have insured the property, which is another cost of buying and owning a home.

EXAMPLE 1

Hilda Mikon is buying a home for $74,000. She will make a 20% down payment and estimates closing costs as: legal fees, $950; title insurance, $140; property survey, $250; inspection, $175; loan processing fee, $84; recording fee, $740. What amount of mortgage loan will she need? What amount of cash will she need when she buys the house?

MATH TIP

When you multiply a number by two different percents, you may add the percents and do one multiplication to find the answer.

SOLUTION

Multiply the purchase price by the down payment percent.

20% × $74,000 = 0.2 × $74,000 = $14,800 amount of down payment

Subtract the down payment from the purchase price.

$74,000 − $14,800 = $59,200 amount of mortgage loan

Add the closing costs to find their total.

$950 + $140 + $250 + $175 + $84 + $740 = $2,339 total closing costs

Add the down payment and the total closing costs.

$14,800 + $2,339 = $17,139 cash needed to buy house

CHECK YOUR UNDERSTANDING

A. Ricky Alberts' lender requires him to make a 25% down payment to get a mortgage on a home that costs $86,000. What amount will Ricky have to borrow to purchase the home? $64,500

B. Terri Wilburn will be able to purchase a condominium by making a 5% down payment on its $64,000 purchase price. She estimates her closing costs to be 3.5% of the purchase price. What amount of money will Terri need to pay the down payment and closing costs? $5,440

■ **Apply Goal 1**

Work through the math of Example 1 at the board and have students complete the calculations at their desks.

Point out that closing costs are estimated to give the homebuyer an idea of how much cash will be needed to buy the home. The real estate agent handling the sale of the home can give buyers a fairly good estimate of what types of closing costs can be expected.

Assign Check Your Understanding problems A and B for class work. Review student work at their desks to identify any difficulties they have in solving problems.

Lesson 6.1 Borrowing to Buy a Home ■ **223**

■ *CHECK YOUR UNDERSTANDING SOLUTIONS*

A. 0.25 × $86,000 = $21,500;
$86,000 − $21,500 = $64,500

B. 0.05 × $64,000 = $3,200;
0.035 × $64,000 = $2,240;
$3,200 + $2,240 = $5,440

■ Teach Goal 2

Emphasize to students that a fixed-rate mortgage means that the interest rate is constant for the term of the mortgage. It does not change over time.

Point out that the interest rate on a variable-rate mortgage is fixed for only a short period, often 5 years or less. At the end of the term, the lender adjusts the interest rate based on the performance of U. S. Treasury notes or some other basis.

Discuss the chart that shows how much of a monthly payment goes for interest at the beginning, middle, and near the end of a mortgage's term.

Show students how the $I = PRT$ formula calculates the interest for the first month. Thus, $\$70{,}000 \times 0.0975 \times \frac{1}{12} = \$568.75$. Tell students that the amount of the monthly payment is figured by a different formula that computes interest and amortizes the loan over its term.

■ Mortgage Loan Interest Costs

There are many different types of mortgages. Two of the most common types are fixed rate mortgages and variable rate mortgages. With a *fixed rate mortgage*, the same rate of interest is paid for the life of the loan. With a *variable rate mortgage*, the rate of interest is not guaranteed and may be increased or decreased.

Most mortgages are repaid gradually, or *amortized*, over the life of the mortgage in equal monthly payments. Each payment pays off part of the principal plus the interest due each month.

At first, most of the monthly payment goes to pay interest. As time passes, the amount that goes to repay the principal increases. The following table shows the amounts of interest and principal paid in different months on a 30-year, $70,000 loan at 9.75% interest. The monthly payment is $601.41.

Payment Breakdown	Month In Which Payment Is Made		
	No. 1	No. 180	No. 358
Interest	$568.75	$462.39	$ 14.40
Principal	$ 32.66	$139.02	$587.01
Total Payment	$601.41	$601.41	$601.41

Most lenders allow customers to make additional payments toward the principal so the mortgage can be paid off earlier. These added payments reduce the total interest paid.

The amortization table below shows the monthly payments needed to amortize mortgage loans over different periods of time using interest rates of 6%, 7%, and 8%. To use the table to find a monthly payment, locate the box where the interest rate, the term of loan, and the amount of loan cross, or intersect.

AMORTIZATION TABLE MONTHLY PAYMENTS NEEDED TO PAY A LOAN									
	Interest Rate								
	6.00%			7.00%			8.00%		
Dollar Amount of Loan	Term of Loan								
	20 yrs	25 yrs	30 yrs	20 yrs	25 yrs	30 yrs	20 yrs	25 yrs	30 yrs
$ 40,000	$286.57	$257.72	$239.82	$310.12	$282.71	$266.12	$334.58	$308.73	$293.51
45,000	322.39	289.94	269.80	348.88	318.05	299.39	376.40	347.32	330.19
50,000	358.22	322.15	299.78	387.65	353.39	332.65	418.22	385.91	366.88
60,000	429.86	386.58	359.73	465.18	424.07	399.18	501.86	463.09	440.26
70,000	501.50	451.01	419.69	542.71	494.75	465.71	585.51	540.27	513.64
80,000	573.14	515.44	479.64	620.24	565.42	532.24	669.15	617.45	587.01
90,000	644.79	579.87	539.60	697.77	636.10	598.77	752.80	694.63	660.39
100,000	716.43	644.30	599.55	775.30	706.78	665.30	836.44	771.82	733.76
110,000	788.07	708.73	659.51	852.83	777.46	731.83	920.08	849.00	807.14

DIFFERENT LEARNING ABILITIES Visually Impaired Learners

When reading the amortization table, visually impaired learners may find it helpful to lay a blank sheet of paper below the row containing the information they need. They can also place another blank sheet of paper to the right of the column that contains the information they need. Then the last entry in the lower right-hand corner (just above and to the left of the blank papers) is the required information.

EXAMPLE 2

Amira Okano wants to buy a home that costs $83,000. She has $13,000 for the down payment, and her bank will lend her $70,000 on a 25-year, 8% mortgage. Find Amira's monthly payments and the total amount of interest she would pay over the term of the mortgage.

SOLUTION

On the $70,000 line of the amortization table in the 25-year column under 8% is the amount $540.27, the monthly payment.

Multiply the number of months in a year by the number of years in the loan to find the total number of months the loan will last.

$25 \times 12 = 300$ months

Multiply the number of months in the loan by the monthly payment to find the total amount needed to pay off the loan over 25 years.

$300 \times \$540.27 = \$162,081$ total payments

Subtract the amount of the mortgage from the total monthly payments to find the total interest paid over 25 years.

$$
\begin{array}{ll}
\$162,081 & \text{total payments} \\
- \underline{70,000} & \text{amount of mortgage} \\
\$\ 92,081 & \text{interest paid over the 25-year period}
\end{array}
$$

■ CHECK YOUR UNDERSTANDING

C. Marvin Zack bought a used home for $95,000 with a $15,000 down payment. His mortgage of $80,000 is for 20 years at 7%. Find Marvin's monthly payments and the total amount he will pay in interest over the 20-year loan period. $620.24, $68,857.60

D. Joseph and Rhoda Flynn bought a modular home as a future retirement home. The Flynn's made a $25,000 down payment and got a $40,000 loan to pay for the home. If the loan is for 25 years at 6%, what monthly payment will they make? What total interest will they pay on the loan over the 25 years? $257.72, $37,316

■ Refinancing a Mortgage

When interest rates go down, business firms and property owners often refinance or replace their fixed rate mortgages with another mortgage at a lower interest rate. Owners also exchange their variable rate mortgages for a fixed rate mortgage that provides a fixed interest rate for the loan's term.

When you refinance a mortgage, you take out a new mortgage and use that money to pay off the old mortgage. When you refinance your mortgage, you also pay closing costs on the new loan. There may also be other fees, such as the application costs for a loan or a prepayment penalty charged for paying off the first mortgage before it is due.

> **BUSINESS TIP**
>
> Due to loan costs, the savings in the first year is small. Finding the difference between loans over several years will show the total savings of refinancing.

■ Apply Goal 2

Work through Example 2 at the board with students completing the math at their desks.

Remind students that multiplying the monthly payment by the number of months in the loan gives the total amount paid, which includes principal and interest. The original principal must be subtracted to find the amount of interest paid.

Relate this process to finding the compound amount and deducting the original deposit amount to find interest earned on savings deposits.

Assign Check Your Understanding problems C and D for class work. Circulate in the classroom and examine student work for any difficulty they may be having with the problems.

■ ONGOING ASSESSMENT

Check that students know how to use the amortization table by having them find the monthly payments for different loan amounts at various rates and terms.

■ Teach Goal 3

Point out that fixed-rate mortgages are often refinanced after interest rates have fallen significantly. However, mortgages are not refinanced every time rates fall because closing costs may eliminate potential savings, at least in the short run.

■ *CHECK YOUR UNDERSTANDING SOLUTIONS*

C. $620.24 monthly payment; $20 \times 12 = 240$ months; $240 \times \$620.24 = \$148,857.60$; $\$148,857.60 - \$80,000 = \$68,857.60$

D. $257.72 monthly payment; $25 \times 12 = 300$ months; $300 \times \$257.72 = \$77,316$; $\$77,316 - \$40,000 = \$37,316$

E. $12 \times \$597 = \$7,164$; $12 \times \$465 = \$5,580$; $\$7,164 - \$5,580 = \$1,584$; $\$1,584 - \$836 = \$748$ savings

F. $12 \times \$982 = \$11,784$; $12 \times \$876 = \$10,512$; $\$11,784 - \$10,512 = \$1,272$; $\$1,272 - (\$716 + \$485) = \$71$ saved

225

Work Example 3 at the board and have students complete calculations at their desks. Explain that the prepayment penalty is a charge made by the original lender to cover the costs of closing the original loan before the end of its term.

Assign Check Your Understanding problems E and F for class work. Examine student work at their desks. Identify errors and help students make corrections.

Wrap Up

Review the Start Up. Remind students of the importance of location when buying property. Discuss why lakefront property costs more than lake access property.

TEAM MEETING

Have team members share their reports with the class and list on the board the interest rates they found. Have the class give possible reasons for the differences in rates.

EXAMPLE 3

The Rowes had a fixed rate mortgage at 9.65% with an unpaid balance of $40,000. The monthly payment on the old mortgage was $511.09. They got a new mortgage at 7.98% for the amount of the unpaid balance from another lender. Their new monthly payment is $340.73.

To get the new mortgage, they had to pay closing costs of $935. To pay off the old mortgage before it was due, they had to pay a prepayment penalty of $500. How much did they save during the first year by getting the new mortgage?

SOLUTION

Multiply the old monthly payment by the number of months in a year.

$12 \times \$511.09 = \$6,133.08$ one year's payment under old mortgage

Multiply the new monthly payment by the number of months in a year.

$12 \times \$340.73 = \$4,088.76$ one year's payment under new mortgage

$\$6,133.08 - \$4,088.76 = \$2,044.32$ difference in yearly payments

$\$935 + \$500 = \$1,435$ total of closing costs and prepayment penalty

$\$2,044.32 - \$1,435 = \$609.32$ amount saved in first year

■ **CHECK YOUR UNDERSTANDING**

E. Nancy Ouimet's monthly mortgage payment is $597. She can refinance her loan with a new mortgage with monthly payments of $465. The total cost of getting a new mortgage is $836. What net first-year savings will she have with the new mortgage? $748

F. Will Ryan can refinance a mortgage by paying $716 in closing costs and $485 for a prepayment charge. His current monthly mortgage payment is $982. The monthly payment for the refinanced mortgage will be $876. If he refinances the mortgage, how much will he save in the first year? $71

Wrap Up

The location of property is usually the most important factor in determining its value. The increased traffic, the exhaust odors, and the noise may make the home near the parking lot less desirable.

TEAM MEETING

Form a team with three to four students. Make an appointment with the manager of a local bank to find the current interest rates for variable rate mortgages. Ask these questions: For how long is the interest rate guaranteed? How will future rates be set? What special rules apply to variable rate mortgages that make them different from fixed rate mortgages. Summarize your findings and report to them to the entire class.

COMMON ERRORS

Students may be confused when solving refinancing problems because the length of the mortgage is not given. Students need to focus on the problem's question that usually asks for a one-year comparison. Thus, any payments stated in the problem need to be multiplied by 12, the number of months in one year.

EXERCISES

Find the sum.
1. $128 + $65 + $902 $1,095
2. $3,404 + $1,783 $5,187

Find the product.
3. 12 × 15 180
4. 12 × 40 480
5. 12 × $653.87 $7,846.44
6. 180 × $326.85 $58,833
7. 20% × $184,600 $36,920
8. 2.5% × $78,400 $1,960

Find the difference.
9. $145,874 − $60,000 $85,874
10. $4,329.34 − $2,508.85 $1,820.49

The Colburns want to buy a condominium priced at $135,700. They will need to make a down payment of 15% and pay closing costs of 3% of the purchase price.

11. How much cash will they need for the down payment? $20,355

12. How much of the purchase price will they have to borrow? $115,345

13. How much cash will they need for the closing costs? $4,071

Ethel and Hector Ward bought a house at its market value of $82,000. They made a 5% down payment and paid these closing costs: legal fees, $550; property survey, $310; title insurance, $275; inspection fees, $240; points, $1,558.

14. What was the amount of the down payment? $4,100

15. What was the total of the closing costs? $2,933

16. How much of the purchase price will they have to borrow? $77,900

17. How much cash will they need to pay the down payment and closing costs? $7,033

Use the loan amortization table to help solve problems 18–23.

	Loan Amount	Interest Rate	Loan Term	Monthly Payment	Total Interest Paid Over Loan Term
18.	$45,000	6%	30 yrs	$269.80	$52,128
19.	$60,000	8%	20 yrs	$501.86	$60,446.40
20.	$110,000	7%	25 yrs	$777.46	$123,238
21.	$90,000	7%	30 yrs	$598.77	$125,557.20
22.	$50,000	6%	20 yrs	$358.22	$35,972.80
23.	$100,000	8%	30 yrs	$733.76	$164,153.60

Lesson 6.1 Borrowing to Buy a Home ■ **227**

Assign

Assignment: Exercises 1–26 and 28–40. Begin with the basic arithmetic problems. They review the underlying arithmetic operations used in the exercises.

Assess

Check student answers to exercise problems by calling on them in class, collecting and grading selected problems, or by observing student work at their desks.

Reteach

STUDENT WORKBOOK If students need help in calculating the down payment, closing costs, and mortgage loan amount, work Exercise 1 in the workbook with them. Then have them do Exercises 2–4.

Some students may require help to find the total interest cost of a mortgage. Work Exercise 5 with them and assign Exercises 6–8 for them to solve.

To help students calculate the refinancing of mortgages, work Exercise 9 with them and assign Exercise 10 for independent work.

SELECTED SOLUTIONS

11. 0.15 × $135,700 = $20,355

13. 0.03 × $135,700 = $4,071

18. $269.80 monthly payment;
12 × 30 = 360; 360 × $269.80 = $97,128;
$97,128 − $45,000 = $52,128

20. $777.46 monthly payment;
12 × 25 = 300; 300 × $777.46 = $233,238;
$233,238 − $110,000 = $123,238

Enrich

Ask students to research other types of mortgages such as balloon, rapid repayment, and reverse mortgages.

Close

Call on students to define these terms in their own words: mortgage, amortize, down payment, closing costs, and refinancing. Encourage other students to add other items that complete the definition.

Assign Exercise 27, Critical Thinking. Make sure students address (1) how low down payments mean less money is needed at the time of purchase, yet more money is borrowed resulting in higher interest costs over the term of the loan and (2) how a longer term means more total interest is paid.

Your old $47,000, 30-year, 12.8% mortgage has a monthly payment of $512.58. Over the 6 years since you took out the loan, mortgage rates have dropped. You can now get a mortgage at 9.05%, which will result in a new monthly payment of $369.36. To refinance, you must pay $1,020 in closing costs and a $480 prepayment penalty.

24. Find the net amount you will save in the first year. $218.64

25. Find the net amount you will save in the second year. $143.22 × 12 = $1,718.64 second year saving

26. After being in effect for 4 years, the rate of interest on Syd Mutin's variable rate mortgage increased to 6.48% from 4.7%. Syd's old monthly payment was $259.32. His new monthly payment is $327.18. How much more will Syd pay in one year at the new mortgage rate? $814.32

27. CRITICAL THINKING What do you think are the advantages and disadvantages of low down payments and long-term loans? See Close section for answers.

28. CRITICAL THINKING When do you think that refinancing a mortgage may not be a good idea? Small difference between original and new interest rates; few years left in mortgage

MIXED REVIEW

29. $ 78,412.23
$129,808.49
$ 3,642.01
$211,862.73

30. $283,371 − $127,319 $156,052

31. Round to the nearest hundred: 5,565.17 5,600

32. Write $12\frac{1}{2}\%$ as a decimal. 0.125

33. $2\frac{1}{8} + 3\frac{3}{8}$ $5\frac{1}{2}$

34. A sales slip's total is $89.52 and includes $53.12 of non-taxable food items. What sales tax should be charged if the rate is 4%? $1.46, Lesson 5.3

35. Benjamin Toomey borrowed $4,200 from his bank for two years at 10.5% annual interest. What total amount must he pay his bank at the end of two years? $5,082, Lesson 4.5

36. The finance charge on an $800 loan for 6 months was $46. Use the Simple Interest table to find the annual percentage rate of the loan. $19\frac{1}{2}\%$, Lesson 4.3

37. Lee Moore began the day with $104.76 in cash. During the day she cashed a paycheck for $130 and spent $189.56 for lumber. How much money did she have left at the end of the day? $45.20, Lesson 2.6

38. You can buy a TV for $275 cash or pay $50 down and the balance in 18 monthly payments of $18.70. What is the installment price? By what percent, to the nearest tenth percent, would your installment price be greater than the cash price? $386.60, 40.6% Lesson 4.4

39. Felicia Delaney uses her credit card to take a cash advance on September 6. She pays off the loan on Novermber 3. For how many days did she borrow money from her credit card company? 58 days, Lesson 4.3

40. What is the price per foot of cloth that sells for $3.59 a yard? $1.20, Lesson 5.3

TEACHING STRATEGIES Cooperative Learning

Students may have heard about VA loans and FHA loans. Have students form teams to find what the letter abbreviations of these loans mean, who is eligible to receive them, whether they have an insurance component, and how the interest rates of these loans compare to the rates of conventional loans.

6.2 Renting or Owning a Home

GOALS

- Calculate the costs of home ownership
- Calculate the cost of renting a home or apartment
- Compare the costs of renting vs. owning

Start Up

Several students who will attend the same college next fall plan to rent apartments. They have been talking about pooling the money they will be paying for rent and using it instead to buy an old, large house in which all of them could live. They believe they could save money by making monthly mortgage payments instead of paying rent. One of the students thinks his father would be willing to sign for the loan. What advice would you give the students?

Math Skill Builder

Review these math skills and solve the exercises that follow.

1. **Add** money amounts.
   Find the sum: $3,600 + $180 + $1,267 + $683 = $5,730

   1a. $5,120 + $1,568 + $462 $7,150   **1b.** $12,874 + $1,236 + $658 $14,768

2. **Subtract** money amounts.
   Find the difference: $11,005 − $1,643 $9,362

   2a. $12,905 − $1,238 $11,667   **2b.** $12,858 − $11,983 $875

3. **Multiply** money amounts by percents and whole numbers.
   Find the product: 2% × $78,400 = 0.02 × $78,400 = $1,568

   3a. 3.5% × $126,900 $4,441.50   **3b.** 1.75% × $56,513 $988.98

   Find the product: 12 × $764 = $9,168

   3c. 12 × $45.60 $547.20   **3d.** 12 × $567 =$6,804

■ Costs of Home Ownership

After the home is bought, a homeowner has many ongoing expenses. Cash has to be paid out for property taxes, repairs, maintenance, utilities, insurance, mortgage interest, and special services such as trash pickup. Two other less obvious expenses are depreciation and the loss of income on the money invested in the home.

Lesson 6.2 Renting or Owning a Home ■ 229

Work through Example 1 with students and have them do the calculations at their desks.

Point out that the mortgage interest and property taxes total $7,594, which is less than the $7,800 standard deduction for married couples. The $1,428 income tax savings means that the Hansen family had other deductions, as well.

Assign Check Your Understanding problems A and B. Observe student work to determine if they have problems in completing the assignment.

Depreciation is the loss in value of property caused by aging and use. The loss in value may be caused by the wearing out of parts of the home, such as the roof. It may also occur as home styles change or if the home becomes too expensive to heat and cool as energy costs rise. Most housing depreciates slowly at about 1% to 4% of its original value per year.

The amount of depreciation cannot be calculated until a house is sold. Until that time, depreciation must be estimated. Estimates of depreciation are often shown as a percent of the original purchase price.

Loss of income occurs because the money initially invested in buying the property (down payment and closing costs) could have been deposited in a savings account or other investment and earned interest.

One financial benefit homeowners have is that they may include the interest they pay on their home mortgage and the property taxes they pay on their property as itemized deductions on their income tax return. This reduces the income tax they pay. Homeowners also build equity in their homes. *Equity* is the difference between what is owed on a home and its value.

EXAMPLE 1

The Hansens want to buy a home. The interest they will pay on their mortgage in the first year will be $5,244. The annual property taxes on the home are $2,350, and an insurance policy on the home will cost $360 a year. They estimate that the home will depreciate $1,240 the first year, utilities will cost $1,710, and maintenance and repairs will cost $1,535. They lose $1,270 interest on their down payment.

They estimate that they will save $1,428 in income taxes in the first year because the mortgage interest and property taxes will raise their itemized deductions above the standard deduction allowed. What will be the net cost of owning the home in the first year for the Hansens?

SOLUTION

Add all the expense items.   Subtract the tax savings.

$5,244	mortgage interest	$13,709	total expenses
2,350	property taxes	− 1,428	tax reductions
360	insurance	$12,281	net cost for the first year
1,240	depreciation		
1,710	utilities		
1,535	maintenance, repairs		
+ 1,270	lost interest		
$13,709	total expenses		

■ CHECK YOUR UNDERSTANDING

A. The Krafts want to buy a home. Their estimated first-year expenses are: mortgage interest, $6,848; property taxes, $3,782; insurance, $560; depreciation, $1,790; utilities, $1,300; maintenance and repairs, $2,050. They estimate lost interest income on savings to be $1,562. Income tax savings are estimated to be $1,320. Find their net cost of home ownership for the first year. $16,572

■ *CHECK YOUR UNDERSTANDING SOLUTIONS*

A. $6,848 + $3,782 + $560 + $1,790 + $1,300 + $2,050 + $1,562 = $17,892; $17,892 − $1,320 = $16,572

B. 0.02 × $87,000 = $1,740; $5,788 + $1,904 + $347 + $1,140 + $1,740 + $900 + $1,860 = $13,679; $13,679 − $1,050 = $12,629

B. The Khurana family is building a home for $87,000 on a lot they own. They estimate their expenses for the first year to be: mortgage interest, $5,788; property taxes, $1,904; insurance, $347; lost interest income, $1,140; depreciation, 2% of the home's cost; maintenance and repairs, $900. The cost of heating, electricity, and water is estimated to be $1,860. The Khurana's expect to save $1,050 in income taxes as a result of owning the home. What will be the net cost of the home the first year? $12,629

■ Costs of Property Rental

Some people rent until they can afford to buy a home. Others prefer to rent. Many people prefer not to worry about the expense and effort of maintaining a property. There are financial advantages and disadvantages to renting as well.

FINANCIAL ADVANTAGES OF RENTING Advantages include not having to pay a significant down payment to rent; earning interest on money that would be used for a down payment; and having more predictable housing costs. Renters do not have to worry about major unplanned housing expenses, such as a leaking roof or a cracked foundation. Renters of apartments do not have the maintenance costs associated with home ownership. Renters of homes may be expected to perform routine maintenance, such as mowing the lawn as part of their lease. Apartment renters may find that utilities are included in the monthly rent.

FINANCIAL DISADVANTAGES OF RENTING Renters receive no federal income tax benefits. (However, some states let renters claim a portion of their rent as a tax deduction.) In addition, renters do not build equity on the housing they rent.

Renters usually pay a one-time security deposit in addition to their first month's rent when they sign a *lease*, or rental agreement. Return of the security deposit at the end of the lease is not guaranteed. The property owner may keep the security deposit to pay for repairs to the rental property or to clean the property, if the renters have not done so.

EXAMPLE 2

Mary Beth Berkovic plans to rent an apartment for $710 a month, including heat and water. The security deposit will be one-month's rent. She estimates that other annual costs connected with the apartment will be: insurance, $110; utilities, $600; covered parking space, $240. What is Mary Beth's first-year cost of renting the apartment?

SOLUTION
$12 \times \$710 = \$8,520$ yearly rent

$\$8,520 + \$710 + \$110 + \$600 + \$240 = \$10,180$ total first-year cost

■ CHECK YOUR UNDERSTANDING

C. Rick Cassell rented an apartment for one year and paid $625 monthly rent. His other apartment-related costs for the year were: security deposit of $625; insurance, $85; utilities, $1,210; replacement of lost mailbox key, $10. What was the cost of renting the apartment for the one year? $9,430

Lesson 6.2 Renting or Owning a Home ■ **231**

■ *CHECK YOUR UNDERSTANDING SOLUTIONS*

C. $12 \times \$625 = \$7,500$;
$\$7,500 + \$625 + \$85 + \$1,210 + \$10 = \$9,430$

D. $12 \times \$1,250 = \$15,000$;
$12 \times 100 = \$1,200$; $\$15,000 + \$1,250 + \$1,200 + \$136 + \$1,700 = \$19,286$

Students are likely to be aware of the different categories of costs in owning and renting dwellings. Remind them that comparisons are approximate because the sizes and locations of homes and apartments and the terms of lease contracts differ widely.

Also remind students that people have valid reasons for renting or owning that have nothing to do with costs.

Inform students that the term dwelling is often used because it best describes the wide variety of places in which people live.

Work Example 3 at the board while students do calculations at their desks. Tell students that this example combines the processes they have already used in this lesson.

Assign Check Your Understanding problems E and F for class work. Monitor student progress at their desks to ensure they are following correct procedures for solving the problems.

D. Belinda Pryor's monthly rent on a house she is leasing is $1,250. The security deposit is one month's rent. Belinda is responsible for mowing the lawn and clearing snow and estimates she will spend $100 a month to have this done. Her other annual costs include $136 for insurance and $1,700 for utilities. What will be her first-year costs of renting this home? $19,286

■ Comparing Renting and Owning Homes

When you buy or rent property you have some expenses that are similar, such as insurance and utilities. Most other expenses are quite different as are the sizes of the properties and their locations. For these reasons, it is very difficult to compare the purchase of a home to the rental of an apartment. However, the costs of owning a home and renting a similar home can be compared.

EXAMPLE 3

Cedric Thorne has $17,000 he can use as a down payment on a house that sells for $85,000. The interest for a year on his mortgage would be $5,184. He estimates his property taxes to be $1,720. Other costs of home ownership would total $3,270. He would lose $680 interest on his down payment and closing costs, but would save $895 on income taxes. Cedric can rent a similar home for $850 a month with a $1,200 security deposit.

His other annual expenses of renting would be $130 for insurance and $1,400 for utilities. Is it less expensive for Cedric to buy or rent a home, and what is the difference?

SOLUTION
Find the net cost of home ownership.

($5,184 + $1,720 + $3,270 + $680) − $895 = $9,959 cost of home ownership

Find the cost of renting.

12 × $850 = $10,200 annual rent

$10,200 + $1,200 + $130 + $1,400 = $12,930 cost of renting

Find the difference between owning and renting.

$12,930 − $9,959 = $2,971

Buying is $2,971 less expensive than renting for the first year.

■ CHECK YOUR UNDERSTANDING

E. Lynette Wolfe estimates her loan interest, taxes, insurance, and maintenance to be $9,100 on a house she bought for $83,600. She estimates her house would depreciate $2,926 a year. Lynette would lose $560 interest on the cash invested in her home, but would pay $1,600 less in income taxes. She could have rented the house for $785 a month, paid insurance of $115, utilities of $1,150, and not had any maintenance expenses except for the cost of routine cleaning. She also would have paid a security deposit of $200. For the first year, would it have been cheaper to rent or buy the house? Rent, $101 cheaper

CONNECTION TO LANGUAGE ARTS

Students use and see a variety of terms that refer to housing. To be sure they understand their differences, have students find and write in complete sentences the definitions of these housing terms: single-family, condo, duplex, townhouse, apartment, studio apartment, manufactured home, and mobile home.

F. If Roscoe Tippin bought a manufactured home instead of continuing to rent an apartment, these expenses would increase by the amount shown: insurance, $276; utilities, $980. His annual interest on the mortgage would be $4,060, and he would have to rent a lot on which to place the home for $240 a month. The current monthly rent on his apartment is $510. Depreciation on the home is estimated to be $764. If he bought the home he would lose $57 interest on the cash invested, pay yearly property taxes of $945, and have income tax savings of $274. Is it more expensive for Roscoe to rent the apartment or buy the home, and how much more? Buying is $3,568 more expensive

Wrap Up

Buying a house instead of just renting an apartment presents several problems when expenses are shared. There is no guarantee that all the students will remain in school, and some will be in school longer than others. All would have to cooperate in maintaining the property to keep up its value. Also, the student group may not be able to afford to pay the cost of major, unexpected repairs. The purchase of a home also requires money up front to make the down payment and pay closing costs. Finding a parent willing to make such a financial investment may be a possibility, but not a certainty.

COMMUNICATION

The monthly rent for a large luxury apartment in an exclusive high-rise building in New York City is $7,000 a month. An apartment of the same size located in a mid-western city costs only $2,000 a month. Write the reasons you think could account for the difference in rents. Share your thoughts with other class members in class discussion.

EXERCISES

Find the sum.
1. $12,876 + $1,003 $13,879
2. $284 + $128 + $265 $677

Find the difference.
3. $12,736 − $9,375 $3,361
4. $1,680 − $735 $945

Find the product.
5. 2.5% of $140,300 $3,507.50
6. 1.5% of $67,200 $1,008
7. 12 × $578 $6,936
8. 12 × $67.50 $810

9. Mort and Jackie Silver own a home. They estimate their expenses to be mortgage interest, $10,180; property taxes, $3,690; insurance, $833; depreciation, $3,800; maintenance and repairs, $900; lost interest income, $2,375; utilities, $2,450. They expect to save $3,700 in income taxes from home expense. What is their net cost of home ownership? $20,528

Lesson 6.2 Renting or Owning a Home ■ 233

ENRICHING SELECTED PROBLEMS

Students may not be familiar with the term subsidized housing in Exercise 11. Explain that this is a federal program to provide low-income individuals or families with quality, affordable housing, usually apartments. The occupants pay part of the monthly rent and the federal government *subsidizes* or pays the rest of the rent.

10. Joyce Navarro-Martin wants to buy a home for $73,200. She estimates her first-year expenses to be mortgage interest, $6,810; lost interest of $971; property taxes, $1,585; insurance, $395; depreciation at $1,098; maintenance and repairs, $1,800; utilities, $1,250. She expects to save $1,847 in taxes. What will be the net cost of owning the home in the first year? $12,062

11. Patricia McCarthy lives in a subsidized apartment complex for low-income senior citizens. She pays monthly rent of $297 for a unit that could rent for $650 a month elsewhere. The monthly rent provides heat and water, but does not cover the $42 average monthly cost of electricity. She carries no insurance on the contents of the apartment. What are her annual costs of renting the apartment? $4,068

12. Tyrone Northrup pays monthly rent of $1,240 for a one-bedroom apartment in a large city. He pays an extra monthly charge of $160 to the rental company for a parking space in an attended lot. His other costs are: electricity, $90 a month; other utilities, $860 a year; insurance, $170 a year. What is his annual cost of renting? $18,910

13. Sybil Kline rents a home for $970 a month. Her other annual expenses of renting total $1,305. If she buys the home, her estimated yearly expenses would be mortgage interest, $5,100; property taxes, $1,890; depreciation, $2,400; maintenance, $1,100; insurance, $479; utilities, $1,470; lost interest income, $1,020. She would save $1,536 in income taxes. Are her net annual costs of housing lower by renting or buying? How much is saved? Buying, $1,022 lower

Carole Finney rents an apartment for $640 a month and pays $120 for insurance and $820 for utilities yearly. She can buy a home with about the same space for $52,000. If she buys the home, she must withdraw $10,400 from her savings account and lose $624 interest. Her other home ownership expenses are estimated to be $9,300. She also estimates that owning a home will save her $1,428 in income taxes.

14. What is her total cost of renting for the year? $8,620

15. Which costs more, renting or owning? How much more? Renting; $124 more

16. **INTEGRATING YOUR KNOWLEDGE** Stephanie Larken presently rents an apartment for $580 a month. She estimates that her rent will increase 4% each year and that she will make total rent payments of $207,592.68 over 20 years. Her insurance and utility bills will average $800 a year over the 20 years. Stephanie has savings that she could use to buy a home with the same space as her apartment for $62,000. If she makes a 5% down payment and pays closing costs of $1,900, she can get a 20-year mortgage with a monthly payment of $465.53. Stephanie estimates her average annual ownership expenses as: depreciation, $1,150; maintenance, $1,400; insurance, $280; property taxes, $1,970, utilities, $1,390. Her income tax savings would average $965 a year. Interest of $310 a year could be earned on the money used for the down payment and closing costs. What is the total amount Stephanie might pay out over 20 years for renting the apartment and buying the home? Which plan do you think would work best for Stephanie? Renting, $223,592.68; Buying, $227,427.20 Although slightly more money ($3,834.52) is required to buy the home, Stephanie ends up owning the home at the end of 20 years.

SELECTED SOLUTIONS

9. $10,180 + $3,690 + $833 + $3,800 + $900 + $2,375 + $2,450 − $3,700 = $20,528

12. 12 × $1,240 = $14,880; 12 × $160 = $1,920; 12 × $90 = $1,080; $14,880 + $1,920 + $1,080 + $860 + $170 = $18,910

14. 12 × $640 = $7,680; $7,680 + $120 + $820 = $8,620 cost of renting

15. $9,300 + $624 − $1,428 = $8,496 cost of owning; $8,620 − $8,496 = $124 renting costs more

17. **CRITICAL THINKING** Assuming your monthly rent and mortgage payments would be identical, would you prefer to buy or rent a home? Make a list of five reasons for your choice. Number them from 1–5 in order of importance, with 1 being the most important. Answers will vary. Students should give reasons.

18. **CRITICAL THINKING** Many homes are worth more now than when they were purchased. These homes are said to have appreciated, or increased in value. In this lesson you calculated the estimated depreciation on homes. Can homes appreciate and depreciate at the same time? See Enrich section for answer.

MIXED REVIEW

19. $92.75 + $11.49 + $102 + $42.11 + $905.72 $1,154.07

20. Find the estimated and actual product of 93.59 × 406. 36,000; 37,997.54

21. 10¢ × 152 $15.20

22. Write 316% as a decimal. 3.16

23. Round to the nearest 10,000: 129,817 130,000

24. Lou Miller paid $39 interest on a loan of $1,200 for 3 months. Find the interest rate he paid. 13%, Lesson 4.1

25. Use the Simple Interest Table in Lesson 4.3 to find the interest on a $1,400 loan at $12\frac{1}{2}$% for 29 days. $13.90, Lesson 4.3

26. Stella Sabo worked these weekly hours in February: $27\frac{1}{2}$, $30\frac{3}{4}$, $38\frac{1}{2}$, $31\frac{1}{2}$. What average number of hours did she work per week for these four weeks, to the nearest tenth hour? 32.1, Lesson 1.2

27. Stuart Chapman repaid a 9-month, Rule of 78 loan for $3,000 at the end of 6 months. The total finance charge for the loan was $310. What was the amount of his earned and unearned finance charges? Use the Chart in Lesson 4.5 to help solve the problem. earned, $268.68; unearned, $41.32, Lesson 4.5

28. Tischa Fogoros' credit card statement for June showed no previous balance on June 1. A purchase of $263.18 was posted on June 9, and a $15.85 credit for returned merchandise was posted on June 17. Tischa's credit card company uses the average daily balance method to compute finance charges based on a 1.52% monthly APR. Find the finance charge for June and the new balance. $2.82, $250.15, Lesson 4.8

29. What amount of tax will be owed on an income of $63,280 if the city income tax rate is 1.5% of all income? $949.20, Lesson 2.4

30. What are the gross earnings of an employee who works 43 hours and is paid $11.23 an hour? $482.89, Lesson 1.1

31. Find the finance charge per $100 on a loan of $8,260 with a finance charge of $1,230. $14.89, Lesson 4.6

32. Luann Weber is paid a salary of $520 a week and commission of 4.5% on all sales. Her sales last week were $8,600. Find her total earnings for the week. $907, Lesson 1.4

33. Felicia Delaney uses her credit card to take a cash advance on September 6. She pays off the loan on November 3. For how many days did she borrow money from her credit card company? 58 days, Lesson 4.3

Lesson 6.2 Renting or Owning a Home ▪ 235

CONNECTION TO FINANCE

Remind students that when people buy a home for their own use, they earn no income on their investment. So, in financial terms, the home is called a non-income producing investment. People who buy property to rent to someone else expect to earn income on their investment. So they make an income-producing investment.

GOALS

- Calculate the decimal tax rate
- Calculate property taxes for tax rates per $100 or $1,000
- Calculate property taxes for tax rates in mills or cents per $1

Start Up

Renters of apartments or homes do not own the property they rent. Do the renters have to pay any property taxes?

Math Skill Builder

Review these math skills and solve the exercises that follow.

1 **Multiply** money amounts by decimals.
Find the product. $72,000 \times 0.0587 = \$4,226.40$

  1a. $1,000 \times 0.0564$ 56.40 **1b.** $84,000 \times 0.0642$ $5,392.80

2 **Divide** money amounts by money amounts with end zeros.
Find the quotient. $75,126 \div \$1,000 = 75.126$

  2a. $46,300 \div \$100$ 463   **2b.** $59,317 \div \$1,000$ 59.317

3 **Divide** money amounts and round to four decimal places.
Find the quotient. $507,000 \div \$8,000,000 = 0.06338$, or 0.0634

  3a. $483,200 \div \$6,000,000$ 0.0805   **3b.** $889,600 \div \$9,800,000$ 0.0908

■ Decimal Tax Rate

Property taxes are taxes on the value of real estate such as homes, business property, or farm land. Taxes are collected annually or semiannually by the tax departments of local tax districts such as cities and towns in which the property is located.

Services that are often supported by taxes include schools, government operations, fire and police protection, and parks and road maintenance.

The amount of property tax paid is based on the **assessed value** of a property. Local tax assessors calculate this value. For example, the Watson's tax bill on the next page shows their property has a fair market value of $150,000. It is assessed at 40% of its market value, or $60,000. The assessed values of properties are usually less than their market values. Similar properties in the same community should have similar assessed values.

CONNECTION TO ECONOMICS

Students may not know that not all property in a tax district is subject to property tax. Have students recall that sales taxes sometimes are not charged on certain purchases, such as food. Similarly, property taxes are not charged on the property owned by non-profit organizations such as schools, churches, libraries, and government buildings. These are tax-exempt. Point out the consequences of a community consisting entirely of tax-exempt property: the base would be zero; there would be no local revenue to pay for essential services, such as fire and police protection.

Local tax districts determine the tax rate needed to pay for the services they provide. They estimate their expenses for the coming year and prepare an expense budget. They also estimate income from sources other than the property tax, such as licenses, fees, fines, rents, state aid, and so on. The difference between the total budget and the income from other sources is the amount that must be raised by the property tax.

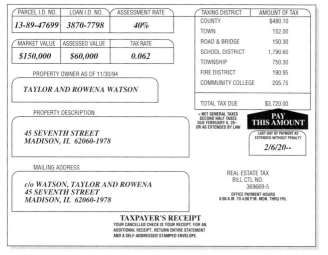

PARCEL I.D. NO.	LOAN I.D. NO.	ASSESSMENT RATE
13-89-47699	3870-7798	40%

MARKET VALUE	ASSESSED VALUE	TAX RATE
$150,000	$60,000	0.062

PROPERTY OWNER AS OF 11/30/94

TAYLOR AND ROWENA WATSON

PROPERTY DESCRIPTION

45 SEVENTH STREET
MADISON, IL 62060-1978

MAILING ADDRESS

c/o WATSON, TAYLOR AND ROWENA
45 SEVENTH STREET
MADISON, IL 62060-1978

TAXING DISTRICT	AMOUNT OF TAX
COUNTY	$480.10
TOWN	152.00
ROAD & BRIDGE	150.30
SCHOOL DISTRICT	1,790.60
TOWNSHIP	750.30
FIRE DISTRICT	190.95
COMMUNITY COLLEGE	205.75
TOTAL TAX DUE	$3,720.00

= NET GENERAL TAXES
SECOND HALF TAXES
DUE FEBRUARY 6, 20--
OR AS EXTENDED BY LAW

PAY THIS AMOUNT

LAST DAY OF PAYMENT AS
EXTENDED WITHOUT PENALTY

2/6/20--

REAL ESTATE TAX
BILL CTL NO.
369669-5
OFFICE PAYMENT HOURS
8:00 A.M. TO 4:00 P.M. MON. THRU FRI.

TAXPAYER'S RECEIPT
YOUR CANCELLED CHECK IS YOUR RECEIPT. FOR AN
ADDITIONAL RECEIPT, RETURN ENTIRE STATEMENT
AND A SELF-ADDRESSED STAMPED ENVELOPE.

Local tax districts then determine the *decimal tax rate*, which is the tax rate at which property is to be taxed. They find the decimal tax rate by dividing the amount to be raised by the property tax by the total assessed value of all property in the district.

$$\frac{\text{Amount to be Raised by Property Tax}}{\text{Total Assessed Value}} = \text{Decimal Tax Rate}$$

EXAMPLE 1

The Columbia School District's total budgeted expenses last year were $6,000,000. Estimated income from other sources was $1,800,000. The total assessed value of all taxable property in Columbia last year was $39,000,000. Find the tax rate needed to meet expenses, correct to five decimal places.

SOLUTION
Subtract the income from other sources from the total budgeted expenses to find the income to be raised from property taxes.

$6,000,000 − $1,800,000 = $4,200,000 property tax income needed

Divide the income to be raised from property taxes by the total assessed value of all property.

$4,200,000 ÷ $39,000,000 = 0.107692 = 0.10769 tax rate

■ CHECK YOUR UNDERSTANDING

A. Filber County's budget for a year is $6,750,000. Of that, $650,000 is raised from other income, and the rest from property taxes. The total assessed value of the county's property is $80,000,000. What is the decimal tax rate, rounded to three places? 0.076

B. The Gayle Fire District must raise $1,950,000 from property taxes. The assessed value of property in the district is $48,200,000. What is the decimal tax rate needed, to four decimal places? 0.0405

Lesson 6.3 Property Taxes ■ 237

Have students look at the top of
page 238 to examine the equivalent ways in which a decimal tax
rate of 0.062 may be stated. Use
the Math Tip to explain what a rate
in mills represents.

Refer to the tax bill on page 237
and show how multiplying the
assessed value of $60,000 by the
decimal tax rate of 0.062 yields a
tax due of $3,720.

Work Examples 2 and 3 at the
board and explain how the
processes are identical except that
the number of units, $100 or
$1,000, differ. Review the Math Tip
that shows how to quickly divide
by 100 or 1,000.

Assign Check Your Understanding
problems C through F for class
work. Check student work at their
desks to ensure they are following
the procedures outlined in the
examples.

In some communities the decimal tax rate is shown as a
rate per $1,000 or $100, cents per $1, or mills per $1. So,
the Watson's tax rate of 0.062 could also be stated as:

$62 per $1,000 (0.062 × $1,000 = $62);

$6.20 per $100 (0.062 × $100 = $6.20);

6.2 cents per $1 (0.062 × 100 cents = 6.2 cents), or as;

62 mills per $1 (0.062 × 1,000 mills = 62 mills).

All the tax rates are equivalent, and the tax due on the Watson's property in all
cases is $3,720.

MATH TIP

A mill is one-tenth of
a cent and one
thousandth of a
dollar.

■ Tax Rates per $100 or $1,000 of Assessed Value

To find the tax due on property when the rate is in $100 or $1,000, first find the
number of $100 units or $1,000 units in the assessed value. Then, multiply the
numbers of units by the tax rate to find the tax due.

EXAMPLE 2

Calculate the property tax due on the Watson's property if
their tax rate is stated as $6.20 per $100.

SOLUTION
Divide the assessed value by $100.

$60,000 ÷ $100 = 600   number of $100 units in the
                        assessed value

Multiply the tax rate per $100 by the number of $100 units.

600 × $6.20 = $3,720   property tax due

MATH TIP

To quickly divide by
100, move the
decimal point two
places to the left;
move the decimal
point three places to
the left to divide by
1,000.

■ CHECK YOUR UNDERSTANDING

C. The tax rate for the town of Beal is $3.736 per $100.
Find Rita's tax bill if her property in Beal is assessed at
$42,000. $1,569.12

D. Find the tax on property assessed at $120,000 if the tax rate is $4.128 per $100.
$4,953.60

EXAMPLE 3

Calculate the property tax due on the Watson's property if their tax rate is stated as
$62 per $1,000.

SOLUTION
$60,000 ÷ $1,000 = 60   number of $1,000 units in the assessed value

60 × $62 = $3,720   property tax due

■ *CHECK YOUR UNDERSTANDING SOLUTIONS*

E. $67,500 ÷ $1,000 = 67.5;
   67.5 × $50.08 = $3,380.40

F. $13,500 ÷ $1,000 = 13.5;
   13.5 × $25.83 = $348.705, or $348.71

G. 52 mills ÷ 1,000 = $0.052;
   $0.052 × $38,400 = $1,996.80

H. 3.8 cents ÷ 100 = $0.038;
   $0.038 × $32,100 = $1,219.80

E. What tax must Art pay on his home, assessed for $67,500 if his tax rate is $50.08 per $1,000? $3,380.40

F. The Gilbey family owns a cabin and land with an assessed value of $13,500. What property tax do they pay if the tax rate on the property is $25.83 per $1,000? $348.71

■ Tax Rates in Mills or Cents per Dollar of Assessed Value

Some communities show the tax rate in mills. A mill is one tenth of a cent, and one thousandth of a dollar. There are ten mills in one cent and 1,000 mills in one dollar.

To find the tax due when the rate is in mills or cents per $1 of assessed value, change the rate to a rate in dollars. Then multiply that rate by the assessed value. To change mills to dollars, divide the number of mills by 1,000. To change cents to dollars, divide the number of cents by 100.

EXAMPLE 4

Calculate the tax due on the Watson's property if their tax rate is stated as either 62 mills or 6.2 cents per $1 of assessed value.

SOLUTION

62 mills ÷ 1,000 = $0.062 (mills rate changed to rate in dollars)

6.2 cents ÷ 100 = $0.062 (cents rate changed to rate in dollars)

$60,000 × $0.062 = $3,720 total tax amount

■ CHECK YOUR UNDERSTANDING

G. The city tax rate in Milser is 52 mills per $1 of assessed value. Find the tax to be paid on property assessed at $38,400. $1,996.80

H. What tax must Michelle Nolan pay on a condominium assessed at $32,100 if her tax rate is 3.8 cents per $1? $1,219.80

Wrap Up

Renters pay property taxes indirectly through the rent they are charged. The owners of the real estate being rented must pay property taxes on its assessed value. The rents the owners charge usually cover their expenses, including property taxes.

COMMUNICATION

Contact your city or town tax office and find out what taxes are charged property owners to support local government services and schools. Also find the rates at which taxes are levied. Write a short report summarizing your findings.

■ Teach Goal 3

Tell students that the public information advertising for local bond issues may be stated in mills, and that a tax proposal to raise 2 mills (two one-thousandths of a dollar) appears to be very small. However, on a home assessed for $50,000, the tax increase is $100 a year.

Tell students the key to solving problems with tax rates in mills or cents is to recall how many mills or cents are in one dollar.

■ Apply Goal 3

Work Example 4 at the board. Ask students to explain why mills are divided by 1,000 and cents are divided by 100.

Assign Check Your Understanding problems G and H for class work. Observe student work at their desks to identify any student errors or difficulties they have in solving the problems.

Wrap Up

Review the Start Up. Point out that a developer may choose not to build rental units in a community with high property tax rates. The high tax will require a higher rent that may be out of line with competitive rents in adjoining areas, with all other factors considered to be equal.

COMMUNICATION

Review student reports and extract tax rate and tax usage information. Write examples on the board for each of the tax rate formats presented in the lesson.

COMMON ERRORS

Students may not remember whether they are to divide by 100 or 1,000 to change a rate in mills to a rate in dollars. Tell them the correct divisor can be calculated. Remind them they already know that 100 cents make $1.

Similarly, they should already know or have to memorize that there are 10 mills in each cent. So, 100 cents × 10 mills in a cent = 1,000, the number of mills in a dollar.

Assign

Assignment: Exercises 1–24 and 26–37. Students are to begin with the basic arithmetic problems at the beginning of the exercises. They review the underlying arithmetic in the exercises.

Assess

Collect student work and check the answers to selected problems except for problems 13–20 which ought to be checked in their entirety.

Reteach

STUDENT WORKBOOK Some students may need more practice in calculating decimal tax rates. Work Exercise 1 with them and then have them complete Exercise 2 a–d independently.

Other students may have difficulty in solving problems for tax rates per $100 or $1,000. Work with them the first two columns of Exercise 3 a. For more practice, assign the first two columns of Exercises 3 b–d, and Exercises 4 and 5.

If students have difficulty with tax rates shown in mills or cents, work the last two columns of Exercise 3 a with them. Then assign the last two columns of Exercises 3 b–d, and Exercises 6 and 7.

EXERCISES

Find the product.
1. 900 × $6.86 $6,174
2. 1,370 × $5.07 $6,945.90

Find the quotient.
3. $125,300 ÷ $100 1,253
4. $467,890 ÷ $1,000 467.89

Find the quotient, correct to four decimal places.
5. $264,000 ÷ $9,300,000 0.0284
6. $1,315,000 ÷ $24,100,000 0.0546

7. Property in the Bello School District has a total assessed value of $98,500,000. The district's budget for next year shows expenses totaling $5,000,000. The district expects to receive $3,200,000 from sources other than property tax. What decimal property tax rate, to four places, will the district use to raise enough money to meet budgeted expenses? 0.0183

Find the amount to be raised by property tax and the tax rate. Show the rate as a decimal, correct to three decimal places.

	Assessed Value	Total Expenses	Other Income	Raised by Property Tax	Tax Rate
8.	$27,000,000	$989,000	$87,000	$902,000	0.033
9.	$36,000,000	$878,000	$97,500	$780,500	0.022
10.	$22,750,000	$382,700	$68,400	$314,300	0.014
11.	$ 7,900,000	$396,300	$45,600	$350,700	0.044

12. Hazel Forest City plans to spend $4,470,000 next year. Income from sources other than property tax will be $1,430,000. The taxable property in the city has an assessed value of $78,000,000. Find the tax rate, correct to five decimal places. 0.03897

Find the tax due for Exercises 13–20.

	Assessed Value	Tax Rate	Tax Due
13.	$18,000	$5.20 per $100	$936
14.	$48,500	$71.10 per $1,000	$3,448.35
15.	$37,000	3.5 cents per $1	$1,295
16.	$25,300	77.3 mills per $1	$1,955.69
17.	$59,100	$4.747 per $100	$2,805.48
18.	$89,000	$87.45 per $1,000	$7,783.05
19.	$60,200	4.28 cents per $1	$2,576.56
20.	$19,800	56.82 mills per $1	$1,125.04

21. The town of Chester has a tax rate of 47.079 mills per $1. Find the tax on property in Chester worth $350,000, assessed at 60% of its market value. $9,886.59

SELECTED SOLUTIONS

7. $5,000,000 − $3,200,000 = $1,800,000;
   $1,800,000 ÷ $98,500,000 = .01827, or 0.0183
13. $18,000 ÷ $100 = 180; 180 × $5.20 = $936
14. $48,000 ÷ $1,000 = 48.5;
    48.5 × $71.10 = $3,448.35

15. 3.5 cents ÷ 100 = $0.035;
    $0.035 × $37,000 = $1,295
16. 77.3 mills ÷ 1,000 = $0.0773;
    $0.0773 × $25,300 = $1,955.69

22. Voters in Harmon approved a library tax of 0.75 mills per $1 of assessed value. What amount of library tax will a business owner pay for property assessed at $240,000? $180

23. Carlos' property is assessed at $92,700. The school tax rate in his district is 1.45 cents per $1. What is Carlos' school tax? $1,344.15

24. Redfield Township levied a property tax of 1.5 mills per $1 to pay for new equipment for its fire department. If the total value of all property in the township is $790 million, what amount will be raised by this tax to pay for new equipment? $1,185,000

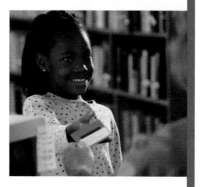

25. **CRITICAL THINKING** Business firms are often given a tax abatement to encourage them to build or expand their operations in a community. The tax abatement usually reduces the amount of tax paid by the business over several years. For example, the abatement could be a 50% reduction in taxes for 20 years. Are such tax abatements to businesses fair to homeowners who do not get such tax reductions? See Enrich section for answer.

26. **INTEGRATING YOUR KNOWLEDGE** Maxine Campau lives in a city that has a flat tax rate of 0.5% on all income. The city property tax rate is 3.43 cents per $1. The county in which Maxine lives also charges tax on property at a rate of 2.3 mills per $1 to pay for county operations. Maxine expects her income this year to be $52,000. Her home has an assessed value of 50% of its market value of $110,000. What total amount will Maxine expect to pay this year in city income tax and property taxes? $2,273

MIXED REVIEW

27. 0.004 × 84.27 0.33708

28. $1\frac{7}{8} \times 6$ $11\frac{1}{4}$

29. Write $\frac{9}{20}$ as a decimal 0.45

30. $4,228 ÷ 7 $604

31. Estimate, then find the exact product: 80.35 × 29 2,400; 2,330.15

32. Round the result of 135.7 ÷ 5.2 to two places. 26.10

33. Winston Chambers borrows $3,000 at 7% exact interest for 43 days. What interest will he pay on the loan? $24.74, Lesson 4.1

34. A futon has a cash price of $650. To buy it on an installment plan, you pay $100 down and $40 a month for 18 months. What finance charge will you pay for this purchase? $170, Lesson 4.4

35. You borrowed $300 for 15 days using your credit card's cash advance feature. The credit card company charges a $5 fee and a daily periodic interest rate of 0.0482% on the cash advance. What was the total finance charge on the cash advance? $7.17, Lesson 4.8

36. Find the total sale for Fred's purchase of 13 boxes of nails @ $4.83 and 6 tubes of caulking @ $4.67. $90.81, Lesson 5.1

37. The Mitchell family's total budget is $58,400. Of their total budget they plan to spend 5% on a summer vacation trip and 4% on entertainment near home. How much do they plan to spend for these two expense items? $5,256, Lesson 2.6

Lesson 6.3 Property Taxes ■ 241

Start Up

Have students read the Start Up. As students discuss the Start Up, point out that mortgage lenders require borrowers to carry adequate home insurance to protect the lender's investment in the property as well.

Math Skill Builder

Students use the skills of addition, multiplication, subtraction, division and rounding of money amounts in this lesson.

Complete all exercises in Math Skill Builder 1–5.

■ Teach Goal 1

Review these general concepts: an insurance policy is a contract between a property owner and the insurance company; insurance rates are based on the degree of risk exposure to the insurer.

Discuss what a basic homeowners policy covers and show students how to calculate the amount of coverage for a category, such as personal property, that is based on the insurance carried on the dwelling.

Point out the additional protection that the purchase of riders and replacement cost insurance provides to policyholders.

GOALS

- Calculate property insurance premiums for homeowners
- Calculate property insurance premiums for renters
- Calculate how much can be collected on insurance claims

Start Up

Some people insure their homes for less than they are worth to save money on their home insurance policy. Is this a wise decision?

Math Skill Builder

Review these math skills and solve the exercises that follow.

1. **Add** money amounts.
Find the sum. $462 + $89 = $551
   1a. $728 + $127 $855
   1b. $327 + $46 $373

2. **Subtract** money amounts.
Find the difference. $58,000 − $750 = $57,250
   2a. $1,284 − $500 $784
   2b. $6,738 − $250 $6,488

3. **Multiply** money amounts by percents.
Find the product. $86,000 × 80% = $86,000 × 0.8 = $68,800
   3a. $75,000 × 90% $67,500
   3b. $42,500 × 80% $34,000

4. **Multiply** money amounts by whole numbers and **round** to the nearest dollar.
Find the product. 762 × $0.83 = $632.46 = $632
   4a. 1,051 × $0.54 $568
   4b. 797 × $ 0.67 $534

5. **Divide** money amounts by money amounts.
Find the quotient, to the nearest thousandth. $38,000 ÷ $56,000 = 0.679
   5a. $43,000 ÷ $60,000 0.717
   5b. $85,000 ÷ $120,000 0.708

■ Property Owners Insurance Premiums

A policy that covers your home and protects you against other risks is called homeowners insurance. Basic homeowners insurance covers:

- *Dwelling*, the home in which you live

- *Other structures*, such as a garage

- *Personal property*, includes the contents of a home

- *Additional living expense*, which pays for the extra costs of living when you cannot use your own home because of damage

242 ■ **Chapter 6** Own a Home or Car

DIFFERENT LEARNING ABILITIES At-Risk Learners

This lesson contains several insurance terms with which students may not be familiar. You may wish to have stu-dents make vocabulary cards showing the word, its defini-tion, and a relevant example.

- *Personal liability*, which protects you in case of lawsuits by persons injured on your property

- *Medical payments to others*, but not to you or your family, for medical expenses in case of injury on your property

The amount for which your home is insured is called the face value of the policy. That amount determines the amount of insurance you have in other categories. For example, if your home is insured for a face value of $60,000, personal property is usually covered for 50% of that amount, or $30,000. Additional living expense coverage is typically 20% of the face value, or $12,000.

Homeowner policies may provide other options as well. For example, a policy may insure personal property when you are away from home. This coverage is called *off premises* and is usually for 10% of the amount of the policy. For example, if the luggage and clothes you take on vacation are stolen, their loss would be covered under the off premises policy feature.

BUSINESS TIP

Basic policies often do not cover the full value of jewelry, cameras, computers, furs, and valuable collections. Special insurance called a personal articles floater is required to insure such items to full value.

REPLACEMENT COST POLICIES   Under replacement cost policies, the insurance company will pay the cost of replacing your property at current prices. If a leather chair that cost $600 is destroyed by fire, the insurer will pay for a replacement chair that now costs $900 even though the cost is higher than the original purchase price.

Before issuing this type of policy, insurers usually require a survey and inspection of the property. Also, the property must be insured for 100% of its current replacement value with automatic annual adjustments for inflation. Premiums for this type of policy are 10–15% higher than a standard policy because of the extra protection it offers.

INSURANCE PREMIUMS   The money paid to an insurance company for property insurance is the **premium**. The premiums you pay depend on many things, such as how much and what kind of coverage you buy, how your house or apartment is built, and where it is located. For example, the premium rates for a brick house near a fire department will be less than for a house made of wood that is far from a fire department.

Some items such as computer systems, jewelry, and expensive entertainment systems may not be covered by a basic policy. You will have to buy additional insurance, called a *rider*, to cover possible loss.

Property insurance rates are usually based on $100 units of insurance.

NOTE: Homeowners insurance premium charges are rounded to the nearest dollar.

EXAMPLE 1

Marion Duval insured his house for $89,000 at an annual rate of $0.51 per $100. Find his premium.

SOLUTION

Find the number of $100 units in the insured amount.

$89,000 ÷ $100 = 890   number of $100 units

Multiply the rate per $100 by the number of $100 units.

890 × $0.51 = $453.90, or $454   premium rounded to the nearest dollar

Lesson 6.4 Property Insurance ■ 243

■ **Apply Goal 1**

Work through Example 1 at the board while students complete the math at their desks.

Remind students to round insurance premiums to the nearest dollar as this is a customary practice of the insurance industry.

Assign Check Your Understanding problems A and B for class work. Move about the classroom and review student work to observe any difficulties they may be having.

■ **ONGOING ASSESSMENT**
Write various policy amounts on the board and have students mentally calculate the number of $100 units in each amount.

COMMON ERRORS

When finding property insurance premiums, students may make simple errors in calculating the number of $100 units or when multiplying by the unit rate to find the annual premium. Remind students to use estimation to check if answers seem reasonable. For instance, answers of $45,390 or $4.539 would not be reasonable for coverage on an $89,000 house with a rate of $0.51 per $100.

Inform students that the insurance carried by landlords does not cover the personal property of renters who must obtain their own insurance.

Tell them that renters may not get insurance on the physical apartment or home they rent because they have no insurable interest; that is, they do not own the property.

Tell students that insurance rates are based not only on the nearness of fire stations, but also how near the property is to a fire hydrant and whether a volunteer or full-time fire department exists in the community.

■ **Apply Goal 2**

Work through Example 2 at the board with students. Explain how to locate the correct column and row in the table.

Assign Check Your Understanding problems C and D to be done in class. Check student work at their desks.

■ **CHECK YOUR UNDERSTANDING**

A. Nolan Harwood insured his home for $61,000. Find the annual premium, to the nearest dollar, he will pay for a policy that costs $0.46 per $100. $281

B. Mandy Wisko insures her home for $43,000. What annual premium will she pay if the policy cost is $0.74 per $100? $318

■ Renters Insurance Premiums

If you rent a house or an apartment, you can buy a **renters policy** that provides nearly the same coverage as a homeowners policy except for loss of the dwelling and other structures. Annual premiums for a renters policy are based on the amount of insurance on the contents of your apartment or rental home. The table below shows the annual premium charged by one company for a basic renters policy.

Maximum Amount of Coverage on Contents	Distance From Fire Station	
	Less Than 5 Miles	5 Miles or More
$ 5,000	$120	$138
$10,000	$129	$148
$15,000	$140	$161
$20,000	$152	$175
$25,000	$165	$190
$30,000	$177	$204

EXAMPLE 2

Myron Segal rents an apartment that is 4.1 miles from a fire station. He insures its contents for $10,000. A computer system Myron owns is also insured, but at an extra cost of $27 per year. What total annual premium will Myron pay for this coverage?

SOLUTION
Locate the correct insurance amount row and distance from fire station column to find the basic premium.

The basic premium is $129.

Add to the basic premium the cost of additional insurance, if any.

$129 + $27 = $156 total annual premium

■ **CHECK YOUR UNDERSTANDING**

C. Ed and Kathryn Bosh want to insure their apartment's contents for $25,000. In addition, they decide to insure jewelry appraised at $3,000 for an additional premium of $31. They live one block from the fire station. Find their total premium for one year. $196

■ *CHECK YOUR UNDERSTANDING SOLUTIONS*

A. $61,000 ÷ $100 = 610;
610 × $0.46 = $280.60, or $281

B. $43,000 ÷ $100 = 430;
430 × $0.74 = $318.20, or $318

C. $165 + $31 = $196

D. $138, directly from the table

D. Samantha Hilliard rents a home that is located 12 miles from the nearest fire station. She insures the home's contents for $5,000. What annual premium will she pay? $138

■ Collecting on Insurance Claims

If your property is damaged by fire or a theft occurs, you have to file a claim with your insurance company. The company will send an adjuster to look at the property and decide on the amount of loss. The amount of the loss your insurance company pays depends on the type of coverage you have.

If you have a basic policy, the company will pay the full amount of the loss up to the face value of the policy. It will not pay more than the amount of your policy.

Your basic policy usually contains a *deductible*. With a $100 deductible, you are responsible for the first $100 of loss. The insurance company pays the full amount less the deductible up to the face value of the policy. The higher the deductible the lower the premium.

BUSINESS TIP

When a loss occurs, coinsurance policies pay only the depreciated value of personal property, not its replacement cost.

EXAMPLE 3

Your policy has a face value of $30,000 with a $1,000 deductible. How much will the insurance company pay if your loss is $7,800?

SOLUTION
Find the amount paid by the insurance company by subtracting the deductible from the loss amount.

$7,800 − $1,000 = $6,800 amount insurance company pays

FIRE STATION

■ CHECK YOUR UNDERSTANDING

E. How much will an insurance company pay for a loss of $10,200 if property is insured for $18,000 with a $250 deductible? $9,950

F. Property insured for $70,000 with a $500 deductible suffers a loss of $82,000. How much will the insurance company pay? $69,500

If you have a *coinsurance policy*, you purchase insurance up to a stated percent of the value of the property. This is usually 80% of the property's value. If you have a property valued at $50,000 and insure it at 80%, the coinsurance coverage is $40,000. Because the property is insured for less, the annual premium will be less also.

If you have a *coinsurance policy* and carry the required insurance, the insurance will pay for losses up to the face value of the coinsurance policy. If the coinsurance carried is less than 80% (or the agreed upon coinsurance percent), an insurance company will pay only a fractional part of the damages. The formula used is:

$$\frac{\text{Amount Paid by}}{\text{Insurance Company}} = \frac{\text{Face Value of Policy}}{\text{Required Amount of Coinsurance}} \times \text{Amount of Loss}$$

Lesson 6.4 Property Insurance ■ **245**

■ Teach Goal 3

Tell students that insurance claims are paid after an insurance adjuster verifies the circumstances and amount of loss.

Inform them that the full amount of loss is reduced first by the deductible amount and then by any coinsurance factor.

■ Apply Goal 3

Work Example 3 at the board. Then refer students to the coinsurance equation at the bottom of page 245. Relate the equation to your explanation of Example 4.

Assign Check Your Understanding problems E through H for class work. Observe student work at their desks and identify any difficulty they have in applying the correct procedures to solve problems.

■ *CHECK YOUR UNDERSTANDING SOLUTIONS*

E. $10,200 − $250 = $9,950

F. $70,000 − $500 = $69,500

G. 0.8 × $65,000 = $52,000;
($41,600 ÷ $52,000) × $4,000 = $3,200

H. 0.8 × $90,000 = $72,000; ($46,800 ÷ $72,000) × $42,000 = $27,300

Wrap Up

Review the Start Up. Ask students if a home can be insured for an amount much greater than its market value and to give reasons for their answers. Based on their replies, remind them that the initial homeowners insurance policy is issued after an inspection and appraisal of the property.

EXAMPLE 4

A building with a value of $50,000 is insured for $24,000 under an 80% coinsurance policy. The building had fire damage of $7,200. What amount did the insurance company pay?

SOLUTION

The face value of the policy is $24,000.

$50,000 \times 80\% = \$50,000 \times 0.8 = \$40,000$ required coinsurance

Divide the face value of the policy by the required amount of coinsurance. Then multiply the result times the loss amount.

$$\frac{\$24,000}{\$40,000} \times \$7,200 = 0.6 \times \$7,200 = \$4,320 \text{ amount insurance pays}$$

■ **CHECK YOUR UNDERSTANDING**

G. Betsy Rowan has an 80% coinsurance policy and insures her home for $41,600. Her home is worth $65,000. What amount will she collect from insurance on a $4,000 loss? $3,200

H. Casey Maynard's home is worth $90,000. He insures his home for $46,800 on an 80% coinsurance policy. What amount will the insurance company pay on a $42,000 loss? $27,300

Wrap Up

Carrying less insurance is one way to save money, but the property owner carries a great risk to save a relatively small amount of money. Since a home is the greatest investment that most people will make in their lifetime, it is good practice to protect the investment and insure the property for full value.

TEAM MEETING

A Homeowners insurance policy that provides additional coverage is known as a Broad Form, HO2 policy. Find out what the HO2 policy covers. Also find out what other forms of homeowners insurance exist and what they cover. Summarize in a paragraph what the general differences are, if any, between the policies. Suggested sources include insurance company sites on the Web, insurance agents, or a search of the Web using the term Broad Form, HO2 policy.

EXERCISES

Find the sum.
1. $820 + $79 $899

2. $455 + $66 $521

Find the difference.
3. $26,870 − $250 $26,620

4. $1,025 − $750 $275

Find the product.

5. $67,000 × 85% $56,950

6. $137,100 × 90% $123,390

Find the quotient to the nearest thousandth.

7. $36,000 ÷ $51,000 0.706

8. $74,000 ÷ $78,000 0.949

Find the quotient.

9. $150,500 ÷ $100 1,505

10. $36,440 ÷ $100 364.4

11. Find the premium, to the nearest dollar, for one year for a $61,000 policy at $0.47 per $100. $287

12. A $31,000 policy costs $0.68 per $100. Find the premium for one year, to the nearest dollar. $211

13. A home valued at $200,000 is insured for $0.56 per $100 on a basic policy. Earthquake insurance costs $850 extra a year. What total premium must be paid to insure this home? $1,970

The Woodman family moved to a new home in the same town. Their new house had the same value as their old home, $129,500. Because the new home is located more than 1,000 feet from a fire hydrant, their homeowners insurance rate increased by $0.11 per $100.

14. Estimate the amount their annual premium will increase? $130

15. Calculate their actual premium increase for a year. $142

16. Glenda Hope insures the basic contents of her apartment for $25,000 at the rate shown in the Renter's Insurance Table. She lives in the city a few blocks from the fire station. Glenda's depression glass collection is not covered by her basic policy and she gets extra coverage at $0.35 per $100 of its $12,500 value. What annual premium does she pay? $209

Your home is valued at $130,000. Your insurance rate is $0.72 per $100. How much does it cost to insure the home for

17. 100% of its value? $936

18. an 80% coinsurance rate of its value? $749

Find the amount paid by an insurer for each loss in problems 19–23.

	Face of Policy	Amount of Loss	Value of Property	Coinsurance Percent	Amount Paid
19.	$45,000	$ 8,000	$75,000	80%	$ 6,000
20.	$63,000	$ 5,600	$90,000	80%	$ 4,900
21.	$40,000	$13,200	$60,000	80%	$11,000
22.	$45,000	$ 7,000	$62,500	80%	$ 6,300
23.	$49,000	$22,500	$70,000	90%	$17,500

Lesson 6.4 Property Insurance ▪ **247**

SELECTED SOLUTIONS

13. $200,000 ÷ $100 = 2,000;
2,000 × $0.56 = $1,120; $1,120 + $850 = $1,970

14. $130,000 ÷ $100 = 1,300;
1,300 × $0.10 = $130 estimate

19. 0.8 × $75,000 = $60,000;
($45,000 ÷ $60,000) × $8,000 = $6,000

23. 0.9 × $70,000 = $63,000;
($49,000 ÷ $63,000) × $22,500 = $17,499.998, or $17,500

Assign Exercise 26, Critical Thinking. Relate to students the extent of the flooding that occurred from March to September 1993 when heavy rains in the Midwest caused rivers in 9 states to over-flow. Use that illustration to stimulate class discussion. Point out that even rains that occur every 100 years and cause major flooding do occur, hence their name, 100-year rains.

Point out that many policies do not cover loss through flooding. Flood insurance is purchased through private companies, but claims are paid through the federal government's National Flood Insurance Program.

Assign Exercise 27, Critical Thinking. Laws generally prohibit insurance companies from discriminating against homeowners because of a property's location; however, higher rates may be charged for property located in higher-risk areas based on loss history.

24. Allison Renfrew had a $750 deductible, replacement cost policy. Her laser printer and fax machine were stolen. Their value was $824. How much did Allison collect from the insurance company? $74

25. Your policy has a face value of $20,000 with a $1,000 deductible. How much will your insurance company pay if your loss is $7,400? $20,500? $24,000? $6,400, $19,500, $20,000

26. **CRITICAL THINKING** A flood plain is an area where floods could possibly occur even though it may be some distance from a river. Why does the insurance on homes within the flood plain cost more even if the area has not been flooded for the past 100 years? See Enrich section for answer.

27. **CRITICAL THINKING** Homes located in certain coastal areas of the United States may be destroyed by hurricanes. Is an insurance company obligated by law or a principle of good business practice to provide insurance even for high risks? See Enrich section for answer.

28. **DECISION MAKING** Benita Lahr insures her home for $60,000 and pays insurance at a rate of $0.50 per $100. She will receive a 2% discount if she installs smoke detectors and dead-bolt locks and has a fire extinguisher. These items will cost $250 to purchase and install. Should she install the safety devices to save 2%? The 2% savings amount to a $6 reduction, which is not a significant amount. Yet, the factor of personal safety makes the investment worthwhile.

MIXED REVIEW

29. $1,429 ÷ 100 $14.29

30. $\frac{1}{5} \times \frac{1}{7}$ $\frac{1}{35}$

31. $5\frac{3}{4} - 3\frac{1}{4}$ $2\frac{1}{2}$

32. 15 − 12.78 2.22

33. 8% of $1,675.40 $134.03

34. Find $\frac{3}{10}$ of 28. 8.4

35. Rewrite 0.44 as a fraction in lowest terms. $\frac{11}{25}$

36. In the number 1,427.589, what is the place value of the 4? the 9? hundred, thousandth

37. A lender discounted a $5,000 note for Nina Garcia at 13% interest for 6 months. What true rate of interest, rounded to the nearest tenth of a percent, did Nina pay on the loan? 13.9%, Lesson 4.2

38. The installment price of a set of golf clubs is $947. You must pay $200 down and make payments for 18 months. What will be your monthly payments? $41.50, Lesson 4.4

39. When Wallace Figueroa checked his March 8 credit card statement, he found a sales charge of $128.30 that was unauthorized. He also found that a sales slip for $36.25 dated March 11 did not appear on the statement. What is Wallace's correct new balance if the new balance listed on the statement is $301.68? $173.38, Lesson 4.7

40. A 50 lb. bag of flour sells for $14.25. What is the cost per pound, to the nearest cent? $0.29, Lesson 5.2

41. The income tax rate for the city of Allenby was 1% last year, and is 1.25% this year. Syd Johnson expects his income this year to be the same as last year, $48,400. What city income tax will Syd owe this year? By what percent did Syd's income taxes increase this year? $605; 25%, Lesson 2.4

42. The Howdy Steak House feeds two children free on Tuesday when an entrée is purchased at regular price. The JP Steak House has children's meals for $2.19 each. When Helena goes to Howdy's the entrée costs $18.99. The entrée she orders at JP's is $13.59. At which steak house is it cheaper for Helena and her two children to eat on a Tuesday? JP Steak House; Lesson 5.4

248 ■ Chapter 6 Own a Home or Car

CONNECTION TO ECONOMICS

Students may wish to explore the Coastal Barrier Resources Act (CBRA) of 1982. The Act tries to discourage development in certain environmentally sensitive areas.

They will find that the Act does not prohibit property owners from building in coastal areas, but transfers the risk of loss to the property owner and not the insurer.

6.5 Buying a Car

GOALS

- Calculate the MSRP for a new car, including optional equipment
- Calculate the delivered price and the balance due for new car
- Calculate the delivered price and the balance due for used car

Start Up

Most people who buy a new car make a down payment, get a loan, and then make regular monthly payments until the loan is repaid. Others make regular payments into a savings account until they have enough money to pay the entire purchase price in cash. Which way is better?

Math Skill Builder

Review these math skills and solve the exercises that follow.

1. **Add** money amounts.
   Find the sum. $23,456 + $938.24 + $198 = $24,592.24$

   1a. $19,276 + 235 $19,511$ **1b.** $187 + $12,390.04$ $12,577.04$

2. **Subtract** money amounts.
   Find the difference. $18,629 - $1,500 = $17,129$

   2a. $14,592 - 500 $14,092$ **2b.** $27,582 - $3,985$ $23,597$

3. **Multiply** money amounts by percents.
   Find the product. $5.5\% \times \$26,780 = 0.055 \times \$26,780 = \$1,472.90$

   3a. $3\% \times \$12,833$ 384.99 **3b.** $20\% \times \$9,384$ $1,876.80$

■ Manufacturer's Suggested Retail Price

Most car buyers are familiar with a car's MSRP (Manufacturer's Suggested Retail Price), or *sticker price*. This is the price printed on a sticker pasted on the window of a new car. The sticker also lists the equipment on the car and mileage information. Car buyers do not usually pay the full MSRP for their car because of discounts given by the car dealer or manufacturer. A car in very high demand may sell for a price higher than the MSRP.

Now assume that you are interested in buying the Thomson MR35, a small sports car. The features found on three MR35 models are shown on the next page. By looking to the right of each feature, you can determine if the feature is standard (S), optional (O), or not available (NA) on each model.

Lesson 6.5 Buying a Car ■ 249

Start Up

Have students read the Start Up. Before discussing the Start Up, ask students when they expect to own their first car, if they don't own one already. Follow up by asking what car they would buy, whether they would buy it new, and how they would pay for the car. Have them evaluate the two car buying approaches described in the Start Up.

Math Skill Builder

In this lesson, students use the skills of adding, subtracting and multiplying money amounts.

Complete Exercises 1–3 in the Math Skill Builder.

CONNECTION TO PERSONAL FINANCE

Students may report that a family member or friend paid less for a new car than the MSRP or sticker price. Point out that car buyers often negotiate a lower price by knowing the cost of the car to the dealer. Refer students to books such as *Edmund's New Car Prices* and the *Kelley Blue Book New Car Price Manual* to find the dealer's cost. Both Edmund's and Kelley's are also on the web.

Point out to students that the laws of all states require new cars to be sold only through dealers. Internet web sites that some believe to sell cars actually contact dealers with whom they have an agreement for price information and then direct you to contact a specific dealer to make the actual purchase. A fee is charged for the service.

Review the tables for the MR35 Sports Sedan that itemize its features and retail prices. Explain the meaning of standard, optional and not available coding in the features table and the meaning of base price and extended warranty in the retail price table. Explain that the price actually paid for a car is likely to be less than the MSRP, but that exceptions do occur.

Remind students that the length and mileage limits of warranties vary among manufacturers who specify maintenance requirements and exclusions in their warranty agreements.

Buyer's Guide to Features

THOMSON MOTOR CAR COMPANY Product Features: MR35 Sports Sedan, 2-door							
	Model				Model		
Features	STD	CTM	PRM	Features	STD	CTM	PRM
Air bags	S	S	S	Power windows	NA	O	S
Air conditioning	S	S	S	Seats, cloth	S	S	S
Alarm system	O	O	O	Seats, leather	NA	NA	O
Cruise control	S	S	S	Side mirror, manual	S	NA	NA
Defogger, rear	S	S	S	Side mirror, electric	O	S	S
Engine, 4 cylinder	S	NA	NA	Ski rack	O	O	O
Engine, 6 cylinder	O	S	S	Sound, standard	S	NA	NA
Light package	S	S	S	Sound, deluxe	O	S	NA
Message center	NA	O	S	Sound, premium	O	O	S
Power brakes	S	S	S	Tilt steering	S	S	S
Power seats	O	O	S	Trim, bright	S	S	S
Power steering	S	S	S	Trim, color matched	NA	NA	O
Code: S–Standard; O–Optional; NA–Not Available							
New Car Warranty On All Models: 12 Months or 12,000 Miles							

The features listed in the table above are available on many cars. The buyer's guide you get from a new car dealer would list more options for you to consider.

The table below shows the MSRP base price for each MR35 model and the prices for longer warranties and optional features. The *base price* is the price paid for a model equipped with all the standard features shown in the buyer's guide. For example, the base price for the STD model is $23,208. The basic new car warranty, abbreviated as 12/12,000, covers the car "bumper to bumper" for 12 months, or 12,000 miles, whichever comes first. The *extended warranty* provides extra coverage for the number of months and miles shown.

Manufacturer's Suggested Retail Price List

THOMSON MOTOR CAR COMPANY MSRP: MR35, Sports Sedan, 2-door			
Car Model	Base Price	Optional Features	Price
Model STD	$23,208	Alarm system	$481
Model CTM	$24,185	Engine, 6 cylinder	$796
Model PRM	$25,096	Message center	$348
Extended Warranty	**Price**	Power seats	$410
		Power windows	$306
24 months; 24,000 miles	$240	Seats, leather	$680
36 months, 36,000 miles	$375	Side mirror, electric	$197
48 months, 48,000 miles	$575	Ski rack	$365
24 months, 30,000 miles	$400	Sound, deluxe	$187
36 months, 45,000 miles	$585	Sound, premium	$246
48 months, 60,000 miles	$750	Trim, color matched	$248

250 ■ Chapter 6 Own a Home or Car

DIFFERENT LEARNING ABILITIES Visually Impaired

If students have difficulty reading the print in the features guide and the MSRP list, make an enlarged photocopy of the tables for students to use. Also prepare a transparency from the enlargement so students may more easily follow your explanations as you point to specific items on the charts. Allow students to keep the enlarged copy for future use.

EXAMPLE 1

A customer wants to buy the MR35 Sports Sedan, STD model with the optional six-cylinder engine and power seats and the 36/36,000 extended warranty. Using the information from the MSRP list, find the price of this car.

SOLUTION

Find the base price of the STD model. Then add the base price and the cost of the optional features and extended warranty, if any.

$23,208   base price

$23,208 + $796 + $410 + $375 = $24,789   MSRP

CHECK YOUR UNDERSTANDING

A. Loretta wants the MR35 PRM model with an alarm system and color matched trim. What is the MSRP of this car? $25,825

B. Jack is interested in the MR35, Model CTM, with the message center and ski rack. What is the car's MSRP? $24,898

BUSINESS TIP

When shopping for a new car, read reports found in libraries or through an Internet search that compare the repair and insurance costs and the safety features of various makes of cars. Also ask owners for their opinion about the car you may want and take a test drive to make sure the car suits your needs.

■ Apply Goal 1

Work through Example 1 with students using a transparency of the tables on page 250 to show students how to locate items within the tables.

Assign Check Your Understanding problems A and B for class work. When students complete their work, use the transparency again to show students where the features and prices may be found in the tables.

■ ONGOING ASSESSMENT

Use the tables on page 250 and call out models and features at random and ask students to identify if the feature is standard, optional, or not available on that model. Then have them locate the cost of that feature, if any, in the retail price table.

■ STUDENT PORTFOLIO

Students should consider including in their portfolio the car pricing problems they will solve or the Team Meeting research chart they will complete in this lesson.

■ Teach Goal 2

Remind students that the selling price negotiated with the dealer is not the total price paid for the car. Review how items such as sales taxes and registration fees add to the price and how rebates subtract from the negotiated price to arrive at a delivered price. Point out that cash or a trade-in of a vehicle may be used for the down payment.

■ Cost of New Car Purchases

The key items in a new car purchase are listed below.

PURCHASE PRICE   The price negotiated by the dealer and the buyer. The price includes the car and any options installed by the dealer.

SALES TAX   Tax computed on the purchase price.

REGISTRATION FEES   License and title transfer fees.

NON-TAXABLE ITEMS   Any items such as extended warranties that may be exempt from sales tax depending on state tax laws.

REBATES   Discounts, if any, given by the manufacturer or car dealer.

DELIVERED PRICE   Often called the "out-the-door" price. It is the total of the purchase price, sales tax, registration fees, and non-taxable items, less any rebates.

DOWN PAYMENT   A cash payment made by the customer or the value of a vehicle given as a trade-in.

BALANCE DUE   The amount the customer has left to pay. This amount is usually borrowed from the car dealer or other lender.

To find the delivered price and balance due on a new car purchase,

Delivered Price = Purchase Price + Sales Tax + Registration Fees + Non-taxable Items − Rebates

Balance Due = Delivered Price − Down Payment

Lesson 6.5 Buying a Car ■ **251**

■ *CHECK YOUR UNDERSTANDING SOLUTIONS*

A. $25,096 + $481 + $248 = $25,825

B. $24,185 + $348 + $365 = $24,898

Work Example 2 at the board with students completing the math at their desks. Relate the solution of the example to the delivered price and balance due equations on page 251.

Emphasize that the delivered price must be found by working the problem in the correct sequence. Sales tax is figured on the car's purchase price. Adding the registration fees and other non-taxable items to the purchase price and then calculating sales tax would result in the wrong sales tax calculation and the wrong delivered price.

Assign Check Your Understanding problems C and D for class work and observe student work at their desks.

Work Example 3 at the board. Have students tell why certain items are added or subtracted to calculate the delivered price and the amount due.

Assign Check Your Understanding problems E and F for class work. Move about the classroom and observe student work to identify difficulties they have.

EXAMPLE 2

The purchase price on a new car bought by Gretchen Cerna is $23,340. She is charged a 5% sales tax on the purchase price. She received a manufacturer's rebate of $1,250. Registration costs were $128. Gretchen's down payment was a trade-in of $4,300 given for her old car. Find the delivered price and the balance due.

SOLUTION

Find the sales tax on the purchase price.

$5\% \times \$23,340 = 0.05 \times \$23,340 = \$1,167$ sales tax

Add the purchase price, sales tax, and registration costs. Then deduct the rebate.

$(\$23,340 + \$1,167 + \$128) - \$1,250 = \$23,385$ delivered price

Subtract the down payment from the delivered price.

$\$23,385 - \$4,300 = \$19,085$ balance due

■ CHECK YOUR UNDERSTANDING

C. Tim Garner and a car dealer agreed on a $20,067 price for a car. Tim then decided to buy an extended service warranty for $250 extra. He used his old license plates, but still had to pay registration and title fees of $134.85. A 4.5% state sales tax is charged on all purchases, except warranties. Tim made a cash down payment of $6,000. Find the delivered price and the balance due for this purchase. $21,354.87, $15,354.87

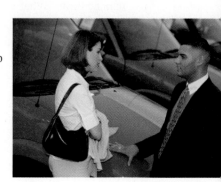

D. Lillian Weinstein's purchase price for an economy car is $16,238. Sales tax is charged at 6% in her state. Plates, title transfer, and other fees totaled $186. Lillian made a down payment of 10% of the purchase price of the car. Find the delivered price and the balance due. $17,398.28, $15,774.48

■ Cost of Used Car Purchases

Used cars may be purchased from new car dealers who resell trade-ins, used car dealers, car rental agencies, and individual car owners. The used cars are generally sold "as is," without warranty.

The *purchase price* for a used car refers to the price on which the buyer and the seller agree and is the price on which sales tax is figured.

The *delivered price* of used cars is equal to the sum of the purchase price, sales tax, and registration fees. The balance due is the delivered price less the down payment.

BUSINESS TIP

A used car seller may give a limited warranty to the buyer to make the sale. Buyers of used cars with part of the manufacturer's warranty still in effect are often allowed to transfer the warranty to their name.

EXAMPLE 3

The purchase price of a 3-year old used car is $12,450. Other costs include registration fees of $128 and sales tax of 4%. The buyer made a down payment of $3,800. What is the delivered price of the car and the balance due?

■ *CHECK YOUR UNDERSTANDING SOLUTIONS*

C. $0.045 \times \$20,067 = \$903.02$;
$\$20,067 + \$903.02 + \$250 + \$134.85 = \$21,354.87$ delivered price; $\$21,354.87 - \$6,000 = \$15,354.87$ balance due

D. $0.06 \times \$16,238 = \$974.28$;
$\$16,238 + \$974.28 + \$186 = \$17,398.28$ delivered price; $0.10 \times \$16,238 = \$1,623.80$; $\$17,398.28 - \$1,623.80 = \$15,774.48$ balance due

SOLUTION

Find the sales tax on the purchase price.

$4\% \times \$12,450 = 0.04 \times \$12,450 = \$498$ sales tax

Add the purchase price, sales tax, and registration fees.

$\$12,450 + \$498 + \$128 = \$13,076$ delivered price

Subtract the down payment from the delivered price to find the balance due.

$\$13,076 - \$3,800 = \$9,276$ balance due

■ **CHECK YOUR UNDERSTANDING**

E. Arnold Knapp agreed to buy a 1-year old car for $16,500 cash. Sales tax of 7% is charged on the sale. Other costs included license plates, $85; title transfer, $47. What was the total cost of the car? $17,787

F. The purchase price of a used van bought by Frances Sauger was $11,370. She paid $200 extra for a 2-year warranty on the transmission. In her state, warranties are exempt from the 5% sales tax charged on merchandise. Registration costs were $129. What is the balance due that Frances needs to finance if she makes a down payment of 25% of the purchase price? $9,425

Wrap Up

People who need a car now and have little money must buy a car on the monthly payment plan. Those who are able to save money and pay cash for a car earn interest on their savings and do not pay interest on their loan. The best way is the one that fits the circumstances.

TEAM MEETING

Visit the "make your own car" portion of the Web site of one of the major car manufacturers. Select three different car lines and find the price of the most basic model within each car line. Then find the price for the same basic model with every option. Prepare a chart showing the prices you found and calculate the amount and percent of increase from the lowest to the highest prices in a car line. Share your findings with the rest of the class.

EXERCISES

Find the sum or difference.

1. $\$18,458 + \$239$ $18,697

2. $\$456 + \$318 + \$148$ $922

3. $\$28,346 - \$7,086.50$ $21,259.50

4. $\$34,829 - \$14,340$ $20,489

Find the product.

5. $4\% \times \$36,784$ $1,471.36

6. $30\% \times \$29,006$ $8,701.80

Lesson 6.5 Buying a Car ■ 253

■ **CHECK YOUR UNDERSTANDING SOLUTIONS**

E. $0.07 \times \$16,500 = \$1,155$;
$\$16,500 + \$1,155 + \$85 + \$47 = \$17,787$

F. $0.05 \times \$11,370 = \$568.50$;

$\$11,370 + \$568.50 + \$200 + \$129 = \$12,267.50$;
$0.25 \times \$11,370 = \$2,842.50$;
$\$12,267.50 - \$2,842.50 = \$9,425$ balance due

Reteach

STUDENT WORKBOOK Work Exercise 1 with students who need help with calculating the MSRP. For independent practice, change Exercise 1 in this way: new MSRP of $17,210; larger tires and leather seats options are not purchased. Have students calculate the new MSRP, $18,530.

If students need help in finding the delivered price and amount due for new cars, work Exercise 2 with them. Assign Exercise 3 for independent work.

If students have difficulty with calculating the delivered price and amount due for used cars, work Exercise 4 with them and assign Exercise 5.

Use the buyer's guide and MSRP table given in the lesson to solve Exercises 7–11. (Hint: For Exercises 7–10, if the features the customer wants are either standard features or are not available for the model, do not include their cost in the MSRP you calculate.)

	Car Model	Features Wanted	Warranty Wanted	MSRP
7.	STD	alarm system, air conditioning, tilt steering	24/24,000	$23,929
8.	PRM	color matched trim, leather seats	48/60,000	$26,774
9.	CTM	premium sound, alarm system, leather seats	12/12,000	$24,912
10.	PRM	power brakes, seats, steering, windows	48/48,000	$25,671

11. A customer wants to buy the STD model with the three features that are standard on the CTM model but optional on the STD model. Would the customer save money by buying the base CTM model instead? If so, how much would be saved? Yes, $203

12. The purchase price of a new car bought by Kay Terchek is $30,875. The car's MSRP was $32,560. Her other costs were: sales tax at 7%, non-taxable extended warranty at $390, registration fees at $128. Kay got a $250 rebate and made a $4,300 down payment. What was the delivered price of the car and the amount due? $33,304.25, $29,004.25

13. Herman Ollender's purchase price for a new car was 95% of the $21,400 MSRP. Sales tax was figured at 5%. Registration fees totaled $284. He received a customer loyalty rebate of $500. A trade-in value of $3,170 for Herman's old car was used for the down payment. Find the car's delivered price and the amount due. $21,130.50, $17,960.50

14. A new car's usual purchase price of $21,480 was reduced by $1,007 because it had been used as a demonstrator car. Eugene Basanese paid a 3.5% sales tax, registration fees of $172, and made a $3,200 down payment. What is the balance due on the car? $18,161.56

15. A used car's price is $4,850. The buyer pays a combined city/state sales tax of 4.6%. Registration fees are $85 for license plates and $31 for title transfer. If the buyer pays for the car in cash, how much will be due? $5,189.10

16. A car that was bought for $23,700 nine years ago was offered for sale at $4,125. Because the car had some body rust, the buyer asked the seller to reduce the price by $350. The seller agreed. The buyer paid $167 in registration fees and a 6% sales tax. What was the total cost of this car to the buyer? $4,168.50

17. **CRITICAL THINKING** Tom believes that most new cars are very reliable and should run with no problems for 125,000 miles. He also believes that buying extended warranties is a waste of money since they will never be needed. What do you think? Answers will vary. Pro: Mechanical designs of cars are good; proper care can extend life of car even further. Con: Major repairs may far exceed cost of extended warranty; warranty is like an insurance policy.

SELECTED SOLUTIONS

7. $23,208 + $481 + $240 = $23,929

11. $23,208 + $796 + $197 + $187 = $24,388;
$24,388 − $24,185 = $203

12. 0.07 × $30,875 = $2,161.25;
$30,875 + $2,161.25 + $390 + $128 − $250 =

$33,304.25 delivered price;
$33,304.25 − $4,300 = $29,004.25 amount due

15. 0.046 × $4,850 = $223.10;
$4,850 + $223.10 + $85 + $31 = $5,189.10

18. **DECISION MAKING** Betty is offered $7,400 for her old car as a trade in on a new car. She looks in the want ads and sees that many cars the same age as hers sell for up to $3,000 more. Should Betty trade the car or try to sell it herself for a higher price? *Betty must decide if she has the time and skill to sell the car. She also must confirm that she can get a much higher price.*

MIXED REVIEW

19. Round 10.09 to the nearest tenth and to the nearest unit. *10.1, 10*

20. Multiply $5\frac{1}{4}$ by $2\frac{1}{3}$ *$12\frac{1}{4}$*

21. $2,142 \div 9$ *238*

22. Rewrite $1\frac{1}{8}$ as a decimal. *1.125*

23. 0.17×0.34 *0.0578*

24. Colin Marshall's $2,500 note at 14% interest for 2 months was discounted by his bank. Find the proceeds of the note. *$2,441.67, Lesson 4.2*

25. Find the maturity date of a 90-day note dated July 17. *October 15, Lesson 4.3*

26. Carmen Rizzo opened an Any-Mall charge account in January. She paid an annual card fee of $35 and a transfer fee of $27 to move another credit card's balance to the Any-Mall account. The finance charges she paid during the year were: Feb., $1.08; Mar., $2.12; June, $6.25; Sep., $3.85. What was Carmen's total annual cost of the Any-Mall charge account? *$75.30, Lesson 4.7*

27. Inkjet printer paper sells for $4.30 a ream. A special 5-pack sale allows you to buy four reams at the regular price and get the fifth ream free. How much would you save by buying the 5-pack instead of buying five reams, one at a time? *$4.30 Lesson 5.4*

28. Stan and Chris Folson's gross income is $68,127. They are allowed a $3,100 per person exemption for themselves and their three children. Their standard deduction is $9,700. Their itemized deductions total $4,172. What is their taxable income? *$42,927, Lesson 2.3*

29. Use the Partial APR table to find the annual percentage rate on a 15-month, $1,800 installment loan that had a finance charge of $176. *$14\frac{1}{4}$%, Lesson 4.6*

30. Frank Rozier worked five days last week and was paid a per diem rate of $109.50. If his workday is 7.5 hours, how much does Frank earn per hour of work? *$14.60, Lesson 1.5*

31. Gilbert Conroy withdrew $200 from his bank's ATM. On a shopping trip he bought an office chair for $120.87 in cash and paid $75.11 cash for groceries. He then used his ATM card to pay for: $136.50 in painting supplies; $66.52 for lawn mover repair. What amount was left in Gilbert's account if it had a balance of $740.12 at the start of the day? *$337.10, Lesson 3.1*

32. Find the unit price of 1 vacuum bag @ 3 for $5.99. *$2, Lesson 5.3*

Moira Birnbaum has a sound system installed in her car. Her sales receipts shows that the subtotal for the parts for the system cost $389.99, and their installation cost $75. Her state has a sales tax rate of 4.5% that is not applied to labor or service. *Lesson 5.1*

33. How much sales tax will she pay? *$17.55*

34. What is the total amount of the sales slip? *$482.54*

CONNECTION TO ECONOMICS

Point out to students that many years ago it was easy to identify cars sold in the U. S. as domestic (made in America) or imported (made in foreign countries). The distinction has blurred because many of the original imported carmakers have built auto plants in the U. S. Have students research what it would take to advertise a car or car-related product as Made in America without deceiving consumers or violating any laws against misrepresentation.

6.6 Depreciating a Car

GOALS
- Calculate average annual depreciation on a car
- Calculate the rate of depreciation

Start Up

What do you think has more value: a 3-year old car with 30,000 miles or a 1-year old car of the same make and style with 80,000 miles? List at least one source where you could verify your answer.

Math Skill Builder

Review these math skills and solve the exercises that follow.

1. **Divide** money amounts by whole numbers.
   Find the quotient. $14,240 \div 8 = $1,780$

   1a. $23,580 \div 9$ $2,620   **1b.** $12,438 \div 3$ $4,146

2. **Divide** money amounts by money amounts to find a percent.
   Find the percent, to the nearest tenth. $540 \div $10,500 = 0.0514$, or 5.1%

   2a. $1,260 \div $9,400$ 13.4%   **2b.** $5,200 \div $28,600$ 18.2%

■ Average Annual Depreciation

A car loses value as it grows older. This loss of value is called *depreciation*. The total depreciation on a car is the difference between its original cost and its resale, or trade-in, value. **Resale value** is the market value, or the amount you get when you sell the car to someone else. The **trade-in value** is the amount you get for your old car when you trade it in to buy a new car.

Original Cost − Trade-in Resale Value = Depreciation

When you buy a car, you can only estimate what the depreciation will be. The actual amount of depreciation will be known only when the car is sold or traded in. However, by making some good guesses about your car's future value, you can calculate the estimated *average annual depreciation*.

To calculate the *estimated* average annual depreciation on a car or other motor vehicle follow these steps:

> **BUSINESS TIP**
>
> Cars depreciate much more quickly in their first few years of use than in their last years of use. Cars with many defects or those of poor design will depreciate even more quickly. Cars of high quality depreciate less.

DIFFERENT LEARNING ABILITIES Gifted Learners

Students may be assigned a research project to calculate approximate rates of depreciation for cars they select. They may use references such as the *Official Used Car Guide* published monthly by the National Automotive Dealer's Association to gather comparative price data for cars of varying ages. Suggest that they begin with the MSRP of their selected car and calculate the actual rate of depreciation for each year of a 6-year period. Then they should calculate the average annual depreciation for the 6 years. They should prepare a chart and a report to be presented to the class.

1. Estimate the number of years the car will be kept.

2. Estimate the value of the car when it is resold or traded in.

3. Subtract trade-in value from the original cost to estimate total depreciation.

4. Divide the total depreciation by the number of years the car will be kept.

To calculate the *actual* average annual depreciation, also follow these four steps, keeping in mind that you are using actual, not estimated, amounts. For example, you do not have to estimate the length of time you keep the car or its resale or trade-in value. You use the actual time and dollar amounts.

EXAMPLE 1

LaWanda Turgill bought a car for $14,800. She estimates its trade-in value will be $5,800 at the end of 4 years. Find the estimated total and the estimated average annual depreciation of the car.

SOLUTION
Subtract the estimated trade-in value from the original cost.

$14,800 − $5,800 = $9,000 estimated total depreciation

Divide the estimated total depreciation by the number of years.

$9,000 ÷ 4 = $2,250 estimated average annual depreciation

BUSINESS TIP

Go to used car websites to get data that will help you find the estimated depreciation for a car.

■ CHECK YOUR UNDERSTANDING

A. Roland Corbett bought a new car for $19,500. He has been told that his car will probably be worth $9,800 at the end of two years. What will be his estimated total and average annual depreciation for two years? $9,700, $4,850

B. Genevieve Prekova bought a car 9 years ago for $14,130. She sold it recently for $1,800. What was the total and average annual depreciation on the car? $12,330, $1,370

This way of calculating average annual depreciation is called the *straight-line method*. It assumes the car depreciates the same amount each year.

■ Rate of Depreciation

When the straight-line method of finding depreciation is used, the average annual depreciation may be shown as a percent of the original cost. The percent is called the *rate of depreciation*.

Rate of Depreciation = Average Annual Depreciation ÷ Original Cost

EXAMPLE 2

A $12,000 car is sold 3 years later for $6,960. What is the rate of depreciation?

SOLUTION
Find the total depreciation.   Find the average annual depreciation.

$12,000 − $6,960 = $5,040 $5,040 ÷ 3 = $1,680

Divide the annual depreciation by the original cost to find the rate of depreciation.
$1,680 ÷ $12,000 = 0.14, or 14% rate of depreciation

Lesson 6.6 Depreciating a Car ■ **257**

■ **Apply Goal 1**

Work through Example 1 on the board with students completing the math at their desks. Label all calculations done on the board and remind students to label theirs as well.

Assign Check Your Understanding problems A and B for completion in class. Check student work at their desks to identify any difficulties.

■ **ONGOING ASSESSMENT**
Have students identify the phrases in the first two sentences of Check Your Understanding problems A and B that indicate that depreciation is either estimated or actual.

■ **Teach Goal 2**

Explain that the average rate of depreciation implies that a car depreciates the same rate each year. Further explain that while cars may depreciate more in the earlier years, the average rate is true for the time period measured.

■ **Apply Goal 2**

Use the board to work through Example 2 with students completing the math at their desks. Ask students whether the rate calculated is actual or estimated.

Assign Check Your Understanding problems C and D for completion in class. Move about the classroom to check student work.

■ *CHECK YOUR UNDERSTANDING SOLUTIONS*

A. $19,500 − $9,800 = $9,700; $9,700 ÷ 2 = $4,850

B. $14,130 − $1,800 = $12,330;
   $12,330 ÷ 9 = $1,370

C. $23,000 − $16,100 = $6,900;
   $6,900 ÷ $23,000 = 0.30, or 30%

D. $9,200 − $368 = $8,832; $8,832 ÷ 12 = $736;
   $736 ÷ $9,200 = 0.08, or 8%

C. A new car that cost $23,000 is worth $16,100 a year later. What was the rate of depreciation for the one year? 30%

D. Billy Macon sold his car for $368. He paid $9,200 for the car when he bought it 12 years ago. What was the annual rate of depreciation? 8%

Wrap Up

The value of a used car depends not only on its age and the miles it has been driven, but also on its overall condition and how it has been maintained. After the two cars are seen and their service records examined, their true value is determined by what price they will bring in the market. The Blue Book is one source that provides used car pricing information. You may also want to look at the want ad prices for similar cars or check the prices posted on used car web sites or the Blue Book site.

TEAM MEETING

Meet with three to four members of your class and select one specific make and model that would fit into each of these vehicle categories: luxury car, luxury SUV, economy car, economy SUV. Find the approximate selling price of each vehicle a year ago and what each vehicle would sell for today as a one-year old vehicle. Calculate the percent of depreciation for each vehicle. Study the depreciation percents and write a paragraph about any differences you find.

EXERCISES

Find the difference or quotient.

1. $28,459 − $14,286 $14,173
2. $34,120 − $20,875 $13,245
3. $16,457 ÷ 7 $2,351
4. $18,372 ÷ 12 $1,531

Find the percent, to the nearest percent.

5. $2,368 ÷ $18,300   13%
6. $1,280 ÷ $15,340   8%

Find the total depreciation.

	Type of Vehicle	Original Cost	Resale or Trade-in Value	Total Depreciation
7.	Mid-size Car	$21,606	$9,375	$12,231
8.	Sports Utility	$28,461	$12,225	$16,236
9.	Pickup Truck	$14,187	$1,560	$12,627
10.	Luxury Car	$43,597	$20,150	$23,447
11.	Mini Van	$20,500	$12,800	$7,700

12. Brandon Merritt paid $11,300 for a car 7 years ago. He bought a new car recently at a total cost of $11,100 after deducting the $950 he got as a trade-in for his old car. What was the total depreciation on the 7-year old car? $10,350

SELECTED SOLUTIONS

7. $21,606 − $9,375 = $12,231
13. $12,800 − $6,710 = $6,090; $6,090 ÷ 3 = $2,030

19. $14,500 − $5,600 = $8,900;
$8,900 ÷ 4 = $2,225; $2,225 ÷ $14,500 = 0.153, or 15%

Wrap Up

Review the Start Up and ask the student volunteers to present the information they found. Verbally summarize the student reports and ask the class to vote again on which car they now believe to have the greatest value. Share the results of the voting in the Start Up.

Ask for student volunteers to contact a used car dealer to get an informed opinion on which car might have greater value, research want ads, or consult the Blue Book.

TEAM MEETING

Have students summarize their findings about the amount and rate that each of the selected vehicles depreciated. Have the class discuss possible reasons why vehicles in one category might have depreciated at a faster rate than vehicles in another category.

Ask students to share with the class the sources they used to collect depreciation data.

Assign

Assignment: Exercises 1–25, 27–32. Have students solve the basic arithmetic problems before completing the rest of the exercises.

Find the average annual depreciation for each.

		Resale or Trade-in Value		Average Annual Depreciation
	Original Cost	At end of	Amount	
13.	$12,800	3 years	$6,710	$2,030
14.	$23,100	7 years	$7,210	$2,270
15.	$19,750	2 years	$10,120	$4,815
16.	$28,980	5 years	$10,800	$3,636

Trudy Winslow bought a car for $8,850 three years ago. A car dealer offered Trudy $3,825 as the trade-in value, but she feels she can sell the car for $4,500.

17. What will be the average annual depreciation if she takes the trade-in offer?
$1,675

18. What will be the average annual depreciation if she is able to sell the car at the price she wants? $1,450

Find the rate of depreciation. Round answers to the nearest percent.

		Resale or Trade-in Value		Rate of Depreciation
	Original Cost	At end of	Amount	
19.	$14,500	4 years	$ 5,600	15%
20.	$28,350	3 years	$14,700	16%
21.	$ 9,450	6 years	$ 1,800	13%
22.	$12,680	2 years	$ 7,700	20%

23. A bakery bought a truck for $21,088. After four years a new truck was bought that cost $23,420. A trade-in value of $4,790 was given for the old truck. To the nearest dollar, find the average annual depreciation of the old truck. $4,075

24. A van that costs $24,444 is estimated to be worth $6,300 after four years. Find the rate of depreciation on the van, to the nearest percent. 19%

25. **STRETCHING YOUR SKILLS** Nora sold her car for $3,100 after owning it for five years. She found the average annual depreciation was $1,860 and the rate was 15%. What did Nora pay for the car when it was new? $12,400

26. **CRITICAL THINKING** A new car may depreciate as much as 35% of its original cost in the first year of use. Would it make more sense not to buy the car new but to wait one year and buy it used for less money?
See Enrich section for answer.

MIXED REVIEW

27. Find the average of 8, 11, 15, 3, 27. 12.8

28. $\frac{5}{6} - \frac{2}{3}$ $\frac{1}{6}$ 29. $\frac{2}{9} + \frac{11}{18}$ $\frac{5}{6}$ 30. $\frac{7}{12} \div \frac{5}{6}$ $\frac{7}{10}$

31. Nell Burton borrows $4,500 at 6% banker's interest for 24 days. What amount of interest does she pay? $18, Lesson 4.1

32. Alex Sims borrowed $750 on a one-year simple interest installment loan at 18%. His monthly payment on the loan was $68.76. Find the amount of interest, amount applied to the principal, and new balance for the first monthly payment.
$11.25, $57.51, $692.49, Lesson 4.4

Lesson 6.6 Depreciating a Car ∎ **259**

Assess

Have students check their own answers to selected problems as other students write solutions on the board and explain their solutions to Exercises 7, 13, 14, 18–19, 21, and 26.

Reteach

STUDENT WORKBOOK If students encounter difficulty with average annual depreciation calculations, work Exercise 1 with them. Then assign Exercises 2 for independent work.

Work Exercise 3 with students who need help in calculating the rate of depreciation. Assign Exercises 4 and 5 as class work.

Enrich

Assign Exercise 26, Critical Thinking. When discussing the question, emphasize that many cars depreciate far less than 35% in the first year. Point out that the first-year depreciation rate doesn't matter to an owner who plans to keep the car for some time.

Close

Ask students to define in their own words what total depreciation, estimated depreciation, actual depreciation, and rate of depreciation mean. Then ask how each is calculated.

CONNECTION TO PERSONAL FINANCE

Have students discuss what the impact might be on a family that purchases a new car each year and trades in the car the following year at an average depreciation rate of 25%. Have them consider the family's budget, the prob- ability of major mechanical repairs or replacement of con- sumable items such as tires, and any additional aspect they wish to consider.

6.7 Car Insurance

GOAL

■ Calculate car insurance premiums

Start Up

Insurance companies charge young drivers below age 25 much higher premiums for insuring their cars than they would older drivers. Are there any factors that they especially consider in setting their rates for young people?

Math Skill Builder

Review these math skills and solve the exercises.

1 **Rewrite** a percent as a decimal.
Rewrite as a decimal. 80% = 0.8

   1a. 25%   0.25   **1b.** 5%   0.05

2 **Multiply** money amounts by percents.
Find the product. 20% × $387 = 0.20 × $387 = $77.40

   2a. 5% × $468 $23.40   **2b.** 10% × $763 $76.30

■ Car Insurance Premiums

There are four basic types of insurance or coverage for motor vehicles that protect you against the risk of financial loss:

- **Bodily injury** Covers your liability for injury to others.
- **Property damage** Covers damage to other people's property, including their vehicles.
- **Collision** Covers damage to your own motor vehicle.
- **Comprehensive damage** Covers damage or loss to your vehicle from fire, theft, vandalism, hail, and other causes.

States require car owners to carry minimum amounts of car insurance. Some states combine bodily injury and property damage coverage into one minimum amount of insurance required. The insurance applies regardless of whether there is injury to one or more persons or whether there is damage to property of others in a single accident.

In addition to requiring minimum amounts of the basic types of insurance coverage, states may require car owners to carry additional coverage.

> ### BUSINESS TIP
>
> The minimum car insurance you must carry by law for bodily injury and property damage may not offer the financial protection you need.

CONNECTION TO PERSONAL FINANCE

As students discuss the Start-Up question, they may focus on age as being a key factor in how much insurance premiums cost. Ask them to list other factors such as the driving record of the individual, a drunk driving citation or conviction, the driver's sex, and the type of car that is driven. Also, some models of cars are stolen frequently while others cost more to repair than the average.

A car owner may be required to buy *uninsured motorists insurance*, which protects against damage to the car or injury to persons in the car caused by a driver who carries no insurance.

Premiums for automobile insurance may vary from state to state and within a state. Each insurance company sets its own rates following state regulations. Premiums may be higher in large cities than in small cities and rural areas. Premiums may also be higher on cars used for business than those used for pleasure driving. Premiums are usually higher for drivers under 25 years of age than for those over 25.

Sample car insurance annual premiums are found in the table below. As you study the table, notice how the premium changes depending on the use of the car, the coverage limits, and the deductible amount.

BUSINESS TIP

Some insurance companies bill semiannually, or twice a year. This allows them to change rates more frequently and be able to review the insured's driving record every six months.

Sample Annual Car Insurance Premiums

Type of Insurance Coverage	Coverage Limits	Annual Premiums for:		
		Pleasure Use Only	Driving to Work	Business
Bodily Injury	$25/50,000	$ 20.58	$ 22.84	$ 29.71
	50/100,000	30.88	34.27	44.68
	100/300,000	53.95	59.35	79.74
Property Damage	$25,000	$ 135.80	$ 150.74	$ 196.50
	50,000	161.67	179.44	233.92
	100,000	190.19	211.11	274.44
Collision	$100 deductible	$ 466.53	$ 517.84	$ 574.70
	250 deductible	324.03	358.24	461.81
	500 deductible	261.95	290.77	378.01
Comprehensive	$50 deductible	$ 125.32	$ 137.85	$ 179.21
	100 deductible	93.99	104.33	135.62

EXAMPLE

Emma Jane Cooke wants a basic insurance policy for her car that she uses only for pleasure driving. She chooses this coverage: bodily injury, $25/50,000; property damage, $25,000; collision, $500 deductible; comprehensive, $100 deductible. Using the rates in the premiums table above, what annual premium will Emma Jane pay for car insurance?

SOLUTION

Find the premiums in the pleasure use only column.

$20.85 + $135.80 + $261.95 + $93.99 = $512.59 annual premium

■ CHECK YOUR UNDERSTANDING

A. Oliver Trainor insures the car that he drives to work. His coverage is $25/50,000 bodily injury, $50,000 property damage, $250 deductible collision, and $100 deductible comprehensive. Using the premiums shown in the premiums table, what will be Oliver's annual car insurance premium? $664.85

B. Harriet Driscoll's car is insured for business use. She chooses the highest coverage limits for bodily injury and property damage and $100 deductibles for both collision and comprehensive. Using the rates shown in the premiums table, what is her annual premium? $1,064.50

Lesson 6.7 Car Insurance ■ **261**

■ **Apply Goal 1**

Work through Example 1 on the board and use a transparency to display the car insurance premium table. Show students how to identify the column and the line that contains the rate that matches the coverage. Have students complete the math at their desks.

Assign Check Your Understanding problems A and B for completion in class. Circulate around the classroom and check student work.

■ **ONGOING ASSESSMENT**
Have students refer to the car insurance premium table to find the annual premium for a coverage, coverage limit, and driving category that you select at random. Give several examples for students to find.

■ *CHECK YOUR UNDERSTANDING SOLUTIONS*

A. $22.84 + $179.44 + $358.24 + $104.33 = $664.85   B. $79.74 + $274.44 + $574.70 + $135.62 = $1,064.50

Wrap Up

Ask students who drive whether they own a car or use a family car. Ask the class how much they think insurance costs increase when a young driver begins driving the family car. Inform them that the insurance company must be notified when another driver other than the insured owner will also be driving the car.

TEAM MEETING

Have students compare their findings with other students to self-check that the correct types of required insurance were included.

Ask students to give rates for certain coverage and write them on the board. Have students calculate the range of rates, which is the difference between the greatest and smallest premium amounts.

Assign

Assignment: Exercises 1–16, 19–26. Begin with the basic arithmetic problems to ensure that students understand the underlying arithmetic in the exercises.

Explain the meaning of the word *justify* in Exercise 16, Critical Thinking. Tell students to answer the question using complete sentences, not phrases.

Assess

Check student answers to the exercises by observing their work at their desks or by collecting and grading the problems. Make or write a comment regarding the clarity of their responses to Exercise 16.

Wrap Up

Insurance companies base their insurance rates on statistics that show that young drivers in the 16–25 years age group are more likely to be involved in accidents, especially fatal accidents. Higher rates are charged to cover the increased damage payments insurance companies will have to make for the young driver group as a whole compared to the general population. Some companies decrease their rates for good students and for those who have taken approved driver's education training.

TEAM MEETING

Form a small group and find out what types and amounts of car insurance are required in the state in which you live. Contact a local insurance agent or your state's car registration office, or search insurance Web sites to access the information you need. Present your findings to the class.

EXERCISES

Write as a decimal.

1. 5% 0.05

2. 2.5% 0.025

3. 10.35% 0.1035

Find the product correct to the nearest cent.

4. 2% × $563.98 $11.28

5. $3\frac{1}{4}$% × $762.37 $24.78

For the car insurance problems in this textbook, use the premiums table to find the cost of insurance. If the insurance coverage is not given, assume it is one of these standard coverages: bodily injury, $25/50,000; property damage, $25,000; collision, $100 deductible; comprehensive, $50 deductible. The same rate will apply to all types of motor vehicles unless otherwise indicated.

6. What is the total premium for standard insurance coverage on a car driven to work? $829.27

7. On a truck he drives to work, Norbert carries bodily injury insurance of $50/100,000 and $250 deductible on collision. Other coverage is standard. Find his annual premium. $681.10

June Driscoll uses her truck for business and insures the truck with standard coverage.

8. What annual premium does she pay? $980.12

9. If June took the highest deductibles, what amount would she save annually on her total car insurance bill? $240.28

10. Wasaburo Sumida owns two cars. One car, used for pleasure only, is insured at standard coverage. His business car is insured for the greatest amount of bodily injury and property damage coverage and the highest deductibles. Because he insures both cars with the same company, he gets a 10% discount on his total premium. Find the premium for insuring both cars for one year. $1,454.44

262 ■ Chapter 6 Own a Home or Car

SELECTED SOLUTIONS

6. $22.84 + $150.74 + $517.84 + $137.85 = $829.27

8. $29.71 + $196.50 + $574.70 + $179.21 = $980.12

10. $20.58 + $135.80 + $466.53 + $125.32 = $748.23 pleasure car premium; $79.74 + $274.44 + $378.01 + $135.62 = $867.81

business car premium; $748.23 + $867.81 = $1,616.04; 0.10 × $1,616.04 = $161.60 discount; $1,616.04 − $161.60 = $1,454.44 total premium

11. $22.84 + $150.74 + $517.84 + $137.85 = $829.27; $829.27 × 2.2 = $1,824.39

11. Because of her three speeding tickets, Louella Burchette cannot get car insurance unless she pays a premium of 2.2 times the rate for standard coverage. She uses her car to drive to work. What is her premium for one year? $1,824.39

12. Owners of cars with antilock brakes and an alarm system get a 3.5% discount on their total insurance premium. What premium would they pay for standard coverage if they used their car to drive to work? $800.25

13. A truck used on a farm is insured at the same rate as if it were being driven to work. It has standard coverage with the highest deductibles. Since the truck is seldom driven outside the farm, it can be insured for 70% of the usual rate. Find the annual premium. $398.08

Karl Trattner is 16 years old and owns his car. Because of his age and the type of car he owns, Karl must pay four times the usual rate for his insurance.

14. What annual premium must he pay with standard coverage? $2,992.92

15. To reduce the amount he must pay, Karl is considering not covering his car for collision and comprehensive damage. What would be his annual premium with this reduced coverage? $625.52

16. **CRITICAL THINKING**   Insurance companies offer discounts to owners of cars that have features such as air bags, anti-lock brakes, and alarm systems. How can they justify giving such discounts? May reduce injuries, accidents, and theft. Fewer claims = lower costs and premiums.

17. **CRITICAL THINKING**   Insurance companies may charge higher rates to very old drivers or give them insurance with restrictions, such as allowing them to drive only in daylight hours. Is this a form of age discrimination? See Enrich section for answer.

18. **DECISION MAKING**   A car that you drive to work is worth about $1,200. If you did not insure your car for comprehensive and collision coverage, you would save about $500 a year in insurance costs. Should you drop these two coverages to save money? See Enrich section for answer.

MIXED REVIEW

19. $12 \div \frac{1}{4}$ 48

20. Rewrite 1.75 as a percent.   175%

21. $1,236 + $0.78 + $12.37 + $672.99 + $5.82 $1,927.96

22. Round to the nearest cent: $0.876, $15.027, $45.514 $0.88, $15.03, $45.51

23. Marcus Ridley signed a promissory note for $10,200 at 9% ordinary interest for 180 days. Find the interest and amount due he will pay when the note is due. $459, $10,659, Lesson 4.1

24. Find the number of days from March 18 to July 5.   109, Lesson 4.3

Delphine Salmer's credit card statement for August showed a previous balance of $658.18, new purchases and fees of $583.10 posted on August 10, and payments and credits of $218.40 posted on August 22. Her charge card company's monthly APR is 1.5%, and the company uses the previous balance method to figure the finance charge.

25. What is Delphine's finance charge for August and her new balance? $9.87, $1,032.75, Lesson 4.8

26. What would be the finance charge and new balance if the company used the adjusted balance method of computing finance charges? $6.60, $1,029.48, Lesson 4.8

Lesson 6.7 Car Insurance ■ **263**

TEACHING STRATEGIES Cooperative Learning

Some states have car insurance laws mandating no-fault insurance. Have students collaborate to do research to find what no-fault insurance means, what coverage is required, how claims against underinsured and uninsured drivers are handled, and whether there are any specific limitations on claims. Suggest that students contact their family's insurance agent if they live in a no-fault state or search the Web using the keyword no-fault.

Start Up

Have students read the Start Up.
Take a poll through a show of
hands to determine how many students agree with Bob. Allow students to have an informal debate
between those who agree with
Bob's views and those who disagree.

Math Skill Builder

The skills of adding, subtracting,
and multiplying money amounts
are used in this lesson.

Complete all exercises in Math Skill
Builder 1–3.

■ **Teach Goal 1**

You may want to review installment
loans in Lesson 4.4 to refresh student understanding of how car purchases are financed.

Point out to students that many
automobile manufacturers have a
credit division that provides car
financing to buyers of their products. The credit division competes
with banks and other lenders.

6.8 Car Purchases and Leases

GOALS

- Calculate the total amount paid and the finance charge for installment loan car purchases
- Calculate the cost of leasing cars
- Compare the costs of leasing and buying cars
- Calculate the cost of operating cars

Start Up

Bob tells you that he doesn't like his family's cars because they are kept too long, for 8–10 years. He claims that he will always lease cars so he can drive a new car all the time. He asks you whether you agree with him. What would you say?

Math Skill Builder

Review these math skills and solve the exercises that follow.

1 **Add** money amounts.
Find the sum. $24,875 + $3,100 + $450 = $28,425

  1a. $180 + $570 + $43 $793   **1b.** $24,765 + $1,250 $26,015

2 **Subtract** money amounts.
Find the difference. $34,279 − $33,892 = $387

  2a. $18,367 − $17,907 $460   **2b.** $38,431 − $8,400 $30,031

3 **Multiply** money amounts by whole numbers and percents.
Find the product. $24 \times \$582 = \$13,968$
Find the product. $13\% \times \$16,300 = 0.13 \times \$16,300 = \$2,119$

  3a. $48 \times \$648$ $31,104   **3b.** $60 \times \$610.45$ $36,627

  3c. $21\% \times \$19,250$ $4,042.50   **3d.** $17\% \times \$9,670$ $1,643.90

■ Financing Car Purchases

The delivered price of a car purchase may be paid in cash. Most buyers, however, make a down payment and take out an installment loan.

EXAMPLE 1

The delivered price of Lydia Zollner's new car is $23,560. She makes a $2,000 down payment and pays the balance in 48 monthly payments of $560. What total amount did Lydia pay for the car? What was the finance charge?

TEACHING STRATEGIES Cooperative Learning

To apply what they have learned in this lesson, have students bring in copies of car lease ads that contain data
about the lease deal offered. After the study of car leases

is concluded, have students discuss what they found in
the ads and calculate the total costs of leasing using the
data from one of the ads.

SOLUTION

Add the total of the monthly payments and the down payment.

$48 \times \$560 = \$26,880$ $\quad\quad \$26,880 + \$2,000 = \$28,880$ total paid

Subtract the cash price from the total paid.

$\$28,880 - \$23,560 = \$5,320$ finance charge

■ CHECK YOUR UNDERSTANDING

A. Steve Ruhlin bought a used truck for \$9,650. He paid for the truck with a \$2,650 down payment and 36 monthly payments of \$234.30. What total amount did the truck cost? $\$11,084.80$

B. Iris DiNeise bought a luxury car for \$47,851 and made a \$4,500 down payment. She got a special loan rate of 2.1% for 60 months. Iris' monthly payments were \$805.47. What was her finance charge on this car? $\$4,977.20$

■ Costs of Leasing

People who lease cars sign a lease. A **lease** is a contract made between the company that owns the car (the lessor) and the person who will be given the right to use the car (the lessee). Leasing a car is similar to renting a car. You use the car for a time and once the lease period is over you turn in the car and walk away.

Before signing a lease, be sure you understand the lease contract, including how many miles you are allowed to drive the car each year.

A LEASE CONTRACT Leasing is based on the idea that you agree to make a monthly payment that covers the depreciation, finance charges, prepaid mileage, and other fees. An additional payment may also be required at the time the lease is signed. The typical lease contract includes these items:

LEASE PRICE The price negotiated by you and the dealer. It is the price on which the monthly lease payments are usually figured.

DOWN PAYMENT This is an amount that may be required by the lease contract or voluntarily paid by a buyer. A down payment reduces the lease price and results in smaller monthly lease payments.

RESIDUAL VALUE The expected value of the car at the end of the lease period. This may also be thought of as the depreciated value of the car.

INTEREST RATE The rate used to compute the finance charge.

LEASE TERM The length of the lease, usually stated in months.

SECURITY DEPOSIT Money held by the dealer to pay for any possible damage to the leased car. The security deposit is refundable.

LOAN FEE A charge for processing the lease contract and making credit checks.

REGISTRATION FEES The cost of license plates and title registration.

MILEAGE ALLOWED The number of miles the car may be driven each year for the term of the lease.

> **BUSINESS TIP**
>
> Most leases are closed-end leases that have a fixed residual value regardless of what the market price of the car may be at the lease end.

■ **Apply Goal 1**

Work through the procedures for solving Example 1 at the board and have students complete the calculations at their desks. Ask them to calculate the percent (about 20%) that the finance charge adds to the cost of the vehicle.

Assign Check Your Understanding problems A and B as class work. Review student work at their desks to identify any difficulties and answer questions they may have about the problems.

■ **Teach Goal 2**

Point out that a lease is a convenient way to get a new car without investing much money in a down payment and making monthly payments that are smaller than payments on loans. Many businesspersons lease cars, especially if the cost of the lease is a deductible business expense on federal income tax returns.

Discuss the terms found in a typical lease contract. Point out that no refund is given if fewer miles are driven than the mileage allowed by the lease agreement.

Explain that a lessee has the option of increasing the annual mileage allowance by paying for extra miles at the time of lease signing. The cost of buying extra miles in this way is less than the mileage charge at the end of the lease.

If the lessee does not use all the extra miles, their cost may be refunded at the end of the lease.

■ *CHECK YOUR UNDERSTANDING SOLUTIONS*

A. $36 \times \$234.30 = \$8,434.80$;
$\$8,434.80 + \$2,650 = \$11,084.80$

B. $60 \times \$805.47 = \$48,328.20$;
$\$48,328.20 + \$4,500 = \$52,828.20$;
$\$52,828.20 - \$47,851 = \$4,977.20$

C. $2 \times 12 = 24$; $24 \times \$528 = \$12,672$ lease payments;

$30,850 - (2 \times 12,000) = 6,850$; $6,850 \times \$0.20 =$
$\$1,370$ excess miles charge; $\$12,672 + \$1,370 =$
$\$14,042$ total cost

D. $4 \times 12 = 48$; $48 \times \$332 = \$15,936$ lease payments;
$4 \times 3,000 = 12,000$; $12,000 \times \$0.07 = \$840$ extra
miles; $\$15,936 + \$840 + \$418 = \$17,194$ total cost

■ **Apply Goal 2**

Work Example 2 at the board and have students do the math at their desks.

Assign Check Your Understanding problems C and D for class work. Point out that Problem D presents a situation where extra miles are purchased. Monitor student work to check that correct procedures are used and answers are labeled.

■ **ONGOING ASSESSMENT**
Ask students to explain these terms: lessee, lessor, lease, security deposit, and mileage allowed.

■ **Teach Goal 3**

Point out that if only the amount of cash paid out per month is considered, leasing is likely to cost less than buying a vehicle. Emphasize the flaw in this comparison in that the purchaser is acquiring equity in the car through monthly payments whereas the lessee is not.

Point out that the comparative method used in the textbook assumes that the lessee will purchase the car at the end of the lease for its residual value.

■ **Apply Goal 3**

Work Example 3 at the board and have students complete the math at their desks. Point out the two purchase costs in the solution: cost to purchase the leased car and cost to purchase outright.

Assign Check Your Understanding problems E and F for class work. Check student work.

When you lease a car you must buy insurance and pay for gas, oil, and other routine maintenance expenses.

EXAMPLE 2

Jay Sluman leased a car at $307 a month for 48 months with a $995 down payment. At the end of the lease he was charged $0.22 a mile for the 2,800 miles he drove over his lease mileage allowance. What were his total lease costs?

SOLUTION
Find the total of the monthly lease payments and the excess miles charge. Then add the two answers to the down payment.

$48 \times \$307 = \$14,736$ total lease payments

$\$0.22 \times 2,800 = \$616$ excess miles charge

$\$14,736 + \$616 + \$995 = \$16,347$ total lease costs

■ **CHECK YOUR UNDERSTANDING**

C. Candace Ortisi had a two-year car lease with $528 monthly payments. Her lease had a mileage limit of 12,000 miles a year and charged 20 cents a mile for each mile over the limit. Her total mileage for the two years was 30,850 miles. What was the total cost of the lease over its term? $14,042

D. Terrance Duggan's 4-year lease cost $332 a month and allowed him to drive 12,000 miles a year. He bought 3,000 extra miles each year for an additional charge of 7 cents a mile. Lease processing fees and a down payment totaled $418. What was the four-year cost of the lease? $17,194

■ Comparing Leasing and Buying

When you buy a car you pay for its total cost and end up owning a car that still has some value. When you lease the car you pay for only part of its cost, so your monthly payments are lower, but you have no ownership claim on the car.

When you lease a car you have the option to buy the car at the end of its lease. The price you would pay is the *residual value,* which is the estimated value of the car. The method used in this book to compare leasing and buying will be to calculate the total cost of buying the car under both plans.

EXAMPLE 3

Wilbur Frye and his dealer negotiated a price of $27,400 for a new car. Wilbur can lease the car for $496 a month for 36 months and buy it at the end of the lease for its residual value of $16,200. If he buys the car now his monthly loan payment will be $82 for three years after making a $2,000 down payment. What is the total cost of purchasing the car under each plan? Which plan is less expensive?

CONNECTION TO ECONOMICS

Point out to students that carmakers often stimulate car leasing by promoting the smaller monthly cash outlay required for leasing than for buying. In this way, they hope to increase the total units they lease and sell. One of the ways the monthly lease charge can be reduced is to figure less depreciation by establishing a high residual price for the leased car. However, the resulting lower lease charge leads to leasing being more expensive than buying when the total costs of buying a car outright and leasing and then buying the leased car are calculated.

SOLUTION

Find the total of the monthly lease payments. Then add the residual value and the down payment, if any.

$36 \times \$496 = \$17,856$ total lease payments

$\$17,856 + \$16,200 = \$34,056$ total cost to purchase leased car

Find the total of the monthly loan payments, add the down payment amount, and find the difference.

$36 \times \$822 = \$29,592$ total monthly loan payments

$\$29,592 + \$2,000 = \$31,592$ total cost to purchase outright

$\$34,056 - \$31,592 = \$2,494$ difference between two costs

The outright purchase cost is $2,494 less expensive.

■ **CHECK YOUR UNDERSTANDING**

E. A car that costs $18,500 can be leased for $436 monthly with a $500 down payment and an $11,000 residual value. The monthly loan price cost is $728 with a $3,100 down payment. The lease and loan terms are 24 months. Which is less expensive, leasing or buying, and how much less? buying is $1,392 less

F. A car that sells for $37,960 today is expected to have a residual value of $19,050 in four years. With a $3,800 down payment the loan payments for four years will be $873 monthly. The monthly lease price for four years with a $995 down payment is $623. Does leasing or buying cost more? How much more? leasing costs $4,245 more

■ Costs of Operating Cars

The total operating cost for a car is the sum of all the annual expenses of using the car. These expenses may include insurance, gas, oil, license and inspection fees, tires, repairs, garage rent, parking fees, taxes, and general upkeep. They also include depreciation and interest lost on a down payment.

EXAMPLE 4

Gerri Forbes paid $18,700 for her car. Her annual payments for insurance, gas, oil, repairs, and other expenses total $2,300. The car depreciates 16% a year. Gerri could have earned $145 interest on her investment in the car. What was her total annual cost of operating the car?

SOLUTION

Find the annual depreciation on the car. Then add to that amount the annual expenses and lost interest.

$16\% \times \$18,700 = 0.16 \times \$18,700 = \$2,992$ annual deprecation

$\$2,992 + \$2,300 + \$145 = \$5,437$ annual cost of car operation

■ **STUDENT PORTFOLIO**
Students should consider including in their portfolio the solutions to problems comparing the costs of leasing and buying vehicles.

■ **Teach Goal 4**

Relate the costs of operating cars to the costs of owning a home. Review how depreciation and lost interest are included as costs of home ownership and inform students they are included in the costs of car operations as well, and for the same reasons.

■ **Apply Goal 4**

Work Example 4 at the board and have students make calculations at their desks.

Assign Check Your Understanding problems G and H for class work. Observe student work at their desks to identify any student errors or difficulties they have in solving the problems.

■ *CHECK YOUR UNDERSTANDING SOLUTIONS*

E. $24 \times \$436 = \$10,464$; $\$10,464 + \$500 + \$11,000 = \$21,964$ lease; $24 \times \$728 = \$17,472$; $\$17,472 + \$3,100 = \$20,572$ purchase; $\$21,964 - \$20,572 = \$1,392$ buying is less

F. $4 \times 12 = 48$; $48 \times \$873 = \$41,904$; $\$41,904 + \$3,800 = \$45,704$ purchase cost; $48 \times \$623 = \$29,904$; $\$29,904 + \$995 + \$19,050 = \$49,949$ lease; $\$49,949 - \$45,704 = \$4,245$ leasing costs more

G. $0.12 \times \$12,480 = \$1,497.60$; $\$1,497.60 + \$1,070 + \$512 + \$981 + \$83 + \$561 = \$4,704.60$, or $4,705

H. $0.10 \times \$600 = \$60$; $\$610 + \$780 + \$630 + \$63 + \$60 + \$15 = \$2,158$

G. Conrad bought a used car for $12,480. His expenses for the first year were gas and oil, $1,070; repairs, $512; insurance, $981; license plates, $83; loss of interest on his car investment, $561; depreciation, 12%. Find the total operating cost for the year, rounded to the nearest dollar. $4,705

H. Ester McHugh, a high school student, bought an old, used car for $600. Her expenses for the year were gas, $610; maintenance and repairs, $780; property damage and liability insurance, $630; license plates, $63; depreciation, 10%; lost interest, $15. What was Ester's annual cost of operating the car? $2,158

Wrap Up

Having a fairly new car all the time is one of the appealing features of leasing if you are willing to pay the cost. Bob should realize that his family has to make a choice on how they spend their money. Perhaps they know that buying and keeping a car for 10 years costs less than leasing 5 different cars for 2 years at a time.

COMMUNICATION

Select the car you would most like to own. Then find a list that ranks cars by the number of miles per gallon they get. List the names and mileage information for four cars: the car you selected, the most efficient car, the least efficient car, and the average car. Assume that all the cars will be driven 15,000 miles in a year and their owners will buy fuel at your local gas station. Calculate how much would be spent per year on fuel for each car listed. Write a one-page report, including a chart, about your findings.

EXERCISES

Find the sum.
1. $47 + $167 + $476 $690
2. $12,450 + $1,250 + $1,800 $15,500

Find the difference.
3. $31,374 − $29,857 $1,517
4. $26,473 − $23,826 $2,647

Find the product.
5. 72 × $457 $32,904
6. 24 × $518 $12,432
7. 14% × $21,560 $3,018.40
8. 11% × $19,870 $2,185.70

9. Maggie Holden's 2-year car lease costs $597 a month. She had to pay a $600 security deposit that she got back at the end of the lease. She made a down payment of $500 and paid fees of $125 to get the lease. What was the net cost of the lease to Maggie at the end of the lease? $14,953

Wrap Up

Review the Start Up. Read the last sentence of the Wrap Up to the class and ask how they could prove this to be true.

The procedure they might use is to assume the car was purchased for $20,000. The average annual depreciation is $2,000 a year assuming the car has no value at the end of 10 years. The annual cost of leasing could be compared to the annual cost (average depreciation) of the purchased car to arrive at one solution.

COMMUNICATION

Have students exchange reports and check the calculations of fuel costs for accuracy. Have them write corrected solutions, if required, on another sheet of paper.

Discuss how the differences in fuel costs might be of special importance to individuals and families who are on a tight budget.

Assign

Assignment: Exercises 1–18, 20–34. Have students solve the basic arithmetic problems before completing the rest of the exercises. Alert students that while Exercise 18, Decision Making, may require a simple response to the second question, they are also to include a reason for their answer.

COMMON ERRORS

When finding total expenses, students may be in a hurry and incorrectly add the numbers in a problem, even when one is a percent. For instance, in Example H, students may find the total operating costs to be $2,108 by adding 10% as $10 instead of finding 10% of $600. To avoid this error, you might recommend that students scan the problem and first do the percent calculations.

Amy Stiles bought a new car for $24,300. She made a $1,800 down payment. Her monthly loan payments for four years are $569. Had she bought the car two months later and made the same down payment, she would have received a $1,250 rebate that would have lowered her monthly loan payments to $538.

10. What total amount will she pay for the car? $29,112

11. What total amount would she have paid if she could have received the rebate and the lower loan payment rate? $27,624

Mike Huber bought a car for $24,300. He wants to make a maximum down payment of $3,000. Two deals are available to Mike, both for 48-month loans. In the first deal, with a factory rebate his down payment will be $1,000. His monthly loan payments would be $590 at 8.4% interest. In the second deal, he gets no rebate and makes a $3,000 down payment, but his interest rate is 0.9% resulting in a $551 loan payment.

12. What total amount will Mike pay with the first deal? $29,320

13. What total amount will Mike pay with the second deal? $29,448

14. A 3-year lease costs $324 a month and a 2-year lease costs $392 a month for the same car. On the lease signing date Matt Grove makes a $990 down payment and pays lease application costs of $175. How much more would Matt pay for leasing during the first year under the more expensive plan? $816 more under the 2-year plan

15. A car that costs $20,990 can be bought for $1,800 down and 48 monthly loan payments of $488. It can be leased for $354 a month for 48 months with $760 down and a residual value at lease end of $9,445. Looking at the total purchase costs, will buying or leasing cost more? How much more? leasing costs $1,973 more

16. The monthly payment is $356 for a 36-month lease with a $250 down payment for a car that sells for $18,042. Its residual value is $10,284. With a $1,700 down payment, the monthly payments on a 48-month loan would be $546. Compare the total purchase costs of leasing vs. buying. Which costs more over a 3-year period, and how much more? leasing costs $1,994 more

17. After buying a car for $12,230, JoAnn Zimmer estimates her first-year car expenses as: gas, $1,458; maintenance and repairs, $312; license plates, $64; insurance, $511; depreciation, 10% of the car's purchase price; lost interest, $305. Find JoAnn's total cost of operating the car for the first year. $3,873

18. **DECISION MAKING** A dealer offers you a 2-year lease with no money down at $675 a month for a car that costs $29,100. The estimated residual value of the car is $18,915 at the end of the 2-year lease. You want to buy the car over four years with a $1,200 down payment. The monthly loan payment would be $712. What is the difference between the total cost of buying the car under both plans? Would you choose the less expensive plan? Lease plan costs $261 less than purchase plan. Lease deal should not be made because all money is paid in two years making it more expensive per year.

19. **CRITICAL THINKING** When you lease a car you are responsible for returning the car in good condition that has only the normal amount of wear and tear. How would you define what is normal "wear and tear?" Do you think your lease contract defines it in the same way? See Enrich section for answer.

Lesson 6.8 Car Purchases and Leases ▪ **269**

SELECTED SOLUTIONS

9. 2 × 12 × $597 = $14,328;
$14,328 + $500 + $125 = $14,953

10. 4 × 12 × $569 = $27,312;
$27,312 + $1,800 = $29,112

14. 12 × $324 = $3,888; 12 × $392 = $4,704;
$4,704 − $3,888 = $816 more for 2-year plan

18. 2 × 12 × $675 = $16,200;
$16,200 + $18,915 = $35,115 lease cost;
4 × 12 × $712 = $34,176;
$34,176 + $1,200 = $35,376 purchase cost;
$35,376 − $35,115 = $261

Assign Exercise 19, Critical Thinking. Ask students to define normal wear and tear in regard to the condition of the interior and exterior of the car, mechanical soundness, wear on tires, and service record.

Point out that most leases specify that leased cars are to have "normal wear and tear," the most visible of which is the exterior of the car which may have minor scratches and dings consistent with its age, but no broken glass.

Close

Write on the board the heading "operating costs" and beneath the heading two columns: "leased car" and "purchased car." Ask students to list in each column the operating costs that a lessee and a car owner might have. When the list is complete, have students identify the differences and similarities between the lists.

MIXED REVIEW

20. Estimate, then find the actual quotient of $27,414 \div 9$ 3,000, 3,046

21. Divide 4.37 by 0.023. 190

22. $7\frac{1}{2} + 1\frac{3}{5}$ $9\frac{1}{10}$

23. Divide 5,639 by 0.1 and by 1,000.
    56,390; 5.639

24. $48.32 decreased by $\frac{1}{8}$ of itself $42.28

25. $52.44 increased by $\frac{1}{3}$ of itself $69.92

26. $19.45 decreased by $\frac{2}{5}$ of itself $11.67

27. The interest charge per $100 is $0.8630 at $10\frac{1}{2}$% interest for 30 days and $0.4315 per $100 for 15 days. What interest will be paid on a $700 loan for 45 days at $10\frac{1}{2}$%? $9.06, Lesson 4.3

28. A home entertainment center sells for $3,200 cash. It may be purchased for $400 down and monthly payments of $89 for 48 months. By what percent is the installment price greater than the cash price, to the nearest tenth percent?
    46%, Lesson 4.4

29. Mike Ruskey's charge statement showed these figures: previous balance, $346.90; new balance, $684.70; cash advance limit, $750; credit limit, $1,250; minimum payment due, $19.12. If Mike makes the minimum payment, what is the most he can charge next month and not exceed his credit limit? $584.42, Lesson 4.7

30. Ella Rankin sells printer paper to retail stores. She is paid a commission of 1.25% on all sales for a month. What are her commission earnings for a month where her sales are $382,000? $4,775, Lesson 1.4

31. You can buy a package of six, 1.5 oz. boxes of raisins for $1.53 or a 1 lb. box of raisins for $2.24. Does the package or box cost less per ounce? How much less per ounce? Box, 3¢ less per oz., Lesson 5.3

Last year, Chandna Venkatraman was paid a salary of $700 a week for 52 weeks. Her federal taxable income for the same period was $21,200. She paid to the city of Carthage in which she worked an income tax of 3.5% on her taxable income. She could have worked at another firm in the city of Hamden. Her annual salary at the other firm would have been $39,000. The city in which the other firm is located charges an income tax of 1.8% on the gross salary. Lesson 2.4.

32. In which city would Chandna have paid more city income taxes? Carthage

33. How much more money would she have paid in city income taxes? $40

34. Lori Schneider can buy a large TV for $700 cash. On the installment plan, Lori must make a down payment of $100 and pay $54.50 for 12 months. How much more is the installment price than the cash price? $54, Lesson 4.4

DIFFERENT LEARNING STYLES Print Learner

When students complete the Close activity, ask them to say aloud first those expenses that are common to both leasing and purchasing. Write the expenses in each column and draw an arrow to connect them. Then write the expenses that are unique to leasing or purchasing. Have the learners check your chart against theirs and copy your chart if they are dissimilar. Remind learners to keep the chart for future reference.

Chapter Review

Lesson 6.1 Borrowing to Buy a Home
- Subtract down payment from home price to find amount borrowed.
- Add down payment and closing costs to find cash needed to buy home.
- Multiply monthly payments by number of payments to find total mortgage payments.
- Subtract original loan amount from total payments to find total interest paid.
- Subtract closing costs from difference of original and new payments to find refinancing savings.

Vocabulary Review

assessed value	homeowners insurance	property taxes
bodily injury	lease	renters policy
closing costs	manufacturer's suggested	resale value
collision	retail price (MSRP)	security deposit
comprehensive damage	mortgage loan	trade-in value
depreciation	premium	
down payment	property damage	

Fill in the blanks with the term that best completes the statement.

1. The money paid to purchase an insurance policy is called the __?__. premium

2. A contract that allows you to use property, such as a car, for a certain period is known as (a, an) __?__. lease

3. A type of car insurance that covers your liability for injury to other persons is called __?__. bodily injury

4. The money paid in addition to a down payment to complete the purchase of a home is __?__. closing costs

5. The gradual reduction in the value of a home due to aging and use is referred to as __?__. depreciation

6. A home's estimated worth used for tax purposes is called __?__. assessed value

7. The insurance usually obtained by tenants to cover the things they own and to provide personal liability protection is known as (a, an) __?__. renters policy

8. The protection you get from car insurance that covers possible damage to your car is known as __?__. collision

9. An amount of money kept by a landlord to cover any damage you may cause when renting property is called the __?__. security deposit

10. The money you pay to a government unit based on the value of the property you own is called __?__. property taxes

LESSON 6.1

11. Chester Thornton plans to buy a home for $105,700 with a 15% down payment. He estimates his closing costs as inspections, $360; property survey, $250; legal fees, $1,300; title insurance, $220; loan administration fee, $115; recording fee, $180. What amount will Chester have to borrow to buy the home? What amount of cash will he need? $89,845, $18,280

12. LuAnne Wiggins is buying a home for $167,000. She will make a 10% down payment and borrow the balance for 30 years at 8.23%. Her monthly mortgage payments will be $1,127.04. What total amount of interest will she pay over 30 years? $255,434.40

13. Robbie Whitaker's monthly mortgage payment is $823. His new monthly payment will be $694 if he refinances the mortgage loan. The refinancing costs are closing costs of $1,074 and a prepayment penalty of $421. How much will Robbie save in the first year by refinancing his mortgage? $53

Chapter 6 Review ■ 271

TEACHING STRATEGIES Chapter Review

Prior to assigning the Vocabulary Review, pronounce each word on the vocabulary list and have students write the words. Have them check their spellings against those in the list, rewriting any words they misspelled. Then have students place a check next to each term associated with car insurance to give them practice in grouping terms by content.

Chapter Review

LESSON 6.2

14. Muriel Voegel plans to buy a home. She estimates her annual home ownership expenses to be: mortgage interest, $4,873; property taxes, $2,156; home insurance, $418; depreciation, $1,800; utilities, $1,835; maintenance and repairs, $825. She will lose $1,410 interest on her down payment and save $640 in income taxes. What will be Muriel's net cost of owning the home in the first year? $12,677

15. Rafael Gonzalez rents a home for $1,400 a month. The security deposit he paid is two months' rent. Renters insurance costs $210 a year. Rafael expects utilities to average $136 a month. What will be the cost of renting the home for the first year? $21,442

16. Heather Rayburn estimates that she would pay $4,150 a year for taxes, insurance, and maintenance on a home she bought. Other annual home costs would be $8,800 in mortgage loan interest and $1,300 in estimated depreciation. During the year, Heather would lose $820 interest on her down payment, but her income taxes would be $1,145 less. Heather could have rented the home for $1,300 a month and had annual expenses of $205 for insurance and $1,780 for utilities. Her security deposit would have been $1,200. For the first year, would it have been less expensive to buy or rent the house, and how much less? Buying, $4,860 less

LESSON 6.3

17. The Wabeek County Library System's total budgeted expense for a year is $8,240,000. Of that total, $1,970,000 will come from various sources. The rest must be raised by a property tax. The total assessed value of all property in the county is $8,500,000,000. What tax rate is needed to cover budgeted expenses, correct to five decimal places? 0.00074

18. What property tax is due on a home assessed at $210,000 if the tax rate is $4.23 per $100? $8,883

19. The property tax rate is $34.67 per $1,000. Find the tax due on a business whose property is assessed at $540,000. $18,721.80

20. The property tax rate to maintain a park is 0.18 mills per $1 of assessed value. What tax will be paid on a home assessed at $42,500? $7.65

21. A vacant lot is assessed at $26,000. What property tax must be paid on the lot if the tax rate is 2.8 cents per $1? $728

LESSON 6.4

22. Virgil Tulley insured his home for $123,000 at an annual rate of $0.76 per $100. What premium did he pay? $934.80

23. Cecilia Emeg's apartment is located 6 miles from a fire station. She insured the apartment's contents for $15,000 and paid $49 extra for insuring a diamond ring. Use the renter's premium table to find the total insurance premium paid. $210

24. Jeremy O'Brien's homeowners policy has a face value of $56,400 and a $750 deductible. How much will the insurance company pay on a $1,612 loss? $862

TEACHING STRATEGIES Chapter Review

After students complete problem solutions, have them read the goals for each lesson and examine each review problem to see how it matches one or more of the lesson goals.

25. A warehouse with a value of $240,000 is insured for $144,000 under an 80% coinsurance policy. A fire loss of $84,000 occurs. How much of the loss will the insurance company pay? $63,000

LESSON 6.5

26. Find the MSRP of a MR35 sports sedan, Model CTM with these options: power seats and windows, ski rack, and 36/45,000 warranty. $25,851

27. Libby Coulson agreed to a purchase price of $32,568 for a new SUV. She made a down payment of $7,500. Libby is charged 4% sales tax on the purchase price and paid $183 in registration costs. She also received a $1,500 manufacturer's rebate. Find the delivered price and the balance due on this purchase. $32,553.72; $25,053.72

28. The purchase price of a used car Wade Hatcher bought was $6,140. Sales tax of 6.5% was charged on the purchase. Registration fees were $116. Wade paid cash for the car. What was the delivered price and balance due on this purchase? $6,655.10; $0

LESSON 6.6

29. A new car bought for $28,240 is estimated to have a value of $6,100 after 6 years. What is the car's estimated average annual depreciation? $3,690

30. A used car bought for $16,230 was sold for $1,200 after 9 years of use. What was the car's rate of depreciation, to the nearest tenth percent? 10.3%

LESSON 6.7

31. Kendra Busby drives her car to work. She wants to insure the car with $100 deductibles for collision and comprehensive coverage. Kendra also wants to carry $100/$300,000 bodily injury and $100,000 property damage coverage. Use the premiums table to find the premium she must pay. $892.63

LESSON 6.8

32. Archie Beane bought a used van for $8,127. He paid for the van with a $1,500 down payment and 24 monthly payments of $327.86. What total amount did he pay for the van and what was the finance charge on the loan? $9,368.64; $1,241.64

33. Pattie Truitt made a $2,000 down payment on a 60-month SUV lease contract. Her monthly payments were $485.30. At the end of the lease she was charged $0.19 per mile for 1,800 excess miles. What was Pattie's total cost of leasing? $31,460

34. A car that costs $25,007 can be leased for $414 monthly over 4 years with a $2,100 down payment. The car's residual value is estimated to be $11,050. If the car is purchased with $2,100 down, the monthly payments will be $594 for 4 years. Which is less expensive, leasing or buying, and how much less? buying is $2,410 less expensive

35. Bernie Kuykendall bought a used car for $7,300. His expenses for the first year were: gas and oil, $1,184; insurance, $620; repairs, $217; lost interest, $296; license plates, $56; depreciation, 11%. What was Bernie's annual cost of operating the car? $3,176

Chapter 6 Review ■ 273

TEACHING STRATEGIES Chapter Review

If the chapter review is assigned as class work, have selected students work at the board so that seated students can compare the steps they used to solve the problems with others. As students finish at the board, discuss each board solution in terms of the answers and the steps used to solve it. Try to select students for board work that you are reasonably sure will do the problem correctly.

The Tasks

Students need spreadsheet file tech6-1.xls for Tasks 1 and 2.

Task 1 Students enter data into a spreadsheet template that calculates for a mortgage the monthly payments, the total payments made over its term, and the total interest paid on the loan.

Task 2 Students answer questions about the results of Task 1. They also key in new data and answer questions about the results.

Task 3 Students design and create a spreadsheet to calculate the amount of loss paid by an insurer.

Task 4 Students answer questions about the results of calculations and how the spreadsheet might be modified.

Teach and Apply Task 1

Task 1 Point out that only the digits in the loan amount are entered in Cell B3 and that the interest rate without the % sign is entered in Cell B4.

If students should ask, inform them that the mortgage factor is the result of an intermediate calculation in the mortgage formula.

Teach and Apply Task 2

Assign questions 1–5 and have students write down their answers. Then discuss the answers.

Next have students change the data in Cell B4 before they answer questions 6–7. Ask students to read question 8 in its entirety before they change any data.

Task 1: Calculating Mortgage Payments

Enter data into a template that calculates the monthly mortgage loan payments and the total interest paid on the loan. You may use the template to compare the effects of changes in the interest rate and loan term on the total interest paid.

Open the spreadsheet for Chapter 6 (tech6-1.xls) and enter the data shown in blue (cells B3-5) into the spreadsheet. The spreadsheet will calculate the monthly loan payment, total amount paid on the loan, and the total interest paid on the loan.

Your computer screen should look like the one shown below when you are done.

	A	B
1	**MORTGAGE LOAN CALCULATOR**	
2	**Mortgage Loan Data**	
3	Amount	$110,000.00
4	Interest Rate (%)	8.160
5	Term (in years)	30
6	**Mortgage Payment Data**	
7	Mortgage Factor	0.9128142
8	Number of Payments	360
9	Monthly Payment	$819.44
10	Total Amount Paid	$294,998.40
11	Less Original Mortgage	$110,000.00
12	Total Interest Paid	$184,998.40

Task 2: Analyze the Spreadsheet Output

Answer these questions about the mortgage loan calculations.

1. For how many years was the loan made? 30 years

2. What amount was borrowed? $110,000

3. What was the monthly payment? $819.44

4. What total amount was paid on the mortgage loan? $294,998.40

5. What total amount of interest was paid on the loan? $184,998.40

Now move the cursor to cell B4, which holds the mortgage interest rate. Enter the rate 8.66%, which is $\frac{1}{2}$% higher than the rate you first entered. Enter the new rate of 8.66% without the percent symbol.

Answer these questions.

6. What total interest would be paid on the loan at the higher interest rate? $198,991.60

7. Approximately how much more would be paid in interest over 30 years at the $\frac{1}{2}$% higher interest rate? $14,000

TEACHING STRATEGIES Task 1

Before students begin entering data into the mortgage payments spreadsheet, have them display and print the formulas used. They will find that a lengthy formula is used to calculate the amount of the mortgage payment.

You may assign the finding of a simpler formula that yields the same mortgage payment calculation as an extra-credit assignment.

8. Assume you changed the loan term to 25 years and kept the rate at 8.66%. Over which term, 25 years or 30 years, do you think you would pay the greatest total amount of interest? Now, change the term to 25 years and check your thinking. You would pay about $40,000 less interest by taking a 25-year loan.

Task 3: Design an Insurance Loss Payment Spreadsheet

You are to design a spreadsheet that will calculate the amount of loss paid by an insurance company under a coinsurance policy. Also calculate the required amount of coinsurance.

The spreadsheet should have two sections, one for input data, and another for calculated data. Design your spreadsheet so the amount of loss paid is never greater than the insurance carried on the property.

SITUATION: Dewayne Clayton owns a home worth $50,000. He insures it for $35,000 under an 80% coinsurance policy. His roof was damaged by high winds, and its repair will cost $2,000. Find the amount of this loss that will be paid by the insurance company.

Task 4: Analyze the Spreadsheet Output

Answer these questions about your completed spreadsheet:

9. What amount of loss did the insurance company pay? $1,750

10. What coinsurance amount should have been carried on the home? $40,000

11. How much of the loss will Dewayne have to pay? $250

12. If the policy had a deductible, what change would you have to make in your spreadsheet? Add a row to input the deductible; subtract the deductible from the loss before calculating the amount paid by the insurance company.

TEACHING STRATEGY Task 3

After students complete and print the spreadsheet they developed, display the spreadsheet tech6-3.xls that provides a sample solution. Have students compare the sample to their spreadsheet solution and make suggestions of ways in which both spreadsheets might be improved.

Assess

■ **HOW TIMES HAVE CHANGED**

1. $12,400 × 0.45 = $5,580
$12,400 − $5,580 = $6,820
Helen needed to take out a mortgage of $6,820.

2. 106 million × 0.683 = 72.398 million
The number of households that owned homes in 2003 was about 72 million.

106 million − 72 million = 34 million
The number of 2003 households that were renters was about 34 million.

■ **WRITE**
Inform students that a personal business letter format should be used. The letter may contain numbered or bulleted items to separate and emphasize points.

■ **SCANS**
Students may collaborate to find a loan calculator. They are to write the rest of their plan independently. A monthly timeline should be used to show payments and income receipts and the savings needed to accumulate money to pay for anticipated large expenses, such as insurance.

■ **ONGOING ASSESSMENT**
STUDENT WORKBOOK The Integrated Project found in the workbook provides a broad, ongoing assessment activity for the goals of this chapter.

How Times Have Changed

For Questions 1–2, refer to the timeline on page 221 as needed.

1. In the early 1900s, it was not uncommon for a homebuyer to be required to pay a down payment of 50%. If in 1914 Helen Bogart wanted to buy a home that cost $12,400, and her lender required her to make a 45% down payment, what was the amount of the mortgage that Helen needed?
2. The number of households consists of the number of homeowners and the number of renters. The number of households in 2003 was about 106 million. About how many households owned homes in 2003? About how many 2003 households were renters?

WRITE

Write a letter to an adult, such as your parent, grandparent, or uncle, to convince them that you are ready to own your own car. (If you already have a car, write a letter about your wanting a different car.) Include in your letter information that shows you understand the steps involved in buying a car and paying for its operation. Discuss such items as down payment, monthly payments, insurance and your understanding of depreciation.

Include a spreadsheet where you show a financial summary of how you will afford a down payment, monthly payments, and other expenses associated with owning and operating a car.

SCANS

Workplace Skills—*Allocate Money*

You must be able to analyze costs and forecast expenditures when preparing a budget. You must also keep detailed records of the amounts you spend on each budget item so you may track how closely the budget is being followed. Following a budget requires a personal commitment on your part to stay with the plan.

Test Your Skills Create a spreadsheet that displays the costs associated with buying a car and the costs associated with operating and maintaining a car. For the car purchase, assume you are buying a used car for $6,500 and get a 36-month loan at 6.8% interest for the car's purchase price. Use a loan calculator you find on the Internet to calculate the monthly payment amount. For costs of operating the car, include all annual, monthly, weekly, and daily payments.

Make a Plan Review your spreadsheet and create a timeline that will show when the costs are incurred. Then show how you plan to pay for the costs.

Summarize Write a paragraph justifying your reasons for includng each car buying and operating cost. Also provide the details of your payment plan. Explain how, if your wish to own a car becomes a reality, you will use the following skills and abilities.

arithmetic	*decision making*	*problem solving*	*responsibility*
reading	*self-management*	*integrity/honesty*	*self-esteem*

PORTFOLIO ASSESSMENT

Have students read the first paragraph of their letters so that the class may reflect on the different approaches used. Have them decide, in their own mind, which approaches they thought were most creative and effective. Students need to prepare their letters for their student portfolios. Also have them include their reflections about the other students' letters. To complete the entry for the portfolio, students should write a self-evaluation of their own letter in comparison to those they heard presented to the class.

Chapter-Test Correlation

Question	Lesson
11	6.1
12	6.2
13	6.3
14	6.4
15	6.4
16	6.5
17	6.6
18	6.7
19	6.8

Chapter Test

Answer each question.

1. $1,057 + $186.20 + $595.86 $1,839.06
2. $248,112 − $162,905.70 $85,206.30
3. 360 × $918.47 $330,649.20
4. 2.45% × $137,000 $3,356.50
5. $1\frac{3}{5}$ × $24,000 $38,400
6. $6,840 ÷ 0.5% $1,368,000
7. 18 is what percent of 360? 5%
8. $542 increased by $\frac{1}{4}$ of itself is? $677.50
9. $6\frac{1}{2} + 1\frac{3}{5} + 4\frac{3}{4}$ $12\frac{17}{20}$
10. Divide to four places: $118,400 ÷ $10,500,000 0.0113

Applications

11. The home that Hilda Vaughan wants to buy sells for $213,000. She plans to make a 5% down payment and borrow the balance at 7.67% for 25 years. Her monthly mortgage payments will be $1,517.80. What total interest will Hilda pay over 25 years? $252,990

12. Eldon Hudspeth estimates that the cost of taxes, insurance, and maintenance on a home he bought is $4,980 a year. His other yearly costs would be $12,760 in mortgage loan interest and $2,050 in estimated depreciation. For a year, he would lose $1,030 interest on his down payment and save $2,400 on his income taxes. Eldon could have rented a similar home for $1,400 a month and had annual expenses of $302 for insurance and $2,760 for utilities. The security deposit on the rented home would have been $500. For the first year, which would have been less expensive, buying or renting a home? How much less? Buying, $1,942 less

13. Find the property tax due on a building assessed at $360,000 if the tax rate is $37.40 per $1,000? $13,464

14. Wanda Frey insured her home for $156,400. Her annual insurance rate is $0.83 per $100. What annual premium did she pay? $1,298.12

15. Kerry Molloy's homeowners policy has a face value of $78,200 and a $250 deductible. How much of a $4,783 loss will the insurance company pay? $4,533

16. Janese Mosby bought a new car for $27,437. She made a down payment of $4,200. Janese must pay 5% sales tax on the purchase and $121 in registration costs. She received a $500 rebate from the manufacturer when she bought the car. Find the delivered price and the balance due on this car purchase. $28,429.85; $24,229.85

17. A car bought for $18,216 was sold for $12,870 after 2 years of use. What was the car's rate of depreciation, to the nearest tenth percent? 14.7%

18. Edward Laffin uses his car for pleasure driving. The insurance coverages he wants and their costs are: collision, $368.12; comprehensive, $146.89; bodily injury, $164.14; property damage, $186.34. Edward receives a 5% discount on the total premium because he drives the car less than 7,500 miles a year. What annual premium will Edward pay? $822.22

19. A car costing $34,000 can be leased for $473 monthly over 5 years with a $2,420 down payment. The car's residual value is estimated to be $16,400. If the car is purchased with a $5,000 down payment, the monthly loan payments will be $623 for 60 months. Is buying or leasing less expensive, and how much less? buying is $4,820 less expensive

Chapter 6 Assessement ■ **277**

TEACHING STRATEGIES Chapter Test

Remind students to show each step in the solution of problems and to label intermediate and final results. Also remind them that you will be evaluating not only their solutions, but also the neatness and organization of their work. Remind them that numbers are to be clearly written and aligned.

Test Taking Strategies

■ MULTIPLE CHOICE

In exercise 7 two of the choices may be eliminated by the addition and subtraction only of the known digits in the thousands position. So, the estimated solution might be $18,000 - 2,000 - 1,000 = 15,000$. Since sales tax and fees remain to be added, the answer cannot possibly be C and A appears to be too high. That leaves B, D, and E as possible answers, with B as the most likely answer of the three.

Chapters 5–6 Cumulative Review

MULTIPLE CHOICE

Select the best choice for each question.

1. A lawnmower sells for $489. The sales tax is 5.1%. What is the total cost of the mower? A
   - **A.** $513.94
   - **B.** $513.45
   - **C.** $489.00
   - **D.** $24.94
   - **E.** $464.06

2. You bought 6 pairs of socks @ $4.25 and 3 shirts at $18.95. The sales tax is 3%. What was the total amount of the purchase? C
   - **A.** $82.35
   - **B.** $23.90
   - **C.** $84.82
   - **D.** $45.78
   - **E.** $79.88

3. The regular price of a quart of motor oil is $1.84. You can buy a 12-quart case of motor oil for $16.99. How much will you save by buying oil by the case? D
   - **A.** $11.08
   - **B.** $22.08
   - **C.** $39.97
   - **D.** $5.09
   - **E.** $5.15

4. A document you want to download from the Internet is 64.8 KB in size. If the true speed of the Internet connection is 38 kbps, how many seconds will it take to download the file, to the nearest tenth second? B
   - **A.** 1.7
   - **B.** 13.6
   - **C.** 17.05
   - **D.** 17.1
   - **E.** 3.3

5. You are thinking of buying a home for $104,300 and making an 18% down payment. You estimate closing costs will be 2.5% of the home's purchase price. How much cash will you need to buy the home? D
   - **A.** $16,166.50
   - **B.** $2,607.50
   - **C.** $18,774
   - **D.** $21,381.50
   - **E.** $20,800

6. A home worth $105,000 is insured for $85,000 under a 90% coinsurance policy. How much of a $28,000 loss would an insurance company pay? E
   - **A.** $20,000
   - **B.** $28,000
   - **C.** $26,444.44
   - **D.** $25,200
   - **E.** $25,185.18

7. Vicky Zielinski bought a truck on these terms: purchase price, $18,240; down payment, $2,500; rebate, $1,200; sales tax, 5%; registration fees, $117. What was the balance due? B
   - **A.** $20,579
   - **B.** $15,569
   - **C.** $13,745
   - **D.** $17,805
   - **E.** $17,979

8. Charles Codwell bought a used car for $7,195. He made an $800 down payment and paid the balance in 24 payments of $318.47 a month. What was the finance charge on the loan? C
   - **A.** $448.28
   - **B.** $1,258.32
   - **C.** $1,248.28
   - **D.** $351.72
   - **E.** $1,428.28

9. A car bought new for $27,118 is sold for $950 after 14 years of use. What is the average annual depreciation? A
   - **A.** $1,869.14
   - **B.** $67.86
   - **C.** $1,937
   - **D.** $2,854.52
   - **E.** $1,689.14

TEACHING STRATEGIES Cumulative Review

Remind students to keep in mind that time can be saved by combining amounts whenever possible. For example, a state sales tax rate of 4% and a city sales tax rate of 1% can be combined by mentally adding the rates to give 5%. Thus, one multiplication and one rounding are done instead of two.

OPEN ENDED

10. A pack of 4 toothbrushes sells for $8.69. Another pack of 6 toothbrushes sells for $11.89. Which pack costs less per toothbrush? How much less, to the nearest cent? 6-pack costs 19¢ less

11. A package of 6 water filters sells for $26.99. Find the price per filter, to the nearest cent? $4.50

12. A sales tax of 4.3% applies to all purchases, except food. Phil Chambers made these purchases at a supermarket: household supplies, $24.18; packaged meats, $29.42; fruit, $12.18; CD, $15.14; book, $11.98. What was the total cost of the purchase? $95.11

13. A wallpaper steamer rents for $12 an hour or $72 a day. You need the steamer for 8 hours a day for 3 consecutive days. How much would you save by renting the steamer by the day instead of by the hour? $72

14. The basic annual cost of an auto insurance policy on Kara Malgren's car is $726. She gets a 2% discount for having a theft alarm and side impact air bags. She also gets a 4% discount for her safe driving record. What annual premium will Kara pay? $682.44

15. Ewald Farleigh's ISP charges a $30 installation fee, $80 for a network connection card, and a monthly access fee of $47.95. In addition, Ewald bought a modem for $180 and antivirus software for $34.98. What will be Ewalds's total cost for the first year of his connection to the Internet? $900.38

16. A home may be bought for $72,000 with a 15% down payment. The monthly payments on a 20-year loan at 7.61% will be $497.15. What total interest will be paid on the loan? $58,116

17. A town needs $580,000 to maintain its parks. Park use fees raise $124,000 of that amount. The total assessed value of property in the town is $10,900,000. What tax rate is needed to provide enough money to maintain the parks, to four decimal places? 0.0418

18. A home's assessed value is $185,410. If the property tax rate is $29.18 per $1,000 of assessed value, what tax is due on the home? $5,410.26

19. A tax rate of 24 mills per $1 of assessed value is equivalent to what rate in dollars? $0.024

20. Bess Ambrose owns a car whose average monthly cost of gas, oil, and repairs is $184. The annual costs include insurance, $842; depreciation, $1,080; license plates, $68; lost interest, $48. What is the total annual cost of operating the car? $4,246

21. Yong's Flower Shop purchased a delivery van for $32,599. The salesperson guaranteed that the dealership would buy back the van after four years for $12,550. What is the expected rate of depreciation? about 15.4%; Lesson 6.6

CONSTRUCTED RESPONSE

22. A car can be leased for $289 a month for 36 months with no money down. The same car could be bought for $15,680 with $1,700 down and 36 monthly payments of $453. Write a note to a friend explaining why even with the $164 monthly payment difference, leasing the car may be more expensive than buying. The lease pays for only part of the car's price; the purchase pays for the entire price of the car. Also, the cost to purchase the leased car is unknown. Adding that amount to the lease costs would give a fairer comparison of which plan is more expensive.

TEST-TAKING STRATEGIES Constructed Response

Students may calculate only the cash paid in the transactions, but they may wonder about the great difference between the amounts. The discrepancy may prompt them to recall that the residual value of the leased car must be added to total lease costs to provide a valid comparison to the car's total purchase costs. Explain how finding an error in a problem may lead to better understanding the reason why it occurred.

Chapter 7 reviews addition, subtraction, multiplication, percents, fractions, rounding, and division to solve problems pertaining to insurance and investments.

Lesson 7.1 Life Insurance
Students find life insurance premiums, cash surrender values, and the net cost of insurance.

Lesson 7.2 Health Insurance
Students find health insurance premiums, coinsurance, and benefits.

Lesson 7.3 Disability Insurance
Students calculate disability insurance benefits.

Lesson 7.4 Buying Bonds
Students find the market price of bonds and their total investments.

Lesson 7.5 Bond Interest
Students find bond income, yield, and the total cost of bonds.

Lesson 7.6 Stocks
Students find the cost of stock purchases, dividends, yield, and proceeds from the sale of stocks.

Lesson 7.7 Mutual Funds
Students find mutual fund investments, commissions, and profit or loss from investments.

Lesson 7.8 Real Estate
Students find the net income on investments and find the rent tenants need to be charged.

Lesson 7.9 Retirement Investments
Students find retirement income.

CHAPTER 7

Insurance and Investments

7.1 Life Insurance

7.2 Health Insurance

7.3 Disability Insurance

7.4 Buying Bonds

7.5 Bond Interest

7.6 Stocks

7.7 Mutual Funds

7.8 Real Estate

7.9 Retirement Investments

Statistical Insights

Health Insurance Coverage in United States

Year	1990	1994	1998	2002
Population (Thousands)	248,886	262,105	271,743	285,933
Percent Covered by Health Insurance	86.1	84.8	83.7	84.8

Use the data shown above to answer each question.

1. About how many people in the United States were covered by health insurance in 1998? 227,449,000

2. About how many people in the United States were not covered by health insurance in 2002? 43,462,000

3. What is the percent increase in the total population from 1990 to 2002? about 14.9%

Statistical Insights

There are a number of retirement planning sites on the Web that help workers plan their retirement investments and estimate their retirement income. These include brokerage web sites, insurance web sites, and non-profit organizations like the American Association of Retired People, or AARP. You might have students search these web sites, and list the features that they provide. Have students report their findings in class and discuss them.

NetCheck

Looking for Real Estate

To get into the business of being a landlord, one should do extensive research to determine the types of rental properties that offer a good return on the original investment. Most major metropolitan areas have a network of real estate services known as the Multiple Listings Service. Real estate agents of single-family homes, land for both residential and commercial development, and rental property for sale use this network. When you locate the web site of your area's Multiple Listings Service, you will be able to browse the available real estate for sale in or near your city.

Looking for Insurance

Many major insurance companies are competing for everyone's business via the Internet. You can locate web sites that will let you fill in your needs for insurance and then shop for the most cost-efficient policy with the best coverage.

Look into web sites that help you shop for life, health, dental, vision, and short-term and long-term disability insurances. You may find that one type of insurance company is better equipped to offer comparable quotes online than others.

How Times Have Changed

The origin of the New York Stock Exchange can be traced to 1792. Since 1896, the Dow Jones Industrial Average—the Dow—has been used to indicate the trend of the NYSE. At its inception in 1896, the Dow was 40.74 points. About 100 years later on December 31, 1999, the Dow reached a record high of 11,497.12 points.

Teaching Resources

Lesson Plans, Ch. 7
Chapter 7 Test Forms A and B
Workbook, Ch. 7
Explore Algebra and Geometry Activities
Technology Activities
Competitive Events Prep
Data Activities CD, Ch. 7
ExamView® Pro CD, Ch. 7

NetCheck

Looking for Real Estate Investments Help students locate multiple listing service web sites that serve your area. If you can use a computer lab or display a computer screen in class, bring up a web site and show students how to navigate it for the information they need.

Looking for Insurance Ask students for key words that, if used in a search engine, are likely to locate insurance web sites. Write the key words on the board and discuss the utility of each with the class.

Answer to research item:

The Dow's 1929 high was 381.17 points. As a result of the stock market crash, the Dow plummeted to a 1929 low of 198.69 points.

HOW TIMES HAVE CHANGED

Lead the class into a discussion about the stock market. Possible question to ask:

Have you heard it reported on the news that the "market is up" or "the Dow is down"? What do you think that means?

Turn the students' attention to the timeline. Have them do their own research to discover a significant event that happened in 1929 that relates to the stock market. Also have them find the Dow in 1929.

See page 342 for assessment questions related to the timeline.

Life Insurance

GOALS

- ■ Calculate life insurance premiums
- ■ Calculate the net cost of life insurance
- ■ Calculate the cash and loan values of a life insurance policy

Start Up

How important, on a scale of 1-10, is life insurance to the following people:

a. A single person with no dependents who attends school.

b. A single person who supports an aging parent.

c. A working couple with one child.

d. A working couple with no children.

e. A couple with two children, where one parent works and the other takes care of the children.

f. A widow with two self-supporting, adult children.

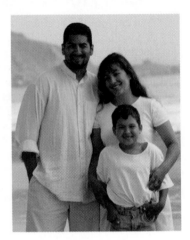

Math Skill Builder

Review these math skills and solve the exercises that follow.

1 **Divide** by 1,000.
Find the quotient. $250,000 ÷ 1,000 = $250

1a. $125,000 ÷ 1,000
$125

1b. $335,000 ÷ 1,000
$335

1c. $1,678,200 ÷ 1,000
$1,678.20

1d. $89,000 ÷ 1,000
$89

2 **Multiply** by percents.
Find the product. $225 × 30% = $225 × 0.30 = $67.50

2a. $189 × 10% $18.90

2b. $210 × 15% $31.50

2c. $549 × 25% $137.25

2d. $92 × 5% $4.60

3 **Divide** to find percents.
Find the percent. $350 is what percent more than $300? $50 ÷ $300 = $16\frac{2}{3}$%

3a. $300 is what percent more than $250?   20%

3b. $280 is what percent more than $240? $16\frac{2}{3}$%

Life Insurance Premiums

Life insurance is a way of protecting your family from financial hardship when you die. If your income supports your family, they will need to replace that income when you die. If you are a homemaker, your surviving spouse may need to pay someone to care for your children and home. In both cases, money is needed to pay funeral costs. Life insurance may also be bought to repay debts when you die, such as a home mortgage or a car loan.

A life insurance *policy* is a contract between the *insured*, the person whose life is covered, and the insurer, the insurance company. The contract states the amount of insurance to be paid on the death of the insured, or the *death benefits* of the policy. The death benefits are usually equal to the face amount (or *face value*) of the policy.

The money paid to an insurance company for life insurance is the *premium*. When the insured dies, death benefits are paid to the beneficiary. The *beneficiary* is the person named in the policy to receive the death benefits.

There are two basic types of life insurance policies: term life insurance and permanent life insurance. Insurance companies have designed many variations of these two types for people with different needs and budgets.

Term life insurance offers protection for a fixed period of time, such as 1, 5, or 10 years. If you die within that time, your beneficiary receives the face value of the policy. Term insurance can usually be renewed after the fixed term expires, but usually the policy premiums will be higher because you are older and more likely to die. Term insurance is the least expensive kind of life insurance.

One variation of term life insurance is *decreasing term life insurance*. With decreasing term life, the face amount of the policy decreases over time. Decreasing term life insurance is popular with homeowners who use the policies to cover their mortgage loans. Because the amount of insurance declines over time, the premiums are lower than with standard term life insurance.

Permanent life insurance insures you for your whole life, and is often called *whole*, or *straight life insurance*. Premiums usually are paid for your whole life.

A variation of permanent life insurance is universal life insurance. *Universal life insurance* allows you limited ability to change the amount of the death benefit and how much you pay in premiums. A certain amount of each premium payment is invested and earns tax-free income. In years when you can, you may pay in more than the premium. The overpayment is invested. In years when your money is tight, you can pay in less than the premium or skip it entirely. The premium is then paid from the invested funds.

Annual Premiums per $1,000 of Life Insurance				
Age of Insured	10-Year Term		Whole Life	
	Male	Female	Male	Female
20	1.12	1.08	9.84	8.92
25	1.14	1.10	11.61	10.56
30	1.17	1.13	14.08	12.81
35	1.30	1.26	17.44	15.86
40	1.54	1.49	22.60	20.55
45	1.97	1.91	27.75	25.24

Lesson 7.1 Life Insurance ■ **283**

Choose at random a series of ages that appear on the life insurance premium chart, type of policy, and gender and ask selected students to calculate the premiums at the board. When the students have completed the calculations, ask the class to audit their work for errors in arithmetic, omission of labels, or incorrect procedures.

■ **Teach Goal 2**

Stock insurance companies issue stock and are owned by the stock-holders, who receive dividends, if declared. The stockholders elect a board of directors who govern the company.

A mutual insurance company does not issue stock. The policyholders elect a board of directors who govern the company. Policyholders are members of the company and receive dividends, if declared, usually in amounts proportionate to how much insurance they carry.

In recent years, a number of mutual insurance companies have "demutualized" and become stock insurance corporations. Policyholders of demutualized insurance companies are given stock in the new company, usually in proportion to the amount of insurance they carry.

■ **Apply Goal 2**

Work through Example 2 at the board while students do the math at their desks.

Assign Check Your Understanding problems C and D to do in class. Look over students' shoulders to check on their work.

The table at the bottom of the previous page shows the premiums an insurance company might charge for each $1,000 of life insurance. Different rates are given for men and women at different ages. The rates shown are for nonsmokers. To find the annual premium for a policy, divide the face amount by $1,000 and then multiply the result by the cost per $1,000 in the table.

$$\frac{\text{Face of Policy}}{\$1,000} \times \text{Cost per \$1,000}$$

EXAMPLE 1

Shelly Burnam buys a $25,000 whole life insurance policy at age 25. Shelly does not smoke. What is her annual premium?

SOLUTION
Divide the face of the policy by $1,000.

$25,000 \div \$1,000 = 25$ number of $1,000 units

Multiply the number of $1,000 units by the cost per unit found in the table.

$25 \times \$10.56 = \$264$ annual premium

■ **CHECK YOUR UNDERSTANDING**

A. Bob Walzcek bought a $135,000 term life insurance policy. He is 35 years old and does not smoke. Using the insurance premium table, find his annual premium. $175.50

B. Risa Belvador bought a $150,000 whole life insurance policy at age 20. Risa does not smoke. Using the insurance premium table, find her annual premium. $1,338

■ Net Cost of Insurance

Some insurance companies may return part of your premium to you as a *dividend*. You may deduct the dividend from the premium due or leave the dividend with the company to buy more insurance or to earn interest. The total premium for the year less the dividend is the net cost of the insurance for the year.

Total Premiums − Dividends = Net Cost of Insurance

EXAMPLE 2

Tom Fisher paid $57 quarterly for a life insurance policy. His policy also paid a dividend of $14.80 at the end of the year. What was the net cost of his insurance policy for the year?

SOLUTION
Multiply the quarterly premium by 4.

$57 \times 4 = \$228$ total premiums for year

Subtract the dividend from the total premiums.

$228 − \$14.80 = \$213.20$ net cost of insurance for year

BUSINESS TIP

Many insurance companies have web sites that let you get rate quotes for different types of life insurance policies.

■ *CHECK YOUR UNDERSTANDING SOLUTIONS*
A. $135,000 \div \$1,000 = 135; 135 \times \$1.30 = \$175.50$ **B.** $150,000 \div \$1,000 = 150; 150 \times \$8.92 = \$1,338$

C. Ricardo Ballas received a premium notice from his insurance company for his life insurance policy. The policy listed an annual premium of $856 and also a dividend of $38.56. Ricardo decided to deduct the dividend from the premium and pay the difference. What was the net premium he paid? $817.44

D. Yolanda Pagan doesn't smoke. Five years ago, when she was 30, she bought a whole life insurance policy for $150,000. This year her policy paid a dividend of $23.16. Using the insurance premium table, find her annual premium and the net cost of her policy for this year. $1,898.34

■ Life Insurance Cash Values

If you cancel a term policy, you get nothing. Whole life policies build cash value after premiums have been paid for a few years. Cash value is the money that you get if you cancel the policy. The policy may give you a choice of taking the cash, or using it to buy a small amount of whole life insurance that is totally paid up, or to buy term insurance.

The policy may also allow you to borrow up to the total amount of the cash value, often at a lower interest rate than that offered by other lenders. If you don't pay back the loan, it will be subtracted from the amount paid to your beneficiaries when you die.

A whole life policy that builds cash value would have a table much like the one shown at the right. The cash values of universal life insurance policies will vary with the current value of the investments that have been made.

Cash Value Table	
Year	Cash/Loan Values per $1,000
1	0
5	10
10	42
15	80
20	124
25	174

EXAMPLE 3

Using the cash value table, find the maximum amount you can borrow against your $100,000 policy if you had the policy for 20 years.

SOLUTION
Divide the face value of the policy by $1,000.

$100,000 ÷ $1,000 = 100   number of $1,000 units in the policy

Multiply the number of units by the appropriate table amount.

100 × $124 = $12,400   maximum loan amount of policy

■ CHECK YOUR UNDERSTANDING

E. Using the cash value table, how much can you borrow against a 10-year policy with a face value of $300,000? $12,600

F. Using the cash value table, how much would you receive if you cancelled a 15-year policy with a face value of $150,000? $12,000

Lesson 7.1 Life Insurance ■ 285

■ *CHECK YOUR UNDERSTANDING SOLUTIONS*

C. $856 − $38.56 = $817.44

D. $150,000 ÷ $1,000 = 150;
150 × $12.81 = $1,921.50;
$1,921.50 − $23.16 = $1,898.34

E. $300,000 ÷ $1,000 = 300; 300 × $42 = $12,600

F. $150,000 ÷ $1,000 = 150; 150 × $80 = $12,000

Wrap Up

Review the Start Up. Ask students to explain what factors lead them to choose a higher rating for one situation than another. Some of these factors are given in the Wrap Up.

COMMUNICATION

Help students identify web sites, credit unions, banks, and insurance agents (use yellow pages) as resources. Discuss how they might approach area companies to get information; e.g., what questions they might ask in a site interview.

Combine and write on the board the data that students locate. Discuss the range of interest rates found.

Wrap Up

Look at the list of situations in the Start Up question at the beginning of this lesson. When you rated the importance of insurance, did you consider the (a) number of dependents, (b) need for insurance to cover a mortgage, (c) need for insurance to protect against the loss of income for both working partners, or (d) need for money to cover the cost of burial?

COMMUNICATION

Investigate the interest rates charged for a car loan from one credit union and one bank. Then find the interest rate charged for borrowing from a whole life insurance policy's cash surrender value. Prepare a chart of your results and present your findings to the class.

Some sources for gathering information include:

- the Web
- a credit union
- a bank
- an insurance agent

EXERCISES

Find the quotient or product.

1. $104,580 ÷ 1,000 $104.58
2. $59,320 ÷ 1,000 $59.32
3. $28 × 25% $7
4. 412 × $0.76 $313.12
5. $339 × 20% $67.80
6. 78 × $1.54 $120.12

Divide to find the percent.

7. $500 is what percent more than $400?   25%

8. $750 is what percent more than $500?   50%

Use the insurance premium table to solve Exercises 9–12.

	Policy Type	Age and Sex	Policy Face	Annual Premium
9.	Whole Life	20, female	200,000	$1,784
10.	10-Year Term	30, male	150,000	$175.50
11.	10-Year Term	40, female	400,000	$596
12.	Whole Life	25, male	50,000	$580.50

13. How much more is the annual premium on a $50,000, whole life policy for a male at age 45 than at age 25? $807

14. How much more is the annual premium on a $100,000, whole life policy than a 10-year term policy for a 30-year old female? $1,168

286 ■ Chapter 7 Insurance and Investments

TEACHING STRATEGIES Cooperative Learning

Have teams of students research the difference between stock insurance companies and mutual insurance companies. Each team should prepare a report that lists and briefly describes the features of each type of insurance company. Have student teams report their findings orally in class and have the whole class discuss each feature that is reported.

15. Paul Poncelli, age 30, is comparing the premium for a $100,000, whole life policy he may take now and the premium for the same policy taken out at age 35. Find the difference in total premium costs over 20 years for this policy at the two age levels. $6,720

16. STRETCHING YOUR SKILLS   Because she smokes, Valerie Corini pays 20% more for life insurance. How much more will Valerie pay for $150,000 of 10-year term insurance at age 45 than a nonsmoker would pay at the same age? $57.30

17. STRETCHING YOUR SKILLS   To the nearest percent, what percent greater is the cost of a whole life policy taken out by a male at age 45 than at age 35?   59%

STRETCHING YOUR SKILLS   Rollie Collins, age 25, wants to pay no more than $600 a year in life insurance. In even thousands of dollars, what is the largest policy he can buy without spending more than $600 annually on a

18. whole-life policy? $51,000

19. 10-year term insurance policy? $526,000

20. Melva Davis paid an annual premium of $12.80 per $1,000 for an $8,000 life insurance policy. Her policy also paid a dividend of $18.90, which she used to reduce her premium. What net premium did Melva pay? $83.50

21. Trent Coleman pays a premium of $18.80 per $1,000 for a $120,000 life insurance policy. During the year, his policy paid a dividend of $11.90. What is the net cost of the policy for the year? $2,244.10

22. Alicia Ronzetti bought a 30-year decreasing term life insurance policy to repay her 30-year, $150,000 mortgage in the event of her death. The insurance company's annual rate per $1,000 for the policy was $0.76. What was her annual premium? $114

23. Silvia Olivares takes out a universal life policy for $50,000 and pays $490 in annual premiums. What total amount will she pay in premiums in 20 years? $9,800

Use the table of cash values to solve Exercises 24–28.

24. How much cash would you get if you canceled a $50,000 whole life policy after paying premiums for ten years? $2,100

25. You have paid annual premiums of $242 on a $75,000 policy for ten years. What amount could you borrow on your policy? $3,150

26. What amount could you borrow on a $200,000 policy that was 25 years old? $34,800

27. How much could you borrow on a 15-year old policy with a face value of $50,000? $4,000

28. What amount would you receive if you cancelled a $150,000 policy that you had held for 20 years? $18,600

Lesson 7.1 Life Insurance ▪ **287**

Assign

Assignment: Exercises 1–29, 32–45. Start with the basic arithmetic problems to be sure that students understand the underlying arithmetic in the exercises.

Assess

Ask students these questions:

1. How do you use the premium table to find the annual premium? **Find rate for age, gender, insurance type and multiply by the number of $1,000 units of insurance wanted.**

2. What steps do you use to find a policy's cash surrender value? **Find policy year in table and multiply by number of $1,000 units of policy face value.**

3. What steps do you take to find net cost of insurance? **Subtract dividends from annual premium.**

Reteach

STUDENT WORKBOOK To reteach Goal 1, demonstrate how to solve Exercise 1a. Then have students do Exercises 1b–1e.

To reteach Goal 2, demonstrate how to solve Exercise 5. Then have students do Exercise 6.

To reteach Goal 3, demonstrate how to solve Exercise 7. Then have students do Exercise 8.

SELECTED SOLUTIONS

13. $50,000 ÷ $1,000 = 50;
   50 × $27.75 = $1,387.50;
   50 × $11.61 = $580.50;
   $1,387.50 − $580.50 = $807

15. $17.44 − $14.08 = $3.36;
   $100,000 ÷ $1,000 = 100;
   $3.36 × 100 = $336; $336 × 20 = $6,720

16. $150,000 ÷ $1,000 = 150;
   150 × $1.91 = $286.50; $286.50 × 0.20 = $57.30

Bring in premium charts from term insurance ads from the mail, found on the Internet, or provided by an insurance agent. Discuss with students the factors these charts reveal that affect premiums such as smoking, gender longevity, occupation, etc.

Assign Exercise 30, Critical Thinking. Answers will vary depending on what students perceive are the insured's *needs* and *wants*. In general, the need for insurance varies with the number and type of dependents. A single person with no dependents may have *need* only for a small whole life policy that will cover burial. However, the person may *want* to carry a larger policy with a favorite charity as beneficiary.

The discussion should use the common purposes of insurance (see last sentence of gifted learner assignment, p. 282). A married couple, both working, with children, may choose a decreasing term policy to cover their home mortgage, a term policy to recover the spouse's lost income, and whole life policies to cover the costs of burial.

Assign Exercise 31, Critical Thinking. Student answers should include loss of death benefits to beneficiaries if loan is outstanding at death and how loan will be repaid since no monthly payments are usually required.

29. STRETCHING YOUR SKILLS Bill Woolsley paid annual premiums on a $50,000 whole life policy at a rate of $17.20 per $1,000. After ten years, he canceled the policy and found that its cash value was $49 per $1,000. Over the ten years, he received dividends of $318.55. For the time Bill had the policy, find the net cost of the insurance he held. $5,831.45

30. CRITICAL THINKING Four different types of life insurance were discussed in this lesson. Return to the list of insurance situations presented at the start of this lesson. Which type of life insurance, if any, would you recommend in each situation and why? See Enrich section for answers.

31. CRITICAL THINKING What concerns should a person have for borrowing money from the cash surrender value of their insurance policies?
See Enrich section for answers.

MIXED REVIEW

32. Write $128\frac{3}{5}\%$ as a decimal. 1.286

33. Find $12\frac{1}{2}\%$ of $184. $23

34. Multiply $217.80 by 22%, to the nearest hundredth. $47.92

35. $30.20 increased by 30% of itself is? $39.26

36. The average of 14, 28, 19, 22, and 18 is? 20.2

37. $\frac{2}{5} \div \frac{1}{8} = ?$ $3\frac{1}{5}$

38. Charlie Evers is paid $12.56 an hour and time-and-a-half for overtime. Last week he worked 40 regular and 4.5 overtime hours. What was his gross pay for the week? $587.18, Lesson 1.3

39. Sonia Ortiz earned $1,500 last year at her part-time job. Her parents claimed her as a dependent on their federal income tax return. What taxable income did Sonia have last year? $0, Lesson 2.3

40. Rosie McFarland's check register balance on October 31 was $374.60. In making a reconciliation statement, she found that a check for $17 was incorrectly recorded in the register as $71; she had no record in her register of a service charge of $2.80, earned interest of $0.71, and a deposit of $68.74. What was her correct check register balance? $495.25, Lesson 3.4

41. Umeki Akita repaid a loan of $3,200 in 15 monthly installments of $232.80 each. Use the annual percentage rate table in Chapter 4 to find the APR on his loan. $13\frac{1}{4}\%$, Lesson 4.6

42. The regional library system tax rate in Odell County is 2.5 mills per dollar of assessed value. Find the tax to be paid on property assessed at $87,000.
$217.50, Lesson 6.3

Lesson 7.1

Vi Foe is 25 and doesn't smoke. She owns a $200,000 whole life insurance policy.

43. Using the insurance premium table, what is her annual premium? $2,112

44. During this year, her policy paid a dividend of $62.10. What was the net cost of her policy for the year? $2,049.90

45. Roger canceled his $250,000 whole life policy. The cash/loan value for his policy at the time was $95 per $1,000 of insurance. How much did Roger receive when he cancelled his policy? $23,750

288 ■ **Chapter 7** Insurance and Investments

SELECTED SOLUTIONS

18. $600 ÷ $11.61 = $51.679586;
$51.679586 × $1,000 = $51,679.59, or $51,000

19. $600 ÷ $1.14 = $526.31578;
$526.31578 × $1,000 = $526,315.78, or $526,000

20. $8,000 ÷ $1,000 = 8; 8 × $12.80 = $102.40;
$102.40 − $18.90 = $83.50

24. $50,000 ÷ $1,000 = 50; 50 × $42 = $2,100

26. $200,000 ÷ $1,000 = 200; 200 × $174 = $34,800

7.2 Health Insurance

GOALS

- Calculate health insurance premiums
- Calculate health insurance benefits and coinsurance

Start Up

Wilbur Bradley has just entered college as a freshman. As part of the enrollment procedures, he is offered a health plan that covers him while he is enrolled as a student. Wilbur doesn't think he should spend the money on the premiums because he is young and healthy. He asks you for advice. What would you tell him?

Math Skill Builder

Review these math skills and solve the exercises that follow.

1. **Add** dollar amounts.
    Find the sum. $378 + $108 + $2,823 = $3,309

    1a. $4,298 + $218 + $48 $4,564

    1b. $376 + $294 + $1,397 $2,067

2. **Subtract** dollar amounts from dollar amounts.
    Find the difference. $3,298.28 − $1,089.27 = $2,209.01

    2a. $1,703.93 − $727.19 $ 976.74

    2b. $7,319.29 − $3,519.07 $3,800.22

3. **Multiply** dollar amounts by whole numbers and percents.
    Find the products. $45 × 12 = $540 and $798 × 35% = $798 × 0.35 = $279.30

    3a. $59.20 × 12 $710.40   **3b.** $197 × 6 $1,182

    3c. $488 × 65% $317.20   **3d.** $1,497 × 72% $1,077.84

■ Health Insurance Premiums

Health insurance, like other insurance, protects against financial loss. In this case, the financial loss is from medical bills. Employers often provide *group health insurance* as a job benefit for employees and their families. The employee usually pays part of the cost of the group policy. If you are not covered by a group policy, you may buy individual health insurance for yourself and your family, but it is usually more expensive.

Lesson 7.2 Health Insurance ■ **289**

Apply Goal 1

Do Example 1 at the board while students do the math at their desks.

Assign Check Your Understanding problems A and B to do in class. Walk about your classroom and check student work for errors and difficulties.

Teach Goal 2

Point out that major medical insurance offers more protection by paying higher maximum benefits than basic insurance pays. It is usually offered as an option to traditional health insurance plans.

Note that coordinated benefits clauses usually appear in health and accident insurance policies. This ensures that benefits and payments for services are not duplicated if parents and family members are covered by competing insurance plans

■ ONGOING ASSESSMENT

Call on students to explain these terms: group health insurance, annual deductible, and coinsurance.

Group health policies usually provide *basic health coverage*, including:

- *Hospitalization insurance*, which helps pay expenses of a hospital stay, such as hospital room, medicine, lab tests, X-rays, operating room.
- *Surgical insurance*, which covers the fees of doctors who do surgery or who help with surgery in or out of a hospital.
- *Medical insurance*, which pays the fees of other doctors who see you in or out of the hospital, as well as some other medical expenses, such as physical therapy.

You may supplement your basic health coverage with **major medical insurance**. It helps pay for hospital, surgical, medical, or other health care expenses due to a major illness or an injury. Often basic health insurance and major medical insurance policies are combined into one comprehensive health package.

Your employer may also have group plans for other health areas, such as dental insurance and vision insurance.

EXAMPLE 1

Lela Wendt's employer offers a health insurance plan that covers Lela, her husband and their child. The total monthly premium is $285, of which the employer pays 26%. How much does Lela pay for the health insurance for one year?

SOLUTION

Multiply the total monthly premium by 12.

$285 × 12 = $3,420   total annual premium

Multiply the total annual premium by 26%.

$3,420 × 0.26 = $889.20   part of annual premium paid by employer

Subtract the employer's share of the premium from the total premium.

$3,420 − $889.20 = $2,530.80   Lela's share of health insurance for year

> **PROBLEM SOLVING TIP**
>
> To find the employee share of the premium, deduct the employer's percentage share from 100%. The difference is the employee's percentage share. Then multiply the total premium by the employee's percentage share.

■ CHECK YOUR UNDERSTANDING

A. Ted Larkin's employer pays 50% of his annual health insurance premium. If the total monthly premium for the insurance is $57, what is Ted's share of the annual premium? $342

B. An employer provides dental health insurance to employees. The monthly premium cost per employee is $36. If the employees pay 65% of the premium, what is the total annual premium paid by an employee for the dental insurance? $280.80

■ Health Insurance Benefits and Coinsurance

Basic health insurance plans usually include an *annual deductible amount* for each insured person. When the health bills for a person covered by the plan exceed the deductible amount for that person, the insurance company begins to pay benefits.

■ *CHECK YOUR UNDERSTANDING SOLUTIONS*

A. $57 × 12 = $684; $684 × 0.50 = $342
B. $36 × 12 = $432; $432 × 0.65 = $280.80
C. $2,964 − $2,583 = $381; $2,583 − $500 = $2,083; $2,083 × 0.21 = $437.43; $381 + $500 + $437.43 = $1,318.43

D. $525 − $450 = $75; $450 × 0.10 = $45; $75 + $45 = $120

Major medical insurance plans usually have a deductible amount for *each* treated illness or injury. For example you may be required to pay the first $500 of a health bill for an injury before the insurance company begins to pay benefits.

Once the deductible amount has been met, you usually must pay part of the remaining health bills out of your own pocket. These part payments are called **coinsurance**, or *co-payments*. For example, you may be required to pay as coinsurance 15% of a surgery bill. Or, you may be required to pay a $10 co-payment for each visit to a doctor's office.

Usually coinsurance is stated as a percent and co-payments as a dollar amount. Both coinsurance and co-payments amount to the same thing. They are your share of the bill.

Finally, the total health bill may not be covered by your policy. For example, a psychiatrist may charge $85 for each office visit but your insurance policy may set a maximum benefit of $70 for such visits.

To find how much of a health bill you will have to pay, you must first determine how much of the bill is covered by your policy. Next, you must determine if you have any deductible amount left to pay for the year. Then you must know what coinsurance percent you are responsible for.

Total Bill − Covered Amount = Uncovered Amount

(Covered Amount − Deductible) × Coinsurance Rate = Coinsurance Amount

Uncovered Amount + Deductible + Coinsurance = Amount Patient Must Pay

EXAMPLE 2

Jolene Ridgeway underwent surgery for an injury. The hospital portion of the bill was $5,298, of which only $4,875 was covered by Jolene's group medical insurance policy. In addition, the coinsurance amount of the bill was 18%, and the remaining deductible she had for the year was $300. How much of the hospital bill must Jolene pay?

SOLUTION
Subtract the covered portion from the total bill.

$5,298 − $4,875 = $423   uncovered amount

Subtract the deductible from the covered amount.

$4,875 − $300 = $4,575

Then multiply by the coinsurance rate.

$4,575 × 0.18 = $823.50   coinsurance amount

Add the uncovered amount, the deductible amount, and the coinsurance amount.

$423 + $300 + $823.50 = $1,546.50   amount Jolene must pay

■ **Apply Goal 2**

Work through Example 2 at the board while students work with you at their desks.

Assign Check Your Understanding problems C and D for classwork. Check student work for difficulties by looking over their shoulders.

BUSINESS TIP

Indemnity plans allow you to choose your own doctors and hospitals but the coinsurance amounts are usually higher than HMOs. HMOs usually require you to use specified doctors and hospitals.

BUSINESS TIP

Group policies are issued on a group of people, such as all the employees in a firm. Group policies usually do not require the employee to take a physical examination.

COMMON ERRORS

Students may forget to subtract the deductible amount from the covered amount before they apply the coinsurance rate. Another common error is that students correctly find the coinsurance but then forget to add the deductible to the coinsurance amount and the uncovered amount to find the total that the insured must pay. Remind students to follow the exact order of the procedures shown in the examples.

Wrap Up

Review the Start Up. Compare the advice given in the Wrap Up to the earlier class discussion. Lead into a discussion of the health care needs of people in various stages of their lives.

TEAM MEETING

Assign the Team Meeting. Help students to identify key words to use in search engines. Have selected students report their findings to the class orally. Student teams should submit their lists, the web addresses of the Internet sources they used, and the name and insurance company of the agent interviewed.

■ CHECK YOUR UNDERSTANDING

C. The surgery portion of Ruiz Alicea's total medical bill was $2,964. Only $2,583 was covered by his group medical insurance policy. Ruiz's coinsurance for the surgery was 21%, and his remaining annual deductible was $500. What amount of the surgery bill must Ruiz pay? $1,318.43

D. Elisa Renteria's dental insurance plan pays a maximum of $450 for a crown. It also requires her to pay 10% coinsurance. Her policy does not have a deductible. The bill she receives for a crown from her dentist is $525. How much of that bill will Elisa pay? $120

Wrap Up

You might tell Wilbur that accidents can happen to anyone at anytime. Also, while he is less likely than older people to become seriously ill, the possibility still exists. By taking out the policy, he will be insuring against the risk of large health bills with a relatively small amount of insurance premium.

TEAM MEETING

With two other students, investigate the advantages and disadvantages of health maintenance organization health plans, or HMOs, and indemnity health plans. You should use Internet search tools and talk to at least one health insurance agent to obtain your information.

You need to define a health maintenance organization plan. Name the requirements and the general premise under which they operate. Also define an indemnity health plan and its requirements and how they function.

List the advantages and disadvantages of each. It is a good idea to question adults who participate in each type of program and get their opinions.

EXERCISES

1. $298 + $12,216 + $4,228
$16,742

2. $9,039 − $457.89
$8581.11

3. $3,158 × 12%
$378.96

4. Bella Melino elects to be covered by her employer's vision health insurance program. The program covers part of the expense of eye examinations, eye glasses or contact lenses, and office visits. The total monthly premium is $105.36, of which the employer pays 45%. Bella's share of the monthly premium is deducted from her monthly paycheck. What is the amount of the deduction? $57.95

The annual premium for Chi Kuo's health insurance plan is made up of $2,844 for hospitalization and medical; $1,649 for surgery; and $428 for major medical. Chi's employer pays 42% of the premium.

5. What is the total annual premium for Chi's health plan?
$4,921

6. What is Chi's share of the total annual premium?
$2,854.18

292 ■ Chapter 7 Insurance and Investments

SELECTED SOLUTIONS

4. 100% − 45% = 55%; $105.36 × 0.055 = $57.95   **6.** 100% − 42% = 58%; $4,921 × 0.58 = $2,854.18

5. $2,844 + $1,649 + $428 = $4,921

Rosa Suarez pays for a general health plan, a dental health plan, and a vision health plan through her employer. The monthly premiums are: general health, $209; dental health, $265; vision health, $59. Her employer's share of these plans is: general health, 35%; dental health, 45%; vision health, 75%.

7. What is the total monthly premium for all of Rosa's health plans? $533

8. What is her employer's share of that total monthly premium? $236.65

Stanislov Pulkin works for a county agency as an accountant. His employer provides group health policies for basic health care, major medical health care, and dental health care. The annual premium for Stanislov consists of $3,190 for basic health, $518 for major medical, and $2,875 for dental. The county picks up 57% of his basic, 60% of his major medical, and 32% of his dental health premiums.

9. What is the total annual premium for all of Stanislov's health plans? $6,583

10. What is his share of the total annual premium? $3,533.90

11. If the county deducts his share from his weekly paycheck, what is the amount of the deduction? $67.96

Zena Tubicek can buy a group major medical insurance plan from her employer at a monthly premium of $56 or buy an individual policy with similar coverage from another insurance company for $938 annually.

12. What is the difference in annual premiums between the employer's group policy and the individual policy? $266

13. By what percent, to the nearest tenth of a percent, does the individual policy premium exceed the group policy premium? 39.6%

14. Frank Duval was hospitalized for an illness for 12 days. The cost of his hospital room was $458 a day. The cost of medical services was $2,492. His insurance company covered the full amount of the medical services but allowed only 8 days of hospitalization for his illness. The policy also requires $250 in deductible and 15% coinsurance for the remaining hospital room and medical services costs. What amount did Frank have to pay for his illness? $2,967.90

Davey's major medical policy has a $1,000 deductible feature and he must pay 10% coinsurance. He is injured in an accident and his health care bills amount to $21,700.

15. What amount will be paid by his insurance company? $18,630

16. What amount will he pay? $3,070

Molly Nairah had three x-rays taken at a total cost of $230. Under her major medical coverage, the insurance company paid 80% of the cost of X-rays after a $25 deductible fee for each x-ray.

17. What was the company's share of the cost of the x-rays? $124

18. What was Molly's share of the cost? $106

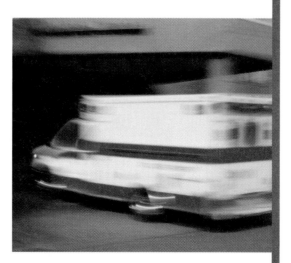

Lesson 7.2 Health Insurance ■ **293**

Assign

Assignment: Exercises 1–21 and 23, 25–35. Start with the beginning problems to be sure students understand the underlying arithmetic in the Exercises.

Assess

Check student answers to the exercises by calling on them in class, collecting and grading selected problems, or by observing students at work.

Ask students to define the bolded and italicized terms in the lesson and use them in sentences.

Reteach

STUDENT WORKBOOK
Redemonstrate the steps in Example 1 using Exercise 1. Then have students complete Exercise 2 at their desks. Redemonstrate the steps in Example 2 using Exercise 3 paying special attention to student problems listed in Common Errors. Then have students complete Exercises 4–5 at their desks.

SELECTED SOLUTIONS

7. $209 + $265 + $59 = $533

8. $209 × 0.35 = $73.15; $265 × 0.45 = $119.25;
$59 × 0.75 = $44.25;
$73.15 + $119.25 + $44.25 = $236.65

14. 12 − 8 = 4;
4 × $458 = $1,832; 8 × $458 = $3,664;

$3,664 + $2,492 = $6,156;
$6,156 − $250 = $5,906; $5,906 × 0.15 = $885.90; $1,832 + $250 + $885.90 = $2,967.90

17. $25 × 3 = $75; $230 − $75 = $155;
$155 × 0.80 = $124

Assign and discuss with students Exercise 24, Critical Thinking. Some possible ideas: reduced rates for people who take care of their health (such as people who do not smoke, maintain a stable weight, etc.), health insurance rates set up like car insurance (the higher the deductible or co-payment, the less your premium).

Have students investigate health insurance coverage in countries that have national health care programs, such as Canada.

Close

Have students tell you how to do Exercise 22, step by step, while you write on the board or transparency. Make them spell out the labels for each part of the answer.

With their books closed, have them tell you the formula for finding the solution to Exercise 21.

■ STUDENT PORTFOLIO

Students might consider placing the lists they prepared in the Team Meeting in their portfolios. They might also consider placing a copy of Exercise 21 and the labeled solution to it in their portfolios.

Eve and Ollie Dunbar's major medical policy pays 90% of covered expenses for each of them in any year. A $500 deductible feature applies to each person's claim. Last year the Dunbars made two medical claims. Eve's claim was for $1,230; Ollie's claim was for $1,870. The insurance company did not cover $170 of Eve's claim and $225 of Ollie's claim. What amount did the Dunbars receive from their insurance company for

19. Eve's claim? $504

20. Ollies's claim? $1,030.50

21. Julie Crane required lengthy hospital and medical care. The fees of her doctors were $128,700 and covered at 90% by her major medical policy. Her hospital expenses were $44,460, and the policy covered 85% of the hospital bills beyond a $500 deductible. After Julie left the hospital, a physical therapist made 15 visits to her home at $95 a visit. Julie's policy paid 70% of the therapy bills. Of the total expenses, what amount did Julie have to pay? $20,391.50

22. Mehta Goldberg was hospitalized for 12 days. Her total bill for medical care was $21,570. Mehta's major medical coverage pays for 85% of medical expenses above a $750 deductible. How much of the bill does Mehta owe after the insurance company pays its share? $3,873

23. **STRETCHING YOUR SKILLS**   An employee's share of a vision insurance policy premium was $130. This was 65% of the policy premium. What was the policy premium? $200

24. **CRITICAL THINKING**   The costs of health care and insurance have gone up sharply in recent years. What might insurance companies do to reduce health insurance costs? See Enrich section for answer.

MIXED REVIEW

25. Add $34.12 + $19.98 + $108.29 + $72.07 + $2,781. $3,015.46

26. Multiply 208.108 × 0.28, to the nearest hundredth. 58.27

27. Divide 642 by 46 to the nearest thousandth. 13.957

28. $1\frac{5}{8} - 1\frac{1}{4} = ?$ $\frac{3}{8}$

29. How many days are there from July 17 to September 28? 73

30. $13.30 is what percent greater than $10.64? 25%

Ben Arnold worked 48 hours last week. He earned $11.72 per hour for the first 37.5 hours. For time worked over 37.5 hours, he earned time-and-a-half. Deductions of $172.29 were made from his paycheck.

31. Find Ben's gross pay for the week. $624.09, Lesson 1.3

32. Find his net pay for the week. $451.80, Lesson 2.1

33. You added a deck to your home. The materials cost $1,796 and the labor cost $2,398. In your area there is a 4.5% state and a 1.5% city sales tax on the materials. What was the total bill for the deck? $4,301.76, Lesson 5.1

34. A truck which originally cost $16,450 is traded in eight years later for $3,290. What was the average annual depreciation on the truck? $1,645, Lesson 6.6

35. After 10 years, Lisa Myers canceled her $35,000 life insurance policy and took the cash value of $57 per $1,000. The annual premiums on the policy were $370. While the policy was in effect, she received a total of $217.90 in dividends. What was the net cost of the policy? $1,922.90, Lesson 7.1

SELECTED SOLUTIONS

19. $1,230 − $170 = $1,060; $1,060 − $500 = $560;
$560 × 0.90 = $504

21. 100% − 90% = 10%; 100% − 85% = 15%;
100% − 70% = 30%;
$128,700 × 0.10 = $12,870;

$44,460 − $500 = $43,960;
$43,960 × 0.15 = $6,594; 15 × $95 = $1,425;
$1,425 × 0.30 = $427.50;
$12,870 + $500 + $6,594 + $427.50 = $20,391.50

23. $130 ÷ 0.65 = $200

7.3 Disability Insurance

GOAL

- Calculate disability insurance benefits

Start Up

Ghayda Meguid is 35 and has 2 children. She has purchased as much term life insurance as she thinks she needs. However, she has no disability insurance. She works as a systems programmer for a software company and doesn't believe she is at risk for injuries. What would you advise her to do?

Math Skill Builder

Review these math skills and solve the exercises that follow.

1 **Divide** dollar amounts by whole numbers.
Find the quotient. $280,000 \div 4 = $70,000

1a. $105,000 \div 3
$35,000

1b. $325,000 \div 4
$81,250

1c. $1,286,700 \div 20
$64,335

2 **Multiply** dollar amounts by percents.
Find the product. $25,000 \times 60\% = $25,000 \times 0.6 = $15,000

2a. $18,290 \times 30\%
$5,487

2b. $21,800 \times 45\%
$9,810

2c. $54,790 \times 65\%
$35,613.50

3 **Subtract** dollar amounts.
Find the difference. $1,560 - $253 = $1,307

3a. $2,250 - $314 $1,936

3b. $1,230 - $428 $802

3c. $1,548 - $217 $1,331

3d. $2,830 - $139 $2,691

■ Disability Insurance Benefits

Disability insurance pays you a portion of the income you lose if you cannot work due to a health condition or an injury.

One form of disability insurance is *short-term disability insurance*. This policy pays you a portion of your income for a short period of time, such as 13–26 weeks. Usually there is a maximum amount that can be paid out per week or month. Some people choose to buy an accident policy or rely on their savings instead of buying short-term disability insurance.

Another form of disability insurance is *long-term disability insurance*. This type of policy may cover you for several years or until you reach retirement age. The longer the term of coverage, the higher the premium.

> **BUSINESS TIP**
>
> The portion of your income paid by insurance is usually stated as a percentage of your income. It is called the *benefits percentage*.

Lesson 7.3 Disability Insurance ■ 295

Do Example 1 at the board or on a transparency while students do the math at their desks.

Assign Check Your Understanding problems A and B for in class work. Walk around your classroom and examine student work for errors and problems.

■ **ONGOING ASSESSMENT**

Place the following annual wages on the board and ask students to calculate the average: $24,800, $25,600, and $26,400 **($25,600)**. Then ask students to multiply the average by 55% **($14,080)**.

Call on students to explain the meaning of average wages for 3 years **(sum ÷ 3)** and a benefit percentage **(the portion of your average predisability income paid as benefits)**.

Disability insurance is usually bought through a group plan offered through your employer. You can also buy individual rather than group disability insurance, but it is usually more expensive.

If your job is covered by social security, you also may be eligible for disability insurance through the federal government. Your annual social security statement shows how much monthly disability benefits you are eligible to receive.

If you are injured on the job, you may be covered by *Worker's compensation insurance*. This insurance covers lost wages and medical expenses from on-the-job injuries. It is usually required by state governments and for work on federal contracts and paid for by the employer.

The benefits you receive from disability insurance depend on whether you are totally or partially disabled, how long you have worked, your wages, percent of your wages that are paid as benefits, and other factors. Also, the benefits you receive may be reduced by the benefits you receive from worker's compensation and social security disability insurance.

EXAMPLE 1

Phil Kustin injures himself in an accident and can no longer work. His disability policy will pay 60% of his average annual wages for the last 3 years. His wages were $28,500, $29,070, and $29,940. What is Phil's monthly disability benefit.

SOLUTION
Add the annual wages, then divide the total by the number of years.

$28,500 + $29,070 + $29,940 = $87,510

$87,510 ÷ 3 = $29,170   average wages for last 3 years

Multiply the average wages by the benefit percentage.

$29,170 × 0.6 = $17,502   annual disability benefit

Divide the annual disability benefit by 12.

$17,502 ÷ 12 = $1,458.50   monthly disability benefit

■ **CHECK YOUR UNDERSTANDING**

A. Yan Kaponovich becomes totally disabled. His group disability policy's benefit percentage is 65% of his average annual salary for the last 3 years. His annual salaries were $45,200; $48,300, and $49,900. What monthly benefit amount will he receive? $2,589.17

B. Kelly O'Hara is injured and is covered by a group disability policy and by social security disability insurance. Her group policy pays 45% of her average wages for the last 4 years, less any other disability benefits she receives from other policies. Social security disability will pay her $225 a month. If her wages for the last 4 years were $34,600; $34,900; $40,800, and $42,000, what is the total amount Kelly will receive a month from her group policy? $1,202.81

■ *CHECK YOUR UNDERSTANDING SOLUTIONS*

A. $45,200 + $48,300 + $49,900 = $143,400;
$143,400 ÷ 3 = $47,800;
$47,800 × 0.65 = $31,070;
$31,070 ÷ 12 = $2,589.17

B. $34,600 + $34,900 + $40,800 + $42,000 = $152,300; $152,300 ÷ 4 = $38,075;
$38,075 × 0.45 = $17,133.75;
$17,133.75 ÷ 12 = $1,427.81;
$1,427.81 − $225 = $1,202.81

You might advise Ghayda that she can be injured in her home and in her car, too. About one third of all Americans will suffer a serious disability between the ages of 35 and 65 and 1 in 5 of all Americans will become disabled to some extent during their lives. If she becomes totally or partially disabled, her family will lose her income. She should consider buying disability insurance and she should check to see if she has coverage through worker's compensation and social security.

COMMUNICATION

Life insurance policies provide income to your survivors when you die. Disability insurance policies provide income to you and your dependents if you become unable to work due to injury or illness. Use the Internet to find answers to these questions:

1. What percent of employees of US companies are offered group life insurance policies and what percent are offered group disability insurance?

2. What is the chance that a person who is 21 years of age will die versus the chance that that person will become disabled?

Prepare a report of your findings. The report should include the web page addresses of your sources of information.

EXERCISES

Perform the indicated operation.

1. $569,400 ÷ 12 $47,450
2. $45,800 ÷ 5 $9,160
3. $5,884 − $885 $4,999
4. $22,509 × 10% $2,250.90
5. $31,770 × 60% $19,062
6. $12,929 − $4,228 $8,701

Louisa Tibaldi's group disability policy has a benefit percentage of 65% of her average annual salary for the last 2 years. Her annual salary for the last 2 years was $65,200 and $68,300.

7. What is Louisa's average annual salary for the last 2 years? $66,750

8. What monthly benefit amount will she receive? $3,615.63

9. Fayad Mehkta is insured under a disability policy that calculates his benefits percentage at 2.25% for each year he has worked for his company. If Fayad has worked 12 years at the company, what is his benefits percentage? 27%

Trisha Dabney's disability insurance policy will pay her 45% of her average annual wages for the last 4 years. It will reduce the benefits paid by any amounts Trisha receives from worker's compensation insurance. Trisha's wages for the last 4 years were $24,560; $25,100; $25,820; and $26,200.

10. What was Trisha's average annual wage for the last 4 years? $25,420

11. If she receives $467 monthly from worker's compensation, what monthly income will her disability insurance company pay her? $486.25

Lesson 7.3 Disability Insurance ■ **297**

SELECTED SOLUTIONS

7. $65,200 + $68,300 = $133,500;
$133,500 ÷ 2 = $66,750

8. $66,750 × 0.65 = $43,387.50;
$43,387.50 ÷ 12 = $3,615.63

9. 2.25% × 12 = 27%

12. 17 × 2.5% = 42.5%;

13. $3,500 × 0.425 = $1,487.50

Renaldo Rodriguez's group disability policy pays a benefit percentage of 2.5% for each year that he has worked for his company. The benefit percentage is applied to his average monthly compensation for the last 36 months. Renaldo worked for 17 years for the company at an average monthly wage of $3,500 for the last 36 months.

12. What is his disability benefit percentage? 42.5%

13. What monthly benefit amount would he receive? $1,487.50

A college provides short-term disability insurance for its employees. The benefits depend on years of service at the college and the benefit percentage the employee chooses. The chart below shows the number of weeks employees would receive benefits for depending on whether they chose to receive 100%, 80%, or 60% of their weekly income.

The Number of Weeks an Employee Will Receive Benefits			
Benefit Percentage Chosen			
Years of Service	**100% of Wages**	**80% of Wages**	**60% of Wages**
Less than 5	1	4	5
5 but less than 10	5	5	10
10 but less than 15	5	10	15
15 but less than 26	5	15	20

14. How many weeks of benefits will an employee who has worked for 7 years receive if the employee chooses a benefit percentage of 80% of his or her salary? 5

15. Kim Lucas has worked at the college for 12 years. How many weeks of coverage would she receive if she chose a benefit percentage of 60%? 15

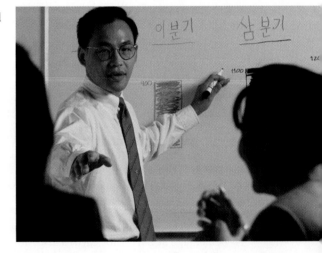

16. Jose Fuentes worked for 21 years at the college before being injured. If Jose needs to receive benefits for 20 weeks, what benefits percentage should Jose choose? 60%

STRETCHING YOUR SKILLS A worker receives $27,830 in monthly disability benefits based on the average of her last 3 years of salary. If her salary for the last 3 years was $49,300; 50,300; and $52,200

17. What was her average salary for the last 3 years? $50,600

18. What benefits percentage did she receive? 55%

298 ■ Chapter 7 Insurance and Investments

19. **CRITICAL THINKING** What reasons might be used to explain why disability payments are usually less than the last salary or wages of an employee?
See Enrich section for answer.

MIXED REVIEW

20. Write $1\frac{1}{3}$ as a percent. $133\frac{1}{3}\%$

21. What percent is 77.25 of 618? 12.5%

22. Divide 592 by 1.06, to the nearest tenth. 558.5

23. $60.40 is what percent less than $78.52, to the nearest tenth percent? 23.1%

24. Find the average of $1,250, $1,280, $1,297, and $1,320. $1,286.75

25. Divide $\frac{3}{8}$ by $\frac{2}{5}$. $\frac{15}{16}$

26. Alberto Viña is paid $13.20 an hour for the first eight hours of work each day and time-and-a-half for overtime past 8 hours. Last week Alberto worked these hours: Mon., 8; Tues., 10; Wed., 6; Thurs., 7; Fri., 10. What was Alberto's gross pay for the week? $567.60, Lesson 1.3

27. Ivy Washington had a balance of $259.12 in her checking account at the start of the day. During the day she wrote a check for $35, withdrew $100 using her ATM card, and deposited a rebate check for $25 she received from a recent purchase. What is her new balance after her bank processes the items? $149.12, Lesson 3.2

Tony Giardino borrowed $525 for one year from his bank using a non-interest bearing promissory note. The rate of discount was 16%.

28. What amount did Tony receive? $441, Lesson 4.2

29. What true rate of interest did Tony pay, to the nearest percent? 19%, Lesson 4.2

30. Sally Parker's Internet service provider charges $15 a month for an unlimited dial-up Internet connection. She also paid $25 to start the service. To allow her to have a concurrent voice and Internet connection, Sally had another phone line installed in her home. The installation fee was $75 and the monthly basic charge is $16.75 for the phone line. What was Sally's total cost for the phone and Internet connections during the first 12 months? $481, Lesson 5.5

31. Tom Wilson received a $2,300 trade-in for a car that he originally paid $12,500 for six years ago. What was the average annual depreciation on the car? $1,700, Lesson 6.6

32. Sean O'Leary bought a $200,000 term insurance policy. The annual premium was $1.07 per $1,000 of insurance. What was Sean's annual premium for the policy? $214, Lesson 7.1

33. Rosa Carlotto's employer pays 65% of his health insurance premium. If the total monthly premium for the insurance is $127, what is Rosa's share? $44.45, Lesson 7.2

Roger Tulane invested $10,000 in a 4-year CD that paid 6% annual interest. When he withdrew $500 at the end of 3 years, he was charged an early withdrawal penalty of 6 months' interest.

34. What was the amount of the penalty? $15, Lesson 3.7

35. What net withdrawal will Roger receive? $485, Lesson 3.7

36. Tom O'Malley wants to download a document that is 95.6 KB in size over the Internet. If Tom has a true Internet connection speed of 44 kbps, how long will it take to download the file, to the nearest second? 17, Lesson 5.5

Lesson 7.3 Disability Insurance ■ **299**

TEACHING STRATEGIES Communication

Assign each student a writing problem. They are to assume that they are employed in the human resource department of a firm that carries a group disability insurance policy on its workers similar to the facts presented in Exercises 7–8 on page 297. Each student is to prepare a memo addressed to new human resource employees describing how the benefits for Louisa Tibaldi should be calculated. Have students use one of the memo templates provided by their word processing software and keep their memos to no more than 1 page in length.

Start Up

Have students read the Start Up. Discuss with students the advice they would give Vanessa.

Math Skill Builder

The addition and multiplication of money amounts are skills that are used in the lesson. So is the ability to rewrite percents as decimals.

Have students complete all exercises in Math Skill Builder 1–4.

■ Teach Goal 1

Point out that bonds are issued in par values that will appeal to those who the issuer wants and expects to buy them. Bonds may be issued with par values of $10,000 if it is expected that financial institutions are likely to be the predominant buyers. Face values of $1,000 or $500 will be able to attract buyers with fewer financial resources.

Students should understand that before investing in bonds, they should have enough accessible savings to live on for at least 3 to 6 months, have investment goals, develop an investment strategy, and be familiar with different investment options and their associated risks.

7.4 Buying Bonds

GOALS

- Calculate the market price of bonds
- Calculate the total investment in bonds

Start Up

Vanessa Olemkov earns $44,500 a year. She is considering investing all of her savings in the stock market because she has been told that the market provides the most return for your dollar over the long run. What advice might you give Vanessa?

Math Skill Builder

Review these math skills and solve the exercises that follow.

1 **Multiply** dollar amounts by whole numbers.
Find the product. $1,075 \times 4 = $4,300

    1a. 504×6 $3,024   **1b.** $1,085 \times 9$ $9,765   **1c.** 509×8 $4,072

2 **Multiply** dollar amounts by percents.
Find the product. $1,000 \times 106\% = $1,000 \times 1.06 = $1,060

    2a. $500 \times 97\%$ $485   **2b.** $1,000 \times 95\%$ $950   **2c.** $500 \times 101\%$ $505

    2d. $1,000 \times 103.2\%$ $1,032   **2e.** $500 \times 6.5\%$ $32.50   **2f.** $1,000 \times 7.8\%$ $78

3 **Add** dollar amounts.
Find the sum. $1,050 + $55 = $1,105

    3a. $512 + 28 $540   **3b.** $1,040 + 65 $1,105   **3c.** $519 + 632 $1,151

4 **Write** percents as decimals.
Write 103\% as a decimal. 103\% = 1.03

    4a. 106\%   1.06   **4b.** 108.9\%   1.089   **4c.** 98\%   0.98   **4d.** 96.4\%   0.964

■ Market Price of Bonds

Bonds are a form of long-term promissory note. **Bonds** are a written promise to repay the money loaned on the due date. *Bondholders*, or the people who own the bonds, may keep them until the due date or sell them to other investors.

Bonds are usually issued with a face, or par value of $1,000 (see table on next page). Bonds may also be issued with other par values, such as $500, $5,000, or $10,000. Par value is the amount of money that the *issuer*, or the organization that sells the bonds, agrees to pay the bondholder on the due date.

COMMON ERRORS

Some students will have more difficulty expressing as decimals the prices of bonds selling at a premium than the prices of bonds selling at a discount. Stress that expressing a percent as a decimal means moving the decimal to the left two places, whether the percent is 97.xxx% or 103.xxx%. Students also may have more difficulty with bonds that have face values of $500 rather than $1,000. Stress that the market price of a bond with a par value of $500 is found in exactly the same way as one with $1,000: multiply the par value by the decimal price.

The *market value* of a bond is its selling price and may be different from par value. If the market value is more than par value, the bond is selling at a **premium**. If the market value is less than the par value, the bond is selling at a **discount**. The amount of the premium or discount is the difference between the market value and the par value.

The market price, or market value, of a bond is quoted as a percent of the par value. For example, a price quotation of 97.056 means 97.056% of the par value. This bond is selling at a discount. To find a bond's market price, multiply its par value by the percent. If the price of a $500 par value bond is 102.182, the market price is 102.182% of $500, or $510.91. This bond is selling at a premium.

EXAMPLE 1

Edgewood School Bonds are selling at 97.223. What is the price of one of the school's $1,000 bonds? Are these bonds selling at a discount or a premium?

SOLUTION

Convert the market price to a decimal and multiply by the bond's par value.

$97.223 = 0.97223; 0.97223 \times \$1,000 = \$972.23$ market price

The bond is selling at a discount because the price is less than the par value.

■ CHECK YOUR UNDERSTANDING

A. AGL Industries $1,000 bonds are quoted at 103.883. What is the market price of the bonds? Are they selling for a discount or premium? $1,038.83; premium

B. Millville Water District bonds are selling at 96.225. What is the market price of one of their $500 bonds? What is the amount of discount on each bond?
$481.13; $18.87

■ Total Investment in Bonds

Bonds are usually bought and sold through a broker, who is a dealer in stocks and bonds. *Full service* brokers provide advice on what and when to buy and sell. They charge a *broker's commission* or brokerage fee but the commission is usually included as part of the price the buyer pays for a bond and not shown separately. *Discount* and *online brokers* usually offer less financial help but also charge less commission. They usually show their commission rates on their web sites.

Lesson 7.4 Buying Bonds ■ 301

■ Apply Goal 1

Work through Example 1 with students completing the math at their desks.

Note to students that bond market prices are commonly stated as percents to three decimal places and that these are rewritten to decimals of five places.

Assign Check Your Understanding problems A and B for completion in class. Examine student work at their desks for errors or problems.

■ Teach Goal 2

Discuss with students why bonds are relatively more secure than stocks. Compare bonds to mortgages in that physical assets usually secure both.

Explain the difference between municipal bonds and corporate bonds and provide examples of municipal bonds in your area (roadway bonds, water plant bonds, etc.) Point out that some municipal bonds are insured, which means that if a municipality fails to support its bonds, the insurance policy will repay the principal and interest due bondholders.

Work through Example 2 with students working at their desks.

Assign Check Your Understanding problems C and D for classwork. Check student deskwork for difficulties.

■ **ONGOING ASSESSMENT**
Ask students if Clara paid any commission when she bought Xnet bonds in Check Your Understanding C (yes, it was included in purchase price).

Wrap **Up**

Review the Start Up. Ask students why people invest in bonds rather than in stocks or other investments. Factors such as greater security of the principal and steady income should surface.

Ask students to research the highs and lows of the stock market in each of the last 3 years. Have them use the Web as a source and the Dow Jones Industrial average to measure the market's highs and lows. If possible, have them print out a chart portraying the DJIA during the 3 years. Suggest they start their search looking at a brokerage firm's web site. Help them interpret their search results and use the data to affirm or discount their advice to Vanessa given in the Start Up.

WORKPLACE WINDOW

Invite a financial advisor to speak about the topics in Workplace Window. Have students complete their work first so that they can ask intelligent questions.

To find the total investment in bonds, you must find the market price of one bond, add the commission if it is known, and multiply by the number of bonds bought.

Total Bond Investment = (Market Price + Commission) × Number of Bonds

EXAMPLE 2

Leroy Walker bought 10, $1,000 Regis, Inc. bonds at 104.113 from a broker. The broker charges $4 per bond commission. What was Leroy's total investment?

SOLUTION
Convert the market price to a decimal and multiply by the par value.

104.113 = 1.04113; $1,000 × 1.04113 = $1,041.13   market price of 1 bond

Add the commission charge to the market price.

$1,041.13 + $4 = $1,045.13   total price of bond plus commission

Multiply the total price of 1 bond by the number of bonds bought.

10 × $1,045.13 = $10,451.30   total investment

■ **CHECK YOUR UNDERSTANDING**

C. Clara Maliszewski bought 10, $1,000 Xnet Corporation bonds at 97.297. No commission was shown. What is the total investment Clara has in the bonds? $9,729.70

D. Taylor Wilson bought 15, $1,000 Maryville Sewer District bonds at 103.228. The broker charged $3 per bond commission. What total investment did Taylor make in the bonds? $15,529.20

Wrap **Up**

Look at the Start Up problem at the start of this lesson. While it is true that the stock market has been a good investment over the long run, Vanessa may need money in the short run for emergencies or job loss. Placing all her savings in the stock market may mean that she must make withdrawals for emergencies when the market is low. Many financial experts advise keeping enough money in savings accounts, money market accounts, and short-term CDs to cover at least 3-6 months of your income. They may also recommend putting some savings into income producing investments like bonds.

WORKPLACE WINDOW

FINANCIAL ADVISOR Investigate the job of financial advisor in your state. Describe the typical duties of the job. Identify the typical education requirements, if any. Check to see if your state requires any licensing, testing, or certification of people with that job title. Use the resources of the Web. Some tips: go to the Web sites for the Dictionary of Occupational Titles, the Certified Financial Planner Board of Standards, and the National Association of Securities Dealers Regulation. Prepare a report of your findings and list your sources of information.

CONNECTION TO FINANCE

Have small teams of students research bond ratings. The research should include what rating indicates the maximum safety and what rating indicates substantial risk, who rates bonds, and how the ratings or changes in ratings affect bond prices.

EXERCISES

Find the product or sum.

1. $629 × 10 $6,290

2. $2,198 × 9 $19,782

3. $1,000 × 102.7% $1,027

4. $500 × 93.6% $468

5. $1,108 + $77 $1,185

6. $521 + $48 $569

State the market price, in dollars and cents, of each $1,000 bond below. Also state whether the bond is selling at a discount or premium.

7. 92.877 $928.77; disc.

8. 89.231 $892.31; disc.

9. 103.088 $1,030.88, prem.

10. 102.662 $1,026.62; prem.

11. 109.836 $1,098.36; prem.

12. 88.114 $881.14; disc.

Find the amount of money invested in each bond purchase below.
Madison County, $1,000 bonds:

13. 5 @ 91.445 $4,572.25

14. 12 @ 88.331 $10,599.72

15. 20 @ 106.292 $21,258.40

Eggleston Power Company, $1,000 bonds:

16. 6 @ 99.323 $5,959.38

17. 15 @ 94.494 $14,174.10

18. 18 @ 102.313 $18,416.34

Teasdale Transportation Authority, $500 bonds:

19. 24 @ 114.673 $13,760.76

20. 8 @ 92.555 $3,702.20

21. 12 @ 79.447 $4,766.82

22. Rob Adams invested in 25 bonds with a par value of $1,000 each. The quoted price for each bond was 110.345. His broker charged $3.50 per bond commission. How much did Rob invest? $27,673.75

23. Simone Tremont bought 8, $1,000 bonds at 88.563. No commission was shown. What was her total investment in the bonds? $7,085.04

24. Olaf Hansen bought 4, $1,000 bonds at 88.559. Two days ago the price of the bonds was 87.443. What was the amount of Olaf's investment in the bonds? $3,542.36

Leslie Ikwelugo buys a $1,000 bond at 105.874. The broker charges $3 commission per bond with a minimum of $30 commission per order.

25. What commission was Leslie charged? $30

26. What was the total amount she invested in the bond? $1,088.74

27. What is the amount of premium she paid on the bond? $58.74

Henry Schmidt bought 6, $500 bonds at 98.580.

28. What is his total investment in the bonds? $2,957.40

29. What discount did he receive on each bond? $7.10

30. **CRITICAL THINKING**   If a bond promises a bondholder a guaranteed price at the maturity date, why may the market value be more or less than the par value?   See Enrich section for answer.

31. **CRITICAL THINKING**   Corporations often use their land, buildings, or equipment as collateral for the money they borrow. If the loan is not repaid, the bondholders may take over the corporation's property. Since the collateral of a company backs these bonds, does that mean there is no risk involved in purchasing a bond?   See Enrich section for answer.

Lesson 7.4 Buying Bonds ▪ 303

SELECTED SOLUTIONS

22. 110.345 = 1.10345; $1,000 = $1,103.45;
$1,103.45 + $3.50 = $1,106.95;
$1,106.95 × 25 = $27,673.75

23. 88.563 = 0.88563; $1,000 × 0.88563 = $885.63;
$885.63 × 8 = $7,085.04

26. 105.874 = 1.05874; $1,000 × 1.05874 = $1,058.74;
$1,058.74 + $30 = $1,088.74

27. $1,058.74 − $1,000 = $58.74

MIXED REVIEW

32. Find the sums and grand total.

$$24.0 + 16.0 + 12.5 + 9.2 \qquad 61.7$$
$$\underline{12.6 + 22.7 + 18.6 + 6.3} \qquad 60.2$$
$$36.6 + 38.7 + 31.1 + 15.5 = \qquad 121.9$$

33. Divide 1,560 by 27 to the nearest hundredth. 57.78

34. Divide 23.67 by 100. 0.2367

35. Add: $\frac{3}{8} + \frac{5}{6}$. $1\frac{5}{24}$

36. What fractional part of 56 is 8? $\frac{1}{7}$

37. Multiply $2\frac{3}{4}$ by $2\frac{2}{7}$. $6\frac{2}{7}$

38. Janice Ludlow bought the following number of bonds in a week: Mon., 4; Tues., 6; Wed., 6; Thurs., 5. How many bonds did she buy on Friday if the average number of bonds she bought each day was 5? 4 bonds, Lesson 1.2

39. Tomas Reynoso spent 35.6% of his total income last year on housing. If his income last year was $67,800, how much did he spend on housing?
$24,136.80, Lesson 2.7

Reiko Wakui wants to buy a home for $175,000. She expects to make a 20% down payment and estimates her closing costs as: legal fees, $1,350; title insurance, $331; property survey, $275; inspection, $175; loan processing fee, $96; recording fee, $540.

40. What amount of mortgage loan will she need? $140,000, Lesson 6.1

41. What amount of cash will she need when she buys the house? $37,767, Lesson 6.1

42. Vic Davis paid an annual premium of $11.80 per $1,000 for a $30,000 life insurance policy. His policy also paid a dividend of $29.50, which he used to reduce his premium. What net premium did Vic pay? $324.50, Lesson 7.1

43. Risa Levine was injured and hospitalized for 8 days. Her total medical bill was $16,360. Risa's major medical coverage pays for 80% of medical expenses above a $500 deductible. How much does Risa have to pay? $3,672, Lesson 7.2

44. Juan Imalgo was billed $125 for an office visit and eye examination and $339 for new eyeglasses. His group insurance policy had a deductible of $75 and a coinsurance rate of 25% on the visit and exam, but only allowed a maximum amount of $275 for glasses. What amount of the bill did Juan pay? $151.50, Lesson 7.2

304 ■ **Chapter 7** Insurance and Investments

DIFFERENT LEARNING ABILITIES At Risk Learners

Students who are having difficulty rewriting bond quotes may do better if you make them place a percent sign after the quote, as in 97.887%. Many students have had exten- sive repetition in changing percents to decimals in grade school and adding the percent sign makes the problems more familiar to them.

7.5 Bond Interest

GOALS

- Calculate bond income
- Calculate bond yield
- Calculate total cost of bonds

Start Up

Have students read the Start Up. Remind them about the meaning of true rate of interest when they studied discounted promissory notes. Ask how what they have already learned applies to bonds.

Discuss their results to the Start Up question.

Start Up

You can buy a $1,000, 9.5% bond for 97.000 or a $1,000, 10.5% bond for 108.000. Which offers the highest true rate of interest?

Math Skill Builder

Review these math skills and solve the exercises.

1. **Rewrite** percents as decimals.
   Rewrite 95.141% as a decimal. 0.95141

   1a. 102.597% $\quad$ 1.02597 $\qquad$ **1b.** 97.289%
   $\qquad\qquad\qquad\qquad\qquad\qquad\qquad\qquad$ 0.97289

2. **Add** dollar amounts.
   Find the sum. $2,890.80 + $395 = $3,285.80

   2a. $5,190 + $56.16 $\quad$ $5,246.16 $\quad$ **2b.** $11,390.56 + $298.88 $\quad$ $11,689.44

3. **Multiply** dollar amounts by percents, whole numbers, and fractions.
   Find the product. $500 × 99.567% = $500 × 0.99567 = $497.835, or $497.84
   Find the product. $1,000 × 8% × $\frac{1}{2}$ = $1,000 × 0.08 × $\frac{1}{2}$ = $40
   Find the product. $26.59 × 2 = $53.18

   3a. $1,000 × 105.295% $\qquad$ **3b.** $49.50 × 2 $\quad$ $99
   $\quad\quad$ $1,052.95
   3c. $500 × 97.114% $\quad$ $485.57 $\quad$ **3d.** $1,000 × 9.5% × $\frac{1}{2}$ $\quad$ $47.50

4. **Divide** dollar amounts by dollar amounts to find percents.
   Find the percent, to the nearest tenth. $83 ÷ $946.80 = 0.0876, or 8.8%

   4a. $94.60 ÷ $1,200 $\quad$ 7.9% $\qquad$ **4b.** $37.94 ÷ $10,000 $\quad$ 0.4%

■ Bond Income

Investors in bonds receive interest payments as income. Bond interest is often paid semiannually. The interest rate of a bond is based on the bond's par value. Since the par value is the principal, the interest formula is:

Par Value × Rate × Time = Interest

To find your bond income, find the interest you receive for one bond. Then multiply that result by the number of bonds you own.

Math Skill Builder

Use the Math Skill Builder to prepare students for the addition, multiplication, division, fraction, and percentage tasks in the lesson. You may also use it to get the class started while attendance is taken or while materials are handed out.

Complete all exercises in Math Skill Builder 1–4.

■ Teach Goal 1

Stress that bond interest is a fixed percent of a bond's par value.

Lesson 7.5 Bond Interest ■ 305

TEACHING STRATEGIES Expand Beyond the Classroom

Have students bring to class a current bond quotation table and one about a month old. By comparing price data for the same bond, students can see that items such as volume and price fluctuate. Items such as the maturity date and interest rate of the bond remain the same because these are fixed at the time a bond is issued. Bond quotation tables may be obtained from the financial sections of newspapers, the Web, and brokerage firms.

Apply Goal 1

Work through Example 1 with students doing the math at their desks.

Assign Check Your Understanding problems A and B for completion in class. Check student work at their desks for problems.

Teach Goal 2

Emphasize that when the amount of bond interest is for less than one year, the annual amount must be found before dividing the interest amount by the market price of the bond to find the current yield.

Point out that when the bond face value is not mentioned, students should assume that it is $1,000.

Apply Goal 2

Work through Example 2 at the board while students do the math at their desks.

Remind students that bond interest for less than a year must be changed to an annual amount to calculate bond yields accurately.

Assign Check Your Understanding problems C and D for completion in class. Move about your classroom and check student work for difficulties.

EXAMPLE 1

Find the interest for one year on 5, $1,000 par value, 9% bonds.

SOLUTION
Rewrite the interest rate as a decimal and multiply by the par value.

$1,000 \times 0.09 \times 1 = \$90$ interest for 1 year on 1 bond

Multipy the interest for 1 bond by the number of bonds owned.

$5 \times \$90 = \$450$ interest for 1 year on 5 bonds

If the interest is paid semiannually, the amount of each interest payment for this bond would be $45.

$\$1,000 \times 0.09 \times \frac{1}{2} = \$45$ semiannual interest on 1 bond

■ CHECK YOUR UNDERSTANDING

A. Alif Guilak owns 10, $1,000, 9% bonds. What is his semiannual interest on the bonds? $450

B. Beatrice Grezlak bought 20, $500, 8.5% bonds. What is her annual income from the bonds? $850

■ Bond Yields

One way to compare bond investments is to find the current yield of bonds. The **current yield** of a bond is found by dividing the bond's annual interest income by the bond's price.

Current Yield = Annual Income ÷ Bond Price

EXAMPLE 2

What is the current yield on a $1,000, 7% Elgin Transit Company bond priced at 96.462? Round your answer to the nearest tenth of a percent.

SOLUTION
Multiply the face value of the bond price times the bond's interest rate.

$0.07 \times \$1,000 = \$70$ annual income

Multiply the bond's face value times the bond price.

$0.96462 \times \$1,000 = \$964.62$ bond price

Divide the annual income by the bond price.

$\$70 \div \$964.62 = 00.0725 = 7.3\%$ current yield

■ CHECK YOUR UNDERSTANDING

C. Crescent Company $1,000, 9% bonds are offered at 101.585. What is the current yield, to the nearest tenth percent? 8.9%

D. The semiannual interest on Lancaster Housing bonds is $47.50. If you buy the bonds at 94.598, what is the current yield? 10%

■ *CHECK YOUR UNDERSTANDING SOLUTIONS*

A. $1,000 × 0.09 × $\frac{1}{2}$ = $45; 10 × $45 = $450

B. $500 × 0.085 = $42.50; 20 × $42.50 = $850

C. $1,000 × 0.09 = $90; 101.585 = 1.01585;
1.01585 × $1,000 = $1,015.85;
$90 ÷ $1,015.85 = 0.0885, or 8.9%

D. $47.50 × 2 = $95; 94.598 = 0.94598;
0.94598 × $1,000 = $945.98;
$95 ÷ $945.98 = 0.1004, or 10%

■ Total Cost of Bonds

When a bond is sold, whoever owns the bond on the next interest date receives the full amount of interest for the entire past interest period. When you buy a bond, you may have to pay the market price of the bond plus any interest that the bond has earned from the last interest date.

For example, if on April 1 you buy a bond that pays interest semiannually, you have to pay the seller for the interest that he or she has already earned on the bond from January 1 through March 31. On July 1, the bond will pay you interest for the full 6 months. The interest for that first three months is called *accrued* interest.

EXAMPLE 3

Ed Martin buys 5, $1,000, 8% bonds through a dealer at 102.797 plus accrued interest of $20 per bond. The dealer charged $3 commission per bond. What is the total cost of the bonds to Ed?

SOLUTION

Change the market price to a decimal and multiply by the par value.

102.797% = 1.02797; 1.02797 × $1,000 = $1,027.97   price of one bond

Add the accrued interest, commission, and the price of one bond.

$1,027.97 + $20 + $3 = $1,050.97   cost of each bond

Multiply the total cost of each bond by the number of bonds purchased.

5 × $1,050.97 = $5,254.85   total cost of bond purchase

■ CHECK YOUR UNDERSTANDING

E. Reba Neel buys 10, $1,000, 9.7% bonds through a dealer at 97.272 plus accrued interest of $24.25 per bond and commission of $4 per bond. What is the total cost of the bonds to Reba? $10,009.70

F. Julio Pujols buys 20, $1,000, 8% bonds on April 1 at 105.288 plus accrued interest from January 1. Commission was not shown. What is Julio's total cost for each bond? $1,072.88

Wrap Up

Look at the Start Up problem at the start of this lesson. The interest rate of both bonds is based on the par value of the bonds. You will receive $1,000 × 9.5%, or $95 as annual interest on the first bond. You will receive $1,000 × 10.5%, or $105 on the second bond. However, the market price of the first bond is only $97. If you buy that bond, the true rate of interest is $95 divided by the market price of the bond, or 9.8%, rounded to the nearest tenth percent. The true rate of interest on the second bond is $105 divided by $1,080, or 9.7%, rounded to the nearest tenth percent.

■ Teach Goal 3

Explain that when an investor buys a bond between two interest dates, the interest that has accrued from the last interest date to the date of purchase must be paid in addition to the price of the bond and commission. On the next interest date, however, the buyer receives the full interest for the period and so is reimbursed for the accrued interest.

Since bonds are bought every day, accrued interest is a factor in the total cost of most bonds purchases.

■ Apply Goal 3

Work through Example 3 with students completing the math at their desks.

Assign Check Your Understanding problems E and F for completion in class. Move about your classroom and check student work for difficulties.

Wrap Up

Review the Start Up. Point out that changes in the true rate of interest do not affect the actual amount of interest paid. This is important to those who hold bonds to earn a specific amount of interest income each quarter or year.

■ *CHECK YOUR UNDERSTANDING SOLUTIONS*

E. 97.272 = 0.97272; $1,000 × 0.97272 = $972.72; $972.72 + $24.25 + $4 = $1,000.97; 10 × $1,000.97 ÷ $10,009.70

F. $1,000 × 0.08 = $80; $80 ÷ 4 = $20; 105.288 = 1.05288; 1.05288 × $1,000 = $1,052.88; $1,052.88 + $20 = $1,072.88

COMMUNICATION

Help students use the Web, library sources, or an area broker to find answers to the questions. Answers should include the fact that municipal, or muni bond interest is often lower because it is not taxed at the federal level and may not be taxed at the state level if purchased within the same state of the municipality.

If muni bond interest was taxed, it would take a higher rate of interest to earn the same amount.

The major advantage to muni bonds is that interest is not included as taxable income on federal income tax returns. Another advantage may be that they are insured.

Assign

Assignment: Exercises 1–27 and 29, 31–35. Start with the basic arithmetic problems at the beginning of the exercises to ensure that students understand the underlying arithmetic in the exercises.

Assess

Check student answers to the exercises by calling on them in class, collecting and grading selected problems, or by viewing their work as you move about the room.

Ask students to define the bolded and italicized terms in the lesson and use them in sentences.

COMMUNICATION

Municipal bonds are bonds that are issued by state and local governments and government agencies. Write complete sentences to answer each of the following questions.

1. Why is the interest rate paid on municipal bonds often lower than the interest rates paid on bonds of comparable quality issued by corporations?

2. What is the advantage of buying municipal bonds?

Write a brief memo to another person that includes the answers to these questions.

EXERCISES

Find the annual income in each problem.

1. 14, $1,000, 6% bonds $840
2. 6, $1,000, 10% bonds $600
3. 8, $1,000, 12% bonds $960
4. 2, $500, 7.25% bonds $72.50
5. 20, $500, 9% bonds $900
6. 15, $1,000, $8\frac{1}{2}$% bonds $1,275
7. 5, $1,000, 9.25% bonds $462.50
8. 12, $1,000, 11.5% bonds $1,380

9. What is the semiannual income from six $1,000, 5.5% bonds? $165

10. You own 30 bonds with a par value of $1,000 each and paying 9.75% interest. Find your semiannual income from these bonds. $1,462.50

Find the total investment and the total annual income from the investment.

	Bonds Owned	Par Value per Bond	Price Paid	Total Investment	Interest Rate	Annual Income
11.	5	$1,000	99.246	$4,962.30	9%	$450
12.	10	1,000	104.932	$10,493.20	12%	$1,200
13.	30	1,000	107.253	$32,175.90	$12\frac{1}{2}$%	$3,750
14.	45	1,000	94.342	$42,453.90	8.7%	$3,915

Find the current yield on each bond to the nearest tenth of a percent.

	Par Value	Interest Rate	Price Paid	Current Yield
15.	$1,000	10%	91.899	10.9%
16.	$1,000	8.5%	104.363	8.1%
17.	$1,000	$9\frac{1}{2}$%	112.008	8.5%
18.	$500	7.8%	92.826	8.4%

308 ■ Chapter 7 Insurance and Investments

SELECTED SOLUTIONS

10. $1,000 × 0.0975 × $\frac{1}{2}$ = $48.75;
30 × $48.75 = $1,462.50

15. $1,000 × 0.10 = $100;
$1,000 × 0.91899 = $918.99;
$100 ÷ $918.99 = 0.1088, or 10.9%

25. $1,000 × 0.0925 = $92.50; $1,850 ÷ $92.50 = 20;

103.976 = 1.03976; 1.03976 × $1,000 = $1,039.76;
20 × $1,039.76 = $20,795.20

29. 95.089 = 0.95089; $1,000 × 0.95089 = $950.89;
$1,000 × 0.08 = $80; $80 ÷ 4 = $20;
$950.89 + $20 = $970.89;
20 × $970.89 = $19,417.80

19. How much is each interest payment on a $500, 8% bond if the interest is paid semiannually on June 1 and December 1? $20

20. What estimated and actual annual interest would you get from 10, $1,000 par value bonds that pay 6.8% interest? $700; $680

21. A $1,000 bond, paying 8% interest, was bought at 78.569. What is the current yield to the nearest tenth percent?   10.2%

22. A $1,000, 12% bond was bought at 114.936. The previous day the bond sold at 112.72. Find the current yield on the bond to the nearest tenth percent.   10.4%

23. What is the current yield, to the nearest tenth percent, on a $1,000, 11.2% bond bought at 108.289?   10.3%

24. What is the current yield, to the nearest tenth percent, on a $500, 9% bond bought at 95.976?   9.4%

25. **STRETCHING YOUR SKILLS** EPrint, Inc. $1,000, $9\frac{1}{4}$% bonds can be purchased at 103.976. How much money must be invested in the bonds to produce an annual income of $1,850? $20,795.20

26. **STRETCHING YOUR SKILLS** What amount must be invested in Poe County $1,000, 9% bonds at 80.360 in order to earn an annual income of $2,250? $20,090

27. Denny Lensing bought 10 Brittle Company $1,000 par value, 13% bonds at 150.883. Interest on these bonds is paid semiannually on January 1 and July 1. What semiannual interest payment will Denny receive from this investment? $650

28. Julie Margolis buys 10, $1,000, 12% bonds on October 1 at 102.814 plus accrued interest from July 1 and a commission of $4 per bond. What is Julie's total cost for each bond? $1,062.14

29. On April 1, Alan Durston buys 20, $1,000, 8% bonds at 95.089, plus accrued interest from January 1. No commission is shown. What total amount does Alan spend for the bonds? $19,417.80

30. **DECISION MAKING** You can invest in a 15-year bond with a current yield of 8.5% or a 6-month CD with an APR of 6.5%. Why might you invest in the CD? Why might you invest in the bond?   See Enrich section for answer.

MIXED REVIEW

31. Subtract $\frac{2}{5}$ from $\frac{4}{9}$. $\frac{2}{45}$

32. What number is 10% greater than 55?   60.5

33. Divide $5\frac{1}{5}$ by $2\frac{1}{2}$. $2\frac{2}{25}$

34. June Riebold's taxable income last year was $45,380. She paid state income taxes of 5.5% and city income taxes of 1.3%. What was the total of her state and city income taxes for the year? $3,085.84, Lesson 2.4

35. On July 1, Laura Knolls deposited $540 in a bank account that paid 4% interest per year, compounded semiannually. Interest was added on January 1 and July 1. Find her balance on July 1 of the next year if she made no other deposits or withdrawals. $561.82, Lesson 3.6

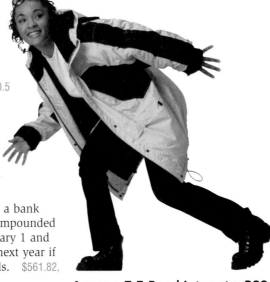

Lesson 7.5 Bond Interest ■ **309**

CONNECTION TO ALGEBRA

Have students compare finding bond interest or yield with finding simple interest. (Both use the formula $I = PRT$, with p representing the principal in simple interest and the par value in bond interest.)

Start Up

Have students read the Start Up. The problem is designed to let students see the difference between real and "paper" profits. It also allows you to bring up the subject of commissions, which are studied in the first goal of the lesson.

Math Skill Builder

Assign all exercises in the Math Skill Builder 1–2 to prepare students for the multiplication, division, rounding, and rewriting used in the lesson. You may also use it to get the class started while attendance is taken or while materials are handed out.

■ Teach Goal 1

Stress the element of risk in making investment decisions. Some people like to take risks; others prefer safer investments.

Point out that stock may be issued with a par value or as a no par stock. Par value is the value of a share of stock that is printed on the certificate. This may be any value that the corporation wants to set. The par value may be as low as $1, $10, $35, or $50. It is seldom more than $100. All the shares of an issue of stock have the same par value. Many corporations issue stock without giving the shares any value. Such stock is called no par stock. The purchase price of any share of stock is its market value.

Read through the stock table on page 311 with students and discuss each of the items on the table that are identified. Alternatively, you may wish to make a transparency of part of a stock quotation page of the financial section of an area newspaper and help students interpret the information on the page.

You may wish to discuss the difference between discount and full-service brokers in terms of the help they provide and the fees they charge.

310

7.6 Stocks

GOALS

- Calculate the cost of stock purchases
- Calculate annual stock dividends
- Calculate the yield on stock investments
- Calculate the proceeds from the sale of stock

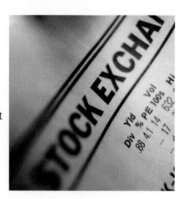

Start Up

You and a friend are reading a newspaper article describing an Internet music provider. The article states that the company's stock started last year at $21 and rose to $53 at the end of the year. Your friend said, "Boy, if I had bought 100 shares of that stock, I would have made $3,200." Is your friend right?

Math Skill Builder

Review these math skills and solve the exercises that follow.

❶ **Multiply** dollar amounts by percents and whole numbers.
Find the product. $14.50 × 200 = $2,900
Find the product. $100 × 2.4% =
$100 × 0.024 = $2.40

1a. $72.58 × 100 $7,258   **1b.** $117 × 500 $58,500

1c. $1,000 × 4.5% $45   **1d.** $100 × 2.14% $2.14

❷ **Divide** dollar amounts by dollar amounts to find percents, to the nearest tenth.
Find the quotient. $14 ÷ $350 = 0.04, or 4%

2a. $8.25 ÷ 200   4.1%   **2b.** $15.23 ÷ $428   3.6%

■ Purchasing Stock

Companies issue shares of stock to raise money, which might be used to expand or to offer new products. Investors who buy the shares are called *stockholders*. Each stockholder gets a stock certificate that shows on its face the number of shares it represents. A stock certificate is shown at the top of the next page.

> **BUSINESS TIP**
>
> Stockholders are also called shareholders.

310 ■ Chapter 7 Insurance and Investments

CONNECTION TO FINANCE

Show students how to go to an Internet portal, such as Excite or Yahoo, or an online broker, such as Charles Schwab, and locate the stock tracking section of the site. Then have each student pick a different company, identify its stock symbol, and get a quote. Have students find the last quote of the day for their stock for 5 days and record them in a table. Then have them find the difference between the price on the first and last days and state that as a percent gain or loss. On the sixth day, call on students to find those with the biggest percentage gains and losses.

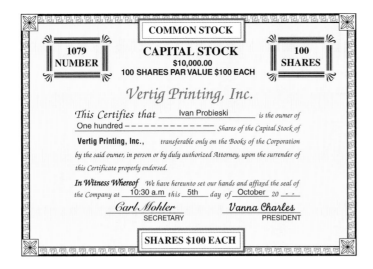

Stockholders usually buy and sell their shares through a broker. The price at which a stock sells is called the **market price** or *market value* and is shown in stock tables in many daily newspapers.

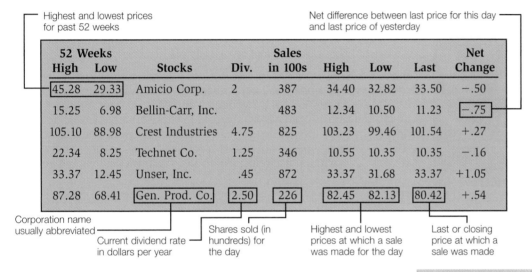

Highest and lowest prices for past 52 weeks

Net difference between last price for this day and last price of yesterday

52 Weeks		Stocks	Div.	Sales in 100s	High	Low	Last	Net Change
High	Low							
45.28	29.33	Amicio Corp.	2	387	34.40	32.82	33.50	−.50
15.25	6.98	Bellin-Carr, Inc.		483	12.34	10.50	11.23	−.75
105.10	88.98	Crest Industries	4.75	825	103.23	99.46	101.54	+.27
22.34	8.25	Technet Co.	1.25	346	10.55	10.35	10.35	−.16
33.37	12.45	Unser, Inc.	.45	872	33.37	31.68	33.37	+1.05
87.28	68.41	Gen. Prod. Co.	2.50	226	82.45	82.13	80.42	+.54

Corporation name usually abbreviated

Current dividend rate in dollars per year

Shares sold (in hundreds) for the day

Highest and lowest prices at which a sale was made for the day

Last or closing price at which a sale was made

When you buy stock through a broker, the total cost of the stock is the market price of the stock plus the broker's commission.

Market Price + Commission = Total Cost

The amount of a broker's commission depends on the services the broker provides, the price of the stock and the number of shares bought. As in bonds, discount and online brokers usually charge lower commissions but give less service to customers than full service brokers.

■ Teach Goal 3

Stress that the yield earned on a stock investment is always stated on an annual basis. If a dividend is paid quarterly or semiannually, the total dividend paid for a year must be found to calculate yield.

Point out to students that the cost of stock includes its price and the commission and other fees that were charged to purchase it.

■ Apply Goal 3

Do Example 3 at the board while students follow along doing the math at their desks.

Assign Check Your Understanding problems E and F for completion in class. Check student work at their desks for problems.

■ ONGOING ASSESSMENT

Call out easy-to-calculate quarterly and semiannual dividends and ask students to calculate the annual dividends mentally **(quarterly: $10 = $40; $15 = $60; $20 = $80; semiannual: $25 = $50; $35 = $70).**

■ Teach Goal 4

Point out that trading on stock exchanges is done in round lots of 100 shares. Orders of less than 100 shares are called odd lots and are handled by odd-lot dealers.

Note that when a broker buys or sells stock for a customer, the customer is given a written notice of the transaction that lists the stock name, the number of shares bought or sold, unit price, total market value, commission, any other charges or fees, and the net amount owed the broker or due the customer.

EXAMPLE 1

Velma D'Anglico bought 500 shares of Vesta stock at $15. The broker charged her $106 commission. Find the total cost of the stock.

SOLUTION

Multiply number of shares times price.

$500 \times \$15 = \$7,500$ total price of shares

Add the broker's commission to the price of the shares.

$\$7,500 + \$106 = \$7,606$ total cost of shares

■ CHECK YOUR UNDERSTANDING

A. Trent Vallow purchased 200 shares of stock from his broker at $24.50. The broker charged $123.51 commission. What is the total cost of the stock? $5,023.51

B. A broker sold Lisa Colon 400 shares of Roly Plastics, Inc. stock at $31.89. Lisa's broker charged $246.89 commission. Find the total cost of the stock to Lisa. $13,002.89

■ Stock Dividends

Unlike bondholders' investments, the money invested in stock does not have to be repaid. Stockholders are owners of the company, not lenders. However, stockholders have a right to share in company profits. These profits are distributed to shareholders as *dividends* and are usually paid quarterly.

Many corporations issue two classes of stock—common stock and preferred stock. A corporation sets a *preferred stock's* dividends when it is first issued. *Common stock* is the ordinary stock of a corporation and does not have a set dividend. There is no guarantee that dividends will be paid to either class of stockholder. When dividends are paid, they go first to shareholders of preferred stock. Dividends may be shown either as a percent of a stock's par value or as an amount of money per share. For stock with no par value, the dividend is always an amount per share.

EXAMPLE 2

Cecile Ware owns 100 shares of Teleos Communications common stock, par value $100. If a dividend of 2.5% is declared, how much should Cecile get in dividends?

SOLUTION

Change the dividend percent to a decimal and multiply by the par value.

$2.5\% \times \$100 = 0.025 \times \$100 = \$2.50$ dividend on one share

Multiply the dividend on one share by the number of shares.

$100 \times \$2.50 = \$250$ total dividend

■ CHECK YOUR UNDERSTANDING

C. Emile Van Tassel owns 600 shares of Brunis Imaging Co. common stock with a par value of $100. Brunis Imaging declares a dividend of 3.7% on the par value to shareholders. How much in dividends will Emile receive? $2,220

D. Dome Petroleum preferred stock pays a quarterly dividend of $1.50 per share. If Sara Karadic owns 800 shares of the stock, what amount will she receive in dividends for the year? $4,800

■ *CHECK YOUR UNDERSTANDING SOLUTIONS*

A. 200 × $24.50 = $4,900;
$4,900 + $123.51 = $5,023.51

B. 400 × $31.89 = $12,756;
$12,756 + $246.89 = $13,002.89

C. 600 × $100 = $60,000; $60,000 × 0.037 = $2,220

D. 800 × $1.50 × 4 = $4,800

■ Stock Yields

The yield, or rate of income, received from an investment is found by dividing the annual income from the investment by the amount invested. For stocks, the investment is the total cost of the stock, including any expenses or commission paid in obtaining the stock. The income is the amount of annual dividends.

Yield = Annual Dividends ÷ Total Cost of Stock

EXAMPLE 3

Sandra bought 10 shares of Calcon, Inc. stock at $25. Her broker charged her $28 commission. If the stock pays an annual dividend of $1.20, what is its yield?

SOLUTION
Multiply the number of shares by share price and add commission.

(10 × $25) + $28 = $278   total cost of the stock

Multiply the annual dividend by the number of shares.

10 × $1.20 = $12   total annual dividend

Divide the total annual dividend by the total cost of the stock. State the yield as a percent to the nearest tenth percent.

$12 ÷ $278 = 0.0431, or 0.043, or 4.3%   annual yield to nearest tenth percent

■ CHECK YOUR UNDERSTANDING

E. Vladan Kortic bought 600 shares of stock at $11.35. His broker charged $182.60 commission. The stock pays a quarterly dividend of $0.12. What is the annual yield, to the nearest tenth percent?   4.1%

F. Penina Kabamba purchased 1,000 shares of Peltor, Inc. stock at $20.80. Her broker charged her $408.23 commission. If the stock pays an annual dividend of $0.62, what is its annual yield, to the nearest tenth percent?   2.9%

■ Stock Sales

When you sell stock through a broker, you pay a commission. You may also pay charges such as a service fee and a *Securities and Exchange Commission (SEC) fee*. Your state may charge a transfer tax. When you buy stock, you do not pay a transfer tax or an SEC fee. When you sell stock, the net proceeds is the market price less the commission and all other charges (service fee, SEC fee, transfer tax).

Market Price − (Commission + Other Charges) = Net Proceeds

EXAMPLE 4

Find the net proceeds from the sale of 100 shares of Danbury Corporation stock at $30.25 with commission and other charges of $86.

SOLUTION
Multiply number of shares by market price.   100 × $30.25 = $3,025   total sale

Subtract the commission and other charges from the total sale.

$3,025 − $86 = $2,939   net proceeds

Lesson 7.6 Stocks ■ 313

Point out that special charges or fees occur when stocks are sold. The seller pays a small Security and Exchange Commission fee and, in some states, a transfer tax. Some brokerage firms add a separate charge to cover the cost of postage and handling of the transaction.

■ Apply Goal 4

Work through Examples 4 and 5 with students completing the math at their desks.

Assign Check Your Understanding problems G and H for completion in class. Check student work at their desks for errors or problems.

■ ONGOING ASSESSMENT
Call out stock purchases or sales using simple stock prices and commissions and ask students if they should add or subtract the commission and to give the result. For example, purchase: $100 price, $10 commission, add, $110 total cost; sale: $300, $30 commission, subtract, $270 net proceeds. Make sure that students use the correct terms to identify the elements of the purchase or sale.

■ CHECK YOUR UNDERSTANDING SOLUTIONS

E. 600 × $11.35 = $6,810;
$6,810 + $182.60 = $6,992.60; 4 × $0.12 = $0.48;
600 × $0.48 = $288; $288 ÷ $6,992.60 = 0.0411, or 4.1%

F. 1,000 × $20.80 = $20,800;
$20,800 + $408.23 = $21,208.23;
1,000 × $0.62 = $620;
$620 ÷ $21,208.23 = 0.0292, or 2.9%

The profit or loss on a sale of stock is the difference between the total cost of purchasing the stock and the net proceeds. If the amount of the net proceeds is greater than the total cost, there is a profit. If it is less than the total cost, the result is a loss.

Net Proceeds − Total Cost = Profit   or   **Total Cost − Net Proceeds = Loss**

EXAMPLE 5

Find the profit or loss from the sale of the Danbury Corporation stock in Example 4. You bought the 100 shares of stock originally at $21.50 a share and paid a commission of $68.55.

SOLUTION
Multiply the price per share by the number of shares and add the commission.

$100 \times \$21.50 = \$2,150$ total price of stock

$\$2,150 + \$68.55 = \$2,218.55$ total cost of stock

Subtract the total cost of the stock from the net proceeds of the sale.

$\$2,939 - \$2,218.55 = \$720.45$ profit from sale of stock

■ CHECK YOUR UNDERSTANDING

G. You bought 100 shares of Pendel preferred stock at $14.70. The commission charge was $54. You sold the same shares later at $21.45. The commission and other fees on the sale were $71. What was the profit or loss on the stock? $550 profit

H. Jorge Venteria bought 300 shares of Silver Forge common stock at $41.80 and was charged a commission of $243. He later sold the stock for $39.12. The commission and fees on the sale were $235. What was Jorge's profit or loss? $1,282 loss

Wrap Up

Look back at the Start Up problem. Your friend overlooks the commission on the purchase of the shares and commission and fees on the sale of the shares. The profit would be reduced by these amounts. Also, you don't make a profit or loss until you actually sell the shares. If your friend checked the current price of the stock, he or she might find that the price had fallen to $15 a share. Unless the stock was sold at year-end, your friend would have made no profit. Unless the stock is sold now, your friend would suffer no loss on the stock.

COMMUNICATION

An old technique for buying stocks is called "dollar cost averaging." Financial advisors often recommend this technique for investors who cannot follow the market closely. What is this technique and why is it useful to investors? Using the Internet or information gathered by visiting a stockbroker, write a brief memo to a friend answering these two questions. Include a description of your sources at the end of the memo.

■ *CHECK YOUR UNDERSTANDING SOLUTIONS*

G. $100 \times \$14.70 = \$1,470$; $\$1,470 + \$54 = \$1,524$;
$100 \times \$21.45 = \$2,145$; $\$2,145 - \$71 = \$2,074$;
$\$2,074 - \$1,524 = \$550$ profit

H. $300 \times \$41.80 = \$12,540$; $\$12,540 \times \$243 = \$12,783$; $300 \times \$39.12 = \$11,736$; $\$11,736 - \$235 = \$11,501$; $\$12,783 - \$11,501 = \$1,282$ loss

EXERCISES

Perform the indicated operation.

1. $5,478 + $56.88   2. $45,298 − $1,497   3. $2,500 × 1.5%
   $5,534.88 $43,801 $37.50
4. Find the percent, to the nearest tenth: $5.60 ÷ $500   1.1%

Find the total cost of each stock purchase.

	Number of Shares	Name of Stock	Market Price	Commission	Total Cost
5.	300	Reinhold	$41.55	241.55	$12,706.55
6.	100	Seibold	22.44	69.80	$2,313.80
7.	100	Danville	17.52	39.20	$1,791.20
8.	50	Net Managers	61.28	76.30	$3,140.30
9.	200	BPM	110.58	143.90	$22,259.90
10.	800	Monterey	14.75	268.85	$12,068.85
11.	400	Nextsand	5.88	42.20	$2,394.20
12.	150	Streiser	32.94	71.20	$5,012.20
13.	35	Tolker	44.26	40.80	$1,589.90
14.	200	Newdays	58.44	116.40	$11,804.40

15. Diane was charged a commission of $119.60 to buy 200 shares of Kirby Products stock at $63.50. What was her total investment in the stock? $12,819.60

16. **STRETCHING YOUR SKILLS** A discount broker offers 40% off the $117 commission charged by a full service broker to handle the purchase of 200 shares of Epsonique at $22.50. How much could a buyer save by purchasing from the discount broker? $46.80

Find the total annual dividend received by each shareholder.

	Shares Owned	Par Value per Share	Annual Dividend Rate	Dividend
17.	100	$100	5%, annually	$500
18.	800	100	8%, annually	$6,400
19.	120	50	4.5%, annually	$270
20.	500	—	$0.75 per share, quarterly	$1,500
21.	100	—	$1.50 per share, quarterly	$600

22. Sun Fabrications declares a dividend of $3.50 per share on its common stock. If Jules Kortel owns 400 shares of the stock, what amount will he receive in dividends? $1,400

23. Karen Hedrick owns 300 shares of Tilden Electronics preferred stock. If the stock pays a quarterly dividend of $1.20 a share, what is the total amount that Karen will receive in a year? $1,440

Lesson 7.6 Stocks ■ 315

Assign

Assignment: Exercises 1–44 and 46–56. Start with the basic arithmetic problems at the beginning of the exercises to ensure that students understand the underlying arithmetic in the exercises.

Assess

Check student answers to the exercises by calling on them in class, collecting and grading selected problems, or by observing student work at their desks.

STUDENT WORKBOOK If students need help with total cost of stock purchase problems, do Exercise 1 with them. Then have them complete Exercises 2–4 during class time so you can be available for help.

To reteach finding annual stock dividends, do Exercise 5 with students. Then have them complete Exercise 6 at their desks.

To reteach finding the yield on stock investments, do Exercise 7 with students, and then have them complete 8–9 at their desks.

To reteach finding the proceeds from the sale of stock, do Exercise 10 at the board with students. Then have them do Exercises 11–14 at their desks.

Find the yield on the investment in each of the following stocks. Round all answers to the nearest tenth of a percent.

	Total Cost per Share	Par Value per Share	Dividend Rate	Dividend Payable	Yield
24.	$120	$100	6%	Annually	5%
25.	80	100	3%	Annually	3.8%
26.	50	—	0.62 per share	Quarterly	5%
27.	26	—	0.40 per share	Quarterly	6.2%
28.	32	—	0.55 per share	Quarterly	6.9%

29. Norm Edmunds owns a share of stock that cost $36 and pays a quarterly dividend of $0.63. Find the yield for that stock. 7%

Tien Niu bought 500 shares of stock at $47.75 a share. She paid a discount broker a commission of $26 for the purchase. The stock pays an annual dividend of 5% on a par value of $100.

30. What total dividend does Tien get from the 500 shares? $2,500

31. What yield, to the nearest tenth percent, does Tien earn on this investment? 10.5%

Sobal Chemical Company preferred stock sells for $38 and pays an annual dividend of 2.7% on a par value of $100. Elgin Equipment Corporation preferred stock has a market price of $18.25 and pays a quarterly dividend of $0.19.

32. Which stock earns a higher yield? Sobal

33. How much higher, to the nearest tenth percent? 2.9%

34. **STRETCHING YOUR SKILLS** What is the rate of income on a share of preferred stock that costs $180 and pays a semiannual dividend of $7.20 a share? 8%

INTEGRATING YOUR KNOWLEDGE Aegis Security Company common stock pays a regular annual dividend of $2.50 a share.

35. How many shares must you buy to get an annual income of $1,000 from the investment? 400

36. What total investment will you make in the stock if you buy the amount of shares in Exercise 35 at $52.50 and pay $78 per 100 shares for commission? $21,312

Common stock paying a quarterly dividend of $0.32 a share sells at 38.

37. How many shares must you buy to get an annual dividend income of $640? 500

38. What total investment, without calculating commissions, would you have to make to earn the dividend income you want? $19,000

SELECTED SOLUTIONS

24. $100 × 0.60 = $6; $6 ÷ $120 = 0.05, or 5%

31. 500 × $47.75 = $23,875; $23,875 + $26 = $23,901; $2,500 ÷ $23,901 = 0.1045, or 10.5%

34. $7.20 × 2 = $14.40; $14.40 ÷ $180 = 0.08, or 8%

37. 4 × $0.32 = $1.28; $640 ÷ $1.28 = 500

Find the profit (+) or loss (−) in each of these sales.

	Name of Stock	Shares Traded	Selling Price	Commission & Other Fees	Total Cost of Purchase	Profit/ Loss
39.	RMB Plastics	200	42.44	$172.88	$7,628.12	+$687
40.	eBuy, Inc.	300	11.50	115.73	$1,809.25	+$1,525.02
41.	Solaris Corp.	400	17.10	165.97	$7,118.90	−$444.87
42.	DigiNet	50	28.25	58.60	$1,178.34	+$175.56
43.	Roces Mfg.	100	37.40	29.95	$3,165.22	+$544.83

44. Terry Vance bought 600 shares of stock for a total cost of $6,398. He later sold the stock at $15 a share and had selling expenses of $94. What was his profit or loss from this sale of stock? $2,508; profit

45. **CRITICAL THINKING**   Explain the difference between a bond holder and a stockholder of a corporation.   See Enrich section for answer.

STRETCHING YOUR SKILLS   You bought 400 shares of stock for a total cost of $8,120 and kept the stock for 3 years during which time you received quarterly dividends of $0.26 per share. You sold the stock and received net proceeds of $9,215.

46. What total dividends did you receive while you owned the stock? $1,248

47. What is your profit on the sale of the stock? $1,095

48. What is your total gain from owning and selling the stock? $2,343

Maria Fuentes bought 500 shares of Apollo Corporation preferred stock at $12.87. The commission on the purchase was $184.38. Maria later sold the stock at $20.15. The commission and fees on the sale were $228.

49. What was the total cost of the stock to Maria? $6,619.38

50. What were the net proceeds of the sale? $9,847

51. What was the amount of profit or loss on the sale? $3,227.62 profit

MIXED REVIEW

52. Divide 3,600 by 21.4, rounded to the nearest tenth.   168.2

53. $482 is what percent of $24,800, to the nearest tenth percent?   1.9%

54. 42 increased by 11.25% of itself is what number?   46.725

55. June Silva borrows $450 and agrees to repay the loan in 36 payments of $15.50 each. How much is the finance charge on the loan? $108, Lesson 4.4

56. Louise Alvarez bought 200 shares of 8% preferred stock with a par value of $100. What is her annual dividend income? $1,600, Lesson 7.6

Lesson 7.6 Stocks ■ **317**

Enrich

Assign Exercise 45, Critical Thinking, and discuss student responses.

The discussion should identify that for bondholders, their bond is a promissory note from a company or municipality to repay the face of the bond. However, stockholders own part of a company. They have no guarantee that their investment will be returned. They could lose all their money or they could earn much more if the company is profitable.

Close

Select one or more problems from the textbook or workbook lesson and call on students to describe how they would solve each part of the problem.

If you haven't already done so, call on students to define and use in a sentence each of the bolded and italicized terms in the lesson.

COMMON ERRORS

A common error made by students is to add the commission to the sale price of stock. Stress that commissions are added to the stock purchase price and subtracted from the stock sale price.

Start Up

Have students read the Start Up. Then have them close their books and form small teams of 2–3 students each and try to identify strategies. Have them write down their strategies on a sheet of paper and hand it in along with the names of team members.

Math Skill Builder

The addition and multiplication of money amounts are skills used in the lesson. So is the ability to calculate percents.

Have students complete all exercises in Math Skill Builder 1–3.

■ Teach Goal 1

Point out that mutual funds have become popular investments because they offer diversification of risk with a single purchase. But, as with other investments, the mutual fund company must be selected carefully to minimize the potential risk of capital loss.

Load funds are bought through brokers who share in the commission charge. No-load funds are bought directly from the investment company that manages the mutual fund. Note that commission or not, most funds charge management fees.

Investors purchase an even number of dollars worth of a fund, such as $5,000. They then receive an odd number of shares, which companies calculate to the nearest thousandth of a share; e.g., $5,000 invested in a fund at 12.89 NAV equals 387.8975, or 387.898 shares. Exercises 2 and 6 in the Workbook have problems of this type.

7.7 Mutual Funds

GOALS

- Calculate the total investment in a mutual fund
- Calculate the amount and rate of commission
- Calculate profit or loss from mutual fund investments

Start Up

Assume you collect baseball cards. Identify strategies you might use to have a good chance of ending up with the trading card of a future superstar.

Math Skill Builder

Review these math skills and solve the exercises that follow.

1 **Subtract** dollar amounts.
Find the difference. $1,542 − $1,312 = $230

  1a. $2,078 − $1,993 $85   **1b.** $12,307.87 − $4,110.57 $8,197.30

2 **Multiply** dollar amounts by decimals.
Find the product. $35.17 × 45.135 = $1,587.397, or $1,587.40

  2a. $14.29 × 325.112 $4,645.85   **2b.** $8.31 × 28.922 $240.34

3 **Divide** dollar amounts to find a percent.
Find the quotient as a percent, to the nearest tenth.
$32.28 ÷ $460 = 0.07, or 7.0%

  3a. $34.80 ÷ $625 5.6%   **3b.** $19.77 ÷ $822 2.4%

■ Total Investment in a Mutual Fund

Mutual fund investment companies use the money from investors to buy stock in many companies. By investing in many companies, the mutual fund increases its chances of buying stocks that will be profitable.

There are many different kinds of mutual fund companies. Some have aggressive growth goals. Others choose to maximize the income from shares held. Some mutual funds specialize in certain sectors of the economy, such as the health sector. Others buy stock from many different types of organizations and from many different sectors of the economy. You will want to invest in a mutual fund that fits your investment requirements and financial goals.

Mutual fund shares are traded based on their net asset values. The net assets are the total value of the fund's investments less any debts it has. The **net asset value**, or NAV, is found by dividing the net assets by the number of shares held by stockholders.

318 ■ Chapter 7 Insurance and Investments

COMMON ERRORS

Students may fail to realize that the result of computations indicates a loss rather than a profit. Emphasize the need to estimate an answer before completing any computation and the need to compare the answer to that estimate.

For example, a fund with net assets of $10,000,000 and 500,000 shares issued will have a net asset value of $20 ($10,000,000 ÷ 500,000 = $20).

Mutual fund NAVs are published on the financial pages of daily newspapers.

Fund Name	NAV	Offer Price
Ameris Growth	10.12	10.96
Banner Income	29.70	30.88
Jantzen High Yield	11.85	12.38
Mercer International	16.58	N.L.
Overland Technology	7.27	N.L.
Parkson Equity	9.27	N.L.
Strand Balanced	10.15	10.47
Tubman Health	32.23	N.L.

Two types of mutual funds are shown in the table: *no-load funds* and *load funds*. The term *load* means commission. No-load funds are sold without a commission and have the abbreviation "N.L." in the Offer Price column. When you buy load funds, you pay the amount shown in the Offer Price column, which includes a commission charge.

To find the total investment made in no-load funds, multiply the number of shares by the NAV. For load funds, multiply the number of shares by the offer price.

Total Investment in No-Load Funds = No. Shares × NAV

Total Investment in Load Funds = No. Shares × Offer Price

EXAMPLE 1

Alberto Allende bought 300 shares of Parkson Equity Fund (see table above) and 500 shares of Ameris Growth Fund. What is Alberto's total investment in these mutual funds?

SOLUTION

Multiply the number of shares of Parkson Equity by its NAV.

300 × $9.27 = $2,781   total investment in no-load fund

Multiply the number of shares of Ameris Growth by its offer price.

500 × $10.96 = $5,480   total investment in load fund

Add the investments in the two mutual funds.

$2,781 + $5,480 = $8,261   total investment in mutual funds

■ **CHECK YOUR UNDERSTANDING**

A. Shizu Wakichi purchased 400 shares of no-load Mellon Technology Fund at its NAV of $17.35. What was her total investment in the fund? $6,940

B. Nicolas Davila bought 1,000 shares of a load fund, Allied Industries Fund, at its offering price of $26.74. What was his total investment in the fund? $26,740

Lesson 7.7 Mutual Funds ■ **319**

■ *CHECK YOUR UNDERSTANDING SOLUTIONS*

A. 400 × $17.35 = $6,940

B. 1,000 × $26.74 = $26,740

C. $9.87 − $9.45 = $0.42; $0.42 ÷ $9.87 = 0.0425, or 4.3%

D. $45.18 − $43.86 = $1.32; $1.32 ÷ $45.18 = 0.0292; or 2.9%

■ **Apply Goal 1**

Work through Example 1 with students completing the math at their desks.

Assign Check Your Understanding problems A and B for completion in class. Examine student work at their desks for errors or problems.

Teach Goal 2

Point out that load fund commission rates may vary substantially. However, rates have typically been between 3% and 8%.

A popular practice of mutual fund investors is to allow dividends to be used to purchase new shares automatically. The practice is called dividend reinvestment, and it avoids commissions on the purchase of the new shares. However, the investor must pay taxes on the dividends, even though the investor has not taken them in cash.

Apply Goal 2

Work through Example 2 with students doing the math at their desks.

Assign Check Your Understanding problems C and D for completion in class. Examine student work at their desks for difficulties.

■ ONGOING ASSESSMENT
Call on students to describe the major difference between load and no load funds, which is the commission. Then ask students to describe the steps to take to calculate the commission.

Teach Goal 3

Tell students that mutual funds pay out dividends and share capital gains with shareholders. If students show interest, you may wish to invite a financial advisor to class to provide information to students about these topics.

■ Amount and Rate of Commissions

When you buy no-load funds, you are not charged a commission. For load funds, the commission is the difference between the net asset value and the offer price. To find the rate of commission on a load fund's purchase, divide the commission by the offer price.

Offer Price − Net Asset Value = Commission

Commission ÷ Offer Price = Rate of Commission

EXAMPLE 2

What is the rate of commission, to the nearest tenth percent, on Banner Income Fund with a net asset value of $29.70 and an offer price of $30.88?

SOLUTION
Subtract the net asset value from the offer price.

$30.88 − $29.70 = $1.18   amount of commission

Divide the commission amount by the offer price.

$1.18 ÷ $30.88 = 0.0382, or 3.8%   rate of commission

■ CHECK YOUR UNDERSTANDING

C. Rosser Midcap Fund has a NAV of $9.45 and an offer price of $9.87. What is the rate of commission, to the nearest tenth percent?   4.3%

D. Tanella Yaou bought Security Real Estate Fund for $45.18. The fund's NAV was $43.86 at the time. What rate of commission, to the nearest tenth percent, did Tanella pay?   2.9%

■ Profit or Loss from Mutual Fund Investments

When shares are *redeemed*, or sold back to the mutual fund company, the investor is paid the net asset value. The proceeds from the sale are found by multiplying the net asset value by the number of shares redeemed.

Proceeds = Number of Shares × Net Asset Value

The profit or loss from owning mutual fund shares is calculated by finding the difference between the proceeds and the total amount invested. If the proceeds exceed the investment, there is a profit. If the amount invested is larger than the proceeds, there is a loss.

Proceeds − Amount of Investment = Profit

Amount of Investment − Proceeds = Loss

EXAMPLE 3

Find the proceeds from the sale of 100 shares of a mutual fund with a net asset value of $8.50. Find the amount of the profit or loss if the total investment in the 100 shares is $675.

COMMON ERRORS

Students may use the NAV as the denominator to find the rate of load fund commission. Emphasize that the denominator must be the offering price.

SOLUTION

Multiply the number of shares by the net asset value.

$100 \times \$8.50 = \$850$ proceeds

Subtract the amount of investment from the proceeds.

$\$850 - \$675 = \$175$ profit

■ **CHECK YOUR UNDERSTANDING**

E. Upon graduation, Todd redeemed 300 shares of a mutual fund at $17.22. His total investment in the shares was $4,391.10. What was his profit or loss? $774.90 profit

F. Ping-lin Sheng redeemed his 500 shares of Madison Capital Fund for $39.45 a share. His total investment in the shares was $19,922.25. What was his profit or loss on the redemption? $197.25 loss

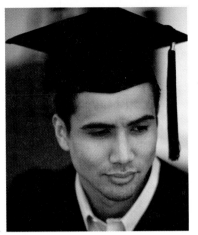

■ **Apply Goal 3**

Work through Example 3 with students doing the math at their desks.

Assign Check Your Understanding problems E and F for completion in class. Examine student work at their desks for difficulties.

Wrap Up

Look back to the Start Up problem. One strategy might be to purchase every trading card for a season, which is similar to the diversification strategy practiced by many mutual funds. Another strategy might be to buy only the cards of players on those teams that were contenders for the playoffs, which is similar to mutual funds investing in businesses that are in sectors that are likely to do well in a year. Another strategy might be to purchase the trading cards of players who show early success, which is similar to a mutual fund's practice of investing in companies with demonstrated potential.

Wrap Up

Review the Start Up. Discuss key items from student papers that may apply to mutual funds. For example, relate the strategy of purchasing every trading card for a year to the diversification strategy practiced by many mutual funds. Relate the purchase of trading cards of players who show early success to a mutual fund's practice of investing in companies with demonstrated potential.

TEAM MEETING

Some problems are simplified if you can find a pattern and use it to solve problems or answer questions.

Suppose you own some stock and are thinking of selling it. You could look for patterns that might help you make a decision. You have tracked its selling price and dividends. You find these results:

	Selling Price	Dividends
Jan. 1	25.25	2.1%
April 1	22.50	1.4%
July 1	20.87	0.5%
Oct. 1	18.38	3.2%
Dec. 31	19.25	3%

Form a team with another student to discuss the following questions: (a) What patterns do you see? (b) Would you have sold the stock in July? (c) If today were January 2, would you sell the stock? Explain your reasoning.

TEAM MEETING

Finding a pattern is a useful problem-solving strategy. Ask students why, when dealing with stock, identifying patterns might help investors to make better decisions.

Answers will vary. Some students may suggest that the pattern may have different meanings depending on the objective of the investor. For example, the fact that the price of the stock has dropped 4 of 5 quarters is especially important knowledge to a trader. However, the fact that the dividend rate has increased substantially during the last 2 quarters is especially important to those investing for income.

Lesson 7.7 Mutual Funds ■ **321**

■ *CHECK YOUR UNDERSTANDING SOLUTIONS*

E. $300 \times \$17.22 = \$5,166$;
   $\$5,166 - \$4,391.10 = \$774.90$ profit

F. $500 \times \$39.45 = \$19,725$;
   $\$19,922.25 - \$19,725 = \$197.25$ loss

Assess

Check student answers to the exercises by calling on them in class, collecting and grading selected problems, or by observing student work as you circulate.

Ask students to define the bolded and italicized terms in the lesson and use them in sentences.

Reteach

STUDENT WORKBOOK If students need help calculating the total investment in a mutual fund, do Exercise 1a with them. Then have them do Exercises 1b–1e.

If students need help with finding the rate of commission, do Exercise 3a with them. Then have them do Exercises 3b–3e.

If students need help finding the profit or loss from a mutual fund investment, do Exercise 4 with them. Then have them do Exercises 5 and 6.

EXERCISES

Find the difference.

1. $4,089 − $3,415 $674

2. $34,551 − $29,796 $4,755

Find the product.

3. $16.32 × 108.55 $1,771.54

4. $7.24 × 44.784 $324.24

Find the percent, to the nearest tenth.

5. $45.12 ÷ $193   23.4%

6. $62.19 ÷ $525   11.8%

Using the information given in the table earlier in the lesson, find the total investment in these mutual fund purchases.

Mutual Fund	Number Shares	Total Investment
7. Ameris Growth	400	$4,384
8. Banner Income	132	$4,076.16
9. Jantzen High Yield	800	$9,904
10. Mercer International	260	$4,310.80
11. Overland Technology	100	$727
12. Parkson Equity	200	$1,854
13. Strand Balanced	500	$5,235

14. Allie Jenkins bought these technology sector shares of New Economy Fund, a no-load mutual fund, on different days: 70 shares, NAV $39.78; 200 shares, NAV $41.52; 80 shares, NAV $42.15. What was her total investment in the fund? $14,460.60

15. Wilson Growth, a no-load fund, has a net asset value of $42.52. Wilson Income, a load fund, is quoted with a net asset value of $30 and an offer price of $32.12. What total investment would be made if 100 shares each of Wilson Growth and Wilson Income were purchased? $7,464

16. Ridge Health Sector Fund is quoted at 12.16 NAV, 12.48 offer price. To the nearest tenth of a percent, what commission rate is charged?   2.6%

17. Your broker quotes Stamper International Fund at these prices: NAV, 7.03; offer price, 7.40. Find the rate of commission.   5%

Find the amount of commission and the rate of commission, to the nearest tenth percent, for each of these mutual fund shares.

Mutual Fund	NAV	Offer Price	Amount of Commission	Rate of Commission
18. Cyber Net Fund	18.87	19.26	$0.39	2%
19. Draper Energy Fund	51.12	53.76	$2.64	4.9%
20. Ethan Pacific Fund	88.75	97.00	$8.25	8.5%
21. Wu Equity Fund	68.64	71.84	$3.20	4.5%

SELECTED SOLUTIONS

14. 70 × $39.78 = $2,784.60; 200 × $41.52 = $8,304;
80 × $42.15 = $3,372;
$2,784.60 + $8,304 + $3,372 = $14,460.60

16. $12.48 − $12.16 = $0.32;
$0.32 ÷ $12.48 = 0.0256, or 2.6%

23. 1,280 × $47.48 = $60,774.40

24. $60,774.40 − $42,792 = $17,982.40 profit

22. A commission of $3.52 is charged for a mutual fund with an offer price of $45.25. What is the actual rate, to the nearest tenth percent?   7.8%

The Bradford Energy Fund has a current NAV of $47.48. Edward Carter redeemed the 1,280 shares that he had bought for a total cost of $42,792.

23. What were Edward's proceeds?
$60,774.40

24. Find his profit or loss.
$17,982.40 profit

The Columbia Fund had a NAV of $47.64 and an offer price of $48.60 on the day that Sally Worth bought 500 shares of the fund. Six months later, the fund was quoted at these prices when Sally redeemed her shares: NAV, $48.66; offer price, $49.68.

25. What proceeds did Sally receive? $24,330

26. What amount of profit or loss did Sally make? $30 profit

MIXED REVIEW

27. 250 is what part greater than 200?   25%

28. Estimate the cost of 5.1 oz. at $8.85. $45

29. 420 is what percent of 4,800?   8.75%

30. Write $\frac{44}{30}$ as a decimal, rounded to the nearest tenth.   1.5

31. Find the cost of 2,600 lb @ 18¢ per cwt. $468, Lesson 5.2

32. Suba Jaidka is a waitress and earned these tips last week: Tues., $55; Wed., $75; Thurs., $80; Fri., $120; Sat., $135. What is the average amount of tips she earned per day? $93, Lesson 1.5

33. The cash payments for Danny McKay for the week of June 6 are: June 6, lunch $12.98; June 7, groceries $148.45; June 7, videos $8.50; June 8, rent $545; June 9, savings $150; June 10, power bill $235; June 12, car payment $378.99. Find Danny's total cash payments for the week. $1,478.92, Lesson 2.6

34. Velma Reese's March 31 bank statement balance was $281.73. Her outstanding checks were for these amounts: $25.17, $19.75, $27.89. Velma deposited $125 late on March 31 in the bank's night deposit box. It was not opened by bank employees until the next day and did not appear on the bank statement. Reconcile the bank statement. $333.92, Lesson 3.5

The Roswell Income Fund trades at a net asset value of $34.88 and an offer price of $36.46.

35. What commission amount is paid per share? $1.58, Lesson 7.7

36. To the nearest tenth percent, find the commission rate.   4.3%, Lesson 7.7

37. Manfred Tulley bought 300 shares of Tempe Growth Fund for $21,577.50. Two years later he sold his shares at a $65.25 NAV. What was his profit or loss?
$2,002.50 loss, Lesson 7.7

Gazi Ecevit purchased 200 shares of common stock in the Rivalo Company at $43.68 through an online broker. The commission was $29.95. He later sold the same stock at $41.25, paying commission and fees of $32.25.

38. What was Gazi's total cost for the stock? $8,765.95

39. What amount did Gazi receive as net proceeds from the sale? $8,217.75

40. What was Gazi's profit or loss on the sale? $548.20 loss

Lesson 7.7 Mutual Funds ▪ **323**

Start Up

Have students read the Start Up. If there are students whose family or friends rent houses, ask them to share the benefits and pitfalls of renting with the class.

List the factors on the board that are discussed by the class and ask a student to record them at the same time. Save the list for the Wrap Up discussion.

Math Skill Builder

Use the Math Skill Builder to prepare students for the addition, subtraction, multiplication, and division used in the lesson.

Have students do all exercises in Math Skill Builder 1–4.

7.8 Real Estate

GOALS

- Calculate net income from real estate investments
- Calculate the rate of return on real estate investments
- Calculate the monthly rent to be charged

Start Up

Janice and Jim Canter would like to move to a larger house. They are considering keeping and renting their present house as an investment. They wonder whether renting the house would be a good investment for them financially. What factors might they consider in making this decision?

Math Skill Builder

Review these math skills and solve the exercises that follow.

1. **Add** dollar amounts.
   Find the sum. $450 + $2,398 + $941 = $3,789

   1a. $1,290 + $4,208 + $638 + $2,108 $8,244

   1b. $289 + $6,792 + $749 + $3,184 $11,014

2. **Subtract** dollar amounts from dollar amounts.
   Find the difference. $9,600 − $7,895 = $1,705

   2a. $11,893 − $9,215 $2,678

   2b. $6,182 − $4,297 $1,885

3. **Multiply** dollar amounts by whole numbers and percents.
   Find the product. $249.20 × 12 = $2,990.40
   Find the product. $246,500 × 3% = $246,500 × 0.03 = $7,395

   3a. $487 × 12 $5,844   **3b.** $134,800 × 2.5% $3,370

   3c. $629 × 12 $7,548   **3d.** $89,345 × 2.7% $2,412.32

4. **Divide** dollar amounts by dollar amounts to find a percent.
   Find the quotient, to the nearest tenth percent.
   $2,400 ÷ $45,000 = 0.0533, or 5.3%

   4a. $3,680 ÷ $56,700   6.5%   **4b.** $2,734 ÷ $38,400   7.1%

324 ■ Chapter 7 Insurance and Investments

TEACHING STRATEGIES Expanding Beyond the Classroom

Consider asking a real estate agent that specializes in rental properties to address the class on rental properties as investments, including current market rents for residential houses, common expenses, and some tools to estimate common expenses. Prepare students for the visit by assigning and discussing the Start Up problem the previous class period.

Net Income from Real Estate

When you invest in real estate, the rent you receive is your gross income from the investment. Your net income is the amount left after you pay all the expenses of owning the property.

The following table shows that only part of the money you collect as rent is profit. The rest of the money is usually used to pay for taxes, repairs, insurance, and interest on a mortgage. Since buildings wear out because of age and use, you will also have to calculate depreciation.

You usually calculate your income and expenses on an annual basis. The annual net income is the amount left after deducting the annual expenses from the annual rental income.

Annual Rental Income − Annual Expenses = Annual Net Income

EXAMPLE 1

Chieko Beppu bought a house and lot for $150,000. She made a $30,000 cash down payment and got a $120,000 mortgage for the balance. She rented the house to a tenant for $1,500 a month. Her annual payments for taxes, repairs, insurance, interest, depreciation, and other expenses totaled $14,100. What annual net income did she earn?

SOLUTION
Multiply rent by 12.

$12 \times \$1,500 = \$18,000$ annual rental income

Subtract the annual expenses from annual rental income.

$\$18,000 - \$14,100 = \$3,900$ annual net income

■ CHECK YOUR UNDERSTANDING

A. Ursula Pavlok bought a building with four stores in it and the lot on which it stands for $850,000. During the first year, she received $2,300 a month in rent for each store unit. Her expenses for the year were: mortgage interest, $102,000; 2% depreciation on the building valued at $650,000; taxes, repairs, insurance, and other expenses, $74,500. Find her net income or loss for the year. $79,100 net loss

---

■ *CHECK YOUR UNDERSTANDING SOLUTIONS*

A. $4 \times 12 \times \$2,300 = \$110,400$;
$\$650,000 \times 0.02 = \$13,000$;
$\$102,000 + \$13,000 + \$74,500 = \$189,500$;
$\$189,500 - \$110,400 = \$79,100$, net loss

B. $12 \times \$3,800 = \$45,600$;
$\$198,000 \times 0.03 = \$5,940$;
$\$19,200 + \$5,940 + \$15,750 = \$40,890$;
$\$45,600 - \$40,890 = \$4,710$

■ **Teach Goal 2**

Point out the relationship between the general level of interest rates and the rate of income that should be earned on real estate investments. Ordinarily, higher returns should be achieved through real estate investments than can be earned by leaving money on deposit in a bank, primarily as a reward or incentive for taking risks.

Stress that only the cash investment is used to find the rate of return on real estate.

Note to students that the rate of return on a real estate investment is also called yield, just as in other investments.

■ **Apply Goal 2**

Do Examples 2 and 3 with students while they do the math at their desks.

Assign Check Your Understanding problems C and D for completion in class. Move about your classroom and check student work for difficulties.

■ **ONGOING ASSESSMENT**

With their books closed, call out, in random order, the two types of capital investments and three types of expenses listed in the last sentences of the paragraphs following the Example 2 solution. As you do so, ask students to identify them as capital investments or expenses.

B. Melvin Weisbaum bought a house and lot in a resort area for $288,000. He paid $72,000 in cash and got a mortgage for the rest. He rented the house to a tenant for $3,800 a month. For the first year, Melvin's expenses were: mortgage interest, $19,200; 3% depreciation on the house, valued at $198,000; taxes, repairs, insurance, and other expenses, $15,750. What was his net income for the year? $4,710

■ Rate of Return on Real Estate

The rate of return on a real estate investment is based on the money or cash invested in the property. It is found by dividing the annual net income by the cash investment.

Rate of Return = Annual Net Income ÷ Cash Investment

EXAMPLE 2

Find the rate of return for Chieko Beppu's house in Example 1.

SOLUTION
Divide the annual net income by the cash invested.

$3,900 ÷ $30,000 = 0.13 or 13%   rate of return

As a property owner, you will spend money on both capital investments and expenses. **Capital investment** is the amount of cash you originally invested plus anything you spent for improvements that make the property more valuable. Adding a room or a garage to a rental house are examples of capital investments.

Money spent for repairing or replacing broken items does not increase the value of property. It is an expense of owning the property. The money paid returns the property to its original condition. Expenses include repainting the house, replacing a broken sidewalk, and repairing leaking faucets.

To find the return on investment after you have made capital investment improvements in a property, you must add the cash spent on the improvements to your original cash investment.

EXAMPLE 3

Suppose that on buying the rental house, Chieko (see Example 1) spent an additional $2,700 in cash to add a deck to her rental house. What would the rate of return on her real estate investment be?

326 ■ Chapter 7 Insurance and Investments

BUSINESS TIP

The rate of return on an investment is also called the *yield*. It is also called the *rate of income* on an investment.

BUSINESS TIP

Capital investment is an investment in anything that cannot easily be turned into cash and which is usually held by the investor for longer than one year.

COMMON ERRORS

Students may confuse capital investments and expenses. Have them reread the relevant paragraphs on page 326. Then suggest that they make a list of possible capital investment and expense items and mark each with the proper label.

SOLUTION

Add the two cash amounts invested in the house.

$30,000 + $2,700 = $32,700   capital investment in house

Divide the annual net income by the capital investment.

$3,900 ÷ $32,700 = 0.119, or 11.9%   rate of return

■ CHECK YOUR UNDERSTANDING

C. Talibu Mbasa bought a house with a $25,000 down payment. He added a basement room and bath for $14,600. He spent $2,600 to paint the exterior and $2,300 to repair the plumbing. What is Talibu's capital investment in the house? $39,600

D. Ida Silvers purchased a cottage and lot for $85,000, paying $17,000 down and using a mortgage for the rest. The lot is estimated to be worth $5,000. She added a room by remodeling the attic for $12,600. She estimates that she will be able to rent the cottage for $1,200 a month. Her annual expenses will be $5,400, mortgage interest; 2.5% depreciation on the cottage and its capital improvements, and $4,800 other expenses. What is Ida's estimated return on her investment, to the nearest tenth percent? 6.4%

■ Finding What Monthly Rent to Charge

To find the amount to charge for rent, first find the total annual expenses. Then find the amount you want to earn as net income on your investment. Add those two amounts and divide the sum by 12 to find the monthly rent to charge.

Annual Net Income + Annual Expenses = Annual Rental Income

Annual Rental Income ÷ 12 = Monthly Rent

EXAMPLE 4

Ezra wants to earn 15% annual net income on his $10,000 cash investment in property. His annual expenses of owning the property are $2,700. What monthly rent must Ezra charge?

SOLUTION

Change the percent to a decimal and multiply by the cash investment.

15% × $10,000 = 0.15 × $10,000 = $1,500   desired annual net income

Add the desired annual net income and the annual expenses.

$1,500 + $2,700 = $4,200   annual rental income

Divide the annual rent income by 12. $4,200 ÷ 12 = $350   monthly rent

■ CHECK YOUR UNDERSTANDING

E. Sid Weisbaum bought a vacant warehouse with a $24,000 down payment. He estimates that expenses will be $8,640 the first year. Sid wants to earn a rate of income of 8% on his investment. To do that, what monthly rent must he charge? $880

F. Ellie Burns wants to earn 15% annual net income on her $30,000 cash investment in a property. Her annual expenses of owning the property are $8,100. What monthly rent must Ellie charge? $1,050

Lesson 7.8 Real Estate ■ 327

■ Teach Goal 3

Point out that the expenses of owning rental property are similar to those of being a homeowner. The total of ownership expenses plus the desired income from the investment are used to calculate the monthly rent to be charged.

Note to students that it would be tempting to simply raise rents to increase net income. However, real estate owners who charge rents that are much higher than the going market are not likely to be able to reach the occupancy level needed to reach investment goals. At the same time, if rates are set too low, they may not be able to pay their obligations or reach their goals.

■ Apply Goal 3

Do Example 4 with students while they do the math at their desks.

Assign Check Your Understanding problems E and F for completion in class. Move about your classroom and check student work for difficulties.

■ STUDENT PORTFOLIO

Students may wish to consider placing their solutions to the Check Your Understanding problems C–F in their portfolios.

■ CHECK YOUR UNDERSTANDING SOLUTIONS

C. $25,000 + $14,600 = $39,600

D. $17,000 + $12,600 = $29,600; 12 × $1,200 = $14,400; $85,000 − $5,000 = $80,000; $80,000 + $12,600 = $92,600; $92,600 × 0.025 = $2,315; $5,400 + $2,315 + $4,800 = $12,515; $14,400 − $12,515 = $1,885; $1,885 ÷ $29,600 = 0.0636, or

6.4%

E. 0.08 × $24,000 = $1,920; $1,920 + $8,640 = $10,560; $10,560 ÷ 12 = $880

F. 0.15 × $30,000 = $4,500; $4,500 + $8,100 = $12,600; $12,600 ÷ 12 = $1,050

Wrap Up

Review the Start Up. Then compare the list of factors used to decide whether to rent or not that were prepared in the Start Up to those listed in the Wrap Up. Discuss the differences and ask if students wish to add more factors to their lists.

COMMUNICATION

With their permission, make transparencies of one or more student charts to show and discuss with the class. You might ask those students to present their charts. In either case, ask the class to discuss why the rates for the different investments vary.

Assign

Assignment: Exercises 1–25 and 28–33, 36–46. Start with the basic arithmetic problems at the beginning of the exercises to be sure that students understand the underlying arithmetic in the exercises.

Wrap Up

Look at the Start Up question at the start of this lesson. One factor to consider is how the return on the rental property compares to the return on other investments they might make with the cash from the sale of the old house. The Canters might estimate their gross income using rents charged for similar properties in their neighborhood. They can subtract from that gross income the expenses they know they will have with the house and find the likely return on their investment. They should then compare their return on the house to returns on other investments, such as bonds, stocks, or mutual funds.

COMMUNICATION

Visit or call a real estate agent to determine the typical return on investment percentages for rental housing in your area. Also, call a local bank to find the APR for a 3-year CD, and the APR for a savings account. Finally, call a local stockbroker to find the annual yield on a high quality corporate bond. Prepare a chart showing the various percentages you found.

EXERCISES

Perform indicated operation. Round to nearest tenth, if needed.

1. $19 + $927 + $638 $1,584
2. $842 + $72 + $604 $1,518
3. $18,598 − $16,223 $2,375
4. $8,450 ÷ $97,922 8.6%
5. $362 − $53 $309
6. $361 × 14 $5,054
7. $187,526 × 1.8% $3,375.47
8. $422 ÷ $7,121 5.9%

Find the annual net income for each real estate owner.

	Monthly Rent Income	Taxes	Repairs	Insurance	Interest	Depreciation	Other	Annual Net Income
					Annual Expenses			
9.	$420	$1,204	$329	$350	$1,470	$910	$35	$742
10.	620	1,900	720	760	2,200	1,120	80	$660
11.	420	1,400	105	295	1,500	1,025	45	$670
12.	1,080	3,260	1,680	720	3,740	2,400	150	$1,010

13. Marvin bought a house and lot for $72,000. He paid $18,000 cash and got a mortgage for the balance. He rented the house to a tenant for $950 a month. For the first year, Marvin's expenses were: mortgage interest, $4,800; 3% depreciation on the house valued at $58,000; taxes, repairs, insurance, and other expenses, $3,750. What was his net income for the year? $1,110

328 ■ Chapter 7 Insurance and Investments

COMMON ERRORS

When completing complicated exercises, such as Exercises 13 and 14, students may leave out one or more essential calculations. Encourage students to work systematically through problems. Keeping work neat is also essential. Finally, students should always check to see if their answer is reasonable.

14. Fatou Keita bought an eight-unit apartment building for $165,000. During the first year of ownership, she received $480 a month for the rent of each apartment unit. Her expenses for the year were: mortgage interest, $20,700; 2.5% depreciation on the building valued at $125,000; taxes, repairs, insurance, and other expenses, $14,200. Find her net income for the year. $8,055

Find the rate of return, to the nearest tenth percent, on each cash investment. Show losses, or negative rates of return with a minus sign.

	Annual Expenses				
	Cash Investment	**Monthly Rental Income**	**Interest on Mortgage**	**Other**	**Rate of Income**
15.	$23,000	$600	$2,800	$2,100	10%
16.	35,000	800	1,800	3,100	13.4%
17.	41,000	1,600	10,200	9,800	−2%
18.	13,000	400	2,100	1,550	8.8%
19.	33,000	700	2,500	2,050	11.7%

20. Mario Valente took out a $58,400 mortgage on a two-family house after making a down payment of $14,600. During the first year, he rented one unit at $550 a month and the other unit at $580 a month. For the year, he paid $5,800 in mortgage interest and $6,300 in other expenses. To the nearest tenth of a percent, what rate of income did Mario earn on his cash investment?   10%

21. For $390,000, Bella Leipsen can buy an office building and lot that rents for $2,600 a month. Taxes, insurance, and repair expenses average $19,500 annually. Depreciation is estimated at $6,000 a year. Bella plans to pay $78,000 cash as a down payment. To the nearest tenth of a percent, find the rate of income she will make on her cash investment.   7.3%

22. Bill Walsh made a $7,000 down payment on a condominium apartment that cost $35,000. He rented the condo at $510 monthly for the first year. During the year he had these expenses: taxes, $1,090; insurance, $370; interest, $2,400; repairs, $1,200; depreciation, $700. What was Bill's rate of income on his cash investment, to the nearest tenth percent?   5.1%

23. Marla Rios bought a six-unit apartment house for $140,000 and made a cash down payment of $40,000. The first year, she rented each of the 6 apartments at $500 a month. Her expenses for the year were: mortgage interest, $9,600; depreciation at 3% of the house's value of $110,000; taxes, insurance, and other expenses, $12,600. Find Marla's rate of income on her cash investment, to the nearest tenth percent.   26.3%

24. Alan Weiss wants to buy a vacant 4-unit apartment by paying $21,000 in back taxes due the city. To meet current building and safety codes, he will have to spend $28,000 in capital improvements. Alan calculates that each unit can be rented for $400 a month and that total annual expenses for all units will be $8,900. If he buys the apartment, what rate of income will Alan earn, to the nearest tenth of a percent?   21%

25. Wendy Baughm bought a five-year old condominium for $136,000. She paid $27,200 in cash and immediately spent $4,400 to install a deck. Wendy also spent $3,200 to paint the interior and make minor repairs. What was her capital investment in the condo? $31,600

Lesson 7.8 Real Estate ■ 329

SELECTED SOLUTIONS

14. $12 \times 8 \times \$480 = \$46,080$;
$0.025 \times \$125,000 = \$3,125$;
$\$20,700 + \$3,125 + \$14,200 = \$38,025$;
$\$46,080 - \$38,025 = \$8,055$

20. $\$550 + \$580 = \$1,130$; $12 \times \$1,130 = \$13,560$;
$\$5,800 + \$6,300 = \$12,100$;
$\$13,560 - \$12,100 = \$1,460$;
$\$1,460 \div \$14,600 = 0.10$, or 10%

25. $\$27,200 + \$4,400 = \$31,600$

Assign Exercise 34, Critical Thinking. Although the questions posed in Exercise 34 are open-ended, many of the problems that students identify will relate to profitability. Answers should focus on procedures that will reduce the occurrence of events that impact negatively on profitability. These may include damage done by tenants, non-payment of rent, disruptions that drive out other tenants, illegal conduct, etc.

Assign Exercise 35, Critical Thinking, and discuss it in class. Student responses should include such factors as risk, time and effort involved in maintaining investment, capital appreciation potential, and liquidity of investment.

Close

Have students read Exercises 26 and 27. Then ask them the steps needed to arrive at the solutions. Have them complete the Exercises and monitor their progress.

Marvin makes a down payment of $45,600 to buy a house. He also spends $14,000 to improve the property by adding a room and paving the driveway. Marvin estimates the total annual expenses of owning the house to be $16,200.

26. What would be Marvin's capital investment in the house? $59,600

27. What monthly rent will he have to charge in order to make a net income of 7% on his total capital investment? $1,697.67

Find the monthly rent the owner must charge.

	Cash Investment	Desired Annual Net Income	Annual Expenses	Monthly Rent
28.	$25,000	12% of investment	$3,900	$575
29.	18,000	8% of investment	2,990	$369.17
30.	35,000	11% of investment	9,430	$1,106.67
31.	46,000	7% of investment	8,600	$985

Bea Tompkins bought two lots for $16,000 at a tax sale. She estimates that her yearly expenses of owning these lots will be $740. A nearby factory wants to use the lots for parking trucks overnight. To earn a 12% rate of income on her investment:

32. What annual rent should Bea charge? $2,660

33. What monthly rent should Bea charge? $221.67

34. **CRITICAL THINKING** Assume you want to buy a small apartment building. What problems do you expect to have by being a landlord? Can you think of ways to prevent or solve those problems? Will you have to work full time at being a landlord? Based on your answers to these questions, what do you think are some of the advantages and disadvantages of investing in real estate?
See Enrich section for answer.

35. **CRITICAL THINKING** Which rate of return would you rather earn: 7% from a rental house or 7% from a bond? Explain your answer.
See Enrich section for answer.

MIXED REVIEW

36. Divide 96 by $\frac{3}{4}$. 128

37. Find 105% of 120. 126

38. Rewrite 4.5 as a percent. 450%

39. 24 is what percent of 75? 32%

40. Find 3% less than $38.25. $37.10

41. Subtract $\frac{1}{16}$ from $\frac{5}{8}$. $\frac{9}{16}$

42. Multiply 45.076 by 100. 4,507.60

43. Multiply 4.017 by 1,000. 4,017

44. Nellie O'Brien earns a salary of $1,500 a month plus 5% commission on all sales. Last month her sales were $40,000. What was her gross income for the month? $3,500, Lesson 1.4

45. Zed Hargrove withdrew $1,200 from a time-certificate account that paid 7% annual interest. Because he withdrew his money before the end of the term, the bank charged a penalty of 2 months' interest. What was the amount of the penalty? $14, Lesson 3.7

46. A 956 KB file was downloaded over the Internet using a dial-up line with a true speed of 40 kbps. How many seconds did the download take? 191.2, Lesson 5.5

330 ■ Chapter 7 Insurance and Investments

SELECTED SOLUTIONS

28. $25,000 × 0.12 = $3,000;
$3,000 + $3,900 = $6,900;
$6,900 ÷ 12 = $575

32. $16,000 × 0.12 = $1,920;
$1,920 + $740 = $2,660

33. $2,660 ÷ 12 = $221.666, or $221.67

7.9 Retirement Investments

GOALS

- Calculate your retirement income
- Calculate your pension income
- Calculate the required minimum payout from a pension fund
- Calculate the penalty for early withdrawal from an individual retirement account

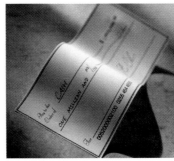

Start Up

Some working people do not save money for retirement, counting on their Social Security benefits to provide their retirement income. Is this a wise plan?

Math Skill Builder

Review these math skills and solve the exercises that follow.

1 **Subtract** dollar amounts.
Find the difference. $4,290 − $2,978 = $1,312

1a. $5,398 − $3,148 $2,250   **1b.** $11,408.23 − $8,971.93 $2,436.30

2 **Multiply** percents by whole numbers and dollar amounts.
Find the product. 2.4% × 40 = 0.024 × 40 = 0.96
Find the product. 96% × $75,000 = 0.96 × $75,000 = $72,000

2a. 1.7% × 30   0.51   **2b.** 2.3% × 40   0.92

2c. $84,500 × 82.4% $69,628   **2d.** $49,300 × 75.9% $37,418.70

3 **Divide** dollar amounts by decimals and dollar amounts.
Find the quotient. $360,000 ÷ 21.8 = $16,513.76
Find the quotient to the nearest tenth percent. $5,500 ÷ $420,000 = 1.3%

3a. $459,600 ÷ 18.4 $24,978.26   **3b.** $277,500 ÷ 12.7 $21,850.39

3c. Divide $3,670 by $248,900 to the nearest tenth percent.   1.5%

■ Retirement Income

You may receive retirement income from several sources: Social Security benefits, your own pension plan, a company, union, or organization pension plan, and income from other investments.

The income taxes on the amount you invest and the income your investment earns may be deferred until you retire, depending on the type of investment. This allows your retirement funds to grow much faster.

Lesson 7.9 Retirement Investments ■ 331

Stress that your retirement funds grow much faster if they are not taxed as they grow. Have students examine the chart comparing taxed and untaxed investments. Ask them to find the difference at 20 years ($54,426) and 40 years ($313,559). Relate the differences to the concept of compound interest.

Emphasize the importance of continual, *early*, investment in a retirement account. Use the Tech7-1 Excel spreadsheet to demonstrate how it is almost impossible to catch up later for lack of consistent investment early on in a worker's life.

Point out that the $5,000 taxable deduction will not be in place fully until 2008.

■ Apply Goal 1

Work through Example 1 with students completing the math at their desks.

Assign Check Your Understanding problems A and B for completion in class. Roam the classroom and check student work for errors and problems.

For example, one type of retirement investment is the **individual retirement account**, or IRA. There are many types of IRAs. The traditional IRA allows individuals earning less than a certain annual amount to invest up to $5,000 each year by the year 2008. The tax on the money invested and any earnings may be deferred until you retire. When you retire, the money you withdraw from your IRA will be taxed at the current tax rate.

Advantage of Tax Deferred Investments		
Years	Nontaxed Investment	Investment Taxed at 20%
5	28,187	22,016
10	65,906	49,846
15	116,382	85,028
20	183,931	129,505
25	274,327	185,731
30	395,297	256,810
35	557,182	346,667
40	773,820	460,261

The table shows the results of investing $5,000 each year from 5 to 40 years. The chart assumes that a $5,000 investment is made at the beginning of each year and that the investment grows at 6% a year. Notice that if you invest in a tax deferred IRA, your total investment would grow to $773,820 in 40 years. If you place your money in a taxable investment, your balance would only be $460,261. Your money would have grown 68% more by being in a tax deferred IRA instead of an investment taxed yearly!

BUSINESS TIP

The maximum amount a person under 50 can contribute to an IRA will increase from $3,000 to $5,000 by 2008. After 2008 the maximum amount will be adjusted for inflation.

BUSINESS TIP

Taxpayers earning less than a certain amount a year may deduct from taxable income up to $5,000 by investing in a traditional IRA. The amount of investment that can be deducted is phased out as annual income rises.

EXAMPLE 1

Sam Weisbrunner is retiring at age 65. At age 65, his company pension will pay him $1,560 a month and social security will pay him $800 a month. He has $120,000 in an IRA fund. What percent, to the nearest tenth of the fund must Sam withdraw each month to raise his monthly retirement income to $3,600 ?

SOLUTION
Add the monthly company pension and social security.

$1,560 + $800 = $2,360   retirement income

Subtract the non-IRA income from the desired monthly income.

$3,600 − $2,360 = $1,240   amount needed from IRA

Divide the amount needed from the IRA by the amount of the IRA fund.

$1,240 ÷ $120,000 = 0.0103, or 1.0%   percent to withdraw each month

TEACHING STRATEGIES Cooperative Learning

Have teams of 2–3 students investigate ERISA, or the Employee Retirement Income Security Act. They should prepare a report that describes the major features of the Act, especially how it protects employee pension plans established by their employers.

■ **CHECK YOUR UNDERSTANDING**

A. Jane Eiler will receive $1,620 in pension and $900 from social security each month when she retires at age 65. She wants her monthly retirement income to be $4,000. What percent, to the nearest tenth percent, of her $350,000 IRA must she withdraw monthly to reach the monthly income she wants? 0.4%

B. Abner Duncan started investing $5,000 in an IRA when he was 30. The account has earned a steady 6% growth each year. Find how much money Abner has in his IRA at age 60. $395,297

■ **Pension Income**

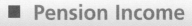

There are two basic types of pension funds: *defined contribution plans* and *defined benefit plans*. Under defined contribution plans, you, your employer, or both contribute to your pension fund, often a percent of your annual wages. The amount you receive depends on how well the investments in your plan do over the years.

A defined benefit plan pays you a specific amount on retirement. The amount you receive from your pension fund usually depends on a number of factors, including how old you are when you retire, how many years you contribute to that pension plan, and how much money you put in the pension fund over the years.

You may be penalized by retiring early. For example, you may receive a reduced benefit for retiring before age 65 or 67. You may also have to contribute for a minimum number of years to a pension plan to collect any money. You may also be given a choice of how much money you can put into the fund each year.

EXAMPLE 2

John Baker's pension fund will pay him a pension rate of 2.2% of his average salary for the last four years for each year of service with his organization. If John plans to retire after 30 years of service, what percent of his final salary will he receive? If his final average salary is $56,000, what annual amount will he receive?

SOLUTION
Multiply the yearly pension rate by the number of years of service.

2.2% × 30 = 66%   total pension rate

Multiply the total pension rate by the final average salary.

66% × $56,000 = 0.66 × $56,000 = $36,960   amount of pension

■ **CHECK YOUR UNDERSTANDING**

C. Keisha Turner is retiring after 30 years with her firm. Her pension fund pays 1.9% of her average salary for the last four years for each year of service. Her annual salary for the last four years was $71,000, $74,000, $75,000, and $77,000. What is her average salary for the last four years? What is the total pension rate? What monthly pension amount will she receive? $74,250; 57%; $3,526.88

D. Juan Vellano's union pension fund provides for $5 a month at age 65 for each $130 he has contributed. When Juan retired at age 65, he had contributed $96,000 to the fund. What is his monthly pension amount? $3,692.31

Lesson 7.9 Retirement Investments ■ **333**

■ *CHECK YOUR UNDERSTANDING SOLUTIONS*

A. $1,620 + $900 = $2,520; $4,000 − $2,520 = $1,480; $1,480 ÷ $350,000 = 0.0042, or 0.4%

C. 71,000 + $74,000 + $75,000 + $77,000 = $297,000; $297,000 ÷ 4 = $74,250 average salary; 30 × 1.9% = 57% pension rate; $74,250 × 0.57 =

$42,322.50; $42,322.50 ÷ 12 = $3,526.88 monthly pension

D. $96,000 ÷ $130 = 738.46153; 738.46153 × $5 = $3,692.307, or $3,692.31

■ **Teach Goal 2**

Point out that many state pension plans are defined benefit plans and that many corporate pension plans are defined contribution plans.

Discuss with students the risk of defined contribution plans that depend on the value of the investment during retirement. Have them consider what can happen if the person's plan is invested heavily in stock and a recession occurs. Relate the risk of defined contribution plans to the investment risks discussed in the previous lessons in Chapter 7.

■ **Apply Goal 2**

Work through Example 2 with students completing the math at their desks.

Assign Check Your Understanding problems C and D for completion in class. Check student work at their desks for errors or problems.

Note that problem C uses a percent per year of service and that D uses a monthly dollar amount.

Teach Goal 3 & 4

Both Goals 3 and 4 deal with withdrawals from retirement investments. Goal 3 and Example 3 deal with the minimum withdrawals from IRA investments required of people $70\frac{1}{2}$ years or older by the federal government.

Goal 4 and Example 4 deal with early withdrawal of amounts from IRA investments and the penalties that are applied by the federal government to this practice, except in specified cases.

Emphasize that regardless of when or how much a person withdraws from an IRA investment, the amount withdrawn is subject to federal income taxes if the amount was deducted from taxable income originally. The taxes on amounts invested in an IRA are not eliminated, but *deferred* until the amounts are withdrawn from the account.

Apply Goal 3 & 4

Work through Examples 3 and 4 with students doing the math at their desks.

Assign Check Your Understanding problems E and F to do in class. Check student work for errors and problems.

ONGOING ASSESSMENT
With the textbook closed, ask students to describe the two ways the lesson shows how a person's pension rate can be determined **(dollars or percent per year of service)**.

With the textbook closed, ask students to describe the procedure for finding the minimum IRA withdrawal amount for those $70\frac{1}{2}$ or more in age **(divide IRA balance by table divisor)**.

Withdrawals from a Retirement Investment

With few exceptions, you can't withdraw funds from a traditional IRA before you reach age $59\frac{1}{2}$. If you do, you will pay a 10% penalty on the amount you withdraw. You will also have to pay federal and state income taxes on the withdrawal.

A person who has a private pension fund, such as an IRA, must withdraw a minimum amount each year from the fund when that person reaches $70\frac{1}{2}$. The minimum amount of the withdrawal required by law depends on the age of the person withdrawing funds and is found using the chart shown below. To use the chart, find your age at retirement. Then divide the divisor for that age into the total value of your IRA. The result is the required minimum you must withdraw each year.

Age	Divisor	Age	Divisor
70	26.2	78	19.2
71	25.3	79	18.4
72	24.4	80	17.6
73	23.5	81	16.8
74	22.7	82	16.0
75	21.8	83	15.3
76	20.9	84	14.5
77	20.1	85	13.8

BUSINESS TIP

Some exceptions to the early IRA withdrawal penalty are if the money is used for a first-time home purchase, higher education, health insurance premium, certain medical expenses, or if you become disabled. The money withdrawn will still be subject to federal and state income taxes.

EXAMPLE 3

Lu-yin Huang's IRA balance is $428,000 at age 75. What amount must she withdraw from her IRA during the year?

SOLUTION
Divide the IRA balance by the divisor in the table for age 75.

$428,000 ÷ 21.8 = $19,633.03   minimum amount to be withdrawn

EXAMPLE 4

Tito Carlocci withdrew $3,000 from his IRA at age 41. What penalty did he pay?

SOLUTION
Multiply the amount withdrawn before the age of $59\frac{1}{2}$ by 10%.

$3,000 × 10% = $3,000 × 0.10 = $300   amount of penalty

■ CHECK YOUR UNDERSTANDING

E. Prasam Shinawatra is 72 and his IRA investment totals $396,100. What minimum amount must he withdraw this year? $16,233.61

F. Karl Schmidt withdrew $12,500 from his IRA at age 46. What penalty did Karl pay? $1,250

■ *CHECK YOUR UNDERSTANDING SOLUTIONS*
E. $396,100 ÷ 24.4 = $16,233.606, or $16,233.61   **F.** $12,500 × 0.10 = $1,250

Look back at the Start Up question. The Social Security Act provides only *supplemental* retirement benefits and should not be counted on to pay enough for a person to live on in retirement. It is important that you save money in a retirement account or pension plan other than social security if you wish to have enough money to retire.

WORKPLACE WINDOW

Many retired people who invest in apartment houses hire others to manage them so that they do not have to be involved in the day-to-day operation. Use the web or real estate agents to identify the following:

1. job titles of these managers

2. typical duties

3. ways in which they are paid

EXERCISES

1. Eileen Rustio started investing $5,000 in an IRA when she was 40. The account has earned a steady 6% growth each year. Use the table in the lesson to find how much money Eileen has in her IRA at age 65. $274,327

2. Use the table in the lesson to find, to the nearest whole percent, by how much the nontaxed investment amount is greater than the investment taxed at 20% after 30 years.   54%

3. Rod Schweiger receives $1,150 in monthly pension and $650 monthly from social security at retirement. He wants his monthly retirement income to be $3,000 a month. What percent of his $275,000 IRA must he withdraw to reach the monthly income he wants?   0.4%

4. Salvador Nuncio's monthly retirement income is made up of $1,900 from his employer-based pension fund and $900 from social security. He also has an IRA worth $150,000. What percent of his IRA must he withdraw if he wants his total retirement income to be $42,600 a year?   6%

5. Tony Conte is retiring after 40 years of work at age 65. He will receive the following monthly amounts: $1,400 from his union pension and $840 from social security. What is his annual retirement income? $26,880

Kelly O'Malley's pension fund pays 2.1% of her average salary for the last three years for each year of service. Her annual salary for the last three years was $87,000, $90,000, and $95,000. Kelly has contributed to her pension fund for 25 years.

6. What is her average salary for the last three years? $90,666.67

7. What is Kelly's total pension rate?   52.5%

8. What monthly pension amount will she receive if she retires this year? $3,966.67

Wrap Up

Review the Start Up. Ask students to identify from their study of the lesson the sources of retirement income that can augment social security to provide retirees with enough funds to live on.

WORKPLACE WINDOW

After students complete the assignment, call on them and make a list of the duties they identify on the board. Discuss the payment methods they found in relation to the duties identified to assess whether the payment methods fit the duties.

Assign

Assignment: Exercises 1–9 and 11–15, 17–24. Point out to students that Rod Schweiger (Exercise 3) and Salvador Nuncio (Exercise 4) do not need to be concerned about early withdrawal penalties because they are both more than $59\frac{1}{2}$ years old. At the same time, they do not need to worry about minimum withdrawals because they are less than $70\frac{1}{2}$ years of age.

Assess

Check student answers to the exercises by calling on them in class, collecting and grading selected problems, or by observing student work at their desks.

Ask students to define the bolded and italicized terms in the lesson and use them in sentences.

SELECTED SOLUTIONS

2. $395,297 − $256,810 = $138,487;
$138,487 ÷ $256,810 = 0.539, or 54%

3. $1,150 + $650 = $1,800;
$3,000 − $1,800 = $1,200;
$1,200 ÷ $275,000 = 0.0043, or 0.4%

6. $87,000 + $90,000 + $95,000 = $272,000;
$272,000 ÷ 3 = $90,666.67

7. 25 × 2.1% = 52.5%

8. $90,666.67 × 0.525 = $47,600; $47,600 ÷ 12 = $3,966.67

STUDENT WORKBOOK To reteach calculating retirement income, do Exercise 1 with students. Then have them do Exercises 2 and 3 independently during class time so you can be available for help.

To reteach calculating pension income, do Exercise 4 with them. Then have them complete Exercises 5 and 6 during class.

To reteach calculating minimum pension payouts, do Exercise 7 with them. Then have them do Exercises 8 and 9 during class.

To reteach calculating early withdrawal penalties from IRAs, do Exercise 11 with students and then have them do Exercise 12 independently at their desks.

Assign Exercise 16, Decision Making, and have students tell you how to solve the problem as you write the arithmetic on the board or a transparency.

Use Exercise 16 to lead into a discussion of (a) the impact of withdrawals on the compounding effect of retirement investing and (b) the alternatives people might consider for borrowing money in addition to life insurance cash value.

Pablo Gonzales contributed $48,000 to his pension fund over 20 years of service to his company. The fund pays $4 a month for each $100 of pension funds contributed if he retires at age 65.

9. What is his monthly pension amount at age 65? $1,920

10. **STRETCHING YOUR SKILLS** How many months will it take Pablo to recover the amount of his contributions? 25

11. Peter True's pension fund reduces the total pension rate he is to receive by $\frac{1}{2}$% for each year that he retires before the age of 67. If Peter retires at age 62, by what percent will he be penalized? 2.5%

12. Marla Pezweski is age 82 and has a $1,289,350 IRA. What amount must she withdraw, as a minimum, from her IRA this year? $80,584.38

13. Jake Reilly has a total of $529,200 in his IRA. If Jake is 76, what minimum amount must he withdraw from his IRA this year? $25,320.57

14. Amoni Rahum is age 78. Her IRA investment is $738,300. What minimum amount must she withdraw this year? $38,453.13

15. Rich Vanegan withdraws $4,350 from his IRA when he is only 35. What penalty must he pay? $435

16. **DECISION MAKING** Bea Roche is 48 years old. She wants to withdraw $5,125 from her IRA for a period of one year. Her friend suggests that she borrow the money from the loan value of her life insurance company. The loan would be at a rate of 7.5%. Which plan will cost Bea less? insurance loan, $128.12 less

MIXED REVIEW

17. Divide 569 by 16 to the nearest tenth. 35.6

18. Divide 104.68 by 4.5 to the nearest hundredth. 23.26

19. What is $\frac{3}{4}$ of $660? $495

20. Divide 54.358 by 100. 0.54358

21. Add: $1\frac{3}{4} + 41\frac{2}{5}$. $43\frac{3}{20}$

22. Rewrite $\frac{3}{8}$ as a decimal. 0.375

23. Tomas Mendosa borrowed $250 for 30 days on his credit card using a cash advance. His card company charged a cash advance fee of $25 and a daily periodic interest rate of 0.0514%. What was the total finance charge on the cash advance? $28.86, Lesson 4.8

24. Xavier Morrero paid for a cable connection to StarNet, an ISP. The ISP charged a $15 installation fee, $65 for a network connection card for his computer, a monthly rental fee of $4 for a modem, and a monthly online access fee of $49.95 for an unlimited connection. Xavier also bought antivirus software for $29.99. What will be Xavier's total cost to connect to the Internet for the first year? $757.39, Lesson 5.5

336 ■ Chapter 7 Insurance and Investments

SELECTED SOLUTIONS

9. $48,000 ÷ $100 = 480; 480 × $4 = $1,920

10. $48,000 ÷ $1,920 = 25

11. 67 − 62 = 5; 5 × $\frac{1}{2}$% = 2.5%

12. $1,289,350 ÷ 16 = $80,584.38

15. $4,350 × 0.10 = $435

Chapter Review

Vocabulary Review

bond discount
bond premium
bonds
capital investment
cash value
coinsurance

current yield on bonds
disability insurance
health insurance
Individual Retirement
    Account (IRA)
life insurance

major medical insurance
market price
mutual fund
net asset value

Fill in the blanks with one of the terms above.

1. If you cannot work due to a health condition or an injury, __?__ pays a portion of the income you lose.   *disability insurance*

2. __?__ protects your family against financial loss due to your death.   *life insurance*

3. __?__ helps pay for hospital, surgical, medical, or other health care expenses due to a major illness or an injury.   *major medical insurance*

4. __?__ provides basic protection against financial loss from medical bills.   *health insurance*

5. The money you get if you cancel a life insurance policy is called __?__.   *cash value*

6. __?__ are a form of long-term promissory note.   *bonds*

7. Annual interest income divided by a bond's price is called __?__.   *current yield on bonds*

8. The price at which a stock sells is called the __?__.   *market price*

9. __?__ companies use money from investors to buy stock in many companies.   *mutual fund*

10. The price at which mutual fund shares are traded is called __?__.   *net asset value*

11. The amount of cash you originally invest plus what you spend for improvements in real estate is called (a, an) __?__.   *capital investment*

12. A popular form of retirement investment is called __?__.   *Individual Retirement Account*

LESSON 7.1

13. Bob Walzcek bought a $135,000 term life insurance policy. He paid an annual premium of $1.65 per $1,000 of insurance. What annual premium did he pay?   *$222.75*

14. Ava Leland pays $145.80 quarterly for a whole life insurance policy. This year, her policy paid a dividend of $43.71. Find her annual premium and the net cost of her policy for the year.   *$583.20; $539.49*

15. Using the cash value table, how much can you borrow against a 15-year policy with a face value of $100,000?   *$8,000*

16. Using the cash value table, how much would you receive if you cancelled a 10-year policy with a face value of $50,000?   *$2,100*

Chapter Summary

Lesson 7.1 Life Insurance
- Divide face value of life insurance policy by $1,000 to find number of $1,000 units.

- Multiply number of $1,000s by cost per unit to find premium.

- Multiply quarterly premium by 4 to find total yearly premium.

- Subtract dividends from total premium to find net cost of insurance for the year.

- Multiply number of $1,000s of face value by table amount to find cash or loan value.

Lesson 7.2 Health Insurance
- Multiply total monthly premium by 12 to find annual premium.

- Multiply annual premium by employer's percentage share for employer's premium share.

- Subtract employer's share of annual premium from total annual premium to find employee's share.

- Subtract covered amount of medical bill from total medical bill to find uncovered portion.

- Subtract deductible from covered amount and multiply by coinsurance rate to find coinsurance amount.

- Add deductible, coinsurance, and uncovered amounts to find total patient must pay.

Lesson 7.3 Disability Insurance
- Find average wage, multiply by benefit percentage to find annual disability benefit.

- Divide annual disability benefit by 12 to find monthly benefit.

DIFFERENT LEARNING STYLES   Visual Learners

Once students complete the Vocabulary Review, have them complete the Term Puzzler for this chapter in the workbook. The term puzzler will visually reinforce the spelling of the terms used in the chapter.

- Multiply bond's decimal market price by bond's par value to find market price in dollars.

- Multiply market price by number bought and add commission to find total investment.

Lesson 7.5 Bond Interest
- Multiply interest rate by par value to find annual interest.

- Multiply year's bond interest by number of bonds owned to find total income from bonds.

- Divide annual bond interest by 2 to find semiannual interest payment on bond.

- Divide annual income by market price to find current yield.

- Add price, commission, if shown, and accrued interest on one bond to find total cost.

- Multiply total cost of each bond by number bought to find total cost of bonds.

Lesson 7.6 Stocks
- Multiply number of shares by market price and add commission to find total cost of stock purchase.

- Multiply dividend percent by stock's par value to find dividend on one share.

- Multiply dividend on one share by number of shares to find total annual dividend.

- Divide total annual dividend by total stock cost to find yield.

- Multiply number of shares of stock by market price and subtract commission and other charges to find net proceeds from sale of stock.

- Subtract total cost of stock from net proceeds from sale of stock to find profit or loss from sale of stock.

Lesson 7.7 Mutual Funds
- Multiply number of shares of no-load mutual fund by NAV to find total investment.

- Multiply number of shares of load mutual fund by offer price to find total investment.

338

LESSON 7.2

17. Alan Lester's employer pays 60% of his annual health insurance premium. If the total monthly premium for the insurance is $86, what is Alan's share of the annual premium? $2,100

18. Louisa Corita's total medical bill was $3,989. Only $3,583 was covered by her group medical insurance policy. Louisa's coinsurance for the bill was 21%, and her remaining annual deductible was $300. What amount of the medical bill must Louisa pay?
$1,395.43

LESSON 7.3

19. Boris Raskonov is totally disabled. His group disability policy's benefit percentage is 60% of his average annual salary for the last 3 years. His annual salary for the last 3 years was $55,300; $58,600, and $59,700. What monthly disability benefit amount will he receive? $2,893.33

LESSON 7.4

20. Tenco Foundry $1,000 bonds are quoted at 101.379. What is their market price?
$1,013.79

21. Tessalee Lightner bought 10, $1,000 Montgomery County bonds at 102.682. The broker charged $3 per bond commission. What total investment did Tessalee make in the bonds? $10,298.20

LESSON 7.5

22. Victor Armound bought 50, $1,000, 7.5% bonds. What is his annual income from the bonds? $3,750

23. Tara Sebring owns 100, $1,000, 8.25% bonds. How much does she earn semiannually from the bonds? $4,125

24. The semiannual interest on Laclede Airport $1,000 bonds is $62.50. If you buy the bonds at 98.487, what is the current yield, to the nearest tenth percent?   12.7%

25. Vaughnie Kinder buys 20, $1,000, 9.4% bonds through a dealer at 102.775 plus accrued interest of $23.50 per bond and commission of $4 per bond. What is the total cost of the bonds to Vaughnie? $21,105

26. Timothy O'Hane buys 10, $1,000, 7% bonds on April 1 at 101.528 plus accrued interest from January 1. Commission was not shown. What is Timothy's total cost for each bond? $10,327.80

LESSON 7.6

27. A broker sold Octavia Relenza 200 shares of stock at $23.19. Octavia's broker charged $199.13 commission. Find the total cost of the stock to Octavia. $4,837.13

28. Reality Films common stock pays a quarterly dividend of $3.50 per share. If Vincente Guillermo owns 500 shares of the stock, what amount will he receive in dividends for the year? $7,000

TEACHING STRATEGIES Chapter Review

Have students complete each problem in the Chapter Review. After students complete all the problems for each lesson, check student answers for each problem by calling on students. As you do so, have students who got the correct answers place their work on the board.

29. Diane Limbaugh bought 100 shares of stock at $10.78. Her broker charged her $47.30 commission. If the stock pays a quarterly dividend of $0.14, what is its annual yield, to the nearest tenth percent?   5.0%

30. Pedro Lamas bought 200 shares of common stock at $31.50 and was charged a commission of $134. He later sold the same stock for $38.20. The commission and fees on the sale were $143. What was Pedro's profit or loss? $1,063 profit

LESSON 7.7

31. Hisako Matsunaga purchased 400 shares of a no-load fund at its NAV of $11.73. She also purchased 300 shares of a load fund at its offer price of $23.77. What was her total investment in the funds? $11,823

32. A mutual fund has a NAV of $6.94 and an offer price of $7.22. What is the rate of commission, to the nearest tenth percent?   3.9%

33. You redeemed 300 shares of a mutual fund at their NAV of $14.72. Your total investment in the shares was $3,910.10. What was your profit or loss on the sale?
$505.90 profit

LESSON 7.8

34. Zebulon Poke bought a house and the lot it is on for $250,000. During the first year, he received $2,150 a month in rent. His expenses for the year were: mortgage interest, $12,800; 2% depreciation on the building valued at $200,000; taxes, repairs, insurance, and other expenses, $5,500. Find his net income or loss for the year. $3,500 net income

35. Bineka Zaheer bought a house with a $20,000 down payment. She also added a carport for $4,600. She estimates that she will be able to rent the house for $1,000 a month and that her first-year expenses will be mortgage interest, $5,600; taxes, $896; depreciation, $1,450; other expenses, $1,288. What is Bineka's estimated return on her investment, to the nearest tenth percent?   11.2%

36. Ollie Breem wants to earn 10% annual net income on his $25,000 cash investment in a property. His annual expenses of owning the property are $8,100. What monthly rent must Ollie charge? $883.33

LESSON 7.9

37. Jeanne Wilder is retired and receives $1,870 in monthly pension and $1,100 monthly from social security. She wants her monthly retirement income to be $4,500. What percent, to the nearest tenth, of her $250,000 IRA must she withdraw monthly to reach the monthly income she wants?   0.6%

38. Keiko Yoshino is retiring after 30 years with her firm. Her pension fund pays 2% of her average salary for the last three years for each year of service. Her annual salary for the last three years was $57,400, $59,200, and $61,600. What is her average salary for the last three years? What is the total pension rate? What monthly pension amount will she receive? $59,400; 60%; $2,970

39. Karl Lamour withdrew $22,000 from his IRA at age 49. What penalty did he pay?
$2,200

Chapter 7 Review ■ 339

(Lesson 7.7 cont'd)

- Subtract NAV from offer price to find amount of commission.

- Divide commission by offer price to find commission rate.

- Multiply number of mutual fund shares sold by NAV to find net proceeds from sale.

- Subtract total investment in fund from proceeds to find profit or loss on sale.

Lesson 7.8 Real Estate
- Multiply monthly rent by 12 and subtract annual expenses from annual rental income to find net annual income.

- Divide annual net income by cash to find rate of return.

- Multiply desired percentage of annual net income by investment for desired net income.

- Add desired net income and annual expenses to find annual rental income desired.

- Divide annual income desired by 12 to find monthly rent.

Lesson 7.9 Retirement Investments
- Add monthly pension and social security to find non-IRA pension income.

- Subtract monthly non-IRA pension income from the desired income to find withdrawal amount from IRA.

- Divide amount needed from IRA by total IRA investment to find percent to withdraw.

- Multiply yearly pension rate by number of years of service to find total pension rate.

- Multiply total pension rate by final average salary to find amount of pension.

- Divide IRA fund by divisor in table to find minimum withdrawal required by law.

- Multiply amount withdrawn from IRA before age $59\frac{1}{2}$ by 10% to find penalty.

PORTFOLIO ASSESSMENT

Students should review the materials they have created in this chapter and select those they wish to place in their portfolios. If students complete the Write or SCANS assign- ments, have them consider placing these assignments in their portfolios.

Students need spreadsheet file tech7-1.xls for Tasks 1 and 2.

Task 1 Students enter data into an IRA calculator template.

Task 2 Students answer questions about the results of Task 1. They also change data and answer questions about the new results.

Task 3 Students design and create a spreadsheet that calculates major medical expenses paid by insurer and insured.

Task 4 Students answer questions about data entered and about spreadsheet design. They also change data and answer questions about the new results.

Teach and Apply Task 1

Point out that at a 20% tax rate, a $5,000 IRA investment really only costs you $4,000 in after-tax income. Thus, saving $5,000 in an IRA has the same impact on your spending money as saving $4,000 in a non tax deferred investment.

Technology Workshop

Task 1: Enter Data In An IRA Calculator Template

Complete a template that estimates the future value of investments you make in an IRA.

Open the spreadsheet for Chapter 7 (tech7-1.xls) and enter the data shown in the blue cells (cells B3 through B5). Your computer screen should look like the one shown below when you are done.

The spreadsheet calculates the value of your investments in the future. For example, suppose that you invest $5,000 each year for 40 years starting at age 25. Suppose also that you estimate that the annual earnings of your investment will be 8%. The

	A	B
1	**IRA Calculator**	
2		
3	Estimated Annual Growth Rate	8.0%
4	Annual Investment	$5,000
5	Number of Years	40
6		
7	Future Value	$1,295,304.32

spreadsheet calculates that the *future value* of your IRA at the end of 40 years will be $1,295,304.32.

Calculating the future value of investments is no different than calculating compound interest when deposits are made at the end of each year. Spreadsheets make these laborious calculations quick and easy to do.

Task 2: Analyze The Spreadsheet Output

It is important to recognize that you must contribute as early as possible to have a large IRA balance when you retire. Small amounts invested over long periods of time are equal to much larger amounts invested over short periods of time. Unfortunately, some people wait until they are in their forties to save for retirement. Enter 20 years in cell B5 to show what the future value of the IRA would be if a person started saving at age 45.

Answer the following questions.
1. What is the future value of the 20-year IRA? $228,814.48

2. Estimate the difference in the balances between the 20-year and 40-year contributions.
   $1,000,000

3. What is the exact difference in the balances? $1,066,489.84

4. Keep raising the annual investment amount until you get close to the future value, $1,295,304 shown in the original spreadsheet. What approximate annual amount must be contributed to some type of retirement investment starting at age 45 to reach the same value (about $1,295,000) as a $5,000 annual investment started at age 20?   ≈$28,350

5. What spreadsheet function is used in cell B7?   FV

6. Re-enter 40 years in cell B5 and $5,000 in cell B4. What would be the future value of the contributions if the estimated growth rate was 10% instead of 8%? $2,213,008.04

TEACHING STRATEGIES Task 1

The formula used in the spreadsheet contains the future value (fv) function. The formula is explained and examples are given for it in Excel's help program. While in Excel, click on Help and search for "future value." The fv function can be used to find compound interest and the compound amount given the original principal, the interest rate, and how often per year it is applied.

Task 3: Design a Major Medical Coverage Spreadsheet

You are to design a spreadsheet that will calculate the amount of medical expenses paid by the insurer and the amount paid by the insured for a major medical insurance policy.

SITUATION: You work in the personnel office of a small company that provides major medical insurance for its employees. The major medical policy pays 85% of all bills after a $1,000 deductible is paid. An employee has $50,000 in major medical expenses after a serious accident.

Task 4: Analyze the Spreadsheet Output

Answer these questions about your completed spreadsheet.

7. How much of the employee's major medical expenses does the insurance company pay? $41,650

8. How much does the employee pay? $8,350

9. What formula did you use to find the amount that the insurance company paid? (expenses − deductible) × coinsurance rate

10. What formula did you use to calculate the employee share? coinsurance amount + deductible

11. Suppose an employee had major medical expenses of $25,500. How much of the employee's major medical expenses does the insurance company pay? $20,825

12. How much does the employee pay? $5,675

Teach and Apply Task 2

Assign questions 1–6.

Point out the difference in the future value of an IRA when investing occurs over 20 years rather than 40 years.

Discuss the results of Question 4 to stress the need for early contributions.

Teach and Apply Task 3

Assign Task 3. You may wish to have students work in groups and plan the format of the spreadsheet on paper first.

Suggest to students that they return to Lesson 7.2 and use the formulas on page 291 to help them design the spreadsheet.

Teach and Apply Task 4

Assign Questions 7–12. Make sure students answer Questions 7–10 before they enter new data for Question 11.

Students may submit disks with their spreadsheets, printouts of the results for Questions 7–12, and a printout of the spreadsheet formulas.

TEACHING STRATEGIES Task 3

An example solution to Task 3 is provided in the file tech7-3.xls. Display the design used in tech7-3.xls and have students compare it to the designs they used. Discuss means for improving the readability, ease of data entry, and organization of the sample spreadsheet and their spreadsheets. Also, discuss with students what changes would be necessary to make the example spreadsheet be usable for other types of health insurance claims.

■ **HOW TIMES HAVE CHANGED**

1. 7,000,000,000,000 ÷ 48,000,000,000 = 145.8$\overline{3}$
   The assets of all mutual funds have increased about 14,583% since 1969.

   10,000 ÷ 270 = 37.$\overline{037}$
   The number of mutual funds has increased about 3,704% since 1969.

2. 1,000 − 100 = 900
   900 ÷ 100 = 9
   9 × 100 = 900
   The Dow increased 900% from 1906 to 1972.

   10,000 − 1,000 = 9,000
   9,000 ÷ 1,000 = 9
   9 × 100 = 900
   The Dow increased 900% from 1972 to 1999.

■ **WRITE**

Before you assign Write, consider discussing with students the advantages of saving in a tax deferred retirement account early and consistently, such as tax deductions, tax-free investment growth, and additional income on retirement.

■ **SCANS**

Have selected students make their presentations to the class.

■ **ONGOING ASSESSMENT**

STUDENT WORKBOOK Use the Integrated Project in the workbook as an assessment activity for the chapter goals.

How Times Have Changed

For Questions 1-2, refer to the timeline on page 281 as needed.

1. In 1925, the Massachusetts Investors Trust mutual fund had $392,000 in assets and about 200 individual investors. By 1969, there were about 270 mutual funds with $48 billion in assets. Today there are over 10,000 mutual funds with over $7 trillion assets and about 83 million individual investors. By what percentage have the assets of all mutual funds increased since 1969? By what percentage has the number of mutual funds increased since 1969?

2. What was the approximate percent of increase in the Dow Jones Industrial Average from 1906 to 1972? What was the approximate percent of increase in the Dow Jones Industrial Average from 1972 to 1999?

WRITE

Write a persuasive essay convincing workers to save for retirement. Use examples of potential results to show how saving as little as $20 a week can grow into a large retirement fund. List the reasons that people should not rely solely on social security and corporate retirement plans.

Include options for how to save and invest to maximize savings growth over different periods of time.

SCANS

Workplace Skills—*Teaches Others*

You must be able to help others learn. Buying insurance and making investments, as well as saving for retirement, are often confusing topics for people to understand.

Test Your Skills Create a presentation to help others learn the main terms of this chapter and review the main concepts.

Make a Plan Review your presentation and determine what would need to be added or removed to modify the presentation for an adult audience. Consider whether adults are insuring themselves and actively investing for their futures.

Summarize Write a summary of the differences between your presentation of this chapter to students and the presentation to adults. Note which of the following skills are used in understanding insurance and investments.

arithmetic	*decision making*	*problem solving*	*self-management*
creative thinking	*knowing how to learn*	*integrity/honesty*	*seeing things in the "mind's eye"*

TEACHING STRATEGIES Write

Have students share their essays and rate each other on a scale of 1–10, with 10 being the highest rating of how convincing an essay is. Students should justify their rat-ings by pointing to the features of the essays that made them choose the ratings they did.

Chapter Test

Answer each question.

1. $235,000 \div \$1,000$ 235
2. $26 \times \$38.89$ $1,011.14
3. $125\% \times \$78$ $97.50
4. $80\% \times \$1,600$ $1,280
5. $1,354 - \$600$ $754
6. $1,050 \times \$0.49$ $514.50
7. $\frac{1}{4} \times \$42,100$ $10,525
8. $37 + \$28 + \$376 + \$73$ $514

Applications

9. Pamela Hopkins has a life insurance policy for $15,000. She pays a premium rate of $23.48 per $1,000 annually. This year the insurance company paid a dividend of $33.60. What is Pamela's premium for the year after deducting the dividend? $318.60

10. Tia's major medical policy has a $1,000 deductible feature and a 15% coinsurance feature. Last month she spent $10,300 for medical expenses, $700 of which were not covered under her policy. How much did Tia pay? $2,990

11. Tito Tortelli becomes totally disabled. His group disability policy's benefit percentage is 60% of his average annual salary for the last 3 years. His annual salaries were $35,800; $38,500, and $39,800. What monthly benefit amount will he receive? $1,901.67

12. Find the yield, to the nearest tenth percent, on a $1,000, 11.5% bond bought at 106.   10.8%

13. Park Lee bought 300 shares of stock at 26.45, plus commission of $182.50. What was the total cost of the purchase? $8,117.50

14. Jolene Williams owns 800 shares of TRI, Inc. common stock paying a quarterly dividend of $0.57 per share and 400 shares of TRI preferred stock, $100 par value, paying an annual dividend of 7.2%. Find the total annual dividend she gets from the common and preferred stock. $4,704

15. Bev Jorald bought 500 shares of a stock at a total cost of $12,762. She sold the shares at 40.76 and was charged a commission and other costs of $374. What was her profit or loss from the sale of the stock? $7,244 profit

Ted Ling made a $37,000 down payment on a resort condominium that sold for $185,000. His average monthly rental income will be $1,850. His total annual expenses will be $18,800.

16. Find his annual net income. $3,400

17. Find his rate of income earned, to the nearest tenth of a percent.   9.2%

Laura Barn's pension fund pays her 1.9% of her average salary for the last three years for each year of service. In the last three years, she earned $57,000, $59,800, and $62,500.

18. What is her average salary for the last three years? $59,766.67

19. If she retired after 30 years of service, what is the total pension rate?   57%

20. What monthly pension amount will she receive? $2,838.92

Chapter 7 Assessment ■ **343**

Chapter-Test Correlation

Question	Lesson
9	7.1
10	7.2
11	7.3
12	7.5
13	7.6
14	7.6
15	7.6
16	7.8
17	7.8
18	7.9
19	7.9
20	7.9

Test Taking Strategies

■ **OPEN-ENDED**

Emphasize that students should label the items used for calculations on their scratch sheets so they will be less likely to mix up questions as the scratch sheets become filled with figures. To save time, students can heavily abbreviate the labels.

TEACHING STRATEGIES Chapter Test

Remind students to show each step in the solution of problems and to label intermediate and final results. Also remind them that you will be evaluating not only their solutions, but also the neatness and organization of their work. Remind them that numbers are to be clearly written and aligned.

Business Data Analysis

8.1 Measures of Central Tendency
8.2 Probability
8.3 Bar and Line Graphs
8.4 Circle and Rectangle Graphs
8.5 Economic Statistics

Statistical Insights

Salary Increases and Consumer Price Index Changes: 1993–2003

Year	Average Salary Increase	Consumer Price Index
1993	4.6%	3.0%
1994	4.2%	2.5%
1995	4.2%	2.8%
1996	4.1%	2.9%
1997	4.1%	2.3%
1998	4.1%	1.6%
1999	3.4%	2.2%
2000	4.1%	3.4%
2001	3.8%	2.8%
2002	3.3%	1.6%
2003	2.9%	2.3%

Use the data shown above to answer each question.

1. What year had the greatest difference between the percent of the average salary increase and percent of the Consumer Price Index? 1998

2. In what year were the percent of the average salary increase and percent of the Consumer Price Index closest in value? 2003

3. Identify the range of years in which the percent of average salary increase nearly remained unchanged. 1994–1998

4. Does the trend for the Consumer Price Index percents during those years also remain about the same? No

Statistical Insights

Some people believe that wage increases cause higher consumer prices. Ask students to compare for each year the percent of salary increase to the percent increase in the Consumer Price Index. Ask what might be the reason why prices did not increase as much as wages. Point out that salaries are only one part of the total wage structure and that productivity gains in other areas may offset the impact of salary increases on consumer prices.

NetCheck

Online Help with Math

Have you ever wished that you had a private tutor when you are working on homework and have a question? The Internet has many sites that make it seem like you do have a tutor. Some web sites allow you to post a question and receive a reply in about a day. Many helpful sites invite you to search a topic, explore a skill or obtain a definition of a term with an example. The next time you forget the meaning of a math or business term or how to solve a math or business problem, try finding a tutor online.

To find a tutor, enter "math tutor" or "business tutor" into a search engine.

Business Graphs

You can visit the web sites of most major corporations and see examples of business statistics in their annual reports. Locate a corporation with which you are familiar. Find the web pages at the company's site that display and describe the data on the company's annual report.

Another place that business statistics are found is in newspapers. Most newspapers also provide their editions online. Locate an online nationally-known newspaper such as the New York Times or Wall Street Journal, and find the web pages at the site that contain statistical information about businesses and the economy.

How Times Have Changed

The timeline shows prices for selected goods in the United States throughout the last century, illustrating the effects of inflation.

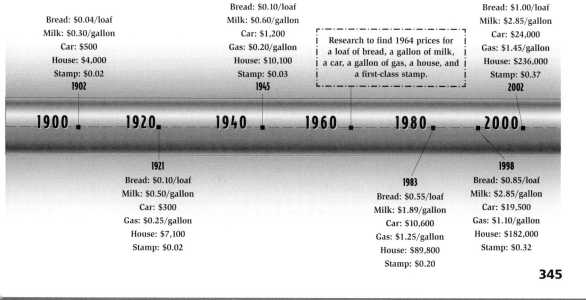

Bread: $0.04/loaf
Milk: $0.30/gallon
Car: $500
House: $4,000
Stamp: $0.02
1902

Bread: $0.10/loaf
Milk: $0.60/gallon
Car: $1,200
Gas: $0.20/gallon
House: $10,100
Stamp: $0.03
1945

Research to find 1964 prices for a loaf of bread, a gallon of milk, a car, a gallon of gas, a house, and a first-class stamp.

Bread: $1.00/loaf
Milk: $2.85/gallon
Car: $24,000
Gas: $1.45/gallon
House: $236,000
Stamp: $0.37
2002

1900 1920 1940 1960 1980 2000

1921
Bread: $0.10/loaf
Milk: $0.50/gallon
Car: $300
Gas: $0.25/gallon
House: $7,100
Stamp: $0.02

1983
Bread: $0.55/loaf
Milk: $1.89/gallon
Car: $10,600
Gas: $1.25/gallon
House: $89,800
Stamp: $0.20

1998
Bread: $0.85/loaf
Milk: $2.85/gallon
Car: $19,500
Gas: $1.10/gallon
House: $182,000
Stamp: $0.32

345

Start Up

Have students read the Start Up. Ask them how many hours they sleep daily. Use their responses to lead into a discussion of the question in the Start Up.

Math Skill Builder

Students use the skills of adding, subtracting, and multiplying money amounts and whole numbers in this lesson.

Complete all exercises in Math Skill Builder 1–3.

■ Teach Goal 1

Remind students that they have already found an average when calculating average pay and will use the same process in this lesson to calculate the mean for various types of data.

Write the data set 2, 2, 3, 4, 5, and 8 on the board and provide a brief overview of how the mean (4), median (3.5), and mode (2) differ.

GOALS

- Find the mean, median, mode, and range for a set of data
- Construct a frequency distribution table and calculate the mean, median, mode, and range

Start Up

A magazine article states that the average person sleeps 8 hours a day. Suppose you sleep about $6\frac{3}{4}$ hours a day. One of your friends sleeps 9 hours a day. Do you think that you are getting too little sleep and your friend too much sleep compared to the average person?

Math Skill Builder

Review these math skills and solve the exercises that follow.

1 **Add** money amounts and whole numbers.
Find the sum. $1,801 + $1,796 + $2,094 = $5,691

1a. $238 + $189 + $197 $624   **1b.** 18 + 12 + 23 + 24 77

2 **Divide** money amounts and whole numbers.
Find the quotient. $48,780 ÷ 6 = $8,130

2a. $348 ÷ 12 = $29   **2b.** 825 ÷ 15 55

3 **Multiply** dollar amounts and whole numbers.
Find the product. 3 × $58 = $174

3a. 4 × $93 $372   **3b.** $7 × 16 $112

■ Mean, Median, and Mode

In the study of statistics there are three types of averages called the mean, median, and mode. As a group, these averages are called *measures of central tendency*.

The **mean**, or *arithmetic average*, is found by adding a group of numbers and dividing the sum by the number of items added. The mean is the best known and most used measure of central tendency. The group of numbers is sometimes referred to as the *data* or *data set*.

EXAMPLE 1

During the second quarter, the Furman Company reported these profits: April, $48,000; May, $64,000; June, $47,000. Find the mean profit per month.

346 ■ Chapter 8 Business Data Analysis

COMMON ERRORS

Students may confuse the terms mean, median, and mode. Have students make a study card for each term that defines the term and gives an example of how to find that particular measure of central tendency.

SOLUTION

Add monthly profits.

$48,000 + $64,000 + $47,000 = $159,000   total profits

Divide the total profits by the number of months.

$159,000 ÷ 3 = $53,000   mean profit per month

The **median** is the middle number in a set of data that is arranged in either ascending or descending order. One-half of the numbers will be on either side of the median.

To find the median, arrange the numbers in order. If the group has an odd count of numbers, the number in the middle is the median. If the group has an even count of numbers, add the two middle numbers and divide by 2 to find the median.

EXAMPLE 2

Find the median for each set of data.

a. 12, 18, 17, 10, 15, 23, 12, 23, 9   **b.** 9, 0, 1, 9, 5, 4, 9, 2

SOLUTION

a. Arrange the numbers in order; there are 9 numbers. Since 9 is an odd number, the number in the middle is the median.

9 10 12 12 15 17 18 23 23   numbers arranged in order
            ↑ The middle number is the median.

b. Arrange the numbers in order; there are 8 numbers. Since 8 is an even number, average the two middle numbers.

0 1 2 4 5 9 9 9   The two middle numbers are 4 and 5.

(4 + 5) ÷ 2 = 9 ÷ 2 = 4.5   median

The **mode** is the number that occurs most frequently in a group of numbers arranged in order. There may be no mode or more than one mode in a set of data.

EXAMPLE 3

Find the mode of the data sets in Examples 1 and 2.

SOLUTION

Identify the number that occurs most frequently, if any.

Example 1: There is no mode. Each profit amount appears once.

Example 2a: Both 12 and 23 are modes. Both appear twice.

Example 2b: The 9 is the mode. It appears three times.

Often when you work with measures of central tendency, you also find the range, which is not a measure of central tendency, rather a *measure of dispersion*. The **range** is the difference between the highest and lowest numbers in a set of data.

Highest Number − Lowest Number = Range

In Example 1, the mean of three monthly profits, the range was

$64,000 − $47,000 or $17,000.

BUSINESS TIP

Company profits are usually reported at the end of each quarter. For a calendar year, the ending dates of each quarter are March 31, June 30, September 30, and December 31.

MATH TIP

Commonly used abbreviations are
Mn = Mean
Md = Median
Mo = Mode

■ **Apply Goal 1**

Work through the math of Examples 1, 2, and 3 at the board and have students complete the calculations at their desks.

Point out that the data in Examples 2 and 3 may be arranged in either ascending or descending order and that either way will produce the same mean, median, or mode.

Inform students that when two modes appear as shown in Example 2a, the set of data is said to be bimodal. Indicate that when each datum is unlikely to be repeated, the mode is not a very good measure of central tendency.

Assign Check Your Understanding problems A through C for class work. Review student work at their desks to identify any difficulties they have in solving the problems.

DIFFERENT LEARNING ABILITIES At-Risk Learners

Some students may not relate to the examples and problems used in the textbook. Have students use data from their personal interests to calculate measures of central tendency. For example, a baseball box score could be used to calculate the mean number of hits for the total at-bats. Also, the running time of several videos could be tabulated to find the median and mode.

■ CHECK YOUR UNDERSTANDING

Find the mean, median, mode, and range for each.

A. A bakery was open six days last week and had these numbers of customers per day: 212, 187, 220, 196, 262, 315 232, 216, no mode, 128

B. The number of books read during the summer by 21 fourth-grade students were: 23, 15, 6, 21, 20, 31, 7, 18, 23, 20, 25, 20, 16, 13, 18, 26, 29, 11, 8, 22, 27 19, 20, 20, 25

C. The daily high temperatures for a two-week period were: 58, 64, 67, 73, 71, 61, 59, 52, 63, 67, 77, 80, 67, 65 66, 66, 67, 28

■ Frequency Distribution

When you work with larger sets of data, it may be difficult to list them in order. Making a **frequency distribution** is one way of arranging numbers. List all the units of data. Every time a unit of data is used, make a vertical mark next to it. Make every fifth mark a slash to group the marks in sets of five. This method called tallying makes counting easier. From the frequency distribution table, you can calculate the mean, median, mode, and range.

EXAMPLE 4

During a 17-day period, daily sales of lawnmowers were: 28, 23, 20, 28, 28, 24, 29, 20, 28, 21, 24, 28, 20, 29, 28, 23, 24. Make a frequency distribution table. Then find the mean, median, mode, and range.

SOLUTION
List each number in order. Place a tally mark next to the number each time it appears in the daily sales list.

29 ‖	24 ‖|	21	
28 卌		23 ‖	20 ‖|

There are 17 tally marks.

Mean: Multiply each number in the table by the number of tally marks next to the number. Then add the products and divide their total by the total number of tally marks.

$(29 \times 2) + (28 \times 6) + (24 \times 3) + (23 \times 2) + (21 \times 1) + (20 \times 3) = 425$

$425 \div 17 = 25$

Median: Locate the middle number (ninth) in the table. Do this by counting the number of tally marks in the table, starting from either the top or bottom until you get to the middle.

The ninth number is 24, which is the median.

Mode: Locate the number that has the most tally marks. The number 28 has 6 tally marks; 28 is the mode.

Range: Subtract the smallest number from the greatest number.

$29 - 20 = 9$

> **MATH TIP**
>
> The frequency distribution table may be arranged in either descending or ascending order. Either order yields the same results.

348 ■ Chapter 8 Business Data Analysis

■ CHECK YOUR UNDERSTANDING SOLUTIONS

A. 1,392 ÷ 6 = 232 mean;
(212 + 220) ÷ 2 = 216 median;
no mode; 315 − 187 = 128 range

B. 399 ÷ 21 = 19 mean; 20 median; 20 mode;
31 − 6 = 25 range

C. 924 ÷ 14 = 66 mean; (65 + 67) ÷ 2 = 66 median;
67 mode; 80 − 52 = 28 range

D. The number of posters sold daily during an eleven-day exhibit were: 23, 28, 19, 28, 21, 24, 26, 28, 17, 19, 20. Find the mean, median, mode, and range. 23, 23, 28, 11

E. In a 10-day period a school club sold these numbers of stadium seat cushions: 25, 22, 24, 26, 24, 22, 25, 22, 20, 20. Find the mean, median, mode, and range. 23, 23, 22, 6

Wrap Up

The average is just an arithmetic calculation. It is not intended to produce a number that everyone should fit. It is likely that many students get less or more than exactly 8 hours sleep per night. The amount of sleep needed varies from one person to the next.

TEAM MEETING

Form a team to survey students as to how much time, to the nearest quarter hour, they spend each week doing homework. Survey 20 students from at least three grade levels. Make a frequency distribution table and calculate the mean, median, and mode of each grade level's data set. Write a summary about any differences you notice between the averages for the grade levels. Be sure that your summary compares the means, medians, and modes of the grade levels. Tell the different messages you could get across by using each of these measures of central tendency.

EXERCISES

Find the sum.

1. $34 + $42 + $39 + $37 $152

2. 65 + 52 + 67 + 55 239

Find the quotient.

3. $1,825 ÷ 25 $73

4. 210 ÷ 14 15

Find the mean, median, mode, and range for Exercises 5–8.

5. Data set: 17, 12, 18, 22, 12, 11, 23 16.429; 17, 12, 12

6. Data set: 16, 25, 19, 29, 18, 25 22, 22, 25, 13

7. Data set: 2,184; 8,105; 19,238; 9,053 9,645; 8,579; no mode; 17,054

8. Data set: 0.2, 0.18, 1.5, 0.7, 0.2, 0.7, 0.9, 1.3 0.71; 0.7; two modes, 0.2 and 0.7; 1.32

9. Nine workers at a small business were paid these amounts per hour: $8; $8.25; $8.45; $8.25; $8; $8.40; $8.20; $8; $8.10. Find the mean, median, mode and range. $8.18; $8.20; $8; $0.45

10. Seventeen apartments in a certain area rented for these monthly rates: $420; $410; $405; $435; $455; $425; $450; $410; $400; $350; $320; $420; $440; $425; $410; $450; $430. Find the mean, median, mode, and range. $415, $420, $410, $135

Make a frequency distribution. Then find the mean, median, mode, and range.

11. The number of cabinet doors built by a carpenter per day in a ten-day period were: 28, 19, 28, 21, 24, 26, 28, 17, 19, 20. 23; 22.5; 28; 11

Lesson 8.1 Measures of Central Tendency ■ **349**

Wrap Up

Review the Start Up. Point out the risk of treating a statistic as a "one size fits all" fact. Show how knowing the average height of basketball players is meaningless as it relates to a player's success since it does not consider factors such as skill, decision making, conditioning, and reaction time.

TEAM MEETING

If several teams worked on the project, prepare a matrix on the board showing three grade levels at the side and mean, median, and mode at the top. Within the matrix, enter data from each team. Then discuss differences between the results of teams.

Have a member from each team report how they interpreted the central tendency measures they calculated.

Assign

Assignment: Exercises 1–15, 17–28. Begin with the basic arithmetic problems that review the underlying arithmetic operations used in the exercises.

If rounding directions are not given for exercises in this lesson, have students round answers to three decimal places.

Assess

Check student answers to exercise problems by calling on them in class and asking them to provide intermediate results and final answers.

■ CHECK YOUR UNDERSTANDING SOLUTIONS

D. 17 + (2 × 19) + 20 + 21 + 23 + 24 + 26 + (3 × 28) = 253; 253 ÷ 11 = 23 mean; 23 median; 28 mode; 28 − 17 = 11 range

E. (2 × 20) + (3 × 22) + (2 × 24) + (2 × 25) + 26 = 230; 230 ÷ 10 = 23 mean; (22 + 24) ÷ 2 = 23 median; 22 mode; 26 − 20 = 6 range

Reteach

STUDENT WORKBOOK If students need help with finding the mean, median, mode, and range, do Exercise 1a with them. Then assign Exercises 1b and 1c.

To help students with frequency distributions, have them first create a list of numbers for the tally of data in Exercise 2. Check their work and have them correct their errors before proceeding.

Now have them tally the applicants. Check their work and have them make corrections as you did before. Continue the process until the problem is solved.

Enrich

Revisit Exercise 15. Ask students to share their experiences in learning a new computer game. Ask if beginning levels take longer to learn, if the game becomes progressively more difficult, and whether software glitches add to learning time.

Finding mean time is a logical choice, but the median may be better because it eliminates the effects of extra time spent at the early and advanced levels or in handling software problems.

Close

Assign Exercise 16, Critical Thinking. Students are likely to know that a different average measure must have been used to arrive at the different average hourly pay amounts. There also may have been differences in the way employees are counted. One measure may have included managers in calculating average hourly pay.

Make a frequency distribution, then find the mean, median, mode, and range.

12. These number of surveys per hour were completed by a researcher during two days of interviews at a shopping mall: 15, 14, 11, 16, 18, 14, 17, 12, 9, 10, 12, 14, 16, 11, 17, 10. 13.5; 14; 14; 9

13. During a recent month, a repair shop had these daily numbers of customers: 14, 21, 16, 18, 14, 20, 19, 20, 14, 27, 17, 22, 18, 14, 21, 14, 19, 20, 14, 27, 19, 12, 14. 18; 18; 14; 15

14. During a year, the Poole Company bought 15,000 bolts at 1.6¢; 20,000 bolts at 1.54¢; and 5,000 bolts at 1.8¢. Find the mean, median, and mode of the cost per bolt. Show your answers in dollars, rounded to the nearest thousandth of a dollar. $0.016; $0.015; $0.016

15. **CRITICAL THINKING** A computer game has 15 levels of difficulty. You keep track of how long it takes you to master each level. Which measure of central tendency will give you the best measure of the average time you spend in mastering all 15 levels of play? mean

16. **CRITICAL THINKING** The management of a small company claims that its employees earn $14.26 an hour. The workers claim their average pay is $11.74 an hour. A consultant states that the average pay is $12.90 an hour. What are some reasons that may account for the difference in calculations? See the Close section for answer.

MIXED REVIEW

17. $\frac{7}{10} \div \frac{14}{25}$ $1\frac{1}{4}$ 18. $\frac{4}{5} \times \frac{15}{16}$ $\frac{3}{4}$ 19. $11 - 6\frac{2}{3}$ $4\frac{1}{3}$ 20. $\frac{11}{15} + 2\frac{1}{3}$ $\frac{46}{15} = 3\frac{1}{15}$

21. What is $\frac{2}{3}$ of $456.21? $304.14

22. Rewrite 0.675 as a fraction. $\frac{27}{40}$

23. Lavina McLean insured her home for $116,000 at an annual rate of $0.42 per $100. Find her annual premium. $487, Lesson 6.4

24. Mickey Fantini plans to buy a home for $135,000 with a 10% down payment. He estimates his closing costs as: loan origination fee, $260; legal fees, $650; property survey, $225; inspection fee, $300; title insurance, $175; recording fee, $275. Find these amounts: down payment, mortgage loan, and cash needed to buy the home. $13,500; $121,500; $15,385, Lesson 6.1

25. Find the interest paid for 6 months on $1,500 at 3.2% annual interest, compounded quarterly. $24.10, Lesson 3.6

26. Dina Orr had these cash receipts for a week: $862.30, paycheck; $4.57, interest on savings; $26.82, subscription refund; $42.80, cash refund for returned purchase. What were her cash receipts for the week? $936.49, Lesson 2.5

27. Curtis Vanover has disability insurance that pays him 55% of the average of his annual earnings. His earnings for the past three years were: $28,500, $35,100, and $34,800. How much will Curtis receive from his disability policy in one year? $18,040, Lesson 7.3

28. Bradon earns $13.50 an hour. He is paid time-and-a-half for any hours beyond 40 hours per week. What is Bradon's gross wages for a week that he works 57 hours? $884.25; Lesson 1.3

350 ■ Chapter 8 Business Data Analysis

SELECTED SOLUTIONS

5. 115 ÷ 7 = 16.4285, or 16.429 mean; 17 median; 12 mode; 23 − 11 = 12 range

9. $73.65 ÷ 9 = $8.183, or $8.18 mean; $8.20 median; $8 mode; $8.45 − $8 = $0.45 range

14. (15,000 × $0.016) + (20,000 × $0.0154) + (5,000 × $0.018) = $638; $638 ÷ 40,000 = $0.0159, or $0.0160 mean; $0.0154, or $0.015 median; $0.0154, or $0.015 mode

8.2 Probability

GOALS

- Compute the probability of simple events
- Compute experimental probability
- Compute probability based on experience

Start Up

Suppose you ask your teacher if there will be a quiz tomorrow and she says "probably." Do you think you will have a quiz? Is it certain you will have a quiz? Suppose your teacher says she will toss a coin three times. If the results are heads each time, you will have a quiz. Now do you think you will have a quiz?

Math Skill Builder

Review these math skills and solve the exercises that follow.

1 **Multiply** whole numbers and money amounts by fractions.
Find the product. $\frac{1}{8} \times 920 = 115$

1a. $\frac{1}{4} \times 368$ 92   **1b.** $\frac{1}{8} \times \$1,280$ $160

2 **Multiply** whole numbers by percents.
Find the product. $9\% \times 1,200 = 0.09 \times 1,200 = 108$

2a. $5\% \times 28,500$ 1,425   **2b.** $3\% \times 128,700$ 3,861

3 **Divide** whole numbers by whole numbers. Round to the nearest thousandth.
Find the quotient. $43,000 \div 60,000 = 0.717$

3a. $65,000 \div 90,000$ 0.722   **3b.** $36,000 \div 58,000$ 0.621

■ Probability

Probability is a way of mathematically predicting the chance an event will occur.

CHANCE EVENTS You have two marbles that are alike in every way except color. The marbles, one blue and one white, are placed in a bag. Suppose you are asked to pick one from the bag without looking. You have no way of knowing which marble is blue and which marble is white. This means that the marble you pick will be a *random choice*, and the outcome will be a *chance event*.

PROBABILITY OF A CHANCE EVENT With this bag of marbles, what are the chances that your outcome will be to pick the blue marble? Two outcomes are possible: 1) you pick the blue marble or 2) you pick the white marble.

Lesson 8.2 Probability ■ 351

Start Up

Have students read the Start Up. Ask them to giver their definitions of the word "probably." Ask what events might occur that would interfere with the teacher giving the test the next day.

Students may mention school being closed because of weather, an emergency the teacher must handle, or the test duplicator being broken. Ask them to assess how likely it is that these events may occur.

Math Skill Builder

The multiplication of money amounts and whole numbers by fractions and percents, the division of whole numbers, and rounding are skills used in this lesson.

Complete all exercises in Math Skill Builder 1–3.

■ Teach Goal 1

You may wish to dramatize the probability of chance events by obtaining ten marbles in colors that match the textbook presentation (or substitute disks of the appropriate color). Place color groups together so that students may visualize how the outcome of chance events is determined.

CONNECTION TO LANGUAGE ARTS

Students may have heard that it might be possible for the best college football team to beat the worst professional football team, but not probable. Have them discuss the statement's meaning. Then ask them whether the statement's meaning could be reversed so that it is not possible for the college team to win, but probable.

Work through Example 1 with students and have them do the calculations at their desks.

Assign Check Your Understanding problems A and B. Observe student work at their desks to determine if they are having any difficulty in completing the assignment.

Since your pick is a random choice, one outcome is just as likely as the other. The outcomes are *equally likely*. The chance that you will pick the blue marble is 1 out of 2, shown as $\frac{1}{2}$. You may also say that the probability is 0.50, or 50%.

Now suppose that the bag holds 6 blue marbles, 3 white marbles, and 1 red marble, making a total of 10 marbles. Again, the marbles are alike except for color. What are the chances of your picking a blue marble? Since there are 6 blue marbles, there are 6 chances out of 10 that you will pick a blue marble. So, the probability of the event that you will pick a blue marble is $\frac{6}{10}$, which simplifies to $\frac{3}{5}$. This can also be written as 0.6, or 60%.

Since 4 of the marbles are not blue, there are 4 chances out of 10 that you will not pick a blue marble. So, the probability of your not picking a blue marble is $\frac{4}{10}$, which simplifies to $\frac{2}{5}$. This can also be written as 0.4, or 40%.

CERTAIN OR IMPOSSIBLE EVENTS   If a bag holds nothing but 5 yellow marbles, the chances of picking a yellow marble are 5 out of 5, which is $\frac{5}{5}$ or 1. In this case picking a yellow marble is an event that is certain to happen, because no other outcome is possible. Any event that is certain has a probability of 1.

From a bag holding nothing but yellow marbles, the event that you will pick a white marble is an impossible outcome. The chances of picking a white marble are 0 out of 5, which is $\frac{0}{5}$, or 0. Any event that is impossible has a probability of 0.

PROBABILITY AND LARGE NUMBER   The probability of an event occurring tells you about how many times you can expect the event to happen in a large number of tries. For example, if a perfectly balanced coin is flipped, it is as likely to come up heads as it is tails. So, you can say that the probability of heads is $\frac{1}{2}$.

This does not mean that out of 40 flips you are sure to get 20 heads. You may get several more or several less than 20. What it does mean is if you flip the coin many times, say 1,000 times, the number of heads should not be far from $\frac{1}{2}$ of 1,000. The longer you keep flipping, the nearer the number of heads should come to $\frac{1}{2}$ the number of flips. This is called *the principle of large numbers*. It is one of the main concepts of probability. For a large number of tries of the same kind, you can predict the outcome with only a small amount of error.

EXAMPLE 1

You toss a standard six-sided die once. What is the probability of tossing a 3? If you toss the die 900 times, how many times would you expect to get a 3?

SOLUTION
Determine the number of possible outcomes for an event.

6 = Possible outcomes (There are six sides to the die.)

Write the probability of a single event (numerator) occurring out of 6 possible outcomes (denominator).

$\frac{1}{6}$ probability of tossing a 3

Multiply the number of tosses by the probability.

$\frac{1}{6} \times 900 = 150$ expected number of times a 3 will be tossed

> **MATH TIP**
>
> A die is a six-sided cube with each side marked with 1 to 6 dots.

DIFFERENT LEARNING STYLES Kinesthetic Learners

You might suggest that learners, where possible, use physical items such as marbles, disks, or dice to replicate a problem's solution. For example, to replicate Example 1, an actual die may be tossed and the outcomes recorded.

Less than 900 tosses may be used or several students could divide the 900 tosses and pool their results to share with the class.

■ **CHECK YOUR UNDERSTANDING**

A. If a coin is flipped and falls freely, it is as likely to turn up heads as tails. What is the probability of tails? $\frac{1}{2}$

B. A bag holds three plastic disks, 1 green, 1 red, and 1 yellow. One disk is picked at random. After each pick the color of the pick is recorded, the disk is put back into the bag, and another disk is picked. If 600 disks are picked, how many times would you expect that the disks will not be green? 400

■ Experimental Probability

In the examples so far you could calculate the probability of the event from the description of the conditions. In many cases, this information may not be known, and the probability must be based on experiment.

The quality control departments of companies do not test every product they make. They often test a few of the products to see how many are up to standard and how many are not. If these samples are chosen by chance, they are called random samples. Suppose 100 staplers were randomly selected and tested and 3 were found to be defective. The probability of finding a defective stapler is $\frac{3}{100}$, 0.03, or 3%.

On the basis of this test, you could estimate that about 3% of the whole batch of staplers from which the samples were taken will be defective. In a batch of 500 of these staplers, the number of defective staplers will be about 3% of 500, or 15.

EXAMPLE 2

A maker of vases finds that 14 out of 200 glass vases inspected are defective. Assume there are no changes in the way vases are made. How many defective vases could be expected from a month's usual production of 7,000 glass vases?

SOLUTION
Divide the number of defects by the number inspected. Write the result as a percent.

$14 \div 200 = 0.07 = 7\%$ defect rate

Multiply total production by the defect percent.

$7\% \times 7,000 = 0.07 \times 7,000 = 490$ expected number of defects

■ **CHECK YOUR UNDERSTANDING**

C. A maker of school pennants tests 72 pennants. Of that total, the ink did not spread evenly on 6 pennants and the printing on 3 others was crooked. The imperfect pennants were destroyed. Based on this probability, how many defective pennants are likely to occur out of 480 made during a week? 60

D. In a factory, a random sample of 400 computer chips was tested. Eight chips were defective. If 12,000 of these chips are made, about how many will be defective. 240

Lesson 8.2 Probability ■ **353**

■ *Teach Goal 2*

Remind students that the probability of an event occurring does not mean it will actually happen. Probability will only tell you what is likely to happen.

■ *Apply Goal 2*

Work Example 2 at the board. Involve students in the presentation by asking them to help explain the solution procedures. Have students do the math at their desks.

Assign Check Your Understanding problems C and D for class work. Observe student work at their desks to check for any difficulties they have.

■ **ONGOING ASSESSMENT**
Refer to Example 2. Ask students to explain why if one glass vase were selected at random, the vase is likely to pass inspection. Also ask whether the vase picked at random is sure to be acceptable.

■ *CHECK YOUR UNDERSTANDING SOLUTIONS*

A. There are 2 possible outcomes; probability of tails is $\frac{1}{2}$.

B. $\frac{2}{3} \times 600 = 400$

C. $6 + 3 = 9$ defects; $\frac{9}{72} = \frac{1}{8}$ probability of defects; $\frac{1}{8} \times 480 = 60$ defective

D. $\frac{8}{400} = \frac{1}{50}$ probability; $\frac{1}{50} \times 12,000 = 240$

Inform students that the premiums charged by insurance companies are based on the likelihood of loss.

By tracking the number of live births and the ages at which people die, life insurers can calculate the risk their policies carry. The mortality tables they develop are essentially probability tables. Thus, for the table shown in the textbook, the probability of children reaching the age of 10 is 97\100, or 97%.

Work Example 3 at the board while students do calculations at their desks.

Assign Check Your Understanding problems E and F for class work. Monitor student work at their desks to ensure that correct procedures for solving the problems are being used.

■ Probability Based on Experience

Life insurance companies use records of births and deaths to make *mortality tables* that show how many persons in a sample group of 100,000 live babies have reached certain ages. A sample mortality table using numbers rounded to the nearest thousand is shown.

From the mortality table, you can calculate the probability that a person will reach a particular age. For example, 93,000 of the sample of 100,000 people born reached the age of 40. So at birth, the probability of living to be 40 is 93,000 ÷ 100,000 or 93%.

Mortality Table

Age	Number Living
0	100,000
10	97,000
20	96,000
30	95,000
40	93,000
50	90,000
60	82,000
70	66,000
80	39,000

EXAMPLE 3

Using the data given above, calculate the probability of people at age 40 living to age 60, to the nearest percent.

SOLUTION

Divide the number of people living at age 60 by the number of people living at age 40.

$82,000 \div 93,000 = 0.881 = 0.88 = 88\%$ probability of people at age 40 living to age 60

■ CHECK YOUR UNDERSTANDING

Use the data given in the mortality table to answer each question.

E. What is the probability of a 10-year old living to be age 70, to the nearest percent? 68%

F. What is the probability, to the nearest tenth percent, of a 60-year old living to 70 years? 80.5%

Wrap Up

The word "probably" could be defined as likely to happen. So you should assume you will have a quiz tomorrow even though it is not certain. Tossing a coin and having it come up heads three times in a row is not likely to happen. You will probably not have a quiz.

WORKPLACE WINDOW

POLLTAKER A polltaker is a person that conducts public-opinion surveys. Polltakers conduct surveys of different types of random samples. These include *cluster sampling, systematic sampling,* and *convenience sampling.* Polltakers often work for research or marketing companies. Many conduct surveys via telephone, while others meet people face to face.

Investigate these three types of samples and other responsibilities of a polltaker by researching the Internet. Prepare a report describing your research.

354 ■ Chapter 8 Business Data Analysis

■ CHECK YOUR UNDERSTANDING SOLUTIONS

E. 66,000 ÷ 97,000 = 0.680, or 68%   **F.** 66,000 ÷ 82,000 = 0.8048, or 80.5%

EXERCISES

Find the product.

1. $\frac{1}{5} \times \$8,600$ $\$1,720$

2. $\frac{1}{3} \times 762$ 254

3. $4\% \times 35,000$ 1,400

4. $2\% \times 87,000$ 1,740

Find the quotient, to the nearest thousandth.

5. $28,000 \div 72,000$ 0.389

6. $47,000 \div 98,000$ 0.480

For Exercises 7–10, five red disks and four black disks are in a bag. You pick one disk without looking.

7. What is the probability that it will be red? $\frac{5}{9}$

8. What is the probability that it will not be red? $\frac{4}{9}$

9. What is the probability that it will be either red or black? $\frac{9}{9}$, or 1

10. What is the probability that it will be white? $\frac{0}{9}$, or 0

For Exercises 11–13, forty balls, numbered from 1 to 40, are placed in a drum.

11. What is the probability of your picking a ball numbered 4? $\frac{1}{40}$

12. What is the probability of your picking a ball with an even number? $\frac{20}{40}$, or $\frac{1}{2}$

13. What is the probability of your picking a ball that is a multiple of 5? $\frac{8}{40}$, or $\frac{1}{5}$

14. An imperfect coin has a 0.715 probability of coming up heads when tossed. How many heads could you expect to get by tossing the coin 4,000 times? 2,860

During the last 365 days, a weather forecaster's predictions have been right 292 days. They have been wrong 73 days.

15. What is the probability that the forecaster's prediction of tomorrow's weather will be right? 0.8 = 80%

16. Over the next 30 days, about how many times would you expect the forecast to be right? 24

For Exercises 17–18, use the mortality table given in this lesson. Find the probability, to the nearest percent.

17. What is the probability that a person born today will live to be 20? Not live to be 20? 96%, 4%

18. What is the probability that a person 10 years old will live to be age 20? 40? 60? 99%, 96%, 85%

19. **STRETCHING YOUR SKILLS** A company found that the probability of defects is 12%. Each 1% of defects raises costs by $56,000. The company can cut the defect rate to 2% by spending $195,000 on employee training. By what net amount would costs be cut if the defect rate is reduced to 2%? $365,000

20. **CRITICAL THINKING** There is a 90% chance that a county road construction project will be done on time. If done on time, the road builder will get a bonus of 1% of the road's $200,000,000 cost. Should the county instead ask the builder to guarantee a 100% probability of being done on time and add a 1% penalty for being late? yes; See the Enrich section for a more detailed answer.

Lesson 8.2 Probability ■ 355

WORKPLACE WINDOW

Have selected students share their definitions of sampling terms with the class and give examples.

They might mention that in cluster sampling the population is divided into groups or clusters and the sample is randomly selected from each cluster. An example is the school as the population of students and each classroom or grade as the cluster.

In systematic sampling the first person is selected at random. Thereafter, every nth person is selected to be included in the sample.

Convenience sampling is done in the easiest way possible. The people who are easiest to reach comprise the sample.

Assign

Assignment: Exercises 1–19, 21–30. Have students begin with the basic skills exercises first since they review the underlying arithmetic in the exercises.

Assess

Ask students to check their work as you write solutions on the board or display them on a transparency.

Have a student volunteer write on the board the solution to Exercise 19, Stretching Your Skills. Point out that business firms often have to spend more money on improvements in the short term to cut costs in the long term. Money spent for training employees is often viewed as a long-term investment that will continue to pay benefits in the future.

SELECTED SOLUTIONS

9. $5 \div 4 = 9$; $\frac{9}{9} = 1$

15. $\frac{292}{365} = 292 \div 365 = 0.8$, or 80%

16. $80\% \times 30 = 0.8 \times 30 = 24$

17. $96,000 \div 100,000 = 0.96$, or 96%; $100\% - 96\% = 4\%$

19. $12\% - 2\% = 10\%$ defect rate cut; $10\% \div 1\% = 10$; $10 \times \$56,000 = \$560,000$ cost of defects; $\$560,000 - \$195,000 = \$365,000$ net amount cost can be cut

Reteach

STUDENT WORKBOOK If students have difficulty with probability based on chance events, work Exercise 1a and 1b with them. Then have them work alone on Exercises 1c through 1j.

If experimental probability poses a problem to some students, work Exercise 2 with them. Assign Exercise 3 to be done independently.

Work Exercise 4a with students who have difficulty with probability based on experience. Then have them work Exercises 4b through 4e independently.

Enrich

Assign Exercise 20, Critical Thinking. When students discuss this exercise, have them think of the advantages of each plan. Point out the difficulty of completing the road on time when weather doesn't allow construction or there are unforeseen design problems.

Also point out the likelihood that companies may raise their bids for future building projects by 1% to cover the potential penalty.

Close

Refer students to the three goals of the lesson. Have them describe, in their own words, the key terms and the procedures they have learned that are associated with each goal.

MIXED REVIEW

21. $425 × 100 $42,500

22. Find the average: $87.51, $91.89, $24.63, $29.05, $46.32 $55.88

23. Round $18.75 to the nearest dollar. $19

24. Find the estimated product: 5,936 × 37 240,000

25. Stuart Ricci's gross pay was $41,050 last year. He estimated last year's fringe benefits to have been: $1,875, paid vacations and holidays; $3,980, health insurance; $2,280 pension contribution; $720, parking allowance. What were Stuart's total job benefits for last year? $49,905, Lesson 2.2

26. Reuben Tabor drives his car to work. He wants to insure his car for the minimum coverage for bodily injury and property damage and the highest deductibles for collision and comprehensive. Use Car Insurance Premium Table in Chapter 6 to find the annual premium Reuben will pay. $568.68, Lesson 6.7

27. Shannon Ebersohl is paid a commission of 1.5% on all sales and 3.6% on sales above $90,000 in a month. What were her earnings for a month in which her sales were $160,000? $4,920, Lesson 1.4

28. Sylvia McCann buys 8, $1,000, 9.1% bonds through her broker at 104.248 plus $15 accrued interest per bond. The commission is $7.50 per bond. What was the total cost of Sylvia's bond purchase? $8,519.84, Lesson 7.5

29. A worker earns regular pay of $14.12 an hour. What will be the worker's time-and-a-half and double-time pay rates? $21.18; $28.24, Lesson 1.3

30. The Zanin Ore Company declares a quarterly dividend of $0.24 a share on its no-par value common stock. What dividend will Mattie receive on the 805 Zanin shares she owns? $193.20, Lesson 7.6

356 ■ Chapter 8 Business Data Analysis

TEACHING STRATEGIES Cooperative Learning

Have students decide which of the three types of sampling studied in the Workplace Window they would use in each situation and why: poll to find for whom voters will vote (cluster); survey of a store's customers to find how they like the layout of a new charge statement (systematic, but survey only charge customers); survey of how people in general feel about the amount of rain that has recently fallen (convenience). Note that there are no absolutely correct answers. Those in parentheses are possible answers.

Bar and Line Graphs

GOALS

- Interpret and make vertical bar graphs
- Interpret and make horizontal bar graphs
- Interpret and make line graphs

Start Up

A newspaper included the graph at the right with an article that claimed a dramatic rise in crime in a city between April and May. Why might people have thought the graph was misleading?

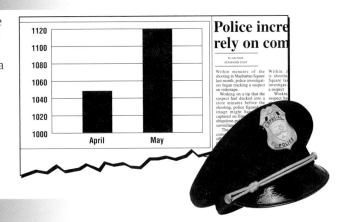

Math Skill Builder

Review these math skills and solve the exercises that follow.

① **Add** money amounts.
Find the sum. $2,600 + $1,900 = $4,500

1a. $4,850 + $3,200 $8,050   **1b.** $3,950 + $2,050 $6,000

② **Subtract** money amounts.
Find the difference. $9,400 − $3,690 = $5,710

2a. $2,300 − $900 $1,400   **2b.** $3,150 − $1,600 $1,550

■ Vertical Bar Graphs

Business firms use graphs to show data about their companies or industries. Graphs often show facts and trends more clearly than do numbers in tables.

The vertical bar graph shown at the top of the next page, with bars running up and down, shows the daily sales of The Building Center for a week. There is a bar for Monday through Saturday. The height of each bar shows the sales for each day. The scale for measuring the bars is on the left side of the graph.

Each vertical block on the graph equals $100 of sales. The lines for $500 and multiples of $500 are labeled. The height of each bar is to the nearest $50. For example, sales for Monday were $842.20. That amount was rounded to the nearest $50, or $850.

Lesson 8.3 Bar and Line Graphs ■ 357

Start Up

Have students read the Start Up. After they give their answers and explanations, ask them how the graph's message might change if the base of the vertical scale began at 1040.

Math Skill Builder

The addition and subtraction of money amounts are skills used in this lesson.

Complete all exercises in Math Skill Builder 1–2.

■ Teach Goal 1

Have students examine the vertical bar graph on page 358. Point out that the horizontal scale is also referred to as the x-axis and the vertical scale as the y-axis.

The horizontal scale usually identifies a constant, such as time. The vertical scale is usually used to show a variable.

Point out that the decision of what amount each block height represents is an important step in making sure the data within the graph are presented fairly. Often a graph will have to be redrawn because it doesn't show data clearly and fairly.

CONNECTION TO ECONOMICS

Indicate to students that graphs are commonly used to present economic data. The reason is that most numerical data are difficult to read and even more difficult to inter-pret. Indicate that most graphs are accompanied by an explanation of the terms and data displayed within the graph.

Work through Example 1 with students. You may wish to use a transparency of the graph so you can point to graph features and data items within the graph.

Assign Check Your Understanding problems A and B for class work. Remind students to show all calculations and label their work.

■ **ONGOING ASSESSMENT**
Ask students to answer the questions that follow.

A piece of graph paper has 4 blocks to an inch. A mark at every fifth block represents 60 employees. (a) How many employees does each block represent? **(12)** (b) How many inches of blocks and how many blocks are necessary to represent 240 employees? **(5 inches, or 20 blocks)**

■ **Teach Goal 2**

Point out that deciding whether to present data with a vertical or horizontal bar graph is often a matter of preference. The horizontal bar graph shown has the advantage of its labels being in the usual reading position.

You might have the students turn their book 90° counter clockwise to get an idea of what the graph shown on page 359 might look like if it were a vertical bar graph.

The heading or title of the graph shows the company name, identifies the data shown, and gives the time period that the graph represents.

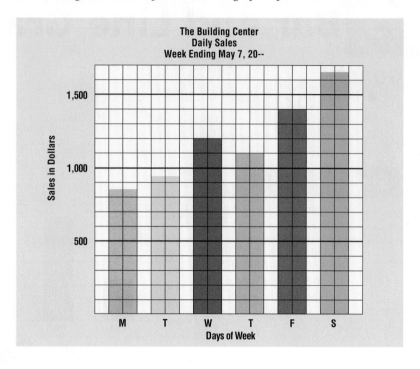

EXAMPLE 1

Use the graph for The Building Center to find the day on which sales were the greatest. What was the amount of sales for that day.

SOLUTION
Determine the sales for each bar. Select the bar that shows the greatest sales amount.

The greatest sales amount is $1,650 for Saturday.

■ **CHECK YOUR UNDERSTANDING**

A. What were The Building Center's sales on the day(s) that sales exceeded $1,300? Friday, $1,400; Saturday, $1,650

B. On which two days was the difference between The Building Center's sales the greatest, and what was the difference? Monday and Saturday, $800

■ Horizontal Bar Graphs

The horizontal bar graph at the top of next page, with bars running left to right, shows the sales by department of The Building Center. It looks like the vertical bar graph except that the bars are horizontal.

Each horizontal block on the graph equals $2,000. The amounts for each bar were rounded to the nearest $1,000 before the graph was made. For example, sales of electrical goods totaled $27,890 but are shown as $28,000.

358 ■ Chapter 8 Business Data Analysis

■ **CHECK YOUR UNDERSTANDING SOLUTIONS**

A. Sales exceed $1,300 on Friday ($1,400) and Saturday ($1,650)

B. $1,650 (Saturday) − $850 (Monday) = $800 difference

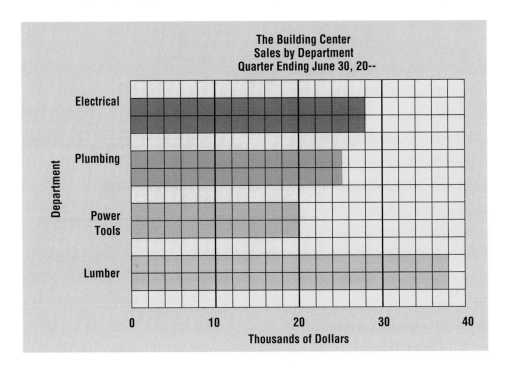

**The Building Center
Sales by Department
Quarter Ending June 30, 20--**

Department

Electrical

Plumbing

Power
Tools

Lumber

0   10   20   30   40

Thousands of Dollars

EXAMPLE 2

Use the graph above to find the department in which the sales for the second quarter were greater than $29,000. Find the total quarterly sales in that department.

SOLUTION

Determine the sales represented by each bar. Identify the department with sales greater than $29,000.

The lumber department's sales were $38,000. This is the only department with sales greater than $29,000.

■ **CHECK YOUR UNDERSTANDING**

C. Use the quarterly sales graph for The Building Center. Which departments had the greatest and smallest quarterly sales, and what were the sales? lumber, $38,000; power tools, $20,000

D. Use the quarterly sales graph for The Building Center. Which department had sales between $26,000 and $30,000? electrical

■ Line Graphs

The line graph shown at the top of the next page shows the sales of The Building Center by months. The time scale runs from left to right and is at the bottom of the graph. The dollar scale runs from bottom to top and is at the left.

The monthly sales were rounded to the nearest $1,000. The line was made by first placing dots showing each month's sales. The dots were then connected by drawing a line with a ruler.

Lesson 8.3 Bar and Line Graphs ■ **359**

359

■ **Apply Goal 2**

Work Example 2 with students by having them look at the graph in their book or at a transparency of the graph.

Assign Check Your Understanding problems C and D for class work. Check student work by asking students to give their answers to the problems.

■ **Teach Goal 3**

Inform students that line graphs are difficult to read when plots are placed between marked lines. For this reason, line graph data for money amounts is often rounded to a multiple that corresponds to a line in the graph.

Work Example 3 with students. Use a transparency or refer students to the line graph for The Building Center.

Assign Check Your Understanding problems E and F for class work. Discuss the answers students provide.

Wrap Up

Review the Start Up. Ask students for their suggestions on how the graph might have been improved or made to be more misleading than it already is.

TEAM MEETING

Review student reports and lead a group discussion to develop rules for making graphs that convey a clear and informative message. List the rules on a blank transparency or write them on the board and have a student copy them for you.

11.

12.

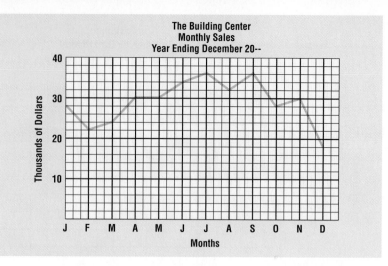

EXAMPLE 3

Use the graph of The Building Center's monthly sales to find the months in which sales were less than $24,000?

SOLUTION
Locate the $24,000 mark on the dollar scale. Locate all the months in which sales were below the $24,000 mark.

February and December were months with sales less than $24,000.

■ CHECK YOUR UNDERSTANDING

E. In the graph of The Building Center's monthly sales, what were the approximate sales for each month from October through December? Oct: $28,000; Nov: $30,000; Dec: $18,000

F. Between which two consecutive months did sales increase the most? March to April

Wrap Up

The graph is misleading since the scale does not begin at 0. The height of the May bar is over twice the height of the April bar. This suggests that crime increased by more than 100%. In fact, the number of crimes committed increased to 1,120 from 1,050, a 6.7% increase.

TEAM MEETING

You and each student in class are to find 3–4 bar graphs or line graphs using magazines, newspapers, books and the Internet as your sources. Form a team and look at the graphs your team collected.

As a team, decide which graphs are especially clear, easy to read, and informative. Prepare a list of the reasons why your team selected certain graphs as being especially good.

Discuss your reasons with those of other teams to develop a set of rules for making quality graphs.

COMMON ERRORS

Students may think that each vertical block represents $1,000 or may find the greatest difference between monthly sales for Check Your Understanding Problem F. Remind them to look at the labels on the vertical axis which show amount of the increment, $10,000. Divide the increment by the number of blocks ($10,000 ÷ 5 = $2,000). Thus, each block represents an additional $2,000 in sales. Also remind them to read problem directions carefully and recognize that if they are looking for increases, all decreases may be ignored.

Find the sum.

1. $1,450 + $2,650 $4,100

2. $550 + $350 + $700 $1,600

Find the difference.

3. $5,700 − $4,350 $1,350

4. $2,050 − $1,700 $350

Refer to the vertical bar graph for The Building Center for Exercises 5–6.

5. On which days were sales below $1,200? Monday, Tuesday, Thursday

6. What were the total sales for Wednesday through Friday? $3,700

Refer to the horizontal bar graph for The Building Center for Exercises 7–8.

7. For which two departments were the sales most nearly the same during the quarter? Electrical and plumbing

8. How much greater were the sales of lumber than the sales of power tools? $18,000

Refer to the line graph for The Building Center for Exercises 9–10.

9. Between which months was there less than a $2,000 difference in sales? April-May

10. What were the total sales for the second quarter of the year? $94,000

For Exercises 11–16, see side column.

For Exercises 11–12, use graph paper with 10 squares to the inch. Include a heading for each graph. In all graphs, make the bars 2 blocks wide; leave 2 blocks between bars.

11. Make a vertical bar graph with each vertical block equal to $20 that shows the daily sales of Unique Pottery. Label each multiple of $100 in the scale at the left.

<table>
<tr><td colspan="6">Unique Pottery
Daily Sales, February 7–12, 20—</td></tr>
<tr><td>Monday</td><td>$440</td><td>Wednesday</td><td>$380</td><td>Friday</td><td>$460</td></tr>
<tr><td>Tuesday</td><td>$340</td><td>Thursday</td><td>$360</td><td>Saturday</td><td>$480</td></tr>
</table>

12. The sales of the True Image Place for 6 months are shown below. Make a vertical bar graph with each vertical block equal to $2,000. Label each multiple of $10,000 in the vertical scale.

<table>
<tr><td colspan="6">True Image Place
Sales for July–December, 20—</td></tr>
<tr><td>July</td><td>$26,000</td><td>September</td><td>$28,000</td><td>November</td><td>$32,000</td></tr>
<tr><td>August</td><td>$18,000</td><td>October</td><td>$22,000</td><td>December</td><td>$46,000</td></tr>
</table>

Lesson 8.3 Bar and Line Graphs ■ **361**

Assign

Assignment: Exercises 1–17, 19–33. Students are to begin with the basic arithmetic problems at the beginning of the exercises. They review the underlying arithmetic in the exercises.

13.

15.

16.

SELECTED SOLUTIONS

Solutions for some of the exercises that require the creation of graphs are shown in the margins on pages 360–361.

14.

Have students read their answers to questions 5–10 and demonstrate the solution to these problems if they caused difficulty for students.

Collect all student work and check the graphs they produced.

Reteach

STUDENT WORKBOOK Some students may need more practice with vertical bar graphs. If so, work Exercise 1 with them. Then assign Exercise 2 to be done independently.

Work Exercise 3 with students who have difficulty with horizontal bar graphs. For independent work, assign Exercise 4.

If some students have difficulty with line graphs, work Exercise 6 with them. Then assign Exercise 7 to be completed independently.

For Exercises 13–14, use graph paper with 10 squares to the inch. Include a heading for each graph. In all graphs, make the bars 2 blocks wide; leave 2 blocks between bars.

13. Make a horizontal bar graph with each horizontal block equal to $100 that shows November sales for the Wall Center. Mark the scale at the bottom of the graph to show each multiple of $1,000.

The Wall Center Sales, November 16–21, 20—			
Paneling	$2,600	Mirror Tile	$1,100
Wall Paper	$2,800	Paint	$1,800
Ceramic Tile	$1,300	Supplies	$2,200

14. Make a horizontal bar graph showing last year's sales in 6 selling areas of the Protect-All Company. Make each block on the horizontal scale equal to $2,000. Round each sales figure to the nearest $2,000 before entering it into the graph.

Home Alarms	$110,365.20	Locks	$58,358.70
Car Alarms	$125,720.10	Steel Doors	$101,395.19
Garage Door Openers	$96,359.22	Repairs	$116,682.44

15. Show the facts below on a line graph. Make each vertical block equal to $10 of sales. Use every fifth vertical line for the days.

The Treasure Map Shop Sales for May 22–28, 20—					
Sunday	$420	Wednesday	$230	Friday	$350
Monday	$270	Thursday	$320	Saturday	$460
Tuesday	$260				

16. The table below shows the number of travel requests received by a visitor's bureau from January through June. Make a line graph with each vertical block equal to 100 requests. Use every fifth vertical line for the months.

Pearl County Visitor's Bureau 6-month Summary of Travel Requests					
January	2,200	March	2,700	May	2,100
February	2,900	April	2,400	June	1,900

17. **CRITICAL THINKING** The graphs you constructed in this lesson used graph paper with 10 blocks to the inch. Assume you did the graphs with the same scales but used graph paper that had 20 blocks to the inch. Would there be any great difference between the 10 and 20 block graphs? The amounts on the graphs would be more difficult to read.

SELECTED SOLUTIONS

17. The graph with 20 blocks to the inch may have the same appearance as the 10 blocks to the inch graph if the number of blocks between amounts on the y-axis and time on the x-axis are doubled. Otherwise, the graphed data would have a flatter and narrower appearance by using the 20 blocks per inch graph.

18. **CRITICAL THINKING** Last week, a department's employees had total gross wages of $45,200, of which $4,800 was from overtime pay. The rest of the wages was from regular time pay. You have similar data for the other 51 weeks of the year and notice that overtime is not worked each week. Your work supervisor wants you to draw a graph with one bar for each week of the year that shows the weekly amounts for regular pay and overtime pay. Are there any problems with making such a chart? Will the chart be understandable? See the Enrich section for answer.

MIXED REVIEW

19. $\frac{4}{5} - \frac{1}{2}$ $\frac{3}{10}$

20. $2\frac{1}{4} \div \frac{7}{8}$ $2\frac{4}{7}$

21. Rewrite 0.6 as a percent. 60%

22. 450 @ $0.10 $45

23. Round to the nearest ten thousand: $11,894 $10,000

24. Rewrite as a decimal: $\frac{1}{8}$ 0.125

25. $3\frac{1}{4} \times 2\frac{1}{2}$ $8\frac{1}{8}$

26. Find the quotient, to the nearest hundredth: 3,647 ÷ 8 455.88

27. Brent Madden's apartment is located 6.8 miles from a fire station. He wants to insure its contents for $5,000. Use the Renters Insurance Premium Table to find the annual premium. $138, Lesson 6.4

28. Fatima Cluett is paid a salary and a commission on all sales. Her sales last month were $43,200. Fatima's total earnings for the month were $2,578, of which $850 was from salary. What rate of commission on sales was Fatima paid? 4%, Lesson 1.4

29. Roxanne Schrader is paid regular pay of $13.78 an hour and time-and-a-half for hours worked beyond 8 hours in a day. She worked these hours last week: $8\frac{1}{2}$, $7\frac{3}{4}$, 8, $8\frac{1}{4}$; $9\frac{3}{4}$. What was her gross pay past week? $599.44, Lesson 1.3

30. A social security tax of 6.2% applies to a maximum wage of $87,900. The Medicare tax rate of 1.45% applies to all wages. What total did Liza pay for these two taxes on her yearly income of $90,000? $6,754.80, Lesson 2.1

31. Jerold Bernard's brain scan cost $1,275. His health insurance policy covered $1,064 of the scan's cost. Jerold's remaining deductible for the year is $184 and he pays 15% coinsurance on all medical tests. What amount must Jerold pay for the scan? $554.60, Lesson 7.2

32. Use the compound interest chart in Chapter 3 to find the compound interest on a $9,000 deposit earning interest at an annual rate of 2% for 30 days. $15.01, Lesson 3.6

33. You can buy a sewing machine for $625 cash or pay $125 down and the balance in 12 monthly payments of $46. What is the installment price? By what percent would your installment price be greater than the cash price, to the nearest tenth percent? $677; 8.3%, Lesson 4.4

COMMON ERRORS

Some students may draw incorrect graphs because they incorrectly round numbers or locate the plot on the graph.

Review procedures for rounding numbers. Allow students to work in pairs to create accurate and correct graphs.

Start Up

Have students read the Start Up. Before getting student responses, ask students what they think of making a circle graph for the actual high temperature recorded each day for 30 days, including any problems or benefits they see in making such a graph.

Math Skill Builder

Students use the skills of division of money amounts, expression of fractions as percents, and multiplication of degrees in a circle by percents.

Complete all exercises in Math Skill Builder 1–3.

■ **Teach Goal 1**

Explain to students that circle graphs show how the items that make up a whole are related to each other. Write H_2O, the chemical formula for water, on the board and ask students how many parts (atoms) of each element, hydrogen and oxygen, are represented by the formula. Then show hydrogen and oxygen as respective parts of a whole (molecule of water), $\frac{2}{3}$ and $\frac{1}{3}$, and their number of degrees in a circle graph.

8.4 Circle and Rectangle Graphs

GOALS
- ■ Make circle graphs
- ■ Interpret and make rectangle graphs

Start Up

Think of all the graphs that you have either interpreted or created in this chapter. Now try to think of them all as a circle graph. Circle graphs are easy to understand. But, some data simply cannot be shown in circle graphs. Make a list of types of data that would not work well in a circle graph. Give a reason why for each type.

Math Skill Builder

Review these math skills and solve the exercises that follow.

1. **Rewrite** fractions as percents.
   Find the percent. $\frac{\$90}{\$450} = 0.20 = 20\%$

   1a. $\frac{\$60}{\$500}$ 12% **1b.** $\frac{\$120}{\$480}$ 25%

   1c. $\frac{\$20}{\$100}$ 20% **1d.** $\frac{\$45}{\$900}$ 5%

2. **Multiply** the degrees in a circle by percents and round to the nearest degree.
   Find the product. $12\% \times 360° = 0.12 \times 360° = 43.2 = 43°$

   2a. $21\% \times 360°$ 76° **2b.** $8\% \times 360°$ 29°

   2c. $15\% \times 360°$ 54° **2d.** $75\% \times 360°$ 270°

3. **Divide** money amounts to find the percent one number is of another.
   Find the quotient. $\$30,000 \div \$120,000 = 0.25 = 25\%$

   3a. $\$120,000 \div \$400,000$ 30% **3b.** $\$5,000 \div \$125,000$ 4%

   3c. $\$150 \div \$1,000$ 15% **3d.** $\$12,000 \div \$60,000$ 20%

■ Circle Graphs

Bar graphs are frequently used to compare quantities to each other. Line graphs show change over time. **Circle graphs** are used to show how parts relate to the whole and to each other.

Circle graphs are based on a full circle of 360 degrees (360°), which is the whole, or 100%. The circle graph is divided into parts, called sectors.

COMMON ERRORS

Some students may fail to find correct central angles when making a circle graph. Some students may simply use the percents, such as 20% = 20°. Others may find the correct number of degrees, such as 20% of 360° = 72°, but then use the protractor incorrectly and draw an angle of 108°. It may be helpful to have students work together to complete such graphs.

EXAMPLE 1

Marvin earns $250 net pay per month from his after-school job. He plans to spend these amounts monthly in each category: Entertainment, $50; Clothes/Personal, $50; Meals, $30; School, $20; Miscellaneous, $25; Savings, $75. Show Marvin's budget in a circle graph.

SOLUTION

Show the budget amounts as percents by dividing the amount budgeted for each category by the total budget. Round percents to the nearest percent, where necessary. Then multiply 360° by the budget percent. Round the degrees to the nearest whole degree.

Budget Category	Amount	Expressed as Percent	Degrees in Sector
Entertainment	$ 50	$\frac{\$50}{\$250} = 0.20$, or 20%	20% of 360° = 72°
Clothes/Personal	$ 50	$\frac{\$50}{\$250} = 0.20$, or 20%	20% of 360° = 72°
Meals	$ 30	$\frac{\$30}{\$250} = 0.12$, or 12%	12% of 360° = 43°
School	$ 20	$\frac{\$20}{\$250} = 0.08$, or 8%	8% of 360° = 29°
Miscellaneous	$ 25	$\frac{\$25}{\$250} = 0.10$, or 10%	10% of 360° = 36°
Savings	$ 75	$\frac{\$75}{\$250} = 0.30$, or 30%	30% of 360° = 108°
TOTALS	$250	$\frac{\$250}{\$250} = 1.00$, or 100%	100% of 360° = 360°

Draw a circle with a compass. Mark the center of the circle. Use a protractor to draw the angles for each category using the degrees calculated above.

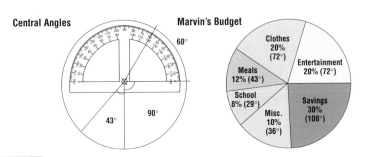

Central Angles   **Marvin's Budget**

MATH TIP

Due to rounding of percents and degrees, it is possible that the percents may not total exactly 100% and the degrees may not total exactly 360°.

■ CHECK YOUR UNDERSTANDING

A. Of the 60 people attending a family reunion, there were 42 adults, 10 teenagers, and 8 children. Show the family reunion attendees in a circle graph. *adults, 252°, teens, 60°, children, 48°*

B. A dealership sold these numbers of vehicles: cars, 300; trucks, 45; vans, 81; SUVs, 24. Show the vehicle sales in a circle graph. *cars, 240°, trucks, 36°, vans, 65°, SUVs, 19°.*

■ Apply Goal 1

Work through Example 1 at the board while students verify the example calculations at their desks.

Remind students that two roundings take place, first to the nearest percent and then to the nearest degree.

Assign Check Your Understanding problems A and B for class work. Move about the classroom and provide assistance to students at their desks.

Note that the solution for problem A shown in the bottom notes uses both percents and fractions to calculate the degrees in a sector. The expression 10 ÷ 60 gives a percent of 16.7%. Using the fractional equivalent of $\frac{1}{6}$ makes the sector degree calculation easier.

Demonstrate the solution and encourage students to choose the easiest expression to work with.

■ ONGOING ASSESSMENT

Have students mentally calculate the degrees in a circle graph for easy-to-calculate percents such as 50%, 25%, 20%, 10%, 5%, and 1%. Write the percents on the board in random order.

■ Apply Goal 2

Work through Example 2 by having students look at the rectangle graphs in their textbook or at a transparency of the graphs. Point out how the graphs are read.

Assign Check Your Understanding problems C and D for class work. Review student work at their desks to identify any difficulties they have in solving problems.

■ Rectangle Graphs

A **rectangle graph** is a single vertical or horizontal rectangular bar that is divided into sections. The entire rectangle represents the whole, or 100%. The sections show the parts of the whole. A rectangle graph shows how the parts relate to each other and to the whole.

Each part is proportional in size to the whole. For example, suppose a 5-inch bar represents $1,000. To show a part equal to $400 you would mark off two inches of the rectangle. ($\frac{\$400}{\$1,000} = \frac{2}{5}$, $\frac{2}{5} \times 5$ inches = 2 inches)

New Solution's Monthly Sales

Rectangle graphs are most often used to show dollars or percents. In the *vertical rectangle graph* shown at the right, the whole rectangle represents New Solution's sales of $2,000,000 for a month. Parts of the rectangle, also shown in dollars, represent each division's contribution to the monthly sales.

The *horizontal rectangle graph* shown above displays the same information as the vertical rectangle graph. However, the data is presented as percents.

EXAMPLE 2

Use the vertical rectangle graph to find the monthly sales of the Text Division. Also find what percent the Text Division's monthly sales are of total monthly sales.

SOLUTION
Find the difference between the amounts shown at the top and bottom of the Text Division part of the graph.

$2,000,000 − $1,600,000 = $400,000 sales for text division

Divide the Text Division's sales by the total sales.

$400,000 ÷ $2,000,000 = 0.20 = 20% sales as a percent of total sales

■ **CHECK YOUR UNDERSTANDING**

C. Use the vertical rectangle graph to find the sales for the Audio Division.
$600,000

D. Use the horizontal rectangle graph to find what percent the Online Division's sales are of total sales. 50%

■ *CHECK YOUR UNDERSTANDING SOLUTIONS*

C. $1,600,000 − $1,000,000 = $600,000 audio division sales

D. 100% − 50% = 50% online division sales

Wrap Up

Different graphs are used to show different types of data. The circle graph is best used to show how each part relates to the whole and to other parts. There may also be a space problem if the data has many parts, some of which are very small percentages of the total. Also, circle graphs are a snapshot of one time period whereas line graphs are best used to show a trend over a longer period of time.

Algebra Connection

A rectangle graph is a visual display of an equation. You can determine the sum by looking at the value at the top or far right of the scale. Each part of the graph is a term of the equation. If you wanted to write an equation for the horizontal rectangle graph on the previous page, let Text $= T$, Audio $= A$, and Online $= L$. The equation is $T + A + L = 100$.

To write the equation using only one variable, let the variable x represent the value of each unit. Text's part of the graph is 4 units so use $4x$ for it. Use $6x$ for Audio Division and $10x$ for Online Division. The equation would be $4x + 6x + 10x = 100$. Then $20x = 100$, so each unit x equals 5.

EXERCISES

Find the percent.

1. $128 \div \$800$ 16%
2. $\$1,200 \div \$60,000$ 2%

Find the product.

3. $40\% \times 360°$ 144°
4. $15\% \times 360°$ 54°

Find the quotient and state it as a percent.

5. $\$240,000 \div \$3,000,000$ 8%
6. $\$60,000 \div \$80,000$ 75%

The LaRowe Company spent $60,000 on advertising as shown.

Newspaper $18,000
Direct mail $15,000
Internet $12,000
Coupons $9,000
Product samples $3,000
Other $3,000

7. Find the percent of advertising spent on each type. newspaper, 30%; Internet, 20%; product samples, 5%; direct mail, 25%; coupons, 15%; other, 5%.

8. Make a circle graph of the LaRowe Company's advertising costs. 108°, 72°, 18°, 90°, 54°, 18°

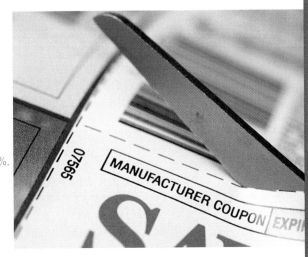

Lesson 8.4 Circle and Rectangle Graphs ■ 367

SELECTED SOLUTIONS

7. $\$18,000 \div \$60,000 = 30\%$;
   $\$12,000 \div \$60,000 = 20\%$;
   $\$3,000 \div \$60,000 = 5\%$;
   $\$15,000 \div \$60,000 = 25\%$;
   $\$9,000 \div \$60,000 = 15\%$; $\$3,000 \div \$60,000 = 5\%$

10. $0.2 \times 360° = 72°$; $0.4 \times 360° = 144°$;
    $0.175 \times 360° = 63°$; $0.06 \times 360° = 21.6$, or 22°;
    $0.165 \times 360° = 59.4$, or 59°

STUDENT WORKBOOK Some students may need help with circle graphs. Work Exercise 3 with them. Assign Exercise 4 for independent work.

Other students may require help with rectangle graphs. Work Exercise 1 with them and then have them solve Exercises 2, 5, and 6 independently.

Enrich

Assign Exercise 16, Critical Thinking. After students finish their discussion, ask them to describe the specific aspect of the question which is to show where profits come from. Since amounts are not needed to answer the question, the percent rectangle graph might be best to use.

Close

Give students problems that are easy to calculate mentally. For a $200 budget, ask what percents and degrees should be shown on a circle graph if these amounts are spent on a category of the budget: $50 (25%, 90°); $20 (10%, 36°).

Out of $500 spent on a trip, ask student what percent would be shown on a rectangle graph for each expense item: $100 (20%); $50 (10%); $150 (30%).

The Crescent Company's proposal to install a book checkout system at a library for $200,000 is divided into these parts: software, $40,000; hardware, $80,000; cabling and installation $35,000; training, $12,000; service contract, $33,000.

9. Find the percent that each part of the proposal represents. 20%, 40%, 17.5%, 6%, 16.5%

10. Make a circle graph showing the parts of the proposal in dollar terms. 72°, 144°, 63°, 22°, 59°

Last year's sales in 4 departments of the Grand Solutions Computer Company were: Training, 50%; Software, 30%; Repair Contracts, 15%; Hardware, 5%.

11. On a circle graph, how many degrees should be used to show the sales of each department? 180°, 108°, 54°, 18°

12. Make a circle graph showing the sales percent for each department.

The cost of a new pair of eyeglasses is made up of these items: examination, $50; lenses, $80; frames, $120.

13. Show the cost items of the eyeglasses on a vertical rectangle graph. Answers will vary.

14. On a horizontal graph, show the percent each part was of the total cost of the eyeglasses, to the nearest percent. exams, 20%; lenses, 32%; frames, 48%

15. **CRITICAL THINKING** If the overall length of a horizontal rectangle graph was reduced to 2 inches from 5 inches, would the graph be misleading? yes

16. **CRITICAL THINKING** A company's profits come from 8 sources. Which would best show where the profits come from in a rectangle graph, dollars or percents? percents; See the Enrich section for a more detailed answer.

MIXED REVIEW

17. Write 87.6% as a decimal. 0.876

18. 2.9×41.25 119.625

19. $4\frac{1}{6} + 3\frac{1}{4}$ $7\frac{5}{12}$

20. $6.4 \div 1,000$ 0.0064

21. $308,000 - 109,266$ 198,734

22. $\frac{3}{4} \times \frac{4}{7}$ $\frac{3}{7}$

23. Find the quotient, to the nearest cent: $612.19 \div 11$ $55.65

24. 96 increased by $\frac{1}{4}$ of itself is? 120

25. Molly Kieffer repays a 12-month, $10,070 Rule of 78 installment loan on the day the sixth payment is due. The monthly installment payments were $940. The total finance charge on the loan was $1,210. How much will Molly's payment be? Refer to Finance Charge Refund Schedule. $6,254.27, Lesson 4.5

26. The county tax rate is 18 mills per $1 of assessed value. Find the tax due on property assessed at $62,500. $1,125, Lesson 6.3

27. A shopper bought 6 packages of dinner napkins at $2.86, 8 rolls of paper toweling at $1.15, and 4 bars of soap at $1.59. A sales tax of 5% was charged. What was the total cost of the purchase? $34.36, Lesson 5.2

28. Marietta and Albert Bilicki, a married couple, have an adjusted gross income of $64,100. They are filing a joint return. Their itemized deductions are $11,450 and they claim six exemptions, one for each spouse and four for their children. What is their taxable income? $34,050, Lesson 2.3

29. A 7%, $1,000 bond may be bought for 98.247, including commission. What is the bond's yield to the nearest tenth percent? 7.1%, Lesson 7.5

DIFFERENT LEARNING ABILITIES Visually Impaired

It is possible that some students may not be able to read the degrees on a protractor to accurately construct a circle graph. What you may do is show students how to divide a circle into 180° degree sectors, then into 90° sectors, 45° degree sectors, and so on. Then have them calculate the degrees in each data item and draw sectors approximately using the circle division technique they were shown. Alternatively, you could enlarge a photocopy of a protractor and have students use scissors to cut out the protractor and use it for making circle graphs.

GOALS

- Interpret consumer price index data
- Calculate rates of inflation
- Calculate the purchasing power of the dollar
- Analyze unemployment data

Start Up

There is one Law of Statistics which states: If the statistics do not support your viewpoint, you obviously need more statistics. What does this statement mean?

Math Skill Builder

Review these math skills and solve the exercises that follow.

1 **Subtract** decimal amounts.
Find the difference. $148.7 - 100.0 = 48.7$

1a. $237.8 - 100.0$ 137.8   **1b.** $107.9 - 100.0$ 7.9

1c. $315.4 - 250.0$ 65.4   **1d.** $118.8 - 10.8$ 108

2 **Divide** decimals and round to the nearest tenth percent.
Find the percent. $4.8 \div 140.5 = 0.0341 = 3.4\%$

2a. $3.7 \div 168.2$ 2.2%   **2b.** $8.4 \div 191.3$ 4.4%

2c. $2.5 \div 35$ 7.1%   **2d.** $10.2 \div 100$ 10.2%

3 **Divide** decimals and round to the nearest thousandth.
Find the quotient. $100 \div 140.2 = 0.7132 = 0.713$

3a. $100 \div 118.6$ 0.843   **3b.** $100 \div 183.5$ 0.545

3c. $100 \div 268.4$ 0.373   **3d.** $100 \div 215.5$ 0.464

■ Consumer Price Index

The **Consumer Price Index (CPI)** is a widely reported measure of how much the prices of goods and services typically bought by consumers have changed when compared to a base period. A **base period** is a period of time with which comparisons are made. The base period for most of the items in the CPI is the 1982-84 period.

Lesson 8.5 Economic Statistics ■ 369

Start Up

Have students read the Start Up. Ask them whether they believe that statistics are used to misinform or mislead others intentionally and, if so, whether that happens rarely, only sometimes, or frequently. Also ask whether they believe that any-one can find a statistic to support his/her views.

Math Skill Builder

In this lesson, students use the skills of subtraction and division of decimals and rounding.

Complete Exercises 1–3 in the Math Skill Builder.

■ Teach Goal 1

Inform students that the CPI cate-gories reflect a "market basket" approach where hypothetical pur-chases are made of a "basket" of goods and services commonly bought by consumers.

CONNECTION TO ECONOMICS

Inform students that the base year or base period changes over time. The current base period of 1982–84 replaced the previous base year of 1967. The base period prior to 1967 was 1957–59. The base period is changed periodi-cally to allow for easier-to-use comparisons. Also, expressing the purchasing power of the dollar as 2¢ of some long-past year sounds much worse than a dollar being worth 60¢ compared to about 20 years ago.

Work through Example 1 with students and have them find the CPI index number and then do the math at their desks.

Assign Check Your Understanding problems A and B for class work. For each problem, ask students to give the number they found in the table, the items they subtracted, and their answer.

■ **ONGOING ASSESSMENT**
Call out the category and year for whichever items you select and have students look up the corresponding index number in the table. Call on students at random to give the number they found.

■ **STUDENT PORTFOLIO**
Students should consider including in their portfolio the problems they will solve in this lesson that require the use of the CPI to calculate rates of inflation and the purchasing power of the dollar.

The CPI uses a single number, called an index number, to compare price changes to the base period. The index number for the base period is always equal to 100.

The Historical Report of the CPI shows index numbers for various categories of consumer goods and services. The All Items column gives an average number considering all categories and is the number commonly used when referring to the CPI. Note that two categories, Recreation and Education & Communication, were added to the CPI in 1997, so 1997 is their base period.

Historical Report—Consumer Price Index, 1994–2003 Categories of Goods and Services									
Years	All Items	Food & Beverages	Housing	Apparel	Transpor- tation	Medical Care	Recrea- tion	Education & Communication	Other
1982-84	100.0	100.0	100.0	100.0	100.0	100.0	—	—	100.0
1994	148.2	147.2	145.4	130.5	137.1	215.3	93.0	90.3	202.4
1995	152.4	150.3	149.7	130.6	139.1	223.8	95.6	93.9	211.1
1996	156.9	156.6	154.0	130.3	145.2	230.6	98.5	97.1	218.7
1997	160.5	159.1	157.7	131.6	143.2	237.1	100.0	100.0	230.1
1998	163.0	162.7	161.3	130.7	140.7	245.2	101.2	100.7	250.3
1999	166.6	165.9	164.8	130.1	148.3	254.2	102.0	102.3	263.0
2000	172.2	170.5	171.9	127.8	154.4	264.8	103.7	103.6	274.0
2001	177.1	175.3	177.6	124.8	149.0	278.3	105.3	106.9	287.0
2002	179.9	177.8	181.1	121.5	154.2	291.3	106.5	109.2	295.8
2003	184.0	184.1	185.1	119.0	154.7	302.1	107.7	110.9	300.2

The CPI may be expressed in several ways. For example, the CPI for "All Items" in 2003 is 184.0. This means that the cost of goods in 2003 was 184.0% of their cost in the base period. The percent increase in prices from the base period to 2003 is 84.0% (184.0 − 100.0). Looking at the relationship in another way, it cost $184 in 2003 to buy the same goods for which you would have paid $100 in the base period.

EXAMPLE 1

Use the table above to find the CPI for All Items for 1995 and the percent the 1995 CPI increased from the base period.

SOLUTION
Copy the index number from the box in the table where the year, 1995, and the "All Items" column meet.

152.4   CPI index number for 1995

Subtract the base period index number from the 1995 index number and add a percent sign to the number.

152.4 − 100.0 = 52.4%   percent CPI increased from base period to 1995

■ **CHECK YOUR UNDERSTANDING SOLUTIONS**

A. 130.5 − 100.0 = 30.5%; 119.0 − 100.0 = 19.0% increase

B. 302.1 − 100.0 = 202.1% increase in medical care; other had the next greatest increase

C. 166.6 − 163.0 = 3.6; 3.6 ÷ 163.0 = 0.0221, or 2.2%

D. 291.3 − 278.3 = 13; 13 ÷ 278.3 = 0.0467, or 4.7%

A. Use the CPI table. By what percent did the CPI for Apparel increase from the base period to 1994? to 2003? 30.5%; 19.0%

B. Refer to the CPI table. Of all the categories whose base period is 1982-84, which one showed the greatest percent increase to 2003? What is the percent increase? Medical care; 202.1%

■ Rate of Inflation

For consumers, business firms, organizations, and the government, inflation means that the prices of goods and services they buy are rising. The U.S. Department of Labor publishes the Consumer Price Index report that tells how much inflation has occurred within the past year. A calculation in the report, called the *rate of inflation*, shows the percent increase in prices from the previous year.

EXAMPLE 2

The CPI table shows an index number of 179.9 for 2002 and an index number of 184.0 for 2003. What was the rate of inflation for 2003, to the nearest tenth percent?

SOLUTION

Find the difference between the two index numbers.

$184.0 - 179.9 = 4.1$

Divide the difference by the index number for the earlier year.

$4.1 \div 179.9 = 0.0228 = 2.3\%$

The rate of inflation for 2003 was 2.3%.

■ **CHECK YOUR UNDERSTANDING**

C. Find the rate of inflation for 1999, to the nearest tenth percent. 2.2%

D. Find the rate of inflation for the Medical Care category for 2002. 4.7%

■ Purchasing Power of the Dollar

When inflation occurs, each dollar buys less than it did in the past. The purchasing power of the dollar is a measure of how much a dollar now buys compared to what it could buy during some base period. The base period is a time period with which all purchasing power of the dollar comparisons are made.

Suppose a Department of Labor report shows that the purchasing power of a dollar in 2003 was $0.54. In the base period, 1982-1984, the dollar was worth its full value of $1.00. In 2003, the dollar was worth $0.54 compared to the base value. This means that a 2003 dollar could buy only about $0.54 worth of the same goods that could have been bought in 1982–84. The 2003 dollar is worth less because of inflation.

Lesson 8.5 Economic Statistics ■ 371

■ **Teach Goal 2**

Inform students that an approximate rate of inflation may be calculated from monthly CPI data. Point out that a 0.3% monthly increase in consumer prices equals an inflation rate of about 3.6% per year (12 × 0.3%).

■ **Apply Goal 2**

Work Example 2 at the board with students completing the math at their desks.

Assign Check Your Understanding problems C and D for class work. Check students' work at their desks.

■ **Teach Goal 3**

Emphasize that the purchasing power of the dollar is a dramatic way of showing how inflation erodes the value of the dollar over time.

Point out that many people understand the meaning of a report stating that today's dollar will buy only 54¢ of what it could have bought 20 years ago.

COMMON ERRORS

Students may divide by the wrong number when finding the rate of inflation or the purchasing power of the dollar. If students are familiar with the concept of base, use base in your explanations. Remind them that finding the rate of inflation means comparing an index number to one in an earlier year. The earlier year is the base and therefore the divisor also. Finding the purchasing power of the dollar involves finding what percent an index is of the base. So the base, 100, is divided by the index number from a later period.

Work Example 3 at the board while students complete work at their desks.

Assign Check Your Understanding problems E and F for class work. Move about the classroom and observe student work to identify difficulties they have.

■ Teach Goal 4

Point out that a national unemployment rate often receives wide publicity as an indicator of how well the U. S. economy is doing. Unemployment data are also available for states and larger cities.

Remind students that national unemployment data is an average number and that unemployment data may vary widely from one area to another. For example, the Midwest, which is more dependent on basic industries, may have a higher unemployment rate during a business slowdown than the southeastern U. S. that has a different mix of industries.

EXAMPLE 3

Use the CPI table to calculate the purchasing power of the dollar for 2000, to the nearest tenth of a cent.

SOLUTION

Divide the CPI index number for the base period by the CPI index number for the year with which a comparison is made, to the nearest thousandth.

172.2 = CPI index for 2000   100 = CPI index for base period

$100 \div 172.2 = 0.5807 = 0.581$ decimal rate

Multiply the decimal rate by $1.

$1 \times 0.581 = \$0.581$ purchasing power of the dollar in 2000

■ CHECK YOUR UNDERSTANDING

E. Use the CPI table to find the purchasing power of the dollar in 2002, to the nearest tenth of a cent. $0.556

F. Use the CPI table to find how much a 1997 dollar is worth compared to 1982-84, to the nearest tenth of a cent. $0.623

■ Unemployment Rate

The **unemployment rate** tells the percentage of the total labor force that is not working. The **labor force** consists of all people who are willing to work and who either have a job or are looking for a job.

The table below shows the unemployment rate for different persons for one month as estimated by the U.S. Department of Labor.

> **MATH TIP**
>
> One meaning of the term "rate" is percent.

August, 2004 Unemployment Rates by Age, Sex, and Race	
Worker Classification	**Unemployment Rate**
All Workers	5.4
Teen Workers	17.0
Male Workers	5.6
Female Workers	5.3
White Workers	4.7
Black Workers	10.4
Hispanic Workers	6.9
Married Male Workers, Spouse Present	3.1
Married Female Workers, Spouse Present	3.5

■ *CHECK YOUR UNDERSTANDING SOLUTIONS*

E. $100 \div 179.9 = \$0.5559$, or $0.556
F. $100 \div 160.5 = \$0.6230$, or $0.623

G. 3.1% is the lowest unemployment rate; married male workers, spouse present
H. 5.6% − 5.3% = 0.3% difference

EXAMPLE 4

Which workers shown in the table above had the highest rate of unemployment? What was the rate?

SOLUTION

Locate the highest rate in the Unemployment Rate column: 17.0%.

Teen workers had the highest unemployment rate.

■ **CHECK YOUR UNDERSTANDING**

G. Refer to the table above to find the workers with the lowest unemployment rate.
married male workers, spouse present

H. What was the difference in the unemployment rate of male and female workers in data shown? 0.3%

Wrap Up

The Law of Statistics tells consumers to be wary of the statistics they hear or read. Almost any viewpoint can be supported by statistics. Individuals, business firms, labor unions, non-profit organizations, and all levels of government use statistics that support their position and ignore those that do not. To believe the statistics used by others, you need to know how the data were collected and analyzed to determine their truthfulness.

COMMUNICATION

Using the Internet or the library, find what types of goods and services are included in the Education and Communication category of the Consumer Price Index. You can begin with your search with any of following keywords. For a more refined search use any of these words joined with the word "and".

- consumer price index
- CPI
- education
- communication
- goods
- services

Identify three types of goods and services within the Education and Communication category in which prices have risen most since the base year.

EXERCISES

Find the difference.

1. 132.9 − 100.0 32.9
2. 287.7 − 100.0 187.7

Find the percent. Round to the nearest tenth percent.

3. 5.8 ÷ 142.7 4.1%
4. 2.6 ÷ 115.4 2.3%

Lesson 8.5 Economic Statistics ■ **373**

■ Apply Goal 4

Ask students to solve Example 4. Remind them to state their answers in complete sentences.

Assign Check Your Understanding problems G and H for class work and check student answers when they are finished with the assignment.

Wrap Up

Review the Start Up. Ask students if they would believe a local store's ad stating that a recent survey showed a 99% satisfaction rating among its customers.

Discuss how the statistic might be true as stated, or how it might be misleading.

COMMUNICATION

Ask students to share their findings with the rest of the class. Have them point out any difficulties they may have had in finding an appropriate source and what led them to locate an informative source.

Assign

Assignment: Exercises 1–18 and 20–22, 23–37. Have students solve the basic arithmetic problems before completing the rest of the exercises.

Remind students to label the results of their calculations.

SELECTED SOLUTIONS

11. 154.0 − 100.0 = 54%
15. 100 ÷ 177.1 = 0.5647, or $0.565 in 2001;
    100 ÷ 172.2 = 0.5807, or $0.581 in 2000;
    $0.581 − $0.565 = $0.16 drop
21. 184.0 − 100.0 = 84.0% CPI increase;

84.0% × $12,000 = 0.84 × $12,000 = $10,080 increase; $12,000 + $10,080 = $22,080 wage in 2003
22. 0.84 × $5 = $4.20 increase; $5 + $4.20 = $9.20 hourly rate in 2003

Assess

Collect student work and check their solutions for these problems: 9, 10, 11, 14, 15, 17, and 22.

Reteach

STUDENT WORKBOOK Work Exercise 1a with students who need help in interpreting CPI data. Assign Exercises 1b–e and 2 for independent work.

Help students having difficulty with calculating rates of inflation by working Exercise 3a with them and assigning Exercises 3b, 3c and 4–7 for independent work.

If students need help in calculating the purchasing power of the dollar, solve Exercise 8a with them. Then assign for independent work Exercises 8b–8d.

If interpreting unemployment data poses a problem for some students, work Exercise 9 with them and assign Exercise 10 for independent work.

Find the quotient. Round to the nearest thousandth.

5. 100 ÷ 236.3 0.423   **6.** 100 ÷ 107.1 0.934

Use the CPI table to solve Exercises 7–17.

7. What was the CPI for Transportation in 1996? 145.2

8. By what percent did the CPI for Food and Beverages increase from the base period to 2003? 84.1%

9. Which category of goods and services showed the smallest price increase between the base period of 1982-84 and 1994? Apparel

10. Which 2 categories of consumer goods and services had price increases greater than those of the CPI from the base period to 1998? Medical Care and Other

11. By what percent did prices for Housing increase from the base period to 1996? 54%

12. What was the rate of inflation in 1995 and 1998, rounded to the nearest tenth percent? 2.8%, 1.6%

13. Of these categories, Food and Beverages, Housing, and Apparel, which had the highest rate of inflation in 1997? What was the rate, to the nearest tenth percent? Housing, 2.4%

14. During the years 1999–2003, in which year was the highest rate of inflation reported, to the nearest tenth percent? What was the percent? 2000, 3.4%

15. What was the purchasing power of the dollar in 2001 and what amount did it drop from the previous year, to the nearest tenth of a cent? $0.565; $0.016

By what amount, to the nearest tenth of a cent, did the purchasing power of the dollar drop?

16. From the base period through 1998? $0.387

17. From 1994 through 2002? $0.119

18. In the Unemployment Rate Table, which gender, male or female, had the highest unemployment rate? Male workers

19. CRITICAL THINKING The CPI index number for Apparel was 130.5 in 1994 and 119.0 in 2003. What might be some reasons for the decrease in Apparel compared to other categories? See the Enrich section for answer.

20. INTEGRATING YOUR KNOWLEDGE Calculate the rates of inflation from 1994 through 2003. Make a vertical bar graph to show the inflation rates. Check student's work.

STRETCHING YOUR SKILLS Marjorie earned $12,000 a year and Timothy earned $5 an hour in the base period of 1982-84. Since then they both have received wage increases equal to the increase in the CPI through 2003.

21. Marjorie should have been earning what annual wage? $22,080

22. Timothy should have been earning what hourly wage, to the nearest cent? $9.20

> **MATH TIP**
>
> The purchasing power of any year's dollar is calculated from the base period.

CONNECTION TO TECHNOLOGY

You may wish to have students create a spreadsheet to calculate the rates of inflation for Exercise 20, Integrating Your Knowledge. They may also use the chart feature of their spreadsheet program to show the inflation rates on a vertical bar graph.

23. $50 − $21.99 $28.01

24. Rewrite as a fraction: 0.005 $\frac{1}{200}$

25. 7.8% of $265 $20.67

26. $\frac{3}{4} \div \frac{3}{8}$ 2

27. $1\frac{1}{3}$ of $183.42 $244.56

28. 10 × $45.18 $451.80

29. What percent of 7,500 is 150? 2%

30. $\frac{3}{4} + \frac{1}{2}$ $1\frac{1}{4}$

31. Round to the nearest cent: $19.9951 $20

32. The Groat family has a fixed-rate mortgage with monthly payments of $682.40. They can refinance their current mortgage with a new loan at a lower interest rate and longer term. The monthly payments on the new loan will be $519.18. To get the new mortgage loan, they had to pay a prepayment penalty of $680 and closing costs of $1,050. How much will they save in the first year by refinancing? $228.64, Lesson 6.1

33. Angie Grosbeck's gross pay is $617.50 a week. How much will Angie earn in one quarter of a year at her current pay? $8,027.50, Lesson 1.1

34. A 13.5 oz. size of body lotion sells for $8.67. A 5.4 oz. size of the same lotion sells for $4.39. Which size of lotion costs more per ounce? How much more per ounce, to the nearest tenth of a cent? 5.4 oz cost more; 17.1¢, Lesson 5.3

35. Cassie Siebert borrowed $5,200 for 24 months to landscape her home. The promissory note carried 14% interest. Find the amount of interest Cassie must pay. Also find the amount she must repay on the due date of the note. $1,456; $6,656, Lesson 4.1

36. The tip income of the seven food servers at a buffet restaurant averages 7% of the food bill. The total of the food bills for one evening was $8,200. How much did each food server earn for the evening? $82, Lesson 1.5

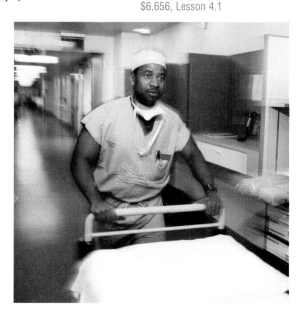

37. After surgery, Gary Schoeffler spent 4 days in the hospital. The hospital room cost of $375 a day was covered for only the two-day stay that his insurance company allowed for the type of surgery Gary had. Other hospital costs related to this surgery were $6,278, of which the insurer approved $5,690. Gary still had $500 of deductible to use and his policy required 12% coinsurance. What amount did Gary have to pay for his surgery. $2,610.80, Lesson 7.2

Lesson 8.5 Economic Statistics ■ **375**

TEACHING STRATEGIES Cooperative Learning

Students may wish to research CPI and unemployment data on the Internet. Both types of data are tabulated by the U. S. Department of Labor, Bureau of Labor Statistics. Its website is www.bls.gov. The website contains a wide variety of related data such as average earnings of workers, duration of unemployment, inflation and consumer spending, and safety and health issues.

Lesson 8.1 Measures of Central Tendency

- Add group of numbers and divide by the number of items to find the mean.

- Arrange numbers in order and locate middle number to find the median. If there is no one middle number, add two middle numbers and divide by two to find the median.

- Arrange numbers in order and locate number or numbers that appear most frequently to find the mode.

- Subtract lowest number from highest number in a group to find the range.

- Arrange numbers in order and mark the total times each number appears to make a frequency distribution.

- Multiply each number in frequency distribution by number of marks, add products, and divide their sum by total marks to find the mean.

- Locate middle number in frequency distribution to find the median.

- Locate number in frequency distribution that has the most marks to find the mode.

Chapter Review

Vocabulary Review

base period	labor force	purchasing power of the dollar
circle graph	line graph	random samples
Consumer Price Index (CPI)	mean	range
frequency distribution	median	rectangle graph
horizontal bar graph	mode	unemployment rate
inflation	probability	vertical bar graph

Fill in the blanks with the term that best completes the statement.

1. The middle number in a group is called the __?__. median

2. A way of predicting the outcome of an event is known as __?__. probability

3. A graph in which bars are drawn left to right is called (a, an) __?__. horizontal bar graph

4. A time period in the past with which comparisons are made is called the __?__. base period

5. A statistical measure of how much a dollar will buy is known as __?__. purchasing power of the dollar

6. The sum of the numbers divided by the number of items is called the __?__. mean

7. A rise in the prices of goods and services in known as __?__. inflation

8. Persons who are employed or who are unemployed and looking for work make up what is called the __?__. labor force

9. A few items selected from a group by chance for testing are called __?__. random samples

10. A single number used to measure changes in the prices of goods and services is called the __?__. Consumer Price Index

LESSON 8.1

11. The Moegel Company reported having these numbers of employees in the past four years: 3,815, 4,210, 4,859, and 3,400. What was the mean number of employees the company had in the 4-year period? 4,071

12. Lucas kept track of his golf scores during July and August. His scores were: 81, 83, 85, 90, 88, 80, 83, 84, 86. Find the median, mode, and range of his golf scores for the two months? 84, 83, 10

13. During the past 12 months, Megan exercised at the health club these number of days: 22, 14, 18, 16, 24, 26, 18, 21, 23, 25, 17, 19. What average number of days per month did Megan exercise for the year, as measured by the median and mode. 20, 18

14. These numbers of employees were absent from work at the Stocker Company during the working days of February: 25, 19, 21, 26, 27, 24, 25, 19, 36, 30, 12, 19, 19, 24, 25, 22, 21, 26, 30, 24. Make a frequency distribution table and find the mean, median, and mode of the days employees were absent from work. Mn = 23.7; Md = 24, Mo = 19

DIFFERENT LEARNING ABILITIES At-Risk Learners

To help students develop skills essential to learning, have them cover the word list in the Vocabulary Review and use their *recall skills* to complete as many statements as they can. If any blanks remain, students may then uncover the list and rely on their *recognition skills* to complete the assignment.

LESSON 8.2

15. A bag contains 20 disks numbered from 1-20. What is the probability you will pick a disk with the numbers 1, 2, 3, 4, or 5? If you picked 500 disks, how many times would you expect to pick disks numbered 1-5? $\frac{1}{4}$, 125

16. In one year, a company found 9 defective parts out of 4,500 parts picked for testing. What was the probability of finding a defect? How many defective parts could be expected from a year's production of 265,000 parts? 0.2%; 530

17. Of 82,000 people living at age 60, 66,000 will be living at age 70. What is the probability that a 60-year old person will live to age 70, to the nearest percent? 80%

LESSON 8.3

18. Refer to the Daily Sales graph to find how much greater Friday's sales were than Wednesday's sales. $200

19. What would be the total annual sales of the Electrical department if the sales for each quarter were exactly the same as those shown in Sales by Department graph? $112,000

20. In Monthly Sales graph, find whether sales for the first or fourth quarter were greater, and how much greater. fourth quarter, $2,000 greater

LESSON 8.4

21. At a football tryout camp, the abilities of 500 players were graded. The players receiving each grade were: A, 25; B, 40; C, 75; D, 160; E, 200. Calculate the number of degrees each letter grade would represent in a circle graph, to the nearest degree. A, 18°; B, 29°; C, 54°; D, 115°; E, 144°

22. Assume the monthly sales of New Solutions' divisions had been Text, $300,000; Audio, $100,000, and Online, $1,600,000. Also assume that sales for each division are recorded as percents in the same order as shown in the horizontal rectangle graph on page 366. Between which percents would the sales for each division have been recorded? 0–15%; 15–20%; 20–100%

LESSON 8.5

23. The Medical Care category for 1994 showed a CPI index number of 215.3. By what percent did medical care prices increase from the base period? 115.3%

24. The CPI index number in 1996 for the Housing category was 154.0. In 1997 the index number for Housing was 157.7. What was the rate of inflation in Housing for 1997, to the nearest tenth percent? 2.4%

25. The CPI index number for 1986 was 109.6. Compared to the base period of 1982-84, what was the purchasing power of the dollar in 1986, to the nearest tenth of a cent? $0.912

26. If the unemployment rate for all workers shown in the Unemployment Rate Table doubled because of an economic slowdown, what would the new unemployment rate be? At the new rate, how many workers would be unemployed out of every one million workers? 10.4%, 104,000

Chapter 8 Review ■ **377**

Lesson 8.2 Probability
- Divide number of times an event may occur by total possible outcomes to find probability of a chance event.

- Multiply probability of an event by number of tries to find expected number of times event will occur.

- Divide defects by total items in sample, then multiply times total production to find expected number of defects.

- Divide number of people living at expected age by number living at comparison age to find probability of living to certain age.

Lesson 8.3 Bar and Line Graphs
- Locate the data plotted on a bar or line graph to interpret the graphs.

Lesson 8.4 Circle and Rectangle Graphs
- Divide each item by total items and multiply that percent by 360° to find degrees in each sector on a circle graph.

- Locate the data plotted on a rectangle graph to interpret the graph.

Lesson 8.5 Economic Statistics
- Subtract base index number from CPI index number for another year to find percent increase in CPI.

- Find difference between index numbers and divide by index number of earlier year to find rate of inflation.

- Divide base index number of 100 by CPI index number for another year to find purchasing power of the dollar.

- Locate appropriate data in an unemployment table to interpret the table and answer questions.

TEACHING STRATEGIES Chapter Review

Assign the review problems to be completed by lesson. Ask students to scan the problems for each lesson and raise their hands if they see any problems they may not know how to solve. Either assign a knowledgeable student to provide assistance or help students at their desks.

Students need spreadsheet file
tech8-1.xls for Tasks 1 and 2.

Task 1 Students enter data into a
spreadsheet template that calculates the purchasing power of the
dollar and the annual rate of inflation for a 15-year period.

Task 2 Students answer questions
about the results of Task 1. They
also key in new data and answer
questions about the results.

Task 3 Students design and create
a spreadsheet that will use the
charting capabilities of software to
graph sales.

Task 4 Students view the graph
they created and answer questions
about the displayed results.

Teach and Apply Task 1

Point out to students that the CPI
index data to be entered includes
more years than appear in the CPI
table shown in Lesson 8-5. Also
note that the procedures for making year-to-year comparisons
remain the same. The additional
years have no effect on such comparisons.

Teach and Apply Task 2

Assign questions 1–6 and have
students discuss their answers.

Now have students change the
data in Cell B10 before they
answer questions 7–10. Question 7
asks students to think of a reason
for a theoretical drop in the CPI
index from the previous year.

Technology Workshop

Task 1: Calculating Inflation Indicators

Enter data into a template that calculates the purchasing power of the dollar and the annual inflation rate. You may use the template to study how the CPI is converted to two common inflation indicators, the purchasing power of the dollar and the rate of inflation.

Open the spreadsheet for Chapter 8 (tech8-1.xls) and enter the data shown in blue (cells B5-20) into the spreadsheet. The spreadsheet will calculate the purchasing power of the dollar for each year, the annual change in the purchasing power of the dollar, and the annual inflation rate. Your computer screen should look like the one shown below when you are done.

	A	B	C	D	E
1			INFLATION INDICATORS		
2-4	Year	CPI Index	Purchasing Power of Dollar	Annual Change In Purchasing Power of Dollar	Annual Inflation Rate Based on CPI
5	1982-84	100.0	$1.000	$0.000	0.0%
6	1985	107.6	0.929	−0.071	7.6%
7	1986	109.6	0.912	−0.017	1.9%
8	1987	113.6	0.880	−0.032	3.6%
9	1988	118.3	0.845	−0.035	4.1%
10	1989	124.0	0.806	−0.039	4.8%
11	1990	130.7	0.765	−0.041	5.4%
12	1991	136.2	0.734	−0.031	4.2%
13	1992	140.3	0.713	−0.021	3.0%
14	1993	144.5	0.692	−0.021	3.0%
15	1994	148.2	0.675	−0.017	2.6%
16	1995	152.4	0.656	−0.019	2.8%
17	1996	156.9	0.637	−0.019	3.0%
18	1997	160.5	0.623	−0.014	2.3%
19	1998	163.0	0.613	−0.010	1.6%
20	1999	166.6	0.600	−0.013	2.2%
21	2000	172.2	0.581	−0.020	3.4%
22	2001	177.1	0.565	−0.016	2.8%
23	2002	179.9	0.556	−0.009	1.6%
24	2003	184.0	0.543	−0.012	2.3%

Task 2: Analyze the Spreadsheet Output

Answer these questions about the inflation indicator calculations.

1. What do the minus signs in front of the output in Column D mean? they show that the purchasing power of the dollar dropped from the previous year

2. What was the purchasing power of the dollar in 1992? $0.713

3. What was the year with the highest annual inflation rate. What was the rate? 1985, 7.6%

4. In which year did the purchasing power of the dollar drop the most? How much was the drop, in cents? 1985, 7.1 cents

5. In which year since 1985 was the annual inflation rate the lowest? What was the rate? 1998 and 2002, 1.6%

TEACHING STRATEGIES Task 1

Explain that a zero amount appears in Cell D5 and a zero percent appears in Cell E5 because there is no prior year shown with which to compare base period data. Ask how the spreadsheet could be changed to bring the data and calculations up-to-date. Point out that the purchasing power of the dollar dropped 1.7¢ from 1985 to 1986 and from 1993 to 1994, yet the annual inflation rates for 1986 and 1994 were different, 1.9% and 2.6%, respectively. Ask students whether they ought to be the same.

6. From 1985 to 1995, in which years was the inflation rate greater than 4.5%? 1985, 1989, 1990

Now move the cursor to cell B10, which holds the CPI index number for 1989. Enter a new index number of 115.0.

Answer these questions.

7. What was the new amount for the purchasing power of the dollar for 1989? $0.870

8. Did the purchasing power of the dollar increase or decrease for 1989? How do you know this? increased in 1989;The change of $0.024 in Cell D10 shows a positive number which means that the purchasing power of the dollar

9. What happened to the annual rate of inflation in 1989? The rate of inflation decreased by 2.8%.

10. What would have occurred in 1989 if the 1989 CPI index number were 115 compared to a 1988 CPI index number of 118.3? The prices of goods and services measured by the Consumer Price Index would have dropped during 1989 from their 1988 level.

Task 3: Design a Spreadsheet to Graph Sales Data

You are to design a spreadsheet that will use the charting features of your software to create a bar graph. The graph will show monthly sales by product line for a two-year period. The monthly sales for each product line are to be printed side-by-side. Round the sales data to the nearest $500 or a multiple of $500 before entering the data into a worksheet. The sales data and the graph are to appear on separate worksheets.

> *SITUATION:* The Clayton Door & Window Company wants a bar graph that shows current year and previous year sales data for its product line. Sales data follows:

Clayton Door & Window Company
Comparative Sales Data
January 2003 and 2004

	January, 2003	January, 2004
Entry Doors	$21,500	$21,050
Garage Doors	$18,900	$15,150
Security Systems	$24,600	$34,025
Windows	$31,112	$25,236

Task 4: Analyze the Spreadsheet Output

Answer these questions about your completed graph.

11. Which product line's 2004 sales were greater than 2003 sales? Security systems

12. Which product line's sales were almost equal in both years? Entry doors

13. Which product line had the greatest amount of sales in 2003? Windows

14. Which product line had monthly sales less than $20,000, and in which year? Garage doors in 2003 and 2004

Chapter 8 Technology Workshop ■ **379**

■ HOW TIMES HAVE CHANGED

1. $177.8 - 100 = 77.8\%$
increase in CPI for Food and Beverages
$\$0.54 \times 0.778 \approx \$0.42$
increase in the price of a loaf of bread
$\$0.54 + \$0.42 = \$0.96$

   $\$1.01 - \$0.96 = \$0.05$
difference

2. $140.7 - 100 = 40.7\%$
increase in CPI for Transportation
$\$1.23 \times 0.407 \approx \$0.50$
increase in the price of a gallon of gas
$\$1.23 + \$0.50 = \$1.73$

   $\$1.73 - \$1.10 = \$0.63$
difference

■ WRITE

Inform students to proofread their writing to make sure that all words are spelled correctly and that complete sentences are used.

■ SCANS

Select a few "before and after" graphs from the Make a Plan assignment that are especially notable and have students present their graphs and how they went about making changes. Have the class decide whether the two graphs impart the same general message and whether the new graph presents data more clearly.

■ ONGOING ASSESSMENT

STUDENT WORKBOOK The Integrated Project found in the workbook provides a broad, ongoing assessment activity for the goals of this chapter.

How Times Have Changed

For Questions 1–2, refer to the timeline on page 345 as needed.

1. According to the CPI table on page 370, how much would you expect a loaf of bread to cost in 2002 based on a price of $0.54 in the base period and on the CPI for Food and Beverages in 2002? What is the difference between this amount and the amount given in the timeline for the price of a loaf of bread in 2002?
2. According to the CPI table on page 370, how much would you expect a gallon of gas to cost in 1998 based on a price of $1.23 in the base period and on the CPI for Transportation in 1998? What is the difference between this amount and the amount given in the timeline for the price of a gallon of gas in 1998?

WRITE

Select a line, bar, circle, or rectangle graph from your local newspaper or a magazine. Study the information displayed. Summarize the information being displayed or conveyed in two to three sentences.

Then label each element of the graph, such as the title, vertical scale, horizontal scale, etc. Refer back to the list your team created in Lesson 8.3's Team Meeting task. Add any elements that are missing that your team decided was necessary for a good graph.

SCANS

Workplace Skills—*Interprets and Communicates Information*

The ability to obtain and evaluate data is an important workplace and life skill. For example in this chapter, you have learned about different types of visual displays of data. You must be able to see what information is needed; to gather information from a variety of sources; and to evaluate the usefulness of the information.

Test Your Skills Locate 3–5 visual displays of data either in newspapers, magazines, the Web, or your textbook. Look at the variety of presentations. Determine if any of the graphs can be presented in a different format to improve its overall effectiveness.

Make a Plan Choose one graph that can be reworked into a different format and create a new graph. Use the same data, but improve the ease of reading the information from the graph. Be sure that you know what message the graph is trying to convey. Be certain that your changes do not affect the message. Prepare the graph for a presentation to the class.

Summarize Prepare a verbal presentation showing the original graph and your "new and improved" graph. Be sure to explain your reasons for the changes you have made. Include as many of the following topics as you can.

reading   *creative thinking*   *problem solving*   *decision making*
mathematics   *speaking*   *seeing things in the mind's eye*

PORTFOLIO ASSESSMENT

Collect graphs and have them on hand for use by students who may have forgotten to bring one to class. Remind students to be sure that their description of the central idea of the graph flows from one sentence to the next, and that complete sentences are used. Upon completion of the chapter, students can review, rewrite, and then evaluate their graphs for placement in their student portfolio.

Chapter-Test Correlation

Question	Lesson
7	8.1
8	8.3
9	8.3
10	8.5
11	8.5
12	8.2
13	8.3
14	8.3
15	8.4
16	8.5
17	8.1

Chapter Test

Answer each question.

1. Rewrite as a percent: $\frac{\$180}{\$900}$ 20%

2. $1\frac{1}{4} + 2\frac{7}{12} + 3$ $6\frac{5}{6}$

3. 90 is $\frac{1}{3}$ greater than what number?   67.5

4. $\$4,000 \times 0.072 \times \frac{30}{360}$ $24

5. 10,400 @ 10¢ $1,040

6. Divide to nearest tenth percent: $3.6 \div 134.6$ 2.7%

Applications

7. For 6 days this week, the number of defective golf clubs produced by a production line were 210, 225, 206, 214, 180, 225. Find the mean number of defects per day.   210

8. In Graph 1 below, how many more health club members were in the 25–35 age group than there were in the 18–24 age group?   75

9. In Graph 1, find the total number of members who were 36 years of age or older.   400

10. The Recreation CPI index number was 93.0 in 1994 and 95.6 in 1995. What was the percent increase in the prices of recreation goods and services for 1995, to the nearest tenth percent?   2.8%

11. During a recession, the unemployment rate was 34.7% for teen workers and 8.7% for male workers. Out of every 1,000 workers in each category, how many more teens were unemployed than males?   260

12. Four cards marked 1, 2, 3, and 4 are put into a hat. A card is picked and then put back 1,200 times. About how many times would be card picked be a 1?   300

13. In Graph 2, in which month(s) were passenger bookings less than 10,000 passengers?   Nov. and April

14. In Graph 2, how many more passengers were booked between the months with the greatest and the least number of passenger bookings?   6,000

15. In a high school with 1,200 students, 240 are seniors. How many degrees in a circle graph would be used to show the senior sector, to the nearest degree?   72°

16. A mortality table based on one million live births shows 810,000 people living at age 58 and 650,000 people living at age 68. What is the probability, to the nearest percent, that a person age 58 will live to be age 68?   80%

17. An employee worked these hours during March: 8.5, 8.0, 8.1, 8.0, 8.3, 8.0, 9.0, 9.0 8.0, 7.8, 8.6, 8.0, 9.0, 9.8, 10.0, 8.0, 8.0, 8.0, 5.1, 9.5, 8.0, 8.0. Find the average hours worked each day as the mean, median, and mode. Find the range. Round answers to the nearest tenth of an hour.   Mean = 8.3; median = 8.0; mode, 8.0; range = 4.9

Graph 1   Graph 2

TEACHING STRATEGIES Chapter Test

Remind students to be sure to read the legend for Graph 1 before answering questions about the graph. The legend provides information that is often necessary to answer questions about the graph.

Test Taking Strategies

■ **MULTIPLE CHOICE**

Exercise 2. The answer may be estimated as $5 \times \$1,000 = \$5,000$. The estimate is greater than the actual answer because the bond sells at a discount. Answers A and D are eliminated because they are too high. Answers B and C appear to be far too low. Thus, answer E appears to be the best choice based on estimation.

Cumulative Review Chapters 7–8

Multiple Choice

Select the best choice for each question.

1. The monthly health insurance premium provided by Lawanda's employer is $448, and Lawanda pays 20% of the cost. What annual amount does she pay for health insurance? A
   - **A.** $1,075.20
   - **B.** $4,300.80
   - **C.** $89.60
   - **D.** $985.60
   - **E.** $1,057.20

2. Crest County 8%, $1,000 par value bonds sell at 95.314. What is the price of 5 bonds? E
   - **A.** $7,625.12
   - **B.** $476.57
   - **C.** $953.14
   - **D.** $5,000
   - **E.** $4,765.70

3. Dean Grigsby was injured on his job. He is insured by a disability policy that pays 35% of his average annual salary of $36,800. What amount does Dean collect monthly? D
   - **A.** $23,920
   - **B.** $12,880
   - **C.** $1,993.33
   - **D.** $1,073.33
   - **E.** $2,142.83

4. The semiannual interest on a $500 par value bond is $20. If the bond now sells at 98, what is its current yield, to the nearest tenth percent? B
   - **A.** 8%
   - **B.** 8.2%
   - **C.** 20%
   - **D.** 4.1%
   - **E.** 20.4%

5. Kristy Chancellor owns 540 shares of FiberQueue $100 par value common stock. The stock pays a dividend of 4%. What total amount will Kristy receive in dividends? D
   - **A.** $2,016
   - **B.** $21.60
   - **C.** $5,184
   - **D.** $2,160
   - **E.** $1,350

6. The mid-day temperatures in your city for 8 days were 78, 85, 82, 90, 98, 87, 82, and 76. What is the average daily temperature, measured by the mean, if you delete two temperatures, the highest and lowest of this data set before finding the mean? A
   - **A.** 84
   - **B.** 84.75
   - **C.** 87.3
   - **D.** 63
   - **E.** 113

7. Out of 250 parts sampled, 2 parts failed a quality control test. How many parts out of 190,000 produced are likely to fail? C
   - **A.** 760
   - **B.** 152
   - **C.** 1,520
   - **D.** 6,700
   - **E.** 2,500

8. The Medical Care CPI index for 2000 was 264.8 and 278.3 in 2001. What was the rate of inflation in Medical Care for 2001, to the nearest tenth percent? D
   - **A.** 5.0%
   - **B.** 178.3%
   - **C.** 278.3%
   - **D.** 5.1%
   - **E.** 13.5%

9. The CPI for the Food category in 1997 was 159.1. What was the purchasing power of the 1997 Food dollar compared to the 1982-84 Food dollar, to the nearest tenth of a cent? C
   - **A.** $1.591
   - **B.** $0.371
   - **C.** $0.629
   - **D.** $0.591
   - **E.** $0.831

TEACHING STRATEGIES Cumulative Review

In Exercise 12, students must remember that patients pay: (1) the difference between total cost of medical care and the approved amount; (2) the deductible, if any; (3) the coinsurance figured on the approved amount less the deductible. Illustrate by a board example how selecting the wrong amounts and following an incorrect procedure yields the wrong answer.

Open Ended

10. Walter Griggs bought a store for $22,000 cash. He paid cash of $36,000 for renovations. The annual expenses of operating the store are estimated at $13,000. What monthly rent must Walter charge to earn a 14% rate of income on his cash investment? $1,760

11. Ann Lee can buy term life insurance for $1.20 per $1,000 less 5% for being a non smoker What annual premium would she pay for $350,000 of term life insurance? $399

12. Virgil Simmons' oral surgery cost $850. His insurance company approved $775 of the cost. Virgil's policy has 25% coinsurance. He has $80 remaining on his deductible for the year. What amount must Virgil pay for this surgery? $328.75

13. Regina Upshaw bought 12, $500 Olan School District bonds at 102.864 through a broker. The broker's charge was $2.50 per bond. The bonds had accrued interest of $14 per bond. What was Regina's total investment in the bonds? $6,369.84

14. Rodney Branch bought 500 shares of Exastent stock at 41.24 plus $186 commission. He later sold the stock for 54.18 and was charged $216 commission. What net profit did Rodney make on this stock investment? $6,068

15. Juanita Denson bought a home for $95,000 with a $12,000 down payment and a mortgage loan for the rest. The lot on which the home stands is valued at $15,000. Juanita spent $11,000 in cash to remodel the home. Annual expenses of owning the home are 1.5% for depreciation, $6,200 in mortgage interest, and $3,900 in other expenses. Juanita estimates she can rent the home for $1,400 a month. What is Juanita's expected return on her investment, to the nearest percent? 24%

16. Find the rate of commission, to the nearest tenth percent, charged by a fund whose shares are quoted as NAV, 29.80, and Offer Price, 30.85. 3.4%

17. Jason Braddock will receive a $1,050 monthly pension from social security and $1,700 monthly from a company pension when he retires at age 65. He wants an income of $4,800 a month when he retires. His IRA's value is $380,000. What percent of the IRA must he withdraw each year to get the income he wants, to the nearest percent? 6%

18. A box holds four cards marked 1, 2, 3, and 4. You pull two cards from the box. What is the probability that the sum of the two cards you pulled is 5? $\frac{1}{3}$

19. Find the median of the data set: 18, 50, 90, 25, 32, 67 41

20. Hisako Akita bought 300 shares of Flag International Fund quoted as 16.42 (NAV) and 400 shares of Nash Equity Fund quoted as 8.26 (NAV) and 8.48 (offer price). What was the total cost of Hisako's purchases? $8,318

21. Helen, age 70, has an IRA worth $468,000. Bruno, her husband, age 73, has an IRA with a $190,000 value. The divisors for this year's minimum distribution are: Helen, 26.2; Bruno, 23.5. Find the total amount of their combined minimum IRA distribution, to the nearest dollar? $25,948

Constructed Response

22. Karl has a job where his hourly pay will be adjusted each year for changes in the CPI. Willa works at a job similar to Karl's. Her employer does not guarantee regular pay increases, but gives merit pay raises instead. These raises often exceed the change in the CPI. Explain in writing whether you would prefer to work for Karl's or Willa's employer. Getting a pay raise tied to the CPI means your pay will keep pace with inflation. Your pay and what it will buy will remain the same from year to year. Getting merit raises means you receive pay increases based on your performance. You will be rewarded for the good work you do, and the pay increases you receive may allow you to raise your standard of living.

Chapter 8 Cumulative Review ■ 383

TEACHING STRATEGIES Cumulative Review

Discuss the meaning of the phrase "merit pay raises" prior to students beginning work on the cumulative review Exercise 22. Point out that one meaning is that pay raises are given to those who deserve them. Another meaning might be that pay raises go only to those whose work performance is excellent or superior. After students write their responses, have a discussion on how the standards workers must meet to get merit pay raises are determined and what evaluation system is in place to judge employee performance.

CHAPTER 9

Business Technologies

9.1 Computer Hardware and Storage
9.2 Software
9.3 Computer System Support
9.4 E-Business
9.5 Wireless Communications

Statistical Insights

Primary Use of Wireless Phones

Friends	11%
Children	20%
Spouse/Significant Other	22%
Business	23%
Other Personal	24%

Use the data shown above to answer each question.

1. The bar graph shows the results of surveying 1,000 wireless phone users. How many more people responded that their primary use of the phone was for business calls than calling their spouse/significant other? 10

2. In this survey how many people does each percentage point represent? 10

3. What percent of use is non business? 77%

Statistical Insights

The use of cell phones in certain European countries exceeds their use in the U.S. Ask students to use the Web to research which European countries have more widespread use of cell phones than the U.S. and to find rea- sons why this is the case. Students may work in teams to prepare a short report of their findings. At the end of each report, teams should list the web sites that provided them with the most information for their report.

NetCheck

Online Technical Support

Consider the application programs you use at home and at school. Have you ever had a question about how to install a program or how to perform a specific task?

Some people like to read the manual that accompanies application software. People who prefer not to use the manual may have another option: Go online. Most major software companies have a means for customers to get assistance via the Internet. This help is not always free.

Try locating the home pages of some of your favorite software programs to determine if you can get help online the next time you have a question.

Looking to Upgrade

Software upgrades are a fact of life. If a company did not regularly improve its software products, the software products would lose their usefulness and the company would probably fail.

Many times minor upgrades and improvements are released free to purchasers. Other times a minimal fee is charged. Either way, you must be able to prove that you originally purchased the software for your own use. These upgrades can usually be downloaded from the web site hosted by the developers. Be aware of the fees for upgrading before you click on the download button.

How Times Have Changed

Individuals and businesses alike increasingly depend on wireless communication. One hundred and fifty years ago, the world did not even have a telephone. Go back only 40 years, and you would not be able to find a cell phone. Wireless communication has come a long way from the days of smoke signals, the Pony Express, and Morse code.

The electric telegraph, invented by Samuel Morse, transmits *signals* over wire, but not the human voice.
1837

The wireless telegraph, which uses radio waves to transmit and receive Morse code, is invented by Guglielmo Marconi.
1895

Research to discover a significant event in 1973 that relates to the history of wireless communication.

The commercial use of cellular phones in the U.S. begins in Chicago.
1983

1850 **1880** **1910** **1940** **1970** **2000**

1876
Alexander Graham Bell invents the telephone, and for the first time speech is transmitted over wire.

1947
The concept of cellular phones arises from mobile car phones, which have been used by police since the 1920s.

1979
The first commercial cellular phone system in the world is put into use in Tokyo.

Start Up

Have students read the Start Up. Discuss their answers to the Start Up question. Make a list of the considerations they propose for Joshua on the board and have a student record them on a sheet of paper that you can save for use with the Wrap Up.

You might use the discussion to lead into a review of the major parts of a typical PC, such as memory, CPU, online storage, monitors, and other peripherals.

Math Skill Builder

The skills of adding and multiplying money amounts as well as multiplying and dividing whole numbers and decimals are used in this lesson. The skill of rounding is also used.

Complete all exercises in Math Skill Builder 1–3.

9.1 Computer Hardware and Storage

GOALS

- Calculate the costs of buying computer hardware
- Calculate the costs of leasing computer hardware
- Calculate the costs and capacities of data storage

Start Up

Joshua Reynolds has an older computer with a slower processing chip. He wants to buy a new computer system with a faster processor. His sister, Julie, doesn't think he should count on the faster processor speeding up her brother's work. What should Joshua consider before he decides on a new computer?

Math Skill Builder

Review these math skills and solve the exercises that follow.

1. **Add** money amounts.
   Find the sum. $2,359.56 + $529.12 + $758.23 + $44.21 = $3,691.12

   1a. $32,106 + $721.48 + $4,192 + $98 + $2,778 $39,895.48

   1b. $893.91 + $544.22 + $298.12 + $5,582.11 + $3,297.19 $10,615.55

2. **Multiply** money amounts, whole numbers, and decimal numbers.
   Find the product. 48 × $28.77 = $1,380.96
   Find the product. 45 × 0.42 = 18.9

   2a. 12 × $35.99 $431.88   **2b.** 36 × $22.56 $812.16

   2c. 5 × 12.8   64   **2d.** 6.8 × 0.58   3.944

3. **Divide** whole numbers and decimals.
   Find the quotient. 25.6 ÷ 1,000 = 0.0256

   3a. 753.9 ÷ 1,000   0.7539

   3b. 19.97 ÷ 1,000   0.01997

   Find the quotient and round up to the next whole number. 6.8 ÷ 0.0063 = 1,079.3, or 1,080

   3c. 14.5 ÷ 0.034   427

   3d. 483.4 ÷ 1.65   293

> **BUSINESS TIP**
>
> The main processing chip of a computer system is called the central processing unit, or CPU. It is often referred to as the "brain" of a computer system.

TEACHING STRATEGIES Finding Patterns

Have student teams research the comparative costs of renting and leasing a computer system. Have the teams select a make and model of a system they would like. Find prices for (a) renting the model daily, weekly and monthly and (b) leasing the model on a yearly and multi-year basis.

Have them prepare charts showing the vendor, the time period, and the rental or lease price. Have selected teams present their charts to the class and discuss the patterns they find in the pricing, such as the relationship between rental or lease term and price.

Buying Computer Hardware

An organization's computer hardware may include different sized devices such as handheld computers, notebook computers, desktop computers, and large computer systems.

Hardware may also include the network servers, cables, and other parts needed to connect these computers. In addition, there are many other hardware devices that organizations typically use, such as printers, scanners, and specialized display screens and data storage systems.

An organization needs to consider many costs when purchasing computer systems. Besides the purchase price of the computers themselves, there is the cost of installing them. For large computer systems, installation costs may include raised flooring, special electrical wiring, cables, and air conditioning.

For desktop computer systems, cables and other equipment may be needed to connect computers to the organization's network. Extra electrical outlets may need to be added.

Other costs include extended warranties, maintenance, repairs, protection against unauthorized access and virus attacks, and backup systems for computer files.

BUSINESS TIP

A network server is a computer system shared by multiple users. Network cards are circuit boards placed in a computer to let it connect to a network.

EXAMPLE 1

A state agency added office space for new employees. To connect the employees to its network, the agency purchased 25 desktop computer systems at $1,689; 25 network cards at $75; network cabling for $625; two other network devices at $96.88; and a network printer for $5,598.

The cost of installing each computer, connecting it to the network, and installing the other network hardware and cabling was $11,890. What was the total cost of the hardware, installed?

BUSINESS TIP

Backup systems make copies of an organization's data for safekeeping.

Lesson 9.1 Computer Hardware and Storage ■ **387**

DIFFERENT LEARNING STYLES Visual Learners

Bring in from home or get from your computer lab staff some of the parts of computer systems included in the problems of this lesson. Most labs have older and sometimes "dead" equipment or supplies that can be used for in-class demonstrations. A CD-ROM disk, DVD disk, Zip Disk, hard drive, memory card, internal modem board, and a network card might be shown to students as they arise in problem work.

Multiply the number of desktop computers, network cards, and other network devices by their unit costs.

$25 \times \$1,689 = \$42,225$ cost of desktop computers

$25 \times \$75 = \$1,875$ cost of network cards

$2 \times \$96.88 = \$193.76$ cost of other network devices

Add costs of all hardware and installation.

$\$42,225 + \$1,875 + \$193.76 + \$625 + \$5,598 + \$11,890 = \$62,406.76$

Total cost of hardware, installed, is $69,406.76.

■ CHECK YOUR UNDERSTANDING

A. Traco, Inc. added a server to be shared by its 56 desktop computer systems. The server cost $24,786. Other costs were network cards for each desktop at $68.99; cabling for each desktop at $14.88; cabling for the server, $76; 4 other network devices at $112.98; a network printer at $3,596; and 42 hours of labor at $119 an hour. What was the total cost of the system, installed? $38,604.64

B. Vical Products decided to protect its new computer network. Vical purchased a backup system to make daily copies of all their computer files for $753; a battery power backup system for $1,589; and antivirus software for $758. Installation of the systems and software took 8 hours at $98. What was the total cost of buying and installing these systems and software? $3,884

BUSINESS TIP

Battery backup systems keep computers running when the power fails. They are designed to run long enough to let all the computer systems shut down safely.

■ Leasing Computer Hardware

Some organizations lease computer systems rather than buy them. Some firms lease computer systems to reduce the need to spend a large amount of money at one time. However, the cost of leasing computer systems for several years may cost more than buying those same computer systems outright.

EXAMPLE 2

Thornton College decides to create a new computer laboratory of 35 networked desktop computers. One company offers to lease the desktops to the college for $38.89 per month each for three years. What would be the total cost of the lease?

SOLUTION

$3 \times 12 = 36$ number of months lease will last

$36 \times \$38.89 = \$1,400.04$ cost of leasing one computer for 3 years

$35 \times \$1,400.04 = \$49,001.40$ total lease cost of all computers for 3 years

■ CHECK YOUR UNDERSTANDING

C. Reality Pictures, Inc. decided to lease 30 notebook computer systems for 3 years for their sales staff. The monthly lease for each system was $78.59. What was the total cost of leasing one notebook? All the notebooks? $2,829.24; $84,877.20

■ *CHECK YOUR UNDERSTANDING SOLUTIONS*

A. $68.99 + $14.88 = $83.87; $112.98 × 4 = $451.92;
$83.87 × 56 = $4,696.72; $119 × 42 = $4,998;
$24,786 + $4,696.72 + $76 + $451.92 + $3,596 +
$4,998 = $38,604.64

B. $98 × 8 = $784;
$753 + $1,589 + $758 + $784 = $3,884

C. $78.59 × 12 × 3 = $2,829.24;
$2,829.24 × 30 = $84,877.20

D. $49.88 × 12 × 3 = $1,795.68;
$49.88 × 4 × 25 = $4,988

Point out that leasing computer equipment has become popular at some nonprofit organizations, because they find it easier to have a smaller, annual budget item for equipment than to have large demands for equipment funds every four or five years. By leasing, the nonprofits insure that they upgrade their equipment regularly. Many universities let students lease computer systems under the same agreement they negotiate with vendors.

Many organizations also find the need to rent, rather than lease, equipment for short periods of time, such as a day, week, or month. They may need the equipment for a conference, for a training session, or to provide computer support to a person temporarily away from the office.

Work through Example 2 at the board with students completing the math at their desks.

Assign Check Your Understanding problems C through D to do in class. Check student work to identify student errors or difficulties.

D. YTek Training, Inc. needs to provide 25 desktop computer systems for a four-month training contract with another company. YTek decides to lease the computer systems at $49.88 a month for three years and use the desktops at their headquarters after the training program ends. What is the cost of leasing one desktop for three years? What is the cost of leasing all the desktops for the four-month training contract? $1,795.68; $4,988

■ **Teach Goal 3**

Point out that computer storage parameters change often. The sizes of hard drives, for example, continue to grow while their prices drop. The measurement of storage space, however, isn't likely to change very soon. It is still measured in increments of bytes.

You may wish to discuss new or emerging storage media with the class. You might also present and discuss the storage capacities of the PCs and servers used in the school labs.

Stress the difference between memory (RAM), fixed storage (hard drives), and removable storage (floppy, CD-R, and Zip drives).

Also stress that when dividing to find the number of media needed, students must round up since partial media are not available.

■ Computer Storage

Computers store data on storage media, which includes hard disks as well as various removable storage media options. Removable data storage options include CD, DVD, Zip, and Jaz disks, as well as external hard drives and USB flash drives.

Transferring data between hard disks and removable storage media is a common business activity. Copying important data to removable disks and then placing these disks in a safe location in another building is one way to insure that the data are not lost.

Computer storage is measured in bytes. One thousand bytes is usually shown as 1KB, a million as 1MB. Large organization data files will contain billions and trillions of bytes of data. These are shown as gigabytes (GB) and terabytes (TB), respectively.

When transferring data from a medium measured in KB to a medium measured in MB, it is helpful to show the storage sizes of both media using in the same measures. For example, restate kilobytes as megabytes.

1 TB = 1,000 GB, 1,000,000 MB, 1,000,000,000 KB

1 GB = 0.001 TB, 1,000 MB, 1,000,000 KB

1 MB = 0.000001 TB, 0.001 GB, 1,000 KB

MATH TIP

1 KB = 1,000 bytes
1 MB = 1,000,000 bytes
1 GB = 1,000,000,000 bytes
1 TB = 1,000,000,000,000 bytes

Notice that to show a capacity measure in terms of the next higher capacity, you divide the lower capacity by 1,000.

1 MB ÷ 1,000 = 0.001 GB

To show a capacity measure in terms of the next lower capacity measure, you multiply by 1,000.

1 MB × 1,000 = 1,000 KB

Suppose you need to know if you can transfer data from three full 700 MB CD-R disks to a hard drive with only 2.5 GB of storage space left on it. You need to show the data to be transferred in GB. That way it is easy to compare the available space on the drive to the space needed to hold the data.

700 MB ÷ 1,000 = 0.7 GB   megabytes restated as gigabytes

3 × 0.7 GB = 2.1 GB   gigabytes of storage space needed for transfer

2.5 GB − 2.1 GB = 0.4 GB   gigabytes of storage left after transfer

So, you have enough space on the drive to hold the three CD-R disks.

Lesson 9.1 Computer Hardware and Storage ■ **389**

COMMON ERRORS

Students are prone to move the decimal point in the wrong direction when restating storage space in a smaller or larger measure. Stress that as you restate a measure in a higher measure, move the decimal point to the left (34 KB is 0.034 MB, or 34 ÷ 1,000 = 0.034). When you restate a measure in a lower measure, move the decimal point to the right (34 MB is 34,000 KB, or 34 × 1,000 = 34,000).

The table shows several capacities of popular storage media.

Type of Storage Media	Capacity	Type of Storage Media	Capacity
3.5-inch floppy disk	1.44 MB	Jaz disk	2 GB
Zip disk	250 MB	DVD-R disk	4.7 GB
CD-R disk	700 MB	Hard drive	80 GB

Work through Example 3 at the board with students doing the math at their desks.

Assign Check Your Understanding problems E and F for in-class work. Walk about the room and examine student work to identify student errors or difficulties.

■ **ONGOING ASSESSMENT**

Call out storage sizes and ask students to restate them in lower or higher measures. For example, call out 1 MB and ask them to restate that in KB **(1,000 KB)** and GB **(0.001 GB)**.

Wrap Up

Review and discuss student responses saved from the Start Up.

The bottom line is that computers are tools that are used to help you with your work and the type of computer system you buy should match the work done.

People should decide on the type of computer system they need based on the type of work they do, not on whether the computer system has the latest bells and whistles, including the latest chip.

EXAMPLE 3

Tetra Consulting Company needs to store 4 TB of data including maps, aerial photographs, engineering drawings, and technical specifications. These data do not change often. So, they decide to store the data on 4.7 GB, DVD disks costing $1 each. How many DVD disks will they need and what will be the total cost?

SOLUTION

Rewrite GB on the DVD disks as TB.

4.7 GB ÷ 1,000 = 0.0047 TB   TB of capacity on a DVD

Divide amount of storage needed by the capacity of one DVD disk.

4 TB ÷ 0.0047 TB ≈ 851.1, or 852   number of DVD disks needed

Since you cannot buy 0.1 of a DVD disc, round up to the next whole number.

852 × $1 = $852   total cost of media needed

■ **CHECK YOUR UNDERSTANDING**

E. The Carrolton Police Department needs to remove 6 GB of old records and reports from their network hard drives to make room for new data. The data still needs to be kept on media that can be read by a computer, however. They decide to use 250 MB Zip disks at $12.89 each. How many Zip disks will they need, and what will be the total cost of the media used?   24; $309.36

F. The Wellston Otters baseball team has 1,367, full 1.44 MB, 3.5 disks that they wish to convert to larger capacity storage media for convenience. They decide to transfer the data to CD-R disks. They will have to buy and install a CD Read/Write device in one of their desktops at $65. How many CD-R disks will be needed, and what will be the total cost of the CD Read/Write device and media if the 700 MB disks are priced at $0.81 each?   3; $67.43

Wrap Up

The speed with which a computer accomplishes tasks depends on the type of tasks it does. A calculation task is directly affected by the speed of the central processor (CPU). The speed at which you view and edit images will be most affected by the type of video card in your computer. The speed at which you download files from the Internet is most affected by the speed of your Internet access. Before Joshua decides to buy a new computer with a faster processor, he should decide which tasks he is performing that are slow. He may need to upgrade his video card or contact an Internet service provider with faster access instead of getting a new computer.

390 ■ Chapter 9 Business Technologies

■ *CHECK YOUR UNDERSTANDING SOLUTIONS*

E. 6 GB × 1,000 = 6,000 MB; 6,000 MB ÷ 250 MB = 24;
24 × $12.89 = $309.36

F. 1,367 × 1.44 MB = 1,968.48 MB;
1,968.48 MB ÷ 700 MB ≈ 2.812 or 3 CD-R disks; 3 × $0.81 = $2.43; $65 + $2.43 = $67.43

WORKPLACE WINDOW

NETWORK ADMINISTRATORS These highly trained employees fill an essential role in the computer operations of both large and small companies. Do research to answer the following questions.

What are the duties and responsibilities of a network administrator? What is the range of salaries for the position? What education is usually required? Prepare a one-page report of your findings. On a second page, list the sources of information you used for your report.

WORKPLACE WINDOW

Ask one student to interview the school's network administrator as a source of information. You might also ask the administrator to address the class on the questions posed in Workplace Window.

Assign

Assignment: Exercises 1–28, 30–41. Start with the basic arithmetic problems to be sure that students understand the underlying arithmetic in the exercises.

EXERCISES

Find the sum.
1. $1,805 + $21.87 + $659.22 $2,486.09
2. $224 + $5,391 + $50.93 $5,665.93

Find the product or quotient.
3. $215 × 24 $5,160
4. 824 × 0.066   54.384
5. 109.3 ÷ 1,000   0.1093
6. 0.0826 ÷ 1,000   0.0000826

Find the quotient and round up to the next whole number.
7. 306.22 ÷ 1.04   295
8. 94.076 ÷ 0.34   277

9. Alison Beamer, Inc. is purchasing 42 desktop computer systems at $1,388 and 14 personal digital assistants at $325 from Leland Technology Corporation. They are considering paying $100 extra for each desktop system and $75 extra for each handheld system to provide an additional two years on the one-year system warranty. If Alison decides to buy the extra warranties, what will be the total cost of the computers and warranty service? $68,096

Mayan Playhouse is a nonprofit entertainment organization. They wish to network their existing 18 desktop computer systems. The company that offers them the best price will charge $27,120 for a file server, $4,259 for a network printer, $2,218 for the other hardware, and $2,488 to install the network.
10. What is the total cost of the hardware, installed? $36,085

11. What is the cost of the network per desktop computer? $2,004.72

Carver Industries signed a three-year lease for 4 notebook computers at $83.89 a month and 17 desktop computers at $42.78 a month.
12. What is the cost of leasing one notebook computer for all three years? $3,020.04

13. How much more, to the nearest tenth of a percent, is the cost of leasing one notebook than one desktop?   96.1%

14. What is the total cost of leasing the notebooks and desktops for three years? $38,261.52

Lesson 9.1 Computer Hardware and Storage ■ **391**

SELECTED SOLUTIONS

10. $27,120 + $4,259 + $2,218 + $2,488 = $36,085
11. $36,085 ÷ 18 = $2,004.722, or $2,004.72
12. $83.89 × 12 × 3 = $3,020.04
13. $83.89 − $42.78 = $41.11;
    $41.11 ÷ $42.78 = 0.9609, or 96.1%
14. $3,020.04 × 4 = $12,080.16;
    $42.78 × 12 × 3 × 17 = $26,181.36;
    $12,080.16 + $26,181.36 = $38,261.52

Check student answers to the exercises by calling on them in class, collecting and grading selected problems, or by observing students at work.

Ask students to define the bolded and italicized terms in the lesson and use them in sentences.

Reteach

STUDENT WORKBOOK To reteach calculating the cost of computer hardware, do Exercise 1 with students. Then have them do Exercises 2 and 3.

To reteach calculating the costs of leasing computer hardware, do Exercise 4 with students. Then have them do Exercises 5 and 6.

To reteach calculating the costs and capacities of data storage, do Exercise 7 with students. Then have them do Exercise 8.

Dugan Manufacturing wants to upgrade its office computer network of 14 desktop computer systems and one server to provide faster service. To do so, they buy 14 faster network cards at $70 each, new network cabling totaling $418, a new server for $16,112, and other devices costing $1,899. Installation was 25 hours at $125 an hour and an extended warranty on the server cost $428.

15. What is the total cost of the hardware, installation, and extended warranty? $22,962

16. What is the cost per desktop of the upgrade? $1,640.14

Tillson Finance Company can lease a notebook computer from Biz-Rent, Inc. for $78.44 a month on a three-year lease. They can buy the same notebook computer from Dolphin Sales for $2,588. Dolphin sales will take the notebook at its fair market value after three years as a trade in for a new computer system. The fair market value of the notebook after three years of use is estimated to be $429.

17. What is the cost of leasing 20 notebook computers from Biz-Rent for three years? $56,476.80

18. What is the net cost of buying 20 notebooks from Dolphin Sales and using them as trade ins on new equipment at the end of three years? $43,180

A network administrator is planning to add a file server that can be used by everyone on the computer network to store data. She estimates that 15 network users each will need 8 gigabytes of file space, 3 more users will need 16 gigabytes each, and 6 users will only need 750 MB each.

19. How much total file space, in gigabytes is needed? 172.5 GB

20. What is the average file space needed per user, in gigabytes? 7.1875 GB

21. How many 40 GB hard drives will the administrator need to serve the users? 5

Morris Real Estate is a regional real estate firm. They need to store 3.74 TB of data files including property listings, property photographs, street maps, sales agreements, and contracts on properties in a seven-state area.

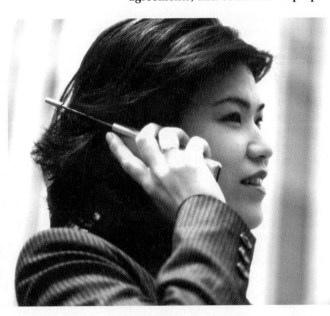

22. If they store the data on 4.7 GB DVD disks, how many disks will be needed? 796

23. If they store the data on 700 MB CD-R disks, how many disks will be needed? 5,343

24. If they store the data on 80 GB hard drives, how many drives will be needed? 47

25. If they store the data on 2 GB flash drives, how many drives will be needed? 1,870

26. If DVD disks cost $0.99, CD-R disks cost $0.40, 2 GB flash drives cost $160, and 80 GB hard drives cost $399, what is the total cost of storing the data on each of the media? $788.04; $21,370.20 $299,200; $18,753

SELECTED SOLUTIONS

19. 15 × 8 = 120 GB; 3 × 16 = 48 GB;
750 MB ÷ 1,000 = 0.75 GB; 6 × 0.75 = 4.5 GB;
120 + 48 + 4.5 = 172.5 GB

20. 15 + 3 + 6 = 24; 172.5 ÷ 24 = 7.1875 GB
21. 172.5 ÷ 40 = 4.3, or 5

INTEGRATING YOUR KNOWLEDGE Shopping for wireless ethernet cards, you find the following prices: $29.99, $54.50, $38.90, $59.00, $29.99, $46.99, $38.79, and $59.99.

27. What are the mean, median, mode, and range for the prices you found?
$44.77; $42.95; $29.99; $30

28. Jack wants to update his computer to have wireless Internet access. He needs to buy a wireless ethernet card and a router. Using the mean price from Exercise 36 for the wireless ethernet card and a price of $65.99 for the router, how much should Jack expect to pay so that he can update his computer to have wireless Internet access? $110.76

29. **CRITICAL THINKING** A company is considering upgrading its computer hardware because a consultant has shown that the replacement of the old computer hardware will increase productivity, customer satisfaction, and will both save the company money and allow it earn more money. The chief financial officer of the company, however, thinks the company should wait a few months before buying because computer hardware prices are falling. If you were the president of the company, would you buy now or wait, and why?

MIXED REVIEW

30. Multiply $16\frac{1}{8}$ by 24.   387

31. Divide 0.042 by 0.006.   7

32. Write 0.7068 as a percent.   70.68%

33. Find 15% of $2,650. $397.50

34. $\frac{1}{3} = \frac{4}{?}$ 12

35. $\frac{5}{12} = \frac{?}{30}$ 12.5

36. $\frac{?}{4} = \frac{15}{10}$ 6

37. Lois Rafferty can buy an MP3 player for $270 cash, or she can make a down payment of $40 and pay $22.50 for 12 months. How much more is the installment price than the cash price? $40, Lesson 4.4

38. Property worth $144,000 is assessed at 35% of its value. The tax rate is $54 per $1,000 of assessed value. What is the tax on the property? $2,721.60, Lesson 6.3

39. Stocks paying quarterly dividends of $1.75 are bought for a total cost of $140 per share. What rate of income is earned on the investment?
5%, Lesson 7.6

40. During the month, a computer help desk received these number of calls: 143, 121, 163, 218, 214, 119, 112, 143, 154, 143, 129, 218, 184, 109, 114, 143, 218, 111, 176, 121, 143. Find the mean, median, and mode for the number of calls received.   152.19; 143; 143, Lesson 8.1

41. Page Discounts, Inc. buys three notebook computers for $2,188 each. An extended warranty for each system costs $189. To connect the notebooks to the Internet, network cards and cables are needed at $143 for each notebook. What is the total cost of the three notebooks? $7,560, Lesson 9.1

Lesson 9.1 Computer Hardware and Storage ■ **393**

Enrich

Assign and discuss Exercise 29, Critical Thinking. Point out that the financial officer is likely to be correct. If the company waits, prices will go down. The problem with this tactic is that it will likely be true for the foreseeable future. That is, if you continue to wait, prices will always be lower. However, while you wait, productivity, customer satisfaction, and company revenue do not increase. If a purchase is cost beneficial now, then the purchase should be made now. Otherwise the benefits will remain on hold indefinitely as the company waits for technology prices to stop falling, which if we can judge from the past, will not happen anytime soon.

Close

Ask students to view the illustration of a network on page 387. Then ask them to identify the hardware elements in the network that will contribute to the cost of the network. Remind students, if necessary, that installation of the network is an important part of the cost. Also, point out that network cards and other hardware, though not shown in the drawing, will also contribute to the cost.

If students suggest the costs associated with training and software, remind them that you asked for hardware costs and that training and software costs will be covered in the next two lessons.

Start Up

Have students read the Start Up. Point out to students that all three copies bought by the other department are in use on their computers. The Start Up should lead to a general discussion of the rise in illegal and unethical copying of software, music, and other copyrighted materials.

Math Skill Builder

The skills of adding, subtracting, and multiplying money amounts are used in this lesson. Also, the skill of finding what percent one number is of another is included.

Complete all exercises in Math Skill Builder 1–4.

■ Teach Goal 1

Ask students to identify common operating systems and application software used in the school labs and in their homes.

Ask students who have home computers to comment on the problems they have had in upgrading to new versions of the software they use. The discussion should include the cost of the upgrades, glitches that occur with the newer version, the new learning that must occur, and new hardware that had to be bought to support the new version.

9.2 Software

GOALS

- Calculate the cost of buying software
- Calculate the cost of developing software

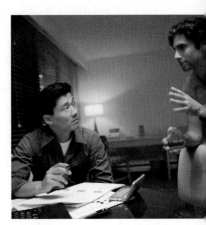

Start Up

Todd Walker received a new computer system at his work place that did not have photo-editing software. He borrowed a photo-editing software CD from a friend in another department of the company. That department had bought three copies of the software for its own use. Was this the right thing for Todd to do? What implications are there for Todd's act?

Math Skill Builder

Review these math skills and solve the exercises that follow.

1. **Add** money amounts.
   Find the sum. $3,498.89 + $108.89 + $929.89 = $4,537.67

   1a $22.89 + $189.99 + $59.79 $272.67 **1b.** $129.88 + $79.59 + $429.78 $639.25

2. **Subtract** money amounts.
   Find the difference. $59,297 − $41,709 = $17,588

   2a. $208.55 − $175.88 $32.67 **2b.** $16,089 − $5,599 $10,490

3. **Multiply** money amounts by whole numbers.
   Find the product. $1,598 × 40 = $63,920

   3a. $19.99 × 500 $9,995 **3b.** $105.59 × 35 $3,695.65 **3c.** $188.98 × 75 $14,173.50

4. Find the **percent** that the smaller amount is of the larger amount.
   Give the percent to the nearest tenth and to the nearest whole percent.
   $39 ÷ $179 = 0.2178, or 21.8% (nearest tenth), 22% (nearest whole percent)

   4a. $450 ÷ $1,895 23.7%, 24% **4b.** $36 ÷ $159 22.6%, 23%

■ Buying Software

Computer systems consist of more than hardware. Computer systems also include **software**, or computer programs.

There are two basic types of computer programs: *operating systems*, which manage computer hardware, and *application software*, which manage data.

> **BUSINESS TIP**
>
> A computer program is instructions that tell a computer system what to do.

394 ■ Chapter 9 Business Technologies

TEACHING STRATEGIES Cooperative Learning

Have students form small teams to investigate software watchdog organizations, such as the Business Software Alliance (www.bsa.org). Students should identify civil and criminal investigations of software piracy underway or recently completed by the organizations. They should also identify how these organizations flag violators. Select some teams to present their findings to the class. Students should see how careless or irresponsible employees can put organizations at risk for large fines or penalties because of the illegal use of licensed software.

You often do not own the software you buy. Instead, you may own a license to use the software. The license may let you use the software on one machine, on a limited number of machines, or on any machine in your organization. The latter is called a **site license** because it allows you to use the software on any and all computers in your company or at your location.

When application software can be used without charge, it is called *freeware*. A large number of programs are available as *shareware*. Shareware can be installed and used without cost to let you see if you like it. If you like it and continue to use it, you are asked to pay for it. Some programs let you try them out for a limited number of times or for a certain number of days before they become unusable. Others rely on the honor system for payment.

There are many other costs to new software in addition to licenses. The software must be installed on computer hardware. Employees must be trained to use it. The software may require hardware upgrades. Existing data may need to be converted so that the new software can use it.

BUSINESS TIP

Some software companies provide a freeware version of their software that does not provide every feature. They hope that you will use it and like it enough to buy a full-featured version.

■ Apply Goal 1

Work through Example 1 at the board while students do the math at their desks.

Assign Check Your Understanding problems A and B to be done in class. Walk about your room and check student work for errors and problems.

EXAMPLE 1

Brandon Glass Corporation is considering upgrading their desktop operating system software from Lenox, version 3.5 to Lenox, version 4.0 for their 43 computer systems. The per-copy cost of the upgrade is $97.89. A 50-workstation upgrade license costs $3,800. How much would Brandon save by buying a 50-workstation upgrade license instead of 43 separate copies of the upgrade?

SOLUTION

Multiply the number of workstations by the price of the software per copy.

$43 \times \$97.89 = \$4,209.27$ cost of upgrading each workstation

Subtract the cost of a 50-workstation license.

$\$4,209.27 - \$3,800 = \$409.27$ savings using 50-workstation license

BUSINESS TIP

The term *workstation* is often used for a computer system used by an employee. The workstation may be a notebook, desktop, or some other computer type.

■ CHECK YOUR UNDERSTANDING

A. Creative Answers, Inc. wants to equip its 74 desktop and notebook computers with word processing and spreadsheet software. It can buy single copies of the word processing software for $129.59 and the spreadsheet software for $94.89. It can also buy a 100-workstation license for a suite of office application software, including word processing, spreadsheet, e-mail, and graphics software for $15,310. Which software deal is the least expensive for all 74 computers? How much less expensive?   100 workstation; $1,301.52

B. The town of Los Mateos purchased new accounting software for $136,800. The Town Supervisor estimates that selected employees will need 16 hours of classroom training on the software at $125 an hour. She also estimates installation costs at $23,880. To convert the data from the old accounting system to the new one will require 36 hours of work by specialists at $80 an hour. What is the estimated cost of changing to the new accounting software? $165,560

■ *CHECK YOUR UNDERSTANDING SOLUTIONS*

A. $129.59 + $94.89 = $224.48;
$224.48 × 74 = $16,611.52;
$16,611.52 − $15,310 = $1,301.52

B. 16 × $125 = $2,000; 36 × $80 = $2,880;
$2,000 + $2,880 + $136,800 + $23,880 = $165,560

C. 25 × 2 = 50; 2,900 ÷ 50 = 58 days;
$29 × 2 = $58; 58 × $58 × 8 hours = $26,912
total cost

D. 15,744 ÷ 96 = 164; 164 ÷ 4 = 41

Point out that organizations have several options for acquiring software. First, they can purchase existing software from commercial software firms (e.g., McAfee's antivirus software) or from other organizations that have developed software for their own needs (e.g., a college that developed student testing software). Second, they can develop the software using their own in-house programmers or use their own programmers to modify existing software. Third, they can outsource development to software development firms. Fourth, they can have software firms modify existing commercial software to meet the needs of the organizations.

You might ask the programming teacher to supply you with the programming code for a small program so that you can display it in class and let students see what a "line" of code looks like.

Work through Example 2 at the board while students do the math at their desks.

Assign Check Your Understanding problems C and D to do in class. Check student work for difficulties.

■ Developing Software

Instead of buying commercial software "off the shelf," an organization may develop specialized programs for its own needs using computer programmers. Computer programs may be made up of thousands of lines of computer instructions, called "lines of code." A good programmer may produce from 20–40 fully tested and finished lines of computer code in one workday.

EXAMPLE 2

A new program contains 3,360 lines of code. Three programmers were paid $47 an hour to work on the program and averaged 28 lines of finished code in an 8-hour day. How long did the project take? What was the programming cost of the project?

SOLUTION
Multiply lines per day for one programmer by number of programmers.

$3 \times 28 = 84$ lines of finished code per day

Divide total lines of code by number of lines completed a day.

$3,360 \div 84 = 40$ number of days the project took

Multiply number of work hours in a day by number of programmers.

$3 \times 8 = 24$ hours programmers worked in a day

Multiply number of hours per day by number of days for the project.

$24 \times 40 = 960$ total hours needed to complete project

Multiply number of hours needed to complete project by cost per hour.

$960 \times \$47 = \$45,120$ total cost of programming for project

■ CHECK YOUR UNDERSTANDING

C. The Information Systems Department of Silver Freight Company was asked to develop a program to keep track of their rail cars. They estimate that the program will require 2,900 lines of code and put 2 programmers to work on it. If programmers at Silver average 25 lines of finished code a day and are paid $29 an hour, how many days will the project take? What will the total cost of the programming be?   58; $26,912

D. It took four programmers 96 days to develop a program containing 15,744 lines of code. How many lines of code a day did each programmer average?   41

CONNECTION TO INFORMATION SYSTEMS

Many students may view careers in information systems narrowly in terms of programming jobs. Consider asking a person from the information systems department at a community college or from an organization's human resource department to address the class on the career opportunities in information systems. Ask the speaker to address the wide range of jobs and industries in the information systems field and the wide variation in skills and abilities needed for these jobs.

Todd has committed theft, plain and simple. There is no difference between stealing a watch from a jewelry store than stealing software from a developer. Illegally copying the software puts Todd's company at risk. The software industry pursues license violations by organizations, including universities, school districts, government agencies, and companies. Todd's firm could be subject to an expensive and embarrassing lawsuit. Todd could have probably found a freeware photo editing program that could be downloaded over the Web to serve his needs. Stealing software also drives up the cost of that software to honest purchasers, including non-profit organizations.

COMMUNICATION

Identify five web sites that provide detailed reviews of application software. Using the reviews from these web sites, critically analyze two spreadsheet programs by comparing their prices and features. Prepare a report that includes a chart of at least 20 features of the two spreadsheet programs. Rate each spreadsheet program on the 20 features using the following scale: Excellent, Good, Average, Below Average, Poor, and Not Available.

EXERCISES

Perform indicated operation.

1. $9,108.34 + $281.87 + $39.88 $9,430.09

2. $3,008.23 + $180.82 + $61.42 $3,250.47

3. $6,088.12 − $5,809.59 $278.53

4. $351.47 − $113.73 $237.74

5. $6.32 × 500 $3,160

6. $385.24 × 50 $19,262

7. $16,709 ÷ 2,400 $6.96

8. $92,512 ÷ 250 $370.05

Find the percent to the nearest tenth.

9. $980 ÷ $3,108   31.5%

10. $65 ÷ $418   15.6%

Find to the nearest whole percent.

11. $803 ÷ $4,580   18%

12. $32 ÷ $520   6%

13. Abbey Graphics, Inc. can buy a spreadsheet program for $89.99 retail. It can also buy a shareware spreadsheet program for $39.99 with fewer features. If they buy the shareware for their 21 computer systems, how much would they save? $1,050

14. The retail price of a full-featured video editing program is $179.89. A shareware version with less features, sells for $59.89. What percent of the full-featured program price does buying the shareware version of the same software save?   67%

15. The Pierce County Clerk's Office buys the following for its 12 computer systems: word processing software at $119.78 a copy; spreadsheet software at $86.59 a copy; image processing software at $68.39 a copy; and operating system software at $95.99 a copy. What total amount did the Clerk's Office pay for the software? $4,449

Lesson 9.2 Software ■ 397

Wrap Up

Review the Start Up. Discuss the ethics of stealing software with students. Stress that illegal use of software can result in substantial penalties to organizations. Also, illegal use reduces profit to developers and thus the incentive to write new software. It also raises the cost of the software. Emphasize the benefits of using freeware or low-cost shareware.

Point out the many web sites that review freeware and shareware, such as the ZDNet and Tucows websites.

COMMUNICATION

Assign the Communication problem. You may wish to have students compare a commercial spreadsheet program, such as Excel or Lotus to a shareware program, such as SpreadPro or GS-Calc. Select one or more of the best reports to be presented to the class.

Assign

Assignment: Exercises 1–22, 24–29. Start with the basic arithmetic problems at the beginning to be sure that students understand the underlying arithmetic in the Exercises.

Assess

Check student answers to the exercises by calling on them in class, collecting and grading selected problems, or by observing students at work.

Ask students to define the bolded and italicized terms in the lesson and use them in sentences.

SELECTED SOLUTIONS

3. $89.99 − $39.99 = $50; $50 × 21 = $1,050

14. $179.89 − $59.89 = $120; $120 ÷ $179.89 = 0.6670, or 67%

15. $119.78 + $86.59 + $68.39 + $95.99 = $370.75; $370.75 × 12 = $4,449

STUDENT WORKBOOK To reteach calculating the costs of buying software, do Exercise 1 with students. Then have them do Exercises 2 and 3.

To reteach calculating the cost of developing software, do Exercise 4 with students. Then have them do Exercise 5.

Enrich

Assign and discuss with students Exercise 23, Critical Thinking. Some reasons are (1) lower cost, since software development costs are spread over many purchasers; (2) a large variety of software already exists and does not require time and effort to develop but can be put to work quickly; (3) the software has been tested by many who have already put it to use as opposed to testing newly developed software in one's own organization; (4) in-house information systems personnel may not have the specialized knowledge or skills required to develop the software needed.

Close

Make a transparency of Check Your Understanding problems A-D. With their books closed, ask students to tell you the steps they would take to solve each problem without actually doing the math. Call on a different student to identify each step.

■ **STUDENT PORTFOLIO**
Students may want to place the report they prepared for Communication or solutions to Exercises 16–22 in their portfolios.

Beeson University bought a site license for software that retails for $149.89 per copy. They paid $268,325 for its use on their 4,520 computer workstations.

16. What would have been the cost of buying the software at the per copy price? $677,502.80

17. What was the per station cost of buying the site license? $59.36

18. Larson Graphics, Inc. estimates that changing to different database software would cost the following: license for the server and workstations, $56,890; employee training, $6,480; conversion of data from the old to new database, $2,950; installation of software, $3,660; hardware upgrades, $12,840. What is the total cost of changing to the new database software? $82,820

19. A programmer, paid $44 an hour, took 900 hours to develop a sales management program made up of 3,000 lines of computer instructions. What was the average programming cost per line? $13.20

20. Six programmers took 54 days to complete a program of 10,692 lines. What was the average number of finished lines per day each programmer wrote? 33

21. **STRETCHING YOUR SKILLS** Vargo Development Corporation has developed and tested a program for tracking customer purchases. The total cost of developing, testing, and advertising the program is $78,350. What minimum number of copies of the software must they sell at $129 to recover their costs and earn $12,000 in profits? 701

22. **INTEGRATING YOUR KNOWLEDGE** The information systems department of your firm orders notebook computer systems at a base price of $1,489. To each notebook they add extra memory costing $198.88, a modem costing $74, a DVD drive costing $94.89, an operating system costing $119.99, and a suite of office software costing $219.78. What is the total cost of the notebook computer system the information systems department bought? $2,196.54

23. **CRITICAL THINKING** What reasons are there for a firm to seek to buy software "off the shelf" instead of developing it on their own? Answers will vary.

MIXED REVIEW

24. Subtract $\frac{1}{6}$ from $\frac{2}{3}$. $\frac{1}{2}$

25. Multiply $1\frac{2}{5}$ by $\frac{3}{8}$. $\frac{21}{40}$

26. Estimate the product. $385 \times \$22.49$ $8,000

27. Divide $388.89 by 100. $3.89

28. Ed Zane invested $10,000 in a 3-year CD that paid 5% annual interest. When he withdrew $1,000 at the end of 2 years, his early withdrawal penalty was 6 months' interest. What was the amount of the penalty and what net withdrawal will Ed get? $25; $975, Lesson 3.7

29. Lillian Reno can buy a DVD player for $350 cash, or she can make a down payment of $50 and pay $27.25 for 12 months. How much more is the installment price than the cash price? $27, Lesson 4.4

SELECTED SOLUTIONS

16. $149.89 × 4,520 = $677,502.80

17. $268,325 ÷ 4,520 = $59.363, or $59.36

18. $56,890 + $6,480 + $2,950 + $3,660 + $12,840 = $82,820

19. $44 × 900 = $39,600; $39,600 ÷ 3,000 = $13.20

20. 10,692 ÷ 6 = 1,782; 1,782 ÷ 54 = 33

Computer System Support

GOALS

- Calculate the total costs of operating computer systems
- Calculate the number and costs of technical support personnel

Start Up

Longwood High School plans to create a second computer lab for its business department. The cost of the lab, including hardware, software, and networking is estimated at $78,500. The school puts that amount in the budget for the coming year. Are they overlooking any other costs for the lab?

Math Skill Builder

Review these math skills and solve the exercises.

1 **Add** money amounts.
Find the sum. $2,089 + $108,338 + $892 + $5,891 = $117,210
1a. $160 + $4,108 + $975 + $89 $5,332   **1b.** $1,784 + $34.59 + $282 $2,100.59

2 **Multiply** money amounts by whole numbers.
Find the product. $112 × 914 = $102,368
Find the product. $95 × 12 × 40 = $45,600

2a. $209 × 19 $3,971   **2b.** $86 × 12 × 112 $115,584

3 **Divide** whole numbers by whole numbers.
Find the quotient. Round up to the nearest whole number. 116 ÷ 25 = 4.64, or 5

3a. 3,188 ÷ 62   52   **3b.** 827 ÷ 70   12

■ Total Cost of Operating Computer Systems

The costs to keep computer systems running properly and to help computer users with problems are often overlooked. Yet, organizations often pay more for computer support than they did to buy computer systems. The costs of installing, operating, and maintaining computer systems are called the total costs of ownership, or *TCO*.

TCO includes 1) purchasing and installing software upgrades; 2) diagnosing and repairing hardware, software, and network problems; 3) replacing hardware and software; 4) paying for increased power and air conditioning; 5) training users and technical support people; and 6) staffing and running technical support departments.

Lesson 9.3 Computer System Support ■ **399**

CONNECTION TO OFFICE TECHNOLOGY

Small teams of students who show an interest in technology may be assigned to identify technical support help within the Windows operating system itself. Ask students to identify the troubleshooting "wizards" within Windows by clicking Start, Help, choosing the Index tab, and then keying in "troubleshooting." Have students explore each of the troubleshooting wizards displayed and prepare a report. The report should list each wizard and provide a brief description of the help the wizard offers. Select one or more of the teams to present their reports to the class.

Work through Example 1 with students doing the math at their desks.

Assign Check Your Understanding problems A and B for classwork. Check student work for errors and problems.

Point out that technical support personnel cannot be expert in all the hardware and software available today. Each operating system, application program, and computer model presents new technical, diagnostic, and user training issues. Each new version of software or hardware upgrade presents the same range of issues. Ongoing training of technical support personnel is critical to a smooth running computer operation or lab.

■ ONGOING ASSESSMENT
Make a transparency of Check Your Understanding problem C or write it on the board. Then with their books closed, have students describe the steps they would take to solve the problem. Ask each student called on to provide one step.

EXAMPLE 1

Janis Markets, Inc. has 96 desktop computers. In March, Janis spent $64,222 on replacement computer parts, $30,707 on the labor to replace the parts, $9,229 on software upgrades, and $6,783 on the labor to upgrade the software. What was the total spent on parts, upgrades, and labor? What was the average spent per machine?

SOLUTION

Add the amount spent on parts, upgrades and labor.

$64,222 + $30,707 + $9,229 + $6,783 = $110,941   total spent

Divide the total amount spent by the number of machines.

$110,941 ÷ 96 = $1,155.64   average spent per machine

■ CHECK YOUR UNDERSTANDING

A. Carlson School District owns 2,189 desktop and notebook computer systems. Last year it spent $415,390 on replacement parts and equipment, $288,083 on software upgrades, and $793,112 on repairs to their systems, user training, and help for their computer users. What amount was spent on technical support per computer system? $683.68

B. The average monthly electricity costs for running the desktop computer systems of Johnson-Wembly Corporation were $63,890. The company estimates that they can save 22% of that cost if the computers are turned off at night, weekends, and holidays. How much do they estimate they can save a year by turning off their desktops? $168,669.60

BUSINESS TIP

The word "support" is used often in information systems. One meaning of the term is providing the resources to keep information systems operating properly. That may mean providing maintenance and repair, training to users, and helping diagnose and solve technical problems.

■ Technical Support

Technical support is an important part of the total cost of ownership. The number of computer technical support people found in business is usually expressed as a ratio, such as 1:50 or 1:75. That is, business usually provides about 1 technical support person per 50–75 computer users.

Besides salaries and benefits, support personnel require frequent training to learn new technologies and to improve their understanding of existing systems. This training may cost $1,500 to $2,000 per year per support person.

Some organizations use outside firms to provide technical support. Using other companies in this way is called outsourcing.

■ *CHECK YOUR UNDERSTANDING SOLUTIONS*

A. $415,390 + $288,083 + $793,112 = $1,496,585;
$1,496,585 ÷ 2,189 = $683.684, or $683.68

B. $63,890 × 12 × 0.22 = $168,669.60

C. 2,500 × 0.80 = 2,000; 2,000 ÷ 60 = 33.3, or 34
technical support people; 34 × $49,228 =
$1,673,752 total salary expense

D. 116 × $94 = $10,904; $10,904 + $3,119.89 =
$14,023.89

EXAMPLE 2

Bi-State Forms, Inc. has 1,864 computer users. They wish to provide a ratio of technical support personnel to computer users of 1:50. How many technical support people will they need? If technical support people average salaries of $4,800 a month, what should be budgeted for their salaries for the year?

SOLUTION

Divide the total number of users by the desired number of users to be served by each technical support worker. Round the quotient up to the nearest whole person.

$1,864 \div 50 = 37.28$, or 38   technical support people needed

Multiply the average monthly salary by 12 and by the number of technical support people needed.

$\$4,800 \times 12 \times 38 = \$2,188,800$ amount budgeted for salaries for year

■ CHECK YOUR UNDERSTANDING

C. AgPa, Inc. plans to expand and needs to add 2,500 workers over the next three years, 80% of whom will need a computer system. They also plan to add one technical support person for each 60 new computer users. How many technical support people will be needed? If the average salary of the support people is $49,228, what will their total salary expense be?   34; $1,673,752

D. Medford County hires ReadyHelp, Inc. to support its desktop and notebook computer systems. ReadyHelp charges $94 an hour, plus materials, for that support. Last month, Medford County required 116 hours of help and $3,119.89 in materials. What total amount did the county spend to support their computers? $14,023.89

Wrap Up

The district is overlooking the technical support costs for the lab, including costs for diagnoses and repair, training, software upgrades, hardware replacements, setup and configuration, and the costs of answering user questions. These costs might run as high as twice the original price of the hardware, software, and networking.

WORKPLACE WINDOW

SUPPORT HELP DESK   A beginning job for many information technology workers is manning a technical support help desk in an organization. What is a help desk? What do help desk workers do? What education and training do help desk workers usually require? What is the average salary for help desk workers?

Lesson 9.3 Computer System Support ■ **401**

CONNECTION TO OFFICE TECHNOLOGY

Assign small teams of students to research TCO using the web as a resource. Students should identify the major costs usually included in TCO. Have each team prepare a report of its findings listing the major costs of TCO it found along with a brief explanation of each cost. You might also have the teams prepare their reports using a presentation software package, such as PowerPoint. Select one or more teams to present their lists to the class.

Assess

Check student answers to the exercises by calling on them in class, collecting and grading selected problems, or by observing student work as you circulate.

Ask students to define the bolded and italicized terms in the lesson and use them in sentences.

Reteach

STUDENT WORKBOOK To reteach calculating the cost of operating computer systems, do Exercise 1 with students. Then have them complete Exercise 2 at their desks independently.

To reteach calculating the number and costs of technical support personnel, do Exercise 3 with students. Then have them complete Exercises 4 and 5 at their desks independently.

EXERCISES

Find the sum.

1. $22,198 + $308 + $71.22 + $5,792 $28,369.22

2. $4,089.56 + $5.92 + $23,009.78 + $418.44 $27,523.70

Find the product.

3. $378 × 104 $39,312

4. $120 × 12 × 98 $141,120

5. $98.50 × 134 $13,199

6. $43 × 12 × 308 $158,928

Find the quotient and round up to the nearest whole number.

7. 847 ÷ 65   14

8. 1,274 ÷ 75   17

9. The Concord Company spent $1,048,800 on computer support for their 608 desktop, notebook, and handheld computers last year. What was the per computer cost of the computer support? $1,725

Rothschild Advertising has 458 desktop and 56 notebook computers. They plan to replace their desktops every 3 years and notebooks every two.

10. **STRETCHING YOUR SKILLS**   How many desktops and notebooks must be replaced each year?   181

11. If the cost of the desktop systems average $1,600 and the notebooks $2,100, what should be budgeted annually? $303,600

12. GeoMetrics, Inc. plans to spend $2,450 per technical support person next year for training. If the company has 78 technical support people, what is the planned training cost for the year? $191,100

Tarrant Medical Company owns 429 desktop and notebook computer systems. They purchased a site license for software upgrades for these systems at $38,605.71. It took an average of 1.75 hours per computer at an average salary of $41 an hour for their technical support people to install and reconfigure the systems. Also, the cost to train the 429 users was $2,500.

13. What was the total cost of the upgrade to the company? $71,886.46

14. What was the average cost of the upgrade per system? $167.57

15. The Gestner Valley Community College District has 1,054 computer users and 11 technical support employees. What is the ratio of technical support personnel to computer users, to the nearest whole person?   1:96

Mecam Foods, Inc. has 2,568 computer users. The information systems department wishes to provide technical support personnel in a ratio of 1 for every 50 users.

16. How many technical support personnel do they need?   52

17. If the average weekly salary for technical support personnel is $1,100, what is their yearly salary cost for technical support personnel? $2,974,400

18. A-B Products, Inc. signs an agreement for technical support with Tech-Help Corporation at $110 an hour for help delivered within a business day and $180 an hour for emergency help delivered within 4 hours. If A-B uses Tech-Help for 45.5 hours of emergency help and 283.25 hours of other help in the year, what is the total amount spent for Tech-Help technical support? $39,347.50

402 ■ **Chapter 9** Business Technologies

SELECTED SOLUTIONS

10. 458 ÷ 3 = 152.6, or 153; 56 ÷ 2 = 28;
153 + 28 = 181

11. $1,600 × 153 = $244,800;
28 × $2,100 = $58,800;
$244,800 + $58,800 = $303,600

13. 1.75 × $41 = $71.75;
$71.75 × 429 = $30,780.75;
$30,780.75 + $38,605.71 + $2,500 = $71,886.46

14. $71,886.46 ÷ 429 = $167.567, or $167.57

Crane Hotels spent $2,300 per worker to train its 39 technical staff last year. This year Crane plans to spend the same amount per worker but also add 14 new staff members.

19. How much did Crane spend on training last year? $89,700

20. How much does Crane plan to spend on training this year? $121,900

21. By what percent, to the nearest tenth, does Crane expect training costs to increase this year?   35.9%

22. **CRITICAL THINKING**   When possible, information systems personnel like to load software onto a server and have computer users use the software off the server instead of loading it on user computer systems. Why is this generally a good idea? What are the disadvantages of it?

MIXED REVIEW

23. Subtract: $9.4501 - 0.419$ 9.0311

24. Add: $1,073.5 + 9.037 + 0.33$ 1,082.867

25. Multiply: 5.108 by 8.02   40.96616

26. Estimate the answer: 56.7×9.8 600

27. 35 is what percent of 80?   43.75%

28. What is 42% of $3,087? $1,296.54

29. 68.16 is 12% of what number?   568

30. Divide $\frac{3}{8}$ by $\frac{1}{6}$. $2\frac{1}{4}$

31. Jamie Vermier bought a portable CD player for $58.89 in an area with 4.5% state and 2.3% city sales taxes. What was the total cost of the CD player? $62.89, Lesson 5-1

32. Masami Soga invested in 40 bonds with a par value of $1,000 each. The quoted price for each bond was 104.674. His broker charged a commission of $3.50 per bond. What was Masami's total investment in the bonds? $4,326.96, Lesson 7.4

33. On a test, a class of 12 students scored 98%, 95%, 91%, 88%, 88%, 88%, 84%, 72%, 71%, 68%, 65%, and 50%. What were the mean, median, and mode of the scores, to the nearest whole percent?   80%, 86%, 88%, Lesson 8.1

34. Jose Martino is paid $1.50 for each unit he assembles. During the week he assembled these units: 64, 68, 59, 62, and 66. What was his gross pay for the week? $478.50, Lesson 1.5

35. Rose D'Marco spent 12% of her gross income last year on entertainment. If her gross income is $89,566 this year and she spends the same percent as last year, what amount will she spend on entertainment? $10,747.92, Lesson 2.7

36. Olive Sanders is insured under a disability policy that calculates her benefits percentage at 2.3% for each year she works for her company. If Olive has worked 22 years at the company, what is her benefits percentage?   50.6%, Lesson 7.3

Lesson 9.3 Computer System Support ■ **403**

9.4 E-Business

GOALS

- Calculate costs of an e-business web site
- Calculate the costs and capacities of high-speed Internet access

Start Up

Your friend, Sara, doesn't think it is safe to buy items over the Internet using a credit card. Is she right to be fearful of online buying?

Math Skill Builder

Review these math skills and solve the exercises that follow.

1. **Add** money amounts.
   Find the sum. $450 + $29 + $1,400 + $650 = $2,529

   1a. $1,690 + $427 + $12,878
   $14,995

   1b. $59.90 + $3,412 + $24,184
   $27,655.90

2. **Multiply** money amounts by whole numbers.
   Find the product. $345 × 12 = $4,140

   2a. $678 × 12 $8,136

   2b. $92.50 × 56 $5,180

3. **Divide** money amounts by whole numbers.
   Find the quotient. $3,498 ÷ 68 = $51.44

   3a. $24,800 ÷ 34 $729.41

   3b. $19,289 ÷ 16 $1,205.56

■ E-Business Web Sites

E-business, or electronic business, is doing business online. Doing business on the Web allows even small companies to reach international customers. To sell on the Web, a firm usually needs a web site, an e-mail address, and the ability to have customers order stock online. Since online orders are usually completed with credit cards, a firm also needs to make access to their files and the order process secure from hackers and thieves.

Large companies usually create and maintain their own web sites. Smaller companies may outsource the web site because they do not have or wish to have people with the special skills and knowledge needed. Firms that supply some or all of these skills are called web-hosting companies.

> **BUSINESS TIP**
>
> The prices for the tools to create and maintain a web site and the rates other companies charge to help businesses develop and run web sites vary widely. Careful comparative shopping is advised.

CONNECTION TO MARKETING

Organizations try to measure if their web expenditures are worthwhile. One measure used is to count the number of times a web page is **hit**, or visited. Other measures include how many *different* people visit a site during a time period or how much online business the site produces. Organizations may show the web site's cost as so much per hit, per customer, or per sales dollar.

EXAMPLE 1

Fido's Fancy makes and sells dog treats. They decide to expand their sales by selling on the Internet. Fido's contracts with E-Biz, Inc. a web hosting service to create and maintain an e-business web site with online ordering. E-Biz charges Fido's $12,450 to create the web pages and $450 a month for server space for the web site and e-mail mailbox. They also charge $650 a month to maintain the web site and $250 a month for high-speed Internet access. What is the first-year cost?

SOLUTION
Multiply the monthly fees by 12.

$12 \times \$450 = \$5,400$ annual fee for server space

$12 \times \$650 = \$7,800$ annual fee for web site maintenance

$12 \times \$250 = \$3,000$ annual fee for Internet access

Add the development fee and annual fees.

$\$12,450 + \$5,400 + \$7,800 + \$3,000 = \$28,650$ total first year cost

EXAMPLE 2

Fido's (see Example 1) hit count for the first year averaged 1,807 visits a month. What is the cost of each hit for the first year?

SOLUTION
Multiply the average monthly hits by 12.

$1,807 \times 12 = 21,684$ hits in first year

Divide the total first year cost by the number of hits in the year.

$\$28,650 \div 21,684 = \$1.32$ cost per hit during first year

■ CHECK YOUR UNDERSTANDING

A. Laver Corporation creates a web site using its own information systems department and outside consultants. The startup costs for the web site are: web server and software, $56,280; e-mail server and software, $48,170; security hardware and software, $25,740; Internet connection hardware and software, $12,300; consulting services, $12,800; web page development, 125 hours at $53 an hour; installation costs, 25 hours at $73 an hour; other costs, $3,590. What is the total cost of starting the web site? $167,330

B. Cassons, Inc. wants to advertise on the Internet but not provide for online orders. Their web hosting firm charges them $2,580 to develop the web site and $65 a month to maintain it. They also charge $25 annually to register the company's web site address and $55 a month for web server space and an Internet connection. What is the total cost for the first year to Cassons? If their web site had 7,356 visitors in the year, what was the cost per hit? $4,045; $0.55

Lesson 9.4 E-Business ■ **405**

■ *CHECK YOUR UNDERSTANDING SOLUTIONS*

A. $125 \times \$53 = \$6,625$; $25 \times \$73 = \$1,825$;
$\$56,280 + \$48,170 + \$25,740 + \$12,300 +$
$\$12,800 + \$6,625 + \$1,825 + \$3,590 = \$167,330$

B. $\$65 + \$55 = \$120$; $12 \times \$120 = \$1,440$;
$\$2,580 + \$25 + \$1,440 = \$4,045$ total cost, first
year; $\$4,045 \div 7,356 = \$0.549$, or $0.55 cost per hit

■ **Apply Goal 1**

Complete Examples 1 and 2 at the board while students do the math at their desks.

Assign Check Your Understanding problems A and B for classwork. Check student work at their desks for errors or problems.

Point out that firms usually connect their whole network of computer systems to the Internet and need much greater capacity than the home user with one or two systems connected.

Point out that when working with access speeds, the values do not need to be written out in full, as in 1.544 Mbps = 1,544,000 bps. It is only necessary to have all values in the same measure. For example, to find how many times 128 Kbps goes into 1.544 Mbps, you can rewrite 1.544 Mbps as 1,544 Kbps. The problem then becomes 1,544 Kbps ÷ 128 Kbps.

■ **Apply Goal 2**

Work through Example 3 with students completing the math at their desks.

Assign Check Your Understanding problems C and D to do in class. Roam your classroom to spot student problems.

■ **ONGOING ASSESSMENT**
With their books closed, have students reread Check Your Understanding problems C and D projected from a transparency. Then call on students to describe the steps they would take to solve the problems. Ask each student called on to describe only one step.

■ High-Speed Internet Access

Organizations need a high-speed connection to their Internet service provider because they want many employees to share the connection. It is less expensive than having each computer individually connected to the organization's Internet service provider.

High-speed Internet access includes digital subscriber line and cable as you learned in Ch. 5. But there are other types of high-speed connections, including *T1* and *T3* telephone lines, and fiber optic cable access, such as *OC1* and *OC3* service.

The types and prices of these connection services change often. Also, these services have many variations. For example, some companies offer *fractional T1* service with speeds ranging from 128 Kbps to 768 Mbps.

> **BUSINESS TIP**
>
> The capacity of a connection is measured by its speed, in bits per second. Capacity is also referred to as *bandwidth*.

Connection Type	Speed (Capacity)
ISDN	128 Kbps–768 Kbps
T1	1.544 Mbps
T3	44.736 Mbps
Optical Cable 1 (OC1)	51.84 Mbps
Optical Cable 3 (OC3)	155.52 Mbps

EXAMPLE 3

To serve their new administration building, Malta County purchased 3, T1 lines at $650 each a month. The connection required hardware and software that cost $7,645, installed. What was the total cost to the County for the first year? What was the total line capacity they purchased? $31,045; 4.632 Mbps

SOLUTION
$650 × 12 × 3 = $23,400   annual connection cost

Add annual connection cost to cost of installed hardware and software.

$23,400 + $7,645 = $31,045   total cost

Multiply the speed of 1, T1 line by 3.

1.544 Mbps × 3 = 4.632 Mbps   total line capacity purchased

■ **CHECK YOUR UNDERSTANDING**

Use the table given above to solve problems C and D.

C. Reisen Glass Works connected its 128 computers to their Internet service provider using 3, T1 lines. Each line cost $825 a month and the hardware and software needed to make the connection cost $11,358, installed. What was the total cost of the connection for the first year? What was the total connection speed they purchased? $41,058; 4.632 Mbps

D. How many times faster is a T3 connection than a T1 connection, rounded to the nearest whole number? 29

■ *CHECK YOUR UNDERSTANDING SOLUTIONS*

C. 3 × $825 = $2,475; $2,475 × 12 = $29,700; $29,700 + $11,358 = $41,058 first-year cost; 1.544 × 3 = 4.632 Mbps

D. 44.736 ÷ 1.544 = 28.9, or 29

Experts recommend that when you buy online you always use your credit card. The reason is that many card companies do not hold you responsible for more than $50 for purchases you did not authorize, if you contact the credit card company soon after noticing the error. Some card companies waive the $50 for online purchases.

Some people feel uneasy having their credit card numbers exposed to hackers and thieves. But, you are likely to be in greater danger by letting your credit card out of sight at a store or restaurant. Dishonest employees can swipe your card into a hand-held card reader that stores the numbers and then create a phony credit card later.

COMMUNICATION

When thieves break into computer files, they may steal your social security number in order to commit identity theft. What is identity theft? What steps can you take to prevent it? What steps should you take if you become a victim of identity theft? Investigate these questions and write a report describing the answers you found.

EXERCISES

Find the sum.

1. $56,389 + $29,124 + $3,288 + $1,450 $90,251

2. $1,329 + $509 + $2,819 + $127 $4,784

Find the product.

3. $128 × 24 $3,072

4. $1,890 × 12 $22,680

5. 36 × $428 $15,408

Find the quotient.

6. $189,350 ÷ 68 $2,784.56

7. $35,280 ÷ 12 $2,940

8. $83,224 ÷ 23 $3,618.43

9. The startup costs for a company's web site are: web server and software, $46,850; e-mail server and software, $35,260; security hardware and software, $18,782; Internet connection hardware and software, $10,253. To develop the web pages, it takes 65 hours of programming time at $61 an hour. Installation and configuration costs take 15 hours at $75 an hour. Other costs are $2,659. What is the total cost of starting the web site? $118,894

Lesson 9.4 E-Business ■ **407**

Wrap Up

Review the Start Up. Ask students if they, their parents or guardians, or friends have experienced credit card theft, and if so, to share what they know about the experience.

COMMUNICATION

Call on students to read their findings and discuss them with the class. Working together, prepare a master list of steps people can take to avoid identity theft and to resolve the problem if it occurs.

Assign

Assignment: Exercises 1–21, 25–40. Start with the basic math exercises at the beginning to make certain that students can handle the arithmetic used in the exercises.

SELECTED SOLUTIONS

9. 65 × $61 = $3,965; 15 × $75 = $1,125;
$3,965 + $1,125 + $46,850 + $35,260 +
$18,782 + $10,253 + $2,659 = $118,894

10. $46 + $45 = $91; $91 × 12 = $1,092;
$1,092 + $1,080 + $15 = $2,187

11. $2,187 ÷ 3,388 = $0.645, or $0.65

12. 12 × $45 = $540; $64 + $20 = $84;
$84 × 12 = $1,008;
$1,008 + $540 + $20 = $1,568

Ask students the following questions to be answered mentally:

1. Convert 142 KB to MB.
   (0.142 MB)

2. How many times faster is a 512 Kbps ISDN line than a 128 Kbps ISDN line? **(4 times faster)**

3. Convert 14 GB to MB.
   (14,000 MB)

Reteach

STUDENT WORKBOOK To reteach calculating the costs of creating and maintaining e-business web sites, do Exercise 1 with students. Then have them do Exercise 2.

If students need help calculating high-speed access line capacities, do Exercise 3a with them. Then have them complete Exercise 3b.

To reteach calculating the costs of high-speed Internet access, do Exercise 4 with them. Then have them complete Exercise 5.

The Montgomery Theatre wants to advertise on the Internet but not sell tickets online. They use a web hosting firm that charges them $1,080 to develop the web site and $46 a month to maintain it. They are also charged $15 annually to register the company's web site address and $45 a month for web server space and an Internet connection.

10. What is the total cost for the first year to the Theatre? $2,187

11. If the total number of site visits in the first year was 3,388, what was the cost per hit, to the nearest cent? $0.65

12. Bullock Accounting, a small firm, paid a web hosting company $20 to register their web site address and $64 a month for an Internet connection, 10 MB of web space and 5 e-mail addresses. Bullock also paid a web developer $45 an hour to develop the web pages and a flat fee of $20 a month to maintain and update them. It took 12 hours for the developer to create the web pages. What is the total cost of the web site for the first year? $1,568

To connect its 26 desktop computer users to the Internet, the Greater Arts Council purchased fractional T1 service at $250 a month. The connection required hardware and software that cost $2,645, installed.

13. What was the total cost to the Council for the first year? $5,645

14. What was the cost per desktop for the year? $217.12

INTEGRATING YOUR KNOWLEDGE Weigand Designs networks its 14 desktop computer systems. It pays $39,500 for a server, $1,590 for network cards and cables, and other devices costing $2,899. Installation will take 22 hours at $95 an hour. It also leases a T1 connection to an Internet service provider for $429 a month and pays $3,150 for the connection's equipment, installed. The Internet service provider charges $195 a month for the connection and e-mail accounts for users.

15. What is the total first-year cost for the network and Internet service? $56,717

16. What is the cost of the network and Internet service per desktop? $4,051.21

Using the table given in the lesson, answer Exercises 17–20.

17. How many T1 lines would it take, to the nearest whole line, to equal the capacity of an OC1 connection? 34

18. How many T3 lines would be needed, to the nearest whole line, to equal the capacity of an OC3 connection? 4

19. By what percent, to the nearest tenth, does an OC1 connection speed exceed a T3 connection speed? 15.9%

20. How many 128 Kbps ISDN lines would be needed, to the nearest whole line, to equal the capacity of one T1 connection? 12

21. The Copy Corner connected its office network to an Internet service provider using a fractional T3 line. The line cost $225 a month and the hardware and software needed to make the connection cost $7,358, installed. The Internet service provider charged $150 to set up the connection and $198 a month for unlimited use, web space, and e-mail accounts. What was the total cost of the connection for the first year? $12,584

SELECTED SOLUTIONS

13. $12 \times \$250 = \$3,000; \$3,000 + \$2,645 = \$5,645$
14. $\$5,645 \div 26 = \$217.115$, or $\$217.12$
17. $51.84 \div 1.544 = 33.5$, or 34

19. $51.84 - 44.736 = 7.104;$
    $7.104 \div 44.736 = 0.1587$, or 15.9%
20. $1.544 \times 1,000 = 1,544; 1,544 \div 128 = 12.06,$ or 12

The home office of a florist store chain connects its network of 18 computers to an Internet service provider using a fractional T1 line. The line cost $110 a month and $3,938 in installed equipment and software. The ISP charged the firm $135 a month for the connection and e-mail accounts. It also charged a setup fee of $350.

22. What was the total first-year cost to the florist chain? $7,228

23. What was the cost per computer for the first year? $401.56

24. **CRITICAL THINKING**   Why might an organization not want to develop their own web site and online order processing themselves? Why might they want to use a web-hosting firm?
See the Enrich section for answer.

MIXED REVIEW

25. Subtract: 41.307 − 1.08   40.227

26. Multiply: 1.52 × 78.03   118.6056

27. Multiply: $1\frac{1}{3} \times 4\frac{1}{2}$ 6

28. Divide: 0.087 ÷ 1,000   0.000087

29. What percent is 5.2 of 340, to the nearest tenth?   1.5%

30. How many days are there between March 16 and June 3?   79

31. Estimate the quotient: 102 ÷ 8   10

32. If a 5% sales tax on a TV is $25, what was the price of the TV? $500

33. What is $\frac{1}{6}$ of $56.88? $9.48

34. Ron Adams earns 5% commission on all sales and 2% commission on sales over $20,000 per week. His sales this week were $24,600. What was Ron's commission for the week? $1,322, Lesson 1.4

Mia Clarke worked 8 hours per day, Monday through Wednesday. She worked 10 hours per day on Thursday and Friday.

35. How many regular hours did Mia work?   40, Lesson 1.3

36. If overtime is based on an 8-hour day, how many overtime hours did she work?
4, Lesson 1.3

37. If she was paid $13.50 an hour, and time and a half for time worked over 8 hours a day, what was her gross pay for the week? $621, Lesson 1.3

38. Yoko Mori's tax return last year showed gross income of $23,412 and adjustments to income of $1,690. What was Yoko's adjusted gross income last year? $21,722, Lesson 2.3

39. Ben Feinberg purchased 400 shares of stock from his broker at $14.75. The broker charged $159.85 commission. What is the total cost of the stock?
$6,059.85, Lesson 7-6

40. A random sample of 375 water sprinklers from a shipment of 25,000 sprinklers was tested. 3 sprinklers were found to be defective. About how many from the entire shipment will be defective?   200, Lesson 8.2

Lesson 9.4 E-Business ■ 409

TEACHING STRATEGIES Cooperative Learning

Have students form small teams to use the Web to investigate credit card theft. Each team should prepare a report listing the major steps people can take to avoid credit card theft. Call on team members to read the steps they found, having each team read only one of their steps to allow for contributions from many teams.

Wireless Communications

GOALS

- Calculate the cost of wireless phone service
- Calculate the cost of paging service

Start Up

Have students read the Start Up and discuss possible answers. Use the Start Up to lead into Goal 1, calculating the cost of wireless phone service.

Math Skill Builder

Use the Math Skill Builder to prepare students for the addition, subtraction, and multiplication of money amounts and whole numbers used in the lesson.

Complete all exercises in Math Skill Builder 1–3.

Start Up

Jose Celera just got a cell phone and dialed several firms with toll-free 1-800 numbers thinking that these calls are free to him. Is he right or wrong?

Math Skill Builder

Review these math skills and answer the questions that follow.

1 **Add** money amounts.
Find the sum. $56.98 + $25.99 + $208.50 = $291.47

1a. $79.99 + $105.30 + $23.88 $209.17

1b. $48.12 + $208 + $15.94 $272.06

2 **Subtract** whole numbers from whole numbers.
Find the difference. 408 − 125 = 283

2a. 159 − 60 99   **2b.** 387 − 250 137   **2c.** 612 − 450 162

3 **Multiply** money amounts by whole numbers.
Find the product. $0.45 × 138 = $62.10

3a. $0.65 × 26 $16.90   **3b.** $0.20 × 120 $24   **3c.** $0.15 × 89 $13.35

■ Wireless Phone Service

Wireless phone service, or *cell phone* service is just that, phone service that does not use wires. The phone companies, or *carriers*, that offer wireless service offer many different *service plans*, or fee schedules. The table on the next page shows the features of several wireless service plans.

Many wireless carriers offer service in one region of the country. If you are traveling outside that region, which is called the **home coverage area**, and wish to make a call, you will pay **roaming charges**. These charges are higher than charges for calls made within your home coverage area.

BUSINESS TIP

Cell phone calls you make are usually billed from the time you press the SEND button until you press the END button.

DIFFERENT LEARNING ABILITIES At Risk Learners

Cell phone rates and fees can get complicated. To help students organize their approach to cell phone exercises, have students copy the row labels in the first column of the cell phone services table on a sheet of paper for each exercise. Then have them work out the charges for each row label. They should enter $0.00 next to any row label that does not apply to the exercise, such as "Each Long Distance Minute" for Vega NationWide. Once the calculation for each row has been completed, students can add the row values to find the total bill.

Some carriers offer service on a national basis and do not charge long distance or roaming fees.

Most carriers offer service plans with a minimum number of calling minutes included at a flat monthly rate. If you make calls beyond the included minutes, the rate for these extra minutes is usually higher. The minutes you spend calling on a cell phone, whether included or extra minutes, are called airtime.

BUSINESS TIP

You are charged airtime for all cell phone calls, including calls to toll-free 1-800 numbers.

■ **Teach Goal 1**

Emphasize that usually national wireless plans do not charge long distance or roaming fees.

Stress that cell phone charges are usually additive. That is, the regular per-minute rate is added to the roaming per-minute rate, etc.

Some service plans split airtime into *peak hours* and *off-peak hours*. Peak hours may be from 6:00 A.M. to 9:00 P.M., Monday through Friday. Off-peak hours may be the remaining hours on weekdays and anytime on Saturday and Sunday. These plans charge higher rates for peak hours.

Some carriers charge a one-time *activation fee* to start your service plan. All carriers will add federal, state, county, or city taxes to your bill.

Wireless Phone Service Plans				
	Teffco	**Wyrless**	**LoadStar**	**Vega NationWide**
Activation Fee	none	$15	$45	$30
Basic Monthly Rate	$19.99	$24.99	$35.99	$59.99
Included Minutes	100	250	500	800
Each Extra Minute	$0.40	$0.42	$0.60	$0.35
Each Roaming Charge Minute	$0.60	$0.40	$0.56	$0.00
Each Long Distance Minute	$0.15	$0.20	$0.15	$0.00
Cancellation Fee	$10 for each remaining month	$200	$10 for each remaining month	$150

Per minute charges are generally additive. If you make a long-distance phone call outside your home coverage area, and have already used up your included minutes, your per minute rate as a Teffco customer would be $0.40 + $0.60 + $0.15, or $1.15.

Telephone handsets may be offered for free or at a reduced price as part of a carrier's service plan. The phone service and handsets may be analog or digital. Many handsets receive both analog and digital phone calls.

Digital handsets and service may let you send and receive text messages, e-mail messages, and digital pictures and may provide you with limited ability to surf the Web.

Service plans usually require you to sign a contract for a year or more. If you cancel your contract, you may pay a cancellation fee. The fee may be a charge for each unused month left in the contract or a flat fee.

BUSINESS TIP

If you call the customer service line for your cell phone company, the minutes of that call may be deducted from your monthly allowance of anytime minutes.

Lesson 9.5 Wireless Communications ■ 411

CONNECTION TO OFFICE TECHNOLOGY

Have small teams of students explore emerging wireless technologies such as wireless Internet access and wireless networking of PCs. Each team should prepare a report listing the emerging wireless technologies they found. The report should also provide a brief explanation of each emerging technology and its possible applications for business and personal use.

EXAMPLE 1

Juanita Callara uses a cell phone provided by her organization that has a service plan from Wyrless for their executives. Juanita used 325 minutes of airtime during February. Use the wireless phone plan table.

Of that total, 176 minutes were for long-distance calls and 128 minutes were made outside her home coverage area. Taxes and other charges totaled $18.48. How much was Juanita's phone bill for February?

SOLUTION

$325 - 250 = 75$ number of extra minutes used

$75 \times \$0.42 = \$31.50$ charge for extra minutes

$176 \times \$0.20 = \$35.20$ charge for long-distance calls

$128 \times \$0.40 = \$51.20$ roaming charge

Add the basic monthly charge, the extra minutes charge, the long-distance charge, the roaming charge, and the taxes and other charges.

$\$24.99 + \$31.50 + \$35.20 + \$51.20 + \$18.48 = \$161.37$ February bill

■ CHECK YOUR UNDERSTANDING

Use the wireless phone plan table to solve problems A and B.

A. Farshid Meguid's company provides him with a cell phone and service plan from Teffco. During May, he used the phone for 136 minutes. Of those minutes, 20 were for long-distance calls and 15 were made outside his home coverage area. Taxes and other charges were $6.50. What was Farshid's Teffco phone bill for May? $52.89

B. Telron, Inc. buys a service plan for 3 cell phones from Vega NationWide. Vega provides free phones to the company, but charges a $30 activation fee for each phone. Each phone was used for less than 800 minutes during the first month. Of the minutes used, 210 minutes were calls made from outside the home coverage area and 114 minutes were long-distance calls. Taxes were 12% of the airtime charges. What was Telron's total phone bill from Vega for the month? $291.57

■ Paging Service

Originally **pagers** were wireless devices that were used to alert people when they had a message waiting for them. Users would then call the paging service and receive the message. Pagers today still perform that function. They can also be much more versatile.

There are one-way pagers that receive only and two-way or interactive pagers that send and receive. There are numeric pagers that receive numbers only, such as a telephone number to call. There are alphanumeric pagers that receive both letters and numbers.

412 ■ **Chapter 9** Business Technologies

■ *CHECK YOUR UNDERSTANDING SOLUTIONS*

A. $136 - 100 = 36$; $36 \times \$0.40 = \$14.40$;
$20 \times \$0.15 = \$3$; $15 \times \$0.60 = \$9$;
$\$19.99 + \$14.40 + \$3 + \$9 + \$6.50 = \$52.89$

B. $3 \times \$30 = \$90$; $\$59.99 \times 3 = \$179.97$;
$\$179.97 \times 0.12 = \$21.596$, or $\$21.60$;
$\$90 + \$179.97 + \$21.60 = \$291.57$

There are also *paging service plans* that provide voice mail and pagers that receive e-mail. Paging services can be added to cell phones and to desktop, notebook, and handheld computers. You can even send a message to a pager using a web browser.

Because all calls are brief, paging services usually charge by the call or message rather than the minute. Pagers can be purchased outright or rented by the month. If you cancel a service within a month, you will usually be responsible for the entire month's fees.

Paging service plans can be local, regional, or nation-wide in scope. You may be able to add one or more local areas or regions to the service plan for an extra charge. For salespeople who live in a city near a state line, getting an extension to the area or region is very helpful. The table shows examples of several alphanumeric paging service plans.

Paging Service Plans			
	MetroPage Paging (Local)	TriState Paging (Regional)	MegaPage Paging (National)
Basic Monthly Rate	$10.99	$24.00	$32.00
Included Calls	300	150	150
Extra Calls	$0.15	$0.25	$0.25
Activation Fee	$15.00	$15.00	$15.00
Monthly Pager Rental	$7.00	$10.00	$8.99
Add 1 Area	$3.00	$4.00	—
Voice Mail Service	$6.99	$8.99	$10.99

EXAMPLE 2

Tomas Barra's company has rented his pager and local paging service from MetroPage since January. Tomas had the company add one local area to his service plan. During July, he had 389 calls. What was the company's total bill for Tomas from MetroPage for the month? Use the table above.

SOLUTION
Subtract the included calls from the total calls.

$389 - 300 = 89$ extra calls

Multiply the extra calls by the extra call rate.

$89 \times \$0.15 = \$13.35$ charge for extra calls

Add the pager rental charge, basic rate charge, extra call charge, and charge for the added area.

$\$7 + \$10.99 + \$13.35 + \$3 = \$34.34$ total bill for July for Tomas

Lesson 9.5 Wireless Communications ■ 413

■ **Apply Goal 2**

Work through Example 2 with students completing the math at their desks.

Assign Check Your Understanding problems C and D for completion in class. Move about your classroom and check student work for difficulties.

■ **ONGOING ASSESSMENT**
Ask students to look at the cell phone services plan table and tell you what 10 extra minutes which are also long distance minutes would cost if Wyrless service was used (10 × ($0.42 + $0.20) = $6.20), if Teffco was used (10 × ($0.40 + $0.15) = $5.50).

CONNECTION TO OFFICE TECHNOLOGY

Have each student create a spreadsheet for calculating the monthly charges for either cell phones or pagers that are rented from the companies shown in the cell phone or pager tables found in the lesson. The spreadsheets should allow the user to enter the number of devices billed so that the total bill for a whole company or department can be calculated.

Wrap Up

Review the Start Up. Stress that usually cell phone service plans charge for all airtime—that includes calls to and from your cell phone—even for 800 number calls. The charges usually start from the time you press SEND until you press END.

TEAM MEETING

After students have completed the Team Meeting, call on the teams to provide their answers to the questions to the class. Discuss the answers.

Ask students to describe events at which they were annoyed when someone's cell phone went off.

Assign

Assignment: Exercises 1–18, 19–25. Start with the basic arithmetic problems at the beginning of the exercises to be sure that students understand the underlying arithmetic in the exercises.

Assess

Make transparencies of Examples 1 and 2. With their books closed, display the transparencies and ask students to spell out the steps needed to solve each problem.

Ask students to explain the meaning of the bolded and italicized terms in the lesson.

■ CHECK YOUR UNDERSTANDING

Use the paging service table to solve problems C and D.

C. Cleo Burris uses a pager and paging service her organization has rented from MegaPage since April. The service has voice mail service. If Cleo used 225 calls during June, what was the bill from MegaPage? $70.73

D. Taxco, Inc. rented pagers and paging service for its 26 salespeople from TriState Paging. The service included one added paging area and voice mail service. They were also charged an activation fee. Taxco had to pay in advance for the first month's service. How much did they pay? $1,611.74

Wrap Up

Cell phone service plans charge for all airtime, even 800 calls. Jose will also be billed land-line charges since he is calling a wired phone. If Jose makes the call from outside his home coverage area, he will be billed for roaming charges, too.

TEAM MEETING

Cell phone use during driving is dangerous. The results of a 1997 study in *The New England Journal of Medicine* disclosed that using a cell phone while driving quadrupled the risk of an accident. Does your city, county, or state regulate the use of cell phones while driving?

Cell phone use can be annoying. In what situations should you turn off your cell phone? With another student answer these questions and prepare a report to be presented to the class.

EXERCISES

Find the sum.

1. $89.23 + $1.50 + $15.99 $106.72   2. $34.99 + $56 + $12.45 $103.44

Find the difference.

3. 458 − 150   308   4. 217 − 175   42   5. 225 − 130   95

Find the product.

6. $0.25 × 26 $6.50   7. $0.34 × 152 $51.68   8. $0.78 × 29 $22.62

9. Z-Link Corporation bought 30 cell phones and service plans for their salespeople. Z-Link got a 45% discount from the $149.99 list price of each cell phone handset. What was the total discount they received? $2,024.87

Use the paging service plan table given to solve Exercises 10–11.

10. Leona Cohen uses a pager her organization rents from TriState Paging. Her service includes one added paging area and voice mail service. Leona used 325 calls during May. What was her paging service bill? $90.74

■ *CHECK YOUR UNDERSTANDING SOLUTIONS*

C. 225 − 150 = 75; 75 × $0.25 = $18.75;
$32 + $18.75 + $8.99 + $10.99 = $70.73

D. $24 + $15 + $10 + $4 + $8.99 = $61.99;
$61.99 × 26 = $1,611.74

11. A company rented pagers and paging service for its 16 field technicians from MetroPage. The service included one added paging area. MetroPage required the company to pay in advance for the first month's service. How much did the company pay in advance? $575.84

Use the wireless phone services table given to solve Exercises 12–15.

12. Yale MaGoo's company lets him use a cell phone and service plan from LoadStar. During October, his total airtime was 552 minutes. Of those, 112 minutes were for long-distance calls and 85 minutes were made outside his home coverage area. Taxes and other charges were 13% of his basic monthly rate and airtime charges. What was Yale's Loadstar phone bill for October? $148.70

13. What would Yale's (see Exercise 12) October phone bill be if his carrier was Wyrless instead of LoadStar and his taxes and other charges were still 13%? $235.30

14. What would Yale's (see Exercise 12) October phone bill be if his carrier was Vega instead of LoadStar and his taxes and other charges were still 13% $67.79

15. Biutta Corporation cancels its service plan for 12 cell phones from LoadStar. There were 4 months to go on the plans. What cancellation fee will LoadStar charge Biutta? $480

BEST BUY Ludlow Electrical Company wants to rent pagers and paging service for its 12 repair specialists. They also want to add voice mail to the service plan. Their specialists use, on average, 63 extra calls per month. Use the paging service table given in the lesson for Exercises 16–18.

16. Which paging company would be the least expensive for the first month: TriState or MegaPage? TriState

17. How much less expensive? $107.88

18. **INTEGRATING YOUR KNOWLEGE** How many months, to the nearest tenth of a month, would it take for the rental of a pager from TriState to equal its purchase price of $245? 24.5 months

MIXED REVIEW

19. Round 56.082 to the nearest tenth. 56.1
20. Round $0.59 to the nearest dollar. $1

21. Multiply 1.289 by 1,000. 1,289
22. Multiply $14.56 × 100. $1,456

23. On Lateesha Wilson's return, the adjusted gross income was $36,057. Lateesha is single and her itemized deductions totaled $3,950. She claimed 1 exemption for herself at $3,100. Find her taxable income. $28,107, Lesson 2.3

24. What tax must Hector Salas pay on his home, assessed for $83,500 if his tax rate is $35.18 per $1,000? $2,937.53, Lesson 6.3

25. A firm needs to remove 4 GB of data from a computer hard drive and store it on removable media. They decide to use 700 MB CD-RW disks. How many CD-RW disks will they need? 6, Lesson 9-1

Lesson 9.5 Wireless Communications ■ **415**

SELECTED SOLUTIONS

10. 325 − 150 = 175; 175 × $0.25 = $43.75;
$43.75 + $24 + $10 + $4 + $8.99 = $90.74
12. 552 − 500 = 52; 52 × $0.60 = $31.20;
112 × $0.15 = $16.80; 85 × $0.56 = $47.60;
$35.99 + $31.20 + $16.80 + $47.60 = $131.59;

$131.59 × 0.13 = $17.106, or $17.11;
$131.59 + $17.11 = $148.70
15. 4 × $10 = $40; 12 × $40 = $480
18. $245 ÷ $10 = 24.5

- Multiply number of computers and network devices by their unit costs and add the results to find total cost of hardware.

- Add hardware and installation costs to find the total cost of hardware after installation.

- Multiply number of months of lease by monthly lease cost to find total cost of lease.

- Multiply total lease cost of one unit by number of units to find total lease cost.

- Divide amount of data by capacity of storage medium (in same units) to find required media.

Lesson 9.2 Software

- Multiply number of workstations by per copy price of software to find total cost.

- Add costs of software, installation, and training to find total cost of new software.

- Subtract price for a multi-station software license from the total cost of software priced per copy to find amount saved.

- Divide number of lines of code written by number of days project took to find average number lines of code written per day.

Lesson 9.3 Computer System Support

- Add amounts spent on installing, running, and maintaining computers to find total cost of system operation.

- Divide total cost of operating computer systems by number of computers to find total operating costs per computer.

- Divide total number of users by number of technical support workers to find ratio.

- Multiply number of technical support hours needed by cost per hour of that support; add that result to cost of materials needed to find total cost of technical support.

Chapter Review

Vocabulary Review

airtime
byte
computer hardware
e-business
home coverage area

outsourcing
pagers
roaming charges
site license
software

storage media
total costs of ownership
Web hosting company

Fill in the blanks with one of the terms above. Use each term only once.

1. A ___?___ is a measure of computer storage.   byte

2. Physical devices, such as desktop computers, cables, and servers, are called ___?___.
   computer hardware

3. Computer data are saved on ___?___, such as CD-R disks.   storage media

4. Computer programs are called ___?___.   software

5. A ___?___ lets you use software on any machine in your organization.   site license

6. The ___?___ include the costs of installing, operating, and maintaining computer systems.
   total costs of ownership

7. Using an outside firm for a business function, such as technical support, is called ___?___.   outsourcing

8. Doing business online is called ___?___.   e-business

9. Firms that provide the special skills and resources to create and maintain web sites are called ___?___.   web hosting companies

10. The geographical area in which your cell phone company operates is called a ___?___.
    home coverage area

11. Cell phone fees that are charged when you make calls outside of your home coverage area are called ___?___.   roaming charges

12. The minutes you spend calling on a cell phone are called ___?___.   airtime

13. Wireless devices whose primary job is to alert you to messages waiting are called _____.   pagers

LESSON 9.1

14. A company decided to network their computer systems. They purchased a network server for $58,359, network cables and network cards for $2,100, a backup system to make daily copies of all their computer files for $1,353; and a battery power backup system for $1,386. Installation of the hardware took 21 hours at a cost of $118 an hour. What was the total cost of buying and installing the hardware for their network? $65,676

15. Hercules, Inc. leased 20 notebook computer systems for 3 years for their marketing staff. The monthly lease for each system was $68.59. What was the annual cost of leasing one notebook? All the notebooks? $823.08; $16,461.60

16. An agency transfers 62.7 GB of data from its network hard drives to 700 MB CD-R disks at $0.68 each. How many CD-R disks did they need, and what was the total cost of the media used?   90; $61.20

DIFFERENT LEARNING ABILITIES Gifted Learners

As an extra-credit project, some students with very good word skills might like to create a crossword puzzle similar to those used in the workbook using the vocabulary terms and definitions in the Chapter Review. Some students might also want to find crossword puzzle software on the web that can be downloaded for use in an educational setting without charge and use it to create the puzzle.

LESSON 9.2

17. A company buys customer management software for $219,400. They estimate that employees will need 11 hours of classroom training on the software at $125 an hour. They also estimate installation costs at $29,170. To convert the data from other systems to the new one will require 27 hours of work by specialists at $128 an hour. What is the estimated cost of adding the new software? $253,401

18. Six programmers took 28 days to develop a program containing 5,880 lines of code. How many lines a day of code did each programmer average? 35

LESSON 9.3

19. The Montgomery County Clerk's Office owns 218 desktop and notebook computer systems. Last year it spent $35,890 on replacement parts and equipment, $27,130 on software upgrades, and $71,316 on repairs to their systems, user training, and help for their computer users. What amount was spent on technical support per computer system? $616.22

20. A school district has 540 computer users and 5 technical support employees. What is the ratio of technical support personnel to computer users, to the nearest whole person? 1:108

LESSON 9.4

21. A dairy equipment company uses the Web to advertise on the Internet. Their web hosting firm charged them $3,150 to develop their web site and $68.50 a month to maintain it. They also charge $20 annually to register the company's web site address and $65 a month for web server space and an Internet connection. What is the total cost for the first year to the company? $4,772

22. To connect 17 desktop computer users to the Internet, a security firm purchased fractional T1 service at $225 a month. The connection required hardware and software that cost $2,198, installed. What was the firm's cost per desktop for the first year?

$288.12

LESSON 9.5

23. Crallo Food Products provided their salespeople with cell phones. The service plan cost $45 a month for 500 included minutes. Extra minutes cost $0.51 each, long-distance minutes cost $0.23 each, and roaming charges were $0.62 a minute. Rose Waterson used 631 minutes during the month. Of those minutes, 59 were long-distance and 72 were made outside her home coverage area. Taxes at 12% were added to the bill. What was Rose's cell phone bill for the month? $190.42

24. Rollins Corporation rented pagers and paging service for its 4 factory floor supervisors. The paging service charged a monthly basic rate of $12.80 for 150 included messages, $0.17 for extra calls, and $8 a month for the pager. During April, the supervisors used 256, 158, 194, and 201 messages. How much was the company's paging bill for April? $118.73

Lesson 9.4 E-Business
- Multiply monthly fees for Internet access, server space and e-mail accounts, and web site maintenance by 12 to find annual cost.

- Add annual cost of fees to fee for web page development to find total first-year cost of web site.

- Divide total first-year cost of web site by number of web site hits in year to find cost per hit for year.

- Multiply monthly cost of Internet access by 12 to find annual cost; add annual cost to installed price of required hardware and software to find total cost of Internet access for first year.

- Multiply speed of Internet access line by number of lines to find the total line capacity.

Lesson 9.5 Wireless Communications
- Subtract included minutes from number of minutes used to find extra minutes used.

- Multiply number of extra minutes, long distance minutes, and roaming minutes by rates, sum results, and add sum to basic charge to find total airtime charges.

- Multiply total airtime charges by tax rate to find taxes. Add tax to total airtime charges to find total bill.

- Subtract included calls from number of calls to find extra calls. Multiply number of extra calls by rate to find total charges for extra calls.

- Add monthly charge for basic rate, extra calls, activation fee, pager rental, added areas, voice mail service to find total first month paging bill.

TEACHING STRATEGIES Chapter Review

Check student accuracy and procedures for solving the problems in this chapter by making transparencies of the solutions to problems 14-24 in the Chapter Review. Then, assign the problems on a lesson-by-lesson basis. Call on students to give the answers and display your transparencies of the correct solutions to the problems in one lesson before assigning problems in the next lesson.

Task 1: Enter Data In A Technical Support Calculator Template

You are to complete a template that calculates the number and total salaries of support personnel needed.

Open the spreadsheet for Chapter 9 (Tech9-1.xls) and enter the data shown in the blue cells (cells B2, B3, and B4). Your computer screen should look like the one shown below when you are done.

	A	B
1	**Technical Support Calculator**	
2	**No. of Users**	256
3	**Support Ratio = 1:**	50
4	**Average Annual Salary for Support Personnel**	$56,000.00
5		
6	**No. of Support Personnel Needed** (rounded up to nearest whole person)	6
7	**Total Salary Cost of Support Personnel**	$336,000.00

You enter the number of users (cell B2), the ratio of support personnel you want (cell B3), and the average annual salary for support personnel (cell B4). The spreadsheet finds the number of support personnel you need (cell B6) and the total salary amount you need to pay those personnel (cell B7). Notice that the number of support personnel is rounded *up* to the nearest whole person.

Task 2: Analyze The Spreadsheet Output

Move your cursor to cell B2 and enter a new number of users: 345. Notice that the number of support personnel and the total salary amount needed changes. Now move the cursor to the support ratio cell B3. Enter 60 instead of 50. Notice how the number of personnel and the salary amount needed change once again.

Return cells B2 and B3 to their original values: 256 and 50. Answer these questions:
  1. How many support people are needed if the number of users is changed to 800 and the support ratio stays at 1:50?   16

  2. What is the total salary cost of providing support personnel for 800 users at a support ratio of 1:60? $784,000

  3. What is the maximum number of support personnel you can employ, with at support ratio of 1:50, and keep total salary costs at $504,000 a year or less?   9

  4. What is the maximum number of users you can serve with 10 technical support people, if the support ratio is 1:60?   600

TEACHING STRATEGIES Task 2

You may wish to have students save the file Tech9-1.xls as Tech 9-1rev.xls. Then have them revise the spreadsheet template to provide answers to problems like Exercise 15 in Lesson 9-3. In this exercise, the spreadsheet must calculate the ratio of technical support staff to users instead of finding the number of technical support staff needed, given specific data.

Task 3: Design a Byte Conversion Spreadsheet

Design a spreadsheet that will convert terabytes, gigabytes, megabytes, and kilobytes into one another. Your spreadsheet should let you enter a number in one column and see that number automatically converted into each of the other byte measures.

> *DATA:*
>
> To test your spreadsheet, enter into different cells:
>
> - 10 terabytes
> - 10 gigabytes
> - 10 megabytes
> - 10 kilobytes
>
> Your results should be
>
> - 10 terabytes = 10,000 gigabytes
> - 10 gigabytes = 10,000 megabytes
> - 10 megabytes = 10,000 kilobytes

Task 4: Analyze the Spreadsheet Output

Answer these questions about your completed spreadsheet:

5. What formula did you use to convert terabytes into gigabytes?   × 1,000

6. What formula did you use to convert gigabytes into terabytes?   ÷ 1,000

7. How many megabytes are 45 terabytes?   45,000,000

8. How many megabytes are 254 kilobytes?   0.254

9. How many gigabytes are 55 megabytes?   0.055

10. How many gigabytes are 12 terabytes?   12,000

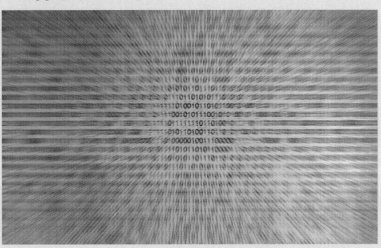

Chapter 9 Technology Workshop ■ 419

■ HOW TIMES HAVE CHANGED

1. 300,000 × $3,995 =
$1,198,500,000
about $1.2 billion

2. $60 × 12 months = $720 per
year per subscriber
$720 × 1.2 billion = $864
billion

■ WRITE

If students are having difficulty
with the assignment, have them
review ads for cell phones or
pagers on the Web to get ideas
about how they might proceed.

Alternatively, you might select a
poorly designed cell phone or
pager ad, duplicate it, and ask students to rewrite and redesign the
ad to improve it.

■ SCANS

Suggest that students prepare for
the "Test Your Skills" assignment
by looking at the factors used to
rate hardware and software on
such web sites as ZDNet, PC World,
and CNET.com.

■ ONGOING ASSESSMENT

STUDENT WORKBOOK The
Integrated Project found in the
workbook provides a broad, ongoing assessment activity for the
goals of this chapter.

Chapter Assessment

How Times Have Changed

For Questions 1–2, refer to the timeline on page 385 as needed.

1. When cellular phones were introduced in the U.S. in 1983, each phone weighed 28 ounces and cost $3,995. By 1984, the number of cell phone subscribers was approximately 300,000. If each subscriber bought a $3,995 phone, about how much would have been spent on the phones alone?
2. Today there are more than 1.2 billion cell phone subscribers in the world. If each subscriber pays an average monthly rate of $40 for the service and incurs an additional $20 per month for roaming charges, extra minutes, and other fees, how much is spent per year for 1.2 billion cell phone service plans?

WRITE

Write a commercial for one of the wireless phone service plans or pager service plans listed in the tables in Lesson 9.5. Be sure to provide all the necessary information about charges and usage. Remember you are trying to sell the company's service so be creative and persuasive.

SCANS

Workplace Skills—*Select Technology*

You must be able to make smart choices when selecting technical equipment and services. It is important that you evaluate procedures, tools, machines, and services against the results you desire. You need to establish a rating system that allows you to compare different equipment and services on the same criteria.

Test Your Skills   Create an evaluation tool, such as a spreadsheet or questionnaire, to use when making decisions about purchasing equipment and services.

Make a Plan   Review advertisements for at least three different computer systems or technical support companies. Use the evaluation tool that you create for comparison. Be sure to support your comments with facts and examples.

Summarize   Write a summary from your comparison that makes a recommendation about which system or service best achieves the results you want. Be aware that your recommendation may be that none of the systems or services reviewed is a good match and that more comparison shopping is necessary. Be sure to identify which, if any, of the following were used in reaching a decision about your recommendation.

arithmetic	*creative thinking*	*problem solving*	*self-management*
responsibility	*knowing how to learn*	*integrity/honesty*	*reasoning*

PORTFOLIO ASSESSMENT

Ask students to review the materials they have created in this chapter and select those they wish to place in their portfolios. Have students write a paragraph about why they selected the entry they have and what skills they are showcasing.

Chapter Test

Answer each question.

1. $436 + 13.8 + 0.36 + 7.36$ 457.52
2. $25\% \times \$578$ $144.50
3. $64.085 - 41.792$ 22.293
4. $1\frac{1}{2} \times \$12.80 \times 6$ $115.20
5. $\$1,354 - \$600$ $754
6. $\$520 \div \frac{1}{4}$ $2,080
7. $24 \times \$18.90$ $453.60
8. Round 458.98 up to the nearest hundred.   500
9. $5,337,000 \div 1,000$ 5,337
10. 50 is $\frac{1}{4}$ greater than what number?   40

Applications

11. Trico, Inc. leased 15 desktop computer systems for 3 years. The monthly lease for each was $48.99. What was the total cost of leasing all the notebooks for three years? $26,454.60

12. A public library removes 12.7 GB of data from its network hard drives to 250 MB Zip disks at $7.99 each. How many disks did they need, and what was the total cost ?   51; $407.49

13. The retail price of a photo editing program is $149.99. A shareware version with less features, sells for $39.79. What percent of the full-featured program price, to the nearest tenth, does buying the shareware version of the same software save?   73.5%

14. Two programmers developed a 6,800 line program. One programmer spent 380 hours on the program and was paid $21.50 an hour. The other sent 370 hours and was paid $17.50 an hour. What was the average programming cost per line for the program? $2.15

15. A college spent $929,300 on computer support for their 580 computers last year. What was the per computer cost of the computer support? $1,602.24

16. HiFiFo Stereo, Inc. has 1,308 computer users. If they provide a ratio of technical support personnel of 1 for every 60 users, how many technical support personnel do they have, to the nearest whole person?   22

17. A firm paid a web hosting company $15 to register their web site address and $56 a month for an Internet connection, 10 MB of web space and 5 e-mail addresses. The firm also paid a web developer $48 an hour to develop the web pages and a flat fee of $25 a month to maintain and update them. If it took 14 hours for the developer to create the web pages, what is the total cost of the web site for the first year? $1,659

18. Arve Trucking connected its 88 computers to their Internet service provider using 3, 1.544 MB, T1 lines. Each line cost $625 a month and the hardware and software needed to make the connection cost $9,957, installed. What was the total cost of the connection for the first year? $32,457

19. Regatta, Inc. cancels its service plans for 8 cell phones from a company that charges a cancellation fee of $10 a month for each remaining month on the service plan. There were 3 months to go on the plans. What cancellation fee will there be? $240

20. LaTonya Walters uses a pager she rents for $10.00 a month. Her paging service monthly basic rate is $25.90 which includes 175 calls. Her service includes one added paging area at $4 a month, voice mail service at $8.50 a month, and extra calls cost $0.20. LaTonya used 325 calls during May. What was her paging service bill? $78.40

Chapter 9 Assessment ■ 421

TEACHING STRATEGIES Chapter Test

Remind students that they must provide all calculations for all steps in every solution to the Applications test items and that their solutions must be fully labeled. To motivate students to do so, set aside points that can be earned for complete and fully labeled solutions.

CHAPTER 10

Manage People and Inventory

10.1 Employee Recruitment Costs
10.2 Wage and Salary Increases
10.3 Total Costs of Labor
10.4 Tracking and Reordering Inventory
10.5 Inventory Valuation
10.6 Ordering and Carrying Inventory

Statistical Insights

Top 15 Largest U.S. Businesses

Rank	Company	Location of Headquarters	Revenues in 2003 (millions of dollars)
1	Exxon Mobil Corporation	Irving, TX	$246,738
2	Wal-Mart Store, Inc.	Bentonville, AR	$244,524
3	General Motors Corporation	Detroit, MI	$186,763
4	Ford Motor Company	Dearborn, MI	$164,196
5	Blue Cross and Blue Shield Association	Chicago, IL	$162,800
6	General Electric Company	Fairfield, CT	$134,187
7	ChevronTexaco Corporation	San Ramon, CA	$120,032
8	ConocoPhillips	Houston, TX	$105,097
9	American International Group, Inc.	New York, NY	$92,654
10	Internation Business Machines (IBM)	Armonk, NY	$89,131
11	Altria Group, Inc.	New York, NY	$81,832
12	Citigroup Inc.	New York, NY	$77,442
13	Hewlett-Packard Company	Palo Alto, CA	$73,061
14	Verizon Communications Inc.	New York, NY	$67,752
15	Cargill, Incorporated	Wayzata, MN	$59,894

Use the data shown above to answer each question.

1. Exxon Mobile was the largest U.S. business by how much revenue?
   $2,214,000,000
2. What was the range of revenue of the top 15 businesses in 2003?
   $186,844,000,000
3. What two firms had the least amount of difference in their revenues?   firm 4 and 5

Statistical Insights

Ask students to sort the companies listed into 5 or 6 industrial categories, such as automotive, financial, technology, and retail. After they make their first sort, ask them to do a web search of each company to get more informa-

tion about the types of products and services they offer. Based on this more detailed information, ask students if they need to make changes in the category titles and in their sorting.

NetCheck

Management Software

Most companies today manage their inventory and human resource records using software. Companies have a large variety of software products from which to choose for inventory and human resource management. Many of the software firms that make these products have web sites that showcase their programs. To locate these sites, enter key terms into a search tool such as, "inventory management software" or "human resource management software." Some web sites offer demonstration software packages that can be downloaded for examination. Others offer online "tours" of their programs.

Government Agencies

The government regulates many of the practices in the management of human resources. The government implements these regulations through agencies such as the Equal Employment Opportunity Commission, Office of Workers' Compensation Programs, and the Social Security Administration. A good starting point is the Department of Labor's web site or the Social Security Administration's web site. Typically, these sites use .gov instead of .com in their web addresses.

How Times Have Changed

A Pennsylvania company introduced the first profit sharing plan in 1797; however, it was not until the early twentieth century that profit sharing plans gained wide acceptance. Today, profit sharing plans play a part in the recruitment of employees. One of these plans, the 401(k), allows employees to contribute money to a retirement fund, and also allows companies to contribute a matching amount.

Procter & Gamble is the first company to contribute stock to employee profit sharing plans.
1903

The IRS passes Section 401(k), which becomes the name of the popular savings and profit sharing plan.
1978

Research to find the maximum annual amount that individuals can contribute to their 401(k) in 2004.

1900 — 1920 — 1940 — 1960 — 1980 — 2000

1921
Congress enacts legislation granting tax benefits to profit sharing plans.

1950s
The Studebaker company goes bankrupt, and employee retirement accounts, which consist entirely of company stock, go broke as well.

1986
The maximum annual amount that individuals can contribute to their 401(k) is $7,000.

2001
The maximum annual amount that individuals can contribute to their 401(k) is $10,500.

423

10.1 Employee Recruitment Costs

GOALS

- Calculate the cost of employment advertising
- Calculate the cost of hiring an employee
- Calculate the cost of outside agency recruitment

Start Up

You read in the newspaper that a company paid $500,000 to an executive recruiting firm to search for a new CEO. Was the search worth the cost considering the number of people who are probably interested in the CEO position?

Math Skill Builder

Review these math skills and solve the exercises that follow.

1. **Add** money amounts.
   Find the sum. $1,238 + $156 + $442 = $1,836

   1a. $218 + $176 + $39 $433   **1b.** $83,100 + $2,176 $85,276

2. **Multiply** money amounts by whole numbers and percents.
   Find the product. $12 \times \$125 = \$1,500$
   Find the product. $38\% \times \$1,200 = 0.38 \times \$1,200 = \$456$

   2a. $6 \times \$134$ $804   **2b.** $26 \times \$157$ $4,082

   2c. $24.6\% \times \$36,100$ $8,880.60   **2d.** $41.3\% \times \$184,000$ $75,992

■ Employment Advertising

One of the ways that employers recruit future employees is through advertising. They place ads in *print media* such as local newspapers, national publications, or trade magazines. Ads may also be posted on Internet job sites.

The cost of an ad depends on its size and the number of days it will run. Other costs include the costs of preparing the ad.

EXAMPLE 1

The XTR Company placed an ad for quality control employees for its new plant. The cost of designing the ad was a one-time charge of $230. The ad appeared in a local newspaper for two days during the week and again on Sunday. The newspaper's charge for the ad was $680 a day during the week and $810 on the weekend. What amount did XTR spend for advertising?

SOLUTION

Multiply the daily charge by the number of days.

$2 \times \$680 = \$1,360$ cost of weekday ad

Add charges.

$\$1,360 + \$810 + \$230 = \$2,400$ total spent on ad

■ **CHECK YOUR UNDERSTANDING**

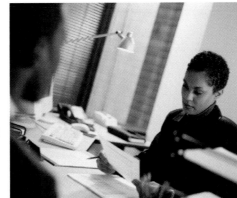

A. Fenton Financial Advisors plans to use print media to recruit new employees over the next year. They decide to buy one ad each month in a financial publication at a monthly cost of $5,400. Because of the number of ads Fenton will run, they receive a 25% discount per ad. What is the cost of running one employment ad per month for a year? $48,600

B. For employment ads in a special section, a newspaper's daily charges are $56 for one inch of a column for weekday and $82 for one inch of a column for weekend. What is the cost of running a weekday ad, four inches long in a column, for two days? $448

■ Hiring Costs

There are two basic classifications of employees: exempt and nonexempt. **Exempt employees** are usually paid a salary and do not qualify for overtime pay. **Nonexempt employees** are usually paid by the hour and do get paid overtime pay. Nonexempt employees may include skilled and unskilled workers in a factory, support employees in an office, or service workers, such as security guards.

The hiring costs for exempt employees are generally greater than those for nonexempt employees. Also, the hiring costs for high-level executives are much greater than those for lower-level exempt employees.

Labor costs are a large part of the hiring costs for many employees. Human resource staff members process applications, verify prior employment, check references, conduct interviews, and complete the paperwork necessary to add an employee to the payroll.

Employers may also spend money to recruit employees when they hold job fairs or send staff to interview graduates on college campuses. Employers may also pay the costs of relocating employees to a new area.

EXAMPLE 2

The Human Resource department hired a new factory worker. The hiring costs included: 0.5 hours, application processing; 1.5 hours, check references; 0.6 hours, interview; 1.4 hours, budget approval and benefit processing. These costs were charged at $80 an hour. General or *overhead* costs of $250 apply to each new worker hired. What was the total cost of hiring this worker?

BUSINESS TIP

In many companies a Human Resource (HR) department hires employees. The HR department may also be known as the Personnel Department.

BUSINESS TIP

Overhead costs are not directly related to a specific activity, such as interviewing an applicant. They include such costs as a manager's time, heat, power, light, office space, and depreciation on furniture and equipment.

■ **Teach Goal 2**

Emphasize to students that advertising a job opening is only one of the costs incurred in hiring new employees. First-line managers often interview several screened applicants to determine which applicant's knowledge and experience will best fit the job's requirements. The cost of a manager's time spent in all interviews is calculated into the cost of filling the job opening.

■ **Apply Goal 2**

Work through Example 2 at the board with students completing the math at their desks.

Review the Business Tip on page 425 with students to ensure they understand the meaning of overhead costs.

Assign Check Your Understanding problems C and D for class work. Circulate about the classroom and examine student work for any difficulty they may have in solving assigned problems.

■ **ONGOING ASSESSMENT**
Review the multiplication of dollar amounts by decimals. Write these problems on the board and have students do the multiplication:
1.25 × $68; **$85** 2.3 × $37; **$85.10** 3.45 × $55; **$189.75** 13.75 × $71; **$976.25**

■ *CHECK YOUR UNDERSTANDING SOLUTIONS*

A. 0.25 × $5,400 = $1,350;
   $5,400 − $1,350 = $4,050; 12 × $4,050 = $48,600

B. 2 × 4 × $56 = $448

Compare a recruiter's contingency fee to a salesperson being paid on a commission basis only. If no placements or sales are made, neither the recruiter nor the salesperson receives a payment. Contrast a contingency fee with a retainer fee that is paid to a recruiter even if an employee is hired through another recruiter.

Point out that recruiters build a pool of potential recruits by always seeking new contacts.

Inform students that contract employees usually receive their pay and benefits from the employment agency since they are employees of the agency and are in effect rented to other companies.

SOLUTION

Add the hours spent hiring: $0.5 + 1.5 + 0.6 + 1.4 = 4$ hours

Multiply the cost per hour by the hours spent in hiring. Then add overhead costs.

$(4 \times \$80) + \$250 = \$320 + \$250 = \$570$ total cost of hiring

■ **CHECK YOUR UNDERSTANDING**

C. Five applicants went through the first round of screening for one opening as an accounts payable supervisor at Wilkins Aircraft Products. The average amount spent by Wilkins of bringing each applicant in for interviews was $1,610 per applicant. Managers spent two hours interviewing each applicant at a cost of $65 an hour. Background and reference checks took 12 hours per applicant at a cost of $41 an hour. Overhead costs were $500 per applicant. What total amount did Wilkins spend on first-round screening for the supervisor job? $13,660

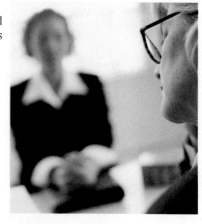

D. A large company received 150 applications for two receptionist job openings. Bobbie Elder took two, 8-hour days to review and sort the applications into the 15 best applicants. The cost of Bobbie's time is $28 an hour. Bobbie spent 45 minutes per applicant to contact and briefly interview each of the 15 applicants. She then spent 1.5 hours per applicant checking the references of each of the 5 applicants who appeared to be best suited for the job. What was the cost of Bobbie's time on this project, to date? $973

■ Employment Agency Recruitment

Some employers use an employment agency to do some employee recruitment. For example, some employers may use **executive recruiters**, often called *headhunters*, to find full-time employees for management or specialized technical positions.

Executive recruiters make all the contacts with potential employees, screen their suitability for the position, determine their level of interest in a new position, and identify their salary and benefit requirements. These recruiters are paid either a contingency fee or a retainer fee.

Recruiters who are paid a *contingency fee* get paid only if they find a suitable employee. The recruiters who are paid a *retainer fee* get paid even for an unsuccessful search.

Instead of recruiting permanent employees, some firms use temporary help agencies. These are companies that have a pool of people who will accept work as contract employees. **Contract employees** are temporary employees who receive their paychecks and benefits from the temporary help agency. The employer who hires contract employees pays a fee to the agency for each contract employee.

■ *CHECK YOUR UNDERSTANDING SOLUTIONS*

C. $2 \times \$65 = \$130$; $12 \times \$41 = \$492$;
$\$1,610 + \$130 + \$492 + \$500 = \$2,732$;
$5 \times \$2,732 = \$13,660$

D. $2 \times 8 \times \$28 = \$448$;
$\frac{45}{60} \times 15 \times \$28 = 0.75 \times 15 \times \$28 = \$315$;
$1.5 \times 5 \times \$28 = \$210$;
$\$448 + \$315 + \$210 = \$973$

EXAMPLE 3

The Tonnel Company hired a contract accountant from the Triple-Star Employment Agency at a total cost of $224 a day. A regularly employed accountant at Tonnel is paid $182 a day. What is the difference between the costs of the contract and regular accountants in wages only for a five-day workweek?

SOLUTION

Multiply the daily rate for each employee by 5 days.

$5 \times \$224 = \$1,120$ contract employee wages

$5 \times \$182 = \$910$ regular employee wages

Subtract employee wage from contract wage.

$\$1,120 - \$910 = \$210$ wage difference

BUSINESS TIP

One of the benefits of using outside agencies is that employers pay for the recruiting services of executive recruiters or for the cost of contract employees only when they are needed.

■ **Apply Goal 3**

Work Example 3 at the board and remind students that the procedures for finding the pay of contract employees is the same as finding the pay of per diem employees.

Work Example 4 on the board and point out that a recruiter's fee is often stated as a percent of the wages paid to the placed employee.

Assign Check Your Understanding problems E and F for class work. Examine student work at their desks and help them make any corrections needed.

EXAMPLE 4

An executive recruiting firm recruited a new accounting manager for the Tonnel Company. The recruiter's contingency fee was 35% of the manager's annual salary of $91,500. The recruiter also charged for $1,900 in travel expenses. What total amount did Tonnel pay the recruiting firm?

SOLUTION

Multiply the annual salary by the contingency fee percent.

$35\% \times \$91,500 = \$32,025$ contingency fee

Add the fee and the travel expenses.

$\$32,025 + \$1,900 = \$33,925$ total amount paid

■ **CHECK YOUR UNDERSTANDING**

E. Use the facts from Example 3. Assume the regular employee receives benefits of 27.5% of wages. For which employee, contract or regular, will it cost more per day considering wages and benefits? How much more? regular employee, $8.05 more

F. A headhunter, Boyd Carron, is recruiting a plant manager for Exwell Manufacturing on a contingency fee basis. Exwell will pay Boyd a 22% fee based on the expected $150,000 salary the manager will earn plus another 3.2% of the manager's salary to cover recruiting expenses. What total fee will Exwell pay Boyd if the search is successful? $37,800

Wrap Up

Review the Start Up. Point out that executive recruiters often make informal contact with candidates to determine their level of initial interest without revealing the name of the company looking for a CEO. Since an outside agency is doing the screening, the hiring company may deny it has contacted individuals named in a speculative report about potential candidates.

Wrap Up

Although many people may be interested in the CEO position, the recruiting firm would likely have a list of highly qualified people to consider because of the high-level contacts it can make. The recruiting firm is paid for its expertise and its discretion. From the company's viewpoint, the $500,000 expense is small compared to the financial growth a company can make by getting the ideal person for the CEO position.

Lesson 10.1 Employee Recruitment Costs ■ **427**

■ *CHECK YOUR UNDERSTANDING SOLUTIONS*

E. $0.275 \times \$182 = \$50.05$; $\$50.05 + \$182 = \$232.05$ cost for regular employee; $\$232.05 - \$224 = \$8.05$ more

F. $22\% + 3.2\% = 25.2\%$; $0.252 \times \$150,000 = \$37,800$

Summarize team findings by posting a tally beneath headings that match those reported by students. As an extra-credit assignment, ask for volunteers to research web sites or other sources for similar reports showing how people get jobs.

Assign

Assignment: Exercises 1–13 and 15–24. Begin with the basic arithmetic problems that review the underlying arithmetic operations used in the exercises.

Assess

Check student answers to exercise problems by calling on them in class. Have students work the problems at the board and ask others to check their own work.

TEAM MEETING

Each class member must join a team of 4-6 students. Each team member needs to interview ten employed people in the general community to determine how they got their current job.

Then the team should look at the responses received and summarize them into 6–10 categories, such as want ads or referred by a friend or relative.

Teams are to present their findings to the class. The class should identify patterns and trends in how people got their jobs and the job types. Summarize all the team findings into 6–10 categories.

EXERCISES

Find the sum.

1. $8,500 + $1,280 + $575 $10,355

2. $1,110 + $355 + $720 $2,185

Find the product.

3. 5 × $127.50 $637.50

4. 52 × $876 $45,552

5. 65% × $240,000 $156,000

6. 20% × $35,550 $7,110

7. A trade journal prints four editions monthly, one each for four different parts of the United States. The cost of a small ad in the job postings section of one of the editions is $1,400 per month. A 17% discount is given if an ad is placed in all editions in a month. What is the total cost of the ad if it is placed in all editions in the same month? $4,648

8. A newspaper charges $67.20 a line per day for employment advertising. The Color-True Paint Company placed a 13-line ad for a polymer chemist in the newspaper for two days. What was the total cost of the ad? $1,747.20

9. The Grix Company spent $108,000 on employment advertising for technical positions. Grix hired 25 technical employees as a direct result of the ad. How much did Grix spend on employment advertising for each technical employee hired? $4,320

10. Trex Graphics Company estimates it spends these amounts to hire each new employee: recruiting, $1,750; 15 hours personnel staff time at $31 an hour; 8 hours interview time at $84 an hour; 5 days employee orientation and training at $360 a day. What is the total cost of hiring an employee? $4,687

11. A law firm spent $18,000 to screen and interview recent college graduates for one job opening. The company hired Gabriella Coates, the top student in her class. Gabriella received an annual salary of $85,000, 41% in benefits, payment of her college student loan of $29,000, and a $10,000 signing bonus. What is the total cost of hiring and employing Gabriella for the first year? $176,850

428 ■ Chapter 10 Manage People and Inventory

SELECTED SOLUTIONS

7. 4 × $1,400 = $5,600; 0.17 × $5,600 = $952;
$5,600 − $952 = $4,648

10. 15 × $31 = $465; 8 × $84 = $672;
5 × $360 = $1,800;
$1,750 + $465 + $672 + $1,800 = $4,687

11. 0.41 × $85,000 = $34,850;
$18,000 + $85,000 + $34,850 + $29,000 +
$10,000 = $176,850

13. 2 × (0.23 × $49,000) = $22,540;
$114,000 + $22,540 = $136,540

12. A plastic molding company with 300 employees has to replace 5% of its employees each year. The average cost of hiring one new employee is $3,900. What total amount does the company pay a year to hire new employees? $58,500

13. Mayfair Industries paid Rosman Recruiting a retainer fee of $114,000 to recruit a chief financial officer who will be paid a salary of $235,000 a year. Rosman was also used to recruit two purchasing agents, each of whom will be paid an annual salary of $49,000. Rosman's contingency fee for recruiting each purchasing agent was 23% of annual salary. What total amount in recruiting fees did Mayfair pay Rosman? $136,540

14. **CRITICAL THINKING**   A job fair for a new store had 500 applicants for 10 jobs. The one recruiter assigned had hoped to interview applicants at the job fair, but was overwhelmed by the response. The recruiter now has to review all the applications and call back certain applicants for an interview. How could the recruiting have been handled better?   See Enrich section for answer.

To meet a deadline, Ronan Products hired four contract employees for 80 total hours at $27.50 an hour. Ronan estimates that regular employees could have done the same work in 60 hours by working overtime at time-and-a-half pay. Regular employees receive $19.20 an hour and benefits of 25% of their wages. By hiring the contract employees, Ronan did not have to pay 60 hours of overtime.

15. What was the cost of using contract employees? $2,200

16. What would have been the cost if regular employees had been used instead of contract employees? $2,160

17. **INTEGRATING YOUR KNOWLEDGE**   Conrad Harris took a new job 700 miles from where he now lives. Conrad's new employer agreed to pay his relocation expenses which were: $3,800 moving bill, $4,200 in closing costs on a new home purchase, and the 7% agent's commission on the sale of his old home at $156,000. What total relocation costs did Conrad's employer pay? $18,920

MIXED REVIEW

18. Rewrite $\frac{1}{2}$ as a decimal.   0.5

19. $3\frac{3}{5} \times 1\frac{7}{8}$ $6\frac{3}{4}$

20. $2,142 \div 9$ 238

21. Find 8% of $23.50. $1.88

22. Inez Folz agrees to a purchase price of $23,050 for a new car. The sales tax is 3.5% of the purchase price and registration fees are $118. Inez made a 20% down payment of the purchase price. What is the delivered price of the car? $23,974.75, Lesson 6.5

23. The CPI for the Recreation category was 102.0 in 1999 and 103.7 in 2000. By what percent did Recreation prices increase from 1993 to 1994, to the nearest tenth percent?   1.7%, Lesson 8.5

24. We Have Puppets, a retail store, plans to sell its puppets online. E-Market will design an e-business web site for $14,800. Server use and storage space will cost $410 a month while high-speed Internet access will cost $275 a month. E-Market will maintain the web site for $780 a month. What is the first-year cost of the site to We Have Puppets? $32,380, Lesson 9.4

Lesson 10.1 Employee Recruitment Costs ■ **429**

CONNECTION TO TECHNOLOGY

Companies routinely use technology in employee recruitment. A job specification may be posted first on an internal web site so employees may apply for the job. Then it may be posted on external web sites or advertised outside the company. When applications are received, systems can scan resumes or applications for key words and match them with the job's description. Also, applicants may attach a resume as a Microsoft Word file that may be searched for key words that match a database without having to print the document.

10.2 Wage and Salary Increases

GOALS

- Calculate Cost-of-Living Adjustments (COLA)
- Calculate bonuses
- Calculate profit sharing

Start Up

An employer offers to pay a wage increase of 4% in one payment at the end of a year. The employees want a 1% wage increase on the first day of each quarter starting at the beginning of the year. The employer argues that 1% for 4 quarters is 4%. Is there any difference between the wage plans?

Math Skill Builder

Review these math skills and solve the exercises that follow.

1 **Add** money amounts.
Find the sum. $0.86 + $17.41 = $18.27

   1a. $0.39 + $10.64 $11.03   **1b.** $1,806 + $31,098 $32,904

2 **Multiply** dollar amounts by percents. Round to the nearest cent.
Find the product. 1.9% × $18.10 = 0.019 × $18.10 = $0.3439, or $0.34

   2a. 3.8% × $14.39   **2b.** 0.6% × $38,400   **2c.** 15% × $3,100,000
   $0.55 $230.40 $465,000

3 **Divide** money amounts by whole numbers.
Find the quotient. $390,000 ÷ 600 = $650

   3a. $86,000 ÷ 215 $400   **3b.** $28,000 ÷ 40 $700

■ Cost-of-Living Adjustments

Some employers pay their employees a Cost-of-Living Adjustment (COLA), which is a wage increase based on changes in the Consumer Price Index (CPI). COLA pay increases may be written into wage contracts made between a company's management and a labor union.

COLA is designed to help employee wages keep up with inflation. COLA wage adjustments are usually made annually, semiannually, or quarterly. Wage adjustments often become a permanent part of the regular hourly pay or salary earned by employees.

Since the Consumer Price Index reports price increases that have already happened, COLA adjustments often lag behind inflation. Because of this, some employers give *retroactive pay*. They compute the amount employees should have been paid since the last COLA wage adjustment.

CONNECTION TO ECONOMICS

EXAMPLE 1

The Skrynn Company gives its employees a COLA equal to the CPI's 2.6% increase in the previous year. Its employees now earn an average rate of $14.50 an hour. What will be the average hourly pay rate after the COLA is given?

SOLUTION

Multiply the hourly rate by the percent increase. Round to the nearest cent.

2.6% × $14.50 = 0.026 × $14.50 = $0.377, or $0.38   COLA

Add the COLA to the old hourly pay.

$0.38 + $14.50 = $14.88   new pay rate

■ CHECK YOUR UNDERSTANDING

A. Omer Brombach earns $11.80 an hour. His employer gives him a COLA based on the 0.8% the CPI rose last quarter. What amount of raise will Omar get, to the nearest cent? What will be his new hourly pay rate? $0.09; $11.89

B. Marsha Ahlquist earned a salary of $56,200 last year. Her employer gave her a COLA pay raise equal to the 4.8% increase in the CPI. What is the amount of the COLA? What is her salary after the COLA?
$2,697.60; $58,897.60

■ Bonuses

Some companies may give their employees a bonus. A **bonus** is pay given to reward employees who make a significant contribution to the success of the company or whose work record is exceptional. A rating system may be used to determine which employees deserve bonuses.

Bonuses may be a stated dollar amount or a percentage of an employee's regular pay. They may also be given in addition to other forms of pay raises, such as COLA. Bonuses may become a permanent part of an employee's pay or they may be only a one-time payment.

EXAMPLE 2

The TSU Company decides to give a bonus to Lowell Hurst. The bonus is 3.5% of his annual earnings of $38,500 a year. What amount of bonus will Lowell receive?

SOLUTION

Multiply the annual earnings by the bonus percent.

3.5% × $38,500 = 0.035 × $38,500 = $1,347.50   bonus

Lesson 10.2 Wage and Salary Increases ■ **431**

■ Apply Goal 1

Work through Example 1 with students and have them do the calculations at their desks.

Assign Check Your Understanding problems A and B. Inform students that COLA may be figured on hourly, weekly, monthly, quarterly, or annual wages.

■ Teach Goal 2

Inform students that a bonus may be based only on regular pay, excluding overtime pay, or on total pay. Some companies give bonuses to all employees while others reward only exceptional performance.

■ Apply Goal 2

Work Example 2 at the board and have students describe the solution in their own words

Assign Check Your Understanding problems C and D for class work. Observe student work at their desks to check for any difficulties they have with the assignment.

■ ONGOING ASSESSMENT

Have students find the total bonus pay for two years of two employees who each earn $40,000 in the first year and receive a 5% bonus each year. Employee #1's bonus becomes a permanent part of annual wages. Employee #2's bonus is an additional payment.
#1 gets $4,100; #2 gets $4,000

■ *CHECK YOUR UNDERSTANDING SOLUTIONS*

A. 0.008 × $11.80 = $0.094, or $0.09;
$11.80 + $0.09 = $11.89

B. 0.048 × $56,200 = $2,697.60;
$56,200 + $2,697.60 = $58,897.60

■ **Teach Goal 3**

Inform students that many profit sharing plans are negotiated in labor contracts with publicly traded companies that are required to publish financial results of their operations, including net profit data. Contrast that with the sole owner of a business who regards the amount of profit earned by the business as privileged information not to be shared with employees.

■ **Apply Goal 1**

Work Example 3 at the board while students do calculations at their desks. Point out that in other situations certain levels of employees, such as managers, may receive greater shares of profits than those earned by subordinates.

Assign Check Your Understanding problems E and F for class work. Monitor student work at their desks and assist those who need help in completing the assignment.

Wrap **Up**

Review the Start Up. Ask students why the employees want the 1% pay raise built into their wages. Also have them check the 4.06% effective rate by compounding a quarterly, 1% pay raise for four quarters. Ask students to make comparisons to compound interest.

C. Althea Gannon received a bonus of 2% of total sales for being the top salesperson in the company. Her sales for the year were $850,000. What bonus did Althea receive? $17,000

D. Four team members received a bonus of $2,000 each for finishing a project two months ahead of schedule. Twelve support team members each received a $1,200 bonus. What total bonus did the employer pay to all team members?
$22,400

■ Profit Sharing

Some companies offer profit sharing to their employees. **Profit sharing** means that employees get part of the profit earned by a company. An employee's share is usually based on the amount of profit and the number of employees eligible for it.

Many profit sharing plans make payments in cash to employees. Employees owe income tax on those payments. Others allow employees to place their shares of the profits in pension programs. When the pension plan is used, the payment is not taxable until it is taken out at retirement.

The idea behind profit sharing plans is to motivate employees to be productive, cut costs, and make suggestions for improvements because they benefit directly from higher profits. Employees share only in the profits of a company, not its losses.

EXAMPLE 3

A company plans to share 20% of its annual profit of $5,000,000 with 250 employees. What profit sharing amount will each employee get?

SOLUTION
Multiply the annual profit by the profit sharing percent.

$20\% \times \$5,000,000 = 0.2 \times \$5,000,000 = \$1,000,000$ profit to be shared

Divide the profit to be shared by the number of employees.

$\$1,000,000 \div 250 = \$4,000$ profit sharing amount per employee

■ **CHECK YOUR UNDERSTANDING**

E. A total of $13,500 profit is to be shared equally by a company's 18 purchasing and warehouse staff. What amount will each employee receive? $750

F. The management of a company shared 20% of its $511,875 profit with its 65 employees. How much did each employee receive? $1,575

Wrap **Up**

By getting the 1% wage increase each quarter, employees would have use of part of their raise throughout the year. The wage increase could be spent or invested. Also, if the wage increase becomes part of regular pay, the 1% raise per quarter would be compounded. So, the actual percent increase would be 4.06% instead of 4%.

■ *CHECK YOUR UNDERSTANDING SOLUTIONS*

C. $0.02 \times \$850,000 = \$17,000$
D. $(4 \times \$2,000) + (12 \times \$1,200) = \$8,000 +$
$\$14,400 = \$22,400$

E. $\$13,500 \div 18 = \$750$
F. $0.20 \times \$511,875 = \$102,375$;
$\$102,375 \div 65 = \$1,575$

COMMUNICATION

Use the Internet or do library research to find a company that pays profit sharing. You could use General Motors, Ford, Daimler-Chrysler, or any other company you find. Find the average amount of profit sharing each hourly-rated employee received for each of the last five years. Find the percent that profit sharing was of the average pay of hourly-rated employees. Write a short report summarizing your findings.

EXERCISES

Find the sum.

1. $0.57 + $14.83 $15.40

2. $1,847 + $38,141 $39,988

Find the product, to the nearest cent.

3. 0.9% × $18.72 $0.17

4. 2.4% × $950,000 $22,800

Find the quotient.

5. $17,920,000 ÷ 28,000 $640

6. $18,512 ÷ 26 $712

7. Viola Forberg earns $19.50 an hour. On April 1, she received an 0.8% COLA. What is her new hourly pay rate, to the nearest cent? $19.66

8. The total payroll of a company whose workers receive COLA is $11,200,000. The CPI is expected to rise 3.46% this year. What total amount of payroll should the company expect to pay this year after COLA, to the nearest ten thousand dollars?
$11,590,000

A company's annual payroll for 400 hourly workers is $14,000,000 and for its 40 salaried workers, $1,800,000. Each worker gets a 3% COLA raise that will be paid at one time as retroactive pay.

9. What retroactive pay will each hourly worker get on average? $1,050

10. What retroactive pay will each salaried worker get on average? $1,350

11. What total retroactive payment will the company make to all workers? $474,000

12. The four top-rated employees in six departments of the Roth Company each received a $1,250 bonus. What total amount of bonus did the Roth Company pay? $30,000

13. **CRITICAL THINKING**   A company has paid COLA for the past 10 years. The company expects a slight loss this year and an even greater loss the next year. The company asks its employees to give up the COLA increase until business improves. What should the employees do? See Enrich section for answer.

Lesson 10.2 Wage and Salary Increases ■ 433

SELECTED SOLUTIONS

8. 0.0346 × $11,200,000 = $387,520;
$11,200,000 + $387,520 = $11,587,520 or
$11,590,000

9. $14,000,000 ÷ 400 = $35,000;
0.03 × $35,000 = $1,050

12. 4 × 6 × $1,250 = $30,000

14. 0.12 × $2,250,000 = $270,000;
$270,000 ÷ 118 = $2,288.135, or $2,288.14

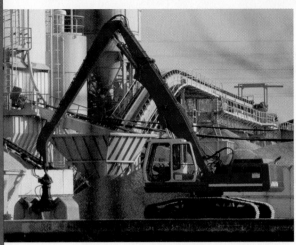

STUDENT WORKBOOK If students have difficulty with COLA wage increases, do Exercise 1 with them. Then assign Exercises 2–4 to be done independently.

Work Exercise 5 with students having problems with bonus calculations. Then have them do Exercises 6–8.

If figuring profit sharing poses a problem to students, work Exercise 9 with them. Assign Exercises 10–12 for independent work.

Enrich

Assign Exercise 13, Critical Thinking. In the discussion, have students consider the impact that giving up COLA will have on individual employees, on a labor contract that may be in place, and on the future of the company.

Revisit Exercise 17 involving Decision Making. Ask for a show of hands to determine which job students would accept. Discuss whether their answers would change if they were planning to keep the job for only one year, for a few years, or for a long time.

Close

Ask students to define these terms in their own words: COLA, CPI, retroactive, bonus, and profit sharing.

Then ask them to explain from memory how to calculate: COLA increases, retroactive pay, bonus pay, and profit sharing for individual employees.

14. Cromwell Electronics set aside 12% of its annual profit of $2,250,000 to share with its 118 employees. What profit sharing check did each employee receive, to the nearest cent? $2,288.14

15. All the workers in a factory received a bonus of 2% of their annual pay for finishing a project on time and below expected cost. The average annual pay of the workers is $49,200. What average bonus was paid per employee? $984

16. A company issued profit sharing checks averaging $3,180 per employee to its 218 employees. The largest check was for $5,008. The smallest check was for $2,117. What total amount of profit did the company share with its employees? $693,240

17. **DECISION MAKING**   You have a choice between two similar jobs, both paying $20,000 a year. One job offers you automatic pay raises of $500 every six months until your reach the maximum pay of $25,000 for the job's classification. The other job does not offer automatic pay increases, but will give increases up to $2,000 a year to employees who do good work. Which job would you take? Why?   Answers will vary; choice between assured increases vs. self-confidence in own ability.

18. **INTEGRATING YOUR KNOWLEDGE**   An employee was paid for an average of 44.5 hours a week for 52 weeks last year. His regular-time pay rate was $15.10 an hour. Time-and-a-half is paid for hours worked over 40 hours a week. His profit sharing check was 4% of his regular time wages for the year. What was his total gross pay for the year from all sources? $37,964.42

MIXED REVIEW

19. $6.6 + 1.76 + 0.9 + 1.875$ 11.135
20. $12 \times 5,400$ 64,800
21. $\frac{3}{4} - \frac{5}{8}$ $\frac{1}{8}$
22. $3\frac{1}{2} \div 4\frac{2}{3}$ $\frac{3}{4}$

23. Find the estimated product of 989×62.   60,000

24. Find the average of 414, 917, 582, 336, and 712.   592.2

25. Flavian Gendron's check register showed a balance of $782.29 at the beginning of the day. During the day he wrote checks for $89.39, $585.87, and $193.92. He also transferred $200 from savings to checking. What was the balance of Flavian's check register after these transactions? $113.11, Lesson 3.1

26. What annual interest is earned by 6, $1,000, 8.25% interest bonds? $495, Lesson 7.6

27. You are using graph paper that has 10 blocks to the inch. How many blocks would you need to make a graph to plot $2,000,000 in sales if each block was equal to $50,000 in sales? to $20,000 in sales?   40; 100, Lesson 8.3

28. The Fleider Company is replacing its 76 desktop computers. The company plans to lease new desktop computers for 36 months at $41.80 a month for each computer. What will be the total cost of leasing per month and over the life of the lease? $3,176.80, $114,364.80, Lesson 9.1

TEACHING STRATEGIES Cooperative Learning

Have students form teams to find companies that pay COLA. Each team should do a different search. One team might search the Internet, another team may do library research, and still another may survey working relatives or friends to ask if they are paid COLA. Each team should attempt to find how the COLA plans are implemented. When all teams have finished their search, they should share the information through classroom discussion.

10.3 Total Costs of Labor

GOALS
- Calculate cost of full-time employees
- Calculate cost of part-time employees

Start Up

A company restricts the hours that several of its employees work to a maximum of 34 hours a week. If the employees worked 40 hours a week, they would be full-time employees and receive the benefits of paid medical insurance and tuition reimbursement. Is this business policy of limiting the hours worked fair to the employees who work less than 40 hours?

Math Skill Builder

Review these math skills and solve the exercises that follow.

1 **Add** money amounts.
Find the sum. $12,345 + $1,888 + $210 = $14,443

   1a. $27,458 + $5,292 $32,750   **1b.** $312.47 + $34.87 $347.34

2 **Multiply** money amounts by percents and whole numbers.
Find the product. 7.65% × $45,600 = $3,488.40
Find the product. 32 × $14.10 = $451.20

   2a. 0.8% × $1,245 $9.96   **2b.** 4.3% × $6,500 $279.50

   2c. 16 × $9.45 $151.20   **2d.** 52 × $269.34 $14,005.68

■ Cost of Full-Time Employees

The cost of full-time employees consists of the wages they are paid and the benefits they receive. Employees may consider only their wages to be income and benefits as only a non-cash incentive for working. Employers consider benefits to be costs, or expenses, because they actually pay the benefits.

Some of the benefits paid by employers are required to be paid by law. For example, employers must match employee payments of FICA taxes that include a 6.2% social security tax on annual wages up to $87,900 and a 1.45% Medicare tax on all wages.

In addition the Federal Unemployment Tax Act (FUTA) requires employers to pay a FUTA tax on the first $7,000 of earnings of each employee.

Lesson 10.3 Total Costs of Labor ■ **435**

Start Up

Have students read the Start Up. Ask them what alternatives an employer might have for lowering labor costs besides reducing benefit payments by keeping employees at a part-time level.

Ask students to contact an adult they know who works in a situation similar to the Start Up about their feelings regarding this practice and report back to the class when the Wrap Up is discussed.

Math Skill Builder

The addition and multiplication of money amounts by percents and whole numbers are skills used in this lesson.

Complete all exercises in Math Skill Builder 1–2.

■ Teach Goal 1

Ask students who work how they feel about paying FICA taxes. Remind them that employers are legally required to deduct FICA taxes from wages and that FICA taxes, unlike income taxes, are not eligible to be refunded at the end of the year based on one's level of income.

Point out that employers must match the employees' FICA contributions, thus making this tax, and others, a cost of hiring employees.

CONNECTION TO TECHNOLOGY

Inform students that one of the costs of employees is the continual training they need to improve their skills to enable them to do their job better. In traditional training programs, each employee received the same training even in areas in which they might already be proficient. To save time and money, many companies now use online training to supplement traditional classroom training. Employees use a computer to study only those portions of the program that relate to specific skills that they need to develop.

Work through Example 1 on the board with students doing the math at their desks.

Assign Check Your Understanding problems A and B for class work. Assist students who have difficulty solving the problems.

Review the Math Tip and explain that the calculations are rounded to the nearest cent because they are separate payments.

■ ONGOING ASSESSMENT

Review how to rewrite percents as decimals by having students state the rule (move decimal point two places to the left and drop the percent sign). Then have them write these percents as decimals: 112% **1.12**; 78.4% **0.784**; 7.54% **0.0754**; 0.85% **0.0085**.

Each state has an unemployment tax law, called the State Unemployment Tax Act, or SUTA. SUTA also levies taxes to be paid by the employer.

SUTA pays cash to workers who are temporarily unemployed. These cash payments are called unemployment compensation. FUTA taxes are primarily used to pay the cost of running the unemployment compensation program.

Other employee benefits commonly provided by employers include retirement plans, medical and related insurance, life insurance, vacation pay, holiday pay, and sick leave. Still other benefits may include a company car, tuition reimbursement, child care, paid parking, employee discounts, and legal services.

BUSINESS TIP

The effective FUTA tax rate is 6.2% − 5.4%, or 0.8%. This is because the federal government lets a firm deduct a maximum 5.4% credit if it pays its SUTA taxes on time, regardless of the SUTA tax rate.

EXAMPLE 1

The Todd Production Company pays Charlene Mitchell a salary of $47,000 a year. The benefits that Todd pays include a 7.65% FICA tax, an 0.8% FUTA tax and 4.5% SUTA tax on the first $7,000 of wages, medical insurance of $4,120 a year, and a retirement contribution of 5% of Charlene's salary. What was the total cost of the benefits the Todd Company provided to Charlene? What total amount did it cost the Todd Company to employ Charlene for the year?

MATH TIP

Round to the nearest cent the results of all tax and benefit calculations involving percents.

SOLUTION

Multiply the annual salary by the FICA and retirement percents.

7.65% × $47,000 = 0.0765 × $47,000 = $3,595.50   FICA taxes paid

5% × $47,000 = 0.05 × $47,000 = $2,350   retirement contribution

Multiply the first $7,000 of wages by the FUTA and SUTA percents.

0.8% × $7,000 = $56   FUTA tax paid

4.5% × $7,000 = $315   SUTA tax paid

Add benefits.

$3,595.50 + $2,350 + $56 + $315 + $4,120 = $10,436.50   total benefits

Add the annual salary and the total benefits.

$47,000 + $10,436.50 = $57,436.50   total cost of employment

■ **CHECK YOUR UNDERSTANDING**

A. Tek-Power pays its employees an average of $540 a week. It also provides these benefits at no cost to employees: medical insurance worth $73.07 a week, life insurance worth $2.80 a week, and pension plan contribution, 3% of wages. FICA taxes of 7.65% and unemployment taxes of 4.7% of wages are paid by Tek-Power. What is the average cost of the benefits of one employee for one week? $158.76

B. The total wages paid by Rizzo Restaurant Supply Company for the second week in January are $10,350. Total benefits paid to employees average 32% of wages. What was the total cost of labor for Rizzo for the week? $13,662

■ *CHECK YOUR UNDERSTANDING SOLUTIONS*

A. 0.03 × $540 = $16.20; 0.0765 × $540 = $41.31;
0.047 × $540 = $25.38; $73.07 + $2.80 +
$16.20 + $41.31 + $25.38 = $158.76

B. 0.32 × $10,350 = $3,312;
$10,350 + $3,312 = $13,662

Cost of Part-Time Employees

Part-time employees are those employees who work less than 40 hours a week. Part-time employees are often paid the same rate of pay as full-time employees, but they do not receive the same benefits. At the minimum, part-time employees receive the benefits required by law. Their employer may also provide a few additional benefits.

EXAMPLE 2

Quintin Napier, a college student, works 25 hours a week during evening hours at the help desk of the Renner Software Company. Renner pays Quintin $11.25 an hour and provides him with tuition reimbursement benefits of $500 a year. The Renner Company's benefits include the 7.65% FICA tax and total unemployment taxes of 4.2% on the first $7,000 of earnings. What total benefits does Renner provide? What is the total cost of Quintin's employment for 52 weeks?

SOLUTION

Multiply the weekly hours worked by the hourly wage and by 52 weeks.

$25 \times \$11.25 \times 52 = \$14,625$ annual earnings

Multiply the annual earnings by the FICA tax rate and the $7,000 of earnings by the unemployment tax rate

$7.65\% \times \$14,625 = \$1,118.81$ FICA tax

$4.2\% \times \$7,000 = 0.042 \times \$7,000 = \$294$ unemployment tax

Add the annual earnings, FICA and unemployment taxes, and the tuition reimbursement.

$\$14,625 + \$1,118.81 + \$294 + \$500 = \$16,537.81$ total cost of employment

■ CHECK YOUR UNDERSTANDING

C. A fast food restaurant pays Carrie Ernst $7.90 an hour and gives her a meal allowance of $3.10 a day. Taxes paid by the restaurant include a 7.65% FICA tax and 5.1% in unemployment taxes. What is the maximum amount the restaurant will spend for Carrie's benefits if she works seven hours a day, four days a week? $40.60

D. The Boot Fitter Shop filled a vacancy by hiring two part-time employees who each work 20 hours a week at the regular pay of $10.85 an hour. As a result, the shop will not have to pay medical benefits that average 14% of employee wages for full-time employees. For each 40-hour week, how much less will the Boot Fitter Shop spend by hiring the two part-time employees than it would have spent by hiring one full-time employee at the same rate? $60.76

Wrap Up

One of the methods employers use to cut costs is reducing the amount they spend on employee benefits. By hiring more employees to work 40 hours a week, the employer is likely to increase costs by $2,000 to $4,000 a year, per employee. While such a policy appears to be unfair to employees, the policy is legal.

Lesson 10.3 Total Costs of Labor ■ **437**

■ Teach Goal 2

Emphasize that FICA taxes are legally mandated even for part-time employees.

Note that part-time employees may complain that they receive no benefits. The truth is that they receive benefits, but they are not in a form (health plan, pension plan) that employees would like.

■ Apply Goal 2

Work Examples 2 at the board and have students do the calculations at their desks. Explain that companies often make small benefit payments (tuition reimbursement, loyalty pay for remaining with an employer, bonus for attendance) to part-time employees to provide them with an incentive to remain with the company.

Assign Check Your Understanding problems C and D for class work. Check student work at their desks to ensure they are solving the problems correctly.

Wrap Up

Review the Start Up. Ask students to report on any contacts they may have made with part-time employees who wish to become full-time employees.

Have student discuss whether a legal practice is a fair practice. Ask what they might do if they were an employer faced with the task of keeping employee costs low.

■ *CHECK YOUR UNDERSTANDING SOLUTIONS*

C. $4 \times 7 \times \$7.90 = \$221.20$;
$0.0765 \times \$221.20 = \$16.92$;
$0.051 \times \$221.20 = \$11.28$;
$(4 \times \$3.10) + \$16.92 + \$11.28 = \$40.60$

D. $2 \times 20 \times \$10.85 = \$434$; $0.14 \times \$434 = \$60.76$

437

COMMUNICATION

Use the Internet or do print media research to find how many people in the United States are working full time and part time in manufacturing, restaurants, and in retail stores. Plot your findings on a graph and write a paragraph summarizing any differences you find.

Remember a complete graph includes:

- A descriptive title
- Titles for each axis
- A reasonable scale for each axis
- A key or legend

EXERCISES

Find the sum.

1. $12,451 + $781 + $26.02 $13,258.02
2. $68,260 + $12,573 $80,833

Find the product to the nearest cent.

3. 2.06% × $762 $15.70
4. 3.98% × $1,071 $42.63
5. 29 × $14.43 $418.47
6. 52 × 23 × $8.92 $10,668.32

7. Eldon Schaff earns wages of $780 a week. His non-tax benefits include medical, dental, and vision insurance worth $4,110 a year; employer pension plan contribution of $2,250 a year; three weeks of vacation and holiday pay, and a paid annual physical exam worth $800. What total benefits does Eldon receive? $9,500

8. Erika Fogarty is allowed to contribute 6% of her annual pay of $73,200 to a retirement savings program. Her employer adds to the retirement program $1 for every $2 that Erika contributes. What is the employer's cost for this benefit? $2,196

9. Edgar Henneman earned $96,000 in wages last year. What was the cost to Edgar's employer of providing these legally required benefits: net FUTA tax of 0.8% on the first $7,000 of wages, SUTA tax of 7.6% of the first $9,500 of wages, social security tax of 6.2% on the first $87,900 of wages, and a Medicare tax of 1.45% on all wages? $7,619.80

The Lentag Company spent $3,750 per employee this year to provide a medical insurance benefit for its 1,100 employees. The insurance company notified Lentag that medical insurance costs would increase 12% next year. Lentag's management decides to keep the same medical coverage but will require employees to pay 15% of the total cost of the medical insurance increase.

10. What will be the new cost of medical insurance per employee? $4,200

11. What amount will each employee pay a year for medical insurance? $67.50

12. What total amount more will Lentag pay for the medical insurance benefit next year than it did this year for all employees? $420,750

438 ■ Chapter 10 Manage People and Inventory

SELECTED SOLUTIONS

8. 0.06 × $73,200 = $4,392; $4,392 ÷ 2 = $2,196
10. 0.12 × $3,750 = $450; $3,750 + $450 = $4,200
11. 0.15 × $450 = $67.50

14. 0.28 × $15.12 = $4.233, or $4.23;
$15.12 + $4.23 = $19.35 full time;
0.09 × $15.12 = $1.360, or $1.36;
$15.12 + $1.36 = $16.48 part time

13. A company employs 60 part-time workers and pays them $12.40 an hour for working an average of 30 hours in a 5-day week. To keep its employees, the company plans to raise the pay rate to $12.95 an hour. It will also give each employee a $4 a day parking allowance and free coffee or juice at an estimated cost of $0.90 a day per employee. What total amount more will it cost the company per week when these pay and benefit changes are made? $2,460

14. The Sure-Freeze Company pays its full and part-time employees the same hourly pay, an average rate of $15.12 an hour. The cost of benefits per full-time employee is 28% of hourly pay and 9% of hourly pay for part-time employees. To the nearest cent, what is the total labor cost per hour for full-time employees? For part-time employees? $19.35, $16.48

15. **DECISION MAKING**   You are the owner of a small company with six part-time employees who each work 36 hours a week. To improve staff morale you would like to have full-time employees even though the benefits would cost $2,000 a year per employee. To keep costs in line you would have to let one person go. The five employees would have to work 43 hours a week to get the same work done. What should you do?
See Enrich section for answer.
16. **CRITICAL THINKING**   To reduce labor costs, a company offers a retirement incentive for employees who are at least 59 years of age and have 30 years of service with the company. A 45-year old employee complains that this program favors older workers and is an example of age discrimination. Do you agree or disagree? Why?   See Enrich section for answer.

MIXED REVIEW

17. 862.7 − 149.34   713.36

18. Write 0.12 as a fraction. $\frac{3}{25}$

19. $\frac{3}{14} \div \frac{5}{7}$ $\frac{3}{10}$

20. 1,000 × 2.07   2,070

21. 10¢ ÷ 1,000   0.0001

22. 35 is what percent of 50?   70%

23. Find the number of days from July 9 to October 15.   98

24. Find the average: $129.43, $241.89, $851.13, $197.43 $354.97

25. Katrina Stovall needs a $60,000 mortgage loan to buy a home. Her bank gives her a 7%, 25-year mortgage. Use the Amortization Table in Chapter 6 to find Katrina's monthly payments. Then find the total interest she will pay on the loan over 25 years. $424.07, $67,221, Lesson 6.1

26. A school's office education club had these receipts from fundraisers: flower sales, $2,500; candy sales, $1,800; notepads, $420. Find the percent that notepad sales were of total sales, to the nearest percent. Then find the number of degrees on a circle graph the notepad sector would take, to the nearest degree.
9%, 32°, Lesson 8.4
27. Chuck Boyce signed a two-year cell phone lease with Vega NationWide. He estimates he will use 850 minutes of airtime a month. Using the Wireless Phone Service Plans Table in Chapter 9, find the estimated cost of the lease over two years, including the activation fee. $1,889.76, Lesson 9.5

Lesson 10.3 Total Costs of Labor ■ **439**

439

GOALS
- Calculate inventory balances
- Calculate the stock reorder point

Start Up

Assume you are responsible for buying food and household items for your home. Some items, such as fresh fruit, will be used quickly. Other items, such as a bottle of furniture wax, are likely to be used over a long period of time. What method would you use to make sure you did not run short of any items needed to feed a family or use around the home?

Math Skill Builder

Review these math skills and solve the exercises that follow.

1 **Subtract** whole numbers.
Find the remainder. $592 - 187 = 405$

   1a. $83 - 29$ 54   **1b.** $118 - 47$ 71   **1c.** $1,276 - 345$ 931

2 **Divide** whole numbers by whole numbers.
Find the quotient. $6,270 \div 22 = 285$

   2a. $527 \div 31$ 17   **2b.** $4,290 \div 30$ 143   **2c.** $5,382 \div 6$ 897

3 **Multiply** whole numbers by whole numbers.
Find the product. $120 \times 7 = 840$

   3a. 230×13 2,990   **3b.** 520×3 1,560   **3c.** 55×21 1,155

■ Inventory Records

All businesses keep a record of the **stock** they have on hand. The stock on hand may be merchandise that is resold to others or a part that will be used in the making of a product. Stock is often referred to as *inventory*.

Businesses are able to keep track of stock on hand by using a stock record form. A **stock record** shows how much of an item has been received, issued, and how much remains. A sample stock record is shown.

Stock Record			
Item: Digital Camera Stock No. DC-106		Reorder Point: 20 Unit: Each	
Date	Quantity Received	Quantity Issued	Balance
March 1			53
March 2		31	22
March 4		18	4
March 6	51		55
March 10		36	19

CONNECTION TO OCCUPATIONS

Some companies hire stock records clerks to keep track of inventory. Stock records clerks often use handheld computers that may have a wand or built-in device to scan a product's bar code. The quantity of the product on hand is then counted and entered into the computer via a keyboard. The stock number may also be entered through the keyboard. When finished, the clerk transfers the data from the handheld computer to a larger computer system. Smaller companies may keep paper records of inventory similar to that shown in this lesson.

The Togan Company is a wholesaler and sells only to retail stores. It does not sell to the general public. The sample stock record shows the number of digital cameras the Togan Company received from a manufacturer and the number of digital cameras it issued, or sold, to retailers. The unit for digital cameras is "each." This means that each camera is sold individually.

In the sample stock record, a balance was found after each transaction was entered in the stock record. The system of keeping a running balance of stock on hand is called **perpetual inventory**. The perpetual inventory system allows you to maintain an up-to-date record of stock on hand. The method used to find stock balances is similar to the one you used to find check register balances.

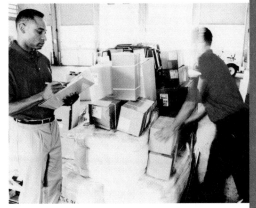

As stock arrives from suppliers, it is inspected, counted, and stored by receiving department employees. Records of stock issued may include sales slips or other records that show the quantity and description of items issued from stock.

EXAMPLE 1

Refer to the sample stock record given. If 36 more digital cameras were received on March 15 and 17 more cameras were issued on March 17, what was the balance in the stock record on March 15 and March 17?

SOLUTION
Add quantity received on March 15 to the stock balance.

$19 + 36 = 55$ stock balance on March 15

Subtract the quantity issued on March 17 from the balance on March 15.

$55 - 17 = 38$ stock balance on March 17

■ CHECK YOUR UNDERSTANDING

A. A wholesaler's stock record for garage doors showed a balance of 38 doors on June 5. The numbers of garage doors issued in June were: June 8, 6; June 14, 28; June 30, 8. Eighteen garage doors were received on June 16. What was the stock record balance on June 30?   14

B. A manufacturer showed a bicycle tire's stock record balance to be 1,389 on April 1. These tire sales were made: April 12, 417 tires; April 26, 874 tires. 900 more bicycle tires were produced on April 29 and added to stock. What were the balances in the stock record after each transaction was recorded?   April 12, 972; April 26, 98; April 29, 998

■ Reorder Point

When the stock of an item runs low, it must be reordered. On the Sample Stock Record the reorder point is 20 units. The **reorder point** is the minimum stock level at which an order must be placed. When the balance on the stock record form is equal to or is less than 20 digital cameras, stock must be reordered.

Lesson 10.4 Tracking and Reordering Inventory ■ **441**

■ **Apply Goal 1**

Work through Example 1 at the board while students complete the math at their desks.

Remind students that the balance found after each transaction is called a running balance.

Assign Check Your Understanding problems A and B for class work. Move about the classroom and review student work for any difficulties they may be having.

■ **ONGOING ASSESSMENT**
Have students find the running balance of garage doors for each date and transaction listed in Check Your Understanding A. **June 5, 38; June 8, 32; June 14, 4; June 16, 22; June 30, 14**.

■ **Teach Goal 2**

Inform students that most companies know from experience what the minimum quantity of stock on hand ought to be before more stock is ordered.

Indicate that all the elements of calculating the reorder point may change within a year. The possibility of bad road conditions due to snow may extend the lead-time and increase the amount of safety stock carried. Even lead-time may be stretched if the supplier has labor problems or if goods shipped from another country are delayed because of closer scrutiny at borders.

■ *CHECK YOUR UNDERSTANDING SOLUTIONS*

A. $38 + 18 = 56$; $6 + 28 + 8 = 42$; $56 - 42 = 14$ **B.** $1,389 - 417 = 972$, April 12; $972 - 874 = 98$, April 26; $98 + 900 = 998$, April 29

Work through Example 2 at the board with students completing the math at their desks.

Assign Check Your Understanding problems C and D to be done in class. Check student work at their desks.

Wrap **Up**

Review the Start Up. Ask students to rate the methods described in terms of how practical each method might be to implement and maintain.

Companies designate a person, usually called a buyer, to order stock. A document that lists the items to be ordered and their prices is sent to the supplier. The document is called a purchase order.

For items in regular demand, most companies know the average number of units they sell or use per day. This average number is called *daily usage*. Companies also know the *lead time*, or the average number of days it will take for ordered stock to arrive. It is possible that an order may be late in arriving. To reduce the possibility of having no stock left at all because of delays, most companies will order additional stock, called *safety stock*.

The reorder point formula shows how the daily usage, lead time, and safety stock are related:

Reorder Point = (Daily Usage × Lead Time) + Safety Stock

> **BUSINESS TIP**
>
> By calculating a realistic reorder point, companies hope to avoid a *stockout* condition. This happens when there is no inventory left to fill orders or meet production needs.

EXAMPLE 2

The Appland Company, a wholesaler, sells 5,280 dishwashers each month in 22 working days. A supplier's lead time for delivery of dishwashers is 5 working days from the time an order is received. Appland wants to keep a safety stock of 50 dishwashers. What is Appland's reorder point for dishwashers?

SOLUTION
Divide the number of dishwashers sold by the number of working days.

$5{,}280 \div 22 = 240$ daily usage (average number of dishwashers sold per day)

Multiply daily usage by the lead-time. Then add the safety stock quantity.

$(240 \times 5) + 50 = 1{,}200 + 50 = 1{,}250$ reorder point

■ CHECK YOUR UNDERSTANDING

C. The Floor Care Place sells 90 floor polishers every 30 days. It takes 10 days' lead time to replace floor polisher stock. Safety stock is 2 polishers. What is the reorder point?   32

D. A lamp manufacturer uses 8,280 of an electrical component every 45 days. The lead time for the component is 13 days. Safety stock is three days' usage. What is the reorder point?   2,944

Wrap **Up**

A number of methods may be used. The simplest is to write down an item on a shopping list when you first notice that it completely used or soon will be. You could also use your computer and print a list of all the essential food and household items and check off needed items.

Stores also have shopping lists that you could bring home. You could also buy two of everything you need and put an item on your list when you reach one item left. In any case, all the methods suggested require that you make a written record of your needs.

■ *CHECK YOUR UNDERSTANDING SOLUTIONS*

C. $90 \div 30 = 3$; $(3 \times 10) + 2 = 30 + 2 = 32$

D. $8{,}280 \div 45 = 184$; $(184 \times 13) + (184 \times 3) =$
$2{,}392 + 552 = 2{,}944$

TEAM MEETING

Form a small team and interview the manager of a store. Select three different products the store sells and ask how the reorder point is calculated for each product.

Also ask if the store ever runs out of stock for a particular item and what the reasons might be for this happening. Present your findings to the class.

Techniques of a good interview you should use include the following.

- Be prepared with questions before you arrive.
- Be prepared with paper and pencil. Before you go to the interview, practice writing without looking at your paper.
- Make frequent eye contact with the person being interviewed.
- Follow up the interview with a thank you note or phone call.
- Offer to share your written summary with the person you interviewed.

TEAM MEETING

Help students draft the interview questions they will ask. Have them practice asking the questions in a conversational tone instead of simply reading the questions aloud.

Also ask students to draft a thank you note. Edit the note and have students make corrections before the note is sent.

Depending on the number of teams, have all or some of the teams report their findings.

EXERCISES

Find the difference.

1. $1,805 - 687$ 1,118
2. $58 - 25$ 33

Find the product or quotient.

3. 39×7 273
4. 31×18 558
5. $6,030 \div 5$ 1,206
6. $810 \div 30$ 27

7. A truck supply store had 18 bed liners in stock on February 1. These number of bed liners were sold in four weeks: Week 1, 11; Week 2, 6; Week 3, 9; Week 4, 16. A shipment of 34 bed liners was received on February 8. What was the stock record balance of bed liners at the close of business on February 28?   10

A manufacturer buys and stores engines to be used in assembling lawn mowers. On Monday, March 6, 800 engines were in stock at the start of the day. From March 6–10, these quantities of engines were taken from storage to a production line: March 6, 315; March 7, 308; March 8, 318; March 9, 298; March 10, 285. These numbers of engines arrived from a supplier: March 7, 750; March 10, 750. How many engines were on hand at the end of the day:

8. on Wednesday?   609
9. on Friday?   776

10. An auto parts store sells 10,350 bottles of windshield washer fluid during the first 90 days of winter. The store does not let stock of washer fluid get below 50 bottles during this period. New stock can be obtained within two days of ordering. What is the reorder point?   280

Lesson 10.4 Tracking and Reordering Inventory ▪ **443**

Assign

Assignment: Exercises 1–13, 16–28. Students are to begin with the basic arithmetic problems that review the underlying arithmetic presented in the lesson.

Assess

Call on students to write their solutions to the exercises on the board. Point out that in Exercises 12–13, the supermarket and supplier use different units, bags vs. cases. Thus, the supermarket must buy a case of 12 bags of flour instead of the 8 bags needed to replenish stock.

SELECTED SOLUTIONS

8. $800 + 750 - 315 - 308 - 318 = 609$ on Wednesday
9. $609 - 298 + 750 - 285 = 776$ on Friday
11. $16,800 \div 6 = 2,800$; $(2,800 \times 3) + (2,800 \times 8) = 8,400 + 22,400 = 30,800$
12. $120 \div 30 = 4$; $4 \times 2 = 8$ bags
13. Minimum order is 12 bags

STUDENT WORKBOOK Some students may require help with calculating inventory balances. If so, work Exercise 1 with them. Assign Exercise 2 for independent work.

Work Exercise 4 with students who need help in calculating the stock reorder point. Assign Exercise 5 for individual solution.

Enrich

Assign Exercise 15, Critical Thinking. Discuss student rankings and the reasons for the rankings. If not mentioned previously, have students consider the impact on lead time for items that are commodities (motor oil) vs. custom order (sofa), and those that might be imported from another country (digital cameras) vs. those that might be produced in the U. S. (refrigerators).

Close

Assign Exercise 14, Critical Thinking. Be sure that the discussion reinforces the benefits of objective record keeping and reordering of stock and how records may show how successful a business is to potential buyers should the business be sold.

11. A manufacturer uses 16,800 fasteners in six days. Safety stock is 8 days' usage. Fasteners usually arrive within three days of ordering. What is the reorder point for fasteners? 30,800

A supermarket carries four brands of general-purpose flour. It sells 120 bags of Winnie's unbleached flour every 30 days. More bags of Winnie's flour can be ordered and received in two days but only in a cases of 12 bags. The supermarket carries no safety stock of Winnie's flour.

12. What is the reorder point for Winnie's flour? 8 bags

13. How many bags must be ordered once the reorder point is reached? 12

14. **CRITICAL THINKING** Lorna Vogt owns a small store and believes that she doesn't need any written perpetual inventory system. She claims she has memorized all the inventory records and can walk down each aisle and know what to order. Should Lorna keep the inventory and ordering system she claims to be working or change to another system? See Close section for answer.

15. **CRITICAL THINKING** Rank these products sold by retailers according to the lead time required to obtain them from a supplier: digital camera, motor oil, sofa, refrigerator. Rank the product with the shortest lead time as "1." Give reasons for your rankings. See Enrich section for answer.

MIXED REVIEW

16. Rewrite 1.8 as a percent. 180%   17. 35×10¢ $3.50

18. Rewrite $\frac{5}{8}$ as a decimal. 0.625   19. $8 \times 2\frac{1}{4}$ 18

20. Find the quotient to the nearest tenth: $2,045 \div 9$ 227.2

21. What number is $1\frac{1}{2}$ of $218.96? $328.44

A box of chocolate candies contains 5 with pecans and 7 without any nuts in them. If you picked a candy from the box without looking, what is the probability you would pick a: Lesson 8.2

22. candy with pecans? $\frac{5}{12}$ 23. candy without pecans? $\frac{7}{12}$

24. candy with walnuts? 0   25. chocolate candy? 1

26. Ila Behrle bought a car for $11,200. She drove the car 12,000 miles last year. Her car expenses for the year were insurance, $786; gas and oil, $960; repairs, $125; license plates, $72; depreciation, 14%; loss of interest on original investment, $442. What was Ila's operating cost per mile of owning this car, to the nearest cent? $0.33, Lesson 6.8

27. Nettie Tindle bought 400 shares of Exoway stock at $54.37. Her broker charged a commission of $186. What was the total cost of the stock purchase? $21,934, Lesson 7.6

28. Brightman Inc. purchased a 50-workstation license for DollarSafe financial software for $4,200. In a survey of software on all its workstations, a software publisher's association audit found that DollarSafe was installed on 86 computers. The penalty is $125 for each unlicensed installation of DollarSafe. What total amount did Brightman Inc. pay to use DollarSafe software? $8,700, Lesson 9.2

DIFFERENT LEARNING STYLES Visual Learners

Some learners understand stock reorder point better by a visual presentation. Use a calendar and draw a border around each working day (Mon.–Fri.) of the month. Write 40 as the daily usage in each workday space. Lead-time for delivery of more stock from a supplier is 4 business days. Safety stock is 2 days of usage. Have students assume that more stock is ordered on the first Monday. Count the number of units used from Tuesday to Friday, the lead-time period, and the following Monday and Tuesday for safety stock. The sum is the reorder point.

10.5 Inventory Valuation

GOALS

- Calculate inventory value on FIFO basis
- Calculate inventory value on LIFO basis
- Calculate inventory value on weighted average basis

Start Up

Suppose you found a package of saw blades with a price of $5.95 on them. You know the current price of similar blades is about $17. If you were asked to state the value of the blades you found, what would you say and why?

Math Skill Builder

Review these math skills and solve the exercises that follow.

1 **Add** whole numbers and money amounts.
Find the sum. $2,450 + $886 = $3,336

   1a. $763 + $827 $1,590   **1b.** 490 + 53   543   **1c.** 215 + 85   300

2 **Multiply** money amounts by whole numbers.
Find the product. 180 × $18 = $3,240

   2a. 218 × $7.50 $1,635   **2b.** 187 × $12.36 $2,311.32

3 **Divide** money amounts by whole numbers.
Find the quotient, to the nearest cent. $18,300 ÷ 650 = $28.15

   3a. $1,280 ÷ 58 $22.07   **3b.** $46,370 ÷ 1,570 $29.54

■ First In, First Out

Companies usually calculate the value of their inventory at a certain time, such as the end of a quarter or end of a year. The inventory's value is often needed for financial records and reports. An inventory's value may also be the basis for calculating the amount of personal property tax due to a city or state. The exact value of inventory is found by multiplying the quantity of items in stock by their cost.

There are several methods of finding the value of the ending inventory. Three widely used methods are: First In, First Out; Last In, First Out; and weighted average.

The First In, First Out (FIFO) method assumes that goods purchased first are sold or used first and the value of inventory is based on the cost of the most recently purchased items. The FIFO method is widely used because the value of the inventory using FIFO is close to the cost of replacing the inventory.

Lesson 10.5 Inventory Valuation ■ **445**

Work through Example 1 with students examining the inventory record in the textbook or a transparency of the record. Have students do the math at their desks.

Assign Check Your Understanding problems A and B for class work. When students complete their work, demonstrate the solutions to both problems.

■ **ONGOING ASSESSMENT**
For a beginning inventory of 64 units, have students calculate the ending inventory in units (77) where the plus marks indicate stock received and the minus marks indicate stock issued: +85, −21, −45, −9 + 90, −87.

■ **STUDENT PORTFOLIO**
Students might consider including in their portfolio the FIFO problems they solved.

ZPM Business Products			
Stock Item: Paper Shredders			Stock No. PS108
Inventory Period: January 1, 20— to March 31, 20—			
	Units	**Unit Cost**	**Total Value**
Beginning Inventory			
January 1	40	20.00	$800
Purchases			
January 13	100	21.00	2,100
February 7	80	22.00	1,760
March 1	160	22.50	3,600
March 20	120	24.00	2,880
Total	500		$11,140
Ending Inventory			
March 31	160		???

The illustration above shows an inventory record for paper shredders. In the FIFO method, the 40 shredders in the beginning inventory would be issued first to fill orders. The 100 units from the January 13 order would be issued next, and so on. Since the units bought first are issued first, the 160 units in the ending inventory must be part of the units purchased last.

EXAMPLE 1

Use the FIFO method to find the value of the ending inventory of paper shredders shown in the illustration above.

SOLUTION
The number of units in the ending inventory: 160 Units

Starting with the last purchase, find the quantities and the cost of the 160 units. Multiply the units by their unit cost and add their products.

March 20 = 120 units at $24	= $2,880
March 1 = 40 units at $22.50	= 900
160 units	$3,780 value of ending inventory

Using the FIFO method, the value of 160 shredders is $3,780.

■ **CHECK YOUR UNDERSTANDING**

These units were purchased by the OPC Company in February.

2-3 140 units @ $36.50   2-14 170 units @ $37.00   2-26 110 units @ $36.00

2-7 110 units @ $38.00   2-18 60 units @ $37.25

A. Assume the beginning inventory was 112 units and the ending inventory is 142 units. Find the ending inventory's value on the FIFO basis. $5,152

B. Now assume the beginning inventory was 234 units and the ending inventory is 196 units. Find the ending inventory's value on the FIFO basis. $7,157

446 ■ **Chapter 10 Manage People and Inventory**

> **BUSINESS TIP**
>
> The unit cost of an item often changes. The item may be bought from different suppliers who have different prices. Also, a discount may be given. The way in which goods are shipped also affect unit costs.

■ **CHECK YOUR UNDERSTANDING SOLUTIONS**

A. (from 2–26), 110 × $36 = $3,960; 142 − 110 = 32; (from 2–18), 32 × $37.25 = $1,192; $3,960 + $1,192 = $5,152

B. (from 2–26), 110 × $36 = $3,960; 196 − 110 = 86; (from 2–18), 60 × $37.25 = $2,235; 86 − 60 = 26; (from 2–14), 26 × $37 = $962; $3,960 + $2,235 + $962 = $7,157

Last In, First Out

The Last In, First Out (LIFO) method assumes that goods purchased last are issued first. The value of the ending inventory is based on the cost of goods purchased first. Some companies use LIFO especially when prices are rising. In that case, LIFO results in the lowest value for inventory and that leads to a lower net income for the company. The company generally pays less in income taxes by using LIFO.

Look back at the illustration at the top of the previous page. Using the LIFO method, the last shredders purchased, which are the 120 units bought on March 20, would be the first to be issued. The 160 units bought on March 1 would be issued next, and so on. Since the units bought last are issued first, the 160 units in the ending inventory must be made up of the units in the beginning inventory and the units purchased in January and February.

BUSINESS TIP

The LIFO method is used only to find the value of the ending inventory. This does not mean that the newest stock is sold first. In fact, where possible companies rotate stock, and use the oldest stock first in the same way that the newest canned goods are moved to the back of the shelf in a supermarket.

EXAMPLE 2

Use the LIFO method to find the value of the ending inventory of paper shredders shown in the illustration at the top of the previous page.

SOLUTION
The number of units in the ending inventory: 160 Units

Starting with the beginning inventory and the first purchases, find the quantities and the costs of 160 units. Multiply the units by their costs and add the products.

January 1 =	40 units at $20 =	$ 800
January 13 =	100 units at $21 =	2,100
February 7 =	20 units at $22 =	440
	160 units	$3,340 value of ending inventory

Under the LIFO method, the value of 160 shredders is $3,340.

■ CHECK YOUR UNDERSTANDING

The Davis Alam Company purchased smoke detectors in November as follows.

11-5   32 units @ $14.60

11-11   40 units @ $14.85

11-18   20 units @ $14.90

11-25   25 units @ $15.10

C. The beginning inventory was 12 units valued at $14.20 per unit. The ending inventory is 32 units. Find the ending inventory's value on the LIFO basis. $462.40

D. The beginning inventory was 6 units valued at $14.55 per unit. Use the LIFO basis to find the value of the ending inventory of 49 units.
$717.85

Lesson 10.5 Inventory Valuation ■ 447

■ Teach Goal 2

Use the same transparency and procedure you used in Teach Goal 1, but start issuing stock from the last units purchased.

Assume that 340 units were shipped on March 22. The shipped units were the 120 March 20 units, the 160 March 1 units, and 60 of the February 7 units.

The remaining units are 40 in the beginning inventory, 100 from January 13, and 20 from February 7.

■ Apply Goal 2

Work Example 2 using the transparency of the inventory record and having students complete the math at their desks.

Assign Check Your Understanding problems C and D for class work and observe student work at their desks. When students are finished solving the problems, demonstrate the solution on the board.

■ *CHECK YOUR UNDERSTANDING SOLUTIONS*

C. (from 11-1), 12 × $14.20 = $170.40; 32 − 12 = 20; (from 11-5), 20 × $14.60 = $292; $170.40 + $292 = $462.40

D. (from 11-1), 6 × $14.55 = $87.30; 49 − 6 = 43; (from 11-5), 32 × $14.60 = $467.20; 43 − 32 = 11; (from 11-11), 11 × $14.85 = $163.35; $87.30 + $467.20 + $163.35 = $717.85

Relate the finding of an average unit cost using the weighted average method to the finding of the mean of a frequency distribution on page 348 in Lesson 8.1.

■ **Teach Goal 3**

Relate the finding of an average unit cost using the weighted average method to the finding of the mean of a frequency distribution on page 348 in Lesson 8.1.

■ **Apply Goal 3**

Work Example 3 at the board. Have students make calculations at their desks.

Assign Check Your Understanding problems E and F for class work. Move about the classroom and observe student work to identify difficulties they have.

■ Weighted Average

In the **weighted average** method, the ending inventory is valued at the average cost of the beginning inventory plus the cost of all purchases during the time period.

The weighted average method is useful when the cost of stock varies a lot and frequently. In that case, the weighted average method may represent the cost of inventory better than some other methods.

EXAMPLE 3

Use the weighted average method to find the value of ending inventory of ZPM Business Products paper shredders.

SOLUTION

Multiply the units in the beginning inventory and those purchased during the quarter by their unit cost. Add the products. Also add the number of units.

$$40 \times \$20.00 = \$\ \ \ 800$$
$$100 \times \$21.00 = \$\ 2,100$$
$$80 \times \$22.00 = \$\ 1,760$$
$$160 \times \$22.50 = \$\ 3,600$$
$$\underline{120} \times \$24.00 = \underline{\$\ 2,880}$$
$$500 \qquad\qquad \$11,140$$

Total units = 500; Total value of 500 units = $11,140

Divide the total value by the total units.

$11,140 ÷ 500 = $22.28   average unit cost

Multiply the ending inventory by the average unit cost.

$22.28 × 160 = $3,564.80   value of ending inventory

Using the weighted average method, the value of the ending inventory of 160 shredders is $3,564.80.

■ CHECK YOUR UNDERSTANDING

The July purchases of tractor tires by the Holwith Manufacturing Company follow. Use these data for Problems E and F. For both problems, use the weighted average method to find the unit cost of the beginning inventory and July's purchases, to the nearest dollar.

7-1   312 units @ $208   7-18 940 units @ $199

7-10 786 units @ $202   7-29 515 units @ $205

E. The beginning inventory of 607 tires was valued at $201 per tire. What is the weighted average unit cost of the beginning inventory and July purchases, to the nearest dollar? What is the value of the ending inventory of 308 units?
$202; $62,216

F. Using the weighted average method, find the unit cost of the beginning inventory of 416 units valued at $205 per tire and the July purchases, rounded to the nearest dollar. Also find the value of the 702 units in the ending inventory. $203; $142,506

■ *CHECK YOUR UNDERSTANDING SOLUTIONS*

E. 607 × $201 = $122,007; 312 × $208 = $64,896;
786 × $202 = $158,772; 940 × $199 = $187,060;
515 × $205 = $105,575; $122,007 + $64,896 +
$158,772 + $187,060 + $105,575 = $638,310;
607 + 312 + 786 + 940 + 515 = 3,160;
$638,310 ÷ 3,160 = $201.99 or $202;

308 × $202 = $62,216

F. 416 × $205 = $85,280; $85,280 + July purchases
from E = $601,583;
416 + sum of July unit purchases = 2,969;
$601,583 ÷ 2,969 = $202.62 or $203;
702 × $203 = $142,506

Assuming the old saw blades were not used, their value to you is probably slightly less than their replacement cost of $17. They would have a lower value if they were sold to someone else because they would be thought of as being old blades. They may also be worth less than new blades because of design changes that make the new blades better than the old blades.

COMMUNICATION

Another way of assigning a value to the ending inventory is to use the *specific identification method.* Refer to a college accounting textbook or do an Internet search to find the information about this method. Keywords for your search include inventory and valuation and method.

Specifically, find how unit costs are assigned in the specific identification method, the types of goods the method is best used for, and how it compares with the three methods you studied in this lesson. Prepare a short written report on your findings.

EXERCISES

Find the sum.

1. 564 + 183   747

2. $8,016 + $2,917 $10,933

Find the product or quotient to the nearest cent.

3. 97 × $18.20 $11,765.40

4. $168,000 ÷ 424 $396.23

The Zonex Plumbing and Supply Company purchased these quantities of water heaters from April 1 to June 30: April 28, 41 @ $146; May 19, 53 @ $139; June 23, 21 @ $149. The April 1 beginning inventory of 27 units was valued at $141 each. Find the value of the ending inventory of 35 water heaters:

5. using the FIFO method $5,075

6. using the LIFO method $4,975

7. using the weighted average method, to the nearest cent $5,000.80

Jessup's Trailer Sales purchased utility trailers from a manufacturer at these quantities and unit costs over a two-month period: April 4, 20 at $376; May 2, 34 at $340; May 29, 18 at $381. The beginning inventory of 9 utility trailers had a total value of $3,159. Find the value of the 31 utility trailers in the May 31 ending inventory:

8. using the FIFO method $11,278

9. using the LIFO method $11,359

10. using the weighted average method (round the unit cost of the beginning inventory and purchases to the nearest dollar.) $11,129

Lesson 10.5 Inventory Valuation ■ **449**

SELECTED SOLUTIONS

5. (from 6–23), 21 × $149 = $3,129;
35 − 21 = 14, (from 5–19), 14 × $139 = $1,946;
$3,129 + $1,946 = $5,075

6. (from 4–1), 27 × $141 = $3,807; 35 − 27 = 8;
(from 4–28), 8 × $146 = $1,168;

$3,807 + $1,168 = $4,975

7. 27 × $141 = $3,807; 41 × $146 = $5,986;
53 × $139 = $7,367; 21 × $149 = $3,129; sum of costs = $20,289; sum of units = 142; $20,289 ÷ 142 = $142.88; 35 × 142.88 = $5,000.80

Assess

Collect student work and check the procedures used to find inventory values in Exercises 5–10. Make a list of the errors students made in solving the problems.

Reteach

Distribute student work on assigned exercises. Demonstrate the correct solution to Exercises 5–7 and point out the sources of the errors detected when assessing student work. Have students rework Exercises 5–7 as needed so they have an accurate copy from which to study for tests.

STUDENT WORKBOOK Work Exercises 1–3 with students who need help with calculating the value of an ending inventory using FIFO, LIFO, and weighted average methods. Assign Exercises 4–6 for independent work.

Enrich

Assign Exercise 11, Critical Thinking. Remind students to consider goods where one unit is not easily distinguishable from another, if at all. Examples of such goods might be coal, milk collected from various dairy farms, wheat, and crude oil.

Close

Ask students to explain which inventory units are used to value the ending inventory in FIFO and LIFO, and why. Also ask why it is necessary to calculate the value of all the units in stock during a certain period when using the weighted average method.

11. **CRITICAL THINKING** The weighted average method of valuing inventory is often used to find the value of a product such as gasoline that is mixed together and whose costs cannot be individually identified. What other products would be suited for being valued by the weighted average method?

INTEGRATING YOUR KNOWLEDGE A wholesaler had an inventory of 850 fishing rods valued at $49,946 on May 1. Shipments of fishing rods received from a manufacturer were: May 15, 2,300 rods at $52.50; June 12, 3,400 rods at $47.75. During May and June 6,100 rods were issued from stock and shipped to retailers. There were no other transactions in May and June. See Enrich section for answer.

12. What was the wholesaler's ending inventory of fishing rods on June 30? 450

13. What was the value of the fishing rod inventory on June 30 using the LIFO method? $26,442

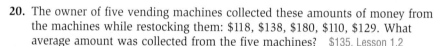

MIXED REVIEW

14. Find the quotient, to the nearest tenth: $15.015 \div 0.7$ 21.5

15. What number is 30% more than $81.19? $105.55

16. $9,184 - 4,079$ 5,105   17. $\frac{2}{3} \times \frac{5}{6}$ $\frac{5}{9}$

18. $4\frac{1}{3} - 1\frac{2}{3}$ $2\frac{2}{3}$ 19. Find 15% of $17.80. $2.67

20. The owner of five vending machines collected these amounts of money from the machines while restocking them: $118, $138, $180, $110, $129. What average amount was collected from the five machines? $135, Lesson 1.2

21. The Carlisle family borrowed $2,000 on a one-year simple interest installment loan at 18%. The monthly payments were $183.48. For the first monthly payment, find the amount of interest, amount applied to the principal, and the new balance. $30, $153.48, $1,846.52, Lesson 4.4

22. The number of miles a rental limousine was driven over a 14-day period is: 225, 260, 105, 182, 176, 238, 395, 320, 256, 287, 316, 290, 238, and 310. Find the range of miles driven and the average number of miles driven a day as measured by the mean, median, and mode. 290, 257, 258, 238, Lesson 8.1

23. A hospital has a network of 150 computers and 600 computer users. The hospital wants to provide one computer support staff member for every 120 users. The average annual wage paid a computer support staff member is $48,600. What will be the annual cost of providing support service to the hospital's computer users? What is the average annual cost per user? $243,000, $405, Lesson 9.3

CONNECTION TO ACCOUNTING

Inform students that a company may select FIFO, LIFO, weighted average, or specific identification to value inventory. However, companies must use the methods consistently so that financial reports may be compared from year-to-year. A business may change its method, but only after getting permission from the IRS. Changing methods frequently is discouraged.

10.6 Ordering and Carrying Inventory

GOALS
- Find the ordering costs of inventory
- Find the carrying costs of inventory

Start Up

On five days a week you drive to a store three miles away to do 15 minutes of grocery shopping on each trip. What factors should you consider to determine what the cost is of each shopping trip?

Math Skill Builder

Review these math skills and solve the exercises that follow.

① **Multiply** dollar amounts by whole numbers.
Find the product. $8 \times \$35.50 = \$284$

   1a. $52 \times \$5,600$ $291,200$

   1b. $12 \times \$3,765$ $45,180$

② **Find a percent** of a number.
Find the product. $12\% \times \$56,000 = \$6,720$

   2a. $6\% \times \$156,000$ $\$9,360$ **2b.** $8.5\% \times \$236,800$ $\$20,128$

③ **Divide** money amounts by whole numbers.
Find the quotient, to the nearest cent. $\$268,000 \div 33,000 = \$8.12$

   3a. $\$1,458,290 \div 980,000$ $\$1.49$ **3b.** $\$180,304 \div 16,000$ $\$11.27$

■ Ordering Costs

The **ordering costs** of inventory include the expenses connected with creating and sending a purchase order to a supplier and handling stock.

Costs of creating purchase orders include the cost of personnel in the purchasing department, office costs, and overhead costs. Office costs include the costs of forms, envelopes, telephones, faxes, copiers, and computers. Overhead costs include such items as heat, power, light, and maintenance.

The costs of handling stock include unloading and checking stock shipments and placing stock in storage areas. Handling costs are usually stated as a cost per hour. Office costs and overhead costs may be stated as a percentage of total office costs or total overhead costs.

Lesson 10.6 Ordering and Carrying Inventory ■ 451

■ **Apply Goal 1**

Work through Example 1 on the board with students completing the math at their desks. Label all calculations done on the board and remind students to label theirs as well.

Assign Check Your Understanding problems A and B for completion in class. Move about the classroom to monitor the work of students at their desks.

■ **ONGOING ASSESSMENT**

Ask students to close their books and give examples of these purchasing cost elements: personnel, office costs, overhead, and handling costs.

■ **Teach Goal 2**

Ask students to determine which costs a retailer more to keep: a 500-unit order of a popular game priced at $45 that sells within a day of delivery or 10 dozen tank tops that sell for $11 and take all summer to sell. Then ask students to explain their answers.

Point the ensuing discussion to include the typical carrying costs listed in the textbook.

Many organizations calculate ordering costs as a cost per purchase order. The average ordering cost does not include the value of the items bought. So, it costs the same to order a box of printer paper worth $36 as it does to order a $16,000 computer workstation.

The cost per order increases if specifications have to be written, bids have to be compared, products have to be tested before purchase, or if the product purchased has special handling or storage requirements.

EXAMPLE 1

The Linkman Company issues 500 purchase orders a month. The company estimated these monthly costs of issuing purchase orders: 60% of the company's office personnel costs of $4,600; $150 an hour for 12 hours for handling incoming stock; 10% of overhead costs of $1,400. What is the average monthly cost of issuing a purchase order?

SOLUTION

Multiply the monthly cost for each item by the percent rate or the number of hours.

$60\% \times \$4,600 = 0.6 \times \$4,600 = \$2,760$ cost of office personnel

$12 \times \$150 = \$1,800$ cost of handling incoming stock

$10\% \times \$1,400 = 0.1 \times \$1,400 = \$140$ overhead costs

$\$2,760 + \$1,800 + \$140 = \$4,700$ total monthly cost of purchasing

Divide the monthly purchase cost by the number of purchase orders issued.

$\$4,700 \div 500 = \$9.40$ average cost of issuing purchase orders

■ CHECK YOUR UNDERSTANDING

A. A retail chain of drugstores has two purchasing agents and one assistant who work full time on stock orders. Their annual wages total $128,100. These employees process 15,000 orders a year. Of the total warehouse cost of $250,000 a year, 60% is charged to ordering. The total office costs are $54,000 a year, 35% of which is allocated to ordering. What is the average cost of each stock order? $19.80

B. The ExaSol Company estimates the basic cost of processing any purchase order to be $12 per order. Each year 125 special orders must be handled at these extra costs: 5.5 hours of staff time per order to write specifications at $43 an hour; 2.5 hours per order at $32 an hour for staff to review the bids received. What are the total and average costs of handling these special purchase orders?
$41,062.50; $328.50

■ Carrying Costs

Carrying costs include all the costs of holding inventory until it is issued. You usually show carrying costs by how much it costs to hold one unit of inventory for a year. A large part of carrying costs is interest on money borrowed to buy the inventory. Other costs include personal property taxes on the inventory's value, insurance, storage costs, and loss from theft, damage, or obsolescence.

■ *CHECK YOUR UNDERSTANDING SOLUTIONS*

A. 0.60 × $250,000 = $150,000;
0.35 × $54,000 = $18,900;
$128,100 + $150,000 + $18,900 = $297,000;
$297,000 ÷ 15,000 = $19.80

B. 5.5 × $43 = $236.50; 2.5 × $32 = $80;
$236.50 + $80 + $12 = $328.50, average cost of one order; $328.50 × 125 = $41,062.50

EXAMPLE 2

The Turned Page carries an inventory of 40,000 books valued at $22.50 per book. It pays 11% annual interest on its inventory and an annual property tax of 1% of inventory value. Each year, about 0.5% of the inventory is damaged and must be discarded. The total of other carrying costs is $8,000 a year. What is the average carrying cost, per book?

SOLUTION

Multiply the number of books by the value per book.

$40,000 \times \$22.50 = \$900,000$ annual value of inventory

Multiply the inventory's value by the interest rate, the property tax rate, and the damage rate.

$11\% \times \$900,000 = 0.11 \times \$900,000 = \$99,000$ annual interest

$1\% \times \$900,000 = 0.01 \times \$900,000 = \$9,000$ annual property tax

$0.5\% \times \$900,000 = 0.005 \times \$900,000 = \$4,500$ annual damage

Add the annual amounts for interest, property tax, and damage.

$\$99,000 + \$9,000 + \$4,500 = \$112,500$ annual carrying costs

Divide annual carrying costs by the number of books.

$\$112,500 \div 40,000 = \$2.812$, or $\$2.81$ average carrying cost per book

■ CHECK YOUR UNDERSTANDING

C. A food wholesaler's cost for Happy House frozen vegetables is $1.05 per bag for the 600,000 bags handled each year. The wholesaler pays 8% interest on one-half of the frozen vegetables inventory value for a year. Each year, 0.25% of the bags tear and must be thrown out. The cost of freezers and electricity to run the freezers is $90,000 a year. What is the carrying cost for one bag of frozen vegetables, to the nearest tenth of a cent? $0.195

D. A fruit retailer's average weekly inventory is valued at $7,200. Annual interest of 9% is paid on one-fourth of the inventory's annual value. About 4% of the annual inventory spoils and must be thrown out. Other costs related to inventory total $2,000 a year. What is the carrying cost for each one dollar of annual inventory, to the nearest tenth of a cent? $0.068

Wrap Up

The most visible cost per trip would be the operating cost per mile of your car. Another cost would be the value of the time you spend in driving and shopping and the alternative cost of what else you could be doing with your time.

■ Apply Goal 2

Use the board to work through Example 2 with students completing the math at their desks. Point out that whether a cost is stated as a percent or fixed dollar amount varies among companies, usually by how cost data were collected.

Assign Check Your Understanding problems C and D for completion in class. Move about the classroom to check student work.

■ Apply Goal 1

Review the Start Up. Illustrate the concept of alternative cost by asking students to consider what it would cost an attorney who charges $125 an hour in legal fees to do one hours' worth of grocery shopping. **$125**

Point out that the attorney might hire a shopping firm at $20 an hour to do the shopping, thereby saving $105. **$125 − $20 = $105** Explain that the idea of alternative cost is based on an assumption that time spent on other activities is in lieu of working for pay.

■ *CHECK YOUR UNDERSTANDING SOLUTIONS*

C. $1.05 \times 600,000 = \$630,000$; $\$630,000 \div 2 = \$315,000$; $0.08 \times \$315,000 = \$25,200$; $0.0025 \times \$630,000 = \$1,575$; $\$25,200 + \$1,575 + \$90,000 = \$116,775$; $\$116,775 \div 600,000 = \$0.1946$, or $\$0.195$

D. $7,200 \times 52 = \$374,400$; $\$374,400 \div 4 = \$93,600$; $0.09 \times \$93,600 = \$8,424$; $0.04 \times \$374,400 = \$14,976$; $\$8,424 + \$14,976 + \$2,000 = \$25,400$; $\$25,400 \div 374,400 = \$0.0678$, or $\$0.068$

COMMUNICATION

Have students share their definitions of the prime rate of interest. Stress that each definition ought to contain one key element, namely that prime is the rate given to borrowers whose credit standing is so high that making the loan carries little risk. Point out that loans at prime are short-term and may be given to individuals or corporations.

Assign

Assignment: Exercises 1–16, 18–24. Have students solve the basic arithmetic problems before completing the rest of the exercise.

Assess

Call on students for their answers to the exercises. Demonstrate the solution of any problems with which students may have had difficulty.

Have students draw a single line through any incorrect solution or result that appears on their work and write above that line the correct procedure or answer. Collect student work and examine it to see what types of errors they made to provide a basis for future explanations you may give to individual students.

COMMUNICATION

The cost of borrowing money is one of the costs of carrying inventory. Organizations with good credit ratings or who are good customers of a lender may borrow money at or near the *prime rate of interest.*

Through research, find a definition for the prime rate of interest, how the prime rate is determined, and what the current prime rate is. Write a one-page summary of your research.

EXERCISES

Find the product.
1. $12 \times \$34,580$ $414,960
2. $26 \times \$78,192$ $2,032,992
3. $7.3\% \times \$124,600$ $9,095.80
4. $0.75\% \times \$1,300,000$ $9,750

Find the quotient.
5. $\$186,200 \div 9,500$ $19.60
6. $\$54,316 \div 734,000$ $0.074

7. These percents are charged to ordering: 100% of the purchasing department's annual wages of $86,400 and 40% of warehouse costs of $285,000 a year. Other ordering costs amount to $27,000 a year. If 13,000 purchase orders are placed each year, what is the cost per order to the nearest cent? $17.49

The Kroban Company's cost breakdown for the average purchase order is: 15 minutes at $28 an hour, 6 minutes stocking at $96 an hour; office costs of $1.18 per order; overhead costs of $0.86 per order.

8. What amount does Kroban spend per order? $18.64

9. What total amount is spent if 7,600 purchase orders are issued each year? $141,664

10. The Sensun Fabric Company finds its average stock order costs $16. Sensun plans to allow some departments to place supply orders through the online ordering system of various suppliers instead of through the Sensun purchase order system. The company expects to save 23% of order costs on an estimated 4,100 supply orders. What will be the total estimated annual savings of changing the ordering procedure? $15,088

11. A company issues 65,000 stock orders a year. The total costs assigned to handling are: $450,000, warehouse employee wages; depreciation on equipment, $29,000; 13% of overhead warehouse costs of $260,000. To the nearest cent, what is the average cost of handling per stock order? $7.89

12. Brent Custom Products pays 7.6% annual interest on one-half of its $3,000,000 annual inventory value. It also pays 0.65% personal property tax on the total value of inventory. Other carrying costs include $26,000 insurance, $51,000 in labor costs, and $19,000 in overhead costs. What is the carrying cost per $1 of annual inventory, to the nearest tenth of a cent? $0.077

SELECTED SOLUTIONS

7. $0.40 \times \$285,000 = \$114,000$;
$\$86,400 + \$114,000 + \$27,000 = \$227,400$;
$\$227,400 \div 13,000 = \$17.492$, or $17.49
10. $0.23 \times \$16 = \$3.68$; $\$3.68 \times 4,100 = \$15,088$
12. $\$3,000,000 \div 2 = \$1,500,000$;
$0.076 \times \$1,500,000 = \$114,000$;

$0.0065 \times \$3,000,000 = \$19,500$;
$\$114,000 + \$19,500 + \$26,000 + \$51,000 + \$19,000 = \$229,500$; $\$229,500 \div \$3,000,000 = 0.0765$, or 0.077; $0.077 \times \$1 = \$0.077$
13. $0.17 \times \$1 = \$0.17$

The Stone Heating Company has an annual inventory value of $1,500,000. Because of financial problems, Stone has to finance its entire inventory at 17% annual interest. If Stone had been able to maintain an excellent credit rating, it would have had to borrow money for only 40% of the inventory's annual value. The interest rate charged by a lender would have been 8.2%.

13. What amount must Stone now pay for the interest portion of carrying costs per each dollar of inventory? $0.17

14. To the nearest cent, what amount could Stone have paid for the carrying charges of interest for each dollar of inventory if it had an excellent credit rating? $0.033

15. Gerald's Blooms carries a weekly inventory valued at $26,000. Due to spoilage, 15% of the stock of flowers must be thrown out each week. What is the carrying cost of spoilage per dollar of weekly inventory? $0.15

16. **STRETCHING YOUR SKILLS**   The New Markets Company updated its stock ordering system by installing $580,000 of new hardware and buying new software at a cost of $230,000. New Markets expects the new system will reduce ordering costs by 20%. The company now spends $19.70 per purchase order to process 60,000 purchase orders a year. How many years will it take New Market to recover the costs of the new ordering system, to the nearest tenth year?   3.4 years

17. **CRITICAL THINKING**   A painting company uses 3,000 gallons of paint a year. If the company bought all the paint at one time, it would have high storage, or carrying costs. If it bought paint, say every working day, the time and effort put into frequent ordering would result in higher ordering costs. How do companies such as this strike a balance between the two costs? See Enrich section for answer.

MIXED REVIEW

18. Rewrite 0.73 as a percent.   73%

19. 62.5 ft @ 10¢ a foot $6.25

20. 0.724 + 8.516 + 15.73   24.97

21. $\frac{4}{5} - \frac{3}{8}$ $\frac{17}{40}$

22. Round these to the nearest cent: 7.68¢ and 39.15¢   8¢, 39¢

23. The Estes are a married, retired couple. Harold Estes earned $4,387.50 last year working as a crossing guard. His wife, Eva, earned $8,100 as a greeter at a chain store. They file a joint city income tax return and are allowed deductions that reduce their taxable income by $9,750. On the remainder of their income they pay a city income tax rate of $1\frac{1}{2}$%. What was their city income tax? $41.06, Lesson 2.4

24. Adrian Parnell borrowed $6,000 for 18 months to buy materials to remodel his house. Adrian signed a promissory note at his bank to repay the loan at 13.5% interest. Find the amount of interest Adrian must pay. Then find the amount Adrian must pay his bank when the note is due. $1,215, $7,215, Lesson 4.1

Lesson 10.6 Ordering and Carrying Inventory ▪ 455

Lesson 10.1 Employee Recruitment Costs

- Multiply daily employment ad cost by number of days less discounts to find cost of ad.

- Multiply hours spent hiring by hourly rate and add overhead cost to find cost of hiring.

- Multiply period pay rate by periods worked to find cost of contract employees.

- Multiply percentage fee by wages and add expenses to find cost of recruiter.

Lesson 10.2 Wage and Salary Increases

- Multiply hourly rate by COLA percent increase; add to old hourly rate to find new rate.

- Multiply wages earned since last wage adjustment by COLA percent increase to find retroactive pay.

- Multiply annual wages by bonus percent to find amount of bonus pay.

- Divide profits set aside for sharing by number of employees to find profit sharing amount per employee.

Lesson 10.3 Total Costs of Labor

- Multiply gross wages by FICA, FUTA, SUTA, and other mandated rates to find cost of required benefits.

- Multiply gross wages by optional benefit rates to find cost of non-required benefits.

- Add gross wages, required and non-required benefits to find total cost of full-time and part-time employees.

Chapter Review

Vocabulary Review

bonuses
carrying costs
contract employee
Cost of Living Adjustment (COLA)
executive recruiter

exempt employee
First-In, First Out
Last-In, First Out
nonexempt employee
ordering costs
part-time employee

perpetual inventory
profit sharing
reorder point
stock
stock record
weighted average

Fill in the blanks with the word or words that best completes the statement.

1. The expenses of creating purchase orders and handling stock are called __?__. ordering costs

2. Payments that employees get for exceptional job performance are known as __?__. bonuses

3. A listing of the units received, issued, and on hand for a specific item of merchandise is called (a, an) __?__. stock record

4. Someone who works for one organization but is paid by another is called (a, an) __?__. contract employee

5. A type of employee who is not usually paid overtime is called (a, an) __?__. exempt employee

6. A pay system that gives wage increases based on inflation is known as __?__. COLA

7. An inventory valuation system that uses the unit cost of goods bought first to calculate the value of ending inventory is called __?__. LIFO

8. The expenses involved in storing inventory until it is issued are called __?__. carrying costs

9. A person who tries to find full-time employees for an employer and gets paid only for successful searches is known as (a, an) __?__. executive recruiter

LESSON 10.1

10. The Keller Company runs a newspaper employment ad each Sunday. The ad should cost $1,400 a day. Because of the number of ads it runs, Keller receives a 22% discount off the usual price. What is the cost for Keller to run ads for one year? $56,784

11. A company hired Joanna Neech through an executive recruiter. The recruiter's fee was 26% of all money paid to Joanna in her first year of employment. Joanna agreed to a salary of $65,000 a year. She also was paid an $11,000 signing bonus. What was the cost of using the recruiter? $19,760

LESSON 10.2

12. Helmut Nemzek received a COLA of 2.3% on his weekly gross wages of $760. How much will Helmut earn per week after the pay increase? $777.48

13. Kruse Products, Inc. shared 15% of its $2,000,000 profit with its 120 hourly employees. What was the total amount of profit shared? What was each employee's share? $300,000, $2,500

TEACHING STRATEGIES Chapter Review

Before assigning the Vocabulary Review, have students close their books. Pronounce each word on the vocabulary list and have students write the words. When finished, have students check their spelling with the spelling in the textbook. Have them rewrite any misspelled words. Have students keep the lists and two days later ask a friend or someone at home to read the misspelled words so they may get additional practice in spelling the words from memory.

LESSON 10.3

14. Becky Dressler earns $42,000 a year. The benefits her employer pays in taxes include 7.65% FICA tax and a combined FUTA and SUTA tax of 7.1% of the first $8,000 of income. Becky also receives medical benefits worth $3,890 a year. Her employer pays 3.4% of her annual pay into a retirement program. What is the employer's total cost of providing these benefits? $9,099

15. Lyle LeBlanc completed his first month of work at a restaurant. He was paid $7.75 an hour for the 118 hours he worked. Lyle received a $25 loyalty bonus for staying with the restaurant for at least one month. The restaurant paid FICA taxes of 7.65%, FUTA taxes of 6.2%, and SUTA taxes of 2.1% on Lyle's wages. What was the total cost of employing Lyle for one month? $1,085.36

LESSON 10.4

16. A wholesaler showed a stock balance of 812 units of WT-45 electric shavers on Nov. 1. WT-45 shavers were shipped to retailers on these dates: Nov. 2, 415 units; Nov. 12, 570 units; Nov. 28, 605 units. The wholesaler received 900 shavers from a manufacturer on Nov. 10. What was the stock record balance of shavers on Nov. 30? 122

17. On average, Parts Source, a wholesaler, sells 28 electric motors a day to repair shops. It takes six days for Parts Source to get new motors from a manufacturer. Safety stock is $1\frac{1}{2}$ times the daily motor sales. What is the reorder point? 210

LESSON 10.5

Davis & Simpson, a distributor, purchased kitchen shears from different manufacturers.

September 3	700 @ $7.30	September 18	300 @ $7.62
September 12	1,200 @ $6.90	September 28	500 @ $7.41

18. The unit value of the beginning inventory of 600 shears was $7.28. Find the value of the ending inventory of 700 shears using FIFO. $5,229

19. The beginning inventory was 160 units with a unit value of $6.85. Use LIFO to find the value of the ending inventory of 300 units. $2,118

20. The total value of a beginning inventory of 450 units was $3,253.50. Use the weighted average method to find the value of the ending inventory of 610 units. $4,385.90

LESSON 10.6

21. The Piper Company issues 120 stock orders a week. A purchasing agent earning $700 a week spends 100% of her time on ordering. Her assistant earns $112 a day and spends 10% of his time entering orders into a computer system. Warehouse and office costs are calculated at $5.17 per order. What is the cost of issuing each stock order? $11.47

22. A retailer's annual inventory value is $720,000. He borrows money at 17% for three-tenths of the inventory's annual value. Customer theft is 3% of inventory. Other costs related to holding stock are $28,000. What is the carrying cost per $1 of inventory? $0.12

Chapter 10 Review ▪ **457**

Lesson 10.4 Tracking and Reordering Inventory

- To beginning stock balance add quantity received and subtract quantity issued to find stock on hand.

- Divide stock used by number of days to find daily usage.

- Multiply daily usage by lead-time and add safety stock to find reorder point.

Lesson 10.5 Inventory Valuation

- Multiply ending inventory units by unit cost of most recent purchases to find ending inventory value by FIFO.

- Multiply ending inventory units by unit cost of beginning inventory and first purchases to find LIFO inventory value.

- Divide total cost of stock by total units in beginning inventory and purchases to find average cost per unit.

- Multiply ending inventory units by average cost per unit to find value of ending inventory by weighted average.

Lesson 10.6 Ordering and Carrying Inventory

- Add personnel, stock handling, and overhead costs to find total cost of purchasing.

- Divide total cost of purchasing by number of purchase orders issued to find average purchase order cost.

- Multiply inventory value by interest, tax, and damage rates; add products to find annual carrying costs.

- Divide annual carrying costs by units in inventory to find average carrying cost per unit.

TEACHING STRATEGIES Chapter Review

After students complete the Chapter Review exercises, collect their work and check their answers. Return their papers and ask students that are likely to have the correct solution to place their solutions on the board. Seated students should check the board work against their work and make corrections as needed. If they don't know why a certain procedure was done, encourage them to ask questions or place a check next to the procedure so they may ask you for an explanation later.

Task 1: Calculating COLA

Enter data into a template that calculates Cost of Living Adjustment (COLA) for employees of the Canton Manufacturing Company. You may use the template to study the effect of wage increases on a company's total wage costs.

Open the spreadsheet for Chapter 10 (tech10-1.xls) and enter the data shown in blue (cells C3–4) into the spreadsheet. The percent change in the CPI, which is calculated for you, is also known as the rate of inflation. A new hourly wage rate for employees, total annual wages based on the new wage rate, amount of wage increase for each employee, and the total of the wage increases are also calculated. Your computer screen should look like the one shown when you are done.

	A	B	C	D	E
1	Canton Manufacturing Company				
2	Projected COLA Wage Increase, January, 20--				
3	CPI Year-End Data:	Old CPI	179.9		
4		New CPI	184.0		
5		% Change	2.3%		
6		Old Hourly	New Hourly	New Annual	Amount of
7	Employee	Pay Rate	Pay Rate	Cost of Wages	Wage Increase
8	Bealer, Timothy	16.75	17.13	35630.40	790.40
9	Creslin, Ronald	17.20	17.59	36587.20	811.20
10	Eggert, Diane	16.90	17.29	35963.20	811.20
11	Fujiwara, Ritsuko	18.34	18.76	39020.80	873.60
12	Liston, Skip	17.05	17.44	36275.20	811.20
13	O'Brien, Sean	17.56	17.96	37356.80	832.00
14	Quincey, Roxanne	17.86	18.27	38001.60	852.80
15	Ramirez, Maria	19.45	19.89	41371.20	915.20
16	Zollig, Conrad	18.90	19.33	40206.40	894.40
17	TOTAL				7592.00

Task 2: Analyze the Spreadsheet Output

Answer these questions about the COLA wage calculations.

1. What was the CPI at the end of the year? 184.0

2. By what percent did the CPI change during the year to the nearest tenth percent? 2.3%

3. How was the percent change in the CPI calculated?
   The difference between the CPI figures was divided by the old CPI figure.

4. By what amount will wages increase in the coming year due to the change in the CPI? $7,592

5. The annual cost of wages calculation assumes that employees work 52 weeks, 40 hours a week. How many total hours are used in the calculation? 2,080

6. Which employee will have the lowest hourly pay rate after the raise? What is the rate?
   Bealer, $17.13

458 ■ Chapter 10 Manage People and Inventory

7. Which employee will have the greatest annual earnings at the new pay rate? What are the earnings?   Ramirez, $41,371.20

Now move the cursor to cell C4, which holds the new CPI index number. Enter a new index number of 187.5.

8. What is the total percent change in the CPI with the new data?   4.2%

9. Compare the total wage increase with the CPI at 187.5 to your total from Question 4. How much more will Canton have to pay its employees at the higher CPI? $6,448

10. Now enter a new CPI of 179.9 in cell C4. Will the employees get COLA? What is the reason?   No, employees did not get COLA because the CPI showed no change

11. Now enter a new CPI of 177.2 in cell C4. What does the lower CPI figure mean? Explain what happened to the hourly pay rate of employees?   When the CPI index is lower than the previous CPI figure, consumer prices have fallen. The hourly pay rate of employees did not drop to match the percent drop in the CPI. One reason why this happened is that the employer only figures COLA increases, not decreases.

Task 3: Design a Spreadsheet to Find an Ending Inventory's Value

You are to design a spreadsheet to find the value of the ending inventory using the weighted average method. Your spreadsheet should include columns for the date, the number of units, their unit cost, and total value. Where possible, use spreadsheet functions to calculate the ending inventory's unit cost and value.

SITUATION: A wholesaler, Storage Products, Inc., keeps an inventory record for steel utility shelving. Use the weighted average method to calculate the value of the ending inventory. Inventory and purchase data are to the right.

Storage Product, Inc.
Inventory Period: April 1, 20— to June 30, 20—
Stock Item: Steel Utility Shelving

April 1 beginning inventory, 58 units with a unit cost of $48.12.
June 30 ending inventory, 31 units.

Purchases: April 10, 35 units @ $53.90
                April 23, 56 units @ $50.10
                May 11, 21 units @ $58.12
                June 1, 65 units @ $46.05
                June 20, 44 units @ $52.80

Task 4: Analyze the Spreadsheet Output

Answer these questions about your spreadsheet output.

12. What was the unit cost of the ending inventory? $50.25

13. What was the value of the ending inventory? $1,557.75

14. How did you calculate the value of the ending inventory?
    Multiplied the units in the ending inventory by the weighted average unit cost
15. What functions did you use to calculate the unit cost of the ending inventory?   ROUND, SUM

Chapter 10 Technology Workshop ■ **459**

1. $36,470 × 0.06 = $2,188.20
   $2,000 + $2,000 = $4,000

   $4,000 + $2,188.20 = $6,188.20

2. $87,530 × 0.08 = $7,002.40
   $7,002.40 × 2 = $14,004.80
   $7,002.40 + $14,004.80 = $21,007.20

   $15,000 − $14,004.80 = $995.20

■ **WRITE**
Inform students that their proposals should appear in business memo format. Tell students that they will receive extra credit if they also cite non-financial benefits to the firm of using recruiters.

■ **SCANS**
Some students may also wish to explore other less visible areas of school operation such as cleaning the building, making repairs, or maintaining a computer lab.

■ **ONGOING ASSESSMENT**
STUDENT WORKBOOK An Integrated Project found in the workbook provides a broad assessment of the goals of the chapter.

Chapter Assessment

How Times Have Changed

For Questions 1–2, refer to the timeline on page 423 as needed.

1. Douglas Kerr's employer will match his contribution to a 401(k). The matching amount will be a dollar-for-dollar match not to exceed 6% of his salary. In 2004, Douglas's salary was $36,470. If he contributed $2,000, what would be the total amount contributed to the plan? What would be the total amount contributed to the plan if he contributed $4,000?
2. The maximum annual amount that individuals can contribute to their 401(k) in 2006 is $15,000. Sondra Jameson's employer will match 50% of every dollar that she contributes to a 401(k) up to 8% or her salary. If Sondra earns $87,530 in 2006 and she contributes only the amount her employer will match, what would be the total amount contributed to the plan? How much more could Sondra have contributed?

WRITE

Suppose that you work in the human resource department of a company. Your company is preparing to hire 5 middle managers that will have the same responsibilities, but in different departments. You think that your company should hire a recruiting firm to handle this task. Your boss thinks that is too expensive, but is willing to look at a proposal comparing costs.

Prepare a proposal for your boss comparing the costs of the hiring the managers using a recruiting firm versus using your human resource department.

SCANS

Workplace Skills—*Understanding Systems*

The ability to know how systems work is a critical skill and makes you valuable to an employer. You need to be able to demonstrate that you can operate effectively within social, organizational, and technological systems.

Test Your Skills Consider three areas or services that are available in your school, such as the bookstore or cafeteria. Describe a system that is in place in each of the three areas. An example of a system in a school bookstore may be how the decisions are made on what to stock. A system in a school cafeteria may be how classes are released to go to lunch.

Make a Plan Choose one area where you think you understand the reasons for the system and how it operates. Write a brief instructional guide, as if you were training someone new to work in the area you chose.

Summarize Prepare a visual or verbal presentation showing how the system you are analyzing works. Be sure to explain the reasons why you think it operates effectively or ineffectively. Include references to as many of the following as you can.

reading   *listening*   *problem solving*   *decision making*
mathematics   *speaking*   *self management*   *integrity/honesty*

TEACHING STRATEGIES Chapter Assessment

Have students explain how the SCANS skills of listening, problem solving, and self management were used in the completion of this assessment.

Chapter Test

Answer each question.

1. Add: $45,384 + $3,482 + $2,005.34 $50,871.34
2. Subtract: 1,748 − 985   763
3. Multiply: 0.6% × $1,480 $8.88
4. Divide $1,479,400 by 260 $5,690
5. $\frac{3}{4} \div 1\frac{1}{2}$ $\frac{1}{2}$
6. 4.8 ÷ 0.006%   80,000
7. What percent of $50,400 is $1,260?   2.5%
8. $225 + (11% × $225) $249.75

Applications

9. The board game Skribin has daily sales of 12 units. It takes 28 days to receive a new shipment. No safety stock is purchased. What is the reorder point for the game?   336

10. Five percent of a company's profits of $472,000 are to be shared with 4 supervisors. Thirty percent of the profits are to be shared with 48 hourly employees. What profit sharing amount did each of the supervisors and hourly employees get? $5,900; $2,950

11. A contract employee is paid $24 an hour for the same work done by a full-time employee who earns $19 an hour plus 37% in benefits. Which employee costs more to hire per hour, and how much more?   The full-time employee costs $2.03 more per hour

12. Bear County will pay a COLA equal to the 0.7% rise in the CPI last quarter. If Tabatha is now paid $18.70 an hour by the county, what will be her new hourly rate when the raise is given? $18.83

13. The unit cost of a beginning inventory of 405 units is $15.16. The unit cost of the last 600 units purchased is $16.81. Use FIFO to find the value of the ending inventory of 170 units. $2,857.70

14. MXV Products uses a computer program to screen job applications at a cost of $1.40 per application. Screening used to be done by an employee who took ten minutes at an average cost of $36 an hour. How much will computer screening save MXV for the 426 applications it expects to receive this month? $1,959.60

15. A weekend employment ad costs $36 a column inch per day. Find the cost of a 3-inch ad that runs on Saturday and Sunday. $216

16. Linus received a $750 bonus in April. In the same year he received a bonus of 1% of his annual pay of $38,900. What total amount did Linus receive in bonuses during the year? $1,139

17. Marta Lind received a notice showing that her employer paid these benefits based on her $53,000 annual salary: 8.7%, required tax benefits, 6%; medical insurance; 3%, pension plan contribution; 5%, vacation and holiday pay. What total benefits did Marta's employer provide? $12,031

18. The total value of 680 units of beginning inventory and purchases in a quarter is $28,900. What is the value of an ending inventory of 76 units using the weighted average method? $3,230

Chapter 10 Assessment ■ 461

PORTFOLIO ASSESSMENT

Have students review the materials they have created in this chapter and select those they wish to place in their portfolios. Students should include a description of the work that includes what they found most challenging and what they were the most proud of regarding the work. They should also include a self-evaluation of the portfolio entry.

Cumulative Review–Lesson Correlation

Question	Lesson
1	9.5
2	10.2
3	10.3
4	10.1
5	9.2
6	9.3
7	9.1
8	10.2
9	10.2
10	9.1
11	9.1
12	10.4
13	9.5
14	10.6
15	9.2
16	10.6
17	10.4
18	9.3
19	10.3
20	9.4
21	10.3

Test Taking Strategies

Multiple Choice, Exercise 7. Students may find it easier to solve Exercise 7 by listing all the factors needed to solve Exercise 7, such as: $34.12, monthly cost of one computer; 12, number of months in a year; 3, number of years in lease; 20, number of computers leased.

Chapters 9–10 Cumulative Review

MULTIPLE CHOICE

Select the best choice for each question.

1. A wireless service provider charges $0.25 for each minute of service, $0.70 a minute for roaming charges, and $0.18 a minute for long-distance calls. What is the charge for a 6-minute, long-distance call within the home coverage area? E
   A. $1.08   B. $0.18   C. $1.13   D. $6.78   E. $2.58

2. A $20.12 hourly rate is increased by a COLA of 2.9%. What is the new hourly rate? B
   A. $0.58   B. $20.70   C. $58.35   D. $2.07   E. $5.83

3. On Elmer Byrnes' first $7,000 of earnings, his employer must pay FICA tax of 7.65%, FUTA tax of 6.2%, and SUTA tax of 0.5%. How much does the employer pay in legally required taxes on Byrnes' $7,000 of earnings? C
   A. $535.50   B. $434   C. $1,004.50   D. $35   E. $6,027

4. A headhunter agreed to a contingency fee of 25% of wages to recruit employees for the XMS Company. Two recruited employees were hired by XMS. The average of their annual wages is $58,500. What fee amount must XMS pay the headhunter? A
   A. $29,250   B. $14,625   C. $7,312.50   D. $2,925   E. $292.50

5. A 50-workstation license for Valley DB software costs $10,200. A single copy of the software costs $320. DB software is needed for 43 workstations. How much can be saved by buying a 50-workstation license instead of 43 single copies? B
   A. $13,760   B. $3,560   C. $23,960   D. $8,772   E. $275.20

6. A company wants to provide one technical support staff member for every 50 computer users. The company now has 1,000 computer users. In the next 3 years the company plans to hire 1,000 additional employees, 80% of whom will use computers. How many support staff should the company have at the end of 3 years? D
   A. 20   B. 40   C. 16   D. 36   E. 68

7. It costs $34.12 a month to lease a computer on a three-year lease. A hospital leased 20 computers. What is the annual cost of leasing 20 computers? A
   A. $8,188.80   B. $24,566.40   C. $2,047.20   D. $409.44   E. $1,228.32

8. Ninety employees share a company's profit of $325,350. The share is to be paid in two equal payments. What amount will each employee receive in the first payment? D
   A. $3,615   B. $361.50   C. $18,075   D. $1,807.50   E. $162,675

9. Felicia was given a 0.25% attendance bonus and an extra bonus of 8% for developing a patent, both based on her annual pay of $61,500. What total bonus did she receive? E
   A. $153.75   B. $4,920   C. $20,295   D. $1,230   E. $5,073.75

10. A USB flash drive stores 256 MB of data. How many USB flash drives are needed to store a 1 GB file? C
    A. 0.004   B. 40   C. 4   D. 2,500   E. 0.25

TEACHING STRATEGIES Cumulative Review

Remind students that they have solved problems where different words or phrases are used in place of a technical term. For example, in Exercise 17, the term lead-time is not used. Instead, the sentence "More cereal will arrive within three days of ordering." is used. Both mean the same.

OPEN ENDED

11. A network required 20 minitower computer systems at $1,718; 20 network cards at $81; network cabling, $460; network printer, $12,280; file server, $18,100. The cost of installing and connecting all hardware was $9,118. What total amount was spent on hardware-related costs of the network? $75,938

12. A wholesaler had a beginning inventory of 683 blenders on February 1. A total of 1,340 blenders were added to stock in February. Stock shipments of blenders were: Feb. 5, 280; Feb 13, 459; Feb 19, 580; Feb 26, 387. What was the ending inventory? 317

13. In the first month of his pager service contract, Wesley made 238 calls. Wesley paid an activation fee of $15, pager rental of $8, and a monthly service charge of $11.99 that allows him a maximum of 150 calls a month. Calls beyond the maximum cost $0.20 per call. What was Wesley's cost for the first month of pager service? $52.59

14. An appliance repair company carries a $41,000 annual parts inventory. The company pays 8.2% interest on 50% of the inventory and a 0.4% personal property tax on the inventory's full annual value. The annual cost of storage and insurance is $2,665. What is the carrying cost of inventory per $1 of inventory? $0.11

15. Twenty-five programmers worked 9 hours a day at $41 an hour to complete a program containing 51,850 lines of code. The programmers each averaged 34 lines of finished code per day. What was the programming cost of the project? $562,725

16. An office manager earns a salary of $41,500 and spends 15% of his time ordering stock. Other costs of ordering are: 6% of warehouse costs of $61,000, 15% of general office costs of $19,000, and 10% of office building rental and maintenance of $42,000. What is the cost per order if 1,200 orders are placed each year? $14.11

17. A store sells 45 boxes of Crunch cereal daily. More cereal will arrive within three days of ordering. Safety stock is 16 boxes. What is the reorder point for Crunch cereal? 151

18. A regional library system supports 1,620 desktop computer systems in 42 locations. Last year, it spent $58,000 for new printers, $486,000 for computer upgrades, $51,150 on repairs, and $112,000 on user training. What amount was spent on each computer system to the nearest dollar? $437

19. Marilee spends 20% of her time training part-time employees. What is the cost of training if Marilee earns $46,500 a year and receives benefits valued at 30.5% of gross pay? $12,136.50

20. The Rare Coin Association created a web site to provide information but not make online sales. A web hosting company charged them $4,812 for developing the web site and $196 a month to maintain it. Web server space and an Internet connection cost $95 a month. What is the total first year cost of the web site? $8,304

CONSTRUCTED RESPONSE

21. The management of a company believes that it is less expensive in the long run to hire co-op students and interns to do the work of full-time employees. Explain in writing whether you agree or disagree with management. Full-time employees receive wages and benefits not given to part-time employees. A hidden cost of employing co-op students and interns is the cost of training. Training may be informal and usually done by a manager or a coworker. While they are providing training they are not doing the job they were hired to do, resulting in **Chapter 10 Cumulative Review ■ 463** lost productivity that cannot be made up.

Test Taking Strategies

■ OPEN-ENDED
Explain to students that a technique for gaining confidence in taking a test is to scan quickly a few test items and search for key words such as bonus, reorder point, COLA, or cost of pager service that are associated with problems that students know how to solve.

■ PORTFOLIO ASSESSMENT
Have students review the materials they have created in this chapter and select those they wish to place in their portfolios.

TEST-TAKING STRATEGIES Constructed Response

When students consider training costs they may also note the percentage of time spent in training. A 40-hour training session is about 2% of a full-time employee's annual work schedule, but about 4% for a part-time employee working 20 hours a week. Also, part-time employees may leave for another job that pays slightly more since income is of key importance to them. Their training leaves with them as well.

Business Costs

11.1 Manufacturing Costs
11.2 Break-Even Point
11.3 Depreciation Costs
11.4 Shipping Costs
11.5 Office Costs
11.6 Travel Expenses

Statistical Insights

CARRIERS' RESTRICTIONS FOR WEIGHT AND DIMENSIONS

Girth is the distance all the way around the package, or twice the height plus twice the width of the package.

Carrier/Service	Maximum Weight	Maximum Dimensions
United Parcel Service	Up to 150 lb	Length: 108 in. Length + girth: 130 in.
United States Postal Service Parcel Post	Greater than 1 lb Up to 70 lb	Length + girth: 130 in.
United States Postal Service Priority Mail	Up to 70 lb	Length + girth: 108 in.
United States Postal Service Express Mail	Up to 70 lb	Length + girth: 108 in.
FedEx	Up to 150 lb	Length: 119 in. Length + girth: 165 in.
Airborne Standard	Up to 150 lb	Length: 56 in. and less then 29,100 cubic in.
Airborne Next Day Afternoon Service	Up to 5 lb	Length: 56 in. and less then 29,100 cubic in.

Use the data shown above to answer each question.

1. What carriers can be used if a package weighs 72 lb and has dimensions of 5.5 ft long, 10 in. wide, and 8 in. deep.   United Parcel Service, FedEx

2. A box is 18 in. × 14 in. × 20 in. The box does not show which way is right side up. So it is not known which number goes with which dimension. Can this box be shipped by all carriers listed no matter which dimension given is the length?   Yes

Statistical Insights

Discuss with students why carriers use weight and girth to screen packages. The discussion should include the fact that packages must be delivered door to door. Thus, delivery people must be able to carry them in their hands or with a hand truck. Weight is also important because of the weight limitations imposed by governments on trucks or the limitations imposed on airplanes by the laws of aeronautics.

NetCheck

Fixed Assets Depreciating

Fixed assets must be reported regularly on income statements and tax reports each year. Companies may have developed their own software to prepare depreciation schedules. They may also use software developed by others to ensure that depreciation is calculated in a way that is consistent with federal tax regulations.

Keeping accurate records means that a business can quickly value its fixed assets. Automating these records should result in fewer calculation errors and precise timetables for depreciating an expense. Several Internet sites offer such software.

Employee Expenses

Companies often establish expense guidelines for employees who travel for business purposes. The guidelines usually follow the allowable business expenses established by the Internal Revenue Service, including the type of receipts needed and how employees will be reimbursed for out-of-pocket expenses.

Point your browser to the web site of the Internal Revenue Service to view a list of charges that businesses can claim on their federal income tax returns. This is the starting point for any company that is preparing its own guidelines.

How Times Have Changed

People have been manufacturing things since civilization began in the New Stone Age around 8000 B.C. Following stone, copper was discovered, then bronze, and then around 2000 B.C., iron. Four thousand years later, the dependence on steel for so many things means people are still considered as living in the Iron Age.

465

Teaching Resources

Lesson Plans, Ch. 11
Chapter 11 Test Forms A and B
Workbook, Ch. 11
Explore Algebra and Geometry
    Activities
Technology Activities
Competitive Events Prep
Data Activities CD, Ch. 11
ExamView® Pro CD, Ch. 11

NetCheck

Fixed Assets Depreciating
Download demonstration depreciation software from the Internet or locate sites on which these software packages are reviewed. Have students evaluate these programs and list their key features. Compare the features they found by listing them on the board and discussing them.

Employee Expenses Help students find and use web sites that display the travel guidelines for organizations. A search on business travel expenses will reveal many sites listing helpful guidelines. Some public university sites list state travel expense guidelines. A search on state travel guidelines will reveal many of these sites.

Answer to research item:

cost of a hot-rolled steel bar per 100 pounds in 1998: $18.75

HOW TIMES HAVE CHANGED

Lead the class into a discussion about business costs, with a special emphasis on the cost of raw materials used in manufacturing. Possible questions to ask:
    Which raw materials do you think are some of the most common? most expensive? least expensive?

Turn the students' attention to the timeline. Have them do their own research to find the cost of a hot-rolled steel bar per 100 pounds in 1998.
See page 498 for assessment questions related to the timeline.

Start Up

Have students read the Start Up. Then ask them what Mr. Dabney might do at work to consider himself "overhead." Write down the responses on the board and have one student record what you write on paper. Save the paper for use in the Wrap Up.

Math Skill Builder

The skills of adding and multiplying money amounts by fractions and dividing money amounts and rounding the results to the nearest cent are used in this lesson.

Complete all exercises in Math Skill Builder 1–2.

■ Teach Goal 1

Explain that prime cost includes those costs directly tied to the product being manufactured. Overhead costs are costs that cannot be tied directly to a product.

Point out that accounting systems for factories usually separate direct labor by product so that the direct labor costs of making a specific product can be identified. This is information that is extremely helpful in deciding what to produce.

11.1 Manufacturing Costs

GOALS

- Calculate prime cost and total manufacturing costs
- Distribute factory expenses to units

Start Up

Mr. Dabney, your friend's dad, walked by you on his way home from work one day. Trying to be friendly, you asked him what he did at work that day. He answered, "Oh, I just tried to keep out of the way today." Puzzled, you asked him what he meant by that and he answered: "You see, I am part of the overhead down at the plant." Now you were really puzzled, but before you could ask him another question, he had walked on. What did he mean when he said he was part of the "overhead" at the plant?

Math Skill Builder

Review these math skills and solve the exercises that follow.

❶ **Divide** money amounts by whole numbers.
Find the quotient, to the nearest cent. $238,674 \div 4,200 = \$56.827$, or $56.83

1a. $560 \div 30$ $18.67

1b. $372,000 \div 600$ $620

❷ **Multiply** money amounts by fractions.
Find the product. $\frac{10,000}{50,000} \times \$358,000 = \$71,600$

2a. $\frac{5,000}{15,000} \times \$138,400$ $46,133.33

2b. $\frac{12,000}{72,000} \times \$598,300$ $99,716.67

■ Prime Cost and Total Cost of Manufacturing

Manufacturers make the products they sell. They must keep records of their factory costs so that they can control those costs and set selling prices that will produce a net income instead of a net loss.

There are three kinds of factory costs:

1. *Raw materials* costs are the costs of materials which are used in manufacturing and which become part of the finished product.

2. *Direct labor costs* are the wages of all the workers who work directly on the products as they move through the factory.

3. *Factory overhead* includes the expenses that cannot be directly tied to producing a product. For example, it includes salaries and wages of the factory managers, supervisors, inspectors, and other workers who do not work directly on the manufactured products. It also includes building rent, depreciation of equipment, heat, power, insurance, and factory supplies.

466 ■ Chapter 11 Business Costs

CONNECTION TO ACCOUNTING

Accountants in manufacturing plants must keep track of three types of inventories: raw materials, goods in process, and finished goods. Have students use the Web or other sources to describe and distinguish between these inventories. Also, have students create an example of the three inventories in their school or home environment. For example, students might identify dirty clothes as raw materials; clothes that are being washed, dried, or folded as goods in process, and clean, dried, and folded clothes as finished goods.

The costs of raw materials and direct labor are called the **prime cost** of manufacturing a product. The prime cost plus **factory overhead** are the **total manufacturing cost** of a product.

Prime Cost = Raw Materials + Direct Labor

Total Manufacturing Cost = Prime Cost + Factory Overhead

EXAMPLE 1

The costs of manufacturing 1,000 computer monitors are $15,000 for raw materials, $25,000 for direct labor, and $5,000 for factory overhead. What is the prime cost of the computer monitors? What is the total manufacturing cost of the monitors?

SOLUTION

Add the costs for raw materials and direct labor.

$15,000 + $25,000 = $40,000   prime cost

Add prime cost and factory overhead.

$40,000 + $5,000 = $45,000   total manufacturing cost

CHECK YOUR UNDERSTANDING

A. The records of a bicycle factory show these costs for the goods produced in the first quarter of a year: raw materials, $861,980; direct labor, $1,976,200; factory overhead, $387,950. What was the prime cost of the goods produced during the quarter? What was the total manufacturing cost of the goods? $2,838,180; $3,226,130

B. To make 150 telephones, ComTech, Inc. had these manufacturing costs: materials, $1,282.29; labor, $1,975.26; factory overhead, $1,234.31. What was the prime cost of making the telephones? What was the total manufacturing cost of each phone, on average, to the nearest whole cent? $3,257.55; $29.95

Distribute Factory Overhead to Units

A manufacturer needs to know the costs of running each of its divisions, departments, or other units. So, factory expenses, or overhead, are often distributed or charged to each unit.

The way they are distributed varies with the company and the kind of expense. For example, rent may be distributed in proportion to the floor space used by the units. Taxes and insurance on equipment may be distributed based on the value of the equipment in each unit. Cleaning expenses may be distributed on the basis of floor space. Management salaries may be distributed based on the number of factory workers in a unit.

Lesson 11.1 Manufacturing Costs ■ 467

Work through Example 2 at the board with students completing the math at their desks.

Assign Check Your Understanding problems C and D for completion in class. Move about the classroom and examine student work to identify student errors or difficulties.

■ **ONGOING ASSESSMENT**

Make a transparency of Check Your Understanding C. Then, with their textbooks closed, ask students to describe the steps needed to solve the problem. Spread the task around by limiting each student to one step.

Wrap Up

Review the Start Up. Read the statements on the paper that the students created earlier. Discuss and evaluate each statement in light of what students have learned in the lesson.

COMMUNICATION

Help students to use search tools to find the answers to the three questions. Discuss possible key terms that can be used. The Dictionary of Occupational Titles is one place to start.

EXAMPLE 2

Mayforge, Inc. pays $30,000 a month rent for its factory and distributes the rent on the basis of floor space. What amount should be charged to each of its three departments? Department A has 2,000 sq. ft of floor space; Department B, 5,000 sq. ft; and Department C, 3,000 sq. ft.

SOLUTION

Add the floor space for each department.

$2,000 + 5,000 + 3,000 = 10,000$ sq. ft.   total floor space

Divide the floor space for each department by the total floor space. Then multiply the result by the monthly rent

$\frac{2,000}{10,000} \times \$30,000 = \$6,000$ monthly rent charged to Dept. A

$\frac{5,000}{10,000} \times \$30,000 = \$15,000$ monthly rent charged to Dept. B

$\frac{3,000}{10,000} \times \$30,000 = \$9,000$ monthly rent charged to Dept. C

> **MATH TIP**
>
> Square feet may be abbreviated to sq. ft or ft^2.

■ **CHECK YOUR UNDERSTANDING**

C. The four divisions of Panasol Electronics, Inc., use this floor space: Printers, 6,000 ft^2; Scanners, 2,800 ft^2; Copiers, 5,000 ft^2; Faxes, 2,200 ft^2. The yearly maintenance cost of the building, $28,000, is distributed based on the floor space of each division. How much is each division charged annually?
$10,500; $4,900; $8,750; $3,850

D. Biosfeer, Inc. pays its managers a total of $500,000 a year. This expense is charged to the four sections of the company on the basis of the number of workers in each section. The number of workers is: Fabrication, 120; Testing, 20; Painting, 46; Assembly, 64. What amount is charged to each section?
$240,000; $40,000; $92,000; $128,000

Wrap Up

Your friend's dad probably meant that in his job he did not directly produce products. He might be an accountant, manager, supervisor, or any of a number of people who provide support for those who actually build and assemble products. The wages and salaries of such workers go to make up the overhead costs of a manufactured product.

COMMUNICATION

A term that is likely to be heard in discussions of manufacturing costs is *cost accounting*.

- What is cost accounting?
- What are common job titles of people who perform cost accounting?
- How does cost accounting relate to the topics included in this lesson?

Answer these questions in a brief report. Attach to the report a list of the sources you used to complete the report.

■ *CHECK YOUR UNDERSTANDING SOLUTIONS*

C. $6,000 \text{ ft}^2 + 2,800 \text{ ft}^2 + 5,000 \text{ ft}^2 + 2,200 \text{ ft}^2 = 16,000 \text{ ft}^2$; $\frac{6,000}{16,000} \times \$28,000 = \$10,500$ Printers; $\frac{2,800}{16,000} \times \$28,000 = \$4,900$ Scanners; $\frac{5,000}{16,000} \times \$28,000 = \$8,750$ Copiers; $\frac{2,200}{16,000} \times \$28,000 = \$3,850$ Faxes

D. $120 + 20 + 46 + 64 = 250$; $\frac{120}{250} \times \$500,000 = \$240,000$ Fabrication; $\frac{20}{250} \times \$500,000 = \$40,000$ Testing; $\frac{46}{250} \times \$500,000 = \$92,000$ Painting; $\frac{64}{250} \times \$500,000 = \$128,000$ Assembly

EXERCISES

Find the quotient to the nearest cent.

1. $40,908 ÷ 112 $365.25

2. $586,883 ÷ 105 $5,589.36

3. $382,400 ÷ 420 $910.48

4. $1,483,800 ÷ 720 $2,060.83

Find the product, to the nearest cent.

5. $\frac{45,000}{90,000}$ × $890,300 $445,150

6. $\frac{25,000}{125,000}$ × $308,800 $61,760

In March of last year, manufacturing costs of Eder Stamping Company were: raw materials, $529,926; direct labor, $756,416; factory overhead, $157,344.

7. What was Eder's prime cost? $1,286,342

8. What was Eder's total manufacturing cost? $1,443,686

For August, Santoni, Inc. had these manufacturing costs: raw materials, $139,648; direct labor, $324,814; overhead, $106,584. In that month, Santoni manufactured 4,000 units of their product.

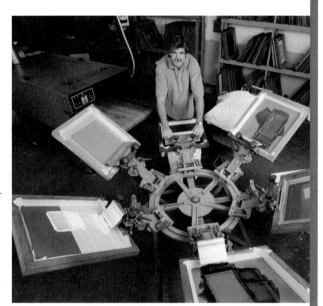

9. What was Santoni's prime cost for manufacturing the units? $464,462

10. What are Santoni's total manufacturing costs? $571,046

11. Estimate the average cost per unit. $150

12. What was the actual average cost per unit, to the nearest cent? $142.76

13. An auto parts factory had this overhead for September: supervisory wages, $108,342; rent, $7,278; depreciation, $23,207; power, $7,725; maintenance and repairs, $12,465; other, $3,674. What was the total factory overhead? $162,691

The factory records of Glaser Sheetrock show these costs for the last quarter: raw materials, $517,912.80; direct labor, $635,724.80; supervisory salaries and wages, $59,538.47; rent, $27,235; depreciation and repairs, $32,105.67; power, $18,181.30; factory supplies, $15,945.74; other factory expense, $7,209.82.

14. What was the total factory overhead for the quarter? $160,216

15. What was the prime cost for the quarter? $1,153,637.60

16. What was the total manufacturing cost? $1,313,853.60

Lesson 11.1 Manufacturing Costs ■ 469

Assign

Assignment: Exercises 1–18, 24–32. Start with the basic arithmetic problems at the beginning to be sure that students understand the underlying arithmetic in the exercises.

Assess

Using the board or a blank transparency, ask students to lead you through the creation of the formulas for prime cost and total manufacturing cost.

Ask students to define the bolded and italicized terms in the lesson and use them in sentences.

Reteach

STUDENT WORKBOOK For students who need help with calculating prime and total manufacturing costs, complete Exercise 1 with them. Then have them do Exercise 2.

If students need help with distributing factory expenses, do Exercise 5 with them. Then have them do Exercise 6.

Close

Assign Exercises 19–22, Integrating Your Knowledge. After students finish doing the problem, have them lead you through the solution to Exercises 20 and 21 at the board or on a blank transparency.

17. A firm's $4,500 electric power bill is distributed by the number of horsepower-hours used by the equipment in each division. This is found by multiplying the horsepower of each motor by the number of hours it is used. The horsepower-hours of each division are: Division X, 3,000; Division Z, 7,500; Division Y, 4,500. What is the amount to be charged to each division? $900; $2,250; $1,350

18. The annual sales of Eberle Press, Inc. are $4,300,000. The cost of Eberle's insurance on its manufacturing equipment is $2,890, which is 27% of the total insurance costs of the company. The equipment insurance cost is distributed in proportion to the value of the equipment in each department. Those equipment values are: Department G, $36,125; Department R, $86,700; Department K, $21,675. How much insurance should be charged to each department?
$722.50; $1,734; $433.50

INTEGRATING YOUR KNOWLEDGE   During June, Radion Products had these manufacturing costs: raw materials, $419,754; direct labor, $1,329,784; overhead, $384,598. In that month, Radion manufactured 24,600 units of their product, 1% of which were found to be defective by their quality control department.

19. How many defective units were there?   246

20. What was the total manufacturing cost for June? $2,134,136

21. What was the average manufacturing cost for each non-defective item? $87.63

22. If Radion produces 28,900 units in July, how many units are likely to be defective?   289

23. **CRITICAL THINKING**   One of the ways to lower manufacturing costs is to improve worker productivity. How might you improve worker productivity in the factory?   training to upgrade skills; better equipment and tools

MIXED REVIEW

24. Add 275 + 0.04 + 7.202 + 28.1.   310.342

25. Multiply $\frac{3}{5} \times \frac{8}{9}$. $\frac{8}{15}$

26. Rewrite 60% as a fraction and simplify. $\frac{3}{5}$

27. Divide $81.20 by 140%. $58

28. Divide 10 by $\frac{2}{5}$.   25

29. 45 is what percent of 150?   30%

30. The Knabe family's income on which they must pay state tax is $68,540. The tax rate is 5.8%. What is their state tax? $3,975.32, Lesson 2.4

31. Tom Wu bought a light truck for $12,900 and drove it 15,000 miles in the first year. His expenses in that year were: depreciation, 20% of the cost of the truck; interest at 12% of the cost of the truck; gas, oil, insurance, and other expenses, $1,860. Find the operating cost of the truck per mile, to the nearest tenth of a cent.   39.9 cents, Lesson 6.6

32. After Ursala retired she starting receiving a social security check for $835 each month. She needed $20,100 to meet her yearly expenses. How much did she need to withdraw from her IRA account each month to cover these expenses? $840; Lesson 7.9

470 ■ Chapter 11 Business Costs

SELECTED SOLUTIONS

17. 3,000 + 7,500 + 4,500 = 15,000;
$\frac{3,000}{15,000} \times \$4,500 = \$900$ X;
$\frac{7,500}{15,000} \times \$4,500 = \$2,250$ Y;
$\frac{4,500}{15,000} \times \$4,500 = \$1,350$ Z

19. 24,600 × 0.01 = 246
20. $419,754 + $1,329,784 + $384,598 = $2,134,136
22. 28,900 × 0.01 = 289

11.2 Break-Even Point

GOALS
- Calculate the break-even point for a product in units
- Calculate the break-even point for a product in sales dollars

Start Up

Imagine that your company has just invented a product that is so new it has never been offered on the market before. What factors might you use to help you set the price of the product?

Math Skill Builder

Review these math skills and solve the exercises that follow.

1 **Subtract** dollar amounts from dollar amounts. Find the difference. $45.49 − $23.78 = $21.71

   1a. $108.39 − $74.19 $34.20   **1b.** $358.12 − $286.87 $71.25

2 **Multiply** dollar amounts by whole numbers. Find the product. $16.88 × 3,500 = $59,080

   2a. $3.89 × 38,970 $151,593.30   **2b.** $98.30 × 42,670 $4,194,461

3 **Divide** dollar amounts by dollar amounts. Find the quotient. $34,500 ÷ $12 = 2,875

   3a. $174,000 ÷ $15 11,600   **3b.** $83,300 ÷ $35 2,380

Break-Even Point in Units and Sales Dollars

To plan their operations, manufacturing firms must decide:

- How many units they expect to sell
- How many units to produce
- How much to spend to produce and sell these units
- At what price they must sell the units to make the profit they want

To make these decisions, firms may calculate the break-even point. The **break-even point** is the point at which income from sales equals the total cost of producing and selling goods. It is the point at which the business will make no profit or suffer a loss.

When sales exceed the break-even point, there is a profit. When sales are less than the break-even point, there is a loss.

Start Up

Have students read the Start Up. They will have fun trying to come up with a new idea for a product. Pick one of their ideas and ask them to suggest factors that could be used to set its price. Record the factors on the board and have one student record them on a sheet of paper. Save the paper for use in the Wrap Up.

Math Skill Builder

The skills of subtracting and dividing money amounts are used in this lesson. So is the skill of multiplying dollar amounts and whole numbers.

Complete all exercises in Math Skill Builder 1–3 to have students review these skills.

■ Teach Goals 1 & 2

Stress that the break-even point is the point at which you neither make a profit or a loss.

Ask students to look at the formula for finding the break-even point in units. Point out that when they subtract the per-unit variable costs from the per-unit sales price, the result is the per-unit fixed cost. Dividing the total fixed costs by the per-unit fixed cost results in the number of units needed to break even.

DIFFERENT LEARNING ABILITIES At-Risk Learners

Some students may have difficulty solving the problems in this lesson because they don't really understand the difference between fixed and variable costs. Discussing fixed and variable costs for a lemonade stand or a coke machine might help students see the difference in settings that are more realistic to them than the manufacturing world.

To find the break-even point, you need to know the:

- Fixed costs for manufacturing the product
- Variable costs for manufacturing each unit of the product
- Expected selling price of each unit of the product

Fixed costs are costs such as rent, salaries, heat, insurance, advertising, and other overhead costs that remain the same no matter how much of the product is manufactured or sold. Variable costs are costs such as raw materials, direct labor, and energy that vary or change directly with the amount of product produced and sold.

The formula used to calculate the number of units that must be sold to break even is:

Break-Even Point in Units =
Fixed Costs ÷ (Sales Price per Unit − Variable Cost per Unit)

To calculate the amount of sales needed to break even, multiply the number of units that must be sold to break even by the sales price of each unit.

Break-Even Point in Dollars = Break-Even Point in Units × Sales Price per Unit

EXAMPLE 1

BF Corporation plans to produce porcelain bowls that will be sold at $10 per unit. Manufacturing any quantity of bowls will cost an estimated $12,000 in fixed costs. The variable costs of producing each bowl are estimated to be $5. How many bowls must they sell to break even? What sales must BF earn on the bowls to reach the break-even point?

SOLUTION
Divide the fixed costs by the difference between the selling price of each bowl and the variable costs for each bowl.

$12,000 ÷ ($10 − $5) = $12,000 ÷ $5 = 2,400   bowls that must be sold to break even

Multiply the number of bowls needed to break even by the selling price of each bowl.

2,400 × $10 = $24,000   sales needed to break even

■ **CHECK YOUR UNDERSTANDING**

A. Rally Co.'s fixed costs to produce toy trucks are $200,000. The variable costs to produce each truck are $4. They will price the trucks at $20. How many trucks must they sell to break even? What sales must they reach to break even?
12,500; $250,000

B. Grossi Corporation estimated their fixed cost of producing aluminum baseball bats at $105,900 and their variable costs at $39 per bat. If they plan to sell the bats at $89, how many bats do they need to sell to break even? How much more than the break-even point will their income be if they sell 3,000 bats for $89?   2,118; $78,498

■ *CHECK YOUR UNDERSTANDING SOLUTIONS*

A. $20 − $4 = $16; $200,000 ÷ $16 = 12,500 toy trucks; 12,500 × $20 = $250,000 sales

B. $89 − $39 = $50; $105,900 ÷ $50 = 2,118 bats; 3,000 − 2,118 = 882; 882 × $89 = $78,498 more

Setting a price on a new product is not easy. Setting the price too high might drive customers away. Setting the price too low might result in a loss. Factors to use in setting the price are the cost of producing the product, how many units you expect to sell, and how much people can be expected to pay for it. These factors are also interdependent. The more you produce, the lower the cost per unit. The lower the price, the more of it you will sell.

COMMUNICATION

Mass production in manufacturing has allowed companies to produce goods at low prices. However, mass production tends to limit the diversity of the manufactured product. Henry Ford described it best when he said, "Any customer can have any car painted any color that he wants, so long as it is black." Information technology, however, is changing manufacturing. One change is the ability to provide for *mass customization*. What is mass customization? How does it differ from mass production? How can it benefit the consumer? How can it benefit the manufacturer? Prepare a report on mass customization for presentation to your class.

EXERCISES

Find the difference.
1. $74.56 − $42.88 $31.68
2. $126.90 − $89.56 $37.34

Find the product.
3. $28.70 × 10,200 $292,740
4. $5.87 × 25,800 $151,446

Find the quotient.
5. $108,800 ÷ $8.50   12,800
6. $20,160 ÷ $4.20   4,800

Boldfinch, Inc. plans to make patio chairs and sell them at $75 each. They estimate their fixed costs to produce the chairs at $300,000 and variable costs of $45 per chair.

7. How many chairs must Boldfinch sell to break even?   10,000

8. What sales amount must they reach to break even? $750,000

9. If they sold 25,600 chairs, how much over the break-even point will their sales income be? $1,170,000

A manufacturer produced 6,000 video games and sold them at $20 each. Fixed costs were $18,000 and the variable cost of each game was $5.

10. What were the production costs to produce the games? $48,000

11. How many games did they need to sell to break even?   1,200

12. How much over the break-even point was their sales income? $96,000

Lesson 11.2 Break-Even Point ■ **473**

SELECTED SOLUTIONS

7. $75 − $45 = $30; $300,000 ÷ $30 = 10,000
8. $75 × 10,000 = $750,000
9. 25,600 − 10,000 = 15,600;
   15,600 × $75 = $1,170,000

13. $500,000 + $250,000 = $750,000;
    $750,000 ÷ 40,000 = $18.75

Assign and discuss with students Exercises 15 and 16, Critical Thinking.

For Exercise 15, explain to students that the production of any product involves materials and labor. The more produced, the more materials and labor required. Thus, these two costs vary with the number of products made.

For Exercise 16, point out that while retail firms do not require raw materials as do manufacturers, they do require merchandise to be resold. The cost of the latter is known as the cost of the goods sold. Furthermore, there are many expenses that retailers must pay to operate their stores, such as paying salesclerks, etc. The cost of the goods they sell is subtracted from the total sales to find their gross profit. The operating expenses are then subtracted from the gross profit to find their net profit. When gross profit equals operating expenses, there is no net profit.

Close

Have students read Exercise 13. Call on students to describe the steps they must follow to solve the problem.

Ask students to define or explain the following terms: break-even point, fixed costs, and variable costs.

■ **STUDENT PORTFOLIO**
Students might want to consider placing the solutions to Exercises 7–12 in their portfolios.

13. **STRETCHING YOUR SKILLS** To produce and sell 40,000 copies of a novel, Beardsley-Martin Publishing Company will have fixed and variable costs totaling $500,000. The company wants to make a profit of $250,000 on the books. At what price must the books be sold to make the profit they want? $18.75

14. **STRETCHING YOUR SKILLS** Newlet Tracker Corporation plans to manufacture and sell 25,000 units of a computer printer. They estimate their fixed costs will be $3,750,000 and their variable costs $4,900,000. At what price each must they sell the printers to break even? $346

15. **CRITICAL THINKING** Why can't you simply divide the fixed costs by the number of items produced to find the break-even point? Break-even point includes both fixed costs and variable costs.

16. **CRITICAL THINKING** How would you calculate the break-even point for a retail business? Break-even point is when gross profit equals operating expenses.

MIXED REVIEW

17. $82 \times 21\frac{1}{2}$ 1,763

18. $6.95 \times 1,000$ $6,950

19. $2\frac{1}{4} \div 18$ 0.125

20. $160\frac{1}{2}\% \times \$280$ $449.40

21. Find the due date of a 38-day note dated May 2.   June 9, Lesson 4.3

22. $25\frac{3}{4}\%$ of 800   206

23. Muhammed Rahum owns 50 bonds with a par value of $1,000 each that pay 8.75% interest. Find his semiannual income from these bonds. $2,187.50, Lesson 7.5

24. Juanita's lot and house are assessed at $76,800. The school tax rate in her district is 2.13 cents per $1. What is Juanita's school tax? $1,635.84, Lesson 6.3

25. A mill uses 4,300 brass rods in five days. Safety stock is 6 day's usage. Rods usually arrive within three days after ordering. What is the reorder point for brass rods?   7,740, Lesson 10.4

26. The Daily Sentinel charges $45.80 a line for job advertising on any weekday. Your company places an 11-line ad for a systems analyst in the newspaper for Monday through Friday. What was the total cost of the ad? $2,519, Lesson 10.1

27. Will a 40GB hard drive be adequate to store data for three employees that each use 12 gigabytes of file space and five employees that each use 650 MB of file space? Explain. yes, 12 (3 = 36 and 5 (650 = 3,250. 3,250 MB = 3GB and 250 MB. All together the employees have 39 GB 250 MB; Lesson 9.1

28. A factory had this overhead for June: supervisory wages, $218,834; rent, $16,726; depreciation, $45,187; power, $15,125; maintenance and repairs, $25,165; other, $7,367. What was the total factory overhead? $328,404, Lesson 11.1

474 ■ **Chapter 11 Business Costs**

DIFFERENT LEARNING STYLES Visual Learners

In Exercises 13 and 14, students may be confused about why they add fixed costs, variable costs, and profits to find the total sales needed to break even. To help students visualize total sales, you might construct a rectangle on the board and divide it into two parts, roughly approaching the relative sizes of the combined fixed and variable costs, and profits.

11.3 Depreciation Costs

GOALS

- Calculate depreciation using declining-balance method
- Calculate depreciation using sum-of-the-years-digits method
- Calculate depreciation using modified accelerated cost recovery system method

Start Up

Business property loses value over time from wear and tear. Can you think of another reason why business property might lose value over time?

Math Skill Builder

Review these math skills and solve the exercises that follow.

1 **Subtract** money amounts.
Find the difference. $13,500 − $2,560 = $10,940

  1a. $24,850 − $6,520 $18,330 **1b.** $14,208 − $11,078 $3,130

2 **Multiply** money amounts by percents.
Find the product. $24,800 × 20% = $24,800 × 0.20 = $4,960

  2a. $14,780 × 8.5% $1,256.30   **2b.** $86,480 × 19.5%
                                      $16,863.60

■ Declining-Balance Method

The depreciation of property that has a life of more than one year is a major expense for many businesses. The Internal Revenue Service regulates the calculation of depreciation. They allow depreciation to be calculated in several ways, including the straight-line method that you have already learned.

Businesses may use depreciation methods that deduct greater amounts in the early years than in later years. Two such methods are the declining-balance method and the sum-of-the-years-digits method. When calculating depreciation, the term book value is used. Book value is the original cost of the property less the total depreciation to date.

The declining-balance method uses a fixed rate of depreciation for each year. Because the rate is applied to a declining or decreasing balance, the amount of depreciation decreases each year.

EXAMPLE 1

A van costing $16,000 is estimated to depreciate 20% each year. What is the estimated book value of the truck at the end of the first and second years?

Start Up

Have students read the Start Up. Discuss with them possible answers to the question posed.

Math Skill Builder

The skills of adding, subtracting, and multiplying money amounts are used in this lesson. So is multiplying money amounts by percents and fractions.

Complete all exercises in Math Skill Builder 1–2 to have students review many of these skills.

■ Teach Goal 1

Point out that depreciation is simply a method of spreading the cost of a property over its estimated life. Land is not considered an expense. It does not wear out and cannot be depreciated.

If a firm owns a mine, however, it can be depleted. If students are interested in depletion, assign the Connection to Accounting project in Lesson 11-3.

Remind students that the straight-line method of depreciation results in the same amount of depreciation each year. The declining-balance method and the sum-of-the-years-digits method give a more realistic picture of the value of properties.

Point out that with the declining-balance method, there will always be a book value, even at the end of the useful life. That last book value is considered to be the salvage or trade-in value.

CONNECTION TO ACCOUNTING

Some forms of depreciation are treated differently by the rules of accounting and by the Internal Revenue Service. One form of depreciation is the reduction in value of a mine through removal of the accessible ore. This form of depreciation is called depletion. You may want students to research depletion and prepare a brief written report on the topic. The report should include a definition or explanation of depletion, how depletion differs from depreciation, and the sources used to research the topic.

$0.20 \times \$16,000 = \$3,200$ first year depreciation

$\$16,000 - \$3,200 = \$12,800$ book value, end of first year

$0.20 \times \$12,800 = \$2,560$ second year depreciation

$\$12,800 - \$2,560 = \$10,240$ book value, end of second year

■ **CHECK YOUR UNDERSTANDING**

A. A forming machine that cost $45,000 is depreciated each year at the rate of 8%. What is the book value of the machine at the end of the second year? $38,088

B. LB Forging buys a drill press for $7,500. The estimated life is 12 years, and the annual depreciation rate used is 8%. What will be the book value of the press at the end of 3 years? $5,840.16

■ Sum-Of-The-Years-Digits Method

Another way to calculate depreciation is the **sum-of-the-years-digits method**. This is a variable-rate method. Like the declining-balance method, the sum-of-the-years-digits method provides the greatest amount of depreciation in the first year and smaller amounts of depreciation after that.

For example, if you estimate to use a machine for five years, the amount of depreciation is calculated by adding the years together: $1 + 2 + 3 + 4 + 5 = 15$ years. Then you depreciate the machine $\frac{5}{15}$ of the total depreciation for the first year, $\frac{4}{15}$ of the total depreciation for the second year, $\frac{3}{15}$ for the third year, $\frac{2}{15}$ for the fourth year, and $\frac{1}{15}$ for the fifth year.

EXAMPLE 2

A lathe costing $16,000 will be used for 5 years, and then traded in for an estimated $8,500. Find the book value of the lathe at the end of the second year.

SOLUTION

Subtract the estimated trade-in value from the original cost.

$\$16,000 - \$8,500 = \$7,500$ total depreciation

Find the sum-of-the-years-digits: $1 + 2 + 3 + 4 + 5 = 15$

Find the depreciation for the first year: $\frac{5}{15} \times \$7,500 = \$2,500$

Find the book value at the end of the first year: $\$16,000 - \$2,500 = \$13,500$

Find the depreciation for the second year: $\frac{4}{15} \times \$7,500 = \$2,000$

Find the book value at the end of the second year: $\$13,500 - \$2,000 = \$11,500$

■ **CHECK YOUR UNDERSTANDING**

C. Yankee Products bought a hydraulic winch for $23,600. They plan to use it for 6 years and then trade it for $4,500. Find the book value of the winch at the end of the second year. $13,595.24

D. Roberto Bros. bought a loader for $80,000. The firm estimates that the loader will be used for 7 years and then traded in for $6,000. What will the book value of the loader be at the end of the first and third years? $61,500; $32,428.57

Sidebar (left column)

Work through Example 1 with students completing the math at their desks.

Assign Check Your Understanding problems A and B for completion in class. Walk about your classroom and examine student work for errors and problems.

Stress that the sum-of-the-years-digits method applies the depreciation fraction to the total depreciation of the property, not the original cost of the property.

Show students how to find the sum-of-the-years-digits for other depreciation periods. 10 years = $1 + 2 + 3 + 4 + 5 + 6 + 7 + 8 + 9 + 10 = 55$. For the first year, you use $\frac{10}{55}$ or $\frac{2}{11}$ of the total depreciation (original cost less trade-in value).

■ **ONGOING ASSESSMENT**

Call out a number, such as 9 and ask students to find the sum of its digits. **45.** Then call out an amount, such as $20,000 and ask students to find the depreciation on it for the first year using the sum-of-the-years-digits method. $\frac{9}{45} = 0.2$; $0.2 \times$ **$20,000 = $4,000**

Do Example 2 with students doing the math at their desks.

Assign Check Your Understanding problems C and D for in-class work. Move about the room to check student work.

■ *CHECK YOUR UNDERSTANDING SOLUTIONS*

A. $45,000 × 0.08 = $3,600;
$45,000 − $3,600 = $41,400;
$41,400 × 0.08 = $3,312;
$41,400 − $3,312 = $38,088

B. $7,500 × 0.08 = $600; $7,500 − $600 = $6,900;
$6,900 × 0.08 = $552; $6,900 − $552 = $6,348;
$6,348 × 0.08 = $507.84; $6,348 − $507.84 = $5,840.16

Modified Accelerated Cost Recovery System Method

For federal income tax purposes, the modified accelerated cost recovery system (MACRS) must be used to calculate depreciation for most business property placed in service after 1986. The MACRS method allows you to claim depreciation over a fixed number of years depending on the *class life* of the property. The class life means how long the Internal Revenue Service (IRS) will let you depreciate the property.

The Internal Revenue Service (IRS) categorized the lives of different types of property into a number of classes, including 3, 5, 7, 10, 15, and 20 years. For example, the IRS puts cars, trucks, and most office equipment into a 5-year class life and office furniture into a 7-year class life. The rate of depreciation to be used for each year of a property's life is set by the IRS and varies with each class life.

You calculate the depreciation deduction for any one year by multiplying the original cost by the rate of depreciation for that year. Trade-in value, or salvage value, is not used in the MACRS method.

The table of depreciation rates for properties with class lives of 5 and 7 years is shown. Notice that 5-year properties and 7-year properties are depreciated over six and eight years, respectively.

> **BUSINESS TIP**
>
> The MACRS method allows businesses to depreciate their property fully and at a faster rate than they might otherwise. Congress passed the MACRS to encourage business to invest in new equipment.

EXAMPLE 3

Elena Suarez bought a business truck for $19,000. Find the depreciation for each year. What is its book value at the end of its class life?

SOLUTION
Multiply the original cost by the rate of depreciation for each year.

	Cars, Trucks, Office Equipment	Office Furniture and Fixtures
Class Life	*5-Years*	*7-Years*
First Year	20.0%	14.29%
Second Year	32.0%	24.49%
Third Year	19.2%	17.49%
Fourth Year	11.52%	12.49%
Fifth Year	11.52%	8.93%
Sixth Year	5.76%	8.92%
Seventh Year		8.93%
Eighth Year		4.46%

First Year   0.20   × $19,000 = $3,800.00

Second Year   0.32   × 19,000 = 6,080.00

Third Year   0.192 × 19,000 = 3,648.00

Fourth Year   0.1152 × 19,000 = 2,188.80

Fifth Year   0.1152 × 19,000 = 2,188.80

Sixth Year   0.0576 × 19,000 = 1,094.40

Total Depreciation $19,000.00

> **MATH TIP**
>
> To check your calculations for MACRS, add the depreciation for each year. If you did your work correctly, the total depreciation should equal the original cost.

Subtract the total depreciation from the original cost.

$19,000 − $19,000 = $0   book value at end of class life

■ CHECK YOUR UNDERSTANDING SOLUTIONS

C. $1 + 2 + 3 + 4 + 5 + 6 = 21$; $23,600 − $4,500 = $19,100; $\frac{6}{21} \times$ $19,100 = $5,457.14; $23,600 − $5,457.14 = $18,142.86; $\frac{5}{21} \times$ $19,100 = $4,547.62; $18,142.86 − $4,547.62 = $13,595.24

D. $1 + 2 + 3 + 4 + 5 + 6 + 7 = 28$; $80,000 − $6,000 = $74,000; $\frac{7}{28} \times$ $74,000 = $18,500; $80,000 − $18,500 = $61,500; $\frac{6}{28} \times$ $74,000 = $15,857.14; $61,500 − $15,857.14 = $45,642.86; $\frac{5}{28} \times$ $74,000 = $13,214.29; $45,642.86 − $13,214.29 = $32,428.57

477

■ CHECK YOUR UNDERSTANDING

E. LaBeck, Inc. paid $14,200 for a copier that had a class life of 5 years. What amount of depreciation was allowed on the copier for each of the first 5 years? $2,840; $4,544; $2,726.40; $1,635.84; $1,635.84

F. A suite of office furniture cost $15,900. What total depreciation is allowable for the first year's use? Using MACRS table, what is the book value of the furniture after the third year? $2,272.11; $6,953.07

Wrap Up

One reason that business property might lose value over time is obsolescence. New equipment might do the work faster and cheaper, for example. New equipment might also perform functions that were not performed by the older equipment.

COMMUNICATION

Another way that the Internal Revenue Service allows businesses to depreciate property is through *first-year expensing*.

- What is first-year expensing of property?

- Is there a limit to the value of property that can be expensed?

- Are there some types of property that can't be expensed?

- How does this benefit small business?

EXERCISES

1. $1 + 2 + 3 + 4 + 5 + 6$ 21   **2.** $3,108 + $1,397 $4,505

3. $180,380 − $83,700 $96,680   **4.** $16,338 − $11,089 $5,249

5. $245,700 × 19.2% $47,174.40   **6.** $375,990 × 20% $75,198

7. A truck that cost $15,000 is depreciated in value each year at the rate of 8%. What is the book value of the machine at the end of the second year using the declining-balance method? $12,696

8. Syncom Corporation buys a machine for $23,800. The rate of annual depreciation is 12%. How much will be the book value of the press at the end of 3 years using the declining-balance method? $16,219.03

■ *CHECK YOUR UNDERSTANDING SOLUTIONS*

E. $14,200 × 0.20 = $2,840 first year;
$14,200 × 0.32 = $4,544 second year;
$14,200 × 0.192 = $2,726.40 third year;
$14,200 × 0.1152 = $1,635.84 fourth year;
$14,200 × 0.1152 = $1,635.84 fifth year

F. First year: $15,900 × 0.1429 = $2,272.11 deprec.;
$15,900 − $2,272.11 = $13,627.89 book value.
Second year: $15,900 × 0.2449 = $3,893.91 deprec.;
$13,627.89 − $3,893.91 = $9,733.98 book value.
Third year: $15,900 × 0.1749 = $2,780.91 deprec.;
$9,733.98 − $2,780.91 = $6,953.07 book value.

Copy and complete the table using the declining-balance method of depreciation.

	Property	Original Cost	Rate of Depreciation	Book Value At End of First Year	Book Value At End of Third Year
9.	Sprayer	$1,400	8%	$1,288	$1,090.16
10.	Fork Lift Truck	$11,200	15%	$9,520	$6,878.20
11.	Press	$8,600	12%	$7,568	$5,860.66
12.	Die Cutter	$45,000	14%	$38,700	$28,622.52
13.	Hydraulic Punch Press	$22,800	13%	$19,836	$15,013.87

14. L. Diaz, Inc., bought a boring machine for $18,900. The company plans to use the borer for 7 years and then sell it. The company estimates the resale value will be $3,800. Find the depreciation for each of the first 3 years using the sum-of-the-years-digits method. $3,775; $3,235.71; $2,696.43

15. Bellevue Farms bought 5 items of office equipment, weighing 14 metric tons, for $84,200. The company plans to use the equipment for 16 hours daily for 12 years and then scrap it for no value. Using the sum-of-the-years-digits depreciation method, what will be the book value of the equipment at the end of 3 years? $48,576.92

Use the MACRS table given in the lesson to solve Exercises 16–19.

A property costs $250,000 and is classified as a 5-year class life property under MACRS.

16. What is the total amount of depreciation allowed for its first year of use? $50,000

17. What is the total amount of depreciation allowed for the life of the property? $250,000

18. What is the book value of the property after the first year's use? $200,000

19. What is the book value of the property after two years' use? $120,000

20. **CRITICAL THINKING**   Another method of depreciation is called the *unit of performance* (or production) *method*. What do you think this means and how do you think you calculate depreciation using this method?   Depreciate equipment on basis of use, e.g., hours of use, number of products produced, miles run.

21. **CRITICAL THINKING**   Why is there an advantage to a company to have a larger tax deduction for depreciation in the early years of a property than having depreciation spread evenly over each year of a property's life?   Company has longer use of larger amount of money

MIXED REVIEW

22. Write $\frac{1}{8}$ as a decimal to the nearest hundredth.   0.13

23. Red Frankel deposited $20,000 in a three-year certificate of deposit that pays simple interest at a fixed annual rate of 6.7%. What total interest will Red have earned at the end of three years? $4,020, Lesson 3.7

24. To make 600 book covers, the costs are: materials, $7,289; labor, $12,828; factory overhead, $1,723. What is the average cost of each cover, to the nearest cent? $36.40, Lesson 11.1

Lesson 11.3 Depreciation Costs ■ **479**

Enrich

Assign and discuss Exercise 20, Critical Thinking. Depreciation using unit of performance or production methods is found by the number of hours a machine has operated, units it has produced, or how many miles it has run. Plane and boat motors are often depreciated using hours operated. Factory cutting tools may be depreciated using the number of items cut. To find the depreciation for one year, divide the actual number of hours, miles, or units in that year by the estimated total. Multiply the result by the depreciable cost of the machine (original cost less salvage value).

Assign Exercise 21, Critical Thinking. Point out the time value of money they learned by compounding interest and the future value of IRA funds. High depreciation results in lower taxes early on and allows a firm to invest or use that money for a longer period of time.

Close

Give students an ad for office equipment and a depreciation schedule. Divide students into groups. Have each group depreciate the property using one of the methods studied. Then have students discuss the implications of the different depreciation amounts on a firm's taxes in the first and third years of ownership.

■ **STUDENT PORTFOLIO**
Students may wish to place the solutions to Exercises 20 and 21 in their portfolios.

Start Up

Have students read the Start Up. Bring an empty box from the school office or elsewhere to class and demonstrate how to measure its girth using a ruler or yardstick.

Math Skill Builder

The addition and multiplication of money amounts by whole numbers are skills that are used in the lesson. So are the abilities to divide amounts by 100 and round up any answer with a remainder to the next 100.

Have students complete all exercises in Math Skill Builder 1–4 so that they are ready for the problems in the lesson.

■ Teach Goal 1

You may wish to make a transparency of part of a current U.S. Postal Service rate table for parcel post or part of a current rate table for United Parcel Service and use one or both of those tables to solve Example 1 and Exercises 12–20.

Explain to students that zones refer to arbitrary circles that radiate out from a given point, such as a city, that are used to calculate rates for shipping distances from the city. Draw on the board a dot to represent a city and then a few circles, each increasing in size, around the city to help students visualize the concept.

Point out that e-business has boosted the amount of shipping substantially since buying from online stores requires shipping.

11.4 Shipping Costs

GOALS

- Calculate shipping charges
- Calculate freight charges

Start Up

Julia Martino wants to ship a present to her dad. When she calls a shipping service for help they ask her for the weight and girth of the package. She doesn't know how to measure for girth and she doesn't have a scale for weighing packages. What help can you give her?

Math Skill Builder

Review these math skills and solve the exercises that follow.

1 **Add** dollar amounts.
Find the sum. $148 + $12.50 + $34.89 = $195.39

1a. $24.50 + $89.10 + $1.56 $115.16   **1b.** $108 + $38.22 + $16.75 $162.97

2 **Multiply** dollar amounts by dollar amounts and whole numbers.
Find the product. $0.76 × 456 = $346.56 $4.87 × 34 = $165.58

2a. $0.53 × $580 $307.40   **2b.** $1.56 × $750 $1,170

2c. $6.78 × 125 $847.50   **2d.** $2.16 × 1,560 $3,369.60

3 **Divide** dollar amounts and whole numbers by 100.
Find the quotient. $1,250 ÷ 100 = $12.50
Find the quotient. 45,600 ÷ 100 = 456

3a. $25,900 ÷ 100 $259   **3b.** 145,800 ÷ 100   1,458

4 **Round** whole numbers up to the next 100.
Round up to the next 100. 14,356, or 14,400.

4a. 289   300   **4b.** 1,978   2,000   **4c.** 28,084   28,100   **4d.** 87,219   87,300

■ Shipping Charges

Businesses use the U.S. Postal Service, private carriers, and other shippers to deliver products to their customers. Businesses may also pay shipping costs when they purchase items. Before deciding how to ship, a firm must consider the speed and distance the package will travel, and the size, weight, and shape of the package. The firm may also want insurance, special handling, C.O.D. (collect on delivery), weekend delivery, and door-to-door pickup and delivery. These services raise the cost of shipping the goods.

480 ■ Chapter 11 Business Costs

DIFFERENT LEARNING ABILITIES Visually Impaired Learners

If you expect that some students will have difficulty reading the rate tables in the lesson, consider making copies of the tables using a copy machine that can enlarge images. Run off enough copies of the enlarged tables for the students that need them.

A package may be sent by the U.S. Postal Service by *parcel post* service if the package weighs not more than 70 pounds and is not more than 130 inches in combined length and *girth*. Other shipping services use different limitations. When measuring weight, most services consider a fraction of a pound as a full pound.

A table of rates for a shipping company is shown below. These rates are for delivery within two business days and are charged for each package delivered. Distance is shown in *zones*, or circular bands of miles around the shipping point. The number of miles wide each zone is may vary with each shipper.

MATH TIP

Girth is the measurement around a package at its thickest part. If a package is 30 inches long, 10 inches wide, and 4 inches deep, the girth is 10 + 4 + 10 + 4, or 28 inches. The combined length and girth is 30 + 28, or 58 inches.

■ **Apply Goal 1**

Do Example 1 at the board or on a transparency while students do the math at their desks.

Assign Check Your Understanding problems A and B for completion in class. Examine student work at their desks for errors or problems.

EXAMPLE 1

Clarion Corporation ships a 14-lb package to zone 6. Insuring the package costs $7.50 more. What is the total cost to ship the package using shipping rate table below?

SOLUTION

Find the shipping charge by moving down to the row for the package weight and over to the right for the column of the destination zone.

$33.25   shipping charge

Add the shipping charge and the insurance charge.

$33.25 + $7.50 = $40.75   total cost of shipping

Package weight (lb)	Destination Zones						
	1 & 2	3	4	5	6	7	8
1	$7.50	$8.25	$9.00	$9.75	$10.75	$11.25	$11.50
2	$8.00	$8.75	$10.00	$11.00	$12.00	$12.75	$13.00
3	$8.50	$9.25	$11.00	$12.75	$13.75	$14.25	$14.75
4	$9.25	$10.00	$12.00	$13.75	$15.25	$16.00	$16.75
5	$10.00	$11.00	$13.25	$15.25	$17.25	$18.25	$18.75
6	$10.75	$11.75	$14.25	$16.75	$19.25	$20.50	$21.00
7	$11.25	$12.75	$15.50	$18.00	$21.25	$22.25	$23.00
8	$12.00	$13.50	$16.50	$19.50	$23.00	$24.00	$25.00
9	$12.50	$14.25	$17.75	$21.00	$25.00	$26.00	$26.75
10	$13.00	$15.00	$18.50	$22.25	$26.50	$27.75	$29.00
11	$13.75	$15.75	$19.50	$23.50	$28.00	$29.75	$30.50
12	$14.50	$17.00	$20.50	$25.00	$30.00	$30.75	$32.00
13	$15.25	$17.75	$21.50	$26.50	$31.25	$32.25	$33.75
14	$15.75	$18.25	$22.75	$27.75	$33.25	$34.25	$35.25
15	$16.50	$19.00	$23.75	$28.75	$34.25	$35.50	$36.50
16	$16.75	$19.75	$24.75	$29.50	$35.25	$36.50	$38.25

National Shipping Company Rates for 2-Day Delivery

COMMON ERRORS

Students may use the wrong rate because they have gotten off track when reading across the rate table from the package weight to the destination zone they seek. To avoid these mistakes, have students use a ruler or the edge of a piece of paper to help them locate data in the rate table.

Obtain the freight rates for one or more freight shippers who use trucks in your area. Make transparencies of the rates and display them to the class. Ask students to compare the rates and the rate structures of area shippers with those in the textbook. You might also have students solve some of the problems using the rates from area shippers.

Stress that when partial hundredweight amounts are shipped, the amounts are rounded up to the next hundredweight.

■ **Apply Goal 2**

Do Example 2 at the board or on a transparency while students solve it at their desks.

Assign Check Your Understanding problems C and D to do in class. Circulate through your classroom and examine student work for difficulties.

■ **ONGOING ASSESSMENT**
Make a transparency of Check Your Understanding problem D. Then with their books closed, call on students to describe the steps they must take to solve the problem. Ask each student called upon to describe one step.

■ **CHECK YOUR UNDERSTANDING**

A. Tosco Imaging, Inc. ships 3 packages weighing $5\frac{1}{2}$, 12, and 15 pounds to zone 3 using National Shipping's 2-Day service (see shipping rate table). Insurance costs were $31.89. Since the second day falls on Saturday, $15 extra per package is charged. What was the total cost of the shipment? $124.64

B. Ridgeway, Inc. ships and insures 5 packages worth $1,800 each by SpeediAir for same day delivery. SpeediAir charges $159 for each package. They also charge $0.50 per $100 of value for insurance. What is the total cost of the shipment?
$840

■ Freight Charges

Freight is often used for shipping heavy, bulky goods. Freight shipments may be sent by airplane, truck, train, barge, or ship. Many shipping companies that deliver letters and small parcels handle freight, too. Sample rates for a freight company are shown.

Curry Freight and Express Company							
3-Day Delivery—Rates Per Pound							
Weight in Pounds	**Destination Zones**						
	1 & 2	**3**	**4**	**5**	**6**	**7**	**8**
151–499	0.50	0.90	1.10	1.19	1.66	2.08	2.34
500–999	0.49	0.88	1.07	1.19	1.61	1.97	2.34
1000–1999	0.47	0.85	1.04	1.14	1.56	1.97	2.28
2000+	0.45	0.83	1.03	1.09	1.51	1.92	2.23

The term **f.o.b.**, or **free on board**, may be used by sellers to show who pays the shipping costs. For example, a seller in New York quotes a buyer in St. Louis a price, f.o.b. St. Louis. This means that the seller will pay the transportation charges to St. Louis, or that the goods will travel "free on board" to the buyer in St. Louis. If the seller quotes a price, f.o.b. New York, the buyer pays the transportation costs from New York to St. Louis.

Shipping charges may be calculated on the basis of weight per 100 pounds, or *cwt* (*hundredweight*). To find the charge, divide the weight of the shipment by 100 and multiply by the rate per cwt. Any amount less than 100 pounds is usually charged at the full 100-pound rate. So, a 532-pound parcel would be charged as if it were 600 pounds.

EXAMPLE 2

A 1,500-pound package is to be delivered in three days by Curry Freight and Express to a firm in zone 5. What is the freight charge?

SOLUTION
Using the freight table, find the price per pound by moving down to the row for the package weight and then over to the column for destination zone.

$1.14   price per pound

Multiply the weight of the package by the price per pound.

1,500 × $1.14 = $1,710   freight charge

■ *CHECK YOUR UNDERSTANDING SOLUTIONS*

A. 3 × $15 = $45; $45 + $11.75 + $17 + $19 + $31.89 = $124.64

B. $1,800 ÷ 100 = 18; 18 × $0.50 = $9; 5 × $9 = $45; 5 × $159 = $795; $45 + $795 = $840

C. 2 × 850 = 1,700; 1,700 × $1.07 = $1,819

D. 42,350 ÷ 100 = 423.5 or 424; 424 × $19.45 = $8,246.80; f.o.b. Toledo means Montez, in Mayfield, pays the freight charge.

C. Gomez Bros. ships two 850-pound packages to zone 4 by Curry Freight in three days. What is the freight charge? $1,819

D. Louisa Montez, Inc. of Mayfield ships 42,350 pounds of steel rods by freight to Carlson Forging Corporation of Toledo, f.o.b. Toledo. The freight company charges $19.45 a cwt. What is the freight charge? Who pays it? $8246.80; Montez

Wrap Up

Girth is measured by the distance around a package. For cartons or boxes, a ruler can be used to measure all four sides around the package. For round packages or oddly shaped packages, a tape measure will usually do. To weigh a package without a regular parcel scale, Julia can use a standard home scale. Julia should step on the scale and weigh herself. Then she should hold the package and weigh herself again. The difference in weights is the weight of the package.

TEAM MEETING

With two other students, compare the cost of shipping a 30 lb. package worth $750 overnight to a city in a nearby state by the U.S. Postal Service's parcel post and two other shipping firms. The shipping cost should include enough insurance to cover the value of the package. Prepare a chart comparing the costs of shipping, insuring, and the total cost for the three shippers. The package has a combined length and girth of 80 inches.

EXERCISES

1. $2.59 × 359 $929.81
2. $0.24 × 5,480 $1,315.20
3. $4,810 ÷ 100 $48.10
4. 89,340 ÷ 100   893.4
5. Round up to the next even 100: 32,876   32,900
6. $369.28 + $12.89 + $83.19 $465.36

Which of the packages below may be sent by the U.S. Postal Service's parcel post service?

	Length	Width	Depth	Weight	
7.	23 inches	8 inches	14 inches	16 lb	yes
8.	50 inches	12 inches	7 inches	75 lb	no
9.	30 inches	6 inches	8 inches	$42\frac{1}{2}$ lb	yes
10.	60 inches	15 inches	12 inches	50 lb	yes
11.	70 inches	12 inches	14 inches	65 lb	yes

Lesson 11.4 Shipping Costs ■ **483**

SELECTED SOLUTIONS

22. 12 × $6.40 = $76.80; $76.80 + $48.90 = $125.70   **23.** 16 × $2.25 = $36; $590 ÷ 100 = 5.9, or 6; 6 × $0.35 = $2.10; $36 + $2.10 + $25 = $63.10

STUDENT WORKBOOK To reteach calculating shipping charges, do Exercise 1 with students. Then have them do Exercises 2–11.

To reteach calculating freight charges, do Exercise 12 with students. Then have them do Exercises 13–22.

Have students locate the rate tables used by the U.S. Postal Service and at least two other shippers on the Internet.

Ask a school employee or an employee of an area business who handles package shipping and deliveries to address the class about shipping "horror stories" the employee has experienced and how the problems were handled. For example, the employee might describe a shipment that contained damaged goods. The employee might then describe how they handled the damaged shipment with the vendor and the shipper.

Use the shipping table given in the lesson to find the shipping charges for each package in Exercises 12–21.

	Weight in Pounds	Destination in Zone	Shipping Charge		Weight	Destination in Zone	Shipping Charge
12.	6	8	$21.00	**13.**	$13\frac{1}{2}$ lb	6	$33.25
14.	10	3	$15.00	**15.**	3.25 lb	4	$12.00
16.	16	7	$36.50	**17.**	9 lb 4 oz.	7	$27.75
18.	5	2	$10.00	**19.**	4 lb 8 oz.	5	$15.25
20.	8	5	$19.50	**21.**	7 lb 3 oz.	8	$25.00

22. The U.S. Postal Service charges $6.40 each to ship 12 parcels of reel film by parcel post. The company that is shipping the film insures the contents with a private insurer for $48.90. What is the total cost of the shipment? $125.70

23. A shipping service charges $2.25 per pound to deliver a 16-pound package on a weekend. Insurance costs an additional $0.35 per $100, or fraction of $100 of value. The company values its parcel at $590. Weekend delivery costs $25 additional. What is the cost to ship the package? $63.10

BEST BUY A company wants to ship 3 parcels weighing 12 lbs. each to zone 7. They can have the packages delivered in three days using National Shipping (see shipping rate table) or a week to ten days using the U.S. Postal Service's parcel post. The parcel post rates are $15.15 per package.

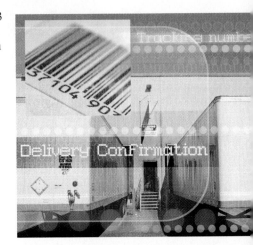

24. What will it cost to ship the packages in 3 days using National? $92.25

25. What will it cost to ship the packages in 7–10 days using parcel post? $45.45

26. How much will the company save by shipping the packages by parcel post? $46.80

Use the freight table to calculate the freight charges for each shipment.

	Weight in Pounds	Destination in Zone	Freight Charge		Weight in Pounds	Destination in Zone	Freight Charge
27.	386	2	$193	**28.**	513	8	$1,200.42
29.	1,370	6	$2,137.20	**30.**	725	4	$775.75
31.	160	3	$144	**32.**	919	7	$1,810.43
33.	584	8	$1,366.56	**34.**	499	5	$593.81
35.	1,809	5	$2,062.26	**36.**	2,598	3	$2,156.34

SELECTED SOLUTIONS

24. 3 × $30.75 = $92.25
25. 3 × $15.15 = $45.45
26. $92.25 − $45.45 = $46.80

46. $79,104 − $7,800 − $9,000 = $62,304
47. $62,304 × 0.035 = $2,180.64

37. Crayco, Inc. of Madison ships 12,635 pounds of metal bars by freight to Sisco Manufacturing Company of Roswell, f.o.b. Madison. The freight company charges $12.49 a cwt. What is the freight charge? Who pays it? $1,586.23; Sisco

The freight rate to Hammond for a certain type of item is $38.87 per cwt or any remaining fraction of the total shipment. A customer wants to ship 9 crates weighing 95 pounds each and 11 cartons weighing 22 pounds each.

38. Estimate the total weight of the shipment. 1,200 lb

39. Estimate the freight charge. $400

40. What is the exact freight charge? $427.57

41. **INTEGRATING YOUR KNOWLEDGE** Johnson Electric Company buys 380 electrical switches @ $1.88 and 20 pre-cut cables @ $2. The switches and cables are shipped in one box weighing 14 pounds to zone 6 using National Shipping. What is the total cost of the switches to Johnson? $787.65

MIXED REVIEW

42. Multiply 28 by 5. 140

43. What amount is 140% greater than $34? $47.60

44. Find the number of days from May 1 to October 5. 157

45. Show 0.0975 as a percent. 9.75%

The Bernsteins' gross income for a year was $79,104. From that amount they subtracted a standard deduction of $9,700, and 3 exemptions at $3,100 each to find their taxable income. Lesson 2.4

46. What was their taxable income? $60,104

47. What was the amount of their state income tax in a state with an income tax rate of 3.5% on taxable income? $2,103.64

48. Yang Su's online checking account balance was $437. In the past seven days, she had these transactions in her account: deposit, $362.18; debit card purchase of $43.68; one check written for $162. Today Yang is making online payments for car insurance, $278; charge card, $48.92; power bill, $164.55. What will be the balance of her online checking account after all the transactions and online payments are entered? $102.03, Lesson 3.3

49. Ahmed Tahil bought a car for $15,600. He estimates its trade-in value will be $5,200 at the end of 4 years. What is the estimated average annual depreciation of the car? $2,600, Lesson 6.6

50. A computer that cost $2,400 is estimated to depreciate 20% each year. Using the declining-balance method, find the book value of the computer at the end of the third year. $1,228.80, Lesson 11.3

51. Tolson, Ltd. ships and insures 3 packages worth a total of $840 for same day delivery. The shipper charges $125 to deliver each package and $0.35 per $100, or fraction of $100 of the value of the total shipment for insurance. What is the total cost of the shipment? $378.15, Lesson 11.4

Lesson 11.4 Shipping Costs ■ **485**

Close

Use Exercise 24, Best Buy, to review the steps to calculate shipping costs.

Use Exercise 41, Integrating Your Knowledge, to review the steps to calculate freight costs.

■ **STUDENT PORTFOLIO**
If you assign the Team Meeting project, have students consider including their charts in their portfolios.

SELECTED SOLUTIONS

38. 9 is rounded to 10, 95 to 100; 10 × 100 = 1,000; 11 is rounded to 10, 22 to 20; 10 × 20 = 200; 1,000 + 200 = 1,200 lbs.

39. $38.87 is rounded to $40; 1,200 is rounded to 1,000; 1,000 ÷ 100 = 10; 10 × $40 = $400

40. 9 × 95 = 855; 11 × 22 = 242; 1,097 ÷ 100 = 10.97, or 11; 11 × $38.87 = $427.57

41. 380 × $1.88 = $714.40; 20 × $2 = $40; $714.40 + $40 + $33.25 = $787.65

11.5 Office Costs

GOALS

- Calculate the costs of office space
- Calculate the cost of a unit of office work

Start Up

Ruby Lake recently found that the firm for which she works can monitor the e-mail messages that she receives and sends. She felt this was a violation of her privacy and was illegal. What do you think?

Math Skill Builder

Review these math skills and solve the exercises that follow.

1. **Subtract** money amounts from money amounts.
   Find the difference. $89.12 − $77.64 = $11.48

   1a. $159.35 − $140.98 $18.37   **1b.** $207.44 − $56.29 $151.15

2. **Divide** money amounts by whole numbers.
   Find the quotient. $108,245 ÷ 36,000 = $3.007, or $3.01

   2a. $29,800 ÷ 2,500 $11.92   **2b.** $310,780 ÷ 5,500 $56.51

■ Office Space

Office space is a major office expense. The costs for providing office space may include rent, light, heat, air conditioning, insurance, cleaning, and maintenance. If the office is owned instead of rented, the costs may include depreciation of the building, mortgage interest, and real estate taxes.

EXAMPLE 1

A 4,500 sq ft office area rents for $62,250 a year. Utilities cost $4,800 a year. What is the total yearly cost of this office space per square foot? If a clerk's workstation is 64 sq ft, how much does this workstation space cost per year?

SOLUTION

Add the costs for rent and utilities.

$62,250 + $4,800 = $67,050   total annual cost of office space

Divide the total annual cost of the office space by the square feet.

$67,050 ÷ 4,500 = $14.90   cost of office space per square foot

Multiply the cost per square foot by the workstation square feet.

$14.90 × 64 = $953.60   annual cost of workstation space

A. An office with 2,600 ft² rents for $49,400 a year. Power, natural gas, and maintenance are estimated to cost $4,940 a year. What is the total monthly cost of this office space per square foot? If one workstation's area is 32 ft², how much does this workstation cost per year? $20.90; $668.80

B. A 40,000 ft² building contains a warehouse and offices. The offices occupy 10% of the building. The rent, power, maintenance, insurance, and other costs for the entire building are $1,289,600 per year. How many square feet does the office occupy? What is the annual cost of the office space per square foot?   4,000 ft²; $32.24

■ Unit Costs of Office Work

Owners and managers often need to know the cost of one job, of each workstation, or of a unit of work, such as a letter or report. These costs can then be compared to the costs of other firms and industry averages.

EXAMPLE 2

Last year an office spent these amounts on three workstations: salaries, $42,824; rent and utilities, $8,200; depreciation of equipment, $7,140; supplies, repairs, postage, and telephone, $9,420. Estimate the total amount spent on the three workstations. What was the average annual amount spent on each workstation?

SOLUTION

Round off and add the amounts spent on the workstations.

$40,000 + $8,000 + $7,000 + $9,000 = $64,000   estimated total spent

Add the exact amounts spent on the workstations.

$42,824 + $8,200 + $7,140 + $9,420 = $67,584   total spent on 3 workstations

Divide the total spent on workstations by the number of workstations.

$67,584 ÷ 3 = $22,528   average spent on each workstation

■ CHECK YOUR UNDERSTANDING

C. Three workers in a document center produced this number of lines of text in a week: Emma LeCono, 15,600; Edwin Rosen, 13,600; Jose Cruziero, 12,800. The total cost of running the center for the week was $2,257. How much did each document line cost, to the nearest cent? $0.05

D. Copy paper costs $4.15 per ream (500 sheets). When bought in a case of 10 reams, the same paper costs $38 per case. What is the cost per ream when buying a case? What is the savings per ream when buying a case? $3.80; $0.35

Wrap Up

Unless the employer promises employees that their e-mail messages are off limits to the firm, it is perfectly legal for the firm to view the messages, as it would be legal for them to open a worker's filing cabinet and view paper documents. The e-mail messages were created using the firm's computer system, network and the other resources, including paid time. If the employee has private messages on the computer system, then the employee may have used the firm's workstation for personal use.

Lesson 11.5 Office Costs ■ **487**

■ *CHECK YOUR UNDERSTANDING SOLUTIONS*

A. $49,400 + $4,940 = $54,350; $54,350 ÷ 2,600 = $20.903, or $20.90 total annual cost per ft²; $20.90 × 32 = $668.80 cost of workstation per year

B. 40,000 ft² × 0.10 = 4,000 office ft²; $1,289,600 × 0.10 = $128,960; $128,960 ÷ 4,000 = $32.24

C. 15,600 + 13,600 + 12,800 = 42,000; $2,257 ÷ 42,000 = $0.053, or $0.05

D. $38 ÷ 10 = $3.80 cost per ream; $4.15 − $3.80 = $0.35 savings per ream

TEAM MEETING

An office manager wants to increase the number of workstations that can be put in a space 40 feet wide by 30 feet long. That space now contains 4 rows of 5 workstations each. Each workstation requires a minimum of 30 square feet of space. Aisles must be 3 feet wide. Movable partitions can be used to separate workstations, but you must be able to get to each workstation without going through another.

With another student, use graph paper to draw a diagram that shows how you would rearrange the workstations. Then answer these questions.

1. If the office space rents for $22,400 per year, what is the annual rent per workstation with the old arrangement? $1,120

2. What is the annual rent per workstation with your new arrangement?   Answers will vary.

3. By what percent has your new arrangement increased the number of workstations in the same space?   Answers will vary.

EXERCISES

1. $56.78 − $45.49 $11.29
2. $1,597 − $997.45 $599.55
3. $288,560 ÷ 10,800 $26.72
4. $83,480 ÷ 3,280 $25.45

One office in an office building has an area of 5,200 ft². The office costs are $87,360 a year including rent, heating, cooling, lighting, and maintenance.

5. What is the annual cost of the office per square foot? $16.80

6. What is the annual cost of a supervisor's workstation that is 100 ft² in area? $1,680

A manager wants to increase the number of workstations that can be put in a space 43 feet wide by 58 feet long. That space now contains 6 rows of 10 workstations each. The manager wants to increase floor space by placing every two rows of desks together so that the aisle between them is eliminated.

7. How many aisles will be eliminated?   3

8. If the aisles are 3 feet wide, how much floor space, in square feet, is gained?   522 ft²

9. If two more rows of 10 workstations are added, by what percent has the manager increased the number of workstations in the same space? $33\frac{1}{3}$%

10. If the office space rents for $49,680 per year, what is the annual rent per workstation with the old arrangement? $828

11. What is the annual rent per workstation with the new arrangement? $621

12. What is the total cost of equipping a workstation with this equipment? $2,396.77

1 desk @ $359.89	1 letter tray @ $19.50
1 chair @ $119.50	1 computer system @ $1,695
1 calculator @ $15.99	1 telephone @ $86.99
1 lamp @ $69.95	1 floor mat @ $29.95

SELECTED SOLUTIONS

5. $87,360 ÷ 5,200 = $16.80
6. 100 × $16.80 = $1,680
7. 6 rows of single desks become 3 rows of 2 desks placed together, eliminating 3 aisles

8. 3 × 58 = 174 ft²; 174 × 3 = 522 ft² saved
9. 20 ÷ 60 = 0.33$\frac{1}{3}$, or 33$\frac{1}{3}$%
11. 60 + 20 = 80; $49,680 ÷ 80 = $621

Tomas Figuero works in an advertising copy center and keys in 585 lines of text per day, on average.

13. In 7.5 hours of work per day, how many lines per minute does he key in? 1.3

14. If he earns $10.80 an hour, what is the labor cost per line, to the nearest tenth of a cent? $0.138

A policy clerk can sort and file 170 original, signed insurance policies per hour.

15. How many policies would the clerk file in $7\frac{1}{2}$ hours of work? 1,275

16. At a wage rate of $9.20 per hour for the clerk, what does it cost to file each policy, to the nearest tenth of a cent? $0.054

17. An office manager supervises five data-entry workstations. The cost of each workstation is as follows: wages, 1,950 hours per year @ $10.80; fringe benefits, 25% of wages; space, 60 square feet @ $18.50 per square foot per year; data terminal rental, $50 per month; supplies, $275 per year; other costs, $1,300 per year. What is the total yearly cost of the five stations? $148,050

18. An office manager found that these amounts were spent to produce and mail 100 first-class letters: creation time, $278; materials, $12; postage, $34; equipment and space, $217; other, $94. What was the average cost per letter? $6.35

STRETCHING YOUR SKILLS When mailing 5,000 letters to customers, a mail clerk put 58 cents postage on each letter instead of the right amount, 55 cents.

19. What amount of postage was wasted on this mailing? $150

20. If the clerk was paid $10 per hour, how many hours of wages were wasted? 15

STRETCHING YOUR SKILLS A manager needed 20 copies of a 30-page report. The copy clerk ran 25 copies of the report so that they would have extras. The cost of the copy paper was $4.20 per ream (500 sheets).

21. What was the cost of the paper for the 25 copies? $6.30

22. How much could have been saved by running only as many copies as were needed? $1.26

MIXED REVIEW

23. Multiply $16\frac{1}{8}$ by 12. $193\frac{1}{2}$ **24.** What is 12% of $4.30? $0.52

25. Divide 0.042 by 0.006. 7 **26.** 16 is what percent of 20? 80%

27. Find the number of days from March 10 to May 6.
    57, Lesson 4.3

28. Find exact interest on $800 at 12% for 3 months.
    $24, Lesson 4.1

29. Three departments of a store use this floor space: home furnishings, 2,400 ft²; patio furniture, 1,200 ft²; lighting, 400 ft². Cooling costs are charged to departments on the basis of floor space. What is each department's share of the $1,200 summer cooling costs? $720, $360, $120, Lesson 11.1

30. A building valued at $200,000 was insured for $120,000 under an 80% coinsurance clause policy. A fire caused a loss of $25,600. How much did the insurance company pay? $19,200, Lesson 6.4

Lesson 11.5 Office Costs ■ 489

Enrich

Invite an office manager or an office management instructor at an area college to class to address students on layout principles. You might also have the manager review some of the answers to the Team Meeting assignment.

Close

Ask students to identify why finding the costs of office space on a square foot basis and why finding the unit costs of office work is helpful to organizations. Make sure that the discussion identifies the importance of comparisons within an organization, between organizations, and to an industry.

■ **STUDENT PORTFOLIO**
Consider having students place their Team Meeting solutions in their portfolios.

Start Up

Have students read the Start Up and describe situations that they feel are and are not the employer's responsibility. Abbreviate their responses on the board and have a student record them for use in the Wrap Up.

Math Skill Builder

Assign all exercises in the Math Skill Builder 1–3 to prepare students for the addition, multiplication, rounding, and rewriting used in the lesson.

■ Teach Goal 1

Emphasize that the IRS requires careful and concurrent record keeping of mileage and other travel expenses. Many companies issue log forms for this purpose.

Point out that if you keep records of your actual car expenses, you still need a record of the mileage to calculate what fraction of your car expenses can be allocated to business use.

Stress that students should not round mileage or the reimbursement rate when computing the reimbursement.

■ Apply Goal 1

Work through Example 1 at the board or on a transparency with students completing the math at their desks.

Assign Check Your Understanding problems A and B for completion in class. Move through the classroom and check student work for errors.

11.6 Travel Expenses

GOALS

- Calculate mileage reimbursement
- Calculate business travel expenses

Start Up

Beverly O'Hara used her car to deliver a package for her employer. However, she parked in a no parking zone and also dented her car when she accidentally hit the no parking sign. Since she was using her car for her employer, she feels the employer should pay for these expenses. Do you think she is right?

Math Skill Builder

Review these math skills and solve the exercises that follow.

1 **Add** money amounts.
Find the sum. $398 + $12.58 + $98.31 + $43 + $3.75 = $555.64
$451.29
1a. $598 + $18.90 + $125 + $315.78 $1,057.68   **1b.** $31.64 + $397 + $22.65

2 **Multiply** money amounts by whole numbers.
Find the product. $112 × 4 = $448   2,498 × $0.38\frac{1}{2} = $961.73
2a. $135.78 × 8 $1,086.24   **2b.** 5,078 × $0.40\frac{1}{2} $2,056.59

3 **Multiply** money amounts and whole numbers by percents.
Find the product. $389 × 85% = $330.65   24,875 × 38% = 9,452.50
3a. $1,970 × 76.5% $1,507.05   **3b.** 32,089 × 42.5% $13,637.83

■ Mileage Reimbursement

Companies may pay back, or *reimburse* employees on a per mile basis when personal cars are used for business. The IRS also allows people to deduct car mileage when they use their car for business, if the employer doesn't reimburse them fully.

Often, the rate per mile paid by businesses matches the rate allowed by the IRS. If the firm pays employees less per mile than the IRS, employees can deduct the difference on their tax returns.

> **BUSINESS TIP**
>
> The IRS allows you to keep records of your actual car expenses and use these for the tax deduction instead of using the per mile rate.

EXAMPLE 1

Rosa Lazare is a salesperson for Trumble Publishing Company and uses her own car to make sales calls. Trumble reimburses her for the use of her car at $0.34\frac{1}{2} per mile. If Rosa drove 1,268 miles on company business last month, how much did Trumble reimburse her for the use of her car?

490 ■ Chapter 11 Business Costs

CONNECTION TO ACCOUNTING

You may wish to assign some students who are interested in accounting careers to research the IRS rules for keeping travel expense logs. These students may use the IRS Internet web site as a source. They may also visit a CPA who does personal income taxes to get the information for the project. Have students prepare a brief report of the rules and attach a sample travel expense log, such as a mileage log. Select one or more of the reports for presentation and discussion in class.

SOLUTION

Multiply the business miles by the rate per mile.

$1{,}268 \times \$0.345 = \$437.46$ reimbursement amount

■ CHECK YOUR UNDERSTANDING

A. Erica Rosenberg drove her car 986 miles in May, 35% of which were for her job. The company reimburses Erica $0.32 a mile for business use. What did Erica receive as reimbursement for the use of her car in May? $110.43

B. Sateesh Alwash drove his car 19,308 miles last year. Of those miles, 28% were reimbursed by his company at $0.30 a mile. The IRS mileage rate for that year was $0.33 a mile. How much did Sateesh receive from his company for mileage? What amount might Sateesh use as a tax deduction? $1,621.87; $162.19

■ Business Travel Expenses

In addition to mileage, often employees are reimbursed for other **travel expenses**. These include hotel fees, meal charges, airfares, taxi fares, rental car charges, expenses for entertaining customers, and related expenses.

Some businesses reimburse employees for their actual expenses, and some reimburse employees on a **per diem**, or per day basis regardless of how much was spent.

Many organizations set limits on certain types of expenses, such as maximums for hotel charges and meals. Many organizations also do not reimburse employees for personal expenses that they consider unrelated to the employee's travel, such as the cost of personal entertainment.

> **BUSINESS TIP**
>
> The IRS also allows you to deduct mileage when you use your car in the service of a charity. The rate per mile that they allow for charitable use is lower than for business use.

EXAMPLE 2

Marta Guzman is a technical support specialist for 100-Com Communications. 100-Com sent Marta to a desktop operating system seminar in another city. 100-Com paid the seminar fees directly to the seminar company. They also paid Marta $459 to reimburse her for airfare and $120 per diem for the three days she attended the seminar. How much did Marta receive as reimbursement?

SOLUTION

Multiply the per diem rate by the number of days.

$3 \times \$120 = \$360$ per diem reimbursement

Add the per diem and airfare reimbursements.

$\$360 + \$459 = \$819$ total amount of reimbursement

> **BUSINESS TIP**
>
> Porterage is the tip amount you give to have your bags carried by airport limousine drivers, hotel bellhops, and others.

■ CHECK YOUR UNDRSTANDING

C. Po-ling Shen attended a business conference in another state. His approved expenses were: airfare, $582; meals, $224; taxis, $38; airport parking, $42; porterage, $12; conference registration fee, $275; mileage to and from airport, 32 miles; hotel charges, $216; other expenses, $54. If his company pays $0.35 a mile for use of personal cars, how much was Po-ling reimbursed? $1,454.20

Lesson 11.6 Travel Expenses ■ **491**

■ *CHECK YOUR UNDERSTANDING SOLUTIONS*

A. $986 \times 0.35 = 345.1$; $345.1 \times \$0.32 = \$110.432$, or $110.43

B. $19{,}308 \times 0.28 = 5{,}406.24$; $5{,}406.24 \times \$0.30 = \$1{,}621.872$, or $1,621.87 reimbursement; $5{,}406.24 \times \$0.33 = \$1{,}784.059$, or $1,784.06; $1{,}785.06 - \$1{,}621.87 = \$162.19$ tax deduction

C. $32 \times \$0.35 = \$11.20$; $\$11.20 + \$582 + \$224 + \$38 + \$42 + \$12 + \$275 + \$216 + \$54 = \$1{,}454.20$

D. $315 \times \$0.38 = \$119.70$; $3.5 \times \$125 = \$437.50$; $\$119.70 + \$437.50 = \$557.20$

491

■ **Teach Goal 2**

Discuss with students the various types of business expenses that occur when traveling to a conference. If you have traveled to a conference recently, go through your trip, step by step, to show students what events are involved. For example, driving to the airport, parking, checking in at the gate, taking a taxi or airport limo to your hotel, etc.

■ **Apply Goal 2**

Do Example 2 at the board while students do the math at their desks.

Assign Check Your Understanding problems C and D to do in class. Check student work at their desks for errors or problems.

■ **ONGOING ASSESSMENT**

With the textbook closed, call on students to name possible expense items for travel to a business conference.

WORKPLACE WINDOW

Call on different students to answer each of the questions posed in the problem. Point out that airlines have their own web sites and some have joined together to offer their own travel site that competes with existing Internet travel sites, independent of the airlines.

Assign

Assignment: Exercises 1–15, 17–20. Start with the basic arithmetic problems at the beginning of the exercises to be sure that students understand the underlying arithmetic in the exercises.

Assess

Check student answers to exercise problems by calling on them in class, collecting and grading selected problems, or by observing student work at their desks.

D. Susan O'Bannion spent $3\frac{1}{2}$ days at a conference. She was reimbursed for traveling the 315 miles to and from the conference by personal car at $0.38 a mile. She was also paid $125 per diem. What was her total reimbursement for the conference? $557.20

WRAP UP

Most organizations will not pay for parking fines or car accidents that are the direct fault of the employee even though the car was being used for business purposes.

WORKPLACE WINDOW

Some companies run their own travel departments to provide help for employees when they travel on company business. Other companies outsource the travel function to commercial travel agencies. What kinds of services do commercial travel agents offer? How are commercial travel agents typically paid? How have travel agencies been affected by Internet travel sites? Prepare a brief report that answers these questions. Your resources may include interviews with travel agents, Internet travel sites, library materials, and sources found through web searches.

EXERCISES

1. Add: $189 + $42.16 + $15 + $68.26 $314.42

2. Multiply 8,497 by $0.42. $3,568.74

3. Multiply $109 by $6\frac{1}{2}$. $708.50

4. Multiply 13,597 by 75%. $10,197.75

5. Clarice Johnson put 1,489 miles on her car in June. Of those miles, 27% were for her job. The company reimburses Clarice $0.35 a mile for business use. What did Clarice receive as reimbursement for the use of her car in June? $140.71

6. Julio Valliente drove his car 23,188 miles last year, 32% of which were reimbursed by his company at 0.33\frac{1}{2}$ a mile. The IRS mileage rate for that year was $0.35 a mile. How much did Julio receive from his company for mileage? What amount might Julio use as a tax deduction? $2,485.75, $111.30

7. LaDonna White works in the human resource department of Valatia Corporation and attended a conference on health insurance. Her approved expenses were: airfare, $768; meals, $267; taxis and limousines, $43; airport parking, $54; porterage, $16; registration fee, $175; mileage to and from airport, 26 miles; hotel charges, $368; other expenses, $41. If her company pays 36.5¢ a mile for use of personal cars, how much was LaDonna reimbursed? $1,741.49

8. Felicia Ryan spent $2\frac{1}{2}$ days at a business show. She was reimbursed for traveling the 173 miles to and from the show by personal car at 0.36\frac{1}{2}$ a mile. She was also paid $146 per diem. What was her total reimbursement for the show? $428.15

9. Don Dykstra attended a business conference for his company. His approved expenses were: $734 for airfare; $257 for meals; $29 for limousines and taxis, $389 for his hotel room, $400 in conference fees, and $215 in other charges. What was the amount of his reimbursement? $2,024

492 ■ Chapter 11 Business Costs

SELECTED SOLUTIONS

5. 1,489 × 0.27 = 402.03;
402.03 × $0.35 = $140.71

6. 23,188 × 0.32 = 7,420.16; 7,420.16 × $0.335 = $2,485.753, or $2,485.75 reimbursement; 7,420.16 × $0.35 = $2,597.056, or $2,597.06; $2,597.06 − $2,485.75 = $111.31 tax deduction

7. 26 × $0.365 = $9.49; $9.49 + $768 + $267 + $43 + $54 + $16 + $175 + $368 + $41 = $1,741.49

8. 173 × $0.365 = $63.145, or $63.15; 2.5 × $146 = $365; $63.15 + $365 = $428.15

10. Calvin Jones spent the following on a 3-day business trip: airfare, $586; airport limousines, $24; porterage and other tips, $28; taxis, $45; movie, $8.95; hotel, $145 a night; meals, $58 a day. His employer did not reimburse entertainment expenses and has a maximum hotel charge of $130 a night. What was Calvin's total reimbursement amount? $1,247

11. Seela Alwaif drove her personal auto 176 miles last year while helping a charity in a clothes drive. The IRS in that year allowed a deduction of $0.14 per mile for charitable use of a personal car. What was the amount of Seela's tax deduction? $24.64

Last year Yolanda paid $25,800 for a light truck and drove it 21,000 miles in the first year. She spent these amounts: $1,120, gas; $578, repairs and maintenance; $1,277, insurance; $64, truck washes; $1,200, interest on truck loan; other, $156.

12. **INTEGRATING YOUR KNOWLEDGE** Using a 20% rate and the declining balance method, what is the depreciation for the first year? $5,160

13. What was the total cost of owning and operating the truck last year, including depreciation? $9,555

14. What was the cost per mile of owning and operating the truck last year, to the nearest tenth of a cent? $0.455

15. Yolanda used her truck 23% of the time to deliver products for her employer who reimbursed her $0.39 a mile. How much did Yolanda receive for the use of her car from her employer? $1,883.70

16. **DECISION MAKING** Elvis Clarke is self-employed and uses a new van that cost $22,500 exclusively in his business. The van was driven 12,700 miles. When preparing his income tax return, Elvis had a choice of declaring his actual expenses for the car or using that year's IRS per mile rate of $0.39. Which method is likely to offer Elvis the largest tax deduction for the first and second years of use? Why?   actual; more depreciation

MIXED REVIEW

17. Divide 56.7 by 8.9 rounded to three decimal places.   6.371

18. What percent is 136 of 1,700?   8%

19. A disk caddy holds four floppy disks with the following unused space on them: 1, 70 Kb; 2, 15 Kb; 3, 789 Kb; and 4, 416 Kb. One disk is picked at random. What is the probability that the disk will contain more than 70 Kb of unused space?   50%, Lesson 8.2

20. Yallow Appliances, Inc. owns 680 desktop and notebook computer systems. Last year it spent $255,390 on replacement parts and equipment, $143,788 on software upgrades, and $493,714 on repairs to their systems, user training, and help for their computer users. What amount was spent on technical support per computer system? $1,313.08, Lesson 9.3

Lesson 11.6 Travel Expenses ■ 493

SELECTED SOLUTIONS

12. $25,800 × 0.20 = $5,160
13. $1,120 + $578 + $1,277 + $64 + $1,200 + $156 + $5,160 = $9,555
14. $9,555 ÷ 21,000 = $0.455
15. 21,000 × 0.23 = 4,830; 4,830 × $0.39 = $1,883.70

Chapter Summary

Lesson 11.1 Manufacturing Costs

- Add costs of materials and direct labor to find prime cost.

- Add prime cost and factory overhead to find total manufacturing cost.

- Add floor space, number of workers, or other bases for distributing overhead costs to find their total.

- Divide total by each department or division's part. Multiply by total overhead costs to find each unit's share.

Lesson 11.2 Break-Even Point

- Subtract variable cost from sales price per unit and divide into total fixed costs to find break-even point in units.

- Multiply number of units needed to break even by sales price of units to find break-even point in dollars.

Lesson 11.3 Depreciation Costs

- Multiply property's cost by declining-balance rate to find amount of depreciation.

- Add digits for each year of property's estimated use to find sum-of-the-years-digits.

- Subtract estimated trade-in value from original cost to find estimated amount of depreciation.

- Divide last year's digits by sum-of-the-years-digits. Multiply amount of depreciation by result to find first-year depreciation.

- Identify MACRS depreciation rate for property's class life. Multiply property's original cost by depreciation rate to find amount of depreciation.

- Subtract amount of depreciation from original cost to find book value.

Lesson 11.4 Shipping Costs

- Find shipping cost for package weight and distance from shipping rate table.

Vocabulary Review

book value	freight	total manufacturing cost
break-even point	modified accelerated cost	travel expenses
declining-balance method	recovery system method (MACRS)	sum-of-the-years-digits
factory overhead	per diem	method
fixed costs	prime cost	variable costs
free on board (f.o.b.)		

Fill in the blanks with one of the words above.

1. Prime cost plus factory overhead is called ___?___. total manufacturing cost

2. Expenses not directly tied to producing goods are called ___?___. factory overhead

3. The point at which income from sales equals the total cost of producing and selling goods is called ___?___. break-even point

4. The costs that remain no matter how much of a product is produced are called ___?___. fixed costs

5. Costs that change directly with the number of units produced are called ___?___. variable costs

6. The ___?___ of depreciation uses a fixed rate of depreciation for each year. declining-balance method

7. The depreciation method required by the IRS for most business properties is called ___?___. MACRS

8. A method of shipping heavy, bulky goods, often by rail, truck, barge, or ship is called ___?___. freight

9. ___?___ is a term used to determine who pays shipping costs. f.o.b.

10. A daily reimbursement rate used by some employers is called ___?___ per diem

LESSON 11.1

11. An electric appliance factory had these costs for the goods produced in the first quarter of a year: raw materials, $1,671,680; direct labor, $2,168,320; factory overhead, $684,850. What was the prime cost of the goods produced during the quarter? What was the total manufacturing cost of the goods? $3,840,000; $4,524,850

12. The 3 departments of Aranson's Auto Repair use this floor space: Body, 3,000 ft^2; Repair/Service, 2,000 ft^2; Painting, 1,000 ft^2. The annual insurance cost of the building is $2,800. It is distributed on the basis of the floor space of each department. How much should each department be charged annually for insurance, to the nearest whole dollar? Body, $1,400; Repair/Service, $933; Painting, $467

LESSON 11.2

13. Balen Operating Corporation plans to produce cowlings that will be sold at $20 per unit. Manufacturing any cowlings will cost an estimated $24,000 in fixed costs. The variable costs of producing each cowling are estimated to be $10. How many cowlings must they sell to break even? What sales must Balen earn on the cowlings to reach the break-even point? 2,400 cowlings; $48,000

494 ■ Chapter 11 Business Costs

TEACHING STRATEGIES Chapter Review

Choose students to copy their solutions to Exercises 11–23 on the board. Have students compare their answers to the board answers and discuss any differences in answers or solution steps. Make certain that board solutions are fully labeled.

LESSON 11.3

14. A factory machine that cost $164,000 is depreciated each year at the rate of 12% using the declining-balance method. What is the book value of the machine at the end of the first year? $144,320

15. The original cost of a stamping press was $152,600. The factory plans to use it for 5 years and then trade it in for $44,600. Find the book value of the press at the end of the first year using the sum-of-the-years-digits method. $116,600

16. A business van costs $21,000. Using the MACRS table, find the depreciation for the first year. What is its book value at the end of the first year? $4,200; $16,800

LESSON 11.4

17. A company wants to ship a package that weighs 10 pounds to zone 5, using National Shipping Company's two-day service (see the shipping table). Insuring the package will cost $6.75 more. What is the total cost to ship the package? $29

18. Belcro, Inc. in Madison ships 42,350 pounds of lumber by freight to True-Time, Inc. in Pine Valley, f.o.b. Pine Valley. The freight company charges $21.19 a cwt. What is the freight charge? Who pays it? $8,984.56, Belcro

LESSON 11.5

19. An office with 2,500 ft^2 rents for $48,000 a year. Light, heat, insurance, and maintenance are estimated to cost $4,500 a year. What is the total annual cost of this office space per square foot? If one workstation's area is 30 ft^2, how much does this workstation cost per year? $21; $630

20. The total annual cost of an office is $158,000, including wages, fringe benefits, rent, insurance, and power. If the office has 5 workstations, what is the average annual cost of each workstation? $31,600

21. A clerk can sort and file 1,125 invoices per day. If the clerk earns $10.20 per hour and works for $7\frac{1}{2}$ hours a day, how much does it cost to file each invoice, to the nearest tenth of a cent? $0.068

LESSON 11.6

22. Sandra Duarte attended a business conference in another state. Her approved expenses were: airfare, $485; meals, $267; taxis, $28; airport parking, $34; porterage, $15; conference registration fee, $150; mileage to and from airport, 62 miles; hotel charges, $258; other expenses, $76. If her company pays $0.37 a mile for use of personal cars, how much was Sandra reimbursed? $1,335.94

23. Rick Belle spent $2\frac{1}{2}$ days at a business seminar. He was reimbursed for traveling the 250 miles to and from the seminar by personal car at $0.38 a mile. He was also paid $135 per diem. What was his total reimbursement for the seminar? $432.50

- Find freight rate for package weight and distance shipped. Multiply package weight by rate to find freight cost.

- If rate is by hundredweight, divide package weight by 100. Round answer up to next higher number of cwt.

- Add amounts for insurance, special delivery, and other charges to shipping or freight costs to find total charges.

Lesson 11.5 Office Costs
- Add costs of rent or depreciation, mortgage interest, and real estate taxes to cost of power, insurance, cleaning, and maintenance to find total cost of office space.

- Divide total cost of office space by square feet of office space to find cost of space per square foot.

- Multiply square feet of work area by cost of office space per square foot to find cost of work area space.

- Add costs of producing a type of office work to find total cost of producing that office work.

- Divide total cost of office work by number of units of office work produced to find cost per unit of office work.

Lesson 11.6 Travel Expenses
- Multiply total mileage by percent of business use to find amount of business mileage.

- Multiply amount of business mileage by mileage reimbursement rate to find amount of reimbursement.

- Subtract amount of mileage reimbursement paid by organization from reimbursement amount allowed by IRS to find tax deduction amount.

- Multiply number of days of business travel by per diem rate to find amount of per diem reimbursement.

- Add approved costs of business travel and, where paid, per diem reimbursement, to find total amount reimbursed by organization.

TEACHING STRATEGIES Chapter Review

When students experience problems in completing an exercise in the Chapter Review, have them return to the lesson from which the exercise was drawn and study the appropriate example problem in the lesson. Then have them return to the Chapter Review and retry solving the problem. After solving the problem, have students return to the example and compare their solution steps and labels to those in the example.

Task 1 Students enter data into a MACRS depreciation template.

Task 2 Students answer questions about the results of Task 1. They also change data and answer questions about the results.

Task 3 Students design and create a spreadsheet that calculates the break-even point in units and dollars.

Task 4 Students answer questions about the formulas they used in their spreadsheets. They also answer questions about the situation described in Task 3.

Technology Workshop

Task 1: Enter Data In A MACRS Depreciation Template

Complete a template that calculates the amount of MACRS depreciation and book value for properties with 5-year and 7-year class lives.

Open the spreadsheet for Chapter 11 (Tech11-1.xls) and enter 10,000 in the blue cell, B5. Your computer screen should look like the one shown below when you are done.

	A	B	C	D	E
1	**MACRS Depreciation Calculator**				
2					
3		**Class Life**			
4		**5-Year**	**7-Year**		
5	Cost	$10,000.00	$0.00		
6					
7		**Depreciation and Book Value Calculation**			
8		**5-Year**		**7-Year**	
9	Year	**Depreciation**	**Book Value**	**Depreciation**	**Book Value**
10	1	$2,000.00	$8,000.00	$0.00	$0.00
11	2	$3,200.00	$4,800.00	$0.00	$0.00
12	3	$1,920.00	$2,880.00	$0.00	$0.00
13	4	$1,152.00	$1,728.00	$0.00	$0.00
14	5	$1,152.00	$576.00	$0.00	$0.00
15	6	$576.00	$0.00	$0.00	$0.00
16	7			$0.00	$0.00
17	8			$0.00	$0.00
18	**Total**	$10,000.00		$0.00	

Notice that when you enter the cost of a 5-year class property into cell B5, the spreadsheet automatically calculates the annual depreciation and book values of the property.

Task 2: Analyze the Spreadsheet Output

Move your cursor to cell C5 and enter 20,000. Notice that the annual depreciation and book values of a 7-year class property are automatically calculated.

Answer these questions about your updated spreadsheet.

1. What function is used in cell D18? sum function

2. What arithmetic is done in cell D11? property cost multiplied by MACRS rate

3. What arithmetic is done in cell E11? depreciation subtracted from book value

4. Now enter 10,000 in both cells B5 and C5. Look at the row for year 3 for both the 5-year and 7-year properties. Which property depreciated the most that year? How much more? Why? 5-year; $171; MACRS rate higher for 5-year property

5. What is the book value for both properties, 5-year and 7-year, by the end of their class life? $0

496 ■ Chapter 11 Business Costs

TEACHING STRATEGIES Task 2

As an optional assignment to Task 2, you may wish to have some students design a spreadsheet for the declining balance method of depreciation. The spreadsheet should calculate depreciation and book value by year. Have one or more of the students present the spreadsheet to the class, pointing out the formulas and functions used in key cells. If a computer projector is available, have each presenter demonstrate the use of the spreadsheet by solving a problem from the Exercises in the textbook.

Task 3: Design a Break-Even Point Spreadsheet

Design a spreadsheet that will calculate the break-even point in units and in dollars.

SITUATION: Brainard Furniture, Inc. plans to make computer desks and sell them at $175 each. They estimate their fixed costs to produce the desks at $600,000 and variable costs of $90 per chair. You need to find the number of units Brainard must produce and sell to break even. You also need to find the total sales needed to break even.

Task 4: Analyze the Spreadsheet Output

Answer these questions about your completed spreadsheet.

6. How did you calculate the break-even point in number of units? subtract variable cost from sales price and divide fixed cost by difference
7. How did you make the spreadsheet round up the number of units to the nearest whole unit? use roundup function

8. How many desks must Brainard produce and sell to break even? 7,059

9. How did you calculate the amount of sales needed to break even? multiply break-even point in units by unit sales price
10. What is the minimum amount of desk sales Brainard needs to break even? $1,235,325

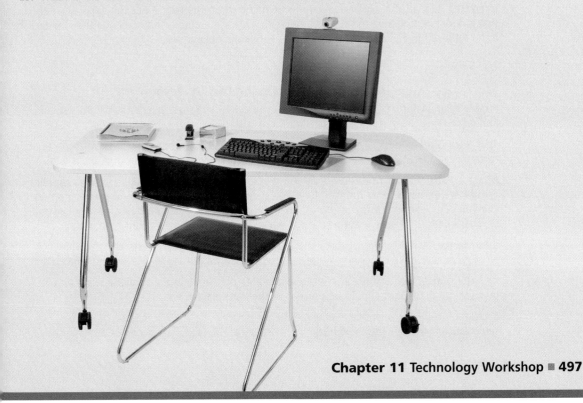

Chapter 11 Technology Workshop ■ 497

Teach and Apply Task 1

Point out that users only have to enter the original cost of the property in the correct cell. No other data entries are needed to find each year's depreciation and remaining book value.

Teach and Apply Task 2

Assign questions 1–5. Point out that the sum of the depreciation columns for 5- and 7-year properties must equal the original cost of the property because MACRS allows the full depreciation of a property without any residual salvage or trade-in value.

Teach and Apply Task 3

Assign Task 3. You may wish to have students work in small groups.

Refer students to the formulas for finding the break-even point in units and dollars in the textbook as the starting point in their design.

Teach and Apply Task 4

Assign questions 1–5. Each student should submit a disk with the completed spreadsheet, or a printout of the results of the data for questions 1–5, and a printout of the spreadsheet formulas.

TEACHING STRATEGIES Task 3

Select one or more templates designed by students and have them display their spreadsheets to the class. If a computer projector is not available for use, have students print out their spreadsheets with data entered into them and also print out the formulas used. Make transparencies of the spreadsheet printouts and have students display these and explain their designs to the class. Make sure that the discussion includes possible improvements to the design of each spreadsheet.

1. 40 tons × 2,000 lb = 80,000 lb
   80,000 ÷ 100 = 8,000
   8,000 × $1.48 = $1,184

2. 57,000 tons × 2,000 lb = 114,000,000 lb
   114,000,000 ÷ 100 = 1,140,000
   1,140,000 × $1.58 = $1,801,200

Note: The total cost of the Empire State Building, including the price of the land, was $49,948,900.

Have one or more students present the itineraries to the rest of the class. Discuss each presenter's list of expenses and how they were classified: reimbursed or not reimbursed.

With the student's permission, select one student's work for presentation and discussion in class. As the procedures for identifying reordering needs, organizing supplies, distributing supplies, and handling requests for items not in stock are presented, ask class members to offer alternative procedures that they used in their plans.

The Integrated Project found in the workbook provides a broad, ongoing assessment activity for the goals of this chapter.

Chapter Assessment

How Times Have Changed

For Questions 1–2, refer to the timeline on page 465 as needed.

1. Before the mass-production of steel, railroad tracks had to be replaced or repaired often because the wrought iron would crack or deform. In 1905, if a company that manufactured new steel railroad tracks ordered 40 tons of hot-rolled steel bars, how much would the steel cost the company?
2. The steel skeleton of the Empire State Building is made up of about 57,000 tons of steel. Using $1.58 per 100 pounds, the 1932 price of a hot-rolled steel bar, how much did 57,000 tons of steel cost?

WRITE

As a class, create an itinerary and a daily schedule for an executive's business trip to New York City. The executive will be in staff meetings from 8:30 A.M. to 12:00 Noon, Monday through Thursday. On the first and last day of the trip, there will be a luncheon meeting with clients until 3:00 P.M. On the other days, a one-hour working lunch with managers is planned followed by an information systems meeting until 4:00 p.m. on Tuesday, and a 60-minute conference call with the San Diego office on Wednesday. After scheduled meetings, the executive wants to see some of New York's attractions.

Individually, prepare a list of the attractions and theaters in which the executive may be interested. List all the expenses likely to be incurred on the trip. Place the expenses into two groups, reimbursed and not reimbursed. Write a statement that explains the standards to be followed in reimbursing employees for business expenses.

SCANS

Workplace Skills—*Allocating Materials and Facility Resources*

Supply management skills include locating sources of supplies, negotiating with vendors, and organizing the storage and distribution of materials, tools, and equipment.

Test Your Skills Think of yourself as a supply manager for a business. It is your job to be certain that office supplies are available when needed and stored in an organized way.

Make a Plan Write a procedure that you would put into place to make sure that supplies are always on hand. Also indicate how you would organize the storage of office supplies such as pens, staplers, stick-on notes, etc. You also need to explain how the supplies will be distributed, and how a request for a special item not in stock would be handled.

Summarize Based on your procedures, list the elements of your plans about which employers may have concerns. Write statements you might use to answer the concerns.

Be sure to make procedures and write statements that include the thinking skills and personal qualities that should be present in the workplace.

decision making	*problem solving*	*reasoning*	*creative thinking*
self-management	*responsibility*	*integrity/honesty*	*social skills*

PORTFOLIO ASSESSMENT

Ask students to review the itinerary they have created to place in their portfolios. Students should write a description of their assignment to be included with the finished product. Include comments about the parts of the assignment they liked and disliked with reasons for each.

CHAPTER TEST

Answer each question.

1. $1,574 − $560 $1,014

2. $1,237 + $28.79 + $746 + $175.37 $2,187.16

3. $0.26 × 1,589 $413.14

4. 12,350 ÷ 100   123.5

5. 37% × 42,718   15,805.66

6. $1,599 ÷ $82   19.5

7. 1,000 × $34.49 $34,490

8. $\frac{3}{4}$ × $64,800 $48,600

9. $22,050 ÷ 2,100 $10.50

10. 0.36 × $3,800 $1,368

Applications

11. A factory had these costs for the products produced in one year: raw materials, $1,468,190; direct labor, $2,365,100; factory overhead, $539,850. What was the prime cost of the goods produced? What was the total manufacturing cost of the goods? $3,833,290; $4,373,140

12. Four departments of a company use this floor space: Dept. A, 12,000 sq. ft; Dept. B, 5,600 sq. ft; Dept. C, 10,000 sq. ft; Dept. D, 4,400 sq. ft. The yearly maintenance cost of the building, $36,000, is distributed based on the floor space. How much of the annual maintenance cost is each department charged?   A, $13,500; B, $6,300; C, $11,250; D, $4,950

13. A company's fixed costs to produce a product are $150,000. The variable costs to produce each product are $6. They will sell the product at $18. How many products must they produce and sell to break even?   12,500

14. Trical Manufacturing buys a machine with an estimated life of 6 years for $28,500. They use an annual depreciation rate of 15%. What will be the book value of the machine at the end of one year using the declining-balance method? $24,225

15. A van costing $26,000 will be used for 5 years, and then traded in for an estimated $8,000. Find the book value of the van at the end of the first year using the sum-of-the-years-digits method. $20,000

16. Benton Corporation ships and insures 3 packages worth $600 each using a shipping company for next-day delivery. The shipper charges $56 for each package. They also charge $0.45 per $100 of value for insurance. What is the total cost of the shipment? $176.10

17. Travers, Inc. ships 3 packages weighing 400 lb each by freight, f.o.b., customer. The shipping company charges $36 per cwt plus $18.50 for insurance. What is the total cost to ship the packages? $450.50

18. An office has an area of 2,500 ft². The office costs $76,500 a year including rent, power, insurance, and maintenance. What is the annual cost of the office per square foot? $30.60

19. Grace Larke spent 5 days at a business conference. She was reimbursed for traveling 434 miles to and from the conference by personal car at 0.37\frac{1}{2}$ a mile. She was also paid $130 per diem. What was her total reimbursement for the conference? $812.75

Chapter 11 Assessment ■ 499

Chapter-Test Correlation

Question	Lesson
11	11.1
12	11.1
13	11.2
14	11.3
15	11.3
16	11.4
17	11.4
18	11.5
19	11.6

Test Taking Strategies

■ **BASIC ARITHMETIC**

The fast way to multiply by 1,000 is to move the decimal place three places to the right.

The fast way to divide by 100 is to move the decimal place two places to the left.

TEACHING STRATEGIES Chapter Test

For test questions that require more than one answer, you may wish to give more credit. For example, question 11 requires two answers and question 12 requires four. You might consider treating these two questions as 6 questions and weight them accordingly in your test-grading scheme.

Chapter Overview

Chapter 12 reviews the math skills of addition, multiplication, percents, and rounding to solve problems in sales records, discounts, pricing, and marketing.

Lesson 12.1 Cash Sales and Sales on Account
Students prove cash and calculate invoices, credit memos, and customer accounts.

Lesson 12.2 Cash and Trade Discounts
Students calculate cash and trade discounts, cash and invoice prices, and rates of discount.

Lesson 12.3 Series Trade Discounts
Students find the invoice price and the single discount equivalent for a series of discounts.

Lesson 12.4 Markup and Markdown
Students calculate cost and selling price for markup on selling price, rate of markup on cost, and selling price on markdown.

Lesson 12.5 Marketing Surveys
Students find the response rate and analyze survey results.

Lesson 12.6 Sales Forecasts
Students find future sales based on trends and forecast methods.

Lesson 12.7 Market Share
Students calculate market share.

Lesson 12.8 Advertising
Students calculate the total and per person cost of advertising.

Statistical Insights

Restaurant Advertising Expenditures, U.S.

Category	Expenditures (Millions of Dollars)
Magazines	$37
Sunday Magazines	$3
Newspapers	$89
Network Television	$1,166
Spot Television	$1,296
Syndicated Television	$183
Cable Networks	$364
Radio	$24
Total	**$3,162**

Use the data shown above to answer each question.

1. On what type of ad is the least and most money spent? Name amounts spent, written in full.   Sunday Magazine, $3,000,000; Spot Television, $1,296,000,000

2. Which category has about 10% of the total amount spent of restaurant advertising?   cable networks

3. To the nearest percent, what percent of all restaurant advertising appears in printed publications?   4%

Statistical Insights

Have students calculate the amount of money spent for advertising on radio and all television including cable. Ask them to identify on which of the two media was the greatest amount spent (television). Then have them calculate the ratio of television expenditures to radio expenditures, to the nearest whole number (125:1). Ask them to state the ratio in sentence form (the amount spent on television advertising is 125 times greater than the amount spent on radio advertising).

NetCheck

Forecasting Next Year's Sales

Technology is available to help sales and marketing managers generate accurate sales forecasts. You can locate forecasting software by searching the Internet, using keywords such as forecast, sales, predicting sales, and sales management. You will find more than one type of software, and most likely you will be able to download a trial version of many programs. Each program will have its own type of reporting structure, so each company must evaluate several software products to find one that most closely fits its needs.

Methods of Surveying

Many universities and market research companies study human behavior. Along with these studies, information is generated about how individuals react in certain situations and how they respond to marketing approaches. Information is available on the Internet about surveying methods and interpreting survey results. You can browse the web sites of universities, especially those known for their study of human behavior. You may also use keyword searches for human behavior, predicting behavior, customer responses, and target marketing.

How Times Have Changed

Retailers are continually looking for new ways to improve the checkout procedure, both for themselves and for customers. With the help of technology, and the Universal Product Code (UPC) and the European Article Numbering (EAN) symbols, the process has become more efficient than ever before.

The cash register is invented by James Ritty. **1879**

NCR has over 90% of the market share of brass-encased cash registers. **1910**

Research to discover a significant event in 1974 that relates to the history of UPC symbols and cash registers.

All U.S. companies must be capable of scanning EAN symbols. **2005**

1875 **1900** **1925** **1950** **1975** **2000**

1884 National Cash Register Company (NCR) becomes first manufacturer of cash registers.

1973 The grocery industry selects the UPC symbol as the industry standard for marking products.

1976 The EAN symbol expands the UPC barcode for international use.

2003 About 90% of U.S. supermarkets use scanners.

501

12.1 Cash Sales and Sales on Account

GOALS

- Complete a cash proof form
- Calculate sales invoice and credit memo totals
- Calculate a customer account balance

Start Up

You buy a new sweater and charge the purchase. A day later you decide you don't like the sweater and return it to the store. Will the store give you a cash refund if you request one, or will you get a credit against your charge account?

Math Skill Builder

Review these math skills and solve the exercises that follow.

1 **Add** money amounts.
Find the sum. $1,284.74 + $827.47 = $2,112.21

1a. $386.12 + $182.34 + $78.28 $646.74

1b. $2,980 + $34.78 $3,014.78

2 **Subtract** money amounts.
Find the difference. $7,492.92 − $234.87 = $7,258.05

2a. $18,472.87 − $12,852.48 $5,620.39   **2b.** $1,273.48 − $28.47 $1,245.01

3 **Multiply** money amounts by whole numbers.
Find the product. 18 × $12.87 = $231.66

3a. 125 × $18.40 $2,300   **3b.** 65 × $118.72 $7,716.80

■ Proving Cash

Cash registers provide a place to keep cash and a means to record cash sales and payments. Employees who use cash registers are called cash register clerks or cashiers.

Most cash registers are really computer terminals with a display screen and a scanner that is connected to a computer. The scanner reads bar codes printed on the items being purchased. The *bar codes* tell the computer the department, brand, size, and price of each item bought. This information is shown on the display screen and printed on a cash register receipt.

The computer also finds the sales tax, totals the sale, and updates inventory records. When the clerk keys in the amount received from the customer, the correct change is displayed on the screen. The computer also keeps a running total of sales.

Cashiers put money in the cash register drawer when they start work so they can make change. This money is called a *change fund*. While they work, they take in and pay out cash. At the end of their work period, cashiers take a reading of total sales for their register. Then they have to prove cash.

Proving cash means counting the money in the drawer and checking this amount against the cash register readings to see if the right amount is on hand. A *cash proof form* is used for this purpose. If you have less cash than you should, you are *cash short*. If you have more cash than you should, you are *cash over*.

EXAMPLE 1

Gretchen Roth works as a cashier for Tri-City Markets. When she started work on June 11, she put $100 in her cash register drawer as a change fund. At the end of her work period, her register readings showed total cash received, $4,672.98, and total cash paid out, $68.42. When she counted the cash in her drawer, she found $4,702.56. Prove cash using a cash proof form.

SOLUTION

Add the change fund to the register's record of cash received. Record the total and then subtract the total cash paid out.

Compare the cash that should be in the drawer with the actual cash in the drawer. Enter the difference on the appropriate cash short or cash over line.

Gretchen's cash proof showed cash short of $2.

Tri-City Markets Cash Proof Form		
Change fund	100	00
+ Register total of cash received	4,672	98
Total	4,772	98
− Register total of cash paid out	68	42
Cash that should be in drawer	4,704	56
Cash actually in drawer	4,702	56
Cash short	2	00
Cash over		

Date : *June 11, 20--*   Cash Register No.: *7*
Cash Register Operator: *Gretchen Roth*

CHECK YOUR UNDERSTANDING

A. At the start of his morning work period on January 8, Avery Nugent put $120 in change into his cash register drawer. When his work period finished, Avery's cash register totals showed $5,289.76 received and $76.30 paid out. Avery counted the money in the register and found he had $5,334.81 cash. Was the cash short or over? How much?   Over, $1.35

B. On August 3, Coletta Butzel put an $80 change fund into her cash register. When she read the cash register totals at the end of her working day, they showed cash received of $3,102.45 and cash paid out of $34.87. The actual cash in the drawer was $3,144.83. Prepare a cash proof form. $2.75 short

Sales Invoice and Credit Memo

When a seller sells goods to a buyer on credit, the seller gives the customer a sales invoice. A **sales invoice** lists the goods sold and delivered to the buyer. The buyer calls this form a *purchase invoice*.

On the sales invoice the unit price is multiplied by the quantity to find the price extension. The price extensions are added together to find the total amount of the invoice.

Lesson 12.1 Cash Sales and Sales on Account ▪ 503

▪ Apply Goal 1

Do Example 1 at the board and have students complete the calculations at their desks.

Point out that the change fund is not included in the register total of cash received. The register totals report customer transactions only.

Assign Check Your Understanding problems A and B. Check student work.

▪ Teach Goal 2

Remind students that finding the price extension for an invoice is the same as finding the extension for sales receipts as was done in Lesson 5.2. Extensions are rounded to the nearest cent, where necessary.

Discuss the Business Tip on page 504 and emphasize that a credit may be received in business-to-business transactions even if the physical goods are not returned to the seller. This happens when goods arrived damaged or spoiled.

It may also be less expensive for the seller to give a price adjustment instead of paying the cost of shipping.

▪ CHECK YOUR UNDERSTANDING SOLUTIONS

A. $120 + $5,289.76 − $76.30 = $5,333.46 should be in cash drawer; $5,334.81 − $5,333.46 = $1.35 cash over

B. $80 + $3,102.45 − $34.87 = $3,147.58 should be in cash drawer; $3,147.58 − $3,144.83 = $2.75 cash short

Work through Examples 2 and 3 at the board with students completing the math at their desks.

Inform students that the unit price of the product listed in the credit memo is taken from the invoice. Point out how the credit memo includes the invoice number to provide a cross reference for both the buyer and seller.

Assign Check Your Understanding problems C and D. Move about the classroom and provide individual help as needed.

■ **ONGOING ASSESSMENT**
Small parts such as bolts may have unit prices shown to three or more decimal places.

Have students find the extensions for these: 51 × $0.035; **$1.79** 875 × $0.0257; **$22.49** 1,025 × $0.783; **$802.58**

A sales invoice that Garden Products, a wholesale yard equipment firm, sent to Yard-N-Stuff, a retailer, is shown.

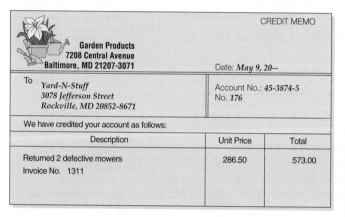

When merchandise bought on credit is returned, the seller does not return the buyer's money. Instead, the seller reduces the buyer's account balance by the amount of the return. The seller notifies the buyer about the reduction by sending the buyer a credit memorandum, or **credit memo**.

For example, when Yard-N-Stuff returned two defective mowers from Invoice #1311, Garden Products sent a credit memo.

EXAMPLE 2

Garden Products sold Yard-N-Stuff 45 watering cans @ $9.31 and 60 lawn sprinklers @ $7.89 on Invoice #1604. What was the total amount of the sales invoice?

SOLUTION
Multiply the unit cost of each item by its quantity. Then add the price extensions for each item.

45 × $9.31 = $418.95   cost of watering cans

60 × $7.89 = $473.40   cost of lawn sprinklers

$418.95 + $473.40 = $892.35   sales invoice amount

504 ■ **Chapter 12 Sales and Marketing**

CONNECTION TO MANAGEMENT

Point out that credit memos are usually issued after a distributor and retailer negotiate the amount of credit to be given. Retailers, on the other hand, issue refunds only when the merchandise is returned within a specified time period, in good order, and with the original receipt. The retailer may deduct a restocking charge of 10–30% of the original cost from the refund. The charge is made to pay for the cost of placing the item back in stock. Another reason for the charge is to minimize frivolous purchases and returns.

EXAMPLE 3

Two watering cans and one lawn sprinkler bought on
Invoice #1604 as described in Example 2 were
defective. They were returned by Yard-N-Stuff to
Garden Products. What was the total of the credit memo
issued by Garden Products to cover these returns?

SOLUTION

Multiply the unit cost of each returned item by its quantity. Then
add the price extensions.

$2 \times \$9.31 = \$18.62$ watering can credit

$1 \times \$7.89 = \$7.89$ sprinkler credit

$\$18.62 + \$7.89 = \$26.51$ credit memo total

■ CHECK YOUR UNDERSTANDING

C. Cellamation, an electronics wholesaler sold these items to CellNow, a mall
retailer: 150 Model NP-4 cell phones @ $85.15 and 75 Model CR-12 charging
kits @ $14.80. What was the total of the sales invoice? $13,882.50

D. Of the items purchased in Problem C, CellNow returned 12 phones due to a
wrong model being sent. CellNow also returned 2 charging kits because of
damage. What is the amount of the credit memo that Cellamation issues for
these returns? $1,051.40

■ Customer Account Balance

Most people use credit cards when they do not pay cash for a purchase. Businesses
whose customers are other businesses often let them buy on credit, or **on account**.
The seller then keeps records for each customer to show how much each customer
owes. A common form of *customer account* is shown below. This account shows the
transactions between Garden Products (the seller) and Yard-N-Stuff (the customer).

EXAMPLE 4

Prepare a customer account for Yard-N-Stuff to show: balance owed to Garden
Products on May 1 was $12,763.87; Invoice #1311 for $10,312.30 charged on May 1;
Credit Memo #176 for $573 credited on May 9; payment of $12,763.87 received on
May 20; payment for the May 20 account balance received on May 31.

SOLUTION

Enter the May 1 balance in the
balance column. Then enter the
invoice amount in the charges
column and the credit memo
amount in the credits column,
taking a balance after each
entry.

Record the May 20 payment in
the credits column. Find the
account balance. Enter as the
May 30 payment the May 20 balance.

Account:
Yard-N-Stuff
3078 Jefferson Street
Rockville, MD 20852-8671

Account No.: *45-3874-5*

Date	Description	Charges	Credits	Balance
5/1	*Balance Forward*			12,763.87
5/1	*Invoice No. 1311*	10,312.30		23,076.17
5/9	*Credit Memo No. 176*		573.00	22,503.17
5/20	*Payment*		12,763.87	9,739.30
5/31	*Payment*		9,739.30	0.00

Lesson 12.1 Cash Sales and Sales on Account ■ **505**

■ *CHECK YOUR UNDERSTANDING SOLUTIONS*

C. 150 × $85.15 = $12,772.50; 75 × $14.80 =
$1,110; 12,772.50 + $1,110 = $13,882.50

D. 12 × $85.15 = $1,021.80; 2 × $14.80 = $29.60;
$1,021.80 + $29.60 = $1,051.40

Wrap Up

Review the Start Up. Ask students to recall how cash advances on a credit card are handled and how they might relate to receiving an interest-free loan from a cash refund on a charge purchase.

COMMUNICATION

Before students do the interview, remind them that companies may use different terms when referring to cash proof, cash short, or cash over. Remind them to ask for explanations of terms or procedures they do not understand in addition to asking the questions listed in the directions for the activity.

Assign

Assignment: Exercises 1–15, 18–28. Start with the basic arithmetic problems that review the underlying arithmetic operations used in the exercises.

■ **CHECK YOUR UNDERSTANDING**

E. The customer account for Retro Hardware showed a balance of $2,384.76 on August 1. Sales to Retro were Invoice #1823 for $500.15 on August 3 and Invoice #1956 for $841.56 on August 9. A payment of $2,884.91 was received on August 13. Credit memo #112 was issued to Retro for $56.73 on August 16. There were no other transactions in August. What was Retro's account balance on August 31? $784.83

F. Mint Wholesale's customer account for Laurel Place Markets showed a balance of $29,379 on November 1. On November 13 a payment of $21,893 was received from Laurel. Laurel was charged $8,112 for purchases made on Invoice #1876 on November 16. On November 25 Mint issued Laurel a credit memo for $2,570 for stock that was recalled by the manufacturer. What was Laurel's account balance on November 25? $13,028

Wrap Up

If you charge a purchase, stores will issue a credit against your charge. Since you did not pay cash, they will not give you a cash refund. If they gave you cash, you would have use of the cash until your charge bill had to be paid. This would be the same as getting an interest-free loan.

COMMUNICATION

Interview a store manager or head cashier to discuss the store's policies about proving cash.

Ask questions such as

1. How frequently is it done?

2. Who verifies a cashier's cash proof?

3. Does the cashier have to make up any cash shortages?

4. What happens to cash overages?

Prepare a summary to share with the entire class.

EXERCISES

Find the sum.
1. $34,281.82 + $23,183.09 $57,464.91   2. $1,283 + $412.83 $1,695.83

Find the difference.
3. $4,284.84 − $231.07 $4,053.77   4. $12,899 − $8,243.18 $4,655.82

Find the product.
5. 120 × $23.87 $2,864.40   6. 512 × $3.76 $1,925.12

506 ■ **Chapter 12** Sales and Marketing

■ *CHECK YOUR UNDERSTANDING SOLUTIONS*

E. $2,384.76 + $500.15 = $2,884.91 (Aug. 3); $2,884.91 + $841.56 = $3,726.47 (Aug. 9); $3,726.47 − $2,884.91 = $841.56 (Aug. 13); $841.56 − $56.73 = $784.83 (Aug. 16 and Aug 31 balance).

F. $29,379 − $21,893 = $7,486 (Nov. 13); $7,486 + $8,112 = $15,598 (Nov. 16); $15,598 − $2,570 = $13,028 (Nov. 25)

7. At the start of the day, March 6, Marsha Vaught put a $100 change fund in her cash register. The cash register readings at the end of the day showed total cash received, $3,283.86, and total cash paid out, $45.31. The cash in the register at the end of the day was $3,338.37. Prepare a cash proof form. 18¢ short

8. When Kyle Timmons opened his shop on December 3, he put $80 in change in his cash register drawer. At the end of the day, the cash register readings showed that $4,924.67 had been taken in, that $328.17 had been paid out in cash refunds, and that Kyle had taken out $40 for his personal use. The cash on hand in the drawer at the end of the day was $4,637.90. Was the cash short or over? How much? Over, $1.40

9. Annette had $140 in change in her cash register at the start of work on March 19. At the end of her work period, there was $2,961.19 in the cash register. The register totals showed that she received $2,983.27 and paid out $159.76 during the period. How much was the cash over or short? $2.32 short

10. Risco Products sold these items to Sponson's Flooring: 60 cases floor tile @ $24.54 a case, 12 gallons adhesive @ $31.89 a gallon, and 12 tile cutters @ $48.23 each. What was the total of the sales invoice? $2,433.84

All-Marine Products sold 28 Model XV-450 outboard engines at $1,682.60 to Key Boats, Inc. on Invoice #4523. Key Boats had financial problems and returned 10 engines to All-Marine for credit. All-Marine issued Credit Memo #624 after deducting a 25% restocking charge for each returned engine.

11. What was the total of Invoice #4523?
$47,112.80

12. For what amount was Credit Memo #624 issued? $12,619.50

13. HairGlo shampoo was recalled for safety reasons. The manufacturer will issue a credit memo to each retailer for 120% of the original cost of the shampoo to cover the expenses of removing the item from store shelves. A retail chain of 8 stores returned 1,230 bottles of HairGlo whose original cost was $2.95 each. What amount of credit should the chain receive? $4,354.20

14. Make an account form like the one shown in the solution to Example 4. Record these facts about Alexea Co.'s account with Derstin Supply Company. Alexea's address is 708 Gower St., Greenville, SC 29611-3381.

Nov   1   The balance in Alexea's account was $5,372.38

      3   Alexea paid the November 1 balance $0

      5   Sold goods to Alexea, $4,182.89; Inv. #7021 $4,182.89

      17   Alexea returned $619 of the goods from Inv. #7021; Credit Memo #671 $3,563.89

      18   Sold goods to Alexea, $2,278.36; Inv. #7287. $5,842.25

      25   Alexea paid Inv. #7021, less Credit Memo #671 $2,278.36

      26   Alexea returned $89.01 of the goods on Inv. #7287;
           Credit Memo #709. $2,189.35

Lesson 12.1 Cash Sales and Sales on Account ■ 507

SELECTED SOLUTIONS

7. $100 + $3,283.86 − $45.31 = $3,338.55;
$3,338.55 − $3,338.37 = $0.18 cash short

10. 60 × $24.54 = $1,472.40;
12 × $31.89 = $382.68;

12 × $48.23 = $578.76;
$1,472.40 + $382.68 + $578.76 = $2,433.84

13. 120% = 1.2; 1.2 × 1,230 × $2.95 = $4,354.20

Assign Exercise 16, Critical Thinking. Students might point out that while 50% of new businesses fail, 50% succeed, and may continue to do business with a supplier for many years. Also point out that even large, well-established companies fail.

Assign Exercise 17, Critical Thinking. If not mentioned by students, indicate that consistently being cash over means that the cashier is not doing the job correctly. Customers who are overcharged for their purchases may stop shopping at the store.

15. Make an account form like the one shown in the Example 4 solution. Record these transactions between Bay Sales and a customer, Earp Products, Inc. Earp is located at 5302 Post Road, Warwick, RI 02886-9898. Calculate all balances.

Mar 1   The balance of Earp's account was $3,145.50.

     8   Sold goods to Earp, $1,892.32; Inv. #3369; terms, 30 days. $5,037.82

    16   Earp returned $71.45 of the goods sold on March 8; Credit Memo #277. $4,966.37

    20   Earp paid the March 1 balance of $3,145.50. $1,820.87

    26   Sold goods to Earp, $2,574.36; Inv. #3502; terms, 30 days. $4,395.23

    31   Earp paid the invoice of March 8, less Credit Memo #277 $2,574.36

Apr 12   Sold goods to Earp, $916.76; Inv. #3689; terms, 30 days. $3,491.12

    15   Earp returned $12.56 of the goods sold on April 12;

          Credit Memo, #388. $3,478.56

    25   Earp paid Inv. #3502 $904.20

16. **CRITICAL THINKING**   Up to 50% of businesses fail in their first year of operation. Why would a supplier give any new business credit? See Enrich section for answer.

17. **CRITICAL THINKING**   If an employee is consistently cash over when proving cash, should the employer be pleased or concerned? See Enrich section for answer.

MIXED REVIEW

18. Find $\frac{1}{8}$ of $54.80. $6.85

19. 36% less than $700 is what number? $448

20. $57.5 \times 1,000$ 57,500

21. $7.82 \div 1,000$ 0.00782

22. $78 \div 2\frac{1}{2}$ $31\frac{1}{5}$

23. $\frac{1}{2} \times 9 \times \frac{2}{3}$ 3

24. A city has taxable property assessed at $540,000,000. To meet expenses, $28,000,000 must be raised by property tax. What is the decimal tax rate to four places?   0.0519, Lesson 6.3

25. A $300,000 term life insurance policy is sold at a rate of $1.18 per $1,000 of insurance. What is the annual premium? $354, Lesson 7.1

26. Tracy Voisene earns $18.15 an hour. What will be her new hourly rate if she receives a COLA of 0.75%? $18.29, Lesson 10.2

27. The records of XD Products show these costs for producing 12,000 garden hoses: raw material, $14,460; direct labor, $23,760; overhead, $8,112. What was the prime cost of making the hoses? What was the manufacturing cost of a hose, to the nearest cent? $38,220, $3.86, Lesson 11.1

28. A retailer's stock record for a certain model modem showed a balance of 23 modems on August 1. The numbers of modems issued in August were: August 5, 4; August 13, 2; August 23, 8. Fifteen modems were received on August 18. What was the stock record balance on August 31?   24, Lesson 10.4

TEACHING STRATEGIES Cooperative Learning

Have students in each row think of all the possible items in a cash register drawer. The first student in a row writes one item on a sheet and passes it to the next student. That student adds another item and passes the paper. The row with the most acceptable answers wins this friendly competition. Answers might include: cash fund, cash received from customers, cash paid out to customers, checks, credit card and debit card slips, gift certificates, coupons, vouchers, and food stamps.

Cash and Trade Discounts

GOALS

- Calculate cash discount and cash price
- Calculate trade discount and invoice price
- Calculate the rate of discount

Start Up

Have students read the Start Up. Ask them what they might do if a retailer offered them an immediate 3% discount if they paid cash for an item and did not charge the purchase. Also ask them to give reasons for their answers.

Start Up

Imagine that you recently started your own business and a supplier offers you a 3% discount if you pay cash when you make a purchase. Would you pay cash for each purchase from this supplier? Why, or why not?

Math Skill Builder

Review these math skills and solve the exercises that follow.

1 **Multiply** money amounts by percents.
Find the product. $3\% \times \$21,780 = 0.03 \times \$21,780 = \$653.40$

1a. $1.5\% \times \$4,692$ $70.38

1b. $35\% \times \$129$ $45.15

2 Find what **percent** one number is of another number.
Find the percent. $\$1.16 \div \$5.80 = 0.2$, or 20%

2a. $\$52.20 \div \$116$ 45%

2b. $\$2,000 \div \$80,000$ 2.5%

Math Skill Builder

The subtraction and multiplication of money amounts, finding what percent one number is of another number, and multiplying money amounts by percents are skills used in this lesson.

Complete all exercises in Math Skill Builder 1–2.

■ Cash Discounts

Most business-to-business transactions begin with a *purchase order* from the buyer that identifies the goods ordered, the agreed upon price, and delivery terms. The purchase order may be written or verbal. After the order is filled, the seller issues a *sales invoice*. Both documents include the details of the purchase.

At the right is an invoice for Farwell Paints from Everyday Textures. While the placement of items on an invoice may vary, the information shown is typical. The main portion of the invoice contains detailed information on the order. This includes the unit price of each item, the price extension, and the total of the extensions, or *total due*.

			Original invoice GB4302
Remit payment to: **Everyday Textures** **2382 Bingham Road** **Freemont, OH 43420**			

Shipping: *FOB Fremont*

Sold to: *Farwell Paints* Ship to: *Same address*
231 Grove Avenue
Clyde, OH 43410

Refer to:

Order Number	Date Entered	Date Shipped	Invoice Date	Terms of Sale
56827	06/07/20--	06/07/20--	06/10/20--	2/10, 1/30, n/60

Quantity	Unit	Description	Unit Price	Amount
36	each	*Brush, Nylon, 2 inch*	2.90	104.40
48	each	*Brush, Bristle, 3 inch*	4.52	216.96
12	each	*Ladder, wood, 6-foot*	42.67	512.04
50	pkg	*Painting gloves, latex*	3.84	192.00
		Total Due		$1,025.40

Lesson 12.2 Cash and Trade Discounts ■ **509**

■ Teach Goal 1

Direct students to look at the invoice on page 509. Emphasize that the top part of the form gives important information about the sale, some of which will be used in making calculations. Remind students that the terms of sale impact the cost of the purchase. Just like consumers, businesses must shop to get the best terms.

Explain that the calculation of price extensions is identical to those done earlier where a unit price is multiplied by a quantity.

Remind students that sales taxes are not charged on business-to-business sales. Only the end user, the retail customer, pays sales taxes.

Discuss with students the meaning of the terms cash discount and f.o.b.

CONNECTION TO MANAGEMENT

Remind students that businesses exist to make a profit for their owners or shareholders. The term *list* price used in this lesson refers to the retail price a retailer might charge. Most wholesalers or distributors sell goods to retailers at a discount from list price because retailers must make a profit on items they sell. Other discounts may be given by distributors to encourage retailers to purchase in large quantities or remain as customers.

Work through Examples 1 and 2 with students while they do the calculations at their desks.

Remind students that to find discount or due dates, they begin counting on the day following the invoice date.

After the due date is calculated, refer students to the Business Tip on page 510. Relate the interest that may be paid by businesses for late payments to the interest paid by charge account owners who do not pay the total amount due by the due date.

Assign Check Your Understanding problems A through D for class work. Check student work at their desks to ensure they are using correct procedures to solve the problems.

■ **ONGOING ASSESSMENT**
Have students assume that four invoices dated July 25 have the credit terms that follow. Find the discount date for each:
2/5, n/30 **July 30**
1/10, n/45 **August 4**
2/20 EOM **August 14**
n/45 **none**

Notice that the top portion of the invoice includes information about when the order was made. The top portion of the bill also identifies the terms of the sale. *Terms of sale* specify how and when an invoice will be paid. Usually businesses sell to other businesses *on account*. This means the customer will be billed later for purchases. The time a purchaser has to pay a bill, usually 30 to 90 days, is called the *credit period*.

Businesses frequently offer **cash discounts** as a way to encourage their business customers to pay their invoices early. Cash discounts are figured on the *invoice price* that is shown on the invoice as the *total due*. The terms of sale tell how much of a discount will be given.

For example, the terms of Farwell Paints' invoice are 2/10, 1/30, n/60. That means that 2% may be deducted from the invoice price if it is paid within 10 days of the invoice date. If the invoice is paid within 30 days, 1% may be deducted. The full amount is due within 60 days.

Sometimes a term such as 3/10 EOM is used. This means that the buyer can claim a 3% discount if the bill is paid within 10 days after the end of month shown on the invoice.

To find the due date of the invoice and the last day for receiving a discount, count ahead, from the date on the invoice, the number of days shown in the terms.

> ### BUSINESS TIP
> Buyers who do not pay their bills by the due date may be charged interest on the amount owed or a late payment fee.

EXAMPLE 1

The credit terms are 2/10, 1/30, n/60, and the invoice date is June 10. Find the last date for taking each cash discount and the date on which the invoice is due.

SOLUTION
Add 10 days to the invoice date.

June 10 + 10 days = June 20 Last day for 2% discount

Count 30 days from the invoice date.

20 Days = June 10 to June 30
10 Days = July 1 to July 10
30 Days   July 10 Last day for 1% discount

Count 60 days from the invoice date.

20 Days = June 10 to June 30
31 Days = July 1 to July 31
 9 Days = August 1 to August 9
60 Days   August 9 Due date of invoice

■ **CHECK YOUR UNDERSTANDING**

A. Credit terms of 1/15, n/30 appear on an invoice dated November 28. What are the discount date and the due date of the invoice? *Dec. 13, Dec. 28*

B. An invoice dated March 20 has credit terms of 3/15, 1/30, n/45. Find the discount dates and due date of the invoice. *Apr. 4, Apr. 19, May 4*

■ *CHECK YOUR UNDERSTANDING SOLUTIONS*

A. 2 days in November + 13 days in December = December 13, discount date; 2 days in November + 28 days in December = December 28, due date

B. 11 days in March + 4 days in April = April 4, first discount date; 11 days in March + 19 days in April = April 19, second discount date; 11 days in March + 30 days in April + 4 days in May = May 4, due date

If the customer pays the invoice within the discount period and deducts a cash discount from the invoice price, the amount paid is called the *cash price*.

Cash Discount = Invoice Price × Rate of Cash Discount

Cash Price = Invoice Price − Cash Discount

Sometimes shipping charges appear on the invoice. If so, they must be added to the cash price to find the total amount due to the seller. Cash discounts are not allowed on shipping charges. If the terms of sale show f.o.b. destination, or f.o.b. customer, this means the seller will pay the shipping charges. Terms of sale such as f.o.b. factory, or f.o.b. shipping point, mean the buyer will pay shipping costs.

BUSINESS TIP

The shipping charge may be identified on the invoice as shipping and handling or freight.

EXAMPLE 2

Find the amount of cash discount Farwell Paints would get if the invoice price of $1,025.40 were paid within the 2% discount period. Also find the cash price of the invoice Farwell would pay after taking the discount.

SOLUTION
Multiply the invoice price by the discount percent.

2% × $1,025.40 = 0.02 × $1,025.40 = $20.508, or $20.51 cash discount

Subtract the cash discount from the invoice price.

$1,025.40 − $20.51 = $1,004.89 cash price

■ **CHECK YOUR UNDERSTANDING**

C. Find the cash discount and the cash price of an invoice whose total is $23,747 if the invoice is paid within the first discount period. The credit terms are 4/5, 1/30, n/60. $949.88, $22,797.12

D. The total due for an invoice dated July 28 is $12,836. Credit terms are 2/15, 1/30, n/45. If the invoice is paid on August 13, what are the cash discount and the cash price? $128.36, $12,707.64

■ Trade Discounts

Many businesses offer **trade discounts**. These are reductions from the list price to their business customers. Trade discounts are usually figured on each item within the invoice since it is possible for a different trade discount to apply to different items on an invoice. Also, the trade discounts offered to customers may differ.

Trade discounts are always based on the list price of the items being purchased. To find the trade discount, multiply the list price times the rate of discount. To find the *invoice price*, or net price, subtract the trade discount amount from the list price.

Rate of Discount × List Price = Trade Discount

List Price − Trade Discount = Invoice Price

Lesson 12.2 Cash and Trade Discounts ■ **511**

■ **Teach Goal 2**

Inform students that the unit prices shown in the invoice on page 509 are net prices after trade discounts have been taken. Each item listed on the invoice may have had a different trade discount.

If the same trade discount was applied to all invoice items, the list price of each item could have been used as the unit price for calculating extensions. The trade discount would then be taken off the total of the extensions, listed on a separate line, and subtracted to find the invoice price.

■ ***CHECK YOUR UNDERSTANDING SOLUTIONS***

C. $23,747 × 0.04 = $949.88 discount; $23,747 − $949.88 = $22,797.12 cash price

D. 3 days in July + 12 days in August = August 12 last day to take first discount; $12,836 × 0.01 = $128.36 discount; $12,836 − $128.36 = $12,707.64 cash price

Work through Example 3 at the board. Have students do the math at their desks.

Assign Check Your Understanding problems E and F for class work. Observe student work at their desks to check for any difficulties they have.

Work Examples 4 and 5 at the board and have students do the calculations at their desks.

Assign Check Your Understanding problems G and H to be done in class. Monitor student work at their desks to ensure they are using correct procedures and labeling answers.

EXAMPLE 3

The list price of an air compressor is $480. The trade discount given to a retailer is 40%. What invoice price will a retailer pay for the compressor?

SOLUTION

Multiply the list price by the rate of discount.

$40\% \times \$480 = 0.4 \times \$480 = \$192$ trade discount

Subtract the trade discount from the list price.

$\$480 - \$192 = \$288$ invoice price

■ CHECK YOUR UNDERSTANDING

E. The list price of a gas grill is $249 with a 35% trade discount to retailers. What trade discount would a retailer get on the grill? What invoice price would be paid? $87.15, $161.85

F. A water filter system has a list price of $172. What trade discount would a retailer get if a $37\frac{1}{2}\%$ trade discount is given? What is the invoice price of the filter system? $64.50, $107.50

■ Rate of Discount

If you know the discount amount and the total amount on which a discount is based, you can find the *rate of discount*. For example, the cash discount divided by the invoice price (invoice amount) will give the rate of cash discount. The trade discount divided by the list price will give the rate of trade discount.

Rate of Cash Discount = Cash Discount ÷ Invoice Price

Rate of Trade Discount = Trade Discount ÷ List Price

EXAMPLE 4

By taking advantage of a cash discount, a retailer paid $2,522 to settle a $2,600 invoice. Find the amount of the cash discount and the rate of cash discount.

SOLUTION

Subtract the cash price from the invoice price.

$\$2,600 - \$2,522 = \$78$ cash discount

Divide the cash discount by the invoice price.

$\$78 \div \$2,600 = 0.03$, or 3%   rate of cash discount

EXAMPLE 5

A garage door opener is listed in a wholesaler's catalog at $220. The opener is sold to retailers at an invoice price of $154. What is the rate of trade discount?

SOLUTION

Subtract the invoice price from the list price.

$\$220 - \$154 = \$66$ trade discount

Divide the trade discount by the list price.

$\$66 \div \$220 = 0.3$, or 30%   rate of trade discount

■ *CHECK YOUR UNDERSTANDING SOLUTIONS*

E. $0.35 \times \$249 = \$87.15$ trade discount;   **F.** $0.375 \times \$172 = \$64.50$ trade discount;
    $\$249 - \$87.15 = \$161.85$ invoice price $\$172 - \$64.50 = \$107.50$ invoice price

G. An invoice totaling $5,200 was paid within the discount period. The amount paid was $5,070. What was the rate of cash discount? 2.5%

H. A swimsuit with a list price of $75 was sold to a retailer for $41.25. What was the amount and rate of trade discount? $33.75, 45%

Wrap Up

Many new businesses may not have the cash available to take advantage of an immediate cash discount and will buy merchandise on credit. As they sell the stock they buy they use that money to pay the invoice when it is due. For this reason it is unlikely that a new business will choose to take an immediate cash discount.

TEAM MEETING

If you could buy an item directly from a factory, you would save part of the markup that distributors, such as wholesalers and retailers, charge. Distributors get a markup on the products they sell because they perform an important economic function of creating time utility, place utility, and form utility.

Form a team and do library or Internet research to find the meanings of these terms. Then give an example of how the terms apply to distributors. Present your findings to the class.

EXERCISES

Find the difference.
1. $7,117 − $213.51 $6,903.49
2. $99.98 − $29.99 $69.99

Find the product.
3. $1\frac{1}{2}\% \times \$6,027.45$ $90.41
4. $33\frac{1}{3}\% \times \$480$ $160

Find the percent.
5. $18.20 ÷ $910 2%
6. $0.91 ÷ $2.60 35%

Find the date on which each invoice must be paid.

	Invoice Date	Terms			Invoice Date	Terms	
7.	August 16	10 days	Aug. 26	8.	April 24	60 days	June 23
9.	March 5	30 days	Apr. 4	10.	October 28	75 days	Jan. 11
11.	November 14	90 days	Feb. 12	12.	January 7	45 days	Feb. 21

Lesson 12.2 Cash and Trade Discounts ■ **513**

■ CHECK YOUR UNDERSTANDING SOLUTIONS

G. $5,200 − $5,070 = $130; $130 ÷ $5,200 = 0.025, or 2.5%

H. $75 − $41.25 = $33.75; $33.75 ÷ $75 = 0.45, or 45%

Ask students to self-check their work as you write answers on the board or display them on a transparency.

Have student volunteers write the solutions to Exercises 8, 13, 15, 20, and 21 on the board or on a transparency. Discuss student responses to Exercise 29, Critical Thinking.

■ **STUDENT PORTFOLIO**
Remind students to consider including in their portfolio some of the problems they solve in this lesson, especially 16–19 and 30–33.

13. An invoice with a total due of $3,400 is paid within the discount period. Credit terms are 2/30. Find the cash discount and the cash price. $68, $3,332

14. The credit terms of an invoice dated June 23 are 2/10, 1/20, n/30. The total amount due on the invoice is $3,106. Find the cash discount and cash price if the invoice is paid July 5. $31.06, $3,074.94

15. The usual cost to ship men's shirts is $16 a dozen. A retailer in Peoria bought 6-dozen men's shirts on March 16 from a wholesaler in Chicago at $16.32 per shirt. The terms of the sale were 2/15, n/30; f.o.b. Chicago. The invoice was paid by check on March 29. What was the amount of the check? $1,151.54

Carrie Osterman, a storeowner whose shop is on a boardwalk by the Atlantic Ocean, buys 250 beach towels with a list price of $18.20 each. She receives a 40% trade discount.

16. What amount of discount will she get on the entire order? $1,820

17. What will be the invoice price of the order? $2,730

18. How much would a retailer pay for 30 dozen work gloves if the wholesaler's list price is $62 a dozen, less 28%? $1,339.20

19. Josh Hill, the owner of Hill's Auto Parts, paid $6,873.75 to settle Invoice #B-2826 after taking a cash discount. The original invoice amount was $7,050. What rate of cash discount was given? 2.5%

An invoice of $1,230 was paid within the discount period with a check written for $1,211.55.

20. What cash discount was received? $18.45

21. What was the cash discount rate? 1.5%

Carlos Durbin paid an invoice on February 16. The invoice for $783.20 was dated January 7 with credit terms of 3/20 EOM.

22. What was the last day on which a discount could be taken? Feb. 20

23. If a discount could have been taken, what amount was sent when the invoice was paid? $759.70

24. A rocking chair with a list price of $245 is offered to a retailer for $98. What rate of trade discount is offered? 60%

A retailer ordered 8-dozen casual slacks for $14.50 each. The list price of the slacks is $25.

25. What trade discount was given per slack? $10.50

26. What was the rate of trade discount? 42%

27. What will be the amount of the invoice when it is received? $1,392

28. **BEST BUY** Pearl Keating, a storeowner, gets prices on a curio cabinet from two wholesale firms. The Trill Company offers a cabinet for $800, less 40%. Pender Products offers the same cabinet for $650, less 30%. From which firm should Pearl buy the cabinet in order to get the lowest price? How much less will the lower price be? Pender, $25 less

514 ■ **Chapter 12** Sales and Marketing

SELECTED SOLUTIONS

13. 0.02 × $3,400 = $68; $3,400 − $68 = $3,332

16. 250 × $18.20 = $4,550; $4,550 × 0.4 = $1,820

17. $4,550 − $1,820 = $2,730

20. $1,230 − $1,211.55 = $18.45

21. $18.45 ÷ $1,230 = 0.015, or 1.5%

29. **CRITICAL THINKING** Name three things that you consider when you buy a product and rank them in order of importance. Next list three things that you think a business considers when it buys a product and rank them in order of importance. What are the similarities and differences between the lists and the rankings? *Answers will vary, but price, availability, and quality of goods are important.*

STRETCHING YOUR SKILLS On November 6, Owen Tormo bought $28,000 worth of goods with terms of 3/10, n/30. To pay the invoice on November 16 and get the 3% discount, Owen borrowed the cash price of the invoice at his bank for 20 days at 12%, ordinary interest.

30. What was the cash price of the invoice? $27,160

31. What was the cost of interest on the loan? $181.07

32. What cash discount did Owen receive? $840

33. How much did Owen save by borrowing money to take the cash discount?
$658.93

MIXED REVIEW

34. Write 1.93 as a percent. 193%

35. Find $\frac{2}{5}$ of 550. 220

36. Estimate: 3,016 ÷ 18 150

37. $\frac{2}{3} \div 48$ $\frac{1}{72}$

38. Find the quotient of 9.5 ÷ 2.4 to the nearest hundredth. 3.96

39. The Bremmers want to buy a home. They estimate these home operating expenses: property tax, $3,400; insurance, $485; utilities, $1,480; maintenance, $1,200; mortgage interest, $6,400; lost interest on down payment, $420. Their estimated income tax savings are $1,800. What will be the net cost of owning the home in the first year? $11,585, Lesson 6.2

40. Seletha Payne bought 150 shares of Regal Building Materials preferred stock. The stock paid a quarterly dividend of 1.25% on a par value of $100. What total amount in dividends did Seletha receive from owning this stock for one year? $750, Lesson 7.6

41. A store had 62 bags of lawn fertilizer on hand on May 1. New shipments of fertilizer arrived on May 19, 120 bags, and on June 9, 200 bags. Fertilizer sales for May were 146 bags, and for June, 198 bags. How many bags of fertilizer should be in stock on June 30? 38, Lesson 10.4

42. Nanno Metal Products estimated that the fixed costs of producing filing cabinets are $111,300 and their variable costs are $65 a cabinet. The filing cabinets will sell for $118. How many cabinets must be sold to break even, to the nearest unit? 2,100, Lesson 11.2

43. Ridgeway Industries buys a planer for $3,500. The estimated life is 8 years, and the annual depreciation rate used is 12%. What will the book value of the planer be at the end of 3 years? $2,385.15, Lesson 11.3

44. What is the girth of a box that is 40 inches long, 10 inches wide, and 5 inches deep? 30 inches; Lesson 11.4

Lesson 12.2 Cash and Trade Discounts ▪ **515**

Reteach

STUDENT WORKBOOK If students have difficulty in calculating the discount date and due date, do Exercises 1a, 1b with them. Assign 1c–1f for individual work.

If finding a cash discount and a cash price are areas of difficulty for students, work Exercises 1a and 1b with them. Have them do Exercises 1c–1f for independent practice.

Help students find the trade discount and invoice price by working Exercise 2 with them and assign Exercises 3 and 6.

If students need help with finding the rate of trade discount, do Exercise 4 with them. Have them work Exercise 5 independently.

Enrich

Review student answers to Exercises 30–33, Stretching Your Skills. Point out that borrowing money to take advantage of a cash discount is a powerful tool for business owners.

Assume the transaction is repeated every 20 days and that there are about 18 periods of 20 days in a year. Total annual savings would be 18 × $658.93, or $11,861, to the nearest dollar. An approximate annual rate of return on a $28,000 investment would be 42.4% ($11,861 ÷ $28,000).

Close

Have students provide definitions to the bolded and italicized terms in the lesson.

CONNECTION TO ECONOMICS

Students already know that retailers do not have to charge the suggested list price for an item. In the early part of the twentieth century fair trade laws were passed by states to protect small retailers. The laws applied to intrastate commerce. Eventually, the laws were repealed because enforcement was difficult and the basis of fair trade and related laws were challenged in courts. In 1975, Congress passed an act that reaffirmed that agreements to fix prices were a violation of federal antitrust laws.

Start Up

Have students read the Start Up. Ask them if they recall seeing any products labeled with a manufacturer's suggested price. You might remind them that new cars have stickers with an MSRP. Review the reasons why cars may be sold for less than the MSRP and apply those reasons to other consumer products.

Math Skill Builder

The subtraction and multiplication of money amounts and percents are skills used in this lesson.

Complete all exercises in Math Skill Builder 1–3.

■ Teach Goal 1

Tell students that series discounts are just another form of trade discount. Illustrate the inverse relationship of trade discount rates and prices. An increase in a trade discount rate results in a lower invoice price for buyers; a decrease in a trade discount rate results in higher prices for buyers.

Point out that prices are often raised or lowered simply by changing the last discount in the series.

GOALS

- Calculate the invoice price for a series of discounts
- Calculate the single discount equivalent to a series of discounts

Start Up

Have you ever seen or been offered a product at a price less than the suggested retail price printed on the package? How can a retailer afford to sell for less than the suggested price?

Math Skill Builder

Review these math skills and solve the exercises that follow.

1 **Subtract** money amounts and percents.
Find the difference. $1,807 − $36.14 = $1,770.86$
Find the difference. $82\% − 8.2\% = 73.8\%$

1a. $545.60 − 163.68 381.92 **1b.** $281.32 − 4.22 277.10

1c. $90\% − 13.5\%$ 76.5% **1d.** $95\% − 9.5\%$ 85.5%

2 **Multiply** money amounts by percents.
Find the product. $15\% \times $759.29 = 0.15 \times $759.29 = 113.893, or 113.89

2a. $35\% \times 17.12 5.99 **2b.** $7\% \times 763.11 53.42

3 **Multiply** percents by percents.
Find the product. $80\% \times 90\% = 0.8 \times 0.9 = 0.72$, or 72%

3a. $70\% \times 90\%$ 63% **3b.** $85\% \times 90\%$ 76.5%

■ Series Discounts

In the previous lesson, you saw that businesses frequently offer business customers trade discounts. Companies, such as wholesalers, often publish a catalog that lists items offered for sale and their prices. The price in the catalog is called the **list price**, which is the price that a consumer might pay. The price the retailer pays after the trade discount is given is called the **invoice price**.

To save the cost of reprinting their catalog when list prices change, wholesalers simply change the trade discount percent to raise or lower the prices they charge retailers.

Some wholesalers may give a trade discount that has two or more discounts, called a **discount series** or a series of discounts. For example, the trade discount may be 20%, 15%, 10%. This means that three discounts are given on an item.

COMMON ERRORS

Students may try taking series discounts by adding them together and finding a single amount. For instance, they might come up with an invoice price of $104 ($260 − (0.6 × $260)) for Check Your Understanding Problem A rather than $131.04. Remind students that series discounts must be taken sequentially or an appropriate equivalent used.

To find the invoice price, the first discount is based on the list price. The second discount is based on the remainder after deducting the first discount. The third discount is based on the remainder after deducting the second discount, and so on.

EXAMPLE 1

The list price of a display case is $2,100, less 25%, 10%, and 5%. Find the invoice price and the amount of trade discount.

SOLUTION

Multiply the list price by the rate of the first discount. Subtract the amount of discount from the list price. Use each remainder you get to repeat the process until all discounts have been taken.

$2,100.00	List price
− 525.00	First discount (25% of $2,100)
$1,575.00	First remainder
− 157.50	Second discount (10% of $1,575)
$1,417.50	Second remainder
− 70.875	Third discount (5% of $1,417.50)
$1,346.625	Third remainder

$1,346.625 = $1,346.63 invoice price

Subtract the invoice price from the list price.

$2,100 − $1,346.63 = $753.37 trade discount amount

> **MATH TIP**
>
> Note that amounts are rounded to the nearest cent ONLY after all computations are done.

> **MATH TIP**
>
> Check your work by taking the series discounts in a different order.

■ CHECK YOUR UNDERSTANDING

A. What are the invoice price and the amount of discount for a kitchen cabinet that has a list price of $260, with discounts of 30%, 20%, and 10%? $131.04, $128.96

B. A faucet with a list price of $140 is offered to retailers with discounts of 20%, 20%, and 5%. Find the invoice price and the amount of discount. $85.12, $54.88

■ Single Discount Equivalent

If you buy regularly from one vendor and always receive the same discount series, you can calculate the invoice price faster by using one discount that is equal to the series of discounts. That one discount is called the *single discount equivalent*.

EXAMPLE 2

Use the three methods below to find the single discount equivalent and the invoice price for a pair of hiking boots that have a list price of $80. They are offered to retailers with a series discount of 20%, 10%, and 10%.

a. percent method   b. table method   c. complement method

Lesson 12.3 Series Trade Discounts ■ **517**

■ **Apply Goal 1**

Do Example 1 on the board while students do the math at their desks. Show how the first Math Tip on page 517 is applied in the Example 1 solution.

Review the second Math Tip on page 517 and assign rows of students to take the 25%, 10%, and 5% discount series in a different order to demonstrate how they can arrive at the same invoice price.

Assign Check Your Understanding problems A and B for work in class. Assist students who have difficulty solving the problems.

■ **ONGOING ASSESSMENT**

Remind students that a combination of decimals and fractions may be used to calculate series discounts. Have students identify what fraction they might use in place of these percents: $33\frac{1}{3}$%; $\frac{1}{3}$ $16\frac{2}{3}$%; $\frac{1}{6}$ 20%; $\frac{1}{5}$ and 25%. $\frac{1}{4}$

■ **Teach Goal 2**

Remind students that three methods are presented to find the single discount equivalent to a discount series. If the series discount values are in the table shown on page 518, the Table Method is the simplest to use provided that the textbook is available to use as a reference. The next simplest method is the Complement Method.

Inform students that they must learn all three methods since problem directions may require them to use a specific method.

■ *CHECK YOUR UNDERSTANDING SOLUTIONS*

A. $260 × 0.30 = $78; $260 − $78 = $182 first remainder; $182 × 0.20 = $36.40; $182 − $36.40 = $145.60 second remainder; $145.60 × 0.10 = $14.56; $145.60 − $14.56 = $131.04 invoice price; $260 − $131.04 = $128.96 discount

B. $140 × 0.20 = $28; $140 − $28 = $112 first remainder; $112 × 0.20 = $22.40; $112 − $22.40 = $89.60 second remainder; $89.60 × 0.05 = $4.48; $89.60 − $4.48 = $85.12 invoice price; $140 − $85.12 = $54.88 discount

Work Example 2 at the board with students following your presentation and verifying the calculations for each step of the three methods presented. Emphasize that exactly the same invoice price equivalent, invoice price, and single discount equivalent are obtained with each method.

Assign Check Your Understanding problems C through E for class work. Check student work at their desks to ensure they are using the method indicated. If students need more practice, have them solve problems C through E again using at least one different method.

SOLUTION

a. The Percent Method: To find the single discount equivalent for a series discount of 20%, 10%, and 10% follow these steps.

Step 1:	100%	List price
	− 20%	First discount (20% of 100%)
	80%	First remainder
	− 8%	Second discount (10% of 80%)
	72.0%	Second remainder
	− 7.2%	Third percent (10% of 72%)
	64.8%	Third remainder, or invoice price

Step 2: 64.8% × $80 = 0.648 × $80 = $51.84   invoice price

Step 3:	100.0%	List price
	− 64.8%	Invoice price
	35.2%	Single discount equivalent

b. The Table Method: To find the single discount equivalent for a series discount of 20%, 10%, and 10% follow these steps.

The table shows the invoice price equivalents for a variety of series discounts.

Rate	5%	10%	15%	20%	25%	30%
5%	0.9025	0.855	0.8075	0.76	0.7125	0.665
5%, 5%	0.85738	0.81225	0.76713	0.722	0.67688	0.63175
10%	0.855	0.81	0.765	0.72	0.675	0.63
10%, 5%	0.81225	0.7695	0.72675	0.684	0.64125	0.5985
10%, 10%	0.7695	0.729	0.6885	0.648	0.6075	0.567

Step 1: Locate the 20% column. Then find the 10%, 10% row. The invoice price equivalent is 0.648, or 64.8%

Step 2: 64.8% × $80 = 0.648 × $80 = $51.84   invoice price

Step 3: 100.0% − 64.8% = 35.2%   single discount equivalent

c. The Complement Method: To find the single discount equivalent for a series discount of 20%, 10%, and 10% follow these steps.

The complement of any discount rate is the difference between that rate and 100%. For example, if the discount rate is 30%, the complement of the discount rate is 70%.

Step 1: Multiply the complements of the discounts.
0.80 × 0.90 × 0.90 = 0.648 = 64.8%   invoice price equivalent

Step 2: 64.8% × $80 = 0.648 × $80 = $51.84   invoice price

Step 3: 100% − 64.8% = 35.2%   single discount equivalent

DIFFERENT LEARNING ABILITIES At-Risk Learners

Some students may not understand how the conversion table on page 518 works. Explain that the horizontal line of rates at the top of the table may be thought of as representing the first discount in a series. The rate(s) at the left of the table represent the remaining discounts in the discount series. The point at which the rates intersect is the invoice price equivalent. That equivalent may be multiplied by the list price to find the invoice price.

Look back to the previous examples, parts a, b, and c. In Step 1 you found the percent that the invoice price is of the list price. In Step 2 you multiplied the list price by the percent (invoice price equivalent) to calculate the invoice price.

In Step 3 you subtracted the percent that is the invoice price equivalent from 100%. The result is a single discount, 35.2%, which is equivalent to the series discount of 20%, 10%, and 10%. If you know the single discount equivalent, you may also calculate the invoice price this way:

$35.2\% \times \$80 = \$28.16$ discount amount

$\$80 - \$28.16 = \$51.84$ invoice price

■ **CHECK YOUR UNDERSTANDING**

Find the single discount equivalent to the series discount, the amount of trade discount, and the invoice price for Problems C, D, and E, using the method indicated.

C. Percent Method: series discount, 20%, 10%, 5%; list price $900.   31.6%, $284.40, $615.60

D. Table Method: series discount, 30%, 5%, 5%; list price, $34.16.   36.825%, $12.58, $21.58

E. Complement Method: series discount, 10%, 25%, 5%; list price, $12.80.   35.875%, $4.59, $8.21

Wrap Up

The retailer pays less than the suggested retail price for goods. As long as the actual selling price is greater than the retailer's invoice price, a gross profit is made on the sale. Also, the "suggested price" is just that, a suggested price, not a required price.

TEAM MEETING

Some manufacturers sell only through authorized dealers. A new company that wishes to become an authorized dealer is told that there are enough dealers in the area already. The new company states that this policy is unfair, and that anyone should be able to buy and sell any product they wish.

Two teams should be formed to debate the issue that manufacturers have the right to use authorized dealers.

• One team should take the *pro position* and agree with the issue.

• The second team should take the *con position* and argue against the issue.

The debate should be held in class. The class members who listen to the debate will decide which team wins the debate.

■ *CHECK YOUR UNDERSTANDING SOLUTIONS*

C. 100% − 20% = 80% first remainder; 80% − (10% × 80%) = 72% second remainder; 72% − (5% × 72%) = 68.4%; 100% − 68.4% = 31.6% single discount; 0.316 × $900 = $284.40 trade discount; $900 − $284.40 = $615.60 invoice price

D. From table, 0.63175, or 63.175%; 100% − 63.175% = 36.825% single discount; 0.36825 × $34.16 = $12.579, or $12.58 trade discount; $34.16 − $12.58 = $21.58 invoice price

E. 100% − (90% × 75% × 95%) = 35.875%; 35.875% × $12.80 = $4.59; $12.80 − $4.59 = $8.21

Assign

Assignment: Exercises 1–21, 24–33. Students are to begin with the basic arithmetic problems at the beginning of the exercises. They review the underlying arithmetic in the exercises.

Assess

Have students read their answers to Exercises 1–6. Then have two students place their solutions for Exercise 7 on the board. Have one student do the problem as indicated while the other student provides the check solution.

For Exercises 11–16, place three columns on the board, one for each method. Ask the class to give the answers for each method and write their answers in the appropriate column. Review the answers to reinforce the idea that the same answer is obtained regardless of the method used.

Reteach

STUDENT WORKBOOK Some students may need help in calculating the invoice price. If so, do Exercise 1 with them and assign Exercises 2–4.

If students need help in finding the single discount equivalent, work Exercise 5 with them using the percent and complement methods. Assign Exercises 6 and 7 as independent work. Tell students to use the method stated in the problem and one other method of their choosing.

EXERCISES

Find the difference.

1. $2,689 − $672.25 $2,016.75

2. 88% − 13.2%   74.8%

Find the product.

3. $12\frac{1}{2}\% \times \$205.37$ $25.67

4. $45\% \times \$87.90$ $39.56

5. $80\% \times 85\% \times 75\%$ 51%

6. $95\% \times 95\% \times 80\%$ 72.2%

Find the invoice price and the amount of trade discount. Check your work by taking the discounts in a different order.

	List Price	Trade Discount	Invoice Price	Amount of Trade Discount
7.	$120	20%, 10%	$86.40	$33.60
8.	$ 87	20%, 10%, 10%	$56.38	$30.62
9.	$315	30%, 15%, 10%	$168.68	$146.32

10. Xavier, Inc. sells a computer chair for $238, with discounts of 20%, $12\frac{1}{2}\%$, and 7%. Find the invoice price. $154.94

For Exercises 11–16, use any method you choose to find the single discount equivalent for each. Use each method at least once. Show your work.

11. 10%, 10%   19%

12. 20%, 25%   40%

13. 20%, 12.5%   30%

14. 10%, $33\frac{1}{3}\%$ 40%

15. 25%, 20%, 5%   43%

16. 30%, 20%, $12\frac{1}{2}\%$ 51%

17. A jade bracelet has a list price of $460 and series discounts of 30%, 10%, and 5%. Find the invoice price. $275.31

18. What invoice price will a retailer pay for a book with a list price of $35 and series discounts of 20%, 20%, and 15%? $19.04

19. A garden hose with a list price of $32 is offered for series discounts of 15%, 15%, and 10%. What are the amounts of the invoice price and trade discount? $20.81, $11.19

20. **BEST BUY** Newland Distributing offers to deliver an order of 30 sets of patio furniture for $14,000 list price, less 30%, 20%, and 5%. Ingle Wholesale offers the same furniture at 25%, 20% and 10%. Which is the best offer, and how much would be saved by taking the better offer?   Newland, $112

SELECTED SOLUTIONS

7. 20% × $120 = $24; $120 − $24 = $96; 10% × $96 = $9.60; $96 − $9.60 = $86.40 invoice price; $120 − $86.40 = $33.60 trade discount

11. Percent Method: 10% × 100% = 10%; 100% − 10% = 90%; 10% × 90% = 9%; 90% − 9% = 81%; 100% − 81% = 19%

12. Complement Method: 80% × 75% = 60%; 100% − 60% = 40%

21. CRITICAL THINKING The order in which a series of discounts are taken may be changed and the answer will be the same. Why is this so? *Multiplication is commutative.*

INTEGRATING YOUR KNOWLEDGE A hotel wants to buy a new ice machine. Three vendors were asked to submit bids. The terms of their bids are shown in the chart below. Assume the hotel will take the highest cash discount offered. Copy and complete the chart by finding the invoice price and the total due. Then answer these questions:

22. Which vendor offers the best package price? B

23. If the purchase is made on March 18, what is the due date of the invoice?
May 17

	Vendor A	Vendor B	Vendor C
List Price	$1,600	$1,650	$1,930
Cash Discount	1/30, n/60	2/30, n/60	2/10, 1/30, n/60
Trade Discount	5%	3%, 7%	10%
Shipping Terms	FOB Factory	FOB Factory	FOB Seller
Delivery Charges	$175	$203	$175
Invoice Price	$1,520	$1,487.64	$1,737
Total Due	$1,679.80	$1,660.89	$1,877.26

MIXED REVIEW

24. $\frac{1}{6}$ of $468.30 is what number? $78.05

25. Write $\frac{1}{10}$% as a decimal. 0.001

26. $87\frac{1}{2}$% of $2,480 $2,170

27. 30% less than $570 $399

28. Round 0.1896 to the nearest hundredth. 0.19

29. Fiona Adams is paid a salary of $187 a week and a commission of 2% on sales. Last week her sales were $58,120. What were her total wages for the week?
$1,349.40, Lesson 1.4

30. On October 1, Dwight's check register had a balance of $943.06. His bank statement balance on the same date was $773.55. Checks outstanding were #259, $56.71; #261, $33.78. A line on the bank statement showed that the bank charged his account $260 for the October car loan payment due the bank. Reconcile the statement. $683.06, Lesson 3.4

31. The beginning inventory of work gloves was 35 pair with a value of $72.45. The most recent purchase of work gloves was 70 pair for $136.50. Use the LIFO method to find the value of the ending inventory of 18 gloves.
$37.26, Lesson 10.5

32. The preparation of a job description and job specifications for a college recruiter position took 12 hours of human resources staff time. The direct costs were: wages at $23.60 an hour, fringe benefits at 35% of wages, and 2 hours of computer time at $12.60 an hour. What was the total direct cost of this project?
$407.52, Lesson 11.5

33. A random sample of 300 lamps was tested at a lamp factory. Six lamps were found to be defective. If 24,000 of these lamps were made, about how many are likely to be defective? 480, Lesson 8.2

Lesson 12.3 Series Trade Discounts ■ **521**

DIFFERENT LEARNING STYLES Auditory Learners

The calculation of series discounts by the percent method requires one basic step to be repeated until all discounts are taken. The approach that follows may help auditory learners remember the percent method process. In Solution a. on page 518, state that the first discount gives the first remainder, the second discount gives the second remainder, and the third discount gives the third remainder. The known price, the list price, is used to find the first discount. Then, each successive remainder is used in place of the list price.

521

12.4 Markup and Markdown

GOALS

- Calculate cost and selling price when markup is based on selling price
- Calculate the rate of markup based on cost
- Calculate markdown and selling price

Start Up

Often new products appear on the market and there are no competitors in sight. Because of this, a very high price may be charged for the item. Would the manufacturer or seller of the product be better off by charging a lower price so as to put it into the price range of more buyers?

Math Skill Builder

Review these math skills and solve the exercises that follow.

① Subtract money amounts and percents.
Find the difference. $120 − $56.80 = $63.20
Find the difference. 100% − 37.5% = 62.5%

1a. $87 − $65.10 $21.90   **1b.** $199.95 − $59.99 $139.96

1c. $100\% − 33\frac{1}{3}\%$ $66\frac{2}{3}\%$ **1d.** 100% − 38.5%   61.5%

② Multiply money amounts by percents.
Find the product. 60% × $118 = 0.6 × $118 = $70.80

2a. 85% × $6.24 $5.30   **2b.** 55% × $18.95 $10.42

③ Divide money amounts by money amounts.
Find the quotient. $63 ÷ $180 = 0.35, or 35%

3a. $16.25 ÷ $65   25%   **3b.** $45 ÷ $50   90%

■ Markup Based on Selling Price

Businesses have to decide what price to charge for an item. The price must cover the cost of the item, all expenses, including overhead, and generate a profit.

One way businesses price items is to use *markup pricing*. With markup pricing, an amount is added to the cost of the goods to cover all other expenses plus a profit. This is known as the **markup** or *margin*. The *selling price* is the price at which the item is actually sold.

Retailers often sell goods in *price lines*. For example, an auto supply store may stock three price lines of car batteries. One price line sells for $79.99; another line

522 ■ Chapter 12 Sales and Marketing

sells for $69.99; a third line sells for $59.99. The different price lines are expected to appeal to the different needs of buyers.

When batteries are bought by a retailer for a price line, such as $59.99, the selling price is already known. The problem is to find the highest price the retailer can pay for the batteries and still get the markup it wants. If the cost of the batteries is too high, the retailer will make too little profit in selling them.

EXAMPLE 1

Ida Schrader owns the Luggage Place and has to buy carry-on luggage for a line she sells for $90. She knows that her markup must be 40% of the selling price to cover expenses and get the net income she wants. What is the highest price she can afford to pay for each piece of luggage?

SOLUTION
Method 1:

Multiply the selling price by the markup rate to find the markup.

$40\% \times \$90 = 0.4 \times \$90 = \$36$

Subtract the markup from the selling price to find the cost: $\$90 - \$36 = \$54$

Method 2:

Subtract the markup rate from 100% to find the cost as a percent: $100\% - 40\% = 60\%$

Multiply the selling price by the cost as a percent to find the cost.

$60\% \times \$90 = 0.6 \times \$90 = \$54$

■ CHECK YOUR UNDERSTANDING

A. A wholesaler wants to sell a drill to retailers for $45 and earn a markup of 20% on the selling price. What is the most the wholesaler can pay a drill manufacturer and get the desired markup? $36

B. Marion Cassidy, a jeweler, wants to set a price of $600 for a bracelet. The markup he wants is 60% of the selling price. What is the most he can pay for the bracelet?
$240

Retailers also buy goods without a specific selling price in mind. However, since they know the cost of an item and the rate of markup *on the selling price* they want, they can calculate the selling price. The selling price is found by dividing the cost of an item by the percent that cost is of the selling price.

100% − Rate of Markup = Cost as a Percent of Selling Price

Cost ÷ Cost as a Percent of Selling Price = Selling Price

EXAMPLE 2

A retailer bases its markup of shoes on their selling price. What is the selling price of a shoe with a cost of $56 and a 30% markup on the selling price?

SOLUTION
$100\% - 30\% = 70\%$ cost as a percent of selling price

$\$56 \div 70\% = \$56 \div 0.7 = \$80$ selling price

Check: $30\% \times \$80 = 0.3 \times \$80 = \$24$ amount of markup
$\$80 - \$24 = \$56$ cost

Lesson 12.4 Markup and Markdown ■ **523**

■ Apply Goal 1

Work through Examples 1 and 2 at the board. Remind students that in Example 1, the selling price is known, but the cost is unknown and must be calculated. Then emphasize that in Example 2 the selling price is the unknown. Have students complete the math at their desks.

Assign Check Your Understanding problems A and B for class work. Have students solve these problems using both methods.

Next assign Check Your Understanding problems C and D. Remind students to include in their solutions the check step shown in the solution for Example 2.

■ ONGOING ASSESSMENT
Have students calculate the selling price for an item that costs $100 for these rates of markup on selling price: 10%; **$111.11** 20%; **$125** 25%; **$133.33** 35%. **$153.85**

■ *CHECK YOUR UNDERSTANDING SOLUTIONS*

A. $0.20 \times \$45 = \$9; \$45 - \$9 = \$36$

B. $100\% - 60\% = 40\%; 40\% \times \$600 = 0.4 \times \$600 = \$240$

C. The cost of $\frac{1}{2}$ oz. of a perfume is $18. The markup is 60% of the selling price. What is the selling price? $45

D. A birdbath costs $20.30. A retailer wants a markup of 42% of the selling price. What is the selling price of the birdbath? $35

■ Markup Based on Cost

While many businesses use the selling price to figure markup, others use the cost. When the cost price is used, you find the rate of markup by dividing the markup by the cost.

$$\text{Rate of Markup} = \frac{\text{Markup}}{\text{Cost}}$$

EXAMPLE 3

The cost of a rain suit that Emil Shulman bought for his store is $120. Emil wants to sell the jacket for $162. What is the rate of markup on the cost of the rain jacket?

SOLUTION
Subtract the cost from the selling price.

$162 − $120 = $42   markup

$42 ÷ $120 = 0.35, or 35%   rate of markup

■ CHECK YOUR UNDERSTANDING

E. The cost of a comb is $0.80. A retailer wants to sell the comb for $1.28. What rate of markup based on cost will the seller have to use? 60%

F. A grocer pays $2.50 for a half gallon of milk. The grocer wants to sell the milk for $2.70. What is the milk's rate of markup on cost? 8%

■ Markdown

In some cases, retailers reduce prices by applying a **markdown** to their *marked price*, or original selling price. The marked price is the price that is marked on the item. Recall that the selling price is always the price the item actually sold for.

A markdown may be taken on the marked price at the end of a season or on items that are not selling well. Markdowns might also be done to attract customers to the store for a sale or to be more competitive.

Markdown, which is also known as *discount*, is stated as a percentage of a marked price. The markdown formulas we will use are:

Rate of Markdown × Marked Price = Markdown

Marked Price − Markdown = Selling Price

EXAMPLE 4

To move an overstocked item, a discount of 15% is given on a backpack with a marked price of $70. Find the amount of the discount and the selling price.

■ Teach Goal 2

In addition to finding the rate of markup on cost, show students how to find the selling price when the cost and rate of markup are known. For instance, if a puzzle costs $3 and the rate of markup is 45% on cost, the selling price is $4.35, which is the result of $3 + (0.45 × $3).

■ Apply Goal 2

Work through Example 3 at the board with students and have them verify the calculations.

Assign Check Your Understanding problems E and F to be done in class. Check student work at their desks.

■ Teach Goal 3

Inform students that the calculation of markdown is similar to discount problems they have already solved. Ask students to describe the various ways that retail stores indicate a markdown (original price may be crossed off and a new price written; a 25% off sign notifies customers that discounts will be calculated at the register).

■ Apply Goal 3

Do Example 4 at the board. Relate the solution to the markdown formulas on page 524.

Assign Check Your Understanding problems G and H to be done in class. Walk around the class and check student work at their desks.

524

■ *CHECK YOUR UNDERSTANDING SOLUTIONS*

C. 100% − 60% = 40%;
   $18 ÷ 40% = $18 ÷ 0.4 = $45
D. 100% − 42% = 58%;
   $20.30 ÷ 58% = $20.30 ÷ 0.58 = $35

E. $1.28 − $0.80 = $0.48;
   $0.48 ÷ $0.80 = 0.6, or 60%
F. $2.70 − $2.50 = $0.20;
   $0.20 ÷ $2.50 = 0.08, or 8%

SOLUTION

Multiply the marked price by the rate of discount.

$15\% \times \$70 = 0.15 \times \$70 = \$10.50$ discount, or markdown

Subtract the amount of discount from the marked price.

$\$70 - \$10.50 = \$59.50$ selling price

■ CHECK YOUR UNDERSTANDING

G. A man's suit with a marked price of $270 is being offered at a 20% discount. What is the selling price of the suit? $216

H. At the end of the selling season a flat of flowers marked at $12.50 is discounted 50%. What is the selling price of the flat? $6.25

Wrap Up

It is possible that the new item has a very high manufacturing cost and must be sold at a high price. It is also possible that the company has a marketing strategy of first charging the highest price possible knowing they will attract some buyers. The next step in their strategy would be to cut the price so as to bring in the most anxious buyers at that price level, and so on until the item is widely distributed.

COMMUNICATION

Investigate what it would take for anyone to become a wholesaler. Use the library, Internet, or informational sources such as the Small Business Administration. Determine how the prospective wholesaler would establish contact with manufacturers in order to receive wholesaler's pricing and terms. Also determine how new wholesalers would begin building their business since they will be competing against established companies.

Present your findings in a short report that can be shared with the class.

EXERCISES

Find the difference.

1. $\$4.56 - \$4.04$ $0.52
2. $\$1,276 - \$982$ $294
3. $100\% - 92\frac{1}{2}\%$ $7\frac{1}{2}\%$
4. $100\% - 26.5\%$ 73.5%

Find the product.

5. $72.5\% \times \$10.76$ $7.80
6. $28\% \times \$1,764$ $493.92

Lesson 12.4 Markup and Markdown ■ **525**

Review the Start Up. Remind students that companies use different strategies in deciding how to run the company, including how to price products. Point out that the strategy described in the Wrap Up is one used by stores that are going out of business where progressively greater discounts are given to attract different types of customers.

COMMUNICATION

Have two to three students present their findings to the class. After the presentations are made, ask the rest of the class to add any additional information they found. Summarize the students' remarks.

Assign

Assignment: Exercises 1–38. Have students begin with the basic arithmetic problems that review the underlying arithmetic presented in the lesson.

■ *CHECK YOUR UNDERSTANDING SOLUTIONS*

G. $0.2 \times \$270 = \$54; \$270 - \$54 = \$216$

H. $0.5 \times \$12.50 = \$6.25; \$12.50 - \$6.25 = \$6.25$

Assess

Before collecting student work for checking, call on selected students to write on the board their solutions to exercises 9, 12, 18, 23, 24, and 26.

Reteach

STUDENT WORKBOOK Some students may need help with finding the cost and selling price when markup is on selling price. If so, work Exercises 1 and 4 with them. For independent work assign Exercises 2–3 and 5–6.

For students who have difficulty in finding the rate of markup based on cost, do Exercise 8 with them and assign Exercises 9 and 10 for independent solution.

Work Exercise 11 with students who may need help with finding markdown and selling price. Then have them solve Exercises 12 and 13 by themselves.

Find the quotient, as a percent.

7. $0.24 ÷ $2   12%

8. $21.09 ÷ $56.24   37.5%

9. Margaret Kogut buys golf bags for a line with a selling price of $80. What is the most she can pay for a golf bag if the markup must be at least 45% of the selling price? $44

10. A wholesaler has a line of rugs that sell for $129.50 each. What is the highest price the wholesaler can pay for the rugs and make a markup of 44% of the selling price? $72.52

11. What is the most that a store owner should pay per dozen for slippers with a selling price of $28.75 each if the owner needs a markup of 34% on the selling price? $227.70

For Exercises 12–16, markup is based on selling price. Find the cost as a percent of selling price. Also find the selling price.

	Item	Cost	Rate of Markup	Cost as a Percent of Selling Price	Selling Price
12.	Mattress	$562.50	55%	45%	$1,250
13.	Framed Print	112.70	54%	46%	$245
14.	Sandals	4.51	45%	55%	$8.20
15.	Trailer Mirror	26.22	31%	69%	$38
16.	Sleeping Bag	46.78	$37\frac{1}{2}$%	$62\frac{1}{2}$%	$74.85

17. Lori McCabe owns a hardware store and figures markup based on selling price. For a special sale, she buys 500 rolls of masking tape at 48¢ each. Lori wants a markup of 20%. What is the selling price of each roll? $0.60

For Exercises 18–22, find the markup and the rate of markup based on cost.

	Stock Number	Cost	Selling Price	Markup	Rate of Markup On Cost
18.	501-A	$ 77.25	$101.97	$24.72	32%
19.	501-B	150.00	225.00	$75	50%
20.	503-AA	720.00	864.00	$144	20%
21.	556-M	110.25	147.00	$36.75	$33\frac{1}{3}$%
22.	576-V	42.00	60.90	$18.90	45%

SELECTED SOLUTIONS

9. 0.45 × $80 = $36; $80 - $36 = $44

12. 100% − 55% = 45%; $562.50 ÷ 45% =
   $562.50 ÷ 0.45 = $1,250

18. $101.97 − $77.25 = $24.72; $24.72 ÷ $77.25 =
   0.32, or 32%

24. $1,285 − $1,050 = $235; $235 ÷ $1,285 = 0.182,
   or 18%

23. A retailer paid $220 for an end table plus $28 for delivery charges. What is the lowest price at which the table may be sold if a 48% markup, based on cost, is wanted? $367.04

24. Amy Hearns' bicycle shop regularly sells a racing bike for $1,285. At the end of the season, Amy reduces the price of the bike to $1,050. What is the rate of markdown, to the nearest percent? 18%

25. A catalog store discounts the price of a pool liner to $215 from $280. The cost of shipping the liner is $34.50. What is the rate of markdown, to the nearest tenth percent? 23.2%

26. **INTEGRATING YOUR KNOWLEDGE** Barry Waldo, a retailer, purchased 25 cooler chests for $28.10, less 30% and 10%. Barry priced the coolers at a markup of 35% on the selling price. What are the cost price and the selling price of each cooler? $17.70, $27.23

27. **INTEGRATING YOUR KNOWLEDGE** A wholesaler buys a shop vacuum from a manufacturer for a 30% trade discount from its list price of $100. What rate of markup on selling price will the wholesaler have to charge so the vacuum sells for the $100 list price? 30%

MIXED REVIEW

28. $0.87 \div 10$ 0.087

29. Write 0.034% as a decimal.   0.00034

30. $4\frac{11}{12} + 6\frac{5}{6}$ $11\frac{3}{4}$

31. $1.274 \div 4.9$ 0.26

32. What is 12% more than $842? $943.04

33. $856 - 0.427$ 855.573

34. The Sorgen Delivery Company hires per diem workers during busy periods at $96 a day. Last year, Sorgen hired 4 per diem workers for six weeks in the winter and 8 per diem workers for one week in the spring. The workweek at Sorgen is Monday through Friday. What total amount did Sorgen spend in the year on per diem workers? $15,360, Lesson 1.5

35. Eight cars are parked in a lot. Four of the cars are blue, 3 are red, and 1 is white. What is the probability that the first car leaving the lot will be blue, assuming no other cars enter? 0.5, Lesson 8.2

36. The Mallen Printing Company estimates the costs of issuing 4,100 purchase orders a year to be: office personnel costs, 30% of $118,000 annual wages and benefits; warehouse costs, $4,428; office costs, $9,800; overhead costs, $3,148 a year. What is the average cost of a purchase order, to the nearest cent? $12.87, Lesson 10.6

37. Zeppa Electronics uses National's two-day service (see Lesson 11.4) to ship customer purchases. On Tuesday, Zeppa shipped 20 identical packages, each weighing 1.75 lb, to customers in zone 3. Insurance will cost $2.10 per package. What is the total cost of Tuesday's shipment? $217, Lesson 11.4

38. You can buy a TV for $275 cash or pay $50 down and the balance in 18 monthly payments of $18.70. What is the installment price? By what percent, to the nearest tenth of a percent, would your installment price be greater than the cash price? $386.60, 40.6%, Lesson 4.4

Lesson 12.4 Markup and Markdown ■ 527

Start Up

Have students read the Start Up. Ask them to relate any personal experiences they might have had with surveys of any type. Discuss the types of questions asked during the survey and the type of demographic data requested.

Ask students how they feel about providing personal information to survey takers. Remind students that they should never give their social security, charge card, or driver's licenses numbers to anyone doing a survey.

Math Skill Builder

In this lesson, students use the skills of adding, subtracting, and dividing whole numbers.

Complete Exercises 1–2 in the Math Skill Builder.

■ Teach Goal 1

Discuss with students how it is often too costly and impractical for an organization to survey an entire population. Review with students the sampling techniques discussed in Chapter 8.

Point out that an organization may apply different criteria in deciding whether a survey is valid. An analogy might be the range of criteria proposed to hand-count ballots in Florida in the 2000 presidential election.

Stress that when a sample is used for surveys, great care is taken to ensure that the sample is typical of the total population.

12.5 Marketing Surveys

GOALS

- Calculate the response rate of surveys
- Calculate the results of surveys

Start Up

You just completed a 10-minute telephone survey covering your opinions about your bank. At the end of the survey you are asked for the amount of your total income. When you hesitate, the interviewer tells you that your survey can't be counted unless you answer all questions. Why would your income be important to the survey's results?

Math Skill Builder

Review these math skills and solve the exercises that follow.

1 Add whole numbers.
Find the sum. $1,282 + 281 = 1,563$

    1a. $238 + 94$ 332   **1b.** $3,879 + 1,082$ 4,961

2 Divide whole numbers to find a percent.
Find the percent. $84 \div 560 = 0.15$, or 15%

    2a. $180 \div 720$ 25%   **2b.** $2,883 \div 4,650$ 62%

■ Response Rate

Businesses survey customers to find what they think about products and services. Mail, Internet, telephone, or personal contact may be used. The total potential number of people or organizations that may be surveyed is called the *population*. Organizations such as the Bureau of Census try to survey every person in the U.S. To save time and money, most organizations survey only part of the total population, called the *sample*, or *sample population*.

To insure that the people in the sample represent the people in the whole population, demographic data about the people in the sample are collected. *Demographic data* may include age, sex, education, marital status, occupation, and income.

People who complete surveys are called **respondents**. Surveys are complete and *valid* when all questions are answered and demographic data are collected. Some responses may not be counted if a quota for respondents with certain characteristics has been filled. The response rate to a survey is found by dividing the number of responses by the number of surveys attempted.

Response Rate = Responses ÷ Surveys Attempted

TEACHING STRATEGIES Cooperative Learning

Students may wish to explore the ways in which researchers try to remove bias from surveys. Bias is a factor in surveys that provides misleading data. As an example, consumers may be asked to taste a low-fat bread. Some consumers may equate low-fat with low-taste, thereby introducing bias into the survey. Have interested students research the use of control and experimental groups or the use of double-blind tests. Encourage them to report the meanings of these terms in their own words and to give examples.

EXAMPLE 1

The Danton Company mailed 25,000 surveys to users of its Silk Smooth Soap. Of the 1,257 returned surveys, 57 were discarded as incomplete. What was the survey's response rate?

SOLUTION

Subtract the discarded surveys from the total surveys returned.

$1,257 - 57 = 1,200$ valid surveys

Divide the valid surveys by the total surveys.

$1,200 \div 25,000 = 0.048$, or 4.8% response rate

■ CHECK YOUR UNDERSTANDING

A. An auto research firm mailed questionnaires to the 240,000 buyers of a certain car model. Replies were received from 149,050 buyers, but 250 incomplete surveys were not counted. What was the response rate to the mailing?   62%

B. A manufacturer surveyed 80,000 buyers who registered their new printers online. There were 34,387 respondents to the initial e-mail survey request and 28,113 respondents to an e-mail reminder. Of that total, 4,100 surveys did not have enough information and were not counted. How many valid surveys were there? What was the response rate?   58,400, 73%

■ Survey Results

The results of surveys are tabulated to provide information about the respondents. Companies use this information to improve their products or to plan more effective ways to sell products or services. The results of a product satisfaction survey are shown.

<table>
<tr><th colspan="6">Danton Company
Silk Smooth Satisfaction Survey</th></tr>
<tr><th></th><th colspan="5">Product Rating</th></tr>
<tr><th>Ages</th><th>Excellent</th><th>Good</th><th>Average</th><th>Poor</th><th>Total</th></tr>
<tr><td>18–30</td><td>78</td><td>185</td><td>118</td><td>15</td><td>396</td></tr>
<tr><td>31–45</td><td>145</td><td>190</td><td>31</td><td>37</td><td>403</td></tr>
<tr><td>46–60</td><td>203</td><td>135</td><td>52</td><td>11</td><td>401</td></tr>
<tr><td>Totals</td><td>426</td><td>510</td><td>201</td><td>63</td><td>1,200</td></tr>
</table>

BUSINESS TIP

Business people often tabulate data to make them easier to understand. *Tabulate* means to place data in columns and rows and take totals of the columns and rows.

EXAMPLE 2

What percent of all respondents gave Silk Smooth soap a rating of better than average?

SOLUTION

Add the totals of the excellent and good rating categories.

$426 + 510 = 936$ total respondents, better than average rating

Divide the above total by the total number of respondents.

$936 \div 1,200 = 0.78$, or 78% rating, better than average

Lesson 12.5 Marketing Surveys ■ 529

■ **Apply Goal 1**

Work Example 1 with students. Explain that while a response rate of 4.8% may seem low, it may represent the total population.

Assign Check Your Understanding problems A and B for class work. Give individual help to students if they encounter any problems in completing their work.

■ **ONGOING ASSESSMENT**

Ask students to calculate the response rate for the following to the nearest percent and to the nearest tenth of a percent:

Surveys	Responses	Rate
20,000	4,232	**21%, 21.2%**
860	97	**11%, 11.3%**

■ **Teach Goal 2**

Discuss the table showing the results of the Danton Company's survey.

Also ask them to identify the purpose of finding a total of each column and row and then calculating a grand total (calculations may be done with row and column totals; the corner total is a check on the accuracy of the row and column totals).

■ **Apply Goal 2**

Work Example 2 at the board with students completing the math at their desks.

Assign Check Your Understanding Problems C and D for completion in class. Move about the classroom and check student work at their desks.

■ *CHECK YOUR UNDERSTANDING SOLUTIONS*

A. $149,050 - 250 = 148,800$; $148,800 \div 240,000 = 0.62$, or 62%

B. $34,387 + 28,113 - 4,100 = 58,400$; $58,400 \div 80,000 = 0.73$, or 73%

C. What percent of all respondents rated Silk Smooth as average, to the nearest tenth of a percent? 16.8%

D. What percent of respondents in the 31–45 age group gave Silk Smooth a poor rating? 9.2%

Wrap Up

Income, along with other demographic data, gives the bank a profile of your personal characteristics to see if your views about the bank are typical of other people with the same characteristics. However, you are under no obligation to provide such personal information especially to a person you don't know.

TEAM MEETING

You and your team members are to conduct a survey of 200 people to determine what they think about a movie. First, select a relatively new movie that would appeal to a wide audience. Then construct a simple questionnaire to determine whether the respondents like or do not like the movie, or have not seen the movie. Demographic data should be the age of the respondent in five-year segments, such as 13–17, 18–22, and so on. Also ask for the number of movies seen in a year within these categories: once a week, once a month, less than once a month.

Tabulate the data from the survey of your 200-person population. Then randomly select 20 surveys and tabulate their results. Compare the results of the population and sample surveys. Discuss the reasons for any differences you find in the results.

EXERCISES

Find the sum.

1. 738 + 183   921

2. 1,583 + 192 + 3,192   4,967

Find the percent, to the nearest tenth percent.

3. 237 ÷ 1,815   13.1%

4. 32,717 ÷ 187,512   17.4%

5. A researcher at a shopping mall stopped 214 young people who wore certain brands of clothing. Fifty-four people refused to be interviewed and 27 people did not answer enough questions to complete the survey. The rest answered all the questions. What was the total number of respondents? What was the response rate, to the nearest tenth of a percent?   133, 62.1%

6. A mail survey of 8,400 households received a 8.5% response rate. How many households responded to the survey?   714

7. A car manufacturer invited a group of customers to evaluate a new shade of red paint. The results showed that 500 people liked the new color, 315 liked the old shade better, 975 thought both colors looked alike, and 613 did not like the color red at all. To the nearest tenth of a percent, what percent of the respondents could not tell the difference between the old and new shades of red?   40.6%

530 ■ **Chapter 12 Sales and Marketing**

Wrap Up

Review the Start Up. Inform students that research companies may know a great deal about survey respondents even if they do not provide personal data. For example, if a home address is known, research data banks provide information about the home's value, from which a rough estimate of the homeowner's annual income may be derived.

Census data collected by the federal government provides much data relating to income, education, family size, and ethnicity of the respondents.

TEAM MEETING

Students should be responsible for planning the survey. The entire class may serve as the team for this activity. Each student should be assigned a quota of people to survey by age group.

Suggest that individual survey data be placed on 3 × 5 index cards to facilitate tabulation and sample drawing.

■ **STUDENT PORTFOLIO**

Students should consider including the Team Meeting survey results in their portfolios.

Assign

Assignment: Exercises 1–14, 16–22. Have students solve the basic arithmetic problems first. Remind students to show problem solutions in a systematic way and to label their answers.

The results of a survey asking people whether they liked the fragrance of a new shampoo are shown at the right. In Exercises 8–11, show any percent answers correct to the nearest tenth percent.

	Yes	No	No opinion
Female	570	211	109
Male	270	386	212

8. What was the total number of respondents? 1,758

9. What percent of the respondents had no opinion? 18.3%

10. What percent of the females liked the new fragrance? 64%

11. What percent of the respondents did not like the new fragrance? 34%

The Yard Pal Mower Company asked 550 customers to rate its newest lawnmower in three categories on a scale of 1–5, with 5 being the highest. The chart shown below summarizes the results of the survey.

Yard Pal Mower Company: Ratings of Selected Features						
	Rating (5 = highest; 3 = average; 0 = lowest)					
Feature	5	4	3	2	1	Totals
Easy to start?	350	117	40	14	29	550
Easy to change oil?	240	130	64	46	70	550
Easy to operate?	364	92	54	31	9	550

12. Which feature received the greatest number of average ratings? easy to change oil

13. What percent of respondents gave the "easy to change oil" category a rating of average or better, to the nearest percent? 79%

14. What percent of respondents gave the "easy to operate" category a below-average rating, to the nearest tenth of a percent? 7.3%

15. **CRITICAL THINKING** How do companies doing surveys select the people they survey to make sure they get accurate data? See Enrich section for answer.

16. **DECISION MAKING** Drew Enterprises mailed a 90-question survey to 6,000 businesses in 12 states. Drew selected its sample population by taking every fifth business listed in a directory. They received 135 responses, mainly from small businesses. What was the response rate? Can the new company make any business decisions based on the survey? 2.25%; No. The sample was not selected properly. Also, the lack of response makes it unlikely that the results represent the 6,000 businesses surveyed very well.

MIXED REVIEW

17. $5.41 \times 1,000$ 5,410

18. $\frac{4}{9} \div \frac{5}{20}$ $1\frac{7}{9}$

19. 920×400 368,000

20. $3\frac{1}{2} \times 4\frac{2}{3}$ $16\frac{1}{3}$

21. Lance Bader earned $6,200 in January. He paid an overall FICA tax rate of 7.65% that consists of a 6.2% social security tax and a 1.45% Medicare tax. Federal income taxes withheld from his wages were $1,512. What total amount of taxes was deducted from his pay in January? $1,986.30, Lesson 2.1

22. What property tax is due on a home assessed for $213,000 if the tax rate is $2.85 per $100? $6,070.50, Lesson 6.3

Lesson 12.5 Marketing Surveys ■ 531

SELECTED SOLUTIONS

5. 214 − 54 − 27 = 133 respondents; 133 ÷ 214 = 0.6214, or 62.1% response rate

7. 500 + 315 + 975 + 613 = 2,403 total respondents; 975 ÷ 2,403 = 0.4057, or 40.6% can't tell difference in red colors

8. 570 + 211 + 109 + 270 + 386 + 212 = 1,758 total respondents

9. 109 + 212 = 321 total no opinion respondents; 321 ÷ 1,758 = 0.1825, or 18.3%

10. 570 + 211 + 109 = 890 total female respondents; 570 ÷ 890 = 0.6404, or 64.0%

Start Up

Have students read the Start Up. Before discussing the Start Up, ask students whether the score they get on the first exam or quiz in a class is a good indicator of what their performance will be on future tests. Have them identify the variables that affect the test score. Similarly, have them identify variables affecting Darlene's annual wage projection.

Math Skill Builder

In this lesson, students use the skills of adding, subtracting and multiplying money amounts and finding a percent of an amount.

Complete Exercises 1–2 in the Math Skill Builder.

■ Teach Goal 1

Point out how a small company may show dramatic increases in sales and use the data to project future sales.

For example assume a company had sales of $200,000 last year and $800,000 of sales this year. The amount of sales increase is $600,000, and the one-year rate of growth in sales is 300%.

Ask students to calculate sales for next year by applying this year's growth rate. Thus, next year's projected sales increase would be $2,400,000 and projected total sales would be $3,200,000

Discuss how such rapid growth is possible over the short run but is unlikely to be sustained over the long run.

12.6 Sales Forecasts

GOALS

- Calculate future sales using trend data
- Calculate future sales using forecast methods

Start Up

During winter break week, Darlene Silvin, a high school student, earned $232 in gross wages at her part-time job. At that gross wage rate, Darlene figures that she will earn $12,064 in wages for a full year. She plans to buy a car with the money she will make. Do you agree with Darlene's forecast and plans?

Math Skill Builder

Review these math skills and solve the exercises.

1 **Multiply** money amounts by percents.
Find the product. $2,340,500 \times 13\% = \$2,340,500 \times 0.13 = \$304,265$

1a. $60,100,000 \times 3.5\%$ $2,103,500   **1b.** $381,000 \times 7.7\%$ $29,337

2 **Multiply** whole numbers by whole numbers and money amounts.
Find the product. $12 \times 1,800 = 21,600$
Find the product. $\$9.12 \times 58,000 = \$528,960$

2a. $48 \times 6,780$ 325,440   **2b.** $35 \times 2,736$ 95,760

2c. $\$24.05 \times 12,200$ $293,410   **2d.** $\$7.34 \times 31,900$ $234,146

■ Sales Trends

Many companies try to estimate their future sales. They may call these estimates sales forecasts, sales predictions, or sales projections. The sales forecast allows them to plan for future expansion and prepare annual budgets based on expected sales.

One way that companies may forecast future sales is by analyzing sales trends. A trend is a historical relationship between sales and time. For example, a trend may show that over 12 years sales have increased 10% each year, on average. A forecast based on this trend is that sales will be 10% higher next year than they are this year.

Using trends to forecast sales assumes that all the factors that influence sales remain the same. Some factors that may influence sales include consumer spending habits, new competition, and the general condition of the United States and world economies. Also, the longer the time period analyzed, the more accurate is the forecast.

TEACHING STRATEGIES Cooperative Learning

Have students form teams to conduct a search of newspapers, magazines, and Internet sources to find articles where companies forecast future sales. Have each team prepare a short report that lists the company, the nature of the forecast, and the specific reasons given to justify the forecast. Also have each team identify the contributions each member made to the final product. Have students share their findings in a class discussion. List the reasons for projected sales increases and decreases on the board so students may see the variety of factors that affect sales.

EXAMPLE 1

Sales of Morning Treat cereal increased an average of 20% a year over the past six years. This year's sales of Morning Treat were $6,500,000. Based on this trend, what are the forecasted sales for next year?

SOLUTION

Multiply current sales by the average percent of sales increase.

$20\% \times \$6,500,000 = 0.2 \times \$6,500,000 = \$1,300,000$ forecasted sales increase

Add the forecasted sales increase to current sales.

$\$1,300,000 + \$6,500,000 = \$7,800,000$ forecasted next year's sales

◼ CHECK YOUR UNDERSTANDING

A. The sales of Dentmile, a new toothpaste produced by Universal Brands, were $2,820,000 last year. Based on Universal's historical pattern of new product sales, Dentmile's sales are projected to be $2\frac{1}{2}$ times greater this year. What is the projection for this year's sales? $7,050,000

B. Last year's sales of an antivirus software package were 215,000 units to the business market and 98,000 units to the school market. Software sales to both markets are expected to increase by an average of 8% this year. What are the predicted total unit sales of the software to businesses and schools this year?   338,040

◼ Forecasting Methods

In addition to analyzing sales trends, companies use other methods to forecast sales. These include market tests, surveys, sales projections, and management opinion.

Market tests involve the actual sale of a new product in a small geographic area, such as a large city. Based on the success of the product in the test market, a projected sales figure for all markets is calculated.

Surveys may ask consumers to examine a product and state whether or not they intend to buy the product. *Sales force projections* are made from reports filed by sales staff about their customer's future spending plans. *Management opinion* may be used to forecast sales for new products that have no sales history. Whatever method is used, the data you get do not guarantee actual sales.

EXAMPLE 2

The Useful Products Company developed a clip-on carrying case that holds two pair of eyeglasses. In one test market, Useful Products sold 7,200 cases at $3.80 a case. Useful Products now wants to sell the cases nationally in all 60 of its markets, all of which are similar in size. Based on sales in the test market, what total unit and dollar sales are forecast for the first year?

SOLUTION

Multiply the test market unit sales by the number of markets.

$60 \times 7,200 = 432,000$ unit sales forecast for first year

Multiply the unit sales forecast by the unit price

$\$3.80 \times 432,000 = \$1,641,600$ dollar sales forecast for first year

Lesson 12.6 Sales Forecasts ◼ 533

◼ *CHECK YOUR UNDERSTANDING SOLUTIONS*

A. $2,820,000 × 2.5 = $7,050,000

B. 215,000 + 98,000 = 313,000; 0.08 × 313,000 = 25,040; 313,000 + 25,040 = 338,040

Wrap Up

Review the Start Up. Ask students to review what average means, how it is calculated, and how it is used. Discuss whether an annual wage projection based on two months' pay provides valid data for decision-making.

Algebra Connection

Ask students if they found the meaning of the equation $Y = bx$, which is a simple linear equation. Have them share their answers with the class.

Their answers might explain Y as the increase in sales, b as the product of the sales at the point of origin multiplied by the rate of increase or decrease, and x as the number of time periods projected forward from the point of origin. So, in applying $Y = bx$ we get $Y = (0.05 \times \$45,000) \times 1$, or $Y = \$2,250$, the projected increase for the next month.

Assign

Assignment: Exercises 1–12, 14–21. Have students do the basic arithmetic skill problems first before solving any other exercises.

■ **CHECK YOUR UNDERSTANDING**

C. Sales of House-Glow dish soap increased by 2.5% in a test market due to a new bottle color. Total sales in all markets are now $16,115,000. House-Glow plans to change the color permanently and predicts total sales to increase by the same percent as in the test market. By what amount are sales predicted to increase? What are the total predicted sales once the color change is made?
$402,875; $16,517,875

D. The sales staff of an office products dealer expects to sell 31 more copiers next year than this year. This year 176 copiers were sold at an average price of $16,400. Assume the sales projections are correct and the average price will remain the same. What is the total projected copier sales next year, in dollars?
$3,394,800

Wrap Up

Darlene may have worked more hours than usual during winter break week because she didn't have to go to school. If so, her estimate of earning $12,064 in annual wages is wrong. She should calculate her annual wages on a typical week or on her wages over a longer period, such as two months. She may have to reconsider her car buying plans.

Algebra Connection

The formula $Y = bx$ may be used to calculate a sales forecast based on a trend. Search the Internet or locate a statistics book to find the meanings of the factors in the formula and the method of calculation. Write short sentences to describe the factors and then show how you applied the formula to forecast sales if next month's sales are expected to increase by 5% from this month's sales of $45,000.

EXERCISES

Find the product.

1. $13.5\% \times \$346,700$ $46,804.50
2. $4.25\% \times \$41,200$ $1,751
3. $15 \times \$12,800$ $192,000
4. $42 \times \$117,985$ $4,955,370

Total sales of the Worland Markets were $8,200,000 two years ago and $9,020,000 last year.

5. By what percent did sales increase last year?   10%

6. If the same trend continues, what are sales likely to be this year? $9,922,000

7. Sales of a wood picnic table have dropped an average of 5% each year for the past 6 years. Last year, 220 tables were sold. Based on the trend, how many tables will be sold this year?   209

8. Based on past sales records, the sales of Uncle Stan's Original Sauce are expected to increase by 6% a year for the next two years from $270,000 this year. What are sales forecasted to be in each of the next two years? $286,200; $303,372

534 ■ **Chapter 12** Sales and Marketing

■ *CHECK YOUR UNDERSTANDING SOLUTIONS*

C. $0.025 \times \$16,115,000 = \$402,875$; $\$16,115,000 + \$402,875 = \$16,517,875$

D. $176 + 31 = 207$; $207 \times \$16,400 = \$3,394,800$

9. A child's toy was recalled as being unsafe. Before the recall, sales of the toy were 16,760 units. The toy has been redesigned, and the company expects unit sales to be only 40% of what they were before the recall. What unit sales should the toy maker expect?   6,704

10. Canfield Medical Supply sold 2,312 units of a new blood pressure reader last year. Canfield's management expects sales of the reader to increase 250% this year. What are the projected sales for this year?   5,780

A survey showed that 22% of the people in a test market who sampled Sweet Delite ice cream said they preferred Sweet Delite to other brands and would buy it. In the test market area, 68,000 gallons of ice cream were sold last year.

11. How many gallons of ice cream might the makers of Sweet Delite expect to sell in the test market area based on the survey results?   14,960

12. Assume that only 25% of the respondents who said they would purchase Sweet Delite actually did so. How many gallons of Sweet Delite will be sold?   3,740

13. **CRITICAL THINKING**   Because of a business slowdown that lasted three years, the sales of replacement batteries for older cars increased by 17% a year during that time. The battery production manager wants to build his budget based on battery sales for the past three years. Higher-level management wants budgets to be developed based on average sales for the past 12 years. Select the plan to be used and give reasons for your choice.   See Enrich section for answer.

14. **INTEGRATING YOUR KNOWLEDGE**   A survey of 260 store customers yielded 78 respondents who said they would buy cut flowers more often if the price was 25% lower. The store estimates they have 10,000 different customers who buy 2,200 bouquets of flowers a year. What would bouquet sales be if prices were cut by 25% and the survey results were true?   3,000

MIXED REVIEW

15. Find the average of 119, 203, 89, and 417.   207

16. $89.28 + $193.38 + $38 + $40.01 $360.67

17. What is $8.19 ÷ 10 rounded to the nearest cent? $0.82

18. Billie Renner is paid time-and-a-half for hours worked over 40 hours in a week. Her regular hourly pay is $16.15. What gross pay did Billie earn in a week where she worked 46.2 hours?
$796.20, Lesson 1.3

19. A used car's purchase price is $8,100. Other costs are registration fees of $97 and a sales tax of 6%. The buyer made a $2,100 down payment. What is the delivered price of the car and the balance due? $8,683; $6,583, Lesson 6.5

20. The Midland Tech Fund has a NAV of 5.89 and an offer price of 6.14. Neil Przybilski bought 2,000 shares of the fund. What was his total investment? $12,280, Lesson 7.7

21. A golf course owner bought a mower for $12,619. The mower has a class life of 5 years. Using the MACRS schedule find the first year's depreciation and the book value of the mower at the end of the first year. $2,523.80; $10,095.20, Lesson 11.3

Lesson 12.6 Sales Forecasts ■ **535**

Assess

Have students collaborate to find their errors if their answers do not agree. Before collecting student work, discuss their solutions and answers to Exercise 14, Integrating Your Knowledge.

Reteach

STUDENT WORKBOOK Work Exercise 1 with students who need help with calculating future sales using trend data. Assign Exercise 2 for independent work.

If students have difficulty with calculating future sales based on forecast methods, do Exercise 3 with them. Then have them do Exercises 4–6 independently.

Enrich

Assign Exercise 13, Critical Thinking. Remind students to consider the cost of carrying inventory (Lesson 10.6) in deciding which plan to select.

Also point out that when economic downturns occur consumers often hold off on major purchases, such as cars. They keep and repair old cars much longer than they would otherwise.

Taking the conservative approach might work best for the battery maker since it is likely that 100% of production will be sold.

Close

Have students describe what it means to base sales forecasts on trend data. Then have them describe other forecast methods.

SELECTED SOLUTIONS

5. $9,020,000 − $8,200,000 = $820,000;
   $820,000 ÷ $8,200,000 = 0.1, or 10%
6. 0.1 × $9,020,000 = $902,000;
   $9,020,000 + $902,000 = $9,922,000

8. 0.06 × $270,000 = $16,200; $270,000 + $16,200 =
   $286,200; 0.06 × $286,200 = $17,172;
   $286,200 + $17,172 = $303,372
11. 0.22 × 68,000 = 14,960
12. 0.25 × 14,960 = 3,740

Start Up

Have students read the Start Up. Ask whether they have seen or heard of the impact that large stores moving into the immediate area has had on small stores in that area.

Ask them about the fairness of a situation where a new store, possibly much larger, takes business away from older, smaller stores. Based on their responses, discuss the concept of competition and whether it is fair to consumers to deprive them of the greater selection and lower prices a larger store might offer.

Math Skill Builder

In this lesson, students use the skills of multiplying whole numbers and money amounts by percents and calculating percents.

Complete Exercises 1–2 in the Math Skill Builder.

■ Teach Goal 1

After a discussion of what market and market share mean, ask students what the market might be for a local gas station, a regional shopping mall, a long-distance phone company, and a virtual bank.

12.7 Market Share

GOAL
- Calculate market share

Start Up

Two stores each with local owners shared equally the market for clothing sales in Green City. A large chain store that sells everything at discount prices will open soon. What is likely to happen to the total market for clothing and to market share of each store when the chain store opens?

Math Skill Builder

Review these math skills and solve the exercises that follow.

① **Calculate** a percent.
Find the percent. $8,820 \div 49,000 = 0.18$, or 18%

1a. $17,360 \div 56,000$ 31%   **1b.** $\$96,000 \div \$2,400,000$ 4%

② **Multiply** whole numbers or money amounts by percents.
Find the product. $12\% \times 136,000 = 0.12 \times 136,000 = \$16,320$

2a. $37\% \times 43,200$ 15,984   **2b.** $12\% \times \$13,600,000$ $\$1,632,000$

■ Market Share

A **market** is the total of all the persons or organizations that are potential customers. The market for corn seed, for example, consists of all farmers and home gardeners who grow corn. **Market share** tells what percentage of the total market's sales one seller has.

An individual company's market share may be very high. For example, a local bakery in a very large city where few people drive cars may have 80–90% of the market for baked goods in the few blocks surrounding the bakery.

Other companies may have a relatively small market share, yet be financially successful. For example, a pharmaceutical company that sells medical equipment may have only a 5% share of the worldwide export market. However, if the worldwide market is $5 billion a year, the 5% market share equals $200,000,000 in annual export sales.

Market share is usually stated as a percent and may be based on the number of units sold or their dollar value.

536 ■ Chapter 12 Sales and Marketing

CONNECTION TO ECONOMICS

Point out to students that companies vie for market share because of the great leverage a market leader may exert on the total market. A company with a large market share may dictate industry standards, be able to use pricing as a competitive tool, and build customer loyalty through name recognition alone. Because of its greater sales, the market-leading company has more money to spend on research and product development. Also point out that market leaders may fail in the long run if they should lose track of customer needs because of their size and arrogance.

EXAMPLE 1

In one year, an airport served 450,000 passengers. One airline served 315,000 of the passengers. What market share did the airline have?

SOLUTION
Divide the airline's passengers by the total passengers.

$315,000 \div 450,000 = 0.7$, or 70%   market share

EXAMPLE 2

The retail stores in Hartwell had estimated total annual sales of $3,180,000 last year. Stengel's Department Store is estimated to have a 44% share of Hartwell's retail market. What amount of sales is Stengel's estimated to have?

SOLUTION
Multiply the total annual sales by the market share.

$44\% \times \$3,180,000 = 0.44 \times \$3,180,000 = \$1,399,200$ Stengel's estimated sales

■ CHECK YOUR UNDERSTANDING

A. Two publishers sell daily newspapers in the City of Wilson. Each day, the Wilson Post sells 16,240 papers and the Wilson Daily News sells 11,760 papers. What market share of daily newspaper sales does the Wilson Post have?   58%

B. A chain of tire stores is estimated to have 21% of the new tire market in a county. If new tire sales in the county are 126,000 tires, how many new tires are likely to have been sold by the chain?   26,460

Wrap Up

Because of its lower prices it is likely that the chain store will gain the greatest share of the clothing market in Green City. Since the chain store may draw customers from a wider area, it is possible that total clothing sales in Green City may increase. However, even though total sales may increase, the two stores that are locally owned are likely to have lower sales because of their reduced market share.

COMMUNICATION

Use the Internet or do library research to determine the market share held by the top three companies in each of the industries listed below. In a short report list in order each company's name and its market share. The name of the industry is to appear in the report's heading. Also list the source you used and the date on which the source's data was compiled.

Research these industries: personal desktop computers, refrigerators, and breakfast cereals.

Lesson 12.7 Market Share ■ **537**

■ *CHECK YOUR UNDERSTANDING SOLUTIONS*

A. 16,240 + 11,760 = 28,000; 16,240 ÷ 28,000 = 0.58, or 58%

B. 0.21 × 126,000 = 26,460

537

Assignment: Exercises 1–12 and 14–26. Have students solve the basic arithmetic problems before completing the rest of the exercises.

Remind students to label the results of calculations.

STUDENT WORKBOOK Work Exercise 1 with students who need help with calculating the percent of market share. Then assign Exercises 2 and 3 for individual work.

Do Exercise 4 with students to practice finding market share in dollars and assign Exercise 5.

Do Exercise 6 with students to help them find market share in units. Assign Exercise 7.

EXERCISES

Find the percent.

1. $1,330 \div 26,600$ 5%

2. $\$125,000 \div \$625,000$ 20%

Find the product.

3. $21.5\% \times 86,000$ 18,490

4. $27\% \times \$1,327,000$ $358,290

5. The industry forecast for next year is that 2,800,000 pairs of leather slippers will be sold. The Comfort-Wear Company expects to sell 1,008,000 pairs of leather slippers. What market share does Comfort-Wear expect to have? 36%

6. The annual sales of dishwasher soap in an eleven-state region are estimated to be $90,000,000 a year. The Blair Company expects its brand of dishwasher soap to have annual sales of $8,670,000. What market share, to the nearest tenth of a percent, does Blair expect to have? 9.6%

7. The manufacturers of replacement car floor mats expect to sell 120,000 mats in a certain state. Of that total, the Binko Company expects to sell 46,500 mats and Solwell Products expects to sell 31,000 mats. What market share does the Binko Company expect to have, to the nearest tenth of a percent? 38.8%

8. There are six companies that sell and clean work uniforms. Their combined revenues for the year are $4,120,500. Two of the companies have combined annual revenues of $2,940,000. What market share do the four remaining companies have, to the nearest percent? 29%

9. A new company hopes to get a 15% share of a $2,400,000 school supply contract. What is the dollar value of the contract the new company hopes to get? $360,000

10. The Perton Company increased its market share from 15% two years ago to 16% last year. Perton expects to gain another 1% of market share this year. What total sales can it expect if total industry sales are $48,500,000? $8,245,000

11. Sales of used ski equipment through Internet ads are expected to reach a 7% market share this year. The value of used ski equipment sold through all types of ads is estimated to be $7,000,000. What is the value of the ski equipment sold through Internet ads? $490,000

538 ■ **Chapter 12** Sales and Marketing

SELECTED SOLUTIONS

5. $1,008,000 \div 2,800,000 = 0.36$, or 36%

8. $\$4,120,500 - \$2,940,000 = \$1,180,500$;
$\$1,180,500 \div 4,120,500 = 0.286$, or 29%

10. $0.17 \times \$48,500,000 = \$8,245,000$

14. $0.001 \times \$40,000,000 = \$40,000$ gain in sales which is less than $150,000 cost of promotion plan

12. The total market for specialty woodworking tools sold through catalogs is $14,000,000 annually. Wilkin Wood Works is the industry leader with a 45% market share in catalog sales. What annual catalog sales does Wilkin have? $6,300,000

13. **CRITICAL THINKING** The executives of Landry Enterprises believe they can start a new division that within five years will have a 10% share of the one billion dollars a year modular office furniture market. Is this a realistic goal? See Enrich section for answers.

14. **DECISION MAKING** A company's share of a $40,000,000 market has remained at 6.1% for the past 11 years. The company's planners estimate they can gain an additional 0.1% market share gain by spending $150,000 each year to promote aggressively their products. Should the company go ahead with the promotion plan? No, they would spend $150,000 to gain only $40,000 in sales

MIXED REVIEW

15. $345 + 254 + 378 = 977$
   $692 + 235 + 758 = 1,685$
   $843 + 718 + 698 = 2,259$
   $1,880 \quad 1,207 \quad 1,834 = 4,921$

16. $3,007$
   $- 1,849$
   $1,158$

17. $\frac{3}{4} \times \frac{7}{12} \times \frac{8}{21}$ $\frac{1}{6}$

18. $14 - 4\frac{3}{8}$ $9\frac{5}{8}$

19. Find the number of days from January 13 to February 27.   45

20. Round 42.95¢ to the nearest cent.   43¢

21. Darla Runnels began the day with a bank balance of $356.32. Her employer direct deposited her weekly pay of $512.10. After work she made an ATM withdrawal of $75 and made two debit purchases for $61.15 and $119.04. What was Darla's bank balance at the end of the day? $613.23, Lesson 3.2

22. Merle Croswell's employer provides a health insurance plan that covers him and three family members. Merle pays 15% of the $238 monthly premium. How much does Merle pay in one year for health insurance? $428.40, Lesson 7.2

23. Rison Manufacturing calculates the average cost of replacing a non-exempt employee at $780 per employee. What is the annual cost of replacing employees if 10% of Rison's 70 non-exempt employees leave each year? $5,460, Lesson 10.1

24. Connie Alpern drove her truck 21,470 miles last year. She uses her truck 40% of the time on her job, installing dishwashers and gas ranges. Her employer reimburses business mileage at the rate of 32.8¢ a mile. What total reimbursement for mileage did Connie receive last year? $2,816.86, Lesson 11.6

25. Rosanna Zerwig paid $418 for a dishwasher and $120 for its installation. The sales tax of 4.2% in her state applies only to goods and not services. What was the total cost of the dishwasher? $555.56, Lesson 5.5

26. Stock paying quarterly dividends of $1.80 is bought for a total cost of $45 per share. What rate of income is earned on the investment?   16%, Lesson 7.6

Lesson 12.7 Market Share ■ **539**

CONNECTION TO FINANCE

Alert students not to confuse market share increases with sales increases. Explain how a company that increased its sales by 20% from the previous year may have lost market share if overall industry sales increased by more than 20%. Review the solution to Exercise 14, Decision Making, to illustrate how a company could become so focused on growing market share that it neglects to look at the bottom line, the profit it makes.

Start Up

Have students read the Start Up. Have them consider the types of stands they see in malls before they give their answers.

Math Skill Builder

In this lesson, students use the skills of adding, multiplying, and dividing whole numbers and money amounts.

Complete Exercises 1–3 in the Math Skill Builder.

■ Teach Goal 1

Refer students to the illustration on page 541. Point out to students that newspapers come in different sizes and may have more than six column widths and be longer than 21 inches. Regardless of page size, advertising space is still sold by the column inch.

Inform students that ads are often sold as ROP (run of paper or run of press). ROP means that the publisher may place an ad anywhere in the paper where there is room.

An advertiser may request an ad to be placed in a preferred position such as the top outside corner of a page or in a special section, both at extra cost.

12.8 Advertising

GOALS

- Calculate the cost of advertising in print media
- Calculate the cost of advertising in other media
- Calculate the advertising cost per person reached

Start Up

Imagine that your friend, Sheila, just opened a sunglass stand in a shopping mall. Sheila thinks that she ought to advertise her business, but doesn't know where she should advertise. What advice might you give Sheila?

Math Skill Builder

Review these math skills and solve the exercises that follow.

1 **Add** money amounts.
Find the sum. $3,120 + $790 = $3,910

   1a. $458 + $1,235 $1,693   **1b.** $774 + $2,560 $3,334

2 **Multiply** money amounts by whole numbers.
Find the product. 12 × $62 × 3 = $2,232

   2a. 7 × $34.50 × 5 $1,207.50   **2b.** 14 × $468 $6,552

3 **Divide** money amounts by whole numbers.
Find the quotient to the nearest tenth of a cent. $846 ÷ 1,980 = $0.427

   3a. $56,300 ÷ 980,000 $0.057   **3b.** $615 ÷ 46,000 $0.013

■ Cost of Print Ads

Advertising is a way of communicating a message about an organization, or its products and services, to a target audience through advertising media. A *target audience* consists of all possible customers for a product or service. *Media* refers to the different forms of advertising.

Print ads are ads that appear in printed publications such as newspapers. Most advertisers purchase *general ads*, also known as *display ads*. General ads usually contain large type and an illustration.

General ads are often sold by column inch. A *column inch* is a space one column wide by one inch deep.

> **BUSINESS TIP**
>
> Newspapers may charge a lower rate for ads from local retail stores than for ads from national manufacturers.

CONNECTION TO FINANCE

Point out to students that advertising rates of print media are generally based on circulation. Audited circulation data is provided by the Audit Bureau of Circulations, a non-profit organization that objectively examines a publisher's records and reports the circulation of print media, such as newspapers and magazines. The information is shared with sellers and buyers of print advertising. The Audit Bureau of Circulations also does audits of trade shows and web sites.

The illustration shows one column inch on a newspaper page that is 6 columns wide and 21″ deep.

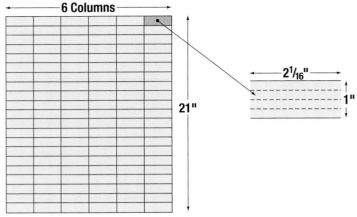

The formula for determining an ad's cost based on column inch is:

Ad Cost = Column Inches × Cost per Inch × Number of Columns Width

EXAMPLE 1

A newspaper charges $237 per column inch for a one-column width general ad. What is the cost of an ad that is 4 column inches long and one column width wide?

SOLUTION
Multiply the cost per column inch by the number of column inches and by the number of column widths.

$4″ × \$237 × 1 = \$948$ cost of ad

Print ads may also be sold by *page size*, such as a full page or part of a page. An example of an advertising rate card shown below gives the per-issue costs for a magazine that sells ads by page size. A discount is given when the advertiser agrees to run ads in more than one issue. The 1X, 3X, etc. refer to the *frequency rate*, or the number of times the ad will run.

ADVERTISING RATE CARD				
SIZE	**1X**	**3X**	**5X**	**12X**
Full page	$3,095	$2,940	$2,725	$2,570
$\frac{2}{3}$ page	2,045	1,945	1,800	1,700
$\frac{1}{2}$ page	1,555	1,475	1,370	1,290
$\frac{1}{3}$ page	1,085	1,030	955	900
Special Charges: Add to page rate				
4-color	$1,460	$1,390	$1,285	$1,210
2-color	525	500	465	435
Inside Cover	3,875	3,680	3,410	3,215

To calculate the total cost of an ad, find the base price by matching the ad size with the frequency rate. Then add any special charges for color or a preferred location, such as the inside cover. Multiply the total by the number of times the ad will run.

Lesson 12.8 Advertising ■ 541

CONNECTION TO LANGUAGE ARTS

By this stage of the course, students should recognize that the various aspects of business use a specialized vocabulary. To build their vocabulary, have students research and report the definitions of these advertising terms: ad copy, billings, cooperative advertising, fringe time, holdover audience, insert, make good, overrun, renewal rate, split run, and tracking studies.

Ask students to think of other places where advertising appears in addition to those listed in the textbook.

Remind students that ads may appear on refrigerator magnets, during the previews at movie theaters, in theater playbills, on license plate frames, and even on the clothes they wear.

■ Apply Goal 2

Work Example 3 at the board with students completing the math at their desks. Relate the solution of the example to the price extensions they have already calculated.

EXAMPLE 2

Find the cost of a full-page, 4-color ad that runs 5 times using the advertising rate chart.

SOLUTION

Add the base rate and the 4-color rate of a full-page in the 5X (times) column.

$2,725 + $1,285 = $4,010   cost of single issue ad

Multiply the single-issue ad cost by the number of times the ad runs.

5 × $4,010 = $20,050   cost of ad

■ CHECK YOUR UNDERSTANDING

A. Your local newspaper charges $135 a column inch for a one-column width general ad. What would you pay for an ad that is 3 column inches long and 2 column widths wide. $810

B. Find the total cost of a $\frac{1}{3}$ page, two-color ad that runs 1 time. $1,610

■ Cost of Other Ads

In addition to print media, advertisers frequently use TV, radio, direct mail, billboards, and the Internet to reach their target audience. The total cost of an ad is found by multiplying the cost of the ad by the number of times the ad will run.

EXAMPLE 3

An Internet service provider charges $5,000 a week for an ad on its home page. What would be the total cost of an Internet ad that runs for 6 weeks?

SOLUTION

Multiply the weekly cost of the ad by the number of weeks it runs.

6 × $5,000 = $30,000   total cost of ad

■ CHECK YOUR UNDERSTANDING

C. The cost of a 20-second, afternoon ad on a local radio station is $120 per ad, per day. What will be the ad's total cost if it runs once a day for 10 weekdays? $1,200

D. A network charges $875,000 for a 30-second ad at a major sports event televised nationally. The advertisers must agree to purchase a minimum of four ads during the telecast. What is the advertiser's total cost of buying the minimum number of ads? $3,500,000

■ *CHECK YOUR UNDERSTANDING SOLUTIONS*

A. 3 × 2 × $135 = $810

B. $1,085 + $525 = $1,610

C. 10 × $120 = $1,200

D. 4 × $875,000 = $3,500,000

■ Cost per Person Reached

Advertising rates are based on an ad's reach through a particular media. **Reach** refers to how many people see or hear an ad. The number of people reached by an ad is usually a measurable number. It may be the number of subscribers, readers, listeners, households in a geographic area, or cars passing a certain location. Internet sites may define reach as the number of hits, registrations, or searches beyond the home page.

The cost per person of an ad is found by dividing the ad's cost by the number of people reached. The per person cost of the ad may be impressively small. However, the ad is likely to reach people who are not interested in the product. So, the actual cost of the ad, per person, to reach the target audience is likely to be much greater.

EXAMPLE 4

The cost of an advertising insert in a daily newspaper delivered to one zip code is $1,600 per edition. There are 7,920 households that receive the newspaper. What will be the cost of the ad per household, to the nearest tenth of a cent?

SOLUTION
Divide the cost of the ad by the number of households.

$1,600 ÷ 7,920 = $0.202   cost per household

■ CHECK YOUR UNDERSTANDING

E. A direct mailer inserts 30 ads in an envelope and bulk mails them to 24,300 households in a city. The cost of each ad is $825. To the nearest tenth of a cent, what is the cost per household reached to an advertiser who places one ad? $0.034

F. A furniture store spent $3,640 on a newspaper ad featuring a sale on leather sofas. In the next two days, 130 people who looked at the sofas said they saw the ad. What was the cost of the ad for each shopper who was attracted by the ad? $28

Wrap Up

Since the sunglass stand is likely to be fairly small, it probably wouldn't pay to place ads in the usual places. Sheila might consider placing an ad in the local Yellow Pages or getting her stand's name listed on an electronic message board at the mall, if there is one. She may also print one-page flyers and hand them to shoppers entering the mall if she is allowed to do so by the mall's management.

TEAM MEETING

Contact your local newspaper and find the cost of a full-page daily ad and the daily circulation of the paper. Also contact a local or nearby radio station to find the cost of 30-second ad in the most expensive part of the day. Determine how many listeners the radio station has at that time of day.

For each type of media, calculate the cost per person reached. Write a short paragraph describing any differences you find.

■ *CHECK YOUR UNDERSTANDING SOLUTIONS*

E. $825 ÷ 24,300 = $0.0339, or $0.034   **F.** $3,640 ÷ 130 = $28

Assignment: Exercises 1–16 and 18–32. Have students solve the basic arithmetic problems before completing the rest of the exercises.

Remind students to do their work in an organized manner and to label the results of calculations.

Assess

Before collecting student work, have three students write their solutions to Exercises 18–20 on the board. Have the rest of the class review the solutions and ask them to point out the similarities and differences among the solutions.

Reteach

STUDENT WORKBOOK Work Exercise 1 with students who are having difficulty in finding the cost of print ads. Assign Exercises 2 for independent work.

Some students may have difficulty with finding the cost of other media. If so, do Exercise 3 with them and have them solve Exercise 4a independently.

Do Exercise 4b with students who may have difficulty with calculating the cost of advertising per person reached. Assign Exercises 4c, 5b, 5c, and 6 to be done independently.

EXERCISES

Find the sum or product.

1. $238 + $784 $1,022
2. $990 + $1,360 $2,350
3. 14 × $183 $2,562
4. 8 × $23.25 × 14 $2,604

Find the quotient, to the nearest tenth of a cent.

5. $230 ÷ 78,000 $0.003
6. $554,000 ÷ 12,000,000 $0.046

7. A newspaper charges $148.75 for a one-column inch, one-column wide display ad. Ads that run for more than four consecutive days receive a 5% discount. What is the cost of a 4-column inch, one-column ad that runs from Monday through Friday? $2,826.25

8. The Sunshine Journal's weekday ad rates are $98.50 per one-column inch, per one-column width. The rates increase 40% on Saturdays and Sundays. An 8-column inch, 3-column width ad runs for 7 consecutive days. What is the cost of this ad space? $18,439.20

Use the advertising rate card to solve Exercises 9–10.

9. Find the cost of a $\frac{1}{3}$ page ad with four colors that runs 12 times? $25,320

10. How much more would it cost to buy four sets of $\frac{2}{3}$ page ads that run 3 times each than to buy the same sized ad to run 12 times? $2,940

11. Nextbid.com, an Internet auction site, pays $3,270 a week to an ISP for a banner ad that will automatically link to Nextbid's web site. Nextbid signed a contract with the ISP that runs for 13 weeks. What is the cost of the ad? $42,510

12. The Internet edition of the Marval County Daily Tribune charges $75 a day for display ads on its home page. What income will Marval receive from Internet ads in June if it sells 3 ads daily? $6,750

13. A billboard rents for $128 a day with a 30-day minimum rental. What is the cost of renting the billboard for one rental period? $3,840

The Daily Press sells 230,000 newspapers daily. Through surveys it found that 2.3 persons read each newspaper sold.

14. What total number of people read the newspaper daily?   529,000

15. What is the cost per reader, to the nearest tenth of a cent, of an ad that sells for $3,200? $0.006

544 ■ Chapter 12 Sales and Marketing

SELECTED SOLUTIONS

7. 4 × $148.75 = $595; $595 × 5 = $2,975; $2,975 × 0.05 = $148.75; $2,975 − $148.75 = $2,826.25
9. $900 + $1,210 = $2,110; 12 × $2,110 = $25,320

11. 13 × $3,270 = $42,510
14. 2.3 × 230,000 = 529,000
15. $3,200 ÷ 529,000 = 0.0060, or $0.006

16. An online magazine charges $45,000 for a 3-month contract for a banner ad displayed above its weekly feature article. The magazine has 120,000 subscribers and gets 195,000 hits per day. What is the banner's cost per subscriber if a banner ad was taken for a year? $1.50

17. **CRITICAL THINKING** An Internet web site claims it gets 240,000 hits per day and wants to charge an advertiser a daily advertising rate based on 3¢ for each hit the web site records. What questions might the advertiser ask before agreeing to the rate? See Enrich section for answer.

INTEGRATING YOUR KNOWLEDGE Stephanie Hagan, an artist, has a successful business making ink sketches of infants for $80 a sketch. To expand her business she plans to mail an announcement to the families of the 200 children born each month in areas near her home. She estimates that 10% of the families will respond to the ad and that 50% of the respondents will order a sketch. Stephanie estimates the total annual cost of preparing, printing, and mailing the announcements to be $4,680.

18. How much will Stephanie spend on her ads per family in a year? $1.95

19. How many orders does Stephanie expect to receive each year? 120

20. Will Stephanie make a profit or loss on her advertising campaign, and how much will her profit or loss be? Profit, $4,920

MIXED REVIEW

21. $\frac{3}{4} - \frac{1}{2}$ $\frac{1}{4}$

22. $72 + 83 + 46 + 54$ 255

23. Rewrite 0.007 as a percent. 0.7%

24. 78 ft @ $0.01 $0.78

25. $5\frac{1}{4}$% of $729 $38.27

26. $\frac{1}{8} \times \$15,000$ $1,875

27. Estimate the quotient of $9,217 \div 8.9$. 1,000

28. Estimate the product of 675×23. 14,000

29. Lonnie Erhardt borrowed $4,000 at 7% exact interest for 170 days. What amount of interest did he pay? $130.41, Lesson 4.1

30. Rodger Cleary bought 120 shares of Fleider Oil at $78.12. His broker charged $176 commission. Fleider Oil pays an annual dividend of $1.35 a share. What is the annual yield to the nearest tenth percent? 1.7%, Lesson 7.6

31. A wireless carrier offers a wireless phone plan that includes 450 minutes per phone for $65.45 a month. Each extra minute costs $0.14. The plan allows unused minutes on one phone to cover extra minutes on other phones under contract. A business owner leased a phone for himself and three employees. The minutes used in March on all four phones are 468, 564, 390, and 420. What should be the amount of the owner's monthly bill for March? $267.68, Lesson 9.5

32. An office printer uses 26 inkjet cartridges a year @ $26.50 each. The annual maintenance contract on the printer is $195. Annual depreciation on the printer is $125. What is the total cost of operating the printer for a year? $1,009, Lesson 11.5

Lesson 12.8 Advertising ■ **545**

Lesson 12.1 Cash Sales and Sales on Account

- Add change fund to cash received, subtract cash paid out; compare result to register to find cash over or short.

- Multiply quantity by unit cost, add extensions to find total.

- Multiply quantity of each item returned by unit price and add extensions to find credit memo amount.

- Add charges and subtract credits to find customer account balance.

Lesson 12.2 Cash and Trade Discounts

- Count forward from invoice date the number of days in terms of sale to find discount and due dates.

- Multiply invoice price by discount rate to find discount.

- Subtract cash discount from invoice to find cash price.

- Multiply invoice price by discount rate for trade discount.

- Subtract trade discount from list price to find invoice price.

Lesson 12.3 Series Trade Discounts

- Multiply list price by first discount, subtract result to find amount after first discount; repeat process for all other discounts for invoice price.

- Use percent, table, or complement method to find series invoice price equivalent.

- Subtract invoice price equivalent from 100% to find single discount equivalent.

Chapter Review

Vocabulary Review

cash discount	markdown	reach
credit memo	market	respondent
discount series	market share	sales invoice
forecast	markup	trade discount
invoice price	on account	trend
list price	prove cash	

Fill in the blanks with the term that best completes the statement.

1. A reduction of the invoice price given for early payment is known as __?__.   cash discount

2. The number of people who see or hear an ad is called __?__.   reach

3. The relationship between time and data, such as sales, is referred to as (a, an) __?__.   trend

4. The selling price of an item less its cost is called the __?__.   markup

5. A price for goods that is published in a catalog is called the __?__.   list price

6. Price reductions, such as 10%, 10%, and 5%, are called (a, an) __?__.   discount series

7. All the people interested in buying a certain product are referred to as the product's __?__.   market

8. A form sent to retailers showing the value of returned merchandise is called (a, an) __?__.   credit memo

9. A prediction, projection, or estimate of future sales is also called (a, an) __?__.   forecast

LESSON 12.1

10. A cashier began the day with a $140 change fund. His cash register totals were $4,529 cash received and $389.15 in cash paid out. There was $4,278.15 cash in the register. How much was cash over or short?   Cash short, $1.70

11. Mendrin Markets bought these items from a wholesaler: 24 cases canned vegetables @ $80.16 and 120 bags of sugar @ $2.31. What was the total of the sales invoice? $2,201.04

12. Mendrin Markets found that four of the bags of sugar purchased in Problem 11 were ripped and unusable. What should be the amount of the credit memo the wholesaler issues? $9.24

13. A wholesaler recorded these transactions in April for Rasher Hardware's account: April 1, balance forward, $3,482; April 7, Invoice #358 for $4,233; April 12, payment of $3,482; April 13, Credit Memo #98 for $78.40; April 28, Invoice #427 for $1,873. What was the account's balance on April 30? $6,027.60

LESSON 12.2

14. An invoice dated March 11 has terms of sale of 1/10, n/45. What are the discount date and the due date of the invoice?   March 21, April 25

15. An invoice for $3,410 dated November 6 has terms of 2/10, 1/20, n/60. What is the amount of the cash discount and cash price if the invoice is paid on November 23? $34.10; $3,375.90

16. A straw hat has a list price of $26 and is offered at a 45% trade discount. What is the amount of the trade discount and the invoice price? $11.70; $14.30

TEACHING STRATEGIES Chapter Review

Before assigning the Vocabulary Review, conduct an impromptu spelling exercise. Pronounce each word on the vocabulary list and have students write the words. Have them self-check their spellings against those in the list. They should rewrite any words they misspelled.

LESSON 12.3

17. A box of party streamers has a list price of $15.70. The series discount offered is 20%, 15%, and 5%. What is the invoice price of the box of streamers? $10.14

18. What are the invoice price and single discount equivalents written as percents for a series discount of 10%, 15%, and 20%?   61.2%; 38.8%

LESSON 12.4

19. A store carries women's suits in a $400 price line. The markup is 47% of the selling price. What is the highest amount the store may pay for suits to get the desired markup? $212

20. Multi-Sports sold a hockey jersey for $112. The cost of the jersey was $85. What rate of markup on cost did Multi-Sports earn on the jersey, to the nearest percent?   32%

21. At the end of a season a ski sweater with a marked price of $140 was offered at a 60% discount. What is the selling price of the sweater? $56

LESSON 12.5

22. A research firm mailed 12,500 surveys to a company's shareholders. The number of valid surveys returned was 4,872. What was the response rate, to the nearest percent?   39%

23. The respondents to a theater lobby survey rated a movie as follows: 4 stars, 125; 3 stars, 86; 2 stars, 31; 1 star, 47. What average star rating did the movie get? What percent of the raters gave the movie 3 or more stars, to the nearest percent?   3 stars; 73%

LESSON 12.6

24. A four-year old company's sales last year were $3,120,000. The average sales increase over the past four years is 32.5%. Based on that rate, project this year's sales? $4,134,000

25. Sales of a security scanner were 240 in a test market. There are an estimated 54 similar sized markets in the United States and another 280 in foreign countries. What are the expected unit sales for the scanner when it is marketed worldwide?   80,160

LESSON 12.7

26. A hardware chain's total annual sales were estimated to be $5,200,000 out of a total of $18,000,000 in estimated sales of all hardware stores in an area. What market share does the chain have, to the nearest tenth percent?   28.9%

27. Of the 600,000 gallons of gasoline sold annually in a town, 34% are sold by Blue's Garage. What are Blue's gasoline sales for a year?   204,000 gallons

LESSON 12.8

28. A weekly newspaper charges $82 a column inch and one column width. What is the cost of an ad that runs 2 column inches and 2 column widths? $328

29. The cost of advertising during a fifteen-minute radio news program is $150 a day. What amount would an advertiser pay for one ad daily during the month of March? $4,650

30. A magazine has 45,000 subscribers. What is the cost per subscriber of an ad that costs $3,890, to the nearest tenth of a cent? $0.086

Chapter 12 Review ▪ 547

TEACHING STRATEGIES Chapter Review

Inform students that the problems for each lesson in the Chapter Review reflect the lesson's goals. Students may wish to review the goals to get an overview of the problems they will be solving.

The Tasks

Students need spreadsheet file tech12-1.xls for Tasks 1 and 2.

Task 1 Students enter sales data into a spreadsheet template that calculates annual and average percent increases in sales over nine years to forecast sales for Year 10.

Task 2 Students answer questions about the results of Task 1 and the functions used. They also key in new data and answer questions about the new results.

Task 3 Students design and create a spreadsheet to calculate series discounts.

Task 4 Students answer questions about the results shown in the spreadsheet and how it might be modified.

Teach and Apply Task 1

Assign Task 1. Inform students that they might arrive at a different percent for average sales increases and a different projection for Year 10 sales if they calculated sales increases based on a simple average.

Technology Workshop

Task 1: Forecasting Sales

This chapter showed how business firms forecast future sales by various methods. Another method used is a statistical method called "least squares." The FORECAST function in Excel and Lotus 1-2-3 calculates trends using the least squares method. It produces different projections of future sales than you would get by calculating a simple average.

Enter data into a template that uses the FORECAST function to project sales for Year 10 based on sales in Years 1–9. In statistical work, time in years is often identified by a numeral instead of the actual year.

Open the spreadsheet for Chapter 12 (tech12-1.xls) and enter the data shown in blue (cells B5–13) into the spreadsheet. The spreadsheet will calculate the amount and percent of sales increase for each year based on a year-to-year comparison. The FORECAST function will project sales for Year 10 based on the value of sales for the entire nine previous years. Your computer screen should look like the one below.

	A	B	C	D
1		Buchanan Products, Inc.		
2		Sales Data, Electric Motor Division		
3			Sales Increase From Previous Year	
4	Year	Sales	Dollar Increase	Percent Increase
5	1	568,000	---	---
6	2	637,864	69,864	12.30%
7	3	687,043	49,179	7.71%
8	4	695,287	8,244	1.20%
9	5	791,724	96,437	13.87%
10	6	875,647	83,923	10.60%
11	7	939,043	63,396	7.24%
12	8	1,019,332	80,289	8.55%
13	9	1,068,565	49,233	4.83%
14	10	???		
15	Average of Percent Increases, Years 1-9			8.29%
16	Sales Forecast for Year 10			$1,128,419

Task 2: Analyze the Spreadsheet Output

Answer these questions about the sales forecast calculations.

1. In which year from 1–9 did the lowest percent year-to-year sales increase occur? Year 4, 1.20%
2. In which year from 1–9 did the year-to-year percent increase in sales the greatest? Year 5, 13.87%
3. What was the average of the percent increases for Years 1–9? 8.29%

4. What spreadsheet functions were used to calculate the average of percent increases? ROUND, AVERAGE

TEACHING STRATEGIES Task 1

Before students begin entering data into the forecasting spreadsheet, have them display the formula in Cell D16 to view the use of the FORECAST function. Inform students that if the average annual percent increase of 8.29% had been used instead of the FORECAST function, the projected Year 10 sales would have been $1,157,149 (1.0829 × $1,068,565).

5. What amount of sales was forecast for Year 10? $1,128,419

6. In which years was the year-to-year percent increase within 1% plus or minus of the average of the percent increases for Years 1–9?   Years 3 and 8

Now assume that sales in Year 1 were $818,000. Move the cursor to cell B5, which holds the sales for Year 1. Enter sales of 818,000.

7. What is the new figure for the average of the percent increases?   4.00%

8. What was the new figure for the Year 10 sales forecast? $1,072,864

9. Did the year-to-year sales percent change for any year other than Year 2? Why?
   No. The sales percent changes are compared year-to-year, not to the first year.

10. In which year did sales recover to equal or exceed the Year 1 sales?   Year 6

11. What might be some reasons why sales decreased $180,136 in Year 2 and did not recover for some time?   Several reasons may be given: the general economy may have been poor for several years, the product may have had quality problems or had to be recalled resulting in a negative image that took time to overcome, or the products produced did not meet the needs of a changing marketplace.

Task 3: Design a Spreadsheet to Calculate Series Discounts

Design a spreadsheet that will calculate series discounts. The spreadsheet should allow a list price and up to three series discounts to be entered. The spreadsheet should calculate the single discount equivalent to the series discounts, the amount of the trade discount, and the invoice price.

If there are less than three discounts in the series, enter 0 for the missing discount. Calculate the single discount equivalent as a percent to four decimal places.

> *SITUATION:* A dishwasher with a list price of $480.54 is offered to retailers with series discounts of 15%, 10%, and 5%. Find the single discount equivalent, trade discount, and invoice price of the dishwasher.

Task 4: Analyze the Spreadsheet Output

Answer these questions about your completed spreadsheet:

12. What is the single discount equivalent to the 15%, 10%, and 5% series discount?   27.3250%

13. What is the amount of the trade discount? $131.31

14. What is the invoice price of the dishwasher? $349.23

15. Enter the discounts in a different order. Do you get the same results?   Yes

16. How can you use the spreadsheet's results to calculate the invoice price equivalent of the series discounts?   Subtract the single discount equivalent from 100%

You may use the series discount spreadsheet to verify the examples, and exercises in Lesson 12-3 that required the use of series discounts.

TEACHING STRATEGIES Task 3

After students complete, test, and print the spreadsheet they developed, display the spreadsheet tech12-3.xls that provides a sample solution. Have students compare the sample solution to their spreadsheet solution and make suggestions of ways in which both spreadsheets might have been designed differently to improve them.

■ HOW TIMES HAVE CHANGED

1. 800,000 × 0.9 = 720,000
800,000 − 720,000 = 80,000

2. $200 × 0.2 = $40
$200 − $40 = $160
$160 × 0.1 = $16
$160 − $16 = $144
$144 × 0.5 = $7.20
$144 − $7.20 = $136.80

■ WRITE

Inform students that they might include a brief explanation of how to calculate a simple discount as an introduction to calculating series discounts. Remind them to include a practice problem to be solved by the person who will test their instructions.

■ SCANS

Students may collaborate to estimate the time needed to complete the training plan. Remind them that they are training the person only for a specific task and not to develop all the skills an employee may need.

■ ONGOING ASSESSMENT

The Integrated Project found in the workbook provides a broad, ongoing assessment activity for the goals of this chapter.

Chapter Assessment

How Times Have Changed

For Questions 1–2, refer to the timeline on page 501 as needed.
1. If NCR sold 800,000 brass-encased cash registers in 1910, how many brass-encased registers did all of their competitors combined sell?
2. The price of Ritty's first telegraphs was $100 each. He sold two of them to the eventual founder of NCR, John Patterson. If Ritty offered Patterson a series trade discount of 20%, 10%, 5%, how much would Patterson have paid for the cash registers?

WRITE

Suppose it is your job to train new employees in the procedures for calculating the single discount equivalent to a series discount. Write step-by-step instructions in sentence form together with sample figures.

Include statements that warn of possible "trouble spots" in making calculations. Also include advice on how to remember the steps to be followed.

Test your instructions with a student who is not taking this course or an adult at home who is not familiar with the topic. Make revisions as indicated by the comments and the success of the student or adult who tests your instructions.

SCANS

Workplace Skills—*Teaches Others*

The ability to train coworkers is a valuable skill to have because companies often hire inexperienced people as new employees. Companies also retrain current employees to upgrade their skills or provide them with the new skills they need for other jobs within the company.

Test Your Skills Consider the step-by-step instructions that you prepared in the Write section. Describe how you determined the steps to be included and how you assured yourself that the instructions were complete and accurate.

Make a Plan Write a training plan you would have each employee follow. Keep in mind that you are preparing them for a job where they are entrusted with finding the single discount equivalent to a series of discounts quoted by a supplier. Describe the phases of training that are needed, including a review of essential background information. Provide an estimate of the time needed to train for each phase.

Summarize Decide how you would verify that employees have successfully completed the training and are prepared to work on their own. If this verification includes testing, describe what will be a passing score on the test. Be sure to include any of the following skills that play a part in a successful training sequence.

reading	*listening*	*problem solving*	*decision making*
speaking	*arithmetic*	*knowing how to learn*	*responsibility*

550 ■ Chapter 12 Sales and Marketing

PORTFOLIO ASSESSMENT

Ask students to review the materials they have created in this chapter and select those they wish to place in their portfolios. Then have students select one entry from Chapters 7–12 that displays their best work. Students should explain why this piece is the best.

Chapter Test

Answer each question.

1. $3,412.80 + $1,815.09 + $212.18 $5,440.07

2. $16,090.18 − $436.77 $15,653.41

3. $1\frac{1}{2} \times $978,000 $1,467,000

4. Rewrite 3.25% as a decimal. 0.0325

5. 250 @ $26.12 $6,530

6. 85% × 90% × 72% 55.08%

7. 1 − 0.64125 0.35875

8. 4.65% × $2,367 $110.07

9. Find the percent: $234.90 ÷ $522 45%

10. Round $2,838,922 to the nearest thousand. $2,839,000

Applications

11. What is the invoice price for the purchase of a tractor with a list price of $18,560 and terms of 10%, 15%, and 4%? $13,630.46

12. An advertiser bought space for 12 ads at a list price of $680 per ad, less a 7% discount. What was the cost of the ads? $7,588.80

13. After two markdowns a pair of boots has a marked price of $38.95. A retailer marks down the boots another 15%. What is the marked price of the boots after the third markdown? $33.11

14. An invoice for 56 shirts @ $22.46 dated August 2 was paid on September 6. Credit terms were 1/10 EOM, n/60. What amount should be sent to pay the invoice? $1,245.18

15. A survey of a sample population of 1,800 households out of a population of 75,000 households resulted in 1,247 valid responses. What was the response rate, to the tenth percent? 69.3%

16. A cashier began a work period with a $180 change fund. At the end of the work period, the register showed cash received of $8,359.29 and cash paid out of $400.16. Actual cash in the register was $8,141.85. Was cash over or short? Cash over, $2.72

17. The overall trend of sales increases is 4.2% a year. Forecast next year's sales to the nearest ten thousand dollars based on last year's sales of $76,428,500. $79,640,000

18. A nursery is estimated to have a 35% market share of the landscaping market. Total market sales are $1,000,000. What is the nursery's market share in dollars? $350,000

19. The cost of a desk telephone is $56.12. A retailer plans a markup of 36% on cost. What is the selling price of the telephone? $76.32

20. What is the single discount equivalent to a discount series of 20%, 10%, and 6.5%? 32.68%

21. A customer's account had a balance of $2,680.65 on September 1. Transactions recorded in September are: Invoice #1211, $3,583; Credit Memo #129, $23.80; Payment, $656.85; Invoice #1387, $1,452; Payment, $3,196. What was the account's balance on September 30? $3,839

22. A company's owner set a sales goal for next year that each of 3 salespersons would sell 20% more lawn watering systems than they did this year. This year's sales averaged 75 systems per salesperson. How many watering systems are projected to be sold next year? 270

Chapter 12 Assessment ▪ 551

TEACHING STRATEGIES Chapter Test

Remind students to show each step in their problem solutions and to label all results. Inform them that you will be evaluating their solutions and the neatness and organization of their work.

Test Taking Strategies

■ IN MULTIPLE CHOICE

Exercise 4, students may eliminate some choices. They can estimate depreciation at about $1,000 (10% × $10,000). Thus, the book value is around $9,000. Choices A and E are too low and D is greater than the original cost. The problem then breaks down to two choices, B and C.

Multiple Choice

Select the best choice for each question.

1. The monthly rent on a 4,000 sq. ft. office is $12,000. The sales area is 1,400 sq. ft. Rent is allocated on the basis of space used. What amount of monthly rent is charged to sales? C

   A. $350   B. $4,850   C. $4,200   D. $8,570   E. $3,600

2. An invoice dated April 13 has terms of 3/12, 1/30, n/60. What is the invoice's due date? A

   A. June 12   B. May 12   C. May 13   D. April 25   E. June 14

3. Stellar Sports has a price line for a bowling ball of $120 with a 35.5% markup on selling price. What is the most that Stellar can pay for the bowling ball? E

   A. $74.40   B. $42.60   C. $84.50   D. $78   E. $77.40

4. A commercial-grade riding lawnmower that costs $10,800 is estimated to depreciate 13% a year. What is the book value of the mower at the end of the first year? B

   A. $1,404   B. $9,396   C. $8,619   D. $12,204   E. $3,348

5. A hunting cap originally priced at $18.29 was marked down 15% for a preseason sale. What is the selling price of the cap? D

   A. $18.14   B. $13.72   C. $2.74   D. $15.55   E. $21.03

6. Rita used her van at work for 25% of the 26,112 miles she drove last year. Her employer reimbursed work mileage at 28¢ a mile. What reimbursement did Rita receive? E

   A. $1,958.40   B. $6,528   C. $5,483.52   D. $7,311.36   E. $1,827.84

7. The MACRS depreciation rates for 7-year class life equipment are 14.29% the first year and 24.49% the second year. What total depreciation would there be for the first two years on a copier that costs $34,500 and has a 7-year class life? A

   A. $13,379.10   B. $21,120.90   C. $4,930.05   D. $26,050.95   E. $8,449.05

8. What is the single discount equivalent to a series discount of 12%, 20%, and 5%? B

   A. 66.88%   B. 33.12%   C. 32.5%   D. 37%   E. 63%

9. For one package weighing 6 lb, the shipping charge is $11.75 to Zone 3 and $19.25 to Zone 6. Ten, 6 lb packages are to be shipped, 8 to Zone 3 and 2 to Zone 6. Insurance costs are $1.45 a package. What is the total cost of shipping the packages? D

   A. $133.95   B. $132.50   C. $192   D. $147   E. $184.25

10. Five percent of the 620 survey returns to a mail survey were not valid. If 3,400 surveys were mailed, what was the response rate, to the nearest percent? C

    A. 5%   B. 18%   C. 17%   D. 9%   E. 13%

11. A company's share of a $390,000,000 market is 1.75%. What is the company's share of the market in dollars? E

    A. $6,630,000   B. $7,800,000   C. $2,925,000   D. $68,250,000   E. $6,825,000

TEACHING STRATEGIES Cumulative Review

Remind students to use estimation wherever possible to judge whether their answers are reasonable. They should also think of what type of answer is likely to result from the procedure they use. For example, if they are finding a percent of a number, the result should be an amount smaller than the original amount if the percent used is less than 100%. Similarly, multiplying an amount by a number greater than one will give an answer that is greater than the original amount.

Open Ended

12. Trexx Products wants to produce camera cases that will be sold at $16 a unit. The fixed costs are estimated at $19,200. The variable costs of producing each case are estimated to be $6. How many cases must be sold by Trexx to break even?   1,920

13. A picnic basket with a list price of $46 is sold to a retailer for $29.90. What rate of trade discount was the retailer given?   35%

14. The freight charge for a 786 lb shipment is $185 per hundredweight. What is the freight charge? $1,480

15. Wedamor Products had these manufacturing costs in March: raw materials, $265,190; direct labor, $717,080; overhead, $241,800. What were Wedamor's prime cost and total manufacturing costs for March? $982,270; $1,224,070

16. What is the invoice price of an item with a list price of $520 and a discount series of 15%, 15%, and 10%? $338.13

17. The usual rate of a one-half page ad is $1,800. An advertiser signs a contract to run a one-half page ad weekly for 52 weeks and receives a $12\frac{1}{2}$% discount off the usual rate. What annual amount will the advertiser pay for the ads? $81,900

18. Ben's Hardware bought a hand vacuum for $16.70 and marked it for sale at $23.38. What rate of markup based on cost did Ben's Hardware use?   40%

19. A building with 50,000 sq. ft. is divided into a production area, warehouse, and offices. Production occupies 60% of the total building. The rent, maintenance, insurance, power, and other costs are $1,460,000 a year for the entire building. How many square feet does production occupy? What is the cost of the production area per square foot?   30,000 sq. ft.; $29.20

20. The Kite House had sales of $192,300 this year. The Kite House's 6.1% average annual sales growth is expected to continue. What is the forecast for next year's sales, to the nearest thousand? $204,000

21. A cash proof form shows these facts: change fund, $110; cash receipts, $2,986.20; cash paid out, $112.45; cash in the drawer, $2,981.90. Was cash short or over, and by how much?   Cash short, $1.85

22. Cecile Doran attended a trade show for her employer. Her expenses for a four-day, three-night trip were: airfare, $528; hotel, $139 per night; meals, $327; show registration, $250, taxis, $86; other expenses, $190. What was the amount of her reimbursement? $1,798

23. A retailer bought 240 knit shirts @ $19.84. Because the shirts arrived late for a special sale, the wholesaler gave the retailer a 3% credit on the total order. What is the amount of the credit memo the retailer should have received? $142.85

24. Out of 312 people surveyed, 79 gave a product a superior rating, 207 gave it an average rating, and 26 gave it a poor rating. What percent of the ratings were average or better, to the nearest tenth percent?   91.7%

Constructed Response

25. The owner of a company tells you to cut each expense item by 5% next year. You tell him   Expenses consist that he has given you an impossible assignment. He threatens to fire you unless you give a   of variable and good explanation. Explain to the owner in writing why the plan will not work.   fixed expenses. Some fixed expenses, such as property taxes and an employer's FICA contributions are set by governmental units or by law. These expense items may not be cut. **Chapter 12 Cumulative Assessment ▪ 553**

CHAPTER

Chapter Overview

Chapter 13 reviews the math skills of addition, subtraction, multiplication, fractions, percents, rounding, and division. These skills are applied to income statements and balance sheets, the distribution of partnership income, and bankruptcy.

Lesson 13.1 Preparing Income Statements
Students learn to find net sales, cost of goods sold, gross profit, and net income.

Lesson 13.2 Analyzing Income Statements
Students learn to use percents and ratios to analyze income statements.

Lesson 13.3 Partnership Income
Students learn to distribute partnership income in proportion to investments, in a fixed ratio or percent, and after paying interest on partnership investments.

Lesson 13.4 Preparing Balance Sheets
Students learn to calculate total assets, liabilities, and capital.

Lesson 13.5 Analyzing Balance Sheets
Students learn to find the current ratio, debt-to-equity ratio, and return on equity.

Lesson 13.6 Bankruptcy
Students learn to calculate the percent and amount of bankruptcy claims.

Statistical Insights

U.S. Bankruptcy Filings
1980–1999

Year	Business Filings	Non-Business Filings	Year	Business Filings	Non-Business Filings
1985	71,277	341,233	1995	51,959	874,642
1986	81,235	449,203	1996	53,549	1,125,006
1987	82,446	495,553	1997	54,027	1,350,118
1988	63,853	549,612	1998	44,367	1,398,182
1989	63,235	616,226	1999	44,367	1,281,581
1990	64,853	718,107	2000	38,109	1,263,096
1991	71,549	872,438	2001	35,992	1,271,865
1992	70,643	900,874	2002	39,845	1,464,961
1993	62,304	812,898	2003	37,548	1,573,720
1994	52,374	780,455	2004	36,785	1,618,062

Use the data shown above to answer each question.

1. In which years did the number of non-business bankruptcy filings decrease from the previous year?   1993, 1994, 1999, 2000

2. What year had the greatest increase in business bankruptcy filings? in non-business filings?   1986, 1996

Statistical Insights

Discuss with students economic and noneconomic factors that may lead to varying rates of consumer bankruptcies from year to year. The discussion might include consumer debt levels, which has shown a high positive correlation to consumer bankruptcy rates in the past. Other factors may include changes in bankruptcy laws, divorce rates, drops in personal income, rises in the unemployment rate, and recession.

NetCheck

Bankruptcy

Individuals and businesses that are burdened with a great amount of debt may decide to file for bankruptcy. There are several types of bankruptcy including personal bankruptcy for individuals. Bankruptcy is not a simple process.

When you search the Internet for guidelines or help in filing for bankruptcy, check the accuracy of the information on these web sites carefully. Government sites should contain the most accurate information about the bankruptcy laws, but may not provide assistance. Sites offering assistance will probably do so for a fee.

Annual Reports

Businesses must provide annual reports to their investors. These reports show the financial health of the company and the prospects for its future. Companies whose stock is traded publicly make their annual reports public. Since the Internet is widely available, annual reports are often published online.

Identify a company that you have seen in the news and try to locate its annual report. Once you find it, see how many of the statements and vocabulary terms included in this chapter you can find in the annual report.

Teaching Resources

Lesson Plans, Ch. 13
Chapter 13 Test Forms A and B
Workbook, Ch. 13
Explore Algebra and Geometry
    Activities
Technology Activities
Competitive Events Prep
Data Activities CD, Ch. 13
ExamView® Pro CD, Ch. 13

NetCheck

Bankruptcy Have students evaluate two web sites hosted by firms offering help on filing for bankruptcy. Students should prepare a report listing each web site visited and possible inaccuracies and misleading claims or data they encountered. Display selected sites from student reports using a computer projector or transparencies of the web pages. Have report authors discuss their findings with the class.

Annual Reports Help students find web sites that display the annual reports for the organizations they have seen in the news. You might also help them navigate one or more of these sites to find the annual reports of the organizations. Point out to students that a number of web sites provide a database of annual reports for many companies world wide, such as aReport.com and edgar-online.com

How Times Have Changed

The largest bankruptcies in history have occurred in recent years. These events have dramatically illustrated the importance of the accounting profession. From thousands of small businesses to mega-corporations, people depend on accounting statements to accurately portray the financial health of a company.

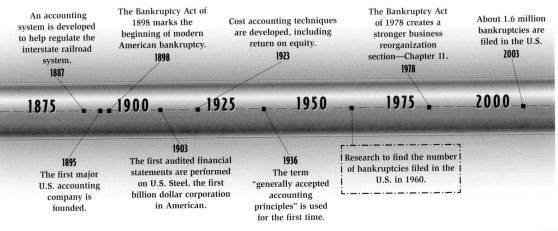

An accounting system is developed to help regulate the interstate railroad system.
1887

The Bankruptcy Act of 1898 marks the beginning of modern American bankruptcy.
1898

Cost accounting techniques are developed, including return on equity.
1923

The Bankruptcy Act of 1978 creates a stronger business reorganization section—Chapter 11.
1978

About 1.6 million bankruptcies are filed in the U.S.
2003

1875   **1900**   **1925**   **1950**   **1975**   **2000**

1895
The first major U.S. accounting company is founded.

1903
The first audited financial statements are performed on U.S. Steel, the first billion dollar corporation in American.

1936
The term "generally accepted accounting principles" is used for the first time.

Research to find the number of bankruptcies filed in the U.S. in 1960.

Answer to research item:

About 110,000 bankruptcies were filed in the U.S. in 1960. (The statistics for 1960 and 2003 include the total number of individual and business bankruptcy filings.)

555

HOW TIMES HAVE CHANGED

Lead the class into a discussion about accounting and bankruptcy. Possible question to ask:
  What major companies have been in the news the past few years because of bankruptcy and questionable accounting practices?

Turn the students' attention to the timeline. Have them do their own research to find the number of bankruptcies filed in the U.S. in 1960.
See page 588 for assessment questions related to the timeline.

Start Up

Have students read the Start Up. Ask them what factors a business might use to determine if a profit is being made. Write down student responses on the board and have one student record them on paper. Save the paper for use in the Wrap Up.

Math Skill Builder

The skills of adding and subtracting money amounts are used in this lesson. Complete all exercises in Math Skill Builder 1–2 to review these skills.

■ Teach Goal 1

Explain that revenue includes all sources of income for a business but that sales include only sales of goods produced, goods resold, or services provided.

In addition to sales, firms may generate revenue from a variety of activities that are not their primary business activities. These might include interest and dividends on idle cash invested and profit from the sale of property.

Ask student to identify what might generate sales returns and allowances. The discussion should include damaged goods, wrong goods sent, and lost goods.

13.1 Preparing Income Statements

GOALS

- Calculate net sales
- Calculate cost of goods sold
- Calculate gross profit
- Calculate net income

Start Up

If you are the owner of a small business, how do you know if you are making a profit? Would looking at the amount of cash in the cash register at the close of a business day tell you if you are making a profit?

Math Skill Builder

Review these math skills and solve the exercises that follow.

1 **Add** money amounts.
Find the sum. $25,149 + $4,509 + $108,558 = $138,216

1a. $145,345 + $87,981 + $16,129 $249,455

1b. $340,288 + $72,465 + $1,598 $414,351

1c. $38,265 + $45,107 + $4,967 $88,339

1d. $16,983 + $8,297 $25,280

2 **Subtract** larger money amounts from smaller money amounts. Show negative differences in parentheses.
Find the difference. $45,608 − $64,733 = ($19,125)

2a. $84,891 − $101,397   ($16,506)

2b. $12,793 − $24,197   ($11,404)

2c. $735,978 − $1,000,783   ($264,805)

2d. $72,197 − $98,288   ($26,091)

■ Net Sales

To stay in business for many years, every business must make a profit for its owners. That means a business must bring in more money than it spends. An **income statement** shows how much money is earned and spent during a period of time, such as a month, quarter, or year. If more money is earned than spent, there is a profit. If more money is spent than earned, there is a loss.

> **BUSINESS TIP**
> An income statement is also called a *profit and loss statement* and an *earnings report*.

There are five major sections to an income statement: revenue, cost of goods sold, gross profit, operating expenses, and net income or loss.

The revenue section starts with *sales*, or the total value of goods sold in the period covered by the statement.

556 ■ Chapter 13 Business Profit and Loss

CONNECTION TO ACCOUNTING

Accountants usually prepare income statements for businesses. Many small businesses can't afford to hire accountants full time, so they pay accounting firms to create their accounting records, prepare reports, and audit their records. You might ask students to identify accounting firms that serve businesses in the area and prepare a report about the services that they offer. The data for the report might come from Internet web sites of accounting firms or from interviews.

Some goods may be returned for refunds by customers, and allowances or price reductions may be given to customers for damaged goods.

These *sales returns and allowances* decrease sales, so they are subtracted from revenue. The amount left is called *net sales* (see A).

Net Sales = Sales − Sales Returns and Allowances

Two income statements are shown below, Petrie's Gift Shop and Cepeda Manufacturing.

■ **Apply Goal 1**

Do Example 1 at the board while students do the math at their desks.

Assign Check Your Understanding problems A and B for class work. Check student work for problems.

Petrie's Gift Shop Income Statement For the month ended July 31, 20—			
Revenue			
Sales		75,952	
Less sales returns and allowances		1,900	
Net sales		**(A)**	74,052
Cost of goods sold			
Beginning inventory, July 1	211,638		
Purchases	31,548		
Goods available for sale	**(B)** 243,186		
Ending inventory, July 31	196,920		
Cost of goods sold		**(C)** 46,266	
Gross profit on sales		**(D)** 27,786	
Operating expenses			
Salaries and wages	10,567		
Rent	3,194		
Taxes	1,864		
Utilities	1,678		
Advertising	780		
Depreciation of equipment	726		
Insurance	253		
Other expenses	854		
Total operating expenses		19,916	
Net income		**(E)** 7,870	

Cepeda Manufacturing Income Statement For the month ended July 31, 20—			
Revenue			
Sales		205,000	
Less sales returns and allowances		8,552	
Net sales		**(A)** 196,448	
Cost of goods sold			
Beginning inventory, July 1	21,148		
Add costs of goods manufactured	145,280		
Goods available for sale	**(B)** 166,428		
Ending inventory, July 31	24,511		
Cost of goods sold		**(C)** 141,917	
Gross profit on sales		**(D)** 54,531	
Operating expenses			
Salaries	18,250		
Office expenses	2,800		
Payroll taxes	2,452		
Depreciation	2,688		
Total operating expenses		26,190	
Net income		**(E)** 28,341	

■ **ONGOING ASSESSMENT**

Ask students how to find net sales **sales − sales returns and allowances.**

■ **Teach Goal 2**

Point out to students that the terminology on the two income statements shown varies slightly. Merchandisers use purchases while manufacturers use the cost of goods manufactured. Both are costs of acquiring new goods.

Point out that the basic concept is that goods on hand at the beginning of the period (beginning inventory) plus goods bought or produced during the period give you the total cost of the goods that could have been sold during the period. If you subtract the cost of the goods that are left at the end of the year (ending inventory), you find the cost of the goods that were sold during the period.

EXAMPLE 1

Regal Book Shop's sales for the year were $156,790. Sales returns and allowances for the same year were $2,398. What were Regal's net sales for the year?

SOLUTION
Subtract the sales returns and allowances from sales.

$156,790 − $2,398 = $154,392   net sales

> **BUSINESS TIP**
>
> *Revenue* is income from all sources. For most businesses, the main revenue is income from the sale of goods produced, services rendered, or goods resold.

■ **CHECK YOUR UNDERSTANDING**

A. The Cycle Shop's sales for the first quarter of the year were $307,892. Sales returns and allowances for the quarter were $14,640. What were the net sales for the quarter? $293,252

B. Crestwood Products had sales of $45,240 in May. Sales returns and allowances in the same month were $1,125. What were Crestwood's net sales? $44,115

Lesson 13.1 Preparing Income Statements ■ **557**

■ *CHECK YOUR UNDERSTANDING SOLUTIONS*

A. $307,892 − $14,640 = $293,252
B. $45,240 − $1,125 = $44,115
C. $317,800 + $219,900 = $537,700;
     $537,700 − $275,300 = $262,400

D. $630,750 + $1,682,900 = $2,313,650;
     $2,313,650 − $673,580 = $1,640,070

Work through Example 2 at the board while students complete the math at their desks.

Assign Check Your Understanding problems C and D for class work. Move about the classroom and examine student work to identify student errors or difficulties.

■ ONGOING ASSESSMENT
Ask students to identify how to find goods available for sale. **beginning inventory + purchases or goods produced** Then ask them how to find cost of goods sold. **goods available for sale − ending inventory**

■ Teach Goal 3

Point out that gross profit is the profit a firm makes from the sale of goods or services without considering the costs of operating the business.

■ Cost of Goods Sold

The cost of goods sold is expenses directly related to buying or producing the goods sold. For a retailer, these are the costs of purchasing merchandise. For a manufacturer, the cost of goods sold is the prime cost, or the sum of the raw materials costs and direct labor costs.

Each income statement has a *beginning inventory*, or the dollar value of all goods on hand at the beginning of the period. Companies add the cost of the goods purchased or made during the time period to the beginning inventory to find the goods available for sale (see B) for the period. The value of the inventory on hand at the end of the period is called the *ending inventory*.

The ending inventory is subtracted from goods available for sale. The difference is the cost of goods sold (see C) for that period. For a retailer, the formula is

Cost of Goods Sold = Beginning Inventory + Purchases − Ending Inventory

For a manufacturer, the formula is

Cost of Goods Sold = Beginning Inventory + Cost of Goods Manufactured − Ending Inventory

EXAMPLE 2

On May 1, Agle Farm Implements had an inventory of merchandise costing $1,895,200. During May, goods costing $497,800 were bought. Merchandise inventory at the end of May was $1,038,700. What was the cost of goods sold for May?

SOLUTION
Add the beginning inventory and the purchases for May.

$1,895,200 + $497,800 = $2,393,000   goods available for sale in May

Subtract the ending inventory from the goods available for sale.

$2,393,000 − $1,038,700 = $1,354,300   cost of goods sold for May

■ CHECK YOUR UNDERSTANDING

C. On January 1, The Shoe Palace had an inventory of merchandise costing $317,800. During the quarter, merchandise costing $219,900 was bought. Merchandise inventory on March 31 was $275,300. Find the cost of goods sold for the quarter. $262,400

D. Rogers Products Company records show these amounts for the year: beginning inventory, January 1, $630,750; cost of goods produced during the year, $1,682,900; ending inventory, December 31, $673,580. Find the cost of goods sold for the year. $1,640,070

■ Gross Profit

Gross Profit (see D) is the difference between the net sales and the cost of goods sold.

Gross Profit = Net Sales − Cost of Goods Sold

COMMON ERRORS

Students may forget to place a minus sign before a net loss. Also, students may subtract a smaller gross profit from larger operating expenses but still call the result net income. Stress the need to determine which amount is larger first. Then have students place the minus sign and the label, net loss, on their papers before they do the subtraction.

EXAMPLE 3

Main Street Appliances had net sales of $34,590 in July. The cost of goods sold in July was $19,670. What was Main Street's gross profit on its sales?

SOLUTION

Subtract the cost of goods sold from the net sales.

$34,590 − $19,670 = $14,920   gross profit for July

■ CHECK YOUR UNDERSTANDING

E. The Tee's net sales of golf equipment for the year were $589,280. The cost of the goods sold for the same period was $298,100. What is the Tee's gross profit for the year? $291,180

F. On July 1, Robles Metal Products had a beginning inventory of $505,700. During the quarter, goods costing $290,900 were manufactured. The inventory at the end of September was $485,300. During the quarter, Robles' net sales were $759,200. What was the cost of goods sold for the quarter? What was Robles' gross profit for the quarter? $311,300; $447,900

■ Net Income

Operating expenses are the costs of running a business and may include salaries and wages, taxes, advertising, rent, depreciation of equipment, utilities, and insurance. Operating expenses are usually listed and totaled on the income statement.

Total operating expenses are deducted from gross profit to determine a company's **net income** (see E). Net income may also be called *net profit*. This is the actual profit earned after all costs are accounted for. Both Petrie's Gift Shop and Cepeda Manufacturing reported a net income at the bottom of their statements.

Net Income = Gross Profit − Operating Expenses

If operating expenses are greater than gross profit on sales, subtract the gross profit from total operating expenses. The result, or difference, is a **net loss**.

Net Loss = Operating Expenses − Gross Profit

For example, suppose your business had a gross profit of $15,000 for a month, and the operating expenses were $20,000 that month. You had a net loss of $5,000. When a net loss occurs, write Net Loss instead of Net Income at the bottom of the income statement. Put parentheses around the amount ($5,000) to show it is a loss, or negative amount.

> **BUSINESS TIP**
>
> Utilities may include many different commodities or services, such as gas, electricity, telephone, cable, and online services.

EXAMPLE 4

A store had a gross profit of $37,200 and total expenses of $28,500 in October. What was the store's net income or loss?

SOLUTION

Subtract the total expenses from the gross profit.

$37,200 − $28,500 = $8,700   net income

Lesson 13.1 Preparing Income Statements ■ **559**

■ Apply Goal 3

Work through Example 3 at the board while students complete the math at their desks.

Assign Check Your Understanding problems E and F for class work. Move about the classroom and examine student work to identify student errors.

■ ONGOING ASSESSMENT

Ask students to identify how to find gross profit. **net sales − cost of goods sold**

■ Teach Goal 4

Stress that before subtracting operating expenses from gross profit, students should see which amount is larger. They should always subtract the smaller amount from the larger amount. If gross profit exceeds operating expenses, there is a net income. If operating expenses exceed gross profit, there is a net loss.

■ Apply Goal 4

Work through Example 4 at the board while students complete the math at their desks.

Assign Check Your Understanding problems G and H for class work. Move about the classroom and examine student work to identify student errors.

■ ONGOING ASSESSMENT

Ask students how to find net income. Then ask them how to find net loss.

■ *CHECK YOUR UNDERSTANDING SOLUTIONS*

E. $589,280 − $298,100 = $291,180

F. $505,700 + $290,900 = $796,600;
$796,600 − $485,300 = $311,300;
$759,200 − $311,300 = $447,900

Wrap Up

Review the Start Up. Read the possible factors on the paper created in the Start Up. Discuss and evaluate each possible factor in light of what students have learned in the lesson.

COMMUNICATION

Select income statements from one or more student reports and make transparencies of them. Then discuss with students the differences between them and the income statements in the Lesson.

Assign

Assignment: Exercises 1–13, 15–22. Start with the basic arithmetic problems at the beginning to be sure that students understand the underlying arithmetic in the exercises.

Assess

Using the board or a blank transparency, ask students to lead you through the creation of the major items included in the income statements used in the lesson. Then ask students to define or explain each of the income statement items.

■ **CHECK YOUR UNDERSTANDING**

G. The Pet Corner had a gross profit of $29,400 in June. It also had these expenses for the month: salaries and wages, $7,400; rent, $1,300; taxes, $550; utilities, $390; advertising, $125; depreciation, $270; insurance, $105; other expenses, $420. What were the store's total expenses? What was the store's net income or loss? $10,560; $18,840 net income

H. Leo's Card Shop had a gross profit of $3,300 in April. It also had these expenses for the month: salaries and wages, $1,340; rent, $1,570; taxes, $450; utilities, $290; advertising, $175; depreciation, $170; insurance, $155; other expenses, $552. What were the shop's total expenses? What was the shop's net income or loss? $4,702; $1,402 net loss

Wrap Up

The amount of cash in the cash register tells you only the amount of cash receipts you had in one day. That is important information. However, to figure whether you made a profit or loss, you must find all the money your business earned and all the money your business spent during a time period, such as a month. If what the business earned was more than what it spent, you made a profit.

COMMUNICATION

Use the web to find the income statements for a retail firm and a manufacturing firm. Most large companies maintain a web site that contains what are called the annual reports to stockholders. The annual reports contain the current income statement for the companies. Identify and list the major sections of the income statement for each company and compare them to the major income statement sections used in this chapter. What differences did you find? What sections were the same? Prepare a brief written report of your findings.

EXERCISES

Find the sum.
1. $19,803 + $28,809 + $12,490 $61,102
2. $389,122 + $15,967 + $1,488 $406,577

Find the difference.
3. $89,220 − $67,208 $22,012
4. $108,893 − $82,415 $26,478
5. $45,280 − $65,820   ($20,540)
6. $348,199 − $399,286   ($51,087)

7. Fleigle Supplies, Inc. had sales of $258,440 in February. Sales returns and allowances in the same month were $2,256. What were Fleigle's net sales? $256,184

■ *CHECK YOUR UNDERSTANDING SOLUTIONS*

G. $7,400 + $1,300 + $550 + $ 390 + $125 + $270 + $105 + $420 = $10,560; $29,400 − $10,560 = $18,840 net income

H. $1,340 + $1,570 + $450 + $290 + $175 + $170 + $155 + $552 = $4,702; $4,702 − $3,300 = $1,402 net loss

8. T-R Roofing Manufacturing Company's beginning inventory on January 1 was $1,530,470. The cost of the goods it produced during the year was $3,828,200. Its ending inventory on December 31 was $1,463,850. What was the cost of goods sold for the year? $3,894,820

9. A company's net sales for the month were $1,498,780. The cost of goods sold for the same period was $849,400. What is the company's gross profit for the month? $649,380

Kemper Foundry had a beginning inventory of $355,700 on July 1. During the quarter, goods costing $1,124,300 were manufactured. The inventory at the end of September was $385,600. During the quarter, Kemper's net sales were $1,675,600.

10. What was the cost of goods sold for the quarter? $1,094,400

11. What was Kemper's gross profit for the quarter? $581,200

Cardwell, Inc. had a gross profit of $459,568 during January. During the same month it had these expenses: salaries and wages, $397,588; loan interest, $21,569; taxes, $5,498; utilities, $4,491; advertising, $5,458; insurance, $11,522; other expenses, $18,945.

12. What was the total of the expenses? $465,071

13. What was the net income or loss?   Net loss, $5,503

14. **CRITICAL THINKING**   Rob Dougherty listened to a local TV news program that claimed that a new shoe store on Main Street had made a net income of 12% last year. Rob thought that was high since most of the local banks only paid 1.5% on interest-bearing accounts and corporate bonds were only paying 7.8% interest. Is Rob right? Why might a net income of 12% from the store be reasonable?   Operating a store is a risk; many new companies fail; store owner might lose everything; bank accounts are less risky and are insured, bonds have claim on firm's assets

MIXED REVIEW

15. What amount is 150% of $84? $126

16. What percent is 144 of 96? 150%

17. What amount is 1% of $1,000,000? $10,000

18. $298.80 is what percent less than $360?   17%

19. Write 57.3% as a decimal, rounded to the nearest hundredth.   0.57

20. Last year, Chandna Venkatraman was paid a salary of $700 a week for 52 weeks. Her federal taxable income for the same period was $21,200. She paid to the city of Carthage in which she worked an income tax of 3.5% on her taxable income. How much did Chandna pay in city income taxes? $742, Lesson 2.4

21. You discount a 6-month, noninterest-bearing note for $3,000 at a bank at 18%. What true rate of interest, to the nearest tenth percent, do you pay?   19.8%, Lesson 4.2

22. A company spent $785,600 on computer support for their 460 desktop, notebook, and handheld computers last year. What was the per computer cost of the computer support? $1,707.83, Lesson 9.3

Lesson 13.1 Preparing Income Statements ▪ 561

Reteach

STUDENT WORKBOOK To reteach finding net sales, do Exercise 1 with students. Then have them do Exercise 2.

To reteach finding cost of goods sold, do Exercise 3 with students. Then have them do Exercise 4 in class.

To reteach finding gross profit, do Exercise 5 with students. Then have them do Exercise 6.

To reteach finding net income and net loss, do Exercise 7 with students. Then have them do Exercise 8.

Enrich

Assign Exercise 14, Critical Thinking. This is an excellent exercise through which students can consider the importance of risk on investment return. The discussion should consider the possible returns for alternative investments that are less risky, such as insured bonds and savings accounts. The discussion should also include the comparative risks of starting a business, such as the high failure rate of new businesses.

Close

Call on students to define and explain the bolded terms in the lesson.

Alternatively, have them complete Exercise 9 in the workbook.

SELECTED SOLUTIONS

8. $1,530,470 + $3,828,200 = $5,358,670;
$5,358,670 − $1,463,850 = $3,894,820

9. $1,498,780 − $849,400 = $649,380

12. $397,588 + $21,569 + $5,498 + $4,491 +
$5,458 + $11,522 + $18,945 = $465,071

13. $465,071 − $459,568 = $5,503 net loss

Start Up

Have students read the Start Up. Ask them for reasons why Juanita might be skeptical. If you taught the section on mutual funds, draw an analogy to it by asking students if they would invest in a mutual fund if they knew it rose in value by 15% in one year. Record the reasons on the board and have one student record them on a sheet of paper. Save the paper for use in the Wrap Up.

Math Skill Builder

The skills of adding, subtracting and dividing money amounts are used in this lesson. So are the skills of dividing dollar amounts to find percents and averages.

Complete all exercises in Math Skill Builder 1–3.

■ **Teach Goal 1**

Point out that percentage analysis of income statements allows one period's statement to be compared to previous statements, to other firms, and to industry averages. The percentages of gross and net profit margins are often used in analyzing a business's progress over the years and in comparing it to other businesses.

Point out that more information than one period's income statement is needed to know how a firm is doing. Current income statements should be compared to previous income statements.

Stress that what is considered a good net income for one type of business may not be good for another type of business. Remind students of the importance of risk in assessing return.

13.2 Analyzing Income Statements

GOALS

- Use percentages to analyze income statement items
- Use ratios to analyze income statement items

Start Up

Jason told Juanita about a company listed on the stock market in which he had decided to invest. Jason was excited because the company had earned a 15% net income for last year. Juanita didn't seem too thrilled, however, at the net income percentage. Why might Juanita be skeptical of the net income percentage?

Math Skill Builder

Review these math skills and solve the exercises that follow.

1 **Divide** dollar amounts by dollar amounts.
Find the quotient. $420,000 \div $60,000 = 7

   1a. $55,352 \div $6,512   8.5   **1b.** $461,900 \div $74,500   6.2

2 **Divide** dollar amounts to find percents.
Find the quotient. $70,000 \div $350,000 = 0.2, or 20%

   2a. $35,235 \div $652,500   5.4%   **2b.** $3,588 \div $89,700   4%

3 **Average** dollar amounts.
Find the average of $38,500 and $36,300.
$38,500 + $36,300 = $74,800; $74,800 \div 2 = $37,400

   3a. Average $12,080 and $14,280. $13,180   **3b.** Average $58,280 and $63,120. $60,700

■ Percentage Analysis of Income Statements

Businesses use income statements to report their income. They also use them to analyze a business. One way to analyze a business using income statements is to compare each item on the statement to net sales using percentages. That means dividing each item by the net sales amount. For Cepeda Manufacturing (see Lesson 13-1) net income, $28,341, as a percent of net sales, $196,448, is found this way:

$28,341 \div $196,448 = 0.1443, or 14.4%

Two important percentage comparisons are the comparisons of gross profit to net sales and net income to net sales. These comparisons are called the **gross profit margin** and the **net profit margin**.

COMMON ERRORS

Students may use the wrong numbers to calculate the percents when analyzing income statements. A common mistake is to use sales as opposed to net sales as the basis of the percentages. Stress that net sales should be used as the denominator in calculating the percentages for items on the income statement, because they are the true sales of the company.

Converting income statement items to percents lets you compare a company's income statements from one year to the next. It also lets you compare a company's income statement to the statements of other companies.

For example, a percentage comparison of key items on the Petrie's Gift Shop (see Lesson 13-1) income statements for two years is shown in the table.

The comparison shows that Petrie's net income as a percent of net sales has risen from 5.9% to 10.6%. There appear to be two reasons for this increase. Petrie has lowered the price his merchandise costs him from 65.2% to 62.5% of net sales and lowered the expenses of operating his business from 28.9% to 26.9% of net sales.

Item	Amount This Year	Percent of Net Sales	
		This Year	Last Year
Net Sales	$74,052	100.0%	100.0%
Cost of Goods Sold	$46,266	62.5%	65.2%
Gross Profit	$27,786	37.5%	34.8%
Operating Expenses	$19,916	26.9%	28.9%
Net Income	$7,870	10.6%	5.9%

EXAMPLE 1

Landau Mechanics, Inc. had gross sales of $543,370, sales returns and allowances of $5,370, and net income of $28,640 last year. What was the company's net profit margin to the nearest whole percent?

SOLUTION

Subtract sales returns and allowances from gross sales.

$543,370 − $5,370 = $538,000   net sales

Divide net income by net sales.

$28,640 ÷ $538,000 = 0.053, or 5%   net profit margin

MATH TIP

The relationship of two numbers such as 1 and 2 can be shown as 1:2, $\frac{1}{2}$, or 50%.

■ CHECK YOUR UNDERSTANDING

A. A vacuum cleaner dealership's net sales were $238,180 last year. Its operating expenses for the same period were $17,700. What were the operating expenses as a percent of net sales, to the nearest tenth percent?   7.4%

B. Cliver Telecommunications, Inc. had net sales of $1,589,300 and cost of goods sold of $1,032,850 this year. Last year the amounts were $1,453,200 and $960,300, respectively. What is the company's gross profit margin, to the nearest tenth percent, for each year? Is the percent rising or falling, and by how much?   35%, 33.9%, rising, by 1.1%

■ Ratio Analysis of Income Statements

Ratio analysis compares items on an income statement. One ratio, the merchandise turnover rate, can be helpful in analyzing a business.

The merchandise turnover rate is the number of times per period that a store replaces, or turns over, its average stock of merchandise. The period is often a month, quarter, or year. Different kinds of businesses have different acceptable turnover rates. Businesses that sell durable and expensive goods such as furniture or large appliances have low turnover rates. Businesses that sell perishables such as food have high turnover rates. The formula for merchandise turnover rate is:

$$\text{Merchandise Turnover Rate} = \frac{\text{Cost of Goods Sold for Period}}{\text{Average Merchandise Inventory for Period}}$$

Lesson 13.2 Analyzing Income Statements ■ **563**

■ **CHECK YOUR UNDERSTANDING SOLUTIONS**

A. $17,700 ÷ $238,180 = 0.074, or 7.4%
B. $1,589,300 − $1,032,850 = $556,450;
$556,450 ÷ $1,589,300 = 0.3501, or 35% gross profit margin this year; $1,453,200 − $960,300 =

$492,900; $492,900 ÷ $1,453,200 = 0.3391, or 33.9% gross profit margin last year; 35.0% − 33.9% = 1.1% rising

■ **Apply Goal 2**

Do Example 2 at the board or transparency while students do it at their desks.

Assign Check Your Understanding problems C and D for class work. Check student work for errors and problems.

■ **ONGOING ASSESSMENT**
With their books closed, ask students to describe the formula for finding the merchandise turnover rate. Also ask students to explain or define each term in the formula.

Wrap **Up**

Review the Start Up. Then read the list of reasons they produced in the Start Up. Have students compare the list and the items listed in the Wrap Up. Discuss the differences with them.

TEAM MEETING

Assign the Team Meeting activity. Have selected students read their reports and discuss their findings with the class. Make sure that student suggestions are more specific than merely increase income and decrease expenses. For example, a student might suggest that Cepeda expand its product line or that the firm examine the use of information systems to reduce office expenses.

■ **STUDENT PORTFOLIO**
Students might want to consider placing their Team Meeting reports in their portfolios.

EXAMPLE 2

Calculate the merchandise turnover rate for Cepeda Manufacturing based on the July income statement.

SOLUTION

Add the beginning and ending inventories for July and divide by 2.

$21,148 (Merchandise inventory, July 1) + $24,511 (Merchandise inventory, July 31) ÷ 2 = $22,829.50   average merchandise inventory for July

Divide the cost of goods sold for July by the average inventory for July.

$141,917 ÷ $22,829.50 = 6.22, or 6.2   merchandise turnover rate for July

The turnover rate may be used not only on an entire inventory but also on each item of inventory. Doing so lets you identify goods that are moving more slowly than others or moving more slowly than they have in the past. To prevent these items from becoming over-stocked, you may decide to discount them.

■ **CHECK YOUR UNDERSTANDING**

C. Rock Creek Stores had a beginning inventory on January 1 of $168,350. The ending inventory on December 31 was $155,490. The Stores' cost of goods sold for the year was $945,280. What was its merchandise inventory turnover rate, to the nearest tenth, for the year?   5.8

D. A fabric manufacturer had an inventory of a stock item costing $34,200 on July 1 and $39,400 on September 30. The cost of goods sold for that inventory item for the quarter was $295,200. What was the turnover rate for the item for the quarter, to the nearest tenth?   8.0

Wrap **Up**

Juanita might be skeptical of the net income percentage for many reasons. One reason is that there is no information against which the percentage can be compared. Several questions should be asked to get the missing information. What has the company's net income percentage been for the last 5 or 10 years? What is the net income of similar companies in the same industry? What forecasts for growth are there for the industry? Company income statement data from a single period need to be compared to other years and other firms to become really useful.

TEAM MEETING

With two other team members, examine the income statement for Cepeda Manufacturing found in Lesson 13.1. Identify steps the firm might consider taking to increase its net income. Prepare a brief report explaining to your class the steps you have identified and how each step will affect net income.

■ *CHECK YOUR UNDERSTANDING SOLUTIONS*

C. $168,350 + $155,490 = $323,840; $323,840 ÷ 2 = $161,920; $945,280 ÷ $161,920 = 5.83, or 5.8

D. $34,200 + $39,400 = $73,600; $73,600 ÷ 2 = $36,800; $295,200 ÷ $36,800 = 8.02, or 8.0

EXERCISES

1. What percent is $9,216 of $76,800? 12%

2. Find the average of $62,780 and $58,270. $60,525

Prepare a percentage analysis of the items below to net sales using Cepeda Manufacturing's income statement. Find each percent to the nearest tenth.

3. Cost of Goods Sold 72.2%   4. Gross Profit on Sales 27.8%

5. Operating Expenses 13.3%   6. Net Income 14.4%

A business had net sales of $140,000. The cost of goods sold was $84,000.

7. The cost of merchandise sold was what percent of net sales? 60%

8. What was the gross profit margin? 40%

The records of the Carlson Company last year showed these data: net sales, $220,000; cost of merchandise sold, $143,000; operating expenses, $52,800.

9. Find the gross profit and the net income for last year. $77,000; $24,200

10. Find the gross profit margin for last year. 35%

11. Find the net profit margin for last year. 11%

From January through June, Dollar Appliance Center took 3 inventories of merchandise: $88,000, $188,200, and $124,600. The cost of merchandise sold during the 6-month period was $601,200.

12. What was Dollar's average merchandise inventory? $133,600

13. What was the merchandise turnover rate for the 6 months? 4.5

14. What is the equivalent merchandise turnover rate for a year? 9

INTEGRATING YOUR KNOWLEDGE ReAlarm Sales purchased alarm systems from a wholesaler at these quantities and unit costs during June: June 5, 20 at $3,760; June 10, 24 at $4,752; June 29, 28 at $5,572. The beginning inventory of 9 systems had a total value of $1,683.

15. Find the value of the 26 alarm systems in the June 30 ending inventory using the FIFO method. $5,174

16. If the cost of the alarm systems sold was $10,593, what was the turnover rate, to the nearest tenth, for the alarms for the month? 3.1

MIXED REVIEW

17. $0.45 \times 1,000$ 450

18. $3.108 \div 100$ 0.03108

19. Rewrite $\frac{7}{8}$ as a percent. $87\frac{1}{2}\%$

20. How many days are there between May 5 and July 16? 72

21. The senior class of Ekersville High School ran a dart game at the town's 3-day homecoming event. The class collected $250.50 on Friday, $242.75 on Saturday, and $224.25 on Sunday. What was the average amount collected by the class each day? $239.17, Lesson 1.3

Lesson 13.2 Analyzing Income Statements ■ 565

Assign

Assignment: Exercises 1–21. Start with the basic arithmetic problems at the beginning so that students understand the underlying arithmetic in the exercises.

Assess

Check student answers to Exercise problems by calling on them in class. Then have selected students place the answers to Exercises 9–11 and Exercises 12–14 on the board. Have the class compare their solutions to those on the board and discuss any differences in the solutions.

Reteach

STUDENT WORKBOOK To reteach finding percentages to analyze income statement data, do Exercise 1a-e with students. Then have them complete Exercises 1f–j, 2, and 3 independently.

To reteach finding merchandise turnover rates, do Exercise 4 with students. Then have them do Exercises 5 and 6 independently.

Enrich

Bring an income statement from an annual report or the Web and calculate a percentage analysis of the items at the board with students helping you by telling you what steps to take.

Close

Ask students to define or explain the following terms: gross profit margin, net profit margin, merchandise turnover rate.

SELECTED SOLUTIONS

3. $141,917 ÷ $196,448 = 0.7224, or 72.2%

8. $140,000 − $84,000 = $56,000;
$56,000 ÷ $140,000 = 0.40, or 40%

12. $88,000 + $188,200 + $124,600 = $400,800;
$400,800 ÷ 3 = $133,600

13. $601,200 ÷ $133,600 = 4.5

16. $1,683 + $5,174 = $6,857; $6,857 ÷ 2 = $3,428.50; $10,593 ÷ $3,428.50 = 3.08, or 3.1

Start Up

Have students read the Start Up. Discuss possible problems that could occur in a partnership without a written agreement. These problems might include bad feelings over the division of profits, division of labor, and amount of investment. Also, problems can arise when one partner wants to get out of the partnership or if a partner dies.

Math Skill Builder

The skills of adding, subtracting, and multiplying money amounts are used in this lesson. So is multiplying money amounts by percents and fractions.

Complete all exercises in Math Skill Builder 1–2 to have students review many of these skills.

■ Teach Goal 1

Discuss with students some of the ways partners have divided profits using the bulleted list on page 566. Ask students to suggest other ways. These might include paying partners salaries or basing the division on the amount of time spent at the partnership business.

Point out that some partners are called "silent partners" because their contribution to the partnership is only an investment of funds. Silent partners usually do not take an active part in running the business.

13.3 Partnership Income

GOALS

- Distribute partnership income in proportion to investments
- Distribute partnership income in a fixed ratio or fixed percent
- Distribute partnership income after paying interest on investments

Start Up

Sally's friend, Ralph, told her he was forming a partnership with another friend to start a photography business. Sally asked Ralph what lawyer was drawing up the partnership agreement. Ralph said he had known his friend for many years and trusted him. Sally thought that was suspicious. Is Sally right to be suspicious?

Math Skill Builder

Review these math skills and solve the exercises that follow.

❶ **Subtract** money amounts.
Find the difference. $135,800 − $75,000 = $60,800

   1a. $84,500 − $15,400 $69,100   **1b.** $138,540 − $63,470 $75,070

❷ **Multiply** money amounts by percents and fractions.
Find the product. $120,000 × 8% = $120,000 × 0.08 = $9,600
Find the product. $350,000 × $\frac{3}{5}$ = $210,000

   2a. $560,800 × 7% $39,256   **2b.** $280,500 × 9.5% $26,647.50

   2c. $\frac{4}{5}$ × $750,000 $600,000   **2d.** $\frac{\$20,000}{\$50,000}$ × $280,000 $112,000

■ In Proportion to Investments

Firms owned by one person are called *sole proprietorship*. A firm owned by two or more people that is not a corporation or other form of business is called a **partnership**. When you form a partnership, you may sign a partnership agreement. The agreement tells how much money the partners invested and how they will share net income or net loss. Ways to distribute income or loss are:

- Equally between the partners
- In proportion to the partners' investments
- Paying interest to the partners on their investments
- In a fixed ratio or percent
- Combining two or more of the above methods

If no way is specified, income or loss may be distributed equally.

BUSINESS TIP

The IRS expects profits and losses to be distributed according to each partner's percentage interest in the business. Even if there is a written agreement, the partners may have to justify how they divide profits and losses.

COMMON ERRORS

Students may not understand ratios and percentages sufficiently and may make illogical assumptions in calculating partnership shares of net income. For instance, if net income of $10,000 is to be split in the ratio of 4 to 3, students might write answers of $4,000 and $3,000 without realizing that the entire $10,000 must be distributed. Recall for students how factory overhead was distributed and compare the arithmetic used in that process to the process of distributing partnership income in proportion to the amount invested.

To find how much each partner receives when net income is shared in proportion to investments, show each partner's investment as a fractional part of the total investment. Then, multiply the total partnership net income by each partner's fraction.

EXAMPLE 1

Matsumi and O'Conner invest $300,000 and $200,000, respectively, in a partnership. They agree to share net income in proportion to their investments. At the end of the first year, the partnership earns a net income of $52,000. Find each partner's share of the net income.

SOLUTION

Add the investments of each partner.

$300,000 + $200,000 = $500,000   total investment

Multiply the net income by the fraction that shows each partner's investment of the total investment.

$\frac{\$300,000}{\$500,000} \times \$52,000 = \$31,200$ Matsumi's share

$\frac{\$200,000}{\$500,000} \times \$52,000 = \$20,800$ O'Conner's share

MATH TIP

Check your work by adding each partner's share of net income together. They should equal the total net income from the partnership.

■ CHECK YOUR UNDERSTANDING

A. Aguilar and Trent share their partnership net income in proportion to their investments. Aguilar has $180,000 and Trent $120,000 invested. What is each partner's share of this year's $64,000 net income? $38,400; $25,600

B. Silverstein, Clark, and Salinas have invested $250,000, $200,000, and $150,000 in a partnership that had a net income of $90,000 last year. If the partners share the net income in proportion to their investments, what is each partner's share, to the nearest dollar? $37,500; $30,000; $22,500

■ Fixed Ratio or Fixed Percent

In some partnerships, net income is shared in a fixed ratio, such as 5 to 4. In this case, the net income is divided into nine equal parts with five parts going to one partner and four parts to the other partner. In other partnerships, each partner's share may be a certain percent of the net income, such as 55% to one partner and 45% to the other.

EXAMPLE 2

Yeater and Wilson, business partners, agree to divide a net income of $120,000 in the ratio of 5 to 3. What is each partner's share?

SOLUTION
Add the shares.

$5 + 3 = 8$

Form fractions for each partner that show their part of the total shares and multiply the fractions by the net income

$\frac{5}{8} \times \$120,000 = \$75,000$ Yeater's share

$\frac{3}{8} \times \$120,000 = \$45,000$ Wilson's share

Lesson 13.3 Partnership Income ■ 567

■ Apply Goal 1

Do Example 1 with students at the board while they complete the math at their desks.

Assign Check Your Understanding problems A and B for class work. Walk about your classroom to help students who have difficulties solving the problems.

■ Teach Goal 2

Reteach the concept of ratios by pointing out that ratios may be shown in several ways. When discussing Example 2, point out that 5:3, $\frac{5}{8}$, and $62\frac{1}{2}$% all express the same relationship. That is why the ratio of 5:3 is often restated as $\frac{5}{8}$ or 0.625 since the latter are easier to work with arithmetically for most people.

■ ONGOING ASSESSMENT
Call out ratios of 2 numbers, such as 9:3, and ask students to express the ratio as fractions ($\frac{3}{4}$ and $\frac{1}{4}$) and percents (75% and 25%). Another to use might be 3:2 ($\frac{3}{5}$ and $\frac{2}{5}$)(60% and 40%)

■ Apply Goal 2

Do Example 2 at the board while students do the math at their desks.

Assign Check Your Understanding problems C and D for class work. Move about the room to check student work.

■ *CHECK YOUR UNDERSTANDING SOLUTIONS*

A. $180,000 + $120,000 = $300,000;
$\frac{\$180,000}{\$300,000} \times \$64,000 = \$38,400$ Aguilar's share;
$\frac{\$120,000}{\$300,000} \times \$64,000 = \$25,600$ Trent's share

B. $250,000 + $200,000 + $150,000 = $600,000;
$\frac{\$250,000}{\$600,000} \times \$90,000 = \$37,499.99$, or $37,500 Silverstein's share; $\frac{\$200,000}{\$600,000} \times \$90,000 = \$29,999.99$, or $30,000 Clark's share; $\frac{\$150,000}{\$600,000} \times \$90,000 = \$22,500$ Salinas's share

■ **Apply Goal 3**

Work through Example 3 with students at the board while they complete the math at their desks.

Assign Check Your Understanding problems E and F to do in class. Check student work for errors as you walk about the room.

■ **CHECK YOUR UNDERSTANDING**

C. Tandjung and Sikorski share the net income of $24,000 from their partnership in the ratio of 6 to 5. What is each partner's share? $13,090.91; $10,909.09

D. Cerkez and White share their partnership income 58% and 42%, respectively. If their net income this year is $130,500, what is each partner's share? $75,690; $54,810

■ Interest on Investments

When partners invest different amounts, they may be paid interest on their investments. The rest of the net income may then be divided equally, or by other means.

EXAMPLE 3

Thome and Dulay form a partnership, investing $170,000 and $160,000, respectively. They agree to pay each partner 8% interest on their investment and to divide the remainder of the net income equally. The net income for the first year is $40,000. Find each partner's share of the net income.

SOLUTION
Multiply the interest rate by each partner's investment.

$8\% \times \$170,000 = \$13,600$ Thome's interest

$8\% \times \$160,000 = \$12,800$ Dulay's interest

Add each partner's interest payment.

$\$13,600 + \$12,800 = \$26,400$ total interest paid

Subtract the total interest from the net income.

$\$40,000 - \$26,400 = \$13,600$ remainder of net income

Divide the remainder of net income by the number of partners.

$\$13,600 \div 2 = \$6,800$ each partner's share of remainder

Add each partner's share of remainder to their interest payment.

$\$13,600 + \$6,800 = \$20,400$ Thome's total share of net income

$\$12,800 + \$6,800 = \$19,600$ Dulay's total share of net income

■ **CHECK YOUR UNDERSTANDING**

E. Zeigler and Soga are partners with investments of $250,000 and $375,000, respectively. The partners receive 10% interest annually on their investments. The rest of the net income is divided equally. What is each partner's total share of a net income of $96,000? $41,750; $54,250

F. Volmer and Ramos invested $400,000 and $500,000 in a partnership, respectively. The partners agreed to pay 8% interest on their investments and to divide the remainder of any net income equally. The first year's net income was $240,000. What was each partner's share? $116,000 Volmer; $124,000 Ramos

568 ■ Chapter 13 Business Profit and Loss

■ *CHECK YOUR UNDERSTANDING SOLUTIONS*

C. $6 + 5 = 11$; $\frac{6}{11} \times \$24,000 = \$13,090.909$, or $13,090.91 Tandjung's share; $\frac{5}{11} \times \$24,000 = \$10,909.090$, or $10,909.09 Sikorski's share.

D. $130,500 \times 0.58 = \$75,690$ Cerkez's share; $130,500 \times 0.42 = \$54,810$ White's share.

E. $250,000 \times 0.10 = \$25,000$; $375,000 \times 0.10 = \$37,500$; $25,000 + \$37,500 = \$62,500$; $96,000 - \$62,500 = \$33,500$; $33,500 \div 2 = \$16,750$; $25,000 + \$16,750 = \$41,750$ Zeigler's share; $37,500 + \$16,750 = \$54,250$ Soga's share

Wrap Up

Look back at the Start Up problem. Sally is very right to be suspicious. There are too many problems that can crop up to ruin friendships in a partnership. Most states have laws governing partnerships that take effect if no partnership agreement exists. Ralph and his partner might not like the way that those laws affect their partnership arrangements. The best advice is to agree on who will do what and who will get paid what at the beginning and put those conditions in a partnership agreement.

COMMUNICATION

How are the net incomes from partnerships taxed? Are partnerships taxed differently from sole proprietorships? If one partner dies, how are the partnership properties distributed according to the partnership laws in your state? Is one partner responsible for the business debts made by the other partner? Research the answers to these questions using the library, Internet sources, or talking to an attorney. Prepare a brief report containing the answers you found to each question. List the sources you used, including Internet sources.

Wrap Up

Review the Start Up. If any students have information about partnership problems that have occurred in family partnerships or with partnerships that their friends know about, have them share these problems with the class.

COMMUNICATION

Select one or more students to read their reports to the class and discuss their findings. Ask other students whose reports contained different findings to share those with the class.

Assign

Assignment: Exercises 1–25. Start with the basic arithmetic problems at the beginning of the exercises.

Assess

Ask students how they can check their distribution calculations (add distributions to see if they add to total partnership income).

EXERCISES

1. $45,689 − $23,185 $22,504

2. $134,288 − $53,718 $80,570

3. $375,500 × 7% $26,285

4. $745,850 × 9.5% $70,855.75

5. $\frac{3}{5}$ × $37,500 $22,500

6. $\frac{5}{8}$ × $91,000 $56,875

For Exercises 7–8, the partners distribute income in proportion to their investment. Find the net income each partner will get to the nearest dollar.

	Investments				
	Partner X	Partner Y	Partner Z	Net Income	
7.	$260,000	$180,000		$68,400	$40,418; $27,982
8.	$280,000	$270,000	$86,000	$162,600	$71,585; $69,028; $21,987

9. In the partnership of Mallory and Reese, Mallory's investment is $225,000 and Reese's is $130,000. Net income is divided in proportion to their investment. Their net loss for the first year is $18,900. What is each partner's share of the loss? $11,978.87; $6,921.13

10. **INTEGRATING YOUR KNOWLEDGE** The investments of 3 partners are: Medina, $120,000; Douglass, $136,000; and Sanchez, $144,000. Each year net income is distributed in proportion to the partners' investments. Last year, the firm's net sales were $660,400. The cost of merchandise sold was $420,800, and the operating expenses were $129,600. The partners estimate that the business could be sold for $850,000. How much of last year's net income did each partner get? $33,000; $37,400; $39,600

Lesson 13.3 Partnership Income ■ **569**

SELECTED SOLUTIONS

7. $260,000 + $180,000 = $440,000;
$\frac{\$260,000}{\$440,000}$ × $68,400 = $40,418.175, or $40,418 X's share; $\frac{\$180,000}{\$440,000}$ × $68,400 = $27,981.817, or $27,982 Y's share

11. $98,500 × 0.40 = $39,400 Premmel's share; $98,500 × 0.60 = $59,100 Tratia's share

12. 7 + 4 = 11; $\frac{7}{11}$ × $97,400 = $61,981.814, or $61,982 Berrios's share; $\frac{4}{11}$ × $97,400 = $35,418.175, or $35,418 Gruber's share

Reteach

STUDENT WORKBOOK To reteach distributing partnership income in proportion to investments, do Exercise 1 with students. Then have them do Exercises 2 and 3 independently.

To reteach distributing partnership income in a fixed ratio or percent, do Exercise 4 with students. Then have them do Exercises 5 and 6 independently.

To reteach distributing partnership income after paying interest on investments, do Exercise 7a with students. Then have them do Exercises 7b and 8.

Enrich

Bring a partnership agreement form from an office supply store or an area attorney to class and discuss the form with students.

Close

Ask students to describe each of the methods by which partnership income can be distributed that are covered in the lesson. The description should include the arithmetic processes involved in each method.

■ **STUDENT PORTFOLIO**
Students may wish to place the solutions to one or more of the exercises or the reports they completed in the Communication activity in their portfolios.

11. The partnership agreement of Premmel and Tratia states that Premmel should receive 40% of any net income and Tratia should get 60%. The net income last year was $98,500. Find each partner's share of the net income. $39,400; $59,100

12. Berrios and Gruber formed a partnership. They agreed to divide net income in the ratio of 7 to 4, with Berrios receiving the larger share. Last year's net income was $97,400. Find each partner's share, to the nearest dollar. $61,982; $35,418

Find each partner's share of the net income in each problem to the nearest dollar. Interest is paid on investments. The rest of the net income is divided equally.

	Investments			Interest on Investment	Net Income for Year
	Partner A	Partner B	Partner C		
13.	$50,000	$30,000		7%	$83,000
14.	$22,000	$37,000	$46,000	9%	$137,500
15.	$82,000	$58,000	$69,000	12%	$195,000

13: $42,200; $40,800   14: $44,663; $46,013; $46,823   15: $66,480; $63,600; $64,920

16. Riccio, Delgado, and Saburo invested $150,000, $160,000, and $190,000, respectively, in a partnership. For the first year, their gross profit was $208,400 and their expenses were $86,300. The partners got 7% on their investment, and the rest of the net income was shared equally. What was each partner's total share of the net income for the first year, to the nearest dollar? $39,533; $40,233; $42,333

17. **CRITICAL THINKING**   When the partners' shares of net income are written as ratios or as percents, what should the sum of the shares be?   1, or 100%

MIXED REVIEW

18. Round: $567,398.45 to the nearest thousand dollars. $567,000

19. Rewrite $1\frac{3}{5}$ as a percent.   160%

20. Add: 5.078 + 0.005 + 45.1 + 7,870.02 + 0.033   7,920.236

21. Divide to the nearest cent: $208,984 ÷ 34.5 $6,057.51

22. Estimate the quotient: 284.6 ÷ 54.078   6

23. If 20% of a number is 40, what is the number?   200

24. Tom Raymond bought 1,000 shares of a load fund, International Health Fund, at its offering price of $35.87. What was his total investment in the fund? $35,870, Lesson 7.7

25. A company bought a site license for software that retails for $49.99 per copy. They paid $134,486 for use on their 3,200 computer workstations. How much did they save by buying the site license? $25,482, Lesson 9.2

SELECTED SOLUTIONS

13. $50,000 × 0.07 = $3,500; $30,000 × 0.07 = $2,100; $3,500 + $2,100 = $5,600; $83,000 − $5,600 = $77,400; $77,400 ÷ 2 = $38,700; $3,500 + $38,700 = $42,200 (A); $2,100 + $38,700 = $40,800 (B).

16. $208,400 − $86,300 = $122,100; $150,000 × 0.07 = $10,500; $160,000 × 0.07 = $11,200; $190,000 × 0.07 = $13,300; $10,500 + $11,200 + $13,300 = $35,000; $122,100 − $35,000 = $87,100; $87,100 ÷ 3 = $29,033.33; $10,500 + $29,033.33 = $39,533 Riccio; $11,200 + $29,033.33 = $40,233 Delgado; $13,300 + $29,033.33 = $42,333 Saburo

13.4 Preparing Balance Sheets

GOAL
- Calculate total assets, liabilities and capital

Start Up

Have students read the Start Up. Ask them to suggest reasons why a person or business would be a poor loan risk to a bank. The reasons might include current bills overdue, declared bankruptcy in the past, too much debt for current income, pattern of slow payment of previous loans, debts exceed assets.

List the reasons on the board as students respond. Have one student copy the board list. Save the list for the Wrap Up.

Start Up

"I don't understand why the bank won't lend me the money," complained Tom Westman. Tom had asked a bank for a business loan. He had two other business loans from two other banks. "I always pay my bills as soon as I can!" Can you think of any reasons why Tom could not get a bank loan for his business?

Math Skill Builder

Review these math skills and solve the exercises that follow.

BUSINESS TIP
The balance sheet is often called a "snapshot" of a business because it reports data on the business for one specific day.

1 **Add** money amounts.
Find the sum. $24,809 + $17,362 + $54,672 = $96,843

  1a. $10,689 + $21,765 + $28,510 + $3,592 + $5,221 $69,777

  1b. $74,562 + $52,214 + $79,603 + $22,132 + $582 $229,093

2 **Subtract** money amounts.
Find the difference. $107,329 − $45,228 = $62,101

  2a. $274,656 − $132,109 $142,547   **2b.** $92,176 − $53,737 $38,439

  2c. $198,341 − $127,335 $71,006   **2d.** $452,867 − $227,186 $225,681

Math Skill Builder

The addition and subtraction of money amounts are used in the lesson.

Have students complete all exercises in Math Skill Builder 1–2 so that they are ready for the problems in the lesson.

■ Calculate Total Assets, Liabilities and Capital

A balance sheet is prepared at least once a year and shows a company's financial status on a specific day, usually the end of the month, quarter, or year.

Notice that the balance sheet shown on the next page is divided into three categories: assets, liabilities, and capital.

Assets are the things that are owned by a business that have value. Assets may be classified as current or long term. *Current assets* can be turned into cash or used within a year. Current assets include cash, accounts receivable, inventory, and supplies.

Accounts receivable are the accounts of customers who owe the business money for the merchandise that was sold to them on credit. Petrie's Gift Shop's current assets included cash, merchandise inventory, and store supplies.

Long-term assets are property, such as machinery, land, and buildings that have a useful life of more than 1 year. Petrie's Gift Shop's long-term asset is store equipment.

BUSINESS TIP
Long-term assets are also called *fixed assets.*

■ Teach Goal 1

Stress that assets and liabilities listed on the balance sheet are financial assets and liabilities. Point out that financial assets are items owned by a business that can be valued in monetary terms. Financial assets differ from social assets and physical assets, such as muscle strength.

Point out that a balance sheet is normally only accurate for one day in a period. Ordinarily, assets, liabilities, and capital change on a daily basis as a business completes buying, selling, and other activities.

Lesson 13.4 Preparing Balance Sheets ■ 571

COMMON ERRORS

Students incorrectly identify items as assets and liabilities. Discuss categorizing items to help students avoid these errors. For example, accounts receivable is an asset, accounts payable is a liability, and wages or salaries are an expense and not included in either category.

Stress that current assets and liabilities differ from long-term assets and liabilities by time. Ordinarily, one year is used as the criterion to differentiate between current and long-term assets and liabilities.

Read through the items on the balance sheet for Petrie's Gift shop and ask students to give examples of items that would be considered merchandise, store supplies, and store equipment for the gift shop. Make certain that students can differentiate between store supplies and merchandise inventory.

Point out to students that a bank loan may be either a current or a long-term liability depending on its term.

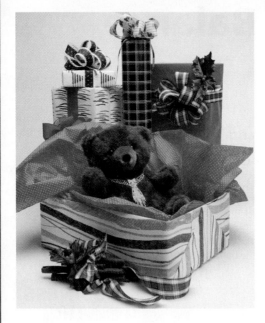

Petrie's Gift Shop
BALANCE SHEET
July 31, 20--

Assets

Cash	$16,300
Merchandise Inventory	196,920
Store Supplies	5,380
Store Equipment	24,500
Total Assets	$243,100

Liabilities

Accounts Payable	$51,560
Bank Loan	45,200
Total Liabilities	$96,760

Capital

Tom Petrie, Capital	146,340
Total Liabilities and Capital	$243,100

The total assets of a business are the sum of its current and long-term assets.

Total Assets = Current Assets + Long-Term Assets

Liabilities are the debts of a business. Businesses often get some of their assets by buying them on credit and promising to pay later. The persons to whom the money is owed are called the *creditors* of the business.

Like assets, liabilities may be *current* or *long term*. An example of a current liability is *accounts payable*. Accounts payable are the companies that sold Petrie merchandise on credit. An example of a long-term liability would be a 25-year mortgage on a building or a three-year bank loan.

Petrie's current liabilities were accounts payable. The store's long-term liability is the bank loan.

The total liabilities of a business are the sum of its current and long-term liabilities.

Total Liabilities = Current Liabilities + Long-Term Liabilities

The owner's share of the business is called capital. If all the assets of a business are owned free of debt, the owner's share of the business is equal to the total value of the assets. If there are liabilities, the value of the owner's share is found by subtracting the liabilities from the assets. Since Tom Petrie is the owner of the gift shop, the capital account is written in his name. The total capital of $146,340 is Petrie's claim against the assets of the business and is found this way:

Assets − Liabilities = Capital

> **BUSINESS TIP**
> Long-term liabilities are also called fixed liabilities.

> **BUSINESS TIP**
> Capital may also be called *owner's equity* or *proprietorship*.

572 ■ Chapter 13 Business Profit and Loss

CONNECTION TO ACCOUNTING

In this lesson, the only assets discussed are tangible assets, such as cash and equipment. But, there are also intangible assets on which a business may place a value. Students interested in the subject of accounting may wish to explore intangible assets. This would include how intangible assets are defined, common examples of intangible assets, and how some common intangible assets are valued. Students may use the Web, an accounting text, an accountant, or an accounting teacher as resources. Students should prepare a report of their findings.

EXAMPLE 1

Petrie's Gift Shop has assets worth $243,100. It also owes creditors $96,760. Find the capital or owner's equity of the business.

SOLUTION
Subtract the total liabilities from the total assets.

$243,100 − $96,760 = $146,340   capital for Petrie's Gift Shop

■ CHECK YOUR UNDERSTANDING

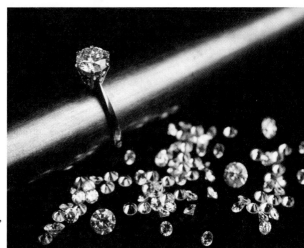

A. TriCity Jewelry Suppliers had these assets on April 30, 20—: Cash, $14,746.10; Accounts Receivable, $63,754.65; Merchandise Inventory, $537,562.50; Supplies, $8,196.00; Equipment, $39,163.00; building, $167,470.00. The company owed $310,799 in accounts payable and $75,000 to the Luzerne County Bank. What were the company's assets, liabilities, and capital? $830,892.25; $385,799; $445,093.25

B. On October 31, 20—, Tremont Brothers, Inc. had these assets: Cash, $5,850; Accounts Receivable, $14,750; Store Equipment, $7,430; Delivery Equipment, $32,540; Supplies, $1,150. The company owed $16,790 in accounts payable. The brothers also owed $7,500 to a local bank for a 4-year truck loan. What were Tremont's assets, liabilities, and capital? $61,720; $24,290; $37,430

Wrap Up

Tom needs to make sure that he makes his loan and bill payments on time to receive the confidence of banks. Tom may also have total liabilities that are getting close to or exceeding the total of his assets. Tom may need to pay off some of his current debt before he asks for another loan.

Algebra Connection

Create a formula that represents the arithmetic of the balance sheet. Include a statement that indicates what each variable represents.   A = L + C; A = Assets, L = Liabilities, C = Capital

■ Apply Goal 1

Do Example 1 at the board or on a transparency while students do the math at their desks.

Assign Check Your Understanding problems A and B for completion in class. Examine student work at their desks for errors or problems.

■ ONGOING ASSESSMENT
Make a transparency of the balance sheet for Petrie's Gift Shop, without the amounts for total assets, liabilities, or capital. Then call on students to describe the steps they must take to complete the balance sheet. Ask each student called on to describe only one step.

Wrap Up

Review the Start Up. Display the list of reasons that came out in the Start Up discussion. Ask students to compare their list with that in the Wrap Up. Discuss any differences.

Algebra Connection
Ask students how the formula might be varied if the format of the balance sheet were not followed (**A − L = C, A − C = L**).

■ CHECK YOUR UNDERSTANDING SOLUTIONS

A. $14,746.10 + $63,754.65 + $537,562.50 + $8,196 + $39,163 + $167,470 = $830,892.25 assets; $310,799 + $75,000 = $385,799 liabilities; $830,892.25 − $385,799 = $445,093.25 capital

B. $5,850 + $14,750 + $7,430 + $32,540 + $1,150 = $61,720 assets; $16,790 + $7,500 = $24,290 liabilities; $61,720 − $24,290 = $37,430 capital

EXERCISES

1. **Add:** $38,297 + $67,110 + $3,207 + $763 $109,377

2. **Subtract:** $257,383 − $131,105 $126,278

John Graber's business had these assets on December 31, 20—: Cash, $2,482; Accounts Receivable, $5,275; Merchandise Inventory, $87,650; Store Supplies, $3,732; Store Equipment, $22,647; Delivery Equipment, $21,582.

3. What were John's current assets? $99,139

4. What were John's long-term assets? $44,229

5. What were John's total assets? $143,368

A business owed the following creditors for merchandise and store supplies: Richard's Landing, Inc., $3,489; Tree-Top Supplies, $4,121; Denson Wholesale Distributors, $8,522; and Abner Products, $3,971. The business also owed Macon Bank $78,300 on a 30-year mortgage, and Crevor National Bank $12,670 on a 3-year loan for store equipment.

6. What were the business's current liabilities? $20,103

7. What were the business's long-term liabilities? $90,970

Tal Benrique owns a flower shop with these assets: Cash, $4,200; Merchandise, $103,400; Store Equipment, $15,600; Store Supplies, $1,860. He has accounts payable of $10,050 and a bank loan of $3,500.

8. What are Tal's total assets? $125,060

9. What are his total liabilities? $13,550

10. What is his capital? $111,510

Ama Rawini owns a tire store. She has these assets: Cash, $5,775; Merchandise, $63,000; Store Supplies, $780; Store Equipment, $13,800; Delivery Van, $12,600; Land and Building, $90,000. She owes the State Bank $12,900 and the Logan Manufacturing Company $35,700.

11. What are Ama's total current assets? $69,555

12. What are Ama's total assets? $185,955

13. What are Ama's total liabilities? $48,600

14. What is her capital? $137,355

Vicente Lopez has an art store with these assets: Cash, $3,500; Accounts Receivable, $4,600; Merchandise, $73,500; Store Equipment, $8,700; Land and Buildings, $125,500. His liabilities are accounts payable, $13,200 and Lassiter Bank, $89,400.

15. What are Vicente's assets $215,800

16. What are Vicente's liabilities $102,600

17. What is Vicente's capital? $113,200

574 ■ Chapter 13 Business Profit and Loss

SELECTED SOLUTIONS

3. $2,482 + $5,275 + $87,650 + $3,732 = $99,139

4. $22,647 + $21,582 = $44,229

5. $99,139 + $44,229 = $143,368

6. $3,489 + $4,121 + $8,522 + $3,971 = $20,103

7. $78,300 + $12,670 = $90,970

Kassie Burns owns a delivery company. She has 6 employees whose total annual wages are $114,000. On December 31 last year, her assets were: Cash, $3,620; Office Supplies, $2,185; Delivery Equipment, $32,950. On that date, she owed $6,358 in accounts payable and $14,280 to Valley Bank.

18. What were Kassie's current assets? $38,755

19. What were Kassie's current liabilities? $20,638

20. What was Kassie's capital? $18,117

21. On December 31, Anthony Fouts, a small engine repair shop owner, had these assets and liabilities. Complete his balance sheet by calculating his total assets, total liabilities, capital, and total liabilities and capital.

Downtown Engine Repair, Inc.
Balance Sheet, December 31, 20-

Cash	$ 2,834	Liabilities:	
Inventory	43,713	Accounts Payable	$ 7,530
Shop Supplies	2,570	Reston National Bank	12,780
Shop Equipment	28,800	Total Liabilities	$20,310
		Chieko Kimura, Capital	57,607
Total Assets	$77,917	Total Liabilities and Capital	$77,917

22. **CRITICAL THINKING** Look at the balance sheet for Petrie's Gift Shop. Suppose that every amount was the same except for the bank loan, which was changed to $200,000. How would Petrie's credit be affected? How would you show the new capital on the balance sheet? credit affected adversely; capital shown as negative amount

23. **CRITICAL THINKING** Why might a bank or other lender want to know a firm's current assets as well as the total assets? current assets can be used to make loan payments

MIXED REVIEW

24. 3.6×15 54

25. $260 \times 1\frac{3}{8}$ $357\frac{1}{2}$

26. $1,486.72 - $978.37 $508.35

27. 40×275 11,000

28. Estimate the product: 875×48 $45,000

29. What part of 360 is 90? $\frac{1}{4}$

30. Find the average, to the nearest tenth: 8, 9, 7, 8, 10, 7.   8.2

31. Luis Bartolemo wants to earn 12% annual net income on his $60,000 cash investment in a business property. His annual expenses of owning the property are $12,000. What monthly rent must Luis charge? $1,600, Lesson 7.8

32. The inflation index for 1996 was 156.9 and 160.5 for 1997. What was the rate of inflation for 1997, to the nearest tenth percent?   2.3%, Lesson 8.5

33. Towson Enterprises, Inc. decided to lease 20 notebook computer systems for 3 years for their technical staff. The monthly lease for each system was $62.88. What was the annual cost of leasing one notebook? All the notebooks? $754.56; $15,091.20, Lesson 9.1

34. The Clearview Window and Door Company increased its market share from 6% to 8% in one year's time. Clearview expects to gain another 3% next year. What is the company's sales goal next year if the window and door industry sales per year are $44 billion? $4.84 billion; Lesson 12.7

Lesson 13.4 Preparing Balance Sheets ■ **575**

Enrich

Assign Exercise 23, Critical Thinking, and discuss possible answers. The discussion should bring out that long-term assets might be difficult to convert to cash quickly to repay a bank loan.

Close

Assign Exercise 22, Critical Thinking, to review the steps to calculate assets, liabilities, and capital. Discuss the impact of the increase in the bank loan on Petrie's borrowing ability. Also, discuss at least three ways to show a negative value on a balance sheet (minus sign, red ink, parentheses).

■ **STUDENT PORTFOLIO**
Have students consider including the solutions to the following exercises in their portfolios: Exercises 3–5 and 11–14.

GOALS

- Calculate the current ratio
- Calculate the debt to equity ratio
- Calculate return on equity

Start Up

Patricia was thinking about starting her own business and was asked by a friend how much she expected to make on her investment in the business. She was not sure how to answer the question. What might Patricia use as a guide?

Math Skill Builder

Review these math skills and solve the exercises that follow.

① **Divide** money amounts and show as a decimal, to the nearest tenth. Find the quotient. $155,600 ÷ $85,400 = 1.82, or 1.8

   1a. $42,500 ÷ $102,840 0.4   **1b.** $5,308 ÷ $2,408 2.2

② **Divide** money amounts and show as a ratio, to the nearest tenth. Find the ratio. $450,000 ÷ $200,000 = 2.3:1

   2a. $65,750 ÷ $31,200 2.1:1   **2b.** $245,900 ÷ $120,400 2.0:1

③ **Divide** money amounts and show as a percent, to the nearest tenth. Find the quotient. $24,500 ÷ $130,000 = 18.8%

   3a. $84,560 ÷ $956,300 8.8%   **3b.** $45,870 ÷ $325,560 14.1%

■ Current Ratio

Like the income statement, items on the balance sheet can be compared to one another as ratios or percents. There are a number of ratios and percents that can be used: the current ratio, the debt-to-equity ratio, and return on equity.

The **current ratio** compares current assets to current liabilities. It is a means of testing whether the business has enough cash, or items that can be turned into cash quickly, to pay its short-term debts. The formula for finding the current ratio is:

$$\text{Current Ratio} = \frac{\text{Current Assets}}{\text{Current Liabilities}}$$

A current ratio of 2:1 means you have twice as many current assets as current liabilities. A current ratio of 2:1 or better is usually considered good. The ratio may be expressed as 2:1, or simply 2.

TEACHING STRATEGIES Cooperative Learning

Ask students to search the Web using the following key phrase: debt-to-equity ratio. Then have them examine any ten web sites that result from the search to see whether the sites use long-term or total liabilities to find the debt-to-equity ratio. They should keep a tally. When students have finished their search, call on them to provide the results of their tallies to find which method is used more frequently on the web pages they reviewed.

EXAMPLE 1

Petrie's Gift Shop has current assets of $218,600 and current liabilities of $51,560. What is the shop's current ratio?

SOLUTION
Divide the current assets by the current liabilities, to the nearest tenth.

$218,600 ÷ $51,560 = 4.2, or 4.2:1   current ratio

■ **CHECK YOUR UNDERSTANDING**

A. A wholesale firm has $289,130 in current liabilities and $428,410 in current assets. What is its current ratio, to the nearest tenth?   1.5:1

B. A camping equipment store has the following current assets: cash, $2,580; accounts receivable, $2,380; merchandise inventory, $87,450; store supplies, $4,730. It owes the following current liabilities: accounts payable, $35,260; 30-day promissory note to the bank, $4,500. What is the store's current ratio, to the nearest tenth?   2.4:1

■ **Apply Goal 1**

Do Example 1 at the board while students do the work at their desks.

Assign Check Your Understanding problems A and B to do in class. Check student work at their desks for problems.

■ **ONGOING ASSESSMENT**
With their textbooks closed, ask students to give you the formula for finding the current ratio. Then ask them to define the terms used in the numerator and denominator of the formula.

■ Debt to Equity Ratio

The **debt-to-equity ratio** is found by dividing the long-term liabilities of a firm by the firm's capital. The ratio helps measure the amount of financial risk a business faces. A debt-to-equity ratio shows the level of debt the firm is carrying. That allows others to determine if the level is appropriate for the business considering such factors as the level of debt similar firms are carrying and the overall condition of the economy at the time. A high debt-to-equity ratio, such as 1:1, may indicate that a firm's borrowing is excessive. The formula for the ratio is:

$$\text{Debt-To-Equity Ratio} = \frac{\text{Long-Term Liabilities}}{\text{Capital}}$$

Debt-to-equity ratio is often expressed as a percent. Thus, a debt-to-equity ratio of 1:1 would be shown as 100%. Whether a given debt-to-equity ratio is high or low depends on the industry within which the firm operates. In some industries, such as leasing and office technology, debt-to-equity ratios of 1:1 or higher are common. In others, ratios of 1:2, or 50% are more frequently found.

BUSINESS TIP
Some people use total liabilities rather than long-term liabilities to find debt-to-equity ratio.

■ **Teach Goal 2**

You may wish to point out that the use of long-term liabilities to find debt-to-equity ratio is well accepted. However, a search of the Web or a discussion with an accountant will disclose that many people use total liabilities instead.

The advantage of using long-term debt, and the reason it was selected for use in this book, is that it provides a measure of the long-term debt risk to the firm while the current ratio provides a measure of the short-term debt risk to the firm.

EXAMPLE 2

Petrie's Gift Shop has $45,200 in long-term debt in the form of a bank loan. Petrie's capital is $146,340. What is its debt-to-equity ratio, shown as a percentage, to the nearest tenth?

SOLUTION
Divide the long-term liabilities by the capital.

$45,200 ÷ $146,340 = 0.3089, or 30.9%   debt-to-equity ratio

■ **Apply Goal 2**

Do Example 2 at the board while students complete the math at their desks.

Assign Check Your Understanding problems C and D to do in class. Check student work for difficulties.

Lesson 13.5 Analyzing Balance Sheets ■ **577**

■ *CHECK YOUR UNDERSTANDING SOLUTIONS*

A. $428,410 ÷ $289,130 = 1.48, or 1.5:1

B. $2,580 + $2,380 + $87,450 + $4,730 = $97,140;
$35,260 + $4,500 = $39,760;
$97,140 ÷ $39,760 = 2.44, or 2.4:1

Teach Goal 3

Point out that calculating the return on equity allows a person to compare the return from a business investment to alternative investments.

Firms with more than one division, branch, or other subdivision may use the return on equity for each subdivision as one measure when deciding which subdivisions to drop or expand.

Apply Goal 3

Do Example 3 at the board while students complete the math at their desks.

Assign Check Your Understanding problems E and F to do in class. Check student work for difficulties.

■ CHECK YOUR UNDERSTADING

C. Johnson's Creamery has long-term debts of $356,890 and capital of $745,200. What is its debt-to-equity ratio, shown as a percent, to the nearest tenth? 47.9%

D. Kriege's Steel Products has a mortgage on its factory for $450,300 and a 3-year bank loan for $250,000. Its total capital is $1,205,500. What is its debt-to-equity ratio, shown as a percent, to the nearest tenth? 58.1%

■ Return on Equity

Some ratios use information from both the balance sheet and income statement. One such ratio, return on equity, compares net income, taken from the income statement, to capital, or owner's equity taken from the balance sheet. The ratio lets you know what you've earned on your investment in a business during a period. Return on equity is usually shown as a percent.

BUSINESS TIP

Return on equity is often called return on investment, ROI.

$$\text{Return on Equity} = \frac{\text{Net Income}}{\text{Capital, or Owner's Equity}}$$

You can compare the return on equity from a business to what the same money might have made in other investments during the same time period. For example, you can compare your return on equity with what a savings account, bond, stock, or money market fund would have paid you. If you are making less by owning and operating a business than you could make in less risky investments, such as savings accounts or bonds, you should question if continuing to operate the business is the best investment of your time and money.

However, new businesses may take some time before they begin to "pay off." Also, many businesses are seasonal. That is, they make much greater net incomes in some months than others. A gift shop, for example, may make much more net income during the Christmas season than they do in the summer months.

EXAMPLE 3

Petrie's Gift Shop had net income of $7,870 and capital of $146,340 on July 31, 20—. What was its return on equity, to the nearest tenth percent?

SOLUTION
Divide net income by capital.

$7,870 ÷ $146,340 = 0.054, or 5.4%   return on equity

■ CHECK YOUR UNDERSTADING

E. Gulliver Travel Agency had a net income of $67,280 on its December 31 income statement. The balance sheet on the same day showed capital of $121,500. What is its return on equity, to the nearest tenth percent? 55.4%

F. Driger Sales, Inc.'s income statement showed these amounts on December 31: net sales, $248,400; cost of goods sold, $145,650; and operating expenses of $65,800. Its balance sheet showed capital of $246,300. What was its return on equity, to the nearest tenth percent? 15.0%

578 ■ Chapter 13 Business Profit and Loss

■ CHECK YOUR UNDERSTANDING SOLUTIONS

C. $356,890 ÷ $745,200 = 0.4789, or 47.9%
D. $450,300 + $250,000 = $700,300;
$700,300 ÷ $1,205,500 = 0.5809, or 58.1%

E. $67,280 ÷ $121,500 = 0.5537, or 55.4%
F. $248,400 − $145,650 = $102,750;
$102,750 − $65,800 = $36,950;
$36,950 ÷ $246,300 = 0.1500, or 15.0%

There are many ways to evaluate what a person makes on an investment, including an investment in one's own business. One guideline is to compare the return from the business to the return on other investments that could be made. Starting a business is risky. Many new businesses fail. Patricia could lose all the money she put into it. So, she should expect a return that is greater than less riskier investments, such as savings accounts, CDs, or money market funds.

WORKPLACE WINDOW

Research the job title, "investment analyst." What does an investment analyst do? What types of businesses employ investment analysts? What education is required of an investment analyst?

Do you think you would like to be an investment analyst? Why or why not? Use the web, library sources, or visit a stockbroker or the trust office of a bank to find answers to these questions. Write a brief report that includes the answers to each question.

EXERCISES

1. **Add**: $67,308 + $10,845 + $93,070 + $23,189 $194,412

2. **Divide**: $45,688 by $23,418 and show as a decimal, to the nearest tenth.   2.0

3. **Divide**: $58,320 by $28,590 and show as a ratio, to the nearest tenth.   2.0:1

4. **Divide**: $194,335 by $352,187 and show as a percent, to the nearest tenth.   55.2%

5. The balance sheet of Corida Manufacturing, Inc. shows $1,168,560 in current liabilities and $2,486,150 in current assets. What is its current ratio, to the nearest tenth?   2.1:1

6. A golf equipment store has the following current assets: cash, $1,958; accounts receivable, $1,080; merchandise inventory, $27,560; store supplies, $1,350. It owes these current liabilities: accounts payable, $15,890 and a 90-day promissory note for $2,400. What is the store's current ratio, to the nearest tenth?   1.7:1

7. Tane's Nursery has long-term debts of $136,910 and capital of $241,020. What is its debt-to-equity ratio, shown as a percent, to the nearest tenth?   56.8%

8. Nieves Foundries has a mortgage on its factory for $845,400 and a 3-year bank loan for $1,500,000. Its total capital is $2,278,150. What is its debt-to-equity ratio, shown as a percent, to the nearest tenth?   103%

Vitaleze Markets' income statement showed these amounts at the end of a year: net sales, $324,700; cost of goods sold, $214,530; and operating expenses of $98,400. Its balance sheet showed capital of $362,800.

9. What was its return on equity, to the nearest tenth percent?   3.2%

10. Vitaleze's owner can earn 2.5% in a one-year CD. Is this more or less than the business's return on equity for the year? How much more or less?   less; 0.7%

Lesson 13.5 Analyzing Balance Sheets ■ 579

Wrap Up

Review the Start Up. Point out that evaluating an investment return usually includes at least two factors: what you can get in alternative investments and how risky your investment is compared to the alternatives. In general, the greater the risk, the higher return you should expect.

WORKPLACE WINDOW

Select one or more students to report on their findings to the rest of the class. Discuss the duties, education requirements, and business locations of investment analysts.

Assign

Assignment: Exercises 1–26. Start with the basic arithmetic problems at the beginning of the exercises to be sure that students understand the underlying arithmetic in the remaining exercises.

Assess

Select students to place their answers to exercises on the board. Have the class compare their answers with those on the board. Discuss board answers that are incorrect or lack complete labels.

SELECTED SOLUTIONS

6. $1,958 + $1,080 + $27,560 + $1,350 = $31,948;
$15,890 + $2,400 = $18,290;
$31,948 ÷ $18,290 = 1.74, or 1.7:1

8. $845,400 + $1,500,000 = $2,345,400;
$2,345,400 ÷ $2,278,150 = 1.0295, or 103%

9. $324,700 − $214,530 = $110,170;
$110,170 − $98,400 = $11,770;
$11,700 ÷ $362,800 = 0.0324, or 3.2%

10. 3.2% − 2.5% = 0.7% less

STUDENT WORKBOOK If students need help with finding the current ratio, do Exercise 1 with them. Then have them complete Exercises 2 and 3.

If students need help with finding the debt-to-equity ratio, do Exercise 4 with them. Then have them complete Exercise 5.

If students need help with finding the return on equity, do Exercise 6 with them. Then have them complete Exercise 7.

With their textbooks closed, ask students to define or explain the bolded terms presented in the lesson. Also ask them to recall and explain the formulas for current ratio, debt-to-equity ratio, and return on equity.

■ **STUDENT PORTFOLIO**
Consider having students place their Workplace Window results in their portfolios.

11. Fiddler Toy Store had a net income of $176,780 on its December 31 monthly income statement. The balance sheet on the same day showed capital of $712,800. What is its return on equity, to the nearest tenth percent? 24.8%

12. **CRITICAL THINKING** A business earns a net income of $345,288 on owner's equity of $3,785,240. What is its return on equity, to the nearest tenth percent? Is this return a good one for the owner? Justify your answer. 9.12%, depends on return of alternate investments

INTEGRATING YOUR KNOWLEDGE During one month, a firm had net sales of $1,358,000, cost of goods sold of $831,070, and operating expenses that were 30% of net sales. The firm's balance sheet showed total assets of $4,568,000 and total liabilities of $3,000,300.

13. What was the firm's gross profit margin, to the nearest whole percent? 39%

14. What was the firm's return on equity, to the nearest whole percent? 8%

MIXED REVIEW

15. $\frac{3}{4} + \frac{4}{5}$ $1\frac{11}{20}$

16. $49.08 - 23.4$ 25.68

17. $400.7 \div 1,000$ 0.4007

18. 56.08×0.003 0.16824

19. Estimate the product of 432.10×328. $120,000

20. $120 is 60% of what amount? $200

21. Ted Wallach earns $12.50 an hour. His employer gives him a COLA based on the 2.8% the CPI rose last year. What will be his new hourly pay rate? $12.85, Lesson 10.2

22. Trish Rothstein drove her car 2,356 miles in October, 22.5% of which were for her job as a salesperson for a firm. The firm reimbursed Trish $0.35 a mile for business use. What did Trish receive as reimbursement for the use of her car in October? $185.54, Lesson 11.6

23. The sales of a product were $11,268,000 last year. Sales are projected to be $1\frac{1}{2}$ times greater this year. What is the forecast for this year's sales? $16,902,000, Lesson 12.6

24. Reece and Nitobe share partnership net income in proportion to their investments. Reece invested $351,000 and Nitobe $429,000 in the partnership. What is each partner's share of a net income of $160,000, to the nearest cent? $72,000; $88,000, Lesson 13.3

25. Ricki Berra worked 12 hours at time-and-a-half pay last week. Her regular-time pay rate was $10.90 an hour. What was Ricki's total overtime pay for the week? $196.20, Lesson 1.3

26. A company bought 150 plastic chairs at $12.80, 240 plastic chairs at $12.40, and 320 plastic chairs at $13.50. What was the average price paid per chair, to the nearest cent? $12.98, Lesson 8.1

SELECTED SOLUTIONS

11. $176,780 ÷ $712,800 = 0.2480, or 24.8%
13. $1,358,000 − $831,070 = $526,930;
    $526,930 ÷ $1,358,000 = 0.388, or 39%

14. $1,358,000 × 0.30 = $407,400;
    $526,930 − $407,400 = $119,530;
    $4,568,000 − $3,000,300 = $1,567,700;
    $119,530 ÷ $1,567,700 = 0.076, or 8%

13.6 Bankruptcy

GOAL

■ Calculate the percent and amount of bankruptcy claims

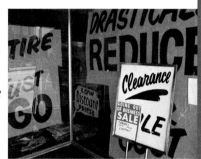

Math Skill Builder

Review these math skills and solve the exercises that follow.

1 **Subtract** money amounts.
Find the difference. $154,780 − $85,259 = $69,521

1a. $256,733 − $192,076 $64,657
1b. $34,199 − $18,228 $15,971

2 **Multiply** money amounts by percents.
Find the product. $3,540 × 41% = $3,540 × 0.41 = $1,451.40
Find the product. 100¢ × 35% = 100¢ × 0.35 = 35¢

2a. $52,368 × 23.5%
$12,306.48
2b. $1,809 × 15.9%
$287.63
2c. 100¢ × 12.5%
12.5¢

3 **Divide** money amounts to get a percent.
Find the percent, to the nearest tenth. $134,500 ÷ $245,600 = 0.5476, or 54.8%

3a. $456,200 ÷ $1,500,200   30.4%
3b. $39,980 ÷ $86,630   46.2%

■ Bankruptcy Claims

When a business keeps operating at a loss, the amounts it owes may become more than its assets are worth. When this happens, the business becomes *insolvent* and a court may declare it **bankrupt**. The court then appoints a trustee or receiver to sell all the assets and pay the debts.

After selling the assets, the trustee must pay the legal costs of the bankruptcy, any other claims that the law says must be paid first, and *secured creditors*, such as banks that hold a mortgage. Then the money that is left is paid to all other creditors in proportion to their claims. The percent to be paid to each creditor is found by dividing the total cash available for the creditors by the total of all creditors' claims.

> **BUSINESS TIP**
>
> People, as well as businesses, can declare bankruptcy. States usually have personal bankruptcy laws to cover this situation.

$$\text{Claim Percent Paid} = \frac{\text{Cash Available for Creditors}}{\text{Total Creditors' Claims}}$$

Lesson 13.6 Bankruptcy ■ 581

CONNECTION TO CONSUMER ECONOMICS

Have students use the Web to find alternatives to declaring personal bankruptcy. For example, persons can work out their debts by making arrangements with creditors to extend the debts. They can also use the assistance of non-profit credit counselors. Financial counseling is offered by some banks, credit unions, universities, housing authorities, military bases, and other organizations. Students should list the alternatives they found and the organizations they found that can help those in debt.

Wrap Up

Review the Start Up. Students should understand that there are very unpleasant effects of bankruptcy for both businesses and persons who declare it.

COMMUNICATION

Call on selected students to read their answers to questions 1–5 in the activity. Each student should read the answer to only one question. Discuss the answers and have students with different answers share them with the class.

Assign

Assignment: Exercises 1–21, 23–27. Start with the basic arithmetic problems at the beginning of the exercises to be sure that students understand the underlying arithmetic in the exercises.

Inform students to round off claim percents to the nearest whole percent.

EXAMPLE 1

The court declared a landscaping firm bankrupt. The trustee sold the firm's assets for $23,000. Legal costs of bankruptcy and other claims the court required to be paid first totaled $8,000. Creditors' claims totaled $37,500. What percent of the creditors' claims can the trustee pay? How many cents on the dollar will creditors get on their claims? How much will a creditor get who has a claim of $3,200?

SOLUTION

Subtract the legal costs and claims that must be paid first from the proceeds of the sale of the firm's assets.

$23,000 − $8,000 = $15,000   amount available to creditors

Divide the amount available to creditors by the total of the creditors' claims.

$15,000 ÷ $37,500 = 0.40, or 40%   percent paid on each claim

Multiply 100 cents by the percent paid on each claim.

100¢ × 0.4 = 40¢   cents on the dollar creditors will get

Multiply the creditor's claim by the percent paid on each claim.

$3,200 × 0.4 = $1,280   amount creditor will get

■ CHECK YOUR UNDERSTANDING

A. A store is declared bankrupt. Creditors' claims total $420,000. After the assets are sold and bankruptcy costs are paid, $150,800 is left for creditors' claims. What percent of their claims will the creditors get?   36%

B. Fairmount, Inc. was declared bankrupt, and its assets sold for $261,900. Legal costs of bankruptcy and other claims that must be paid first totaled $71,600. The total of creditors' claims was $420,000. Tricol, Inc. had a claim for $2,700. How many cents on the dollar will creditors get? How much will Tricol get?   45¢; $1,215

Wrap Up

When a firm goes bankrupt, creditors take the firm's assets, the bankrupt person's credit rating is impaired, and the owners may be held criminally liable if fraud was intended.

COMMUNICATION

Research the personal bankruptcy laws in your state to answer these questions. Write your answers in complete sentences.

1. Under what conditions is a person allowed to declare bankruptcy?
2. What kinds of creditors might have secured claims on the assets of the bankrupt person?
3. Who would be notified about a personal bankruptcy?
4. What property, if any, is a bankrupt person allowed to keep?
5. What are the disadvantages to a person who declares bankruptcy?

582 ■ Chapter 13 Business Profit and Loss

■ *CHECK YOUR UNDERSTANDING SOLUTIONS*

A. $150,800 ÷ $420,000 = 0.359, or 36%

B. $261,900 − $71,600 = $190,300;
$190,300 ÷ $420,000 = 0.453, or 45%;
100¢ × 0.45 = 45¢; $2,700 × 0.45 = $1,215

EXERCISES

1. $158,929 − $45,216
$113,713

2. $187,225 × 19.4%
$36,321.65

3. 100¢ × 28%
28¢

4. Divide $87,380 by $422,500, to the nearest tenth percent.   20.7%

Find what percent of the creditors' claims the trustee can pay.

		Total Creditors' Claims	Cash Available for Creditors
40%	**5.**	$ 68,000	$ 27,200
30%	**6.**	37,200	11,160
35%	**7.**	146,700	51,345
65%	**8.**	288,000	187,200

Find how many cents on the dollar can be paid to the creditors.

	Total Creditors' Claims	Cash Available for Creditors	
9.	$ 83,600	$53,504	64¢
10.	71,760	25,116	35¢
11.	196,000	82,320	42¢
12.	54,300	8,688	16¢

13. A shoe discount store is declared bankrupt. Creditors' claims total $230,000. After the assets are sold and bankruptcy costs are paid, $85,100 is left for creditors' claims. What percent of their claims will the creditors get?   37%

14. A bankrupt wholesaler has debts totaling $124,250. The cash available for the creditors is $57,155. How many cents on the dollar will creditors get?   46¢

The trustee for a bankrupt home builder paid off the builder's debts at the rate of 42¢ on the dollar. A creditor filed a claim with the trustee for $48,958.

15. What estimated amount will the creditor get? $20,000

16. What actual amount will the creditor get? $20,562.36

17. The creditors of a bankrupt manufacturer are paid at the rate of 16.3¢ on the dollar. There are 40 creditors with total claims of $94,557. How much will a creditor get on a claim of $2,560? $417.28

Trail Bikes, Inc. was declared bankrupt, and its assets were sold for $174,600. Legal costs of bankruptcy and claims that must be paid first totaled $47,625. The total of creditors' claims was $370,000. Klesko, Inc. had a claim for $750. Torrant Corporation had a claim for $23,000.

18. How much money was available for all creditors? $126,975

19. What percent of each creditor's claim was paid?   34%

20. How much did the Klesko get? $255

21. How much did Torrant get? $7,820

22. CRITICAL THINKING   Can you think of reasons why personal bankruptcy has increased in the last few years?   easy credit from credit card companies; economic

MIXED REVIEW

23. What part of $1,500 is $75? $\frac{1}{20}$

24. Find 3.7% of $43,930. $1,625.41

25. Estimate 4.87 × 30.68.   150

26. Estimate $9,215 ÷ 18.9. $500

27. The monthly charge for leasing a small luxury car is $379. For all miles driven over 10,000 miles in 1 year, a 20¢ per mile charge is made. What is the yearly cost of leasing the car if it is driven 21,000 miles in a year? $6,748, Lesson 6.8

Lesson 13.6 Bankruptcy ▪ **583**

SELECTED SOLUTIONS

5. $27,200 ÷ $68,000 = 0.40, or 40%

9. $53,504 ÷ $83,600 = 0.64, or 64%;
100¢ × 0.64 = 64¢

18. $174,600 − $47,625 = $126,975

19. $126,975 ÷ $370,000 = 0.343, or 34%

20. $750 × 0.34 = $255

21. $23,000 × 0.34 = $7,820

- Subtract sales returns and allowances from sales to find net sales.

- Add purchases to beginning inventory to find goods available for sale.

- Subtract ending inventory from goods available for sale to find cost of goods sold.

- Subtract cost of goods sold from net sales to find gross profit.

- Subtract operating expenses from gross profit to find net income.

- Subtract gross profit from operating expenses to find net loss.

Lesson 13.2 Analyzing Income Statements

- Divide any item on the income statement by net sales to find its percent of net sales.

- Divide gross profit and net income by net sales to find gross profit margin and net profit margin.

- Divide cost of goods sold by average merchandise inventory for period to find merchandise turnover rate.

Lesson 13.3 Partnership Income

- Multiply net income by each partner's investment divided by total partner investment to find each partner's share of net income.

- Multiply net income by each partner's share divided by total partner shares to find each partner's share of net income.

- Multiply net income by each partner's percentage to find each partner's share of net income.

- Multiply each interest rate by each partner's investment to find interest on partnership investment.

- Add each partner's interest on investment and subtract the sum from net income to find amount remaining.

584

Chapter Review

Vocabulary Review

assets	debt-to-equity ratio	net loss
balance sheet	gross profit	net profit margin
bankrupt	gross profit margin	net income
capital	income statement	partnership
cost of goods sold	liabilities	return on equity
current ratio	merchandise turnover rate	

Fill in the blanks with one of the terms above.

1. A report that shows how much money has been earned and spent during a period of time is called (a, an) __?__. income statement

2. Expenses directly related to producing or buying the goods sold are called __?__.
   cost of goods sold

3. Total operating costs are deducted from gross profit to determine a company's __?__.
   net income

4. The percentage that gross profit is of net sales is called the __?__. gross profit margin

5. The number of times per period that a store replaces its average stock of merchandise is called the __?__. merchandise turnover rate

6. Things that are owned by a business that have value are called __?__. assets

7. The owner's share of the business is called __?__. capital

8. The __?__ compares current assets to current liabilities. current ratio

9. A comparison of net income to capital is called __?__. return on equity

10. When a business becomes *insolvent* a court may declare it __?__. bankrupt

LESSON 13.1

11. A small business's sales for the year were $56,980. Sales returns and allowances for the same year were $1,308. What were the net sales for the year? $55,672

12. Tom's TV Lot had an inventory of merchandise costing $96,300 in April. During April, goods costing $147,200 were bought. Merchandise inventory at the end of April was $88,500. What was the cost of goods sold for April? $155,000

13. Lee's Interiors had net sales for the year of $459,840. The cost of the goods sold for the same period was $268,700. What was Lee's gross profit for the year? $191,140

14. The Furniture Factory had a gross profit of $368,220 and operating expenses of $293,100 in October. What was its net income? $75,120

LESSON 13.2

15. Eddars Bottled Gas Company had net sales of $592,300 and cost of goods sold of $332,450 this year. What is Eddars' gross profit margin, to the nearest tenth percent?
    43.9%

16. The Bookshelf had net sales of $287,900 and net income of $38,220 last year. What was its net profit margin, to the nearest tenth percent? 13.3%

TEACHING STRATEGIES Chapter Review

For students who complete the Chapter Review early, ask them to write "fill in the blank" questions for those vocabulary terms not used in the Vocabulary Review. On page 584, the unused vocabulary words are: balance sheet, debt-to-equity ratio, gross profit, liabilities, net loss, net profit margin, and partnership. After completing the statements, have the students swap papers and answer each other's questions.

17. Central Marts had a beginning inventory on Jan. 1 of $1,668,450. The ending inventory on Dec. 31 was $1,655,490. The Mart's cost of goods sold for the year was $9,945,160. What was its merchandise inventory turnover rate, to the nearest tenth?   6.0

LESSON 13.3

18. Byrd and Tyne invest $200,000 and $400,000, respectively, in a partnership. They agree to share net income in proportion to their investments. The partnership's net income for the year is $82,000. Find each partner's share of the net income. $27,333.33; $54,666.67

19. The partners Merk and Guterrez agree to divide net income of $270,000 in the ratio of 4 to 5. What is each partner's share? $120,000; $150,000

20. The partners Rich and Matsui agree to share their net income of $350,000 by 45% and 55%, respectively. What is each partner's share? $157,500; $192,500

21. Bril and Sosa are partners with investments of $150,000 and $300,000, respectively. The partners receive 12% annually on their investments. The rest of the net income is divided equally. What is each partner's total share of a net income of $89,000? $35,500; $53,500

LESSON 13.4

22. Bevo Discount Mart had these assets on June 30, 20—: Cash, $28,574.10; Accounts Receivable, $123,574.85; Merchandise Inventory, $1,257,612.80; Supplies, $17,936.00; Equipment, $79,637.00; and building, $362,670.00. The company owed $631,939 in accounts payable and $150,000 to the Maritime Bank. What were the company's assets, liabilities, and capital? $1,870,004.75; $781,939; $1,088,065.75

LESSON 13.5

23. A store has current assets of $428,800 and current liabilities of $115,760. What is the store's current ratio?   3.7:1

24. Watkin Manufacturing has long-term debts of $813,900 and capital of $1,425,800. What is its debt-to-equity ratio, shown as a percent, to the nearest tenth?   57.1%

25. A business had net income of $127,820 on its December 31 income statement. The balance sheet on the same day showed capital of $241,600. What is its return on equity, to the nearest tenth percent?   52.9%

LESSON 13.6

26. A wholesaler was declared bankrupt, and its assets sold for $252,600. Legal costs of bankruptcy and other preferred claims totaled $71,600. The total of creditors' claims was $420,000. What percent, to the nearest tenth, of their claims will the creditors get?   43.1%

27. A business is declared bankrupt. Creditors' claims total $240,000. After the assets are sold and bankruptcy costs are paid, $100,320 is left for creditors' claims. Dunne, Inc. had a claim for $4,800. How much will Dunne get? $2,006.40

28. The cash available for creditors from a bankruptcy is $340,000. The total claims of creditors are $720,000. How many cents on the dollar will creditors receive?   47¢

Chapter 13 Review ▪ 585

- Divide amount remaining by number of partners to find each partner's share of amount remaining

Lesson 13.4 Preparing Balance Sheets
- Add current assets to find total current assets. Add long-term assets to find total long-term assets.
- Add total current assets to total long-term assets to find total assets.
- Add current liabilities to find total current liabilities. Add long-term liabilities to find total long-term liabilities.
- Add total current liabilities to total long-term liabilities to find total liabilities.
- Subtract total liabilities from total assets to find capital.

Lesson 13.5 Analyzing Balance Sheets
- Divide total current assets by total current liabilities to find current ratio.
- Divide total long-term liabilities by capital to find debt-to-equity ratio.
- Divide net income by capital to find return on equity.

Lesson 13.6 Bankruptcy
- Subtract cost of bankruptcy and costs of other legal claims from cash received from sale of assets to find cash available for creditors.
- Divide cash available for creditors by total claims to find claim percentage.
- Multiply claims percentage by 100¢ to find cents on the dollar to be paid to creditors.
- Multiply amount owed to each creditor by claims percentage to find amounts to be paid each creditor.

TEACHING STRATEGIES Chapter Review

If students fail to solve a lesson review problem or label the solution correctly, ask them to compare their work to the appropriate example in the lesson. Then, they should redo the review problem correctly.

Task 1 Students enter data into a balance sheet analyzer template.

Task 2 Students enter new data from the income statement and balance sheet of Petrie's Gift Shop found in Chapter 13. They then answer questions about the results of the data entered.

Task 3 Students design and create a spreadsheet that calculates the major items on an income statement and the percent each income statement item is of net sales.

Task 4 Students answer questions about the formulas they used and the format of their spreadsheets.

Technology Workshop

Task 1: Enter Data In A Balance Sheet Analyzer Template

Complete a template that calculates the current ratio, debt-to-equity ratio, and return on capital.

Open the spreadsheet for Chapter 13 (tech13-1.xls) and enter these amounts in the blue cells from the Wehling Wholesale Company: current assets, $250,000; current liabilities, $95,000; long-term liabilities, $100,000; capital, $455,000; net income, $75,000; and capital, $455,000 again. Your computer screen should look like the one shown below when you are done.

	A	B	C
1	**Balance Sheet Analyzer**		
2			
3	**Current Ratio**		
4	Current Assets	250,000.00	
5	Current Liabilities	95,000.00	
6	Ratio	2.6	:1
7			
8	**Debt-to-Equity Ratio**		
9	Long-term Liabilities	100,000.00	
10	Capital	455,000.00	
11	Debt-to-Equity Ratio	1:	4.6
12			
13	**Return on Equity**		
14	Net Income	75,000.00	
15	Capital	455,000.00	
16	Return on Equity	16.5%	

Notice that the spreadsheet does not automatically calculate capital from the asset and liability data entered. This feature lets you use the spreadsheet to find the debt-to-equity ratio for one company and the return on equity for another at the same time.

Task 2: Analyze The Spreadsheet Output

Calculate or find the amounts needed to fill the blue cells using the data from the income statement and balance sheet for Petrie's Gift Shop shown in Lessons 13-1 and 13-4. Make sure that you show Petrie's bank loan of $45,200 as a long-term liability.

Answer the following questions.

1. What is Petrie's current ratio?   4.2:1

2. What is Petrie's debt-to-equity ratio?   1:3.2

3. What is Petrie's return on equity?   5.4%

4. What spreadsheet function is being used in cell B6?   IF

5. What math is being used in cell B16?   division of amount in cell B14 by amount in cell B15

TEACHING STRATEGIES Task 2

As an extra-credit assignment, have some students add to the balance sheet analyzer template a section for merchandise turnover rate. Students must unprotect the cells in the template first. The added section should let a person enter at least three values for merchandise inventory and calculate the average. It should also let a person enter the cost of goods sold and compute merchandise turnover. Have one or more of the students demonstrate the use of the spreadsheet to the class.

Task 3: Design an Income Statement Analyzer Spreadsheet

Design a spreadsheet that will calculate the major items on an income statement and also calculate the percent each item on the income statement is of net sales.

Use the income statement for Petrie's Gift Shop to provide you with the headings, item labels, and amounts. Use one column for the item labels, one column for the amounts, and one column for the percentages.

Petrie's Gift Shop
Income Statement
For month ended July 31, 20—

	Amounts	Percent
Revenue		
Sales	75,952	102.6%
Less sales returns and allowances	1,900	2.6%
Net sales	74,052	100.0%
Cost of goods sold		
Beginning inventory, July 1	211,638	285.8%
Purchases	31,548	42.6%
Goods available for sale	243,186	328.4%
Ending inventory, July 31	196,920	265.9%
Cost of goods sold	46,266	62.5%
Gross profit on sales	27,786	37.5%
Operating expenses		
Salaries and wages	10,567	14.3%
Rent	3,194	4.3%
Taxes	1,864	2.5%
Utilities	1,678	2.3%
Advertising	780	1.1%
Depreciation of equipment	726	1.0%
Insurance	253	0.3%
Other expenses	854	1.2%
Total operating expenses	19,916	26.9%
Net income	7,870	10.6%

Task 4: Analyze the Spreadsheet Output

Answer these questions about your completed spreadsheet:

6. How did you calculate cost of goods sold? subtracted ending inventory from goods available for sale

7. How did you display percentages that had multiple decimal places? answers will vary, but students should display only 1 decimal place because accuracy beyond that is not needed for analysis

8. How did you display percentages in general? answers will vary, but students should use the spreadsheet's percentage formatting feature

9. What sections of the spreadsheet would have to change if you used it to display Cepeda Manufacturing's income statement from Lesson 13-1? cost of goods sold, operating expenses

Chapter 13 Technology Workshop ■ **587**

Teach and Apply Task 1

Point out that users have to enter data from both the income statement and balance sheet of a firm to complete all formulas shown in the spreadsheet.

Teach and Apply Task 2

Assign questions 1–5.

Display the formulas used in cells B6, C11, and B16. Discuss the formulas with students.

Teach and Apply Task 3

Stress that students should use net sales to find the percents for each item on the income statement. Point out that the percent for net sales is 100%.

Teach and Apply Task 4

Assign questions 6–9.

Each student should submit a disk with the completed spreadsheet, or a printout of the spreadsheet and its formulas.

TEACHING STRATEGIES Task 3

Provide students with copies of the sample template for Task 3, tech13-3.xls. Unprotect the cells in the template before making the copies and rename the file. Then have students redesign the template so that it can handle the data for Cepeda Manufacturing's income statement from Lesson 13-1. Have one or more of the students demonstrate the use of the revised spreadsheet to the class, pointing out the formulas and functions used in key cells.

Assess

■ **HOW TIMES HAVE CHANGED**
1. $1,600,000 \times 0.2 = 32,000$
   about 32,000

2. $\$64,540 \div \$987,400 \approx 0.065$
   or 6.5%

■ **WRITE**
Have one or more students present the companies they chose and the reasons for the choice. As students respond, write the financial reasons on the board. Discuss the financial reasons listed with the class. Ask the class to identify possible sources for the financial information listed.

■ **SCANS**
Help students by discussing with the class possible conflicts that might arise in a work environment, such as conflicts resulting from difference in work quality amongst team members and slowness or inability to keep up with the team.

■ **ONGOING ASSESSMENT**
The Integrated Project found in the workbook provides a broad, ongoing assessment activity for the goals of this chapter.

How Times Have Changed

For Questions 1–2, refer to the timeline on page 555 as needed.
1. Of the approximately 1.6 million bankruptcies filed in 2003, about 98% of them were filed by individuals, not businesses. How many bankruptcies were filed by businesses in 2003?
2. A company had a net income of $64,540 and capital of $987,400 on July 31, 1972. What was its return on equity, to the nearest tenth percent?

WRITE

Choose a company and determine why you would want to work there. Include reasons that relate to the financial status of the company. You may locate a company through want ads, business publications, or the Internet. Whichever company you choose, be sure that you can locate financial information about the company to support your reasons.

SCANS

Workplace Skills—*Participates as a Member of a Team*

Having the ability to collaborate with coworkers to form a goal-oriented team to solve problems is a skill and a quality in demand by employers, especially for today's diverse workplace. Being able to resolve conflicts within a group is another ability that employers also seek in potential employees.

Test Your Skills Describe a situation in a workplace that may result in conflict that will have to be resolved among team members, not by managers.

Make a Plan Write a summary of how the conflict could escalate to the point of creating a disturbance in the workplace. Follow the summary with a plan for resolving the conflict that involves all members of the team.

Summarize Have a working adult review your description of the situation, your summary of how the conflict could progress, and your plan for resolution. Ask for comments about the likelihood of the situation actually occurring and your plan being put to use.

Be sure to get comments from the adult reviewer about which of the following thinking skills and personal qualities you need to resolve the conflict.

decision making   *problem solving*   *reasoning*   *creative thinking*
self-control   *responsibility*   *integrity/honesty* *social skills*

PORTFOLIO ASSESSMENT

Ask students to review the materials that they have created in this chapter and select those they wish to place in their portfolios. Remind them to review work completed for the communication, workplace window, team meeting, and algebra connection projects included in the chapter.

Chapter Test

Answer each question.

1. 3,856 ÷ 1,000   3.856

2. $\frac{2}{3}$ × $20,000 to the nearest cent $13,333.33

3. $299 is what percent of $4,600?   6.5%

4. 52 × $77.78 $4,044.56

5. 250% × $98 $245

6. 75% × $3,200 $2,400

7. $21,524 − $16,800 $4,724

8. 2,080 × $0.29 $603.20

9. $172 + $329 + $136 + $473 $1,110

10. 2.62 × $562 $1,472.44

Applications

Kline Products had a beginning inventory of $635,500 on January 1. During the quarter, goods costing $2,245,600 were manufactured. The inventory at the end of March was $785,400. During the quarter, Kline's net sales were $3,265,800.

11. What was the cost of goods sold for the quarter? $2,095,700

12. What was the gross profit? $1,170,100

13. A discount store took three inventories of merchandise during a quarter: $176,000, $178,820, and $246,600. The cost of merchandise sold during the 3-month period was $1,360,200. What was the merchandise turnover rate, to the nearest tenth?   6.8

14. A firm had net sales of $280,000. The cost of goods sold was $168,000. What was the gross profit margin?   40%

15. Miskai invest $425,000 and Donald $260,000 in a partnership. Net income is divided in proportion to their investment. Their net loss for the first year is $38,600. What is each partner's share of the loss? $23,948.90; $14,651.09

16. The partners Herrera and Rothenberg share net income at 40% and 60%, respectively. Their net income last year was $248,500. Find each partner's total share of the net income. $99,400; $149,100

17. A small store has assets worth $124,800. It also owes creditors $65,860. Find the capital of the business. $58,940

18. Jamask, Inc. has $589,300 in current liabilities and $856,410 in current assets. What is its current ratio, to the nearest tenth?   1.5:1

19. Billows Stores had net income of $158,060 and capital of $1,863,450 on October 31, 20—. What was its return on equity for October, to the nearest tenth percent?   8.5%

20. A firm is declared bankrupt. Creditors' claims total $443,000. After the assets are sold and bankruptcy costs are paid, $178,529 is left for creditors' claims. How much will a creditor with a claim of $14,500 get? $5,843.50

Chapter 13 Assessment ■ **589**

Chapter-Test Correlation

Question	Lesson
11	13.1
12	13.1
13	13.2
14	13.2
15	13.3
16	13.3
17	13.4
18	13.5
19	13.5
20	13.6

Test Taking Strategies

■ **BASIC ARITHMETIC**
To solve question 1, the fast way to divide by 1,000 is to move the decimal place in the amount divided three places to the left.

To solve question 6, it might be easier to take $\frac{3}{4}$ of $3,200 mentally than multiply by 75%.

■ **APPLICATION PROBLEMS**
Students can estimate the answer to problem 13 by rounding the inventories to $200,000 each and cost of goods sold to $1,400,000. The estimated turnover rate is 7.

If students use a calculator to solve application problems 11 and 12, they should leave the cost of goods sold amount in the calculator after recording it. Then they should subtract the net sales from the amount to get gross profit. The amount shown will be negative, but students can either ignore the sign or change it by pressing the +/− key.

TEACHING STRATEGIES Chapter Test

Make sure that students label their solutions completely and correctly. For those that don't, ask them to resubmit test papers that have been graded and returned with the correct solutions. Point them to the example problems in the lessons for help. You may wish to provide extra points for resubmitted papers that are labeled correctly.

Chapter Overview

Chapter 14 reviews the math skills of addition, subtraction, division, multiplication, percents, fractions, rounding, and conversion of metric and customary measures to solve international trade, time, temperature, and measurement problems.

Lesson 14.1 Production, Trade, and Finance
Students calculate per capita income, balance of trade payments or deficits, and currency conversions.

Lesson 14.2 International Time and Temperature
Students calculate time in different time zones and convert Fahrenheit and Celsius temperatures.

Lesson 14.3 International Measures of Length
Students convert metric units of length, do arithmetic operations with metric lengths, and convert metric and customary length measures.

Lesson 14.4 International Measures of Area
Students convert metric units of area, calculate the results of metric area problems, and convert metric and customary measures of area.

Lesson 14.5 International Measures of Capacity and Weight
Students convert metric capacity and weight measures, perform arithmetic calculations with metric capacity and weight, and convert metric and customary units in both measures.

14 CHAPTER

International Business

14.1 Production, Trade, and Finance
14.2 International Time and Temperature
14.3 International Measures of Length
14.4 International Measures of Area
14.5 International Measures of Capacity and Weight

Statistical Insights

U.S. Trade with Selected Countries

Rank	Country	Exports ($ million)
1	Canada	$169,923.6
2	Mexico	$97,411.7
3	Japan	$52,004.3
4	United Kingdom	$33,838.0
5	Germany	$28,831.9
6	South Korea	$24,072.7
7	Netherlands	$20,694.9
8	Taiwan	$17,447.8
9	France	$17,053.0
10	Singapore	$16,560.1

Rank	Country	Imports ($ million)
1	Canada	$221,594.7
2	China	$152,436.0
3	Mexico	$138,060.7
4	Japan	$118,036.7
5	Germany	$68,112.7
6	United Kingdom	$42,795.0
7	South Korea	$37,229.4
8	Taiwan	$31,599.3
9	France	$29,219.2
10	Italy	$25,414.4

Use the data shown above to answer each question.

1. Of the countries listed in both columns, which country has the least difference between U.S. exports and imports? What is the difference? United Kingdom; $8,967,000,000

2. How much greater are U.S. imports from Taiwan than U.S. exports to Taiwan? $14,151,500,000

3. What was the range of exports to the countries shown? $153,363,500,000

Statistical Insights

Have students determine whether the U.S. has a trade deficit or surplus with its top three trading partners (trade deficit in all cases). Then have them calculate the ratio of exports to imports, to the nearest tenth, for each of the top three trading partners (Canada, 1:1.3; Mexico, 1:1.4; Japan, 1:2.3).

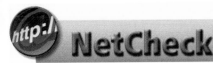

NetCheck

Currency Exchange Rates

Currency exchange rates vary daily based on the economic indicators of both countries involved. There are multiple web sites that provide a currency converter calculator.

A currency converter calculator is helpful if you are planning a trip to a different part of the world where you will be required to exchange your currency for that of the other country or if you are making an online purchase from an Internet retailer that resides in a different country.

Enter the keywords "currency exchange rate" into a search tool to locate a site that offers a conversion calculator.

What Time is It?

There is no "official clock" of the world. Each country establishes its own time.

However, the Internet does have many different sites that provide maps of the world time zones and display the time in any given country. These sites are organized in many different ways. One site may allow you to search a city and will display the city, the country, and the local time. Another may give you the option of sorting the list of countries, either by time or alphabetically.

A simple Internet search of time zones will yield multiple sites to investigate.

Teaching Resources

Lesson Plans, Ch. 14
Chapter 14 Test Forms A and B
Workbook, Ch. 14
Explore Algebra and Geometry
   Activities
Technology Activities
Competitive Events Prep
Data Activities CD, Ch. 14
ExamView® Pro CD, Ch. 14

NetCheck

Currency Exchange Rates Have students search for web sites that provide currency exchange calculators. Have them use at least three calculators and report on any differences in results, ease of use, and variety of foreign currencies listed.

What Time is It? Help students locate web sites that convert time in one zone to time in another zone. Have them report on the differences in the features of each site and whether adjustments are made for daylight saving time.

How Times Have Changed

For most of history, time was not an international concern. Each local area set its own time, based on the position of the sun and kept by a well-known clock in the community. When railroad travel became popular in the nineteenth century, a standardized time keeping system became necessary. This system was the beginning of the international time zones used today.

The use of time zones is introduced in the U.S. and Canada by the railroad industry.
1883

Congress passes the Standard Time Act, which makes the use of time zones mandatory in the U.S.
1918

The international unit of time is defined by the frequency of the cesium atom, which is the atom used in atomic clocks.
1967

The NIST-F1 atomic clock becomes the time standard for the U.S.
1999

1875 · 1900 · 1925 · 1950 · 1975 · 2000

1884
The Meridian Conference selects Greenwich Mean Time to be the official measurement of world time.

Research to discover a significant event in 1949 that relates to the history of atomic clocks.

1972
Coordinated Universal Time, which is based on atomic clocks, becomes the official measurement of world time.

2008
The Primary Atomic Reference Clock in Space (PARCS) is scheduled to fly on the International Space Station.

Answer to research item:

The world's first atomic clock is developed based on the properties of the ammonia molecule. Scientists soon discovered that atomic clocks based on cesium are more reliable.

591

HOW TIMES HAVE CHANGED

Lead the class into a discussion about time keeping. Possible questions to ask:
   If you did not have a clock or watch, how would you know what time it was? Why is an international standardized time necessary?

Turn the students' attention to the timeline. Have them do their own research to discover a significant event in 1949 that relates to the history of atomic clocks. See page 624 for an assessment question related to the timeline.

Start Up

Have students read the Start Up. Discuss the need to equate the currencies. Ask students to identify other workers besides athletes whose pay might be affected by currency exchange rates. These will include those who are paid in their country's national currency, but who work and live in another country. Such workers may include embassy employees, military personnel, and corporate employees assigned to a foreign office.

Math Skill Builder

In this lesson, students use the skills of multiplying and dividing money amounts by whole numbers and decimals and rounding the products and quotients.

Complete all exercises in Math Skill Builder 1–3.

■ Teach Goal 1

Point out that each country calculates Gross Domestic Product (GDP) in its own currency. Comparisons of the GDP of countries may be made only if the GDP is stated in a common measure, such as U.S. dollars. Once GDP is converted to a common measure, per capita GDP may be calculated and compared.

Discuss the Math Tip that shows how to read or write large money amounts. Remind students that the word dollar is not used to write an amount such as $5 million because the $ signifies dollars.

14.1 Production, Trade, and Finance

GOALS

- Calculate a nation's per capita production
- Calculate trade surpluses or trade deficits
- Convert currency using exchange rates

Start Up

Eric, a professional hockey player, signs a contract that pays $1.8 million a year in Canadian dollars. Marcel's contract is for $1.25 million a year payable in U.S. dollars. Which player is paid more per year?

Math Skill Builder

Review these math skills and solve the exercises.

1 **Divide** money amounts by whole numbers.
Find the quotient. $1,200,000,000,000 ÷ 80,000,000 = $15,000

1a. $940,000,000 ÷ 160,000 $5,875   **1b.** $1,910,260,000 ÷ 190,000 $10,054

2 **Multiply** whole numbers by decimals; **round** to the nearest hundredth.
Find the product. 368 × 0.1208 = 44.454, or 44.45

2a. 1,200 × 0.004373   5.25   **2b.** 1,714 × 2.657   4,554.10

3 **Divide** whole numbers by decimals; **round** to the nearest hundredth.
Find the quotient. 1,800 ÷ 3.672 = 490.196 = 490.20

3a. 35 ÷ 0.8975   39.00   **3b.** 96 ÷ 2,302   0.04

■ Gross Domestic Product

The **gross domestic product (GDP)** of a country measures the total market value of the goods and services produced within its borders. Goods sold to other countries (exports) are included in a country's GDP. The goods bought from other countries (imports) are not.

GDP is usually reported annually in dollars. GDP is an indication of the size of a country's economy. In this book, GDP will be shown in United States dollars.

One way to compare GDP among countries is to calculate per capita GDP. *Per capita* means per person. So **per capita GDP** shows the amount of goods and services produced per person by a country. Per capita GDP is often used to measure a country's standard of living.

> **MATH TIP**
>
> Large money amounts may be written in this way:
>
> $1.4 billion for $1,400,000,000
> $1.12 trillion for $1,120,000,000,000
> $0.45 million for $450,000

CONNECTION TO ECONOMICS

Point out to students that the balance of trade does not include all international business transactions, just imports and exports. Other transactions take place when tourists spend money and individuals or companies make financial investments. These transactions combine to form a balance of payments that measures the flow of money coming into a country minus the total flow going out. Like the balance of trade, the balance of payments can be positive or negative.

EXAMPLE 1

In a recent year, Norway had a GDP of $171,700,000,000 ($171.7 billion) and a population of 4,500,000 (4.5 million) people. Find the per capita GDP for Norway in that year to the nearest hundred dollars.

SOLUTION
Divide GDP by the number of people: $171,700,000,000 ÷ 4,500,000 = $38,155.56

To the nearest hundred dollars, Norway's per capita GDP is $38,200.

■ CHECK YOUR UNDERSTANDING

A. Suppose Japan had a GDP of $3.6 trillion and a population of 127 million. What was Japan's per capita GDP, to the nearest dollar? $28,346

B. The GDP of Zimbabwe is $24 billion. Its population is 12.7 million. Find Zimbabwe's per capita GDP, to the nearest dollar. $1,890

■ Balance of Trade

Domestic business is the manufacturing, buying, and selling of goods and services within a country. Many companies conduct international business that includes all the business activities necessary to manufacture, buy, and sell goods and services across national borders. When people talk about *foreign trade*, they are talking about international business.

The two most important international business activities are exporting and importing. Exporting is the selling to other countries of the goods and services produced within your country. Importing is the buying of products produced outside your country. A measure of a country's international business activity is its balance of trade. *Balance of trade* is the difference between a country's exports and imports.

When foreign exports exceed imports, a country has a trade surplus. When foreign imports exceed exports, a country has a trade deficit and may have to borrow money or ask for credit from other countries, thus establishing *foreign debt*. As with individuals, governments must pay interest on money they owe another country.

If the foreign debt is too large, it can affect the country's economy by limiting the amount of money available for necessary work in that country. For example, a large debt could mean a country could not improve public buildings or roads, or provide some services for its citizens.

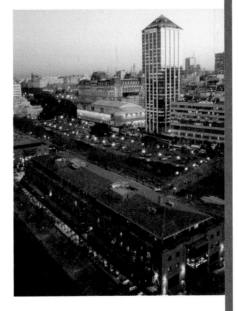

EXAMPLE 2

Recently, Argentina had exports of $29.57 billion and imports of $13.27 billion. Did Argentina have a trade surplus or trade deficit? How much?

SOLUTION
Subtract the smaller number from the larger number.

$13,270,000,000 − $29,570,000,000 = $16,300,000,000

Argentina's exports exceeded imports, so there was a trade surplus.

Lesson 14.1 Production, Trade, and Finance ■ 593

■ Apply Goal 1

Work through Example 1 at the board. Have students do the calculations at their desks.

Remind students that their 8-digit calculators will not accept a 12-digit amount such as $171.7 billion. Show students how, before dividing GDP by population, both numbers may be divided by one million to make them easier to work with. Divide by one million by moving the decimal point six places to the left in both numbers.

Assign Check Your Understanding problems A and B for class work. Review student work to identify any difficulties they have in dividing large numbers.

■ Teach Goal 2

Emphasize that countries desire exports to strengthen their economies, build a trade surplus, and avoid debt.

Point out that local companies in some countries are often restricted in entering new markets due to their lack of raw materials, specialized labor, or financial resources.

Multinational companies, however, often provide the capital to build plants in other countries and train the local labor force.

■ Apply Goal 2

Work through Example 2 at the board with students verifying the math at their desks.

Assign Check Your Understanding problems C and D for class work. Examine student work at their desks.

■ *CHECK YOUR UNDERSTANDING SOLUTIONS*

A. $3,600,000,000,000 ÷ 127,000,000 = $28,346.46, or $28,346

B. $24,000,000,000 ÷ 12,700,000 million = $1,889.76, or $1,890

C. $696.6 billion − $585 billion = $111.6 billion trade surplus

D. $56.73 billion − $37.16 billion = $19.57 billion trade surplus

■ CHECK YOUR UNDERSTANDING

C. In one year, Germany's imports were $585 billion and its exports were $696.6 billion. Did Germany have a trade surplus or trade deficit, and what was the amount? Trade surplus, $111.6 billion

D. Find the amount of trade surplus or trade deficit for the United Arab Emirates in a year when its exports were $56.73 billion and its imports were $37.16 billion. Trade surplus, $19.57 billion

■ Exchange Rates

Most nations have their own kind of money or *currency*. Before a business can buy something in another country, it has to buy their money. How much the business must pay for another country's currency is based on the **foreign exchange rate**, or simply the *exchange rate*.

Foreign exchange is the process of changing or converting the currency of one country into the currency of another country. The exchange rate is the amount of your money you must trade for the currency of another country.

The value of currency like most things is affected by supply and demand. Currency exchange rates are also affected by the country's economic condition and political stability. Exchange rates change daily. The table below shows the exchange rates for sample currencies for one day in a recent year.

Country	Currency	Symbol	Value in U.S. Dollars	Units per U.S. Dollar
Brazil	real	R	$0.3504	2.8540 R
Canada	dollar	$	$0.8167	$1.2244 Canadian
Great Britain	pound	£	$1.8397	£ 0.5436
Hong Kong	dollar	HK$	$0.1285	$7.781 HK
India	rupee	Re	$0.02196	45.530 Re
Japan	yen	¥	$0.009419	106.17 ¥
Kuwait	dinar	KD	$3.3921	0.2948 KD
Thailand	baht	B	$0.02438	41.014 B
Various European	euro	€	$1.2727	0.7857 €

The unit of currency in Brazil is the *real*. The last column shows there are 2.8540 *reais* (plural of real) in one U.S. dollar. The adjacent column states that each *real* is worth $0.3504 in U.S. dollars.

Since January 1, 1999, twelve European countries have replaced their national currencies with a single currency called the *euro*. The euro is now used to settle inter-bank and international commerce payments. Euro currency replaced national currencies on January 1, 2002. This means, for example, that the French franc is no longer used.

There are two ways to find the equivalent amount in U.S. dollars for a given foreign currency amount.

EXAMPLE 3

A businessperson hires a translator in India for 5,000 rupees. How much was the translator paid in U.S. dollars?

CONNECTION TO FINANCE

Foreign exchange rates are often shown in a matrix as cross rates that show rates among several currencies. The matrix may show that the exchange rate in units of currency between a U. S. dollar (USD) and the New Zealand dollar (NZD) is 0.4188; between the New Zealand dollar and the Canadian dollar (CAD) is 1.5309; and between the Canadian dollar and the U. S. dollar is 1.5599. So, $100 USD = 238.78 NZD (100 ÷ 0.4188); 238.78 NZD = 155.97 CAD (238.78 ÷ 1.5309); 155.97 CAD = 99.99 USD (155.97 ÷ 1.5599).

SOLUTION

Method 1: Use the rupee's Value in U.S. Dollars from the table.
$$5,000 \times \$0.02196 = \$109.80 \quad \text{cost in U.S. dollars}$$

Method 2: Use the rupee's Units per U.S. Dollar from the table.
$$5,000 \div 45.530 = \$109.818, \text{ or } \$109.82 \quad \text{cost in U.S. dollars}$$

Since you are converting foreign currency into U.S. dollars, you round to the nearest cent and add a dollar sign to the final answer.

Another way to use the exchange rate table is to calculate how many units of foreign currency you could get in exchange for U.S. dollars.

EXAMPLE 4

On a business trip to England, Maria Cedeno exchanged $120 of U.S. currency to pay for incidental expenses while in England. She got the exchange rate shown in the table. How much money did she receive in return, and in what currency?

SOLUTION

Multiply the pound's units per U.S. dollar by the amount exchanged.

$$\$120 \times 0.5436 = 65.232 \quad \text{amount received in pounds}$$

■ **CHECK YOUR UNDERSTANDING**

E. A manufacturer from Illinois took business clients in Kuwait to dinner. The cost of the dinner was 286 dinar. Find the dinner's cost in U.S. dollars. $970.15

F. Find how many rupees would be received for an exchange of $50 in U.S. currency. 2,276.5 Re

Wrap Up

The only way to compare money amounts in different currencies is to adjust them for the exchange rate. Using the exchange rate table you can calculate that Eric's contract is worth about $1,470,060 in U.S. funds. So, Eric is paid more per year.

COMMUNICATION

Twelve countries in Europe have agreed to use the euro as their currency. Identify the 12 countries. Find the answers to these questions and then write a summary about your findings.

1. May other countries join at a later date?

2. What are the advantages of using a common currency?

3. What are the disadvantages?

4. Is every euro bill and coin identical from country to country?

Lesson 14.1 Production, Trade, and Finance ■ 595

Wrap Up

Review the Start Up. Have students verify the currency conversion given.

Point out that workers from one country may receive a cost-of-living differential to compensate them for the additional amounts they may have to spend to live and work in another country.

Also point out that athletes' contracts may specify payment in constant dollars so that they receive the same relative pay regardless of what happens to exchange rates.

COMMUNICATION

Have student volunteers share their reports with the class. Ask if students encountered any interesting facts about the euro beyond the answers given to the four questions.

Assign

Assignment: Exercises 1–11 and 13–18. Start with the basic arithmetic problems that review the underlying arithmetic operations used in the exercises.

Assess

Call on students to write on the board their solutions to selected problems and, when finished, explain the solutions. Others in the class may self-check their solutions against those presented. Collect student work to determine what difficulties students may have had in solving the exercises.

■ *CHECK YOUR UNDERSTANDING SOLUTIONS*

E. $286 \times \$3.3921 = \$970.1406$, or $970.14

F. $\$50 \times 45.530 = 2,276.5$ Re

STUDENT WORKBOOK If students need help in calculating per capita GDP, do Exercise 1 with them. Assign Exercises 2–5.

If the calculation of trade surpluses or deficits poses a problem to students, work Exercise 6 with them. Assign Exercises 7 and 8 for independent work.

Work Exercise 9 with students who need help with exchange rates. Assign Exercises 10–12.

Enrich

Assign Exercise 12, Critical Thinking. After students give their answers, discuss the need for a central bank to print currency and regulate the money supply, if not already mentioned by students. Also mention that the U. S. dollar is a respected, stable currency that is readily accepted in international transactions.

Close

Call on students to define these terms in their own words: gross domestic product, per capita, domestic business, foreign trade, exports, imports, trade surplus, trade deficit, currency, exchange rate, and euro.

■ **STUDENT PORTFOLIO**
Remind students to consider including their solution to Exercise 12, Critical Thinking, in their portfolios.

EXERCISES

Find the product or quotient, rounded to the nearest hundredth.

1. 23×15.736 361.93
2. 127×88.084 11,186.67
3. $4,500 \div 0.286$ 15,734.27
4. $18.25 \div 0.467$ 39.08

5. Egypt had a GDP of $295.2 billion and a population of 76.1 million. What was Egypt's per capita GDP, to the nearest ten dollars? $3,880

6. New Zealand has a population of 3,993,817 and a GDP of $85.34 billion. What is its per capita GDP, to the nearest dollar? $21,368

7. In one year, Vietnam's GDP was 203.7 billion. Its population was 82.7 million. To the nearest dollar, what was its GDP per capita? $2,463

8. A country's total exports for a year were $3.049 billion. Its imports for the first 6 months of the year were $940 million and $1.08 billion for the last 6 months. What was the amount of the trade surplus or trade deficit for the year? $1.029 billion surplus

Use the Exchange Rate Table for Exercises 9–11. Round to the nearest U.S. dollar.

9. A flying service bought a used airplane in Canada for $140,000 in Canadian dollars. What was the cost of the airplane in U.S. dollars? $114,338

10. A company bought electronics equipment in Japan for 2,400,000 yen. What was the equipment's cost in U.S. dollars? $22,606

11. The purchase of a factory in Finland was settled in euros. The factory's cost was 586,000 euros. What was its cost in U.S. dollars? $745,802

12. **CRITICAL THINKING**   Instead of having their own currency, some countries use U.S. dollars as their currency. Why would they want to do this? See Enrich section for answer.

13. **BEST BUY**   You can buy a sports car in Sweden for 326,400 krona. The krona's exchange rate in U.S. dollars is $0.1403. Shipping the car to the United States would cost 42,340 krona. Once the car arrives in the United States, there would be an additional cost of $800 to get the car transported to your home. Exactly the same car could be bought in a nearby city for $51,840. Which is the better deal?   buying the car in the United States

MIXED REVIEW

14. $2\frac{1}{3} \times \frac{1}{5}$ $\frac{7}{15}$

15. $1\frac{9}{16} \div 1\frac{1}{4}$ $1\frac{1}{4}$

16. Estimate, then find the actual product of 317×9.   2,700; 2,853

17. Round to the nearest 10 million: 543,458,284,009   543,460,000,000

18. Eleanor Scripps has earned exactly the same weekly salary of $1,200 for two years. What is her average monthly salary? $5,200, Lesson 1.2

SELECTED SOLUTIONS

7. $203,700,000,000 \div 82,700,000 = \$2,463.12$, or $2,463

8. $940 million = $0.94 billion; $0.94 billion + $1.08 billion = $2.02 billion imports for year; $3.049 billion − $2.02 billion = $1.029 billion trade surplus

9. $140,000 \times \$0.8167 = \$114,338$

13. 326,400 krona + 42,340 krona = 368,740 krona; $368,740 \times \$0.1403 = \$51,734.22$; $51,734.22 + $800 = $52,534.22 total cost of car bought in Finland; buying in U.S. is less expensive

14.2 International Time and Temperature

GOALS

- Calculate time in different time zones
- Convert Fahrenheit and Celsius temperatures

Start Up

While vacationing in Toronto, Canada, you call the front desk and ask for the outdoor temperature. The clerk answers, "It's 5 degrees." You put on a heavy coat over an extra sweater. When you step outdoors, you are too warm. Why is this so?

Math Skill Builder

Review these math skills and solve the exercises.

1 **Add** or **subtract** hours to or from time.
Find the times. 12:15 P.M. + 7 hours = 7:15 P.M.
3:00 A.M. − 5 hours = 10:00 P.M.

 1a. 9:15 A.M. + 4 hours   1:15 P.M.   **1b.** 7:00 P.M. + 11 hours   6:00 A.M.

 1c. 12:00 Noon − 6 hours   6:00 A.M.   **1d.** 4:10 A.M. − 8 hours   8:10 P.M.

2 **Multiply** numbers by fractions or decimals; **round** to the nearest whole.
Find the products. $\frac{5}{9} \times 68 = 37.7$, or 38
$1.8 \times 54 = 97.2$, or 97

 2a. $\frac{5}{9} \times 72$ 40   **2b.** $\frac{5}{9} \times 29$ 16   **2c.** 1.8×27 49   **2d.** 1.8×-10 −18

■ International Time

Dealing with international travel and customers requires knowledge of international time zones and the International Date Line.

Time Zones The globe is divided into 24 standard time zones based on a 360° circle as shown. The center of each time zone is designated by the standard meridians of longitude. Each time zone is spaced 15° apart. Greenwich, England is designated as the starting point, 0°, or the *prime meridian*.

If you started in Greenwich and moved East one time zone, you would add one hour of clock time for each 15° of longitude. If you moved west one time zone from Greenwich, you would subtract one hour for every 15° of longitude.

In the United States, the mainland is divided into four time zones: Eastern Standard Time (EST), Central Standard Time (CST), Mountain Standard Time (MST), and Pacific Standard Time (PST).

Lesson 14.2 International Time and Temperature ■ 597

CONNECTION TO GEOGRAPHY

Have students identify 30 countries of interest to them. Assign one student to each country to find the type of temperature scale, Fahrenheit or Celsius, used in that country in everyday life. Also, have them find the country's mean temperature in the hottest and coldest months of the year. They should list the hottest and coldest months and report the temperatures in Fahrenheit and Celsius. Collected information may be shared in informal class discussion.

Prepare a transparency of the world map on page 598 and use it to illustrate the solution to Example 1.

Show students how to count the number of time zones from one point on earth to another. In Example 1, count the time just to the left of San Francisco's time zone as 1 and continue counting the time zones up to and including the time zone in which Sydney is located.

Inform them that each time zone is equal to one hour of time difference, so 6 times zones equate to 6 hours time difference. Thus, subtracting 6 hours from the time of 3 P.M. in San Francisco gives a time of 9 A.M. in Sydney.

Assign Check Your Understanding problems A and B. Observe student work to determine how they count time zones and calculate time.

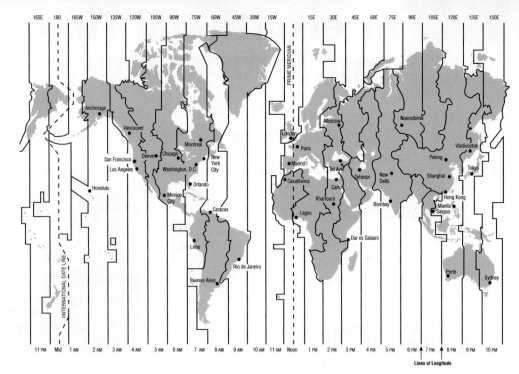

If the time in California is 8:00 A.M. (PST), the time in New York is 11:00 A.M. (EST) If the time in Chicago (CST) is 7:00 P.M., the time in California is 5:00 P.M. (PST).

Remember that when you move across time zones to the *east* you *add* the number of time zones moved to the current time. When you move to the *west*, you *subtract* the number of time zones moved from the current time.

INTERNATIONAL DATE LINE   The International Date Line is an imaginary line located in the middle of the Pacific Ocean. It is halfway around the world from Greenwich, England. When you travel east and cross the date line, you lose a day. If you are traveling east around the world and it is May 15, when you cross the International Date Line it will be May 14. If you were traveling west on May 15, when you cross the International Date Line, it would be May 16.

To determine the time and date in a particular country, calculate the time. Then check the map to see if you need to adjust the date.

EXAMPLE 1

It is 3 P.M., Thurs., in San Francisco. What time and day is it in Sydney, Australia?

SOLUTION
Look at the time zone map and count the number of time zones.

Sydney is 6 time zones to the west of San Francisco.

Subtract the number of time zones from the time you know.

3:00 P.M. − 6 hours = 9 A.M.   time in Sydney

Add 1 day to the current day since the International Date Line was crossed and the direction of travel was to the west.

Thursday + 1 day = Friday

598 ■ **Chapter 14 International Business**

598

TEACHING STRATEGIES Cooperative Learning

Some students may wish to know more about international time zones. If so, consider the following as an extra-credit assignment. Interested students should team together to explore Internet web sites or do library research to determine the history of time zones. Also, have them research the reasons why some countries may not follow the recommended time zones and opt instead to define local time in their own terms. The team should select one member to report the team's findings to the class.

A. It is 7:00 A.M. Thursday in Chicago, Illinois. How many time zones away is Peking, China? What is the day and time in Peking?   10 time zones to the West; Friday, 9:00 P.M.

B. It is 1:30 P.M. Sunday in Vladivostok, Russia. What day and time is it in Anchorage, Alaska? How many time zones were counted and in which direction?   Saturday, 6:30 P.M.; 5 time zones to the east

■ **Teach Goal 2**

Inform students that temperature in the U.S. is reported in Fahrenheit. Celsius is also used in the U.S., mainly in scientific work.

Have students study the graphic of two thermometers showing the comparison of well-known measures in Fahrenheit and Celsius equivalents.

Encourage them to see that there are 180 degrees difference between boiling point and freezing point on the Fahrenheit scale and 100 degrees difference between those two points on the Celsius scale. The ratio 180 to 100 reduces to 9:5 that is the beginning of the conversion formula for Fahrenheit to Celsius.

Temperature Conversion

In the United States, temperature is measured and recorded in the *Fahrenheit scale* in everyday use. Many other countries measure temperature by using the *Celsius scale*. Knowing the differences between the two scales and how to convert from one scale to the other is important to travelers and for business planning. The Fahrenheit and Celsius scales are shown.

As you can see, the Fahrenheit scale is based on a scale of 32° (freezing point) and 212° (boiling point). The Celsius system is based on a scale of 0°C (freezing point) to 100° (boiling point).

To convert between Celsius (C) and Fahrenheit (F) temperatures, you can use one of these two formulas.

$$F = 1.8C + 32$$

$$C = \frac{5}{9}(F - 32)$$

■ **Apply Goal 2**

Work Example 2 at the board. Have students do the math at their desks. Remind students that the arithmetic between the parentheses must be done first before multiplying by $\frac{5}{9}$.

Assign Check Your Understanding problems C and D for class work. Review student work at their desks to check for any errors they might be making.

EXAMPLE 2

The average body temperature in Fahrenheit degrees is 98.6. What is its Celsius equivalent?

SOLUTION

Apply the Celsius conversion formula: $C = \frac{5}{9}(F - 32)$

$\frac{5}{9}(98.6 - 32) = \frac{5}{9} \times 66.6 = 37°C$ body temperature in Celsius

Check your answer by using the Fahrenheit conversion formula: $F = 1.8C + 32$

$1.8(37) + 32 = 66.6 + 32 = 98.6°F$ body temperature in Fahrenheit

■ **CHECK YOUR UNDERSTANDING**

C. The weather report for New York City forecasts a high today of 94°F. What is the equivalent temperature in Celsius, to the nearest degree?   34°C

D. A weather reporter in Naples, Italy states that an overnight low temperature of 15°C is expected. What is the equivalent temperature in Fahrenheit?   59°F

■ **ONGOING ASSESSMENT**
Have students do the temperature conversions that follow, to the nearest degree.

a. $-6°C = ?° F$ **21°F**
b. $0°F = ?° C$ **−18°C**
c. $45°C = ?° F$ **113°F**
d. $104°F = ?° C$ **40°C**

■ *CHECK YOUR UNDERSTANDING SOLUTIONS*

A. Ten times zones to the west; gain a day crossing International Date Line; 7:00 A.M. − 10 hours = 9:00 P.M., Friday

B. Five times zones to the east; lose a day crossing International Date Line; 1:30 P.M. + 5 hours = 6:30 P.M., Saturday

C. $\frac{5}{9}(94 - 32); \frac{5}{9}(62) = 34.4$, or 34°C

D. $(1.8 \times 15) + 32 = 27 + 32 = 59°F$

Review the Start Up. Have students verify the temperature conversion.

The clerk gave the temperature in Celsius, the measure used in Canada. The temperature of 5° Celsius is equal to 41° Fahrenheit. You are warm because your clothing is more suited to a much colder temperature.

Algebra Connection

Have students convert −40° in Fahrenheit to Celsius, and vice versa. Both conversions will equal −40° in the other scale.

Algebra Connection

The temperature conversions you have done show a different number for temperatures in the two scales. However, the Fahrenheit and Celsius thermometers shown in this lesson indicate that the element mercury freezes at −40°F and −40°C.

Use the formulas for converting Fahrenheit and Celsius to prove that the calculation for the freezing point of mercury is correct.

Assign

Assignment: Exercises 1–17, 19–31. Have students work through the basic skills exercises first before solving the rest of the exercises.

EXERCISES

Find the sum or difference.

1. 7:00 P.M. + 10 hours   5:00 A.M.
2. 1:47 A.M. + 11 hours   12:47 P.M.
3. 3:13 A.M. − 9 hours   6:13 P.M.
4. 12:01 A.M. − 4 hours   8:01 P.M.

Find the product, round to the nearest whole.

5. $\frac{5}{9} \times 14$ 8
6. $\frac{5}{9} \times 52$ 29
7. 1.8×6 11
8. 1.8×30 54

9. It is 5:00 A.M. Saturday in Orlando, Florida. What day and time is it in Rio de Janeiro?   2 time zones east; it is 7:00 A.M. Saturday

10. It is 12:00 Noon Greenwich meridian time. What time is it in Khartoum?   2:00 P.M.

11. You are in Vancouver, Canada. Your boss is in Bombay, India. She wants you to call Tuesday at 5:00 P.M. Bombay time. What day and time do you have to make the call?   11 time zones west; Wednesday at 3:00 A.M.

12. You are in Moscow, Russia. You want to call someone in Mexico City at 3:30 P.M., their time. What time is it in Moscow when you place the call?   8 time zones east; call at 11:30 P.M.

13. You imported an exotic bird for display in your pet shop. The exporter tells you the temperature in the area the bird will be housed must always be 30°C or higher. At what Fahrenheit temperature should you set your thermostat?   86°F

14. You receive a shipment of items that includes the warning "Do Not Accept Shipment if Exposed to Temperatures Below 10°C." You know that the package was stalled for several days in a snowstorm where temperatures never got above 20°F. Should you accept the shipment?   No, 50°F was the minimum temperature

600 ■ Chapter 14 International Business

SELECTED SOLUTIONS

9. Two time zones to the east; 5:00 A.M. + 2 hours = 7:00 A.M., Saturday
13. $(1.8 \times 30) + 32 = 54 + 32 = 86°F$

16. $\frac{5}{9}(68 − 32) = \frac{5}{9} \times 36 = 20°C$ winter setting; $\frac{5}{9}(72 − 32) = \frac{5}{9} \times 40 = 22.22°C = 22°C$ summer setting

15. You are sending cargo overseas. The cargo must be kept refrigerated at 45°F. Someone tells you that if you mark the package 32°C it will be kept cool enough. Is the advice correct? Explain.   No, 32°C equals 89.6°F

16. To conserve energy you are advised to set your thermostat to 68°F in the winter and 72°F in the summer. What are the settings in Celsius to the nearest whole degree?   20°C and 22°C

17. **CRITICAL THINKING**   You are flying from Los Angeles, California to Montreal, Canada. Your departure time is 9:30 A.M. PST, and the flight time is 5 hours. What time will it be in Montreal when your flight arrives?   11:30 A.M. EST

18. **CRITICAL THINKING**   The time at the International Date Line is Midnight and 11:00 P.M. one time zone to the west. The days are different. When it is 2:00 A.M. at the International Date Line and 1:00 A.M. one time zone to the west, are the days now the same? Give your reasons.   See Enrich section for answer.

MIXED REVIEW

19. $14 billion ÷ $500 million   28

20. 866 × 10¢ $86.60

21. Rewrite 0.205 as a percent.   20.5%

22. 11.3% of $849.73 $96.02

23. $12\frac{1}{2} + 3\frac{3}{4} + 1\frac{7}{8}$ $18\frac{1}{8}$

24. Show the answer to the nearest hundredth. 874 ÷ 24   36.42

25. Milton Kohl's job pays $39,400 in annual salary and 28% of his salary in fringe benefits. His total job expenses are $940 plus $140 a month for commuting costs. What are Milton's net job benefits? $47,812, Lesson 2.2

26. You signed a promissory note at your credit union to borrow $4,200 for 6 months at 16% annual interest. What was the amount of interest on the loan? What total amount was due at the end of 6 months? $336; $4,536, Lesson 4.1

27. The monthly payments on a $68,500, 30-year mortgage loan are $561.23. Closing costs were $5,113. What total amount of interest was paid on the loan over 30 years? $133,542.80, Lesson 6.1

28. The CPI for 1991 was 136.2. What was the purchasing power of the dollar in 1991, to the nearest cent? $0.73, Lesson 8.5

29. Investments in a partnership were: Goldberg, $84,000; and Makoski, $118,000. The partners agree to pay each partner 6.5% interest on their investment and to divide the remainder of the net income equally. The net income for the year was $117,000. Find each partner's share of the net income. $57,395; $59,605, Lesson 13.3

30. A gallon of low-fat milk is priced at $2.98. A half-gallon of the same milk costs $1.89. How much can be saved by buying 1 gallon of milk instead of buying 2 half-gallons at the same time? $0.80, Lesson 5.3

31. An office estimated that the cost of materials for 25 sets of a report was 5 reams of $8\frac{1}{2}$ inch × 11 inch copy paper @ $4.50; 25, 1-inch binders @ $4.25; 25 sets of dividers @ $2.45; 25, $2\frac{1}{2}$-inch labels @ 3 cents. What was the cost of the materials per report? $7.63, Lesson 11.5

Lesson 14.2 International Time and Temperature ■ 601

TEACHING STRATEGIES Expanding Beyond the Classroom

Identify a person who emigrated to the U.S. and invite that person to speak to the class about life in the country in which he/she lived. Also have them address any difficulties they may have had in adjusting to using U.S. currency and determining whether they receive full value for their purchases of goods and services.

14.3 International Measures of Length

GOALS

- Convert one metric unit of length to another
- Calculate using metric units of length
- Convert metric and customary measurements of length

Start Up

A highway sign in Canada gives the speed limit as 100 km/h. A friend tells you that km is a Canadian expression for miles, so the sign means you can drive at 100 miles an hour. You think you have to drive about 60 miles per hour to be below the speed limit? Who is right? Why?

Math Skill Builder

Review these math skills and solve the exercises that follow.

❶ **Calculate** arithmetic operations on metric lengths.
Find the sum in centimeters. 123 mm + 8.7 cm = 12.3 cm + 8.7 cm = 21 cm

1a. 0.96 km + 1 345 m = ? km   2.305 km   **1b.** 6 cm × 54 = ? cm   324 cm

1c. 79 cm − 286 mm = ? cm   50.4 cm   **1d.** 340 hm ÷ 17 = ? hm   20 hm

❷ **Multiply** whole numbers and decimals.
Find the product. 20 × 3.28 = 65.6

2a. 6.5 × 2.54   16.51   **2b.** 35 × 1.61   56.35

■ Metric Measures of Length

The *metric system* of measurement is used in most countries. In the United States, the *customary system* is used most often. Because a growing variety of products are manufactured in the U.S. for worldwide use, you should be familiar with basic units of metric measurements. These basic units are the meter (length), the liter (capacity), and the gram (weight or mass).

The metric system of is based on the decimal system. Therefore, all relationships among metric units are based on 10. Prefixes before the basic unit indicate smaller and larger units and are used with all of the basic metric measurements. The prefixes and their order are shown in the metric length place value table.

1,000 m	100 m	10 m	1 m	0.1 m	0.01 m	0.001 m
kilo-meter	hecto-meter	deca-meter	meter	deci-meter	centi-meter	milli-meter
km	hm	dam	m	dm	cm	mm

CONNECTION TO HISTORY

Point out that the formalized metric system dates back to the 1790s when the French government asked a group of scientists to begin work on a standard system of measures. The metric system used today, the International System of Units (SI), is a modified version of the original system. Besides having standard units for length (meter), capacity (liter), and mass, (gram), SI also has standard units for time (second), temperature (kelvin), heat (joule), electric current (ampere), and intensity of light (candela), to name a few.

The basic unit of length in the metric system is the **meter**. One meter is equivalent to 3.28 feet, or slightly more than one yard in the customary system. The metric units of length, their symbols, and their values in meters are shown.

	Unit	Symbol	Value in Meters
Parts of a meter	millimeter	mm	0.001 m (one-thousandth meter)
	centimeter	cm	0.01 m (one-hundredth meter)
	decimeter	dm	0.1 m (one-tenth meter)
Basic unit	meter	m	1 m (one meter)
Multiples of a meter	decameter	dam	10 m (ten meters)
	hectometer	hm	100 m (one hundred meters)
	kilometer	km	1000 m (one thousand meters)

(Commonly used units are in **bold** type.)

When writing metric amounts, follow these rules:

1. Write the symbol, not the unit name, in small letters. (18 millimeters = 18 mm)

2. Use the same symbol for singular and plural values. (3 centimeters = 3 cm; 0.03 centimeters = 0.03 cm; 1 centimeter = 1 cm)

3. To break up large numbers, use a space instead of a comma. (1200 meters = 1 200; 4243 kilometers = 4 243 km)

To change or convert metric measurements is easy because the metric system is a decimal system. Each position in the metric system is either 10 times more than, or one-tenth of, the next unit. To change units, multiply or divide by 10 as many times as needed to change to the unit you want.

Another way to change units is by moving the decimal point. When changing from a larger to a smaller unit, move the decimal point to the right. When changing from a smaller to a larger unit, move the decimal point to the left.

EXAMPLE 1

Change 94 m to centimeters.

SOLUTION
Use the metric table to count the number of places to the desired unit.

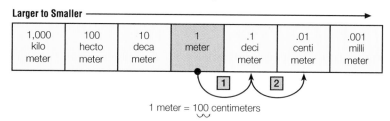

To move from meter (the larger unit) to centimeter (the smaller unit), you must move the decimal point two places to the right of meter (m).

94 m = 9 400 cm

Lesson 14.3 International Measures of Length ■ 603

TEACHING STRATEGIES Cooperative Learning

Have students form teams to explore these aspects of the metric system: the meanings of common prefixes and their sources; the meaning and common examples of derived units; which measure was defined first and what is the standard by which the measure was determined; history of legislative efforts in the U. S. to adopt the metric system. As students search, they may come across items that may be of interest to other teams. Promote cooperation among team members and among teams.

Remind students that if they are calculating distance traveled and one distance is given in feet and the other in miles, either the feet or miles must be converted to the other measure.

Inform students that a similar conversion is required when doing arithmetic with metric measures expressed in different units, such as meters and millimeters.

■ Apply Goal 2

Work Example 4 on the board and remind students that the conversions are to be stated in the larger measure. Thus in 4a, centimeters are changed to meters, the larger measure.

Use the metric length place value table transparency to illustrate the conversion.

Assign Check Your Understanding problems C and D for in-class work. Check student work at their desks to ensure they are following the procedures outlined in the examples.

EXAMPLE 2

Change 9 400 cm to kilometers.

SOLUTION
Use the table to count the number of places needed to move from centimeter to kilometer.

Move the decimal point 5 places to the left.

9 400 cm = 0.094 km

EXAMPLE 3

Which is longer, 4 meters or 485 centimeters?

SOLUTION
4 m = 400 cm   change 4 meters to centimeters

400 cm is less than 485 cm   compare numbers

485 cm is longer than 4 m

■ CHECK YOUR UNDERSTANDING

A. Change 16 m to mm and to hm.   16 000 mm; 0.16 hm

B. Which is longer, 0.45 km or 450 dm?   0.45 km

■ Calculating With Metric Measures

Metric measurements are added, subtracted, multiplied, and divided in the same way as customary values. Before doing any operations, change measurements so that they all are the same unit.

EXAMPLE 4

a. Add 6.85 meters and 70 centimeters.

b. Multiply 3.5 cm by 800.

SOLUTION
a. 70 cm = 0.7 m   change cm to m

6.85 m + 0.7 m = 7.55 m   answer in meters

NOTE: *When computing with more than one metric measure, such as meters and centimeters, state your answer in the largest measure (the meter in this case), unless you are directed otherwise.*

b. 3.5 cm × 800 = 2 800 cm

■ CHECK YOUR UNDERSTANDING

C. Find the difference: 33 cm − 124 mm   20.6 cm

D. Find the quotient: 2 100 km ÷ 7   300 km

■ *CHECK YOUR UNDERSTANDING SOLUTIONS*

A. 16m = 16 000 mm, move decimal point 3 places to the right; 16 m = 0.16 hm, move decimal point 2 places to the left

B. 450 dm = 0.045 km; 4.5 km is longer than 450 dm

C. 124 mm = 12.4 cm; 33 cm − 12.4 cm = 20.6 cm

D. 2 100 km ÷ 7 = 300 km

■ Converting Metric and Customary Measures

Once in a while, you may find it necessary to convert a measurement from the metric system to the customary system or vice versa. Listed are some equivalencies between the metric and customary systems.

Metric to Customary	Customary to Metric
1 cm ≈ 0.39 inches	1 inch ≈ 2.54 cm
1 m ≈ 3.28 feet	1 foot ≈ 0.305 m
1 km ≈ 0.62 miles	1 mile ≈ 1.61 km

MATH TIP

The symbol ≈ means nearly equal and is used when the equivalency of items is not exact, but approximate.

EXAMPLE 5

A sailboat is 8 meters long. What is its length in feet?

SOLUTION
Multiply the meters by the correct equivalency.

1 m   ≈ 3.28 feet
8 × 3.28 ≈ 26.24 feet   sailboat length

EXAMPLE 6

Elaine bicycled 7 miles. How many kilometers did she bicycle?

SOLUTION
Multiply the miles by the correct equivalency.

1 mile   ≈ 1.61 km
7 × 1.61 ≈ 11.27 km   kilometers bicycled

■ CHECK YOUR UNDERSTANDING

E. The length of a ribbon is 243 cm. What length is the ribbon in inches?   94.77 inches

F. The distance from home plate to first base is 90 feet. What is the equivalent distance in meters?   27.45 m

Wrap Up

The 100 km means 100 kilometers an hour, not miles per hour. Since a kilometer is equivalent to about 0.62 miles, the 100 km is equal to about 62 miles per hour.

TEAM MEETING

Form a group and visit retail stores, study catalogs, or do Internet research to find 10 items that are sold by metric measurements of length or that list metric measures on the item's label or its wrapping. Produce a table that gives the name of the item, its metric measurement, and its customary measure. Share your table with the entire class.

■ Teach Goal 3

Remind students that the Start Up solution requires knowing the relationship between miles and meters. Point out that the conversions in the table on page 605 are approximate as shown by the use of the approximately equal (≈) symbol in place of an equals sign.

Indicate to students that multiplication is used to convert metric and customary measures.

■ Apply Goal 3

Work Examples 5 and 6 at the board. Have students look at the conversion table and identify the column and row in which the conversion factor appears.

Assign Check Your Understanding problems E and F for class work. Check that students are using the correct conversion factor for each problem.

Wrap Up

Review the Start Up. Students who looked at car speedometers are likely to report that speedometers show speed in miles and kilometers. The mile scale is likely to be the larger, dominant scale while the kilometer scale is probably smaller and may be more difficult to read at a quick glance.

TEAM MEETING

Select two reports to be presented to the class. Assign one item to each row and have students in that row verify the metric and customary measurements.

■ *CHECK YOUR UNDERSTANDING SOLUTIONS*

E. 243 × 0.39 inches ≈ 94.77 inches

F. 90 × 0.305 m ≈ 27.45 m

Assign

Assignment: Exercises 1–51, 54–64. Students are to complete the basic arithmetic problems, Exercises 1–39, before doing the rest of the exercises.

Assess

Have students give the answers to Exercises 1–39 for self-checking. Them ask selected students to explain their solutions to exercises that students wish to see solved.

Call on students to give their answers to Exercises 40–51 and have all other students mark their own answers as correct or incorrect. Do Exercises 42, 45–47, 50, and 51 on the board and call on students to state each step in solving the exercises.

EXERCISES

Find the unknown length.

1. 1 m = ? cm
100

2. 1 m = ? mm
1 000

3. 1 km = ? m
1 000

4. 1 cm = ? m
0.01

5. 1 dm = ? m
0.1

6. 1 mm = ? m
0.001

7. 6 mm = ? cm
0.6

8. 900 mm = ? m
0.9

9. 368 m = ? km
0.368

10. 7 m = ? cm
700

11. 5 m = ? mm
5 000

12. 9 cm = ? mm
90

13. 3 km = ? m
3 000

14. 700 m = ? km
0.7

15. 290 cm = ? m
2.9

16. 1 085 cm = ? m
10.85 m

Find the result.

17. 56 mm − 14.5 mm
41.5 mm

18. 12 m + 187 cm
13.87 m

19. 4.1 cm × 4
16.4 cm

20. 70 km × 8
560 km

21. 4.8 mm ÷ 12
0.4 mm

22. 7 320 m ÷ 6
1 220 m

23. 23 × 120 cm
2 760 cm

24. 1 280 mm ÷ 64
20 mm

25. (55 m + 45 m) ÷ 2
50 m

26. 3 cm + 4 cm + 1 cm   8 cm

27. 6.2 km − 4 500 m   1.7 km

28. 14.1 km + 930 m   15.03 km

29. 345 cm − 753 mm   269.7 cm

30. 23 m + 74 cm + 6 829 mm   30.569 m

31. 115 m − 960 cm   105.4 m

Find the equivalent measures of length.

32. 2.5 cm ≈ ? inches   0.975 in

33. 2,200 miles ≈ ? km   3 542 km

Which measure is longer?

34. 0.4 km or 4 100 m   4 100 m

35. 0.6 m or 6 000 cm   6 000 cm

36. 53 mm or 53 dm   53 dm

37. 1 040 mm or 1.4 cm   1 040 mm

38. 7 832 m or 78.32 cm   7 832 m

39. 4 700 m or 4.64 km   4 700 m

40. Lena Hailey needed these lengths of rope: 12 m, 3.5 m, 2.6 m. What total amount of rope did Lena need?   18.1 m

41. A company used 312 meters of fiber optic cable from a spool that originally held 1 200 meters of cable. How much cable was left on the spool?   888 m

42. A trip of 600 kilometers was estimated to take 7.5 hours. In the first 6.5 hours, 524 kilometers were driven. How many kilometers must be driven in one hour to meet the trip's estimate?   76 km

43. Four students reported the length of material they used for a project as: 0.5 m, 25 cm, 400 mm, 18.4 cm. What total length of material in meters did they use?   1.334 m

44. Laura Hiller is cutting pieces of tubing to fill an order. The order is for these pieces and lengths of tubing: 12 pieces, 180 cm long; 30 pieces, 54 cm long; 126 pieces, 1.2 m long. What total length of tubing, in meters, does Laura need to fill the order?   189 m

---

SELECTED SOLUTIONS

28. 930 m = 0.93 km; 14.1 km + 0.93 km = 15.03 km

29. 753 mm = 75.3 cm; 345 cm − 75.3 cm = 269.7 cm

33. 2,200 × 1.61 km ≈ 3 542 km

42. 600 km − 524 km = 76 km

44. (12 × 1.8 m) + (30 × 0.54 m) + (126 × 1.2 m) = 21.6 m + 16.2 m + 151.2 m = 189 m

On a business trip, Rudy Komiko drove these distances in three days: 216 km, 237 km, 165 km.

45. How many km did Rudy drive in those three days? 618 km

46. What estimated average number of km did he drive per day? 200 km

47. What actual average number of km did he drive each day? 206 km

48. The length of a car is 5.5 m. What is its length in feet? 18.04 ft

49. A circle has a diameter of 18 cm. What is the circle's diameter in inches? 7.02 in.

50. A four-year old car had been driven for a recorded distance of 105,000 km. What was the distance driven in miles? 65,100 mi

51. A box measures 14 inches long by 8 inches wide by 7 inches tall. Will a book that measures 34 cm by 20.8 cm by 3 cm fit inside the box completely? No

52. **CRITICAL THINKING** Unlike other countries of the world, the United States uses primarily the customary system in everyday life. What would have to happen for this situation to change? See Enrich section for answer.

53. **CRITICAL THINKING** B & K Manufacturing uses customary measures but wants to do business with a company in England that will only purchase items made to metric measure. What problems might this present to B & K? See Enrich section for answer.

MIXED REVIEW

54. What is the value of X when $\frac{10}{15} = \frac{12}{X}$? 18

55. Rewrite $\frac{3}{4}$ as a decimal. 0.75

56. $436 - 27.4$ 408.6

57. $\frac{7}{8} \div \frac{3}{4}$ $1\frac{1}{6}$

58. $1,752 \times 10¢$ $175.20

59. Round $11.947 to the nearest cent and to the nearest dollar. $11.95; $12

60. A van that costs $24,500 and has a residual value of $16,000 can be leased for $520 monthly with a $1,500 down payment. The van may be purchased with a $6,800 down payment and $891 monthly payments. The lease and loan terms are 24 months. Which costs more, leasing or buying? How much more? leasing, $1,796 more, Lesson 6.8

61. A company uses the sum-of-the-years-digits method of calculating depreciation. The company buys a machine for $45,000 and expects to use it for 5 years and then sell it for $21,000. What are the total depreciation and book value of the machine at the end of the first year? $8,000; $37,000, Lesson 11.3

62. The Easy Tread Company had sales of $83,100 in September. Sales returns and allowances for the same month were $315.40. What were Easy Tread's net sales for September? $82,784.60, Lesson 13.1

63. Yetzin and Golub are business partners and share net income in a ratio of 7 to 5, respectively. What is each partner's share of a net income of $12,852? $7,497; $5,355; Lesson 13.3

64. Cheryl Moores works full time for an annual salary of $39,560. She also works part-time 5 hours each week at a job that pays $17.45 an hour. Both jobs pay bi-weekly. What is her gross wages each pay period for the two jobs combined? $1,696.04; Lesson 1.1

Lesson 14.3 International Measures of Length ■ 607

SELECTED SOLUTIONS

45. 216 km + 237 km + 165 km = 618 km

47. 618 km ÷ 3 = 206 km

49. 18 × 0.39 inches ≈ 7.02 inches

51. No; book's width is 20.8 cm; 20.8 × 0.39 in. = 8.112 in. width of book; book is too wide

Start Up

Have students read the Start Up. Ask if they have seen other products that give size in area. Their answers might include wallpaper, tablecloths, rolls of insulation, or coverage area of a gallon of paint. Then discuss their responses to the Start Up question.

Math Skill Builder

Exercises 1–3 may be used as a pretest to find what students know about conversion of metric area measures and performing metric area arithmetic operations.

Complete all exercises in Math Skill Builder 1–3.

GOALS

- Convert one metric unit of area to another
- Calculate using metric units of area
- Convert metric and customary measurements of area

Start Up

You notice that a package of plastic food wrap you bought contains 100 square feet or 9.2 square meters of wrap. You bought the product in the United States. Why would the package give both customary and metric measures?

Math Skill Builder

Review these math skills and answer the questions that follow.

1. **Add** or **Subtract** as indicated. Write answers using the larger unit.
   Find the sum. 2 m + 100 cm = 2 m + 1 m = 3 m
   Find the difference. 12 hm − 38 dam = 12 hm − 3.8 hm = 8.2 hm

   1a. 14 cm + 1 420 mm   156 cm   **1b.** 8 hm^2 + 1.6 hm^2 9.6 hm^2

   1c. 8 km^2 − 5 km^2 3 km^2 **1d.** 6.75 cm − 50 mm   1.75 cm

2. **Multiply** or **Divide** as indicated.
   Find the product. 16 m^2 × 4 = 64 m^2
   Find the quotient. 96 km ÷ 4 km = 24

   2a. 12 mm^2 × 3   36 mm^2 **2b.** 35 × 4 m   140 m

   2c. 45 mm ÷ 5   9 mm   **2d.** 26 cm ÷ 13 cm   2

3. **Multiply** whole numbers and decimals.
   Find the product. 2 × 10.8 ft = 21.6 ft

   3a. 50 × 0.16 in.^{2} 8 in.^{2} **3b.** 3 × 0.4 ha   1.2 ha

■ Metric Measures of Area

The amount of surface an item has is called its area. To find the area of any rectangle, such as a desk or floor, multiply its length by its width.

Area = Length × Width   or $A = L \times W$

Calculating area is a skill used in many businesses. For example, the owner of a paving company must find the area of a parking lot to estimate how much to charge for paving the lot. If a parking lot is 120 feet long by 60 feet wide, its area is 120 ft × 60 ft or 7,200 ft^2.

DIFFERENT LEARNING STYLES Visual Learners

Some students may benefit by being able to visualize the relationship of all the metric measures covered in this textbook. To help them, photocopy the metric place value table for each metric measure and paste the tables onto a single sheet of paper. Show students the similarities that place value has among the measures.

Area measures the space covered by two dimensions, so area is expressed in terms of square units. In the customary system, area may be in square inches, square feet, square yards, or square miles, depending on what is being measured. For example, a tablecloth may cover a certain area measured in square inches. The area covered by a box of floor tiles can be measured in square feet. Carpeting is sold by the square yard, while forests may be measured in square miles.

In the metric system, the basic unit of area is the square meter. The square meter is equivalent to approximately 1.2 square yards in the customary system. Square meter is written as m^2. The word "square" is not written. It is named by the exponent "2" that appears to the right and above the m notation for meter.

	Unit	Symbol	Value in Square Meters
Parts of a square meter	square millimeter	mm^2	0.000 001 m^2 (one-millionth square meter)
	square centimeter	cm^2	0.000 1 m^2 (one-ten-thousandth square meter)
	square decimeter	dm^2	0.01 m^2 (one-hundredth square meter)
Basic unit	square meter	m^2	1 m^2 (square meter)
Multiples of a square meter	square decameter	dam^2	100 m^2 (one hundred square meters)
	square hectometer or **hectare**	hm^2 or **ha**	10 000 m^2 (ten thousand square meters)
	square kilometer	km^2	1 000 000 m^2 (one million square meters)

(Commonly used units are in **bold** type.)

Square centimeter and square meter are the measures of area used most often. Large areas are measured in either hectares (ha) or square kilometers (km^2). Hectare is another name for square hectometer. Hectare is used because it is easier to say and write.

CONVERTING METRIC UNITS OF AREA   In metric measures of area, each square unit is *100 times* the next smaller unit, or *one hundredth* of the next larger unit. This is shown in the illustration at the right. Remember that to determine area, multiply length by width.

$1 \text{ cm} \times 1 \text{ cm} = 1 \text{ cm}^2$

Since 1 cm = 10 mm, the area can also be expressed as:

$10 \text{ mm} \times 10 \text{ mm} = 100 \text{ mm}^2$.

So $1 \text{ cm}^2 = 100 \text{ mm}^2$.

area = 100 mm^2 = 1 cm^2

Metric measures of area may be changed by moving the decimal point in a way similar to changing metric measures of length. A metric area place value table is shown.

1,000,000 m^2	10,000 m^2	100 m^2	1 m^2	0.01 m^2	0.0001 m^2	0.000001 m^2
kilo-meter^2	hectare or hectometer^2	deca-meter^2	meter^2	deci-meter^2	centi-meter^2	milli-meter^2
km^2	ha or hm^2	dam^2	m^2	dm^2	cm^2	mm^2

To change from a metric unit of area to the next smaller unit, you move *one place* on the area place value table and move the decimal point *two places* to the right. To change to the next larger unit of area, move the decimal two places to the left.

Lesson 14.4 International Measures of Area ■ **609**

■ **Teach Goal 1**

Point out that area is found by multiplying a rectangle's length by its width for both customary and metric measures. Review the use of square feet, or ft^2, and m^2 to show the square measure of feet and meters.

Emphasize that the decimal point in a quantity is moved two places for each place moved on a metric area place value table.

Remind students that hectare, ha, is commonly used in place of the square hectometer, hm^2. Have them note that ha is written without an exponent.

COMMON ERRORS

Some students may move the decimal point in the wrong direction to convert from one metric unit to another. Remind them that when they move from larger units to smaller units, the larger measure is broken into many small parts so the number becomes greater. Other students may fail to move the decimal point two places for each place moved in the area place value table. Have them associate the exponent^2 with moving two places.

■ Apply Goal 1

Prepare a transparency of the metric area place value table on page 609 and use it to demonstrate the solutions of the four exercises in Example 1.

Assign Check Your Understanding problems A and B to be done in class. Walk around the classroom and review student work to see what difficulties they may be having.

■ ONGOING ASSESSMENT

Ask students to convert these as indicated:

a. $5 \text{ m}^2 = ? \text{ cm}^2$ **50 000 cm²**
b. $0.8 \text{ ha} = ? \text{ m}^2$ **8 000 m²**
c. $1.5 \text{ m}^2 = ? \text{ dm}^2 = $ **150 dm²**
d. $8\ 750 \text{ mm}^2 = ? \text{ cm}^2$ **87.5 cm²**

■ Teach Goal 2

Remind students that, as was done with length, unlike metric units of area must be expressed in the same unit, the larger unit, before doing calculations.

■ Apply Goal 2

Work through the six exercises in Example 2 at the board and use the place value transparency to illustrate problem solutions. Show how the Math Tip is applied.

Assign Check Your Understanding problems C and D to be done in class. Check student work at their desks.

EXAMPLE 1

Change the metric measures of area shown below to the unit indicated.

a. $1 \text{ cm}^2 = ? \text{ mm}^2$ b. $1 \text{ m}^2 = ? \text{ cm}^2$ c. $100 \text{ mm}^2 = ? \text{ cm}^2$ d. $10\ 000 \text{ cm}^2 = ? \text{ m}^2$

SOLUTION

To change to a smaller unit, move the decimal point two places to the right for each place you move on the metric area place value table.

a. $1 \text{ cm}^2 = 100 \text{ mm}^2$ The decimal point is moved 2 places to the right.

b. $1 \text{ m}^2 = 10\ 000 \text{ cm}^2$ The decimal point is moved 4 places to the right.

To change to a larger unit, move the decimal point two places to the left for each place you move on the metric area place value table.

c. $100 \text{ mm}^2 = 1.00 \text{ cm}^2$ The decimal point is moved 2 places to the left.

d. $10\ 000 \text{ cm}^2 = 1 \text{ m}^2$ The decimal point is moved 4 places to the left.

■ CHECK YOUR UNDERSTANDING

A. Change to the smaller measure indicated: $1 \text{ km}^2 = ? \text{ m}^2$ 1 000 000 m²

B. Change to the larger measure indicated: $1\ 000 \text{ m}^2 = ? \text{ ha}$ 0.1 ha

■ Calculating With Metric Measures

When you add or subtract square units, the unit in the measure remains the same. Remember, measurements must have the same units in order to be added or subtracted.

When two measures in millimeters are multiplied, the result is mm^2. When a square unit, such as cm^2, is multiplied by a number, the answer is given in cm^2. When square units, such as km^2, are divided by a measurement, such as km^2, the quotient is in units, not square units.

EXAMPLE 2

Solve each problem.

a. $12 \text{ km}^2 + 600 \text{ ha}$
b. $18 \text{ cm}^2 - 700 \text{ mm}^2$
c. $8 \text{ cm} \times 4 \text{ cm}$
d. $6 \text{ km}^2 \times 3$
e. $48 \text{ mm}^2 \div 12$
f. $48 \text{ km}^2 \div 24 \text{ km}^2$

SOLUTION

a. $12 \text{ km}^2 + 600 \text{ ha} = 12 \text{ km}^2 + 6 \text{ km}^2 = 18 \text{ km}^2$

b. $18 \text{ cm}^2 - 700 \text{ mm}^2 = 18 \text{ cm}^2 - 7 \text{ cm}^2 = 11 \text{ cm}^2$

c. $8 \text{ cm} \times 4 \text{ cm} = 32 \text{ cm}^2$

d. $6 \text{ km}^2 \times 3 = 18 \text{ km}^2$

e. $48 \text{ mm}^2 \div 12 = 4 \text{ mm}^2$

f. $48 \text{ km}^2 \div 24 \text{ km}^2 = 2$

MATH TIP

When calculating with metric measures, such as km^2 and m^2, state your answer in the largest measure (km^2 in this case), unless you are otherwise directed.

■ *CHECK YOUR UNDERSTANDING SOLUTIONS*

A. $1 \text{ km}^2 = 1\ 000\ 000 \text{ m}^2$; decimal point is moved 6 places to the right

B. $1\ 000 \text{ m}^2 = 0.1 \text{ ha}$; decimal point is moved 4 places to the left

C. What is the sum of 7 cm² and 400 mm²? What is the difference of 13 km² − 1 200 ha?   11 cm²; 1 km²

D. What is the product of 9 mm × 2 mm? What is the product of 5 ha × 11? What is the quotient of 25 km² ÷ 5?   18 mm²; 55 ha; 5 km²

■ Converting Metric and Customary Measures

You may occasionally find it necessary to convert from the metric system to the customary system or vice versa.

Metric to Customary	Customary to Metric
1 cm² ≈ 0.16 in.²	1 in.² = 6.5 cm²
1 m² ≈ 10.8 ft²	1 ft² ≈ 0.09 m²
1 ha ≈ 2.5 acres	1 acre ≈ 0.4 ha

EXAMPLE 3

Alvin bought a roll containing 7 m² of gift-wrap. How many square feet of gift-wrap are in the roll?

SOLUTION
Multiply the number of square feet in one square meter by the number of square meters.

$1 m^2 \approx 10.8\ ft^2$ equivalency for one square meter

$7 \times 10.8\ ft^2 \approx 75.6\ ft^2$ paper in one roll

EXAMPLE 4

A stock clerk found a carpet remnant that covers 360 square feet of floor space. How many square meters will the remnant cover?

SOLUTION
Multiply the number of square meters in one square foot by the number of square feet.

$1\ ft^2 \approx 0.09\ m^2$ equivalency for one square foot

$360 \times 0.09\ m^2 \approx 32.4\ m^2$ size of remnant

■ CHECK YOUR UNDERSTANDING

E. Maria Blasko bought a can of spray paint that will cover a 1.8 m² surface. How many square feet will the paint cover?   19.44 ft²

F. A computer monitor occupies a space of 272 square inches. To how many square centimeters is the space equal?   1 768 cm²

Lesson 14.4 International Measures of Area ■ **611**

■ *CHECK YOUR UNDERSTANDING SOLUTIONS*

C. 400 mm² = 4 cm²; 7 cm² + 4 cm² = 11 cm²;
1 200 ha = 12 km²; 13 km² − 12 km² = 1 km²

D. 9 mm × 2 mm = 18 mm²; 5 ha × 11 = 55 ha;
25 km² ÷ 5 = 5 km²

E. 1.8 × 10.8 ft² ≈ 19.44 ft²
F. 272 × 6.5 cm² ≈ 1 768 cm²

■ **Teach Goal 3**

Remind students to use the approximately equal (≈) sign when showing the equivalency of metric and customary measures. Also remind students that multiplication by the stated factor is used to convert from one measure to the other.

■ **Apply Goal 3**

Do Examples 3 and 4 at the board. Have students identify the column, row, and conversion factor for each measure to be converted in the Examples.

Assign Check Your Understanding problems E and F to be done in class. Circulate about the class and check student work.

Review the Start Up. Discuss the answers given in the Wrap Up.

Bring to class a package that shows the area of its contents in customary and metric measures. Also point out, if present on the package, that product features and instructions are printed in English and other languages, most commonly Spanish.

Algebra Connection

In the first equivalency equation, 1 cm^2 = 0.16 in.^{2}, divide both sides of the equation by 0.16. The result is 1 cm^2 ÷ 0.16 = 1 in.^{2}, or 6.25 cm^2 = 1 in.^{2}, which is the second equation.

Assign

Assignment: Exercises 1–47.
Have students solve the basic arithmetic problems, Exercises 1–26, that provide practice on basic metric conversions and arithmetic operations. When finished, have them complete the rest of the exercises.

Assess

Ask students to give their answers to Exercises 1–26. Select two exercises from each basic skills section and call on students to write their solutions on the board and use the area place value transparency, where appropriate, to explain their solutions.

Collect student work and check their answers to Exercises 27–37.

Wrap Up

Although you purchased the product in the United States, it is possible the product is sold in other countries that use the metric system. Instead of printing two different packages, the manufacturer places all the information on one package and saves the trouble and expense of keeping the packages separate.

Algebra Connection

Two related conversion formulas are shown below. How can you prove the formulas are correct with respect to each other?

$$1 \text{ cm}^2 = 0.16 \text{ in}^2 \qquad 1 \text{ in}^2 = 6.5 \text{ cm}^2$$

If the accuracy of the formulas is not as precise as you might want, search the Internet for equivalencies that show more decimal places.

EXERCISES

Find the missing area.

1. 1 cm^2 = ? mm^2 100 mm^2
2. 1 m^2 = ? cm^2 10 000 cm^2
3. 86 km^2 = ? ha   8 600 ha
4. 960 cm^2 = ? m^2 0.096 m^2
5. 26 ha = ? m^2 260 000 m^2
6. 2 000 mm^2 = ? m^2 0.002 m^2

Find the sum or difference.

7. 3 cm^2 + 900 mm^2 + 1.5 m^2 1.5012 m^2
8. 6 km^2 + 120 ha   7.2 km^2
9. 9 m^2 + 7 000 cm^2 9.7 m^2
10. 10 000 m^2 + 6 ha   7 ha
11. 4.5 km^2 − 18 ha   4.32 km^2
12. 5 cm^2 − 100 mm^2 4 cm^2
13. 4 km^2 − 1 000 000 m^2 3 km^2
14. 1 ha − 6 000 m^2 0.4 ha

Find the product or quotient.

15. 827 mm^2 × 5   4 135 mm^2
16. 100 m × 100 m   10 000 m^2
17. 3 km^2 × 0.5   1.5 km^2
18. 0.4 × 58 cm^2 23.2 cm^2
19. 240 km^2 ÷ 60 km^2 4
20. 0.75 m^2 ÷ 3   0.25 m^2
21. 156 mm^2 ÷ 39 mm^2 4
22. 920 cm^2 ÷ 115 cm^2 8

Find the equivalent measure of area.

23. 25 ha ≈ ? acres   62.5 acres
24. 16 ft^2 ≈ ? m^2 1.44 m^2
25. 140 cm^2 ≈ ? in.^{2} 22.4 in.^{2}
26. 2,000 acres ≈ ? ha   800 ha

27. The Liverpool Home Building Company bought these tracts of land: 9 ha, 140 ha, 73 ha, 1 168 ha. Find the total amount of land they purchased.   1 390 ha

28. Roland wants to buy carpeting for a room that measures 3 m × 4.1 m. What amount of carpeting will he need?   12.3 m^2

SELECTED SOLUTIONS

12. 100 mm^2 = 1 cm^2; 5 cm^2 − 1 cm^2 = 4 cm^2
23. 25 × 2.5 acres ≈ 62.5 acres
27. 9 ha + 140 ha + 73 ha + 1 168 ha = 1 390 ha
28. 3 m × 4.1 m = 12.3 m^2

29. Keisha Beard's yard is 44 meters long by 25 meters wide. She turned part of her yard into a garden 12 meters long by 5 meters wide. She also has a 3 m by 3 m shed on her lawn. She has to mow the rest of the lawn. How much lawn does she mow?   1 031 m²

30. Umberto inherited a 450 ha farm in Argentina. What is the equivalent size of the farm in acres?   1,125 acres

31. A paper mill produced 190 000 m² of card stock last month. What was last month's card stock production in square feet?   2,052,000 ft²

32. Rhonda Issel plans to make and sell decorative pillows that are about 1.5 ft². The pattern for the pillow gives the area of a pillow in centimeters. To the next highest 100, how many cm² are equal to 1.5 ft²?   1 400 cm²

INTEGRATING YOUR KNOWLEDGE   A box holds 45 floor tiles. Each tile measures 30.5 cm by 30.5 cm.

33. What does a tile measure, in inches, to the nearest inch?   12 inches by 12 inches

34. Estimate the area, in cm², covered by a tile?   900 cm²

35. What area, to the nearest square meter, will a box of tiles cover?   4 m²

36. What area, to the nearest ft², will a box of tiles cover?   45 ft.²

37. **DECISION MAKING**   A carpet company quotes an installed price of $5 a square foot for a type of carpeting. Another company quotes an installed price of $50 a square meter for the same type of carpeting. The room to be carpeted measures 24 feet by 15 feet. Which is the better offer? How much will you save by taking the better offer?   m² offer; $180 saved

MIXED REVIEW

38. $\frac{7}{8} \times \frac{16}{35} \times \frac{5}{6}$ $\frac{1}{3}$

39. $6\frac{3}{5} - 3\frac{1}{2}$ $3\frac{1}{10}$

40. How many days are there between June 27 to August 14?   48

41. $27.9 - 15$ 12.9

42. $0.035 \times \$516.12$ $18.06

43. What percent of 90 is 27?   30%

44. Write 1.2 as a fraction. $\frac{6}{5}$

42. Round $872,598 to the nearest ten thousand. $870,000

45. Valerie Clay-Gelen's credit card statement for April showed these items: 4/1, previous balance, $218.06; 4/12, purchase, $119; 4/18, payment, $200. Valerie's credit card company uses a 1.5% monthly periodic rate and the average daily balance method. What is the finance charge for April? What is Valerie's new balance? $3.10; $140.16, Lesson 4.8

46. Zetex provides its employees with a disability policy. The policy pays a benefit of 5% of wages plus $1\frac{1}{4}$% for each of the 14 years that Max Randolph has been employed with the Zetex. What is his benefit percent?   22.5%, Lesson 7.3

47. An invoice for $2,050 dated December 12 has credit terms of 1.5/10, n30. The invoice is paid on December 21. What amount should have been paid? $2,019.25, Lesson 12.2

Lesson 14.4 International Measures of Area ■ 613

SELECTED SOLUTIONS

31. 190 000 × 10.8 ft² ≈ 2,052,000 ft²

35. 45 × (30.5 cm × 30.5 cm) = 45 × 930.25 cm² = 41 861.25 cm²; 41 861.25 cm² = 4.186125 m² or 4 m²

37. 24 ft. × 15 ft = 360 ft²; 360 × $5 = $1,800; 360 × 0.09 m² ≈ 32.4 m²; 32.4 m² × $50 = $1,620; $1,800 − $1,620 = $180 saved by taking offer in square meters

GOALS

- Convert one metric unit of capacity to another
- Convert one metric unit of weight to another
- Calculate using metric units of capacity and weight
- Convert metric and customary measures of capacity and weight

Start Up

You pick up a suitcase in a store and notice its label gives the weight of the case in kilograms. The label on a second suitcase of the same size states its weight in pounds. The second suitcase feels lighter than the first when you pick it up. Might this be your imagination at work? How might you compare the weights?

Math Skill Builder

Review these math skills and solve the exercises.

1. **Convert** one measure of metric capacity to another measure of metric capacity.
   Find the capacity. 21 mL = ? L = 0.021 L

   1a. 134 mL = ? dL   1.34 dL   **1b.** 1.3 kL = ? L   1 300 L

2. **Convert** one measure of metric weight to another measure of metric weight.
   Find the weight. 31 mg = ? dg = 0.31 dg

   2a. 430 cg = ? g   4.3 g   **2b.** 2.1 kg = ? g   2 100 g

3. **Calculate** arithmetic operations on metric capacity and weight.
   Find the sum. 17 cg + 17 mg = 17 cg + 1.7 cg = 18.7 cg

   3a. 9 L + 200 cL   11 L   **3b.** 9 kg − 5 000 g   4 kg

   3c. 960 L ÷ 12   80 L   **3d.** 15 000 g ÷ 600   25 g

■ Metric Measure of Capacity

The basic metric measure of capacity is the **liter**. A liter is slightly larger than a quart. In this textbook, the symbol for the liter is a capital L. Another common symbol for the liter is a small l.

Most small capacity measures are shown in milliliters or as decimal parts of a liter. For example, a measure of 400 mL is equivalent to 0.4 L. Larger measures may be written in liters or kiloliters. For example, 4 000 L is the same as 4 kL. To change from one measure of capacity to another you may move the decimal point as you have done with metric lengths.

DIFFERENT LEARNING ABILITIES At-Risk Learners

Suppose you have three containers: a very large pitcher, a 3-liter jar, and a 5-liter jar. You are given a large amount of juice and need to have exactly 2 liters in the pitcher. How can you get exactly two liters in the pitcher? (Fill the 5-liter jar. From the full 5-liter jar, fill the 3-liter jar. Pour the remaining juice, 2 liters, into the pitcher.) Using the same conditions, how can you get 1 liter of juice in the pitcher. (Repeat the above procedure twice, getting 4 liters in the pitcher. Then, from the pitcher, fill the 3-liter jar, leaving 1 liter in the pitcher.)

Unit	Symbol	Value in Liters
milliliter	**mL**	0.001 L (one-thousandth liter)
centiliter	cL	0.01 L (one-hundredth liter)
deciliter	dL	0.1 L (one-tenth liter)
liter	**L**	1 L (one liter)
decaliter	daL	10 L (ten liters)
hectoliter	hL	100 L (one hundred liters)
kiloliter	**kL**	1 000 L (one thousand liters)

Parts of a liter — milliliter, centiliter, deciliter

Basic unit — liter

Multiples of a liter — decaliter, hectoliter, kiloliter

(Commonly used units are in **bold** type.)

1,000 L	100 L	10 L	1 L	0.1 L	0.01 L	0.001 L
kilo-liter	hecto-liter	deca-liter	liter	deci-liter	centi-liter	milli-liter
kL	hL	daL	L	dL	cL	mL

EXAMPLE 1

Change the metric measures of capacity to the unit indicated.

a. 38 daL to liters

b. 36 000 mL to liters

SOLUTION

To change to a smaller unit, move the decimal point to the right.

a. 38 daL = 380 L   The decimal point is moved one place to the right.

To change to a larger unit, move the decimal point to the left.

b. 36 000 mL = 36 L   The decimal point is moved three places to the left.

■ **CHECK YOUR UNDERSTANDING**

A. Change 4 L to milliliters.   4 000 mL   **B.** Change 180 cL to liters.   1.8 L

■ Metric Measure of Weight

In this text and in everyday conversation, *weight* and *mass* are used interchangeably. Technically, however, mass is a measurement of the quantity of matter. Weight is a force exerted by gravitational pull against a mass. That is why astronauts on the moon weigh approximately $\frac{1}{6}$ of their weight on earth. An astronaut's mass, however, is the same on earth and in space.

Unit	Symbol	Value in Grams
milligram	**mg**	0.001 g (one-thousandth gram)
centigram	**cg**	0.01 g (one-hundredth gram)
decigram	dg	0.1 g (one-tenth gram)
gram	**g**	1 g (one gram)
decagram	dag	10 g (ten grams)
hectogram	hg	100 g (one hundred grams)
kilogram	**kg**	1 000 g (one thousand grams)
metric ton	**t**	1 000 kg (one thousand kilograms)

Parts of a gram — milligram, centigram, decigram

Basic unit — gram

Multiples of a gram — decagram, hectogram, kilogram, metric ton

(Commonly used units are in **bold** type.)

Lesson 14.5 International Measures of Capacity and Weight ■ 615

■ *CHECK YOUR UNDERSTANDING SOLUTIONS*

A. 4 L = 4 000 mL, decimal point is moved 3 places to the right

B. 180 cL = 1.8 L, decimal point is moved 2 places to the left

■ Apply Goal 2

Make a transparency of the metric weight place value table on page 616 and use it to explain the solutions to the two parts of Example 2.

Assign Check Your Understanding problems C and D for class work and observe student work at their desks.

■ ONGOING ASSESSMENT

Assign these conversions:

a. 18 L = ? mL **18 000 mL**
b. 200 L = ? kL **0.2 kL**
c. 51 cg = ? mg **510 mg**
d. 16 hg = ? kg **1.6 kg**

■ Teach Goal 3

Reiterate that arithmetic operations with metric capacities and weights are done in the same way as with customary capacity and weight measures. Emphasize that unlike measures must be converted to a common measure before the math may be done.

Remind students that conversions are to be made to the larger unit, unless problem directions specify otherwise.

■ Apply Goal 3

Have students look at the six parts of Example 3 and point out which of the six parts requires a conversion to a common unit of measure (a and b). Then explain the solutions to the six parts of Example 3.

Assign Check Your Understanding problems E and F for class work. Move about the classroom to observe student work.

In the metric system, the **gram** is the basic unit of weight. One kilogram, or 1 000 grams, is equivalent to approximately 2.2 customary pounds. A *gram* is equivalent to about 0.04 of a customary ounce.

Usually grams or milligrams are used to measure items with a small weight or mass. Kilograms or metric tons are used to measure large items. A metric ton, *t*, is equal to 1 000 kg.

Use the metric weight place value table shown to count the number of places you need to move the decimal point to change from one weight measure to another.

1,000 g	100 g	10 g	1 g	0.1 g	0.01 g	0.001 g
kilo-gram	hecto-gram	deca-gram	gram	deci-gram	centi-gram	milli-gram
kg	hg	dag	g	dg	cg	mg

EXAMPLE 2

Change the metric measures of weight to the unit indicated.

a. 3 g to centigrams   **b.** 762 dag to kilograms

SOLUTION

To change to a smaller unit, move the decimal point to the right.

a. 3 g = 300 cg   The decimal point is moved two places to the right.

To change to a larger unit, move the decimal point to the left.

b. 762 dag = 7.62 kg   The decimal point is moved two places to the left.

■ CHECK YOUR UNDERSTANDING

C. Change 5 cg to milligrams.   50 mg

D. Change 19 000 kg to tons   19 t

■ Calculating With Metric Measures

You can add, subtract, multiply, and divide capacity and weight measures in the same way as other numbers. When measures are in different units, convert them to the same unit. Remember to state your answer in the larger unit.

EXAMPLE 3

Perform the indicated operation.

a. 18 L + 250 cL   **b.** 56 kL − 2 000 L   **c.** 24 L × 15

d. 2 300 g × 1.4   **e.** 620 mg ÷ 0.5   **f.** 625 mg ÷ 4 mg

SOLUTION

a. 18 L + 250 cL = 20.5 L   **b.** 56 kL − 2 000 L = 54 kL

c. 24 L × 15 = 360 L   **d.** 2 300 g × 1.4 = 3 220 g

e. 620 mg ÷ 0.5 = 1 240 mg   **f.** 625 mg ÷ 4 mg = 156.25

■ *CHECK YOUR UNDERSTANDING SOLUTIONS*

C. 5 cg = 50 mg, decimal point is moved 1 place to the right

D. 1 t = 1 000 kg; 19 000 ÷ 1 000 = 19 t

E. Find the sum: 2 L + 400 mL   2.4 L

F. Find the difference: 19 g − 20 mg   18.98 g

■ Converting Metric and Customary Measures

As you did with length and area, use the appropriate conversion figure to convert metric capacity and metric weight measures to customary measures, and vice versa. Commonly used capacity and weight conversions are shown below.

Metric to Customary	Customary to Metric
1 L ≈ 1.06 quarts	1 quart ≈ 0.95 L
1 L ≈ 0.26 gallons	1 gallon ≈ 3.79 L
1 g ≈ 0.035 ounce	1 ounce ≈ 28.3 g
1 kg ≈ 2.2 pounds	1 pound ≈ 0.45 kg

EXAMPLE 4

What is the equivalency in liters of a bottle of bleach whose capacity is 0.75 gallons?

SOLUTION
Multiply the gallons by the correct equivalency.

0.75 gallons × 3.79 ≈ 2.84 L   capacity of bottle

EXAMPLE 5

A jar of olives has a net weight of 70 g. What is the equivalent weight in ounces?

SOLUTION
Multiply the grams by the correct equivalency.

70 g × 0.035 ≈ 2.45 oz   net weight of olive jar

■ **CHECK YOUR UNDERSTANDING**

G. While traveling, you buy 54 liters of gasoline. To how many gallons was this purchase equivalent?   14.04 gallons

H. You calculate from a European recipe that you need 240 kg of flour to bake a certain type of bread for a town fundraiser. How many pounds of flour must you buy?   528 lb

Wrap Up

If there is a sizable difference in the weight of the cases, you may be correct in saying one case is lighter than the other. The best way to make comparisons is to change the weights to the same measure, either metric or customary.

Lesson 14.5 International Measures of Capacity and Weight ■ 617

■ **Teach Goal 4**

Remind students that the equivalencies to convert metric and customary measures are approximate. Also, the table on page 617 combines capacity and weight equivalencies.

■ **Apply Goal 4**

Work Examples 4 and 5 at the board. Have students identify the column and row in which the equivalency factor appears.

Assign Check Your Understanding problems G and H for class work. Move about the classroom to monitor student work.

Wrap Up

Review the Start Up. Point out that people often buy luggage to replace pieces they own that are too heavy. If so, they need to know the weight of their old luggage before shopping for new and lighter luggage.

■ *CHECK YOUR UNDERSTANDING SOLUTIONS*

E. 400 mL = 0.4 L; 2 L + 0.4 L = 2.4 L

F. 20 mg = 0.02 g; 19 g − 0.02 g = 18.98 g

G. 54 × 0.26 gal ≈ 14.04 gal

H. 240 × 2.2 lb ≈ 528 lb

COMMUNICATION

Form a group to conduct a survey of adults outside of school to determine their knowledge of the metric system. Create a short questionnaire that asks people to explain metric measures. Base your questions around 5 items commonly sold by metric measure or found in daily life. Create a scale for evaluating the responses. Combine all the data collected by the group and compose a short report on your research findings.

Describe how prepared the majority the adults you surveyed would be to use metrics should the United States switch to the metric system.

EXERCISES

Change the metric measures to the unit indicated.

1. 1 kL = ? L   1 000 L
2. 1 mL = ? kL   0.000 001 kL
3. 600 mL = ? L   0.6 L
4. 470 L = ? kL   0.47 kL
5. 1 900 mg = ? g   1.9 g
6. 740 g = ? kg   0.74 kg
7. 0.65 kg = ? g   650 g
8. 500 kg = ? t   0.5 t
9. 1 mL = ? L   0.001 L

Perform the indicated operation.

10. 400 mL + 34.6 mL   434.6 mL
11. 3 t + 1.5 t + 54 kg   4.554 kg
12. 35.23 kL − 35 000 L   0.23 kL
13. 7 450 mg − 2.09 g   5.36 g
14. 22 × 23.5 kL   517 kL
15. 4% × 1 800 kg   72 kg
16. 100 mL ÷ 8   12.5 mL
17. 9 t ÷ 0.2   45 t
18. 2 004 t ÷ 12 t   167
19. 913.5 mL ÷ 7 mL   130.5

Find the equivalent measures of capacity and weight.

20. 6 quarts ≈ ? L   5.7 L
21. 12 pounds ≈ ? kg   5.4 kg
22. 2 L ≈ ? quarts   2.12 qt.
23. 24 ounces ≈ ? g   679.2 g

24. A tank holds 150 kL of fuel oil when full. On Monday, the tank was 90% full. These amounts of fuel were pumped from the tank in the next three days: 33 500 L, 27 000 L, and 22 450 L. How many kL of fuel oil were left in the tank at the end of the third day?   52.05 kL

25. Jacob Stearns is providing refreshments for the 12 cast members of a dance group. If Jacob buys 15 liters of juice, how many liters of juice will there be for each cast member?   1.25 L

A 354 mL can of frozen concentrate makes 0.94 liters of lemonade.

26. How many liters of lemonade can you make from 6 cans?   5.64 L

27. How many cans of concentrate would you need to make 4.7 liters of lemonade?   5

618 ■ Chapter 14 International Business

SELECTED SOLUTIONS

12. 35 000 L = 35 kL; 35.23 kL − 35 kL = 0.23 kL
20. 6 × 0.95 L ≈ 5.7 L
24. 0.90 × 150 kL = 135 kL in tank on Monday;
    33 500 L + 27 000 L + 22 450 L = 82 950 L, or
    82.95 kL; 135 kL − 82.95 kL = 52.05 kL

25. 15 L ÷ 12 = 1.25 L
27. 4.7 L ÷ 0.94 L = 5

Northern Products produced 6 kiloliters of syrup. The syrup is poured into one-fourth liter size bottles and is packed 48 bottles to a case.

28. What total number of bottles may be filled with the syrup produced? 24,000

29. If all the bottles are packed in cases, how many cases will there be? 500

30. A box contains 240 writing pads. The pads alone weigh 31.2 kg and the box weighs 3 kg. How many grams does each steno pad weigh? 130 g

31. A full box of crackers weighed 0.410 kg. The box is now $\frac{1}{2}$ full. What is the weight in grams of the crackers left? 205 g

32. Regal hand soap is sold in 8-bar packs. Each pack weighs 1.136 kg. Hand soap made by Rose Mist is sold in 3-bar packs with a total weight of 405 g. What is the average weight in grams of one bar of each brand of soap? 142 g, Regal; 135 g, Rose Mist

33. The Zealan Company is shipping 1,500 roasting timers. The weight of one timer and its shipping box is 730 g. What is the total weight of this shipment in kilograms? 1 095 kg

A certain model of a car used to weigh 1 200 kg. The car has been redesigned so that its total mass is now 1 170 kg.

34. By how many kg was the weight of the car reduced? 30 kg

35. What percent of the car's original weight is this reduction? 2.5%

36. A painting company used 240 gallons of paint last week. How much paint was used in liters? 909.6 L

37. To keep hydrated during a bike race, racers were advised to drink 2.5 L of water during the race. There are 32 ounces in a quart. How many ounces of water should each racer drink? 84.8 oz.

38. CRITICAL THINKING Other countries have adopted the U.S. economic system, but not the customary system of measures. Why do you think this is?
See Enrich section for answer.

39. CRITICAL THINKING Since many products now show customary and equivalent metric measures, do you think that the people who use such products gradually learn metric measures? What are your reasons? See Enrich section for answer.

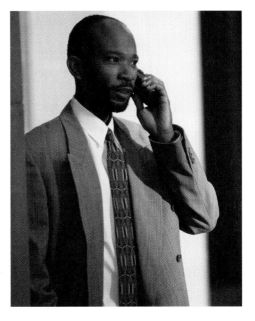

MIXED REVIEW

40. What number is $\frac{3}{8}$ less than $205.68? $128.55

41. A server wrote $5,912 in food checks in a week. If her average tip was 12% of the check, what tip income did she earn for the week? $709.44, Lesson 1.5

42. Cedric Marshall spends 8.5% of his $46,000 annual income on commuting costs. He wants to cut that cost to $40 a week by using the subway instead of driving. How much less will Cedric spend in a year on commuting by making this change? $1,830, Lesson 2.7

Lesson 14.5 International Measures of Capacity and Weight ■ **619**

SELECTED SOLUTIONS

28. 6 kL = 6 000 L; 6 000 ÷ $\frac{1}{4}$ = 24,000 bottles
31. $\frac{1}{2}$ × 0.410 kg = 0.205 kg, or 205 g
33. 1,500 × 730 g = 1 095 000 g, or 1 095 kg
34. 1 200 kg − 1 170 kg = 30 kg weight reduction

35. 30 kg ÷ 1 200 kg = 0.025, or 2.5%
37. 2.5 × 1.06 qts. ≈ 2.65 qts.; 2.65 qts. × 32 oz. ≈ 84.8 oz.

- Divide Gross Domestic Product by total population to find per capita GDP.

- Calculate difference between exports and imports to find trade surplus or deficit.

- Multiply foreign currency by exchange rate in U.S. dollars to find value in U.S. dollars.

- Divide foreign currency by foreign units per U.S. dollar to find value in U.S. dollars.

Lesson 14.2 International Time and Temperature

- Add one hour to current time for each time zone moved east and subtract one hour for each time zone moved west to find time in another time zone.

- Use the formula $C = \frac{5}{9}(F - 32)$ to convert Fahrenheit temperature to Celsius.

- Use the formula $F = 1.8C + 32$ to convert Celsius temperature to Fahrenheit.

Lesson 14.3 International Measures of Length

- Move decimal point to left (or right) one place for each place moved on metric length scale and write correct place value symbol to change smaller unit to larger unit (or larger unit to smaller unit).

- Use customary calculation methods to do metric length arithmetic operations.

- Multiply length by equivalent length to find metric or customary equivalency.

Chapter Review

Vocabulary Review

area	Gross Domestic Product (GDP)	per capita GDP
domestic business	importing	square meter
exporting	international business	trade deficit
foreign exchange rate	liter	trade surplus
gram	meter	

Fill in the blanks with the word or words that best completes the statement.

1. (A, an) __?__ results when a country buys more goods from other countries than it sells to other countries.   trade deficit

2. The basic metric measure for mass is known as the __?__.   gram

3. The purchase of goods and services among countries is referred to as __?__.   international business

4. The basic unit of length or distance in the metric system is called the __?__.   meter

5. The amount of currency of one country that can be exchanged for another country's currency is determined by the __?__.   foreign exchange rate

6. Buying goods from other countries is called __?__.   importing

7. All the trade that takes place within a country's borders is called __?__.   domestic business

8. In the metric system, the basic unit of capacity is known as the __?__.   liter

9. The result you get by multiplying an item's length by its width is called __?__   area

10. The result of dividing a country's Gross Domestic Product by its population is known as __?__.   per capita GDP

LESSON 14.1

11. The GDP of Mongolia is $5.8 billion. Its population is 2.62 million. What is its per capita GDP, to the nearest dollar? $2,214

12. In one year, Saudi Arabia had imports of $30.4 billion and exports of $86.5 billion. What was the amount of their trade surplus or trade deficit? $56.1 billion trade surplus

13. The exchange rate for the Chilean peso is $0.001657. To how many U.S. dollars are 4,000 Chilean pesos equal, to the nearest cent? $6.63

LESSON 14.2

14. A business call is made on Wednesday from Los Angeles, California to Tokyo, Japan at 5:00 P.M. Los Angeles time. Find what time it is in Tokyo.   10:00 A.M. Thursday

15. The average low temperature in January in Green Bay, Wisconsin is 7°F. What is the temperature in Celsius, to the nearest whole degree?   −14°C

16. The high temperature for the day in Dublin, Ireland was reported as 17°C. To what Fahrenheit temperature is this equivalent, to the nearest degree?   63°F

TEACHING STRATEGIES Chapter Review

Have students close their books. Write the first term in the vocabulary review on the board and have students give a very short definition or description of the term as quickly as they can. Go on to the next term and repeat the process. When all terms have been reviewed, have students open their books and complete the Vocabulary Review, under a time limit.

LESSON 14.3

17. How many kilometers are in 5 000 m?   5 km

18. To how many centimeters is 530 mm equal?   53 cm

19. Find the value of a in this equation: $a = 5(2 \text{ m} + 125 \text{ cm})$ 16.25 m

20. Find the value of b in this equation: $b = (23 \text{ km} - 19\,000 \text{ m}) \div 2.5$ 1.6 km

21. Find the number of meters in 25 ft.   7.625 m

22. Find the number of inches in 46.1 cm.   17.979 in.

23. The Just Right Tailor shop buys twelve 500-m spools of black thread every three months. How many kilometers of thread does the shop buy in one year?   24 km

LESSON 14.4

24. A farm measures 40 000 m². What is its measure in hectare?   4 ha

25. The inland waterways of a European country measure 19 km². What is this measure in square meters?   19 000 000 m²

26. Find the value of c in this equation: $c = 3(49 \text{ m}^2 - 15\,000 \text{ cm}^2)$ 142.5 m²

27. Find the value of d in this equation: $d = 160 \text{ ha} - (6 \text{ km}^2 \div 4)$ 0.1 km²

28. Find the number of hectares in 840 acres.   336 ha

29. Find the number of square inches in 540 cm².   86.4 in.²

30. Pam's living room is 14 feet by 16 feet. She has a grand piano that covers of an area of about 4 square meters. Her entertainment center covers about 2.16 square meters. About how much floor space remains for Pam to place other furniture in her living room?   about 157 square feet

LESSON 14.5

31. How many kiloliters are in 24 000 L?   24 kL

32. To what number of centiliters are 212 mL equal?   21.2 cL

33. A shipment weighing 6 700 kg is equal to what number of metric tons?   6.7 t

34. What weight in grams is a packet of spice that weighs 40 000 mg?   40 g

35. Find the value of e in this equation: $e = 36(22 \text{ L} - 1\,200 \text{ cL})$ 360 L

36. Find the value of f in this equation: $f = (62 \text{ g} + (10 \times 400 \text{ mg})) \div 4$ 16.5 g

37. Find the number of liters in 4 quarts and the number of gallons in 12 L.   3.8 L; 3.12 gal

38. Find the number of grams in 16 oz.   452.8 g

39. Find the number of pounds in 250 kg.   550 lb

Chapter 14 Review ■ **621**

Lesson 14.4 International Measures of Area

• Move decimal point to left (or right) two places for each place moved on metric area scale and write correct place value symbol to change smaller unit to larger unit (or larger unit to smaller unit).

• Use customary calculation methods to do metric area arithmetic operations.

• Multiply area by equivalent area to find metric or customary equivalency.

Lesson 14.5 International Measures of Capacity and Weight

• Move decimal point to left (or right) one place for each place moved on metric capacity or weight scale and write new place value symbol to change smaller unit to larger unit (or larger unit to smaller unit).

• Use customary calculation methods to do metric capacity and weight arithmetic operations.

• Multiply capacity or weight by equivalent capacity or weight to find metric or customary equivalencies.

TEACHING STRATEGIES Chapter Review

Have students study the examples for a lesson and then solve the Chapter Review problems corresponding to that lesson without referring back to the lesson. When the review problems for a lesson are completed, give students the correct answers and have them refer to the lesson examples to locate the cause of any errors. Then have them rework the incorrect problems.

Task 1: Currency Exchange

Enter data into a template that will calculate the U.S. currency equivalent to a foreign currency, given an exchange rate in dollars.

Open the spreadsheet for Chapter 14 (tech14-1.xls) and enter the data shown in blue (cells B2-3) into the spreadsheet. The spreadsheet assumes that a hotel room was rented in Berlin, Germany for four days and the total bill came to 686.16 euros. Your computer screen should look like the one shown below when you are done.

	A	B
1	**Currency Exchange Calculator**	
2	Units of Foreign Currency	686.16
3	Exchange Rate in U.S. Dollars	$1.272700
4	U.S. Currency Equivalent	$873.28

Task 2: Analyze the Spreadsheet Output

Answer these questions about the spreadsheet.

1. Why was the hotel bill entered as 686.16 instead of 686.16 €?   Only units need to be entered, not the currency symbol
2. What does the exchange rate mean?   It tells how much in U.S. dollars each unit of foreign currency is worth. One euro is equal to 1.2727 U.S. dollars.
3. To what amount in U.S. currency was the hotel bill equal? $873.28

4. If the hotel room rate does not change during the next year, would the U.S. currency equivalent remain the same for a four-day stay? Give your reasons.   Possibly, but unlikely. Exchange rate changes day-to-day and year-to-year.
5. Why was the U.S. currency output rounded to the nearest cent and not the nearest dollar, as $600?   U.S. currency may be expressed to the nearest cent, so rounding is not used. Also currency exchanges keep records correct to the cent.

Now assume that a currency trader exchanged 300,000,000 euros for U.S. dollars on July 1 at the exchange rate of $1.2727. Move the cursor to B2 and enter 300,000,000 without the commas.

6. What amount of U.S. dollars did the trader receive from this exchange? $381,810,000
7. Now assume that by one week later, on July 8, the value of a euro dropped by 1.5¢ in relation to the U.S. dollar. What would be the new exchange rate? $1.2577
8. Enter the new exchange rate to find the amount in U.S. dollars that could be purchased with 300,000,000 euros. What is the amount? $377,310,000

9. What do the answers to Problems 6 and 8 suggest?   The currency trader owns $381,810,000 U.S. dollars as of July 1. If U.S. dollars are exchanged for euros on July 8, only $377,310,000 U.S. dollars would be needed to buy back the original 300,000,000 euros. The difference $4,500,000 ($381,810,000 − $377,310,000) represents the profit in U.S. dollars that a trader could have made on this transaction.

TEACHING STRATEGIES Task 1

Have students use the currency exchange calculator to rework any example problems, Check Your Understanding problems, or exercises that require currency conversion.

Teach and Apply Task 3

Suggest that students use a calculator to verify spreadsheet calculations.

Teach and Apply Task 4

Have students write their answers to questions 10–13.

Task 3: Design a Spreadsheet to Convert Temperatures

Design a spreadsheet that will convert Fahrenheit temperature to Celsius, and Celsius to Fahrenheit. The spreadsheet should show the equivalent temperature at the right of each temperature entered. Use the conversion formulas that appear in Lesson 14.2.

SITUATION: The low temperature for a day in January in Duluth, Minnesota is expected to be 21°F. You receive an email from a friend who lives in Geneva, Switzerland. She reports that the low temperature in Geneva for the same day is expected to be −2°C. Compare the two temperatures.

Task 4: Analyze the Spreadsheet Output

Answer these questions about your completed spreadsheet.

10. To what Celsius temperature is 21°F equivalent?   −6.1°C

11. What is the equivalent Fahrenheit temperature for −2°C?   28.4°F

12. In which city will it be warmer, at the low temperature for the day?   Geneva

13. At about which whole degree in Fahrenheit will the temperatures in Duluth and Geneva be about the same?   At 28°F which is equal to −2.2°C

You may want to use the spreadsheet to verify the temperature conversions you have already solved in Lesson 14.2.

Chapter 14 Technology Workshop ■ 623

TEACHING STRATEGIES Task 3

After students complete and print the spreadsheet they developed, display the spreadsheet tech14-3.xls that provides a sample solution. Have students compare the sample to their spreadsheet solution. Discuss any differences they note between the spreadsheets.

$60 \times 60 = 3,600$ seconds in one hour

$3,600 \times 20,000,000 = 72,000,000,000$

72 billion years

■ WRITE

Inform students that their speeches may include emotional and factual approaches. Remind them that they must do research to gather the facts they will use.

Suggest that students prepare an outline of their speech and limit speaking time to two minutes.

■ SCANS

Students may work in teams to locate information about how people live and work in other countries. Students may also find it interesting to search for the differences in terms used in English-speaking countries to describe the same item.

In England, for instance, a spanner is a wrench, the hood of a car is called a bonnet, and cars use petrol, or gasoline.

■ ONGOING ASSESSMENT

The Integrated Project found in the workbook provides a broad, ongoing assessment activity for the goals of this chapter.

Chapter Assessment

How Times Have Changed

For the following question, refer to the timeline on page 591 as needed.

The NIST-F1 atomic clock that was put into use in 1999 was the most accurate clock ever. In 20 million years the clock would be off at most by one second. In how many years would it be possible that the clock was off by one hour?

WRITE

Ask yourself which system of measurement you prefer, metric or customary. When you make your decision be sure you think about the positive and negatives aspects of both systems.

Imagine that your class has been given the authority to make a decision that would impact the entire country. Your class gets to decide if the U.S. will continue to use customary measures or change to using metric measures.

Write a persuasive speech that will be presented to the class. Explain your personal decision and state reasons that you think will sway your class members to vote for the same choice as you.

SCANS

Workplace Skills—*Works with Cultural Diversity*

Understanding and respecting how people and cultures differ is an important skill for any employee. Throughout your life, you will work in various situations with various people that have cultural and ethnic backgrounds different from yours. You will be expected to interact with all types of individuals at work, in public places, and in social gatherings.

Test Your Skills Choose a country that you are interested in learning more about. Find out all that you can about how the workplaces in that country differ from the workplaces in the U.S.

Make a Plan Create a summary, (either an outline, a chart, or a report) that compares and contrasts the cultural differences and similarities among employees in the country you selected and employees in the U.S. Include suggestions that U.S. employers can put in place to assist employees to know more about cultural differences.

Summarize Prepare either through visual or verbal presentation the information you found about cultural differences. Explain how this knowledge aids employees in the workplace and what long-term benefits might result. Include references to as many of the following skills, traits, or abilities as you can.

writing	*listening*	*responsibility*	*seeing things in the mind's eye*
social skills	*speaking*	*self-esteem*	*integrity/honesty*

TEACHING STRATEGIES Chapter Assessment

Have those students who prepared a visual summary of cultural differences present their display to the class. Remind students that visual displays help focus attention on a specific topic directly related to the information being presented verbally.

Chapter-Test Correlation

Question	Lesson
11	14.1
12	14.1
13	14.1
14	14.2
15	14.2
16	14.3
17	14.3
18	14.4
19	14.4
20	14.5
21	14.5

CHAPTER TEST

Answer each question.

1. Write out $1.072 million as a numeral. $1,072,000

2. Multiply 55×0.3642 and round to the nearest tenth.   20.0

3. Solve $2,900 \div 0.3642$ and round to the nearest hundredth.   7,962.66

4. Add 7 hours to 10:14 A.M.   5:14 P.M.

5. 15 cm + 900 mm + 0.014 m   1.064 m

6. 60 km ÷ 0.4 km   150   7. 24% of 6.5 kL   1.56 kL

8. What number is $\frac{1}{8}$ more than 160 L?   180 L

9. Find what percent 340 mg is of 200 mg.   170%

10. $1\frac{3}{4} \times 76.2$ kg   133.35 kg

Applications

11. In a recent year, a country had a Gross Domestic Product of $4,200,000,000 and a population of 1,200,000. What was its per capita GDP? $3,500

12. Last year a country had exports of $1.04 billion and imports of $924 million. What was the amount of the trade surplus or deficit? $116 million trade surplus

13. Thailand's currency, the baht (B), has a value in U.S. dollars of $0.02438. Also, there are 41.014 B per U.S. Dollar. To what amount in U.S. dollars are 60,000 B equal?
$1,462.80

14. A telephone call is made at 6:00 A.M. across 6 time zones to the east and across the International Date Line. What time is it in the place where the phone call is received?
12 Noon

15. To what temperature in Celsius is a temperature of 50°F equal?   10° C

16. A store sold 218 cm of gold chain from a roll that originally held 12.5 m of chain. How much chain is left on the roll in centimeters?   1 032 cm

17. One inch ≈ 2.54 cm, and 1 foot ≈ 0.305 m. How many meters are there in a board 7.5 ft long, to the nearest tenth meter?   2.3 m

18. Michelle cut 2 boards for shelving out of a 2.88 m² sheet of wood. One board was cut 20 cm by 120 cm; the other was cut 30 cm by 120 cm. How much wood in m² was left of the larger sheet?   2.28 m²

19. A cabinet top measures 20 inches × 32 inches. If 1 in.² ≈ 6.5 cm², what is the area of the cabinet top in cm²?   4 160 cm²

20. The Hilton family saves 25¢ per liter by buying orange juice in bulk. The family uses 2.5 L of orange juice a week. How much will the Hiltons save in a year by buying juice in bulk? $32.50

21. A deli restaurant chain sells 572 lb of potato salad a week. How many kg of potato salad will the chain sell in 1 year at this rate, to the nearest kg?   13 385 kg

Chapter 14 Assessment ■ **625**

TEACHING STRATEGIES Chapter Test

Remind students to show each step in the solution of problems in a logical sequence. Items are to be labeled as needed. Also remind them to use correct abbreviations including all punctuation.

Test Taking Strategies

■ **MULTIPLE CHOICE**
Exercise 10. Point out that often two conversions are necessary to solve a problem. Since the equivalency is in liters and quarts, the ounces must be converted first to quarts, and then to liters.

MULTIPLE CHOICE

Select the best choice for each question.

1. A day care center has current assets of $60,100 and current liabilities of $32,100. What is the center's current ratio, to the nearest tenth? B

    A. $28.000   **B.** 1.9:1   **C.** 1.3:1   **D.** $46,100   **E.** 0.5:1

2. What is the area of a building that is 15 m × 30 m? E

    A. 450 m   **B.** 90 m^2 **C.** 327 m^2 **D.** 90 m   **E.** 450 m^2

3. On Tuesday, you flew west from Chicago to Australia on a 24-hour flight. You crossed the International Date Line. What day of the week was it when you landed? C

    A. Sunday   **B.** Monday   **C.** Tuesday   **D.** Wednesday   **E.** Thursday

4. Lowen's Books had net sales of $541,290, gross profit of $162,300, and net income of $42,460. What was Lowen's net profit margin, to the nearest tenth percent? C

    A. 7.9%   **B.** 30%   **C.** 7.8%   **D.** 37.8%   **E.** 26.2%

5. A product's beginning inventory on January 1 was $8,400, and its ending inventory on March 31 was $3,600. The cost of goods sold for the product in the quarter was $14,500. What was the product's turnover rate, to the nearest tenth? B

    A. 3.0   **B.** 2.4   **C.** 1.3   **D.** 1.7   **E.** 6.4

6. A business had a net income for a year of $86,580 and capital of $619,900. What was its return on equity, to the nearest tenth percent? D

    A. 6.2%   **B.** 17.3%   **C.** 7.2%   **D.** 14%   **E.** 11.4%

7. The exchange rates in U.S. Dollars for Israel's shekel and Poland's zloty, are $0.2246 and $0.2980, respectively. What would a 149 zloty purchase cost in U.S. dollars? D

    A. $71.04   **B.** $500   **C.** $33.47   **D.** $44.40   **E.** $663.40

8. To how many ha is a field that measures 1 400 m by 860 m equal? A

    A. 120.4 ha   **B.** 4 520 ha   **C.** 4 708 ha   **D.** 123.7 m^2 **E.** 12 040 ha

9. The partners, Boyd and Blake, agree to share equally a $145,000 annual net income after Boyd is paid a salary of $12,000 plus 7.2% interest on his $115,000 investment in the business. What is Boyd's total share of the net income? E

    A. $20,280   **B.** $68,360   **C.** $68,720   **D.** $78,500   **E.** $82,640

10. If there are 32 oz. and 0.95 L in a quart, how many liters would there be in a can that holds 48 oz. of paint thinner? C

    A. 15.2 L   **B.** 45.6 L   **C.** 1.425 L   **D.** 30.4 L   **E.** 50.5 L

11. Wilbur unloaded 80 bags of potatoes from a delivery truck. Each bag weighed 22.5 kg. At 2.2 lb to the kilogram, what was the total weight in pounds of the unloaded potatoes? B

    A. 197.6   **B.** 3,960   **C.** 176   **D.** 1,800   **E.** 49.5

626 ■ **Chapter 14 International Business**

TEACHING STRATEGIES Cumulative Review

Remind students to use their skills of estimation to limit the number of possible choices in the multiple-choice exercises and to test for the reasonableness of answers they calculate for open-ended exercises.

OPEN ENDED

12. Two partners agree to share profits in proportion to their investments. Partner A invested $120,000, and Partner B invested $160,000. What share of a $214,970 annual profit does each partner receive, to the nearest dollar? A, $92,130; B, $122,840

13. A bankrupt firm has $42,500 to pay $250,000 of creditors' claims. How many cents on the dollar will each creditor receive? 17¢

14. A country with a population of 109,000 has a Gross Domestic Product of $156,960,000. What was the per capita GDP in this country? $1,440

15. Pruitt Furnishings had sales of $218,400 and sales returns and allowances of $1,572 in March. The cost of goods sold in March was $130,789. What was the gross profit for March? $86,039

16. Robert Murphy needs these amounts of electrical wire: seven 4 m pieces; four 2.75 cm pieces; six 100 mm pieces. How many meters of wire are needed? 28.71 m

17. U.S. exports to Brazil were $13,202,198,000. U.S. imports from Brazil were $11,313,062,000. Did the U.S. have a trade surplus or trade deficit with Brazil, and what was the amount? trade surplus of $1,889,136,000

18. On a trip to Canada your car breaks down and you are towed 60 kilometers to the Canadian border. The towing service charged you $1.85 per kilometer plus $0.18 for each kilogram of your car's 2,200 lb weight. What was the total towing charge? $289.20

19. LeMoyne's Department Store had these assets on December 31: Cash, $34,288.92; accounts receivable, $123,573.65; store and warehouse, $435,200. The store owed $85,323.05 in accounts payable and a $178,000 loan to Second Street Bank. What were the store's assets, liabilities, and capital? $593,062.57; $263,323.05; $329,739.52

20. One day in a recent year, the euro exchange rate in U.S. dollars was $1.2198. Also, the euro converts as 0.8201 euros per U.S. Dollar. A sale of computers was priced at 2,500,000 euros. What was the sale amount in U.S. dollars, to the nearest thousand dollars? $3,049,000

21. Sylvan Beauty Supply had an inventory valued at $38,200 on February 1. During February, $72,070 of goods was bought. The inventory at the end of February was $44,618. What was the cost of goods sold for February? $65,652

22. A can holds 9.5 L of gasoline. Katrina used 7 full cans of gasoline in her mower to cut her lawn last year. She used 2 full cans to operate her snow blower. If 1 liter is equal to 0.26 gallons, how may gallons of gasoline did Katrina use last year for mowing her lawn and operating her snow blower? 22.23 gal.

CONSTRUCTED RESPONSE

23. You read an article distributed on the Internet discussing how important it is for the United States to have a strong dollar. Explain the effect that you think a strong dollar will have on imports and exports. A strong dollar means that other currencies will be worth less in relation to the U.S. dollar. It will take more units of a foreign currency to buy one dollar's worth of goods produced in the United States. When U.S. goods become more expensive to the rest of the world, U.S. exports are likely to decrease. Similarly, the U.S. will likely import more goods because the goods produced by other countries will have become less expensive.

Chapter 14 Cumulative Review ▪ 627

PORTFOLIO ASSESSMENT

Remind students to review the materials they created in this chapter and select those they wish to place in their portfolios. Students should be that certain the contents of their portfolios show the best selections of their work from the entire year.

CHAPTER 1: GROSS PAY

Lesson 1.1, pages 4–7

Exercises

1. 36.5 **3.** $2,223 **5.** $456 **7.** $10,300
9. $3,239.50 **11.** $112 **13.** $806 **15.** $456
17. $2,248 **19.** $365.25 **21.** $302.40
23. $342 **25.** Answers will vary. Possible answer: ask for a raise.

Mixed Review
27. $42,952 **29.** $70.65

Lesson 1.2, pages 8–13

Exercises

1. $375 **3.** $18,936 **5.** $406.44 **7.** $90
9. $19,900 **11.** $3,245.83, $749.04
13. $9.83 **15.** $1,125 **17.** $375 **19.** $978
21. $21,696 **23.** 33 **25.** $13.26
27. You will lose $3.

Mixed Review
29. $940 **31.** $70,304

Lesson 1.3, pages 14–19

Exercises

1. 18.25 **3.** 0.5 **5.** 43.5 **7.** 17.445
9. $78.44 **11.** $419.10 **13.** $17.925 **15.** 40
17. $480 **19.** $611.40 **21.** $17.055; $22.74
23. $646.39 **25.** experience, background, education, and years of experience

Mixed Review
27. $18 **29.** $34.50 **31.** 60 **33.** 15 **35.** 75
37. $660 **39.** 20 **41.** $616.33 **43.** $696.28

Lesson 1.4, pages 20–25

Exercises

1. 0.0925 **3.** 0.005 **5.** $975 **7.** 18%
9. 4.5% **11.** 11.625% **13.** $600; $592.25
15. $403.34 **17.** $632.30 **19.** $6,144
21. 3.2% **23.** 6%

Mixed Review
27. $70 **29.** 400 **31.** 6% **33.** $2,505

Lesson 1.5, pages 26–31

Exercises

1. 203 **3.** $97.44 **5.** $225 **7.** $37.40
9. $650 **11.** $2,090 **13.** $477.75 **15.** 140, $392.00 **17.** 354, 417.72 **19.** No, only 4%.
21. $580.75 **23.** $96, $116.15; $480, $580.75; $24,960, $30,199

Mixed Review
25. 24 **27.** $2,100 **29.** $840 **31.** $1,935

CHAPTER 2: NET PAY

Lesson 2.1, pages 40–46

Exercises

1. $138.09 **3.** $416.77 **5.** $309.76
7. 0.08 **9.** 0.1206 **11.** 0.89145 **13.** $27.89
15. $36 **17.** $48 **19.** $7 **21.** $45
23. $29.45, $6.89 **25.** $15.46, $3.62
27. $46.45, $10.86 **29.** $17.95, $4.20
31. 46.00; 28.97; 6.78; 82.12; 163.87; 303.42
33. 24.00; 35.85; 8.38; 31.51; 99.74; 478.47
35. 26.00; 33.40; 7.81; 48.22; 115.43; 423.33
37. $471.66 **39.** $465 **41.** $1,305
43. $651 **45.** Taxes go up with income, go down with allowances; exemptions are greater.

Mixed Review
47. $32 **49.** $1\frac{3}{4}$ **51.** 50 **53.** $126.36
55. $432

Lesson 2.2, pages 47–52

Exercises

1. $67,969 **3.** $4,186 **5.** $4,629 **7.** 0.564
9. 0.236 **11.** $11,333.19 **13.** $6,956.30
15. $6,301 **17.** $42,776 **19.** $5,461.56
21. B-Tree **23.** 1

Mixed Review
25. 39% **27.** 0.375 **29.** 0.005 **31.** $\frac{1}{4}$
33. $\frac{1}{10}$ **35.** $448.40 **37.** $48.75 **39.** 65

Lesson 2.3, pages 53–59

Exercises

1. $8,496 **3.** $3,493 **5.** $57,599
7. $21,238 **9.** $15,281 **11.** $39,712.27
13. $8,000 **15.** $20,000 **17.** $2,791
19. $3,056 **21.** $172 **23.** $33,781
25. $31,762 **27.** $3,216 **29.** $800
31. $4,850 **33.** $240 **35.** $263

Mixed Review
37. $27.50 **39.** 25% **41.** 0.432 **43.** $610

Lesson 2.4, pages 60–63

Exercises

1. $1,254 **3.** 0.072 **5.** 0.2498 **7.** $2,160.43
9. $58.63 **11.** $814.50 **13.** $667.60
15. $850 **17.** $2,872.65 **19.** $24,450
21. Tax due: $222.50

Mixed Review

23. $10\frac{11}{12}$ **25.** $2,167.11 **27.** 2,667.50

Lesson 2.5, pages 64–68

Exercises

1. 31 **3.** 295.19 **5.** 20, 24, 18, 17, 19, 26, 13, 21, 79 **7.** 383, 290, 405, 236, 497, 187, 630, 1,314 **9.** $900.75 **11.** $1,481.81 **13.** $28,978.49

Mixed Review

15. $1,814.12 **17.** $17\frac{21}{40}$ **19.** 5 **21.** 3 **23.** $33.85

Lesson 2.6, pages 69–73

Exercises

1. 0.19 **3.** 39% **5.** 70.5% **7.** $\frac{3}{4}$ **9.** $\frac{1}{3}$ **11.** $4,380 **13.** $12,848 **15.** $\frac{2}{25}$ **17.** 12% **19.** 71% **21.** 12.5%, $10,187.50 **23.** 3%, $2,445 **27.** Answers will vary. Tyrone spent 5.4% of his salary. Rosita spent 2.5% of her salary.

Mixed Review

29. $3\frac{5}{8}$ **31.** $5\frac{2}{5}$ **33.** $486 **35.** 66%

CHAPTER 3: BANKING SERVICES

Lesson 3.1, pages 84–89

Exercises

1. $770.62 **3.** $1,260.93 **5.** $140 **7.** $680.95 **9.** $981.75 **11.** $299.94 **13.** $1,354.52 **15.** Answers will vary. Sample answer: 400, save on shipping costs **17.** $593.25 **19.** $1,199.47

Mixed Review

21. $\frac{23}{24}$ **23.** $5\frac{1}{12}$ **25.** 14.859 **27.** $20,944.29 **29.** $36,920 **31.** $49,200

Lesson 3.2, pages 90–93

Exercises

1. $175.61 **3.** $6,951.09 **5.** $252.35 **7.** $123.62 **9.** Answers will vary, but may include that it is easy, the deposit is made on time, and eliminates the theft of a check.

Mixed Review

11. 0.6 **13.** $97.92 **15.** $22.005

Lesson 3.3, pages 94–98

Exercises

1. $15,371.61 **3.** $641.49 **5.** no **7.** $24.82

Mixed Review

9. 616 **11.** $10,578 **13.** $552.50

Lesson 3.4, pages 99–104

Exercises

1. $1,266.49 **3.** $14,906.25 **5.** $2,257.84 **7.** $972.37 **9.** keep track of account balance **11.** Possibly not since many banks honor checks up to 6 months after they are written.

Mixed Review

13. $9\frac{5}{8}$ **15.** $105 **17.** 134.46 **19.** $41,930 **21.** $47.30 **23.** 4%

Lesson 3.5, pages 105–110

Exercises

1. $148.62 **3.** $4,186.56 **5.** $286.30 **7.** $287.14 **9.** $912.61 **11.** Because too much was taken out

Mixed Review

13. $15.60 **15.** $326 **17.** $85 **19.** $696 **21.** 3.1% **23.** $157.50 **25.** $336

Lesson 3.6, pages 111–117

Exercises

1. $874.89 **3.** $16.08 **5.** $5.60 **7.** $3.75 **9.** $0.82 **11.** $1,050.95, $50.95 **13.** $905.64, $5.64 **15.** $696.45, $96.45 **17.** $865.45 **19.** $1,600 $\times$ 3% = $48 estimated; $50.18 actual. **21.** $613 **23.** $817.14 **25.** Answers will vary. Rounding to the nearest cent can increase amounts significantly over the life of loan. This method is more fair to the consumer.

Mixed Review

27. 8 **29.** $\frac{1}{28}$ **31.** $3,218,000 **33.** 7.5% **35.** $0.70 **37.** $428.48 **39.** 5%

Lesson 3.7, pages 118–123

Exercises

3. $7,500 **5.** $30.67 **7.** $13.92 **9.** time deposit, $0.37 more **11.** 5% **13.** money market earns $40.12; CD earns $0 after penalty

Mixed Review

15. $847.29 **17.** $4\frac{1}{5}$ **19.** 188

CHAPTER 4: LOANS AND CREDIT CARDS

Lesson 4.1, pages 132–138

Exercises

1. $93.78 **3.** $660 **5.** 12.5% **7.** $750
9. $20 **11.** $6.75; $156.75 **13.** $29,370
15. $29.00, $29.40 **17.** $47.34, $48
19. $21.60, $21.90 **21.** Estimates will vary;
$600 **23.** $10,591.78 **25.** $1,325 **27.** 9%
29. 8.4% **31.** exact interest lender **33.** 93%

Mixed Review

35. 3.4113 **37.** $1,230.77 **39.** $32.50
41. $480

Lesson 4.2, pages 139–143

Exercises

1. 0.023 **3.** 0.0075 **5.** $126 **7.** $484.50
9. 12.5% **11.** $8,190 **13.** $14,100 **15.** $30
17. $965.15 **19.** 11.6% **21.** $19,250
23. $588 **25.** $8,400 **27.** 1st lender

Mixed Review

29. $6,490.04 **31.** $\frac{6}{7}$ **33.** $\frac{1}{200}$ **35.** $474,
$16,274 **37.** 2%

Lesson 4.3, pages 144–149

Exercises

1. $4.18 **3.** 3,107.90 **5.** 512.80 **7.** 353
9. 70 **11.** $2.19 **13.** $37.91 **15.** $4.68
17. $15.98 **19.** $41.10 **21.** $33.53
23. 66 days **25.** 71 days **27.** 120 days
29. $\frac{3}{12}$ **31.** $\frac{7}{31}$ **33.** $\frac{4}{4}$ **35.** $\frac{3}{16}$ **37.** $\frac{3}{18}$
39. 90 days **41.** $15,554.79 **43.** Answers
will vary; 1st = $2,687.50; 2nd = $2,733.33;
difference of $45.83 buys you two more months

Mixed Review

45. 2,034.912 **47.** $20.25 **49.** August 8
51. $2,788.85 **53.** $335.25 **55.** $336.39

Lesson 4.4, pages 150–155

Exercises

1. $2,589.15 **3.** $575 **5.** $441 **7.** $1,413
9. 0.017 **11.** $1,793.68; $293.68
13. $2,280.60; $130.60 **15.** 6% **17.** $6.25,
$80.77, $419.23 **19.** $12, $61.34, $738.66
21. $60.88 **23.** $72.54 **25.** $24.86
27. $63.81 **29.** Installment plan; interest is
$55.64; interest on note is $86.40

Mixed Review

31. 7.082 **33.** 0.365 **35.** $602.80 **37.** 6.1%

Lesson 4.5, pages 156–160

Exercises

1. 2.456 **3.** $719 **5.** $2,278.44 **7.** $210.02
9. $306 **11.** $1,732.22 **13.** A, $31.73

Mixed Review

17. $750 **19.** 8%

Lesson 4.6, pages 161–164

Exercises

1. $4.56 **3.** $9,820,800 **5.** $10,784.30
7. 0.225 **9.** $15 **11.** $13\frac{1}{2}$% **13.** 13%
15. $184 **17.** $12\frac{3}{4}$% **19.** $7.08 **21.** $13\frac{1}{4}$%
23. $4,320 **25.** $9

Mixed Review

27. $78,800 **29.** $107.80 **31.** 1:4
33. $737.42 **35.** $312.37

Lesson 4.7, pages 165–171

Exercises

1. $25.38 **3.** $321.76 **5.** $9.01
7. $53 **9.** $1,711.74 **11.** 0.000316
13. $322.66 **15.** $3.74, $267.88, $29
17. $51.48 **19.** $338.11 **21.** $391,200.40
23. $I = PRT$, compounding

Mixed Review

25. 3.0225 **27.** $33 **29.** $851.08
31. $54,128

Lesson 4.8, pages 172–179

Exercises

1. $944.51 **3.** $4.63 **5.** $3.07, $162.22
7. $6.96, $244.76 **9.** $3.49, $479.98
11. No, finance charge is less ($1.34) in first;
second is $2.90 **13.** $5.56, $371.08
15. $21.93 **17.** $21.76

Mixed Review

19. 0.06% **21.** 8.6 **23.** $33\frac{1}{3}$%
25. 25 months **27.** $708.27 **29.** $17.21

CHAPTER 5: SPEND WISELY

Lesson 5.1, pages 190–193

Exercises

1. $247.89 **3.** $2.22 **5.** $13.79 **7.** $5.80
9. $18.42 **11.** $20.85 **13.** $683.64
15. $33.50

Mixed Review
19. $0.09 **21.** $\frac{5}{9}$ **23.** 1.75 **25.** 0.000589
27. $3,913 **29.** $1.33

Lesson 5.2, pages 194–198

Exercises
1. 0.0485 **3.** 0.029 **5.** $229.97 **7.** $28.87
9. $594.90 **11.** $257.34 **13.** $521.68
15. $91.72 **17.** $81.39 **19.** $87.25

Mixed Review
21. 16.168 **23.** $1\frac{1}{4}$ **25.** 88 **27.** $766.01
29. $3.13 **31.** $603.03 **33.** $239.17
35. $21,722

Lesson 5.3, pages 199–201

Exercises
1. $5.07 **3.** $0.19 **5.** $0.70 **7.** $1.50
9. $0.67 **11.** $0.12 **13.** $21 **15.** $0.07
17. $5.16 **19.** larger; $0.01

Mixed Review
21. 0.04109 **23.** 5%

Lesson 5.4, pages 202–207

Exercises
1. $37.52 **3.** $153.24 **5.** $30.60 **7.** $10.46
9. 18% **11.** $46.51 **13.** 10% **15.** $99
17. $30 **19.** $66.45 **21.** $0.38 **23.** daily
rental rate **25.** weekly rate **27.** 19 weeks

Mixed Review
29. 16.2 **31.** 73 **33.** $15,664.20

Lesson 5.5, pages 208–213

Exercises
1. $338.98 **3.** 14.77 **5.** $119.88
7. $43.49 **9.** $1,638.88 **11.** $656 **13.** 5
15. 124.8 sec **17.** 240 sec

Mixed Review
19. $0.96 **21.** 10 **23.** 21.9% **25.** $3,528
27. $16.24 **29.** June 13 **31.** $279.12
33. $1,494.50 **35.** $2,767.37

CHAPTER 6: OWN A HOME OR CAR

Lesson 6.1, pages 222–228

Exercises
1. $1,095 **3.** 180 **5.** $7,846.44 **7.** $36,920
9. $85,874 **11.** $20,355 **13.** $4,071
15. $2,933 **17.** $7,033 **19.** $501.86,

$60,446.40 **21.** $598.77, $125,557.20
23. $733.76, $164,153.60
25. $143.22 $\times$ 12 = $1,718.64 second year
saving

Mixed Review
29. $211,862.73 **31.** 5,600
33. $5\frac{1}{2}$ **35.** $5,082 **37.** $45.20
39. 58 days

Lesson 6.2, pages 229–235

Exercises
1. $13,879 **3.** $3,361 **5.** $3,507.50
7. $6,936 **9.** $20,528 **11.** $4,068
13. Buying, $1,022 lower **15.** Renting; $124
more

Mixed Review
19. $1,154.07 **21.** $15.20 **23.** 130,000
25. $13.90 **27.** earned, $268.68; unearned,
$41.32 **29.** $949.20 **31.** $14.89
33. 58 days

Lesson 6.3, pages 236–241

Exercises
1. $6,174 **3.** 1,253 **5.** 0.0284 **7.** 0.0183
9. $780,500; 0.022 **11.** $350,700; 0.044
13. $936 **15.** $1,295 **17.** $2,805.48
19. $2,576.56 **21.** $9,886.59 **23.** $1,344.15

Mixed Review
27. 0.33708 **29.** 0.45 **31.** 2,400; 2,330.15
33. $24.74 **35.** $7.17 **37.** $5,256

Lesson 6.4, pages 242–248

Exercises
1. $899 **3.** $26,620 **5.** $56,950 **7.** 0.706
9. 1,505 **11.** $287 **13.** $1,970 **15.** $142
17. $936 **19.** $ 6,000 **21.** $11,000
23. $17,500 **25.** $6,400, $19,500, $20,000

Mixed Review
29. $14.29 **31.** $2\frac{1}{2}$ **33.** $134.03 **35.** $\frac{11}{25}$
37. 13.9% **39.** $173.38 **41.** $605; 25%

Lesson 6.5, pages 249–255

Exercises
1. $18,697 **3.** $21,259.50 **5.** $1,471.36
7. $23,929 **9.** $24,912 **11.** Yes, $203
13. $21,130.50, $17,960.50 **15.** $5,189.10
17. Answers will vary. Pro: Mechanical designs
of cars are good; proper care can extend life of

car even further. Con: Major repairs may far exceed cost of extended warranty; warranty is like an insurance policy.

Mixed Review

19. 10.1, 10 **21.** 238 **23.** 0.0578
25. October 15 **27.** $4.30 **29.** $14\frac{1}{4}$%
31. $337.10 **33.** $17.55

Lesson 6.6, pages 256–259

Exercises

1. $14,173 **3.** $2,351 **5.** 13% **7.** $12,231
9. $12,627 **11.** $7,700 **13.** $2,030
15. $4,815 **17.** $1,675 **19.** 15% **21.** 13%
23. $4,075 **25.** $12,400

Mixed Review

27. 12.8 **29.** $\frac{5}{6}$ **31.** $18

Lesson 6.7, pages 260–263

Exercises

1. 0.05 **3.** 0.1035 **5.** $24.78 **7.** $681.10
9. $240.28 **11.** $1,824.39 **13.** $398.08
15. $625.52

Mixed Review

19. 48 **21.** $1,927.96 **23.** $459, $10,659
25. $9.87, $1,032.75

Lesson 6.8, pages 264–270

Exercises

1. $690 **3.** $1,517 **5.** $32,904
7. $3,018.40 **9.** $14,953 **11.** $27,624
13. $29,448 **15.** leasing costs $1,973 more
17. $3,873

Mixed Review

21. 190 **23.** 56,390; 5.639 **25.** $69.92
27. $9.06 **29.** $584.42
31. Box, 3¢ less per oz. **33.** $40

CHAPTER 7: INSURANCE AND INVESTMENTS

Lesson 7.1, pages 282–288

Exercises

1. $104.58 **3.** $7 **5.** $67.80 **7.** 25%
9. $1,784 **11.** $596 **13.** $807 **15.** $6,720
17. 59% **19.** $526,000 **21.** $2,244.10
23. $9,800 **25.** $3,150 **27.** $4,000
29. $5,831.45

Mixed Review

33. $23 **35.** $39.26 **37.** $3\frac{1}{5}$ **39.** $0
41. $13\frac{1}{4}$% **43.** $2,112 **45.** $23,750

Lesson 7.2, pages 289–294

Exercises

1. $16,742 **3.** $378.96 **5.** $4,921
7. $533 **9.** $6,583 **11.** $67.96 **13.** 39.6%
15. $18,630 **17.** $124 **19.** $504
21. $20,391.50 **23.** $200

Mixed Review

25. $3,015.46 **27.** 13.957 **29.** 73
31. $624.09 **33.** $4,301.76 **35.** $1,922.90

Lesson 7.3, pages 295–299

Exercises

1. $47,450 **3.** $4,999 **5.** $19,062
7. $66,750 **9.** 27% **11.** $486.25
13. $1,487.50 **15.** 15 **17.** $50,600

Mixed Review

21. 12.5% **23.** 23.1% **25.** $\frac{15}{16}$ **27.** $149.12
29. 19% **31.** $1,700 **33.** $44.45 **35.** $485

Lesson 7.4, pages 300–304

Exercises

1. $6,290 **3.** $1,027 **5.** $1,185 **7.** $928.77;
disc. **9.** $1,030.88, prem.
11. $1,098.36; prem. **13.** $4,572.25
15. $21,258.40 **17.** $14,174.10
19. $13,760.76 **21.** $4,766.82 **23.** $7,085.04
25. $30 **27.** $58.74 **29.** $7.10

Mixed Review

33. 57.78 **35.** $1\frac{5}{24}$ **37.** $6\frac{2}{7}$ **39.** $24,136.80
41. $37,767 **43.** $3,672

Lesson 7.5, pages 305–309

Exercises

1. $840 **3.** $960 **5.** $900
7. $462.50 **9.** $165 **11.** $4,962.30, $450
13. $32,175.90, $3,750 **15.** 10.9% **17.** 8.5%
19. $20 **21.** 10.2% **23.** 10.3%
25. $20,795.20 **27.** $650 **29.** $19,417.80

Mixed Review

31. $\frac{2}{45}$ **33.** $2\frac{2}{25}$ **35.** $561.82

Lesson 7.6, pages 310–317

Exercises

1. $5,534.88 **3.** $37.50 **5.** $12,706.55
7. $1,791.20 **9.** $22,259.90 **11.** $2,394.20
13. $1,589.90 **15.** $12,819.60 **17.** $500
19. $270 **21.** $600 **23.** $1,440 **25.** 3.8%
27. 6.2% **29.** 7% **31.** 10.5% **33.** 2.9%
35. 400 **37.** 500 **39.** $7,628.12, +$687

41. $7,118.90, −$444.87
43. $3,165.22, +$544.83 **47.** $1,095
49. $6,619.38 **51.** $3,227.62 profit

Mixed Review
53. 1.9% **55.** $108

Lesson 7.7, pages 318–323

Exercises
1. $674 **3.** $1,771.54 **5.** 23.4% **7.** $4,384
9. $9,904 **11.** $727 **13.** $5,235 **15.** $7,464
17. 5% **19.** $2.64, 4.9% **21.** $3.20, 4.5%
23. $60,774.40 **25.** $24,330

Mixed Review
27. 25% **29.** 8.75% **31.** $468
33. $1,478.92 **35.** $1.58 **37.** $2,002.50 loss
39. $8,217.75

Lesson 7.8, pages 324–330

Exercises
1. $1,584 **3.** $2,375 **5.** $309 **7.** $3,375.47
9. $742 **11.** $670 **13.** $1,110 **15.** 10%
17. −2% **19.** 11.7% **21.** 7.3% **23.** 26.3%
25. $31,600 **27.** $1,697.67 **29.** $369.17
31. $985 **33.** $221.67

Mixed Review
37. 126 **39.** 32% **41.** $\frac{9}{16}$ **43.** 4,017
45. $14

Lesson 7.9, pages 331–336

Exercises
1. $274,327 **3.** 0.4% **5.** $26,880 **7.** 52.5%
9. $1,920 **11.** 2.5% **13.** $25,320.57
15. $435

Mixed Review
17. 35.6 **19.** $495 **21.** $43\frac{3}{20}$ **23.** $28.86

CHAPTER 8: BUSINESS DATA ANALYSIS

Lesson 8.1, pages 346–350

Exercises
1. $152 **3.** $73 **5.** 16.429; 17, 12, 12
7. 9,645; 8,579; no mode; 17,054
9. $8.18; $8.20; $8; $0.45 **11.** 23; 22.5; 28; 11
13. 18; 18; 14; 15 **15.** mean

Mixed Review
17. $1\frac{1}{4}$ **19.** $4\frac{1}{3}$ **21.** $304.14 **23.** $487
25. $24.10 **27.** $18,040

Lesson 8.2, pages 351–356

Exercises
1. $1,720 **3.** 1,400 **5.** 0.389 **7.** $\frac{5}{9}$
9. $\frac{9}{9}$, or 1 **11.** $\frac{1}{40}$ **13.** $\frac{8}{40}$, or $\frac{1}{5}$
15. 0.8 = 80% **17.** 96%, 4% **19.** $365,000

Mixed Review
21. $42,500 **23.** $19
25. $49,905 **27.** $4,920 **29.** $21.18; $28.24

Lesson 8.3, pages 357–363

Exercises
1. $4,100 **3.** $1,350 **5.** Monday, Tuesday,
Thursday **7.** Electrical and plumbing
9. April-May **17.** The amounts on the graphs
would be more difficult to read.

Mixed Review
19. $\frac{3}{10}$ **21.** 60% **23.** $10,000 **25.** $8\frac{1}{8}$
27. $138 **29.** $599.44 **31.** $554.60
33. $677; 8.3%

Lesson 8.4, pages 364–368

Exercises
1. 16% **3.** 144° **5.** 8% **7.** newspaper, 30%;
Internet, 20%; product samples, 5%; direct mail,
25%; coupons, 15%; other, 5%. **9.** 20%, 40%,
17.5%, 6%, 16.5% **11.** 180°, 108°, 54°, 18°
15. yes

Mixed Review
17. 0.876 **19.** $7\frac{5}{12}$ **21.** 198,734 **23.** $55.65
25. $6,254.27 **27.** $34.36 **29.** 7.1%

Lesson 8.5, pages 369–375

Exercises
1. 32.9 **3.** 4.1% **5.** 0.423 **7.** 145.2
9. Apparel **11.** 54% **13.** Housing, 2.4%
15. $0.565; $0.016 **17.** $0.119
21. $22,080

Mixed Review
23. $28.01 **25.** $20.67 **27.** $244.56
29. 2% **31.** $20 **33.** $8,027.50
35. $1,456; $6,656 **37.** $2,610.80

CHAPTER 9: BUSINESS TECHNOLOGIES

Lesson 9.1, pages 386–393

Exercises
1. $2,486.09 **3.** $5,160 **5.** 0.1093 **7.** 295
9. $68,096 **11.** $2,004.72 **13.** 96.1%

15. $22,962 **17.** $56,476.80 **19.** 172.5 GB
21. 5 **23.** 5,343 **25.** 1,870 **27.** $44.77;
$42.95; $29.99; $30

Mixed Review
31. 7 **33.** $397.50 **35.** 12.5
37. $40 **39.** 5% **41.** $7,560

Lesson 9.2, pages 394–398

Exercises
1. $9,430.09 **3.** $278.53 **5.** $3,160
7. $6.96 **9.** 31.5% **11.** 18% **13.** $1,050
15. $4,449 **17.** $59.36 **19.** $13.20 **21.** 701

Mixed Review
25. $\frac{21}{40}$ **27.** $3.89 **29.** $27

Lesson 9.3, pages 399–403

Exercises
1. $28,369.22 **3.** $39,312 **5.** $13,199
7. 14 **9.** $1,725 **11.** $303,600
13. $71,886.46 **15.** 1:96 **17.** $2,974,400
19. $89,700 **21.** 35.9%

Mixed Review
23. 9.0311 **25.** 40.96616 **27.** 43.75%
29. 568 **31.** $62.89 **33.** 80%, 86%, 88%
35. $10,747.92

Lesson 9.4, pages 404–409

Exercises
1. $90,251 **3.** $3,072 **5.** $15,408
7. $2,940 **9.** $118,894 **11.** $0.65
13. $5,645 **15.** $56,717 **17.** 34
19. 15.9% **21.** $12,584 **23.** $401.56

Mixed Review
25. 40.227 **27.** 6 **29.** 1.5% **31.** 10
33. $9.48 **35.** 40 **37.** $621 **39.** $6,059.85

Lesson 9.5, pages 410–415

Exercises
1. $106.72 **3.** 308 **5.** 95 **7.** $51.68
9. $2,024.87 **11.** $575.84 **13.** $235.30
15. $480 **17.** $107.88

Mixed Review
19. 56.1 **21.** 1,289 **23.** $28,107 **25.** 6

**CHAPTER 10: MANAGE PEOPLE AND
INVENTORY**

Lesson 10.1, pages 424–429

Exercises
1. $10,355 **3.** $637.50 **5.** $156,000
7. $4,648 **9.** $4,320 **11.** $176,850
13. $136,540 **15.** $2,200 **17.** $18,920

Mixed Review
19. $6\frac{3}{4}$ **21.** $1.88 **23.** 1.7%

Lesson 10.2, pages 430–434

Exercises
1. $15.40 **3.** $0.17 **5.** $640 **7.** $19.66
9. $1,050 **11.** $474,000 **15.** $984
17. Answers will vary; choose between assured
increases vs. self-confidence in own ability.

Mixed Review
19. 11.135 **21.** $\frac{1}{8}$ **23.** 60,000 **25.** $113.11
27. 40; 100

Lesson 10.3, pages 435–439

Exercises
1. $13,258.02 **3.** $15.70 **5.** $418.47
7. $9,500 **9.** $7,619.80 **11.** $67.50
13. $2,460

Mixed Review
17. 713.36 **19.** $\frac{3}{10}$ **21.** 0.0001 **23.** 98
25. $424.07, $67,221 **27.** $1,889.76

Lesson 10.4, pages 440–444

Exercises
1. 1,118 **3.** 273 **5.** 1,206 **7.** 10 **9.** 776
11. 30,800 **13.** 12

Mixed Review
17. $3.50 **19.** 18 **21.** $328.44 **23.** $\frac{7}{12}$
25. 1 **27.** $21,934

Lesson 10.5, pages 445–450

Exercises
1. 747 **3.** $11,765.40 **5.** $5,075
7. $5,000.80 **9.** $11,359 **13.** $26,442

Mixed Review

15. $105.55 **17.** $\frac{5}{9}$ **19.** $2.67
21. $30, $153.48, $1,846.52
23. $243,000, $405

Lesson 10.6, pages 451–455

Exercises

1. $414,960 **3.** $9,095.80 **5.** $19.60
7. $17.49 **9.** $141,664 **11.** $7.89
13. $0.17 **15.** $0.15

Mixed Review

19. $6.25 **21.** $\frac{17}{40}$ **23.** $41.06

CHAPTER 11: BUSINESS COSTS

Lesson 11.1, pages 466–470

Exercises

1. $365.25 **3.** $910.48 **5.** $445,150
7. $1,286,342 **9.** $464,462 **11.** $150
13. $162,691 **15.** $1,153,637.60 **17.** $900;
$2,250; $1,350 **19.** 246 **21.** $87.63
23. training to upgrade skills; better equipment
and tools

Mixed Review

25. $\frac{8}{15}$ **27.** $58 **29.** 30% **31.** 39.9 cents

Lesson 11.2, pages 471–474

Exercises

1. $31.68 **3.** $292,740 **5.** 12,800
7. 10,000 **9.** $1,170,000 **11.** 1,200
13. $18.75 **15.** Break-even point includes
both fixed costs and variable costs.

Mixed Review

17. 1,763 **19.** 0.125 **21.** June 9
23. $2,187.50 **25.** 7,740 **27.** Yes,
$12 \times 3 = 36$ and $5 \times 650 = 3,250$.
3,250 MB = 3GB and 250 MB. All together the
employees have 39GB 250 MB.

Lesson 11.3, pages 475–479

Exercises

1. 21 **3.** $96,680 **5.** $47,174.40
7. $12,696 **9.** $1,288, $1,090.16 **11.** $7,568,
$5,860.66 **13.** $19,836, $15,013.87
15. $48,576.92 **17.** $250,000 **19.** $120,000
21. Company has longer use of larger amount
of money

Mixed Review

23. $4,020

Lesson 11.4, pages 480–485

Exercises

1. $929.81 **3.** $48.10 **5.** 32,900 **7.** Yes
9. Yes **11.** yes **13.** $33.25 **15.** $12.00
17. $27.75 **19.** $15.25 **21.** $25.00
23. $63.10 **25.** $45.45 **27.** $193
29. $2,137.20 **31.** $144 **33.** $1,366.56
35. $2,062.26 **37.** $1,586.23; Sisco
39. $400 **41.** $787.65

Mixed Review

43. $47.60 **45.** 9.75% **47.** $2,103.64
49. $2,600 **51.** $378.15

Lesson 11.5, pages 486–489

Exercises

1. $11.29 **3.** $26.72 **5.** $16.80 **7.** 3
9. $33\frac{1}{3}$% **11.** $621 **13.** 1.3 **15.** 1,275
17. $148,050 **19.** $150 **21.** $6.30

Mixed Review

23. $193\frac{1}{2}$ **25.** 7 **27.** 57 **29.** 57

Lesson 11.6, pages 490–493

Exercises

1. $314.42 **3.** $708.50 **5.** $140.71
7. $1,741.49 **9.** $2,024 **11.** $24.64
13. $9,555 **15.** $1,883.70

Mixed Review

17. 6.371 **19.** 50%

CHAPTER 12: SALES AND MARKETING

Lesson 12.1, pages 500–508

Exercises

1. $57,464.91 **3.** $4,053.77 **5.** $2,864.40
7. 18¢ short **9.** $2.32 short **11.** $47,112.80
13. $4,354.20 **15.** $5,037.82; $4,966.37;
$1,820.87; $4,395.23; $2,574.36; $3,491.12;
$3,478.56; $904.20

Mixed Review

9. $448 **21.** 0.00782 **23.** 3 **25.** $354
27. $38,220, $3.86

Lesson 12.2, pages 509–515

Exercises

1. $6,903.49 **3.** $90.41 **5.** 2% **7.** Aug. 26
9. Apr. 4 **11.** Feb. 12 **13.** $68, $3,332
15. $1,151.54 **17.** $2,730 **19.** 2.5%
21. 1.5% **23.** $759.70 **25.** $10.50
27. $1,392 **29.** Answers will vary, but price,
availability, and quality of goods are important.
31. $181.07 **33.** $658.93

Mixed Review

35. 220 **37.** $\frac{1}{72}$ **39.** $11,585 **41.** 38
43. $2,385.15

Lesson 12.3, pages 516–521

Exercises

1. $2,016.75 **3.** $25.67 **5.** 51% **7.** $86.40;
$33.60 **9.** $168.68; $146.32 **11.** 19%
13. 30% **15.** 43% **17.** $275.31 **19.** $20.81,
$11.19 **21.** Multiplication is commutative.
23. May 17; $1,520, $1,487.64, $1,737;
$1,679.80, $1,660.89, $1,877.26

Mixed Review

25. 0.001 **27.** $399 **29.** $1,349.40
31. $37.26 **33.** 480

Lesson 12.4, pages 522–527

Exercises

1. $0.52 **3.** $7\frac{1}{2}$% **5.** $7.80 **7.** 12% **9.** $44
11. $227.70 **13.** 46%; $245 **15.** 69%; $38
17. $0.60 **19.** $75; 50% **21.** $36.75; $33\frac{1}{3}$%
23. $367.04 **25.** 23.2% **27.** 30%

Mixed Review

29. 0.00034 **31.** 0.26 **33.** 855.573 **35.** 0.5
37. $217

Lesson 12.5, pages 528–531

Exercises

1. 921 **3.** 13.1% **5.** 133, 62.1% **7.** 40.6%
9. 18.3% **11.** 34% **13.** 79%

Mixed Review

17. 5,410 **19.** 368,000 **21.** $1,986.30

Lesson 12.6, pages 532–535

Exercises

1. $46,804.50 **3.** $192,000 **5.** 10% **7.** 209
9. 6,704 **11.** 14,960

Mixed Review

15. 207 **17.** $0.82 **19.** $8,683; $6,583
21. $2,523.80; $10,095.20

Lesson 12.7, pages 536–539

Exercises

1. 5% **3.** 18,490 **5.** 36% **7.** 38.8%
9. $360,000 **11.** $490,000

Mixed Review

15. 977; 1,685; 2,259; 1,880; 1,207; 1,834;
4,921 **17.** $\frac{1}{6}$ **19.** 45 **21.** $613.23
23. $5,460 **25.** $555.56

Lesson 12.8, pages 540–545

Exercises

1. $1,022 **3.** $2,562 **5.** $0.003
7. $2,826.25 **9.** $25,320 **11.** $42,510
13. $3,840 **15.** $0.006 **19.** 120

Mixed Review

21. $\frac{1}{4}$ **23.** 0.7% **25.** $38.27 **27.** 1,000
29. $130.41 **31.** $267.68

CHAPTER 13: BUSINESS PROFIT AND LOSS

Lesson 13.1, pages 556–561

Exercises

1. $61,102 **3.** $22,012 **5.** ($20,540)
7. $256,184 **9.** $649,380 **11.** $581,200
13. Net loss, $5,503

Mixed Review

15. $126 **17.** $10,000 **19.** 0.57 **21.** 19.8%

Lesson 13.2, pages 562–565

Exercises

1. 12% **3.** 72.2% **5.** 13.3% **7.** 60%
9. $77,000; $24,200 **11.** 11% **13.** 4.5
15. $5,174

Mixed Review

17. 450 **19.** $87\frac{1}{2}$% **21.** $239.17

Lesson 13.3, pages 566–570

Exercises

1. $22,504 **3.** $26,285 **5.** $22,500
7. $40,418; $27,982 **9.** $11,978.87; $6,921.13
11. $39,400; $59,100 **13.** $42,200; $40,800
15. $66,480; $63,600; $64,920 **17.** 1, or
100%

Mixed Review

19. 160% **21.** $6,057.51 **23.** 200
25. $25,482

Lesson 13.4, pages 571–575

Exercises

1. $109,377   **3.** $99,139   **5.** $143,368
7. $90,970   **9.** $13,550   **11.** $69,555
13. $48,600   **15.** $215,800   **17.** $113,200
19. $20,638   **21.** Total Liabilities, $20,310;
Chieko Kimura, Capital, 57,607; Total Assets,
$77,917; Total Liabilities and Capital; $77,917
23. current assets can be used to make loan
payments

Mixed Review
25. $357\frac{1}{2}$ **27.** 11,000   **29.** $\frac{1}{4}$ **31.** $1,600
33. $754.56; $15,091.20

Lesson 13.5, pages 576–580

Exercises
1. $194,412   **3.** 2.0:1   **5.** 2.1:1   **7.** 56.8%
9. 3.2%   **11.** 24.8%   **13.** 39%

Mixed Review
15. $11\frac{1}{20}$ **17.** 0.4007   **19.** $120,000
21. $12.85   **23.** $16,902,000   **25.** $196.20

Lesson 13.6, pages 581–583

Exercises
1. $113,713   **3.** 28¢   **5.** 40%   **7.** 35%
9. 64¢   **11.** 42¢   **13.** 37%   **15.** $20,000
17. $417.28   **19.** 34%   **21.** $7,820

Mixed Review
23. $\frac{1}{20}$ **25.** 150   **27.** $6,748

CHAPTER 14: INTERNATIONAL BUSINESS

Lesson 14.1, pages 592–596

Exercises
1. 361.93   **3.** 15,734.27   **5.** $3,880
7. $2,463   **9.** $114,338   **11.** $745,802
13. buying the car in the United States

Mixed Review
15. $1\frac{1}{4}$ **17.** 543,460,000,000

Lesson 14.2, pages 597–601

Exercises
1. 5:00 A.M.   **3.** 6:13 P.M.   **5.** 8   **7.** 11
9. 2 time zones east; it is 7:00 A.M. Saturday
11. 11 time zones west; Wednesday at 3:00 A.M.
13. 86°F   **15.** No, 32°C equals 89.6°F
17. 11:30 A.M. EST   **19.** 28

Mixed Review
21. 20.5%   **23.** $18\frac{1}{8}$ **25.** $47,812
27. $133,542.80   **29.** $57,395; $59,605
31. $7.63

Lesson 14.3, pages 602–605

Exercises
1. 100   **3.** 1 000   **5.** 0.1   **7.** 0.6   **9.** 0.368
11. 5 000   **13.** 3 000   **15.** 2.9   **17.** 41.5 mm
19. 16.4 cm   **21.** 0.4 mm   **23.** 2 760 cm
25. 50 m   **27.** 1.7 km   **29.** 269.7 cm
31. 105.4 m   **33.** 3 542 km   **35.** 6 000 cm
37. 1 040 mm   **39.** 4 700 m   **41.** 888 m
43. 1.334 m   **45.** 618 km   **47.** 206 km
49. 7.02 in.   **51.** No

Mixed Review
55. 0.75   **57.** $1\frac{1}{6}$ **59.** $11.95; $12
61. $8,000; $37,000   **63.** $7,497; $5,355

Lesson 14.4, pages 608–613

Exercises
1. 100 mm^2 **3.** 8 600 ha   **5.** 260 000 m^2
7. 1.5012 m^2 **9.** 9.7 m^2 **11.** 4.32 km^2
13. 3 km^2 **15.** 4 135 mm^2 **17.** 1.5 km^2
19. 4   **21.** 4   **23.** 62.5 acres   **25.** 22.4 in.^{2}
27. 1 390 ha   **29.** 1 031 m^2 **31.** 2,052,000 ft^2
33. 12 inches by 12 inches   **35.** 4 m^2
37. m^2 offer; $180 saved

Mixed Review
39. $3\frac{1}{10}$ **41.** 12.9   **43.** 30%   **45.** $3.10;
$140.16   **47.** $2,019.25

Lesson 14.5, pages 614–619

Exercises
1. 1 000 L   **3.** 0.6 L   **5.** 1.9 g   **7.** 650 g
9. 0.001 L   **11.** 4.554 kg   **13.** 5.36 g
15. 72 kg   **17.** 45 t   **19.** 130.5   **21.** 5.4 kg
23. 679.2 g   **25.** 1.25 L   **27.** 5   **29.** 500
31. 205 g   **33.** 1 095 kg   **35.** 2.5%
37. 84.8 oz.

Mixed Review
41. $709.44

A

Access fees Money paid to ISP for usage of Internet.

Adjusted balance method The difference between payments and credits during a month from the balance at the end of the previous month.

Adjusted gross income A tax term meaning gross income less adjustments.

Airtime The minutes you spend calling on a cell-phone.

Annual percentage rate (APR) A percent that shows the ratio of finance charges to the amount financed.

Area The amount of surface an item has.

Assessed value A value put on property as a base for figuring amount of tax.

Assets Things of value owned by a person or business.

Automatic teller machine (ATM) A computer system that lets you withdraw or deposit money in your bank account without a teller's help.

Average A single number used to represent a group of numbers.

Average daily balance method The periodic rate applied to the average daily balance in the account during the billing period.

B

Balance The amount of money in an account; the difference between the two sides of an account.

Balance sheet A statement showing the assets, liabilities, and capital of a person or business for a certain date.

Bank discount Interest collected in advance.

Bank statement A monthly report to a depositor showing deposits, payments, and balance in a checking account.

Bankrupt Legally insolvent and unable to pay debts.

Base period A period in time with which comparisons are made.

Benefits An addition to wages provided by the employer that are of value.

Bodily injury insurance Auto insurance covering liability for injury to other persons.

Bond discount When the amount of market value of a bond is less than the par value.

Bond premium When the market value of a bond is more than par value.

Bonds Written promise to repay the money loaned on the due date.

Bonus Pay given to reward employees who make a significant contribution to the success of the company or whose work record is exceptional.

Book value Original cost less total depreciation to date.

Break-even point The point at which income from sales equals total costs of producing and selling goods.

Budget Future spending goals.

Byte A character stored in a computer system.

C

Capital investment The amount of cash you originally invested plus anything you spent for improvements.

Carrying costs The costs of holding inventory until it is issued.

Cash advance The cash received when money is borrowed on a credit card.

Cash discount Discount given for early payment of a bill.

Cash payments record A written record of money paid out.

Cash receipts record A written record of money received.

Cash value The value of an insurance policy if it is canceled; cash surrender value.

Certificate of deposit (CD) A time deposit or savings certificate.

Check register A record of deposits and checks.

Circle graph A circle showing how parts relate to the whole and to each other.

Closing costs Fees and expenses paid to complete the transfer of ownership of a home.

Coinsurance When the insured and the insurer share losses or costs.

Collision Auto insurance that covers damage to the insured's car.

Commission A payment amount to a salesperson that may be an amount for each item sold or it may be a percent of the dollar value of sales.

Compound amount The total in a savings account at the end of an interest period after compound interest is added.

Compound interest The difference between the original principal and the compound amount; interest figured on interest after it has been added to principal.

Comprehensive damage Insurance that covers damage or loss to your vehicle from fire, theft, vandalism, and other causes.

Computer hardware May include different sized devices such as handheld computers, notebook computers, desktop computers, and large computer systems.

Consumer price index (CPI) A single number used to measure a change in consumer prices compared to a base year.

Contract employees Temporary employees who receive their paychecks and benefits from the employment agency.

Cost of goods sold The amount paid by the seller for the goods sold.

Cost-of-Living-Adjustment (COLA) A wage increase based on changes in the Consumer Price Index (CPI).

Credit memo A form that tells the buyer that the buyer's account has been reduced.

Current ratio Compares current assets to current liabilities.

Current yield on bonds Found by dividing the bond's annual interest income by the bond's price.

D

Declining-balance method A way of figuring depreciation at a fixed rate on a decreasing balance; fixed-rate method.

Debit card A card that lets you pay for purchases using a terminal in a store.

Debt to equity ratio Found by dividing the long term liabilities of a firm by the firm's capital. Helps measure the amount of financial risk of a business.

Deductions Subtractions from gross pay.

Deposit Slip A form used to list all money deposited in a bank.

Depreciation The decrease in value caused by wear and aging.

Direct Deposit Transferring funds by a company directly into their employees bank accounts without writing any checks.

Disability insurance Pays a portion of the income you lose if you cannot work due to a health condition or injury.

Discount series A trade discount that has two or more discounts.

Domestic business The manufacturing, purchasing and selling of goods and services within a country.

Double-time pay Pay that is twice the regular pay.

Down payment The part of a price that is paid at the time of buying on the installment plan.

Download Receive files over the Internet.

E

E-business Electronic business; doing business online.

Earned income Money received from working such as wages, salaries, and tips.

Electronic funds transfer (EFT) When funds are withdrawn from one account and deposited into another using computers.

Employee A person who works for others.

Employer A person or company that an employee works for.

Exact interest method Interest based on exact time and a 365-day year.

Executive recruiters People hired to fine full-time employees for management or specialized technical positions; headhunters.

Exempt employees Paid a salary and do not qualify for overtime pay.

Exemption An amount of income that is free from tax.

Exporting Selling of goods or services produced within your country and sold to other countries.

Extension The total price of each quantity on a sales slip, found by multiplying the quantity by the unit price.

F

Factory overhead The total cost of items such as rent, depreciation, heat, light, power, insurance, supplies, and indirect labor used in a factory.

Finance charge The sum of the interest and any other charges on an installment loan or purchase.

First in, first out (FIFO) A method used to find the value of ending inventory when the exact cost is not known. Merchandise purchased first is used first and the value of the ending inventory is based on the cost of the most recently purchased items.

Fixed costs Overhead items such as rent, salaries, heat, and insurance that remain the same no matter how much is produced and sold.

Flat tax A tax rate that stays the same for every person regardless of the amount of income they earn in a year.

f.o.b. Free on board; a term used in price quotations to tell who will pay transportation costs.

Forecasts Estimate of future sales.

Foreign exchange rate The amount paid for another country's currency.

Freight A service for delivery of heavy, bulky goods.

Frequency distribution A table of numbers arranged in order and with the frequency, or how often they occur, tallied.

Fringe benefits Paid vacations, sick leave, retirement plans, insurance, and other benefits beyond the wage or salary.

G

Graduated commission A pay system in which the rate of commission increases as the base increases.

Gram The basic unit of weight in the metric system.

Grand total The corner total on a columnar table. Used to check accuracy of vertical and horizontal addition.

Gross domestic product (GDP) A system of a country that measures the total market value of the goods and services produced within its borders.

Gross income Total income in a year. Includes wages, salaries, commissions, bonuses, tips, interest, dividends, prizes, pensions, sale of stock, and profit from a business.

Gross pay The total amount that an employee is paid.

Gross profit The difference between the net sales and the cost of goods sold.

Gross profit margin The comparison of gross profit to net sales.

H

Health insurance Protects policyholder from financial loss due to illness.

Hit Number of times a web page is visited.

Home coverage area One region of the country where you have wireless phone service.

Homeowners insurance An insurance policy that covers your home and protects you against risk.

Horizontal bar graph A graph with bars running to the left and right.

Hourly rate An amount of pay for each hour worked.

I

Importing The buying of products produced outside your country.

Income statement Shows how much money has been earned and spent during a period of time.

Individual retirement account (IRA) Retirement investment.

Inflation A rise in the prices of goods and services.

Interest Money paid to an individual or institution for the privilege of using their money.

International business All business activities necessary to manufacture, purchase, and sell goods and services across national borders; foreign trade.

Internet service provider (ISP) An organization that provides access to the Internet in your area.

Invoice price Price the retailer pays after the trade discount is given.

J

Job expenses Money paid out of total job benefits for things such as travel, dues, tools.

K

Kilobyte (kbps) One thousand bytes, or characters.

L

Labor force All persons who are working or looking for work.

Last in, last out (LIFO) A method to find the value of ending inventory when the exact cost is not known. Merchandise purchased last is used first so inventory is based on the costs of goods purchased first.

Lease A rental agreement.

Liabilities Debts of a business.

Life insurance A way of protecting your family from financial hardship when you die.

Line graph A graph on which lines connect dots to show values.

List price A price shown in a catalog.

Liter The basic metric measure of capacity.

M

Major medical insurance Supplements basic health coverage. Designed to help pay the hospital costs or other health care expenses due to a major illness or injury.

Manufacturer's Suggested Retail Price (MSRP) The price printed on a sticker pasted on the window of a new car.

Markdown A reduction in marked or retail price; a discount.

Market The total of all persons or organizations that are potential customers.

Market price The price at which a stock or bond is sold; the price or value of an item in the open market.

Market share Tells what percentage of the total market's sales one seller has.

Markup The amount added to the cost of the goods to cover all other expenses plus a profit.

Maturity date The date that marks the end of the term of a loan. When money must be repaid.

Mean The sum of the numbers divided by the number of items; arithmetic average; a measure of central tendency.

Median The middle number in a group of numbers arranged in order.

Megabyte (Mbps) One million bytes, or characters.

Merchandise turnover rate The number of times per period that a store replaces, or turns over it's average stock of merchandise.

Meter (m) The basic unit of length in the metric system.

Mode The number that occurs most frequently in a group of numbers.

Modified accelerated cost recovery system (MACRS) Allows you to claim depreciation over a fixed number of years depending on the class life of the property.

Mortgage loan A paper signed by a borrower that gives the lender the right to ownership of property if the borrower does not pay the principal or interest.

Mutual fund An investment company that buys stocks and bonds of other companies.

N

Net asset value The value of a mutual fund share found by dividing net assets of the fund by outstanding shares.

Net income The amount left after subtracting operating expenses from gross profit; net profit.

Net job benefits The total value of the benefits received from a job less job expenses.

Net loss When operating expenses are greater than gross profit; net loss equals operating expenses less gross profit.

Net pay The remaining pay after deductions have been subtracted from total or gross wages; take-home pay.

Nonexempt employees Employees who are paid by the hour and get paid overtime.

Net profit margin The comparison of net income to net sales.

O

On account A term indication that payment is to be made at a later date, or describing a partial payment on an amount owed.

Online Being connected to the Internet.

Online banking An electronic banking service that allows you to do your banking by using your personal computer and the Internet.

Ordering costs Inventory costs that include the expenses connected with creating and sending a purchase order to a supplier and handling stock.

Outsourcing Companies using outside firms to provide technical support.

Outstanding checks A check issued but not yet received and paid by the bank.

Overtime Time worked beyond the regular working day or week.

P

Pagers Wireless devices used to alert people.

Part-time employees Employees who work less than 40 hours per week.

Partnership A business owned by two or more persons that is not a corporation or other form of business.

Per capita GDP Shows the amount of goods and services produced per person by a country.

Per diem An employee who is needed and paid by the day.

Periodic rate A daily or monthly rate found by dividing the Annual Percentage Rate (APR) by 365 or 12.

Perpetual inventory The system of keeping a running balance of stock on hand.

Piece rate A wage system in which workers are paid by the number of pieces produced.

Premium The amount paid for insurance; a bond selling above par value is selling "at a premium."

Previous balance method Charges interest on the balance in the account on the last billing date of the previous month.

Prime cost The cost of raw materials and direct labor.

Principal The one for whom an agent acts; the face of a note; the amount on which interest is paid.

Probability A way of mathematically predicting the chance that an event will occur.

Profit sharing Employees get part of the profit earned by a company.

Property damage insurance Auto insurance covering damage to property of others.

Property tax A tax on value of real estate.

Prove cash Count cash on and check accuracy against the record of cash received and paid out.

Purchasing power of the dollar A measure of how much a dollar now buys compared to what it could buy during some base period.

Q

Quota A fixed amount of sales above which commission is paid.

R

Random sample A few items selected by chance from the whole group.

Range The difference between the highest and lowest numbers in a set of data.

Rate of interest Interest shown as a percent.

Reconciliation form A form showing how the checkbook and bank statement balances are made to agree.

Rectangle graph A graph that uses vertical or horizontal rectangles to show how parts relate to the whole and to each other.

Renters policy Similar to homeowners insurance, but not covering loss of building or apartment.

Reorder point The minimum stock level at which an order must be placed.

Replacement cost policy Insurance that pays the cost of replacing a property at current prices.

Resale value The amount you receive when you sell an asset, such as a car.

Respondents People who complete business surveys.

Return on equity Compares net income to capital.

Roaming charges Charges you pay to make a call when you are outside your home coverage area.

S

Sales invoice Lists the goods sold and delivered to the buyer.

Sales returns and allowances The dollar amount of goods sold that were later returned for refunds or for which credit was given because of damage; a decrease in sales.

Sales tax A tax charged by a city, county, or state on the sale of items or services and collected by sellers from buyers.

Security deposit Amount of money given to guarantee a lease.

Service charge A bank charge or deductions for handling a checking account; a charge in addition to interest on an installment purchase.

Site license Allows you to use the software on any and all computers in your company or at your location.

Software Computer programs, a set of instructions that tells the computer what to do.

Square meter The basic unit of area in the metric system.

Standard deduction A fixed amount that can be deducted from taxable income. Used in place of itemized deductions.

Stock Goods or supplies on hand; shares of ownership in a corporation.

Stock record Shows how much of a particular item has been received and issued and how much remains on hand.

Storage media Where computers store data.

Straight commission A pay system in which commission is the only pay; there is no other wage or salary.

Subtotal On a sales slip, the sum of the extensions before taxes are added.

Sum-of-the-years-digits method A variable-rate way of depreciating that provides decreasing amounts of depreciation as an item ages.

T

Taxable income The amount used to figure income tax with a tax-rate schedule.

Term of discount The time during which a bank holds a discounted note; date of discount to date of maturity.

Time For a note, the length of time for which the money is borrowed.

Time-and-a-half-pay Pay that is one and a half times the regular pay rate.

Tips Amount of money given to someone for services they provide.

Total costs of Ownership (TCO) The costs of installing, operating, and maintaining computer systems.

Total manufacturing cost The sum of the costs of raw materials, direct labor, and factory expense.

Trade deficit When foreign imports exceed exports.

Trade discount A reduction or discount given

from a catalog or list price; a discount given "within the trade."

Trade surplus When foreign exports exceed imports.

Trade-in value The amount you get for your old car or other asset when buying a new car or other asset.

Transaction A deposit or withdrawal that has to be recorded.

Travel expenses Expenses incurred while traveling for business; mileage, hotel fees, meal charges, airfares, taxi fares, rental car charges, expenses for entertaining customers, and related expenses.

Trend A historical relationship between sales and time.

U

Unearned income Money received from interest and dividends.

Unit price The price of one item or one measure of the item.

Upload Send a file to another person over the Internet.

V

Variable costs Costs such as raw materials, direct labor, and energy that vary or change with the amount of goods produced and sold.

Vertical bar graph A graph with bars running up and down.

W

Wages The total pay for a day or week of a worker paid on an hourly rate basis.

Web-hosting companies Firms that create and maintain websites for other companies.

Weighted Average Method A method used to find the value of ending inventory when the exact cost is not known. Inventory is priced at the average price per unit of the beginning inventory plus the cost of all purchases during the fiscal year.

Withholding allowance An allowance for a person used to reduce the amount of tax withheld from pay.

Withholding tax A deduction from pay for income tax.

All photos © PhotoDisc, Inc.